Lecture Notes in Computer Science 3768

Commenced Publication in 1973
Founding and Former Series Editors:
Gerhard Goos, Juris Hartmanis, and Jan van Leeuwen

Editorial Board

David Hutchison
　Lancaster University, UK
Takeo Kanade
　Carnegie Mellon University, Pittsburgh, PA, USA
Josef Kittler
　University of Surrey, Guildford, UK
Jon M. Kleinberg
　Cornell University, Ithaca, NY, USA
Friedemann Mattern
　ETH Zurich, Switzerland
John C. Mitchell
　Stanford University, CA, USA
Moni Naor
　Weizmann Institute of Science, Rehovot, Israel
Oscar Nierstrasz
　University of Bern, Switzerland
C. Pandu Rangan
　Indian Institute of Technology, Madras, India
Bernhard Steffen
　University of Dortmund, Germany
Madhu Sudan
　Massachusetts Institute of Technology, MA, USA
Demetri Terzopoulos
　New York University, NY, USA
Doug Tygar
　University of California, Berkeley, CA, USA
Moshe Y. Vardi
　Rice University, Houston, TX, USA
Gerhard Weikum
　Max-Planck Institute of Computer Science, Saarbruecken, Germany

Yo-Sung Ho   Hyoung Joong Kim (Eds.)

Advances in Multimedia Information Processing – PCM 2005

6th Pacific-Rim Conference on Multimedia
Jeju Island, Korea, November 13-16, 2005
Proceedings, Part II

Springer

Volume Editors

Yo-Sung Ho
Gwangju Institute of Science and Technology (GIST)
1 Oryong-dong buk-gu, Gwangju, 500-712, Korea
E-mail: hoyo@gist.ac.kr

Hyoung Joong Kim
Kangwon National University
Department of Control and Instrumentation Engineering
Kangwondaehakgil, Chunchon, Kangwondo, 200-701, Korea
E-mail: khj@kangwon.ac.kr

Library of Congress Control Number: 2005935482

CR Subject Classification (1998): H.5.1, H.3, H.5, C.2, H.4, I.3, K.6, I.7, I.4

ISSN   0302-9743
ISBN-10   3-540-30040-6 Springer Berlin Heidelberg New York
ISBN-13   978-3-540-30040-3 Springer Berlin Heidelberg New York

This work is subject to copyright. All rights are reserved, whether the whole or part of the material is concerned, specifically the rights of translation, reprinting, re-use of illustrations, recitation, broadcasting, reproduction on microfilms or in any other way, and storage in data banks. Duplication of this publication or parts thereof is permitted only under the provisions of the German Copyright Law of September 9, 1965, in its current version, and permission for use must always be obtained from Springer. Violations are liable to prosecution under the German Copyright Law.

Springer is a part of Springer Science+Business Media

springeronline.com

© Springer-Verlag Berlin Heidelberg 2005
Printed in Germany

Typesetting: Camera-ready by author, data conversion by Scientific Publishing Services, Chennai, India
Printed on acid-free paper   SPIN: 11582267   06/3142   5 4 3 2 1 0

Preface

We are delighted to welcome readers to the proceedings of the 6th Pacific-Rim Conference on Multimedia (PCM). The first PCM was held in Sydney, Australia, in 2000. Since then, it has been hosted successfully by Beijing, China, in 2001, Hsinchu, Taiwan, in 2002, Singapore in 2003, and Tokyo, Japan, in 2004, and finally Jeju, one of the most beautiful and fantastic islands in Korea.

This year, we accepted 181 papers out of 570 submissions including regular and special session papers. The acceptance rate of 32% indicates our commitment to ensuring a very high-quality conference. This would not be possible without the full support of the excellent Technical Committee and anonymous reviewers that provided timely and insightful reviews. We would therefore like to thank the Program Committee and all reviewers.

The program of this year reflects the current interests of the PCM's. The accepted papers cover a range of topics, including, all aspects of multimedia, both technical and artistic perspectives and both theoretical and practical issues. The PCM 2005 program covers tutorial sessions and plenary lectures as well as regular presentations in three tracks of oral sessions and a poster session in a single track. We have tried to expand the scope of PCM to the artistic papers which need not to be strictly technical. Since we are living in the age of convergence, we believe that convergence of technology and art is also highly needed. However, we realize that bridging the gap between them has not been easy due to the lack of mutual understanding and lack of fair evaluation criteria. Of course, a few papers widen the horizon of the PCM 2005. Traditional topics of multimedia, such as multimedia communications, audio-visual compressions, multimedia security, image and signal processing techniques, multimedia data processing, and other important works are balanced in the PCM 2005.

We give a special thanks to Prof. Jae-Kyoon Kim, General Chair, for his brilliant leadership in organizing this conference. This was an important work which was dealt with very efficiently and harmoniously. Our thanks must go to all the Organizing Committee members for their precious time and enthusiasm. They did their best in financing, publicity, proceedings, registration, Web and local arrangement. We cannot forget Victoria Kim for her professionalism in managing and assisting us as a Conference Secretary. We express our thanks to the sponsors including the Ministry of Information and Communication, the Institute of Information Technology Assessment, Korea National Tourism Organization, and Korea Society of Broadcast Engineers.

Yo-Sung Ho
Hyoung Joong Kim

Committee List

Technical Program Committee Members

Masao Aizu (Canon, Japan)
John Apostolopoulos (Hewlett-Packard, USA)
Yasuo Ariki (Kobe University, Japan)
Goh Wooi Boon (Nanyang Technological University, Singapore)
Nozha Boujemaa (INRIA Rocquencourt, France)
Hye Ran Byun (Yonsei University, Korea)
Long-Wen Chang (National Tsing Hua University, Taiwan)
Yung-Chang Chen (National Tsing Hua University, Taiwan)
Liang-Tien Chia (Nanyang Technological University, Singapore)
Yoon Sik Choe (Yonsei University, Korea)
Song Chong (KAIST, Korea)
Alberto Del Bimbo (University of Florence, Italy)
Chabane Djeraba (Laboratoire d' Informatique Fondamentale de Lille, France)
Toshiaki Fujii (Nagoya University, Japan)
Patrick Gioia (France Telecom R&D, France)
Yihong Gong (NEC Laboratories America, USA)
Patrick Gros (IRISA-CNRS, France)
William Grosky (University of Michigan - Dearborn, USA)
Irene H. Y. Gu (Chalmers, Sweden)
Ling Guan (Ryerson University, Canada)
Anthony T. S. Ho (Nanyang Technological University, Singapore)
Yo-Sung Ho (GIST, Korea)
Min Cheol Hong (Soongsil University, Korea)
Xian-Sheng Hua (Microsoft, China)
Jenq-Nenq Hwang (University of Washington, USA)
Ichiro Ide (Nagoya University, Japan)
Alejandro Jaimes (FX Pal Japan, Fuji Xerox, USA)
R. C. Jain (Birla Institute of Science and Technology, India)
Kyeong Hoon Jung (Kookmin University, Korea)
Mohan S. Kankanhalli (National University of Singapore, Singapore)
Aggelos Katsaggelos (Northwestern University, USA)
Jiro Katto (Waseda University, Japan)
Roichi Kawada (KDDI R&D Laboratories Inc., Japan)
Dong In Kim (Simon Fraser University, Canada)
Hae Kwang Kim (Sejong University, Korea)
Hae Yong Kim (University of São Paulo, Brazil)
Hong Kook Kim (GIST, Korea)

Hyoung Joong Kim (Kangwon National University, Korea)
Jong Won Kim (GIST, Korea)
Man Bae Kim (Kangwon National University, Korea)
Asanobu Kitamoto (National Institute of Informatics, Japan)
Hitoshi Kiya (Tokyo Metropolitan University, Japan)
Sung-Jea Ko (Korea University, Korea)
Ki Ryong Kwon (Pusan University of Foreign Studies, Korea)
Chil Woo Lee (Chonnam National University, Korea)
Jeong A. Lee (Chosun University, Korea)
Jong Weon Lee (Sejong University, Korea)
Kwan Heng Lee (GIST, Korea)
Yoon Joon Lee (KAIST, Korea)
Yung Lyul Lee (Sejong University, Korea)
Riccardo Leonardi (Università degli Studi di Brescia, Italy)
Jin Jang Leou (National Chung Cheng University, Taiwan)
Michael Lew (University of Leiden, The Netherlands)
Chung Sheng Li (IBM, USA)
Kin Li (Microsoft, USA)
Mingjing Li (Microsoft Research Asia, China)
Rainer Lienhart (University of Augsburg, Germany)
Chia Wen Lin (National Chung Cheng University, Taiwan)
David Lin (National Chiao Tung University, Taiwan)
Weisi Lin (Agency for Science, Technology and Research, Singapore)
Wanquan Liu (Curtin University of Technology, Australia)
Kai Kuang Ma (Nanyang Technological University, Singapore)
Wei Ying Ma (Microsoft Research Asia, China)
Young Shik Moon (Hanyang University, Korea)
Chong Wah Ngo (City University of Hong Kong, Hong Kong)
Vincent Oria (New Jersey Institute of Technology, USA)
Rae Hong Park (Sogang University, Korea)
Peter Pyun (Hewlett-Packard, USA)
Anthony Reeves (Cornell University, USA)
Kang Hyeon Rhee (Chosun University, Korea)
Takahiro Saito (Kanagawa University, Japan)
Philippe Salembier (Universitat Politècnica de Catalunya, Spain)
Peter Schelkens (Vrije Universiteit Brussel, Belgium)
Nicu Sebe (University of Amsterdam, The Netherlands)
Timothy K. Shih (Tamkang University, Taiwan)
Dong Gyu Sim (Kwangwoon University, Korea)
John R. Smith (IBM T. J. Watson Research Center, USA)
Lifeng Sun (Tsinghua University, China)
Luis Torres (Universitat Politècnica de Catalunya, Spain)
Hsiao-Rong Tyan (Chung Yuan Christian University, Taiwan)
Shekhar Verma (Indian Institute of Information Technology, India)
Chee Sun Won (Dongguk University, Korea)

You Jip Won (Hanyang University, Korea)
Lingda Wu (National University of Defense Technology, China)
Changsheng Xu (Agency for Science, Technology and Research, Singapore)
Youngjun Francis Yoo (Texas Instruments, USA)
Lu Yu (Zhe Jiang University, China)
Ley Zhang (Microsoft Research Asia, China)
Xiao-Ping Zhang (Ryerson University, Canada)

Additional Reviewer List

Jeong-Hwan Ahn (Samsung AIT, Korea)
Hee Jun An (Seoul National University of Technology, Korea)
Jaakko Astola (Tampere University of Technology, Finland)
Marcos Avilés Rodrigálvarez (Universidad Politécnica de Madrid, Spain)
Konsung Bae (Kyungpook National University, Korea)
Joong-Hwan Baek (Hankuk Aviation University, Korea)
Hyokyung Bahn (Ewha Womans University, Korea)
Raphaèle Balter (France Telecom R&D, France)
Gaspard Breton (France Telecom R&D, France)
David Cailliere (France Telecom R&D, France)
Kyung-Ae Cha (Daegu University, Korea)
Ching-Han Chen (I-Shou University, Taiwan)
Adrian David Cheok (National University of Singapore, Singapore)
Hoyong Choi (Chungbuk National University, Korea)
Jong-Soo Choi (Chung-Ang University, Korea)
Sumi Choi (Sejong University, Korea)
Ho-Yong Choi (Chungbuk National University, Korea)
Ki Dong Chung (Pusan National University, Korea)
Thomas Di Giacomo (University of Geneva, Switzerland)
Jean-Pierre Evain (European Broadcasting Union, France)
Víctor Fernández (UAM (ES), Spain)
Masaaki Fujiyoshi (Tokyo Metropolitan University, Japan)
Wen Gao (Joint Research & Development Laboratory, China)
Takayuki Hamamoto (Tokyo University of Science, Japan)
JungHyun Han (Korea University, Korea)
Mahnjin Han (Samsung AIT, Korea)
Dongsoo Har (GIST, Korea)
Jun Heo (Konkuk University, Korea)
HyunKi Hong (Chung-Ang University, Korea)
Jin-Woo Hong (ETRI, Korea)
Ki-Sang Hong (POSTECH, Korea)
Eenjun Hwang (Korea University, Korea)
Euee S. Jang (Hanyang University, Korea)
Ju-wook Jang (Sogang University, Korea)
Byeungwoo Jeon (Sung Kyun Kwan University, Korea)

Jechang Jeong (Hanyang University, Korea)
Xiaoyue Jiang (Northwestern Polytechnical University, China)
Xiaogang Jin (Zhejiang University, China)
Nam Ik Joe (Seoul National University, Korea)
Inwhee Joe (Hanyang University, Korea)
Jae Hak Jung (Inha University, Korea)
Soon Ki Jung (Kyungpook National University, Korea)
Sung-Hwan Jung (Changwon National University, Korea)
Dong Wook Kang (Kookmin University, Korea)
Hong-Goo Kang (Yonsei University, Korea)
Hyun-Soo Kang (Chungbuk National University, Korea)
Mun Gi Kang (Yonsei University, Korea)
Sooyong Kang (Hanyang University, Korea)
Mohan Kankanhalli (National University of Singapore, Singapore)
Hirokazu Kato (Osaka University, Japan)
Stefan Katzenbeisser (Technische Universität München, Germany)
Bo Yon Kim (Kangwon National University, Korea)
Chong-kwon Kim (Seoul National University, Korea)
Changick Kim (ICU, Korea)
Doh-Suk Kim (Lucent Technologies, USA)
Gerard Jounghyun Kim (POSTECH, Korea)
HyungJun Kim (Korea University, Korea)
Jaejoon Kim (Daegu University, Korea)
Jong-Nam Kim (Pukyong National University, Korea)
JongWeon Kim (Sangmyung University, Korea)
Keunho Kim (Samsung AIT, Korea)
Laehyun Kim (KIST, Korea)
Mun Chul Kim (ICU, Korea)
Sangwook Kim (Kyungpook National University, Korea)
Sang-Wook Kim (Samsung AIT, Korea)
Weon-Goo Kim (Kunsan National University, Korea)
Whoi-Yul Yura Kim (Hanyang University, Korea)
Won-Ha Kim (Kyung Hee University, Korea)
Wook-Joong Kim (ETRI, Korea)
Yong Kuk Kim (Sejong University, Korea)
Young Yong Kim (Yonsei University, Korea)
Youngseop Kim (Dankook University, Korea)
Hideaki Kimata (NTT Advanced Technology, Japan)
Lisimachos P. Kondi (State University of New York, USA)
Alex C. Kot (Nanyang Technological University, Singapore)
Sunil Kumar (Clarkson University, USA)
No-Yoon Kwak (Cheonan University, Korea)
Gauthier Lafruit (IMEC-DESICS-Multimedia, Belgium)
Chulhee Lee (Yonsei University, Korea)
Haeyoung Lee (Hongik University, Korea)

Heung-Kyu Lee (KAIST, Korea)
Jeong-Gun Lee (University of Cambridge, UK)
MeeSuk Lee (ETRI, Korea)
Minkyu Lee (Lucent Technologies, USA)
Sang Hwa Lee (Seoul National University, Korea)
Sang Wook Lee (Sogang University, Korea)
Sangyoun Lee (Yonsei University, Korea)
Seok-Pil Lee (KETI, Korea)
Seong-Won Lee (Kangwon National University, Korea)
Si-Woong Lee (Hanbat National University, Korea)
Suk-Hwan Lee (Tongmyong University, Korea)
Yugyung Lee (University of Missouri, USA)
Igor Lemberski (Transport and Telecommunication Institute, Latvia)
Jae Hyuck Lim (Yonsei University, Korea)
B. S. Manjunath (University of Califormnia Santa Barbara, USA)
Yannick Maret (École Polytechnique Fédérale de Lausanne, Switzerland)
Jeonghoon Mo (ICU, Korea)
Sang Man Mo (Chosun University, Korea)
Francisco Morán Burgos (Universidad Politécnica de Madrid, Spain)
Hiroaki Morino (Shibaura Institute of Technology, Japan)
Hiroshi Murase (Nagoya University, Japan)
Jae Yul Nam (Keimyung University, Korea)
Jeho Nam (ETRI, Korea)
Yang-Hee Nam (Ewha Womans University, Korea)
Tobias Oelbaum (Technische Universität München, Germany)
Seoung-Jun Oh (Kangwon National University, Korea)
Joonki Paik (Chung-Ang University, Korea)
Sung Bum Pan (Chosun Universirty, Korea)
Zhigeng Pan (Zhejiang University, China)
Raveendran Paramesran (University of Malaya, Malaysia)
Changhan Park (Chung-Ang University, Korea)
Changhoon Park (University of Tokyo, Japan)
Dong-Kwon Park (Ubix System Inc., Korea)
HyunWook Park (KAIST, Korea)
Jong-Il Park (Hanyang University, Korea)
Seung Kwon Park (Hanyang University, Korea)
In Kyu Park (Inha University, Korea)
Fernando Pereira (IST(PT), Portugal)
Sylvain Prat (France Telecom R&D, France)
Marius Preda (Institut National des Télécommunications, France)
Safavi-Naini Rei (University of Wollongong, Australia)
Kyung Hyune Rhee (PuKyong National University, Korea)
Yong Man Ro (ICU, Korea)
Yeonseung Ryu (Myongji University, Korea)
Shin'ichi Satoh (National Institute of Informatics, Japan)

Yong Duk Seo (Sogang University, Korea)
Jaehong Shim (Chosun University, Korea)
Seokjoo Shin (Chosun University, Korea)
Jitae Shin (Sungkyunkwan University, Korea)
Yoan Shin (Soongsil University, Korea)
Kwang-Hoon Son (Yonsei University, Korea)
Sung-Hoon Son (Sangmyung University, Korea)
Wookho Son (ETRI, Korea)
Hwangjun Song (POSTECH, Korea)
Junehwa Song (KAIST, Korea)
Po-Chyi Su (National Central University, Taiwan)
Doug Young Suh (KyungHee University, Korea)
Sanghoon Sull (Korea University, Korea)
Huifang Sun (Mitsubishi Electric Research Labs, USA)
Seyoon Tak (Samsung AIT, Korea)
Tomokazu Takahashi (Nagoya University, Japan)
Rin-ichiro Taniguchi (Kyushu University, Japan)
Ronald M. Tol (Philips Applied Technologies, The Netherlands)
Chun-Jen Tsai (National Chiao Tung University, Taiwan)
Gi-Mun Um (ETRI, Korea)
S. Verma (Indian Institute of Information Technology and Management, India)
Semyung Wang (GIST, Korea)
Lin Weisi (Institute for Infocomm Research, Singapore)
Duminda Wijesekera (George Mason University, USA)
Woontack Woo (GIST, Korea)
Jeong-Hyu Yang (LG Electronics, Korea)
Jianjun Ye (Harbin Institute of Technology, China)
Changhoon Yim (Konkuk University, Korea)
Naokazu Yokoya (Nara Institute of Science and Technology, Japan)
Chuck Yoo (Korea University, Korea)
Hui Zhang (Samsung AIT, China)

Table of Contents – II

Efficient Cache Management for QoS Adaptive Multimedia Streaming Services
   Taeseok Kim, Hyokyung Bahn, Kern Koh 1

An Effective Failure Recovery Mechanism with Pipeline Computing in Clustered-Based VOD Servers
   Dongmahn Seo, Joahyoung Lee, Dongkook Kim, Yoon Kim, Inbum Jung 12

Dynamic and Scalable Caching Algorithm of Proxy Server for Multiple Videos
   Hyung Rai Oh, Hwangjun Song 24

Dynamic Adaptive Architecture for Self-adaptation in VideoConferencing System
   Chulho Jung, Sanghee Lee, Eunseok Lee 36

Scalable and Reliable Overlay Multicast Network for Live Media Streaming
   Eunyong Park, Sunyoung Han, Sangjoon Ahn, Hyunje Park, Sangchul Shin 48

Apollon : File System Level Support for QoS Augmented I/O
   Taeseok Kim, Youjip Won, Doohan Kim, Kern Koh, Yong H. Shin .. 59

Seamless Video Streaming for Video on Demand Services in Vertical Handoff
   Jae-Won Kim, Hye-Soo Kim, Jae-Woong Yun, Hyeong-Min Nam, Sung-Jea Ko 71

MPEG-4 FGS Video Traffic Model and Its Application in Simulations for Layered Video Multicast
   Hui Wang, Jichang Sha, Xiao Sun, Jun Tao, Wei He 83

Dynamic Voltage Scaling for Real-Time Scheduling of Multimedia Tasks
   Yeong Rak Seong, Min-Sik Gong, Ha Ryoung Oh, Cheol-Hoon Lee 94

Class Renegotiating Mechanism for Guaranteed End-to-End QoS over DiffServ Networks
   Dai-Boong Lee, Hwangjun Song 105

Secure and Efficient ID-Based Group Key Agreement Fitted for Pay-TV
Hyunjue Kim, Junghyun Nam, Seungjoo Kim, Dongho Won 117

A Method of Generating Table of Contents for Educational Videos
Gwang-Gook Lee, Eui-Jin Kim, Jung Won Kang, Jae-Gon Kim, Whoi-Yul Kim 129

Study of Inter-effect and Behavior of Multimedia Traffic in a QoS-Enabled Communication Network
Nashwa Abdel-Baki, Hans Peter Großmann 141

Broadcast Synchronizing System Using Audio Watermark
DongHwan Shin, JongWeon Kim, JongUk Choi 153

Realistic Broadcasting Using Multi-modal Immersive Media
Sung-Yeol Kim, Seung-Uk Yoon, Yo-Sung Ho 164

Client System for Realistic Broadcasting: A First Prototype
Jongeun Cha, Seung-Man Kim, Sung-Yeol Kim, Sehwan Kim, Seung-Uk Yoon, Ian Oakley, Jeha Ryu, Kwan H. Lee, Woontack Woo, Yo-Sung Ho 176

Proposal of Cooperative Transmission for the Uplink of TDD-CDMA Systems
Ho Van Khuong, Hyung-Yun Kong 187

A Novel Scheduler for 1xEV-DO Type System Supporting Diverse Multimedia Traffics
Shan Guo Quan, Jeong-Jun Suh, Tae Chul Hong, Young Yong Kim . 200

Proposal of Space-Time Block Coded Cooperative Wireless Transmission in Rayleigh Fading Channels
Ho Van Khuong, Hyung-Yun Kong 212

Downlink Packet Scheduling Based on Channel Condition for Multimedia Services of Mobile Users in OFDMA-TDD
Ryong Oh, Se-Jin Kim, Hyong-Woo Lee, Choong-Ho Cho 224

An Efficient Channel Tracking Method for OFDM Based High Mobility Wireless Multimedia System
Kwanghoon Kim, Haelyong Kim, Hyuncheol Park 235

A Novel Key Management and Distribution Solution for Secure Video Multicast
Hao Yin, Xiaowen Chu, Chuang Lin, Feng Qiu, Geyong Min 246

A Robust Method for Data Hiding in Color Images
  Mohsen Ashourian, Peyman Moallem, Yo-Sung Ho 258

A Color Image Encryption Algorithm Based on Magic Cube
Transformation and Modular Arithmetic Operation
  Jianbing Shen, Xiaogang Jin, Chuan Zhou 270

Selective Video Encryption Based on Advanced Video Coding
  Shiguo Lian, Zhongxuan Liu, Zhen Ren, Zhiquan Wang 281

Key Frame Extraction Based on Shot Coverage and Distortion
  *Ki Tae Park, Joong Yong Lee, Kee Wook Rim,
  Young Shik Moon* 291

Secret Message Location Steganalysis Based on Local Coherences of Hue
  Xiang-Wei Kong, Wen-Feng Liu, Xin-Gang You 301

Feature-Based Image Watermarking Method Using Scale-Invariant
Keypoints
  *Hae-Yeoun Lee, Choong-hoon Lee, Heung-Kyu Lee,
  Jeho Nam* 312

Watermarking NURBS Surfaces
  Zhigeng Pan, Shusen Sun, Mingmin Zhang, Daxing Zhang 325

Digital Watermarking Based on Three-Dimensional Wavelet Transform
for Video Data
  *Seung-Jin Kim, Tae-Su Kim, Ki-Ryong Kwon, Sang-Ho Ahn,
  Kuhn-Il Lee* 337

Using Space-Time Coding for Watermarking of Three-Dimensional
Triangle Mesh
  Mohsen Ashourian, Keyvan Mohebbi 349

Perceptually Tuned Auto-correlation Based Video Watermarking Using
Independent Component Analysis
  Seong-Whan Kim, Hyun-Sung Sung 360

Invertible Watermarking Scheme for Authentication and Integrity
  Kil-Sang Yoo, Mi-Ae Kim, Won-Hyung Lee 371

Adaptive Congestion Control Scheme Based on DCCP for
Wireless/Mobile Access Networks
  Si-Yong Park, Sung-Min Kim, Tae-Hoon Lee, Ki-Dong Chung 382

SARS : A Linear Source Model Based Adaptive Rate-Control Scheme for TCP-Friendly Real-Time MPEG-4 Video Streaming
Eric Hsiao-Kuang Wu, Ming-I Hsieh, Chung-Yuan Knight Chang ... 394

Evaluation of a Crossover Router Based QoS Mechanism in Fast Mobile IPv6 Networks*
Zheng Wan, Zhengyou Wang, Zhijun Fang, Weiming Zeng, Shiqian Wu 405

Adaptive and QoS Downlink Multimedia Packet Scheduling for Broadband Wireless Systems
Seungwan Ryu, Byunghan Ryu, Hyunhwa Seo 417

A Practical Multicast Transmission Control Method for Multi-channel HDTV IP Broadcasting System
Kazuhiro Kamimura, Teruyuki Hasegawa, Haruo Hoshino, Shigehiro Ano, Toru Hasegawa 429

MEET : Multicast Debugging Toolkit with End-to-End Packet Trace
Jinyong Jo, Jaiseung Kwak, Okhwan Byeon 441

Traffic Management for Video Streaming Service over Diff-Serv
Sang-Hyun Park, Jeong-Sik Park, Jae-Young Pyun 453

Scalable and Adaptive QoS Mapping Control Framework for Packet Video Delivery
Gooyoun Hwang, Jitae Shin, JongWon Kim 465

A Frame-Layer Rate Control Algorithm for H.264 Using Rate-Dependent Mode Selection
Jun-Yup Kim, Seung-Hwan Kim, Yo-Sung Ho 477

TCP-Friendly Congestion Control over Heterogeneous Wired/Wireless IP Network
Jae-Young Pyun, Jong An Park, Seung Jo Han, Yoon Kim, Sang-Hyun Park 489

A Balanced Revenue-Based Resource Sharing Scheme for Advance and Immediate Reservations
Dong-Hoon Yi, JongWon Kim 501

Sequential Mesh Coding Using Wave Partitioning
Tae-Wan Kim, Kyoung Won Min, Byeong Ho Choi, Yo-Sung Ho ... 514

Dimension-Reduction Technique for MPEG-7 Audio Descriptors
Jui-Yu Lee, Shingchern D. You 526

Design of an Asynchronous Switch Based on Butterfly Fat-Tree for
Network-on-Chip Applications
  Min-Chang Kang, Eun-Gu Jung, Dong-Soo Har 538

Adaptive Deinterlacing for Real-Time Applications
  *Qian Huang, Wen Gao, Debin Zhao,
  Huifang Sun* 550

Adaptive MAP High-Resolution Image Reconstruction Algorithm Using
Local Statistics
  Kyung-Ho Kim, Yoan Shin, Min-Cheol Hong 561

Energy-Efficient Cooperative Image Processing in Video Sensor
Networks
  Dan Tao, Huadong Ma, Yonghe Liu 572

Mathematical PSNR Prediction Model Between Compressed Normal
Maps and Rendered 3D Images
  Toshihiko Yamasaki, Kazuya Hayase, Kiyoharu Aizawa 584

Fast Adaptive Skin Detection in JPEG Images
  Qing-Fang Zheng, Wen Gao 595

Effective Blocking Artifact Reduction Using Classification of Block
Boundary Area
  Jung-Youp Suk, Gun-Woo Lee, Kuhn-Il Lee 606

Adaptive Rate-Distortion Optimization for H.264
  Kwan-Jung Oh, Yo-Sung Ho 617

Directional Lifting-Based Wavelet Transform for Multiple Description
Image Coding with Quincunx Segmentation
  Nan Zhang, Yan Lu, Feng Wu, Baocai Yin 629

Non-periodic Frame Refreshment Based on the Uncertainty Models of
the Reference Frames
  *Yong Tae Kim, Youngil Yoo, Dong Wook Kang, Kyeong Hoon Jung,
  Ki-Doo Kim, Seung-Jun Lee* 641

Color Quantization of Digital Images
  Xin Zhang, Zuman Song, Yunli Wang, Hui Wang 653

Directional Feature Detection and Correspondence
  Wen-Hao Wang, Fu-Jen Hsiao, Tsuhan Chen 665

An Improvement of Dead Reckoning Algorithm Using Kalman Filter
for Minimizing Network Traffic of 3D On-Line Games
  Hyon-Gook Kim, Seong-Whan Kim 676

IRED Gun: Infrared LED Tracking System for Game Interface
  *SeongHo Baek, TaeYong Kim, JongSu Kim,
  ChaSeop Im, Chan Lim* 688

On the Implementation of Gentle Phone's Function Based on PSOLA
Algorithm
  JongKuk Kim, MyungJin Bae 700

A Novel Blind Equalizer Based on Dual-Mode MCMA and DD
Algorithm
  *Seokho Yoon, Sang Won Choi, Jumi Lee, Hyoungmoon Kwon,
  Iickho Song* 711

Robust Secret Key Based Authentication Scheme Using Smart Cards
  Eun-Jun Yoon, Kee-Young Yoo 723

A Dynamically Configurable Multimedia Middleware
  Hendry, Munchurl Kim 735

Adaptive VoIP Smoothing of Pareto Traffic Based on Optimal E-Model
Quality
  Shyh-Fang Huang, Eric Hsiao-Kuang Wu, Pao-Chi Chang 747

Indoor Scene Reconstruction Using a Projection-Based Registration
Technique of Multi-view Depth Images
  Sehwan Kim, Woontack Woo 759

Image-Based Relighting in Dynamic Scenes
  Yong-Ho Hwang, Hyun-Ki Hong, Jun-Sik Kwon 772

Stippling Technique Based on Color Analysis
  Seok Jang, Hyun-Ki Hong 782

Photometry Data Coding for Three-Dimensional Mesh Models Using
Connectivity and Geometry Information
  Young-Suk Yoon, Sung-Yeol Kim, Yo-Sung Ho 794

Adaptation of MPEG-4 BIFS Scenes into MPEG-4 LASeR Scenes in
MPEG-21 DIA Framework
  Qonita M. Shahab, Munchurl Kim 806

Performance Evaluation of H.264 Mapping Strategies over IEEE
802.11e WLAN for Robust Video Streaming
Umar Iqbal Choudhry, JongWon Kim 818

Reducing Spatial Resolution for MPEG-2 to H.264/AVC Transcoding
Bo Hu, Peng Zhang, Qingming Huang, Wen Gao 830

Low-Bitrate Video Quality Enhancement by Frame Rate Up-Conversion
and Adaptive Frame Encoding
Ya-Ting Yang, Yi-Shin Tung, Ja-Ling Wu, Chung-Yi Weng 841

Face Recognition Using Neighborhood Preserving Projections
Yanwei Pang, Nenghai Yu, Houqiang Li, Rong Zhang, Zhengkai Liu. 854

An Efficient Virtual Aesthetic Surgery Model Based on 2D Color
Photograph
Hyun Park, Kee Wook Rim, Young Shik Moon................... 865

Automatic Photo Indexing Based on Person Identity
*Seungji Yang, Kyong Sok Seo, Sang Kyun Kim, Yong Man Ro,
Ji-Yeon Kim, Yang Suk Seo* 877

Bayesian Colorization Using MRF Color Image Modeling
Hideki Noda, Hitoshi Korekuni, Nobuteru Takao, Michiharu Niimi .. 889

An Efficient Player for MPEG-4 Contents on a Mobile Device
Sangwook Kim, Kyungdeok Kim 900

Conversion Mechanism of XMT into SMIL in MPEG-4 System
Heesun Kim.. 912

Two-Channel-Based Noise Reduction in a Complex Spectrum Plane for
Hands-Free Communication System
Toshiya Ohkubo, Tetsuya Takiguchi, Yasuo Ariki.................. 923

An Efficient Classifier Fusion for Face Recognition Including Varying
Illumination
Mi Young Nam, Jo Hyung Yoo, Phill Kyu Rhee................... 935

Illumination Invariant Feature Selection for Face Recognition
Yazhou Liu, Hongxun Yao, Wen Gao, Debin Zhao 946

Specular Removal Using CL-Projection
Joung Wook Park, Jae Doug Yoo, Kwan H. Lee 958

Oriental Color-Ink Model Based Painterly Rendering for Realtime Application
  Crystal S. Oh, Yang-Hee Nam 970

An Adjusted-Q Digital Graphic Equalizer Employing Opposite Filters
  Yonghee Lee, Rinchul Kim, Googchun Cho, Seong Jong Choi 981

Interactive Transfer of Human Facial Color
  Kyoung Chin Seo, Giroo Shin, Sang Wook Lee 993

Panoramic Mesh Model Generation from Multiple Range Data for Indoor Scene Reconstruction
  Wonwoo Lee, Woontack Woo 1004

A Novel Low Latency Packet Scheduling Scheme for Broadband Networks
  Eric Hsiao-Kuang Wu, Ming-I Hsieh, Hsu-Te Lai 1015

Creative Cartoon Face Synthesis System for Mobile Entertainment
  Junfa Liu, Yiqiang Chen, Wen Gao, Rong Fu, Renqin Zhou 1027

Concept and Construction of the Caddy Robot
  Florent Servillat, Ryohei Nakatsu, Xiao-feng Wu, Kazuo Itoh .. 1039

Rapid Algorithms for MPEG-2 to H.264 Transcoding
  Xiaoming Sun, Pin Tao 1049

A New Method for Controlling Smoke's Shape
  Yongxia Zhou, Jiaoying Shi, Jiarong Yu 1060

A Scene Change Detection in H.264/AVC Compression Domain
  Sung Min Kim, Ju Wan Byun, Chee Sun Won 1072

Author Index 1083

Table of Contents – I

New Panoramic Image Generation Based on Modeling of Vignetting
and Illumination Effects
    Dong-Gyu Sim 1

Virtual Object Placement in Video for Augmented Reality
    Jong-Seung Park, Mee Young Sung, Sung-Ryul Noh 13

Realtime Control for Motion Creation of 3D Avatars
    *Dong Hoon Kim, Mee Young Sung, Jong-Seung Park, Kyungkoo Jun,
    Sang-Rak Lee* 25

Environment Matting of Transparent Objects Based on
Frequency-Domain Analysis
    I-Cheng Chang, Tian-Lin Yang, Chung-Ling Huang 37

Adaptation of Quadric Metric Simplification to MPEG-4 Animated
Object
    Marius Preda, Son Tran, Françoise Prêteux 49

Progressive Lower Trees of Wavelet Coefficients: Efficient Spatial and
SNR Scalable Coding of 3D Models
    Marcos Avilés, Francisco Morán, Narciso García 61

An Adaptive Quantization Scheme for Efficient Texture Coordinate
Compression in MPEG 3DMC
    *Sunyoung Lee, Byeongwook Min, Daiyong Kim, Eun-Young Chang,
    Namho Hur, Soo In Lee, Euee S. Jang* 73

Special Effects: Efficient and Scalable Encoding of the 3D
Metamorphosis Animation with MESHGRID
    *Ioan Alexandru Salomie, Rudi Deklerck, Dan Cernea,
    Aneta Markova, Adrian Munteanu, Peter Schelkens, Jan Cornelis* ... 84

Hardware Accelerated Image-Based Rendering with Compressed
Surface Light Fields and Multiresolution Geometry
    *Masaki Kitahara, Shinya Shimizu, Kazuto Kamikura,
    Yashima Yoshiyuki* 96

Adaptive Vertex Chasing for the Lossless Geometry Coding of 3D
Meshes
    Haeyoung Lee, Sujin Park 108

Analysis and Performance Evaluation of Flexible Marcoblock Ordering
for H.264 Video Transmission over Packet-Lossy Networks
  Changhoon Yim, Wonjung Kim, Hyesook Lim 120

Motion Perception Based Adaptive Quantization for Video Coding
  Chih-Wei Tang 132

Hybrid Deblocking Algorithm for Block-Based Low Bit Rate Coded
Images
  Kee-Koo Kwon, In-Su Jeon, Dong-Sun Lim 144

A Cross-Resolution Leaky Prediction Scheme for In-Band Wavelet
Video Coding with Spatial Scalability
  *Dongdong Zhang, Jizheng Xu, Feng Wu, Wenjun Zhang,
  Hongkai Xiong* 156

Efficient Intra Prediction Mode Decision for H.264 Video
  Seong Soo Chun, Ja-Cheon Yoon, Sanghoon Sull 168

Optimum Quantization Parameters for Mode Decision in Scalable
Extension of H.264/AVC Video Codec
  Seung-Hwan Kim, Yo-Sung Ho 179

A Metadata Model for Event Notification on Interactive Broadcasting
Service
  Kyunghee Ji, Nammee Moon, Jungwon Kang 191

Target Advertisement Service Using TV Viewers' Profile Inference
  Munjo Kim, Sanggil Kang, Munchurl Kim, Jaegon Kim 202

Personalized TV Services and T-Learning Based on TV-Anytime
Metadata
  HeeKyung Lee, Seung-Jun Yang, Han-Kyu Lee, Jinwoo Hong 212

Metadata Generation and Distribution for Live Programs on
Broadcasting-Telecommunication Linkage Services
  *Yuko Kon'ya, Hidetaka Kuwano, Tomokazu Yamada,
  Masahito Kawamori, Katsuhiko Kawazoe* 224

Data Broadcast Metadata Based on PMCP for Open Interface to a
DTV Data Server
  Minsik Park, Yong Ho Kim, Jin Soo Choi, Jin Woo Hong 234

Super-resolution Sharpening-Demosaicking with Spatially Adaptive
Total-Variation Image Regularization
  Takahiro Saito, Takashi Komatsu 246

Gradient Based Image Completion by Solving Poisson Equation
  Jianbing Shen, Xiaogang Jin, Chuan Zhou 257

Predictive Directional Rectangular Zonal Search for Digital Multimedia Processor
  Soon-Tak Lee, Joong-Hwan Baek 269

Motion Field Refinement and Region-Based Motion Segmentation
  Sun-Kyoo Hwang, Whoi-Yul Kim 280

Motion Adaptive De-interlacing with Horizontal and Vertical Motions Detection
  Chung-Chi Lin, Ming-Hwa Sheu, Huann-Keng Chiang, Chishyan Liaw 291

All-in-Focus Image Generation by Merging Multiple Differently Focused Images in Three-Dimensional Frequency Domain
  Kazuya Kodama, Hiroshi Mo, Akira Kubota 303

Free-Hand Stroke Based NURBS Surface for Sketching and Deforming 3D Contents
  Jung-hoon Kwon, Han-wool Choi, Jeong-in Lee, Young-Ho Chai 315

Redeeming Valleys and Ridges for Line-Drawing
  Kyung Gun Na, Moon Ryul Jung, Jongwan Lee, Changgeun Song ... 327

Interactive Rembrandt Lighting Design
  Hongmi Joe, Kyoung Chin Seo, Sang Wook Lee 339

Image-Based Generation of Facial Skin Texture with Make-Up
  Sang Min Kim, Kyoung Chin Seo, Sang Wook Lee 350

Responsive Multimedia System for Virtual Storytelling
  Youngho Lee, Sejin Oh, Youngmin Park, Beom-Chan Lee, Jeung-Chul Park, Yoo Rhee Oh, Seokhee Lee, Han Oh, Jeha Ryu, Kwan H. Lee, Hong Kook Kim, Yong-Gu Lee, JongWon Kim, Yo-Sung Ho, Woontack Woo 361

Communication and Control of a Home Robot Using a Mobile Phone
  Kuniya Shinozaki, Hajime Sakamoto, Takaho Tanaka, Ryohei Nakatsu 373

Real-Time Stereo Using Foreground Segmentation and Hierarchical Disparity Estimation
  Hansung Kim, Dong Bo Min, Kwanghoon Sohn 384

Multi-view Video Coding Using Illumination Change-Adaptive Motion
Estimation and 2-D Direct Mode
   Yung-Lyul Lee, Yung-Ki Lee, Dae-Yeon Kim 396

Fast Ray-Space Interpolation with Depth Discontinuity Preserving for
Free Viewpoint Video System
   *Gangyi Jiang, Liangzhong Fan, Mei Yu, Xien Ye, Rangding Wang,
Yong-Deak Kim* 408

Haptic Interaction with Depth Video Media
   *Jongeun Cha, Seung-man Kim, Ian Oakley, Jeha Ryu,
Kwan H. Lee* 420

A Framework for Multi-view Video Coding Using Layered Depth
Images
   Seung-Uk Yoon, Eun-Kyung Lee, Sung-Yeol Kim, Yo-Sung Ho 431

A Proxy-Based Distributed Approach for Reliable Content Sharing
Among UPnP-Enabled Home Networks
   HyunRyong Lee, JongWon Kim 443

Adaptive Distributed Video Coding for Video Applications in Ad-Hoc
Networks
   Ke Liang, Lifeng Sun, Yuzhuo Zhong 455

High Speed JPEG Coder Based on Modularized and Pipelined
Architecture with Distributed Control
   *Fahad Ali Mujahid, Eun-Gu Jung, Dong-Soo Har, Jun-Hee Hong,
Hoi-Jeong Lim* 466

Efficient Distribution of Feature Parameters for Speech Recognition in
Network Environments
   Jae Sam Yoon, Gil Ho Lee, Hong Kook Kim 477

Magnitude-Sign Split Quantization for Bandwidth Scalable Wideband
Speech Codec
   *Ji-Hyuk You, Chul-Man Park, Jung-Il Lee, Chang-Beom Ahn,
Seoung-Jun Oh, Hochong Park* 489

Self-timed Interconnect with Layered Interface Based on Distributed
and Modularized Control for Multimedia SoCs
   *Eun-Gu Jung, Eon-Pyo Hong, Kyoung-Son Jhang, Jeong-A Lee,
Dong-Soo Har* 500

Enhanced Downhill Simplex Search for Fast Video Motion Estimation
   Hwai-Chung Fei, Chun-Jen Chen, Shang-Hong Lai 512

Camera Motion Detection in Video Sequences Using Motion
Cooccurrences
  Hyun-Ho Jeon, Andrea Basso, Peter F. Driessen 524

A Hybrid Motion Compensated 3-D Video Coding System for Blocking
Artifacts Reduction
  Cho-Chun Cheng, Wen-Liang Hwang, Zuowei Shen, Tao Xia 535

Fast Panoramic Image Generation Method Using Morphological Corner
Detection
  Jungho Lee, Woongho Lee, Ikhwan Cho, Dongseok Jeong 547

Generation of 3D Building Model Using 3D Line Detection Scheme
Based on Line Fitting of Elevation Data
  Dong-Min Woo, Seung-Soo Han, Young-Kee Jung, Kyu-Won Lee ... 559

Segmentation of the Liver Using the Deformable Contour Method on
CT Images
  Seong-Jae Lim, Yong-Yeon Jeong, Yo-Sung Ho 570

Radial Projection: A Feature Extraction Method for Topographical
Shapes
  Yong-Il Kwon, Ho-Hyun Park, Jixue Liu, Mario A. Nascimento 582

A Robust Text Segmentation Approach in Complex Background Based
on Multiple Constraints
  Libo Fu, Weiqiang Wang, Yaowen Zhan 594

Specularity-Free Projection on Nonplanar Surface
  Hanhoon Park, Moon-Hyun Lee, Sang-Jun Kim, Jong-Il Park 606

Salient Feature Selection for Visual Concept Learning
  Feng Xu, Lei Zhang, Yu-Jin Zhang, Wei-Ying Ma 617

Contourlet Image Coding Based on Adjusted SPIHT
  Haohao Song, Songyu Yu, Li Song, Hongkai Xiong 629

Using Bitstream Structure Descriptions for the Exploitation of
Multi-layered Temporal Scalability in H.264/AVC's Base Specification
  *Wesley De Neve, Davy Van Deursen, Davy De Schrijver,
  Koen De Wolf, Rik Van de Walle* 641

Efficient Control for the Distortion Incurred by Dropping DCT
Coefficients in Compressed Domain
  Jin-Soo Kim, Jae-Gon Kim 653

Kalman Filter Based Error Resilience for H.264 Motion Vector Recovery
  Ki-Hong Ko, Seong-Whan Kim 664

High Efficient Context-Based Variable Length Coding with Parallel Orientation
  Qiang Wang, Debin Zhao, Wen Gao, Siwei Ma 675

Texture Coordinate Compression for 3-D Mesh Models Using Texture Image Rearrangement
  Sung-Yeol Kim, Young-Suk Yoon, Seung-Man Kim, Kwan-Heng Lee, Yo-Sung Ho 687

Classification of Audio Signals Using Gradient-Based Fuzzy c-Means Algorithm with Divergence Measure
  Dong-Chul Park, Duc-Hoai Nguyen, Seung-Hwa Beack, Sancho Park 698

Variable Bit Quantization for Virtual Source Location Information in Spatial Audio Coding
  Sang Bae Chon, In Yong Choi, Jeongil Seo, Koeng-Mo Sung 709

The Realtime Method Based on Audio Scenegraph for 3D Sound Rendering
  Jeong-Seon Yi, Suk-Jeong Seong, Yang-Hee Nam 720

Dual-Domain Quantization for Transform Coding of Speech and Audio Signals
  Jun-Seong Hong, Jong-Hyun Choi, Chang-Beom Ahn, Chae-Bong Sohn, Seoung-Jun Oh, Hochong Park 731

A Multi-channel Audio Compression Method with Virtual Source Location Information
  Han-gil Moon, Jeong-il Seo, Seungkwon Beak, Koeng-Mo Sung 742

A System for Detecting and Tracking Internet News Event
  Zhen Lei, Ling-da Wu, Ying Zhang, Yu-chi Liu 754

A Video Summarization Method for Basketball Game
  Eui-Jin Kim, Gwang-Gook Lee, Cheolkon Jung, Sang-Kyun Kim, Ji-Yeun Kim, Whoi-Yul Kim 765

Improvement of Commercial Boundary Detection Using Audiovisual Features
  Jun-Cheng Chen, Jen-Hao Yeh, Wei-Ta Chu, Jin-Hau Kuo, Ja-Ling Wu 776

Automatic Dissolve Detection Scheme Based on Visual Rhythm
Spectrum
  *Seong Jun Park, Kwang-Deok Seo, Jae-Gon Kim,
  Samuel Moon-Ho Song* 787

A Study on the Relation Between the Frame Pruning and the Robust
Speaker Identification with Multivariate t-Distribution
  Younjeong Lee, Joohun Lee, Hernsoo Hahn 799

Auto-summarization of Multimedia Meeting Records Based on
Accessing Log
  Weisheng He, Yuanchun Shi, Xin Xiao 809

Towards a High-Level Audio Framework for Video Retrieval Combining
Conceptual Descriptions and Fully-Automated Processes
  Mbarek Charhad, Mohammed Belkhatir 820

A New Concept of Security Camera Monitoring with Privacy Protection
by Masking Moving Objects
  Kenichi Yabuta, Hitoshi Kitazawa, Toshihisa Tanaka 831

Feature Fusion-Based Multiple People Tracking
  *Junhaeng Lee, Sangjin Kim, Daehee Kim, Jeongho Shin,
  Joonki Paik* 843

Extracting the Movement of Lip and Tongue During Articulation
  *Hanhoon Park, Seung-Wook Hong, Jong-Il Park, Sung-Kyun Moon,
  Hyeongseok Ko* 854

A Scheme for Ball Detection and Tracking in Broadcast Soccer Video
  Dawei Liang, Yang Liu, Qingming Huang, Wen Gao 864

A Shape-Based Retrieval Scheme for Leaf Images
  Yunyoung Nam, Eenjun Hwang 876

Lung Detection by Using Geodesic Active Contour Model Based on
Characteristics of Lung Parenchyma Region
  Chul-Ho Won, Seung-Ik Lee, Dong-Hun Kim, Jin-Ho Cho 888

Improved Automatic Liver Segmentation of a Contrast Enhanced CT
Image
  Kyung-Sik Seo, Jong-An Park 899

Automated Detection of Tumors in Mammograms Using Two Segments
for Classification
  Mahmoud R. Hejazi, Yo-Sung Ho 910

Registration of Brain MR Images Using Feature Information of
Structural Elements
　　Jeong-Sook Chae, Hyung-Jea Cho 922

Cyber Surgery: Parameterized Mesh for Multi-modal Surgery
Simulation
　　Qiang Liu, Edmond C. Prakash 934

Image Retrieval Based on Co-occurrence Matrix Using Block
Classification Characteristics
　　Tae-Su Kim, Seung-Jin Kim, Kuhn-Il Lee 946

Automatic Generation of the Initial Query Set for CBIR on the Mobile
Web
　　Deok Hwan Kim, Chan Young Kim, Yoon Ho Cho 957

Classification of MPEG Video Content Using Divergence Measure with
Data Covariance
　　Dong-Chul Park, Chung-Nguyen Tran, Yunsik Lee 969

Image Retrieval Using Spatial Color and Edge Detection
　　Chin-Chen Chang, Yung-Chen Chou, Wen-Chuan Wu 981

Understanding Multimedia Document Semantics for Cross-Media
Retrieval
　　Fei Wu, Yi Yang, Yueting Zhuang, Yunhe Pan 993

Multimedia Retrieval from a Large Number of Sources in a Ubiquitous
Environment
　　Gamhewage C. de Silva, T. Yamasaki, K. Aizawa 1005

Author Index 1017

Efficient Cache Management for QoS Adaptive Multimedia Streaming Services

Taeseok Kim[1], Hyokyung Bahn[2], and Kern Koh[1]

[1] School of Computer Science and Engineering, Seoul National University,
56-1, Shillim-Dong, Kwanak-Ku, Seoul, 151-742, Korea
{tskim, kernkoh}@oslab.snu.ac.kr
[2] Department of Computer Science and Engineering, Ewha Womans University,
11-1, Daehyun-Dong, Seodaemun-Ku, Seoul, 120-750, Korea
bahn@ewha.ac.kr

Abstract. With the recent advances in the wireless network technologies as well as the explosive usage of small handheld appliances, multimedia streaming services for these appliances have become increasingly important. Caching in a multimedia streaming server is an effective way to improve the performance of streaming systems and reduce the service latency. In this paper, we propose a new multimedia data cache management scheme for different digital multimedia devices such as set-top box, personal digital assistants, etc. Our new scheme exploits the reference popularity of multimedia objects as well as the inter-arrival time between two consecutive requests on an identical object. It also considers the streaming rate of objects to provide QoS (quality of service) adaptive streaming service for various appliances. Through trace-driven simulations, we show that the proposed scheme improves the performance of multimedia streaming systems significantly.

1 Introduction

Using computer technologies in the consumer electronics industry is becoming widespread with the penetration of digital technology into all aspects of society. Analogue TV has been evolving into digital TV and a great variety of computerized devices such as set-top box, PDAs (Personal Digital Assistants), and cellular phones are being diffused. These computerized products enable us to enjoy useful services that could be available only by traditional computer systems such as desktop computers in the past. One example is multimedia streaming service. Nowadays, we can use multimedia streaming service with digital TV, set-top box, PDA, and cellular phone as well as traditional computer systems (Fig.1). Hence, system-level supports for these new appliances have become increasingly important. One type of these supports is the deployment of a caching system in multimedia streaming servers [1-18]. An efficient caching mechanism in the multimedia environment can reduce the service latency as well as allow more streams to be admitted by obviating the need for disk I/O.

Caching mechanisms have been studied extensively in terms of buffer caching and paging systems in the traditional computer systems. However, due to the large volume of multimedia objects and the strictly sequential access pattern, traditional buffer cache management techniques such as Least Recently Used (LRU) will not work well for multimedia server systems. To address this problem, Dan et al. proposed the interval caching policy that exploits the short term temporal locality of accessing the same multimedia object consecutively [1-4]. By caching only the data in the interval between two successive streams on the same object, the following stream can be serviced directly from the buffer cache without I/O operations. Ozden et al. proposed the distance caching policy which is similar to interval caching [5-6].

However, these interval-based caching mechanisms exploit only the short term temporal locality of two consecutive requests on an identical object and do not consider the popularity of objects. Consequently, when the size of a multimedia object is not sufficiently large or when the inter-arrival time of stream requests is too long, there is little opportunity to obtain the effectiveness of interval caching.

In addition to this, as can be seen in Fig.1, clients in multimedia streaming services have heterogeneous capabilities in processing power, display resolution, storage capacity, and network bandwidth. Therefore, multimedia servers should provide multiple quality-of-service (QoS) versions in accordance with the client's capabilities. To this end, different QoS versions of a multimedia object are created and stored for future requests in recent multimedia servers. In this case, even for the same multimedia contents, the streaming rate may not be identical, which should also be considered in caching mechanisms.

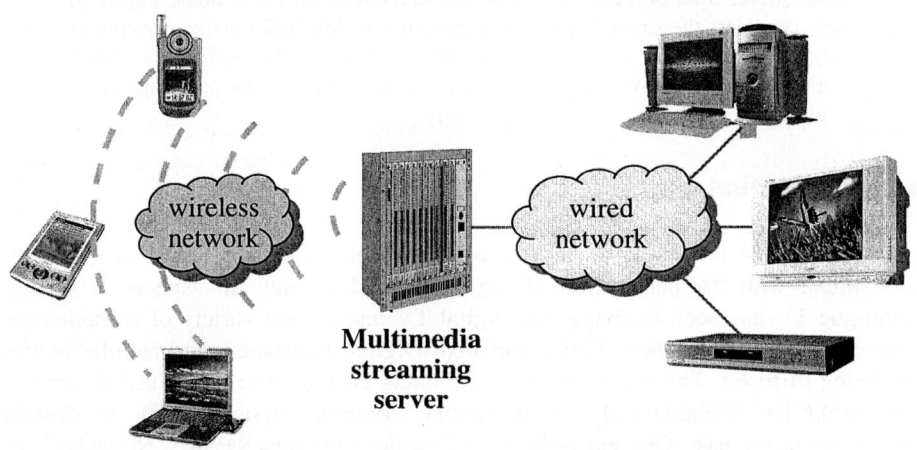

Fig. 1. Multimedia streaming servers for various appliances

In this paper, we propose an efficient cache management scheme in multimedia streaming servers. Our new scheme resolves the aforementioned problems of interval-based caching by considering the popularity and the streaming rate of each object as well as request intervals. We introduce the concept of virtual interval based on the past reference behavior of multimedia objects to exploit the reference popularity. Furthermore, we make use of streaming rates when evaluating the value of caching intervals. Through trace-driven simulations with extensive VOD traces, we show that the proposed scheme performs better than the interval caching policy, the LRU (Least Recently Used) policy, and the MRU (Most Recently Used) policy in terms of the cache hit rate.

The remainder of this paper is organized as follows. In Section 2, we review some existing works on caching algorithms in multimedia environments. Sections 3 and 4 present the system architecture and the proposed caching scheme respectively. We evaluate the performance of the scheme in Section 5. Finally, we conclude the paper in Section 6.

2 Related Works

With the explosive usage of various computing devices providing multimedia services, there have been studies on caching in these environments in recent years. Dan et al. proposed a caching scheme for video-on-demand servers named *interval caching* that exploits temporal locality of accessing the same object consecutively [1-4]. The interval caching policy organizes all consecutive request pairs by increasing order of memory requirements. It then allocates memory space to as many of the consecutive pairs as possible. When an interval is cached, the following stream does not need any disk access since it could be serviced directly from the cache. Ozden et al. proposed a cache replacement algorithm named *distance* algorithm which is similar to the interval caching policy [5-6]. It assigns a distance value to each request based on its distance from the previous request and always replaces the block consumed by the request with the largest distance value over all streams. The interval caching scheme and the distance algorithm only focus on the inter-arrival times between two consecutive requests. Therefore, when the size of a multimedia object is not sufficiently large or when the inter-arrival time of stream requests is too long, there is little opportunity to obtain the effectiveness of caching.

3 System Architecture

Our multimedia server consists of an I/O manager, a buffer manager, and a network manager (Fig. 2). The buffer manager divides the memory buffer into the *cache* and the *read-ahead buffer*. The read-ahead buffer stores data to be sent immediately to clients while the cache stores data already sent to clients which can be reused when requests for the same object arrive. Note that data in the memory buffer do not actually move their physical positions (from the read-ahead buffer to the cache) but just a cache flag is used to indicate whether it is in the cache. For each stream request, when the requested block is not in the cache, the I/O manager acquires a free block, inserts it into the read-ahead buffer, and starts disk I/O. On the other hand, if the requested block is in the cache, the cached block is serviced directly without I/O operations. Finally, the network manager reads necessary data blocks from the memory buffer and sends them to the client through the network.

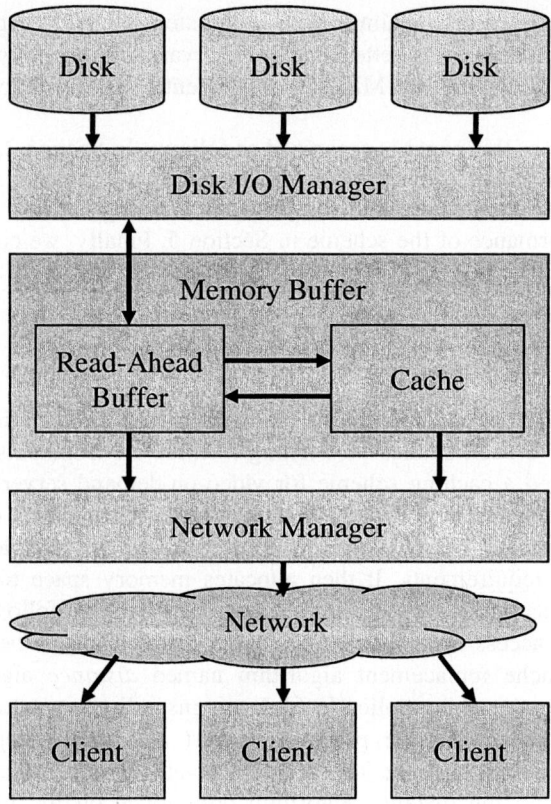

Fig. 2. The multimedia streaming server architecture

4 The Popularity and Streaming Rate Aware Interval Caching Scheme

In this section, we present the Popularity and streaming Rate aware Interval Caching (PRIC) scheme. For any two consecutive requests for the same object, the later request can read the data brought into the memory buffer by the earlier request if the data is retained in the cache until it is read by the later request. Understanding such dependencies makes it possible to guarantee continuous delivery of the later request with a small amount of cache space. In the interval caching (IC) policy, the interval is defined as the offsets between two consecutive requests on an identical object [1-4]. IC aims to maximize the number of concurrent requests serviced from the memory buffer. Hence, with a given cache space, IC orders the intervals in terms of space requirements and caches the shortest intervals.

We use this idea of interval caching and extend the idea by leveraging popularity and streaming rate of each object. Let an *interval* denote the time difference between two consecutive requests on an identical object. Note that the interval is defined as the time difference instead of the offset difference in our scheme. If we assume that object k has the constant streaming rate of r_k (blocks/s), the buffer space requirement of interval I_{ij} between request i and request j is as follows.

$$Buf(I_{ij}) = r_k \cdot I_{ij} \qquad (1)$$

In addition to this, we add the *virtual interval* concept. A *virtual interval* is defined as the time difference between the latest request on an object and the virtual request on that object. A virtual request is not a real request from a client but a predicted request that is expected to be generated at that time based on the past requests on that object. Fig.3 shows an example of the virtual interval. In the figure, a real request is denoted by a solid arrow and a virtual request is denoted by a dotted arrow. In Fig.3, $VReq._1$ is a virtual request and the interval between $Req._3$ and $VReq._1$ is a virtual interval. For example, if we assume that the streaming rate of this object is 2 (blocks/s) and the intervals I_{12}, I_{23} and the virtual interval VI are 4, 2, and 3, the buffer requirements of these intervals are 8, 4, and 6, respectively.

To predict forthcoming requests precisely, we use an exponential average in calculating the virtual interval which puts more weight on the latest interval but also considers previous intervals. Let I be the latest interval and VI_{n-1} be the $(n-1)$-th virtual interval. Then, the n-th virtual interval VI_n is computed as

$$VI_n = \alpha \cdot I + (1-\alpha) \cdot VI_{n-1} \qquad (2)$$

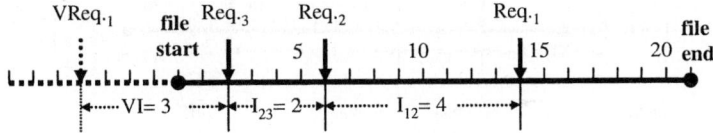

Fig. 3. An example of the virtual interval concept

where α is a constant between zero and one, and determines how much weight is put on the latest interval. We set the default value of α as 0.6 through empirical analysis. Since the virtual interval is updated only when a new request on the object arrives, it may be overestimated when there are no requests for a long time. To resolve this phenomenon, we use an adjustment function. Let t_n be the time since the latest request arrived. Then, the adjusted value should be close to the original value when t_n is small, and it should be large enough when t_n becomes large. The following adjustment function satisfies these requirements.

$$f_n = e^{t_n / VI_n} \qquad (3)$$

After this adjustment, Eq.(2) is replaced by

$$VI_n' = f_n \cdot VI_n \qquad (4)$$

and the adjustment function is invoked periodically.

As mentioned in Section 1, each multimedia object has its own streaming rate and even a single object may have multiple QoS versions for servicing different appliances. In terms of the hit rate, caching an interval with a higher streaming rate is more efficient when buffer requirements are identical. Therefore, we compute the value of an interval as follows.

$$Value(I_{ij}) = r_k / Buf(I_{ij}) \tag{5}$$

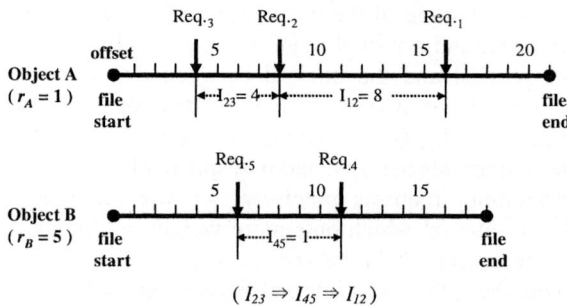

(a) When the cache size is 13, interval caching selects $interval_{23}$ and $interval_{45}$ for caching.

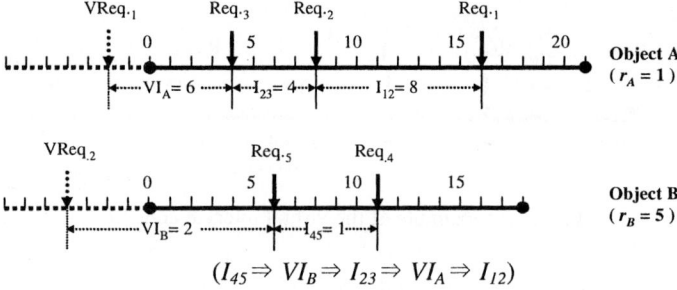

(b) When the cache size is 13, PRIC selects $interval_{45}$ and $virtual\text{-}interval_B$ for caching.

Fig. 4. Comparison of interval caching (IR) and popularity and streaming rate aware interval caching (PRIC)

Our scheme allocates the cache space to intervals (including virtual intervals) by decreasing order of the *Value* of the interval (Fig. 4). Since the cache operations need to find only the interval with the lowest value in the cache when deciding whether a new interval will be cached or not, the intervals do not need to be completely sorted. Hence, we use the heap data structure for an efficient implementation. By allocating the cache to as many intervals as possible, our scheme could maximize the number of concurrent streams serviced from the cache. Furthermore, through the virtual interval concept, our scheme caches the prefix of popular multimedia objects before they are actually requested. This could eventually reduce the start-up latency of popular streams perceived by users which was not possible to the interval caching policy.

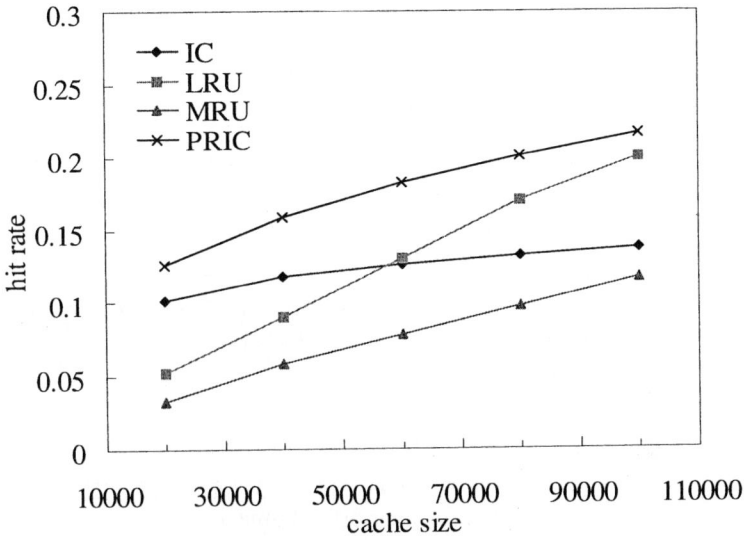

(a) Performance with different cache sizes.

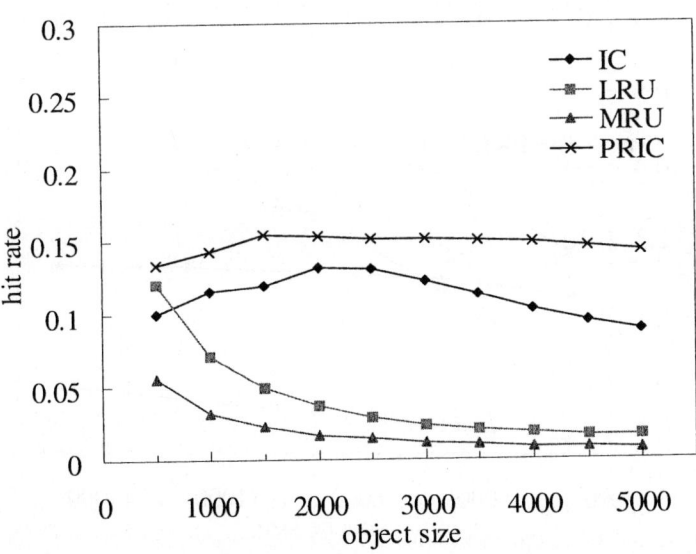

(b) Performance with different object sizes.

Fig. 5. Performance comparison of PRIC and other caching schemes

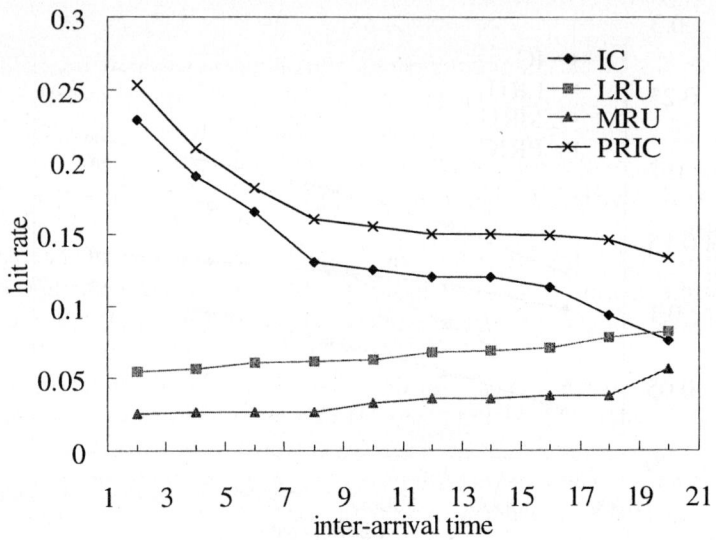

(c) Performance with different inter-arrival times.

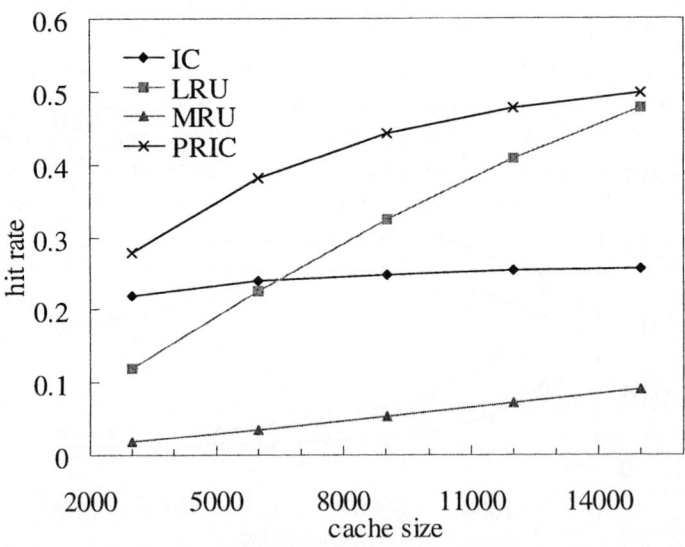

(d) Performance with real world workload.

Fig. 5. Performance comparison of PRIC and other caching schemes (cont'd)

5 Performance Evaluation

In this section, we present the performance results for various streaming conditions to assess the effectiveness of our scheme. We modeled a streaming server architecture with various parameters such as the cache size, the inter-arrival time, and the object size. We conducted extensive simulations to compare the performance of our scheme with those of IC (interval caching), LRU (Least Recently Used), and MRU (Most Recently Used).

Fig. 5(a) illustrates the hit rate of the schemes as a function of the cache size. The trace used in this experiment has 500 video files whose average playback time is 120 seconds and average streaming rate is 24 (bocks/s) with the average inter-arrival time of 5 seconds. As can be seen from the figure, PRIC shows consistently better performance than the other three schemes. Specifically, PRIC performs better than IC, LRU, and MRU by up to 8%, 7%, and 10%, respectively.

Figs. 5(b) and 5(c) show the hit rate of the four schemes as the object size and the average inter-arrival time changes. The traces used in these experiments have 500 video files whose average streaming rate is 24 (blocks/s). We set the cache size 50,000. As mentioned in Section 1, when the object size is small and the average inter-arrival time is long, the interval caching scheme did not show good performance. As we can see, our scheme shows consistently the best performance irrespective of the object size and the inter-arrival time.

We also gathered real world traces from several commercial VOD servers and performed extensive simulations. Among various results, we presented the result for the Myung Film trace [19]. Note that results from other traces are similar. The trace has 274 video files whose average playback time is 167 seconds with an average inter-arrival time of 44 seconds [19]. Fig. 5(d) shows the hit rate of the four schemes as a function of the cache size with this real workload. As we see, the shape of the graph is so similar to that in Fig. 5(a). Our scheme performs better than IC, LRU, and MRU by up to 24%, 16%, and 41%, respectively. The performance of IC is not so good as in [1-4]. This is because the object size is relatively small and the inter-arrival time is long in our traces.

6 Conclusion

In this paper, we presented the Popularity and streaming Rate-aware Interval Caching (PRIC) scheme for multimedia streaming servers. By considering reference popularity and streaming rate as well as the request interval of multimedia objects, our scheme alleviated the performance degradation problem of interval caching when the inter-arrival time is long or the object size is small. The proposed scheme performs better than interval caching, LRU, and MRU in terms of cache hit rate for various traces we considered.

Acknowledgment

The authors thank Myung Films for making their traces available.

References

1. A. Dan and D. Sitaram: Buffer Management Policy for an On-Demand Video Server. IBM Research Report RC19347, T.J. Watson Research Center, Yorktown Heights, NY (1993)
2. A. Dan and D. Sitaram: A Generalized Interval Caching Policy for Mixed Interactive and Long Video Environments. Proceedings of Multimedia Computing and Networking Conference, San Jose, CA (1996)
3. A. Dan and D. Sitaram: Multimedia Caching Strategies for Heterogeneous Application and Server Environments. Multimedia Tools and Applications, vol. 4 (1997) 279-312
4. A. Dan, D. Dias, R. Mukherjee, D. Sitaram, and R. Tewari: Buffering and Caching in Large Scale Multimedia Servers. Proceedings of IEEE COMPCON, San Francisco, CA (1995) 217-224
5. B. Ozden, R. Rastogi and A. Silberschatz: Buffer Replacement Algorithms for Multimedia Storage Systems. Proceedings of International Conference on Multimedia Computing and Systems, Hiroshima, Japan (1996) 172-180
6. B. Ozden, R. Rastogi and A. Silberschatz: Disk Striping in Video Server Environments. Proceedings of International Conference on Multimedia Computing and Systems, Hiroshima, Japan (1996) 580-589
7. M. Andrews, K. Munagala: Online Algorithms for Caching Multimedia Streams, Proceedings of the 8th European Symposium on Algorithms (2000)
8. H. Yan and D. K. Lowenthal: Popularity-Aware Cache Replacement in Streaming Environments. Proceedings of International Conference on Parallel and Distributed Computing Systems (2003)
9. S. Acharya and B. C. Smith: Middleman: A video caching strategy for streaming media files. Proceedings of Multimedia Computing and Networking, (2001)
10. M. Hoffmann, E. Ng, K. Guo, S. Paul, and H. Zhang: Caching techniques for streaming multimedia over the internet. Technical report, Bell Laboratories (1999)
11. Y. S. Ryu, K. W. Cho, Y. J. Won, and K. Koh: Intelligent Buffer Cache Management in Multimedia Data Retrieval. Lecture Notes in Artificial Intelligence, Springer-Verlag (2003) 462-471
12. K. W. Cho, Y. S. Ryu, Y. J. Won, and K. Koh: ABM: Looping Reference-aware Cache Management Scheme For Media-On-Demand server. Lecture Notes in Computer Science, Springer-Verlag, Vol. 2490 (2002) 484-500
13. R. Rejaie, M. Handley, H. Yu, and D. Estrin: Proxy Caching Mechanism for Multimedia Playback Streams in the Internet. Proceedings of Fourth International WWW Caching Workshop, San Diego (1999) 100-111
14. R. Rejaie, H. Yu, M. Handley, and D. Estrin: Multimedia Proxy Caching Mechanism for Quality Adaptive Streaming Applications in the Internet. Proceedings of IEEE Infocom, Tel Aviv, Israel (2000)
15. J. M. Almeida, D. L. Eager, and M. K. Vernon: A hybrid caching strategy for streaming media files. Proceedings of Multimedia Computing and Networking, San Jose, CA. (2001)
16. M. Kamath, K. Ramamritham, and D. Towsley: Continuous Media Sharing in Multimedia Database Systems. Proceedings of International Conference on Database Systems for Advanced Applications, Singapore (1995) 79-86

17. R. Tewari, H. Vin, A. Dan, and D. Sitaram: Caching in Bandwidth and Space Constrained Hierarchical Hyper-media Servers. Technical Report CS-TR-96-30, Department of Computer Sciences, University of Texas at Austin (1997)
18. R. Tewari, H. Vin, A. Dan, and D. Sitaram: Resource-based Caching for Web Servers. Proceedings of SPIE/ACM Conference on Multimedia Computing and Networking, San Jose, CA (1998) 191-204
19. Myung Films Co. Ltd, http://www.myungfilm.com

An Effective Failure Recovery Mechanism with Pipeline Computing in Clustered-Based VOD Servers

Dongmahn Seo, Joahyoung Lee, Dongkook Kim,
Yoon Kim, and Inbum Jung

Department of Computer Information & Telecommunication Engineering,
Kangwon National University, Hyoja-Dong, Chunchon,
Kangwon, 200-701, Korea
{dmseo, jhlee, dkkim, yooni, ibjung}@snslab.kangwon.ac.kr

Abstract. For the actual Video-On-Demand (VOD) service environment, we implement a cluster-based VOD server composed of general PCs and adopt the parallel processing for MPEG movies. For the implemented VOD server, a video block recovery mechanism is designed on the RAID-3 and the RAID-4 algorithms. However, without considering the architecture of cluster-based VOD server, the application of these basic RAID techniques causes the performance bottleneck of the internal network for recovery. To solve these problems, the new failure recovery mechanism based on the pipeline computing concept is proposed. The proposed method distributes the network traffics invoked by recovery operations and utilizes the available CPU computing power of cluster nodes.

1 Introduction

Recent advanced computer and communication technologies have provide economically feasible multimedia services such as VOD, digital library and Education-On-Demand (EOD). Among them, the VOD service is the most prominent multimedia application. It provides online clients with the video data of streaming level by guaranteeing the Quality of Service (QoS) metric [1].

In contrary to traditional file servers, VOD servers are subject to real-time constraints while storing, retrieving and delivering the movie data into the network. Since the ceasing and jittering streaming videos are unmeaningful for VOD clients, the streaming media should be supplied within the QoS metric to each client. To support the QoS, servers must be able to continuously deliver video data at a constant interval to VOD clients. And also, even in the failure of server components, the streaming service should be re-continued within the human acceptable Mean Time To Repair (MTTR) value [2,3].

A cluster server architecture has been exploited in the areas of Internet Web, database, game and VOD server [4]. It has an advantage of the ratio of performance to cost and is easily extended from the general PC equipment. The cluster server architecture usually consists of a front-end node and multiple backend nodes. Since the video data are distributed into several backend nodes, the performance scalability including the storage devices could be achieved accordingly as the number of backend nodes increased. However, even if the cluster server can be scaled by just adding new backend nodes, the probability of the failure of nodes also increases in proportion to the number of backend nodes.

The fault of nodes causes not only the stop of all streaming service but also the loss of the position information of current playing movies. Since the VOD server has to guarantee QoS streams to all clients even in the failure of nodes, the recover mechanisms are necessary for dealing with a realistic VOD service. In this paper, the recovery mechanisms in cluster-based VOD servers are studied to support QoS streams while a backend node is in failure state.

To study the failure events during the actual VOD service, we implement the cluster-based VOD server composed of general PCs and adopts parallel processing for MPEG media to support large scale clients. From the implemented VOD server, it is evaluated that a basic recovery system is composed of the advantages of RAID-3 and RAID-4 algorithms. From experiments, it is found that the basic recovery system causes the performance bottleneck on the input network of the recovery node that consume a few computing resource of CPU. To solve these issues, the new failure recovery system based on pipeline computing is proposed over all survived backend nodes. The proposed system distributes the network traffics across all backend nodes. All survived backend nodes are participated in the recovery operations so that the proposed method provides the improved performance of cluster-based VOD servers as well as the unceasing streaming service even in the failure state of a backend node.

The rest of this paper is organized as follows. Sect. 2 explains the implemented cluster-based VOD server and the management of video blocks in the cluster architecture. Sect. 3 suggests the basic recovery system mixed the advantages of RAID-3 and RAID-4 levels and a new recovery mechanism based on pipeline computing to utilize the resources of backend nodes. In Sect. 4, performances of two recovery systems are measured and discussed. Sect. 5 concludes the paper.

2 Implemented Cluster-Based VOD Server

For large scale VOD services, we implement a cluster-based VOD server called as Video On Demand on Clustering Architecture (VODCA). The VODCA consists of a front-end node named as Head-end Server (HS) and several backend nodes known as Media Management Server (MMS). Throughout the internal network path between a HS node and MMS nodes, they exchange the working states and internal commands each other. The HS node not only receives clients' requests but also manages MMS nodes to support QoS. When new MPEG movies are enrolled, they are split by HS and distributed into each MMS node. To perform these administrative functions, the HS consists of striping module, monitoring module, service-control module and main-daemon module. The MMS nodes transmit their stored movie fragments to clients under the supervision of the HS node. Each MMS node sends the current working status to the HS node periodically. This message operates as a heartbeat protocol between MMS nodes and the HS node. Each MMS node consists of media_management module, media_service module, resource_management module and main_daemon module.

To apply parallel processing for MPEG movies, movie files are striped according to the defined granularity policy. To exploit MPEG media characteristics in parallel processing, a GOP size is used as a striping unit, since each GOP has approximately equal running time in MPEG streams. The MPEG movies are split into GOPs and distributed into each node with their sequence number and size.

3 Proposed Recovery Systems

From the implemented VOD server of previous section, a video block recovery mechanism is designed on the RAID-3 and the RAID-4 algorithms. However, without considering the architecture of cluster-based VOD server, the application of these basic RAID techniques causes the performance bottleneck of the internal network for recovery. To solve these problems, the new failure recovery mechanism based on the pipeline computing concept is proposed.

3.1 Recovery System on Basic RAID Mechanisms

Fig. 1 shows the architecture of the recovery system based on basic RAID-3 and RAID-4 mechanisms. We denote this recovery model as Recover System based on Basic RAID Mechanisms (RS-BRM). This system is implemented on VODCA sever described in Sect. 2. As shown in Fig. 1, two network paths exist: one is used for connecting between the MMS nodes and the VOD clients, and

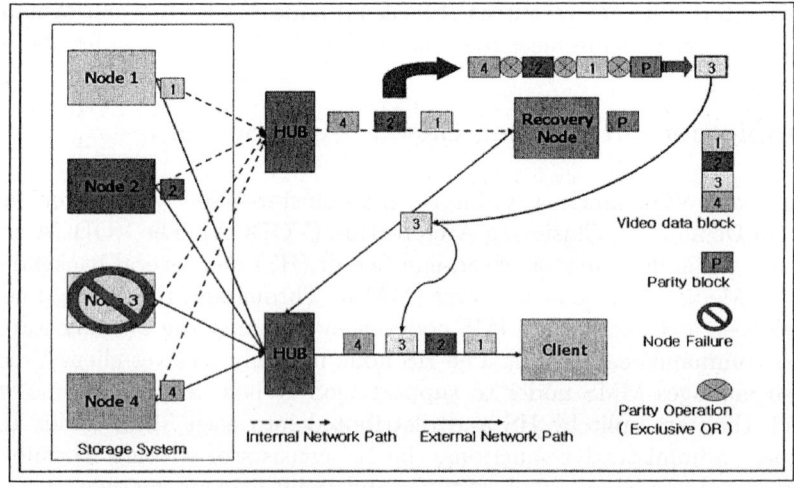

Fig. 1. Architecture and video block flows in RS-BRM

the other is an internal network path installed between all MMS nodes and a recovery node. When a MMS node fails, the video blocks should be transferred to the recovery node. These blocks are transferred on the isolated internal network path. Therefore, the external network path fully focuses on the QoS streams for clients without interference events.

When all MMS nodes are working normally, all MMS nodes transmit their stored video blocks to clients directly through the external network path. On the other hand, when a MMS node fails, the survived MMS nodes send the video blocks to both the clients and the recovery node. Using the video blocks received from the MMS nodes and the parity blocks stored in its own disks, the recovery node regenerates the failed video blocks. Since both MMS nodes and the recovery node use their internal network path for recovery operations, the external network bandwidth can support QoS streams to the VOD clients. For the cluster-based VOD server architecture, we introduce the RAID-4 level to improve the data retrieving performance, and apply the RAID-3 level to the cases of data transferring and recovering operations. Since the RAID-3 level can support smaller stripping units, all video blocks are gradually aggregated in the recovery node so that the abrupt memory shortage could be avoided. By tailoring the advantage of the RAID-3 and RAID-4 mechanisms, this mixed approach improves the performance of recovery system by utilizing the characteristics of individual hardware components. For example, as shown in Fig. 1, when the MMS 3 node fails, the recovery node regenerates the video block 3 by calculating the exclusive OR operation with the received video blocks 1, 2, 4 and its own parity block. Since the regenerated video block 3 is sent to the corresponding client via the external network path, the streaming media service is unceased even in the failure state.

3.2 Recovery System Based on Pipeline Computing

The performance of RS-BRM suffers from the bottleneck of input network on the recovery node. It has been restricted by the number of MMS nodes. To address this problem, the new recovery system based on the pipeline computing is proposed. It is denoted as Recovery System based on Pipeline Computing Mechanism (RS-PCM). The proposed method distributes the network traffics for recovery operations into all survived MMS nodes and utilizes the available CPU computing capacity of MMS nodes.

The exclusive OR operations for video blocks are a major role of parity based RAID algorithms. To rebuild the video blocks stored in the failure MMS node, sequential several exclusive OR stages are necessary. For each stage, the two blocks are needed to compute exclusive OR operation at a time. Based on this characteristic, the stages are distributed into MMS nodes so that the network saturation in the recovery node is solved. In addition, the CPU computing power of MMS nodes can be utilized without impairing the QoS streams.

Fig. 2 shows the architecture of RS-PCM and the flow of video blocks in the VODCA server. The basic algorithm for data recovery is based on the RAID-4,

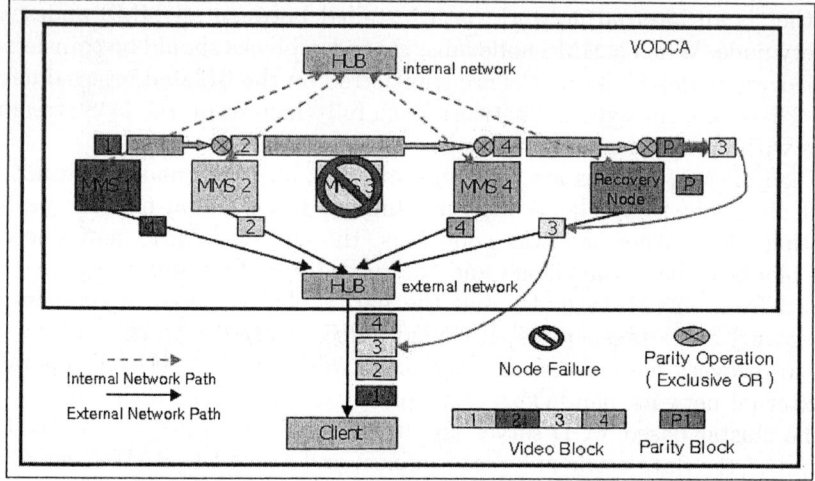

Fig. 2. Architecture and the flow of video blocks in RS-PCM

3 algorithms. As shown in Fig. 2, the RS-PCM distributes the network traffics for recovery processes, and spreads the exclusive OR operations over all MMS nodes.

When a MMS node fails, survived MMS nodes do not send their video blocks to the recovery node directly but transmit the original video block or their own exclusive OR result block to their neighbor MMS node. Each MMS node performs its own fraction of exclusive OR operation with both the video block retrieved from its local disk and the block received from its neighbor MMS node. The blocks received from its neighbor MMS node may be an original video block stored in the disk or the result of exclusive OR operation processed on the neighbor MMS node. The results are sent to the neighbor MMS node successively such as the pipeline process in the instruction level [5].

Finally, the recovery node performs the last exclusive OR operation with its parity block and the aggregate result of all MMS nodes so that the video block of the failure MMS node is rebuilt. After that, the regenerated video block is transmitted to the client through the external network path. For example, as shown in the Fig. 2, when the MMS node 3 fails, the MMS 1 node sends the video block 1 to the MMS 2 node. The MMS 2 node performs the exclusive OR operations with both the video block 1 and the block 2. After that, the result is sent to the MMS 4 node to perform the exclusive OR operation with the video block 4. Finally, after the exclusive OR operations for all survived video blocks are finished, the result is sent to the recovery node. The recovery node regenerates the video block 3 throughout the exclusive OR operation with the parity block.

Fig. 3 shows the recovery operations according to the pipeline concept of the RS-PCM. As a CPU unit executes a step of pipeline to perform an operation in a cycle, each MMS node executes a step of recovery operation using its idle CPU in order to recover a failed movie block in a cycle [5]. This parallel processing for recovering the failed blocks makes a good performance in proposed RS-PCM.

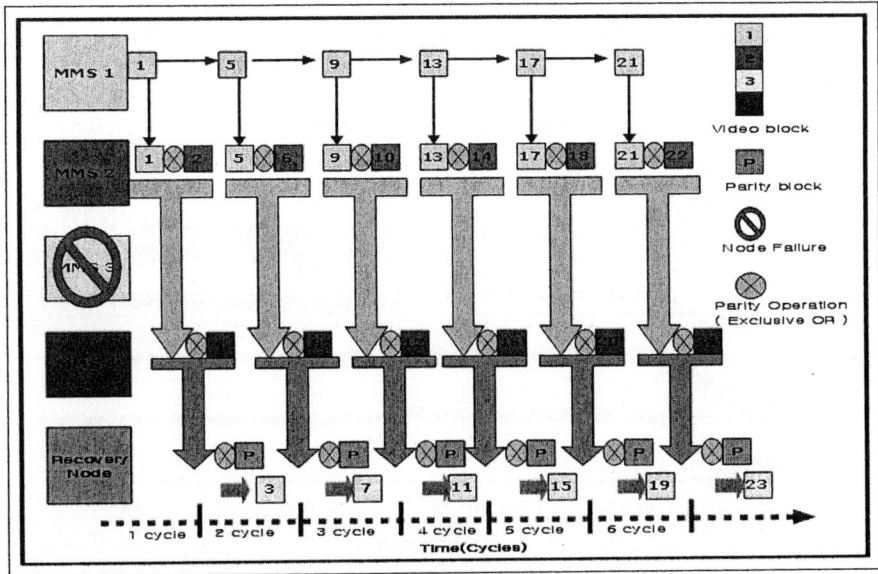

Fig. 3. Recovery steps based on pipeline concept in RS-PCM

As shown in Fig. 3, the failed MMS 3 node has video block 3, 7, 11, 15, 19, 23. These blocks are regenerated in the recovery node every cycle according to the pipeline computing.

4 Performances of Proposed Recovery Systems

The VODCA server for experiments consists of a HS node, 4 MMS nodes and a recovery node. Each node operates on the Linux operating system. The MMS nodes, HS node and clients are connected via a 100 Mbps ethernet switch. All MMS nodes and the recovery node are also connected via the internal network path constructed by a 100 Mbps ethernet switch. The yardstick program is used to measure the performance of the implemented cluster-based VOD server [6]. The yardstick program consists of the virtual load generator and the virtual client daemon. The virtual load generator is located in the HS node and generates client requests based on the Poisson distribution with $\lambda = 0.25$ [7,8]. These requests are sent to each MMS nodes. After that, all MMS nodes concurrently begin streaming media services for satisfying the client's demand.

4.1 Performances of RS-BRM

Fig. 4 shows the amounts of output network traffics transmitted from a MMS node to all clients in the RS-BRM. The results are the averages of the network traffics of each MMS node. As shown in Fig 4, the load generator generates six loads individually. The VODCA server guarantees 1.5 Mbps transmitting rates

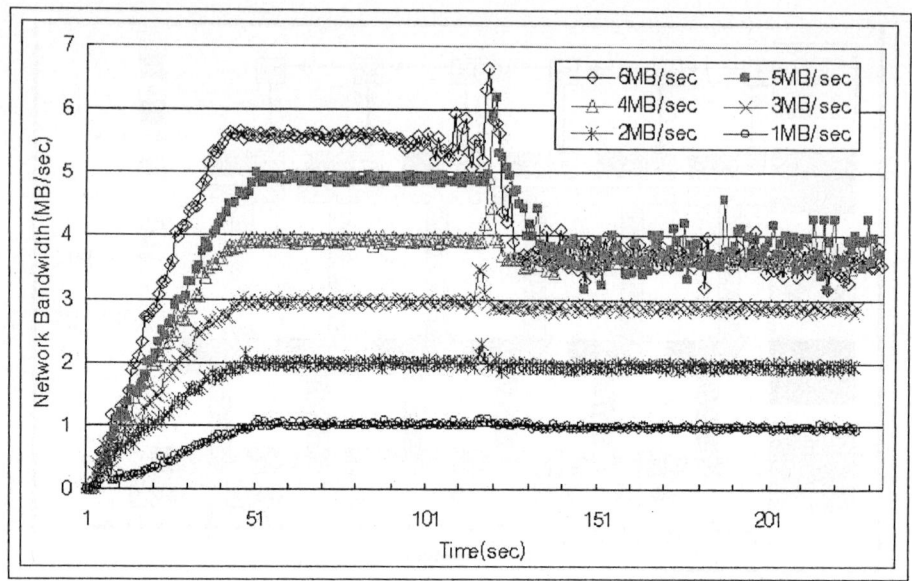

Fig. 4. Output network traffic from a MMS node to all clients

for each QoS stream. The output network traffic of 6 MB/s means that 4 MMS nodes provide 128 clients with QoS stream.

The failure of a MMS node takes place at 120 second of time line. Under the 1 MB/s, 2 MB/s and 3 MB/s traffics, the variations of network traffics are minimal after the failing event. However, in the 6 MB/s, 5 MB/s and 4 MB/s traffics, the fluctuations of network traffics continuously appear in the time line from the 120 second position. In particular, the severely reduced network traffics are incurred in the 6 MB/s and 5 MB/s cases. The reason is that the MMS node can not send the video blocks fully to clients only if the recovery node can not receive more video blocks due to its input network bottleneck. Under the 5MB/s and the 6 MB/s loads, the network traffics from 3 MMS nodes to the recovery node reach to 15 MB/s and 18 MB/s respectively. Since the input network capacity of the recovery node is limited to 12 MB/s, the recovery node suffers from the bottleneck phenomenon of input network path.

From the experiments, we also observe that the CPU usage of MMS nodes is minimal. Since the MMS nodes simply perform the retrieving and transmitting of their own video blocks, the average CPU utilization is measured below 10 %.

Fig. 5 shows the reading times of one GOP in the client side while the streaming service is in progress. Although the failure time of a MMS node is the 120 second of the time line, the fluctuation of reading times in the client side appears in the 156 second of the time line. Since the network delay exists from the VOD server to clients, the time delay takes place due to the buffering mechanism in the client side.

As shown in Fig. 5, when all MMS nodes work normally, the average reading time is about 0.65 seconds and it keeps steady state. However, after a MMS node

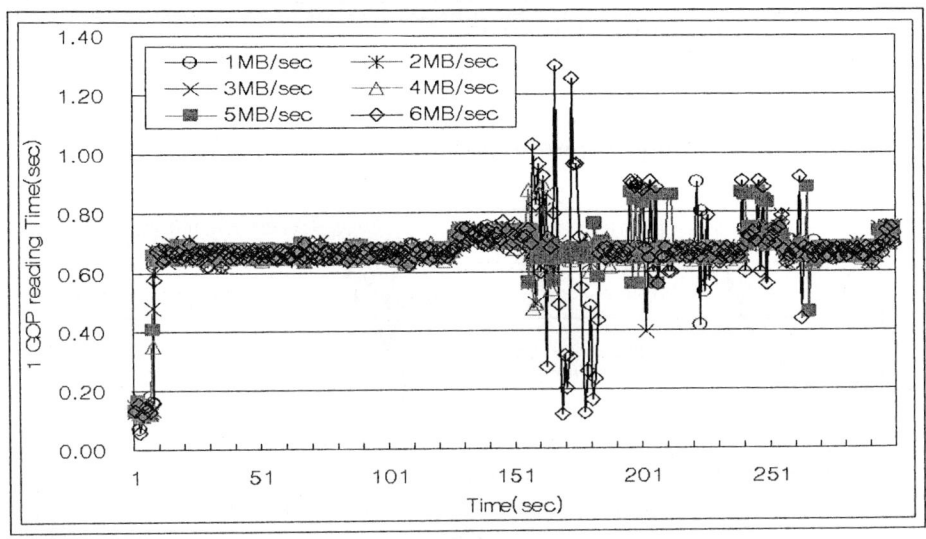

Fig. 5. GOP reading time in the client side under RS-BRM

fails, the reading times vary. These variations are due to the packet data loss, the initial setup time of the recovery node and the data congestion phenomenon of the recovery node. In particular, the fluctuation rates are high at the 5 MB/s and 6 MB/s load. In these work loads, the unsteady state of the reading times comes out between the 156 seconds and the 266 seconds. The difference between the maximum reading time and the minimum reading time is about 1.18 second. After the fluctuation period pass through, the recovery node works normally and the reading times converge into the 0.65 second level again. The MTTR value is 110 seconds [2,3]. It can be regarded as impatient period to VOD clients.

4.2 Performances of RS-PCM

Fig. 6 shows the network traffics in a MMS node and the recovery node when the 12 MB/s network traffic is loaded in the RS-PCM. The failure takes place at the 120 second of the time line. As shown in Fig 6, after the failure occurs, the network traffics from a MMS node to clients decrease from 12 MB/s rates to 9 MB/s rates. The reason is that the video blocks transmitted from the neighbor MMS node occupy the main memory of the MMS node. If many clients are serviced, the video blocks from its neighbor MMS node take a great part of memory. The shortage of memory causes memory swapping overheads. However, the output traffic to clients in a MMS node is over twofold compared with the RS-BRM. In Fig. 4, the RS-BRM shows the maximum 4 MB/s traffics due to the input network bottleneck of the recovery node. In the RS-BRM, even though the 12 MB/s load is generated, the output traffics to clients is 8MB/s rates. This experimental result proves that the RS-PCM provides more clients with the QoS streams than the RS-BSM.

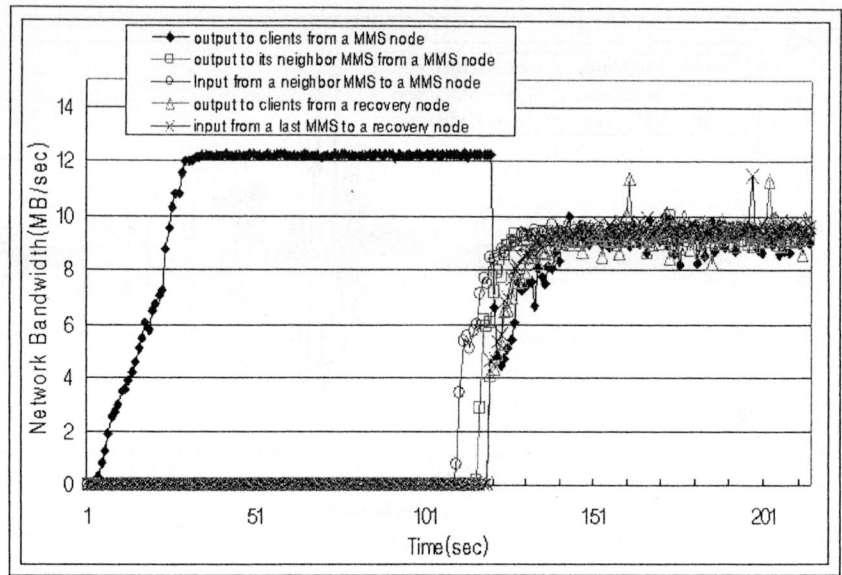

Fig. 6. Network traffic of a MMS node and a recovery node under 12 MB/s load

The square legend mark of this figure represents the amount of output traffic toward the neighbor MMS node. In the RS-PCM, if the current MMS node is not the last MMS node, it transmits its own video blocks or the result blocks of exclusive OR operation to its neighbor MMS. From the circle legend mark, it is found that the amount of input traffics from the neighbor MMS node is almost equal to that of its own output traffics. The amount of input traffics from the last MMS node reaches the 9 MB/s rates so that the recovery node also can rebuild the video blocks as much as 9 MB/s rates. After that, the recovery node transmits them to clients. According to the triangle legend mark of this figure, the output traffics of rebuilt blocks in the recovery node get to the 9 MB/s rates.

When compared with the RS-BRM, the RS-PCM has better performance as much as double streams in the same working environment. The memory swapping problem in the RS-PCM could be simply solved by adding memory units. From additional experiments, after extending the memory capacity, it is confirmed that the output network traffics from a MMS node reached the maximum 12 MB/s. However, even if the amount of memory units increase, the internal network bottleneck of the RS-BRM can not be avoided. Since the RS-PCM utilizes the available CPU resources of MMS nodes and all MMS nodes are participated in the total recovery procedures, it provides the improved performance of cluster-based VOD servers as well as the unceasing streaming services under the failure of a MMS node.

Fig. 7 represents the reading times of one GOP in the client side. The experiments are performed on between the 7 MB/s and 12 MB/s loads. The RS-PCM can support these network traffic loads. The failure of a MMS node takes place in the 120 seconds position. Since there is the network delay between the server

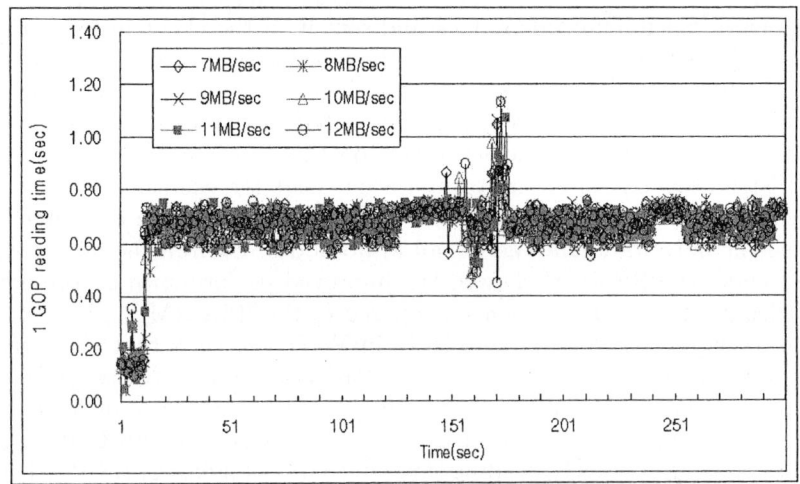

Fig. 7. GOP reading time in the clients side under RS-PCM

and clients, the fluctuations of reading time in the client side begin at the 148 seconds and end at the 176 seconds. After the agitation state, the reading times promptly converge into the steady state with 0.65 seconds levels. The fluctuation period is 28 seconds.

When compared with the RS-BRM, the period of the fluctuation is very short. Since the recovery operations are distributed into all MMS nodes, the recovery node can transmit the rebuilt video blocks in the relatively short time. As shown in the Fig. 5, after a MMS failure happen, the RS-BRM need 110 seconds to return to the steady state. The fluctuation period of RS-PCM is 4 times shorter than the RS-BRM.

Furthermore, as shown in Fig. 7, the difference between the maximum reading time and the minimum time is 0.68 seconds. This result is the half of the difference in the RS-BRM. In the RS-PCM, both the period of fluctuations and the amplitudes of vibration are shorter than those of the RS-BRM. From these results, the RS-PCM results in much better MTTR value than the RS-BRM [2,3].

5 Conclusions

To study the recovery system in the actual VOD service, we implemented the cluster-based VOD servers composed of general PCs and the internal network path. From the implemented VOD server, the RS-BRM was designed with the advantage of RAID-4 in disk retrieving speed and the advantage of RAID-3 in effective memory usage. However, in the RS-BRM, it was found that the input network path of a recovery node was easily saturated with the video blocks transmitted from the survived MMS nodes.

To address these issues, the RS-PCM based on the pipeline computing was proposed over the MMS nodes and a recovery node. In the RS-PCM, the recovery node generated a rebuilt video block and sent it to the client just one time for each cycle. This mechanism is similar to the pipeline process of instructions. The RS-PCM made an efficient use of the available CPU resource of MMS nodes since all survived MMS nodes were participated in the recovery procedures to rebuild the impaired video blocks. Based on this pipeline computing, the RS-PCM distributed not only the computation load for exclusive OR operation but also the network traffics across all MMS nodes. From the experiments, we observed the network traffics across all MMS nodes. Even in the failure state of a MMS node, the RS-PCM showed the improved performance by providing at least twice unceasing QoS streams compared to the RS-BRM.

One of the important characteristics in VOD service is that the streaming media with ceasing, jittering and out of ordered frames are not meaningful. This requirement is deserved even in the partial failure state of VOD server. To satisfy this characteristic, after a failure takes place, the fluctuation period should be short. In the GOP reading times in the client side, the RS-PCM showed the 4 times shorter fluctuation period than the RS-BRM. Due to the relatively short fluctuation period, the streaming media service quickly converged into the normal steady state. As a result, the RS-PCM resulted in much better MTTR value than RS-BSM.

In future work, we plan to evaluate the effectiveness of RS-PCM in the failure of a portion of disks in a MMS node. In that case, since the impaired MMS node can send its heart beat, it is difficult to detect the abnormal MMS node from the point of view of the HS node. And also, there are several issues that the MMS node with the partly failed disks will be participated in the recovery operation. We will investigate the method to detect the partial disk failure from MMS nodes and apply the RS-PCM to the imperfect cluster-based VOD server.

References

1. Dinkar Sitaram, Asit Dan: Multimedia Servers: Applications, Environments, and Design. Morgan Kaufmann Publishers, 2000
2. Armando Fox, David Patterson: Approaches to Recovery Oriented Computing. IEEE Internet Computing, Vol. 9, No. 2, pp.14–16, 2005
3. Dong Tang, Ji Zhu, Roy Andrada: Automatic Generation of Availability Models in RAScard. IEEE International Conference of Dependable Systems and Networks, pp.488–494, June 2002
4. http://www.ieeetfcc.org/
5. David A. Patterson and John L. Hennessy: Computer Organization & Design. Morgan Kaufmann, pp.392–490, 1998
6. Brian K. Schmidt, Monica S. Lam, J. Duane Northcutt: The interactive performance of SLIM: a stateless, thin-client architecture. ACM SOSP'99, pp.31–47, 1999
7. W.C. Feng and M. Lie: Critical Bandwidth Allocation Techniques for Stored Video Delivery Across Best-Effort Networks. 20th International Conference on Distributed Computing Systems, April, pp.201–207, 2000
8. Jung-Min Choi, Seung-Won Lee, Ki-Dong Chung: A Muticast Delivery Scheme for VCR Operations in a Large VOD System. 8th IEEE International Conference on Parallel and Distributed Systems, pp.555–561, June 2001

9. http://www.mpeg.org/
10. T. Chang, S. Shim, and D. Du: The Designs of RAID with XOR Engines on Disks for Mass Storage Systems. IEEE Mass Storage Conference, pp.181–186, March 1998
11. Prashant J. Shenoy, Harrick M. Vin: Failure recovery algorithms for multimedia servers. Multimedia Systems, 8, Springer-Verlag, pp.1–19, 2000
12. Leana Golubchik, Richard R. Muntz, Cheng-Fu Chou, Steven Berson: Design of Fault-Tolerant Large-Scale VOD Servers: With Emphasis on High-Performance and Low-Cost. IEEE Transactions on PARALLEL AND DISTRIBUTED SYSTEMS, Vol.12, No.4, pp.363–386, 2001

Dynamic and Scalable Caching Algorithm of Proxy Server for Multiple Videos[*]

Hyung Rai Oh and Hwangjun Song

Department of Computer Science and Engineering,
Pohang University of Science and Technology (POSTECH),
San 31 Hyoja-dong, Nam-gu, Pohang, Kyungbuk, 790-784, Republic of Korea
{raibest, hwangjun}@postech.ac.kr
http://mcsl.postech.ac.kr

Abstract. This paper presents a dynamic and scalable caching algorithm for proxy servers with a finite storage size. Under a general video traffic condition, it is observed that the amount of decreased client's buffer size and channel bandwidth after caching a video frame depends on the relative frame position in the time axis as well as the frame size. Based on this fact, we proposed an effective scalable caching algorithm to select the cached frames by using the normalized buffer size. The obtained data are saved into the metafile. Now, we study the caching and replacing algorithms for multiple videos that are based on the metafile and effectively reduce both the buffer size and the required bandwidth. Finally, experimental results are provided to show the superior performance of the proposed algorithm.

1 Introduction

In the recent years, the demand of video service over the network has been increasing very fast, and it is feasible due to the fast development of network and digital video processing technologies. Generally, video needs a larger amount of data compared with other media. Thus, it is indispensable to employ the effective video compression algorithm to reduce the amount of data. So far, digital video coding techniques have advanced rapidly. International standards such as MPEG-1, 2 [1] and 4 [2], H.261 [3], H.263/+/++ [4], and H.264 [5] have been established or under development to accommodate different needs by ISO/IEC and ITU-T, respectively. The compressed video data is generally variable-bit-rate due to the generic characteristics of entropy coder, frame type and scene change/inconstant motion change of the underlying video. Generally speaking, the variability of compressed video traffics consists of two components such as short-term variability (or high frequency variability) and long-term variability (or low frequency variability). Buffering is quite effective in reducing losses caused by variability in the high frequency domain while it is not effective for handling variability in the low frequency domain [11]. On the other hand, a

---

[*] This research was supported by the MIC(Ministry of Information and Communication), Korea, under the HNRC-ITRC(Home Network Research Center) support program supervised by the IITA(Institute of Information Technology Assessment).

constant-bit-rate video traffic may be generated by controlling the quantization parameters and it is much easier to handle over the network, but the quality of the decoded video may be seriously degraded. Furthermore, video requires the stringent network quality-of-service (QoS) due to its generic time constrain characteristic for the smooth display. These facts make the problem more challenging. Until now, a large amount of research efforts have been devoted to the networks supporting guaranteed QoS and video coding that is adaptive and robust to network conditions.

Proxy server has been widely employed to reduce the response time delay and improve the network utilization [8, 9]. Proxy server is closely located to clients. When a client wants some data, proxy server intercepts the request message and provides the data if possible. Otherwise it contacts the remote original server, and then saves the received data in storage devices and forwards them to the client. As a result, the response time is significantly reduced in terms of client, the load of server can be reduced, and the network utilization can be improved since the number of duplicated data decreases. Recently, proxy server has been extended to seamless video services over network while Web caching is a dominant application until now. However, it is almost impossible to store all data at the proxy server in the case of video since proxy server generally has a limited storage size. Hence it is very important to determine which parts of data must be stored at proxy server. Caching algorithm handles this problem. Several approaches have been proposed so far. The prefix caching, proposed by Sen et al. [10], is a special form of selective video caching, which involves caching only a group of consecutive frames at the beginning of the video sequence to smooth and reduce the bit-rate of VBR video. Wang et al. proposed a video staging algorithm in [7], which pre-fetches to the proxy a portion of bits from the video frames whose size is larger than a pre-determined cut-off rate, to reduce the bandwidth in the server-proxy channel. Dan and Sitaram proposed a Generalized Interval Caching (GIC) algorithm in [12], which caches short video objects as well as intervals or fractions of large video object. The algorithm orders all intervals in terms of increasing interval size. It allocates cache to as many of the intervals as possible. Hence, the GIC algorithm still maximizes the number of streams served from cache with a larger number video segments and video objects. Yu., et al. proposed QoS-adaptive proxy caching [13], which adapts fairly well to network bandwidth variations and achieves good quality under different network conditions by media-characteristic-weighted replacing algorithm, network-condition-and-media-quality-adaptive resource-management mechanism, pre-fetching scheme and request and send-back scheduling algorithms. Shen, et al. proposed caching strategies in the transcoding-enabled proxy systems [16] that is useful a caching algorithm over heterogeneous network. B. Wang, et al. proposed the proxy-assisted transmission scheme [17] that reduces the initial latency and maximize the utilization of server network bandwidth over multicast for continuous media delivery. And, Miao and Ortega proposed a scalable selective caching [6] that is partial caching strategies specifically designed for streaming video. They proposed Selective Caching for QoS networks (SCQ) and Selective Caching for Best-effort networks (SCB). These algorithms are frame-wise caching schemes in which SCQ algorithm reduces the required maximum buffer size and SCB algorithm prevents underflow at the client.

However, it is observed that the performance of caching algorithm generally depends on the relative frame positions in the time axis as well as the frame size under the general traffic condition. Hence, we consider an effective caching algorithm minimizing the required client's buffer size and the channel bandwidth between the remote original server and client, which is achieved by selecting cached frames minimizing the normalized buffer size defined in the followings, and then the data are stored into a metafile. Now, we propose a dynamic and scalable caching algorithm based on the metafile for multiple video traffics. In the followings, it is assumed that the time delay and the cost between proxy server and client are negligible compared with those between remote server and proxy server, and thus the cached data at the proxy server is almost instantly available for the display at the client. Thus, the client buffers for proxy server can be kept in a very small size. Consequently, the required client's buffer size in the proxy-to-client channel is negligible compared with that in the server-to-client channel. The logical system architecture under the consideration is shown in Figure 1. This paper is organized as follows. Basic definitions are described in Section 2, details of proposed caching and replacing algorithms are presented in Section 3, experimental results are provided in Section 4, and finally concluding remarks are given in Section 5.

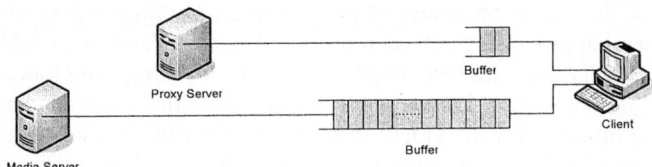

Fig. 1. Logical system architecture under the consideration

2 Basic Definitions

We assume that the number of video contents is V, the j_{th} video consists of N^j frames where $j \in [1, V]$, the size of the i_{th} frame is R_i^j bytes in the j_{th} video, and its temporal sampling rate is T_s^j second (Typical values are 1/25 or 1/30 second.). Hence the total size of the j_{th} video is calculated by

$$R_t^j = \sum_{i=1}^{N^j} R_i^j. \tag{1}$$

And let $\vec{c}^j$ denote the positions of cached frames in the j_{th} video (it is called the cached frame vector in the following), i.e.

$$\vec{c}^j = \left(c_1^j, c_2^j, \cdots, c_{N^j}^j\right), \tag{2}$$

where c_i^j indicates whether the i_{th} frame of the j_{th} video is cached or not, which is defined by

$$c_i^j = \begin{cases} 0 & \text{if the } i_{th} \text{ frame in the } j_{th} \text{ video is not cached} \\ 1 & \text{if the } i_{th} \text{ frame in the } j_{th} \text{ video is cached} \end{cases} \quad (3)$$

Now the following condition must be satisfied when the available storage size of proxy server is M_c.

$$\sum_{j=1}^{V} \vec{c}^j \cdot \left[\vec{R}^j\right]^T \leq M_c, \quad (4)$$

where $\vec{R}^j = (R_1^j, R_2^j, \cdots, R_{N^j}^j)$ and the dot operator is the vector inner product. By the way, some of M_c must be reserved for the instant display before the data from the remote original server arrive, that is, prefix caching is required for at least round trip time between remote original server and client. The required prefix caching size is denoted by M_{prefix}. We also assume that the channel bandwidth is constant-bit-rate BW_{ch}^j for the j_{th} video, and the initial latency of the j_{th} video, the time delay between the display time at client and the time that the transmission begins at the sender, is d, that is, R_i^j is consumed for the display the j_{th} video at time $t = i$. Generally speaking, BW_{ch}^j must be larger than the average rate of the j_{th} video defined by $BW_{avg}^j = R_t^j / N^j \cdot T_s^j$ for the smooth display of the j_{th} video at the client since the compressed video traffic is burst as mentioned earlier. Now, the following equation must be satisfied to avoid the client's buffer underflow to cause the display time delay.

$$BW_{ch}^j \geq BW_{avg}^j. \quad (5)$$

For the simplicity, it is assumed that the client starts to display the first frame of the j_{th} video at $t = 0$ and thus the media server begins transmitting the first packet at $t = -d^j$ since the initial latency is d^j. The cumulative frame rate at time t in the j_{th} video, which means the video data consumption curve at the client at time t, is defined by

$$S^j(t) = \sum_{i=0}^{t} R_i^j. \quad (6)$$

Now, $BW_{ch}^j(\vec{c})$ and $S_{\vec{c}}^j(t)$ indicate the required constant-bit-rate channel bandwidth and the cumulative frame rate at time t in the j_{th} video when the cached frame vector is $\vec{c}^j$, respectively. Thus, $S_{\vec{c}^j}^j(t)$ is defined by

$$S_{\vec{c}^j}^j(t) = \sum_{i=0}^{t} (1 - c_i^j) \cdot R_i^j. \quad (7)$$

And, the slope function of the video j is defined by

$$L_{\bar{c}^j}^j(t) = S_{\bar{c}^j}^j(t) \Big/ t . \tag{8}$$

Since the client retrieves the cached frames from the proxy server at the time when those frames need to be displayed and it is assumed that the time delay is very short between the proxy server and the client, the condition for the smooth display at client can be described as follows.

$$\sum_{i=-d}^{t} BW^j(i) \geq S_{\bar{c}^j}^j(t), \text{ for all } t \in [1, N^j], \tag{9}$$

where $BW^j(i)$ is the channel bandwidth at i^{th} frame's time in the j_{th} video. Actually, $S_{\bar{c}^j}^j(t)$ is thought of as the video data consumption curve at the client when the cached frame vector is $\vec{c}^j$ while $\sum_{i=-d}^{t} BW^j(i)$ is the data supply curve from the server-to-client channel. Under the constant bit rate (CBR) channel whose bandwidth is BW_{ch}^j, $\sum_{i=-d}^{t} BW^j(i)$ is simply calculated by $BW_{ch}^j \cdot (t+d)$. To avoid client's buffer underflow for display the j_{th} video, the following condition must be satisfied.

$$BW_{ch}^j(\vec{c}) = \max_{1 \leq t \leq N^j} \{L_{\bar{c}^j}^j(t)\}, \quad t \in [1, N^j] \tag{10}$$

since $BW_{ch}^j(\vec{c}) \geq L_{\bar{c}}^j(t)$, $t \in [1, N^j]$ must be satisfied. And, the time that the peak bandwidth is required in the j_{th} video is defined by

$$t_{peak}^j = \arg \max_{1 \leq t \leq N^j} \{L_{\bar{c}^j}^j(t)\} \tag{11}$$

The time that the maximum buffer size is needed in the j_{th} video is defined by

$$t_{max}^j = \arg \max_{1 \leq t \leq N^j} \left\{ \sum_{i=-d}^{t} BW^j(i) - S_{\bar{c}^j}^j(t) \right\} \tag{12}$$

3 Proposed Caching Algorithm

In this scenario, we assume that server-to-proxy channel provides guaranteed constant bandwidth service, but the higher bandwidth service is provided at the higher cost. On the other hand, proxy-to-client channel is fast and reliable at the even lower and fixed price. Now, we address how to determine the cached frame vector $\vec{c}^j$, $j = 1, 2, \cdots, V$ minimizing the required client's buffer size $B^j(\vec{c}^j)$ and the channel bandwidth $BW_{ch}^j(\vec{c}^j)$.

Problem Formulation: Determine $\vec{c}^j$, $j = 1, 2, \cdots, V$ to minimize the required client's buffer size and the peak bandwidth subject to $\sum_{j=1}^{V} \vec{c}_{prefix}^{j} \cdot \left[\vec{R}^{j}\right]^{T} \leq M_c - M_{prefix}$, (13)

$$d \leq d_{max},$$

where $\vec{c}_{prefix}^{j}$ is the indicator vector with 1 at the positions of prefix cached frames and d_{max} is the tolerable maximum initial latency. In our previous work [14], we proposed a scalable proxy caching algorithm for only a video traffic to minimize the required buffer size and the required bandwidth at the client. The proposed caching algorithm is summarized as follows (see [14] for the details).

Rule 1: Cache the frame maximizing $B_{norm}^{j}\left(\vec{c}_{aft}^{j}\right)$ for $1 \leq i \leq t_{peak}^{j}$.

Rule 2: When several frames have the same normalized buffer size, cache the frame minimizing $BW_{ch}^{j}\left(\vec{c}_{aft}^{j}\right) - L_{\vec{c}_{aft}^{j}}^{j}(t)$.

Now, we assume that $\vec{c}^{j}, j = 1, 2, \cdots, V$ are found and saved into metafile as shown in Table 1.

Table 1. An example of metafile

Caching Order i	Frame number $O_j(i)$	Required Bandwidth	Required Buffer Size	Frame Rate
1	0(no caching)	10000	7500000	0
2	1	990	7490000	30000
3	2	980	7480000	3000
4	3	970	7470000	3000
5	4	960	7460000	7000
6	876	955	7450000	3000
7	745	950	7440000	30000
8	1023	945	7430000	27000
9	1932	940	7420000	34000
10	534	935	7410000	10000

3.1 Metafile-Based Dynamic and Scalable Caching Algorithm for Multiple Videos

Based on the above metafile, we propose a dynamic and scalable caching algorithm for multiple videos in this section. It is assumed that request is arrived according to a Poisson distribution with an expected inter-arrival time of $1/\lambda$, where λ is request rate. And, video selection follows Zipf-like distribution. Now, the probability of choosing the j_{th} video is calculated by

$$p^{j} = \frac{f^{j}}{\sum_{k=1}^{V} f^{k}}, j = 1, \ldots, V,$$ (14)

where $f^j = 1/j^{1-\theta}$. Here, θ is a parameter to specify the skew factor (θ is typically set to 0.271, which closely matches the popularities generally observed by video store rentals [15]). The request rate for the j_{th} video is calculated by

$$\lambda^j = p^j \lambda. \qquad (15)$$

In the real system, λ^j is estimated by

$$\hat{\lambda}^j = AC^j / T, \qquad (16)$$

where AC^j is the number of request in the j_{th} video during the time interval T. Now, total reduction cost is calculated by

$$\sum_{j=1}^{V} \lambda^j \left(\alpha \cdot \left(BW_{ch}^j(0) - BW_{ch}^j(\vec{c}^j) \right) + (1-\alpha) \cdot \left(B^j(0) - B^j(\vec{c}^j) \right) \right), \qquad (17)$$

where α is the weighting factor between the required bandwidth and the required buffer size.

Now, dynamic caching algorithm for multiple videos is formulated as finding all $\vec{c}^j$ that maximizes the total reduction cost, and thus it looks like the knapsack problem. To solve the knapsack problem, Greed algorithm and Dynamic Programming can be employed. However, the former may provide only a local minimum with a low computational complexity and the latter give the optimal solution with a huge computational complexity. In this work, we propose a dynamic caching algorithm that provides a solution close to the globally optimal solution with a relatively low computational complexity. Now, the beneficial value is defined by

$$\mu^j = \gamma_{O_j(i)}^j / R_{O_j(i)}^j, \qquad (18)$$

$$\gamma_{O_j(i)}^j = \alpha \cdot \lambda^j \cdot \left(BW^j \left(O_j(i-1) \right) - BW^j \left(O_j(i) \right) \right)$$
$$+ (1-\alpha) \cdot \lambda^j \cdot \left(B^j \left(O_j(i-1) \right) - B^j \left(O_j(i) \right) \right),$$

where, $O_j(i)$ is the frame number of the i_{th} cached frame in the j_{th} video. Now, the pseudo code of the proposed dynamic caching algorithm is summarized in the followings.

Dynamic Caching Algorithm

```
The proxy server must cache the first some frames for
initial latency in every videos.
cached size = M_prefix ;
I_j = the number of the prefix-cached frames in the j_th
video, m_j = I_j , j∈[1,V];
while {
    find k = arg max {μ_j^max} ;
              1≤j≤V
```

```
        if (cached size + R_{m_k}^{k} > M_c) break;
        cache m_k th frame of the k_{th} video;
        cached size += R_{m_k}^{k};  m_k = m_k + 1;
}
```

Window Size

```
    if (m_j + W + 1 > N^j)    W = N^j - m_j - 1;
```

where μ_j^{max} is denoted by $\sum_{i=m_j+1}^{m_j+W+1} \gamma_{O_j(i)}^j / \sum_{i=m_j+1}^{m_j+W+1} R_{O_j(i)}^j$.

3.2 Replacing Algorithm

In this section, we propose the replacing algorithm when a user access pattern is changed or a new request is arrived. It is assumed that the proxy server executes the replacing algorithm periodically every T_r. The proposed replacing algorithm can significantly reduce the computational complexity without the performance degradation compared with the re-caching if T_r is well determined considering the user access pattern changing rate. The pseudo code of the replacing algorithm is presented in the followings

Replacing Algorithm

```
    while {
        k = arg max_j {μ_j^max},  j ∈ [1,V | p_j^bef < p_j^aft];
        cached size += R_{m_k+1}^{k};
        while (cached size > M_c) {
            l = arg min_j {μ_j^min},  j ∈ [1,V | p_j^bef > p_j^aft];
            if (μ_k^max > μ_l^min) {
                remove R_{m_l}^{l};  m^l --;  cache R_{m_k+1}^{k};  m^k ++;
            }
            else {
                cached size -= R_{m_k+1}^{k};
                END;
            }
        }
        cache R_{m_k}^{k};  m^k ++;
    }
```

Window Size

```
    if (m_j + W + 1 > N^j)    W = N^j - m_j - 1;
    if (m_j - W < I_j)        W = m_j - I_j;
```

where, μ_j^{min} is denoted by $\sum_{i=m_j-W}^{m_j} \gamma_{O_j(i)}^j / \sum_{i=m_j-W}^{m_j} R_{O_j(i)}^j$, p_j^{bef} is the probability of choosing the j_{th} video at the first previous replacing and p_j^{cur} is the probability at the current.

4 Experiment Results

During the experiment, we used 25 videos (titles are given in Table 2) that are encoded by H.263 [4]. The encoding frame rate is 25 frames per a second, and the encoding structure is IBBPBBPBBPBB (i.e. 1 GOP consists of 12 frames). As a result, the average number of frames is 31,465 and the output traffics are variable-bit-rate. During the experiment, the time interval for prefix caching is set to about 334 milliseconds and thus the corresponding prefix caching size (M_{prefix}) is set to the amount of the first ten frames in every video. The proxy server's space (M_c) is set to 60Mbytes for the dynamic caching, the average request number is 100 for a unit time and the weighting factor (α) is set to 0.8.

Table 2. Titles of test H.263 trace files
(http://mcsl.postech.ac.kr/mcsl/dynamic_caching/table2.htm)

Video ID	Trace Files	Video ID	Trace Files
1	Aladdin	14	VIVA
2	ARD News	15	N3 Talk
3	ARD Talk	16	Parking
4	Mr. Bean	17	Robin Hood
5	Boulevard Bio	18	Silence Of The Lambs
6	The Firm	19	Simpsons
7	Die Hard III	20	Alpin Ski
8	From Dusk Till Dawn	21	Soccer
9	Star Trek – First Contact	22	South Park
10	Office Cam	23	Star Wars IV
11	Formula 1	24	Susi und Strolch
12	Futurama	25	Starship Troopers
13	Jurassic Park I		

The experimental results are presented in figure 2, 3, and 4. Figure 2 shows the performance comparison according to window size. It is observed that Greed algorithm shows the worst performance. On the other hand, the proposed algorithm shows a better performance as the window size increases. Compared with Greed algorithm, the total reduction cost is improved by about 300% when the caching ratio is 100%, where the caching ratio is denoted by the cached size/the storage size. The total reduction cost (Eq. 17) curves are almost same when window sizes are 5, 10, and 20 as shown in Figure 2. Figure 3 shows performance comparison with SCQ algorithm according to window size. The proposed algorithm shows a better

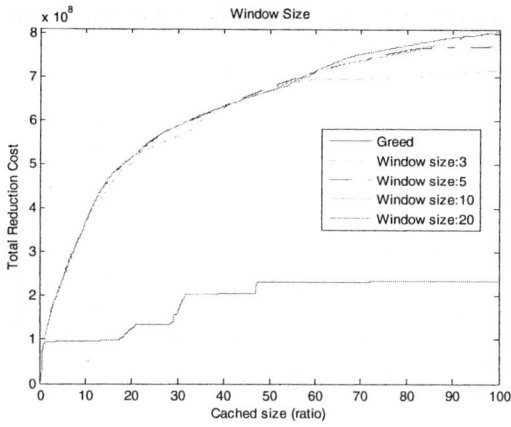

Fig. 2. Performance comparison according to the window size

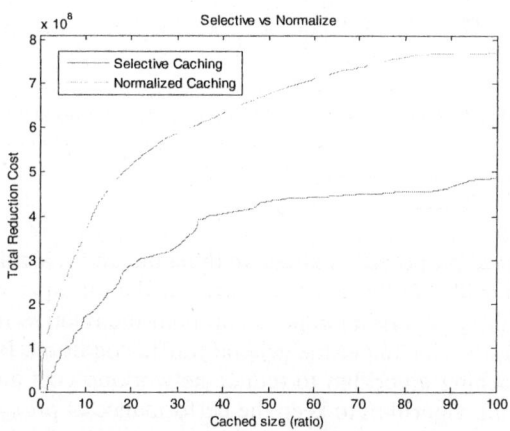

Fig. 3. Performance comparison the selective caching with the proposed caching algorithm when the widow size is 10

performance than SCQ algorithm since it does not consider the general traffic as shown the previous work [14], Actually, the proposed algorithm shows performance improvement by about 80% when the caching ratio is 100% compared with SCQ algorithm.

Figure 4 shows the performances comparison among re-caching algorithm, Greed algorithm, and the proposed replacing algorithm when the request rate is changed. Now, the normalized cost is defined by the total reduction cost/the total cached size. The re-caching means that the proxy server executes the proposed caching algorithm with the new request rate after removing all cached data. As shown in Figure 4, both the re-caching and the proposed replacing algorithm can provide almost same efficiency, but the performance of Greed algorithm seriously deteriorates. By the way, it is empirically observed that the computational complexity of the proposed replacing algorithm is about 10% of that of re-caching although the computational complexity of the proposed replacing algorithm generally depends on the request rates of video contents and video characteristics, etc.

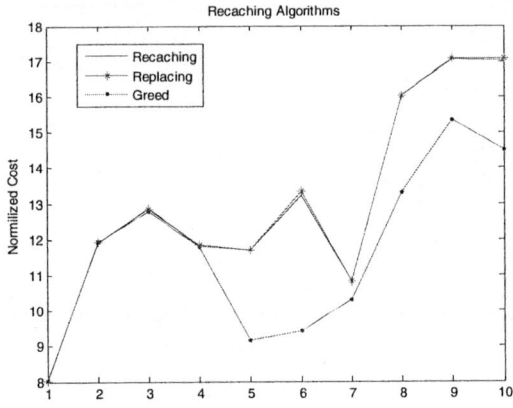

Fig. 4. Performance comparison of replacing algorithms

5 Conclusion

In this paper, we have proposed an effective dynamic and scalable caching algorithm of the proxy server with the finite storage size for the multiple videos. Actually, the performance of caching algorithm depends on both the relative frame position in the time axis and the frame size under the general traffic condition. Based on the fact, we have proposed a caching algorithm to reduce networking cost and the load of proxy server and a replacing algorithm to keep the performance of proxy server almost same as re-caching algorithm with a low computational complexity when user access pattern is changed. The proposed algorithms have shown a superior performance during the whole experiment.

References

1. ISO/IEC 13818 (MPEG-2): Generic coding of moving pictures and associated audio information, Nov. 1994.
2. ISO/IEC JTC1/SC29/WG11, "Overview of the MPEG-4 standard," ISO/IEC JTC1/SC29/WG11 N4030, March 2001.
3. ITU-T Recommendation H.261: Video codec audiovisual service at p*64kbps, March 1993.
4. ITU-T Recommendation H.263 version 2, "Video coding for low bitrate communication," Jan. 1998.

5. Joint Video Team of ISO/IEC MPEG and ITU-T VCEG, JVT-G050, "Draft ITU-T recommendation and final draft international standard of joint video specification (ITU-T Rec. H.264/ISO/IEC 14 496-10 AVC)," 2003.
6. Z. Miao and A. Ortega, "Scalable proxy caching of video under storage constraints," IEEE Journal of Selected Areas in Communications, Vol. 20, No. 7, pp. 1315-1327, Sept. 2002.
7. Z. Zhang, Y. Wang, and D. H. C. Du, "Video staging: A proxy-server-based approach to end-to-end video delivery over wide-area networks," IEEE/ACM Tran. on Networking, Vol. 8, No. 4, pp. 429-442, August 2000.
8. L. Rizzo and L. Vicisano, "Replacing policies for a proxy cache," IEEE/ACM Tran. on Networking, Vol. 8, No. 4, pp. 158-170, April 2000.
9. J. Shim, P. Scheuermann, and R. Vingralek, "Proxy cache algorithms: design, implementation, and performance," IEEE Trans. on Knowledge and Data Engineering, Vol. 11, No. 4, pp. 549-562, Jan. 1999.
10. S. Sen, J. Rexford, and D. Towsley, "Proxy prefix caching for multimedia streams," in Proc. IEEE Infocom. 99, New York, USA, March 1999.
11. Z. Zhang, J. Kurose, J. Salehi and D. Towsley, "Traffic smoothing, statistical multiplexing and call admission control for stored video," IEEE Journal on Selected Areas in Communication, Vol. 15, No. 6, pp. 1148-66, Aug. 1997.
12. A. Dan, and D. Sitaram, "A Generalized Interval Caching Algorithm for Mixed Interactive and Long Video Workloads," Proceedings of SPIE Vol. 2667, page 344-351, Jan. 1996.
13. F. Yu., Q. Zhang., W. Zhu, "QoS-Adaptive Proxy Caching for Multimedia Streaming Over the internet," IEEE Trans. on Circuits and Systems for Video Technology, Vol. 13, No. 3, pages 257 – 269, March 2003
14. Hyung Rai Oh, Hwangjun Song. "Scalable proxy caching algorithm minimizing client's buffer size and channel bandwidth," Accepted for the publication in Journal of Visual Communication and Image Representation, Feb. 2005
15. Aggarwal, C.C., Wolf, J.L., Yu., P.S. "On optimal batching policies for video-on-demand storage server," in Proc. IEEE ICMS, June 1996.
16. Bo Shen, Sung-Ju Lee, Sujoy Basu. "Caching Strategies in Transcoding-Enabled Proxy System for Streaming Media Distribution Network," IEEE Trans. on Multimedia, Vol. 6, No. 2, April 2004.
17. B. Wang, S. Sen, et al, "Optimal Proxy Cache Allocation for Efficient Streaming Media Distribution", IEEE Trans. on Multimedia, Vol. 6, No. 2, April 2004.
18. Video Traces Research Group, http://trace.eas.asu.edu/

Dynamic Adaptive Architecture for Self-adaptation in VideoConferencing System

Chulho Jung, Sanghee Lee, and Eunseok Lee

School of Information and Communication Engineering,
Sungkyunkwan University, 300 Chunchun Jangahn Suwon,
400-746, Korea
{jesus98, neomine}@selab.skku.ac.kr,
eslee@ece.skku.ac.kr

Abstract. Internet-based videoconferencing systems have many variable factors, such as changes in the system operating environment or operating status of the hardware, according to the operator using the system. In this paper, we propose the Self-Adaptive Videoconferencing System, with multi-agents, for efficient videoconferencing, which is able to adapt itself to these various factors. Also, we propose a dynamic adaptive architecture, where the device changes its adaptation architecture according to the circumstance. To this end, we propose an Architecture Manager, which is able to perform this architectural adaptation.

1 Introduction

These days, software is becoming ever more complicated, with the requirement of new technology for the adaptation to different network systems and operating environments. Internet videoconferencing systems are no exception to this rule, and need various structures and languages for their interoperation with various network systems and operating environments, which have resulted in the development of many new technologies [1], such as Self-Adaptive software. The Self-Adaptive software [1] uses technology that is able to understand, monitor and correct changes by program itself; therefore, it should already have data relating to the program needs, the know how to enable evaluation of these data and to the ability to respond to any changes. Hence, an execution code for Self-Adaptive software needs to have the following two elements:

First, Self-Adaptive software has to include a statement of its aim and software structure.

Second, Self-Adaptive software should have a selective algorithm or implementation.

This Self-Adaptive software technology helps clients adapt to the videoconferencing environment. For this reason, Self-Adaptive software research has been applied to many Videoconferencing Systems. [2][6]

In this paper, we propose a videoconferencing system in which the clients are able to adapt to the operator's processing capability and network bandwidth. Also, our system includes specific functions that allow it to adapt to various network situations, operating systems (O.S.'s) and devices. Moreover, the system helps a client communicates with the other clients with a different operating platform. However, it is difficult for a mobile device to adapt itself to the videoconferencing environment, as the adaptation mechanism is optimized for a Desktop PC. Thus, we have designed dynamic adaptive architecture that changes the adaptation architecture of the devices according to the circumstances. For this, we have designed and implemented a system with an Architecture Manager, which decides and manages the client's architecture according to the particular environment.

Section 2 contains a summary of related works, in section 3 we describe the proposed system and section 4 discusses the implementation and evaluation of such software. Section 5 is a presentation of our conclusions.

2 Related Works

2.1 Dynamic Software Architecture

2.1.1 C2 – A Component- and Message-Based Architectural Style for GUI Software. [7]

C2, which was developed at UCI(University of California - Irvine), is an architecture used to support application software development, which uses a component and message based format. A C2 system is composed of a hierarchy of concurrent components interlinked by connectors – message-routing devices – such that each component within the hierarchy can only be aware of those components "above", and completely unaware of components residing at the same level or "beneath". [7] During runtime, C2 can add, delete or rearrange components, and has been optimized for flexible components.

2.1.2 Weave – Using Weaves for Software Construction and Analysis. [8]

Weaves, made by The Aerospace Corporation, are networks of concurrently executing tool fragments that communicate by passing objects, and have a dynamic, object-flow-centric architecture, designed for applications that are characterized by continuous or intermittent voluminous data flows and real-time deadlines.

Weaves embrace a set of architectural principles, known as the laws of blind communication: [8]

- No component in a network is able to recognize the sources of its input objects or the destinations of its output objects;
- No network component is able to recognize the semantics of the connectors that delivered its input objects or transmitted its output objects; and
- No network component is able to recognize the loss of a connection.

Weaves support component manipulation of a like form, emphasize the dynamic distribution, modification and rearrangement of connectors, and has been optimized for flexible connectors.

2.2 Video Conferencing System

2.2.1 JQOS – A QoS-Based Internet Videoconferencing System. [2]

The JQOS system was developed at MCR Laboratory, Ottawa Univ. Canada, an is based on QoS; therefore, a QoS adaptation function is included in the Video Conferencing System

It's functions are as follows:

- First, for the End-User, the Active QoS Self-Adaptive function is now based on the network transportation capability.
- Second, for the Receiver, the smart processing of the requirements from the receiver, and the measurement for proper adaptation of the current system QoS.
- Third, for the Receiver, an expression function of the receiver's interests relating to the transporting stream is required for the QoS adaptation.

The JQOS system limits the Self-Adaptive element to stream the quality of the user, as mentioned above. This system also uses RTPR (Real-time Transport Protocol Report) as a control method, from the RTP (Real-time Transport Protocol) of JMF[4], so the Self-Adaptive function in the JQOS system is only weak.

3 The Proposed System

3.1 Architecture-Based Adaptation

Our self-adaptive videoconferencing system is an "Architecture based approach to Self-Adaptive software"[3], but with the "Enact Change" step slightly revised [3].

The architecture-based approach [3], which mentions the **Enact Change** step, utilizes two tools:

- The *Architecture Editor*, which is used to construct the architectures and describe the modifications
- The *Modification Interpreter*, which acts as a second, companion tool, and is used to interpret the change scripts, written in change-description language, used to describe the primitive actions supported by the AEM (Architecture Evolution Manager)

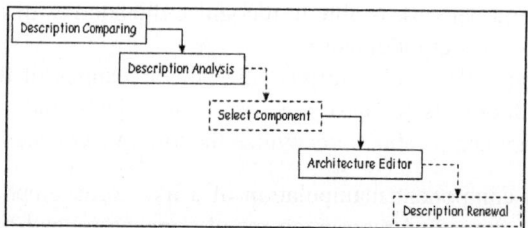

Fig. 1. Description of the "Enact Change"

We reconfigured the "Enact Change" step by adjusting the above tools.

- *Comparing Descriptions*: This can compare the description of the changes with that of the default architecture
- *Description Analysis*: This can interpret and analyze the description
- *Select Component (Optional)*: If a new description has to be used, then the Select Component Step is executed, which selects and rearranges the appropriate components
- *Architecture Editor*: The components rebuilding step. We uses FRACTAL [5] to rebuild the components
- *Description Renewal*: When the new description is used, the default description is renewed

Fig.2. shows the self-adaptive software process, which has been adapted using the above steps. The dark area was modified by us.

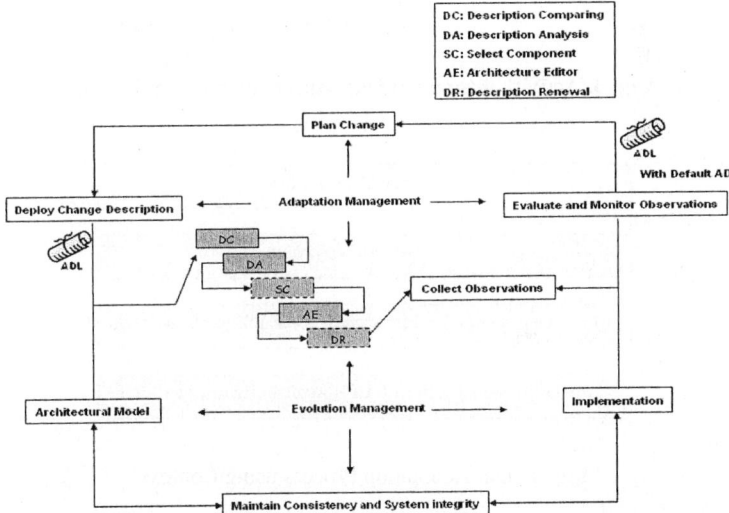

Fig. 2. The Self-Adaptive Software process, which has an adapted revised "Enact Change" step

In this paper, our proposed system is reflected in the above self-adaptive software process.

Also, we developed the Videoconferencing system, which is operated by activity, as follows in Fig.3:

Our adaptation process is shown in Fig.4.

For the adaptation to a dynamic environment, all environment information, such as the system components and theirs interactive environmental information, and the available resources and operating environments, are captured and modeled with respect to several multi-aspects. The term "multi-aspect" refers to four main aspects - an architectural aspect, a behavioral aspect, a resource aspect and an environment aspect. Each aspect is defined as follow:

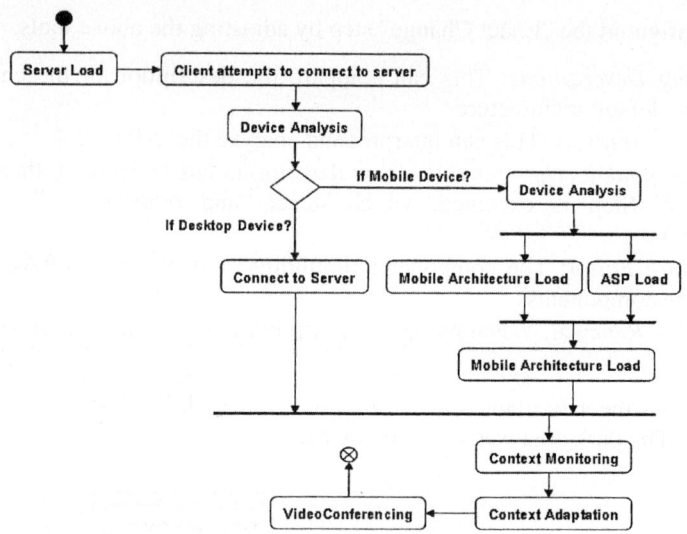

Fig. 3. Activity diagram of Our Videoconferencing System

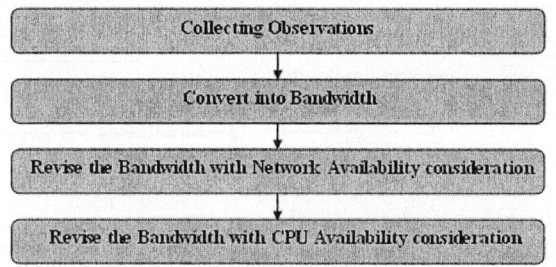

Fig. 4. Out Adaptation Process using Context

The architectural aspect is used to describe configurative entities, such as the software architecture, its configurative elements, each element's operation or role, and the relationship of each element. Each element is represented by a node, referred to as a "Component", with the relationship of each component represented by arcs, which are referred to as 'connectors'. The behavioral aspect defines the 'Interactive' operation end events between components. The resource aspect defines the general system environmental entities that execute the necessary videoconferencing system. The target of a system for modeling the resource aspect is classified into two categories, the static and dynamic contexts. The static contexts are elements that have less dynamic changing characteristics, such as the type of user device, OS, executing software and Player information. The dynamic contexts are dynamic changeable elements, such as the current CPU and memory usage, state of camera and audio devices, network bandwidth and user preference. The Environment aspect defines the external environmental element that is mutually applied or affected by the surroundings of the videoconferencing system.

These four aspects of modeling are graphically and texturally represented using the GME (Generic Modeling Environment) Tool. To adapt for executing system, Modeled elements must be transmitted to be realized by software, so we applied CC/PP technology to recognize system.

3.2 Overall Architecture

Our general approach for supporting the Dynamic Adaptation Architecture consists of several parts: the *Server, Client, Mobile-Client and Adaptation Proxy Server*. Fig.5. show the overall architecture.

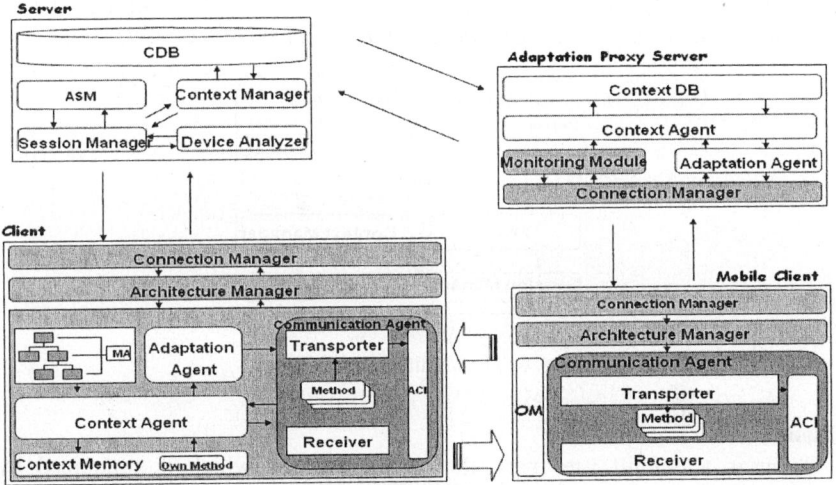

Fig. 5. Overall architecture

The detailed architecture and algorithm of each part can be described as follows:

a) Server

The server is a manager, which manages the session, Adaptive Proxy Server and context, and consists of 1) Context DB, 2) Adaptive Proxy Server Manager (APSM), 3) Session Manager, 4) Context Manager and 5) Device Analyzer.

The Context DB is the stored context, by the Context Manager, of the connected client. The APSM manages the Adaptive Proxy Server. The functions of the APSM are as follows: 1) creates new APS; 2) assigns clients to APS; 3) controls client's number per APS; and 4) manages a session of executing APS. The policy of an APS creation mechanism is as follows:

1. If there is no device with enough resource on the network, the APSM does not create an APS.
2. If there are devices with enough resources on the network, the APSM creates an APS.
3. If the number of clients per APS is larger than 15, the APSM creates a new APS. We investigate the relationships between the APS and the clients. '15' is optimized the number of clients per APS. However, if there is only one device with enough resource on the network, the APSM create another APS in this device.

The *Session Manager* manages a client's sessions, sending session information to the others clients and requests allocation of an APS to the APSM. The *Context Manager* manages the context data in the Context DB, and the *Device Analyzer* analyzes the connecting client's device. The functions of the Device Analyzer are as follows: 1) distinguish between client's devices, 2) when the connecting client's device is mobile, the Device Analyzer requests allocation of an APS to the APSM through the Session Manager. Fig.6. show the architecture of the Server.

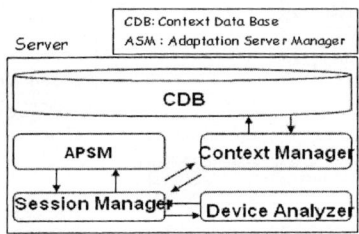

Fig. 6. The architecture of Server

b) Client

The Client is a default user part, the architecture of which is organized by the Architecture Manager. When the client's resource is sufficient, the architecture of Client is structured. In cases where the resource is insufficient, the Adaptive Proxy Server and Mobile Client are used. The main function of the client is videoconferencing. The Client consists of: 1) the Connection Manager, 2) Architecture Manager, 3) Monitoring Agent, 4) Adaptation Agent, 5) Context Agent, 6) Context Memory and 7) Communication Agent.

The Connection Manager is a component that manages the client's connection to the server and sends session information to the server. The Architecture Manager is a component that manages the client's architecture, which is composes of components according to the contexts. If its resources are insufficient for contents adaptation, the Architecture Manager organizes its architecture as that of a Mobile Client's architecture, at which point the Architecture Manager uses a runtime reconfiguration mechanism. Runtime reconfiguration can be performed by altering the connector bindings, as these mediate all component communication. The runtime reconfiguration mechanism has been proposed in many researches [9, 10].

The *Monitoring Agent* gathers the client context. The *Adaptation Agent* decides the method of communication and performs contents adaptation according to information in the Context Memory of other clients. The functions of the Adaptation Agent are as follows: 1) receive the context information of each client from the Monitoring Agent, and 2) determines which communication method is used by the client according to the context information.

The decision of the Adaptation Agent is based on the following policy:

[Monitoring Agent must have only one Parameter each step. (D)(W)(PO)(A) Parameter is Available, (D)(P)(PX)(A) Parameter is disabled.]

Decision Policy

```
If the first Parameter is (P), an application module
for PDA is required. The Default Parameter is (D)

If the second Parameter is not (W), but either (U), (L)
or (S), the Direct Audio Renderer and Capturer must
change. The Default Parameter is (W).

If the second Parameter is (C) or (M), an algorithm
change is needed. The Default Parameter is (M).

If the second Parameter is (S), the environmental
configuration of the client for this Parameter is (W),
change is needed.

If the third Parameter is (PX), a port change algorithm
is executed. The Default Parameter is (PO).

If the forth Parameter is (NA), an algorithm for
synchronizing the vector number with the connect number
is needed. The Default Parameter is (A).
```

The *Context Agent* stores the contexts to the Context Memory and obtains the contexts in the other client's Context Memory through the ACI (Agent Communication Interface). The *Context Memory* stores the client's context and communication methods. The *Communication Agent* communicates with the other clients, and consists of the *Transporter*, *Communication Method* and *Receiver*.

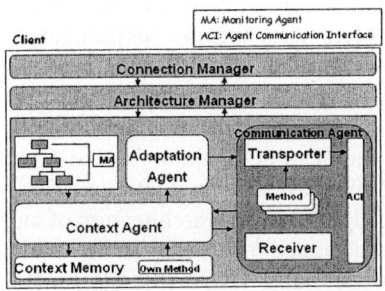

Fig. 7. The architecture of Client

The *Transporter* obtains video and audio information from the system, and communicates this contents to the other clients using the Communication Method. *Communication Method* is a transmission code that is received from the communication target. The *Receiver* receives video and audio information from other clients. Fig.7. show the architecture of the Client.

c) Mobile Client
The Mobile Client is a client with an architecture for mobile users that have insufficient resources for a contents adaptation. The Mobile Client's architecture is decided by the Architecture Manager, which then organizes the Mobile Client's architecture. Fig.8 show the Mobile Client's architecture.

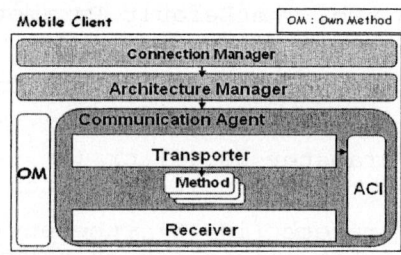

Fig. 8. Architecture of the Mobile Client

A Mobile Client has less functionality then a Client because the contents adaptation function is too heavy for a Mobile Client. Therefore, to support a Mobile Client's contents, adaptation is performed by an Adaptation Proxy Server.

d) Adaptation Proxy Server
The Adaptation Proxy Server is a proxy server, which performs contents adaptation in the place of a Mobile Client, which consists of 1) Context DB, 2) Context Agent, 3) Monitoring Agent, 4) Adaptation Agent and 5) Connection Manager. If a Mobile Client connects to an APS through the Connection Manager, the Monitoring Agent gathers the context and session information of the connected Mobile Client, which are then stored to the Context DB. When a client is connecting to an APS, the Context Agent updates the Context DB in the Server. The Context Agent also obtains each client's Communication Methods using the session information of the Server. The Context Agent also sends the session information, context and Communication Method to the Adaptation Agent. The Adaptation Agent decides the appropriate Communication Method for contents adapted communication. The Adaptation Agent then composes the Communication Method for the Communication Agent of the Mobile Client and the Mobile Client then communicates with each client using this Communication Method. Fig.9. show the architecture of an Adaptation Proxy Server.

In this paper, we have designed a reconfigurable architecture for a Mobile Client using the Fractal [5] libraries and Weave [8]; the Fractal changes the structure of system and reflects the implementation code while the system is in operation, and chooses and rearranges the algorithm component for adapting the system according to the monitored results of the JAVA based Library while a program is working.

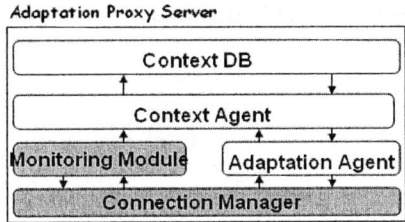

Fig. 9. Architecture of an Adaptation Proxy Server

Weaves, made by The Aerospace Corporation, are networks of concurrently executing tool fragments that communicate by passing objects, and have a dynamic, object-flow-centric architecture designed for applications that are characterized by continuous or intermittent voluminous data floes and real-time deadlines. We have already addressed Weaves [8] in section 2.

4 Implementation and Evaluation

The system proposed in this paper has been implemented based on JAVA SDK in Windows, Linux and Solaris environments. The main code for transmission of the picture information is made using JMF [4], for which the user needs a capturing device to obtain the picture information.

Fig. 10. Screen shot of our system

This system is implemented on a component basis, consisting of adjustable components, where each component is associated with an appropriate algorithm for adaptation to the user's operating environment as well as that of the overall network. This is the basic characteristic of self-adaptive software, which has been implemented using the Fractal [5] library for our proposed system.

Evaluation: According to the location of adaptation, an adaptation system is separated into the client-side, server-side and proxy server-side adaptation systems. [11] First, the client side adaptation system monitors and adapts the environment on its own side [12, 13], which could prevent the exposure of personnel information to the outside, and could also be suitable for performing reconfiguration of a control device configuration or to modify its functionality. Second, the server-side adaptive system monitors each client and performs contents adaptation, involving adaptive modules on their side. [14] Third, the proxy adaptation system has adaptive modules installed, which sets the proxy server between a client and server [15, 16], which can take advantage of being able to adapt, by the addition of the proxy server, without modification to the server or client components. In this paper, the difference between a general videoconferencing system and our proposed system, using the self-adaptive concept, has been evaluated, and the quantitative differences between the use of three adaptation mechanism - Server side, Client side and Proxy Server side adaptation - based approaches and a Dynamic adaptive architecture based approach. In Fig.11, the horizontal axis represents the adaptation time, and the vertical axis the number of clients.

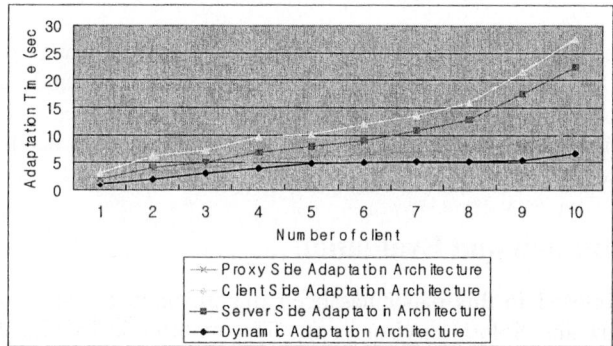

Fig. 11. Comparison of the adaptation and dynamic adaptation architectures when a mobile client is connecting. The use of dynamic adaptation architecture is more effective than those of the three adaptation mechanisms – Server side, Client side and Proxy Server side adaptation.

In Fig.11, the use of the three adaptation mechanisms required more time than that with the Dynamic Adaptive Architecture. Evaluation environment is following.

Server : HP net Server. Os. Windows 2003 Server CPU 3.0G, RAM 1024Mb
Proxy Server : Os. Windows XP Pro, CPU 3.0G G RAM 1024Mb
Client : Os. Windows XP Pro, CPU. 2.4G RAM 512Mb

An almost mobile device has less resources for adaptation; therefore, a mobile device requires a proxy. However, if mobile devices have sufficient resources, they work more efficiently than if the client performs the adaptation themselves. In view of these facts, the use of Dynamic adaptive architecture is more effective. If the number of clients per APS is optimized, our system will spend less time on adaptation.

5 Conclusion

In this paper, an architecture based self-adaptive videoconferencing system, with dynamic adaptive architecture, has been proposed for internet based videoconferencing. The was able to adapt to the user's environment, requests and network surroundings. The proposed system was implemented using JMF and Fractal. These two techniques completely satisfied the requirements of the self-adaptive software structure and have active embodying language according to active changes of the structure. The users of our videoconferencing system are able to utilize a system that is optimized for their environment and network surroundings. Also, this system can operate as a self-configuring and self-healing system, because it is able to cope with new problems by the addition of new components. It also includes monitoring techniques that can deal with problems while the program is running. However, if our system had more optimized client allocating mechanisms, the time required for adaptation could be reduced. Also, our research has not mentioned change management, which is an important issue in runtime software evolution and will be the subject of a future publication.

References

1. R. Laddaga.: Active Software. Lecture Notes in Computer Science, Vol. 1936. Springer-Verlag, Oxford UK(2000)11–26.
2. Wenbiao Zhu, etc. al..: JQOS: a QoS-based Internet videoconferencing system using the Java media framework (JMF). IEEE ECE 2001. Vol. 1, 13-16. Canada (2001)625 - 630
3. Peyman Oreizy, etc. al..: An Architecture-Based Approach to Self-Adaptive Software. IEEE Educational Activities Department, Vol. 14 (1999) 54 - 62
4. Java Media Framework. http://java.sun.com/products/java-media/jmf/index.jsp
5. Pierre-Charles David etc. al.. : Towards a Framework for Self-Adaptive Component-Based Applications. Lecture Notes in Computer Science, Vol. 1936. Springer-Verlag (2003)1-14
6. Sung Doke Lee, etc. al..: Multi-agent based Adaptive QoS Control Mechanism in Flexible videoconferencing System. Advanced Communication Technology 2004. Vol. 2 (2004)745 - 750
7. R.N. Taylor et al..: A Component- and Message-Based Architectural Style for GUI Software. IEEE Trans. Software Eng., Vol. 22, No. 6, (1996)390–406
8. Michael M. Gorlick and Rami R. Razouk. The Aerospace Corporation..: Using Weaves for Software Construction and Analysis
9. Peyman. et al..: Architecture-Based Runtime Software Evolution. ICSE'98 (1998)
10. Quianxian Wang, etc al..: Runtime Software Architecture Based Software Online Evolution. IEEE CIMPSAC'03 (2003)
11. M. Margaritidis, G.C. Polyzos.: Adaptation Techniques for Ubiquitous Internet Multimedia. Wireless Communications and Mobile Computing, Vol.1, No.2, (2001)141-163
12. Brian Noble.: System Support for Mobile, Adaptive Applications. IEEE Personal Communications, Vol.7, No.1 (2000)44-49
13. C.Y. Hsu, A. Ortega, M. Khansari.: Rate control for robust video transmission over burst-error wireless channels. IEEE Journal on. Selected Areas in Communications, Vol.17, No.5, (1999)
14. Friday A., N. Davies, G. Blair and K. Cheverst.: Developing Adaptive Applications: The MOST Experience. Journal of Integrated Computer-Aided Engineering, Vol.6 Num.2, (1999)143-157
15. M. Margaritidis, G.C. Polyzos.: MobiWeb: Enabling Adaptive Continuous Media Applications over 3G Wireless Links. IEEE Personal Communications Magazine, Vol.7, no.6, (2000)36-41
16. IBM WebSphere® Transcoding Publisher, http://www-306.ibm.com/software/pervasive/ transcoding_publisher
17. Gu, X.; Nahrstedt, K.; Messer, A.; Greenberg, I.; Milojicic, D.: Adaptive Offloading for Pervasive Computing. IEEE Pervasive Computing, Vol. 3.(2004)66 - 73

Scalable and Reliable Overlay Multicast Network for Live Media Streaming

Eunyong Park[1], Sunyoung Han[1,*], Sangjoon Ahn[2],
Hyunje Park[2], and Sangchul Shin[3,†]

[1] Dept. of Computer Science and Engineering, Konkuk University,
1 Hwayang-dong, Kwangjin-gu, Seoul, Korea
{eypark, syhan}@cclab.konkuk.ac.kr
[2] Zooinnet, 4F Royal B/D, 1459-12 Seocho 3dong,
Secho-gu, Seoul, Korea
{sjahn, hjpark}@zooin.net
[3] National Computerization Agency, NCA B/D, 77 Mugyodong,
Chung-Gu, Seoul, Korea
ssc@nca.or.kr

Abstract. We have implemented and tested an overlay multicast solution with scalability and reliability that is suitable for a single source live stream distribution such as an IP broadcast service. Our presented solution is independent of a specific streaming server or streaming data and it can distribute multicast data to isolated multicast networks through an unicast tunneling. In order to solve the problems of the peer-to-peer based solutions, we employed dedicated hardware-based solution. We also adopted subnet multicasting to provide scalability so that unlimited number of members could join a multicast group. In the multicast island, the tree depth among the end-users is kept as only one level, which means inherited packet losses can be minimized. To provide reliability, we employ the loosely-coupled TCP connection for unicast-tunneling and FEC (forward error correction) for subnet multicast. We evaluated its performance depending on the bit-rates and PPS (packet per second) of the streams. To verify the efficiency of our solution, we tested it on a real world Internet test-bed and it proved to be more efficient than traditional unicast approaches.

1 Introduction

With the drastic growth of the Internet, convergence of different media into the digital has brought us to an environment where high quality video stream over network is available.[1] An overlay technology, for example, can provide newborn services for the Internet without modifying the existing network infrastructure. Many overlay multicast studies have been introduced [5], [6], [7], [8], [9], [10], [11], [12], [13], [14], and they can be summarized into two categories. One is a peer-to-peer based scheme in which end-users are responsible to distribute multicast data [5]. The other

---

* Corresponding author.
† This work was supported by NCA (National Computerization Agency) of Korea for Project on "Development and Test of Overlay Multicast Transform Device between IPv6 and IPv4".

uses dedicated high-performance hardware servers responsible for distributing multicast data, even though it is still an end-node [7], [13]. Originally, the peer-to-peer technique was developed to share files over the Internet, and has been adapted to the overlay multicast area. In distributing live stream of high bandwidth, however, peer-to-peer technique is not appropriate for some reasons. First, an end-user machine itself might have a very low performance to decode and to play the high quality video stream, which may cause possible missing of packets even though the network bandwidth is enough. Besides, packet losses of a parent will be inherited to all of its child end-users and the children of its children likewise. Since end-users have no obligation to distribute stream data, they can leave and join the group anytime. It makes frequent reconstructions of multicast tree unavoidable. Due to those drawbacks, a dedicated high performance hardware based scheme is necessary for such fields as IP broadcast services.

We employed two types of reliable transmission techniques. When it comes to unicast-tunnels, loosely-coupled TCP connection is used. Loosely-coupled TCP connection is initially introduced by ROMA [14], but our approach is different with it in some ways. ROMA aggregates loosely-coupled TCP connection and FEC algorithm for providing reliable transport but we separate two techniques by its use. We use loosely coupled TCP connections for unicast-tunneling and FEC for subnet multicast.

2 Architectural Model

The drastic growth of the Internet has required network equipments to do more and more functions. With its very high availability, the widely used TCP/IP networks have been stabilized over a long period. In this situation, adding unproved functions to the network can be a very dangerous try and can cost tremendous amount of money. An overlay network technique proposed to solve those problems, however, enables us to use new technologies in the legacy network without any replacement of existing equipments. Up to now, various overlay network applications have been introduced. Among them, CDN (Contents Distribution Network) is the most famous application. It pushes contents to the edges of the network and delivers the contents with massive intelligence and manageability. It employs functions of DNS for end-users to find out the most reachable edge server. Though CDN is widely used, it is suitable only for web contents that do not require real time distribution.

Our implemented platform provides an overlay solution equipped with scalability and reliability for single source live streaming like an IP broadcast service. It can be efficiently done by delivering stream data to end-users through non-multicast networks. And the implementation focuses on the following aspects.

2.1 Components

Manager: A Manager supervises the information of all the deployed Relays and updates its changing conditions immediately. With that updated information, Manager helps clients to locate their nearest Relay. For the same purpose, CDN employs a modification of DNS (Domain Name System), in which a network administrator must create a configuration file manually. In our presented solution, however, a Relay registers its information into the Manager by itself, so the overlay network managers need not to configure the Manager manually, thus zero-configuration could be possible.

To find the nearest Relay, it uses RTT as an evaluation matrix like many other solutions. But, it will take considerable amount of time for an end-user with low performance machine to evaluate all the RTT values. To prevent this kind of problem, we adopted an effective RTT evaluation method whose detail will be introduced at the implementation section.

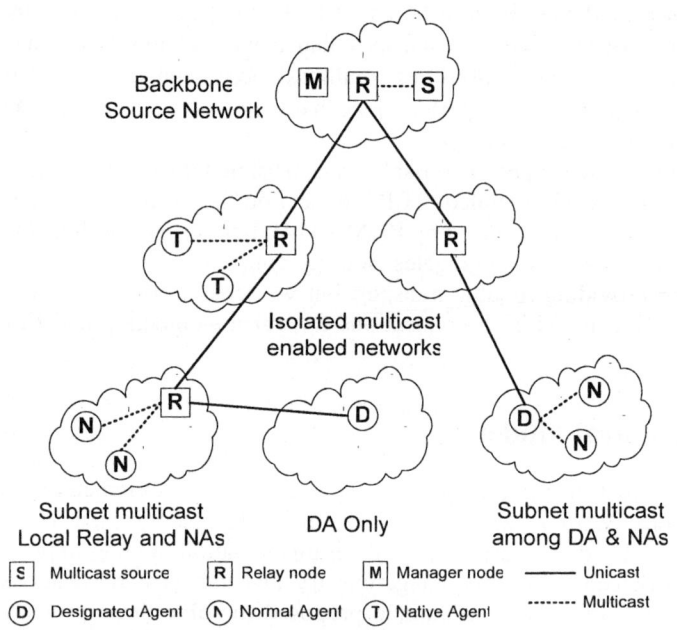

Fig. 1. The architectural model of the suggested overlay multicast network

Relay: A Relay distributes multicast data to its child node through either a unicast tunneling or multicasting depending on the underlying network between parent node and child node. When a Relay receives a connection request from an Agent and it is the first member of the group, it connects to a higher level Relay. In this way, a multicast tree is constructed up to the highest level Relay that receives multicast packets directly from a multicast source or a stream server. When the highest level Relay, also called Root Relay, receives multicast packets from the source, it encapsulates the payload with its overlay multicast header that will be de-capsulated by Agents.

Agent: An Agent is an edge node of the presented overlay multicast network and runs at end-users' machines. It determines the best way to connect to the overlay multicast network and make a connection to a selected node. It also de-capsulates the overlay multicast packets and re-multicasts the original stream to an application like a video stream player at the local host. According to the roles of the Agent, there are 3 types of Agent mode.

- **Source Direct Mode:** In this mode, an end-user node can receive multicast directly from the stream source and Agents do not do any overlay multicasting action because multicast data from source is not modified. The multicast data pass through directly to a stream player.
- **Native Agent Mode:** When a Relay exists in the same multicast island, an Agent enters this mode in which an Agent only plays the role of the unicast tunnel's edge. By advertised multicast packets from a local Relay, an Agent can find where the local Relay is. In this mode, Agents receive data from local Relay through subnet multicasting. In fig. 1, the circled Ts connected to the square Rs are in this mode.
- **Designated Agent Mode:** When an Agent is the only member of the overlay multicast within the multicast domain, it enters DA mode. An Agent of DA mode is responsible for subnet multicasting in the local domain. In fig. 1, the circled Ds are in DA mode.
- **Normal Agent Mode:** If a DA already exists in the local domain, an Agent enters normal Agent (NA) mode. A NA receives data from a DA through subnet multicasting. In fig. 1, the circled N connected to the circled D is a normal Agent.

Fig. 1 depicts the architectural model of our solution. At the top of the overlay network tree, called source network, a multicast source (S), a Manager (M), and a Relay (R) are located. At initial states, there is no connection on the overlay network and no routing information is managed, but the manager only knows the existing Relays location and RTT between Relays and the Manager. The connection is made when the end-user request to join multicast group. After overlay multicast tree is established, the highest level Relay R at the backbone source network receives multicast from source S and send packets to the connected child Relays through TCP connections. If the child Relays have group members in the same multicast island, it send packets via subnet multicast and it also send to the child node in the other multicast island in the same manner of the highest level Relay.

2.2 Features

Our new model has the following features.

- **Scalability:** The influence of concurrent connections on the performance must be minimal. To support scalability, the deployed Relays construct a hierarchical tree structure. And in the multicast enabled network, it uses subnet multicast to distribute data efficiently.[3]
- **Reliability:** A reliable transport scheme must be provided by the overlay network since an IP multicast doesn't support reliable transmission.[2] We employ loosely-coupled TCP connections for reliable transmission between each hop of unicast tunnels. Using TCP, it is possible to use the every functionality of TCP embedded facilities like retransmission and congestion control mechanism. And we also adopted FEC algorithm for subnet multicast areas.
- **High Availability:** Each relay node must be highly available and re-construction of multicast tree should not happen frequently. Our dedicated hardware Relays are very stable compared with the end-users of peer-to-peer-based solutions.

- **Low Latency:** End-to-end delay must be kept small for live streaming. Adopting a high performance hardware-based dedicated server and by minimizing the depth among end-users, this solution supports a high availability and minimizes end-to-end delays.
- **Stream Independency:** An overlay network must be independent of stream server or stream type. Our solution is definitely independent on a stream type and can distribute any kind of stream.

We compare our solution with other overlay solutions that support live stream distribution and reliable transport. Zigzag[5] introduces P2P techniques for single source media streaming. As mentioned above, with P2P-oriented solution, it's impossible to support highly available service. And it doesn't support any reliable transport scheme. Overcast[6] introduces the overlay multicast techniques for single source streaming that employs dedicated service nodes placed at strategic location. The goal of Overcast is to maximize bandwidth to the root for all nodes that leads to "deep" distribution trees. It means that long end-to-end delay is unavoidable. OMNI[7] also deploys a set of service nodes in the network to efficiently implement media-streaming application but it doesn't adopt any reliable transport scheme.

3 Protocols

3.1 Tree Building

If a Relay is not present in the local multicast domain or a statically configured parent Relay is not working properly, child nodes inquire Manager of the nearest Relay information. The information controlled by Manager is collected by static configuration or dynamic registration. Since no static configuration of Manager is required when new Relays are deployed, zero-configuration could be possible and it helps the Manager to easily maintain the overlay multicast network.

Generally, checking the RTT from a client is the most common way of finding the nearest Relay. But with this way, when overlay network becomes so huge in size and the number of Relays becomes tremendous, it will take a lot of time for end-users to check RTT of all the Relays. This could be worse for end-users who have a low performance machine. In order to determine which one of the Relays is the closest, they have to send ping queries sequentially to all the Relays and wait until the timeout ends. To overcome the drawback of this kind of general check routine, we have adopted a server-oriented method. In this way, an Agent sends the Manager an inquiry of the nearest Relay, it gets the first response from the nearest Relay. Thus, it takes very little time to determine the optimal Relay. Details of this algorithm are depicted in Fig. 2. Once the Manager receives an inquiry from an Agent, it commands all of the Relays to response to the Agent exactly after some designated period of time. The time value is calculated by the Manager and all the Relays must synchronize their clock accordingly. Since the Manager is located in backbone and its network condition is usually better than that of end-users, it can send commands to many Relays simultaneously. Although all the Relays must wait some designated period of time, which can be a delay, it is still more efficient and faster than the previous method.

Once the child node selects the best parent node with this method, it sends the result back to the Manager. The feed-back has its network address and the selected Relay's address. Once the Manager saves the information into a cache table, it searches the cache table first when a new request arrives from the same network. If the Manager finds out matching information from the cache, it immediately responds to the Agents. Just like other caches, the stored information will be expired after some designated period.

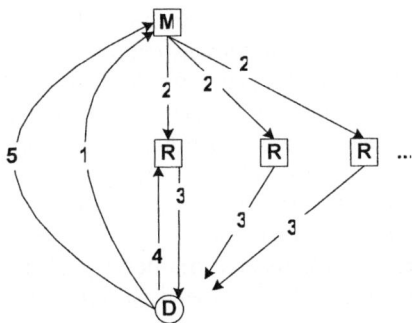

Fig. 2. Server-oriented RTT evaluating scheme

In fig.2, arrow 1 is an inquiry from a designated Agent (D) to seek the nearest Relay. Arrow 2 is the command from Manager (M) to All Relays (R) that orders Relay to respond to the Agent. Arrow 3 means a response from a Relay to the Agent. Arrow 4 is showing that the Agent selects a Relay and sends join messages. If the join query fails, it will try to join the next fastest Relay. Arrow 5 is the feed-back containing the Agent's network address and the finally selected Relay's address that the Agent succeeded to join.

Explicit level numbers according to topological information are assigned to Relays and they are used when a Relay dynamically searches its parent node. These numbers keep Relays from connecting to Relays of lower levels. When a Relay sends its level information along with a request to find a proper higher level Relay, the Manager returns only the information of those Relays from the higher level.

3.2 Reliable Transmitting with TCP-Based Technique

It is commonly believe that TCP is not suitable for real-time streaming services because TCP's use of packet retransmissions incurs unacceptable end-to-end latency. It means, re-sending lost data is not appropriate because the resent data would no arrive at the receiver in time for display. Besides, UDP is also not suitable because UDP's service model doesn't provide enough support to the application for streaming while TCP's provides too much. Consequently, numerous researches on new transport protocol with alternative service-model as more suitable for live streaming are introduced. For example, such service models might provide higher reliability than UDP but not the full-reliability of TCP. Through some combination of accident and design, TCP's congestion avoidance mechanism seems essential to the Internet's scalability and stability. Research on modeling TCP dynamics in order to effectively define the notion of TCP-friendly congestion avoidance is very active. Meanwhile, proposals for vide-oriented transport protocol continue to appear, but they now generally include TCP-friendly congestion avoidance.

To provide reliability, we adopt loosely-coupled TCP techniques between Relay nodes. Use of TCP is clearly desirable, as it is universally implemented, provides built-in congestion control and reliability, and does not raise any questions of fairness. Loosely-coupled TCP connection was introduced from ROMA[14]. Instead of using store-and-forward approach, it adopted a forward-when-feasible approach, where by each intermediary be written into the downstream TCP socket. The most difference between our solution and the ROMA is that we don't accept FEC algorithm.

FEC is well-known techniques developed for reliable IP multicast. It is a very effective algorithm when packets are transmitted using unreliable transport protocols like UDP. On the contrary, with the reliable transport protocol like TCP, the transport protocol already support reliable delivery, burdening FEC overhead to recover packet loss could brings needless congestions on the network. Besides, a FEC encoder (the very first overlay multicast node receive multicast packets from the source) should buffer enough packets to make FEC overhead packets. This also makes unnecessary end-to-end latency.

However, it comes to subnet multicast, it becomes the opposite story. The subnet multicast technique use IP multicast to transfer packet to neighbor overlay node and the possibility of packet losses increase. So we adopt FEC algorithm to provide reliable delivery.

Fig. 3 depicts how the provided reliable transmission mechanism, Loosely-coupled TCP works. When packet arrive, the overlay multicast application checks the each buffer of sockets which are connected with receivers and if there is not enough space for new arrived packet left, it drops the packet. In Fig. 3, TCP send buffer for R1 is the socket buffer for the connections with receiver R1 and it seems to be full and no empty space left, so the newly arrived packet will be dropped. But, R2 will receive the packet because its TCP socket send buffer has enough space for the packet.

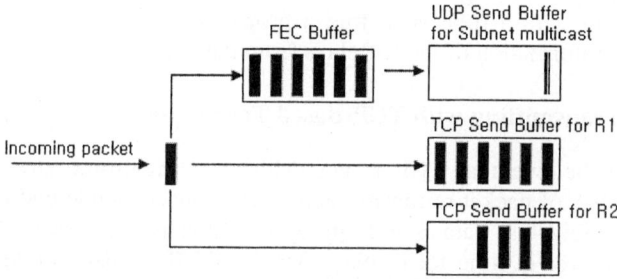

Fig. 3. Implementation of Reliable Transmission

For subnet multicast, when it sends packets to its neighbors in the same multicast island, it encodes packets and makes FEC recovery packets. To do this, it keeps FEC buffers. When enough packets to make FEC over head packets are gathered, send them using to subnet multicast members. If it sends packets to original multicast group, the originally intended multicast application like stream video player could not understand the FEC encoded packets, so it have to send FEC encoded multicast packet to another multicast group address which can be calculated with original group address. The receivers also should listen to the promised multicast group address and re-send it with TTL 0 for the stream player application to display. In Fig. 3, FEC buffer is filled with incoming packets to make FEC encodings.

4 Experiments

We tested the implementation on a test-bed that is deployed on the real Internet not in the lab environment of the limited conditions. The test-bed consisted of 4 isolated multicast domains that were connected through the KOREN (KOrea advanced REsearch Network) backbone. And the real Internet was also connected through the KOREN.

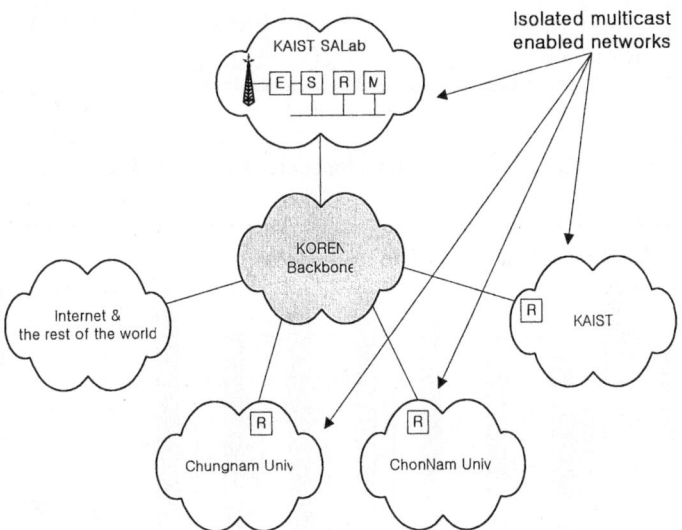

Fig. 4. Test bed constructed on APAN-kr network and Internet

The test was performed using a WMT® stream server of Microsoft®. We accepted participants not from our staffs but from many unspecified end-users on the 4 domains and the Internet. We assumed that most of the end-users were using MS-Windows systems as their OS and the MS media-player was the most common player and basically included in their OS. We implemented an Agent in forms of ActiveX control and it was automatically installed to each end-user's computer once connected. There was no need for them to download and install any other applications.

To gather enough number of end-users, we used a very famous sports event for the streaming content, whose paying time was about 90 minutes. We received the high quality stream using satellite antenna and encoded it in real-time. The encoded output was put to the MS WMT server for multicasting. We chose two bit-rates of 1.5Mbps and 750kbps because most of the home networks' bandwidth were about 2Mbps. In Fig. 4 E is live encoder which receives signal from a satellite dish. S means the WMT stream server as source. A root Relay and a Manager is located at the source network. Session information was given to Agents in HTML codes.

We gathered the information logs after 90 minutes' streaming test. During the streaming, a total of 377 connections were made and the number of concurrent users reached up to 198 while the average number of connections was about 172.

315 out of 377 connections are made from the 4 test-bed networks and the other 62 connections are made from 18 different AS(autonomous systems) through the Internet. The reason the number of users from a non-Relay deployed network is relatively small is because we advertised the sport event streaming only at 3 participating campus' web pages.

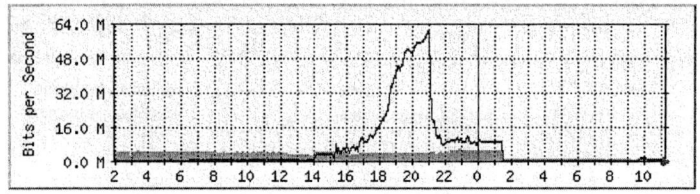

Fig. 5. MRTG analysis for source network traffic

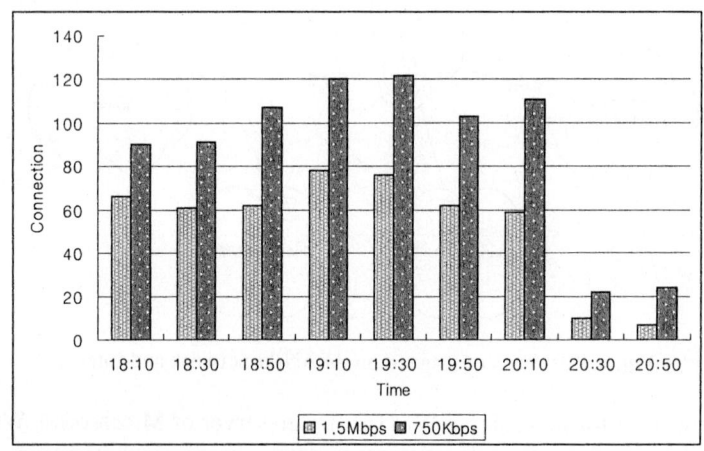

Fig. 6. Connections during the event

The MRTG analysis graph (in Fig. 5) shows the monitored network traffic of the source network during the event. Theoretically, a total of 198 users (1.5Mbps * 78 + 750Kbps * 120) would take 207Mbps traffic but the maximum traffic actually monitored from MRTG was only 64Mbps.

5 Performance Evaluation

The smaller packet size is, the more packets need to be sent and the higher PPS (Packet Per Second) could lower the performance overlay equipments. In fact, Microsoft WMT® generates 11 packets (10 data packets + 1 FEC packet) regardless of bit-rate and single packet size of Kasenna Media Base® is about 1.5k and makes about 350 PPS for a 4Mbps stream. So, we evaluated the performance of the presented solution depending on bit rates and the packet size of streams with gigabit network interface installed Relays. The selected bit-rates consisted of various from 1Mbps for high quality internet video stream to 20Mbps for HDTV quality. And the packet size of the streams varied from 1440bytes of not being fragmented on the Ethernet to 8Kbps. We used MGEN, the packet generator as the source of streams and to monitor the quality of played video we added the DVTS system sending 20Mbps stream. We also placed the multicast listener which checked a latency and packet losses by using the time-stamp and sequence numbers on the MGEN generated packet header.

To guarantee the low latency, which is crucial to live streaming services, we excluded the results that had larger latency than 50 ms from the source to end-users.

Table 1 shows the evaluated performance results which shows our implementation is not affect by the bit-rates or PPS of stream.

Table 1. Performance evaluation with various bit rates and packet size

Result Bit-rates	P.S.=1440		P.S.=2048		P.S.=4096		P.S.=8192	
	CH.	T.P.	CH.	T.P.	CH.	T.P.	CH.	T.P.
1M	500	500	500	500	500	500	200	200
2M	240	480	260	520	260	520	200	400
4M	130	520	140	560	140	560	130	520
6M	86	516	90	540	96	576	90	540
8M	64	512	62	496	64	512	64	512
10M	54	540	58	580	58	580	58	580
20M	26	520	26	520	26	520	26	520

P.S.: Packet Size in Byte, CH.: Number of Channels, T.P.: Throughput of the Relay in Mbps

6 Conclusion

In this paper, we introduced a novel overlay multicast structure suitable for distributing live stream. Focusing on developing practical solution rather than theoretical discussion, we put some features of live stream distribution solutions on the table and apply those to our solution. To overcome the shortcomings of peer-to-peer solution we employed the high-performance hardware based dedicated Relay nodes. We also improved scalability and kept low latency by adopting hierarchical tree structures for multicast distribution network, efficient and fast Relay seeking algorithm, caching technique and subnet multicasting. We employed two types of reliable transmission techniques. When it comes to unicast-tunnels, loosely-coupled TCP connection is used. Loosely-coupled

TCP connection is initially introduced by ROMA [14], but our approach is different with it in some ways. ROMA aggregates loosely-coupled TCP connection and FEC algorithm for providing reliable transport but we separate two techniques by its use. We use loosely coupled TCP connections for unicast-tunneling and FEC for subnet multicast. To prove its usefulness and efficiency, we constructed a test-bed on the real Internet environment and deployed the developed equipment on it. The evaluation broadcasted the famous 90 minutes long sports event to the test-bed and the result has shown that our solution is performing about 3 times better than unicast transport. We had evaluated its performance, differentiating PPS and bit-rates of the stream. The result has shown that our solution is performing well without regards to the PPS or bit-rates. The result shows that it can transport 500 channels concurrently and can process 580Mbps in maximum.

References

1. D. B. Yoffie: Competing in the Age of Digital Convergence. Harvard Business School Press (1997)
2. S. Deering: Host Extensions for IP Multicast. RFC-1112 (1989)
3. J. Y. Park, S. J. Koh, S. G. Kang, D. Y. Kim: Multicast Delivery Based on Unicast and Subnet Multicast. IEEE Communications Letters, Vol 5, no. 4 (2001)
4. RMT Working Group, IETF, http://www.ietf.org/html.charters/rmt-charter.html
5. D. A. Tran, K. A. Hua, and T. T. Do. Zigzag: An efficient peer-to-peer scheme for media streaming. In IEEE INFOCOM 2003, San Francisco (2003)
6. J. Jannotti, D. K. Gifford, K. L. Johnson, M. F. Kaashoek, and J. W. O'Toole Jr. Overcast: Reliable multicasting with an overlay network. In Proceedings of the Fourth Symposium on Operating System Design and Implementation (OSDI) (2000)
7. S. Banerjee, C. Kommareddy, K. Kar, B. Bhattacharjee and S. Khuller: Construction of an Efficient Overlay Multicast Infrastructure for Real-time Applications. IEEE INFOCOM 2003, San Francisco (2003)
8. Y. Chu, S. G. Rao, and H. Zhang: A Case For End System Multicast. In Proc. of ACM SIGMETRICS (2000)
9. P. Francis: Yoid: Extending the Multicast Internet Architecture, White paper at http://www.aciri.org/yoid/ (1999)
10. D. Pendarakis, S. Shi, D. Verma, and M. Waldvogel: ALMI: An application level multicast infrastructure. In Proc. of the 3rd USENIX Symposium on Internet Technologies and Systems (USITS '01) (2001)
11. J. Byers, J. Considine, M. Mitzenmacher, and S. Rost: Informed Content Delivery Across Adaptive Overlay Networks. In Proc. of ACM SIGCOMM (2002)
12. S. Banerjee, B. Bhattacharjee, and C. Kommareddy: Scalable Application Layer Multicast. In Proc. of ACM SIGCOMM (2002)
13. B. Zhang, S. Jamin, and L. Zhang. Host multicast: A framework for delivering multicast to end users. In Proceedings of IEEE Infocom (2002)
14. G. Kwon and J. Byers. ROMA: Reliable Overlay Multicast with Loosely Coupled TCP Connections. Technical Report BU-CS-TR-2003-015, Boston University (2003)
15. Charles Krasic, Jonathan Walpole, Kang Li, and Asvin Goel. The case for streaming multimedia with tcp. Technical report, Oregon Graduate Institute, CSE Technical Report (2001)

Apollon : File System Level Support for QoS Augmented I/O

Taeseok Kim[1], Youjip Won[2], Doohan Kim[2], Kern Koh[1], and Yong H. Shin[3]

[1] School of Computer Science and Engineering, Seoul National University,
56-1, Shillim-Dong, Kwanak-Ku, Seoul, 151-742, Korea
{tskim, kernkoh}@oslab.snu.ac.kr
[2] Division of Electrical and Computer Engineering, Hanyang University,
17, Hangdang-Dong, Seongdong-Ku, Seoul, 133-791, Korea
{yjwon, lissom33}@ece.hanyang.ac.kr
[3] Dept. of Computer Science and Engineering, Seoul National University of Technology,
172, Gongreung-Dong, Nowon-Ku, Seoul, 139-743, Korea
yshin@snut.ac.kr

Abstract. Next generation information appliances are required to handle real-time audio/video playback and in the mean time should be able to handle text based requests such as database search, file recording, etc. Although several techniques are presented to address this problem, most of them are rather theoretical to be employed into practical systems as they are. In this paper, we present our experience in developing the file system which can efficiently handle mixed workload. To this end, we develop practical I/O scheduling mechanism to prioritize the incoming disk I/O requests: deadline-driven I/O scheduler and admission control module. We also discuss some issues on QoS enhanced I/O semantics. The proto-type file system Apollon is developed on Linux Operating System. Compared to legacy system, Apollon exhibits superior performance in guaranteeing the QoS requirement of real-time requests.

1 Introduction

With the penetration of computer technologies into consumer electronics platform, the usage of digital home appliances such as digital TV, set-top box and PVR(Personalized Video Recorder) have explosively increased. These embedded devices enable us to enjoy service such as interactive multimedia presentation without the full fledged computer system, e.g. desktop, laptop computer, etc. They are usually equipped with relatively limited computing capability: smaller amount of main memory and storage. They also have to fulfill new line of constraints which have been applied to consumer electronics platform: reliability, shock-resistance, and energy consumption, etc. Legacy operating systems carry too much weight to be used in these embedded devices. Hence, it is mandatory that the operating system for these embedded devices is carefully tailored to satisfy the specific constraints of the devices.

In this work, we focus our effort on developing file system which can efficiently handle audio/video workload as well as the I/O workload without timing constraints. Developing this file system is motivated by the actual need. ATSC standard requires 19.2 Mbits/sec playback rate[1]. And single set-top box or PVR device is required to handle at least two read and two write sessions of ATSC stream. This type of real-time requirement has not existed in legacy computer systems domain, it should be necessarily considered in designing the I/O subsystem for multimedia embedded devices. In addition, the device needs to handle aperiodic I/O request, e.g. file download, database search, etc. This requirement will be more realistic when TV-anytime or infomercial is combined with real-time database navigation capability.

Due to the head movement overhead of disk and the stringent real-time characteristics of video/audio workload in home appliances, the file system in such embedded devices requires rather sophisticated treatment. The easiest way to overcome this situation is to allocate different device[1] to each type of data. However, this approach cannot use the underlying resources efficiently[2]. In this work, we consider that single device is required to provide streaming service as well as to handle the requests for non-playback related data.

In fact, guaranteeing QoS under mixed workload has been under serious attention for the past few years[3-5]. Most of the techniques including Cello[3] employ period based scheme. Period based approach delivers very sophisticated model and can exploit that underlying resources efficiently. However, it mandates the in-depth knowledge of the disk internals, e.g. the number of cylinders, sectors/cylinder, seek distance vs. seek time curve which are not usually accessible from operating system's point of view. Further worse, it requires more CPU cycles to schedule the request. Another common approach for servicing the mixed I/O requests is to employ a scheduler that assigns priorities to application classes and services disk requests in the priority order[6-7]. Unfortunately, such scheduler may violate service requirements of lower priority requests and induce long-time starvation.

In this paper, we present simple yet efficient method of handling different I/O requests. We first classify all I/O requests into two categories: real-time requests and best-effort requests. And then we develop a deadline-driven I/O scheduler which can not only meet the deadlines of real-time requests but also offer good response time to best-effort requests. For jitter-free service for audio/video under bursty workload environment, we also supplement our scheduling scheme with admission control module. Finally, we discuss some issues on QoS enhanced I/O semantics in commodity operating system. We demonstrate that Apollon is suitable for next generation embedded devices since: (i) it provides the QoS service for audio/video playback requests, (ii) it is so simple to be employed into low capability devices, and (iii) it has practical assumptions to be implemented as it is.

The rest of this paper is organized as follows. First, Apollon architecture and Apollon APIs are presented in Section 2, Section 3, respectively. And then, we discuss the prototype implementation in Section 4 and show the efficacy of Apollon through extensive experiment in Section 5. Finally, we conclude the paper in Section 6.

---

[1] The device denotes the physical device which is a separate scheduling entity.

2 Apollon File System

2.1 Apollon File System Architecture

Apollon file system is designed for embedded device with limited computing capability, e.g. a few hundred MHz at most. It naturally raises two main design philosophy: small code size and less CPU overhead. Apollon is very simple, and yet still successfully guarantees the required bandwidth for multimedia stream. Fig.1 illustrates the architecture of Apollon. We classify all I/O requests into two categories; soft real-time I/O, e.g. I/O request for audio/video playback and best-effort I/O, e.g. file copy, file transfer, or I/O request originated from database search. As is the case for all real-time operations, real-time I/O request should accompany deadline requirement. However, in POSIX standard, file system interfaces do not carry deadline information. Hence, in Apollon file system, we augment I/O system calls with deadline to support real-time I/O. Details on specifying QoS of real-time requests will be discussed in Section 3. System call can also be called without deadline such as best-effort I/O request. When the system call is called without deadline, file system layer assigns infinite value for deadline field. Based this deadline information, we implemented deadline-driven I/O scheduler: Earliest Deadline First with Aging. We also added admission control module to prevent the system from being overloaded. We describe admission control module and deadline-driven I/O scheduler one after another in next subsections.

2.2 Admission Control Module for Apollon

To service a given I/O request satisfying its deadline requirement, the system should not be overloaded. There are a number of levels in determining whether to accept a given I/O request or not: (i) open/close level, (ii) session level, and (iii) I/O request level. When we control the admission in open/close level, the application specifies the deadline requirement(or playback rate of a file) when file is open. The file system computes the resource requirements of a given open system call and rejects that if it cannot guarantee a given deadline. The second approach is at session level. Session is

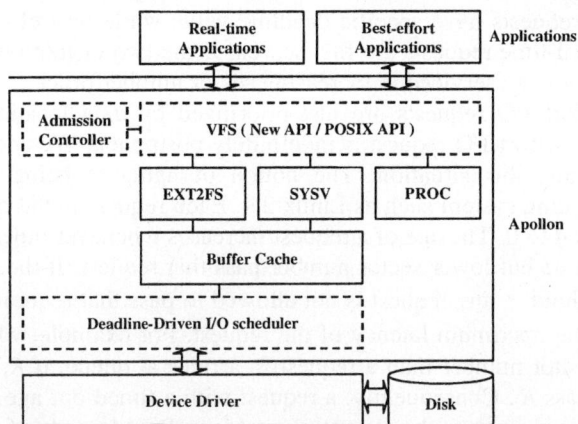

Fig. 1. Architecture of Apollon file system. The dotted line boxes denote the modules which are implemented by Apollon.

a sequence of homogeneous QoS I/O requests. In VCR like operation, user can watch the video in a number of different playback speeds. The admission control module recomputes the resource requirement of the playback when the user updates the playback speed and determines whether to accept the given session or not. Finally, we can determine the admissibility of a request for individual I/O request. In Apollon, we adopt the first approach.

The continuity requirement to maintain jitter-free playback can be represented with two conditions. The first condition is that the number of data blocks retrieved during time T should be greater than the amount of data blocks needed for playback for same period of time. This condition could be denoted by Eq.(1).

$$T \cdot r_i < n_i \cdot b \qquad (1)$$

In Eq.(1), n_i, b, and r_i are the number of data blocks read during T, size of I/O unit, and playback rate of stream i, respectively. This condition should hold for each stream, $i = 1,\ldots, m$. The second condition is that it should take less than time T to retrieve the data blocks for all streams.

$$T \geq \{\sum_{i=1}^{m} \frac{n_i \cdot b}{B_{max}}\} + O(m) \qquad (2)$$

In Eq.(2), m and B_{max} are the number of streams, maximum transfer rate of the disk, respectively. And $O(m)$ is the disk movement overhead such as seek and rotation latency in reading the data blocks for m streams. It is important to note that $O(m)$ is determined by the disk scheduling policy, e.g. EDF, SCAN, FIFO, etc. When the player opens a multimedia file, admission control module is required to compute above two equations and determines whether to accept or reject the I/O requests.

2.3 Deadline-Driven I/O Scheduler: Earliest Deadline First with Aging

Based deadline and data location on disk, we develop novel scheduling strategy. In this scheduling strategy, each request has deadline, location of a requested block on disk, and age. Our I/O scheduler first services the request with the earliest deadline. Since real-time requests have specific deadline value while best-effort requests have infinite value, real-time requests are first served. If the two or more requests have the same deadline, they are serviced in increasing sector number order.

Since best-effort I/O requests are just prioritized by data location on disk, it is possible that best-effort I/O request is indefinitely postponed. We adopt the notion of "age" to overcome this situation. The notion of aging is being widely used in commodity operating system such as Linux 2.4. Each request in the queue has an age and it is initialized to 0. The age of a request increases whenever other requests which have same deadline but lower sector number pass that request. If the age of a request comes to a threshold τ, any request is not allowed to pass that request. This threshold value τ means the maximum latency of the request. For example, when new request R_k with lower sector number than a request R_i arrives at queue, if R_i has a timed out age, R_k cannot pass R_i. Consequently, a request with a timed out age acts as a barrier and this mechanism resolves the starvation problem. Pseudo code of our algorithm is explained in table 1.

Table 1. Pseudo Code of Deadline-driven I/O Scheduler

$R_i \ (d_i, s_i, a_i)$
d_i : deadline of request i
s_i : sector number of request i
a_i : age of request i for preventing long starvation

when new request R_k arrives at queue
for (i := N; i >0; i--) do
    if ($d_k > d_i$) then insert R_k after R_i and return;
    else if ($d_k = d_i$) then
        if ($s_k > s_i$ | a_i = threshold) then insert R_k after R_i and return;
        else a_i ++;
        end if;
    end if;
end for;
insert R_k at head of queue;

2.4 Analysis of Deadline-Driven I/O Scheduling Algorithm

In this section, we discuss the performance analysis of our scheduling algorithm. $T_{service}$, the time required to service N requests in queue is modeled as Eq.(3). In Eq.(3), B_{max} is the maximum data transfer rate which is governed by the rotational speed and magnetic density of the disk plate. n_i, b, N represent the number of blocks to be fetched for ith request operation, the block size and the number of requests in queue, respectively. And δ_i in Eq.(3) is the disk head repositioning overhead for ith request I/O operation.

$$T_{service} = \sum_{i=1}^{N} (\frac{bn_i}{B_{max}} + \delta_i)$$
$$= \sum_{i=1}^{N} \frac{bn_i}{B_{max}} + \sum_{i=1}^{N} \delta_i \quad (3)$$

We can partition Eq.(3) into two parts, namely, the data transfer time, which is $\sum_{i=1}^{N} \frac{bn_i}{B_{max}}$, and the positioning overhead, $\sum_{i=1}^{N} \delta_i$. The data transfer time depends on the total number of blocks to be transferred, while the positioning time is governed by the disk scheduling policy. The positioning time consists of seek time, rotation latency, settle down time, head change, etc. Among all of them, seek operation dominates the disk head positioning time and thus it should be modeled carefully.

We first model the seek time behavior of the disk head movement. A number of experimental measurements have resulted in the following model of seek time behavior. Here, x and C denote the seek distance and threshold value, respectively, in terms of the number of cylinders.

$$\begin{aligned} T_{seek} &= a_1 + b_1\sqrt{x}, \quad \text{if} \quad x \leq C \\ T_{seek} &= a_2 + b_2 x, \quad \text{if} \quad x > C \end{aligned} \quad (4)$$

In FIFO or EDF disk scheduling algorithm, the disk heads read/write the data blocks in a fixed order independent of the location of the data blocks. Due to this property of FIFO or EDF scheduling, the disk head makes a full sweep of the disk platter (N -1) times in the worst case. The corresponding maximum overhead in FIFO or EDF scheduling, $O_{FIFO/EDF}(seek)$ is expressed as in Eq.(5). In Eq.(5), L means the total number of disk cylinders.

$$O_{FIFO/EDF}(seek) = (N-1)(a_2 + b_2 L) \quad (5)$$

In SCAN scheduling algorithm, the disk head scans the cylinder from the center of the platter outwards (or vice versa), and reads the data blocks in cylinder order. Thus, the respective cylinders are visited once in each cycle. The upper bound on the overhead in SCAN algorithm, $O_{SCAN}(seek)$ is expressed as in Eq.(6), given that $\frac{L}{N-1} \leq C$. This formulation is due to the fact that when the inter-cylinder distance is shorter than a certain threshold, seek time is proportional to the square root of the distance.

$$O_{SCAN}(seek) = (N-1)(a_1 + b_1\sqrt{\frac{L}{N-1}}) \quad (6)$$

In SCAN with aging, the disk head scans the cylinders like SCAN algorithm except prior service for requests with timed out age. In this algorithm, due to aging threshold value τ, the set of requests to be serviced in worst case are partitioned into $\left\lceil \frac{N}{\tau+1} \right\rceil$ groups. SCAN scheduling is used within a group and FIFO scheduling is used between the groups. Since there are $\left\lceil \frac{N}{\tau+1} \right\rceil$ groups to be scanned, the disk head makes $\left\lceil \frac{N}{\tau+1} \right\rceil$ sweeps of the disk platter. With this figure, the positioning overhead in SCAN with aging, $O_{SCANA}(seek)$ can be formulated as in Eq.(7). In Eq.(7), when τ is equal to (N-1), $O_{SCANA}(seek)$ becomes the same as $O_{SCAN}(seek)$ and when τ is equal to 0, $O_{SCANA}(seek)$ becomes the same as $O_{FIFO}(seek)$. Given that $\frac{L}{\tau} \leq C$, $O_{SCANA}(seek)$ is expressed as in Eq.(7).

$$O_{SCANA}(seek) = (N - \left\lceil \frac{N}{\tau+1} \right\rceil)(a_1 + b_1\sqrt{\frac{L}{\tau}}) + (\left\lceil \frac{N}{\tau+1} \right\rceil - 1)(a_2 + b_2 L) \quad (7)$$

From above equations, we can derive worst case seek time overhead in our deadline-driven I/O scheduling: Earliest Deadline First with aging. In this algorithm, real-time requests are serviced in EDF order while best-effort requests are serviced in SCAN with aging algorithm order. Let N_r and N_b be the number of real-time requests and the number of best-effort requests in queue, respectively. The disk head makes a full sweep of the disk platter N_r times and then scans the cylinders like SCAN with aging algorithm for N_b best-effort requests. Given that $\frac{L}{\tau} \leq C$, $O_{EDFA}(seek)$ is expressed as in Eq.(8).

$$\begin{aligned} O_{EDFA}(seek) &= (N_r - 1)(a_2 + b_2 L) + (a_2 + b_2 L) \\ &+ (N_b - \left\lceil \frac{N_b}{\tau+1} \right\rceil)(a_1 + b_1\sqrt{\frac{L}{\tau}}) + (\left\lceil \frac{N_b}{\tau+1} \right\rceil - 1)(a_2 + b_2 L) \end{aligned} \quad (8)$$

3 QoS Enhanced I/O Semantics

3.1 QoS Semantics in I/O Operation

To support QoS in I/O subsystem, operating system should harbor proper abstraction of QoS in I/O operation. In fact, the notion of QoS is unpopular in I/O operation. Traditionally, hard disk has been outside the realm of real-time computing. This is because seek time and rotational latency have made it infeasible to guarantee response time in hard real-time environment. I/O subsystem which is based on such disk is not friendly to real-time system and there is no consideration for specifying timing constraints in POSIX. Hence, to support QoS of real-time requests in I/O subsystem, we first have to define abstract mechanism for specifying QoS.

There are several alternatives in specifying QoS requirement of multimedia applications. The simplest way is to add new APIs including QoS related parameter such as deadline. In [8], they implemented new system calls such as cello_open(), cello_read(), etc. and added QoS parameter into those APIs. [9] specifies QoS parameters per file descriptor, and passes the pointer to parameters to each IO request in the disk queue using ioctl().

The mechanism which classifies the requests class by using file expansion, e.g. mpeg, avi, etc. deserves much consideration. In other words, when opening a file, if its expansion name is one of audio/video file expansions, it is possible to prioritize the real-time requests in I/O level. In this scenario, however, the process which opens audio/video files also should be considered with file expansion. It is because, non-multimedia processes such as *copy* also could open the audio/video files. These processes do not require real-time services. It is also possible to classify the file characteristics in I/O level by analyzing the I/O patterns of files. For example, if the access pattern of a file is sequential and periodic, it could be recognized as stream requests. For this autonomous detection of requests class, the intelligent module for analyzing the file access pattern should be embedded in file system.

3.2 Interface in Apollon

Among several techniques, we added new APIs in order to pass the deadline information of multimedia requests into I/O level. The addition of new system calls causes application which is supposed to use new system calls to be changed. In general purpose system, since there exist many kinds of multimedia applications and they are frequently changed, it is not feasible. On the other hand, in embedded devices such as PVR or set-top box, applications are embedded along with operating system, and thus the above mentioned problems do not matter. Note that the addition of new system calls should be carefully handled because system call index is one of system resources. Though Apollon is yet prototype and thus this simple technique is employed, it might be replaced with other techniques such as QoS parameter passing with `ioctl()`. Table 2 lists the interface exported by Apollon.

Table 2. The Description of Apollon APIs

System Call	Purpose
apollon_open	invoke admission controller and if admitted, open the multimedia file
apollon_close	close the opened multimedia file and reset the admission control module related parameters
apollon_read	read multimedia file with its own deadline parameter
apollon_admin	set and modify the admission control related parameters

4 Implementation of Apollon Prototype

We implemented Apollon file system on Linux kernel v.2.4.20. Since Apollon file system enables the application to specify the deadline of I/O request, several kernel components are re-designed to harbor multimedia related information such as deadline, average playback rate. We also replaced Linux elevator disk scheduler with our deadline-driven I/O scheduler. Note that Apollon file system is completely modular and object-oriented. Hence, it can be seamlessly integrated with the existing file systems, e.g. Ext2fs, XFS, NTFS, etc.

5 Experimental Evaluation of Apollon

5.1 Experimental Methodology

Since Apollon exports QoS-enabled APIs, we modified the commodity mpeg2 player to use this feature[10]. The modified player computes the deadline for every I/O request and invokes the system call with that deadline. The objective of Apollon file system is to guarantee deadline of real-time I/O requests so that multimedia player can provide jitter-free playback. When the I/O subsystem is under utilized, it is not much difficult to deliver the requested data block on time. However, when the I/O subsystem is overloaded with various type of request, special care needs to be taken to guarantee the QoS of real-time I/O.

To evaluate the efficacy of Apollon file system, we compare the deadline guarantee behavior of Apollon with that of legacy Ext2fs using SCAN-like disk scheduler. Although several techniques are presented to support QoS enabled I/O, most of them are not fully implemented and thus they could not be used in our experiment. Instead, we show the performance overhead as well as the deadline guarantee behavior of our Apollon using intensive comparison with Ext2fs. To generate various types of request, we use *ftp*, *find* and *IOZONE*. *Ftp*(file transfer protocol) receives the data blocks from TCP socket and copies it to the disk. *Find* searches the directory entry to find the path of a given file. And *IOZONE* is a file system benchmark tool which measures the performance of a given file system[11]. Multimedia file used in this test is 9 Mbits/sec with 30 frames/sec playback rate. The size of the file is 324 MByte. And the testbed for experiments consists of a 2.4GHz Intel Pentium IV machine running Linux 2.4.20, equipped with 256MB RAM and a 40GB IDE disk.

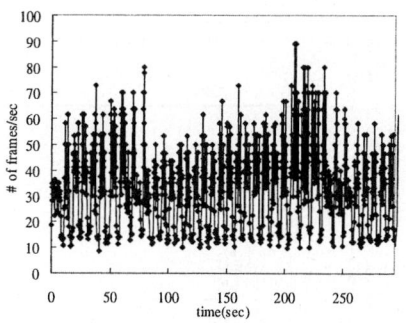 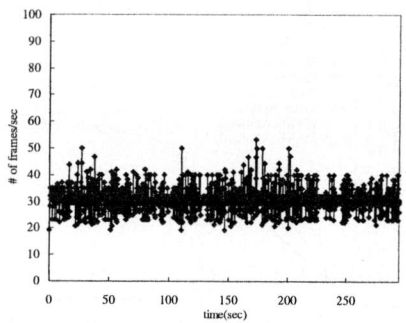

(a) frame rate of Ext2fs with *ftp* workload.   (b) frame rate of Apollon with *ftp* workload.

Fig. 2. Variation in playback frame rate when using *ftp* for background task

5.2 QoS Guarantee Under I/O Intensive Background Workload

We first use *ftp* for I/O intensive background task. Experiment with *ftp* could be regarded as simulation of recording another program during watching a movie in PVR. Fig.2 illustrates the variation of playback rates in both file systems when the *ftp*

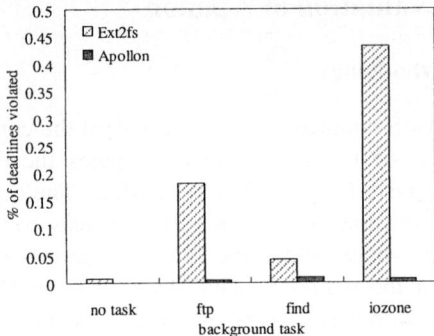

Fig. 3. Deadline violation behavior in different environment. In every case, deadline miss rate in Apollon file system is near zero.

application downloads the 2GB sized file. When we watch the video clip from Ext2fs with *ftp*, the playback speed fluctuates widely and thus it is actually impossible to watch the video clip(Fig.2(a)). However, the variation of playback rate in Apollon is relatively consistent(Fig.2(b)).

Fig.3 illustrates the deadline violation behavior in two file systems using different workload. In Fig.3, Y axis denotes the percentage of I/O requests which do not meet the deadline requirement. For this experiment, we played a movie file when there is no background task, *ftp* application downloads the 2GB sized file, *find* program searches the root file system, and *iozone* benchmark tool is executed with '-a' option, respectively. As can be seen, in every case, the deadline miss rate is near zero in Apollon file system. On the other hand, the deadline miss rate could not be negligible in Ext2fs file system.

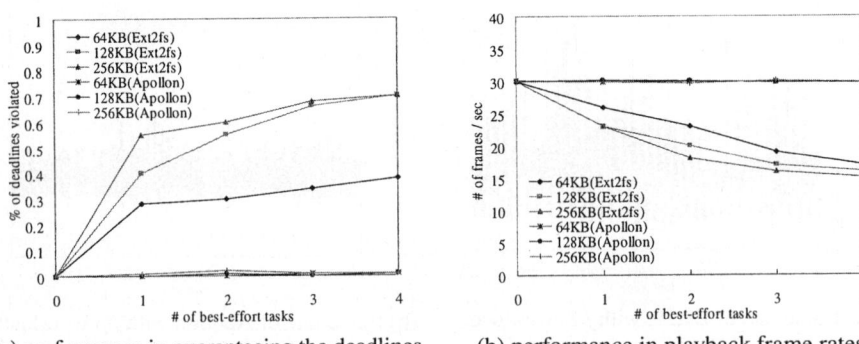

(a) performance in guaranteeing the deadlines   (b) performance in playback frame rates

Fig. 4. QoS guarantee behavior of real-time I/O requests using *IOZONE*. Note that three lines in Apollon file system are overlapped one another. Although the performance is different as I/O size of multimedia player, Apollon exhibits superior performance.

Next, we use *IOZONE* benchmark tool to compare the performance of two file systems under extreme text based workloads. In Fig.4(a), X axis denotes the number of *IOZONE* tasks and Y axis is the percentage of I/O requests which do not meet the deadline requirement. In this figure, one unit of *IOZONE* task means an *IOZONE* session that reads and writes 128MB sized file by 4KB. As can be seen, Apollon file system exhibits superior performance in guaranteeing the deadline of I/O requests. Fig.4(b) plots the average playback frame rates in two file systems. In Ext2fs, the playback rate of player decreases as we increase the number of *IOZONE* tasks. However, in Apollon file system, the playback rate of the player remains constant independent of the number of *IOZONE* background tasks.

Compared with Ext2fs using seek optimized scheduling like SCAN, Apollon file system involves the overhead in disk head moving optimization due to the QoS service for real-time I/O requests. To show the overhead of Apollon, we measure the throughput and the average response time of requests. These measurements are taken under identical conditions with Fig.3. As shown in Fig.5(a), Apollon incurs more overhead than Ext2fs by 3% ~ 14% in throughput. Fig.5(b) also shows that there is little difference in average response time between two file systems. Although Ext2fs is a little better than Apollon in seek optimization performance, it dose not guarantee meeting the deadline requirements of the real-time requests. We have recorded the playback in Apollon file system and Ext2fs. Interested users are referred in [12].

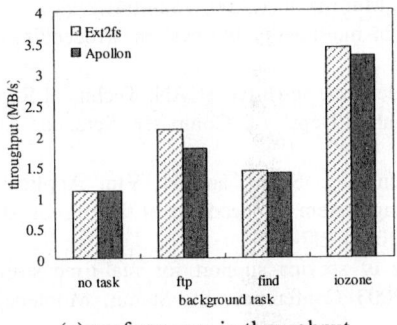
(a) performance in throughput

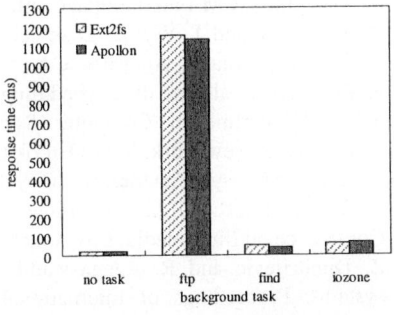
(b) performance in average response time

Fig. 5. The throughput and the average response time in two file systems

6 Conclusion

In this paper, we presented the integrated file system for handling mixed workload. Using admission controller and deadline-driven I/O disk scheduler which prioritizes the different types of requests according to their respective deadline requirements, we were able to successfully meet the soft real-time requirement of audio/video application under mixed workload. We also discussed the limit of POSIX in supporting the real-time characteristics in I/O level and then presented several solutions to relieve that conservative semantics. In the work presented here, we added new system calls for prototype file system, we are currently investigating issues in classifying efficiently the requests class by file expansion or autonomous detection. Apollon file system manifests itself especially when the given system is equipped with relatively low end disk subsystem and the system is required to exploit its capacity. This file system is to be embedded in the digital home appliances, e.g. set-top box, PVR, internet home server, etc.

Acknowledgement

This work is in part funded by KOSEF through Statistical Research Center for Complex System at Seoul National University.

References

1. http://www.atsc.org/standards.html
2. P. Shenoy, P. Goyal, and H. Vin: Architectural considerations for next generation file systems. Proceedings of ACM Multimedia Conference, Orlando, FL, USA (1999) 457-467
3. P. Shenoy: Cello: a disk scheduling framework for next generation operating system. Real Time Systems Journal (2002)
4. R. Wijayaratne and A. L. Reddy: Providing QoS guarantees or disk I/O. Proceedings of ACM/Springer Journal on Multimedia Systems (2000)
5. Y. J. Won and Y. S. Ryu: Handling sporadic tasks in multimedia file system. Proceedings of the eighth ACM International Conference on Multimedia (2000) 462-464
6. A. L. Reddy and J. Wyllie: Disk scheduling in multimedia I/O system. Proceedings of ACM Multimedia'93, Anaheim, CA (1993) 225-234
7. K. Gopalan: Real-time disk scheduling using deadline sensitive SCAN. Technical Report TR-92, Experimental Computer Systems Labs, Dept. of Computer Science, State University of New York, Stony Brook (2001)
8. V. Sundaram, A. Chandra, P. Goyal, P.Shenoy, J. Sahni, and H. Vin: Application performance in the QLinux multimedia operating system. Proceedings of the Eighth ACM Conference on Multimedia, Los Angeles, CA (2000) 127-136
9. Z. Dimitrijevic and R. Rangaswami: Quality of service support for real-time storage systems. Proceedings of International IPSI-2003 Conference, St. Stefan, Montenegro (2003)
10. http://libmpeg2.sourceforge.net
11. http://www.iozone.org
12. http://www.dmclab.hanyang.ac.kr/research/project/hermes-q/hermes-q_overview.htm

Seamless Video Streaming for Video on Demand Services in Vertical Handoff

Jae-Won Kim, Hye-Soo Kim, Jae-Woong Yun,
Hyeong-Min Nam, and Sung-Jea Ko

Department of Electronics Engineering, Korea University,
Anam-Dong Sungbuk-Ku, Seoul, Korea
{jw9557, hyesoo, jyun, min, sjko}@dali.korea.ac.kr

Abstract. Vertical handoff is required to achieve anywhere and anytime internet access in the fourth generation (4G) network providing interoperability between universal mobile telecommunications system (UMTS) and wireless LAN (WLAN). However, video data can be lost due to latency caused by vertical handoff. To solve this problem, in this paper, we propose a video streaming method for video on demand (VOD) services that provides seamless playout at the client in vertical handoff. In the proposed method, the streaming server first predicts the network status by using both the channel modelling and the client buffer status and then selects a proper video transmission method for vertical handoff among pre-transmission, post-transmission, and frame-skipping transmission. Performance evaluations are presented to demonstrate the effectiveness of the proposed method.

1 Introduction

Currently, the research community and industry in the field of telecommunications are considering the possibility of the choice for handoff which could be the solutions for the 4G of wireless communication [1]. The 4G wireless networks will integrate heterogeneous technologies such as WLAN and third generation (3G) network because no single wireless network technology simultaneously can provide a low latency, high bandwidth, and wide area data service to a large number of mobile users [2].

The movement of a user within or among different types of networks is called the vertical mobility. One of the major challenges for seamless service in the vertical mobility is a vertical handoff, where handoff is the process of maintaining a mobile user's active connection by changing its point of attachment [3]. In the 4G wireless systems, seamless handoff with small latency and packet losses should be executed. Handoff latency is one of important factors that decides the quality of service (QoS) in the 4G wireless networks. In the deployment of multimedia services with real-time requirements, the handoff process can significantly degrade the QoS from the user's perspective [4].

In vertical handoff, since video data can be lost due to latency caused by vertical handoff, video quality degradation caused by vertical handoff is the critical problem in video streaming. In order to solve this problem, a successful video streaming solution is required to adapt appropriately to mobile handoff scenarios for maximum user-perceived quality.

There are several methods to achieve seamless vertical handoff for video streaming [5]-[8]. The multimedia transport protocol (MMTP) determines the encoding rate according to the measured available bandwidth for vertical handoff [5]. However, this protocol does not concern packet losses caused by vertical handoff. The method in [6] determines only the required buffer sizes of the client to achieve lossless vertical handoff without QoS control. The QoS based vertical handoff scheme for the UMTS and the WLAN in [7] uses QoS supportable access points (APs) or cells through already connected network in order to achieve seamless connection. However, this scheme requires the support of the system-level design such as the hardware configuration and the lower layer protocol design. The seamless vertical handoff scheme in [8] implements soft handoff based on the stream control transmission protocol (SCTP). However, it needs also the system-level design like [7] and the server should support two IP addresses for the client.

In this paper, we propose a new video streaming method for VOD services that provides seamless playout at the client in vertical handoff between the WLAN and the 3G network without the system-level design. For seamless video playout, the streaming server predicts the network status by using both the channel modelling and the client buffer status. The channel status is estimated by using a two-state Markov model with parameters including the received signal strength indicator (RSSI) in the WLAN and the pilot strength (E_c/I_o) in the 3G network. The client buffer status is estimated by analyzing the RTCP receiver report (RR) and the application-defined packet (APP). Using the predicted network status, the streaming server selects a proper video transmission method for vertical handoff among pre-transmission, post-transmission, and frame-skipping transmission.

The paper is organized as follows. In the next section, we describe the vertical handoff scenario. The channel status prediction method including both the channel modelling and the client buffer status estimation is explained in Section 3. Section 4 presents the proposed video streaming method for vertical handoff. Experimental results are presented in Section 5. Finally, our conclusions are given in Section 6.

2 Vertical Handoff Scenario

Today's wireless access networks consist of several overlapping tiers. The combination of the 3G and WLAN technologies enables the internet access from anywhere and anytime, thereby bringing benefits to both end users and service providers. A horizontal handoff is defined as a handoff between base stations (BSs) that use the same type of wireless network interface. This is the

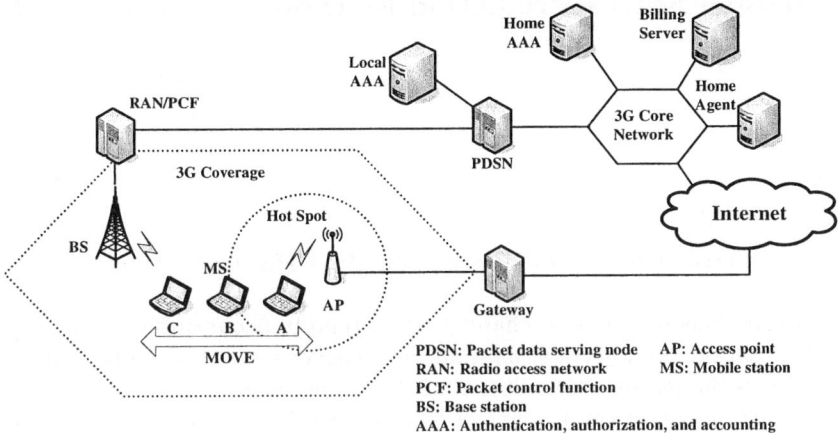

Fig. 1. Vertical handoff scenario

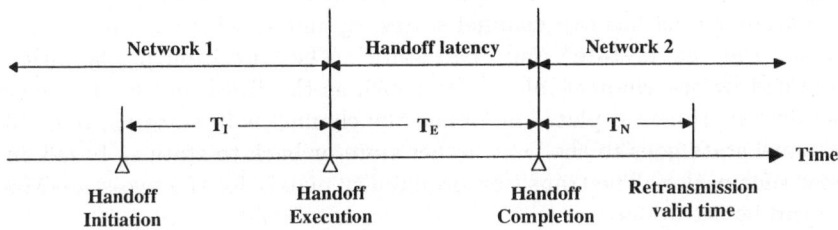

Fig. 2. Handoff procedure

traditional definition of handoff for homogeneous cellular systems. A vertical handoff is defined as a handoff between BSs that use different wireless network technologies such as the WLAN and the 3G network [2]. In our scenario, we focus on the vertical handoff between the WLAN and the 3G network. Figure 1 shows the vertical handoff when the mobile station (MS) moves from location A in the WLAN to location C in the 3G network. As the MS leaves the AP, the strength of the beacon signal received from the AP weakens. If its strength is decreased below a threshold value, the MS tries to connect to the 3G network and starts synchronizing with the system to prepare the handoff.

Figure 2 illustrates the vertical handoff procedure in the heterogeneous network where significant events have been pointed out. The trigger message indicating the handoff initiation for vertical handoff is transmitted to the server. Then, the trigger message indicating the beginning of vertical handoff is transmitted before vertical handoff. Finally, the client informs the server of the handoff completion. These trigger messages are generated by using the RSSI and E_c/I_o. Note that T_I, T_E, and T_N, respectively, are the period for vertical handoff initiation, the handoff latency, and the period for the packet retransmission.

3 Channel Status Prediction Method

In this section, we explain the proposed channel status prediction method which consists of the channel rate estimation and the client buffer prediction. Using the predicted channel status, we can achieve seamless video streaming in vertical handoff.

3.1 Channel Rate Estimation for Vertical Handoff

In the heterogeneous network, channel errors tend to occur in burst during channel fading periods and vertical handoff. The packet losses caused by channel errors result in the quality degradation of streaming video. In order to reduce the video quality degradation in vertical handoff, we first define a wireless channel model. The wireless channel is modelled as a two-state Markov model. Using the wireless channel model, we can develop a video streaming method for the heterogeneous network, as we will discuss in Section 4.

Figure 3 shows the two-state Markov model for vertical handoff. This two-state Markov model has two channel states, s_0 and s_1 where s_0 and s_1, respectively, are the "good state" and "bad state". The transition probabilities can be obtained by the channel information such as the RSSI and E_c/I_o measured in the our experimental platform. When the channel is in state s_n, $n \in \{0,1\}$, the channel state goes to the next higher state or back to state s_0 based on the channel information. The transition probability matrix for the two-state Markov model can be set up as

$$\mathbf{P} = \begin{bmatrix} 1 - p_0 & p_0 \\ p_1 & 1 - p_1 \end{bmatrix}. \quad (1)$$

In the two-state Markov model with transition probabilities in Eq. (1), we define the state probability $\pi_n(k|S(t))$ as the probability that the channel is in state s_n at time k given the channel state observation $S(t)$, where $k > t$. A vector of state probabilities can be written as

$$\vec{\pi}(k|S(t)) = [\pi_0(k|S(t)), \ \pi_1(k|S(t))]. \quad (2)$$

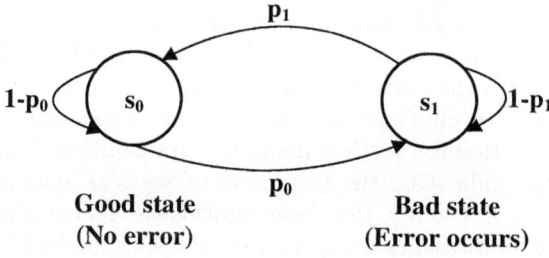

Fig. 3. Two-state Markov model

The initial state probability $\pi_n(t|S(t))$ at time t can be set up as

$$\forall n \in \{0,1\},$$
$$\pi_n(t|S(t)) = \begin{cases} 1, & \text{if } S(t) = s_n, \\ 0, & \text{otherwise.} \end{cases} \quad (3)$$

In the Markov model, the state probabilities $\vec{\pi}(k|S(t))$ at time k can be derived from the state probabilities $\vec{\pi}(k-1|S(t))$ at the previous time slot and the transition probability matrix $\mathbf{P}$ as

$$\vec{\pi}(k|S(t)) = \vec{\pi}(k-1|S(t)) \cdot \mathbf{P}. \quad (4)$$

By recursively using Eq. (4), channel state probabilities at time k, where $k > t$, can then be calculated from $\vec{\pi}(t|S(t))$ and $\mathbf{P}$ as

$$\vec{\pi}(k|S(t)) = \vec{\pi}(t|S(t)) \cdot \mathbf{P}^{k-t}. \quad (5)$$

We consider the heterogeneous wireless channel, where each bandwidth provides the different data rates. Thus, we define the channel transmission rates $\bar{R}$ as the number of bits sent per second as follows:

$$\bar{R} = \begin{cases} R_w^{max}, & \text{for the WLAN,} \\ R_c^{max}, & \text{for the 3G network,} \end{cases} \quad (6)$$

where R_w^{max} and R_c^{max} are the maximum channel rates in the WLAN and the 3G network. In our channel model, packets are transmitted correctly when the channel is in state s_0, while errors occur when the channel is in the other state s_1. Therefore, $\pi_0(k|S(t))$ is the probability of correct transmission at time k. Let $C(k)$ be the future channel transmission rate where $k > t$. The expected channel rate $E[C(k)|S(t)]$ given the observation of channel state $S(t)$ can be calculated as

$$E[C(k)|S(t)] = \bar{R} \cdot \pi_0(k|S(t)). \quad (7)$$

Finally, we define the wireless channel rate $\widehat{R}$ as follows:

$$\widehat{R} = E[C(k)|S(t)]. \quad (8)$$

3.2 Client Buffer Status Prediction

The client buffer status can be predicted by analyzing RTCP RR and APP at the streaming server. Thus, the client buffer fill level, B_C, is given by

$$B_C = \sum_{i=LPSN}^{HTSN} L_i, \quad (9)$$

where L_i is the size of the packet with the ith sequence number, HTSN is the highest transmitted sequence number kept by the server, and LPSN is the last played sequence number which is calculated by using the playout time [12]. The playout time is calculated by using the fields the oldest buffered sequence number (OBSN) and playout delay (PD) contained in the RTCP APP OBSN extension as proposed by 3GPP-SA4 [13].

4 Proposed Video Streaming Method for Vertical Handoff

According to the vertical handoff scenario, the trigger message for the vertical handoff initiation is generated when the client detects the need of vertical handoff. The client transmits the trigger message to the streaming server, where the channel status is predicted. Then, the streaming server selects a proper video transmission method for vertical handoff among pre-transmission, post-transmission, and frame skipping transmission by using the obtained channel information.

4.1 Pre-transmission

In the pre-transmission method, during the vertical handoff initiation period, T_I, the streaming server transmits in advance all the frames that can be lost due to the latency of vertical handoff, achieving seamless playout in the client without packet losses. However, in order to perform the pre-transmission, the following two conditions should be satisfied. First, to transmit in advance all the frames during T_I, the network should guarantee a sufficient channel rate as follows:

$$\hat{R} \cdot T_I > R_C \cdot (T_I + T_E), \qquad (10)$$

where $\hat{R}_E$ is the predicted channel rate at the beginning of the handoff initiation and R_C is the bitrate of the encoded bitstream. Next, the empty space of the client buffer should be also sufficient for the pre-transmitted frames received from the streaming server as follows:

$$B_C^{\max} \geq B_C + R_C \cdot (T_I + T_E) - \mu, \qquad (11)$$

where $B_C^{\max}$ is the maximum level of the client buffer, B_C is the client buffer fill level in Eq. (9) when the vertical handoff initiation trigger message is arrived at the streaming server, and μ represents the sum of the length of packets to be played during T_I in the client buffer, that is given by

$$\mu = \sum_{i=1}^{\lfloor f \cdot T_I \rfloor} L_{LPSN+i}, \qquad (12)$$

where $\lfloor x \rfloor$ represents an integer part of x and f is the frame rate of the video stream.

4.2 Post-transmission

In the post-transmission, the streaming server does not perform anything for vertical handoff in advance and just re-transmits lost packets after vertical handoff. In order to perform the post-transmission, the following two conditions should be satisfied. First, the network should guarantee a sufficient channel rate for re-transmitting lost frames after vertical handoff as follows:

$$\hat{R} \cdot T_N > R_C \cdot (T_E + T_N), \qquad (13)$$

where $\widehat{R}$ is the channel rate after vertical handoff that is predicted by the channel model and T_N is the period maintaining the channel rate, $\widehat{R}$. Note that the condition (13) typically satisfies in the case that handoff is performed from the low bandwidth network to the high bandwidth network. e.g. the 3G network to the WLAN. Next, the client should keep sufficient frames to provide seamless playout during vertical handoff as follows:

$$B_C - \mu \geq 0, \qquad (14)$$

where μ represents the sum of the length of packets to be played during T_E in the client buffer, that is given by

$$\mu = \sum_{i=1}^{\lfloor f \cdot T_E \rfloor} L_{LPSN+i}. \qquad (15)$$

4.3 Frame Skipping Transmission

The frame skipping transmission can be applied when the client buffer does not have enough frames to be played during T_E and the channel rate is also not sufficient for pre-transmission and post-transmission. In order to maintain seamless video playout, during T_I, the streaming server transmits in advance some frames that can be played in handoff latency. Thus, in order to perform frame skipping while minimizing the video quality, the proposed method dynamically skips some frames from all frames that will be assigned for $T_I + T_E$ according to the number of target frames. The maximum number of frames to be transmitted during T_I, N_T, is determined by

$$N_T = \frac{\widehat{R}}{R_C} \cdot f \cdot T_I. \qquad (16)$$

However, if all N_T frames are transmitted to the client, the client buffer overflow may be produced. In order to prevent the client buffer overflow, the modified next rate, $\widehat{R}'$, is determined by

$$\widehat{R}' = \min\left(\max\left(R | B_C^{\max} \geq B_C + \frac{R}{R_C} \cdot T_I - \mu\right), \widehat{R}\right), \qquad (17)$$

where μ is defined as (12). Thus, the modified N_T, N_T', is given by

$$N_T' = \frac{\widehat{R}'}{R_C} \cdot f \cdot T_I. \qquad (18)$$

For the proposed frame-skipping method, we apply the dynamic frame skipping (DFS) scheme according to N_T'. In the proposed DFS scheme, the frame activity, A, is used to determine whether a frame is skipped or not. If a frame is skipped, the activity of the frame is added to the activity of the next frame. If the accumulated frame activity is less than a certain threshold, T, the corresponding frame is skipped. In the proposed method, we use the same activity measure, A, as the complexity measure in MPEG-2 TM5 [14]:

$$A = B \cdot \bar{Q}, \qquad (19)$$

where B is the number of generated bits in a frame and $\bar{Q}$ is the average quantization parameter of a frame. By analyzing the encoded bitstream at the streaming server, the activity measure, A, is calculated as Eq. (19). In the proposed method, we apply the single threshold, T, to all frames that will be assigned for $T_I + T_E$. In order to obtain optimal T, we define $N(T_k)$ that means the number of frames to be encoded when the single threshold is T_k:

$$N(T_k) = \sum_{i=0}^{N-1} I\left(\sum_{j \in F_i} A_j > T_k\right), \tag{20}$$

where T_k is the kth threshold in the range of $(0, T_{max})$, $I(x)$ is one if x holds, and zero otherwise, N is the number of all frames for $T_I + T_E$, F_i is the frame number set including frames from the next frame of the latest encoded frame to the current i^{th} frame, and A_j is the activity of the jth frame in the set F_i. Note that $\sum_{j \in F_i} A_j$ means the accumulated activity of the ith frame. Thus, the optimal threshold for the dynamic frame skipping, T, is determined by

$$T = \{T_k \,|\, N(T_k) = N'_T\}. \tag{21}$$

Using T, the proposed method determines optimal frames to be transmitted. However, video quality will be degraded if selected frames are simply transmitted without the consideration of frame-skipping. Thus, we transcode selected frames to compensate motion mismatching and error drift and then transcoded frames are transmitted to the client. Note that since vertical handoff does not occur frequently, the processing load for transcoding is negligible.

5 Experimental Results

Many experiments have performed in the our experimental platform of Fig. 4 in order to figure out the relationship between PLR and each radio condition: e.g. RSSI in the WLAN and E_c/I_o in the 3G network. Figure 5 shows the experimental result of the relationship between PLR and each radio condition. As shown

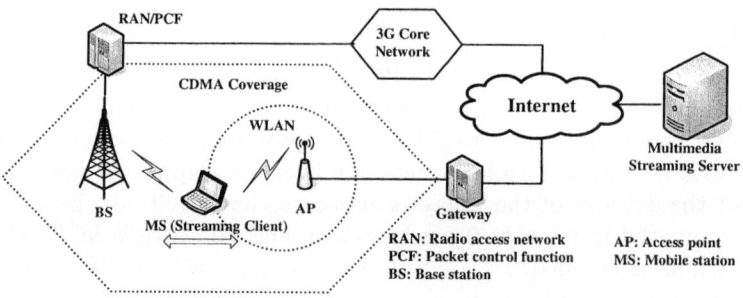

Fig. 4. Experimental platform

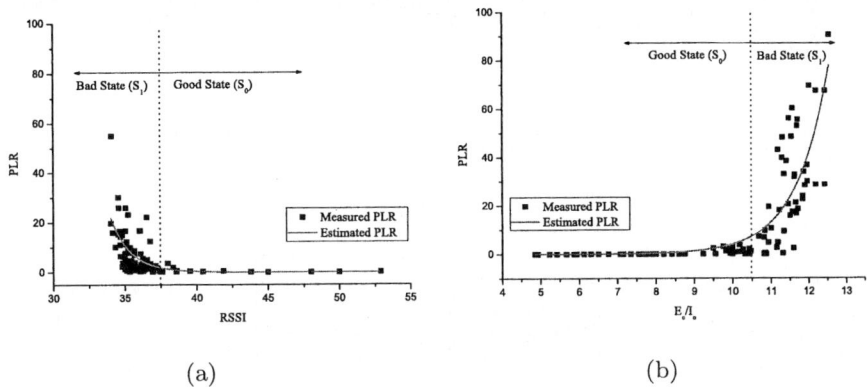

Fig. 5. Channel state determination: (a) PLR vs RSSI in the WLAN and (b) PLR vs E_c/I_o in the 3G network

in Fig. 5, the channel state transition of the proposed wireless channel model is performed by experimental thresholds which are 35 of RSSI and 10.8 of E_c/I_o. Table 1 shows the transition probabilities by using the results in Fig. 5.

Table 1. Transition probabilities in the heterogeneous network

Probability	WLAN	3G network
p_0	0.1875	0.0455
p_1	0.6667	0.4285

With the proposed wireless channel model, we have simulated vertical handoff according to the vertical handoff scenario to show the effectiveness of the proposed video streaming method. The "Foreman" sequence with 300 frames of QCIF format (176×144) is used in our experiments. The test sequence is encoded to the H.263+ CBR bitstream of 128kbps with 30fps. For buffering simulations, a 40KB client buffer is assumed and we specify an 1.25sec pre-buffering time for playout.

In our vertical handoff simulations, there are three times transitions where T_I and T_E, respectively, are 1sec. Each transition is described as follows:

Case 1) 3G → WLAN

The handoff process including the handoff initiation is performed from the 70th frame to the 130th frame. In this case, since each $\widehat{R}$ of the WLAN and the 3G network is not enough for the pre-transmission or the post-transmission, the frame-skipping transmission is performed during T_I where $\widehat{R}$ is 190kbps and N'_T is 44frames.

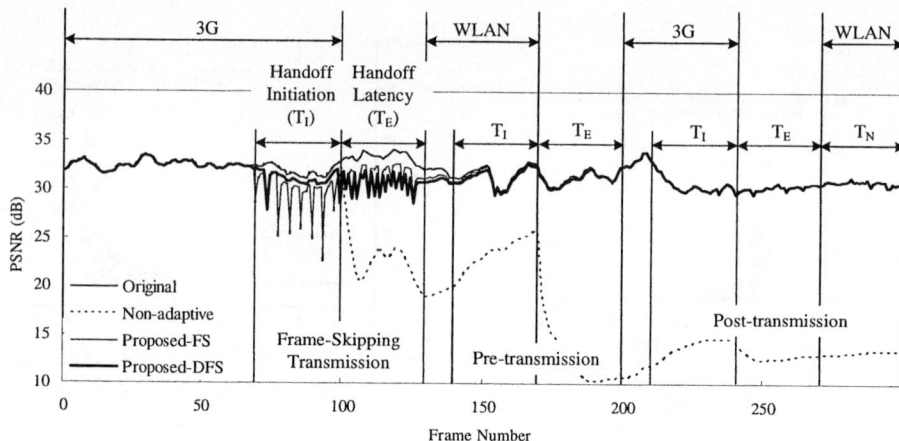

Fig. 6. PSNR performance of the proposed method

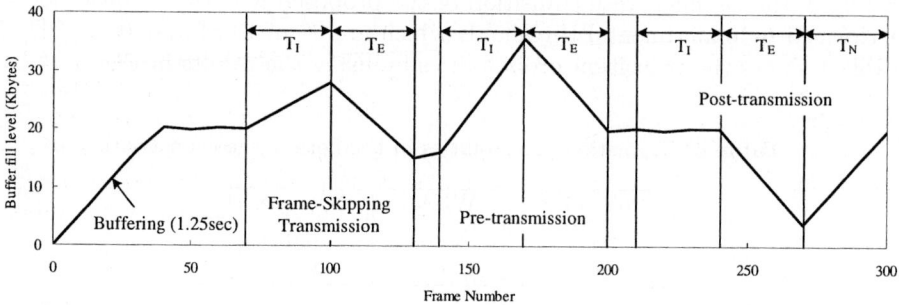

Fig. 7. Client buffer fill level

Case 2) WLAN → 3G

The handoff process is preformed from the 140th frame to the 200th frame. Since $\widehat{R}$ of the WLAN is high enough to transmit in advance all frames that can be lost due to handoff latency and the client buffer has sufficient empty space to receive all frames from the 140th frame to the 200th frame, the pre-transmission is performed during T_I.

Case 3) 3G → WLAN

The handoff process is performed from the 210th frame to the 270th frame. Unlike the first case, in this case, since $\widehat{R}$ of the WLAN is high enough to re-transmit lost frames after vertical handoff, the post-transmission is performed during T_N.

Figure 6 shows the PSNR performance of the proposed method in vertical handoff based on the transition scenario as described before. In Fig. 6, "Non-adaptive" means that the streaming server does not consider vertical handoff.

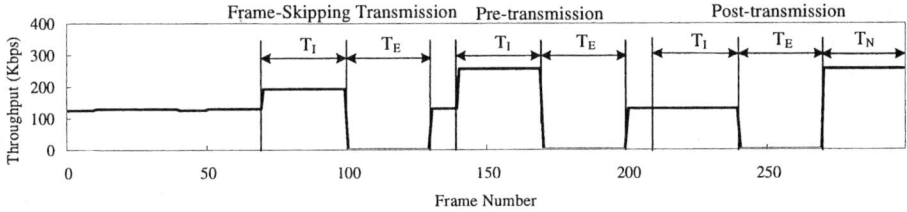

Fig. 8. Throughput graph for the proposed method

The difference between "Proposed-FS" and "Proposed-DFS" is whether frames are skipped dynamically or not. For the "Non-adaptive" case, every transition produces tremendous quality degradation. On the other hand, the proposed methods show that vertical handoff can be effectively overcome. In the first transition, the proposed method based on DFS shows better visual quality than the proposed method that skips frames just periodically. In the other transitions, since all frames are transmitted successfully to the client by the proposed pre-transmission and post-transmission methods, visual quality is maintained well without quality degradation. Figure 7 shows the client buffer fill level of the proposed method. As shown in Fig. 7, despite of three times vertical handoffs, the client buffer is maintained stably without the underflow caused by vertical handoff and the overflow by overtransmission. Figure 8 shows the throughput graph that is the result of the proposed method. It is seen that $\widehat{R}$ is predicted well and each proposed method utilizes the channel bandwidth effectively.

Note that the frame interpolation method can be applied easily to the result of the proposed frame-skipping transmission method in order to conceal skipped frames since skipped frames have high similarity compared with non-skipped frames.

6 Conclusions

In this paper, we have presented a video streaming method for VOD services that provides seamless playout at the client in vertical handoff. For seamless video playout, the streaming server predicts the network status by using both the channel modelling and the client buffer status. The channel status is estimated by the two-state Markov model by using the RSSI and the E_c/I_o. The client buffer status is estimated by analyzing RTCP RR and APP. Using the network status, the streaming server selects the proper video transmission method for vertical handoff among pre-transmission, post-transmission, and frame-skipping transmission. Experimental results show that the proposed method provides seamless video streaming in vertical handoff with both utilizing the channel bandwidth highly and maintaining the client buffer stably.

References

1. Savo, G. G.: Advanced wireless communications 4G technologies. WILEY (2004) 3–3
2. Stemm, M., Katz, R.-H.: Vertical handoffs in wireless overlay networks. ACM Trans. Networking and Applications **3** (1998) 335–350
3. McNair, J., Fang, Z.: Vertical handoffs in fourth-generation multinetwork environments. Wireless Communication. IEEE **11** (2004) 8–15
4. Varshney, U., Jain, R.: Issues in emerging 4G wireless networks. Computer IEEE **34** (2001) 94–96
5. Wu, H., Zhang, Q., Zhu, W.: Design Study for Multimedia Transport Protocol in Heterogeneous Networks. IEEE International Conference on Communications **1** (2003) 567–571
6. Salamah, M., Tansu, F., Khalil, N.: Buffering requirements for lossless vertical handoffs in wireless overlay networks. The 57th IEEE Semiannual Vehicular Technology Conference **3** (2003) 1984–1987
7. Jung, S. K., Cho, D. H., Song, O S.: QoS based vertical handoff method between UMTS systems and wireless LAN networks. 2004 IEEE 60th Vehicular Technology Conference **6** (2004) 4451–4455
8. Ma, L., Yu, F., Leung, V. C. M, Randhawa, T: A new method to support UMTS/WLAN vertical handover using SCTP. IEEE Wireless Communications **11** (2004) 44–51
9. Khansari, M., Jalali, A., Dubois, E., Mermelstein, P.: Low bitrate video transmission over fading channels for wireless microcellular systems. IEEE Trans. Circuits Syst. Video Technol. (1996) 1–11
10. Khansari, M., Jalali, A., Mermelstein, P.: Robust low bitrate video transmission over wireless access systems. in Proc. ICC. **1** (1994) 571–575
11. Ronald, Howard, A.: Dymanic Probabilistic Systems. Wiley, New York (1971)
12. Baldo, N., Horn, U., Kampmann, M., Hartung, F.: RTCP feedback based transmission rate control for 3G wireless multimedia streaming. Personal, Indoor and Mobile Radio Communications, PIMRC 2004. 15th IEEE International Symposium **3** (2004) 1817–1821
13. 3GPP TS 26.234 Rel. 6: Transparent end-to-end packet-switched streaming service (PSS): protocols and codecs
14. ISO/IED-JTC1/SC29/WG11: Test Model 5 (1993)

MPEG-4 FGS Video Traffic Model and Its Application in Simulations for Layered Video Multicast

Hui Wang, Jichang Sha, Xiao Sun, Jun Tao, and Wei He

Multimedia R&D Center, National University of Defense Technology,
47 Deya Road, Changsha, Hunan, China, 410073
huiwang@nudt.edu.cn

Abstract. CBR traffic models are commonly used in simulations to evaluate the performance of the adaptive video multicast protocols. However, more accurate traffic models, such as MPEG-4 FGS models, are necessary to simulate actual video traffic in performance evaluation of adaptive video multicast protocols. We first introduce Markov chain modulated first order autoregressive process to model the statistical properties of FGS layered video traffic, and then implement a layered rate control method based on the proposed FGS traffic model in NS-2. We then design three simulation experiments on RLM, each one adopting the proposed rate control method based on FGS model and one of three typical CBR layered traffic models respectively. The experiments reveal that the result of our scheme differs greatly from those of CBR schemes. Since our FGS model is more accurate than the CBR models, we suggest that layered rate control method based on FGS traffic model is more desirable in the simulations of adaptive video multicast protocols to get more fair and accurate evaluation results.

1 Introduction

Adaptive video multicast has become an essential component of many current and emerging distributed multimedia applications over the Internet, such as videoconferencing, distance learning and video streaming. In recent years, a lot of approaches [1-5] to adaptive video multicast have been proposed, addressing various issues and challenges. Among these solutions, layered video multicast scheme is considered as a promising technique to tackle heterogeneity problem efficiently and its representative protocols are RLM [1], FLID-DL [2], PLM [3] and HALM [4] and so on. The performance comparison and evaluation of fairness, scalability, stability and complexity to those protocols is very significant to confirm an adaptive strategy accommodating to applications' demands. Owing to complexity and poor accuracy of analyzing model method, and high cost in time and money of real practical experiments, computer simulation is commonly considered as an economical and accurate approach to study and evaluate adaptive video multicast protocols. In many simulation tools of networking, the object-oriented simulator, NS-2 with good scalability and simple programming features, has become a widely used simulation tool for assessing the performance of layered video multicast protocols.

There are two fundamental issues we must address in simulation [6]: one is the simulation of traffic load offered by video sources, the other is the performance simulation of video multicast application. For the first problem, using video traffic record file (trace file of frame size) or video traffic model to generate layered video traffic is commonly acceptable. With better accuracy to reflect traffic characteristic of a fixed video source, trace files, however, are less scalable and flexible to reflect statistical characteristic of one kind of video traffic than video traffic models. So video traffic models are desired and appropriate choices to investigate and evaluate the performance of adaptive layered video multicast protocols in heterogeneous networking environment.

For efficiently supporting adaptive delivery of video content over the Internet, scalable video coding has become a promising video coding technology, in which MPEG-4 SNR fine-granular-scalability (FGS) has been accepted as a factual standard of video codec for video streaming applications. FGS coding bitstream can be divided into a base layer and many FGS enhancement layers to support quality scalability where the base layer is elementary bitstream, and if the base layer is destroyed or lost, it can be recovered by means of error correction or error concealment, but due to serious network congestion, the widespread lost base layer data may affect the decoding of the enhancement layer bitstream, and finally induce a undesired video quality. So even if error control technology is adopted, the network bandwidth of the bottleneck link is demanded not to be lower than the average rate of FGS base layer. Because the FGS enhancement layers adopt bit plane coding technology, it becomes very easy to achieve the ideal target rate by truncating the compressed bitstream arbitrarily with very fine granularity rather than to change the quantization step value in encoding phase. The flexible and simple scalable rate control method of FGS encoder is fit well to solve the adaptive video multicast problem in heterogeneous networking environment.

The rest of the paper is organized as follows: Section 2 introduces the commonly used video traffic models in simulations for adaptive video multicast protocols. Section 3 presents a Markov chain modulated first order autoregressive process to model the statistical characteristics of the FGS scalable VBR traffic. In Section 5, we implement a layered rate control mechanism based on our proposed FGS video traffic model in NS-2, then show and compare how this model and three representative CBR layered traffic models have impacts on the performance of RLM protocol by simulation experiments. Section 6 concludes the paper.

2 Traffic Model in Simulations for Layered Video Multicast

2.1 Layered CBR Traffic Models

Layered CBR traffic models are the commonly used in simulations for layered video multicast based on NS-2, including linear layered rate model, exponential layered rate model, and hyperbolic layered rate model and so on. This kind of model has few parameters and is easy to realize. The expression and contrast of these models are shown in Table1.

Table 1. Several kinds of layered CBR traffic models

	Linear layered rate model	Exponential layered rate model	Hyperbolic layered rate model
Base Layer rate	$R_0 = 32 Kbps$	$R_0 = 32 Kbps$	$R_0 = 100 Kbps$
The number of Layers	N	N	N
Rate of i-th enhancement layer	$R_i = (i+1)*R_0, 1 \leq i < N$	$R_i = R_0 * C^i, 1 \leq i < N$	$R_i, R_{i+1} = R_{i-1}/C, 1 \leq i < \lfloor N/2 \rfloor$
Protocols or References	Reference[7]	RLM,FLID-DL,RLC	Reference[7]
Typical layered rate (Kbps) $N=5$	{32,64,96,128,160}	RLM:{32,64,128,256,512},C=2 FLID-DL*:{32,9,13,17,22},C=1.3 RLC*:{32,32,64,128,256},C=2	{100,50,50,25,25},C=2
Rate-adaptation	Linear increase, Linear decrease	Multiplicative increase, Multiplicative decrease	Inverse proportion increase, Inverse proportion decrease

*: The rate of FLID-DL and RLC protocol is an accumulative layered rate

To simulate and assess the congestion control methods for layered video multicast, Layered CBR traffic models borrow the idea of the congestion control in TCP in which the source rate is Additionally Increased and Multiplicatively Decreased (AIMD). Unfortunately, this simple model fails to reflect the nature of real video traffic, specifically, that the instantaneous traffic in each layer varies over time, and that there's a high correlation between the instantaneous traffic in each layer. Hence, they are not real video traffic models.

2.2 Abstract Universal Layered Traffic Model

To capture statistical characteristic of layered video traffic (e.g. burst and correlation), an abstract universal layered traffic model [9] was proposed to evaluate layered video multicast protocol. The model relies on two parameters, A and P, where A is the average number of packets generated per interval, and P characterizes the packet distribution in the interval. When P = 1, the model produces CBR-traffic. As P increases, traffic becomes more bursty (VBR-like). This model can describe both CBR traffic and VBR traffic, so it is called universal layered traffic model. Just as previous layered CBR traffic models, this model is an abstract model, not capturing some statistical characteristics of a kind of video source coding, and is also not a real video traffic model.

2.3 Single-Layer VBR Traffic Model

Researchers have developed numerous traffic models for the single-layer VBR video. Among those models, first order autoregressive model-AR(1) [8] is usually used to model video source traffic in video conferencing system, Markov chain [8] is used to model the switch characteristic of changing video scenes while TES model can precisely capture distribution of VBR traffic and autocorrelation statistical characteristics and so on. Through analysis and comparison among these models, AR(1) has such few parameters gotten easily that it is usually used to model the video traffic of non-change or few-change scenes, and for the trouble of parameterization and the complexity of modeling process, TES tool has seldom been used in modeling multi-layer video traffic although it has been proposed to model single-layer MPEG-4 video traffic [10].

Besides three familiar traffic models above, some other methods can also be used to model layered VBR traffic, such as On/Off model [7]. Nevertheless, to our knowledge, a complex source traffic model for scalable MPEG-4 FGS coding has not been used in existing studies.

3 Modeling FGS Video Traffic

3.1 Basic Modeling Idea

An whole video sequence can be divided into many different scenes which can be further divided into many sequential frames with almost similar background. In one scene, the sizes of the same kind of frames show some similarity because the background image and the foreground moving objects change with a low frequency, so the video traffic generated by the same kind of video frames can be approximatively treated as a stationary stochastic process. Furthermore, all scenes can be clustered to a small number of classes according to their traffic statistical characteristics, then, the changing characteristics of these scene classes can be analyzed and finally modeled using one modeling method.

The modeling methods and results will be present briefly in the following sections.

3.2 Generate Trace File of FGS Coding

We use Microsoft MPEG-4 FGS (version 2.2.0) codec to compress the movie "Jurassic I" with the configure parameters in Table 2, and generate a trace file.

Table 2. Parameters of FGS coding

Parameters	Video format	YUV format	Total frames	Frame rate	scalability	GoP period	I frame quantization step	P frame quantization step	B frame quantization step
Values	CIF	420	27984	30	Quality scalability	12	10	14	16

3.3 Video Scenes Segmentation

After getting the trace file of the FGS coding, we adopt the difference check scheme to segment video scenes. Suppose that the sizes of continuous GoPs in the same scene should be close, namely, if the difference between two sizes of continuous GoPs exceeds a given threshold, a scene switch will be considered happened. As the definition of the scene in base layer is consistent with one in FGS enhancement layer, this paper only uses the GoP video sequence in base layer for scenes segmentation. After calculating the size of each GoP in the base layer, the video sequence then have been segmented into 118 scenes, and it has been found that the duration of each scene approximately obeys geometric distribution [11].

3.4 Video Scenes Clustering

After segmenting video scenes, we use the mean value of each scene as clustering criterion, namely clustering scenes with close mean values into one class by running the K-means clustering algorithm. 118 scenes are clustered into 4 classes which are denoted as class 1, 2, 3, 4 respectively. The clustered scenes sequence is denoted as {33131223212231421132123111111411121321123323213222222222123122222224 21111122111132412241111233333323232223233344444422}.

3.5 Video Scene Modeling

For every class of scenes, one representative scene is chosen to be decomposed to 6 sub-sequences: I frame, P frame, B frame in base layer and I frame, P frame, B frame in FGS enhancement layer, each of which can be modeled as AR(1) respectively. Then, we use MATLAB to calculate the mean, the self-covariance and the variance of each 6 sub-sequences, and then get AR (1) coefficient a, b and η which are shown in Table 3. The detailed formula and calculating procedure have been illustrated in our work [11].

Table 3. AR (1) Model Parameters Table

Frames	Jurassic Park I: Class 1				Frames	Jurassic Park I: Class 2			
	a	b	η	X(1)		a	b	η	X(1)
I	0.818	3137.1	2.255	38128	I	0.723	3133.3	1.928	26400
P	0.469	4598	1.132	14632	P	0.736	4103.3	0.407	1072
B	0.507	2602.4	1.175	2520	B	0.648	3128	0.583	336
FGS_I	0.793	7961.7	2.840	104545	FGS_I	0.759	10776	1.492	89642
FGS_P	0.616	6906.2	7.115	117522	FGS_P	0.778	9350.3	1.847	91565
FGS_B	0.843	5817.7	3.370	104972	FGS_B	0.923	6209.6	0.949	91132
Frames	Jurassic Park I: Class 3				Frames	Jurassic Park I: Class 4			
	a	b	η	X(1)		a	b	η	X(1)
I	0.481	1962.1	8.141	30784	I	0.731	3277.4	4.178	60096
P	0.114	3285.6	0.636	984	P	0.103	2189.7	10.056	19904
B	0.477	1658.5	0.635	504	B	0.225	3241.5	2.551	2200
FGS_I	0.515	4595.1	9.595	94104	FGS_I	0.717	9854.9	4.247	177141
FGS_P	0.672	3960.4	7.904	95908	FGS_P	0.601	10301	6.884	201878
FGS_B	0.823	2935.5	5.726	95384	FGS_B	0.731	3277.4	4.178	60096

3.6 Video Scene Switch

For simulating the switch of the video scenes, we introduce Markov chain states to model the 4 classes of scenes, and the AR (1) model will generate simulated video sequence for each state. The video scene switch will be confirmed by the transformation probability between the states. Suppose that p_{ij} is transformation probability from the state i to the state j, then,

$$p_{ij} = \frac{number(State_i \rightarrow State_j)}{number(State_j \rightarrow Other)}$$

To get the transformation probability, we count the number of transformations of all kinds of states along the clustered video scenes sequence described in sect.3.4. After calculating, the probability vector for generating all 4 classes of scenes is $p = [0.3051 \quad 0.3729 \quad 0.2203 \quad 0.0932]$, further, the one step transformation probability matrix is gained as follow:

$$\pi = \begin{matrix} 1 \\ 2 \\ 3 \\ 4 \end{matrix} \begin{bmatrix} 0.5287 & 0.2778 & 0.1389 & 0.0556 \\ 0.2045 & 0.4773 & 0.2500 & 0.0682 \\ 0.1923 & 0.4231 & 0.3462 & 0.0385 \\ 0.2727 & 0.2727 & 0 & 0.4545 \end{bmatrix}$$

3.7 Verification for FGS Video Traffic Model

To verify the availability of the proposed FGS model, we have compared the traffic generated by the trace file described in sect. 3.2 with the one generated by our proposed FGS model, then find that the simulated traffic can be well fit the real one in terms of the sizes of video frames, the probability distribution and the auto-correlation function. Furthermore, we introduce the both traffic into NS-2, and run a video streaming simulation scenario based on Client/Server mode, then, simulation results reflect that tested packet loss radios and system throughputs induced by both traffic are almost close, which sufficiently verify the availability of our proposed FGS video traffic model [11].

For the lack of space, we introduce here only the methods and results of modeling FGS video traffic from the sect. 3.1 to 3.7. Interested readers may refer to our work in [11] for completed modeling procedure and verification simulations.

4 Simulations for Layered Video Multicast Base on FGS Video Traffic Model

On one hand, the FGS video traffic model can improve the accuracy of the simulations for adaptive video multicast protocols, such as RLM, FLID-DL, PLM, etc.; on the other hand, it can also evaluate layered rate control scheme base on FGS video traffic model.

4.1 Layered Rate Control Scheme Base on FGS Video Traffic Model

As a scalable video codec, the range of FGS rates may be denoted as (R_{min}, R_{max}) where the value R_{min} corresponds to the bit rate under which the received video quality would not be acceptable, and R_{max} to the rate above which there is no significant improvement of visual quality. Because the base layer must be transmitted, we only focus on the rate control of enhancement layers. In order to adapt to the dynamic bandwidth, the rate of enhancement layer can be changed in the range from 0 to $(R_{max} - R_{min})$. The ideal goal of rate control is to try best effort to make the rate of generated video traffic almost be a constant rate under the condition of receiving the best video quality. The base layer of FGS is VBR stream, and after using the rate control scheme to truncate the enhancement layer, the rate of multi-layer FGS traffic can be controlled as semi-CBR. Hence, we implement a layered rate control scheme in NS-2, which is shown in Fig. 1.

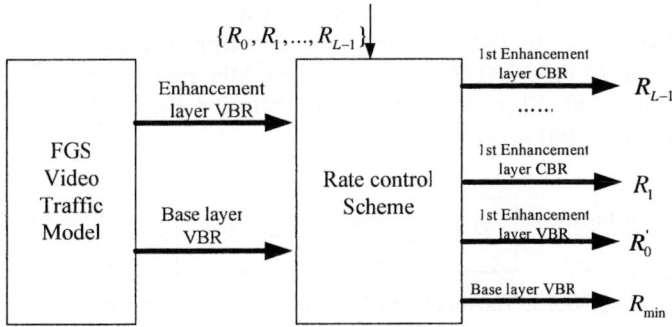

Fig. 1. Layered rate control scheme base on FGS traffic model

(1) Given that the rates of L layers traffic are needed to be generated for a layered video multicast application, which are denoted as $\{R_0, R_1, ..., R_{L-1}\}, R_0 > R_{min}$, $R_0 + R_1 + ... + R_i \leq R_{max}, 1 \leq i \leq L-1$.

(2) As shown in Fig. 1, the layer with the rate value R_0 is divided into two new layers where the first layer corresponds to FGS base layer with the rate R_{min} generated by FGS traffic model, and the second layer corresponds to the 1st enhancement layer with the rate R_0' where $R_{min} + R_0' \approx R_0$. $R_1, ..., R_{L-1}$ represents the average rate of the 2nd to the L-th enhancement layer respectively. So the number of actually generated layers is L+1.

(3) We adopt the FGS traffic model to generate the traffic of the I, P, B frame and introduce a rate control scheme. The base layer of all frames should be transmitted totally, and the truncation scheme of the 1st enhancement layer of all frames is to firstly allocate the rate R_0 averagely to all GoPs in per second, then, to calculate the result of the target rate allocated to every GoP minus the sum of the base layers rate in the GoP. If there are bandwidth remains, the residual rate will be allocated into each

frame of the GoP averagely which can generate the 1st enhancement layer with the rate R_0'. This allocation scheme is not the rate-distortion optimal one, but our video traffic model can easily support the rate allocation scheme based on optimal rate-distortion.
(4) The rates from the 2nd to the L-th enhancement layers are directly allocated from the traffic generated by our FGS model to match the demanded rates.

4.2 Simulation Experiments

1. Simulation Scenario and Objectives

The topology of the simulation experiments is shown in Fig. 2. We use a single video session with FGS or CBR traffic as source across the bottleneck link (between router R1 and R2) with 1 Mbps of bandwidth and 10 milliseconds of delay. Each exterior link is set to 10 Mbps of bandwidth and 10 milliseconds of delay. We start the multicast source at time 0 and start its sink running RLM protocol after 3 seconds. At time 50 seconds, we start a CBR source sharing over the bottleneck link at rate 500 Kbps to use half of the bottleneck bandwidth. At time 100 seconds, we increase the rate of the CBR source to 750 Kbps and leave 250 Kbps available bandwidth for the multicast session. At time 200 seconds, we decrease the rate of the CBR source to 250 Kbps and leave 750 Kbps available bandwidth for the multicast session. The simulation is run for 300 seconds.

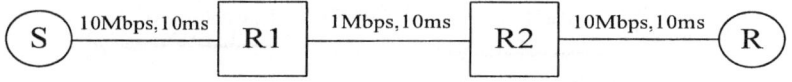

Fig. 2. The topology of the simulation experiments

We have done three groups of simulations, each of which is consisted of two simulations with one FGS layered traffic and CBR layered traffic respectively, the grouping is showed in Table 4..

Through the three groups of the simulations, the objective is to investigate difference on fast convergence, packet loss ratio, RLM throughput of FGS model and CBR models when the available bandwidth changes during a session.

Table 4. Three groups of simulations

Groups	CBR model(Kbps)		FGS model(Kbps)	
1st group	CBR-Linear (CBR-1)	{250,280,310,340,370}	FGS-1	{530,310,340,370}
2nd group	CBR-Exponential(CBR-2)	{250,75,98,127,165},C=1.3	FGS-2	{325,98,127,165}
3rd group	CBR-Hyperbolic (CBR-3)	{250,125,125,63,63}	FGS-3	{375,125,63,63}

2. Analyses of the Simulation Results

The FGS base layer will divide into two VBR streams according to the above layered rate control scheme base on the FGS traffic model. The two streams are new base layer and new 1st enhancement layer where The base layer average rate is 247kbps.

In Fig.3, Fig.4 and Fig.5, graphs of the RLM throughput against the simulation time are plotted. The detailed simulation results of convergence time, packet loss ratio and RLM average throughput are showed in Table 5.

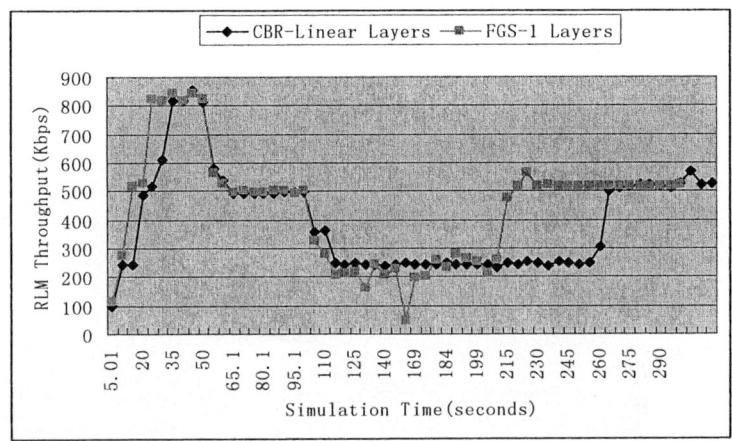

Fig. 3. Comparison of RLM Throughput with CBR-Linear Layers and FGS-1 Layers

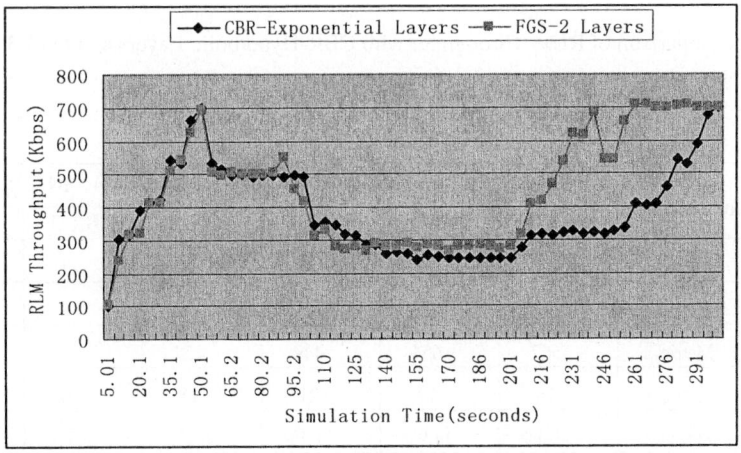

Fig. 4. Comparison of RLM Throughput with CBR-Exponential Layers and FGS-2 Layers

From the results, the changing curves of the two RLM throughputs in each group have great difference, specially existing at the 3rd and 4th phases. Because the bottleneck link bandwidth is decreased to 250Kbps at the 3rd phase, only base layer (1st and 3rd groups) can be transmitted through the bottleneck link. The FGS base layer is VBR stream, and its burst traffic characteristic distinguishes from any one of CBR stream. This difference further affects the RLM throughput at the 4th phase.

As listed in table 5, the simulation results show that the packet loss ratio of FGS traffic is lower than CBR traffic at the 2nd phase in the 2nd and 3rd experiment groups, and is higher at the 3rd and 4th phases in all experiment groups. Anyhow, when bottleneck link bandwidth is more than the total rate of the first two FGS VBR layers, the performances of RLM protocol with FGS model and CBR model are almost the same. Otherwise, they will have great difference. Hence, there will be error if using any one of the three CBR traffic models to simulate the FGS layered traffic, and we suggest that the layered rate control scheme based on our proposed FGS

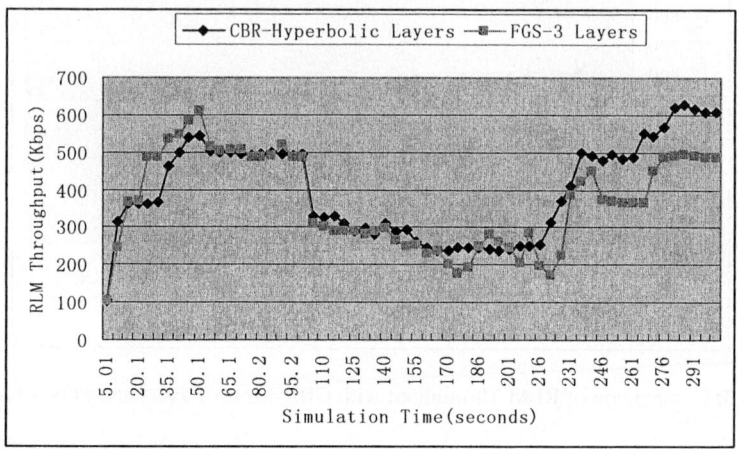

Fig. 5. Comparison of RLM Throughput with CBR-Hyperbolic Layers and FGS-3 Layers

Table 5. The comparison of three simulations' results

Evaluation metrics		1st Group		2nd Group		3rd Group	
		CBR-1	FGS-1	CBR-2	FGS-2	CBR-3	FGS-3
1st Time phase	Metric-1	41	41	40	31	42	42
	Metric-2	0.08%	0.3%	0	0	0	0
	Metric-3	562	654	449	428	401	444
2nd Time phase	Metric-1	16	17	21	15	10	29
	Metric-2	11.3%	11.9%	11.2%	8.4%	9.5%	7%
	Metric-3	519	520	513	506	509	511
3rd Time phase	Metric-1	18	58	60	39	20	53
	Metric-2	6.9%	11.5%	18%	20.2%	16.9%	18.6%
	Metric-3	262	205	281	290	282	267
4th Time phase	Metric-1	45	89	75	10	53	67
	Metric-2	0.04%	0.04%	0	0.09%	0	0
	Metric-3	409	503	416	620	485	385

Metric-1: Convergence time (seconds), Metric-2: Loss ratio, Metric-3: Average throughput (Kbps)

traffic model will generate more accurate and significant results in evaluation the performance of adaptive video multicast protocols.

5 Conclusions

This paper proposes a FGS video traffic model, implements a layered rate control method based on this model, and compares this method with three representative CBR layered traffic models in terms of impacts on RLM protocol performance. By comparisons of simulations, we find that when the bottleneck link bandwidth is lower than the sum of the first two VBR traffic average rate, there are greater diversities to the RLM protocol performances with the three CBR layered traffic model and our FGS layered traffic model respectively. So we suggest that layered rate control method based on FGS traffic model is more desirable in the simulations of adaptive video multicast protocols to get more fair and accurate evaluation results.

Next step, we will employ the layered rate control method based on the FGS traffic model to evaluate more performances (e.g. fairness) of more adaptive video multicast protocols (e.g. PLM and FLID-DL).

References

1. S. McCanne, V. Jacobson, and M. Vetterli, "Receiver-driven layered multicast," in Proceedings of ACM SIGCOMM '96, (Stanford, CA), September 1996. 27
2. J. Byers, M. Frumin, G. Horn and M. Lubby, "FLID-DL: Congestion Control for Layered Multicast", in Proc.ACM Sigcomm '94, London, UK, Sep. 1994, pp. 58-67.
3. A. Legout, "PLM: Fast convergence for cumulative layered multicast transmission scheme". Proceedings of ACM SIGMETRICS 2000, 2000.
4. J. Liu, B. Li, and Y.-Q. Zhang, "A Hybrid Adaptation Protocol for TCP-Friendly Layered Multicast and Its Optimal Rate Allocation," Proc. Ann. Joint Conf. IEEE Computer and Comm. Soc. (Infocom 02), IEEE Press, 2002, pp. 1520-1530.
5. Wang Hui, Zhang Jun, Jiang Zhihong, etc., "ALM: a Novel Adaptive Layer Mapping Algorithm for Intra-Session bandwidth allocation in Layered Video Multicasts," Proc. of 8th IASTED International Conference on Internet and Multimedia systems and Applications, 2004, pp.124-130.
6. J. Liu, B. Li, and Y.-Q. Zhang, "Adaptive Video Multicast over the Internet," IEEE Multimedia, Vol. 10, No. 1, pp. 22-31, January/February 2003.
7. A. Matrawy, I. Lambadaris, and C. Huang, "On Layered Video Fairness on IP Networks", in Proc. of IEEE Global Communications Conference, IEEE GLOBECOM2001, San Antonio, TX, November 2001.
8. Ichael R.Izquierdo, "A Survey of Statistical Source Models for Variable Bit-Rate Compressed Video, " Multimedia System 7:199—213 (1999).
9. S. Bajaj, L. Breslau, and S. Shenker, "Uniform Versus Priority Dropping for Layered Video," Proc. ACM Sigcomm Conf., ACM Press, Sept. 1998, pp.131-143.
10. Ashraf Matrawy, Ioannis Lambadaris, Changcheng Huang, "MPEG 4 Traffic Modeling Using The Transform Expand Sample Methodology," in Proc. of the 4th IEEE International Workshop on Networked Appliances, IWNA4, Gaithersburg, MD, January 2002.
11. He Wei, Wang Hui, "A Video Traffic Model for MPEG-4 FGS", Chinese Computer Simulation, No 3, 2004, 35-40.

Dynamic Voltage Scaling for Real-Time Scheduling of Multimedia Tasks

Yeong Rak Seong[1], Min-Sik Gong[2], Ha Ryoung Oh[1], and Cheol-Hoon Lee[2]

[1] Computer Engineering Lab., School of Electrical Engineering,
Kookmin University, Seoul 136-702, Korea
{yeong, hroh}@kookmin.ac.kr
[2] System Software Lab., Dept. of Computer Engineering,
Chungnam National University, Taejeon 305-764, Korea
{msgong, chlee}@ce.cnu.ac.kr

Abstract. Real-time multimedia applications are usually played back many times. For those applications, the distribution of actual execution time is no longer unknown from the second playback. In this paper, we propose a novel dynamic voltage scaling (DVS) algorithm, called CLDVS, for scheduling real-time multimedia applications. In order to minimize energy consumption, CLDVS determines the processor's operating frequency and supply voltage using the distribution of actual execution time during a time interval at the beginning of the interval. For that, all active tasks in the time interval are identified and incrementally placed on the time vs. scaling factor space in order to reduce variations of the scaling factor for minimum energy consumption. Simulation experiments show CLDVS achieves enormous energy savings and outperforms the existing DVS algorithms with different dynamic workload characteristics.

1 Introduction

Real-time processing is used to control various complex systems containing tasks which have to complete execution within strict time constraints, called deadlines. If meeting time constraints is critical for the system operation, then the deadline is considered to be *hard*. If missing one or a few deadlines degrades the overall performance but causes no serious damage, then the deadline is considered to be *soft*.

Recently there has been a rapid and wide spread of battery-powered mobile computing platforms for hard real-time multimedia processing, such as portable DVD players and MP3 players. Compared to traditional multimedia systems, energy consumption is a major concern due to the available battery life for those devices. The operating system therefore should manage system resources, such as the CPU, in an energy-efficient manner.

Dynamic Voltage Scaling (DVS) is a common technique to reduce CPU energy consumption [1, 2, 3, 4, 5, 6]. It exploits the characteristics of CMOS logic circuits: the maximum operating clock frequency is proportional to the supply voltage, and the energy dissipated per cycle scales quadratically to the supply voltage ($E \propto V^2$) [7]. The major goal of DVS is to reduce energy consumption as much as possible without degrading application performance. Therefore, DVS for real-time multimedia systems should scale the supply voltage and operating clock frequency while still meeting the real-time constraints.

Generally real-time tasks are specified with worst-case computation requirements. However, their actual execution times are much less than the worst-case values for most invocations. [8] reports that the ratio of the worst-case execution time to the best-case execution time can be as high as 10 in typical applications. In most real-time application areas, before a task finishes, its actual computation requirements are unknown. Thus, most existing DVS researches have concentrated on utilizing the difference between worst-case and actual execution times.

Meanwhile, multimedia files have a frame-based structure. Thus, multimedia processing is carried out on a frame-by-frame basis, every invocation yielding a variable amount of actual execution requirement. Unlike traditional real-time applications, however, real-time multimedia applications are usually played back many times. For example, we repeatedly listen to an MP3 audio file, and watch an MPEG movie several times. Thus, if we store workload information of every frame in the files to somewhere, the information can be used to efficiently schedule the tasks from the next playback.

1.1 Related Work

Recently, significant research and development efforts have been made on DVS techniques. We can categorize the DVS techniques into three classes: (i) relying on average processor utilization at periodic intervals [9, 10], (ii) using application worst-case execution times [2, 6], and (iii) using application actual execution times [1, 2, 3, 4]. The first algorithms adjust the processor clock frequency to average of the current processor load. Although the algorithms result in large energy savings, they are inappropriate for real-time applications. The second algorithms schedule tasks by using the worst-case total processor utilization. Thus, they are unsuitable for multimedia applications due to highly irregular actual computation demands.

The third algorithms correspond to DVS in a real-time system's perspective. They can be further categorized into two classes: *intra-task* DVS and *inter-task* DVS. Intra-task algorithms adjust the processor frequency scaling factor within the boundaries of a given task. Considering the actual execution time is smaller than the worst-case execution time, they reduce processor speed as low as possible when a task is dispatched, and gradually accelerate speed to meet real-time constraints. On the other hand, inter-task algorithms determine the scaling factor at task arrival or completion times. Thus, they less frequently change processor speed than the former ones.

Gruian [1] proposed a DVS framework for hard real-time tasks with fixed priorities. It targets energy consumption reduction by using both on-line and off-line decisions, taken both at inter-task and intra-task levels. For that, it employs stochastic data to derive energy efficient schedules.

Pillai and Shin [2] proposed two inter-task DVS algorithms: Cycle-Conserving EDF (ccEDF) and Look-Ahead EDF (laEDF). The algorithms are based on updating and predicting the instantaneous utilization of the periodic task set. While the former initially assumes the worst case and executes at a high frequency until some tasks complete, the latter defers as much work as possible, and sets the operating frequency to meet the minimum work that must be done now to ensure no remaining tasks violate their deadlines.

Aydin et al. [3, 4] proposed a reclaiming algorithm (DRA) and a speculation-based algorithm (AGR). These two inter-task algorithms compare the actual execution history and the worst-case schedule, and then calculate the earliness of the dispatched task to reduce the processor clock frequency. The earliness is computed by using a simple data structure, called α-queue, which totally orders tasks by an extended EDF ordering scheme, called EDF* policy. The later algorithm speculatively assumes that the actual execution time will most probably smaller than the worst-case execution time; and adjusts speed based on the expected workload.

1.2 Paper Organization and Contribution

In this paper, we propose a novel DVS algorithm for real-time multimedia applications called CLDVS. It is based on the fact that the actual execution requirements of the real-time tasks processing multimedia files are no longer unknown after the files are played once. The key idea is that each task executes at the lowest attainable frequency/voltage level by using known actual computation requirements, while guaranteeing feasible execution of all upcoming tasks. In order to minimize energy consumption, CLDVS determines the processor's operating frequency and supply voltage using the distribution of actual execution time during a time interval at the beginning of the interval. For that, all active tasks in the time interval are identified and incrementally placed on the time vs. scaling factor space in order to reduce variations of the scaling factor for minimum energy consumption. Simulation experiments show CLDVS achieves enormous energy savings and outperforms the existing DVS algorithms with different dynamic workload characteristics.

We consider a preemptive hard real-time system in which real-time tasks are scheduled under the earliest-deadline-first (EDF) algorithm [11]. We assume an ideal processor in which the clock frequency and the supply voltage can be changed continuously within its operation range $[f_{min}, f_{max}]$ and $[V_{min}, V_{max}]$. We also assume the processor clock frequency and supply voltage are always scaled with the same processor speed scaling factor α, $0 \leq \alpha \leq 1$, i.e. $\alpha \equiv f/f_{max} = V/V_{max}$, and $f_{min} = V_{min} = 0$.

In [2, 4, 6, 12], some kind of clairvoyant DVS algorithms, which utilize the actual execution time, are considered for performance comparison. However, those algorithms can hardly consider any timing constraints of real-time tasks. Thus, they just provide simple unrealistic lower bounds and are not applicable to schedule hard real-time tasks.

Table 1. Used notation

Notation	Meaning
α	the voltage/frequency scaling factor
τ_i	the i-th task
d_i	the relative deadline of τ_i
p_i	the period of τ_i
p_{max}	the largest period of the given task set ($\stackrel{\text{def}}{=} \max_{i=1}^{n} p_i$)
C_i	the worst-case execution time of τ_i without scaling (i.e., when $\alpha = 1$)
τ_{ij}	the j-th job of τ_i
r_{ij}	the release time of τ_{ij} ($\equiv p_i \cdot (j-1)$)
d_{ij}	the deadline of τ_{ij} ($\equiv r_{ij} + d_i$)
e_{ij}	the actual execution time of τ_{ij} without scaling
$R_{ij}(t)$	the remaining execution time of τ_{ij} at time t without scaling

This paper is organized as follows. In the next section, details of the CLDVS algorithm and an illustrative example are presented. Simulation results are given and analyzed in Section 3. Section 4 concludes the paper with a discussion of practical issues and future works.

Although we will explain used notations when we first introduce them, they are summarized in Table 1 for readers' convenience.

2 The CLDVS Algorithm

In this section, we propose the CLDVS algorithm. This study is based on the classic periodic real-time task model in [11]. In the model, there is a set of tasks $T = \{\tau_1, \tau_2, \cdots, \tau_n\}$, where each task τ_i is defined by a period p_i, and a worst-case execution time (WCET) C_i. The relative deadline d_i of the task τ_i is equal to p_i, and each task starts at time 0. All tasks are fully preemptive and independent, i.e. each task can be preempted anytime and does not depend on the initiation and completion of other tasks. The periodically released instances of a task are called jobs. The j-th job of τ_i, τ_{ij}, is released at time $r_{ij} (\equiv p_i \cdot (j-1))$ and has to be completed until time $d_{ij} (\equiv r_{ij} + d_i = p_i \cdot j)$. Thus τ_{ij} must be completed before τ_{ij+1} releases. The hyperperiod of the task set is defined as the least common multiple of p_i's. The scheduling result within a hyperperiod does not affect others. Thus, in this paper, we will only consider schedules during a hyperperiod. In addition to this traditional model, we assume the actual execution time of a job is already known before it releases in this paper. The actual execution time of τ_{ij} is denoted as e_{ij}. The remaining actual time of τ_{ij} at time t is denoted as $R_{ij}(t)$.

In CLDVS, the frequency and voltage scaling factor during a time interval, called *lookup window*, is calculated at the beginning of the time interval. The length of the lookup window can be arbitrarily determined. In this paper, it is set to the largest period p_{max} of the given task set. Fig. 1 shows the proposed algorithm. When a job τ_{ij} is released, the function $Calculate\_\alpha(\tau_{ij})$ is called.

$WhenRelease(\tau_{ij})$
　　$\alpha = Calculate\_\alpha(r_{ij})$;
　　$SetFrequency(\alpha)$;

$Calculate\_\alpha(t)$
　　// Let τ_{ca} be the current job.
　　// Let Q be the ready queue of the operating system.
　　// Let L be the list of unreleased tasks.
　　// Let Ψ be the scaling table. $\Psi(t)$ returns the scaling value at time t.
　　// Let W be the active work set.
　　$\alpha := \Psi(t)$;
　　if $\alpha < 0$ **then**　　// *alpha* has not been calculated before
　　　　$W := \{\langle \tau_{ca}, t, d_{ca}, R_{ca}(t) \rangle\}$;
　　　　foreach job $\tau_{kb} \in Q$
　　　　　　$W := W \cup \{\langle \tau_{kb}, t, d_{kb}, R_{kb}(t) \rangle\}$;
　　　　foreach job $\tau_{kb} \in L$ such that $t < r_k < t + p_{max}$
　　　　　　$W := W \cup \{\langle \tau_{kb}, max(t, r_{kb}), min(d_{kb}, t + p_{max}),$
　　　　　　　　　　$l_{kb}(max(t, r_{kb}), min(d_{kb}, t + p_{max})) \rangle\}$;
　　　　sort W in ascending order of $(w_t - w_f), w \in W$;
　　　　$\Psi := \emptyset$;
　　　　foreach work $\langle w_{ID}, w_f, w_t, w_l \rangle \in W$
　　　　　　$\Psi[w_f, w_t] \Leftarrow w_l$;
　　　　$\alpha := \Psi(t)$;
　　endif
　　return α;

Fig. 1. The CLDVS algorithm

If the scaling factor α at that time has not been determined before, the scaling table Ψ is constructed.

First, the workload description of each active job in $[t, t + p_{max}]$, which has been released before $t + p_{max}$ but not completed until t, is inserted into the active work set W. A work w is characterized by a tuple $\langle w_{ID}, w_f, w_t, w_l \rangle$, which means workload w_l of the job w_{ID} has to be executed in $[w_f, w_t]$. The inserted works include (i) the current job τ_{ca}, (ii) the jobs in the ready queue Q at time t, and (iii) the jobs, which will be released in $[t, t + p_{max}]$. In the first two cases (i) and (ii), all remain workloads should be executed in $[t, t + p_{max}]$, since the jobs' deadlines are earlier than $t + p_{max}$. However, in the last case (iii), some jobs may have deadlines later than $t + p_{max}$. Then, the only part of workloads has to be assigned in $[t, t + p_{max}]$. $l_{kb}(t_u, t_v)$ denotes the partial workload of the job τ_{kb} in $[t_u, t_v]$.

Then, in order to consider the most time-restricted works first, the works are sorted in ascending order of the lengths of their time ranges. Finally, the scaling table Ψ is constructed by incrementally adding works in W. At this time, to reduce the energy consumption, each work is assigned into the least loaded time zones first, then the next least loaded time zones, and so on. After Ψ is constructed, the operating frequency and the supply voltage are scaled according to the scaling factor α at time t. The overall time complexity of the algorithm is $O(n^2 \log n)$ due to the last **foreach** statement, where $n = |W|$.

Table 2. An example task set

Task (i)	Period (p_i)	Worst-case Execution Time (C_i)	Actual Execution Time					
			e_{i1}	e_{i2}	e_{i3}	e_{i4}	e_{i5}	e_{i6}
1	20	10	2	4	3	3	10	2
2	40	10	4	6	3	-	-	-
3	60	10	10	3	-	-	-	-

2.1 An Illustrative Example

Consider a task set in Table 2. The hyperperiod of this task set is 120 (=LCM(20, 40, 60)). Fig. 2(a) shows the scheduling result generated by CLDVS. Since the length of the lookup window is 60 (= p_{max}), the scaling table Ψ is constructed at $t = 0$ and $t = 60$.

At $t = 0$, $W = \{\langle \tau_{11}, 0, 20, 2 \rangle, \langle \tau_{12}, 20, 40, 4 \rangle, \langle \tau_{13}, 40, 60, 3 \rangle, \langle \tau_{22}, 40, 60, 3 \rangle, \langle \tau_{21}, 0, 40, 4 \rangle, \langle \tau_{31}, 0, 60, 10 \rangle\}$. Note that half of e_{22} is assigned in [40, 60], since τ_{22} can be executed during [40, 80]. The rest will be used in the next lookup

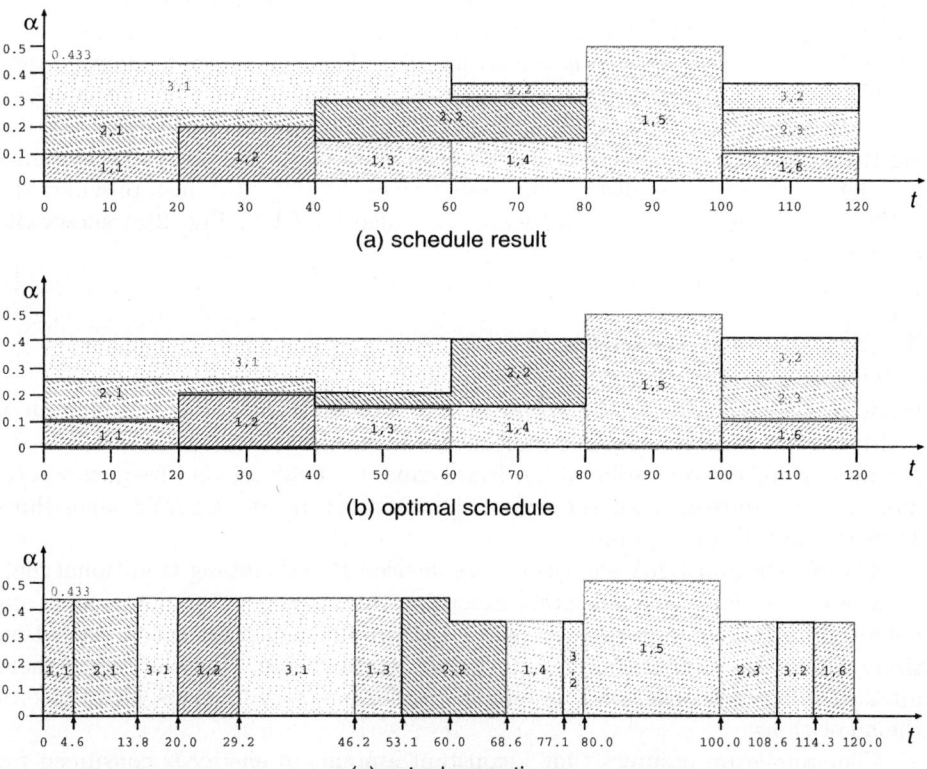

Fig. 2. Example schedule by CLDVS

window. Then, as shown in Fig. 2(a), the scaling table Ψ is constructed by repeatedly placing works in W. Note that, since the previous workloads placed in [0, 20] and [20, 40] were different, $\langle \tau_{21}, 0, 40, 4\rangle$ is placed so that the two time zones become equally loaded. $\langle \tau_{31}, 0, 60, 10\rangle$ is also placed in the same way. Since the workloads are evenly distributed in [0, 60], the resulting schedule is power optimal.

At $t = 60$, $W = \{\langle \tau_{14}, 60, 80, 3\rangle, \langle \tau_{15}, 80, 100, 10\rangle, \langle \tau_{16}, 100, 120, 2\rangle, \langle \tau_{22}, 60, 80, 3\rangle, \langle \tau_{23}, 80, 120, 3\rangle, \langle \tau_{32}, 60, 120, 3\rangle\}$. As shown in the figure, the scaling factor in [80, 100] is much larger than those in the other time intervals. However, since $\langle \tau_{15}, 80, 100, 10\rangle$ has to be executed just in [80, 100], there is no way to reduce the scaling factor in [80, 100]. Thus, the resulting schedule in [60, 120] is also power optimal.

Despite the fact that the above two adjacent schedules are power optimal in their own time ranges, the total schedule in [0, 120] is not power optimal. Fig. 2(b) shows the optimal schedule. The optimal schedule is different from the one by CLDVS. The length of the lookup window does not cause this. Actually, although the size of the lookup window is equal to the hyperperiod, CLDVS generates exactly the same schedule in this example. Until the workloads of τ_{21}, τ_{22}, and τ_{23} are placed, CLDVS produces the optimal result. On placing the workloads of τ_{31} and τ_{32}, the average workload of the time interval [0, 60] becomes larger than that of [60, 120]. For the power optimal schedule, part of workloads of τ_{22} in [40, 60] should be moved to [60, 80]. This means that adding a new workload can change the previous placement of workloads. At the worst-case a newly added workload can affect all the existing placements. Moreover, considering the hyperperiod is generally much longer than p_{max}, the optimal scheduling algorithm is quite unrealistic. The result given in Fig. 2(a) just provides the scaling factor. Actually, the tasks are scheduled by EDF. Fig. 2(c) shows the actual schedule.

3 Simulation Results

In order to evaluate the potential energy saving from voltage scaling in a multiply-reproducible real-time multimedia task scheduling, we have developed a simulator for the operation of hardware capable of voltage and frequency scaling. Also, we implemented the ccEDF [2], DRA [3, 4], and CLDVS algorithms for performance comparison.

The ccEDF and DRA algorithms are devised for scheduling traditional real-time task sets. They assume actual execution time is always unknown, and cannot produce higher performance than CLDVS, which utilizes actual execution time. Thus, the comparison is quite unfair in this sense. However, since there are no comparable ones, we compare the performance of CLDVS with those of the algorithms.

The simulation assumes that a constant amount of energy is consumed for each cycle of operation at a given voltage and frequency level. Only the energy consumed by the processor is computed, and variations due to different types of instructions executed are not considered. The simulator takes as input a task set, specified with the release time, deadline, and the actual execution time of each task. We also assume an ideal machine in that (i) the clock speed and the supply voltage can be adjusted in continuous levels with no switching overhead; (ii) a perfect software-controlled halt feature is provided by the processor, so idle time consumes no energy.

The power consumption for CMOS logic circuitry is dominated by dynamic power dissipation P_d, which is given by: $P_d \propto V_{dd}^2 \cdot f$, where V_{dd} is the supply voltage, and f is the operating clock frequency [7]. As mentioned earlier, V_{dd} and f are always scaled with the same scaling factor α in this paper. Therefore, the processor power consumption, P, can be formulated as: $P = k \cdot \alpha^3$, where k is a constant.

The periodic real-time multimedia task sets are generated randomly as follows. Each task has an equal probability of having a short (1-10ms), medium

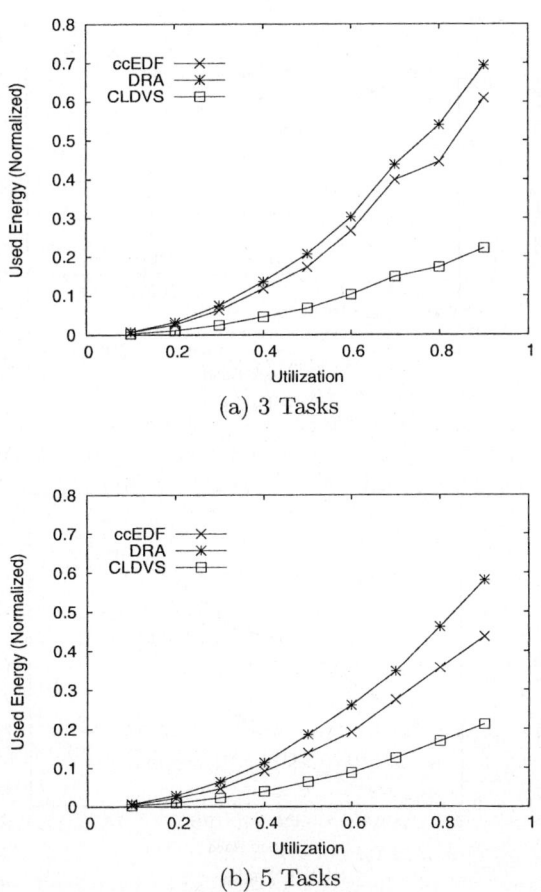

Fig. 3. Normalized energy consumption with load ratio 0.5

(10-100ms), or long (100-1000ms) period. Within each range, task periods are uniformly distributed. The computation requirements of the tasks are randomly assigned using a similar 3 range uniform distribution. The actual computation requirements follow a uniform probability distribution, where the mean is set to *load ratio* × WCET. Finally, the task computation requirements are scaled by a constant chosen such that the total processor utilization becomes a given value.

First, to see how the worst-case utilization of the task set affects the performance of CLDVS, the load ratio is fixed to 0.5, while changing the worst-case total utilization from 0.1 to 0.9 in increments of 0.1. Fig. 3 shows the energy consumption for task sets with 5, 10, and 15 tasks for ccEDF, DRA, and CLDVS. For every case, the average energy consumption of 10 task sets is measured, and those of the non-DVS approach normalize the results. As expected, CLDVS outperforms others in all simulations. Since ccEDF and DRA always have to consider the worst-case situation, they cannot reduce the processor speed to a

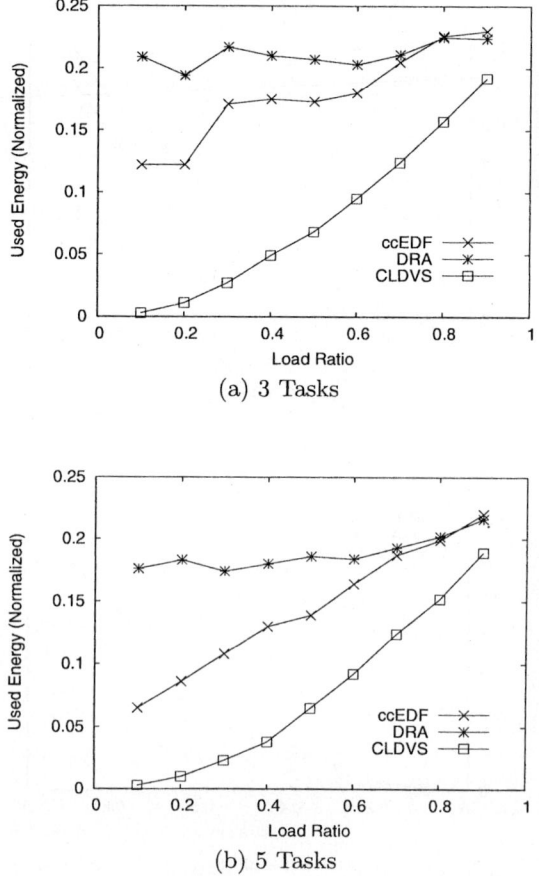

Fig. 4. Normalized energy consumption with utilization 0.5

great extent. However, CLDVS drastically lowers the scaling factor using information on the actual execution time of each job. The performance enhancement becomes larger as the utilization increases.

Secondly, to determine the effects of the load ratio on the performance of CLDVS, we have performed simulations while varying the load ratio. As shown in Fig. 4, we observe that (i) every algorithm reduces energy consumption as the load ratio decreases and (ii) processor's energy consumption can be drastically reduced by use of CLDVS. The performance gap between CLDVS and others also becomes much larger as the load ratio decreases [1].

4 Conclusion

In this paper, we have presented a novel dynamic voltage scaling algorithm for multiply-reproducible real-time multimedia applications. While the most existing traditional DVS algorithms assume the actual execution time of a task is unknown before the task completes, the proposed algorithm does not leave it as an unrevealed value and utilizes the knowledge to further lower the processor clock frequency and supply voltage. Simulation results show that the proposed algorithm achieves much larger energy savings than existing DVS algorithms. Also, the performance gap becomes much larger as the worst-case utilization of the task sets increases and the ratio between the average actual execution time and the worst-case execution time decreases.

The proposed algorithm can be applied to various battery-powered portable devices executing multimedia applications. The algorithm extends battery life of the devices and reduces heat generation. For example, consider a portable DVD player accompanied with a battery which claims to provide two hours of playback. Generally, it plays just one DVD title without recharging the battery. However, if we retrieve actual execution time information of DVD titles beforehand, it can play more DVD titles. Since the information only needs to specify the actual execution time of each frame in the DVD titles, its size will be small. The information would be cached in the flash memory of the DVD player.

We assumed the exact actual execution time of a task is measured beforehand. However, the actual execution time can slightly vary on the same hardware platform due to the effects of cache and other hardware. The difference can cause violation of some hard real-time constraints. In order to avoid this problem, one can use the worst-case actual execution time. In the future, we would like to investigate the effects of the difference. By the way, as opposed to our assumption, commercial variable voltage processors, e.g. Transmeta Crusoe [14] and Intel XScale [15], only have several discrete scaling levels. Expanding this work to the real hardware platform is also our future inquiry.

---

[1] As opposed to the research results in [3,4], DRA outperforms ccEDF only when the load ratio is very high. We suppose that this is caused by the high irregularity of periods and utilizations of tasks in the experimented task sets. When we use lesser irregular task sets, DRA outperforms ccEDF. [13] reports a similar result.

Acknowledgements

This work was supported in part by the Leading R&D Support Project of MIC, Korea.

References

1. Gruian, F.: Hard real-time scheduling for low-energy using stochastic data and DVS processors. In: Proceedings of the 2001 International Symposium on Low Power Electronics and Design. (2001) 46–51
2. Pillai, P., Shin, K.G.: Real-time dynamic voltage scaling for low-power embedded operating systems. In: Proceedings of the 18th ACM Symposium on Operating System Principles. (2001) 89–102
3. Aydin, H., Mejía-Alvarez, P., Mossé, D., Melhem, R.G.: Dynamic and aggressive scheduling techniques for power-aware real-time systems. In: Proceedings of the 22nd IEEE Real-Time Systems Symposium. (2001) 95–105
4. Aydin, H., Melhem, R.G., Mossé, D., Mejía-Alvarez, P.: Power-aware scheduling for periodic real-time tasks. IEEE Trans. Computers **53** (2004) 584–600
5. Zhu, D., Melhem, R.G., Childers, B.R.: Scheduling with dynamic voltage/speed adjustment using slack reclamation in multiprocessor real-time systems. IEEE Trans. Parallel Distrib. Syst. **14** (2003) 686–700
6. Lee, C.H., Shin, K.G.: On-line dynamic voltage scaling for hard real-time systems using the EDF algorithm. In: Proceedings of the 25th IEEE Real-Time Systems Symposium. (2004) 319–327
7. Burd, T.D., Brodersen, R.W.: Energy efficient CMOS microprocessor design. In: Proceedings of the 28th Annual Hawaii International Conference on System Sciences. (1995) 288–297
8. Ernst, R., Ye, W.: Embedded program timing analysis based on path clustering and architecture classification. In: Proceedings of the International Conference on Computer-Aided Design. (1997) 598–604
9. Weiser, M., Welch, B., Demers, A.J., Shenker, S.: Scheduling for reduced CPU energy. In: Proceedings of the First USENIX Symposium on Operating Systems Design and Implementation. (1994) 13–23
10. Pering, T., Burd, T., Brodersen, R.W.: The simulation and evaluation of dynamic voltage scaling algorithms. In: Proceedings of the 1998 International Symposium on Low Power Electronics and Design. (1998) 76–81
11. Liu, C.L., Layland, J.W.: Scheduling algorithms for multiprogramming in a hard-real-time environment. J. ACM **20** (1973) 46–61
12. Zhu, D., Mossé, D., Melhem, R.G.: Power-aware scheduling for AND/OR graphs in real-time systems. IEEE Trans. Parallel Distrib. Syst. **15** (2004) 849–864
13. Shin, D., Kim, W., Jeon, J., Kim, J., Min, S.L.: SimDVS: An integrated simulation environment for performance evaluation of dynamic voltage scaling algorithms. In: Proceedings of the 2nd International Workshop on Power-Aware Computer Systems. (2002) 141–156
14. Transmeta Corporation: http://www.transmeta.com/crusoe/longrun.htm. (2005)
15. Intel Corporation: http://developer.intel.com/design/intelxscale/benchmarks.htm. (2005)

Class Renegotiating Mechanism for Guaranteed End-to-End QoS over DiffServ Networks[*]

Dai-Boong Lee and Hwangjun Song

Department of Computer Science and Engineering,
Pohang University of Science and Technology (POSTECH),
San 31 Hyoja-dong, Nam-gu, Pohang, Kyungbuk, 790-784, Republic of Korea
{boong, hwangjun}@postech.ac.kr
http://mcsl.postech.ac.kr

Abstract. Differentiated-services model has been prevailed as a scalable solution to provide quality of service over the Internet. Many researches have been focused on per hop behavior or a single domain behavior to enhance quality of service. Thus, there are still difficulties in providing the end-to-end guaranteed service when the path between sender and receiver includes multiple domains. Furthermore differentiated-services model mainly considers quality of service for traffic aggregates due to the scalability, and the quality of service state may be time varying according to the network conditions in the case of relative service model, which make the problem more challenging to guarantee the end-to-end quality-of-service. In this paper, we study class renegotiating mechanisms along the path to provide the end-to-end guaranteed quality of service with the minimum networking price over multiple differentiated-service domains. The proposed mechanism includes an effective implementation of relative differentiated-service model, quality of service advertising mechanism and class renegotiating mechanisms. Finally, the experimental results are provided to show the performance of the proposed algorithm.

1 Introduction

The demand of multimedia services over the Internet has been rapidly increasing. In general, networked multimedia services such as Internet telephone and video-on-demand require stringent QoS (quality of service) requirements. As a scalable network solution, DiffServ (differentiated-services) [1] has got a spotlight because it controls the QoS of aggregate flows of a certain class instead of the QoS of individual flow. Hence it generically lacks the end-to-end QoS provision in the end-user point of view although DiffServ is a scalable solution for network QoS. So far, several proposals have been proposed to enhance end-to-end QoS within a single DiffServ domain. An extended approach of PHB(Per Hop Behaviors) tries to define per domain behavior (PDB) [2] as the expected treatment from edge to edge of a single DiffServ domain. That treatment can be described as quantifiable attributes (e.g., delay and packet loss rate) that passing packets experience. But the specific methods to provide

---

[*] This research was supported by the MIC(Ministry of Information and Communication), Korea, under the HNRC-ITRC(Home Network Research Center) support program supervised by the IITA(Institute of Information Technology Assessment).

absolute and statistical bounds for a DiffServ domain still need to be investigated. For controlling the attributes within a DiffServ domain and across DiffServ domains, a domain server (e.g., bandwidth broker (BB) [3]) can be used to perform resource management in its own domain and to communicate with domain servers in the neighboring domains for the negotiation of service level. There are some architectures for enhanced domain server coming from the centralized BB to provide scalable support of guaranteed services [4, 5]. The guaranteed services could be absolutely or statistically bounded services in DiffServ attributes for traffic aggregates. Recently, Christin et al. [6] proposed a quantitative assured forwarding (AF) service with absolute and proportional service differentiation in terms of loss, rates, and delays for traffic aggregates. Also, it is worthwhile to mention a study [7] in the differences of QoS experienced between individual flows and aggregate flows. Then if these extensions are added to the DiffServ architecture that IETF defines basically, it can be expected that each DiffServ domain can provide a certain absolute service ranges (e.g., average packet loss rate with some upper/lower margins) in DiffServ attributes. Another approach to provide absolute QoS [8] tries changing class selection upon feedback information from the receiver if the QoS request is not satisfied.

In this paper, we consider effective class renegotiating mechanisms to provide the guaranteed service to end systems with the minimum price over the multiple domains. In this scenario, the consideration of single DiffServ domain is not sufficient for the end-to-end QoS provision. The experienced QoS state (delay and packet loss rate in this paper) and the price of each class may differ in accordance with domains, and the QoS state may be time-varying according to network conditions. In order to provide the end-to-end QoS, coordination is required among domain servers in DiffServ domains having the linked path between sender and receiver. The problem we address includes how to efficiently advertise time varying QoS state and how to select the classes based on the advertised QoS state so as to satisfy end-to-end QoS request. This paper is organized as follows. Problem formulation of class renegotiating mechanisms, effective implementation method of relative service model, and QoS advertising mechanism are described in Section 2, experimental results and analysis are presented in Section 3, and finally concluding remarks are given in Section 4.

2 Proposed Optimal Class Renegotiating Mechanism

In this paper, we consider delay and packet loss rate as QoS factors. Over multiple domains, the end-to-end delay is the sum of delays caused in the individual domain and the rate that packet successfully arrives at the receiver is the product of the rates that packet is transmitted safely in each domain. Thus, the variance of end-to-end QoS state generally becomes larger compared with QoS state provided by each domain, and thus the increased variance may degrade the video quality seriously. In this case, dynamic class renegotiating mechanism is required. Now, we make the following assumptions.

Assumptions :
1. Each domain supports the different number of classes that provide different QoS states at the different price. And it is assumed that the class i always provides the better QoS than the class $i+1$ with higher price in the domain.

2. The total price is the sum of prices charged by domains along the end-to-end path. (The basic idea of the proposed algorithm in the following can be extended to various pricing mechanisms.)

Before the detail description, we define the CV (class vector) $(c_1, c_2, \cdots, c_N)$ that is the selected classes over multiple DiffServ domains along the path. That is, c_i is the selected class in the domain i. So, the proposed class renegotiating mechanism is to search for the optimal CV.

2.1 Problem Formulation and CV Renegotiation Based on Trellis

First of all, end-to-end guaranteed service problem is formulated into the optimization problem with multiple constraints. Then, optimal approach and fast approach are examined to get the solution of the problem.

2.1.1 Problem Formulation

CV along the path is determined to guarantee QoS with the minimum price. As mentioned earlier, the end-to-end delay is the sum of delays caused in the individual domain, and the rate that packet successfully arrives at the receiver is the product of the rates that packet is transmitted safely in each domain. Now, we can formulate the problem to provide the guaranteed end-to-end QoS state with the minimum networking price as follows.

Problem Formulation: Determine CV (c_1, c_2, c_3, ..., c_N) to minimize

$$\sum_{i=1}^{N} Price(c_i) \tag{1}$$

subject to $$\sum_{i=1}^{N} Delay(c_i) \leq Delay_{req}, \tag{2}$$

$$\prod_{i=1}^{N}(1 - PLR(c_i)) \geq 1 - PLR_{req}, \tag{3}$$

where c_i is the selected class in the domain i, N is the number of DiffServ domains between source and destination, $Price(c_i)$ is the price of the selected class in the domain i, $Delay(c_i)$ and $PLR(c_i)$ are the delay and packet loss rate of the selected class in the domain i, respectively, $Delay_{req}$ and PLR_{req} are the delay and the maximum tolerable packet loss rate required by the end systems, respectively. It is an optimization problem with multiple constraints.

2.1.2 Optimal CV Selection by Viterbi Algorithm

To solve the above problem, dynamic programming algorithm based on Trellis [11] is employed and fast pruning algorithm is used to reduce the computational complexity. It is summarized in Figure 1. As shown in this figure, each domain corresponds to a node and each class is mapped to the circle. When the cumulative QoS state by the domain $(i-1)$ is $\left(\sum_{k=1}^{i-1} Price(c_k), \prod_{k=1}^{i-1}(1 - PLR(c_k)), \sum_{k=1}^{i-1} Delay(c_k)\right)$ and the selected class in the domain i is $(Price(c_i), 1-PLR(c_i), Delay(c_i))$, the cumulative QoS state by the domain i becomes $\left(\sum_{k=1}^{i} Price(c_k), \prod_{k=1}^{i}(1-PLR(c_k)), \sum_{k=1}^{i} Delay(c_k) \right)$. If the cumulative QoS by the domain i does not satisfy the required QoS, then we do not need to check the CV including this part from the domain $(i+1)$ any more. Thus the required computational complexity can be reduced.

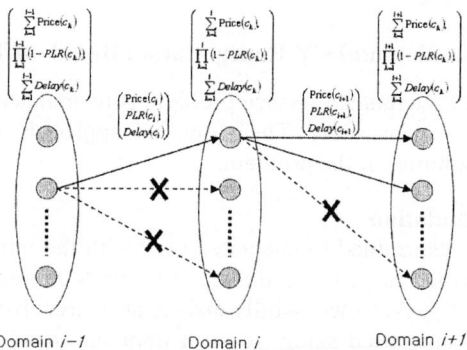

Fig. 1. Trellis for the optimal CV: the dot lines do not satisfy the given constraints

2.2 Relative Service Model and QoS Advertising Mechanism

Now, we consider the case that QoS state is time-varying. First, we address an effective implementation of relative service model, and then describe QoS advertising mechanism in detail. Note that the proposed class renegotiating mechanism can be extended to any other relative service model.

2.2.1 Implementation of Relative Service Model

In the case of assured forwarding (AF) service, queue structure generally consists of four physical queues to which independent forwarding services are provided. Each queue has three virtual queues to support three dropping levels as shown in (a) of Figure 2 [9]. The packets with the same class enter the same physical queue and then these packets are classified into three virtual queues according to their drop precedence. The drop precedence of each class is determined by its policy when packets arrive. The relative service model can be implemented by this queue structure and forwarding mechanism only when routers monitor the QoS state of each class continuously [10]. However, it is a big burden to routers and does not match to the basic idea of DiffServ.

In this paper, the relative service model is simply implemented by changing the queue structure as shown in (b) of Figure 2. One of the unique feature of the proposed method is that the packets with the same precedence are sent to the same physical queue and then they are divided into virtual queue according to the class. Token bucket model is employed as policer type due to the simplicity. In this case, the successfully forwarding packets enter the buffer with the high precedence while the dropping packets move to the buffer with the low precedence. It is achieved by controlling token. An arriving packet is marked with the lower precedence if and only if it is larger than the token bucket. The token rate is controlled to satisfy Eq. 4, and then packet forwarding mechanism makes the relative service model by setting to satisfy Eq. 5 under the assumption that class 1 provides the best service. In this paper, WRR (weighted round robin) is used for packet forwarding mechanism and the weight factors are determined by QoS states of classes.

$$\frac{R_x^y}{R_x^{y+1}} > \frac{R_{x+1}^y}{R_{x+1}^{y+1}} \tag{4}$$

$$\frac{R_x^y}{R_x^{y+1}} < \frac{W_{PQ(y)}}{W_{PQ(y+1)}} \tag{5}$$

where x is the class number satisfying $x \in \{1, 2, \cdots, m-1\}$, y is the drop precedence level number satisfying $y \in \{1, 2, \cdots, n-1\}$, m and n are the possible maximum numbers of class levels and drop precedence levels respectively, R_x^y is the rate of packets assigned to class x and drop precedence level y, and $W_{PQ(y)}$ is the weight of physical queue y. The proposed implementation method does not need to remember the states of router and just forward the incoming packets according to the weighing values of physical queues. Hence the required computational burden of router can be significantly reduced.

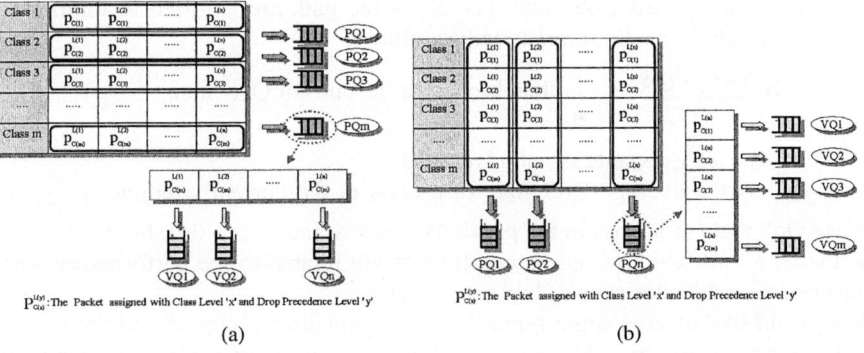

Fig. 2. Performance of queuing structures: (a) RFC 2597 and (b) the proposed method

2.2.2 QoS-State Advertising Mechanism

Since QoS state is random in each DiffServ domain supporting relative service model and end-to-end QoS state is function (sum/product) of these random variables, end-to-end QoS state is also random, whose variances generally become larger as the number of domains between two end systems increases [12]. As a result, the continuous media service can be seriously degraded due to the increased variances. Therefore, our object is to dynamically change CV along the path to provide the guaranteed service with the lowest price.

Now, we need to estimate QoS state for each flow to determine CV. Actually, it is observed that the QoS state of each flow is almost same as that of the class including the flow (See the Figure 5) (The same phenomenon is observed in [10]). The reason is that every individual flow in the same class is handled by the same policy and forwarding mechanism that is designed to provide the guaranteed QoS state to the class, and thus the QoS state experienced by the individual flow is almost same as that of the class. Hence, we can estimate the QoS state of each flow by observing that of the class in each domain. As a result, the computational overhead can be significantly reduced because we do not need to calculate the QoS of each flow. And, we take into account how to advertise QoS state. The more advertisement provides the more accurate QoS state, but increases the signaling overhead and computing load. Thus, we need to investigate effective QoS advertising mechanism and study the relation between the interval of QoS advertisements and the experienced QoS state. In this paper, we study two approaches: periodic approach and aperiodic approach.

2.2.3 Periodic QoS-State Advertisement
Every DiffServ domain calculates the QoS state every fixed time interval and the QoS state is broadcasted to other DiffServ domains. Based on the advertised QoS state, the CV along the path between sender and receiver are recalculated.

2.2.4 A Periodic QoS-State Advertisement
To avoid the unnecessary QoS state advertisements, CV re-searching and control signal overhead, aperiodic QoS state advertisement is examined. In this work, sliding window method is employed. That is, the QoS state is advertised only when the average QoS state in the sliding window abruptly changes more than the threshold value. Based on the advertised QoS state, CV along the path are adjusted to minimize the networking price. It can be summarized as follows.

$$\text{If } \frac{|QoS_{cur} - QoS_{prev}|}{QoS_{prev}} > T, \text{ then broadcast the current QoS state,} \qquad (6)$$

otherwise QoS state is not advertised,

where QoS_{cur} is the average QoS state of a class in the current window, QoS_{prev} is the average QoS state of a class in the previous window and T is a threshold value. Actually, the length of window and its coefficients are related to the performance since it determines the characteristics of low-pass filter.

We would like to give some remarks on the signaling overhead and the computational complexity of the proposed algorithm. In general, aperiodic case needs more computational complexity to continuously monitor QoS states than periodic case, but the signaling load is decreased since the unnecessary advertisements are avoided. As the advertising time interval of the periodic case decreases or the threshold value (Eq. 6) of the aperiodic case decreases, the accuracy of advertisement is improved at the cost of the increases signaling overhead. In the following, we consider two real environments. First of all, if BBs are available, additional computational complexity and signaling overhead to compute the optimal CV is very small since BBs have an effective mechanism to share service states of classes by advisements among them. Secondly, if BBs are not available, edge routers can work instead of BBs. Because edge router checks continuously both agreement and conformity of SLA (service level agreement), it monitors the service state of each class and sends it to other edge routers with a small amount of overhead. Consequently, each edge router can compute the optimal CV based on the updated service state information of each class.

3 Experimental Results

NS-2 is employed to compare the performance. As mentioned earlier, we focus on the QoS advertising mechanism and class renegotiating mechanism. In this paper, three cases are tested in the followings: no CV change, periodic CV change and aperiodic CV change. The numbers of QoS advertisements and CV changes are used as the measure of control signaling overhead. On the other hand, packet loss rate, time delay, and networking price are employed as the performance measures for quality of service. The tested network situation is shown in Figure 3. During the experiment, mean, variance and maximum deviation are employed as performance comparison. The reason that maximum deviation is included is that the instant QoS state deviation can degrade the quality of continuous media. And the test trace files are Star Wars (240*352 size) and Terminator-2 (QCIF size) encoded by MPEG-1, whose lengths are 40,000 frames.

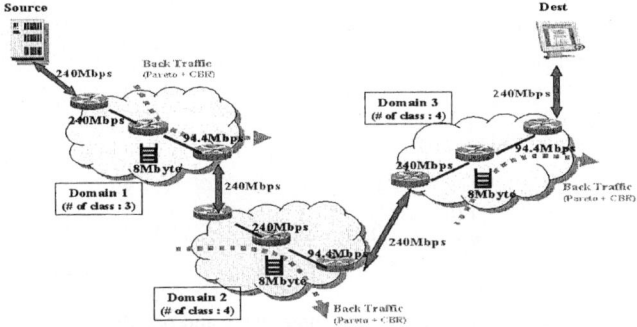

Fig. 3. Tested DiffServ network condition

3.1 QoS Comparison Between Traffic Aggregates and Per-Flow Traffic over Relative Differentiated Service Model

First, the performance of the proposed relative service model is presented. Two cases are tested, i.e. input traffics are constant bit rate (CBR) and variable bit rate (VBR). VBR traffics are generated by Pareto. When the input traffics are Pareto, the QoS state of class 2 always stays between those of class 1 and class 3 in Figure 4. This phenomenon is observed in CBR case too. Based on these observations, the relative service model works successfully. The QoS states of a flow and a class including the flow are given in Figure 5. As shown in the figure, two plots are almost same. Thus, it is reasonable that the QoS state of a class can be used for that of a flow that is aggregated into the class. As a result, the required computational complexity can be significantly reduced since we do not need to calculate the QoS state of each flow.

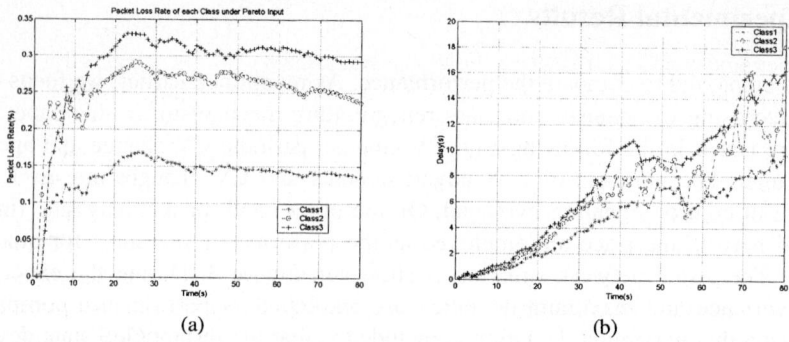

Fig. 4. QoS state comparison of classes when input traffics are Pareto traffics: (a) packet loss rate and (b) time delay

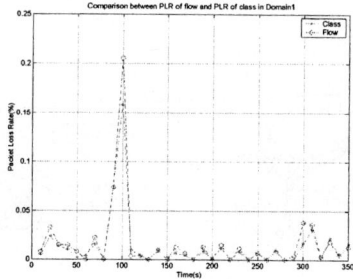

Fig. 5. Packet loss comparison between traffic aggregates and per-flow traffic at the Domain 1

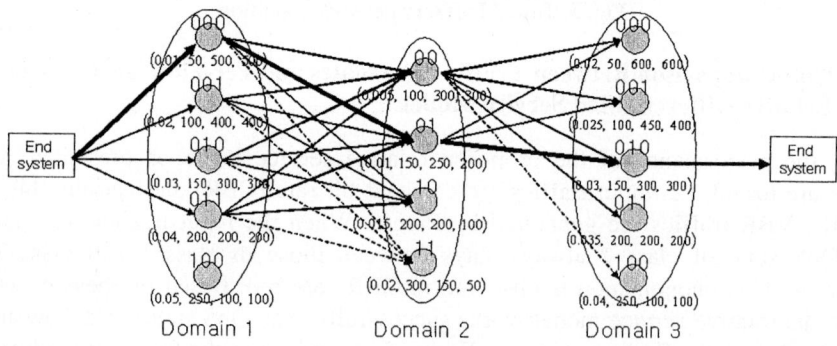

Fig. 6. Simulation result by Viterbi algorithm: The parenthesis of each node (packet loss rate, time-delay, effective bandwidth, price of the selected class), and class identifier (DSCP) is assigned as shown: (000, 001, 010, 011, 100) in the first and the third domains and (00, 01, 10, 11) in the second domains

3.2 CV Searching Method

For an example of performance evaluation, we assume that the requested 3-tuple QoS is {packet loss rate : 0.08, time delay : 400 ms, and effective bandwidth : 200 kbps}. As shown in Figure 6, it is assumed that the path consists of three DiffServ domains, and each domain has different number of classes with different QoS states. By using Viterbi algorithm, we can find that the optimal QoS CV is (000, 01, 010), and the packet loss rate is 0.03465, the delay is 200 ms, the effective bandwidth is 300 kbps, and the price is 1000 units along the path. The details are given in Figure 6. As shown in the figure, the solid lines meet the requested QoS while the dotted lines do not satisfy the requested QoS. The bold line represents the optimal CV. All paths passing the fourth of the domain 2 cannot satisfy the required QoS, thus we do not need to consider any CV passing through this node.

Table 1. Average QoS state comparison between no CV change case and periodic CV change case

	Periodic CV Change					No CV Change		
Interval	No. of CV Changes	Avg. PLR	Avg. Delay	Ave. price	Ave. price	CV	Avg. PLR	Avg. Delay
10s	35	0.0424	0.0941	5.314	6	2-1-3	0.0554	0.0856
						2-3-4	0.0547	0.0872
						3-2-4	0.0558	0.0895
						3-3-3	0.0578	0.0956
30s	12	0.0538	0.0923	4.721	5	2-4-4	0.0724	0.0918
						3-3-4	0.0768	0.0949
						3-4-3	0.0726	0.0957
50s	7	0.0898	0.0959	4	4	3-4-4	0.0898	0.0959

Table 2. Standard deviation and maximum packet loss rate comparison of QoS state between no CV change case and periodic CV change case

	Periodic CV Change					No CV Change		
Interval	No. of CV Changes	MAX. PLR	STDEV of PLR	Ave. price	Ave. price	CV	MAX. PLR	STDEV of PLR
10s	35	0.2085	0.0512	5.314	6	2-1-3	0.4186	0.0736
						2-3-4	0.4455	0.0794
						3-2-4	0.4278	0.0764
						3-3-3	0.4370	0.0751
30s	12	0.3269	0.0722	4.721	5	2-4-4	0.5314	0.0954
						3-3-4	0.5412	0.0966
						3-4-3	0.5347	0.0944
50s	7	0.3777	0.0784	4	4	3-4-4	0.5777	0.0984

3.3 CV Change Case with the Periodic QoS-State Advertisement

We assume that the following QoS is required: the maximum time delay is less than 0.16 sec. and the tolerable packet loss rate is less than 5%. Various time intervals are tested and the experimental results are summarized in Table 1 and 2 and Figure 7. It is observed that average QoS state and QoS state fluctuation are improved as the interval of QoS state advertisement decreases. However, the number of CV changes increases, which makes the control signal overhead larger. As shown in Table 1 and (a) of Figure 7, periodic CV change case can provide the better average end-to-end QoS state with the lower networking price. Furthermore, the performance difference is much more obvious in terms of QoS state fluctuation as shown in Table 2 and (b) of Figure 7. Especially, maximum QoS deviation of periodic CV change case can be significantly reduced compared with that of no CV change. When the advertising time interval is 50 seconds, the standard deviation and maximum deviation are significantly reduced although the average QoS state are same as shown in Figure 7.

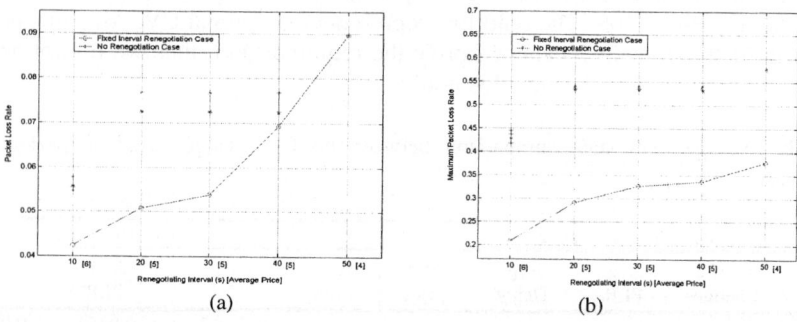

Fig. 7. Performance comparison between no CV change case and periodic CV change case: (a) packet loss rate, and (b) maximum packet loss rate

3.4 CV Change Case with the Aperiodic QoS-State Advertisement

In this section, performance of aperiodic CV change case is compared with those of no CV change case and periodic CV change case. The length of window is set to 3 and the weighting values in the window are set to {2, 3, 5}. The window moves to the right by one second per a time. The performance comparison with no CV change case is summarized in Table 3 and 4 and Figure 8. Compared with no CV change case, average packet loss rate is reduced by more than 30% and standard deviation and maximum deviation are decreased by at least 50% and 70% respectively

Table 3. Average QoS state comparison between no CV change case and a periodic CV change case

Aperiodic CV Change					No CV Change			
Threshold of Adv.	Avg. PLR	Avg. Delay	No. of CV Changes	Ave. price	Ave. price	CV	Avg. PLR	Avg. Delay
10%	0.0385	0.0924	15	5.7451	6	2-1-3	0.0554	0.0856
						2-3-4	0.0547	0.0872
						3-2-4	0.0558	0.0895
						3-3-3	0.0578	0.0956
30%	0.0447	0.0929	12	5.3012	6	2-1-3	0.0554	0.0856
						2-3-4	0.0547	0.0872
						3-2-4	0.0558	0.0895
						3-3-3	0.0578	0.0956
50%	0.0651	0.0975	10	5.1428	5	2-4-4	0.0724	0.0918
						3-3-4	0.0768	0.0949
						3-4-3	0.0726	0.0957

Table 4. Standard deviation and maximum packet loss rate comparison of QoS state between no CV change case and aperiodic CV change case

	Aperiodic CV Change				No CV Change			
Threshold of Adv.	MAX. PLR	STDEV of PLR	No. of CV Changes	Ave. price	Ave. price	CV	MAX. PLR	STDEV of PLR
10%	0.1099	0.0337	15	5.7451	6	2-1-3	0.4186	0.0736
						2-3-4	0.4455	0.0794
						3-2-4	0.4278	0.0764
						3-3-3	0.4370	0.0751
30%	0.1440	0.0356	12	5.3012	6	2-1-3	0.4186	0.0736
						2-3-4	0.4455	0.0794
						3-2-4	0.4278	0.0764
						3-3-3	0.4370	0.0751
50%	0.2920	0.0694	10	5.1428	5	2-4-4	0.5314	0.0954
						3-3-4	0.5412	0.0966
						3-4-3	0.5347	0.0944

Table 5. Average QoS state comparison between periodic CV change case and aperiodic CV change case

	Aperiodic CV Change				Periodic CV Change			
Threshold of Adv.	Avg. PLR	Avg. Delay	No. of CV Changes	Ave. price	No. of CV Changes	Fixed Interval	Avg. PLR	Avg. Delay
10%	0.0385	0.0924	15	5.7451	15	23s	0.0512	0.0962
30%	0.0447	0.0929	12	5.3012	12	30s	0.0538	0.0923
50%	0.0651	0.0975	10	5.1428	10	35s	0.0670	0.0944

Table 6. Standard deviation and maximum packet loss rate comparison of QoS state between periodic CV change case and aperiodic CV change case.

	Aperiodic CV Change				Periodic CV Change			
Threshold of Adv.	MAX. PLR	STDEV of PLR	No. of CV Changes	Ave. price	No. of Path Changes	Fixed Interval	MAX. PLR	STDEV of PLR
10%	0.1099	0.0337	15	5.7451	15	23s	0.3145	0.0714
30%	0.1440	0.0356	12	5.3012	12	30s	0.3269	0.0722
50%	0.2920	0.0694	10	5.1428	10	35s	0.3352	0.0729

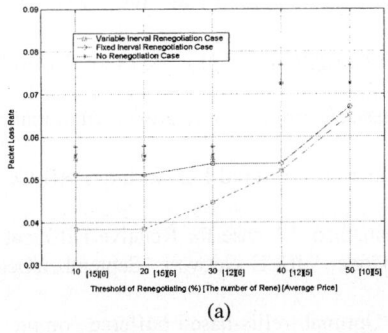
(a)

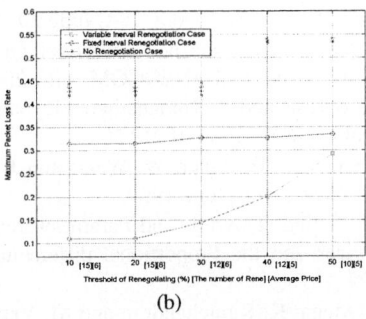
(b)

Fig. 8. Performance comparison among no CV change case, periodic CV change case and aperiodic CV change case: (a) packet loss rate, and (b) maximum packet loss rate

The performance comparison with peroidic CV change case is summarized in Table 5 and 6 and Figure 8. Compared with the periodic case, it is observed that the average packet loss rate of the aperiodic case is maximally reduced by about 25%, and standard deviation and maximum deviation are decreased by about 50% and 65% respectively with the same number of CV changes. Thus, aperiodic CV change case is more efficient that periodic CV change case at the price of computational complexity.

4 Conclusion and Future Work

We have proposed class renegotiating mechanisms for the guaranteed end-to-end QoS over multiple DiffServ domains. The proposed mechanism includes effective relative service model implementation, QoS advertising mechanism, and the class renegotiating mechanism that searches for the optimal CV satisfying the required QoS with the minimum networking price. It has been shown by the experimental results that the dynamic class renegotiating mechanism can significantly improve the average QoS state and the QoS state fluctuation compared with no CV change. Furthermore, we have shown that aperiodic CV change case can provide the better QoS state than periodic CV change case with the same number of CV changes. For the complete solution, the specific control protocols for QoS state advertisement and CV change must be designed and the optimizing process based on these protocols is needed to determine the effective CV changing times. It is under our current investigation.

References

1. S. Blake, D. Blake, M. Carlson, E. Davies, Z. Wang, and W. Weiss, "An architecture for differentiated services," RFC2475, IETF, Dec. 1998.
2. K. Nichols and B. Carpenter, "Definition of Differentiated Services Per Domain Behaviors and Rules for their Specification," RFC3086, IETF, April 2001.
3. K. Nichos, V. Jacobson, and L. Zhang, "A two-bit differentiated service architecture for the Internet, " RFC2638, IETF, July 1999.
4. Z. Zhang, Z. Duan , L. Gao , Y. T. Hou, "Decoupling QoS control from core routers: a novel bandwidth broker architecture for scalable support of guaranteed services," Proc. ACM SIGCOMM, Aug. 2000.
5. E. Nikolouzou et al., "Network Services Definition and deployment in a differentiated services architecture," Proc. IEEE ICC, April 2002.
6. N. Christin, J. Liebeherr, and T. F. Abdelzaher, "A quantitative assured forwarding service," Proc. IEEE INFOCOM, June 2002.
7. Y. Xu and R. Guerin, "Individual QoS versus Aggregate QoS: A Loss Performance Study," Proc. IEEE INFOCOM, June 2002.
8. C. Dovrolis and P. Ramanathan, "Dynamic class selection: from relative differentiation to absolute QoS," Proc. ICNP 2001.
9. J. Heinanen, F. Baker, W. Weiss and J. Wroclawski, "Assured Forwarding PHB Group", RFC2597, IETF, June 1999.
10. Constantinos Dovrolis and Parameswaran Ramanathan, "A case for Relative Differentiated Services and the Proportional differentiation Model," IEEE Network, September/October 1999.
11. A. Ortega, K. Ramchandran and M. Vetterli, "Optimal trellis-based buffered compression and fast approximations," IEEE Trans. On Image Processing, Vol. 3, No. 1, Jan. 1994.
12. A. Papoulis, Probability, Random ariables, and Stochastic Process, McGraw-Hill Inc., 1991.

Secure and Efficient ID-Based Group Key Agreement Fitted for Pay-TV*

Hyunjue Kim, Junghyun Nam, Seungjoo Kim, and Dongho Won

Information security Group, Sungkyunkwan University,
300 Cheoncheon-dong, Jangan-gu, Suwon, Gyeonggi-do, 440-746, Korea
{hjkim, jhnam}@dosan.skku.ac.kr, {skim, dhwon}@ece.skku.ac.kr
http://www.security.re.kr

Abstract. While broadcasting services have witnessed substantial technological developments which are represented by group-oriented applications, an important on-going challenge is to design secure and efficient group key management. A number of protocols targeted for Pay-TV systems have been developed and proposed. However, most of the forward-secure protocols published up to now are not suitable for practical application in mobile devices. In this paper, we propose a secure and efficient two-round protocol which would fit well in Pay-TV systems and, additionally, in mobile environments covering internet stock quotes, audio and music deliveries, software updates and so on. Also we prove its security. The proposed protocol is of simplicity and efficiency and provably secure.

1 Introduction

A number of closely inter-related models and constructions with an aim of securing electronic distribution of digital content have been proposed, and a Pay-TV system provides services that also rely on this kind of distribution. A Pay-TV system is a derivative of commercial TV systems where the broadcaster mainly generates revenue by employing a periodic charge or per-use-charge for Pay-Per-View (PPV) programs. In this situation, a broadcaster needs assurance that only legitimate subscribers who have paid their fee can watch the PPV programs. In order to restrict the flow of PPV programs to a specific set of users, cryptographic mechanisms must be used [1].

In achieving this goal, we must consider the following specific requirements for Pay-TV system:

(1) **Network topology.** A Pay-TV system is a kind of one-to-all broadcasting system where programs are disseminated from a single broadcaster to all subscribers in a network. That network is in the form of a "star network" where each device has a dedicated point-to-point link to a single central controller.

---

* This work was supported by the University IT Research Center Project funded by the Korean Ministry of Information and Communication.

(2) Efficiency.

- **Minimizing the computational load of subscriber:** A Pay-TV system is asymmetric with regard to the computational capabilities between broadcasters and subscribers: The broadcasting server has sufficient computational power while the subscribers' receiving device (digital video receiver, handheld computers, mobile phone, etc.) only bears limited computational resources.
- **Key management:** Certificate-based Public Key Infrastructure (PKI) or ID-based system is commonly used to achieve the assurance of key-sharing with intended users. The former bears high costs necessarily resulting from authentication and management of public keys and the inherent difficulties in managing multiple communities. The latter offers a more attractive alternative solution to such problems [2], thus simplifying key management procedure.

(3) Security.

- **Perfect Forward Secrecy (PFS):** In order to protect programs from illegitimate users, a Pay-TV system should be provided with PFS: The compromise of single or multiple long-term secret keys cannot result in the compromise of past session keys [3].
- **Key contribution:** In order to deploy PFS, contributory key agreement protocols must be used: Each party equally contributes to the key, guaranteeing its freshness [3]. It is often recommended to use key contribution to prevent some parties from having any kind of advantage over others.

In addition, because the PPV system belongs to a derivative of Pay-TV system where frequent membership changes arise as subscribers leave or join the group, rekeying becomes an important problem to solve in order to support secure communications for a dynamic group whose membership can change and the communication party in which can be dynamically configured. Also the computational cost required for group rekeying can be quite substantial. This issue has to be resolved by using a group key agreement protocol.

In this paper, we propose a new scalable two-round ID-based group key agreement protocol, which meets all the specific requirements stated above. This protocol benefits greatly from its simplicity, and only requires two communication rounds minimizing the costs of group rekeying operations associated with group updates. In particular, for the purpose of "minimizing the computational load of subscriber", our protocol shifts much of the computational burden to the broadcaster, who has sufficient computational capability.

2 Related Work

Since Fiat *et al.* [4] first formalized the basic definitions and paradigms of the broadcasting encryption scheme for solving the problem of multi-message encryption, many broadcasting encryption schemes targeted for Pay-TV systems have been proposed [5, 6, 7, 8]. However, these encryption schemes lack an important security property, PFS. Therefore another cryptographic algorithm is required which contains PFS and, at the same time, this algorithm must be compatible with Pay-TV systems. The group key agreement protocol can be the very answer.

Since Ingemarsson et al. [9] presented the idea of group key agreement protocol, much works [10, 11, 12, 13, 14] have followed them with varying levels of complexity. However, all of these suffer from at least one drawback of $O(n)$ or $O(\log n)$ rounds of communication, $O(n)$ broadcasts per round, or lack in PFS.

The constant-round group key agreement protocol with PFS was proposed by Katz et al. [15] in 2003 and Bresson et al. [16] in 2004. However, their character of full symmetry negatively impacts overall performances of the protocol in Pay-TV systems: As the number of subscribers grows, the computational costs of equipment used by subscribers increases quite rapidly.

Similar to the present protocol proposed in this paper, the computationally asymmetric protocol was proposed by Bresson et al. [14] in 2003 and Nam et al. [17, 18] in 2005. However, the protocol [14] dose not support PFS and the protocol [17] and [18] requires certificate-based PKI in order to verify the validity of subscribers, giving rise to the problems of high costs and additional difficulties stated above, whereas an ID-based system offers an easier alternative solution to such problems. In 2004, a two-round ID-based group key agreement protocol providing batch verification was proposed by Choi et al. [19]. This protocol is completely computationally symmetric and adaptively constructed from the pairings based on the protocol by Katz et al. [15]. Therefore, this protocol is not well suited for Pay-TV systems like that of [15, 16].

3 The Protocol ID-AGKA

In this section, an ID-based authenticated group key agreement protocol is presented. This protocol is denoted by ID-AGKA. A group $\mathcal{U} = \{U_1, \cdots, U_n\}$ of n users who wish to establish a group key by participating in protocol ID-AGKA is assumed. We note that user $U_n \in \mathcal{U}$ can act as a broadcaster and the other users $U_i \in \mathcal{U}$ ($1 \leq i \leq n-1$) can act as subscribers in Pay-TV systems in which every subscriber is provided with a device being capable of receiving broadcasted programs. In our protocol ID-AGKA, each user U_i has an unique identity, ID_i, which may be the serial number of device.

The public parameters $e, \mathbb{G}_1$ and $\mathbb{G}_2$ are assumed to be known to all parties in advance. Here, and through this paper, (i) $e : \mathbb{G}_1 \times \mathbb{G}_1 \longrightarrow \mathbb{G}_2$ denotes a pairing[1], (ii) $\mathbb{G}_1$ denotes a cyclic additive group of prime order p, and (iii) $\mathbb{G}_2$ denotes a cyclic multiplicative group of the same order. As depicted in Fig. 1, the protocol ID-AGKA runs in two rounds, the one with $n-1$ unicasts and the other with a single broadcast:

---

[1] A pairing is a bilinear non-degenerate map: Satisfies (i) $e(aP, bQ) = e(P,Q)^{ab}$ for $a, b \in \mathbb{Z}_p^*$ and (ii) $e(P,Q) = 1$ for all $Q \in \mathbb{G}_1$ implies P is identity.

Setup. The Key Generator Center (KGC) runs a Bilinear Diffie-Hellman (BDH) parameter generator, chooses a generator P of $\mathbb{G}_1$, picks a random $w \in \mathbb{Z}_p^*$, sets $P_{pub} = wP$ and chooses the cryptographic hash function $H : \{0,1\}^* \longrightarrow \mathbb{Z}_p$ and $H_Q : \{0,1\}^* \longrightarrow \mathbb{G}_1$, where H and H_Q are considered as random oracles in the security proof. The KGC publishes system parameters $params = \{e, \mathbb{G}_1, \mathbb{G}_2, p, P, P_{pub}, H, H_Q\}$ and keeps w as the master key, which is known only to itself.

Extract. Each user U_i submits his identity information ID_i to KGC. The KGC then computes the user's public key as $Q_i = H_Q(ID_i)$, and returns the private key $D_i = wQ_i$ to the user U_i.

Authenticated key Exchange.

[**Round 1**] Each subscriber $U_i \neq U_n$ chooses a random $r_i \in \mathbb{Z}_p^*$, computes $P_i = r_i P$ and $O_i = H(P_i)D_i + r_i Q_i$, and sends $m_i = (U_i, P_i, O_i)$ to the broadcaster U_n, who chooses random $s, v, z \in \mathbb{Z}_p^*$ and computes $P_S = sP$ and $P_V = vP$.

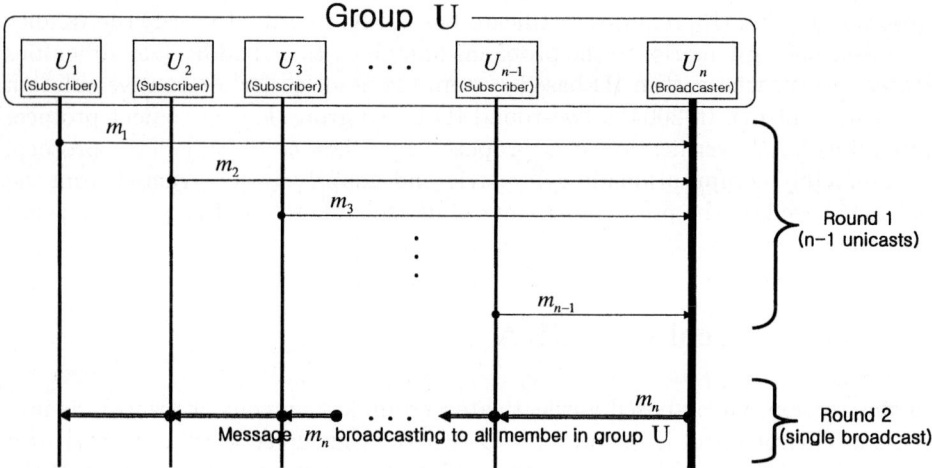

Fig. 1. Group communication sequence diagram for ID-AGKA

[**Round 2**] Having received all the $n-1$ m_i from subscribers, broadcaster U_n verifies

$$e(\sum_{i=1}^{n-1} O_i, P) = \prod_{i=1}^{n-1} e(Q_i, H(P_i)P_{pub} + P_i).$$

If the above equation holds, then the broadcaster U_n computes the set $\Gamma = \{T_i = z \cdot e(P_i, svP) \mid 1 \leq i \leq n-1\}$, and broadcasts $m_n = (P_S, P_V, \Gamma)$ to all subscribers in the group[2], otherwise broadcaster U_n stops.

---

[2] If the subscribers want to do authentication for m_n, the broadcaster U_n broadcasts $m_n^* = (m_n, \sigma)$ instead of m_n, where σ is the signature of m_n.

Key computation. Upon receiving the broadcast, each subscriber $U_i \neq U_n$ computes $z = T_i/e(P_S, P_V)^{r_i}$. All users in $\mathcal{U}$ compute their group key as $K = H(z \parallel \Gamma)$.

4 Security Analysis

In this section, we prove that the security of our group key agreement protocol ID-AGKA relies on the hardness of the DBDH problem in the formal security model, which has been used in [19]. We recall the following definitions:

Definition 1. *The Decisional Bilinear Diffie-Hellman (DBDH) Problem is to distinguish between quadruples $(P, aP, bP, cP, e(P,P)^{abc})$ and $(P, aP, bP, cP, e(P,P)^d)$, where P is a generator of $\mathbb{G}_1$ and $a,b,c,d \in \mathbb{Z}_p^*$. We define the advantage of a distinguisher $\mathcal{D}$ against the DBDH problem like this*

$$\mathsf{Adv}^{BDDH}_{(e,\mathbb{G}_1,\mathbb{G}_2)}(\mathcal{D}) = \left| \begin{array}{l} Pr\left[\mathcal{D}\begin{pmatrix} e, \mathbb{G}_1, \mathbb{G}_2, P, aP, \\ bP, cP, e(P,P)^{abc} \end{pmatrix} = 1 \,\middle|\, \begin{array}{l} (e, \mathbb{G}_1, \mathbb{G}_2) \leftarrow \mathcal{IG}(1^k); \\ P \leftarrow \mathbb{G}_1; a,b,c \leftarrow \mathbb{Z}_p^* \end{array} \right] \\ -Pr\left[\mathcal{D}\begin{pmatrix} e, \mathbb{G}_1, \mathbb{G}_2, P, aP, \\ bP, cP, e(P,P)^d \end{pmatrix} = 1 \,\middle|\, \begin{array}{l} (e, \mathbb{G}_1, \mathbb{G}_2) \leftarrow \mathcal{IG}(1^k); \\ P \leftarrow \mathbb{G}_1; a,b,c,d \leftarrow \mathbb{Z}_p^* \end{array} \right] \end{array} \right|.$$

We say that the DBDH assumption holds in $(e, \mathbb{G}_1, \mathbb{G}_2)$ if $\mathsf{Adv}^{BDDH}_{(e,\mathbb{G}_1,\mathbb{G}_2)}(\mathcal{D})$ is negligible for any probabilistic polynomial time algorithm $\mathcal{D}$.

Definition 2. *The security of group key agreement protocol $\mathcal{P}$ is defined in the following game between the adversary $\mathcal{A}$ and an infinite set of oracles for ID_i. The adversary $\mathcal{A}$ executes the protocol exploiting as much parallelism as possible and any queries allowed in the security model. During execution of the protocol, the adversary $\mathcal{A}$, at any time, asks a Test query to a fresh oracle, gets back a ℓ-bit string in response to this query, and at some later point, outputs a guess bit b'. Such an adversary is said to win the game if $b' = b$ where b is the hidden bit used by the Test oracle. The advantage of $\mathcal{A}$ in attacking protocol $\mathcal{P}$ is defined as*

$$\mathsf{Adv}_\mathcal{P}(k) = 2 \cdot Pr[b'=b] - 1,$$

where k is the security parameter. We say that $\mathcal{P}$ is a secure group key agreement protocol if $\mathsf{Adv}_\mathcal{P}(k)$ is negligible for any probabilistic polynomial time adversaries $\mathcal{A}$.

We shall see that the proposed authentication scheme Λ_1[3] can easily be transformed into an ID-based signature scheme with batch verification [20]; from the

---

[3] We used an authentication scheme Λ_1 defined as follows: (i) **Generation.** Given a secret key D_{ID}, pick a random number $r \in \mathbb{Z}_p^*$ and output an authentication message (rP, O) where $O = H(rP)D_{ID} + rQ_{ID}$. (ii) **Verification.** Given an authentication message (rP, O) for identity ID, the authentication message can be accomplished by simply checking whether $e(O, P) = e(Q_{ID}, H(rP)P_{pub} + rP)$.

proposed protocol we can see the authenticity of ID-AGKA is achieved by authenticators O_i, computed by the subscribers using their private key. O_i can also be considered to be the signature for the message $M_i = NULL$. As a consequence, the authenticity of our protocol is assured by the security of the signature scheme [20]. Therefore scheme Λ_1 is secure against existential forgery on adaptively chosen ID attack in the random oracle model, i.e., $\mathsf{Adv}_{\Lambda_1}(t)$ is negligible, where $\mathsf{Adv}_{\Lambda_1}(t)$ denote the maximum advantage of any adversary attacking Λ_1.

Now, the ID-AGKA is proven to be a secure authenticated group key agreement protocol under the DBDH assumption shown below by Theorem 1.

Theorem 1. *Let* $\mathsf{Adv}_{\mathsf{ID-AGKA}}(t, q_{ex}, q_{se})$ *be the maximum advantage of any active adversary attacking protocol ID-AGKA, where the maximum is over all adversaries that run in time t, and making q_{ex}* Execute *queries and q_{se}* Send *queries. Then we have*

$$\mathsf{Adv}_{\mathsf{ID-AGKA}}(t, q_{ex}, q_{se}) \leq 2q_{ex} \cdot \mathsf{Adv}^{DBDH}_{(e,\mathbb{G}_1,\mathbb{G}_2)}(t) + (n-1) \cdot \mathsf{Adv}_{\Lambda_1}(t),$$

where $\mathsf{Adv}^{DBDH}_{(e,\mathbb{G}_1,\mathbb{G}_2)}(t)$ *is the maximum advantage of any adversary to solve the DBDH problem.*

Proof. Let $\mathcal{A}$ be an active adversary with non-negligible advantages in attacking our protocol ID-AGKA. The proof of this theorem goes with two cases: (1) the one that the adversary $\mathcal{A}$ breaks the protocol ID-AGKA by forging authentication transcripts, and (2) the other that $\mathcal{A}$ breaks the protocol ID-AGKA without altering authentication transcripts.

For the case (1), we reduce the security of protocol ID-AGKA to the security of authentication scheme Λ_1 shown below through Lemma 1.

Lemma 1. *Let* Forge *be the event that adversary $\mathcal{A}$ outputs a valid forgery with respect to Λ_1. Then we have*

$$\Pr[\mathsf{Forge}] \leq (n-1) \cdot \mathsf{Adv}_{\Lambda_1}(t),$$

where t is that in Theorem 1.

Proof. The adversary $\mathcal{A}$ is assumed to gain its advantage by forging authentication transcripts. $\mathcal{A}$ is built into a forger $\mathcal{F}$ generating a valid message pair (ID, rP, O) with respect to Λ_1 as follows: for all other users, $\mathcal{F}$ honestly generates a public/private key pair by running the Extract algorithm. $\mathcal{F}$ then have $\mathcal{A}$ run, simulating the queries from $\mathcal{A}$. This results in a perfect simulation unless $\mathcal{A}$ makes the query Corrupt(ID). If this occurs, $\mathcal{F}$ halts and outputs "`fail`". Otherwise, if $\mathcal{A}$ outputs (ID, rP, O) as a valid forgery with respect to Λ_1, then $\mathcal{F}$ generates the message pair (ID, rP, O). The success probability of $\mathcal{F}$ is $\mathsf{Adv}_{\mathcal{F},\Lambda_1}(t) = \frac{1}{n-1}\Pr[\mathsf{Forge}]$. Then, since $\mathsf{Adv}_{\mathcal{F},\Lambda_1}(t) \leq \mathsf{Adv}_{\Lambda_1}(t)$, we obtain $\Pr[\mathsf{Forge}] \leq (n-1) \cdot \mathsf{Adv}_{\Lambda_1}(t)$. □

Next, for the case (2), the reduction is from the BDDH problem. We assume that $\mathcal{A}$ can guess the hidden bit b correctly with probability $1/2 + \epsilon$. Then from

$\mathcal{A}$ we construct an algorithm solving the BDDH problem in $(e, \mathbb{G}_1, \mathbb{G}_2)$ with probability ϵ/q_{ex}. Let us first consider the distribution defined as follows:

$$\left\{ (W^*, K) \;\middle|\; \begin{array}{l} r_1, \cdots, r_{n-1}, s, v, z \in_R \mathbb{Z}_p^*; \\ P_1 = r_1 P, \cdots, P_{n-1} = r_{n-1} P, P_S = sP, P_V = vP; \\ O_1 = H(P_1)D_1 + r_1 Q_1, \cdots, O_{n-1} = H(P_{n-1})D_{n-1} + r_{n-1} Q_{n-1}; \\ k_1 = e(P,P)^{svr_1}, \cdots, k_{n-1} = e(P,P)^{svr_{n-1}}; \\ T_1 = z \cdot k_1, \cdots, T_{n-1} = z \cdot k_{n-1} \end{array} \right\},$$

where $W^* = (P_1, \cdots, P_{n-1}, O_1, \cdots, O_{n-1}, P_S, P_V, T_1, \cdots T_{n-1})$ and $K = H(z \parallel T_1 \parallel T_2 \parallel \cdots \parallel T_{n-1})$. Note that $\mathcal{A}$ can compute all $r_i Q_i = O_i - H(P_i)D_i$ from the transcripts since $\mathcal{A}$ can obtain all secret keys D_i and hash values $H(P_i)$ ($i = 1, \cdots, n-1$) using multiple Corrupt and H queries, respectively. However, $\mathcal{A}$ does not gain any advantage from $r_i Q_i$ for attacking the protocol ID-AGKA. Therefore the following two distributions are defined:

$$\text{Real} = \left\{ (W, K) \;\middle|\; \begin{array}{l} r_1, \cdots, r_{n-1}, s, v, z \in_R \mathbb{Z}_p^*; \\ P_1 = r_1 P, \cdots, P_{n-1} = r_{n-1} P, P_S = sP, P_V = vP; \\ k_1 = e(P,P)^{svr_1}, \cdots, k_{n-1} = e(P,P)^{svr_{n-1}}; \\ T_1 = z \cdot k_1, \cdots, T_{n-1} = z \cdot k_{n-1} \end{array} \right\},$$

$$\text{Rand} = \left\{ (W, K) \;\middle|\; \begin{array}{l} r_1, \cdots, r_{n-1}, s, v, z, x_1, \cdots, x_{n-1} \in_R \mathbb{Z}_p^*; \\ P_1 = r_1 P, \cdots, P_{n-1} = r_{n-1} P, P_S = sP, P_V = vP; \\ k_1 = e(P,P)^{x_1}, \cdots, k_{n-1} = e(P,P)^{x_{n-1}}; \\ T_1 = z \cdot k_1, \cdots, T_{n-1} = z \cdot k_{n-1} \end{array} \right\},$$

where $W = (P_1, \cdots, P_{n-1}, P_S, P_V, T_1, \cdots T_{n-1})$.

Lemma 2. *Let $\mathcal{A}'$ be an algorithm that, given (W, K) coming from one of the two distributions Real and Rand, runs in time t and outputs 0 or 1. Then we have:*

$$| \Pr[\mathcal{A}'(W, K) = 1 \mid (W, K) \leftarrow \text{Real}] - \Pr[\mathcal{A}'(W, K) = 1 \mid (W, K) \leftarrow \text{Rand}] |$$
$$\leq \text{Adv}_{(e, \mathbb{G}_1, \mathbb{G}_2)}^{\text{BDDH}}(t + (2n-6)t_{smu} + (2n-6)t_{exp} + t_{pa}),$$

where t_{smu} represents the time required to compute a scalar multiplication on $\mathbb{G}_1$, t_{exp} being the time required to compute an exponentiation in $\mathbb{G}_2$ and t_{pa} representing the time required to compute a pairing operation.

Proof. We prove this lemma by using the random self-reducibility of the BDDH problem. Consider the following distribution, constructed from the quadruple $(sP, vP, r_1 P, e(P,P)^{r'}) \subset (e, \mathbb{G}_1, \mathbb{G}_2)$:

$$\mathsf{Simul} = \left\{ (W, K) \;\middle|\; \begin{array}{l} r_2, r_3, z, a_4, \cdots, a_n, b_4, \cdots, b_n, c_4, \cdots, c_n \in_R \mathbb{Z}_p^*; \\ P_1 = r_1 P, P_2 = r_2 P, P_3 = r_3 P, \\ P_4 = (r_1 a_4 + r_2 b_4 + r_3 c_4) P, \cdots \\ \cdots, P_{n-1} = (r_1 a_{n-1} + r_2 b_{n-1} + r_3 c_{n-1}) P, \\ P_S = sP, P_V = vP; \\ k_1 = e(P,P)^{r'}, k_2 = e(P,P)^{svr_2}, k_3 = e(P,P)^{svr_3}, \\ k_4 = e(P,P)^{r' a_4 + svr_2 b_4 + svr_3 c_4}, \cdots \\ \cdots, k_{n-1} = e(P,P)^{r' a_{n-1} + svr_2 b_{n-1} + svr_3 c_{n-1}}; \\ T_1 = z \cdot k_1, \cdots, T_{n-1} = z \cdot k_{n-1} \end{array} \right\},$$

where W and K are as defined above. If $(sP, vP, r_1 P, e(P,P)^{r'})$ is a BDDH-quadruple (i.e., $r' = svr_1$), we have $\mathsf{Simul} \equiv \mathsf{Real}$ since $k_i = e(P, P_i)^{sv} = e(P,P)^{svr_i}$ for all $i \in [1, n-1]$. If instead $(sP, vP, r_1 P, e(P,P)^{r'})$ is a random quadruple, it is clear that $\mathsf{Simul} \equiv \mathsf{Rand}$. □

Lemma 3. *For any (computationally unbounded) adversary $\mathcal{A}$, we have:*

$$\Pr[\mathcal{A}(W, K_b) = b \mid (W, K_1) \leftarrow \mathsf{Rand}; K_0 \leftarrow \{0,1\}^\ell; b \leftarrow \{0,1\}] = 1/2.$$

Proof. In the experiment Rand, the transcript W constrains the value z by the following $n-1$ equations:

$\log_E T_1 = \log_E z + x_1, \log_E T_2 = \log_E z + x_2, \cdots, \log_E T_{n-1} = \log_E z + x_{n-1}$,
where $E = e(P,P)$. Since W does not constrain the value z any further and since the value z is not expressible as a linear combination of the $n-1$ equations above, we have that the value of K is independent of W. This implies that $\Pr[\mathcal{A}(W, z_b) = b \mid (W, z_1) \leftarrow \mathsf{Rand}; z_0 \leftarrow \mathbb{G}; b \leftarrow \{0,1\}] = 1/2$. Since H is a random oracle, the statement of Lemma 3 is immediately as follows. □

The details of construction of distinguisher $\mathcal{D}$ are now given. Assume that without loss of generality $\mathcal{A}$ makes its Test query to an oracle activated by the δth Execute query. The distinguisher $\mathcal{D}$ begins by choosing a random $d \in \{1, \cdots, q_{ex}\}$ as a guess for the value of δ. $\mathcal{D}$ then invokes $\mathcal{A}$ and simulates the queries of $\mathcal{A}$. $\mathcal{D}$ answers all the queries from $\mathcal{A}$ in the obvious way, following the protocol exactly as specified, except if a query is the dth Execute query. In this latter case, $\mathcal{D}$ slightly deviates from the protocol, by embedding the BDDH problem instance given as input into the transcript as follows: Given a quadruple $(sP, vP, r_1 P, e(P,P)^{r'}) \in (e, \mathbb{G}_1, \mathbb{G}_2)$, $\mathcal{D}$ generates (W, K) according to the distribution Simul and answers the dth Execute query of $\mathcal{A}$ with W. The distinguisher $\mathcal{D}$ outputs a random bit if $d \neq \delta$. Otherwise, $\mathcal{D}$ answers the Test query of $\mathcal{A}$ with K. At a later point, when $\mathcal{A}$ terminates and outputs its guess b', $\mathcal{D}$ outputs 1 if $b = b'$, and 0 otherwise.

Applying the Lemma 2 and 3 together with the fact that $\Pr[b = b'] = 1/2$ and $\Pr[d = \delta] = 1/q_{ex}$, we obtain $\Pr[\mathcal{A}(W, K_b) = b \mid (W, K_1) \leftarrow \mathsf{Real}; K_0 \leftarrow \{0,1\}^\ell; b \leftarrow \{0,1\}] = 1/2 + \epsilon$ and $\mathsf{Adv}^{\mathsf{DBDH}}_{(e, \mathbb{G}_1, \mathbb{G}_2)}(\mathcal{D}) = \epsilon / q_{ex}$, which yields the statement in case (2). □

5 Efficiency

In the ID-AGKA of ours, the broadcaster is not required to wait for the last message from subscribers before it can start performing computation: When receiving each message m_i, the broadcaster can compute k_i. Furthermore, if precomputations are possible, all computations in the first round can be performed off-line; thus, only one exponentiation per subscriber is required to be done on-line since, in Round 2, the broadcaster U_n computes $g = e(P, svP)$ and broadcasts, instead of m_n, $m_n^{\dagger} = (g, \Gamma)$ to all subscribers in the group. Therefore the ID-AGKA is well suited for deployment in mobile devices.

Table 1. Complexity comparison with the protocol of Choi et al. and Nam et al.

		Nam et al [17, 18]		Choi et al [19]		Our Protocol	
		Broadcaster	Subscriber	Broadcaster	Subscriber	Broadcaster	Subscriber
Unicast		0	1	0	0	0	1
Broadcast		2	1	2	2	1	0
Message	Send	2	2	2	2	1	1
	Receive	$2(n-1)$	n	$2(n-1)$	$2(n-1)$	$n-1$	1
Signature	Generation	1	1	1	1	1	1
	Verification	$n-1$	1	$n-1$	$n-1$	1	1
Computation[4]		$O(n)$	$O(1)$	$O(n)$	$O(n)$	$O(n)$	$O(1)$
		$O(n^2)$ for total subscribers		$O(n)$ for total subscribers		$O(n)$ for total subscribers	
Round		3		2		2	
Subscribers Join		Yes		No		Yes	
Subscribers Leave		Yes		No		Yes	
Public Key Certificate		Need		No need		No need	

The ID-AGKA improves the three-round group key agreement protocol of Nam et al. [17, 18], resulting in a two-round group key agreement protocol. In addition, this protocol reduces the computational costs of broadcaster, since it simultaneously verifies the validity of transcripts from subscribers. Moreover, using an ID-based system, our protocol provides authentication of subscribers and simplifies key agreement procedures. In addition, unlike [17] and [18], our protocol enhances the computational efficiency and security since our protocol is schemed to select a random number as the information necessary for the generation by broadcaster of relevant group key. In Table 1[4], we compare the performance of our protocol with the protocol presented by Nam et al. and choi et al. [19]. (The protocol of Choi et al., in its basic form, is essentially the protocol of Burmester et al. [21].). With regard to computational costs, the table lists the amount of computation performed per user. To the best of our knowledge, the protocol of Choi et al. is the most efficient protocol among group key agreement protocols published up to date. However, as group size increases, the efficiency of their protocol deteriorates rapidly

---

[4] Note that the computation in [17, 18] does not include the signature computational cost.

since both signature verifications, pairing computations and broadcasts add up. The pairing computation is a critical operation in pairing-based cryptosystems. In the proposed protocol, each subscriber is not required to compute pairing, while there are four pairing computations in that of [19]. As can be seen from Table 1, our protocol is well suited for Pay-TV systems where subscribers have restricted computational capabilities. In addition, our protocol greatly improves the computational efficiency for the broadcaster since the batch verification technique has been adopted in verifying the validity of $n-1$ transcripts P_i. Our batch verification is almost constant for the number of signatures created by single signer unlike [19]. Moreover, the proposed protocol supports dynamic membership operations: Only two communication rounds is required, minimizing the cost of group rekeying operations associated with group updates caused by subscribers' leaving or joining. The protocols representing subscribers' leaving and joining are shown in the Appendix at the end of this paper.

6 Conclusion

In this paper, a new scalable two-round ID-based group key agreement protocol is proposed, suitable for deployment in Pay-TV systems. The protocol meets the strong security requirements while being simple and practical to deploy. Moreover, compared with other provably-secure schemes published up to date, the proposed protocol incurs much lower communication overhead required for an initial group formation and for group updates, in terms of both the number of communication rounds and the number of messages sent by all users.

References

1. B.-M. Macq and J.-J. Quisquater, Cryptology for digital TV broadcasting, Proc. IEEE, 83(6):944–57, 1995.
2. A. Shamir, Identity-based cryptosystems and signature schemes, Advances in Cryptology, Crypto'84, LNCS 196, pp. 47–53, Springer-Verlag, 1984.
3. G. Ateniese, M. Steiner, and G. Tsudik, New multiparty authentication services and key agreement protocols, IEEE Journal on Selected Areas in Communications, 18(4):628–639, 2000.
4. A. Fiat and M. Naor, Broadcast encryption, Advances in Cryptology, Crypto'93, LNCS 773, pp. 480–491, Springer Verlag, 1994.
5. Y. Mu and V. Varadharajan, Robust and secure broadcasting, Advances in Cryptology, Indocrypt'01, LNCS 2247, pp. 223–231, Springer-Verlag, 2001.
6. A. Wool, Key management for encrypted broadcast, Proc. 5th ACM conference on Computer and Communications Security (CCS'98), pp. 7–16, Springer-Verlag, 1998.
7. Y. Mu, W. Susilo and Y.-X. Lin, Identity-Based broadcasting, Advances in Cryptology, Indocrypt'03, LNCS 2904, pp. 177–190, Springer-Verlag, 2003.
8. A. Narayanan, C.P. Rangan, and K. Kim, Practical Pay TV schemes, Proc. 9th Australasian Conference on Information Security and Privacy (ACISP'03), LNCS 2727, pp. 192–203, Springer-Verlag, 2003.

9. I. Ingemarsson and D.C. Wong, A conference key distribution system, IEEE Transactions on Information Theory, 28(5):714–720, 1982.
10. E. Bresson, O. Chevassut, D. Pointcheval, and J.-J. Quisquater, Provably authenticated group Diffie-Hellman key exchange, Proc. 8st ACM Conference on Computer and Communications Security (CCS'01), pp. 255–264, Springer-Verlag, 2001.
11. E. Bresson, O. Chevassut, and D. Pointcheval, Provably authenticated group Diffie-Hellman key exchange — the dynamic case, Advances in Cryptology, Asiacrypt'01, LNCS 2248, pp. 290–309, Springer-Verlag, 2001.
12. E. Bresson, O. Chevassut, and D. Pointcheval, Dynamic group Diffie-Hellman key exchange under standard assumptions, Advances in Cryptology, Eurocrypt'02, LNCS 2332, pp. 321–336, Springer-Verlag, 2002.
13. C. Boyd and J.M.G. Nieto, Round-optimal contributory conference key agreement, Proc. 6th International Workshop on Practice and Theory in Public Key Cryptography (PKC'03), LNCS 2567, pp. 161–174, 2003.
14. E. Bresson, O. Chevassut, A. Essiari, and D. Pointcheval, Mutual authentication and group key agreement for low-power mobile devices, Proc. 5th IFIP-TC6 International Conference on Mobile and Wireless Communications Networks (MWCN'03), pp. 59–62, 2003.
15. J. Katz and M. Yung, Scalable protocols for authenticated group key exchange, Advances in Cryptology, Crypto'03, LNCS 2729, pp. 110–125, Springer-Verlag, 2003.
16. E. Bresson and D. Catalano, Constant round authenticated group key agreement via distributed computation, Proc. 7th International Workshop on Practice and Theory in Public Key Cryptography (PKC'04), LNCS 2947, pp. 115–129, 2004.
17. J. Nam, H. Kim, S. Kim, H. Yang, and D. Won, Practical and provably-secure multicasting over high-delay Networks, Proc. International Conference on Computational Science (ICCS'05), LNCS 3515, pp. 493–501, 2005.
18. J. Nam, J. Lee, S. Kim, and D. Won, DDH-based group key agreement in a mobile environment, Journal of Systems and Software, Elsevier Science Inc, 78(1):73–83, 2005.
19. K.Y. Choi, J.Y. Hwang, and D.H. Lee, Efficient ID-based group key agreement with bilinear maps, Proc. 7th International Workshop on Practice and Theory in Public Key Cryptography (PKC'04), LNCS 2947, pp. 130–134, Springer-Verlag, 2004.
20. J.H. Cheon, Y. Kim, and H.J. Yoon, A new ID-based signature with batch verification, Cryptology ePrint Archive, Report 2004/131, available at iacr.org/2004/131/.
21. M. Burmester and Y. Desmedt, A secure and efficient conference key distribution system, Advances in Cryptology, Eurocrypt'94, LNCS 950, pp. 275–286, Springer-Verlag, 1994.

Appendix

(i) **Subscriber Leave Protocol (SLP):** Assume a scenario where a set of subscribers $\mathcal{L}$ leaves a group $\mathcal{U}$. Then the leave protocol SLP is executed to provide each user in new group $\mathcal{U}_{\mathcal{L}} = \mathcal{U} \backslash \mathcal{L}$ with a new group key. SLP requires only one communication round with single broadcast and proceeds as follows:

[**Round 1**] Broadcaster U_n picks a new random $s', v', z' \in \mathbb{Z}_p^*$ and computes $P'_S = s'P$ and $P'_V = v'P$, then U_n goes through ID-AGKA and broadcasts $m_n = (g', \Gamma')$ to all subscribers in the group $\mathcal{U_L}$, where $g' = e(P, s'v'P)$ and $\Gamma' = \{T'_i = z' \cdot e(P_i, s'v'P) \mid i = [1, n-1]\backslash\{\mathcal{L}\}\}$.

Key computation. Upon receiving the broadcast, each subscriber $U_i \neq U_n$ computes $z' = T'_i / g'^{r_i}$. All users in $\mathcal{U_L}$ compute their group key as $K = H(z' \parallel \Gamma')$.

(ii) **Subscriber Join Protocol (SJP):** Assume a scenario where a set of new j subscribers $\mathcal{J}$ joins a group $\mathcal{U}$ to form a new group $\mathcal{U_J} = \mathcal{U} \cup \mathcal{J}$. Then the join protocol SJP runs to provide the users of $\mathcal{U_J}$ with a group key. SJP takes two communication rounds, the one with j unicasts and the other with single broadcast, and proceeds as follows:

[**Round 1**] Each subscriber $U_j \in \mathcal{J}$ chooses a random $r_j \in \mathbb{Z}_p^*$, then U_n goes through ID-AGKA and sends $m_j = (U_j, P_j, O_j)$ to the broadcaster U_n, who chooses a new random $s', v', z' \in \mathbb{Z}_p^*$ and computes $P'_S = s'P$ and $P'_V = v'P$.

[**Round 2**] Having received all m_j from subscriber $U_j \in \mathcal{J}$, broadcaster U_n verifies $e(\sum_{i=1}^{j} O_j, P) = \prod_{i=1}^{j} e(Q_j, P_{pub} + P_j)$, then U_n goes through ID-AGKA and broadcasts $m_n = (g', \Gamma')$ to all subscribers in the group $\mathcal{U_J}$, where $g' = e(P, s'v'P)$ and $\Gamma' = \{T'_i = z' \cdot e(P_i, s'v'P) \mid i = [1, n-1] \cup \{\mathcal{J}\}\}$.

Key computation. All users in $\mathcal{U_J}$ compute their group key as $K = H(z' \parallel \Gamma')$ as in SLP.

A Method of Generating Table of Contents for Educational Videos

Gwang-Gook Lee[1], Eui-Jin Kim[1], Jung Won Kang[2], Jae-Gon Kim[2], and Whoi-Yul Kim[1]

[1] Division of Electrical and Computer Engineering, Hanyang University,
Haengdang-dong, Seongdong-gu, Seoul, 133-791, Korea
{nohoho, ejkim}@vision.hanyang.ac.kr, wykim@hanyang.ac.kr
[2] Broadcasting Media Research Group, Digital Broadcasting Research Division, ETRI,
161 Gajeong-dong, Yuseong-gu, Daejeon, 305-350, Korea
{jungwon, jgkim}@etri.re.kr

Abstract. The increasing amount of multimedia data enforces the development of automatic video analysis techniques. In this paper, a method of ToC generation is proposed for educational video contents. The proposed method consists of two parts: scene segmentation followed by scene annotation. First, video sequence is divided into scenes by the proposed scene segmentation algorithm which considers the characteristic of educational video. Then each shot in the scene is annotated in terms of scene type, existence of enclosed caption and main speaker of the shot. The experimental result showed that the proposed method can generate ToC for educational video with high accuracy.

1 Introduction

The huge amount of multimedia data increases a need to browse, retrieve and manage them conveniently. Furthermore, the need for generating metadata from large amount of multimedia data is also being increasing accordingly with the rapid development of internet connected STB and user interactive broadcasting. However it is not a trivial task to browse, retrieve, and analyze a video since it is a temporal media in nature. Hence, a structured representation of video, such as a ToC(Table of Contents) or an index, can help users to manage them in a user-friendly manner. In this reason, video analysis techniques which create an effective representation of video become more important in these days.

So far there have been various research efforts in automatic video analysis. Some of them tried to segment a video into scenes, which is a group of shots related to the same semantic meaning [1][2][3]. These previous efforts were mainly focused on dealing with general videos that contain story lines such as movies or dramas. On the other hand, there are many prior works which are dependent on a specific type of videos. In those works, the prior knowledge of a specific domain is utilized to build a model for the structure of videos or for events in the videos [4][5][6]. Algorithms for news story segmentation [4] or sports video indexing [5][6] would be good examples for them.

This paper presents a method to generate a ToC for educational videos. ToC creation for educational videos is highly required because of the increasing demand of educational videos on the network with the expansion of network capacity. In addition, the ToC is also essential to offer user-oriented contents from the entire video. That is, educational contents can be consumed selectively by the level of a user with a ToC. With this goal in mind, in this paper, an educational video is first segmented into scenes, then each shot in this structured representation is annotated automatically. For scene segmentation we consider the characteristics of educational video contents to obtain the structured representation in the scene segmentation process. In the annotation step, on the other hand, every shot is then described by 1) its scene type 2) existence of enclosed caption in the shot, and 3) main speaker of the shot.

The rest of this paper is organized as follows: In section 2, the target video contents are examined and overview of the proposed system is given. In section 3, the utilized scene segmentation method is illustrated. In section 4, the method of scene annotation is described. Section 5 presents the experimental results and conclusion is given in section 6.

2 Overview

In this section, the characteristics of educational videos are observed and the overview of the proposed method is given. Figure 1 shows the structure of a typical educational video. Details of each type of shots are given follows.

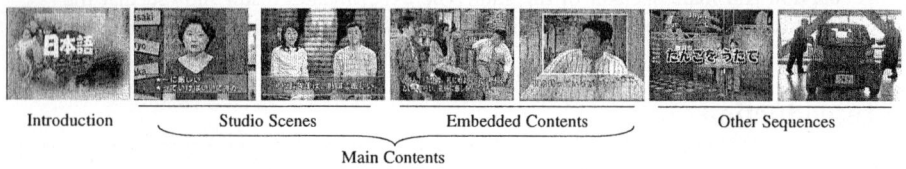

Fig. 1. Typical structure of an educational video

- Intro scenes: Intro scenes usually occur at the transition point between different episodes or topics. They also occur at the very beginning or ending of a program. Those scenes usually contain various graphical effect and large variation in motion.
- Studio scenes: Most scenes of the educational video are taken in a studio. These scenes are generally very static. They are usually captured in real studios, but often taken in virtual studios generated by computer graphics.
- Embedded contents: Embedded contents are the materials that are used to help transmitting the main theme of educational content. It can be video contents or simple static graphical objects. These scenes often interweaved with the main studio shots to suggest the main subject of the video contents.
- Other scenes: Educational contents may contain other episodes except the main topic. This type of scenes can be diverse (indoor/outdoor, graphical/real, and static/dynamic) and even may not exist for some video contents.

As noticed from the above description, no fixed pattern or model exists applicable to any types of educational video contents. For this reason, a model-based approach is not adopted to maintain the generality of the developed algorithm. The framework of the proposed approach developed in this perspective is given in Fig. 2.

The proposed method is composed of two parts: 1) scene segmentation and 2) scene annotation. In scene segmentation process, the video content is divided into scenes which are a collection of semantically correlated shots. This offers a basic structure of a video content. Then each shot in the scene is represented by shot type and speaker in the following scene annotation steps.

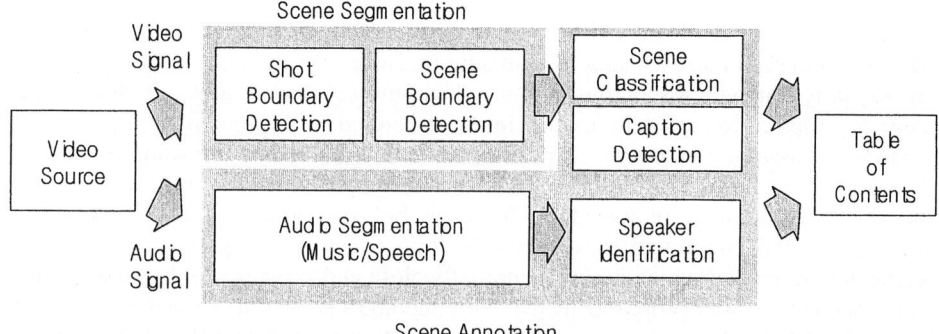

Fig. 2. Flow of the proposed method: input video sequence is first segmented into shots and scenes to give a structured representation of the video content. Then the structured representation is annotated by shot classification and speaker identification.

3 Scene Segmentation

A video itself can be considered analogous to a book since both of them are sequential media. It is in general difficult for a user to browse the contents of the media at a glance and linear search is necessary to look at the contents at a specific location of the media. A structured representation would be helpful for a quick review of the contents by accessing directly to a desired position. In the case of a book, the ToC or index allows to do the task for such role. A user can easily grasp the idea or contents of a book just by browsing the table-of-contents alone and can find a particular contents or subject with an aid from index. A structured representation of video is important and urgently needed for this reason, since the similar mechanism can be applied to a video.

In this paper, a video sequence is structured by scenes and shots. A shot is a group of consecutive frames without any transition effect and a scene is a group of shots having the same semantic meaning. The details of shot/scene segmentation algorithms are described in the following section.

3.1 Shot Segmentation

Prior to scene segmentation, video sequence is segmented into shots. A shot is defined as a set of consecutive frames taken by a single camera and used as a basic building block of video for further processing. The types of shot transition can be classified into two categories: abrupt and gradual transition. In this paper, the methods proposed in [7] and [8] are adopted for detecting abrupt and gradual transitions, respectively. The method proposed in [7] sets its threshold value adaptively to avoid the dependency to specific video contents, and the method suggested in [8] detects gradual transition by investigating the variation in distance domain hence does not dependent on the type of gradual transitions.

3.2 Scene Segmentation

In general, a shot is distinguished by simple the physical discontinuity therefore it does not contain a large amount of semantic meaning. On the other hand, a scene is separated by semantic discontinuity rather than physical discontinuity. In this reason, scene is preferred to represent a video into a structured form in many applications. A scene segmentation method which utilizes a graph to model the transition of shots is proposed in [1]. In this method, similar shots are represented by a node in the graph and their transition is indicated by an edge between nodes. The boundaries of difference scenes are found by detecting cutting edges in this graph. Also a scene segmentation method which groups temporally close and visually similar shots to find scene boundaries was proposed in [2]. This method can be interpreted as a greedy approach of [1]. The scene segmentation method suggested in [3] is based on the algorithm proposed in [2], however, shot features and comparison methods are redesigned to reflect the characteristics of film making techniques.

Those previous works on scene segmentation are based on the same assumptions that 1) shots that belong to the same scene are visually similar (visual similarity) and 2) they also are located closely along the time axis (temporal locality). The first assumption is convincing since shots in the same scenes share the same background or mood. The second assumption indicates that shots located apart may have different meaning in general even though they look very similar. Under those assumptions, scenes are divided by collecting locally similar shots in the previous general-purpose scene segmentation method.

Although these assumptions appear to be very natural and adequate for general video, they may not be enough to reflect the characteristics of the common educational contents hence they often lead to miss-segmentation. Unlike movies or dramas, the educational video contents are taken in a constrained environment. For example, video sequence of all the main studio shots are taken at the same position (i.e., in a studio). Those studio scenes appear in any part of video hence they can be considered the same scenes even though they are far apart along the temporal line. In addition, the repetition of similar shots in a scene may shorter than that of the general video contents or does not exist in the educational video contents. For example, the dialog between two main speakers sometimes contains only two shots (i.e., no repetition of shots in the dialog). Some examples of such situation where the general-purpose methods fail are illustrated in Fig. 3.

In Fig. 3, shot sequences denoted by the same alphabet are visually very similar or identical. In the first scene (Scene 1), the last shot (shot C) can be left out from a group since no links are connected to. In the second scene, even though it is known or learned that two shots A and B belonged to the same scene in the first scene, they cannot be grouped as the same scene because the shots in scene 1 and 2 are treated as different shots due to the temporal locality of the previous works for general video contents.

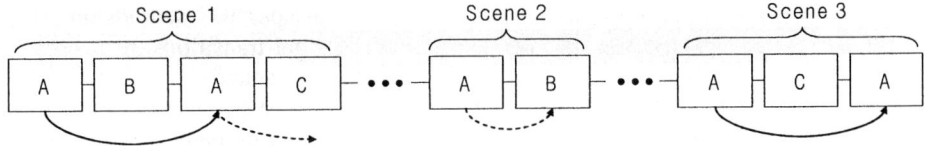

Fig. 3. An example of scene sequences that leads miss-segmentation

However, they can be grouped properly if the known characteristic of educational video is reflected. That is, the shots A, B and C in the first scene can be grouped together if the grouping result of the third scene can be utilized (i.e., shots A and C belong to the same scene). Similarly, relationship between shots A and B in the second scene can also be utilized in grouping scene1. Consequently, analyzing the connectivity of shots globally can improve the accuracy of scene segmentation for educational video. The proposed segmentation method is described below.

Proposed scene segmentation algorithm:

1. Construct a fully connected graph G which has n shots as its nodes. $G = \{V, E\}$, $V = \{s_1, s_2, \ldots, s_n\}$, $E = \{TRUE$ for $\forall (s_i, s_j)\}$
2. Disconnect the edge between two nodes s_i and s_j if the dissimilarity of two nodes is larger then a given threshold. $E(s_i, s_j) = FALSE$ if $d_{shot}(s_i, s_j) > T_{shot}$
3. Repeat step 2 for every node pair in the graph.
4. After step 3, m isolated sub-graphs are obtained. Each sub-graph contains only similar shots hence called a *shot cluster*.
5. Construct a fully connected graph F which has m shots clusters as its nodes. $F = \{W, D\}$, $W = \{c_1, c_2, \ldots, c_n\}$, $D = \{TRUE$ for $\forall (c_i, c_j)\}$
6. Disconnect the edge between two shot clusters c_i and c_j if there is no links between them. A link between two shot clusters is made if a shot in c_i is located between a shot pair in c_j, and the temporal distance between the shot pair becomes shorter than a threshold or vice versa. $D(c_i, c_j) = FALSE$ if $Link(c_i, c_j) = FALSE$
7. After step 6, l isolated sub-graphs are acquired. Every shot in a sub-graph has global connectivity hence belonged to the same scene. The sub-graphs are called *scene clusters* in this reason. Assign the same scene IDs to the shots in the same scene cluster, and segment scenes at the position where scene ID changes.

$$Link(c_i, c_j) = \begin{cases} TRUE & \text{if } index(s_l) < index(s_m) < index(s_{l+1}) \ \& \ index(s_{l+1}) - index(s_l) < k \\ & \text{or } index(s_m) < index(s_l) < index(s_{m+1}) \ \& \ index(s_{m+1}) - index(s_m) < k \\ FALSE & \text{otherwise} \end{cases}$$

These steps of the proposed scene segmentation method are illustrated in Fig. 4. As shown the figure, the shot boundaries of the video are detected first. Then similar shots are grouped together to build shot clusters. The links between different shot clusters are examined to find the scene clusters in the next process. Finally, a scene boundary is declared where the scene is changed in the original video sequence.

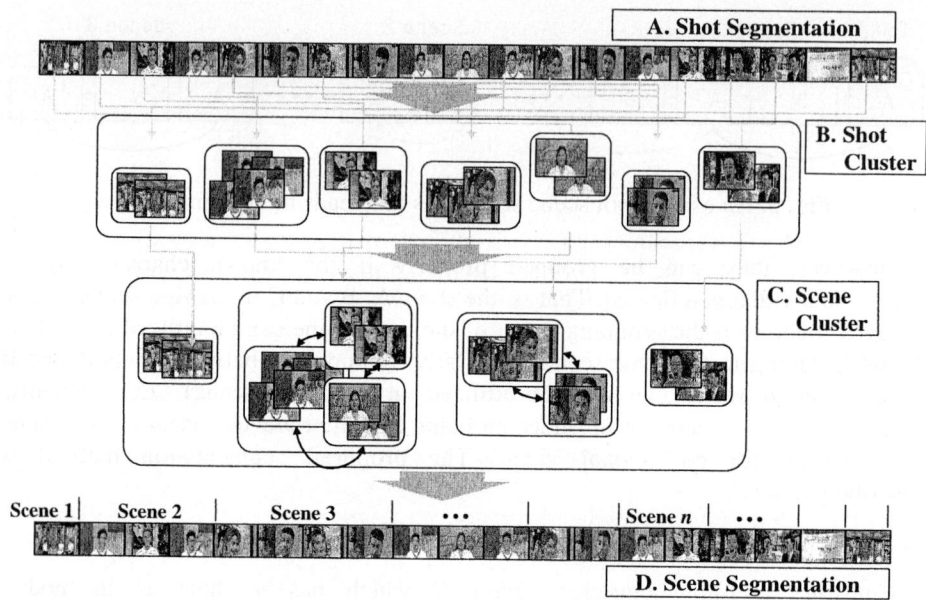

Fig. 4. Proposed scene segmentation method

3.3 Similarity Measure of Shots

To perform scene segmentation described in the previous section, a similarity measure of two different shots must be defined. To compare different shots, key-frames of shots are extracted first. Key-frames are selected by the non-uniform sampling method proposed in [9]. This method chooses a new key-frame when the difference between current frame and last key-fame exceeds a preset threshold. With this method, video can be represented efficiently with only 2 to 5 % frames of the whole number of frames. The dissimilarity between two shots is computed by the average dissimilarity of key-frames. The distance between two key-frames is computed by MPEG-7 color layout descriptor and its distance measure. The MPEG-7 color layout descriptor is adopted for its simplicity and efficiency and also for the extensibility of ToC in XML format.

4 Scene Annotation

Once the structured representation of video sequence is obtained by shot and scene segmentation, each shot is annotated to help users to recognize the contents of a scene. In this annotation process, each shot in a scene is described by 1) the type of scene where the shot belongs, 2) the presence and its position of enclosed caption, and 3) the speaker of the shot.

4.1 Scene Classification

In many researches, scene classification plays an important role in video analysis. In [10], scene classification methods to distinguish dialogs in video sequences are proposed. The proposed method used a sliding window to detect dialogs between two or three characters which are characterized by the repetition of similar shots. In [11], DCT or Hadamard transform coefficients of a video frame are utilized to classify presentation scenes using statistical classifiers such as PCA. Also scene classification is utilized extensively in sport video analysis [5][6].

In this paper, two types of scenes are classified: 1) main studio scenes and 2) intro scenes. Although more than those two types of scenes are mixed in a regular video sequence as investigated in the section 2, only main and intro scenes are considered in this paper to maintain the generality of the algorithm. Other types of scenes cannot be distinguished by general characteristics which is applicable to common educational video. To distinguish main and intro scenes, no specific scene model is used but only common characteristic, which can be easily shown in general videos, are used. In this reason, the proposed scene classification method can be applied to general educational videos. For the scene classification, the characteristics of main studio scenes and intro scenes are examined first and observations below are established.

Characteristics of main studio scenes and intro scenes:

1. The main studio scenes usually occupy the longest part of a video and scattered through the whole video sequence
2. The main studio scenes are usually very static hence contain only small motions
3. The intro scenes are usually not repeated in the video sequence hence occupies only small part of the video sequence
4. The intro scenes regularly contain extreme graphical effect which give rise to large motions

Based on those observation, a function which indicates the probability of a scene to be the main studio scene is designed as Eq.(1). In the equation, S_i represents a scene, and s_j represents a shot respectively. Also $len(s_j)$ denotes the length of shot i, and $activity(s_j)$ stands for the motion intensity of the shot. Therefore, the first term of Eq. (1) indicates the total length of a scene. The second term is the reciprocal of average activity in a scene. Hence long and motionless scene gets high value of P_{main}. With this function, the scene with the highest value of P_{main} is chosen as the main studio scene.

$$P_{main}(S_i) = w_1 \cdot \sum_j len(s_j) + w_2 \cdot \sum_j \frac{N}{activity(s_j)} \qquad (1)$$

The activity of a shot is defined as in Eq. (2). $fr(k_l)$ indicates the frame number of a key-frame k. As described in section 3.3, the key-frame is extracted when the difference between current frame and the last key-frame is largely different. Hence, the difference of frame numbers between two consecutive key-frames will small where the variance of frames or the intensity of motion is large. In this reason, the reciprocal of the frame number difference between two consecutive key-frames can be a simple yet effective measure for the intensity of motion.

$$activity(s_i) = \frac{1}{M} \sum_{l \in s_i} \frac{1}{fr(k_{l-1}) - fr(k_l)} \qquad (2)$$

Similarly, the intro scenes are characterized by high activity and short temporal length. However, unlike the main studio scene which is obtained by finding the maximum value of P_{main}, thresholding is employed to distinguish intro scenes since usually multiple number of intro scene are exist in a video sequence.

4.2 Caption Detection

The enclosed caption of a video is an important means to deliver information to users. Hence localizing the temporal position of enclosed caption can be a good description itself for video contents. For example, a user can watch only shots with enclosed captions for quick review of the content.

In this paper, a filter proposed in [12] is utilized to localize a caption. The filter expressed as in Eq. (3) is designed based on the observation that text region has many vertical strokes. Here, $I(x, y)$ denotes the gray level at spatial coordinate (x, y), and the size of filter is set to $2t + 1$. Since it accumulates gradients in the horizontal direction, high responses are obtained around a vertical stroke.

$$A(x, y) = \sum_{i=-t}^{t} \frac{\partial I}{\partial x}(x+t, y) \tag{3}$$

The result of Eq.(3) is binarized by a threshold and Bayesian decision is taken to decide candidate regions for captions. The size and ratio of bounding rectangle for each binarized region is used as features for the decision. An example of the caption detection result is given in Fig. 5.

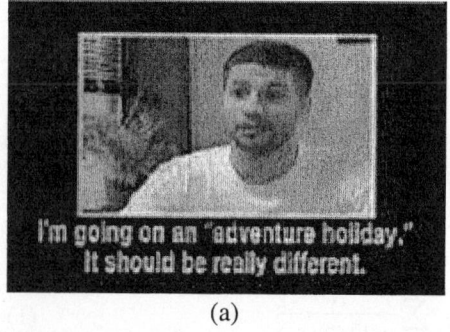
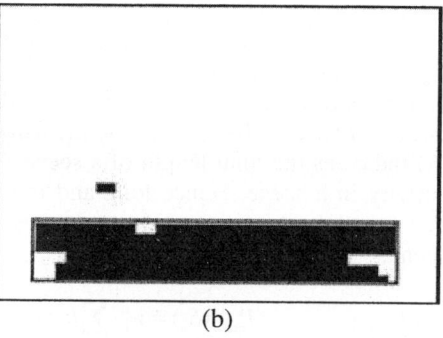

(a)   (b)

Fig. 5. Example of caption detection: (a) original video frame which has enclosed caption on it and (b) caption detection result is bounded by a box

4.3 Speaker Identification

Audio signal is utilized as complementary to the visual signal for video analysis. In [10], audio signal is jointly used with video signal to segment a video sequence into scenes. Also there was an effort to extract events by using only audio signal from a soccer video [13].

In this paper, main speaker of each shot is annotated by the speaker identification module. For the speaker identification, audio signal is divided into music and speech by the algorithm proposed in [14]. Then speaker of each shot is identified by the algorithm proposed in [15]. In both methods, the distribution of each class is modeled by GMM (Gaussian Mixture Model) and classification is performed by maximum likelihood estimation with the developed GMM. Spectral features and MFCC (Mel-Frequency Cepstrum Coefficient) are employed as features for the classification.

5 Experimental Results

In this section, the experimental result of the proposed algorithm is given. Two types of video sequences, "TV English" and "Survival English," are used in the experiment. Both video sequences follow the characteristics of general educational video described in section 2, and their durations are about twenty minutes for both of them. However, they have different characteristics in detail. "TV English" is recorded in a real studio and has only two main speakers. On the other hand, "Survival English" proceeds in a virtual studio hence it has high saturation in its color tone compared to the other video sequence. Also "Survival English" has three main speakers hence it's more difficult to identify speakers compared to the other sequence. For the experiments, 20 video sequences are prepared (10 for each). Between them, six video sequences (3 for each) are utilized to decide appropriate parameters. The same parameters are used for both types of video contents. The last 14 video sequences (7 for each) are utilized in the experiments.

The result of scene segmentation is given in Table 1. The recall and precision of scene boundary is measured for performance evaluation. The definition of recall and precision is represented in Eq. (4) and Eq. (5), respectively. In the equation, N_c stands for the number of correctly found scene boundaries. Also, N_m and N_f denote the number of missed scene boundaries and the number of false positives, respectively. In the result, the precision rate appeared quite low compared to the recall rate.

$$recall = \frac{N_c}{N_c + N_m} \times 100\% \qquad (4)$$

$$precision = \frac{N_c}{N_c + N_f} \times 100\% \qquad (5)$$

Table 1. Results of scene segmentation

	TV English	Survival English	Average
Recall	89.42	85.06	84.71
Precision	58.33	54.52	56.42

About 85% of recall rate is obtained and 55% of precision is achieved through the experiment. The result seems to be somewhat unsatisfactory especially in the precision. However, the low precision rate is not unpredictable. First of all, scene boundary is rather difficult to locate precisely compared to shot boundary since it is determined by semantic discontinuity. Also, one miss-positioned scene boundary induces one false negative and one false positive at the same time. Finally, the number of scene boundary is quite small compared to that of shot boundary, hence even small number of miss detection can degrade the accuracy seriously.

The result of scene classification is given in table 2. Also recall and precision rates were adopted as performance measure in scene classification. The recall and precision were about 90% for main studio scene classification. However, the precision for intro scenes was only 70%. This happened because single isolated shots with high motion were miss-classified into intro scenes.

Table 2. Result of scene classification

	TV English		Survival English		Average	
	Main	Intro	Main	Intro	Main	Intro
Recall	91.36	85.23	83.42	95.32	87.39	90.28
Precision	98.17	55.66	86.54	81.24	92.35	68.45

Table 3 shows the result of speaker identification. The classifier is trained with the samples obtained from a single video sequence and three video sequences are used to create three classifiers (i.e., three classifiers are trained for the experiment). Each classifier is tested on voice signal obtained from test video sequence and the average accuracy is given in table 3. As mentioned above, "TV English" contains two main speakers and "Survival English" contains three main speakers. For the test, bunches of feature vectors with different lengths are used as classifier input. The lengths of buffers used in classification were 1, 10, 30 and 50.

The accuracy was about 85% at the longest length bunch configuration. However, the last class in "Survival English" showed only accuracy of 55%. It is supposed that the low accuracy of the last class was induced by not enough sample numbers used in training, since the character of the last class has relatively fewer speech compared to others.

Table 3. Result of speaker identification

Buffer Length	TV English		Survival English		
	Class 1	Class 2	Class 1	Class 2	Class 3
1	69.73	76.62	64.72	66.75	48.42
10	78.42	78.51	72.65	75.38	52.36
30	83.21	87.11	79.03	83.83	53.73
50	85.46	88.23	82.46	86.21	54.31

6 Conclusion

The need for automatic video analysis is growing to cope with the rapidly increasing amount of multimedia data. In this paper, a ToC generation method is proposed for educational video. The proposed method is based on scene segmentation which considers the characteristics of typical educational video contents. Also the segmented scenes are automatically annotated by scene classification and speaker identification. The experimental result showed that the proposed method effectively generated ToC from educational contents.

Even though the proposed method utilized audio signals to identify speakers, the combined use of both audio and video signals is not considered in this paper yet. For example, shots belonged to the same scene will be share the similar background music or sound. Hence, we are investigating the joint use of audio and video signal to improve the accuracy of scene segmentation or scene classification process for further work.

References

1. M. Yeung, B. L. Yeo.: Time-constrained clustering for segmentation of video into story units. Proceedings of the 13th International Conference on Pattern Recognition, Vol. 3. (1996) 375-380
2. A. Hanjalic, R. L. Legendijk, J. Biemond.: Automated High-Level Movie Segmenation for Advanced Video-Retirieval Systems. IEEE Trans. on Circuits and Systems for Video Technology, Vol. 9. (1999)
3. W. Tavananpong.: Shot Clustering Techniques for Video Browsing. IEEE Trans. on Multimedia, Vol. 6. (2004)
4. W. Hsu, L. Kennedy, C.-W. Huang, S.-F. Chang, C.-Y. Lin, G. Iyengar.: News Video Story Segmentation using Fusion of Multi-Level Multi-modal Features in TRECVID 2003. Proceedings of International Conference on Acoustics, Speech, and Signal Processing, Vol. 3. (2004) 645-648
5. W. Zhou, A. Vellaikal, C. J. Kuo.: Rule-based Video Classification System for Basketball Video Indexing. ACM Multimedia. (2000)
6. A. Ekin, A. M. Tekalp, R. Mehrotra.: Automatic Soccer Video Analysis and Summarization. IEEE Trans. on Image Processing, Vol. 12. (2003) 796-807
7. Y. Yusoff, W. Christmas, J. Kittler.: Video Shot Cut Detection Using Adaptive Thresholding. British Machine Vision Conference. (2000) 362-372
8. J. Bescos, J. M. Menendez, G. Cisneros, J. Cabrera, J. M. Martinez.: A Unified Approach to Gradual Shot Transition Detection. Proceedings of International Conference on Image Processing, Volume 3. (2000) 949-952
9. B. L. Yeo, B. Liu.: Rapid Scene Analysis on Compressed Videos. IEEE Transactions on Circuits and Systems for Video Technology. (1995) 533-544
10. 10 H. Sundaram, S.-F. Chang.: Computable scenes and structures in films. IEEE Transactions on Multimedia, Vol. 4. (2002) 482 – 491
11. A. Girgensohn, J. Foote.: Video Classification using Transform Coefficients. Proceedings of International Conference on Acoustics, Speech, and Signal Processing, Vol. 6. (1999) 3045-3048
12. C. Wolf, J.-M. Jolion, F. Chassaing.: Text Localization, Enhancement and Binarization in Multimedia Document. Proceedings of 16th International Conference on Pattern Recognition, Vol. 2. (2002) 1037-1040

13. M. Xu, N. C. Maddage, C. Xu, M. Kankanhali, Q. Tian.: Creating Audio Keywords for Event Detection in Soccer Video. International Conference on Multimedia and Expo, Vol. 2. 281-284
14. J. Pinquier, C. Senac, R. Andre-Obrecht.: Speech and music classification in audio documents. Proceedings of International Conference on Acoustics, Speech, and Signal Processing, Vol. 4. (2002) 4164-4164
15. D. A. Reynolds.: A Gaussian Mixture Modeling Approach to Text-Independent Speaker Identification. PhD thesis. Electrical Engineering Department, Georgia Institute of Technology. (2000)

Study of Inter-effect and Behavior of Multimedia Traffic in a QoS-Enabled Communication Network

Nashwa Abdel-Baki and Hans Peter Großmann

University of Ulm, OMI, Albert-Einstein-Allee 43, 89081 Ulm, Germany
{nashwa.abdel-baki, hans-peter.grossmann}@uni-ulm.de

Abstract. Multimedia communication systems are rapidly developed during the last decade to reach the technology of streaming applications. Work in this paper analyzes and evaluates the area of multimedia communication services over highspeed networks. The main target is to test the multimedia communication from the applications perspective. This means to test multi-source multi-destination communication and the inter-behavior of multimedia traffic in such an environment. We run a simulation study to examine the network behavior in case of a QoS-enabled architecture, and to introduce establishing the different multi-participant scenarios in multiparty applications. The simulation study in this paper focuses on the inter-effect of varying traffic types generated by distributed traffic sources and injected to distributed groups of destinations. The simulation study examines the responsiveness and performance behavior of the interactive multimedia communication session in the support of QoS architecture with emphasis on DiffServ and MPLS networks.

1 Introduction

Networking infrastructure nowadays encourages to integrate the multimedia services offered over the different networking platforms. Multimedia streaming facilitates efficient interactivity and retrieval of media sources across different platforms and distributed systems. Globally speaking, a multimedia communication system can be classified into a body and its peripherals, or, in other words, a core and edges. The core of the multimedia communication systems refers to the networking infrastructure, the link capacities and the routing protocols. The edges are characterized by the multimedia traffic sources, the multi-participant communication environment and the user interfaces.

The core is actually the communication medium between edges. It is responsible for capturing the services from some edges and delivering the services to other edges. The core must be capable of delivering the multimedia elements efficiently. At the edges, the service delivery has to be performed in an accepted manner suitable for the nature and requirements of each media element.

Evaluating the network performance means to dig into the behavior of both the core and edges of the system. It is mandatory not to focus only on the performance of the transport and application layers and to neglect the effect of the linking and networking layers, and vice versa. This means the process of improving the network performance has to span the whole IP stack targeting improving the performance at the application layer, Figure 1. Actually a multimedia system is an integrated system so that the network infrastructure and topology can affect dramatically the rendering process at the application level. Therefore, to build an integrated system, an important functionality is considered in this study. This is the methodology of improving the performance at both the application level as well as the networking level with its associated Quality of Service architecture.

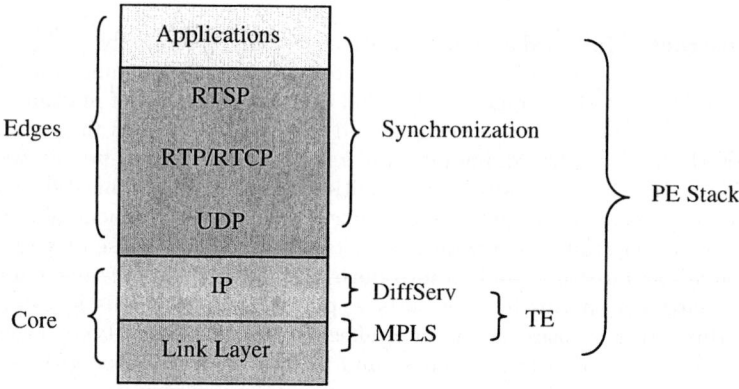

Fig. 1. Multimedia QoS / Performance Evaluation Stack

We have introduced in [1] an algorithm for calling and retrieving multimedia data defined either by their time or event-scheduling or both. This algorithm realizes a new concept of a synchronized event-driven multimedia communication system. The study in our project aims at evaluating and improving the performance of multimedia communication systems as well as enhancing the inter-effect and behavior of the multimedia traffic traversing the networking infrastructure.

The new concept and the developed application can be abstracted mainly in a multiparty multimodal communication environment. Studying the effect of the linking and networking layers on such a kind of applications means in this paper to dig into the behavior of streaming and transporting each media element across the networking infrastructure. This means to study the inter-effect of multimedia transportation. This effect can be classified in two dimensions. The first important parameter to study is the behavior of the traffic type itself in the existence of other traffic types sharing the same communication path. The second dimension of study is the effect of other media traffic types as background traffic on one or more of a certain class of media traffic types.

It is worth to mention that this area of study does not come yet into the focus of the traditional Traffic Engineering (TE) and Quality of Service (QoS) research and studies. The current TE research topics focus on classifying and prioritizing the packets as well as enhancing the routing and switching techniques and algorithms across the multimedia communication platforms and infrastructure.

This paper contributes to the area of digging into the inter-behavior of multimedia traffic itself and the inter-media effect. This study targets shading the light on this new area of the field of multimedia traffic modeling and engineering.

The performance of multiparty multimodal environment is evaluated in a QoS enabled network infrastructure. We have examined the performance of Multicast Routing in [2]. This paper is dedicated to elaborate on the networking infrastructure that supports Multi-Protocol Label Switching (MPLS) and Differentiated Services (DiffServ) architecture.

These techniques and algorithms are lately introduced to the global IP architecture, and they are not widely deployed yet. Therefore, the study considers the performance evaluation and improvement process through a simulation study. The simulation study establishes different multimedia communication scenarios in a distributed environment.

The study defines sample networking topologies suitable for each QoS technique. The sample network topologies are examined with varying different traffic sources in the existence of different background traffic types. The communication scenarios are also examined in classical events of link transitions and bottleneck links.

The rest of this paper is organized into four sections. The second section introduces the simulated network environment. The third and fourth sections demonstrate the topologies and setup of our simulated MPLS and DiffServ architectures respectively. We conclude the work in section 5.

2 Simulation Environment

Internet modeling and simulation is one of the ongoing research topics, [5]. However, this field of study is still in its infancy, [4]. The basics of the study program presented in this paper are to propose a sufficient model with keeping the simplicity. It is obvious for this study that it is mandatory to propose its own models and its justification.

The combination of DiffServ and MPLS presents a very attractive strategy to backbone network service providers with scalable QoS and traffic engineering capabilities using fast packet switching technologies.

The motivations for MPLS and DiffServ support include user demands for consistent QoS guarantees, efficient network resource requirements by network providers, and reliability and adaptation of node and link failures. MPLS and DiffServ are proposed to provide solutions to these problems. DiffServ is defined to provide scalable edge-to-edge QoS, while MPLS performs traffic engineering to evenly distribute traffic load on available links and fast rerouting to route around node and link failures. MPLS can be deployed over a wide variety of networking technologies such as IP, ATM, and Frame Relay.

The simulated network topologies proposed in this paper are examined without and with the support of DiffServ and MPLS with emphasis on multimedia traffic inter-effect and behavior under different transmission conditions. It is compared with the classical Best-Effort (BE) architecture. The throughput, end-to-end delay, jitter, and packet loss are monitored for evaluating the network performance.

Each destination node for UDP traffic is defined as LossMonitor and has the ability to calculate the number of received bytes and number of lost packets per traffic flow. The destination node for TCP traffic is defined as TCPSink and has also the ability to count the number of bytes received where throughput calculation can be performed, [7].

3 MPLS

The MPLS network simulator (MNS), [6], used in this study supports MPLS packet switching, Label Distribution Protocol (LDP), as well as Constraint-based Routing-LDP (CR-LDP). This network simulator does not support RSVP-TE. Therefore, all simulation experiments performed in this paper are based on CR-LDP as the signaling protocol. This version of MNS features data driven and control-driven LSP that trigger with downstream and upstream modes of label creation. In addition, MNS supports CBR with extensive support of ER-LSPs and CR-LSPs.

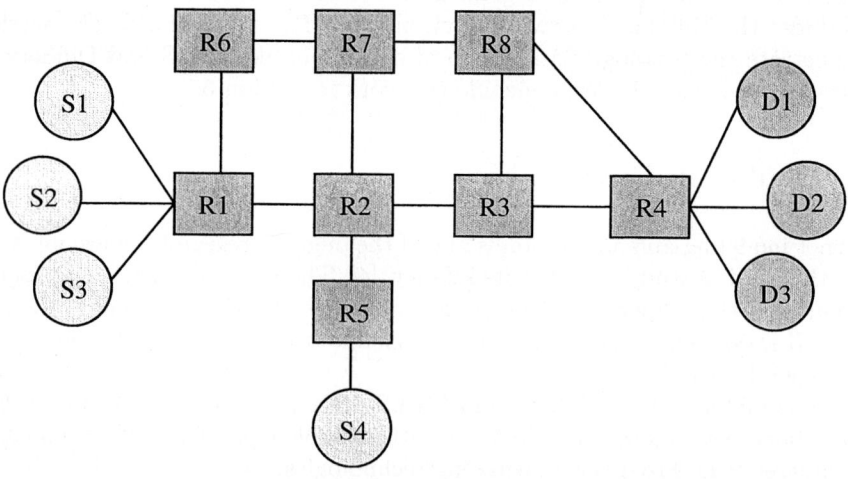

Fig. 2. Multi-Path Sample Network Topology

Node object in the MNS architecture has a reference to a specific classifier called MPLS classifier. This classifier determines whether the received packet is labeled or unlabeled. If labeled, the MPLS classifier does Layer-2 switching instead of Layer-3 routing. If unlabeled and LSP for this packet is not set previously through signaling protocol, the unlabeled packet is processed to add an MPLS label. In this case the node acts as an ingress LSR. Otherwise, the packet is forwarded to the default address classifier for Layer-3 routing.

The sample network topology examined in this study, Figure 2, consists of a mesh of routers connecting four traffic sources, S1 to S4, to three destinations, D1 to D3. The whole network is connected with links of 10Mbps bandwidth with bottleneck link of 2Mbps configured between R3-R4.

The simulation scenarios in this section are classified as follows:

- varying the real time traffic sources
- examining setup of explicit routes and constraint routes
- varying the transmission rates of traffic source generators

3.1 CBR Traffic in MPLS and Best-Effort

The multi-path sample network topology is tested in this scenario with CBR traffic generated by sources S1 to S4 with transmission rates of 8Mbps, 2Mbps, 2Mbps, and 8Mbps respectively.

The MPLS architecture was capable of delivering the first flow, Flow0, with 8Mbps and the fourth flow, Flow3, was delivered with the available bandwidth, i.e., 2Mbps. The second and third flows traversing the constraint-routed path were exchanging the bandwidth, Figure 3. This means, in the period of transient state, Flow1 was first dropped while Flow2 was delivered with 2Mbps. In the steady state, Flow2 was dropped and Flow1 managed to utilize the 2Mbps link. Anyhow this results in a better performance than the Best-Effort architecture, where only Flow3 was delivered and the other three flows were dropped, Figure 3.

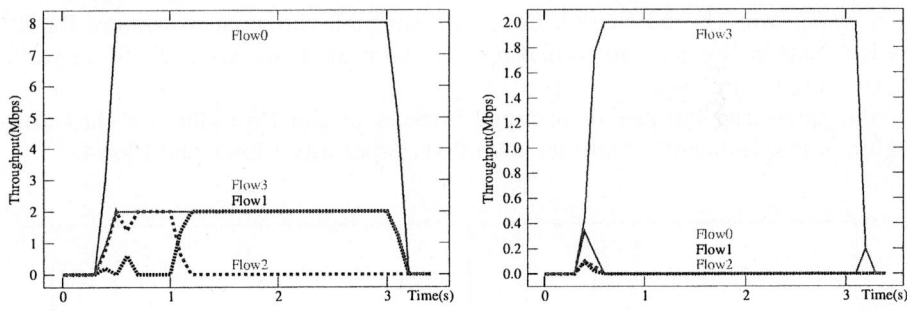

Fig. 3. Performance Improvement with MPLS Network (left) versus BE (right)

3.2 Audio Traffic in MPLS and BE

The same above experiments are repeated with injecting the network with RealAudio traffic connected to S1. The RealAudio source is configured to transmit data with 1Mbps bandwidth. The other three traffic sources were connected to CBR flows as background traffic. The networking and routing conditions were applied without change. In this experiment, the total bandwidth requested is in general in the limits of the available network capacity using the explicit and constraint routed paths.

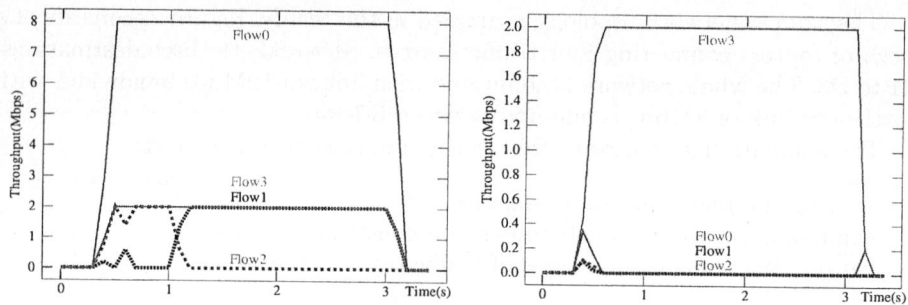

Fig. 4. Throughput of CBR-RealAudio Traffic in MPLS Network (left) and BE Network (right)

In this case, the experiment shows flow stability with MPLS architecture than the Best-Effort, Figure 4. This means the flows across the congested links of the Best-Effort architecture suffer fluctuations between being fully dropped or utilizing the full available bandwidth without sharing with other flows.

3.3 Video Traffic in MPLS and BE

The video source Starwars-IV movie sequence is used with packet size of 200B and peak rate of 1.9Mbps, [3]. MPLS simulation done in this study examines the significance of Traffic Engineering through the MPLS architecture. In the first part of the experiment, all flows are video streams and they are defined to traverse over the bottleneck link, e.g., through the path of routers R1-R2-R3-R4. This is the case of simulating the classical IP network where no traffic engineering is applied.

The measured number of dropped packets in the Best-Effort architecture, Figure 5, is significantly high per each flow, especially Flow1 and Flow4.

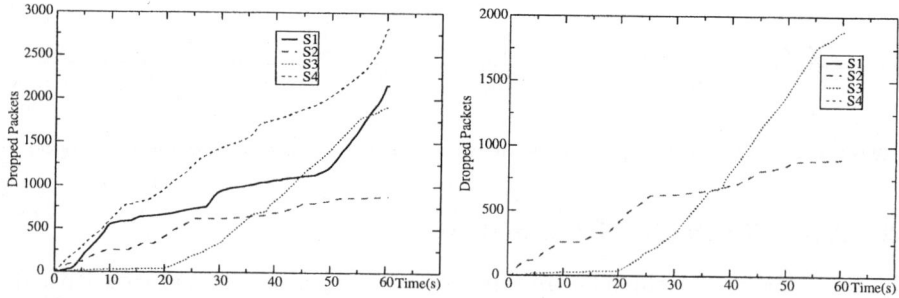

Fig. 5. Video Dropped Packets in non-MPLS Architecture (left) and MPLS Architecture (right)

The simulated network is examined with providing the concept of traffic engineering through defining explicit route for the flow S1-D1 as well as the flow generated by the source S4 to the destination D3. This means the source S1 has to traverse the path of routers R1-R6-R7-R8-R4 while source S4 has to traverse the path R5-R2-R7-R8-R4. The traffic sources S2 and S3 are examined with constrained routed path R1-R2-R3-R4 with controlled bandwidth consumption limited to 2Mbps. Both flows S1 and S4 experience no packet loss, Figure 5, due to the new uncongested paths where all links are underutilized with enough bandwidth for the two flows.

4 DiffServ

The sample network topology, Figure 6, consists of two core routers, C1 and C2, and three edge routers, E1, E2 and E3. The edge routers E1 and E3 are connected to four source nodes, S1, S2, S3 and S4 as traffic generators and the edge router E2 connects three destination nodes, D1, D2 and D3. The whole network is connected with links of 10Mbps bandwidth and 5ms delay.

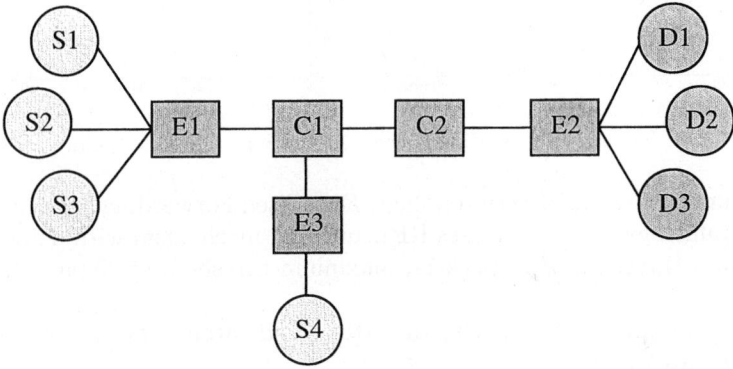

Fig. 6. Sample Multi-LAN Model

Nodes E1 and E3 are defined as boundary ingress routers. Ingress routers are placed at the entry points of the network. In an ingress boundary router a Policy is specified by the network administrator regarding the level of the service that the class of traffic should receive in the network. This means Policy is used to mark the incoming packets and it is established between source and destination nodes. All flows matching that source-destination pair are treated as a single traffic aggregate.

4.1 Video Streaming in DiffServ Architecture Versus BE

The simulation scenario considers all traffic sources are video traffic sources. This means, in this experiment, the DiffServ and Best-Effort topologies are compared when all traffic sources are generating video streams with one video source connected to each node.

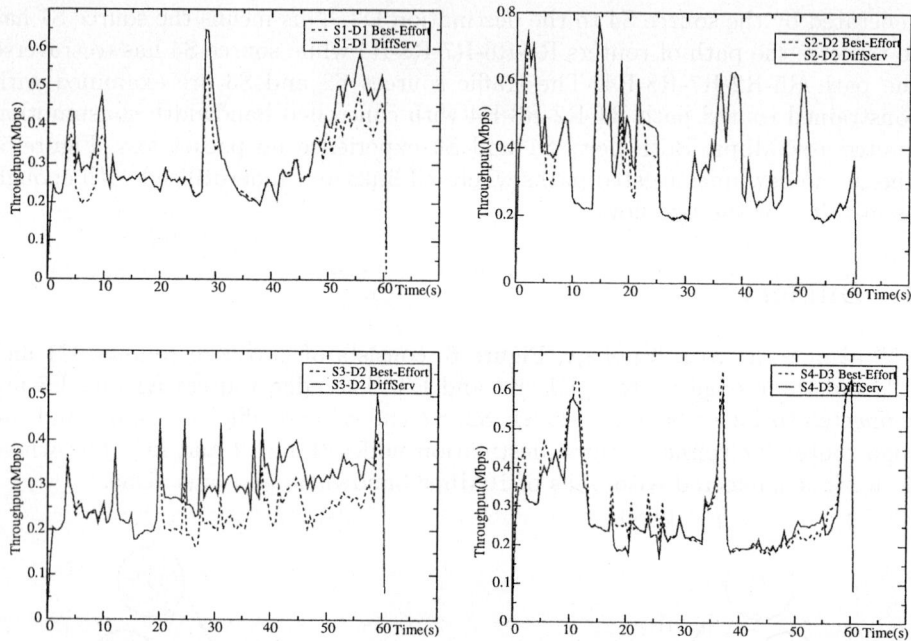

Fig. 7. Throughput of Video Flows in DiffServ and BE Architecture

At router nodes in DiffServ topology, Expedited Forwarding Service is configured as traffic aggregation. It uses RED queuing mechanism with default values of minimum threshold of 10 packets, maximum threshold of 20 packets and 0.1 maximum dropping probability.

Bottleneck link with capacity of 2Mbps and latency of 5ms is configured between nodes C2 and E2.

Monitoring the throughput of each traffic source shows that traffic shaping with DiffServ gives better results than the Best-Effort. Traffic shaping with DiffServ architecture helps to avoid the spikes of the bursty nature of the video traffic.

In order to identify the difference in throughput of BE and DiffServ simulated architecture, the throughput per flow in a DiffServ versus the Best-Effort architecture is displayed in Figure 7. These figures show that DiffServ topology gives better results in performance than the Best-Effort for three sources S1, S2 and S3. This better performance is due to the RED queuing technique which manages efficiently to avoid congestion than the Drop Tail queuing mechanism of Best-Effort.

The simulation shows that the number of packets dropped in DiffServ architecture is higher than the Best-Effort, Figure 8.

This is due to the traffic conditioner that drops the packets that are not within the defined traffic profile. Since all video traffic are defined to be Expedited Forwarding Service (EF), packets that are out-of-profile are discarded. However, to avoid discarding all packets, the minimum parameters of Token Bucket (TB) is defined for this simulation scenario. This means CIR is defined

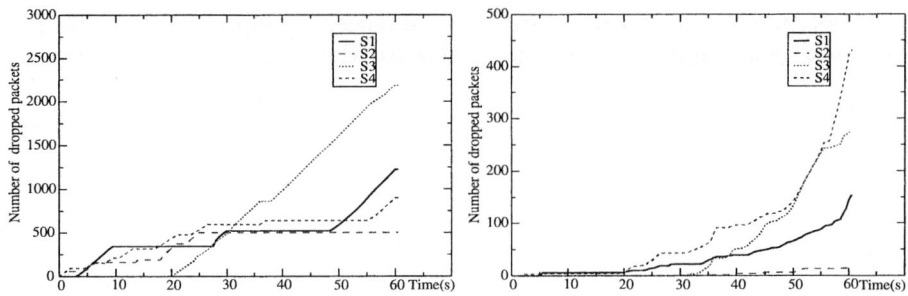

Fig. 8. Number of Dropped Packets in DiffServ (left) and BE (right) Architecture

to the value of 3Mbps and CBS of 200bytes. Despite the loss in DiffServ architecture is much higher, but it shapes the traffic and realizes better performance especially in case of presenting a bottle-neck link within the topology. Jitter calculation and the mean end-to-end delay has shown better results with DiffServ architecture.

4.2 Audio Streaming in DiffServ Architecture Versus BE

The same topology conditions were applied to simulate only audio transmission through connecting RealAudio traffic to the source nodes. Node in this simulation setup simulates a subnet of 100 audio sources where all traffic is RealAudio with peak rate of 100Kbps. The bottleneck link is kept at the same position with bandwidth of 5Mbps. The simulation duration in this case was limited to 20sec.

Throughput measurement shows that, in Best-Effort architecture, one subnet RealAudio traffic source has managed to reach its destination. The rest of flows are fully discarded. The DiffServ architecture manages to deliver three of four flows, Figure 9.

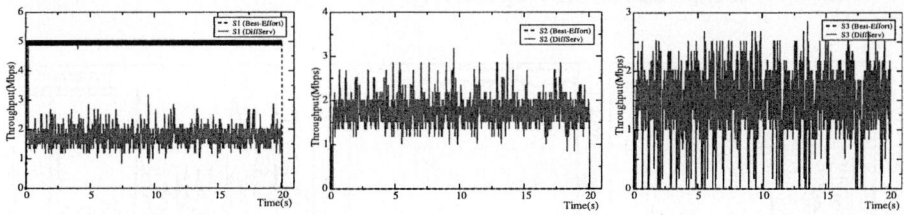

Fig. 9. Throughput of RealAudio Flows

That is a consequence of the bottle-neck link and the bandwidth consuming RealAudio traffic. DiffServ architecture treats this problem and gives significantly better performance.

Still DiffServ topology manages to support three out of four traffic sources. Traffic generated by the fourth source is completely discarded due to bandwidth limitation. On the other hand, Best-Effort manages to support only traffic from one source while intermediate routers discard the packets coming from other traffic generators.

This simulated behavior differs from the reality. In reality the intermediate routers do not process packets per source but just packets regardless of their sources. Consequently, the traffic generated from all sources will be subject to dropping or discarding. Therefore, all traffic sources will not be received in an accepted form from the human perception point of view.

4.3 Streaming of Different Traffic Sources in DiffServ Architecture Versus BE

A mixture of video, audio, and FTP traffic sources were applied to the same topology as follows:

- FTP source is connected to node S1
- Video1 is connected to node S2
- RealAudio is connected to node S3
- Video2 is connected to node S4

Two FTP sources are connected to node S1 with peak rate of 300kbps. Node S3 represents a subnet with 100 established RealAudio traffic generators where each connection has peak rate of 100kbps.

FTP traffic in DiffServ architecture is defined as Assured Forwarding (AF) traffic. Video and audio traffic are defined as Expedited Forwarding (EF) service.

This simulation scenario focuses on the simultaneous influence and behavior of different traffic types. Therefore, the bottleneck link was raised in this section of study.

In this simulation non-conforming EF traffic is dropped and non-conforming AF traffic is remarked to indicate a higher drop probability. The CIR and CBS of AF are set to 0.7Mbps and 200B respectively. For EF traffic the CIR and CBS are defined to 4Mbps and 200B respectively.

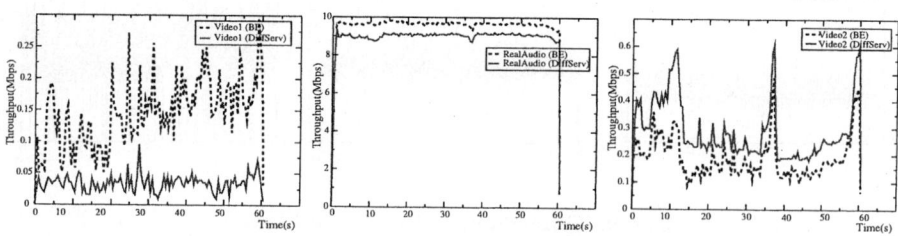

Fig. 10. Media Throughput in a Mixture of Traffic Sources

The results of throughput comparison shows that FTP traffic in Best-Effort is discarded while the DiffServ architecture supports traffic coming from all sources to reach their destinations, Figure 10.

5 Conclusion

This paper contributes to the domain of multimedia communication systems through a simulation study in the area of Traffic Engineering and QoS considerations in the direction of routing and switching protocols concerned with multimedia communication systems.

The objective of the simulation study is not only to examine the networking infrastructure algorithms. More important is to establish the different multi-participant scenarios in multiparty applications. This means to study the effect and behavior of traffic versus traffic. It is to study the inter-behavior of one or more types of multimedia traffic in the existence of other kinds of multimedia traffic. This area of study introduced in this paper hardly exists in the prospective of the research studies on the measurement track and on the simulation track.

The simulation study proves better network performance with MPLS architecture regarding the bandwidth consumption of available network links. Bandwidth utilization is a main issue to consider with the current IP architecture. However, with multimedia traffic delay and jitter are vital parameters to measure the performance of the multimedia communication networks. Therefore, MPLS by itself is not capable to guarantee minimum delay or jitter of a certain flow of a multimedia traffic source. It cannot provide a mechanism to manage for certain flow prioritization. Therefore, it has to be considered with DiffServ. Integrating DiffServ with MPLS is reserved for future publications.

This simulation study has shown that DiffServ architecture can improve the delivering quality of multimedia traffic, even under heavy load conditions. The bandwidth allocation can be managed within different traffic streams which is not the case with Best-Effort architecture where packets of more than one stream are discarded in the presence of a bottleneck link.

Acknowledgement

We would like to thank our colleagues at the department, Ms. Yvonne Günter, Mr. Matthias Rabel and Mr. Andreas Schmeiser. Special thanks are dedicated to Ms. Marija Silajev.

References

1. N. Abdel-Baki, E. Pérez-Soler, B. Aumann, H. P. Großmann: A Simplified Design and Implementation of a Multimedia Streaming System. Proceedings IEEE ICT'2003, International Conference on Telecommunications, Papeete, Tahiti, French Polynesia, February 2003.
2. N. Abdel-Baki, H. P. Großmann: Simulation and Development of Event-Driven Multimedia Session. Lecture Notes in Computer Science, Advances in Multimedia Information Processing - PCM2004, 5th Pacific Rim Conference on Multimedia, Tokyo, Japan, November/December 2004 Proceedings, Springer Verlag, 2004.

3. F. H. P. Fitzek, M. Reisslein: MPEG-4 and H.263 Video Traces for Network Performance Evaluation. Technical Report, TKN-00-02, Technical University Berlin, October 2000.
4. S. Floyd, E. Kohler: Internet Research Needs Better Models. ACM SIGCOMM Computer Communication Review, vol. 33, no. 1, pp. 29-34, January 2003.
5. S. Floyd, V. Paxson: Difficulties in Simulating the Internet. IEEE/ACM Transactions on Networking, vol. 9, issue 4, pp. 392-403, August 2001.
6. The MPLS Network Simulator (MNS) v2.0 for ns-2.1b8(a).
   http://www.isi.edu/nsnam/ns/ns-contributed.html.
7. The Network Simulator ns-2, http://www.isi.edu/nsnam/ns/.

Broadcast Synchronizing System Using Audio Watermark

DongHwan Shin[1], JongWeon Kim[2], and JongUk Choi[3]

[1] Marktek Research Institute. 10F. Ssang-Lim Bldg. 151-11,
Ssang-Lim Dong, Chung-Gu, Seoul, Korea
dhshin@marktek.co.kr
[2] Copy Protection Research Institute, Sangmyung University,
7, Hongji-dong, Jongno-gu, Seoul, 110-743, Korea
jwkim@smu.ac.kr
[3] MarkAny Research Institute. 10F. Ssang-Lim Bldg. 151-11,
Ssang-Lim Dong, Chung-Gu, Seoul, Korea
juchoi@markany.com

Abstract. In this paper, we propose the audio watermarking algorithm based on the critical band of HAS(human auditory system) without audibly affecting the quality of the watermarked audio and implement the detecting algorithm on the BSS(broadcast synchronizing system) for testing the proposed algorithm. According to the audio quality test, the SNR(signal to noise ratio) of the watermarked audio objectively is 66dB above. In the robustness test, the proposed algorithm can detect the watermark more than 90% from various compression (MP3, AAC), A/D and D/A conversions, sampling rate conversions and especially asynchronizing attacks. The BSS automatically switches the programs between the key station and the local station in broadcasting system. The result of reliability test of implemented system by using the real broadcasting audio has no false positive error during 90 days. Because of detecting once processing per 0.5 second, we can judge that the false positive error does not nearly occur.

1 Introduction

Watermarking technologies for audio contents have been developed by many researchers. The spread spectrum technique by Cox et al.[2] is one of the most popular algorithms. As a watermarking method using digital filter, Ciloglu et al.[3] proposed a watermarking method which used phase variation by all pass filtering. But his algorithm included the defect which must synchronize the audio signal for watermark detection.

In this paper, we propose the audio watermarking algorithm and the BSS(broadcast synchronizing system) which automatically switches a program between the key station and the local station in broadcasting system. The proposed watermarking method has the robustness for asynchronizing attacks as well as add-noise, channel conversion and lossy compression. To detect the watermark information effectively, we transform the input signal by fast Fourier transform(FFT), calculate the magnitude spectrum, convert the calculated spectrum in logarithm scale and then detect watermark.

We implement the detecting algorithm on the BSS for testing the proposed algorithm. When the local station sends the self-made program in the middle of broadcasting the program received from the key station, the switching of the program between the key station and the local station should be synchronized[1]. This synchronization is done by detecting the audio watermark embedded in the call sign, broadcasted audio signal. The experiments show the good results in broadcast environments.

2 Proposed Audio Watermark

2.1 Requirements of Watermark for BSS

The watermarking algorithm for BSS, which is proposed in this paper, has been made under the condition mentioned below ;

The first condition is the inaudibility. This condition is generally required in the audio watermarking algorithm. The degradation of the audio quality due to the watermark insertion must not be recognized by consumer. This is somewhat subjective. On the other hand, SNR(signal to noise ratio) is generally used as the objective method.

The second condition is the robustness. The most of audio format serviced at on-line is the lossy compression format such as MP3, AAC, WMA, etc. Therefore, the watermarking algorithm proposed must be robuster for the lossy compression than for any other attacks. Various attacks can be done to remove the watermarks embedded in the original and the lossy compression(MP3, AAC, WMA, etc) is a usual process for listening the music. Also, the original music can be played and copied with microphone or line input. Therefore, watermarks embedded in the audio contents must be alive through attacks such as A/D, D/A, time-scaling, and pitch-shift.

The Third condition is the capability of real-time implementation. In order to detect the watermark embedded in broadcasting signal within short time, 0.5 second, and make a sync control signal, the algorithm must be so simple that the watermark can be detected with a little amount of calculation. Also, the algorithm must require as little amount of memory for program and data as possible because of hardware-restriction and have capability to detect the watermark only with integer operation.

2.2 Frequency Characteristics of HAS

The watermarking algorithm designed in this paper uses the frequency characteristics of HAS(human auditory system) for the imperceptibility. The HAS is largely composed of three parts, outer ear, middle ear and inner ear.

Figure 1 shows basilar membrane(BM) of cochlea in inner ear. The basilar membrane responds more to high frequencies at the entrance to the cochlea. As the sound vibrations penetrate more deeply into the cochlea, BM response becomes more sluggish, corresponding to filters with lower center frequencies. The resonant frequencies of various points along the BM and critical bands of HAS are shown in Figure 1(a) and (b)[7].

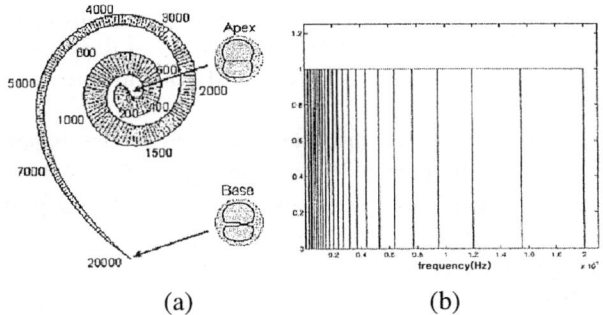

(a) (b)

Fig. 1. Critical band of HAS : (a)resonance frequencies according to the position of basilar membrane in cochlea (b)critical band

Table 1. Critical bands by Zwicker[8]

Bark	f (Hz)	Δ f (Hz)	Bark	f(Hz)	Δ f (Hz)
0	001	100	12	1270	280
1	100	100	13	2000	320
2	200	100	14	2320	380
3	300	100	15	2700	450
4	400	110	16	3150	550
5	510	120	17	3700	700
6	630	140	18	4400	900
7	770	150	19	5300	1100
8	920	160	20	6400	1300
9	1080	190	21	7700	1800
10	1270	210	22	9500	2500
11	1480	240	23	12000	3500

Table 1 shows the critical bands analyzed by Zwicker[8]. The critical bandwidth of 1kHz is 190Hz. But the bandwidth of 4kHz is 900Hz which is broader than that of 1kHz. That is, the critical band becomes broader as the band frequency goes from low to high frequency and the human ear cannot analyze minutely so much.

The filters designed in this paper use the characteristics of the critical bands. The stop bandwidth of the designed notch filter is 100 Hz, which is narrower than the critical bandwidth of 2.8~5.6kHz.

2.3 Structure of the Proposed Algorithm

In this Section, the 4 bits watermark embedding method is proposed. The proposed algorithm requires the design of digital filters in advance. Digital filters are designed by the elliptic filter method in Matlab signal toolbox. Table 2 represents the specification of designed digital filters. With the consideration which the designed system is used in broadcasting system and the watermarked signal is mainly voice, we designed the band stop filters such as Table 2. The energy of the tested voice signal is weak above 6kHz frequency. So, the processing bands of the designed filters are set to 2.8~5.6kHz. The stop bandwidths are set to 100Hz not to perceive the watermarked signal.

The input signal is decomposed into the several frequency bands by the wavelet transform. The needed frequency bands(0~5.5kHz, 5.5~11.1kHz) among the decomposed frequency bands are selected and then filtered by the previously designed filters such as Table 2. It is in order to reduce the side effect which distorts the neighborhood frequency components by filtering.

Table 2. Specification of the designed digital filters

No.	passband[kHz]	stopband[kHz]	Passband ripple(dB)	Stopband decaying ratio(dB)
1	2.85-3.15	2.95-3.05	0.1	74
2	3.30-3.60	3.40-3.50	0.1	75
3	4.00-4.30	4.10-4.20	0.1	77
4	4.60-4.90	4.70-4.80	0.1	78
5	5.30-5.60	5.40-5.50	0.1	80

1) Embedding watermark

Figure 2 shows the structure to embed the watermark into an audio signal, where the cover signal is the original audio signal and the stego signal is the watermarked signal which contains the information embedded on the cover signal. In Figure 2, there is the determination part for embedding the watermark, which decides whether embedding the watermark on cover signal or not for increasing security.

The input signal is decomposed into the several frequency bands by the wavelet transform. And then we do the forward-backward filtering to prevent the phase distortion[5]. Figure 3 shows the procedure of the forward-backward filtering.

Figure 4 shows the embedding watermarks using Figure 2 embedding scheme. The three subband signals are filtered among four subband signals.

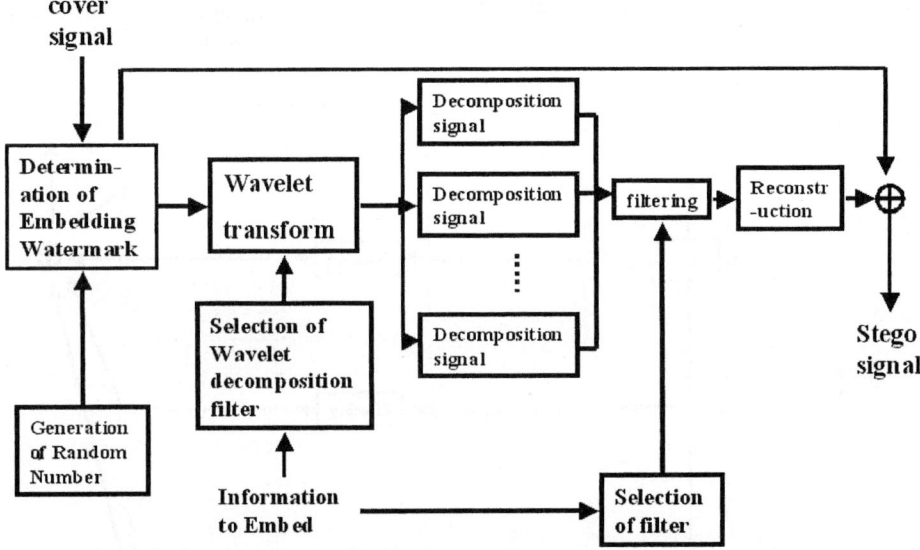

Fig. 2. Structure of the watermark embedding

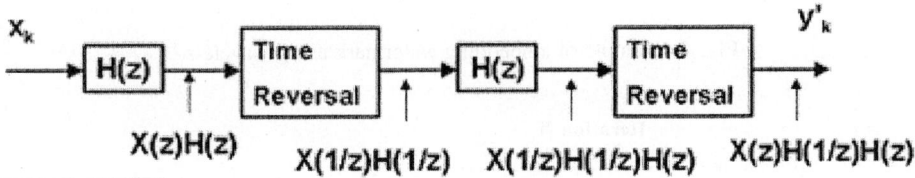

Fig. 3. Procedure of the forward-backward filtering

2) Extracting watermark

Figure5 represents the procedure of extracting the watermark. We can detect the filtering effect clearly by processing 1024 or 2048 samples per frame in 44.1kHz sampling frequency, because the stop bandwidth is about 80Hz. The frame size N = 1024 is set and the watermarked information limited within the maximum threshold is empathized by the logarithmic function. From the empathized frequency peaks, the location of peaks can be known. The embedded watermark is reconstructed by using lookup table in Table2.

Eq. (1) shows that the audio signal is transformed into the frequency spectrum with the logarithm scaling and then we compute the ensemble mean by averaging the sum of N's sequences as

$$M(n) = \frac{1}{N} \sum_{i=0}^{N-1} \log(real(fft(audio(n + i * m)))), \quad (1)$$

where $M(n)$ is n-th ensemble mean, N is a frame number for ensemble mean, m is sample number per frame and audio is audio-sequence played.

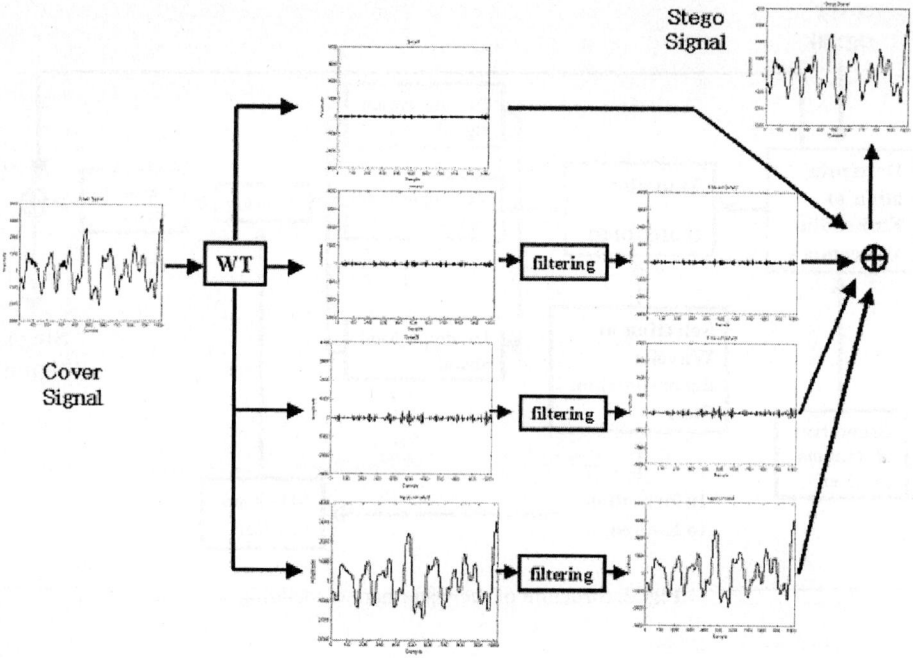

Fig. 4. Example of embedding watermark using wavelets

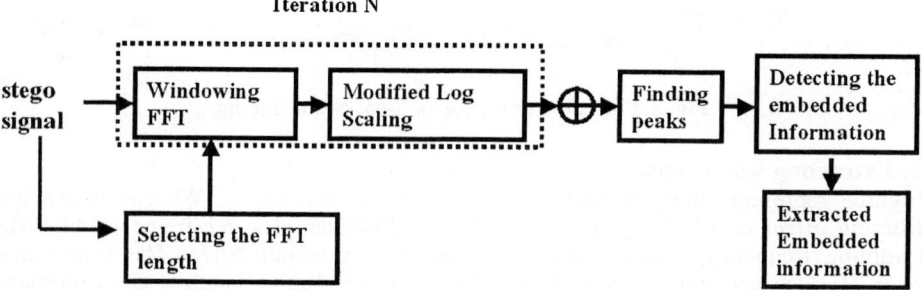

Fig. 5. Structure of extracting the embedded watermarks

3 Broadcast Synchronizing System

3.1 Structure of BSS

The Figure 6 is the structure on the broadcast synchronizing system in the broadcasting system.

In the key station, the watermark is embedded in the audio file to be used on the converting time and this audio file is kept in the digital audio file server.

A program is transmitted from the key station to the local station via the public wave. In the local station, this program is received by the audio receiver and the received audio signal is sent to the synchronized signal detector.

The synchronized signal detector checks whether the watermark is embedded in the input audio signal or not. If the watermark is detected, the local station stops transmitting the key station program and converts to send the self-made local station program.

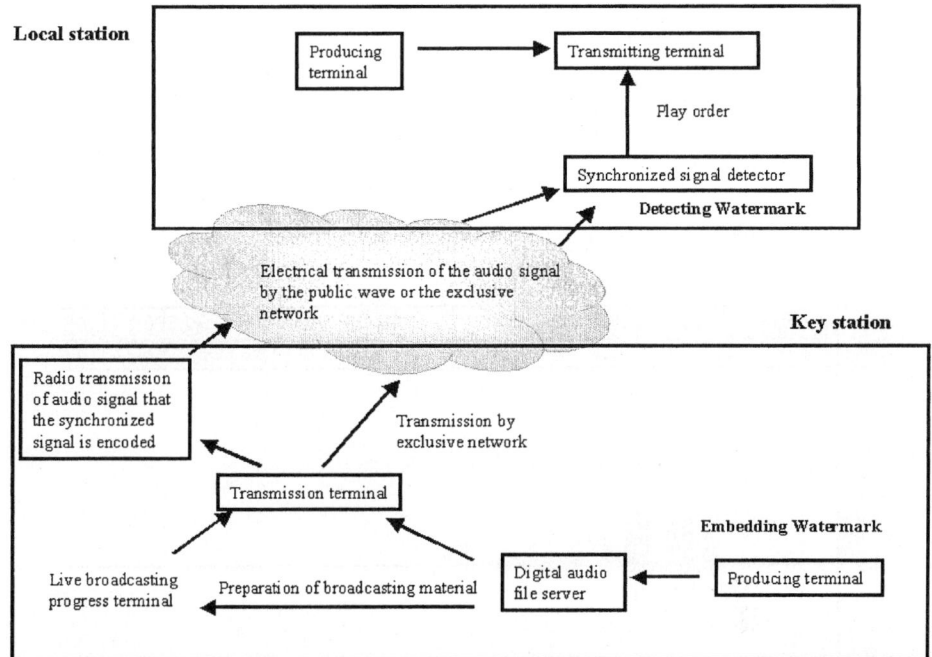

Fig. 6. Structure of the broadcast synchronizing system(Co-worked by MBC)

3.2 Implementation

The dedicated hardware is designed for the system stability and the precise and real-time implementation. The BSS has to detect the sync signal within the short time, at least 0.5 second, and transmit it to the control signal generator. Although the condition mentioned above can be fulfilled under the PC basis, the PC system doesn't guarantee the system stability and the real-time processing. Therefore, we used DSP(digital signal processor) chip so that we get the speedy computation and the stability.

As a DSP chip, TMS320VC5410 -160MIPS (million instructions per second) of TI is used. Figure 7 shows the block diagram of implemented system.

Data converters, such as A/D, D/A, convert the input analog stereo signal to the digital signal of 44.1kHz stereo 16bit ADPCM type and convert the digital stereo signal to the analog stereo signal in the same time. These procedures have been used to generate the loop back signal by which the state of input signal can be monitored.

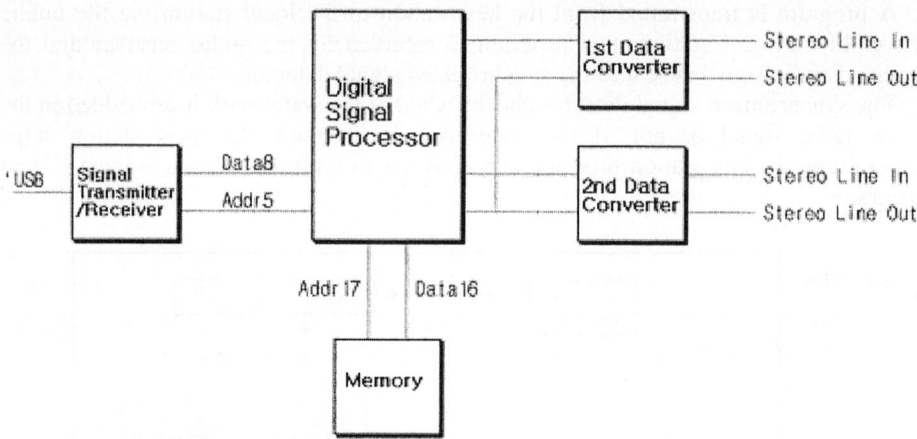

Fig. 7. Block diagram of the implemented system

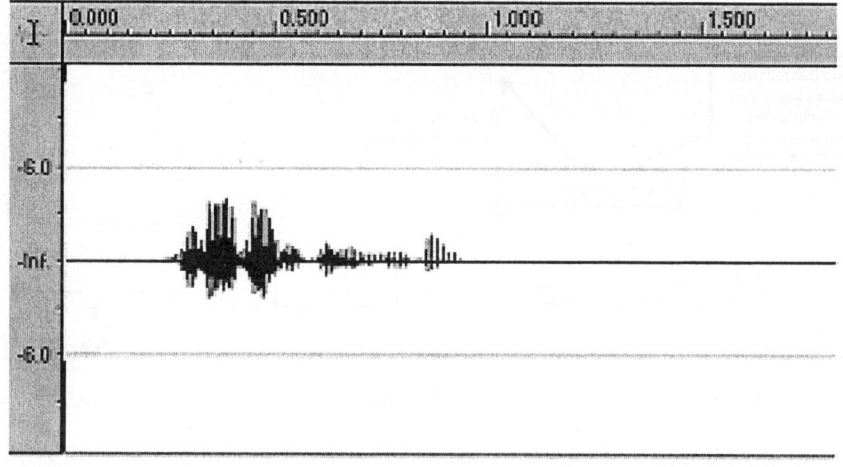

Fig. 8. Used voice signal

The memory block is composed of 128kWords flash memory. This system can process two broadcasting signals simultaneously. The computational power of maximum 40MIPS is consumed per 1 channel.

DSP performs the real-time detection of watermarks in the input broadcasting audio signal with watermark detecting algorithm.

If the watermark information inserted as a sync signal is detected, a sync signal is transmitted to the monitoring PC through USB port. Then, the monitoring PC saves log files which have the information of when the sync signal detected and how many times detected.

Figure 8 shows the voice used in this experiment, which is sampled from the male speaker. Horizontal axis means seconds and vertical axis means the magnitude(dB) of wave. -inf means the absolute silence and 0 dB means the maximum magnitude of which 16 bits data can represent and -90.3dB means the minimum magnitude.

4 Experiments

In this Section, to test the performance of broadcast synchronizing system, the proposed algorithm was tested on the actual broadcasting situations for the false negative error. Also it was tested for compression, A/D, D/A, noise adding and aging test for false positive error during 90 days.

4.1 Audibility Test

The most generally used method for the quantitative evaluation of sound quality is to measure SNR. SNR can be expressed as follows:

$$SNR = 10 \cdot \log_{10}(\frac{Signal}{Noise}) \quad dB \qquad (2)$$

where Signal is signal power and Noise is noise power.

Although SNR test is not sufficient in audibility test, the noise is known not to be detected when SNR is above 60dB.

The watermarks are embedded on the four test audio and SNR values are measured. Table 3 shows the test result. These SNR values are above 66dB, which values mean little degradation of the watermarked audio.

Table 3. Experiment result for 4 sample(SNR, dB)

	Classic	Pop-1	Pop-2	Sound effect
SNR	66.090	67.261	68.056	67.384

4.2 Robustness Test

The proposed algorithm is compared with the spread spectrum method[2][8] to verify the merit of the proposed algorithm. Although there are many methods, the common drawback of the spread spectrum methods is that they must find the sync of each frame to correlate the watermarks with the watermarked audio signal.

Table4 shows a very weak feature about the desynchronizing attacks such as a pitch shift and time scaling. However, the proposed algorithm improves these defects.

The result of reliability test of implemented system by using the real broadcasting audio has no false positive error during 90 days. Because of detecting once processing per 0.5 second, we can judge that the false positive error does not nearly occur.

Table 4. Performance comparison with the spread spectrum and proposed method

attack item		detection rate	
		spread spectrum method	proposed method
amplitude compression		46%	53%
channel conversion		91%	94%
pitch shift	+10%	27%	90%
	-10%	13%	94%
time scaling	+10%	2%	96%
	-10%	2%	96%
noise adding	-36dB	88%	94%
MPEG1 MP3	128kbps	90%	94%
	96kbps	84%	91%
MPEG2 AAC	128kbps	92%	94%
	96kbps	86%	91%

5 Conclusion

We proposed the new audio watermarking algorithm and design the broadcast synchronizing system to automatically switch the programs of the key broadcasting station with those of local stations. The proposed algorithm can embed the watermark by using the band stop filters, which are designed based on critical band of HAS(human auditory system).

The objective audibility test represents 66dB above and there are little degradation of audio quality. In robustness test, the detection rate is 90% over from the various attack such as compression (MP3, AAC), add noise, channel conversion and especially represents robustness about asynchronizing attack (pitch shift and time scaling).

The BSS automatically switches the programs between the key station and the local station in broadcasting system. When the local station sends the self-made program in the middle of broadcasting the program received from the key station, the switching of the program between the key station and the local station should be synchronized. The result of reliability test of implemented system by using the real broadcasting audio has no false positive error during 90 days. Because of detecting once processing per 0.5 second, we can judge that the false positive error does not nearly occur.

Acknowledgement

SoliDeo Gloria. This work was supported by International Cooperation Research Project of Ministry of Science and Technology in Korea.

References

1. D.H. Shin, S.W. Shin, C.K. Ahn, Y.I. Shin, J.W. Kim, and J.U. Choi, "Implementation of Broadcast Synchronizing System using Audio Watermark," Proceedings of the Korean Society of Broadcast Engineers Conference 2001, v.2001, n.2001, pp. 181-185, Nov. 2001.
2. I. Cox, J. Kilian, T. Leighton and T. Shamoon, "Secure Spread Spectrum Watermarking for Multimedia," *IEEE Transactions on Image Processing*, Vol. 6, pp. 1673-1687, Dec. 1997.
3. Tolga Ciloglu and S. Utku Karaaslan, "An Improved All-Pass Watermarking Scheme for Speech and Audio," *Proceedings of the 2000 IEEE International Conference on Multimedia and Expo*, Vol. 2, pp. 1017-1020. 2000.
4. D. J. M. Robinson and M. J. Hawksford, "Time-Domain Auditory Model for the Assessment of High-Quality Coded Audio," *The 107th Conference of the Audio Engineering Society*, Sept. 1999.
5. Fredrik Gustafsson, "Determining the Initial states in forward-backward filtering," *IEEE Transactions on Signal Processing*, vol.44 no.4, pp.988-992, 1996. 4.
6. Burlington R. and May D. Jr., *Handbook of Probability and Statistics with Tables*, Second Edition, McGraw Hill NY, 1970.
7. Udo Zolzer, *Digital Audio Signal Processing*, John Wiley & Sons Ltd, Stuttgart, pp. 252-254, 1995.
8. Bassia, P., Pitas, I., "Robust audio watermarking in the time domain," *In Proc. EUSIPCO 98*, vol. 1, pp. 25-28, 1998.

Realistic Broadcasting Using Multi-modal Immersive Media

Sung-Yeol Kim, Seung-Uk Yoon, and Yo-Sung Ho

Gwangju Institute of Science and Technology (GIST),
1 Oryong-dong, Buk-gu, Gwangju, 500-712, Korea
{sykim75, suyoon, hoyo}@gist.ac.kr

Abstract. Realistic broadcasting is considered as a next generation broadcasting system supporting user-friendly interactions. In this paper, we define multi-modal immersive media and introduce technologies for a realistic broadcasting system, which are developed at Realistic Broadcasting Research Center (RBRC) in Korea. In order to generate three-dimensional (3-D) scenes, we acquire immersive media using a depth-based camera or multi-view cameras. After converting the immersive media into broadcasting contents, we send the immersive contents to the clients using high-speed and high-capacity transmission techniques. Finally, we can experience realistic broadcasting represented by the 3-D display, 3-D sound, and haptic interaction. Demonstrations show two types of broadcasting systems: the system using a depth-based camera and the system using multi-view cameras. From the realistic broadcasting system, we can generate new paradigms for the next generation digital broadcasting.

Keywords: Realistic broadcasting, Immersive media, Technologies of a realistic broadcasting system.

1 Introduction

As the rapid development of telecommunication techniques and high-speed networks, we live in an age of the information revolution and the digital epoch. Humans acquire useful knowledge and information through the Internet since high-speed networks are connected with high-performance personal computers. We cannot only feel deep impressions by a high definition television with a large screen and a high power speaker, but also call to someone using a cellular phone with moving pictures. In addition, banking services and product purchases are possible at home. The digital technologies make a human life more convenient and livelier.

It is not too much to say that the essence of the digital age is the multimedia technologies for digital broadcasting. The digital broadcasting system converts analog multimedia data into digital multimedia data and then transmits the digitized data to the end users. The digital broadcasting is suitable for a high-quality and multi-channel broadcasting in comparison with an analog broadcasting. Furthermore, a digital broadcasting system can make use of the frequency bandwidth effectively and have great advantages for the data broadcasting.

Figure 1 shows the whole development trends of the digital broadcasting [1]. As shown in Fig. 1, the tendency for broadcasting services will change from one-directional services to bi-directional services or interactive services such as a stereoscopic TV, a three-dimensional (3-D) TV, and a realistic broadcasting. In the broadcasting service quality aspect, the next generation broadcasting will be a high quality 3-D broadcasting system.

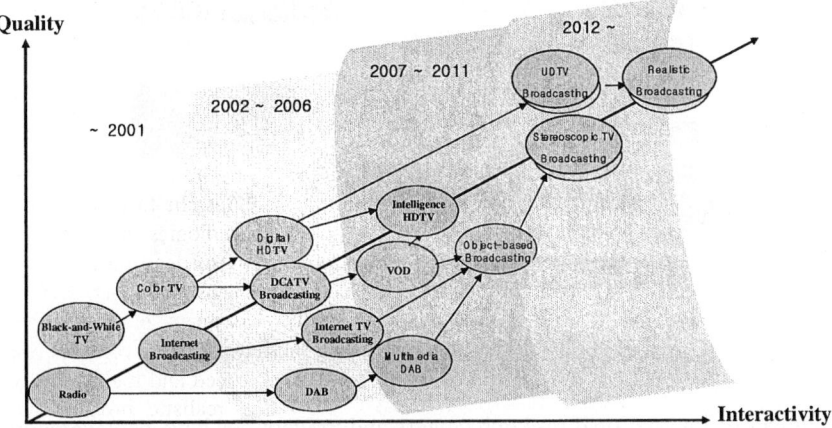

Fig. 1. The trends in digital broadcasting

Especially, realistic broadcasting makes an appearance for the next generation broadcasting. Realistic broadcasting provides not only high quality visual services, but also a variety of user-friendly interactions. Unlike other digital broadcasting systems, we can experience the realism through our five senses.

Several countries have already served 3-D broadcasting experimentally using their satellites. Furthermore, a large number of researchers are interested in developing 3-D displays and 3-D data processing techniques since the scale for 3-D data markets is supposed to be three billion dollars in 2010. In this paper, we will survey the technologies for a realistic broadcasting system, described by Realistic Broadcasting Research Center (RBRC) in Korea, so as to keep pace with this trend.

2 Immersive Media and Realistic Broadcasting

The existing media services focused on 2-D audio-visual data owing to the technological limits. The audio-visual data were not enough to give us the vividness through the five senses of human. However, we can represent and treat high-capacity media easily, as the computer hardware and software progress rapidly.

It is conservative to say that enhanced digital multimedia services lie in the advent of multi-modal immersive media and the technology of realistic broadcasting. Multi-modal immersive media indicate the data overcoming the spatial-temporal limit. As examples of the multi-modal immersive media, there are computer graphic models, 3-D video, multi-channel audio, haptic data, and the information for the sense of smell.

Realistic broadcasting can be defined by a broadcasting service system using multi-modal immersive media so as to endow the end users with the realism. Immersive contents indicate the broadcasting contents with the multi-modal immersive media. Figure 2 shows the conceptual illustration for realistic broadcasting.

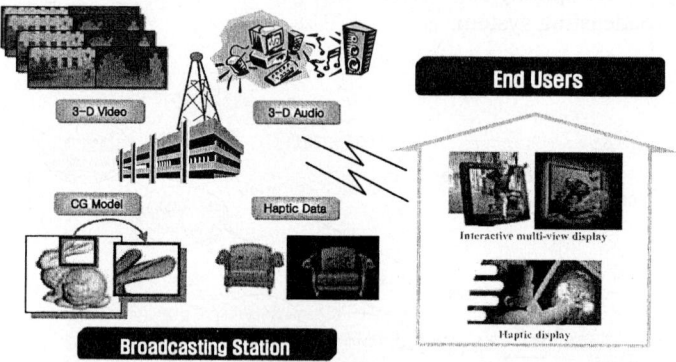

Fig. 2. Realistic broadcasting services

A number of international research centers and universities have persevered in their efforts for developing the core technologies related to realistic broadcasting. Holographic display techniques have been developed in Massachusetts Institute of Technology. The ATTEST project, archived from 2002 to 2004, gave us a possibility for realizing 3-D TV [2]. With a new project named by 3DTV, started in September 2004, the development of the commercial European 3-D broadcasting system has been in progress [3]. O'Modhrain and Oakley [4, 5] discussed the potential role that haptic or touch feedback might play in supporting a greater sense of immersion in the next generation broadcasting system [6]. In recent years, multi-view video coding has been a big issue in MPEG 3DAV standards [7]. Likewise, NHK research center in Japan have been developing 3-D display and 3-D sound technologies [8], and Fraunhofer Heinrich Hertz Institute (FhG-HHI) in Germany exploits the efficient compression scheme based on 3-D object modeling [9].

Previous researches related to realistic broadcasting have been archived by the unit of small group individually. In order to develop a feasible realistic broadcasting, we need to integrate various technologies. In this paper, we will introduce the incorporated technologies to realize a realistic broadcasting system.

3 Technologies for Realistic Broadcasting

The realistic broadcasting system can be divided into four parts largely; the acquisition of immersive media, the editing of immersive contents, the transmission of immersive contents, and the display of immersive media. Figure 3 shows the key technologies of the realistic broadcasting system.

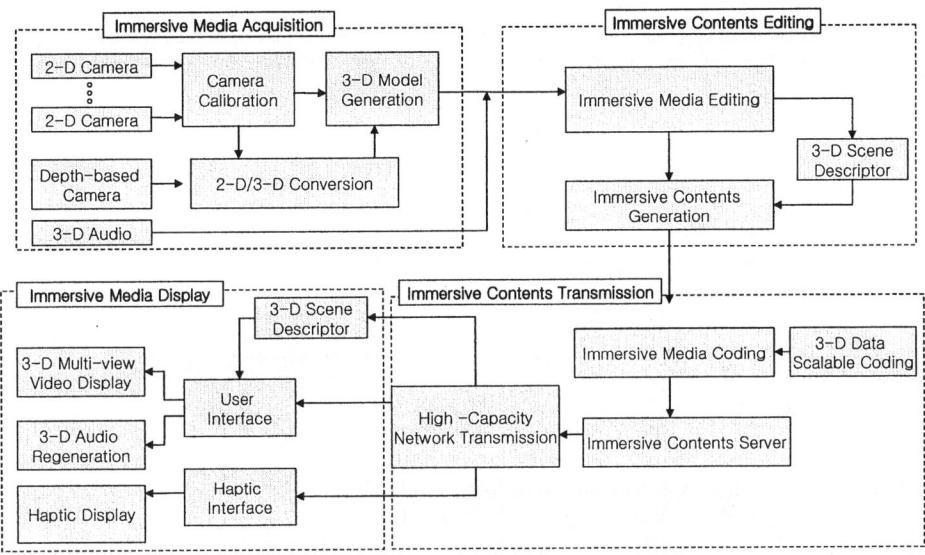

Fig. 3. Overall system of realistic broadcasting

In the process of the acquisition for immersive media, we generate 3-D models and 3-D photo-realistic backgrounds using a number of 2-D stereo cameras or a depth-based camera. Also, we can obtain 3-D sound corresponding to the 3-D models. In general, we pass through a camera calibration so as to obtain the exact 3-D data.

In order to make 3-D scenes, called by the immersive contents, from the acquired 3-D data, we need to edit the immersive media. In the process of the editing for immersive contents, we combine the 3-D video, 3-D audio, and other additional data, such as haptic information.

Basically, the immersive contents require a tremendous amount of data. In order to store the immersive contents compactly and transmit them efficiently, we need to compress the immersive contents. Moreover, we also need to develop a proper network protocol for the high-capacity transmission.

Finally, we display received immersive media with a high definition television. At the client side, we can watch 3-D scenes with stereoscopic displays. Moreover, various user-friendly interactions are supported by a view interaction, a haptic display, and bi- directional data transmission.

3.1 Acquisition of Immersive Media

Before generating immersive contents for realistic broadcasting, we need to acquire immersive media from 3-D data acquisition devices. After obtaining immersive data, we need to do multi-modal immersive media modeling. Figure 4 shows the immersive media acquisition technologies.

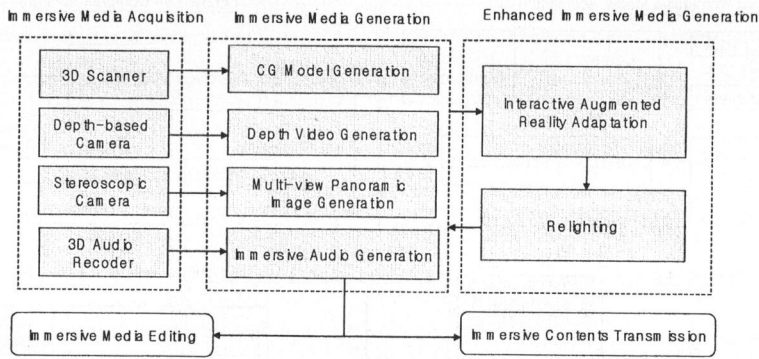

Fig. 4. Immersive media acquisition

3.1.1 Generation of Computer Graphics Models

In order to acquire computer graphics (CG) models, we use 3-D data scanning device or graphic tools. Basically, CG models are composed of 3-D coordinate data and attribute data such as colors, normal vectors, and textures. We need to estimate and compensate the colors and surface materials of CG models since the acquisition environments are various according to lighting and temperature conditions. Figure 5 shows the devices for the immersive media acquisition including a 3-D scanner.

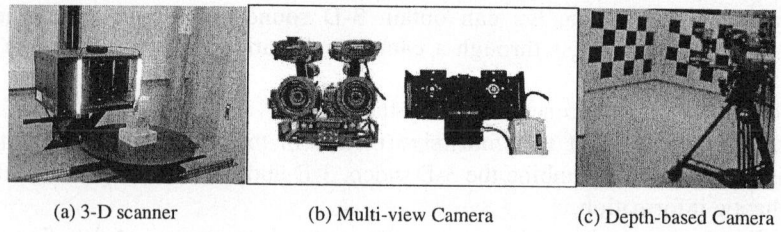

(a) 3-D scanner   (b) Multi-view Camera   (c) Depth-based Camera

Fig. 5. Immersive media acquisition devices

3.1.2 Generation of Depth Video

Depth video indicates a sequence of depth images and texture images. For accomplishing the realistic broadcasting system, we should generate 3-D scenes in real-time. With a depth-based camera and a number of stereo cameras, we can generate 3-D scenes based on depth video. While we can obtain the depth data through stereo matching when we use a set of stereo cameras, we can get the depth information directly by the depth-based camera.

3.1.3 Generation of Multi-view Panoramic Image

Multi-view panoramic images are used for 3-D backgrounds in our realistic broadcasting system. After obtaining images by a set of stereo cameras, we execute the local stitching and the global stitching so as to make a 3-D panoramic image. Finally, we should optimize the geometry data since the stitching can cause errors.

3.1.4 Relighting

When we combine 3-D models and photo-realistic environment, we need to know the similar light conditions with photo-realistic environment to render 3-D scenes naturally. As shown in Fig. 6, after obtaining a high dynamic range (HDR) image by estimating the lighting conditions, light probe, and high-resolution cameras, we adapt the acquired light conditions to 3-D scenes.

Fig. 6. Relighting using HDR

3.1.4 Generation of Immersive Audio

In general, 3-D video data can play a role for realistic broadcasting contents when 3-D audio and 3-D sound are accompanied. Therefore, the generation of immersive audio is an important part in the generation of immersive media. The immersive audio and sound are obtained by evaluating the audio direction and distance using a head related transfer function (HRTF) estimator.

3.2 Editing of Immersive Contents

After acquiring immersive media, we need to edit the immersive media and convert them into immersive contents for realistic broadcasting. As shown in Fig. 7, there are an auto-segmentation, special effects, an editing system for immersive media, and a broadcasting item generation.

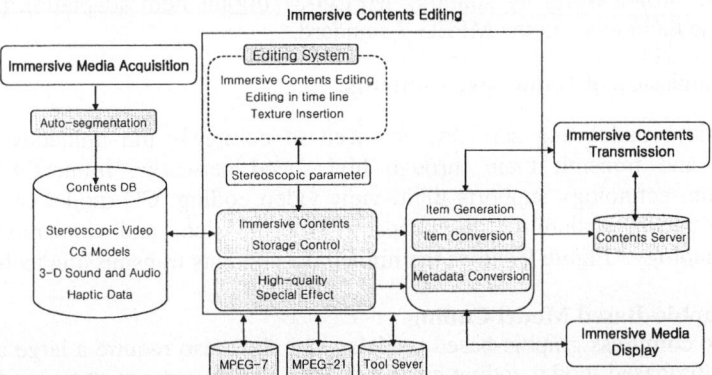

Fig. 7. Immersive Contents Editing

3.2.1 Auto-segmentation and Special Effects

As the essential techniques for immersive content editing, auto-segmentation defines immersive media as a unit of object and extracts the objects from 3-D backgrounds. After the segmented objects are applied by special effects such as warping and morphing techniques according to usages, new immersive contents are generated with combination between the segmented objects and other immersive media.

3.2.2 Editing System

In order to synthesize each immersive media and generate 3-D scenes in timeline, we need to obtain a 3-D scene descriptor. The 3-D scene descriptor indicates the relationship between CG models and generated depth video in each frame. In an editing system for realistic broadcasting, we reallocate the immersive media by 3-D scene editors and generate the 3-D scene descriptor. At the client side, we can regenerate 3-D scenes by analyzing the transmitted 3-D scene descriptor.

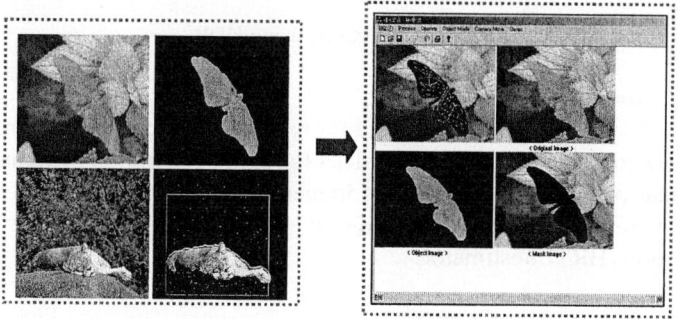

Fig. 8. Auto-segmentation and editing system

3.2.3 Broadcasting Item Generation

The broadcasting item generation is important parts to support an interactive data broadcasting system. In order to communicate broadcasting servers and clients, we should provide a variety of items and metadata. We can generate and convert items for realistic broadcasting by adapting MPEG-21 digital item adaptation (DIA) and stereoscopic techniques in the MPEG-7 standard.

3.3 Transmission of Immersive Contents

For realistic broadcasting services, we need to compress the immersive contents efficiently and transmit them through high-speed networks. Immersive contents transmission technology supports multi-view video coding, CG model compression, immersive media scalability, high-capacity transmission, and immersive content server technology. Figure 9 shows the immersive contents transmission technologies.

3.3.1 Graphic-Based Model Coding

We need to compress graphic-based models since they also require a large amount of data. Graphic-based model coding can be divided into two parts: static model coding and dynamic model coding. For static model coding, we usually use a mesh-based compression scheme provided by the MPEG-4 SHNC standard. Also, we mainly use an interpolator compression (IC) scheme for dynamic models.

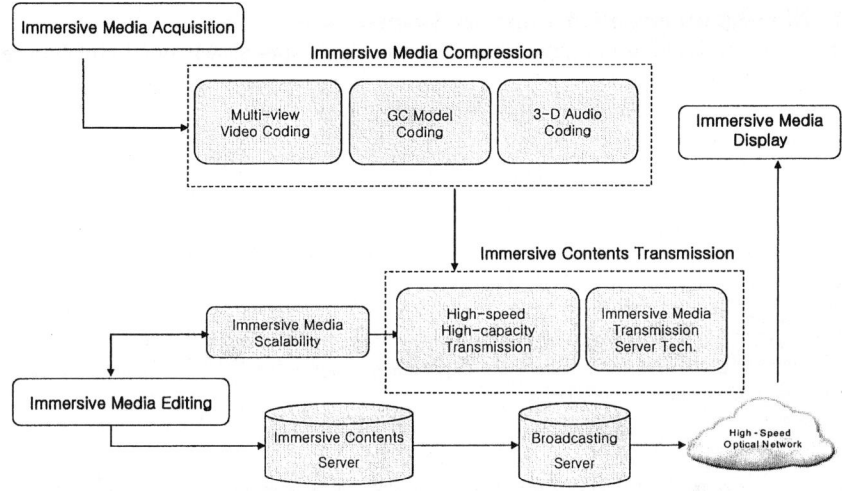

Fig. 9. Immersive contents transmission

3.3.2 Multi-view Video Coding

Realistic broadcasting should provide natural and continuous 3-D video in real-time. In order to support such a multi-view 3-D video, it is beneficial for us to use the 3-D multi-view video. Basically, we develop the multi-view video coding algorithms to transmit the video data within limited-bandwidth networks. In order to compress the multi-view video, we use intermediate view reconstruction (IVR) [10] and layered depth image (LDI) [11].

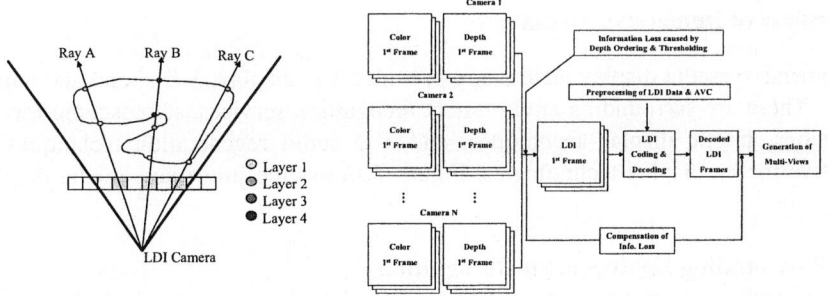

Fig. 10. Multi-view video compression using LDI

3.3.3 Immersive Media Scalability

Immersive media need to be scalable so as to serve the realistic broadcasting according to the capacity and environment of clients. By using the scalability of the immersive media, we can enjoy the realistic broadcasting in anyway and anywhere. We support the immersive media scalability according to the region of interest, view-dependence, and the distance of immersive media.

3.2.4 High-Speed and High-Capacity Transmission

In order to send the immersive content with high speed, we need to change the amount of transmitted data according to the network situation and protocols. We need transcoding schemes and layered representation techniques for immersive media and we consider the robustness and required bandwidth. Furthermore, a priority scheme for determining the order of packets is required for a high-capacity transmission.

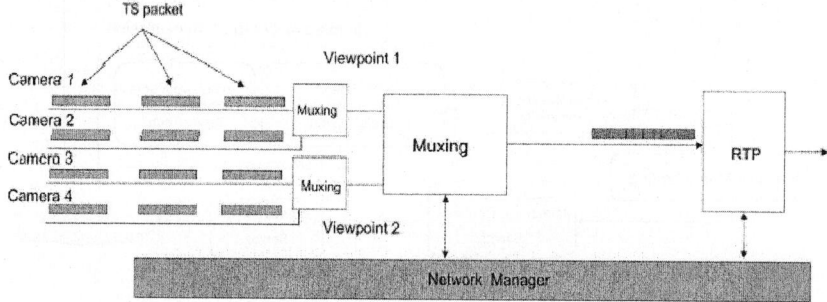

Fig. 11. Immersive contents transmission

3.2.5 Immersive Contents Transmission Server Technology

Since the clients share immersive contents simultaneously in the realistic broadcasting, it is necessary to develop the transmission server technology for supporting the interactive data broadcasting. Moreover, we need to exploit the packet distribution techniques with immersive contents. The content transmission server technologies are composed of server composition and interactive support techniques.

3.4 Display of Immersive Media

The immersive media display technology provides 3-D display, 3-D sound and haptic display. There are surrounding environment recognition services, stereoscopic format conversions, haptic display techniques, and 3-D audio regeneration techniques in immersive media display technologies. Figure 7 shows the immersive media display technologies.

3.4.1 Surrounding Environment Recognition

The surrounding environment recognition is used to trace the eyes of clients. As analyzing the viewpoints and actions of clients, terminals display various stereoscopic images with respect to the viewpoints of the end users. We develop the surrounding environment recognition technique using a head-tacking camera.

3.4.2 Stereoscopic Format Conversions

In order to adapt the existing immersive contents to terminals, we need to develop the 3-D converting techniques. When the input contents are provided by page-flip, interlace, interleave, top-down, side-by-side, and sync double schemes, we convert the input contents into a proper format that is possible to display at a terminal.

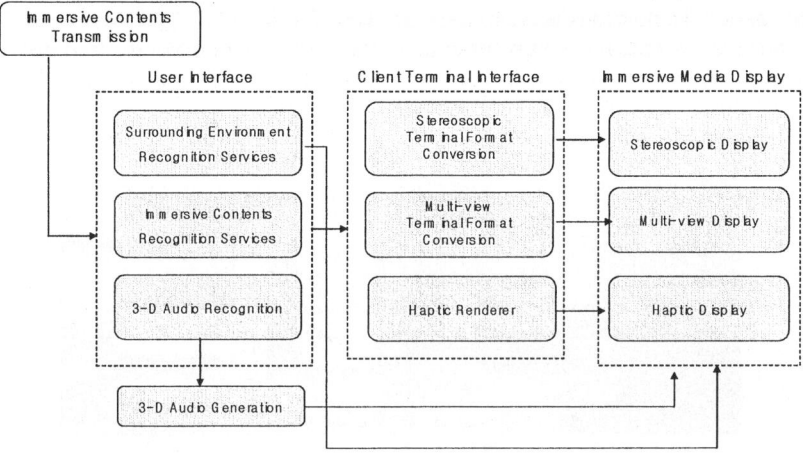

Fig. 12. Immersive media display

3.4.3 Haptic Display

The realistic broadcasting can not only watch and listen to the broadcasting contents by 3-D display and 3-D sound, but also support haptic display so as to touch and control the immersive contents. Haptic information is a sense with human's muscles and skins. We can use the haptic data in educational and entertainment programs such as a scientific documentary and a fishing television program. Also, haptic information can be used for a home shopping channel by supporting surface and shape information of the goods.

3.4.4 Audio Recognition and 3-D Audio Generation

We need to develop an interface using an audio recognition technique for the realistic broadcasting system. We can get useful information from a television by an audio interface, as well as changing a channel and immersive contents. In addition, the acquired immersive audio and sound can be regenerated by 3-D sound techniques.

4 Demonstrations of Realistic Broadcasting

We have evaluated the system using multi-view stereo cameras [12] and the system using a depth-based camera [13] for the realistic broadcasting in the forum provided

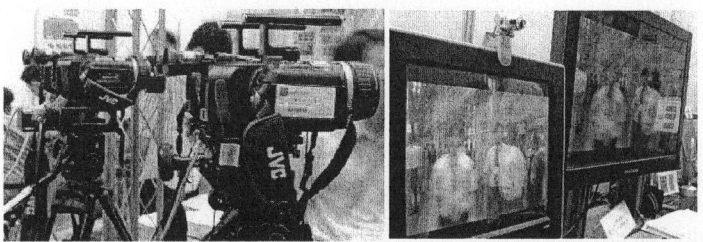

Fig. 13. System using multi-view cameras

by Information Technology Research Center (ITRC) in 2005. The system using multi-view cameras includes the surrounding recognition, high-capacity and high-speed transmission, and stereoscopic conversion techniques. On the other hand, the system using a depth-based camera includes the 3-D data modeling, stereoscopic display and haptic rendering techniques.

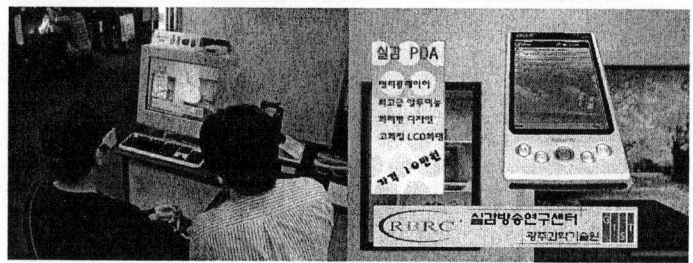

Fig. 14. System using a depth-based camera

5 Conclusions

In this paper, we define a realistic broadcasting system and review the technologies for realistic broadcasting, described in RBRC. In order to generate immersive media, we use the multi-view cameras and a depth-based camera. After converting the immersive media into immersive contents for the 3-D scenes, we send the immersive contents to the client by high-speed and high-capacity transmission techniques. Finally, we can experience the 3-D display, 3-D sound, and haptic display at the client side. The trends of recent broadcasting are changing from one-directional broadcasting systems to interactive bi-directional broadcasting systems. The realistic broadcasting, supporting the interactive bi-directional broadcasting system, is supposed to be the next revolution in the history of television.

Acknowledgements. This work was supported in part by Gwangju Institute of Science and Technology (GIST), in part by the Ministry of Information and Communication (MIC) through the Realistic Broadcasting Research Center (RBRC), and in part by the Ministry of Education (MOE) through the Brain Korea 21 (BK21) project.

References

1. Ministry of Science and Technology of Korea, National Technology Roadmap, 2003.
2. Redert, A., Op de Beeck, M., Fehn, C., IJsselsteijn, W., Pollefeys, M., Van Gool, L., Ofek, E., Sexton, I., Surman, P.: ATTEST–Advanced Three-Dimensional Television System Technologies. Proceeding of International Symposium on 3D Data Processing (2002) 313–319.
3. http://3dtv.zcu.cz/.
4. O'Modhrain, S., Oakley, I.: Touch TV: Adding Feeling to Broadcast Media. Proceeding of the European Conference on Interactive Television (2003) 41-47.

5. O'Modhrain, S., Oakley, I.: Haptic Interfaces for Virtual Environment and Teleoperator Systems. Proceedings of Haptics (2004) 293-294.
6. Cha, J., Ryu, J., Kim, S., Eom, S., Ahn, B.: Haptic Interaction in Realistic Multimedia Broadcasting. Proceeding of Pacific Rim Conference (2004) 482-490.
7. Multi-view Video Coding using Shared Picture Memory and Shared Vector Memory. ISO/IEC JTC1/SC29/WG11 M11570 (2005).
8. McMillan, L.: A List-Priority Rendering Algorithm for Redisplaying Projected Surfaces. University of North Carolina, (1995) 95–105.
9. Duan, J., Li, J.: Compression of the LDI. IEEE Transaction on Image Processing, Vol. 12, No. 3, (2003) 365–372.
10. Bae, J. W., Park, H. J., Kim, E. S., Yoo, J.: An Efficient Disparity Estimation Algorithm Based on Spatial Correlation. Journal of SPIE Optical Engineering Vol.42, No.1, (2003) 176-181.
11. Ho, Y.S., Yoon, S.U., Kim, S.Y., Lee, E.K.: Preliminary Results for Multi-view Video Coding using Layered Depth Image. ISO/IEC JTC1/SC29/WG11 M11916 (2005).
12. Lee, S., Lee, K., Han, C., Yoo, J., Kim, M., Kim, J.W.: Multi-view Stereoscopic High-Definition Video over IP Networks for Next Generation Broadcasting. Proceeding of Pacific Rim Conference (2005).
13. Cha, J., Kim, S., Kim, S.Y., Kim, S., Yoon, S.U., Oakley, I., Ryu, J., Lee, K. H., Woo, W., Ho, Y.S.: Client System for Realistic Broadcasting: A First Prototype. Proceeding of Pacific Rim Conference (2005).

Client System for Realistic Broadcasting: A First Prototype

Jongeun Cha[1], Seung-Man Kim[2], Sung-Yeol Kim[3], Sehwan Kim[4],
Seung-Uk Yoon[3], Ian Oakley[1] Jeha Ryu[1], Kwan H. Lee[2],
Woontack Woo[4], and Yo-Sung Ho[3]

[1] Human-Machine-Computer Interface Lab.,
Gwangju Institute of Science and Technology,
1 Oryong-dong, Buk-gu, Gwangju 500-712 Republic of Korea
{gaecha, ian, ryu}@gist.ac.kr
http://dyconlab.gist.ac.kr
[2] Intelligent Design & Graphics Lab.,
{sman, lee}@kyebek.gist.ac.kr
http://kyebek9.gist.ac.kr
[3] Visual Communication Lab.,
{sykim75, suyoon, hoyo}@gist.ac.kr
http://vclab.gist.ac.kr
[4] U-VR Lab.,
{skim, wwoo}@gist.ac.kr
http://uvr.gist.ac.kr

Abstract. This paper presents a prototype of a client system for Realistic Broadcasting that can receive and process immersive media. It provides a viewer which supports stereoscopic video display and haptic interaction with the displayed media. The structure of the system is introduced and each component is described. In order to show the feasibility of Realistic Broadcasting, a home shopping channel scenario is applied to the system and its demonstration is performed in an exhibition. We also discuss users' comments and directions for improving of Realistic Broadcasting.

1 Introduction

Realistic Broadcasting is a broadcasting service system using multi-modal immersive media in order to provide users with realism, i. e., photorealistic and 3D display, 3D sound, multi-view interaction and haptic interaction. The concept and overview of Realistic Broadcasting is well introduced in [1].

However, new broadcasting and display technologies succeed or fail depending on how they are received by their audience. Now ubiquitous advances to basic broadcast services such as colour display or stereo sound have been well received. Indeed, it is now hard to imagine watching TV in black and white, or listening to music without stereo sound. On the other hand, many technologies that originally appeared promising have experienced a less illustrious history.

The wrap-around displays found in IMAX cinemas have been relegated to a niche domain. Many other advances, such as the primitive smell, touch and stereoscopic displays pioneered by the cinema industry in the 1950's (when it was concerned its popularity would fade as televisions became commonplace) have disappeared completely.

What is clear from this is that it is insufficient to simply develop new broadcasting technologies; the opinions of viewers must be considered from the outset. To achieve this we have developed a prototype system which represents the client side of our proposed Realistic Broadcasting system. It implements only the interface elements and not the technological architecture of the final system and enables us to perform user evaluations of our system early on, potentially feeding into a cycle of iterative development. It is this client system that we describe in this paper.

In order to create a practical example of Realistic Broadcasting, we focused on a home shopping scenario. Home shopping channel is a widespread broadcasting format, and one that, due to its focus on showcasing products for consumers to buy, seems likely to benefit from the additional realism of the media that we aim to create. Imagine being able to not only see, but also feel or interact with the products being described in the program. In the system we describe in this paper, a shopping host introduces a number of items and guides viewers through their features. The audience has a stereoscopic view of the scene and is able to touch the products with a haptic interface.

This paper is organized as follows; Section 2 introduces a client system for Realistic Broadcasting and describes detailed part of the system and its example application, a home shopping. Section 3 explains processes of immersive media acquisition and its edition based on the home shopping application. Section 4 describes a prototype implementation of the client system. Section 5 introduces a demonstration of this prototype in ITRC forum and discusses users' comments and directions for improvement of the client system for Realistic Broadcasting.

2 Client System for Realistic Broadcasting

A typical broadcasting client system receives, processes and displays content in the form of video and audio media. In the case of digital television broadcasting, the client system also serves as an interactive user interface, typically allowing Internet browsing or e-commerce applications. For Realistic Broadcasting, we propose a client system that can receive and process immersive media and provide a viewer which supports stereoscopic video display and haptic interaction with the displayed media. In order to achieve this, the streamed media needs to include a 3D representation. Typically, such representations are generated entirely computationally, and as such only apply to artificial, virtual scenes. Their creation is also laborious and time consuming. In our Realistic Broadcasting system, we are mainly concerned with the capture of real scenes, and so those techniques are largely inappropriate. As an alternative, we use depth imaging techniques to represent 3D information derived from raw camera data for static

178   J. Cha et al.

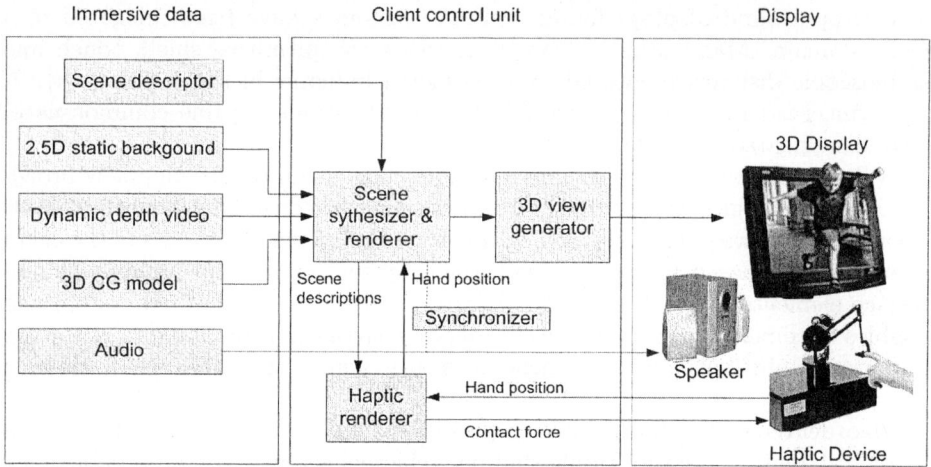

Fig. 1. Client system block diagram

Fig. 2. Home shopping channel scenario

background and depth image captured directly from a depth camera for dynamic part of a scene. However, for objects that are intended for focused, detailed interaction we rely on traditional computer generated models, as they are of a high quality. For haptic rendering of these objects, we augment the graphical models with haptic properties, varying the stiffness, friction and texture as appropriate. Combining this 3D information together with a stereo audio stream yields an immersive media format that we believe will results in viewers attaining increased levels of immersion with the displayed content. These immersive media are then edited and coordinated in 3D space to make meaningful and interesting contents. A scene editor produces a scene descriptor which includes the displayed media identification and the location in the screen. The client system is mainly composed of two parts, a scene renderer and a haptic renderer as shown in Fig. 1. Using the 3D information embedded in the media stream, the scene renderer synthesizes the streamed immersive media by following the scene descriptor instruction and produces a stereoscopic view of the contents. In order to display this view, we simply draw the scene from two virtual camera locations, representing the position of each of the viewer's eyes. We can then use one of a number of 3D display technologies to actually present the image to viewers. In this prototype, we used shutter glasses, as they are an established and reliable technology. The haptic renderer receives the synthesized scene data from the scene renderer and acquires the position of the viewer's hand from a haptic device. It calculates a contact force from these two data, and transmits this back to the haptic device, enabling the viewer to touch the objects and environment shown in the scene. Two different haptic rendering algorithms are used in this prototype, one specifically designed for the depth video [2], the other for the virtual objects [3].

In order to create a practical example of Realistic Broadcasting, we focused on a home shopping scenario. Fig. 2 shows a snapshot of the shopping channel scene. At the beginning of the scenario, a shopping host gives opening comment and starts to introduce a product. While explaining the product appearance and function, the host disappears and the product comes to foreground of the scene. Then, the host guides viewers to touch and manipulate the product with a haptic display. We showcased three products, a PDA, a sofa and a gold mask in the scenario. Viewers are able to touch the depth video as well as the products.

3 Immersive Media Acquisition and Edit

Image acquisition in our system was split into two parts, one encompassing the static and the other the dynamic elements within a scene. In our home shopping scenario the dynamic parts of the scene were essentially limited to the actress playing the show host, while the static parts were the background or setting against which she was situated. Distinguishing between these two elements is commonplace in broadcasting, and is facilitated by "blue screen" systems that enable actors to appear in front of arbitrary backgrounds. The technologies we used to capture depth video for both of these components are discussed below.

3.1 3D Static Background

Image-based 3D reconstruction of the background environment is a crucial factor in creating a visually realistic scene. Furthermore, a photo-realistic background allows an actor to manipulate augmented virtual objects while walking around the generated background by removing/augmenting virtual objects and interacting with them. Fortunately, off-the-shelf multi-view cameras are able to generate a background model of sufficient quality for our prototype.

The process of generating the photo-realistic background model is as follows. First an appropriate physical set is constructed. Lighting is adjusted to match the both the background and dynamic foreground objects. We then use a Digiclops,

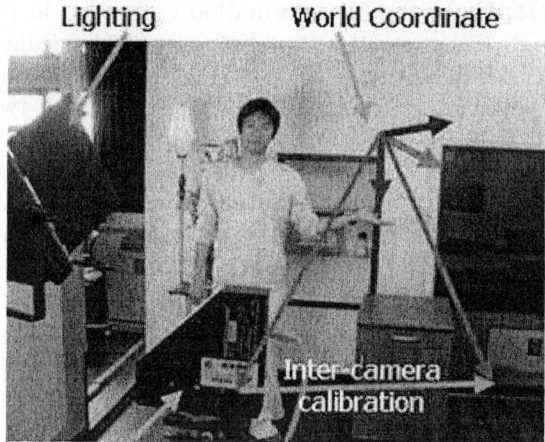

Fig. 3. Environment and System setup for capturing 3D static background

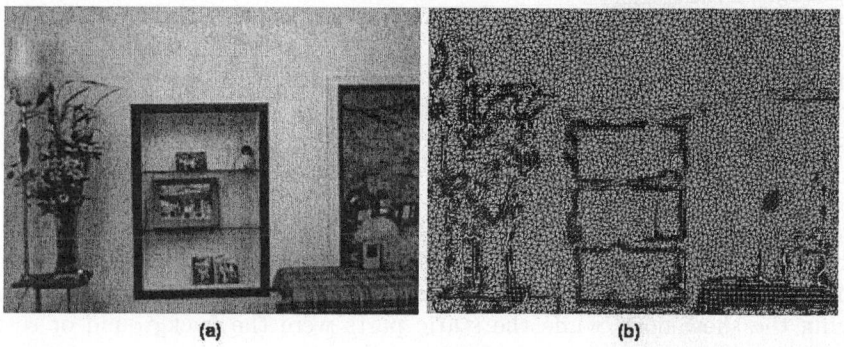

Fig. 4. Captured photorealistic background. (a) Textured view (b) Wireframe view.

a multi-view camera, to acquire a pair of images [4]. The Digiclops calculates 3D coordinates through disparity estimation. After generating a 3D point cloud for each camera position, a projection-based registration method is used to align adjacent 3D point clouds [5], creating a basic depth image. This image is then refined based on the spatio-temporal properties of the 3D point clouds by using adaptive uncertainty regions. Further refinement takes place by searching for correspondences in the projection of the 3D point clouds with a modified KLT feature tracker [6]. Next, the 3D point clouds are fine-registered by minimizing errors. Finally, each 3D point is evaluated with reference to correspondences, and a new color is assigned. In Fig. 3, the process for generating the photo-realistic background is illustrated with a real environment, Fig. 4 (a), one part of the generated background and Fig. 4 (b) the corresponding 3D model.

3.2 Dynamic Depth Video

It is more challenging to acquire depth information from dynamic scenes as they need to be captured and processed in real time. To obtain the dynamic depth stream in our prototype, we used a depth video camera [7] that produces both RGB color and depth signals in real time. Fig. 5 shows the capture system setup in the studio. The depth camera captures a depth value for each screen pixel in its field of view (FOV) using a time-of-flight technique. It is capable of generating an 8-bit (256 level) depth image and makes it possible to record the depth information that pertains to real moving objects at video frame rate.

As we filmed, we set the capture depth range to cover the movement of the actress as illustrated in Fig. 6. For this reason, objects outside of this range were

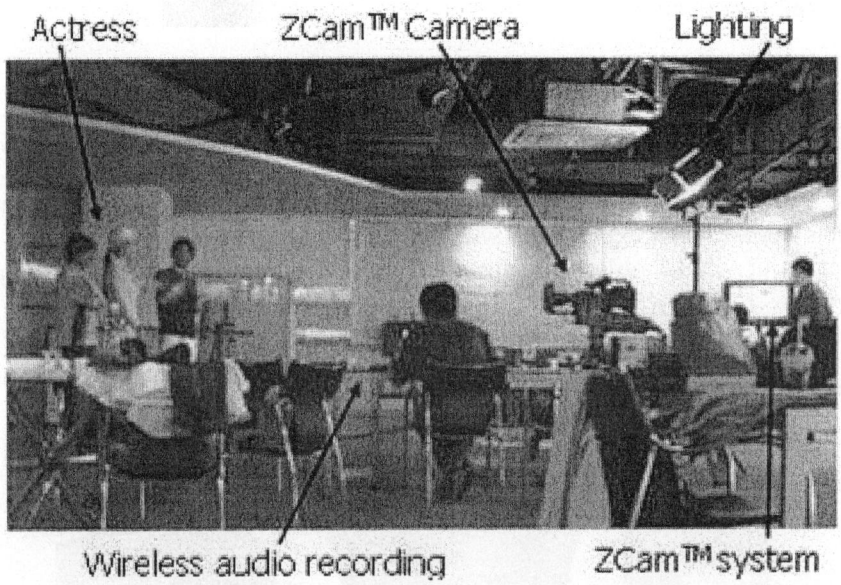

Fig. 5. System setup for capturing the depth video

Fig. 6. Selected images of depth video

not detected, and the depth value is reported to be zero for these pixels. This process ensures our depth image has the highest possible resolution around the objects that we are interested in and allows us to easily segment the data using a threshold histogram.

Each depth image represents the 3D position of the actress, but also contains quantization errors and optical noise as the depth value represents the scaled distance from the camera to the actress in only 8 bits. To increase the quality of the depth image we apply a 3D reconstruction technique [8]. The depth image is processed with segmentation, noise filtering, and adaptive sampling techniques based on the depth variation. From the refined depth image we generate a smooth 3D mesh using the Delaunay triangulation method. We then apply a further Gaussian smoothing technique. Finally, the 3D surfaces are graphically rendered, and we generate a final depth image from Z-buffer produced by this process.

3.3 3D CG Model

In our initial production, the three virtual models in Fig. 7 are the subject of the home shopping segment; the actress describes the features of these objects. The models were purchased on the Internet. The inclusion of these three models allows us to experiment with the effects of 3D display and haptic exploration of virtual objects in our Realistic Broadcasting scenario. Typically,

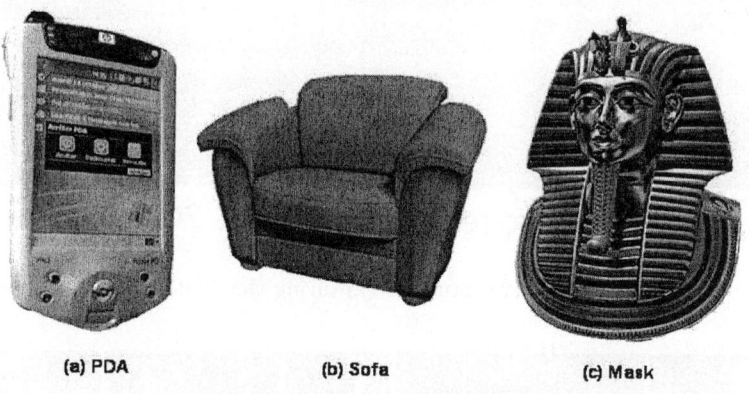

(a) PDA   (b) Sofa   (c) Mask

Fig. 7. CG models are composed into real scene

virtual model data consists of geometrical information and surface properties such as colour and visual texture. For haptic rendering we augmented the models with physical properties such as stiffness, friction, and roughness. We also attached a button force model to the buttons of the PDA virtual object, which enabled the viewers to push against them, and feel the resultant resistance and clicks.

3.4 Immersive Media Editing : Scene Descriptor

In order to synthesize the immersive media into a single timeline, we generated a 3-D scene descriptor. The 3-D scene descriptor specifies the translation and rotation information of the computer graphics models for each frame of the depth video. The structure of a 3-D scene descriptor is summarized by

[NumDepthImage][ObjectUpdateFlag][NumObject][ObjectTag][ObjectData]

```
986  0  1  5  -107.151600  252.144400  -78.404290  0.000000  0.000000  0.000000  0.000000
987  0  1  5  -107.151600  252.144400  -78.404290  0.000000  0.000000  0.000000  0.000000
988  0  1  5  -107.151600  252.144400  -78.404290  0.000000  0.000000  0.000000  0.000000
989  0  1  5  -107.151600  252.144400  -78.404290  0.000000  0.000000  0.000000  0.000000
990  0  1  5  -107.151600  252.144400  -78.404290  0.000000  0.000000  0.000000  0.000000
-1   1  1  5  -107.151600  252.144400  -78.404290  0.000000  0.000000  0.000000  0.000000
-1   0  1  5  -99.408500   241.639200  -70.192460  1.000000  0.000000  0.000000  0.002973
-1   0  1  5  -89.877280   231.999000  -62.852110  1.000000  0.000000  0.000000  0.002973
-1   0  1  5  -78.610710   223.523700  -56.619910  1.000000  0.000000  0.000000  0.002973
```

Fig. 8. A part of the scene descriptor used in our system

NumDepthImage represents the depth image to be rendered in the current frame. The value of NumDepthImage will be NULL when there is no depth image for the current frame. ObjectUpdateFlag indicates whether the 3-D scene is to be updated or not. NumObject is the total number of graphic-based models currently in the scene and ObjectTag is the index of graphic-based model to be rendered in the current frame. Finally, ObjectData indicates the translation and rotation information for the virtual models. Figure 8 shows a part of the 3-D scene descriptor.

4 Client System Prototype Implementation

4.1 Hardware

The prototype was implemented on an Intel based PC (Dual 3.2Ghz Pentium IV Xeon, 3GB DDRRAM, nVidia QuadroFX 4400 PCI-Express) under Microsoft Windows XP. We used PHANToM premium 1.5/3 DOF made by SensAble Technologies as our haptic display as shown in Fig. 9 [9]. The PHANToM provides high-performance 3D positioning and force feedback plus a 3 DOF orientation sensing gimbal. By wearing and moving a thimble attached to end of the device, viewers can move a sphere avatar on screen and touch the virtual scene. The stereoscopic display was provided through CrystalEyes shutter glasses.

4.2 Software

Initially, we experimented with SD (standard definition, 720x486 pixels) depth video. In order to display stereoscopic depth videos with OpenGL, we assigned

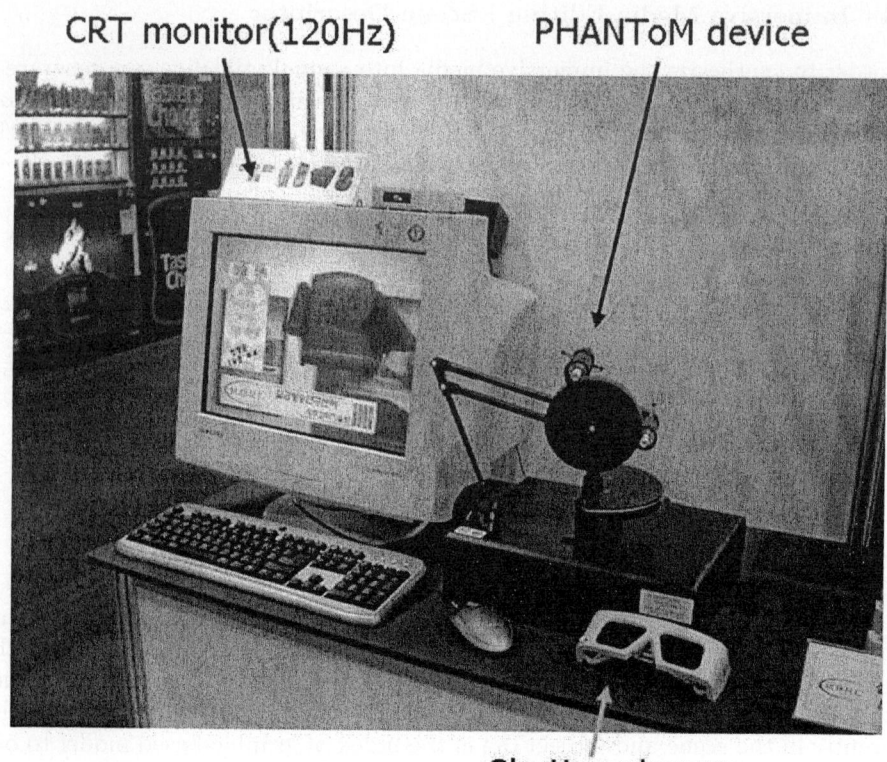

Fig. 9. Client system prototype

column indexes, row indexes and depth values to x, y and z positions. Color information was taken from captured RGB image. Finally, all points were triangulated by adding a diagonal edge. However, after initial tests indicated our system was too slow for real time display, we reduced the graphical resolution to 360x243 pixels. However, we did not reduce the haptic resolution; it remained at SD levels.

The haptic rendering algorithm was implemented using PHANToM Device Drivers Version 4.0 and HDAPI. The HDAPI is a low-level foundational layer for haptics and provides the functions to acquire 3D positions and set the 3D forces at a near real-time 1Khz servo rate.

5 Conclusion

Our prototype was demonstrated at the ITRC Forum held at the COEX exhibition center in Seoul, Korea on the 9th to 11th of June 2005. Figure 10 shows snapshots of the demonstration. Over its three day run, this event attracted many visitors, including IT experts and academics as well school children and the general public. To gain initial impressions of our prototype, we took advantage of this event by creating a questionnaire and attempting to gauge user reactions. While we acknowledge that this sort of evaluation is no replacement for formal empirical study, we found the process useful and informative, and were able to both take encouragement from its results, and to use the comments we received to shape our thinking and influence the next generation of our designs. Most users showed interest in touching both the products and the shopping host. Since the majority of visitors had not experienced force interaction with virtual objects through a haptic device, it was necessary to guide them in their initial explorations. For the most part, young people easily adapted to being able to touch and explore the scene. However, some users had trouble positioning the haptic device on the virtual objects and stated that they found the haptic interaction unnatural.

We attribute this response to a number of factors. The first problem was the display discrepancy between the haptic and graphic workspaces. The graphical display on the screen commands user attention and is the mechanism through which they regulate their position in the virtual scene. However, the workspace of the haptic device they are manipulating in order to perform this control is not coincident to the graphical display. In our system, the haptic device sits to the side of the screen. Although this is a common configuration for haptically enabled VR systems, this discrepancy can be challenging for novice users. The second problem was the use of a sphere avatar to represent the user's fingertip; some users did not immediately understand that it represented their position, which led to some confusion. This problem can be easily solved by substituting the sphere with an avatar that resembles a human hand, or perhaps a simple tool such as a pen. The final problem was simply that it was difficult to perceive the z position, or depth, of the sphere avatar within the scene. Although we provided a stereoscopic view to try to prevent this sort of problem, the differently scaled scene and device positioning made it difficult to precisely locate the depth of the cursor. A potential solution to this problem would be to render shadows, or some other more explicit representation of depth.

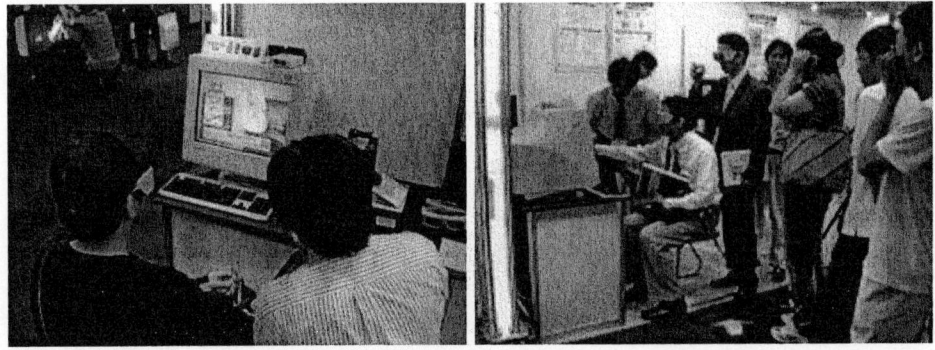

Fig. 10. Demonstration in ITRC forum 2005

Some people also commented that the background scene and the shopping host didn't merge seamlessly. This is due to the different lighting conditions in effect during the filming. Although we attempted to use similar light conditions, this process needs refining before we produce more media segments. Finally, a few users commented that they disliked the shutter glasses. The full value of this prototype can only be appreciated when viewed with a 3D display system. However, we acknowledge that the 3D display used must not negatively impact upon the TV experience to which viewers are accustomed. It must allow them the freedom to sit anywhere, with no need for special glasses, and it must be comfortable for prolonged viewing. We are currently considering the adoption of alternative 3D display systems that meet these requirements.

Acknowledgements

This work was supported by the Ministry of Information and Communication (MIC) through the Realistic Broadcasting IT Research Center (RBRC) at Gwangju Institute of Science and Technology (GIST).

References

1. Kim, S. Y., Yoon, S. U., Ho, Y. S.: Realistic Broadcasting Using Multi-modal Immersive Media, Proc. 6th Pacific-Rim Conf. Multimedia (2005)
2. Cha, J., Kim, S. M., Oakley, I., Ryu, J., Lee, K. H.: Haptic Interaction with Depth Video Media, Proc. 6th Pacific-Rim Conf. Multimedia (2005)
3. Zilles, C., Salisbury, K.: A Constraint Based God-Object Method For Haptic Display, Proc. IEE/RSJ Int. Conf. Intelligent Robots and Systems, Human Robot Interaction, and Cooperative Robots, Vol. 3 (1995) 146-151
4. Point Grey Research Inc., http://www.ptgrey.com/ (2002)
5. Kim, S., Woo, W.: Indoor Scene Reconstruction using a Projection-based Registration Technique of Multi-view Depth Images, Proc. 6th Pacific-Rim Conf. Multimedia (2005)
6. KLT: Kanade-Lucas-Tomasi Feature Tracker,
   http://www.ces.clemson.edu/ stb/klt/ (2005)
7. 3DV Systems, http://www.3dvsystems.com/ (2005)
8. Kim, S. M., Cha, J., Ryu, J., Lee, K. H.: Depth Video Enhancement for Haptic Interaction using a Smooth Surface Reconstruction, Special Issue on Artificial Reality and Telexistence, IEICE Transactions, Jan. (2006) (to appear)
9. SensAble Technologies Inc., http://www.sensable.com/ (2005)

Proposal of Cooperative Transmission for the Uplink of TDD-CDMA Systems[*]

Ho Van Khuong and Hyung-Yun Kong

7-522 Department of Electrical Engineering, University of Ulsan,
San 29, MuGeo-Dong, Nam-Gu, Ulsan, Korea, 680-749
khuongho2001@yahoo.com, hkong@mail.ulsan.ac.kr

Abstract. This paper studies a novel cooperative transmission scheme that allows single-antenna users to benefit from spatial diversity for the uplink of TDD-CDMA systems. In such systems, the chip-synchronous transmission is attainable and thus, using orthogonal spreading codes can completely eliminate MAI in flat Rayleigh fading channels plus AWGN and make the user-cooperation possible. The proposed cooperation scheme is applicable to any constant-envelope modulation and achieves the fullest diversity order, the low implementation complexity and the full data rate. The closed-form outage probability expression was also derived to verify its validity. A variety of numerical results reveal the cooperation significantly outperforms non-cooperative counterpart under the same transmit power constraint.

1 Introduction

TDD-CDMA (Time Division Duplex-Code Division Multiple Access) has been being researched and experimented intensively and extensively to become a standard for the 4th-Generation Mobile Communications System [1] due to its advantages such as design simplicity, efficient bandwidth utilization and high performance. In addition, a very interesting characteristic of TDD-CDMA is feasibility of chip-synchronous transmission in the uplink. The regular TDD slots allow a mobile to precisely detect changes in the propagation delay and to adjust its transmission time such that its signal may arrive synchronously with other users in the same cell. As a result, the orthogonal spreading codes assigned to each mobile can completely remove MAI (Multiple Access Interference) in flat Rayleigh fading channels plus AWGN (Additive White Gaussian Noise).

In wireless networks, signal fading arising from multi-path propagation is a particularly severe channel impairment that can be mitigated through the use of spatial diversity [2]. However, when wireless agents may not be able to support such multiple antennas due to size or other constraints [3], the conventional space-time coding can not be used. To overcome this restriction, a new technique, called cooperative transmission [3]-[7], was born which allows single-antenna mobiles to gain some benefits of spatial diversity. In this paper, we propose a cooperation

---

[*] This research was supported by the MIC (Ministry of Information and Communication), Korea, under the ITRC (Information technology Research Center) support program supervised by the IITA (Institute of Information Technology Assessment).

scheme where two cooperative users share the same spreading code to exchange information together besides their own codes which are used by the base station to distinguish user from one another in the multiple access environment. Even though this waste of spreading code seems unreasonable, the group transmission mode [1] (a few users served in a time slot) in the TDD-CDMA systems makes the redundancy of spreading codes available and thus, taking advantage of redundancy to obtain high performance is very appropriate. In addition, the suggested cooperation scheme offers an appealing signaling structure to facilitate in detecting the signals based on MRC (Maximum Ratio Combining) with negligible implementation complexity of the receiver and to attain both full diversity and full rate. In the cooperation process, each user doesn't perform hard detection on the signal of its partner as in [4] but rather, it simply estimates (by performing the despreading the received signal) and forwards the resultant signal to the destination. This not only reduces the processing time at each user but also avoids the wrong decisions that can adversely affect the overall performance at the destination.

The rest of the paper is organized as follows. Part 2 presents the cooperation scheme and signal analysis in detail. In part 3, we derive the closed-form outage probability expression for the proposed cooperation. Then the numerical results are demonstrated and analyzed in part 4. Finally, the paper is closed in part 5 with many useful comments.

2 Proposed Cooperative Transmission Scheme

As discussed above, a TDD-CDMA system makes the chip-synchronous transmission in the uplink possible and as a result, the orthogonality of the spreading codes is remained for each user's signal to be completely distinguishable at the receiver when the delay among the propagation paths between users and destination is within a chip-duration. Therefore, the performance analysis of the multi-user system can be done in a similar fashion to the case of two users. For this reason, we only investigate a cooperative transmission consisting of two mobiles (MS1 and MS2) communicating with a base station (BS) in a cellular system during each time slot with the assumption that the mobiles can receive and send data simultaneously in the uplink. The basic idea is to construct a system such that signals transmitted by each user arrive at the base station through two independent fading paths while maintaining the same average power as a comparable non-cooperative system.

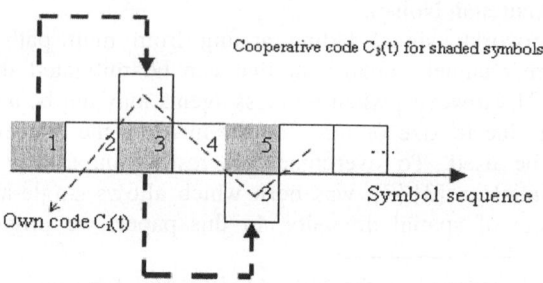

Fig. 1. Transmit symbols distribution in a time slot

Fig. 1 illustrates the chronological order for transmitting the data of each user in a time slot for whom two different spreading codes are allocated: an own code $C_i(t)$ for discriminating between active users and a cooperative code $C_3(t)$ for common usage. All original symbols (represented on the straight line: 1, 2, 3, 4, 5, 6, ...) are spread by the cooperative code in succession to the own code. For example, a symbol sequence numbered 1-2-3-4, ... will be spread by a spreading code sequence C_3-C_i-C_3-C_i, ... However, the repeated symbols (denoted by arrows: 1, 3, ...) always utilize the own code for spreading. Assuming that the echo cancellation at each mobile is perfect, each user only receives the signal from its partner and thus, one spreading code is sufficient to share information for a pair of users. Fig. 1 also indicates a structural reiteration of transmitted signals such that sending two symbols simultaneously (a new one and the replica of the symbol in the previous interval) is interleaved equally with transmitting only a new symbol. Such a repeat facilitates the signal processing at each side. Moreover, source data is sent continuously over the channel and therefore, the system obtains the full rate regardless of cooperation in progress. This is one of the advantages of the proposed cooperation scheme because most cooperation is paid for the loss of the data rate [3]-[7].

Table 1. Summary of transmit and receive signals

Symbol Intervals	User 1 (MS1)		User 2 (MS2)		Base station (BS)
	Transmit	Receive	Transmit	Receive	Receive
1	$\beta_{11}a_{11}C_3$	y_{11}	$\beta_{21}a_{21}C_3$	y_{21}	
2	$-\beta_{12}a_{12}^*C_1 + p_{12}\bar{y}_{11}^*C_2$	y_{12}	$-\beta_{22}a_{22}^*C_2 + p_{22}\bar{y}_{21}^*C_1$	y_{22}	y_{BS2}
3	$\beta_{13}a_{11}C_1 - p_{13}\bar{y}_{12}^*C_2 + \beta_{11}a_{13}C_3$	y_{13}	$\beta_{23}a_{21}C_2 - p_{23}\bar{y}_{22}^*C_1 + \beta_{21}a_{23}C_3$	y_{23}	y_{BS3}
4	$-\beta_{12}a_{14}^*C_1 + p_{12}\bar{y}_{13}^*C_2$	y_{14}	$-\beta_{22}a_{24}^*C_2 + p_{22}\bar{y}_{23}^*C_1$	y_{24}	y_{BS4}
5	$\beta_{13}a_{13}C_1 - p_{13}\bar{y}_{14}^*C_2 + \beta_{11}a_{15}C_3$	y_{15}	$\beta_{23}a_{23}C_2 - p_{23}\bar{y}_{24}^*C_1 + \beta_{21}a_{25}C_3$	y_{25}	y_{BS5}
6	$-\beta_{12}a_{16}^*C_1 + p_{12}\bar{y}_{15}^*C_2$	y_{16}	$-\beta_{22}a_{26}^*C_2 + p_{22}\bar{y}_{25}^*C_1$	y_{26}	y_{BS6}
...	...	...	...	...	y_{BS7}

The new cooperation scheme applicable to MPSK-modulated signals or any kind of constant envelope modulation is illustrated in Table 1 with the assumption that the time delay of signal propagation between two cooperative users is negligible. The notations in Table 1 represent the following quantities.

- a_{ij}: the user i's j^{th} modulated symbol. Without the loss of generality, its amplitude is assumed to be 1 and equally likely.
- $C_i(t)$: the user i's spreading code given by

$$C_i(t) = \sum_{n=1}^{N} c_i(n) p(t - nT_C)$$

where $c_i(n)$: the nth chip of the ith code, p(t): a unit-amplitude rectangular pulse with time duration equal to chip duration and N: the code length.
- β_{ij}: the amplification factor for the ith user's own signal.
- p_{ij}: the amplification factor for the estimated signal of partner of user i.
- $y_{ij}(t)$: the signal of the ith user's partner received during the symbol interval j.
- $y_{BSi}(t)$: the received signal at the base station in the symbol interval i.

Moreover, there are the other channel parameters used throughout the paper such as α_{12}, α_{13}, α_{23} being the path gains of the channels between MS1 and MS2, MS1 and BS, MS2 and BS, respectively. We assume slow and flat Rayleigh fading, hence they are modeled as independent samples of zero-mean complex Gaussian random variables (ZMCGRVs) with variances $\sigma_{12}^2, \sigma_{13}^2, \sigma_{23}^2$ and constant during the two-symbol transmission of any given user, but change independently to the next. Because of slow fading, accurate channel estimation is possible at the receiver [4]. Thus, we will assume perfect channel-state information at all the respective receivers but not at the transmitters. For the inter-user channel, it is also assumed to be reciprocal (the channel characteristics is similar for both directions). The alternative parameters $n_{1ij}(t)$, $n_{0k}(t)$ ($i=1,2$; $j=1,2$; $k=2,3$) are the noise samples corrupting the inter-user channel and MS-BS channel which are modeled as independent ZMCGRVs with variances σ_1^2, σ_2^2, correspondingly. Finally, the Gaussian noise and Rayleigh fading are considered to be statistically independent.

For convenience of exposition, we use complex base-band equivalent models to express all the signals. Now, consider the first three symbol intervals and assume that each user priorly knows the spreading codes of its partner ($C_i(t)$ and $C_3(t)$) while the BS is only interested in users' own codes $C_i(t)$. Due to having two signature sequences, each user must be equipped with two chip-matched filters separately, each of which for one code.

Cooperation process works as follows. In the first symbol interval, users send their own data spread by $C_3(t)$. The received signal at the user i ($i=1,2$) is hence given by

$$y_{11}(t) = \alpha_{12}\beta_{21}a_{21}C_3(t) + n_{111}(t) \qquad y_{21}(t) = \alpha_{12}\beta_{11}a_{11}C_3(t) + n_{112}(t) \qquad (1)$$

At the end of this interval, each user obtains the information of its partner by chip-matched filtering the received signal with the cooperative code. This filter's output is the partner's estimated signal distorted by fade and noise that is of the form

$$\bar{y}_{11} = \frac{1}{NT_C}\int_0^{NT_C} y_{11}(t)C_3(t)dt = \alpha_{12}\beta_{21}a_{21} + \bar{n}_{111}$$

$$\bar{y}_{21} = \frac{1}{NT_C}\int_0^{NT_C} y_{21}(t)C_3(t)dt = \alpha_{12}\beta_{11}a_{11} + \bar{n}_{112} \qquad (2)$$

Without the loss of generality, chip duration can be considered to be 1 time unit ($T_C=1$). Thus, $\bar{n}_{1ij}$ are ZMCGRVs with variance σ_1^2/N hereafter, $i=1,2; j=1,2$.

In the second symbol interval, each user amplifies the information $\bar{y}_{i1}$ received in the previous interval with the gain p_{ij} and sends it along with its own spread data. Therefore, during the second interval, the user i receives

$$y_{12}(t) = \alpha_{12}\{-\beta_{22}a_{22}^*C_2(t) + p_{22}\bar{y}_{21}^*C_1(t)\} + n_{121}(t)$$
$$y_{22}(t) = \alpha_{12}\{-\beta_{12}a_{12}^*C_1(t) + p_{12}\bar{y}_{11}^*C_2(t)\} + n_{122}(t) \qquad (3)$$

where $(.)^*$ denotes complex conjugate operator.

The despread signals produced at the end of the second interval corresponding to the above are given by

$$\bar{y}_{12} = \frac{1}{NT_C} \int_0^{NT_C} y_{12}(t)C_2(t)dt = -\alpha_{12}\beta_{22}a_{22}^* + \bar{n}_{121}$$

$$\bar{y}_{22} = \frac{1}{NT_C} \int_0^{NT_C} y_{22}(t)C_1(t)dt = -\alpha_{12}\beta_{12}a_{12}^* + \bar{n}_{122} \tag{4}$$

In the third symbol interval, the user i constructs a following signal based on three sources of information: current symbol a_{i3}, repeated symbol a_{i1} and the partner's estimated information $\bar{y}_{i2}$ in the previous phase

$$\beta_{i3}a_{i1}C_i(t) - p_{i3}\bar{y}_{i2}^*C_{i'}(t) + \beta_{i1}a_{i3}C_3(t)$$

where i' stands for the index of the partner of user i, for example if $i=1$ and a cooperative pair are user 1 and user 2 then $i'=2$.

Moreover in the last two intervals, the base station starts to receive and process the signals from the mobiles. Those received signals are given by

$$y_{BS2}(t) = \alpha_{13}\{-\beta_{12}a_{12}^*C_1(t) + p_{12}\bar{y}_{11}^*C_2(t)\} + \alpha_{23}\{-\beta_{22}a_{22}^*C_2(t) + p_{22}\bar{y}_{21}^*C_1(t)\} + n_{02}(t) \tag{5}$$

$$y_{BS3}(t) = \alpha_{13}\{\beta_{13}a_{11}C_1(t) - p_{13}\bar{y}_{12}^*C_2(t) + \beta_{11}a_{13}C_3(t)\} + \\ \alpha_{23}\{\beta_{23}a_{21}C_2(t) - p_{23}\bar{y}_{22}^*C_1(t) + \beta_{21}a_{23}C_3(t)\} + n_{03}(t) \tag{6}$$

Now, BS carries out decoding separately the signals for MS1 and MS2 during the second and third symbol-intervals by user-specific spreading codes.

2.1 For User 1

At the BS, the MS1's estimated signals at the output of the chip-matched filter corresponding to the third and second symbol intervals are given by, respectively

$$r_{11} = \frac{1}{NT_C} \int_0^{NT_C} y_{BS3}(t)C_1(t)dt = \alpha_{13}\beta_{13}a_{11} - \alpha_{23}p_{23}\bar{y}_{22}^* + \bar{n}_{031} \\ = \alpha_{13}\beta_{13}a_{11} + \alpha_{23}p_{23}\alpha_{12}^*\beta_{12}a_{12} - \alpha_{23}p_{23}\bar{n}_{122}^* + \bar{n}_{031} \tag{7}$$

$$r_{12} = \frac{1}{NT_C} \int_0^{NT_C} y_{BS2}(t)C_1(t)dt = -\alpha_{13}\beta_{12}a_{12}^* + \alpha_{23}p_{22}\bar{y}_{21}^* + \bar{n}_{021} \\ = -\alpha_{13}\beta_{12}a_{12}^* + \alpha_{23}p_{22}\alpha_{12}^*\beta_{11}^*a_{11}^* + \alpha_{23}p_{22}\bar{n}_{112}^* + \bar{n}_{021} \tag{8}$$

where $\bar{n}_{0ij}$ are ZMCGRVs with variance σ_2^2/N hereafter, $i=2,3; j=1,2$.

We choose

$$\beta_{13} = \beta_{12} \qquad\qquad p_{23}\beta_{12} = p_{22}\beta_{11} \tag{9}$$

Then, (7)-(8) can be rewritten as

$$r_{11} = \gamma_{11}a_{11} + \gamma_{12}a_{12} - \alpha_{23}p_{23}\bar{n}_{122}^* + \bar{n}_{031} \qquad r_{12} = -\gamma_{11}a_{12}^* + \gamma_{12}a_{11}^* + \alpha_{23}p_{22}\bar{n}_{112}^* + \bar{n}_{021} \tag{10}$$

where

$$\gamma_{11} = \alpha_{13}\beta_{13} \qquad \gamma_{12} = \alpha_{23}p_{23}\alpha_{12}^*\beta_{12} \qquad (11)$$

Based on (10), we design a MRC-based combiner to generate the soft decision statistics of a_{11} and a_{12} as follows

$$\bar{a}_{11} = r_{11}\gamma_{11}^* + r_{12}^*\gamma_{12} \qquad \bar{a}_{12} = r_{11}\gamma_{12}^* - r_{12}^*\gamma_{11} \qquad (12)$$

By passing (12) through the M-PSK demodulator, the original symbols a_{11} and a_{12} are easily restored. In addition, (12) illustrates that the detection doesn't require high hardware complexity.

Substituting r_{11} and r_{12} in (10) into (12), we have

$$\bar{a}_{11} = \left(|\gamma_{11}|^2 + |\gamma_{12}|^2\right)a_{11} + n_{11} \qquad \bar{a}_{12} = \left(|\gamma_{11}|^2 + |\gamma_{12}|^2\right)a_{12} + n_{12} \qquad (13)$$

where

$$n_{11} = \left(-\alpha_{23}p_{23}\bar{n}_{122}^* + \bar{n}_{031}\right)\gamma_{11}^* + \left(\alpha_{23}p_{22}\bar{n}_{112}^* + \bar{n}_{021}\right)^*\gamma_{12}$$
$$n_{12} = \left(-\alpha_{23}p_{23}\bar{n}_{122}^* + \bar{n}_{031}\right)\gamma_{12}^* - \left(\alpha_{23}p_{22}\bar{n}_{112}^* + \bar{n}_{021}\right)^*\gamma_{11} \qquad (14)$$

(13) shows that the proposed cooperative transmission scheme can provide exactly the performance as the 2-level receive maximum ratio combining.

2.2 For User 2

Similarly processing the received signals at the base station for user 2, we obtain

$$r_{21} = \frac{1}{NT_C}\int_0^{NT_C} y_{BS3}(t)C_2(t)dt = \alpha_{13}p_{13}\alpha_{12}^*\beta_{22}a_{22} + \alpha_{23}\beta_{23}a_{21} - \alpha_{13}p_{13}\bar{n}_{121}^* + \bar{n}_{032} \qquad (15)$$

$$r_{22} = \frac{1}{NT_C}\int_0^{NT_C} y_{BS2}(t)C_2(t)dt = \alpha_{13}p_{12}\alpha_{12}^*\beta_{21}a_{21}^* - \alpha_{23}\beta_{22}a_{22}^* + \alpha_{13}p_{12}\bar{n}_{111}^* + \bar{n}_{022} \qquad (16)$$

Choose

$$\beta_{23} = \beta_{22} \qquad p_{13}\beta_{22} = p_{12}\beta_{21} \qquad (17)$$

Let

$$\gamma_{21} = \alpha_{23}\beta_{23} \qquad \gamma_{22} = \alpha_{13}p_{13}\alpha_{12}^*\beta_{22} \qquad (18)$$

Then, (15)-(16) are of the following form

$$r_{21} = \gamma_{21}a_{21} + \gamma_{22}a_{22} - \alpha_{13}p_{13}\bar{n}_{121}^* + \bar{n}_{032} \qquad r_{22} = -\gamma_{21}a_{22}^* + \gamma_{22}a_{21}^* + \alpha_{13}p_{12}\bar{n}_{111}^* + \bar{n}_{022} \qquad (19)$$

and the 2nd user's estimated symbols are given by

$$\bar{a}_{21} = r_{21}\gamma_{21}^* + r_{22}^*\gamma_{22} = \left(|\gamma_{21}|^2 + |\gamma_{22}|^2\right)a_{21} + n_{21}$$
$$\bar{a}_{22} = r_{21}\gamma_{22}^* - r_{22}^*\gamma_{21} = \left(|\gamma_{21}|^2 + |\gamma_{22}|^2\right)a_{22} + n_{22} \qquad (20)$$

where

$$n_{21} = \left(-\alpha_{13} p_{13} \bar{n}_{121}^* + \bar{n}_{032}\right) \gamma_{21}^* + \left(\alpha_{13} p_{12} \bar{n}_{111}^* + \bar{n}_{022}\right)^* \gamma_{22}$$
$$n_{22} = \left(-\alpha_{13} p_{13} \bar{n}_{121}^* + \bar{n}_{032}\right) \gamma_{22}^* - \left(\alpha_{13} p_{12} \bar{n}_{111}^* + \bar{n}_{022}\right)^* \gamma_{21} \qquad (21)$$

By carefully observing the signals in Table 1 and the intuitive data distribution shown in Fig. 1, we can find that all entities in the network iterate the signal processing procedure every two-symbol interval since each user transmits the signals of the identical structure in such intervals except the first symbol. This iteration is represented by either shaded or unshaded region in Table 1. It is also noted that the BS only pays attention to the received signal after the first symbol interval. As a consequence, the signal analysis for the next two-symbol intervals is similar to that in the 2nd and 3rd intervals: each mobile gets the information of its partner at the end of "odd" periods and "even" periods by despreading the received signals with the cooperative code $C_3(t)$ and partner's code, respectively; and at the BS's side, it also detects the signals for each user by the user-specific spreading codes $C_i(t)$.

2.3 Selection of Amplification Factors

The amplification factors β_{ij} and p_{ij} are chosen to satisfy the long-term power constraint. Due to the repeating property in the signaling format of each user, the power constraint condition for user *1* (see the transmitted signals of user *1* in Table 1) is given by

$$E\left\{\frac{\beta_{12}^2 |a_{12}|^2 + p_{12}^2 |\bar{y}_{11}|^2 + \beta_{13}^2 |a_{11}|^2 + p_{13}^2 |\bar{y}_{12}|^2 + \beta_{11}^2 |a_{13}|^2}{2}\right\} = P_1$$

and for user 2,

$$E\left\{\frac{\beta_{22}^2 |a_{22}|^2 + p_{22}^2 |\bar{y}_{21}|^2 + \beta_{23}^2 |a_{21}|^2 + p_{23}^2 |\bar{y}_{22}|^2 + \beta_{21}^2 |a_{23}|^2}{2}\right\} = P_2$$

where P_1, P_2 denote average limited powers of user 1 and 2 over two consecutive symbol-intervals, correspondingly; $E\{.\}$ is expectation operator. The values $E\{|\bar{y}_{ij}|^2\}$ can be calculated from (2)-(4):

$$E\{|\bar{y}_{11}|^2\} = \beta_{21}^2 \sigma_{12}^2 + \sigma_1^2 / N \qquad E\{|\bar{y}_{12}|^2\} = \beta_{22}^2 \sigma_{12}^2 + \sigma_1^2 / N$$
$$E\{|\bar{y}_{21}|^2\} = \beta_{11}^2 \sigma_{12}^2 + \sigma_1^2 / N \qquad E\{|\bar{y}_{22}|^2\} = \beta_{12}^2 \sigma_{12}^2 + \sigma_1^2 / N$$

Here $|a_{ij}|^2 = 1$ as assumed before. Thus

$$\beta_{11}^2 + \beta_{12}^2 + \beta_{13}^2 + p_{12}^2 \left(\beta_{21}^2 \sigma_{12}^2 + \sigma_1^2 / N\right) + p_{13}^2 \left(\beta_{22}^2 \sigma_{12}^2 + \sigma_1^2 / N\right) = 2P_1$$
$$\beta_{21}^2 + \beta_{22}^2 + \beta_{23}^2 + p_{22}^2 \left(\beta_{11}^2 \sigma_{12}^2 + \sigma_1^2 / N\right) + p_{23}^2 \left(\beta_{12}^2 \sigma_{12}^2 + \sigma_1^2 / N\right) = 2P_2$$

Using the equalities in (9)-(17), we have

$$\beta_{11}^2 + 2\beta_{12}^2 + 2p_{12}^2 \beta_{21}^2 \sigma_{12}^2 + \left(p_{12}^2 + p_{13}^2\right) \sigma_1^2 / N = 2P_1$$
$$\beta_{21}^2 + 2\beta_{22}^2 + 2p_{22}^2 \beta_{11}^2 \sigma_{12}^2 + \left(p_{22}^2 + p_{23}^2\right) \sigma_1^2 / N = 2P_2 \qquad (22)$$

3 Outage Probability Analysis

Only user 1 is analyzed in the sequel and establishing the expressions for user 2 are followed in the identical manner because of the symmetry. For simplicity in deriving the outage probability, we consider the case that both users have the same transmit power ($P_1=P_2=P$) and choose all β_{ij} and p_{ij} to be equal ($\beta_{ij}=\beta$, $p_{ij}=p$). Thus, (22) can be rewritten as

$$p^2 = \frac{2P-3\beta^2}{2(\beta^2\sigma_{12}^2 + \sigma_1^2/N)} \tag{23}$$

which requires $\beta^2 \leq 2P/3$. The equality "=" of the above expression holds when users stop the cooperation. If we let $\beta^2 = \delta P$ where $0<\delta\leq 2/3$ represents the power sharing level for the cooperation, then (23) has the following form

$$p^2 = \frac{(2-3\delta)P}{2(\delta P\sigma_{12}^2 + \sigma_1^2/N)} \tag{24}$$

In communications systems, a receiver is likely to successfully decode the transmitted data only if the received SNR remains above a certain minimum required (threshold) ratio. Therefore, the outage probability defined as the probability of failing to achieve simultaneously a SNR sufficient to give satisfactory reception is an appropriate measure to evaluate the performance of a communications system.

(13) can be expressed in more compact form

$$\bar{a}_{11} = \lambda a_{11} + n_{11} \qquad \bar{a}_{12} = \lambda a_{12} + n_{12} \tag{25}$$

where

$$\lambda = |\gamma_{11}|^2 + |\gamma_{12}|^2 = \beta^2|\alpha_{13}|^2 + \beta^2 p^2|\alpha_{12}|^2|\alpha_{23}|^2 \tag{26}$$

From (14) and the fact that all r.v.'s $\bar{n}_{ijk}$ are mutually independent of each other, conditioned on the channel realizations, n_{11} and n_{12} are also independent ZMCGRVs with the same variance

$$\varsigma^2 = \left(|\alpha_{23}|^2 p^2\sigma_1^2/N + \sigma_2^2/N\right)\lambda \tag{27}$$

Since α_{ij} are ZMCGRVs with variance σ_{ij}^2, $x=|\alpha_{13}|^2$, $y=|\alpha_{12}|^2$ and $z=|\alpha_{23}|^2$ have exponential distribution with mean value σ_{ij}^2; that is, $f_x(x)=\lambda_x e^{-\lambda_x x}$, $f_y(y)=\lambda_y e^{-\lambda_y y}$, $f_z(z)=\lambda_z e^{-\lambda_z z}$ in which $\lambda_x = 1/\sigma_{13}^2, \lambda_y = 1/\sigma_{12}^2, \lambda_z = 1/\sigma_{23}^2$ and $x, y, z \geq 0$, are pdf's of r.v.'s x, y, z, respectively.

Rewrite (26)-(27) as follows

$$\lambda = \beta^2 x + \beta^2 p^2 z y = x_1 + y_1 \qquad \varsigma^2 = A\lambda$$

where $A = zp^2\sigma_1^2/N + \sigma_2^2/N$. It is natural that x_1 and y_1 are also independent exponentially distributed r.v.'s with parameters $\lambda_1 = \lambda_x/\beta^2 = 1/(\beta^2\sigma_{13}^2)$ and $\lambda_2 = \lambda_y/(\beta^2 p^2 z) = 1/(z\beta^2 p^2\sigma_{12}^2)$, correspondingly.

The pdf of λ, given z, can be computed by using convolution theorem

$$f_{\lambda|z}(\lambda|z) = \int_{-\infty}^{\infty} f_{x_1}(x_1) f_{y_1}(\lambda - x_1) dx_1 = \int_0^{\lambda} \lambda_1 e^{-\lambda_1 x_1} \lambda_2 e^{-\lambda_2(\lambda-x_1)} dx_1 = \frac{\lambda_1 \lambda_2}{\lambda_1 - \lambda_2}\left[e^{-\lambda_2 \lambda} - e^{-\lambda_1 \lambda}\right]$$

with $\lambda \geq 0$.

From (25)-(27), we find that a_{11} and a_{12} are attenuated and corrupted by the same fading and noisy level, their SNR is equal. As a result, outage probability of a_{11} is sufficient to evaluate the performance of user 1.

(25) gives the SNR of user 1 at the BS as $\gamma_1 = \lambda^2/\varsigma^2 = \lambda/A$. Thus, it is easy to deduce the conditional pdf of γ_1 given z from $f_{\lambda|z}(\lambda|z)$.

$$f_{\gamma_1|z}(\gamma_1|z) = A\lambda_1\lambda_2 [\exp(-A\lambda_2\gamma_1) - \exp(-A\lambda_1\gamma_1)]/(\lambda_1 - \lambda_2)$$

with $\gamma_1 \geq 0$.

The outage probability conditioned on the channel realization is defined as the probability that γ_1 is less than or equal to an threshold SNR γ

$$P[\gamma_1 \leq \gamma|z] = \int_0^{\gamma} \frac{A\lambda_1\lambda_2}{\lambda_1 - \lambda_2}\left[e^{-A\lambda_2\gamma_1} - e^{-A\lambda_1\gamma_1}\right]d\gamma_1 = 1 + \frac{\lambda_2 e^{-A\lambda_1\gamma} - \lambda_1 e^{-A\lambda_2\gamma}}{\lambda_1 - \lambda_2}$$

To compute the average outage probability P_{OTG-C}, we take the expectation of the above expression over the parameter z

$$P_{OTG-C} = \int_0^{\infty} P[\gamma_1 \leq \gamma|z] f_z(z) dz = 1 + \int_0^{\infty} \frac{\lambda_2 e^{-A\lambda_1\gamma} - \lambda_1 e^{-A\lambda_2\gamma}}{\lambda_1 - \lambda_2} \lambda_z e^{-\lambda_z z} dz \quad (28)$$

The integral of P_{OTG-C} can be easily calculated by a numerical method [8].

4 Numerical Results and Discussions

In the results presented below, SNR1, SNR2 and SNR3 are the signal-to-noise ratios of inter-user channel (MS1-MS2), MS1-BS channel and MS2-BS channel respectively defined by $SNR1 = \sigma_{12}^2 P/\sigma_1^2$, $SNR2 = \sigma_{13}^2 P/\sigma_2^2$, $SNR3 = \sigma_{23}^2 P/\sigma_2^2$. Moreover, we adopt $P=1, \sigma_1^2 = \sigma_2^2 = 1$ and the system of two active users. All spreading codes are also chosen from Walsh-Hadamard matrix of size 64x64.

First of all, we consider the symmetric scenario where both users have channels of similar quality to the destination. For such symmetric networks, the outage probability of cooperative users is the same. Therefore, the graphs only show the performance of user 1. Fig. 2 shows the average outage probability of the TDD-CDMA systems with and without cooperation under the same transmit power constraint, $\delta=0.55$ and the required SNR of -5dB. Additionally, the quality of inter-user channel changes with SNR1 of -5dB and 5dB. This figure demonstrates that the proposed cooperation scheme significantly outperforms non-cooperative counterpart and the performance improvement also keeps increasing proportionally to the increase of SNR1. For example, at the expected outage probability of 10^{-2} the cooperation achieves a gain of approximately 6dB over the non-cooperation regardless of the severe noise (SNR1=-5dB) of the inter-user channel. In addition, due to the considerably steeper slopes of outage probability curves in the cooperation case than those of non-cooperation[1], the cooperation performance is drastically enhanced with respect to SNR2. As a result, the partnership brings the benefit to both participants with which helps themselves overcome the detrimental effect of fading and noise.

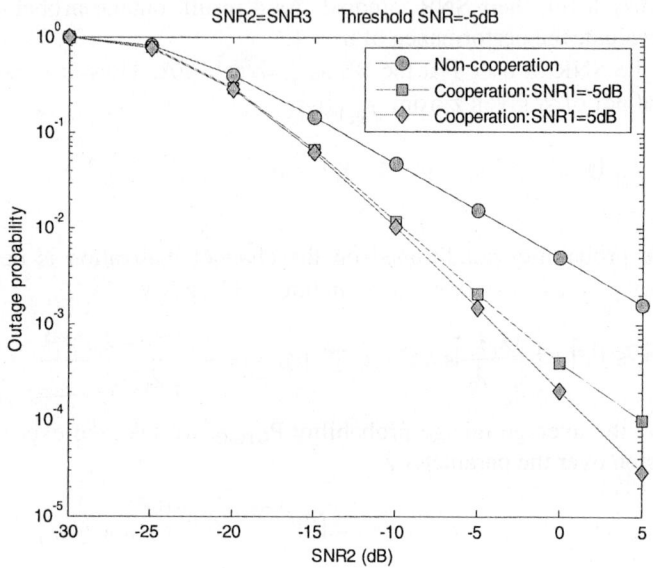

Fig. 2. Outage probability comparison between cooperation and non-cooperation with $\delta=0.55$ and $\gamma=-5$dB in the symmetric case

The influence of the power sharing level δ on the cooperation performance is illustrated in Fig. 3. It is seen that δ dramatically affects the cooperation efficiency. This is obvious because the nature of cooperation is to take advantage of the partner's propagation path as the second independent diversity path to achieve the fullest spatial diversity. If one of two paths is seriously attenuated, the performance must be reduced. In the cooperation scheme, the signal attenuation can be derived from the channel characteristics as well as from the power allocation to transmit each user's own data and its partner's data which is controlled by the coefficients β and p. Therefore, the variation of δ that leads to the changes of β and p certainly causes the significant fluctuation on overall performance. However, in the wide range [0.1, 0.66] of values δ the cooperation always reveals the dominance over the direct transmission. Moreover, there exits an optimum value of δ that minimizes the outage probability. This value as shown in Fig. 3 is almost robust to the changes of the environment and roughly 0.6.

---

[1] It is straightforward to prove the average outage probability of non-cooperative transmission to be $P_{OTG\_N} = 1 - \exp(-\gamma \sigma_2^2 / (NP \sigma_{i3}^2))$.

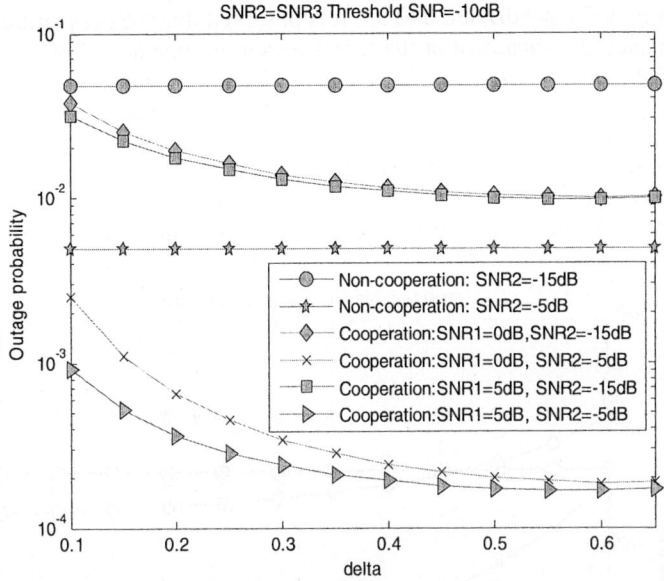

Fig. 3. Outage probability as a function of δ in the symmetric case

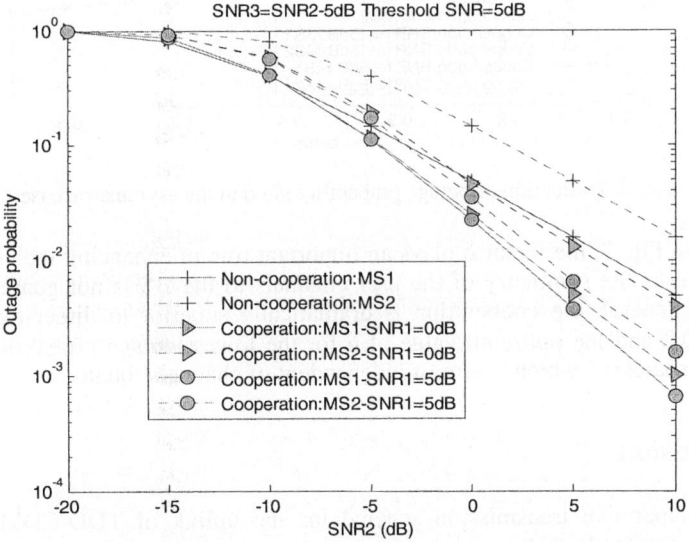

Fig. 4. Outage probability comparison between cooperation and non-cooperation with $\delta=0.55$ and $\gamma=5$dB in the asymmetric scenario

Next, we investigate the asymmetric scenario, where one of the users has a better channel to the BS than the other user, by assigning the average SNR of MS1 to be 5dB higher that of MS2; that is, SNR3=SNR2-5dB. The numerical results are depicted in Fig. 4 for γ=5dB and δ=0.55. It is observed that the cooperation provides a 5dB performance improvement at the target outage probability of 10^{-2} for both users over that of the non-cooperation. Thus, the cooperation proves to be beneficial not only for users with similar channel qualities to the destination, but also in the case when the users have significantly different channel qualities. As a consequence, any user has a motivation to cooperate with the others even though its propagation path's quality is dramatically better than that of its partner. Moreover, the cooperation performance can be enhanced further when the channels' quality is better.

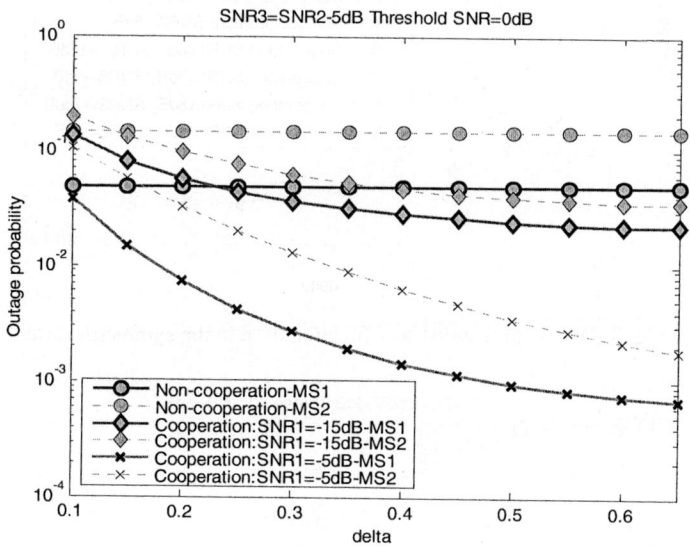

Fig. 5. Evaluation of outage probability via δ in the asymmetric case

Similar to Fig. 3, the factor δ plays an important role in enhancing the cooperation performance as the symmetry of the user channels to the BS is not guaranteed (see Fig. 5). In general, the cooperation is dramatically superior to direct transmission when δ > 0.2 and the optimum value of δ for the lowest outage probability slightly fluctuates around 0.6 which is almost independent of channels' quality.

5 Conclusion

A novel cooperative transmission scheme for the uplink of TDD-CDMA system under flat Rayleigh fading channel plus Gaussian noise was proposed. The cooperation brought a considerable performance improvement over direct transmission in any channel condition. In presented results, the fact that all users have the same transmit power constraint (that means there is no need of power-control mechanism from the BS) exposes another advantage of the cooperation that the system is capable of resisting the near-far phenomenon. In addition, different from other cooperation schemes where the transmission rate is sacrificed to obtain spatial diversity gain, our scheme can get the full rate as non-cooperation. Moreover, we design a MRC-based combiner to achieve the fullest transmit diversity without increasing hardware implementation complexity. Although the results of this paper serve the situation of the two-user system, it is straightforward to verify that the analytical expression is still applicable to the multi-user system without the degradation of performance if the transmission synchronization is remained. Furthermore, this scheme can combine the deployment of multiple receive antennas at the BS to reduce further the outage probability.

References

1. Riaz Esmailzadeh, Masao Nakagawa, "TDD-CDMA for wireless communications", Artech House Inc, 2003.
2. John G. Proakis, "Digital communications", Fourth Edition, McGraw-Hill, 2001.
3. Aria Nosratinia, Todd E. Hunter, "Cooperative Communication in Wireless Networks", IEEE Communications Magazine, Vol. 42, pp. 74-80, Oct. 2004.
4. A. Sendonaris, E. Erkip, B. Aazhang, "User cooperation diversity. Part I-II", IEEE Trans on Communications, Vol. 51, pp. 1927-1948, Nov. 2003.
5. E. Zimmermann, P. Herhold and G. Fettweis, "On the Performance of Cooperative Relaying in Wireless Networks", European Trans. on Telecommunications, Vol. 16, no. 1, Jan-Feb 2005.
6. J.N. Laneman, D.N.C. Tse, G.W. Wornell, "Cooperative diversity in wireless networks: Efficient protocols and outage behavior", IEEE Trans. Inform. Theory, Vol. 50, Issue 12, pp. 3062 – 3080, Dec. 2004.
7. M. Janani, A. Hedayat, T.E. Hunter, A. Nosratinia, "Coded cooperation in wireless communications: space-time transmission and iterative decoding", IEEE Trans. on Signal Processing, Vol. 52, Issue 2, pp. 362-371, Feb. 2004.
8. Marvin K. Simon, and Mohamed-Slim Alouini, "Digital Communication over Fading Channels", Second Edition, John Wiley & Sons, Inc, 2005.

A Novel Scheduler for 1xEV-DO Type System Supporting Diverse Multimedia Traffics

Shan Guo Quan[1], Jeong-Jun Suh[1], Tae Chul Hong[2], and Young Yong Kim[1]

[1] Department of Electrical and Electronic Engineering, Yonsei University,
134 Shinchon-dong, Seodaemun-gu, Seoul, 120-749, Korea
{sgquan, jjun2, y2k}@yonsei.ac.kr
[2] Electronics and Telecommunications Research Institute(ETRI),
161 Gajeong-dong, Yu seong-gu, Daejeon, 305-350, Korea
Taechori@etri.re.kr

Abstract. Many scheduling disciplines have been proposed for the use in CDMA 1xEV-DO like systems. The PF (Proportional Fairness) scheduler proposed by Qualcomm Inc. aims at proportional fairness among users with diverse channel conditions. However, it lacks consideration for the performance of the real time service. To overcome the shortcoming of PF scheduler, Lucent Technologies Inc. suggested M-LWDF (Modified-Largest Weighted Delay First) scheduler for guaranteeing real time service. However, M-LWDF delivers very poor performance for the best effort traffic such as TCP flows. To overcome the shortcomings of available schedulers for 1xEV-DO type environments, we propose a novel scheduler, called BBS (Buffer Based Scheduler), targeting the performance guarantee of real time service without service degradation or starvation of TCP throughput. The simulation results show BBS provides better performance than PF or M-LWDF schedulers for a mixture of realtime and non-realtime data in 1xEV-DO type system.

1 Introduction

1xEV-DO is one of the most widely used data oriented technologies in third generation mobile communication[1]. It can support maximum downlink data rate of 2.4 Mbps, which is much higher than CDMA 1x system. Even though EV-DO throughput is much higher than that of CDMA 1x, EV-DO is not primarily designed to support voice traffic; also neither provides backward compatibility (RF support only), nor handoff. In other words, CDMA2000 1x is not evolved into EV-DO, but EV-DO system is a type of add-on system to CDMA2000 1x for supplemental data service. Therefore, EV-DO is applied to cells where a great amount of data service demand exists. In practice, the deployed HDR(High Data Rate)supporting cell looks more or less like a hot spot cell in the wireless LAN system. Since it is not trivial to support VoIP in EV-DO, and considering that the CDMA 1x system is much better than EV-DO to support voice service, we expect that VoIP service may not attract big popularity in 1xEV-DO system. Instead, most traffic in EV-DO system are in the form of streaming service (e.g. VOD, AOD) and TCP (e.g. Web, Email, FTP). In this paper, we focus on these two services, namely streaming and TCP, which are popular in 1xEV-DO initial stage. Voice and streaming services belong to the group of real time services, but streaming services have different characteristics from interactive real time traffic (e.g. VoIP). Since the delay jitter bound is more important than the absolute value of average delay for the streaming services,initial jitter buffering is used to mitigate the delay jitter. Buffering allows streaming services to tolerate larger delay jitter than ordinary real time service. This characteristic of the streaming service is very important in terms of scheduling. Namely, in case of a streaming service, the scheduler can utilize user diversity further for throughput maximization without degradation of overall performance as in case of interactive real time service. In streaming service, a 'good scheduler' needs intelligent resource management based on information about buffer occupancy, the channel condition of each user, and fairness among different users.

Qualcomm Inc. proposed PF (Proportional Fairness) scheduler[1] which provides a certain notion of 'proportional fairness'. The PF compromises between system throughput and fairness among users with diverse channel qualities. However, the PF scheduler is not designed to meet the performance guarantees of real time services. To overcome the shortcomings of the PF scheduler, Lucent Technologies Inc. suggested M-LWDF (Modified-Largest Weighted Delay First) for guaranteeing real time service[2]. However, M-LWDF delivers very poor performance for the best effort traffic such as TCP flows. The PF scheduler and M-LWDF scheduler will be examined further in section 2. In this paper, we proposed and analyzed a novel scheduling algorithm for the CDMA2000 1xEV-DO type system, called BBS (Buffer Based Scheduler). BBS takes buffer occupancy and delay constraint of each packet into account for scheduling decisions, while achieving the goal of maximizing the throughput of best effort traffic and guaranteeing the performance of a streaming multimedia service. We denote 'PF' for PF scheduler, 'M-LWDF' for M-LWDF scheduler. The proposed BBS algorithm turns out to be a good fit for the mixed traffic of streaming service type and TCP, which is the very current practical situation.

The rest of this paper is organized as follows: In Section 2, we describe PF scheduler and M-LWDF scheduler in detail. In Section 3, we introduce the proposed scheduling algorithm, BBS(Buffer Based Scheduler). In Section 4, we present the comparative results by simulation among PF, M-LWDF, and BBS. Conclusions are drawn in Section 5.

2 Previous Works for Schedulers

2.1 PF (Proportional Fairness) Scheduler

1xEV-DO adopts the AMC (Adaptive Modulation and Coding) scheme, which can select among several data rates according to temporal channel variation. In addition, the 1xEV-DO type system basically works in TDMA mode. In other words, it chooses one user at a time and gives full power to the selected user. 1xEV-DO base station must decide who should transmit data every

1.67 ms. Channel condition (C/I) of each user is a primary factor in determining the data rate, and scheduler should take into consideration this factor when deciding which user to transmit data. Depending on channel conditions, the PF algorithm adopts a notion of fairness known as proportional fairness[3]. PF scheduler maximizes the overall system throughput while maintaining a certain level of fairness. This algorithm maintains a history of each user's RF conditions. The time varying RF condition of a certain user causes the supporting data rates to oscillate in the range of several discrete transmission rates. From the histogram of each user, the scheduler calculates the moving average of rates and serves data when the DRC (Data Rate Request Channel) is equal to or greater than the average, but it does not serve when DRC goes below the average. In other words, PF scheduler decides which user has a relatively good channel compared to his average channel state. The algorithm of PF scheduler[4] can be expressed mathematically as equation(1).

$$f_s = \frac{DRC_i(t)}{R_i(t)} \qquad (1)$$

$DRC_i(t)$ is the instantaneous request rate of user i at slot t, and $R_i(t)$ is the average throughput rate of user i at slot t. Scheduler will select user i who has the largest value of f_s. $R_i(t)$ is a moving average of user i, so the scheduler updates $R_i(t)$ in every slot. We can express $R_i(t)$ as in equation (2). A user who is not currently receiving service has 0 for his current rate of transmission. Even users for whom the scheduler has no data to send also get their average rate updating. In our simulation, we assume $t_c = 1000$ slots.

$$R_i(t+1) = (1 - \frac{1}{t_c}) \times R_i(t) + \frac{1}{t_c} \times (current\ rate\ of\ i) \qquad (2)$$

2.2 M-LWDF (Modified-Largest Weighted Delay First) Scheduler

M-LWDF[2],[5] scheduler is proposed by Lucent Technologies Inc. This scheduler can overcome the shortcoming of PF scheduler. PF scheduler provides fairness to each traffic, but it does not guarantee various requests (e.g. real time traffic) of services. On the contrary, M-LWDF scheduler tries to guarantee various QoS requirements. If a user requests a real time service, the delay of most data packets needs to be kept below a certain threshold. This requirement can be expressed mathematically as follows,

$$P_r\{W_i > T_i\} \leq \delta_i \qquad (3)$$

where W_i is packet delay for user i, T_i and δ_i are delay threshold and maximum probability of outage, respectively. We can also consider a different QoS requirement where average throughput R_i provided to user i should not be less than some predefined value r_i:

$$R_i \geq r_i \qquad (4)$$

These two kinds of QoS requirements can be achieved with M-LWDF scheme. In each time slot t, the scheduler serves the queue j for which is $\gamma_j W_j(t) r_j(t)$ maximized, where $W_j(t)$ is the head-of-line packet delay for queue j, $r_j(t)$ is the channel capacity with respect to flow j and γ_j is arbitrary positive constant. In M-LWDF scheduling, $\gamma_j = a_j/r_j$, $a_j = -(log\delta_j)/T_i$, and r_j is the average channel rate with respect to user i are used. $W_j(t)$ can be substituted with $Q_j(t)$, which represents the queue length of user j. The problem of providing a certain minimum throughput r_j for each user can be also solved by the M-LWDF scheduling algorithm, if it is used in conjunction with token bucket control. A virtual token bucket is associated with each queue j. Token in bucket j arrives at constant rate r_j. In each time slot, the decision of which flow to serve is made according to M-LWDF rule, although $W_j(t)$ is not the delay of actual head-of-line user j packet, but the delay of the longest waiting token in token bucket j. Whenever the service for the certain packet completes, the number of tokens in the corresponding bucket is reduced by the actual amount of data served. Since token arrives at a constant rate, one can readily notice that $W_j(t)$=[Number of tokens in the bucket i]/ r_j. In this paper, we focus on streaming type of service, and compare the performance of our proposed algorithm with M-LWDF criteria for delay guaranteeing only.

3 Proposed Scheduler - BBS (Buffer Based Scheduler)

We expect that 1xEV-DO traffic is composed of mostly streaming and best effort traffic in the early stage. Therefore, it is a safe bet that a scheduler optimized for streaming and best effort service will be an excellent fit for practical services[6].

BBS is optimized for streaming and best effort services. This scheduler considers streaming buffer size and occupancy. In addition, BBS scheduler also uses channel state information. Fig. 1 shows how a base station receives information regarding the status of channel and buffer.

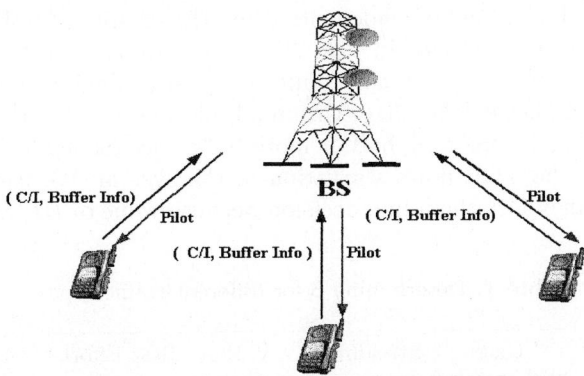

Fig. 1. Delivery of C/I and buffer information from mobile stations

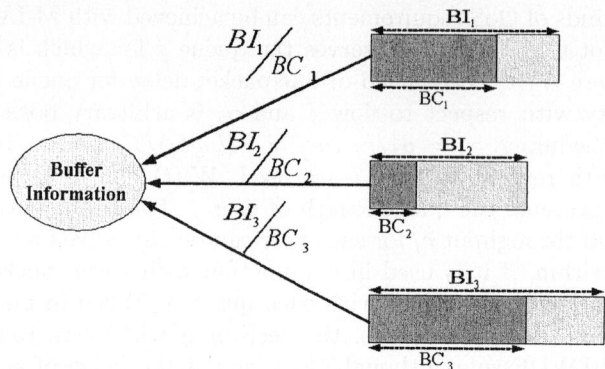

Fig. 2. Buffer information exchanged between BS and mobile stations

A mobile station transmits information about buffer status as well as the information about the channel state every 1.67 ms. Buffer information is composed of the maximum buffer size and current buffer occupancy. BBS scheduling function is defined as follows.

$$arg\ max_j \quad a_j DRC_j\ log(S) \qquad (5)$$

In this procedure, buffer information controls the scheduling priority. Namely, the priority value is inversely proportional to the current buffer occupancy for a given flow (Fig. 2).

The flow, which will be served by scheduler in current time slot, is determined by equation (5) (Table 1).

BI denotes initial buffer occupancy and BC means current buffer occupancy. a_j is defined by service type or service class, and it is 1 by default. In VoIP case, priority is determined by f(Traffic). The value of f(traffic) is changed adaptively by traffic load. The priority of VoIP needs to be determined adaptively by traffic conditions like the case of M-LWDF. Priority of VoIP is not sensitive in lightly loaded situation, but in highly loaded situation, the priority of VoIP must adjust very sensitively to traffic load. In best effort case, we assume that it is higher priority than remaining half or more buffer occupancy amount because streaming services endure large delay jitter through buffering. Furthermore, we assume there always exists a remaining half or more buffer occupancy for some users in order to protect the TCP flows starvation in the system. We use log scale for buffering occupancy for scheduling decision because value of BI/BC is exagger-

Table 1. Determining S for different traffic types

Case	Streaming	VoIP	Best Effort
Value of S	$\frac{BI_j}{BC_j}$	f(traffic)	2

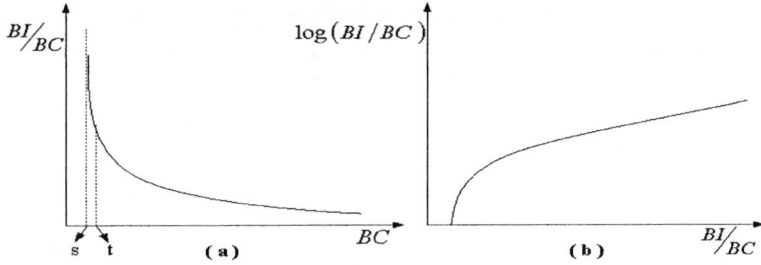

Fig. 3. Effect of using log scale

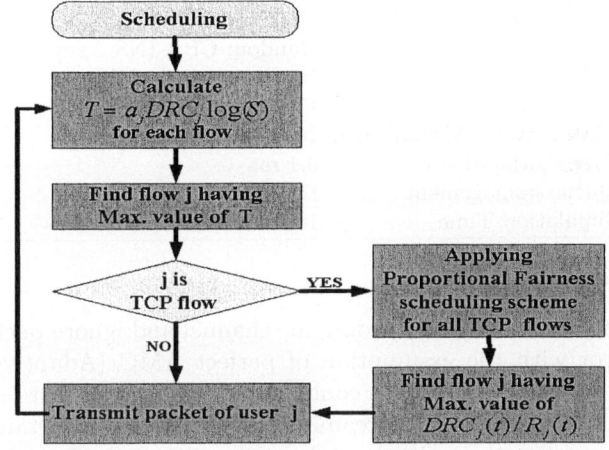

Fig. 4. Scheduling procedure for decoupling streaming and best effort service type

ated when BC becomes very small, as in Fig. 3(a). If we use $log(BI/BC)$, this problem can be remedied as seen in Fig. 3(b).

With the discipline in (5) only, we cannot guarantee fairness of best effort service. For this reason, we use scheduling procedure depicted as in Fig. 4. If TCP flow is selected by scheduling function, scheduler recalculates max. value of users through PF algorithm among TCP flows. In this way, one can decouple guaranteed performance for streaming service users and fairness among best effort service users.

4 Performance Evaluation

We compare the performance of BBS with that of PF and M-LWDF in this section. We carry out a simulation using NS-2[7]. The simulation setup is summarized in Table 2. Packet size is fixed at 1024 bit and streaming frame size is also fixed at 1 packet. HDR system supports 5 rates.

Table 2. Simulation setup

Simulation Parameters	Value
Packet size	1024bits
Streaming frame	1024bits (one packet)
HDR supporting rate	307.2Kbps
	614.4Kbps
	1228.8Kbps
	1843.2Kbps
	2457.6Kbps
Initial buffering time	2 seconds
Wireless channel	Rayleigh Fading
Packet loss	None (Using FEC)
Streaming source	Random CBR (NS-2 support)
TCP version	Reno
TCP source	FTP (NS-2 support)
Link between MS and BS	10 Mbps
Propagation delay	0.1 ms
Queue management	DropTail
Simulation Time	150 seconds

In addition, we use Rayleigh fading for channel and ignore packet loss owing to channel error with the assumption of perfect AMC (Adaptive Modulation and Coding). For the performance comparison, we compare throughput as well as number of buffer exhaustion. Streaming service requires a certain level of minimum throughput together with bounded delay jitter. Buffer exhaustion event means that packet inter-arrival time is over the delay jitter bound when contents in buffer is about to be empty. Therefore, buffer exhaustion frequency (or duration) is an essential performance metric for scheduler performance comparison in case of streaming service type.

4.1 Lightly Loaded Situation

We start with lightly loaded situation, where traffic is composed of 6 streaming sources and 2 TCP sources. The 2 streaming sources have the rate of 125 Kbps, another 2 streaming sources have the rate of 100 Kbps, and the remaining 2 streaming sources have the rate of 75 Kbps. Best effort service uses TCP Reno version.

Fig. 5 shows the simulation results for the performance comparison with those of PF and M-LWDF scheduler. Since PF scheduler focuses on fairness, no guaranteed performance is applicable for streaming service in this case. M-LWDF scheduler prioritizes the performance of streaming service but throughput of TCP flows is severely damaged due to low priority in return. In case of BBS, minimum TCP throughput is maintained while guaranteeing the performance of streaming service.

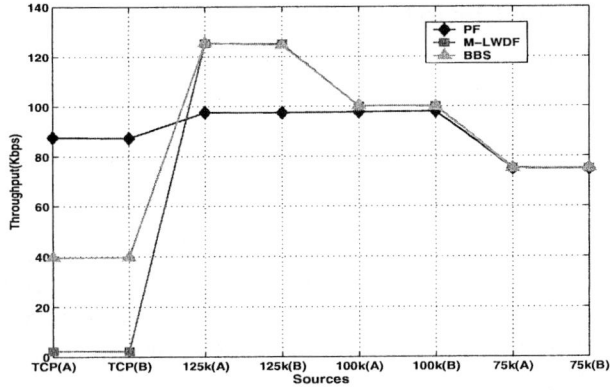

Fig. 5. Comparison of throughput in lightly loaded situation

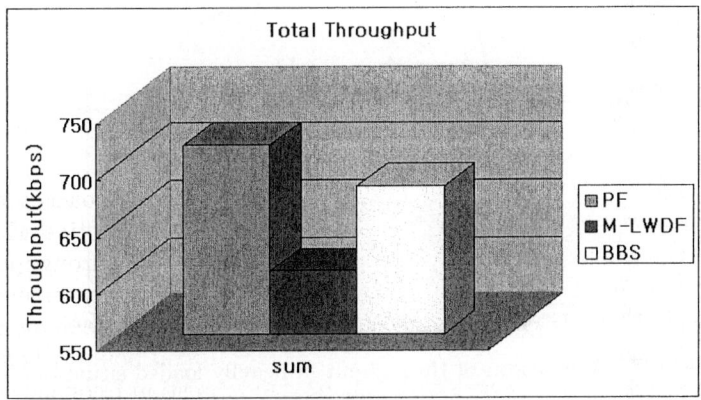

Fig. 6. Total throughput of each scheduler in lightly loaded situation

Fig. 6 shows the comparison of total throughput of each scheduler. Total throughput means bandwidth utilization of scheduler. The PF scheduler has the maximum value of total throughput, and provides a better chance for favorable channel conditions for each user without being constrained by the delay bounds usually found in real-time service. On the other hand, the M-LDWF scheduler gives higher priority to the delay bound of real time services than each channel state. In other words, the M-LDWF scheduler can give a transmitting opportunity to an user with poor channel conditions. However, BBS gives priority adaptively. If a given real time service has the margin of delay bound, BBS gives more priority to best effort traffic. In opposite case, BBS gives higher priority to real time service. Therefore, BBS has larger throughput than that of M-LWDF, but BBS can provide a transmitting chances to a user with poor channel conditions in the case that the delay bounds of a given real time service has no margin. Therefore, total throughput of BBS does not exceed total throughput of PF scheduler.

4.2 Heavily Loaded Situation

We carry out a simulation with total traffic intensity close to system's maximum capacity. Traffic composition is as follows. The 2 streaming sources have the rate of 150 Kbps, another 2 streaming sources have the rate of 100 Kbps, while the remaining 2 streaming sources have the rate of 75 Kbps. In addition, 2 TCP flows are added in.

Fig. 7 shows the simulation results in this heavily load situation. In this case, M-LWDF and BBS both guarantee streaming service rates while PF fails to fulfill the requirements. For best effort service, M-LWDF penalize TCP flows while BBS provides better throughput for the TCP flows.

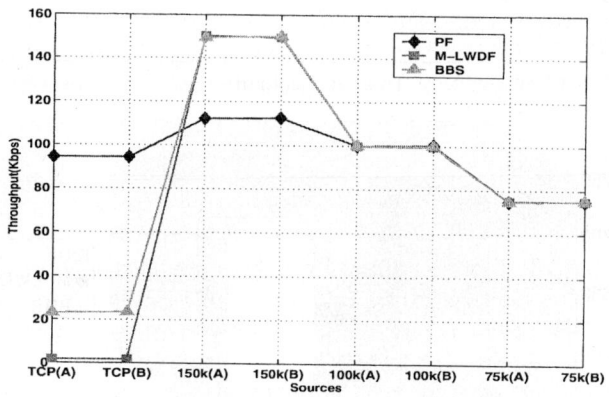

Fig. 7. Comparison of throughput in heavily loaded situation

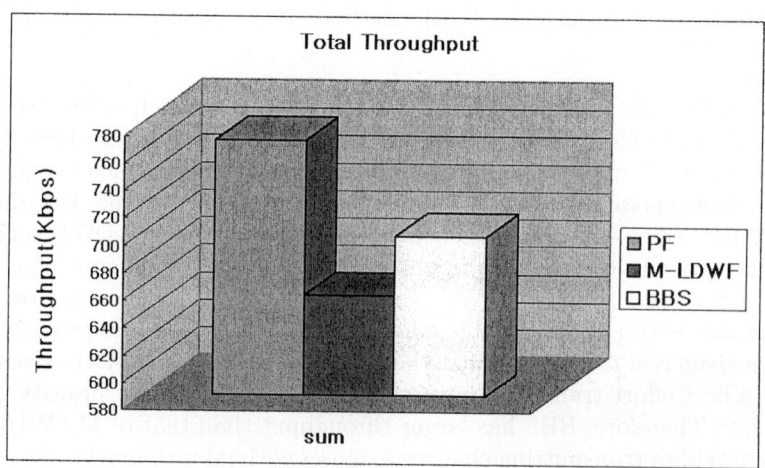

Fig. 8. Total throughput of each scheduler in heavily loaded situation

Table 3. Number of buffer exhaustion in heavily loaded situation

Number of Buffer Emptying	PF	M-LWDF	BBS
150K(A)	759	124	0
150K(B)	756	120	0
125K(A)	24	0	0
125K(B)	28	0	0
100K(A)	0	0	0
100K(B)	0	0	0

In Fig. 8, we show the total throughput performance of each scheduler in a heavily loaded situation. From the results, the comparison of total throughput is quite similar to the results in a lightly loaded situation (Fig. 6).

Table 3 shows the number of buffer exhaustion events. PF scheduler cannot prevent discontinuation of streaming services in heavily loaded situation. Even M-LWDF shows considerable amount of buffer exhaustion for high rate traffic(150kbps), while BBS provides zero buffer exhaustion even with high load.

4.3 Sensitivity of TCP Priority Value in M-LWDF

Since original M-LWDF scheduling discipline does not define the priority for best effort service, we carry out simulation with various priorities (1,10,20,30) of TCP in M-LWDF and compared the results with that of BBS.

Table 4. shows throughput of TCP flows in M-LWDF and BBS. With increasing priority of TCP, throughput of TCP flows in M-LWDF increase. However, when priority of TCP reaches value of 30, QoS of streaming service start to deteriorate which can be checked by nonzero buffer exhaustion events observed as in Table 5. On the other hand, BBS has higher TCP throughput than that of M-LWDF in this case, while the event of empty streaming buffer is nonexistent in BBS case. In other words, in BBS case, TCP throughput is sustained and decoupled with the real time service. We expect that implementation of M-LWDF with minimum guarantee of TCP throughput is very challenging in a real situation, since priority of TCP should be determined dynamically with the time varying traffic situation, while BBS handles the situation without complex fine tuning of priority values.

Table 4. TCP throughput comparison for M-LWDF and BBS

Throughput (Kbps)	M-LWDF (TCP-1)	M-LWDF (TCP-10)	M-LWDF (TCP-20)	M-LWDF (TCP-30)	BBS
TCP(A)	0.942	5.76	10.06	13.85	24.06
TCP(B)	0.935	5.76	10.16	13.99	23.25

Table 5. Number of buffer exhaustion

Number of Buffer Empty	M-LWDF (TCP-1)	M-LWDF (TCP-10)	M-LWDF (TCP-20)	M-LWDF (TCP-30)	BBS
150K(A)	0	0	0	0	0
150K(B)	0	0	0	0	0
100K(A)	0	0	0	12	0
100K(B)	0	0	0	0	0
75K(A)	0	0	0	0	0
75K(B)	0	0	0	0	0

5 Conclusion

In this paper, we proposed and evaluated a novel scheduler for CDMA2000 1xEV-DO like environments with mixed traffic types. Existing schedulers serve their purpose, such as fairness for PF and real time service performance guarantee for M-LWDF. Our proposed BBS aims at the performance guarantee for streaming service types, while preventing starvation for the best effort services. Contrary to PF scheduler, our scheduler (BBS) can guarantee the performance of real time service, and contrary to M-LWDF, our scheduler guarantees TCP throughput not to stifle. The performance of PF, M-LWDF, and BBS scheduler is compared in various aspects. From simulation results, it is clear that BBS with adaptive priority for streaming service shows very good performance in terms of throughput as well as delay jitter.Thererfore, BBS prevents buffer exhaustion. Moreover, it is easier to implement, since BBS can adapt to various environment without manual priority setting.

Acknowledgement

This research was supported by the MIC(Ministry of Information and Communication), Korea, under the ITRC(Information Technology Research Center) support program supervised by the IITA(Institute of Information Technology Assessment).

References

1. Paul Bender, Petet Black, Matthew Grob, Robert Padovani, Nagabhushana Sindushayana, and Andrew Viterbi, "CDMA/HDR: A Bandwidth - Efficient High-Speed Wireless Data Service for Nomadic Users," IEEE Communications Magazine, Vol. 38, No. 7, pp. 70–77, July 2000.
2. Matthew Andrews, Krishnan Kumaran, Kavita Ramanan, Alexander Stoyler, and Phil Whiting, Raijiv Vijayakymar, "Providing Quality of Service over a Shared Wireless Link," IEEE Communications Magazine, Vol. 39, No. 2, pp. 150–154, Feb.2001.

3. QUALCOMM Inc, 1xEV: 1x Evolution, IS-856 TIA/EIA Standard, Air Link Overview, Revision 7.1, May 2001.
4. A.Jalali, R.Padovani, R.Pankaj, "Data Throughput of CDMA-HDR a High Efficient-High Data Rate Personal Communication Wireless System," IEEE VTC 2000-Spring Tokyo.2000 IEEE 51th, Vol. 3, pp. 1854–1858, May 2000.
5. S. Shakkottai and A. Stoyler, "A Study of Scheduling Algorithms for a Mixture of Real-Time and Non-Real-Time Data in HDR", Bell Labs Tech Memo, Aug.2000.
6. http://www.sktelecom.co.kr/telecom lab/sk point tech/ cdma ev do/
7. NS-2 Web Site: http://www.isi.edu/nsnam/ns/

Proposal of Space-Time Block Coded Cooperative Wireless Transmission in Rayleigh Fading Channels

Ho Van Khuong and Hyung-Yun Kong

7-522 Department of Electrical Engineering, University of Ulsan,
San 29, MuGeo-Dong, Nam-Gu, Ulsan, Korea, 680-749
khuongho2001@yahoo.com, hkong@mail.ulsan.ac.kr

Abstract. Space-time block codes (STBC) are well-known for use in the co-located multi-antenna systems to combat the adverse effects of fading channel. However, their application is limited in some scenarios where users can not support multiple transmit antennas. Therefore, we propose a solution of space-time block coded cooperative transmission among single-antenna users in the multiple access wireless environments to obtain the powerful benefits of multi-antenna system without the demand for physical arrays. The closed-form BER expression was also derived and compared to the simulation results to verify the validity of the suggested method. A variety of numerical results demonstrated the superiority of cooperative transmission over direct transmission under flat Rayleigh fading channel plus AWGN (Additive White Gaussian Noise).

1 Introduction

The space-time block coding can achieve the full transmit diversity specified by the number of the transmit antennas while allowing a very simple maximum-likelihood decoding algorithm, based only on linear processing of the received signals [1]. As a result, it has received a great deal of attention in recent years as a powerful coding technique to mitigate fading in wireless channels and improve robustness to interference. However, its advantages are unachievable in some cases where wireless mobiles may not be able to support multiple antennas due to size or other constraints [2]. An efficient way to overcome this problem is to exploit cooperative transmission among single-antenna wireless mobiles to form a virtual antenna array [3]-[5]. Therefore, the Alamouti code [6] was applied in relay networks and wireless sensor networks to acquire the spatial diversity by using two relay terminals to forward the original data from the source node to the destination in the same signaling structure as that for the physical array [7]-[8]. Nevertheless, [7] only mentioned the signal processing from two intermediate nodes to the remote receiver without paying any attention to error transmission caused by the link between the sensor and the intermediate nodes which is faded and noisy in real and generic wireless networks. Such a case was solved by [8] in part but it did not show explicitly the way of detecting the data at the receiver and a closed-form BER expression. This motivates us to apply another space-time block code in such a same scenario but take into consideration the effects of all channels through which the original data can reach the destination and expose a tighter cooperation among the source terminal and two relays. The decoding technique as well as the exact BER expression formulation is also illustrated in our paper.

The rest of the paper is organized as follows. Section 2 presents a cooperative signaling structure as well as the closed-form expression derivation for the error probability. Then the numerical and simulation results that compare the performance of the proposed cooperative transmission with direct transmission are exposed in section 3. Finally, the paper is closed in section 4 with a conclusion.

2 Proposed Cooperative Signaling Structure

Consider a cooperative transmission in a generic wireless network where the information is transmitted from a source terminal S to a destination terminal D with the assistance of two relay terminals. All terminals equipped with single-antenna transceivers share the same frequency band and each terminal cannot transmit and receive signal at the same time. TDM (Time Division Multiplexing) is used for channel access and the signal format of each entity is shown in the Fig. 1.

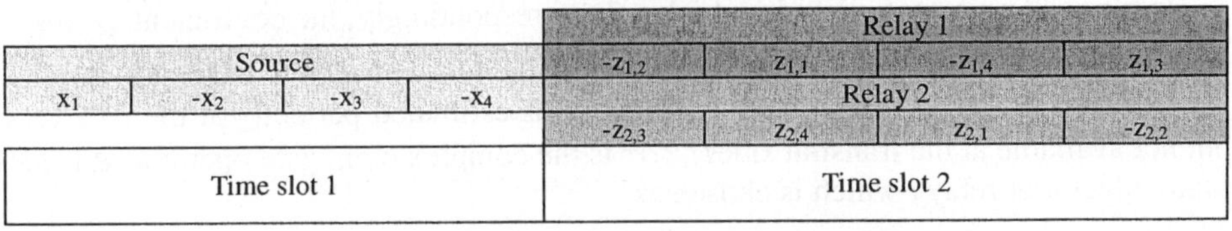

	Source			Relay 1			
x_1	$-x_2$	$-x_3$	$-x_4$	$-z_{1,2}$	$z_{1,1}$	$-z_{1,4}$	$z_{1,3}$
				Relay 2			
				$-z_{2,3}$	$z_{2,4}$	$z_{2,1}$	$-z_{2,2}$
Time slot 1				Time slot 2			

Fig. 1. Proposed cooperative signaling structure

For simplicity of exposition, we use complex baseband-equivalent models to express all the signals. During its own time slot (represented as time slot 1), the source terminal broadcasts four BPSK-modulated symbols x_1, x_2, x_3, x_4 according to the structure x_1, $-x_2$, $-x_3$, $-x_4$ which will be received by the destination and two relays. Assuming that the channels among users (inter-user channels) and between the users and the destination (user-destination channels) are independent of each other. Moreover, all channels experience frequency flat fading and are quasi-static, i.e., they are constant during 4-symbol period but change independently to the next. Therefore, the signals received at the destination and two relays have the common forms as follows

$$y_{Si,1} = \varepsilon_0 \alpha_{Si} x_1 + n_{Si,1} \tag{1a}$$

$$y_{Si,2} = -\varepsilon_0 \alpha_{Si} x_2 + n_{Si,2} \tag{1b}$$

$$y_{Si,3} = -\varepsilon_0 \alpha_{Si} x_3 + n_{Si,3} \tag{1c}$$

$$y_{Si,4} = -\varepsilon_0 \alpha_{Si} x_4 + n_{Si,4} \tag{1d}$$

where

- $y_{Si,j}$ is a signal received at the terminal i from the source S during the jth symbol duration ($i=1, 2, D$ denote relay 1, relay 2 and the destination D, respectively); $j=1, 2, 3, 4$.
- α_{Si} is a fading realization associated with the link from the source S to the target i which is assumed to be an independent zero-mean complex Gaussian random variable (ZMCGRV) with variance λ_{Si}^2.
- $n_{Si,j}$ is a zero-mean additive noise sample of variance σ_{Si}^2 at terminal i in the jth symbol interval.
- $\varepsilon_0 = \sqrt{P_S}$ is an amplification factor at the source where P_S is average source power.

In the second time slot, the relays are to simply amplify the signals received from the source and forward them simultaneously to the destination. These amplified signals obey the format in Fig. 1. Specifically, they are given by

$$z_{i,j} = \varepsilon_i \frac{\alpha_{Si}^*}{|\alpha_{Si}|} y_{Si,j} \qquad (2)$$

Here $i=1, 2$ represent relay 1 and relay 2, correspondingly; the coefficient $\alpha_{Si}^*/|\alpha_{Si}|$ is used to correct the phase distortion caused by the link between S and i (it is implicitly assumed that the channel state information is estimated perfectly at the receivers but not available at the transmit sides); $(.)^*$ is the complex conjugate operator; ε_i is the scaling factor at relay i which is chosen as

$$\varepsilon_i = \sqrt{\frac{P_i}{E\left[|y_{Si,j}|^2\right]}} = \sqrt{\frac{P_i}{P_S \lambda_{Si}^2 + \sigma_{Si}^2}} \qquad (3)$$

where P_i denotes the average power of the relay i and $E[.]$ represents an expectation operator. Selection of ε_i as in Eq. (3) ensures that an average output power is maintained [9].

The signal processing at terminal D must be delayed until the relays have transmitted signal sequences $z_{i,j}$. In order to avoid inter-symbol interference at the destination terminal, we assume that the time delay between the two propagation paths containing a relay is negligible. After collecting all signals from the relays, the D is to simply add the relays' received signals synchronously together with those from the source which are delayed a time-slot duration on the symbol-by-symbol basis. For further simplification, we drop the time indices. Then the signal sequence of 4 consecutive symbols received at the D are given explicitly by

$$r_1 = \underbrace{\left(-\alpha_{1D} z_{1,2} - \alpha_{2D} z_{2,3} + n_{D,1}\right)}_{\text{from relay 1 and relay 2 in the 2nd time-slot}} + \underbrace{\left(\varepsilon_0 \alpha_{SD} x_1 + n_{SD,1}\right)}_{\text{from the source in the 1st time-slot}}$$

$$= \left(-\alpha_{1D}\left[\varepsilon_1 \frac{\alpha_{S1}^*}{|\alpha_{S1}|}(-\alpha_{S1}\varepsilon_0 x_2 + n_{S1,2})\right] - \alpha_{2D}\left[\varepsilon_2 \frac{\alpha_{S2}^*}{|\alpha_{S2}|}(-\alpha_{S2}\varepsilon_0 x_3 + n_{S2,3})\right] + n_{D,1}\right)$$
$$+ \left(\varepsilon_0 \alpha_{SD} x_1 + n_{SD,1}\right)$$

$$= \varepsilon_0 \alpha_{SD} x_1 + \varepsilon_0 \varepsilon_1 \alpha_{1D} |\alpha_{S1}| x_2 + \varepsilon_0 \varepsilon_2 \alpha_{2D} |\alpha_{S2}| x_3 \qquad (4a)$$

$$- \alpha_{1D} \varepsilon_1 \frac{\alpha_{S1}^*}{|\alpha_{S1}|} n_{S1,2} - \alpha_{2D} \varepsilon_2 \frac{\alpha_{S2}^*}{|\alpha_{S2}|} n_{S2,3} + n_{SD,1} + n_{D,1}$$

$$r_2 = \left(\alpha_{1D} z_{1,1} + \alpha_{2D} z_{2,4} + n_{D,2}\right) + \left(-\varepsilon_0 \alpha_{SD} x_2 + n_{SD,2}\right)$$

$$= \left(\alpha_{1D}\left[\varepsilon_1 \frac{\alpha_{S1}^*}{|\alpha_{S1}|}(\alpha_{S1}\varepsilon_0 x_1 + n_{S1,1})\right] + \alpha_{2D}\left[\varepsilon_2 \frac{\alpha_{S2}^*}{|\alpha_{S2}|}(-\alpha_{S2}\varepsilon_0 x_4 + n_{S2,4})\right] + n_{D,2}\right)$$

$$+ \left(-\varepsilon_0 \alpha_{SD} x_2 + n_{SD,2}\right)$$

$$= -\varepsilon_0 \alpha_{SD} x_2 + \varepsilon_0 \varepsilon_1 \alpha_{1D} |\alpha_{S1}| x_1 - \varepsilon_0 \varepsilon_2 \alpha_{2D} |\alpha_{S2}| x_4 \qquad (4b)$$

$$+ \alpha_{1D} \varepsilon_1 \frac{\alpha_{S1}^*}{|\alpha_{S1}|} n_{S1,1} + \alpha_{2D} \varepsilon_2 \frac{\alpha_{S2}^*}{|\alpha_{S2}|} n_{S2,4} + n_{SD,2} + n_{D,2}$$

$$r_3 = \left(-\alpha_{1D} z_{1,4} + \alpha_{2D} z_{2,1} + n_{D,3}\right) + \left(-\varepsilon_0 \alpha_{SD} x_3 + n_{SD,3}\right)$$

$$= \left(-\alpha_{1D}\left[\varepsilon_1 \frac{\alpha_{S1}^*}{|\alpha_{S1}|}(-\alpha_{S1}\varepsilon_0 x_4 + n_{S1,4})\right] + \alpha_{2D}\left[\varepsilon_2 \frac{\alpha_{S2}^*}{|\alpha_{S2}|}(\alpha_{S2}\varepsilon_0 x_1 + n_{S2,1})\right] + n_{D,3}\right)$$

$$+ \left(-\varepsilon_0 \alpha_{SD} x_3 + n_{SD,3}\right)$$

$$= -\varepsilon_0 \alpha_{SD} x_3 + \varepsilon_0 \varepsilon_1 \alpha_{1D} |\alpha_{S1}| x_4 + \varepsilon_0 \varepsilon_2 \alpha_{2D} |\alpha_{S2}| x_1 \qquad (4c)$$

$$- \alpha_{1D} \varepsilon_1 \frac{\alpha_{S1}^*}{|\alpha_{S1}|} n_{S1,4} + \alpha_{2D} \varepsilon_2 \frac{\alpha_{S2}^*}{|\alpha_{S2}|} n_{S2,1} + n_{SD,3} + n_{D,3}$$

$$r_4 = \left(\alpha_{1D} z_{1,3} - \alpha_{2D} z_{2,2} + n_{D,4}\right) + \left(-\varepsilon_0 \alpha_{SD} x_4 + n_{SD,4}\right)$$

$$= \left(\alpha_{1D}\left[\varepsilon_1 \frac{\alpha_{S1}^*}{|\alpha_{S1}|}(-\alpha_{S1}\varepsilon_0 x_3 + n_{S1,3})\right] - \alpha_{2D}\left[\varepsilon_2 \frac{\alpha_{S2}^*}{|\alpha_{S2}|}(-\alpha_{S2}\varepsilon_0 x_2 + n_{S2,2})\right] + n_{D,4}\right)$$

$$+ \left(-\varepsilon_0 \alpha_{SD} x_4 + n_{SD,4}\right)$$

$$= -\varepsilon_0 \alpha_{SD} x_4 - \varepsilon_0 \varepsilon_1 \alpha_{1D} |\alpha_{S1}| x_3 + \varepsilon_0 \varepsilon_2 \alpha_{2D} |\alpha_{S2}| x_2 \qquad (4d)$$

$$+ \alpha_{1D} \varepsilon_1 \frac{\alpha_{S1}^*}{|\alpha_{S1}|} n_{S1,3} - \alpha_{2D} \varepsilon_2 \frac{\alpha_{S2}^*}{|\alpha_{S2}|} n_{S2,2} + n_{SD,4} + n_{D,4}$$

where α_{mD} are path gains of the channels between relay m and the destination D; $m=1, 2$.

In the above expressions, $n_{D,j}$ is an additive noise sample at the destination in j^{th} symbol duration of time slot 2. The quantities $n_{D,j}$ are modeled as ZMCGRVs with variance σ_D^2. Also due to the assumption of slow and flat Rayleigh fading, α_{mD} are independent ZMCGRVs with variances λ_{mD}^2.

We can rewrite the received signals r_j in more compact forms as

$$r_1 = h_1 x_1 + h_2 x_2 + h_3 x_3 + n_1 \qquad (5a)$$

$$r_2 = -h_1 x_2 + h_2 x_1 - h_3 x_4 + n_2 \tag{5b}$$

$$r_3 = -h_1 x_3 + h_2 x_4 + h_3 x_1 + n_3 \tag{5c}$$

$$r_4 = -h_1 x_4 - h_2 x_3 + h_3 x_2 + n_4 \tag{5d}$$

by letting

$$h_1 = \varepsilon_0 \alpha_{SD} \tag{6a}$$

$$h_2 = \varepsilon_0 \varepsilon_1 \alpha_{1D} |\alpha_{S1}| \tag{6b}$$

$$h_3 = \varepsilon_0 \varepsilon_2 \alpha_{2D} |\alpha_{S2}| \tag{6c}$$

$$n_1 = -\alpha_{1D}\varepsilon_1 \frac{\alpha_{S1}^*}{|\alpha_{S1}|} n_{S1,2} - \alpha_{2D}\varepsilon_2 \frac{\alpha_{S2}^*}{|\alpha_{S2}|} n_{S2,3} + n_{SD,1} + n_{D,1} \tag{6d}$$

$$n_2 = \alpha_{1D}\varepsilon_1 \frac{\alpha_{S1}^*}{|\alpha_{S1}|} n_{S1,1} + \alpha_{2D}\varepsilon_2 \frac{\alpha_{S2}^*}{|\alpha_{S2}|} n_{S2,4} + n_{SD,2} + n_{D,2} \tag{6e}$$

$$n_3 = -\alpha_{1D}\varepsilon_1 \frac{\alpha_{S1}^*}{|\alpha_{S1}|} n_{S1,4} + \alpha_{2D}\varepsilon_2 \frac{\alpha_{S2}^*}{|\alpha_{S2}|} n_{S2,1} + n_{SD,3} + n_{D,3} \tag{6f}$$

$$n_4 = \alpha_{1D}\varepsilon_1 \frac{\alpha_{S1}^*}{|\alpha_{S1}|} n_{S1,3} - \alpha_{2D}\varepsilon_2 \frac{\alpha_{S2}^*}{|\alpha_{S2}|} n_{S2,2} + n_{SD,4} + n_{D,4} \tag{6g}$$

Due to the fact that all additive noise r.v.'s are mutually independent of each other, conditioned on the channel realizations, n_j ($j=1, 2, 3, 4$) are also independent ZMCGRVs with the same variance

$$\sigma_n^2 = |\alpha_{1D}|^2 \varepsilon_1^2 \sigma_{S1}^2 + |\alpha_{2D}|^2 \varepsilon_2^2 \sigma_{S2}^2 + \sigma_{SD}^2 + \sigma_D^2 = a\varepsilon_1^2 \sigma_{S1}^2 + b\varepsilon_2^2 \sigma_{S2}^2 + \sigma_{SD}^2 + \sigma_D^2 \tag{7}$$

where $a = |\alpha_{1D}|^2$, $b = |\alpha_{2D}|^2$ are exponentially distributed r.v.'s with mean values $\lambda_{1D}^2, \lambda_{2D}^2$; that is, $f_a(a) = \lambda_a e^{-\lambda_a a}$, $f_b(b) = \lambda_b e^{-\lambda_b b}$ in which $a, b \geq 0$ and $\lambda_a = 1/\lambda_{1D}^2$, $\lambda_b = 1/\lambda_{2D}^2$, are pdf's of r.v.'s a, b, respectively.

Eq. (5) is actually equivalent to the analytical expressions of the STBC of code rate ¾ with transmission matrix given by

$$\begin{bmatrix} x_1 & -x_2 & -x_3 & -x_4 \\ x_2 & x_1 & x_4 & -x_3 \\ x_3 & -x_4 & x_1 & x_2 \end{bmatrix}$$

As a consequence, the maximum likelihood decoding can be applied and results in the decision statistics for the transmitted signals x_i as [1]

$$\bar{x}_i = \sum_{j \in \chi(i)} sig_j(i) r_j h^*_{\phi_j(i)} \tag{8}$$

where $i = 1, 2, 3, 4$; $\chi(i)$ is the set of columns of the transmission matrix in which x_i appears; $\phi_j(i)$ represents the row position of x_i in the jth column and the sign of x_i in the jth column is denoted by $sig_j(i)$. Specifically, we have

$$\bar{x}_1 = r_1 h_1^* + r_2 h_2^* + r_3 h_3^* = \left(|h_1|^2 + |h_2|^2 + |h_3|^2\right)x_1 + h_1^* n_1 + h_2^* n_2 + h_3^* n_3 = \lambda x_1 + N_1 \tag{9a}$$

$$\bar{x}_2 = r_1 h_2^* - r_2 h_1^* + r_4 h_3^* = \left(|h_1|^2 + |h_2|^2 + |h_3|^2\right)x_2 + h_2^* n_1 - h_1^* n_2 + h_3^* n_4 = \lambda x_2 + N_2 \tag{9b}$$

$$\bar{x}_3 = r_1 h_3^* - r_3 h_1^* - r_4 h_2^* = \left(|h_1|^2 + |h_2|^2 + |h_3|^2\right)x_2 + h_3^* n_1 - h_1^* n_3 - h_2^* n_4 = \lambda x_3 + N_3 \tag{9c}$$

$$\bar{x}_4 = -r_2 h_3^* + r_3 h_2^* - r_4 h_1^* = \left(|h_1|^2 + |h_2|^2 + |h_3|^2\right)x_2 - h_3^* n_2 + h_2^* n_3 - h_1^* n_4 = \lambda x_4 + N_4 \tag{9d}$$

Here

$$N_1 = h_1^* n_1 + h_2^* n_2 + h_3^* n_3$$
$$N_2 = h_2^* n_1 - h_1^* n_2 + h_3^* n_4$$
$$N_3 = h_3^* n_1 - h_1^* n_3 - h_2^* n_4$$
$$N_4 = -h_3^* n_2 + h_2^* n_3 - h_1^* n_4$$
$$\lambda = |h_1|^2 + |h_2|^2 + |h_3|^2 = u + v + k$$

$$u = \varepsilon_0^2 |\alpha_{SD}|^2 \tag{10a}$$

$$v = \varepsilon_0^2 \varepsilon_1^2 |\alpha_{1D}|^2 |\alpha_{S1}|^2 = \varepsilon_0^2 \varepsilon_1^2 a |\alpha_{S1}|^2 \tag{10b}$$

$$k = \varepsilon_0^2 \varepsilon_2^2 |\alpha_{2D}|^2 |\alpha_{S2}|^2 = \varepsilon_0^2 \varepsilon_2^2 b |\alpha_{S2}|^2 \tag{10c}$$

Eq. (9) shows that the proposed cooperative transmission protocol can provide exactly performance as the 3-level receive maximum ratio combining.

It is straightforward to infer that N_j ($j=1, 2, 3, 4$) is also independent ZMCGRVs, given the channel realizations, with the same variance

$$\sigma_N^2 = \lambda \sigma_n^2 \tag{11}$$

By observing Eq. (9), we find that x_i are attenuated and corrupted by the same fading and noisy level, their error probability is equal. As a result, BER (bit error rate) of x_1 is sufficient to evaluate the performance of system. For BPSK transmission, the recovered bit of x_1 is given by

$$\hat{x}_1 = sign(\text{Re}\{\bar{x}_1\})$$

where $sign(.)$ is a signum function and $\text{Re}\{.\}$ is the real part of a complex number.

Then the error probability of x_1 conditioned on channel realizations is easily found as

$$P_e = Q(\sqrt{2\gamma}) \qquad (12)$$

where $\gamma = \lambda^2/\sigma_N^2 = \lambda/\sigma_n^2$ can be interpreted as the signal-to-noise ratio at the output of Gaussian channel.

To find the average error probability, we must know the pdf of γ. Expressing γ explicitly results in the following formula

$$\gamma = \frac{\lambda}{\sigma_n^2} = \frac{u+v+k}{\sigma_n^2}$$

Since σ_n^2 is a function of only two r.v.'s a and b, we can find the pdf of $u+v+k$ given a and b. From Eq. (10), we realize that u, v and k have exponential distributions with mean values $\varepsilon_0^2 \lambda_{SD}^2$, $\varepsilon_0^2 \varepsilon_1^2 a \lambda_{S1}^2$, $\varepsilon_0^2 \varepsilon_2^2 b \lambda_{S2}^2$; that is, $f_u(u) = \lambda_u e^{-\lambda_u u}$, $f_v(v) = \lambda_v e^{-\lambda_v v}$, $f_k(k) = \lambda_k e^{-\lambda_k k}$ in which $\lambda_u = 1/(\varepsilon_0^2 \lambda_{SD}^2)$, $\lambda_v = 1/(\varepsilon_0^2 \varepsilon_1^2 a \lambda_{S1}^2)$, $\lambda_k = 1/(\varepsilon_0^2 \varepsilon_2^2 b \lambda_{S2}^2)$ and $u, v, k \geq 0$, are pdf's of r.v.'s u, v, k, correspondingly.

The pdf of $w=u+v$ is computed by using convolution theorem

$$f_{u+v}(w) = \int_0^w \lambda_u e^{-\lambda_u x_1} \lambda_v e^{-\lambda_v(w-x_1)} dx_1 = \frac{\lambda_u \lambda_v}{\lambda_u - \lambda_v}\left[e^{-\lambda_v w} - e^{-\lambda_u w}\right]$$

Then repeating that process, we can obtain the pdf of $\lambda = w+k$ as

$$\begin{aligned}f_\lambda(\lambda) &= f_{u+v}(\lambda) \circ f_k(\lambda) \\ &= \left[\frac{\lambda_u}{\lambda_u - \lambda_v}\lambda_v e^{-\lambda_v \lambda} - \frac{\lambda_v}{\lambda_u - \lambda_v}\lambda_u e^{-\lambda_u \lambda}\right] \circ \left(\lambda_k e^{-\lambda_k \lambda}\right) \\ &= \frac{\lambda_u \lambda_v \lambda_k \left[e^{-\lambda_k \lambda}(\lambda_u - \lambda_v) - e^{-\lambda_v \lambda}(\lambda_u - \lambda_k) + e^{-\lambda_u \lambda}(\lambda_v - \lambda_k)\right]}{(\lambda_u - \lambda_v)(\lambda_v - \lambda_k)(\lambda_u - \lambda_k)}\end{aligned} \qquad (13)$$

where $\circ$ is the convolution operator.

Finally, the pdf of γ given a and b is easily found as

$$f_{\gamma|a,b}(\gamma|a,b) = \frac{\sigma_n^2 \lambda_u \lambda_v \lambda_k}{(\lambda_u - \lambda_v)(\lambda_v - \lambda_k)(\lambda_u - \lambda_k)}\begin{bmatrix}e^{-\lambda_k \sigma_n^2 \lambda}(\lambda_u - \lambda_v) - \\ e^{-\lambda_v \sigma_n^2 \lambda}(\lambda_u - \lambda_k) + e^{-\lambda_u \sigma_n^2 \lambda}(\lambda_v - \lambda_k)\end{bmatrix}$$

Now we can calculate the average error probability as follows

$$P_{eAVG} = \int_0^\infty \int_0^\infty \left[\int_0^\infty P_e f_{\gamma|a,b}(\gamma|a,b) d\gamma\right] f_a(a) f_b(b) da db \qquad (14)$$

where the integral inside the square bracket can be reduced as

$$\int_0^\infty Q(\sqrt{2\gamma}) \sigma_n^2 \lambda_k e^{-\lambda_k \sigma_n^2 \lambda} \frac{\lambda_u \lambda_v}{(\lambda_u - \lambda_v)(\lambda_u - \lambda_k)} d\gamma - \int_0^\infty Q(\sqrt{2\gamma}) \sigma_n^2 \lambda_v e^{-\lambda_v \sigma_n^2 \lambda} \frac{\lambda_u \lambda_k}{(\lambda_u - \lambda_v)(\lambda_v - \lambda_k)} d\gamma$$

$$\int_0^\infty Q(\sqrt{2\gamma}) \sigma_n^2 \lambda_u e^{-\lambda_u \sigma_n^2 \lambda} \frac{\lambda_v \lambda_k}{(\lambda_u - \lambda_v)(\lambda_u - \lambda_k)} d\gamma$$

$$= \frac{\lambda_u \lambda_v}{2(\lambda_v - \lambda_k)(\lambda_u - \lambda_k)}\left[1 - \sqrt{\frac{1}{1+\sigma_n^2 \lambda_k}}\right] - \frac{\lambda_u \lambda_k}{2(\lambda_u - \lambda_v)(\lambda_v - \lambda_k)}\left[1 - \sqrt{\frac{1}{1+\sigma_n^2 \lambda_v}}\right] + \qquad (15)$$

$$\frac{\lambda_v \lambda_k}{2(\lambda_u - \lambda_v)(\lambda_u - \lambda_k)}\left[1 - \sqrt{\frac{1}{1+\sigma_n^2 \lambda_u}}\right]$$

By replacing the term in Eq. (15) into Eq. (14), we obtain the closed-form BER expression for the proposed cooperative transmission scheme. The integrals in Eq. (15) can be easily calculated by a numerical method [10].

For the case of non-cooperation (without relays), the average BER is given by [11]

$$P_{en\_avg} = \frac{1}{2}\left[1 - \sqrt{\frac{P_S \lambda_{SD}^2 / \sigma_{SD}^2}{1 + P_S \lambda_{SD}^2 / \sigma_{SD}^2}}\right] \qquad (16)$$

3 Numerical Results

In the presented results below, we set the noise variances equally as $\sigma_{SD}^2 = \sigma_{S1}^2 = \sigma_{S2}^2 = \sigma_D^2 = 1$. The x-axes of all figures represent the signal-to-noise ratio of the source which is defined as P_S / σ_{SD}^2. Additionally, Monte Carlo simulations are performed to verify the accuracy of the closed-form BER expression in Eq. (14).

For a fair comparison, it is essential that the total consumed energy of the cooperative system does not exceed that of corresponding direct transmission system. This is a strict and conservative constraint; allowing the relays to add additional power can then only increase the attractiveness of the cooperation. Therefore, complying this energy constraint requires $P_1 = P_2 = P_S/2$.

Fig. 2 compares the performance between direct transmission and the proposed cooperative transmission when the quality of user-destination channels is constant $\lambda_{1D}^2 = \lambda_{2D}^2 = \lambda_{SD}^2 = 1$ but that of inter-user channels changes $\lambda_{S1}^2 = \lambda_{S2}^2 = 0.5, 1, 2$. In this figure and those following, the numbers corresponding to the model in the legend box, for example, *Cooperation-Analysis:0.5* mean the performance of the cooperation strategy with respect to the varying parameters; specifically, $\lambda_{S1}^2 = \lambda_{S2}^2 = 0.5$ in this example. As shown in Fig. 2, the performance of the cooperation scheme slightly depends on the inter-user channels since the cooperative transmission must utilize them to achieve the spatial diversity and since using the intermediate nodes to forward the source signal also causes the noise amplification at those nodes. Nevertheless, under any their condition, the cooperation always outperforms non-cooperation and this benefit increases when the channel quality is better. For instance, at the target of BER 10^{-3} the cooperative transmission acquires SNR gains of about 8dB, 8.5dB, 8.7dB correspondingly to $\lambda_{S1}^2 = \lambda_{S2}^2 = 0.5, 1, 2$ relative to the direct transmission. Moreover, due to the steeper BER curves of the cooperation scheme than those of non-cooperation case, the further performance improvement can be yielded when the power of the source (or equivalently, *SNR*) increases. These illustrated results assert that using STBC in the distributed diversity way can also obtain all benefits of transmit diversity as for physically co-located antenna arrays. Furthermore, Fig. 2 also reveals that simulation results perfectly agree with analytical ones (using Eqs. (14)-(16)) and thus, the analysis is proved to be completely exact. As a consequence, only formulas in Eqs. (14)-(16) are used for evaluating the potentials of the cooperation scheme in enhancing the BER performance in comparison to non-cooperation scheme in the sequel.

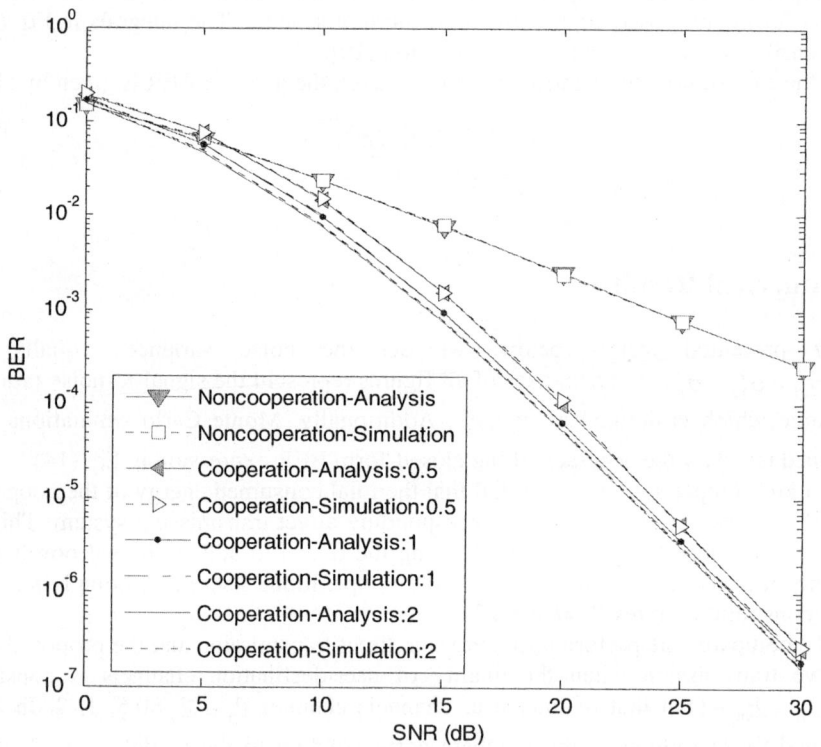

Fig. 2. BER performance via the fluctuation of inter-user channels

It is certain that the direct transmission (non-cooperation) can only obtain low error probability when the channel *S-D* is good. This is demonstrated in Fig. 3 where the fading variances of the user-destination channels vary $\lambda_{1D}^2 = \lambda_{2D}^2 = \lambda_{SD}^2 = 0.5, 1, 2$ while the others are unchanged $\lambda_{S1}^2 = \lambda_{S2}^2 = 1$. Compared to non-cooperation, the proposed cooperative transmission provides a performance benefit of about *8dB* for any value of $\lambda_{1D}^2 = \lambda_{2D}^2 = \lambda_{SD}^2$ at BER of 10^{-3} and this improvement further increases in the quality of user-destination channels. Moreover, the large diversity gain achieved from the cooperation significantly contributes to the performance enhancement as the *SNR* increases.

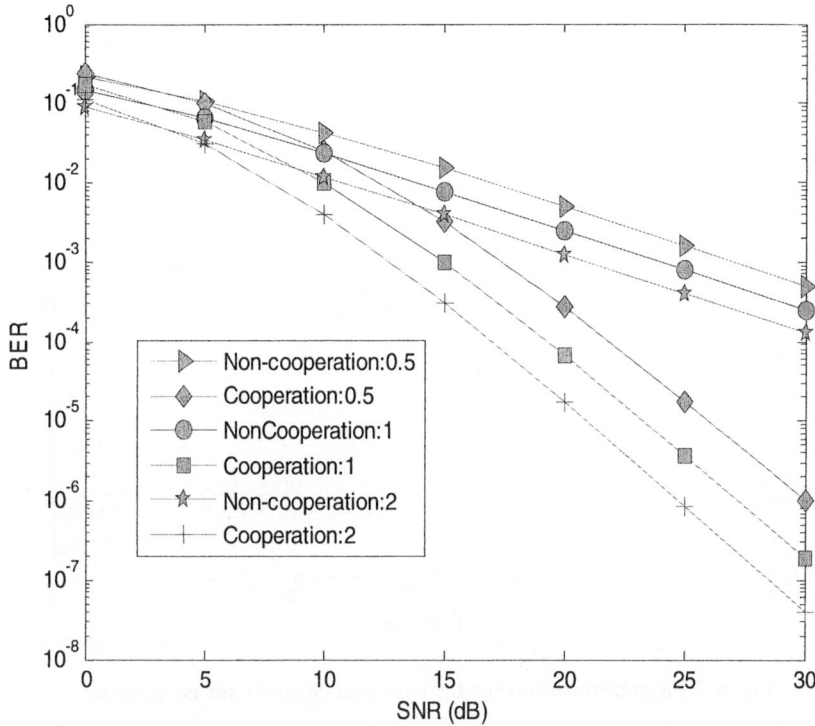

Fig. 3. BER performance via the variation of user-destination channels (the numbers in the legend box denote the values of $\lambda_{1D}^2 = \lambda_{2D}^2 = \lambda_{SD}^2$)

Fig. 4 investigates the impact of asymmetric inter-user channels on the performance of the cooperation. We consider this case by fixing the variances of user-destination channels $\lambda_{1D}^2 = \lambda_{2D}^2 = \lambda_{SD}^2 = 1$ and that of *source-relay 1* channel $\lambda_{S1}^2 = 1$ while changing the quality of *source-relay 2* channel λ_{S2}^2 from 0.5 to 2. Therefore, the numbers in the legend box denote the values of λ_{S2}^2. This figure shows that the cooperative transmission is very robust to the changes of inter-user channels. Specifically, when the source signal experiences the deep fade four times (λ_{S2}^2 from 2 down to 0.5), the performance degradation is just around 0.1dB for any value of *SNR*.

The asymmetry of all possible propagation paths in the cooperative wireless networks is examined in which only λ_{S2}^2 changes from 0.5 to 2 while the others are constant $\lambda_{1D}^2 = 0.5$, $\lambda_{SD}^2 = 1$, $\lambda_{2D}^2 = 2$, $\lambda_{S1}^2 = 1$. The numerical result is depicted in Fig. 5 where the numbers represent the values of λ_{S2}^2. It is recognized that the performance degradation of the cooperation is negligible (less than 0.4dB for any value of *SNR* and λ_{S2}^2). Therefore, the cooperation brings a considerable benefit in combating the adverse effects of fading channels.

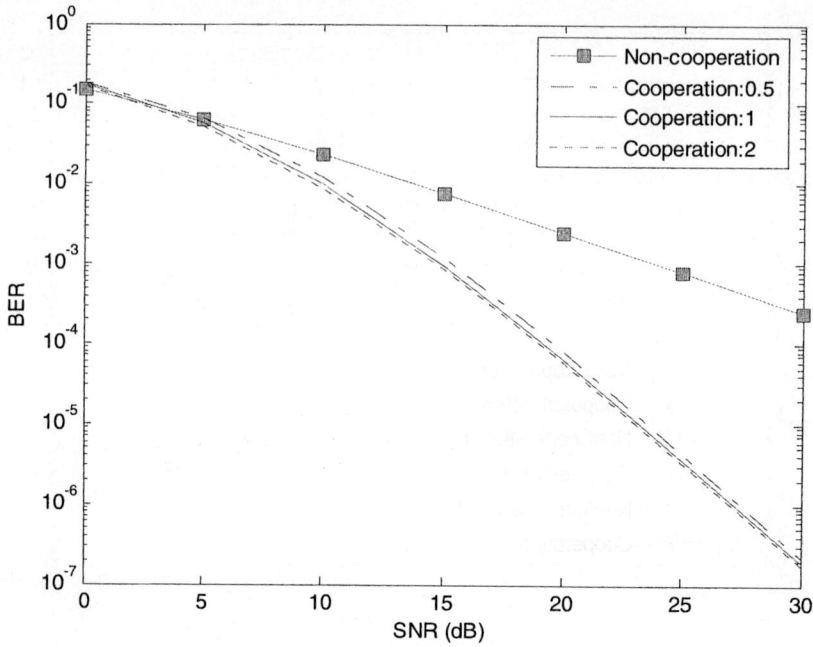

Fig. 4. BER performance when the inter-user channels are asymmetric

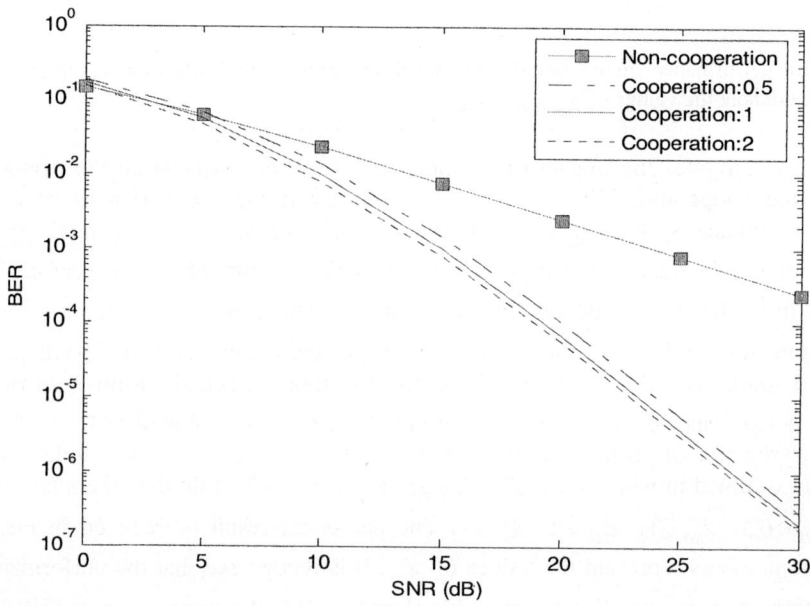

Fig. 5. BER performance when the user-destination and inter-user channels are asymmetric

4 Conclusion

Performance analysis of STBC with rate ¾ in the cooperative transmission scenario was presented and its closed-form error probability expression was also derived. Under the Rayleigh fading channel plus Gaussian noise, the numerical results demonstrate that the proposed cooperation considerably improves the performance over the non-cooperation regardless of the faded noisy inter-user channels. Moreover, the receiver structure with ML detector can be implemented with negligible hardware complexity. Therefore, deploying STBCs in the distributed diversity manner is feasible and is a promising technique for the future wireless networks where there exist idle users to take advantage of system resources efficiently.

Acknowledgement

This work was supported by grant No. (R01-2005-000-10902-0) from Korea Science and Engineering Foundation in Ministry of Science &Technology.

References

1. Branka Vucetic, Jinhong Yuan, "Space-Time Coding", John Wiley & Sons Ltd, 2003.
2. Aria Nosratinia, Todd E. Hunter, "Cooperative Communication in Wireless Networks", IEEE Communications Magazine, Vol. 42, pp. 74-80, Oct. 2004.
3. A. Sendonaris, E. Erkip, B. Aazhang, "User cooperation diversity. Part I-II", IEEE Trans on Communications, Vol. 51, pp. 1927-1948, Nov. 2003.
4. J. N. Laneman and G. W. Wornell, "Distributed space-time-coded protocols for exploiting cooperative diversity in wireless networks," *IEEE Trans. Inf. Theory*, vol. 49, no. 10, pp. 2415 – 2425, Oct. 2003.
5. Zinan Lin, E. Erkip, A. Stefanov, "Cooperative regions for coded cooperative systems", GLOBECOM' 04, IEEE, Vol. 1, pp. 21 - 25, 29 Nov.-3 Dec. 2004.
6. S.M. Alamouti, "A simple transmit diversity technique for wireless communications", IEEE Trans on Communications, Vol. 16, p. 1451–1458, Oct. 1998.
7. Xiaohua Li, "Energy efficient wireless sensor networks with transmission diversity", Electronics Letters, Vol. 39, pp. 1753–1755, 27 Nov. 2003.
8. P.A Anghel, G. Leus, M. Kavehl, "Multi-user space-time coding in cooperative networks", ICASSP 2003, Vol. 4, p. 73-76, April 2003.
9. R.U. Nabar; F.W. Kneubuhler; H. Bolcskei, "Performance limits of amplify-and-forward based fading relay channels", ICASSP 2004, Vol. 4, p. iv-565 - iv-568, 17-21 May 2004.
10. Marvin K. Simon, and Mohamed-Slim Alouini, "Digital Communication over Fading Channels", Second Edition, John Wiley & Sons, Inc, 2005.
11. John G. Proakis, "Digital communications", Fourth Edition, McGraw-Hill, 2001.

Downlink Packet Scheduling Based on Channel Condition for Multimedia Services of Mobile Users in OFDMA-TDD

Ryong Oh[1], Se-Jin Kim[1], Hyong-Woo Lee[2], and Choong-Ho Cho[1]

[1] Korea Univ. Dept. of Computer & Information Science
{orionpia, kimsejin, chcho}@korea.ac.kr
[2] Korea Univ. Dept. of Electronics & Information Engineering
hwlee@korea.ac.kr

Abstract. In this paper, we propose a Wireless Class Based Flexible Queueing (WCBFQ) which is an improved packet scheduling with QoS management based on wireless networks using OFDMA-TDD with adaptive modulation. Under time-varying channel condition, scheduler tries to guarantee required throughput demand for real-time traffic by allocating more channel time to the users in poor channel condition. On the other hand, for non-real time traffic, the scheduler gives lower priority to those experiencing poor channel conditions thereby favoring those having better channel for increased overall system throughput. Simulations are performed to demonstrate the effectiveness of the proposed scheme.

1 Introduction

In the future, broadband wireless networks will be an integral part of the global communication infrastructure. With rapid growth in popularity of wireless data services and increasing demand for multimedia applications, it is expected that future wireless networks will provide services for heterogeneous classes of traffic with different quality of service (QoS) requirements.

Although many mature scheduling algorithms are available for wired networks, they are not directly applicable in wireless networks because of special problems related to time-varying nature of wireless links. The characteristics of wireless communication pose special problems that do not exist in wireline networks. These include: 1) high error rate and bursty errors; 2) location-dependent and time-varying wireless link capacity; 3) scarce bandwidth; 4) user mobility; and 5) power constraint of the mobile hosts. All of the above characteristics make developing efficient and effective scheduling algorithms for wireless networks very challenging [1].

In this paper, we propose a packet scheduling scheme that uses the available radio resource more efficiently while satisfying QoS requirements for multimedia traffic flows. The proposed scheme uses a information such as channel status of mobiles, buffer size of queues, and delay latency. This paper proposes a WCBFQ and Adaptive-WCBFQ which enables flexible tradeoff between delay and throughput of voice traffic as well as data traffic.

The remainder of the paper is organized as follows. Section 2 introduces models for wireless channel, user mobility, and traffic used in the paper. Then section 3 describes in detail our scheduling algorithm and section 4 evaluates the performance of the proposed scheme. Finally, section 5 concludes with a discussion of future studies.

2 Wireless System Model

2.1 Wireless Channel Model

The wireless channel considered in this paper consists of one base station and K wireless terminals or K users. It is assumed that the base station serves the users in a time division fashion, and that the users are distributed uniformly over the cell area with radius R. Each user is dedicated to one or more sessions belonging to one of traffic classes. Under the assumption that the wireless channel of each user is fixed during a scheduling interval, the channel to be described later in this section $H_k(t)$ between the base station and the kth user at the tth scheduling instant may be expressed as [2]

$$H_k(t) = \sqrt{H_k^P(t) \cdot H_k^S(t)} \tag{1}$$

where the path loss is given as $H_k^P(t) = C(\max(r_k(t), r_0))^{-\alpha}$, $C = 10^{-2.86}$ is a constant, $r_k(t)$ is the distance between the base station and the kth user, r_0 is the reference distance, and α is the path loss exponent. The log-normal shadow fading is represented as $H_k^S(t) = 10^{X_k(t)/10}$, where $X_k(t)$ is a zero-mean Gaussian random process with variance σ_S^2. The correlation of shadow fading between two subsequent scheduling instants is modeled using a first-order autoregressive process as $X_k(t) = \rho(d) \cdot X_k(t-1) + \sqrt{1 - \rho^2(d)} \cdot X'$, where X' is an independently generated zero-mean Gaussian random variable with variance of σ_S^2, $\rho(d_k) = \exp(-d_k \ln 2 / d_{\text{cor}})$ denotes the normalized correlation between $X_k(t-1)$ and $X_k(t)$, d_k is the moving distance of the user between the $(t-1)$th and tth scheduling instants, and d_{cor} is defined as the correlation distance of shadow fading [3]. For simplicity, the multipath fading is not considered in this paper.

2.2 Mobility Model

To perform analysis in a mobile environment, we also need to model mobility of the users. This is important for the analysis of throughput and mean delay according to distance, which determins the service rate for users. There are different models for capturing user mobility, such as the fluid model, the Markov model, and user tracking models [4].

In this paper, we use Gauss-Markov model, in which mobile users move randomly in a cell and the variation of the direction and speed of the mobiles is based on Gaussian probability density function [5]. It is proposed that while the mobility patterns are granularly tracked, the modeling parameters can be dynamically adjusted according to the variations observed in the actual movement characteristics. The main merit of applying a Gauss-Markov distribution is its flexibility to control prediction accuracy by adjusting the information feedback frequency.

2.3 Traffic Model

We split up traffic into four types : conversational [6], streaming [7], interactive [8], and background [9] classes. Conversational and streaming classes are real-time traffic flows such as voice and video. Since these traffic classes are delay sensitive, we need to provide sufficient channel resources regardless of users channel conditions. Interactive and background classes are non-real-time traffic flows such as WWW and email. These two classes allow relatively large delay compared with the conversational and streaming classes, but require integrity of information contents. Our scheduling scheme treats all of the traffic classes accordingly to their QoS requirements [10] in an appropriate manner.

3 Proposed Packet Scheduling Scheme with QoS Management

In Section 3.1, an efficient scheduling scheme is introduced based on the wireless class-based flexible queueing (WCBFQ). In Section 3.2, we show another scheduling scheme Adaptive-WCBFQ which is a modification of WCBFQ. Both schemes are proposed for high throughput while satisfy delay constraints of real-time traffic.

3.1 Proposed Packet Scheduling Scheme

The wireless class-based flexible queueing (WCBFQ) algorithm as shown in Fig.1 is a scheduling scheme created to support multiple traffic classes in wireless IP networks, (i.e, conversational, streaming, interactive, and background classes). It should be applied at wireless access points [11]. Our goal of the scheduling algorithm is to take into consideration the high BER in the wireless environment. BER is flow-specific due to the different location of single users and the different states of the air interface. Location-dependent errors are more likely to be expected than uniformly distributed errors over the whole bandwidth of the cell. In such conditions we have to satisfy guaranteed services when they are experiencing high error rate by increasing their share of the bandwidth. On the other hand, it is not desirable to allow flows in the error state to decrease significantly the performances of the entire wireless link.

The base station assigns the traffic flow a channel according to a hierarchy of priorities. The first differentiation of the traffic into two main classes is: real-time traffic class with absolute bandwidth guarantees, and non-real-time class with low error rates. Real-time traffic class consists of conversational and streaming class that each class has its own queue; Non-real-time class also consists of interactive and background classes which have user-based queues. Our scheme tries to

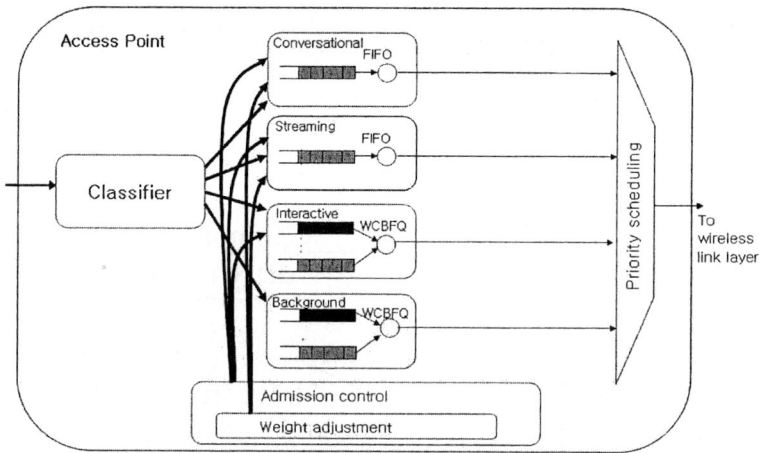

Fig. 1. Model of WCBFQ Scheduler

guarantee QoS of real-time traffic flows firstly because the disconnection of the real-time traffic gives more dissatisfaction to people than non-real-time services.

The conversational class that has strict demands on network delay should have high-priority and the packet belonging to the conversational class will be first served until the buffer for this class is emptied. Streaming is secondly assigned. The assignment of resource for interactive class depends on the channel status of mobiles. Among interactive users, we give higher priority to those under better channel condtions. In order to maintain a certain level of BER performance, those in a poorer channel conditions use more robust modulation and error correction thereby reducing throughput. This class does not have strict demands for delay but it requires low error rates. Background class is served when all the other class buffers are emptied. In short, the scheduler assigns wireless resources orderly like conversational, streaming, interactive, and background.

3.2 Adaptive WCBFQ

When conversational traffic is served, service rate of a slot is determined by channel status. We assume that channel time is divided into contiguous slots of fixed size. Due to variable transmission rate, some of the slots are not fully utilized depending on the channel condition of the users.

After the performance analysis of WCBFQ, we noticied that there is empty space in a slot which is for conversational traffic. This space is just wasted and as a result the more conversational traffic, the bigger wasted channel space. Thus we propose another scheme for conversational traffic only. The algorithm is in Fig.2. Before conversational traffic is served, scheduler makes a decision according to the above algorithm. If RSS(Required Slot Size) which is data size for serving conversation traffic can fill 4/5 of a slot, conversational traffic is served immediately in the current frame. But conversational traffic is lower than 4/5, it is delayed and served with next conversational traffic. In simulation, we delay the conversational

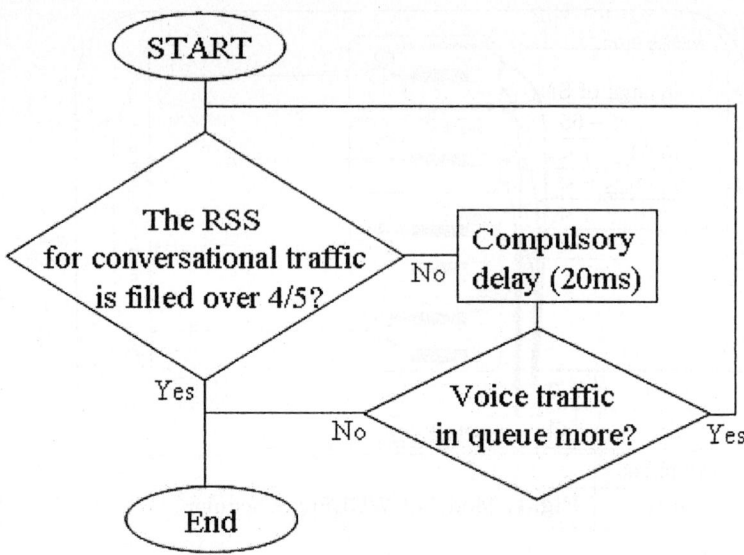

Fig. 2. Algorithmic implementation of A-WCBFQ

traffic 20ms. If more than a slot is used for conversational traffic, this algorithm is applicable for the last slot only. Maximum-delay time depends on the QoS parameter of conversational traffic so scheduler ensures that the sum of delay is within the specified maximum delay. Besides, there is no more conversational traffic arrival after several frames, scheduler recognized that on-period is finished and services delayed conversational traffic. This algorithm can reduce wasted slot for conversational traffic. Simulation results are given in the next section.

4 Performance Evaluation

4.1 Simulation Environment

A simulator is constructed using C++ language. We assume that mobiles can move in a cell only. The cell radius is 1 km and mobiles move in the cell with the average speed of 40km/h. If a mobile could move out of a cell, the direction is changed 180° so that the mobile remains in the cell. OFDMA-TDD is used for multimedia traffic and frame length is 5ms. A frame consists of 12 sub-channels and 8 symbols so the number of total slots is 96. A cell is divided into 5 zones and service rate for users are different. Table 1 shows the parameters for each zone. The service rate is determined by the range of SNR(γ) which is from the channel modeling in section 2.1. Under environments above, this section performances and analyzes the proposed scheme. QoS parameter is shown in Table.2

4.2 Traffic Models

For the conversational class, we adopt the ON/OFF voice traffic model with exponentially distributed ON/OFF durations[6]. The mean durations of ON and

Table 1. Modulation Scheme with channel status

Range of SNR(γ)	Service level	Service rate (bytes)
$\gamma < -65.94$	1	16
$-65.94 \leq \gamma < -64.85$	2	24
$-64.85 \leq \gamma < -63.31$	3	32
$-63.31 \leq \gamma < -60.68$	4	40
$-60.68 \leq \gamma$	5	48

Table 2. QoS Parameter

Service	Traffic Class	Real Time	Loss	Delay
Voice	Conversational	Yes	< 3%	< 80ms
Videophone	Streaming	Yes	< 1%	< 150 ms
WWW	Interactive	No	0	8~10 seconds
E-mail	Background	No	0	Variable

OFF periods are set to 1.0 sec and 1.35 sec, respectively. During each ON period, voice data is generated at a fixed rate of 13Kbps and transmitted in a 20ms cycle. For the streaming class, Autoregressive model[7] whics is suitable for video-telephony is adopted. There is no OFF period after initial video frames are generated. The size of video frame is modeled using a autoregressive distribution. We use the web browsing traffic model[8] as the interactive class. There is a ON, OFF period. If we divide ON period in detail, there is a parsing time, embedded object. OFF period is a reading time. Finally, we use a email traffic model[9] for the background class. The file size of email is modeled using a Truncated Pareto distribution.

4.3 Mobility Model

Fig.3 shows an example trace of a user using Gauss-Markov modeling. We assumes that the cell radius is 1 km and mobiles move in the cell with the average speed of 40 km/h. If a mobile could move out of a cell, the direction is changed 180°.

4.4 Total Throughput

In Fig. 4, total throughput of the proposed packet scheduling scheme(WCBFQ) is compared with that of the FIFO, WFQ, APQ. The graph lines are ordered WCBFQ, APQ, WFQ, FIFO. But APQ and WCBFQ are nearly the same. FIFO uses one queue so real-time traffic is dropped such as conversational and streaming traffic as increasing the number of users. WFQ has four queues for each traffic data. Voice traffic of WFQ has high priority and the second priority is both conversational and streaming traffic. It also has weights between two traffics so that

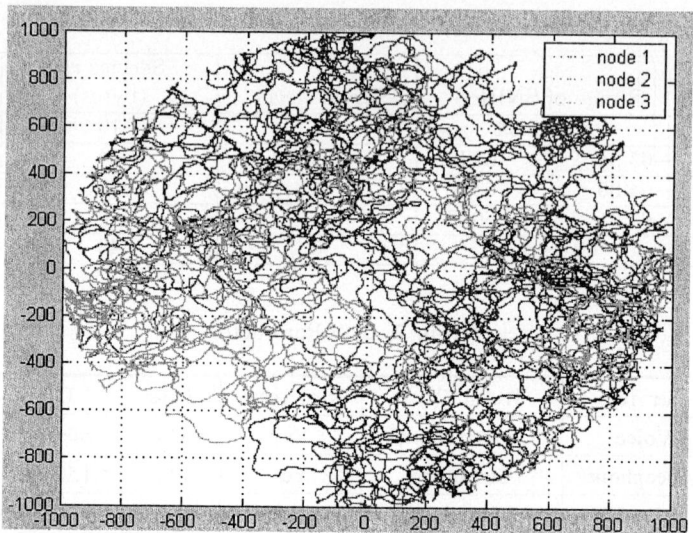

Fig. 3. Mobility simulation

streaming traffic can be dropped when the number of users is bigger. APQ has four queues, each traffic has its own queue and the priority is ordered conversational, streaming, interactive and background. We already described WCBFQ structure. The graph lines of APQ and WCBFQ are almost the same but web delay is different. We will see the performance result later.

4.5 Mean Real-Time Delay

In Fig.5, we examine the delay of real-time traffic such as conversational and streaming traffic as we increase the number of users.

All scheduling scheme give high priority for conversational traffic except FIFO. Thus there is no streaming delay or packet loss for the three schemes. It is reliable that conversational traffic gets high priority because conversational traffic size is normally small and when people get disconnected service, they have more dissatisfaction than other traffic services. Streaming traffic is delayed and dropped with WFQ only among the three schemes except FIFO. When the number of user is 150, streaming traffic of WFQ starts to experience delay. Total throughput of WFQ is a little lower than APQ, WCBFQ in Fig.5 because streaming traffic is dropped. Conversational and streaming traffic of FIFO experience lost packets even with a relatively small number of users. In short, we know that there is no delay and little packet loss with the WCBFQ and APQ as we see in Fig.5.

4.6 Mean Interactive Delay

In Fig.6, we observe the mean delay for interactive traffic as we increase utilization for each scheme. The mean interactive delay of FIFO is lower than that

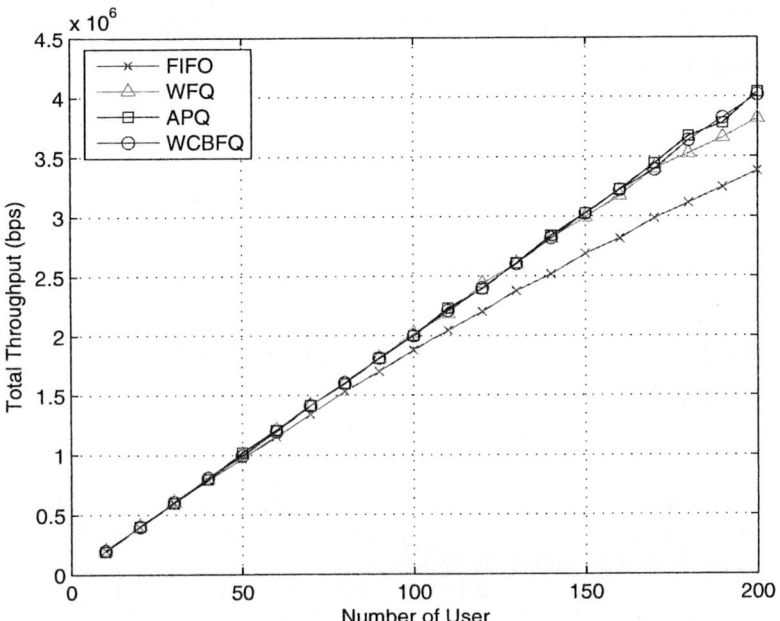

Fig. 4. Total Throughput

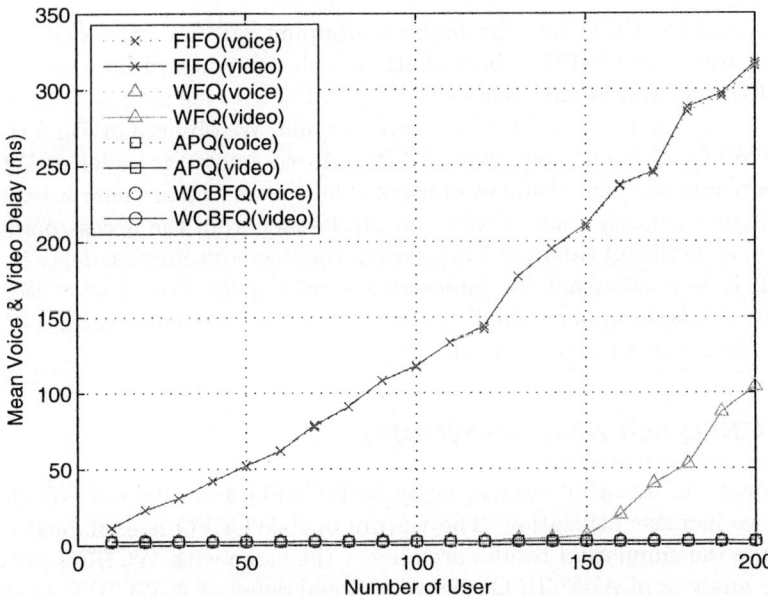

Fig. 5. Mean Real-time Traffic Delay

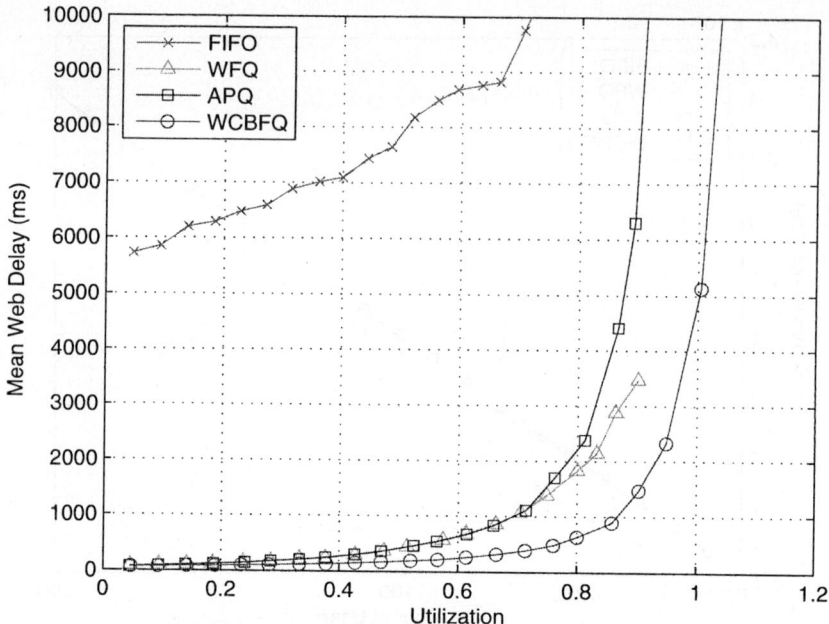

Fig. 6. Mean Interactive Delay

of others because FIFO has the highest dropping rate for conversational and streaming traffic and FIFO is best effort so web delay is still high as we see in Fig.6 WFQ shows streaming delay and drop in Fig.5 so the assigned resource for streaming traffic can be used for interactive traffic. We observe in Fig.5 that the result of WFQ is better than that of APQ. As we know the order of WCBFQ service depends on channel status of users. Thus users who are near access point can get higher priority than others who are farther from the access point. The utilization of WCBFQ can over 1 only when the mean interactive delay is about 5 second. It is known that for interactive service delay over 4 or 8 second in wired network is an upper bound, but we cautiously say that 5 second of delay is not too bad a in wireless network.

4.7 WCBFQ and Adaptive-WCBFQ

We compare the mean interactive delay of WCBFQ and adaptive WCBFQ in Fig.7 as we increase utilization. The feature of A-WCBFQ is explained before. We observe the simulation results are almost the same with WCBFQ after performance analysis of A-WCBFQ. Conversational delay of A-WCBFQ is slightly worse than that of WCBFQ. However, mean conversational delay is much lower than that prescribed for conversational QoS parameter. In Fig.8, the jitter of conversational traffic flow is seen to increase a little. A-WCBFQ can save channel resources at the cost of increased delay. The saved resource is used for interactive

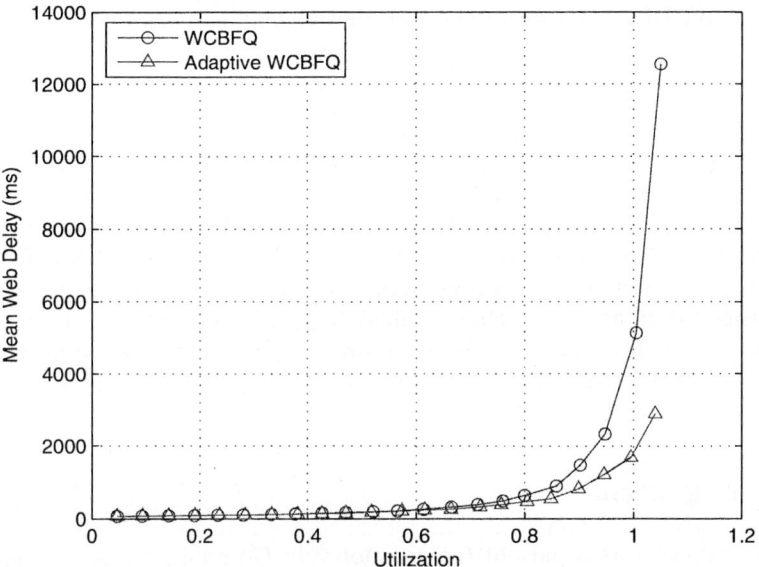

Fig. 7. WCBFQ and A-WCBFQ

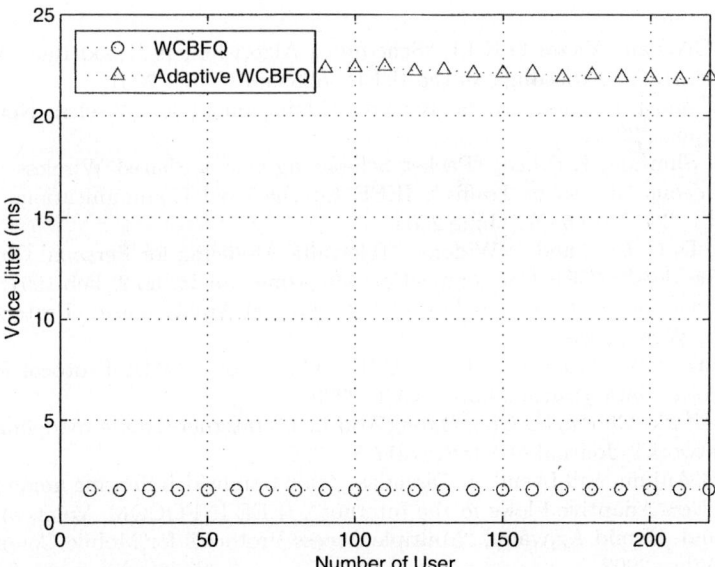

Fig. 8. Jitter

traffic. This implies that interactive traffic of A-WCBFQ can be better served than that of WCBFQ, and as a result interactive traffic delay decreases.

5 Conclusion

This paper has proposed an effective packet scheduling scheme for multimedia traffic for wireless networks. Using realistic traffic, mobility, and channel models and we have shown the proposed scheme is efficient in terms of throughput and delay. Although the proposed scheduler mainly guarantees real-time traffic flows, the simulation results show excellent performance of interactive traffic as well. We also proposed an adaptive scheme called Adaptive-WCBFQ which results in tradeoff between delay and throughput of voice traffic. Future research includes combining the proposed scheme with prediction of mobiles for more efficient channel utilization and treatment of handoff problem.

Acknowledgement

This work was done as a part of Information adn Communication Fundamental Technology Research Program supported by Ministry of Information and Communication in Republic of Korea.

References

1. YAXIN CAO and Victor O.K.LI, "Scheduling Algorithms in Broad-Band Wireless Networks", IEEE Procedings of the IEEE,vol.89,no.1, Jan. 2001.
2. J.Zander and S.L. Kim, "Radio Resource Management for Wireless Networks", Artech House, 2001.
3. Oh-Soon Shin and K.B.Lee, "Packet Scheduling over a Shared Wireless Link for Heterogeneous Classes of Traffic", IEEE International Communications Conference, vol.1, 20-24 pp.58-62, June.2004.
4. Lam, D., D. C. Cox, and J. Widom, "Teletraffic Modeling for Personal Communications Services", IEEE Communication Magazine, vol.35, no.2, Feb.1997.
5. Abbas Jamalipour, "The Wireless mobile Internet:Architectures, Protocols and Services", Wiley, 2003
6. Wonkwang Baik, Hyong woo Lee, "A Hybrid CDMA/TDMA Protocol for Integrated Voice/Data Transmission" JCCI, 2000.
7. Hyekeun Park, Choongho Cho, HyongWoo Lee, "Internet-Traffic modeling in the access network", Journal of KISS, vol17-3, 1999.
8. Farooq M.Anjum, and Leandros Tassiulas, "Fair Bandwidth Sharing among Adaptive and Non-Adaptive Flows in the Internet", IEEE INFOCOM, Vol.3, Mar.1999
9. Alex Brand, Hamid Aghvami, "Multiple Access Protocols for Mobile Communications", Willey,2002
10. "QoS concept and architecture", 3rd Generation Partnership Project (3GPP), TS23.107, V5.0.
11. Toni Janevski, "Traffic Analysis and Design of Wireless IP networks", Artech House,2003.

An Efficient Channel Tracking Method for OFDM Based High Mobility Wireless Multimedia System

Kwanghoon Kim, Haelyong Kim, and Hyuncheol Park

School of Engineering, Information and Communications University (ICU),
P.O.Box77, Yuseong, Daejeon, 305-732, Korea
{hoon0217, seamirr, hpark}@icu.ac.kr

Abstract. Preamble based channel estimation is widely used in OFDM based wireless multimedia system. However, the channel response varies significantly during one transmission packet due to high mobility. We propose new channel estimation method that tracks the channel variation along the time. We take advantage of the pilots occupied for the phase tracking to catch the variation of the channel responses with slightly modified pilot structure. For the accurate channel tracking, the variation trend of the channel is examined by correlation analysis. In here, we see the linear channel variation and so we use the linear interpolation for channel tracking. Without loss of data rate, the method reduces the error floor of bit error rate (BER) dramatically. Simulation results demonstrate the capability of the proposed channel tracking scheme even though the Doppler shift is very large. Moreover, the proposed method shows more competitive performance in convolutional coded systems used in many wireless multimedia application like IEEE 802.11a.

1 Introduction

Orthogonal frequency division multiplexing (OFDM) is the most popular promise for the future high data rate wireless multimedia communication system for its advantages in high-bit-rate transmission over dispersive channel. However, in order to achieve highly spectral efficiency, it is necessary to employ multi-level modulation scheme with non-constant amplitude (e.g., 16-QAM). They require the coherent demodulation that needs to estimate the parameters of fading channel. For this purpose, there are many literatures (see [1]-[3] and the references therein) to achieve a reliable channel estimation with low computational complexity.

The mainstream of recent wireless systems is concentrated on the high mobility system for seamless ubiquitous multimedia services. However, the previous channel estimation methods for OFDM based wireless access system like IEEE 802.11a do not follow the large Doppler shift due to mobility. As a result, the estimated channel can be considerably different to the actual channel of symbols located far away from preamble.

For the sake of mitigating the estimation error, the periodic channel estimation is proposed in [4]. The method estimates the channel frequency response periodically by generating the reference data from received OFDM symbols. With the generated reference data, it uses the time average for the purpose of high estimation accuracy. In addition, the time average with relative magnitude constraint and harmonic average are proposed in [5]. However, these methods can have significant error propagation if the generated reference data are not correct.

In this paper, we propose the channel tracking method without generating the reference data from received data. Instead, we focus on the pilots that occupied for phase tracking since they do not make the error propagation because they are perfectly known in the receiver. By taking the correlation analysis, we verify the linear variation of channel frequency response. The Pearson-correlation-coefficient is adopted to quantify the linear trend. From this verification, the linear interpolation is selected for the channel tracking. For the interpolation, we slightly modify the pilot structure without additional redundancy.

The rest of paper is organized as follows. The next section describes the basic system model and conventional channel estimation for the OFDM wireless access system. We verify the linear variation of channel and propose the channel tracking method that consists of pilot design and linear interpolation in Section 3. Section 4 shows the simulation results that make sure the superior performance of our channel tracking scheme. We conclude this paper in Section 5.

2 System Model and Conventional Channel Estimation

2.1 System Model

We will consider the system depicted in Fig. 1 that consists of N subcarriers. The OFDM transmitter uses an inverse discrete Fourier transform (IDFT) of size N for modulation. Then the transmitted OFDM signal in discrete-time domain can be expressed as:

$$x[t,n] = \frac{1}{N}\sum_{k=0}^{N-1} X[k,n] \exp\left(j2\pi\frac{tk}{N}\right), \quad 0 \leq t \leq N-1 \qquad (1)$$

where t is the time domain sample index of an OFDM signal and n is the order of an OFDM symbol. In order to avoid inter-symbol interference caused by multipath environments and inter-carrier interference, a cyclic prefix (CP) is appended to the OFDM symbol. After passing through a multipath channel and removing the CP, one received discreat time domain OFDM signal $y[t,n]$ is represented by the function of the transmitted signal, the channel transfer function and noise:

$$y[t,n] = x[t,n] \otimes h[t,n] + w[t,n], \quad 0 \leq t \leq N-1 \qquad (2)$$

where $\otimes$ denotes cyclic convolutional operation, $w[t,n]$ is independent and identically distributed additive white Gaussian noise (AWGN) sample in time domain

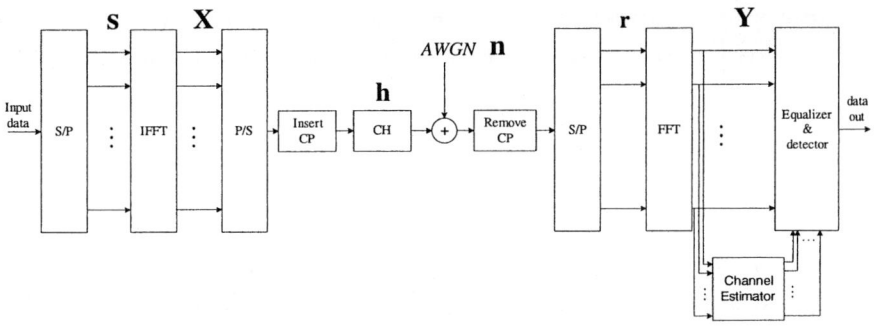

Fig. 1. Base-band OFDM system

with zero mean and variance $\sigma_{wt}{}^2 = E\left[|w[n]|^2\right]$ and $h[t,n]$ is the discrete time channel impulse response given by:

$$h[t,n] = \sum_{l=0}^{L-1} \alpha_l^n \delta[t-l] \quad (3)$$

where α_l^n represents the different path complex gain that is wide-sense stationary (WSS) narrow-band complex Gaussian process, l is the index of the different path delay that is based on sampling time interval that means there is no channel power loss caused by sampling time miss-match [6], and L is index of the maximum channel delay tap. At the receiver, we assume that the guard interval is longer than the maximum channel delay tap and the synchronization is perfect. Then, the k-th subcarrier output in frequency domain can be represented by:

$$Y[k,n] = X[k,n]H[k,n] + W[k,n], \quad 0 \leq k \leq N-1 \quad (4)$$

where $W[k,n]$ is AWGN samples in frequency domain with zero mean and variance $\sigma_{wf}^2 = N\sigma_{wt}^2$ [7], and $H[k,n]$ is the channel frequency response given by:

$$H[k,n] = \sum_{l=0}^{L-1} \alpha_l^n \exp\left(-j2\pi\frac{kl}{N}\right), \quad 0 \leq k \leq N-1. \quad (5)$$

2.2 Channel Estimation

The OFDM based wireless multimedia system conventionally uses the pilot-symbol-aided (PSA) channel estimations that take advantage of known OFDM symbols called channel estimation (CE) symbols included in preamble. Let N_{ce} is the number of CE symbols and $\hat{H}[k,0]$ is the kth estimated sub-channel frequency response of CE symbols. Then, it can be obtained as

$$\hat{H}[k,0] = \frac{1}{N_{cc}} \sum_{l=1}^{N_{ce}} \frac{Y_{ce}[k,l]}{X_{cc}[k,l]}, \quad 0 \leq k \leq N-1 \quad (6)$$

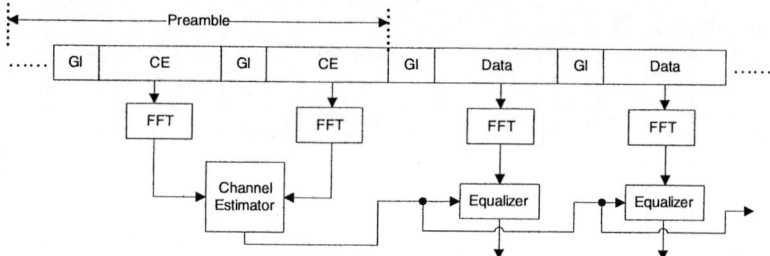

Fig. 2. Process of conventional channel estimation using preamble

where $Y_{ce}[w,l]$ and $X_{ce}[w,l]$ denote the received subcarrier data and know CE data, respectively and this channel estimation method is called the Least square (LS) estimation [8]. Consequent equalized data are achieved by compensating with same response $\hat{H}[w,0]$, and expressed as following equation:

$$X_{eq}[w,n] = \frac{Y[w,n]}{\hat{H}[w,0]} \quad (7)$$

Since the same estimated channel response is used for all OFDM symbols equalization in one transmission packet as shown in Fig. 2, the estimated error becomes significantly large as the index of OFDM symbol increases even if the estimated response of preamble is very accurate. Furthermore, when the time selectivity grows higher, the difference between preamble and data is more severe. Consequently the overall performance can be significantly degraded.

3 Modified Pilot Design and Channel Tracking

3.1 Channel Variation

For the new pilot design and channel tracking, channel frequency response variation should be investigated. First, we execute the correlation analysis of channel frequency response against the symbol time during one transmission packet according to the increase of normalized Doppler frequency $f_d T_s$. In the experiment, we use the exponential decay channel models, where the maximum delay spread is the half of guard interval of OFDM symbol. We calculate the Pearson-correlation-coefficient [9] for each sub-channel that is usually used for verifying the strength of the linear relationship between two variables and expressed as:

$$r = \frac{\sum XY - \frac{\sum X \sum Y}{N}}{\sqrt{(\sum X^2 - \frac{\sum X^2}{N})(\sum Y^2 - \frac{\sum Y^2}{N})}} \quad (8)$$

If two variables have perfect linear relationship, the coefficient r will be ± 1 according as the relation is positive or negative. At other case, r is always from -1 to 1. Since the variation of phase can be compensated by phase tracking, we just consider the variation of amplitude.

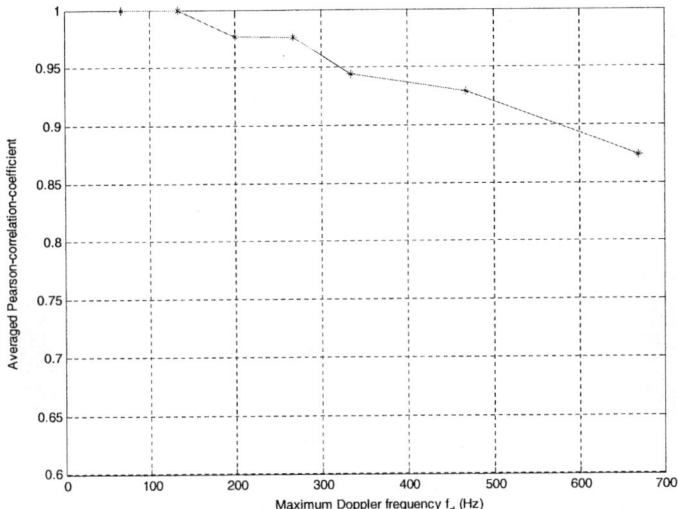

Fig. 3. Averaged Pearson-correlation-coefficient over 1024 bytes/packet data transmissions

Since the linear trend of channel variation is only considered, we take the absolute value of the coefficient of each sub-channel and average it. Fig. 3. shows the averaged Pearson-correlation-coefficient of channel frequency response over various Doppler frequencies from 0 to 670 Hz. Since the averaged-Pearson-correlation-coefficient exceeds 0.9 when the maximum Doppler frequency is 500 Hz, the linear variation model of channel frequency responses is reasonable.

3.2 Proposed Pilot Design

The above linear channel variation over several OFDM symbols makes the possibility of accurate channel tracking by using linear interpolation between the far apart pilots. However, the conventional pilot design of wireless access system like IEEE 802.11a cannot support any channel tracking using them because their positions are fixed for all OFDM symbols [10]. So we slightly modify the pilot design that fits the channel tracking without any redundancy. For the purpose of linear interpolation between sub-channels, we periodically change the pilot position as the order of OFDM symbol increases. Let N is the number of data subcarrier and N_p is the number of pilots. Without losses of generality, the number of data subcarrier is equal to the number of total subcarrier and the number of pilots is a divisor of the number of data subcarrier. If $p_{(k,n)}$ is the position of the $(k+1)$th pilot for nth OFDM symbol and the pilots are equi-spaced within each OFDM symbol, the $(k+1)$th pilot position of t-apart OFDM symbol is

$$p_{(k,n+t)} = (p_{(k,n)} + t)_{\frac{N}{N_p}} + \frac{N}{N_p}k, \quad 0 \leq k \leq N_p - 1 \qquad (9)$$

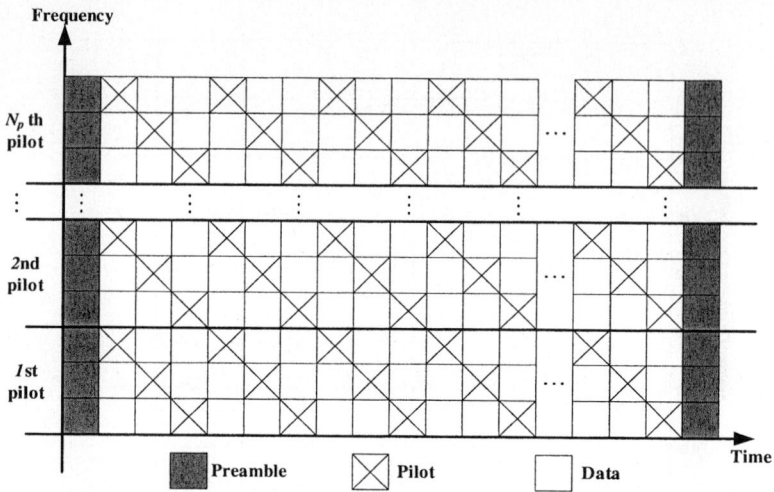

Fig. 4. Modified preamble and pilot structure for channel tracking

where $(\cdot)_N$ represents cyclic shift in the base of N. Then, the position of pilot is cyclicly repeated with a period $\frac{N}{N_p}$. Fig. 4. shows the consequent pilot structure of this modification in time-frequency grid. To maintain equal data rates, the one preamble is shifted in the last of the transmitted packet.

3.3 Channel Tracking

With this pilot and preamble structure, the channel frequency response is periodically updated as shown in Fig 5. From previous notations, let $\hat{H}[w,n]$ is the estimated frequency response of $(w+1)-th$ sub-channel for the n-th OFDM symbol. If w is $p_{(k,n)}$, it is the estimated channel response of that pilot position. The channel estimation of pilot position is another challenging topic, which is beyond the scope of this paper. Since we see the linear variation of each sub-channel, the channel estimation of data position can be achieved by using two consecutive $\frac{N}{N_p}$ spacing estimated pilot responses. Let the two consecutive pilot responses are $\hat{H}[p_{(k,n)}, n]$ and $\hat{H}[p_{(k,n)}, n+\frac{N}{N_p}]$ since $p_{(k,n+\frac{N}{N_p})}$ is equal to $p_{(k,n)}$. Then, the frequency response of data between these two pilots can be estimated as

$$\hat{H}[p_{(k,n)}, n+d] = \hat{H}[p_{(k,n)}, n] + \left\{ \hat{H}[p_{(k,n)}, n+\frac{N}{N_p}] - \hat{H}[p_{(k,n)}, n] \right\} \frac{N}{N_p} d \quad (10)$$

where d $(0 \leq d \leq \frac{N}{N_p})$ is the distance from the nearest same sub-channel pilot position prior to that data position.

Note that, for estimating the data response $\hat{H}[p_{(k,n)}, n+d]$, $(\frac{N}{N_p} - d)$ OFDM symbol delay cannot be inescapable. However, the delay is small enough to wait

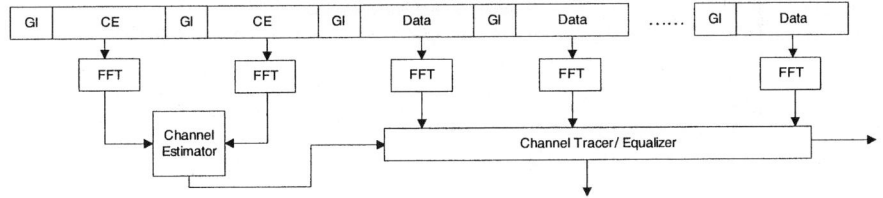

Fig. 5. Process of channel tracking

for many kinds of applications, and even though the delay cannot be acceptable, there is a simple modification. When the delay is severe for some applications, linear extrapolation method can be easily applied instead of the interpolation.

4 Simulations

We investigate the performance of the proposed channel tracking method on multipath channels. An OFDM system with symbols modulated by 16QAM and 64QAM is used on multipath channel. Since the phase tracking that conventional OFDM system used can recover the phase offset caused by channel variation, the constant modulation like QPSK has similar performance without channel tracking. So, we exclude the constant amplitude modulation in simulations. The

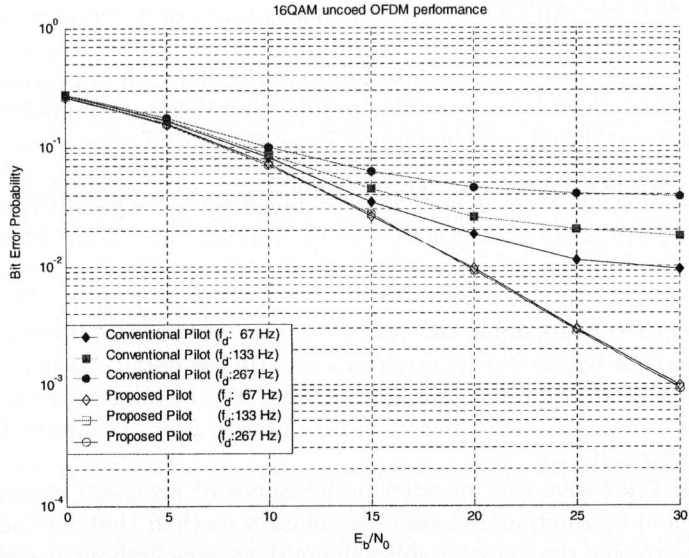

Fig. 6. BER performance of 16QAM uncoded OFDM over 4095 bytes/packet data transmissions

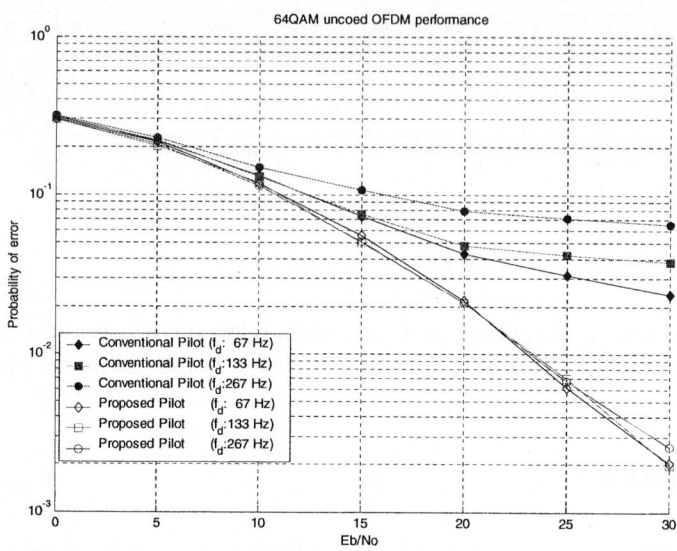

Fig. 7. BER performance of 64QAM uncoded OFDM over 4095 bytes/packet data transmissions

system bandwidth is 20MHz, which is divided into 64 tones with a total symbol period of $4\mu s$, of which $0.8\mu s$ constitutes the guard time, and the carrier frequency is 2.4GHz. An OFDM symbol thus consists of 80 samples containing 16 samples as CP. The simulated channel order is half of the length of CP for ignoring the effect of Inter-symbol interference (ISI) and each tap varies independently with an exponential power delay profile. Unit delay of channel is assumed to be the same as OFDM sample period. Thus, there is no power loss caused by non-sample spaced.

For confirming the effect of channel tracking, 4095 bytes packet that is equal to that of 802.11a is considered and various Doppler shifts from 67 to 267 Hz (equivalent mobile speeds are from 30 to 120 km/h) are used. We adopt the classical Jake's method [11] to implement the various Doppler shifts. The channel estimation method of preamble and each pilot is LS method. Additionally, we use convolutional code with Viterbi decoder to confirm the performance of proposed algorithm in more realistic systems. The encoder use the industry-standard generator polynomials, $g_0 = 133_8$ and $g_1 = 171_8$ of rate $R = 1/2$ adopted in IEEE 802.11a standard [10].

Fig.6 and Fig.7 give the uncoded performance of proposed channel tracking method and conventional channel estimation method that has no channel tracking. As growing the Doppler shift, the performance without tracking experience the severe error floor that is more serious in high order modulated system as shown in Fig.7. However, the floor is almost disappeared with our channel tracking scheme even though the Doppler shift is very high.

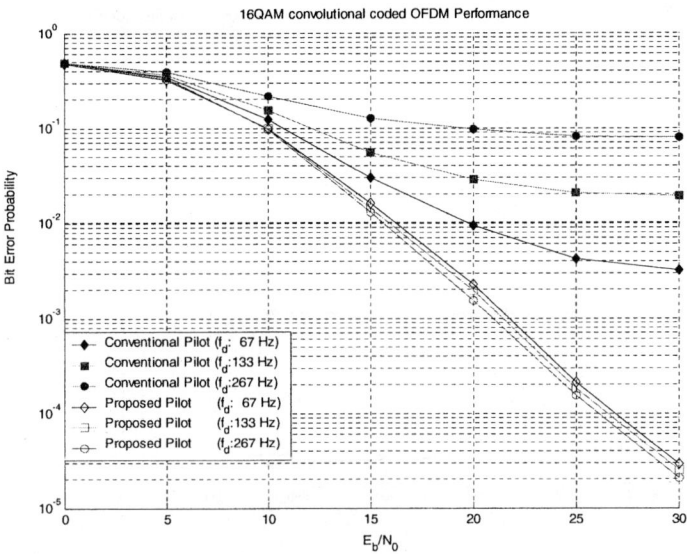

Fig. 8. BER performance of 16QAM convolutional coded OFDM over 4095 bytes/packet data transmissions

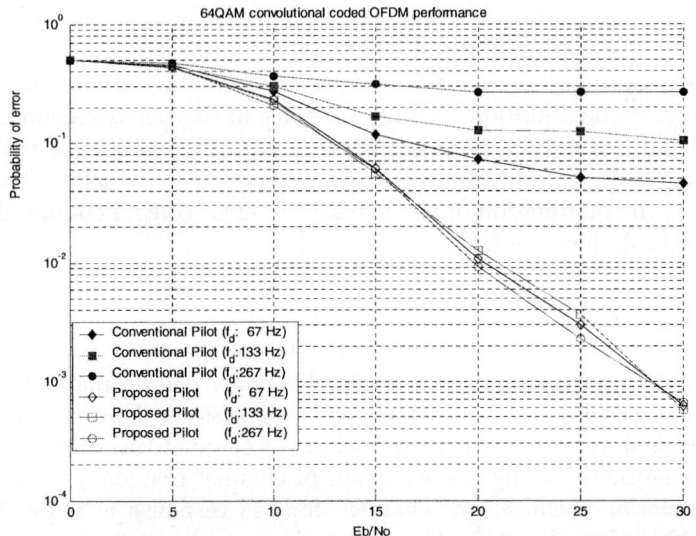

Fig. 9. BER performance of 64QAM convolutional coded OFDM over 4095 bytes/packet data transmissions

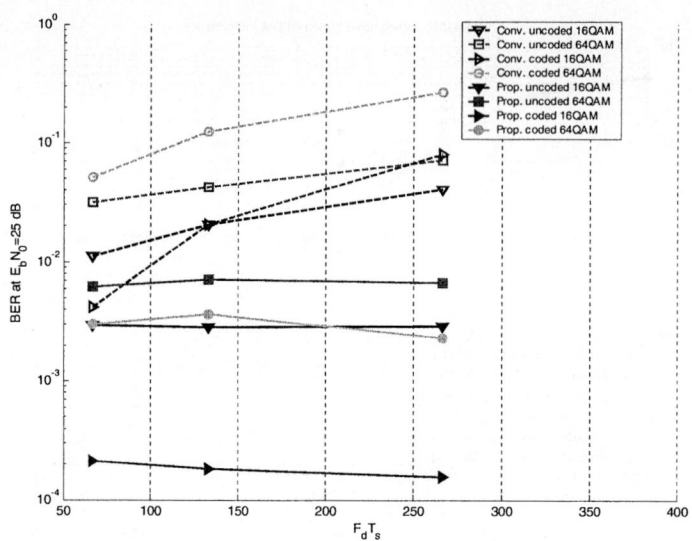

Fig. 10. BER comparison of the proposed channel tracking at $E_b N_0 = 25$dB

Fig.8 and Fig.9 show the convolutional coded performance of the proposed channel tracking. Similar to uncoded system, our method gives robust BER performance regardless of mobility. In coded system, the channel tracking is more crucial as shown in Fig.8 and Fig.9. Demonstrating the superior performance of the proposed method, we compare the BER performance at $E_b N_0 = 25$dB according to increasing the Doppler frequency f_d in Fig.10. The method has little performance degradation for high mobility at any environments, whereas conventional OFDM experiences significant losses of reliability as mobility increases. This result also confirms that the roll of channel tracking has greater importance as the modulation order increases or error control coding like a convolutional code in this case uses.

5 Conclusion

The channel tracking method proposed in this paper can dramatically improve the performance of OFDM based high mobility system. This tracking is fundamentally based on the linear characteristic of channel variation. We use the correlation analysis to verify the variation of channel frequency response. The Pearson-correlation-coefficient of channel impulse response is more than 0.90 even with 500 Hz Doppler shift. This shows the very strong linear trend of variation. Accordingly, the tracking can be performed by using linear interpolation between two consecutive pilots that used the same sub-channel.

Without any data loss, this scheme can track the time variation of fading channel. As a result, there is little error floor of BER performance even with very high Doppler shift. Numerical results show that the proposed scheme performs well for vehicle speed up to 120 km/h. We also confirm that the proposed method gives robust system performance even though using high order modulation like 64QAM. In a convolutional coded system, high mobility system without channel tracking has more severe performance degradation. Moreover, the tracking gives the possibility to increase the size of transmission packet since the tracking can be done by each OFDM symbol.

Acknowledgments

This research was supported by the MIC (Ministry of Information and Communication), Korea, under the ITRC (Information Technology Research Center) support program supervised by the IITA (Institute of Information Technology Assessment)

References

1. O.Edfors, M. Sandell, J.-J. van de Beek, S. K. Wilson and P. O. Borjesson, "OFDM channel estimation by singular value decomposition," *IEEE Trans. Commun.*, vol. 46, pp. 931-939, July 1998.
2. J.-J van de Beek, O. Edfors, M. Sandell, S. K.Wilson, and P. O. Borjesson, "On channel estimation in OFDM systems," *IEEE Veh. Tech. Conf.*, vol. 2, pp. 815-819, July 1995.
3. M. Morelli and U. Mengali, "A comparison of pilot-aided channel estimation methods for OFDM systems," *IEEE Trans. Signal Processing, vol.* 49, pp. 3065-3073, Dec. 2004.
4. R. FUNADA, H. Harada, Y. Kamio, S. Shinoda, and M.Fujise, "A new fading compensation scheme under fast fading environment for OFDM packet transmission system," *IEICE Tehchnical Report*, RCS2000-21. May 2000.
5. R. FUNADA, H. Harada, Y. Kamio and S. Shinoda, "A channel estimation method for a highly mobile OFDM wireless access system," *IEICE Trans. Commun. vol.*E88-B, No.1 pp. 282-291, Jan. 2005.
6. B. Yang, Z. Cao, and K. B. Letaief, "Analysis of low-complexity windowed DFT-based MMSE channel estimation for OFDM systems," *IEEE Trans. Commun.*, vol. 49, pp. 1977-1987, Nov. 2001.
7. C. S. Yeh and Y. Lin, "Channel estimation using pilot tones in OFDM systems," *IEEE Trans. Broadcasting*, vol. 45, no. 4, pp. 400-409, Dec. 1999.
8. L. L. Scharf, *Statistical Signal Processing*, U.S.A, Addison-Wesley Publishing Company, 1991.
9. Douglas C. Montgomery, George C. Runger, *Applied statistics and probability for engineers*, John Wiley Sons, New York, 1999.
10. IEEE 802.11a-1999, "Wireless LAN Medimum Access Control (MAC) and Physical Layer (PHY) Specifications: High speed physical layer in 5 GHz band." 1999 edition.
11. W.C. Jakes, *Microwave Mobile Communications*, New York, Wiley, 1974.

A Novel Key Management and Distribution Solution for Secure Video Multicast*

Hao Yin[1], Xiaowen Chu[2], Chuang Lin[1], Feng Qiu[1], and Geyong Min[3]

[1] Department of Computer Science, Tsinghua University, Beijing, China
{hyin, fqiu, clin}@csnet1.cs.tsinguha.edu.cn
[2] Department of Computer Science, Hong Kong Baptist University, Hong Kong, China
chxw@comp.hkbu.edu.hk
[3] Department of Computing, University of Bradford, Bradford, UK
g.min@bradford.ac.uk

Abstract. In secure video multicast systems, access control is a very important and challenging issue. A common practice is to encrypt the video content using a *group key*, shared only by legitimate clients. Since the clients can join and leave the multicast session frequently, the group key needs to be updated and delivered to the legitimate clients accordingly in order to provide forward/backward secrecy. Therefore, *key management and distribution* plays a crucial role in building a secure and scalable video multicast system. Conventional approaches usually use a dedicated secure channel independent of the video data channel, which is expensive and inefficient. In this paper, we propose a novel and scalable Media-dependent Key Management and Distribution (MKMD) solution that embeds key management messages in video data so as to save network bandwidth and enhance the security level, and most importantly, without sacrificing the quality of video content too much. We have built a prototype system of MKMD, and our extensive experimental results show that MKMD is a secure, scalable, reliable and efficient key management and distribution solution for video multicast system.

1 Introduction

Due to the multi-receiver nature of video programs, real-time video multicast over the Internet has become one of the most important IP multicast applications [1]. However, before the group-oriented video multicast applications can be successfully deployed, it is very important to develop efficient *access control* mechanisms to ensure that only legitimate clients can access the group communications. Unfortunately, the current IP multicast model does not provide any membership management scheme for preventing unauthorized clients from accessing the multicast video data [2]. Therefore *access control* has to be carefully designed at the application layer with the objective to enable only legitimate clients to access the video content.

---

* This research was partly supported by the National Natural Science Foundation of China under contracts 60429202, 60372019, 60473086 and 60432030, and Hong Kong RGC grants under contract No. RGC/HKBU215904 and RGC/HKBU210605.

Access control in multicast system is usually achieved by encrypting the content using an encryption key, known as the group key (GK) that is only known by the content provider and all legitimate group members [3]. However, it is not an easy task to deliver the GK to all the members securely because the group membership is most likely dynamic with clients joining and leaving the group from time to time. Notice that, once a member is not in the multicast session, e.g. before he joins or after he leaves the session, he should not be able to access the video content. The key management and distribution scheme should have the following two security properties: 1) *Forward Secrecy*: to ensure that an expired member cannot access the new GK after he leaves the group. Notice that anyone can receive the IP multicast data at anytime. 2) *Backward Secrecy*: to ensure that when a new member joins the group, he cannot access previous video contents [4].

In order to manage and update GK dynamically, a party responsible for distributing the keys, called the Key Distribution Center (KDC), must securely communicate with all the legitimate clients and find a proper way to enable the legitimate clients to get the new GK. A commonly used solution is that, the KDC assigns a Key-Encrypting Key (KEK) to each legitimate client at the time the client joins the group, and then the KDC can encrypt the GK using the KEK and send the encrypted rekey messages, i.e. the messages used to help the clients get the new GK, to the corresponding clients. The rekey messages can be sent to the n clients one by one using unicast, or be combined as a single huge rekey message and delivered to all the clients by multicast. Neither of the two approaches is scalable because the total size of newly generated rekey messages is $O(n)$.

On the other side, the problem of efficiently delivering rekey messages to the clients has received significant attention in the networking research community. Several different schemes have been proposed with desirable communication properties, which can be divided into two distinct classes: media-independent approach and media-dependent approach [5, 6]. In the former, the rekey messages are conveyed totally disjoint from the video content; while in the latter the rekey messages are embedded in the video content. This paper integrates our early proposed key embedding algorithm [7] and selective multimedia encryption algorithm [8] to implement an efficient, secure, and scalable access control scheme for video multicast applications.

This paper proposes a novel key management and distribution solution called Media-dependent Key Management and Distribution solution (MKMD). Part of our solution is based on a simplified but improved Efficient Large-Group Key Distribution (ELK) protocol [9]. The distinguished properties of our proposed solution include: 1) MKMD is a scalable media-dependent approach which reduces the length of rekey messages significantly by introducing the One-way Function; 2) MKMD is a complete and robust solution and it is resistant to abnormal client leaving actions; 3) MKMD makes a good tradeoff between computation and bandwidth consumption of delivered rekey message. When new clients join, KDC and other clients can get their new GK by local calculation without transmitting any rekey messages; 4) MKMD provides good reliability by an integrated key recovery mechanism; 5) A real-time video encryption algorithm is used to combat the statistical attacks and avoid the Wired Equivalent Privacy error in wireless network [10]; 6) we have built a prototype to validate the feasibility of MKMD.

The rest of the paper is organized as follows. Section 2 outlines the framework of our MKMD solution. Section 3 discusses the key management and distribution mechanism in detail. Section 4 presents our implemented prototype for MKMD, and a series of experimental results are shown in Section 5. Finally, Section 6 concludes the paper.

2 Framework of MKMD

The core of the MKMD is a Key Distribution Center (KDC) which takes charge of member authentications as well as key management and distribution. Member authentication can be derived from many existed schemes, such as Diffie-Hellman [17], PKI [18], etc, which is not the focus of this paper. The distribution of keys employs a media-dependent approach by embedding rekey messages in the multicast video data [7]. The security of transmitting video data is guaranteed by adopting our proposed selective multimedia encryption algorithm [8]. In this section, we present the general framework of MKMD scheme in three aspects: 1) How does a client join the multicast group? 2) How does the KDC distribute rekey messages to the clients? 3) How does a client leave the multicast group?

2.1 Joining the Multicast Group

In secure video multicast, video data are encrypted by the GK. Only legitimate clients can get the valid GK and decrypt the data. A user can become a legitimate client using the follows steps:

1. When a user Jack wants to become a legitimate client, he first sends a JOIN request to the well-known KDC though a secure unicast channel for authentication.
2. KDC receives the JOIN request from Jack, and check the validity of Jack.
3. If Jack is legitimate (maybe after the payment), KDC generates new keys for him and updates the key tree. Details of this process are presented in Section 3.
4. KDC sends back the keys and authentication result to Jack using the secure unicast channel.
5. Jack receives the keys and he can now decrypt the received multicast data.

2.2 During the Multicast Session

After being authorized, Jack receives the encrypted video data and is able to decrypt them with the GK. While Jack is watching the video, there may be some other clients joining or leaving the group. To guarantee the backward secrecy and forward secrecy, KDC needs to updates the GK, and informs all the clients to update their keys by multicasting the rekey messages. The rekey process is as follows:

1. When some clients join or leave the multicast, KDC updates its key tree and generates the rekey messages.
2. As shown in Figure 1, KDC embeds the rekey messages in the video data.
3. The video data are then encrypted by the present GK using our selective encryption algorithm before sending them out by multicast.
4. Jack receives the encrypted data and decrypts them using the present GK.

5. Jack detects the embedded rekey messages and updates his keys, including the new GK.
6. Jack uses the new GK for the decryption of future incoming multicast data.

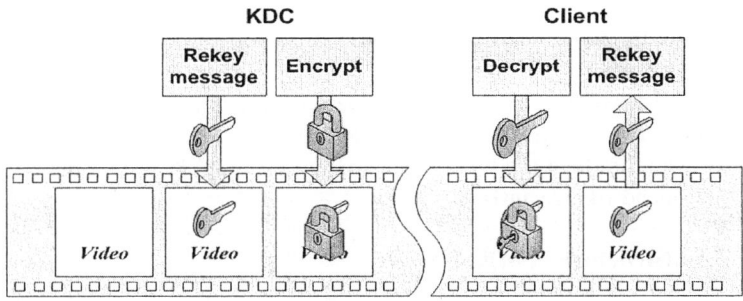

Fig. 1. Secure transmission of rekey messages

With a large number of clients, client join/leave events may occur frequently. Updating the keys immediately when any such event occurs would cause too much computation overhead and waste lots of bandwidth. An effective approach to solve the problem is to divide the time into slices and pipeline the process, as shown in Figure 2. In the first time slice, KDC handles the requests of clients, manages the key tree and generates rekey messages. In the following time slice, rekey messages are distributed and the key updating process is carried out. The new keys will go into effect by the end of this time slice. Therefore the synchronization of the keys between KDC and clients is achieved.

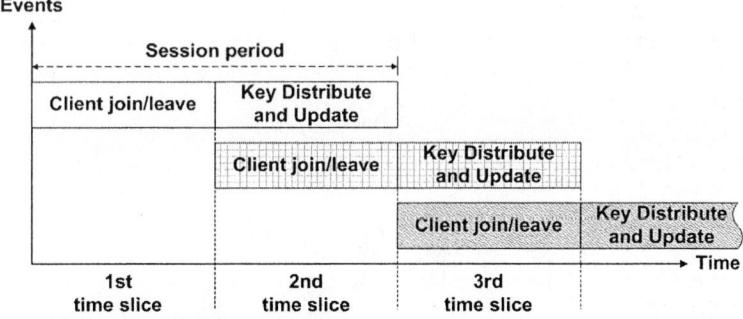

Fig. 2. Time schedule

2.3 Leaving the Multicast Group

If Jack wants to leave, he should go through the following process:

1. Jack sends a *LEAVE* request to KDC.
2. KDC updates the key tree.

3. When a proper time slice comes, KDC generates rekey messages and distributes the rekey messages.
4. After key updating, KDC encrypts the video data using the new GK.

3 Key Management and Distribution

In this section, we describe our MKMD solution in detail. As compared with ELK, our key embedding algorithm can provide efficient error resiliency [7, 8], and therefore we can eliminate the hints mechanism used in ELK so that the computation overhead is reduced significantly.

3.1 Key Tree Structure in MKMD

The MKMD is based on a balanced binary key tree maintained by the KDC. It extends the Logical Key Hierarchy (LKH) and One-way Function Tree (OFT) approaches to achieve an efficient and secure key distribution system. The key tree is used for group key update and distribution. By using the key tree, the size of rekey messages generated by KDC can be decreased from $O(n)$ to $O(\log_2 n)$. In the following, we use an example to illustrate how the key tree works.

Figure 3 shows a sample MKMD key tree. The top node named K_G is assigned with the GK, which is used to encrypt the video data for access control purpose; while other nodes are assigned with KEKs. Each legitimate client is associated with a leaf node in the key tree, and each client knows the keys along the path from his corresponding leaf node to the root node, i.e. the key path. For example, client U_4 maintains a key path $\{K_7, K_6, K_2, K_0, K_G\}$. When client joins or leaves the multicast session, the GK and some of the KEKs have to be updated to achieve the forward secrecy and backward secrecy.

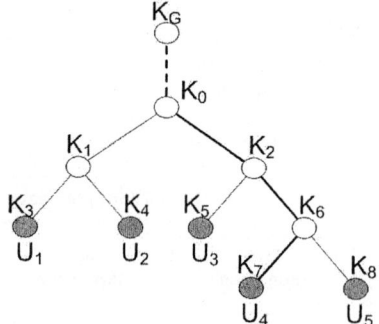

Fig. 3. An example of MKMD key tree

3.2 Pseudo-Random Functions and Notations

In the following, we first introduce a family of pseudo-random functions (PRFs) that use a key K on input M with length m bits, and output a bit stream with n bits: $\mathrm{PRF}^{(m \to n)} : K \times \{0,1\}^m \to \{0,1\}^n$. We simply denote it as $\mathrm{PRF}_K^{(m \to n)}(M)$.

The objective of RPF is to derive different independent keys to be used in different contexts. Especially, the following four new keys are derived from K_i:

$$K_i^{\alpha} = \text{PRF}_{K_i}^{(n \to n)}(1) \, , \, K_i^{\beta} = \text{PRF}_{K_i}^{(n \to n)}(2) \, , \, K_i^{\gamma} = \text{PRF}_{K_i}^{(n \to n)}(3) \, , \, K_i^{\delta} = \text{PRF}_{K_i}^{(n \to n)}(4)$$

In the following, we use $\{M\}_K$ to denote encrypting M with key K, and "|" means the concatenation of two bit streams.

3.3 Key Updating

Since our key embedding algorithm can provide efficient key recovery function, we do not use the hint mechanism in ELK scheme. The consequence is that the computation overhead in our MKMD scheme is decreased by a large margin, while the reliability for key update message is still guaranteed.

3.3.1 Client Joining Event

When a client joins the multicast group, KDC authenticates it and assigns it to a leaf node of the key tree. To preserve backward secrecy, all keys along the corresponding key path to this client need to be independent from any previous keys. Therefore, KDC replaces all old keys on the new client's key path with new random keys and then sends each of these new keys to the whole group. The detailed algorithm is shown in Figure 4.

New client A logins based on authentication;

KDC assigns a new leaf node N_a with a new KEK K_a to the new client A;

If the key tree is empty {

  A new key tree is initialized with node N_a as its root node;

} Else {

  KDC selects a node N_i with its KEK K_i who has the shortest path;

  KDC generates a new node N_p with KEK K_p and inserts it in the place of N_i, where

  $K_p = \text{PRF}_{K_i}^{(n \to n)}(1)$;

  N_i and N_a are inserted as the children of N_p;

  KDC tells N_i to calculate K_p and add the node N_p on his path;

}

KDC and the existing clients update the GK and KEKs synchronously:

  $K_i' = \text{PRF}_{K_i}^{(n \to n)}(K_G) \, , \, K_G' = \text{PRF}_{K_G}^{(n \to n)}(1)$;

KDC tells client A his KEKs on his key path and the new GK K_G' .

Fig. 4. The algorithm for client joining

In MKMD, no rekey message is generated when clients join. But KDC might still need to send a few unicast messages to the clients whose leaf node position has been moved in the key tree.

3.3.2 Client Leaving Event

The client leave, however, is more difficult to handle efficiently. The challenge is to replace the current keys such that only the legitimate clients receive the new key but the leaving client does not. In fact, all keys that the leaving client knows need to be changed to ensure forward secrecy. The keys are replaced sequentially from the leaf up to the root key along the leaving client's key path. The algorithm is described in Figure 5.

If a client wants to update its own K_i, he must know the sequence C_{iLR}. Since the leaving client has been removed from the key tree and his keys are invalidated, he can get nothing from the coming rekey messages. As a result this client loses the chance to get the new GK and can not access the video data any more.

3.4 Key Distribution

In this paper we adopt two media-dependent algorithms for key distribution, in which all the rekey messages are embedded in the video data. Since the number of the rekey messages changes dynamically, KDC also needs to adjust the length of time slice in time. Therefore some timing information is also embedded.

3.4.1 Key Embedding

In our previous work we have designed a reliable key embedding algorithm focusing on the accuracy and reliability against the influence caused by the unreliable transmission and multimedia adaptive mechanism [7, 8].

In this algorithm, the rekey messages are embedded in the I-frames of the GOPs (Group of Pictures). The whole process is carried out in the DCT domain since DCT domain is closer to the video bit stream than the pixel domain. In the concrete, it divides the video image into 200 fields and embeds 1 bit of data in each field by modifying the ALV (Average Luminance Value) of this field in DCT domain. Thus in one I-frame we can embed 200-bit of data, which can be used to carry flag bits, RS codeword, and rekey message. In fact, each I-frame can carry only one piece of fixed size rekey message.

3.4.2 Key Recovery Mechanism

In our key recovery mechanism, there are three recovery approaches integrated in the key distribution when a client fails to get the correct rekey messages during the multicast. First, the RS (Reed-Solomon) code is adopted into our solution [7] to correct the error bits caused by transcoder or unreliable transmission. A small amount of mistakes can be corrected by the RS code. An N-bit RS code can correct at most $N/2$ continuous error bits or at least $N/16$ discrete error bits which are distributed in individual bytes. But if too many bits are mistaken or lost, the rekey messages can never be recovered. Then the client could employ the second approach, i.e., using redundant rekey messages. These messages follow the newly distributed ones. The level of redundancy depends on the network status. Finally, if the client can not recover the key by the above two approaches; he can get the needed rekey messages from KDC by unicast.

For KDC:

A leaving client B with a leaf node N_b logouts based on authentication;

KDC adjusts the key tree: {

  N_b is removed from the key tree;

  If N_b has a parent node: {

  Remove the parent node and promote N_b's sibling node N_s;

  }

  For all the KEKs from N_s up to the root (but except N_s) : {

  KDC derives K'_i from K_i, with its left child key K'_{iL} and right child key K'_{iR}:

  $C'_{iL} = PRF_{K'_\alpha_{iL}}^{<n \to n_1>}(K_i)$, $C'_{iR} = PRF_{K'_\alpha_{iR}}^{<n \to n_2>}(K_i)$;

  $C'_{iLR} = C'_{iL} | C'_{iR}$, $K'_i = PRF_{C'_{iLR}}^{<n \to n>}(K_i)$;

  KDC generates the rekey messages for K_i: $\{\{C'_{iL}\}_{K'^\beta_{iL}}, \{C'_{iR}\}_{K'^\beta_{iR}}\}$

  where $K'^\beta_{iL} = PRF_{K'_{iL}}^{<n \to n>}(2)$, $K'^\beta_{iR} = PRF_{K'_{iR}}^{<n \to n>}(2)$;

  }

}

When the 2nd time slice comes, KDC multicasts all the rekey messages to the clients;

For client:

If the rekey message is for KEK K_i in his path: {

  /* Assume that the client owns the left child key K'_{iL} */

  $K'^\alpha_{iL} = PRF_{K'_{iL}}^{<n \to n>}(1)$, $K'^\beta_{iL} = PRF_{K'_{iL}}^{<n \to n>}(2)$, $C'_{iL} = PRF_{K'^\alpha_{iL}}^{<n \to n_1>}(K_i)$;

  Get C'_{iR} by decrypting $\{C'_{iR}\}_{K'^\beta_{iL}}$ with K'^β_{iL};

  $C'_{iLR} = C'_{iL} | C'_{iR}$, $K'_i = PRF_{C'_{iLR}}^{<n \to n>}(K_i)$;

} Else {

  Drop the rekey message;

}

Fig. 5. The algorithm for client leaving

3.4.3 Adjusting the Time Slice Length

Since lots of clients dynamically join or leave the multicast in a time slice, the number of rekey messages will also change stochastically. The length of a time slice should be long enough for the transmission of the rekey messages; therefore KDC should determine the length of the coming time slice and inform clients in time.

The time slice length depends on the number of rekey messages, the number of I-frames per second, the redundancy level and whether to embed data in P-frames. Among these parameters, the number of I-frames and P-frames per second is always constant in a certain video stream. Hence, the time slice length mainly depends on the number of rekey messages and the requirement for redundancy. In this paper we focus on the former, i.e. we try to make sure that the time slice is long enough for these rekey messages to be sent out completely. Besides this, we also need to increase the time slice length for reliability purpose.

4 Implementation

We have designed and implemented a prototype system for the proposed MKMD, and we have investigated the reliability, feasibility and security of this system. In this section, we describe the experimental platform.

On the top of our system, keys are managed by a KDC server to ensure the security when membership dynamically changes. Rekey messages are then divided into several pieces and embedded in the packets of I-frames. After that the content of each packet is encrypted. All the processes perform certain operations on the video data. At last the prepared video data are sent out by some network protocols, such as RTP/UDP.

We can learn from previous discussion that KDC has two major functions, i.e., video streaming with rekey messages embedded, and key management. In our implementation, KDC consists of two trusted nodes, a video streaming server and a gateway.

When a client event (e.g. join/leave) occurs, the gateway communicates with this client, generates the rekey messages and sends them to the streaming server. Streaming server mainly takes charge of real-time key embedding and also video streaming. It encodes the video and embeds the specific rekey message into the video stream in real-time. The key-embedded video stream is then sent back to the gateway and forwarded to all clients by multicast. The purpose of using both streaming server and the gateway is to separate the two major functions of KDC such that the overhead can be shared.

5 System Performance Study

5.1 Security Study

The security of the system mainly depends on three parts: authentication mechanism, key management mechanism, and multimedia encryption algorithm. The system is considered to be secure only if all three aspects are secure enough. In our solution we can adopt any well-studied authentication approach; therefore, we mainly focus on the latter two aspects.

The key management algorithm in our solution is derived from the ELK scheme, and its security has been validated in [9]. Due to short-term security requirements of IPTV services, the key management mechanism with a 64-bit group key based on the LKH and several pseudo random functions guarantees the key secrecy. Furthermore, getting previous or future group keys for a client with its own keys is computationally impossible in short-term, even by working together with other clients and sharing their keys. Thus the system can guarantee the backward secrecy and forward secrecy, and resist the collusion attack.

5.2 Reliability Study

During the key distribution, the embedded rekey messages may be damaged due to the adaptive mechanism (such as transcoder) or transmission errors. Since the rekey messages need to be precisely transmitted, the reliability of the key distribution mechanism is one of the most important features in our MKMD protocol. It can be obtained by introducing both RS code and rekey message redundancy adopted in our proposed key embedding algorithm [7].

Figure 6 illustrates the error bits distribution by detecting all the 200 bits in an I-frame transcoded with the modulation cycle C. A downscaling transcoder reduces the blocks in each field. The degree how transcoding influences the detection of rekey messages depends on the value of C.

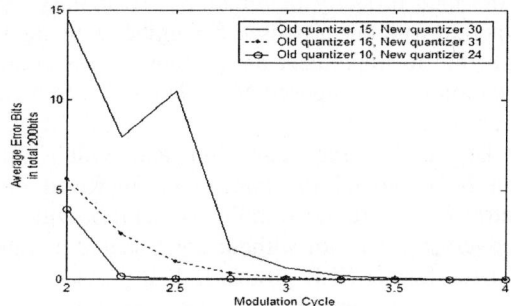

Fig. 6. Average error bits in total 200 embedded bits within an I-frame after transcoding with different modulation cycles and quantizers

Figure 7 (a) shows the average error bits in 200-bit rekey messages caused by the different packet loss rate across the unreliable network without RS code. Evidently the key data error rate of a GOP increases while packet loss rate increases. During the transmission an I-frame is usually divided into more than 10 packets. Thus the lost packets would lead to the missing bits of the rekey messages. RS code in the rekey messages can recover the small amount of errors when the packet loss rate is low. As shown in Figure 7 (b), most of the error bits can be corrected by RS code when the loss rate is lower than 10%.

In our solution some redundant rekey messages are transmitted to further improve the reliability. The number of redundant rekey messages depends on the network status and the time slice length. The transmission of redundant messages not only improves the reliability but also increases the time of the new clients waiting for joining which worsen the feasibility. The KDC should make a tradeoff between reliability and feasibility.

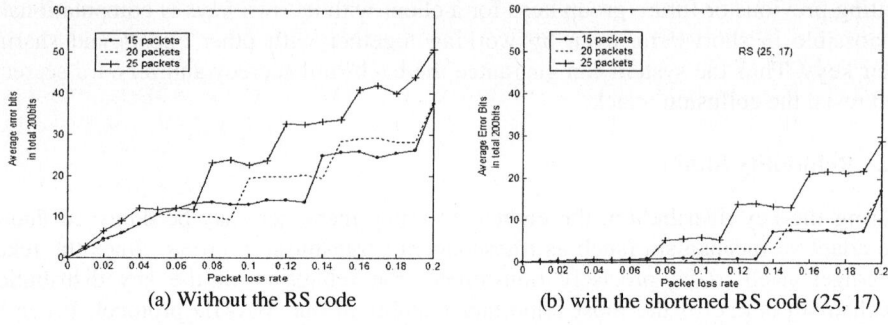

Fig. 7. Average error bits in 200 bit with different packet loss rate

6 Conclusion

This paper proposes a novel key management and distribution solution named MKMD, which has the nice property of reliability, scalability, added security, and efficiency. It can cooperate with our proposed key embedding algorithm and selective video encryption algorithm to implement an efficient access control mechanism for video multicast applications. Our proposed MKMD has the following advantages: 1) it is a complete solution with robustness, efficiency and scalability; 2) it is compatible with our proposed key embedding algorithm and video selective encryption algorithm, which can be exploited to achieve an improved design of a media-dependent access control for secure video multicast; 3) it provides good reliability by an integrated key recovery mechanism without complicated computing and resource consumption derived from former ELK protocol; 4) It provides real-time processing, which is suitable for the deployment of secure video multicast. All these advantages have been validated by our extensive experimental results.

References

1. J.C. Liu, B. Li, and Y.Q. Zhang, Adaptive Video Multicast over the Internet, *IEEE Multimedia*, vol.10, no.1, pp.22-33, January/February 2003.
2. K. Almeroth, The Evolution of Multicast: From the MBone to Inter-Domain Multicast to Internet2 Deployment, *IEEE Network*, vol.14, pp.10-20, January/February 2000.
3. K.-C. Chan and S.-H. Chan, Key Management Approaches to Offer Data Confidentiality for Secure Multicast, *IEEE Network*, vo.17, no.5, pp. 30-39, September/October 2003.
4. S. Rafaeli and D. Hutchison, A Survey of Key Management for Secure Group Communication, *ACM Computing Surveys*, vol.35, no.3, pp.309-329, September 2003.
5. D.M. Wallner, E.J. Harder, and R.C. Agee, Key Management for Multicast: Issues and Architectures, RFC 2627, June 1999.
6. W. Trappe, J. Song, R. Poovendran, and K.J. Liu, Key Management and Distribution for Secure Multimedia Multicast, *IEEE Transaction on Multimedia*, vol.5, no.4, pp.544-557, December 2003.

7. H. Yin, C. Lin, F. Qiu, X.-W. Chu, and G. Min, A Key Embedded Video Codec for Secure Video Multicast, in proceedings of *IFIP Conference on Communications and Multimedia Security (CMS'05)*, Salzburg, Austria, September 2005.
8. H. Yin, C. Lin, F. Qiu, B. Li, and Z. Tan, A Media-Dependent Secure Multicast Protocol for Adaptive Video Applications, in proceedings of *ACM SIGCOMM Asia Workshop*, Beijing, China, April 2005.
9. A. Perrig, D. Song, and J.D. Tygar, A New Protocol for Efficient Large-Group Key Distribution, in proceedings of *IEEE Symposium on Security and Privacy*, Los Alamitos, USA, 2001.
10. N. Borisov, I. Goldberg, and D. Wagner, Intercepting Mobile Communications: The Insecurity of 802.11, in proceedings of *ACM MOBICOM*, 2001.
11. S. Rafaeli, A Decentralized Architecture for Group Key Management, PhD appraisal, Lancaster University, Lancaster, UK, September 2000.
12. M. Waldvogel, G. Caronni, D. Sun, N. Weiler, and B. Plattner, The VersaKey Framework: Versatile Group Key Management, *IEEE Journal on Selected Areas in Communications*, vol. 17, no.9, pp.1614–1631, August 1999.
13. I. Chang, R. Engel, D. Kandlur, D. Pendarakis, and D. Saha, Key Management for Secure Internet Multicast Using Boolean Function Minimization Techniques, in proceedings of *IEEE INFOCOM*, pp.689–698, 1999.
14. C. K. Wong, M. Gouda, and S. S. LAM, Secure Group Communications Using Key Graphs. *IEEE/ACM Transactions on Networking*, vol.8, no.1, pp.16–30, 2000.
15. R. Canetti, J. Garay, G. Itkis, D. Micciancio, M. Naor, and B. Pinkas, Multicast Security: A Taxonomy and Some Efficient Constructions, in proceedings of *IEEE INFOCOM*, pp.708–716, 1999.
16. S. Banerjee and B. Bhattacharjee, Scalable Secure Group Communication over IP Multicast; *IEEE Journal on Selected Areas in Communications*, vol.20, no.8, pp.1511-1527, October 2002.
17. W. Diffie and M.E Hellman, New Directions in Cryptography, *IEEE Transactions on Information Theory*, vol.IT-22, no.6, pp.644-654, November 1976.
18. R. Housley, W. Ford, W. Polk, and D. Solo, Internet Public Key Infrastructure: X.509 Certificate and CRL Profile, RFC 2459, March 1999.
19. J. Song and K.J.R. Liu, A Data Embedded Video Coding Scheme for Error-prone Channels, *IEEE Transactions on Multimedia*, vol.3, no.4, pp.415-423, December 2001.
20. W. Trappe, J. Song, R. Poovendran, and K.J.R. Liu, Key Management and Distribution for Secure Multimedia Multicast, *IEEE Transactions on Multimedia*, vol.5, no.4, pp.544-557, December 2003.

A Robust Method for Data Hiding in Color Images

Mohsen Ashourian[1], Peyman Moallem[1], and Yo-Sung Ho[2]

[1] Faculty of Engineering, Isfahan University,
Isfahan, Iran
mohsena@yahoo.com
[2] Gwangju Institute of Science and Technology,
1 Oryong-dong Puk-gu, Gwangju, 500-712, Korea
hoyo@gist.ac.kr

Abstract. In this paper, we propose a methodology for embedding watermark image data into color images. At the transmitter, the signature image is encoded by a multiple description encoder. The information of the two descriptions are embedded in the host image in the spatial domain in the red and blue components. Furthermore, this scheme requires no knowledge of the original image for the recovery of the signature image, yet yields high signal-to-noise ratios for the recovered output. At the receiver, the multiple description decoder combines the information of each description and reconstructs the original signature image. We experiment the proposed scheme for embedding a gray-scale signature image of 128×128 pixels size in the spatial domain of a color host image of 512×512 pixels. Simulation results show that data embedding based on multiple description coding has low visible distortions in the host image and robustness to various signal processing and geometrical attacks, such as addition of noise, quantization, cropping and down-sampling.

1 Introduction

Various digital data hiding methods have been developed for multimedia services, where a significant amount of signature data is embedded in the host signal. The hidden data should be recoverable even after the host data has undergone some signal processing operations, such as image compression. It should also be retrieved only by those authorized [1, 2, 3, 4].

The main problem of image hiding in another host image is a large amount of data that requires a special data embedding method with high capacity as well as transparency and robustness. Chae and Manjunath used the discrete wavelet transform (DWT) for embedding a signature image into another image, which has high visible distortion in the smooth area of the host image [2]. It is possible to improve their scheme by employing the human visual system (HVS) model in the process of information embedding [3,4]; however, exact adjustment of the HVS model is not easy in many applications. As another approach for improving the robustness of data embedding, Mukherjee et. al. [5] designed a joint source-channel coding scheme for hiding a signature video in a video sequence. However, the channel optimized quantizer is not suitable in image hiding applications, where intentional or non-intentional manipulations, are variable and not known in advance.

In this paper, we suggest to use a multiple description subband coder for encoding the signature image [7,8,9]. The two descriptions are embedded in different part of the host image in red and blue component which are analogies to two communication channel. The algorithm can be used for watermarking color images and has a low complexity compare to many of the color image watermarking schemes [Figure 1 shows the block diagram of the overall system. At the receiver, the multiple description decoder combines the information of each description and reconstructs the original signal. It can decode only one channel, when data on the other channel is highly corrupted; otherwise, it can combine the received information from both channels.

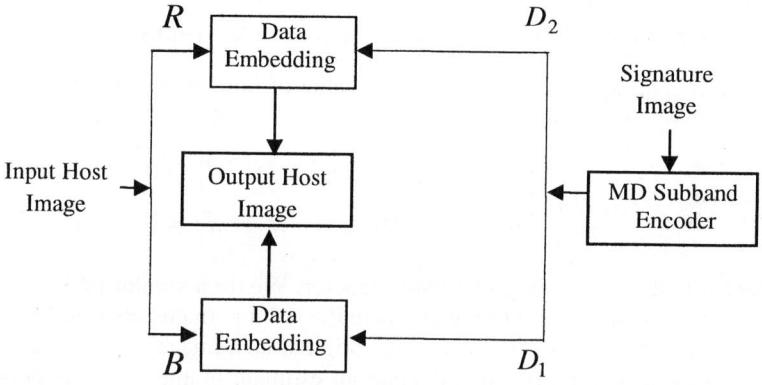

Fig. 1. Overview of the Proposed Scheme

The main advantage of encoding the signature image by two descriptions and embedding these descriptors in the host signal is that with an appropriate strategy, we can reconstruct a good approximation of the signature signal, even when the host signal is severely attacked.

In Section 2, we explain the data embedding and extraction, and in Section 3 we describe encoding and decoding process of the signature image using MDC. In Section 4 the experiments and results of different tests are provided, and finally section 5 summarize the paper.

2 Data Embedding and Extraction

The data embedding in the host image could be in the spatial or frequency domain [10, 11, 12, 13, 14, 15]. While data embedding in the spatial domain is more robust to geometrical attacks, such as cropping and down-sampling, data embedding in the frequency domain usually has more robustness to signal processing attacks, such as addition of noise, compression and lowpass filtering. In this paper, we use data embedding in the spatial domain using the proposed algorithm in [16].

Te data are embedded in one color component of the image based on its luminance. Since human eye is less sensitive to change in blue color, the method suggests modification of the blue component [16]. However the method fails when the image has very low density of blue component. We use MDC and embed in both red and blue components, so that it can survive even for images with low density of blue component. We expect that high resilience of MDC coding of the signature signal can help the data embedding scheme to survive the signal processing attacks.

In order to embed output indices of the signature image into pixel values at point (x, y) of the host image, we scramble and arrange these indices as a binary sequence: $D = d_1, d_2, \cdots, d_n$, where d_k is a binary variable.

We calculate the luminance value of a pixel at (x,y) using its three color components r(x,y), g(x,y) and b(x,y) as

$$l(x, y) = 0.299 r(x, y) + 0.587 g(x, y) + 0.114 b(x, y) \tag{1}$$

We select a group of pixel with higher value of blue components, and change the blue color component using this equation:

$$b'(x, y) = \begin{cases} b(x, y) + \alpha.l(x, y) & if \quad d_i = 0 \\ b(x, y) - \alpha.l(x, y) & if \quad d_i = 1 \end{cases} \tag{2}$$

Where α is the embedding modulation factor. We do a similar process for embedding value in red component of the pixels in the red dominated area of the host image.

For data extraction, we do not need the original host image. For the data embedded in blue components, at first we calculate an estimate of the blue component of the modified pixel using its neighboring pixels in a window size of 3 by 3 pixels (C=1).

$$\hat{b}''(x, y) = \frac{1}{4C} \left(-2b''(x, y) + \sum_{i=-C}^{+C} b''(x+i,y) + \sum_{i=-C}^{+C} b''(x,y+i) \right) \tag{3}$$

Here we use of 3 by 3 pixels (C=1) around each pixel. Now assuming that we embed each bit M times, we can estimate the average of difference using

$$\sigma_k'' = \frac{1}{M} \sum_{l=1}^{M} [\hat{b}''(x_l, y_l) - b''(x_l, y_l)] \tag{4}$$

The bit value is determined by looking at the sign of the difference between the pixel under inspection and the estimated original. In order to increase robustness, each signature bit is embedded several times, and to extract the embedded bit the sign of the sum of all differences is used.

We do a similar process for embedding value in red component of the pixels in the red dominated area of the host image.

3 Encoding and Reconstruction of the Signature Image

We decompose the signature image using the Haar wavelet transform, resulting in four subbands usually referred to as LL, LH, HL and HH. Fig. 2 shows the decomposition scheme.

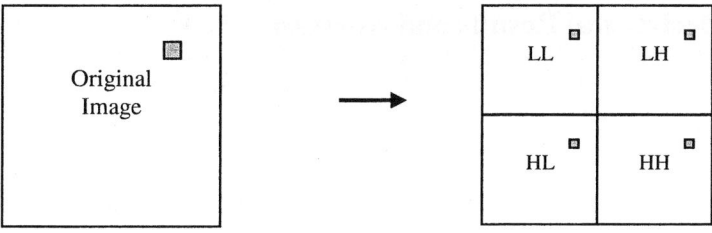

Fig. 2. The wavelet decomposition of the signature image

We use a phase scrambling operation to change the PDF of the lowest frequency subband (LL) to a nearly Gaussian shape [17]. The added random phase could be considered as an additional secret key between the transmitter and the registered receiver.

We encode the subbands using a PDF-optimized two-description scalar quantizer [18,19], assuming the Laplacian distribution for high frequency bands and the Gaussian distribution for the LL subband after phase scrambling. In this paper, we have set the encoding bit-rate at three bit per sample (bps), and obtained PSNR value over 31 dB for different tested images, which is satisfactory in image hiding applications. We use an integer bit-allocation among subbands based on their energies. The information of subband energies (15 bits) can be sent as side information or it can be encoded with a highly robust error correction method and embedded in the host image. We use the folded binary code (FBC) for representing output indices of quantizer to have higher error resilience.

Fig. 3. Host Image- Bird

4 Experimental Results and Analysis

We use a host image of 512×512 pixels and signature image of 128×128 pixels size. The "Cameraman" image is used as signature images, and the two images "Birds" and "Boat" which are shown in Fig. 3 and Fig. 4 are used as the host images.

We set the embedding factors such that their PSNR values stays above 34 dB after data embedding. Fig. 3 shows a sample of reconstructed signature image.

In order to evaluate the system performance, we calculate PSNR values of the reconstructed signature images. The system can be applied to applications such as hiding logo images for copyright protection, where the presence or absence of the signature is important more than the quality of the reconstructed image. In these applications, we usually set a threshold to decide on the amount of the cross correlation between the recovered signature and the original signature [1]. However, in this paper, we concentrate only on image hiding applications and provide PSNR values of reconstructed images.

Fig. 4. Host Image - Boat

Resistance to Baseline-JPEG Compression: The JPEG lossy compression algorithm with different quality factors (Q) is tested. Fig. 5 and Fig. 6 show the recovered signature image before and after JPEG compression of the host image. Fig. 7 shows the PSNR variation for different Q factors. As shown in Fig. 7, the PSNR values drop sharply for Q smaller than 50.

Resistance to JPEG2000 Compression: The JPEG2000 lossy compression algorithm with different output bit rates is tested on the host image. Fig. 8 shows sample of reconstructed image after JPEG-2000 compression of the host image. Fig. 9 shows the PSNR variation of the recovered signature images.

Resistance to Median and Gaussian filtering: Median and Gaussian filters of 3×3 mask size are implemented on the host image after embedding the signature. The PSNR of recovered signature are shown in Table 1. Fig. 10 and Fig. 11 show samples of reconstructed image after Median and Gaussian filtering of the host image.

Fig. 5. Samples of reconstructed signature images

Fig. 6. Samples of reconstructed signature images after JPEG compression of the host image with Q=55

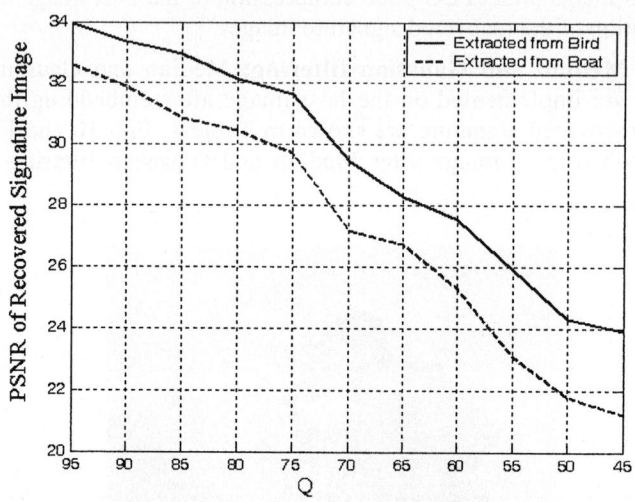

Fig. 7. PSNR variation of recovered signature image due to JPEG-compression of the host image

Fig. 8. Samples of reconstructed signature images after JPEG-2000 compression of the host image at 0.2bps

Table 1. PSNR (dB) values of the recovered signature images after implementing median and Gaussian filters on the host image

	Median Filter	Gaussian Filter
Extracted from Bird Image	20.65	25.80
Extracted from Boat Image	21.65	24.43

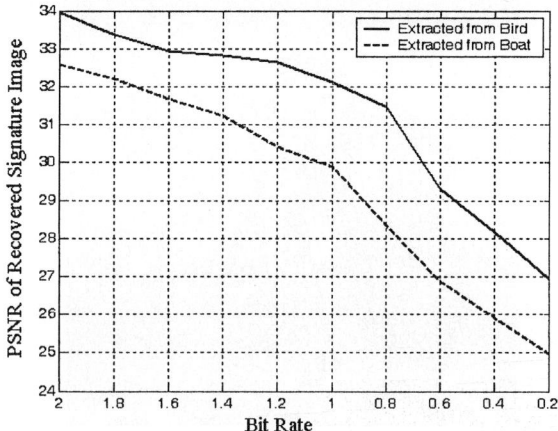

Fig. 9. PSNR variation of recovered signature image due to JPEG2000 compression of the host image

Fig. 10. Samples of reconstructed signature images after Median filtering

Resistance to Cropping: Table 2 shows PSNR values when some parts of the host image corners are cropped. Fig. 12 shows the host image after 10% cropping. Considerably good resistance is due to the existence of two descriptors in the image and scrambling of embedded information, which makes it possible to reconstruct the signature image information in the cropped area from the available descriptor in the non-cropped area. Fig. 13 shows sample of reconstructed image after 10% cropping of the host image.

Fig. 11. Samples of reconstructed signature images after Gaussian filtering the host image

Fig. 12. Sample of the host image after 10% cropping

Table 2. PSNR (dB) values of the recovered signature image for different percentage of cropping the host image

	5%	10%	15%	20%
Extracted from Bird Image	23.48	21.52	20.60	19.82
Extracted from Boat Image	26.25	23.65	20.20	20.70

Table 3. PSNR (dB) values of the recovered signature image after different amount of down-sampling the host image

	1/2	1/4	1/8
Extracted from Bird Image	23.18	19.15	18.27
Extracted from Boat Image	24.33	17.44	16.75

Fig. 13. Samples of reconstructed signature images after cropping the host image

Fig. 14. Samples of reconstructed signature images after down-sampling the host image

Resistance to Down-sampling: Due to loss of information in the down-sampling process, the host image cannot be recovered perfectly after up-sampling. However, it is possible to recover the signature image from those pixels available in the host image, as the two descriptions of the signature image information are scrambled and distributed in the host image. Table 3 lists PSNR values after several down-sampling processes. Fig. 14 shows sample of reconstructed image after down-sampling by 2 of the host image.

5 Conclusions

We have presented a new scheme for embedding a gray-scale image into a color host image. The signature encoding is based on multiple description subband image coding, and the embedding process is performed the spatial domain. The proposed system does not need the original host image for recovering the signature at the receiver. Since the system uses embedding in both red and blue components, it can works well for variety of images with different distribution of colors. We evaluate the reconstructed signature image quality when the host undergone various signal processing and geometrical attacks. The results show the system has good robustness. The developed system has low implementation complexity and can be extended for embedding video in video in real time.

References

1. Petitcolas F.A.P., Anderson R.J., and Kuhn, M.G.: Information Hiding-a Survey. Proceedings of the IEEE, Vol. 87, No.7, (**1999**) 1062-1078.
2. Chae, J.J., and Manjunath, B.S.: A Robust Embedded Data from Wavelet Coefficients. Proc. of SPIE, Storage and Retrieval for Image and Video Databases VI, (**1998**) 308-317.
3. Wolfgang R.B., Podilchuk C.I., and Delp E.J.: Perceptual watermarks for digital images and video. Proceedings of the IEEE, Vol. 87, No. 7, (**1999**) 1108-1126.
4. Swanson M.D., Zhu B., and Tewfik A.H.: Transparent Robust Image Watermarking. In Proceeding of the IEEE International Conference on Image Processing, Vol.2, (**1997**) 676-679.
5. Mukherjee, D., Chae, J.J., Mitra, S.K., and Manjunath, B.S.: A Source and Channel-Coding Framework for Vector-Based Data Hiding in Video. IEEE Trans. on Circuits and System for Video Technology. Vol. 10, No. 6 , (**2000**) 630-645.
6. Ashourian, M., Ho Y. S.: Multiple Description Coding for Image Data Hiding Jointly in the Spatial and DCT Domains. Lecture Notes in Computer Science (LNCS), vol. 2836, (**2003**)179 – 190.
7. Ashourian, M., Ho Y. S.: Multiple Description Coding for Image Data Hiding in the Spatial Domain. Lecture Notes in Computer Science (LNCS), vol. 2869, (**2003**)659-666.
8. Ashourian, M., Ho Y. S.: Blind Image Data Hiding in the Wavelet Domain. Lecture Notes in Computer Science (LNCS), vol. 3333, (**2003**)659 – 666
9. Bas, P.; Le Bihan, N.; Chassery, J.-M.: Color image watermarking using quaternion Fourier transform. IEEE International Conference on Acoustics, Speech, and Signal Processing, vol.3, (**2003**)521-524.
10. Barni, M.; Bartolini, F.; Piva, A.: Multichannel watermarking of color images, IEEE Transactions on Circuits and Systems for Video Technology, Vol. 12, Issue 3, (**2002**) 142 – 156.

11. Ahmidi, N. and Safabakhsh, R.: A novel DCT-based approach for secure color image watermarking. Proceedings Information Technology, Coding and Computing, Vol. 2 , (**2004**)709 – 713.
12. Kutter, M. and Winkler S.: A Vision-Based Masking Model for Spread-Spectrum Image Watermarking. IEEE Transactions on Image Processing, Vol. 11, No. 1, (**2002**) 16-25.
13. Piyu T., Chung C. : A color image watermarking scheme based on color quantization, Elsevier Signal Processing archive, Volume 84 , Issue 1,(**2004**) 95 -106.
14. Parisis, A. Carre, P. , Fernandez, M. C., Laurent, N. : Color image watermarking with adaptive strength of insertion. IEEE International Conference on Acoustics, Speech, and Signal Processing, Vol. 3, (**2004**) 85-88.
15. Hartung F., and Kutter M. : Multimedia watermarking techniques. Proceedings of the IEEE, Vol.87, No.7, (**1999**) 1079–1107.
16. Kutter M., Jordan F., and Bossen F.: Digital watermarking of color images using amplitude modulation. J. Electron. Imaging., vol. 7, no. 2, pp.326–332, (**1998**) 326-332.
17. Kuo C.C.J., and Hung C.H.: Robust Coding Technique-Transform Encryption Coding for Noisy Communication. Optical Eng., Vol. 32, No. 1, (**1993**) 150-153.
18. Goyal, V.K.: Multiple Description Coding: Compression Meets the Network. IEEE Signal Processing Magazine, Vo.18, Issue 5, (**2001**)74-93.
19. Vaishampayan V.A.: Design of Multiple Description Scalar Quantizers. IEEE Trans. on Information Theory, Vol. 39 , No.5, (**1993**) 821-834.

A Color Image Encryption Algorithm Based on Magic Cube Transformation and Modular Arithmetic Operation

Jianbing Shen, Xiaogang Jin, and Chuan Zhou

State Key Lab of CAD&CG, Zhejiang University,
Hangzhou, 310027, P.R., China
{Jianbing Shen, Xiaogang Jin, Chuan Zhou}@cad.zju.edu.cn

Abstract. Permutation-only image ciphers encrypt images by permuting the positions of all pixels in a secret way, which are unfortunately frail under known-text attack. In view of the weakness of permutation-only algorithms, a color image encryption algorithm based on magic cube transformation and a new modular arithmetic operation is designed. First, a natural number chaotic sequence is created with the secret key. For the sake of higher security, all secret keys are generated by different chaotic maps, and thus increase the security for decryption. Second, we implement the position permutation algorithm by magic cube transformation with chaotic sequences. Third, the pixel-substitution algorithm is realized by changing the image pixel value, with a XOR plus mod diffuse operation and a modular arithmetic operation. Finally, experimental results are given to demonstrate the efficiency and high security of our novel algorithm.

1 Introduction

Recent trend in wired/wireless communication has been to include multimedia data such as video, image, voice, music, text, etc. Especially, image and video content is preferred because of its information-implicative property. However, due to the intrinsic characters of images and videos such as bulk data capacity and high redundancy, encryption on which needs their own special requirements.

In order to fulfill such a need, many encryption schemes have been proposed and analyzed as possible solutions in [1, 2, 3, 4, 5, 6, 7], among which most of them are based on chaotic systems [3, 4, 5]. It has been proved that chaotic sequences provide much more additional benefits than pseudo-random sequences in applications of bulk data encryption algorithms [6, 7, 10, 11, 12, 13], which make full use of two special features of chaotic maps, one is the sensitivity to initial conditions and parameters, the other is the mixing property (topological transitivity or ergodicity).

Meanwhile, with the development of more and more encryption schemes and cryptanalysis work, it has been pointed out that some multimedia encryption schemes are insecure [1, 2, 3, 4]. In practical applications, there are three major kinds of methods used for constructing secure encryption algorithms: permutation, substitution, and their combining form, due to its frailty under known-text attack, we need to improve its security and its resistance to hostile attack.

After analyzing the security characteristics of a class of encryption schemes proposed in [1, 2, 3, 4], the present paper continues the same pursuit with further improvement on multimedia encryption security, we propose a novel image encryption algorithm based on magic cube transformation and a modular arithmetic operation, which is essentially motivated by the observation to the rules of magic cube game, totally using the advantages in both of pixel-position permutation and pixel-value substitution, and thus to compose our image encryption scheme.

The rest of the paper is arranged as follows: Section 2 describes the definition of magic cube transformation. Section 3 introduces chaotic sequences generators using various chaotic maps. Section 4 constructs a new image encryption scheme based on magic cube transformation and a new modular arithmetic operation using various nonlinear chaotic maps. Section 5 shows some experimental results with detailed analysis. Finally, in section 6 some characteristics of the proposed algorithm are discussed and summarized.

2 The Definition of Magic Cube Transformation

Based on the present algorithms for image encryption and decryption, inspired by the ideas and rules of magic cube toy, we define a new method for image encryption named as magic cube transformation.

Magic cube game is a process for segmenting the source cube into several sub-cubes, changing the order of the sub-cubes by shifting and rotating them along its cube surface, not only can we make up the desired sequence but also mess up the sequence of sub-cubes.

Consider a magic cube toy of order n, and denote a magic cube matrix $A = a(i,j), 0 \leq i, j \leq n-1$, and then the following properties [8] are obtained: (1) Each of the integers from 1 to $n \times n$ inclusively occurs exactly once among the entries of A; (2) For $0 \leq i \leq n-1$, $0 \leq j \leq n-1$, after magic cube transform, the sum $\sum_{i=0}^{n-1} a_{ij}$, $\sum_{j=0}^{n-1} a_{ij}$ and $\sum_{i=0}^{n-1} a_{ii}$ is independent of and separately.

According to the rules of magic cube game, each row and column of the image matrix can be shifted circularly with given control parameters. Introducing the ideas of circular shifting, rotating a row of the image means shifting $h(k)$ times iteratively in horizontal direction. We define shifting times $h(k)$ as control parameters, which can be obtained by the algorithm described in section 4.1.

A digital image can be regarded as a two-dimensional matrix $I_{M \times N}$, where M and N are the height and width of the image respectively. The parameters used in process of shifting and rotating are defined as control parameters. The magic cube transformation can be described as follows:

$$I'_{M \times N} = f(I_{M \times N}, h(k)) \qquad (1)$$

where $I_{M\times N}$ is the original image and $I'_{M\times N}$ is the ciphered one, $h(k)$ is the shifting times. The symbol denotes the mapping function from to $f(\cdot)$. In practical applications, this magic cube transformation can be shifted iteratively for a certain times to attain a satisfying encrypting result.

3 Chaotic Sequences Generators Using Various Chaotic Maps

Utilizing chaos as a chaotic sequence generator has become an important and exciting study field in the past decade, since it is non-periodic, non-convergent and extremely sensitive to the initial condition. Among the various nonlinear chaotic maps, the most famous and widely used, is the so-called logistic map, which is one of the simplest systems exhibiting order-to-chaos transitions, the basic logistic map is formulated as:

$$\tau(x) = \mu x(1-x) \quad (2)$$

$$x_k + 1 = \mu x_k(1 - x_k) \quad (3)$$

where $k = 0, 1, 2, \cdots$, $0 \leq \mu \leq 4$, μ is called the branch parameter.

All the statistical properties [13] show that the mixing property of the chaotic sequence equals to the effect of adding discrete white noise. This critical issue is what to be needed in the process of image encryption. With some simple variable substitution, logistic map can be redefined within the range of $(-1, 1)$ as the following formula:

$$x_{k+1} = 1 - \lambda \cdot x_k{}^2 \quad (4)$$

where $\lambda \in [0, 2]$, when $\lambda = 2$, the chaotic maps are called the full-maps.

In this paper, we also utilized another two important chaotic dynamic systems; one is so-called exponential chaos system, defined by the following formula:

$$x_{k+1} = \mu^{x_k} mod L \quad (5)$$

The other so-called sin-iteration chaos system is described as follows:

$$x_{k+1} = sin^2(b \cdot arcsin\sqrt{x(n)}) \quad (6)$$

4 Image Encryption and Decryption Algorithm

The thorough encryption/decryption algorithm consists of the following two steps: image pixel-position permutation algorithm using magic cube transformation and chaotic sequences; image pixel-value substitution algorithm by a new modular arithmetic operation.

4.1 Image Pixel-Position Permutation Algorithm

The following four steps achieve the detailed pixel-position permutation algorithm:

Step1: input the plain-image I, which is represented by a matrix $I_{M \times N}$, with a initial secret keys: $(k_0^R, n_r, k_0^G, n_g, k_0^B, n_b)$, where k_0^R, k_0^G, k_0^B is the initial condition of the chaotic maps, n_r, n_g, n_b is the iterated times.

Step2: separately calculate the following three chaotic sequences x_k^R, x_k^G, x_k^B, using formula (7) by three different dynamic chaotic maps: logistic maps (formula 4), exponential chaotic maps (formula 5) and so called sin-iteration chaotic maps (formula 6), respectively for processing the Red, Green and Blue channel in color image.

$$x_k = \{x_k^R, x_k^G, x_k^B | k = 0, 1, 2, \cdots, (M+N)\cdot n - 1\} \tag{7}$$

Now we can directly implement our image pixel-position permutation algorithm by using the above chaotic sequences, which are denoted as the shifting control parameter set $H = \{h(k) | k = 0, 1, 2, \cdots, (M+N)\cdot n - 1\}$ with magic cube transformation.

Step3: shuffle the positions of the plain image rows by rows, columns by columns with control parameter $h(k)$ obtained in step2 using the formula (1).

Step4: after all the pixels' positions have been permutated, we get the permutation-only image noted as I_{pem}.

Obviously, the above permutation-only algorithm just re-arranges the pixel positions without change the pixel's gray value, and there are still some potential weak points existing in these permutation-only algorithms [9], which are frail under known-text attack [3].

However, because different pixels' positions of the image may have the same gray value, the larger the probability of the repetition, the more difficult the decryption will be. To deal with the weakness of pure position permutation, we need further substitution algorithm to change the pixel's gray value to achieve more secure encryption algorithms.

4.2 Image Pixel-Value Substitution Algorithm

Assume that I_{pem} and $I_{pem}^{sub}(i,j)$ are separately the pixel value of the image before and after substitution in the position (i,j), where $0 \leq i \leq M-1$, $0 \leq j \leq N-1$; In order to design a substitution map function which is strong enough to resist the decryption attack and is unpredictable, here we need to define a new modular arithmetic operation as follows.

Considering two integers M and N, where $M < N$, the result of modular arithmetic operation between two integers is the arithmetical compliment obtained through M dividing N, we can get the two modular integers X and Y as follows:

$$Y = (X+M)\%N; M = (Y-X)\%N \tag{8}$$

Now we can realize our pixel-value substitution algorithm with the following two steps:

Step1: do modular arithmetic operation (defined as $p^{mod}(\cdot)$) using formula (8) with the permutation image in section 4.1, and then do XOR plus mod diffuse operation [5] with the chaotic sequence created by the formula (4,5,6), where L is the color level of each channel for color image, the cipher process is as follows:

$$I_{pem}^{mod}(i,j) = P^{mod}(I_{pem}(i,j)) \tag{9}$$

$$C(k) = C(i \times W + j) = I_{pem}^{sub}(i,j)) \tag{10}$$

$$I(k) = I(i \times W + j) = I_{pem}(i,j)) \tag{11}$$

$$C(k+1) = x_k \otimes \{[I(k) + x_k] mod(L)\} \otimes C(k) \tag{12}$$

For the sake of increasing the security of the encrypted image, we need to cut some front numbers in the chaotic sequence, the reserved sequence is $x(k)$ ($k = t, t+1, t+2, \cdots, t + 3\cdot(M+N)\cdot n - 1$, where t is the segment point from which we begin to cut the chaotic sequence.

Step2: the corresponding adverse substitution algorithm is operated with the following inverse XOR plus mod diffusing formula:

$$I(k+1) = \{x_k \otimes C(k+1) \otimes C(k) + L - x_k\} mod(L) \tag{13}$$

Then we do the inverse modular arithmetic operation for decryption.

5 Experiments Results and Security Analysis

We make many experiments with color images of different sizes by applying the new algorithm presented in this paper. The image decrypted with the right key is identical to the original one, while with the wrong key the decrypted one is erroneous. The encrypted image is so disarranged and pixel-changed that it cannot be recognized correctly. The results indicate that the proposed algorithm can get satisfying color image encryption effect.

5.1 Key Sensitive Test and Analysis

We performed a typical key sensitivity test according to changing the least significant bit of the key. A color image is encrypted by using the ciphering test key $k1 = (0.75436285, 10, 0.46270933, 10, 0.22659072, 10)$, where the least significant bit of the key is changed, so the original key becomes the new one $k2 = (0.75436284, 10, 0.46270933, 10, 0.22658172, 10)$. Figures 1, 2 show our key sensitive test results. The image encrypted by $k1$ has 99.99% differences from the one encrypted by $k2$ in terms of pixel values, although there is only one least significant bit difference in the two keys. Moreover, if a key is used to encrypt an image, while another trivially modified key is used to decrypt the ciphered image, and then the decryption does not succeed.

Fig. 1. Plain image and its ciphered one with key sensitive test: result1. Top left: Plain image. Top right: Encrypted image with the key $k1$. Bottom left: Encrypted image with the key $k2$. Bottom right: Difference image. $k1 = (0.75436285, 10, 0.46270933, 10, 0.22658172, 10)$. $k2 = (0.75436284, 10, 0.46270933, 10, 0.22658172, 10)$.

5.2 Key Space Analysis

The key space of a good encryption algorithm should be large enough to make brute-force attack infeasible. Our proposed image encryption algorithm is a 192-bit encryption scheme whose key space size is $2^{192} \approx 5.4526 \times 10^{57}$. An opponent may try to bypass guessing the key and directly guess all the possible combinations of the chaotic sequences, such as the control parameters of the keys. Considering a 512×512 color image, which is encrypted by our algorithm, possible control parameters are $10^8 \times 10^8 \times 10^8 = 10^{32}$, notice this is just for one round of the several iterations. If we use different ciphering keys in each ciphering round, then we will get further larger key space, which is enough to prevent the exhaustive searching.

Fig. 2. Plain image and its ciphered one with key sensitive test: result2. Top left: Plain image. Top right: Encrypted image with the key $k1$. Bottom left: Decrypted image with the correct key $k1$. Bottom right: Decrypted image with the wrong key $k2$. $k1 = (0.75436285, 10, 0.46270933, 10, 0.22658172, 10)$. $k2=(0.75436284, 10, 0.46270933, 10, 0.22658172, 10)$.

5.3 Known-Plaintext Attack Analysis

In known-plaintext attacking scenarios, our proposed method cannot be broken with only one known plaintext and its corresponding cipher-text f', according to the known-plaintext attack method described in [3], the plaintext can not be decrypted by using the mask image $f_m = f \otimes f'$, for our encryption algorithm using a modular arithmetic operation and XOR plus mod diffusing method, which is strong enough to resist the known-text attack.

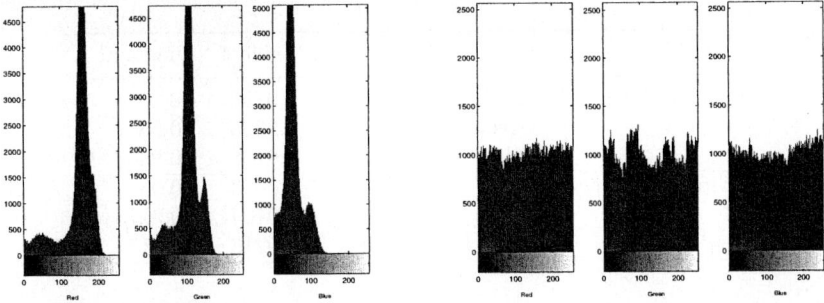

Fig. 3. Histogram of the plain-image and the cipher-image. Left: Histogram of Plain image (Red, Green, Blue) Right: Histogram of Cipher image.

5.4 Statistical Analysis

Statistical analysis [4, 5] has been performed on the proposed image encryption algorithm, demonstrating its superior confusion and diffusion properties, which strongly resist statistical attacks. This is shown by a test on the histograms of the enciphered images and on the correlations of adjacent pixels in the ciphered image.

Histograms of Encrypted Images. Select several color images of size 512× 512 that have different contents, and calculate their histograms. One typical example among them is shown in Fig.3. From the figure, one can see that the histogram of the ciphered image is fairly uniform and is significantly different from that of the original image.

Correlation of Two Adjacent Pixels. To test the correlation between two vertically adjacent pixels, two horizontally adjacent pixels, and two diagonally adjacent pixels, respectively, in a ciphered image, the following procedure was carried out. First, randomly select 1000 pairs of two adjacent pixels from an image. Then, calculate the correlation coefficient of each pair by using the following discrete two formulas from [5]:

$$cov(x,y) = \frac{1}{N}\sum_{i=1}^{N}(x_i - E(x))(y_i - E(y)); r_{xy} = \frac{cov(x,y)}{\sqrt{D(x)}\sqrt{D(y)}}; \quad (14)$$

where x and y are grey-scale values of two adjacent pixels in the image.

Fig.4 shows the correlation distribution of two vertically adjacent pixels in the plain-image and that in the cipher-image: the average correlation coefficients are 0.9799 and 0.0180, respectively, which are far apart. Similar results for diagonal and vertical directions were obtained, which are shown in Table 1:

Table 1. Correlation coefficients of two adjacent pixels in two images

		Horizontal	Vertical	Diagonal
Plain-Image	Red	0.9799	0.9798	0.9775
	Green	0.9809	0.9325	0.9652
	Blue	0.9322	0.9706	0.9403
Ciphered-Image	Red	0.0180	0.0083	0.0324
	Green	0.0099	0.0104	0.0273
	Blue	0.0152	0.0216	0.0177

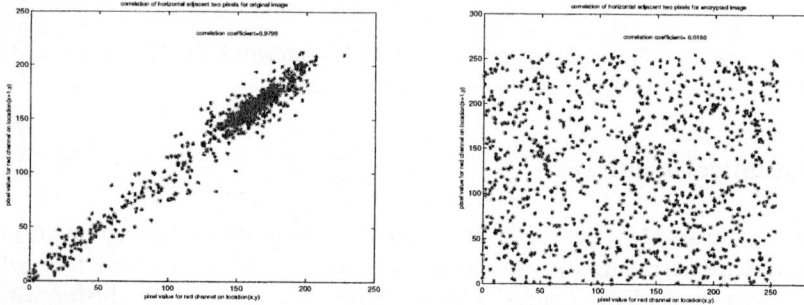

Fig. 4. Correlations of two horizontally adjacent pixels in the plain-image and in the encrypted image

5.5 Attacks and Analysis

Taking into account the variation tolerance of image processing operations, some attack issues on an image encryption scheme are also important, apart from the security consideration. These attacks include ability of surviving from JPEG compression, of Gaussian noise. Here, the PSNR of the noise-contaminated image is 15.08(dB), and the deciphered image cannot be recovered correctly from the Gaussian noise-added encrypted image, JPEG compression also greatly affects decrypted result, as shown in Fig.5, where the quality factor used by JPEG compression is 65, and PSNR =15.82(dB). This test results show that the ciphered image after JPEG compression can still be decrypted with most recovered information.

6 Conclusions

A new color image encryption algorithm based on magic cube transformation and modular arithmetic operation has been proposed in this paper. Chaotic sequence helps to form the magic cube transformation matrix based on keys, while the modular arithmetic operation and XOR plus mod diffusing method increases the security. Our new algorithm is secure enough to resist the following

Fig. 5. Results from attack tests of image processing operations. Top left: Plain image. Top right: Encrypted image. Middle left: Encrypted image with Gaussian noise addition. Middle right: Decrypted image with Gaussian Noise addition. Bottom left: Encrypted image under JPEG Compression. Bottom right: Decrypted image under JPEG Compression.

attacks: the brute-force attack, ciphertext-only attack, known/chosen-plaintext attack and statistical attack. There is no decrease in quality of the original image during encryption. Experimental results and key space analysis have both demonstrated the feasibility and efficiency of our novel algorithm.

Acknowledgement

This work was supported by 973 Program (No.2002CB312101), National Natural Science Foundation of China (No. 60273054, 60340440422) and Fok Ying Tung Education Foundation (No. 91069).

References

1. Li, S., and Zheng, X.: On the security of an image encryption method. In Proc. IEEE Int. Conference on Image Processing. (2002) 925-928
2. Li, S., Chen, G., and Mou, X.: On the Security of the Yi-Tan-Siew Chaotic Cipher. IEEE Transactions on Circuits and Systems. (2004) 665-669
3. Li. C., Li, S., Zhang, D., and Chen, G.: Cryptanalysis of a Chaotic Neural Network Based Multimedia Encryption Scheme. In 5th Pacific-Rim Conference on Multimedia (PCM2004). (2004) 418-425
4. Mao, Y., Chen, G., and Lian, S.: A novel fast image encryption scheme based on 3D chaotic baker maps. International Journal of Bifurcation and Chaos. (2004) 3613-3624
5. Chen, G., Mao, Y., and Charles, K.C.: A symmetric image encryption scheme based on 3D chaotic cat maps. Chaos Solitons and Fractals, (2004) 749-761
6. Kocarev, L., and Jakimovski, G.: Chaos and cryptography: from chaotic maps to encryption algorithms. IEEE Transactions on Circuits and Systems. (2001) 163-169
7. Masuda, N., and Aihara, K.: Cryptosystems with discretized chaotic maps. IEEE Transactions on Circuits and Systems. (2002) 28-40
8. Trenkler, M.: A construction of magic cubes. The Mathematical Gazette. (2000) 36-41
9. Zhao,X.Y., and Chen, G.: Ergodic matrix in image encryption. SPIE. (2002) 4875-4878.
10. Li, S.,lvarez, G., Chen, G., and Mou, X.: Breaking a chaos-noise-based secure communication scheme. Chaos. (2005) 532-534.
11. Li, S., lvarez, G., and Chen, G.: Breaking a chaos-based secure communication scheme designed by an improved modulation method. Chaos, Solitons and Fractals, (2005) 109-120.
12. lvarez, G., Li, S., Montoya, F., Pastor, G., and Romera, M.: Breaking projective chaos synchronization secure communication using filtering and generalized synchronization. Chaos, Solitons and Fractals. (2005) 775-783.
13. Zeng, Z., and Wang. N.: A new method based on chaotic sequence of image encryption. Proceedings of SPIE, the Third International Conference on Photonics and Imaging in Biology and Medicine. (2003) 285-289
14. Schneier, B.: Applied Cryptography - Protocols, algorithms, and source code in C, 2nd edition. New York: John Wiley & Sons, Inc.(1996)

Selective Video Encryption Based on Advanced Video Coding

Shiguo Lian[1,2], Zhongxuan Liu[1], Zhen Ren[1], and Zhiquan Wang[2]

[1] SAMI Lab, France Telecom R&D Beijing,
Beijing, 100080, P.R China
[2] Department of Automation, Nanjing University of Sci. & Tech.,
Nanjing, 210094, P.R. China
sg_lian@163.com

Abstract. Advanced Video Coding is recently announced and widely used, although the according protection means have not been developed thoroughly. In this paper, a selective encryption scheme is constructed on Advanced Video Coding. During AVC encoding, such sensitive data as intra-prediction mode, residue data, inter-prediction mode and motion vector are partially encrypted. This encryption scheme keeps secure against brute-force attack, replacement attack or known-plaintext attack, combines encryption process with compression process with low cost, and keeps the file format unchanged with some direct operations (such as displaying, time seeking, copying, cutting, etc.) supported. These properties make it suitable for secure video transmission.

1 Introduction

With the development of computer technology and Internet technology, multimedia data are used more and more widely. In order to keep secure, multimedia encryption has being studied. For video encryption, the study undergoes two periods: complete encryption and partial encryption. The fist one encrypts raw data or the compressed data directly with traditional or advanced ciphers. For example, some algorithms encrypt raw data directly [1-3], which permute the uncompressed videos and are often used to encrypt TV signals. Some other algorithms encrypt the compressed data directly [4,5], which are of both high security and high complexity. Thus, these algorithms are more suitable for secure video storing. The second one encrypts videos partially or selectively in order to obtain higher efficiency. For example, some algorithms encrypt only the signs of DCT coefficients or motion vectors [6,7,8], some algorithms permute DCT coefficients partially or completely during compression process [9-13], and some algorithms combine encryption process with Variable Length Code (VLC) [14,15]. These algorithms are often of low cost and suitable for video transmission.

The Advanced Video Coding (AVC) [16,17] has some apparent differences compared with MPEG1/2 codec. For example, the video frames are encoded with 4×4 or 2×2 integer DCT in AVC while with 8×8 DCT in MPEG1/2, the intra-macroblocks are encoded with intra-prediction mode according to the adjacent ones while they are encoded independently with only the DCs differentiated, and the inter-macroblocks are encoded with scalable inter-prediction mode while with fixed inter-prediction mode in MPEG1/2. Due to these differences, the AVC codec produces a bit-stream composed of many more parameters than MPEG1/2 does. In AVC, the produced data stream includes synchronization information (sequence-, picture-, slice- syntax), intra-macroblock information (macroblock type, coded block pattern, intra-prediction mode and residue data) and inter-macroblock information (macroblock type, coded block pattern, inter-prediction mode, motion vector difference and residue data). According to these differences, the encryption algorithms used in AVC videos may be different from the ones used in MPEG1/2 videos. For example, encrypting only the residue data may be not secure for some frames because the intra-prediction mode is important to frame's understandability, and encrypting only the macroblock type information is not secure enough because this information can be easily recovered in some frames with plane texture. It is not secure to encrypt only the intra-prediction parameters [18] because attackers can recover the frame's content with replacement attack [19]. For example, Fig. 1(a) is encrypted with intra-prediction permutation, and Fig. 1(b) is the frame with the intra-prediction modes set a certain one. As can be seen, the frame can still be understood. Thus, the parameters to be encrypted should be carefully selected.

(a)   (b)

Fig. 1. Replacement attack of only permuting intra-prediction mode [18]. (a) is the original video, while (b) is the one recovered by setting the intra-prediction mode fixed value.

For a video encryption algorithm, some features are often required, such as security, time efficiency, format compliance, and error robustness. In this paper, we propose a partial-encryption scheme based on AVC codec, which gets a good tradeoff between these requirements. In this scheme, the format information is kept unencrypted, and both the intra-macroblocks and the inter-macroblocks are partially encrypted. In order to reduce the sensitivity to transmission errors, the data stream is encrypted segment by segment with the slice as a unit. The encryption progress is controlled by a key generation and distribution scheme that is used to assign sub-keys to slices.

The rest of the paper is arranged as follows. In Section 2, the encryption scheme is presented based on the analysis of AVC parameters. And this scheme's performances are analyzed in detail in Section 3. Finally, some conclusions are drawn and future work is presented in Section 4.

2 The Proposed Encryption Scheme

In AVC, each frame is partitioned into macroblocks that are encoded with either intra-frame mode or inter-frame mode. In order to protect video data, both the texture information and motion information should be encrypted. For intra-macroblocks, their texture information prefers to be protected, which includes code block pattern, inter-prediction mode and residue data. For inter-macroblocks, the motion vector difference determines the motion information, which prefers to be encrypted. Partial encryption is adopted to obtain high efficiency. Here, we encrypt such parameters as intra-prediction mode, intra-macroblock's residue and motion vector difference (MVD) partially. For intra-prediction mode, the VLC code (Exp-Golomb Entropy coding) [16,17] is partially encrypted with Partial Encryption of Mode (PEM). For residue data, only the DCs and the signs of the ACs are encrypted with Partial Encryption of Coefficients (PEC). For MVDs, only their signs are encrypted with Partial Encryption of Vectors (PEV) in order to keep low cost. Thus, the encryption processes can be combined with the compression process, which is shown in Fig. 2. The decryption processes are symmetric to the encryption ones. All the encryption/decryption operations are under the control of the sub-keys produced by a key generator.

2.1 Partial Encryption of Intra-prediction Mode (PEM)

For intra-prediction encoding, the intra-prediction modes change with the block size. There are 16 modes for 4×4 luma block, 4 modes for 16×16 luma block and 4 modes for 8×8 chroma block, respectively. In AVC, the intra-prediction modes are encoded with Exp-Golomb codes [16]. This kind of codeword is composed of R zeros, one '1'-bit and R bits of information (Y). Thus, the intra-prediction mode is $X=2^R+Y-1$, where $R = \lceil \log_2(X+1) \rceil$. The encryption process is applied as follows: X is firstly encoded into a variable-length code with Exp-Golomb coding, and then only the information Y is encrypted into Z with a stream cipher [20]. Here, a stream cipher supports the plaintext with variable length, which is more suitable for the encoded stream than a block cipher. The decryption process is symmetric to the encryption one.

2.2 Partial Encryption of Coefficients (PEC)

The intra-macroblock's residue data and MVDs are encrypted with a stream cipher. Among them, DCs are first encoded with VLC coding and then encrypted completely, while ACs are first encrypted with sign-encryption and then VLC-encoded. These processes keep the compression ratio and file format unchanged. Here, the stream cipher proposed in [20] is used, which belongs to ciphertext-feedback mode.

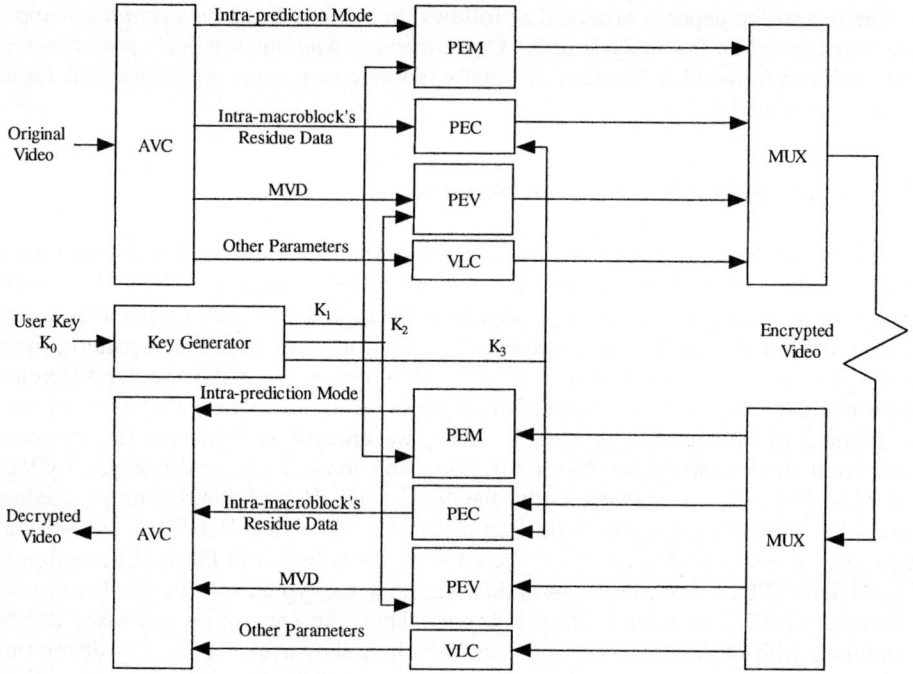

Fig. 2. AVC based encryption and decryption processes. Three encryption operations PEM, PEC and PEV are inserted into encoding process under the control of key generator. The decryption process is symmetric to the encryption one.

2.3 Partial Encryption of Motion Vectors (PEV)

Motion vectors determine the motion information of the video sequence. In order to keep low cost, only the signs of MVDs are encrypted with a stream cipher [20]. The changes in signs do not affect the compression process. For convenience, the encryption process is applied followed with the VLC encoding process. In decryption, the MVDs are firstly decoded, and then decrypted.

2.4 Key Generator

In this encryption scheme, three encryption operations are introduced into AVC encoding or decoding process. In order to keep secure, the three encryption operations can be controlled by different sub-keys. Thus, a key generator is needed to generate these sub-keys. Similarly, data streams can be encrypted segment by segment with multi-keys, which not only strengthen the system but also improve its robustness to transmission errors. Here, we encrypt the video stream with the slice as a segment, and assign each slice a different sub-key. Thus, if errors happen in a slice, then only the according slice is fault-decrypted, while other ones can still be decrypted correctly.

3 Performance Analysis

3.1 Perception Security

Cipher Video. In the proposed encryption scheme, both the texture information and the motion information are encrypted, which make the videos unintelligible. Fig. 3 gives the encryption results of some sample videos. The cipher videos ((c) and (d)) are both too chaotic to be understood. Thus, this encryption scheme is of high perception security.

(a) (b)

(c) (d)

Fig. 3. Results of video encryption. (a) is the original video, (b) is the original video, (c) is the encryption result of (a), and (d) is the encryption result of (b).

Key sensitivity. Taking QCIF Foreman for example, Fig. 4 gives the video encrypted with $k_0=1000$, and the videos decrypted with $k_1=1001$, $k_2=999$ and $k_0=1000$.

Fig. 4. Test of key sensitivity. (a) is the cipher video encrypted with k_0=1000, (b) is the video decrypted with k_1=1001, (c) is the video decrypted with k_2=999 and (d) is the video decrypted with k_0=1000.

As can be seen, slight difference in the key causes great differences in the decrypted videos. This property shows that the encryption scheme is of high key-sensitivity, which increases the difficulty of statistical or differential attacks.

3.2 Ciphertext-Only Attacks

Brute-force attack. Two kinds of brute-force attack may be adopted. The first one is to enumerate the user key, while the second one is to enumerate the encryption space of the internal operations. In this encryption scheme, each slice is encrypted under the control of a sub-key that is generated from the user key. Generally, the user key is bigger than 128-bit, and the brute-force space is more than 2^{128}, which is too large for attackers to break the cryptosystem. The second kind of attackers tries to recover the original videos. That is, to recover the intra-prediction mode, MVD's signs and intra-macroblock's residue data. The difficulty is determined by the encryption scheme. For

W×H frame, if m macroblocks are intra-encoded, and n ones are inter-encoded, then the brute-force space is

$$S_{frame} = (2^2)^n \cdot (2^R \cdot 2^L)^m = 2^{2n+(R+L)m} = 2^{WH/128+(R+L-2)m}$$

Here, m+n=WH/256 and R+L>2, where R is the code parameter mentioned in Section 2 and L is the length of a slice stream. Thus, S_{frame} increases with m. Taking QCIF for example, W×H=176×144, and $S_{frame} \geq 2^{198+m} \geq 2^{198}$. As can be seen, the brute-force space is too large for attackers to recover the original videos.

Replacement attack. Replacement attack [19] is used to break multimedia encryption algorithms under the condition of ciphertext-only attack. That is, the encrypted data can be replaced by some other data, which makes the decoded multimedia data understandable. For example, in wavelet-based codec, only encrypting the coefficients in low frequency is not secure enough because multimedia data can be understood if the encrypted coefficients are replaced by zeros [21]. As has been analyzed in Section 1, encrypting only the intra-prediction mode is not secure enough. In the proposed encryption scheme, both of them are encrypted, which make replacement attack difficult. Fig. 5 shows the video recovered by replacement attack. Here, (a) is the original video, and (b) is the one recovered by replacing all the intra-prediction modes with certain value. As can be seen, the recovered video is too chaotic to be understood, which proves the encryption scheme's security against replacement attack.

(a)　　　　　　　　　　　　　　(b)

Fig. 5. Test of replacement attack. (a) is the original video, and (b) is the video recovered by replacing the intra-prediction mode with certain value.

3.3 Known/Select-Plaintext Attack

If the plain-video is known to attackers, the plain-cipher double can be used to reduce the difficulty of brute-force attacks. In the proposed encryption scheme, the intra-prediction modes, residue data of intra-macroblock and MVD signs are encrypted with stream ciphers. The difficulty to recover the key from the plain-cipher double is determined by the adopted stream cipher. Here, if the stream cipher is of good random property [20], which has been verified difficult to recover the initial-value from only the produced sequence, the plaintext does little help to breaking the key. If the attackers can select various plain-videos, then they can use different plain-cipher doubles to recover the key. In the proposed encryption scheme, different slices are encrypted under the control of different keys, which makes attackers difficult to obtain enough suitable plain-cipher doubles. However, different from text/binary encryption, attackers may adopt video processing methods [19] together with cryptanalysis methods to break video encryption algorithms. Thus, the system's security against some unknown select-plaintext attacks needs to be further studied.

3.4 Computational Cost

The computing complexity of the proposed encryption scheme depends on the encrypted data volumes and the stream cipher's cost. Among them, the data to be encrypted include the intra-prediction mode, the encoded DCs, the signs of ACs and the signs of MVDs. In practice, the encryption data ratio (Edr) is often smaller than 10%, which is defined as the ratio between the encrypted data volume and the whole data volume. Similarly, the operation time ratio between the stream cipher and the encoding process is very small. That is because the encryption process is realized by bit-wise operation, with high time-efficiency. In experiments, we test the time-efficiency of the encryption/decryption process, which is measured by the time ratio between encryption/decryption and compression/decompression. Table 1 gives the experimental results. As can be seen, encryption/decryption makes up no more than 10% percents of the compression/decompression, which shows that the encryption/decryption process does not affect the compression/decompression process greatly.

Table 1. Test of the scheme's time-efficiency

Video	Size	Time ratio	
		Ratio between Encryption and Compression	Ratio between Decryption and Decompression
Foreman	QCIF	0.6%	4.3%
Akiyo	QCIF	0.8%	4.1%
Mother	QCIF	0.9%	5.7%
Mobile	CIF	0.7%	4.2%
Football	CIF	1.1%	5.3%
Akiyo	CIF	0.8%	6.1%

4 Conclusions and Future Work

A video encryption scheme is presented and analyzed in this paper, which encrypts the intra-prediction mode, the intra-macroblock's residue data and the MVD partially and selectively during AVC encoding. It keeps the format information unencrypted, which supports some direct operations. It obtains high time-efficiency through reducing the encrypted data volumes, which makes it practical to incorporate encryption operations in the encoding process. Both the texture information and motion information are encrypted, which makes the scheme not only secure in perception but also secure against brute-force and known-plaintext attacks. Additionally, the segment-based encryption mode makes the scheme of higher robustness to transmission errors. These properties make the scheme suitable for real-time video transmission. The scheme's security against some special attacks and its hardware-implementation will be further studied in the future.

Acknowledgements

This work was supported by the National Natural Science Foundation of China through the grant number 60174005 and the Doctoral Foundation of National Education Ministry through the grant number 20020288052.

References

1. Kudelski, A.: Method for scrambling and unscrambling a video signal. United States Patent 5375168, 20 December (1994)
2. Access control system for the MAC/packet family: EUROCRYPT. European Standard EN 50094, CENELEC, December (1992)
3. Maniccam, S., Nikolaos, G., Bourbakis: Image and video encryption using SCAN patterns. Pattern Recognition 37(4): 725-737 (2004)
4. Qiao, L., Nahrstedt, K.: A new algorithm for MPEG video encryption. In: Proceeding of the First International Conference on Imaging Science, Systems and Technology (CISST'97), Las Vegas, Nevada, July (1997) 21-29
5. Romeo, A., Romdotti, G., Mattavelli, M., Mlynek, D.: Cryptosystem architectures for very high throughput multimedia encryption: the RPK solution. ICECS (1999)
6. Shi, C., Wang, S., Bhargava, B.: MPEG video encryption in real-time using secret key cryptography. In: Proc. of PDPTA'99, Las Vegas, Nevada (1999)
7. Chiaraluce, F., Ciccarelli, L., Gambi, E., Pierleoni, P., Reginelli, M.: A New Chaotic Algorithm for Video Encryption. IEEE Transactions on Consumer Electronics, Vol.48, No.4, Nov (2002)
8. Yen, J.-C., Guo, J.-I.: A new MPEG encryption system and its VLSI architecture. IEEE Workshop on Signal Processing Systems, Taipei, 430-437 (1999)
9. Tang, L.: Methods for encrypting and decrypting MPEG video data efficiently. In: Proceedings of the Fourth ACM International Multimedia Conference (ACM Multimedia'96), Boston, MA, November (1996) 219-230
10. Tosum, A.S., Feng, W.: Efficient multi-layer coding and encryption of MPEG video streams. IEEE International Conference on Multimedia and Expo (I) (2000)
11. Qiao, L., Nahrstedt, K., Tam, I.: Is MPEG encryption by using random list instead of zigzag order secure. IEEE International Symposium on Consumer Electronics, Singapore, December (1997)
12. Shi, C., Bhargava, B.: A fast MPEG video encryption algorithm. In: Proceedings of the 6th ACM International Multimedia Conference, Bristol, UK, September (1998) 81-88

13. Zeng, W., Lei, S.: Efficient frequency domain selective scrambling of digital video. IEEE Trans, Multimedia (2002)
14. Wu, C., Kuo, C.: Fast encryption methods for audiovisual data confidentiality. In: SPIE International Symposia on Information Technologies 2000, Proceedings of SPIE Vol. 4209, Boston, MA, USA, Nov. (2000) 284-295
15. Wu, C., Kuo, C.: Efficient multimedia encryption via entropy codec design. In: SPIE International Symposium on Electronic Imaging 2001, Proceedings of SPIE Vol. 4314, San Jose, CA, USA, Jan. (2001)
16. ITU-T Rec. H.264/ISO/IEC 11496-10. Advanced Video Coding. Final Committee Draft, Document JVT-E022, September (2002)
17. Richardson: H.264/MPEG-4 Part 10, October (2002)
18. Ahn, J., Shim, H., Jeon, B., Choi, I.: Digital Video Scrambling Method Using Intra Prediction Mode. Springer LNCS vol.3333, PCM2004, Nov. (2004) 386-393
19. Podesser, M., Schmidt, H., Uhl, A.: Selective bitplane encryption for secure transmission of image data in mobile environments. In: CD-ROM Proceedings of the 5th IEEE Nordic Signal Processing Symposium (NORSIG 2002), Tromso-Trondheim, Norway, October (2002)
20. Vanstone, S., Menezes, A., Oorschot, P.: Handbook of Applied Cryptography. CRC Press (1996)
21. Lian, S., Sun, J., Zhang, D., Wang, Z.: A Selective Image Encryption Scheme Based on JPEG2000 Codec. In: The 2004 Pacific-Rim Conference on Multimedia (PCM2004), Springer LNCS, 3332 (2004) 65-72

Key Frame Extraction Based on Shot Coverage and Distortion

Ki Tae Park[1], Joong Yong Lee[1], Kee Wook Rim[2], and Young Shik Moon[1]

[1] Department of Computer Science and Engineering,
Hanyang University, Ansan, Republic of Korea
{parkkt, jylee, ysmoon}@cse.hanyang.ac.kr
[2] Department of Knowledge and Industrial Engineering,
Sun Moon University, Chung-Nam, Republic of Korea
rim@sunmoon.ac.kr

Abstract. Key frame extraction has been recognized as one of the important research issues in video information retrieval. Until now, in spite of a lot of research efforts on the key frame extraction for video sequences, existing approaches cannot quantitatively evaluate the importance of extracted frames in representing the video contents. In this paper, we propose a new algorithm for key frame extraction using shot coverage and distortion. The algorithm finds significant key frames from candidate key frames. When selecting the candidate frames, the coverage rate for each frame to the whole frames in a shot is computed by using the difference between adjacent frames. The frames with the coverage rate within 10% from the top are regarded as the candidates. Then, by computing the distortion rate of a candidate against all frames, the most representative frame is selected as a key frame in the shot. The performance of the proposed algorithm has been verified by a statistical test. Experimental results show that the proposed algorithm improves the performance by 13 – 50% over the existing methods.

1 Introduction

The last few years' developments in software tools have made areas such as multimedia databases quite feasible. The incredible rates at which these databases are publishing have exceeded the capabilities of current text base cataloguing. As the number of multimedia contents such as video sequences increase rapidly, the importance of video indexing has been emphasized. Since multimedia contents include a large amount of information, it is difficult to find key issues without searching full data in multimedia contents. To solve the problem, it is necessary to partition multimedia contents into a set of meaningful and manageable segments [1,2]. In order to partition multimedia contents, a video is segmented into shots that are sets of frames generated during a continuous operation and represent continuous action in time and space. After shots are segmented, the most representative frame which can represent the salient content of the shot. Depending on the content complexity of shot, one or more key frames can be extracted from a shot [3]. It is also necessary to extract key frames in each video shot, because key frames are utilized for effectively summarizing, browsing, retrieving, and comparing multimedia contents [4,5,6]. In video sequences, a key frame is the significant frame that indicates the substance of a shot very well. But it is difficult to exactly extract key frames, because methods for extracting key frames utilize low-level features without semantic information, which depends on the subjectivity of users [1,7,8].

2 Related Works

Until now, a lot of research has been carried out regarding the key frame extraction. The method proposed by Nagasaka and Tanka considers key frame as the first frame among frames in a shot after detecting shot boundary [9]. This method is very simple and easy to compute. But regardless of the substance of shot, the number of key frames is limited to one frame per shot. Furthermore, the first frame normally is not stable and does not capture the major visual contents. Zhang and Smoliar proposed a method, which uses the multiple visual criteria such as shot information, color and motion features to extract key frames in a shot [10]. Zhang's method segments the video into shots and selects the first frame of each shot as a key frame. Then, using color and motion features, other frames in the shot that are sufficiently different from the last key frame are marked as key frames as well. Zhang's approach is relatively fast. However, it does not effectively capture the visual contents of the video shot, since the first frame in a shot is not necessarily a key frame. Assuming that the camera position is focused at a significant frame, Wolf proposed a motion based approach to key frame extraction [11]. This method first computes the optical flow for each frame [12], and then computes a simple motion metric based on the optical flow. Finally, this method analyzes the metric as a function of time to select key frames at the local minima of motion. Wolf's method is more sophisticated due to the analysis of motion and extracts key frames without restricting the number of key frames, but it is computationally expensive. Gresle and Huang proposed a shot activity based approach [6]. They first compute the intra- and reference histograms and then compute an activity indicator. Based on the activity curve, the local minima are selected as the key frames. However, its underlying assumption of local minima is not necessarily correct. Also, the computation time is expensive. Han and Tewfik proposed a key frame extraction scheme after detecting shot boundaries using eigenvectors and eigenvalues [13]. This method extracts key frames by reducing the amount of data, but the extracted key frames cannot completely represent the shot because the complexity of shot has not been considered. In spite of a great deal of research efforts on the key frame extraction, methods for extracting representative key frames that represent the major visual contents still need improvement.

3 The Proposed Method

In this paper, we propose a new algorithm for key frame extraction using DC information in video sequences. The proposed algorithm also quantitatively evaluates the key frame selection in terms of the importance of the extracted frames. Our method consists of two steps. In the first step, after computing the similarity among all frames in the shot, the coverage rate of each frame in the shot is computed and the frames with the coverage rate within 10% from the top are selected as candidate key frames. Then, by computing the distortion rate of the candidates against all frames in the shot, the frame that is most representative among candidates is selected as the final key frame. Fig. 1 shows the flowchart of the proposed algorithm.

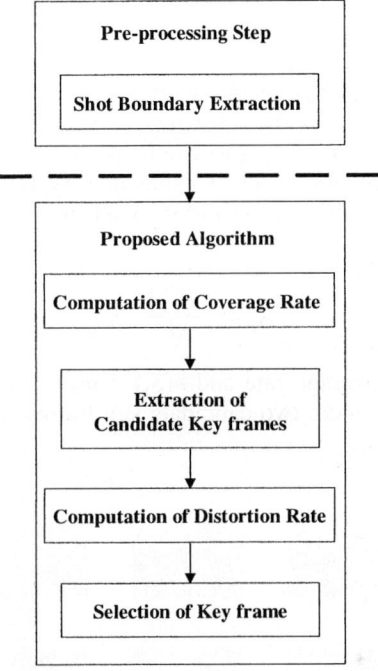

Fig. 1. Flowchart of the proposed algorithm

3.1 Selection of Candidate Key Frames

First, in the process of selecting key frame candidates, we assume that the candidate frames fully represent the contents of a shot focused by camera and appear in the shot repeatedly [1, 4]. By the above assumption, candidate key frames can be selected by computing the coverage rate. The detailed procedures for computing the coverage rate are as follows. First, the similarity between two frames is defined by Equation (1), using the correlation value [14].

$$Corr(x, y) = \frac{Cov(x, y)}{SD(x) \times SD(y)}, \qquad (1)$$

where $Corr(x,y)$ is the covariance value and SD is the standard deviation.

Using the correlation, the mean of the correlation values is computed by Equation (2), which shows how much each frame is similar to all the other frames within a shot.

$$E_x = \frac{1}{N} \sum_{i=1}^{N} Corr(x, i), \qquad (2)$$

where x is the corresponding frame and N denotes the total number of frames in the shot.

Next, the number of frames relevant to each frame is computed by Equation (3) using correlation values and the mean of the correlation values.

$$I \in S_x \quad , \quad if \ Corr(x, I) > E_x, \quad I = x+1, ..., N \tag{3}$$

where I is the frame number in the shot and S_x is the set of frames relevant to the x-th frame. As shown in Equation (3), the number of frames relevant to the corresponding frame is computed by using only the subsequent frames. By doing this, the first frame among all frames with high coverage rate can be declared as a key frame.

In the final step, the coverage rate is calculated by Equation (4) for each frame against all other frames in the shot in order to select candidate key frames that are within 10% from the top.

$$CR_x = \frac{n(S_x)}{N} \quad , \tag{4}$$

where CR_x denotes the coverage rate and $n(S_x)$ denotes the number of frames in S_x. Fig. 2 shows an example where two candidate key frames are selected using the coverage rate.

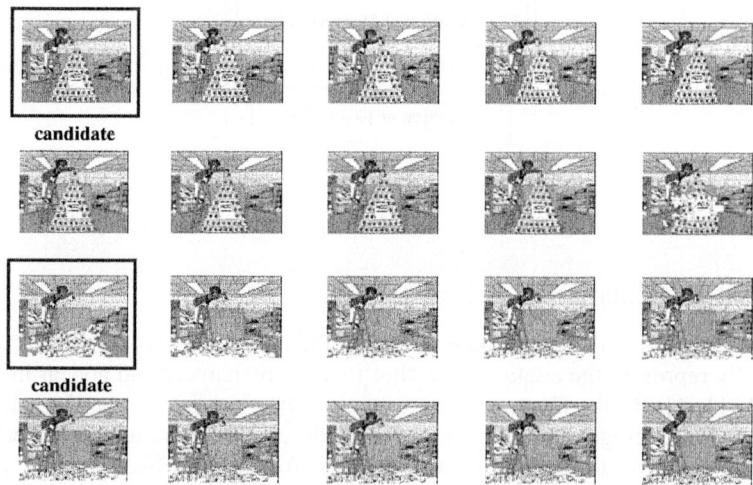

Fig. 2. Selection of candidate key frames using the coverage rate

3.2 Key Frame Extraction

After candidate key frames are selected by the coverage rate, we select the final key frame among the candidates. The coverage rate provides a measure as to how much each candidate is representative for the other frames in the shot. However, it is difficult to determine which frame is the best key frame when several candidate frames have high coverage rates. Thus, in order to determine the key frame, we compute the distortion rate of the candidates against all frames in a shot. After computing the distortion rate, the frame with the lowest distortion rate among the candidates is selected as the key frame. In our method, the distortion rate is computed by the moment of n-th degree, as shown in Equation (5).

$$m = \sum_{i=0}^{L-1} r_i p(r_i) \tag{5}$$

$$\mu_n(r) = \sum_{i=0}^{L-1} (r_i - m)^n p(r_i) \;,$$

where r is a random variable representing discrete gray-levels in the range [0, L-1], $P(r_i)$ denotes an estimate of the probability of occurrence of gray level r, and m is the mean value of r. Using Equation (5), we compute the moment of first, second, and third degree for each frame. Then, each frame in the shot can be represented by a 3- dimensional vector, as in Equation (6).

$$F_n = [\,\mu_1, \mu_2, \mu_3\,]^T \quad n = 1\ldots\ldots N \;, \tag{6}$$

where n denotes the frame number, and μ_1, μ_2, and μ_3 are the mean, variance, and skew, respectively. Then final key frame is determined by computing the partial moment of each candidate frame against the total moment of the shot, as in Equation (7) and (8).

$$AV_{partial} = \frac{1}{n(S_x)} \sum_{j=0}^{n(S_x)-1} F_j[\,\mu_1, \mu_2, \mu_3\,]^T \tag{7}$$

$$AV_{shot} = \frac{1}{N} \sum_{i=0}^{N-1} F_i[\,\mu_1, \mu_2, \mu_3\,]^T \;,$$

where $AV_{partial}$ and AV_{shot} imply the mean vector of frames in S_x and the mean vector of all frames within a shot, respectively.

$$\underset{n}{Arg\max}\left(\frac{AV_{shot} \bullet AV_{partial}^n}{|AV_{shot}| |AV_{partial}^n|}\right) \;, \tag{8}$$

In Equation (8), n implies the frame number of each candidate, $AV_{shot} \bullet AV_{partial}$ is the inner product of two vectors, and $|AV|$ is the amplitude of each vector.

4 Experimental Results and Performance Analysis

For the experiment, we use video sequences of KBS (Korea Broadcasting System), MBC (Moonhwa Broadcasting Company), and SBS (Seoul Broadcasting System) among Korean broadcasting stations. The input videos are in the NTSC format, which are MPEG-1 encoded for the experiment. Also, the experiments have been carried out using IBM Pentium-IV 1.4Ghz computer system and Visual C++ 6.0 compiler. In order to estimate the performance of the proposed algorithm, we compare the results

Table 1. Test video sequences used in the experiment

Type of videos	The number of shots
Advertisement	48
News	52
Drama	45
Animation	55
Movie	50

Fig. 3. Test sequences used in the experiment

with Nagasaka's algorithm and Tewfik' method. These algorithms have been tested using five types of video sequences, as shown in table 1. Fig. 3 shows the test sequences used in the experiment.

In order to evaluate the performance, we carried out a subjective test where 32 graduate students evaluate the satisfaction level of each algorithm into three levels such as best, medium, and worst. If the key frame appropriately represents the substance of a shot, we consider it as "best". If the key frame does not represent the substance at all, it is "worst". In other cases, we consider it as "medium". We first showed the whole frames in the shot to students, and then showed the key frames extracted by various methods including the proposed algorithm. After showing the

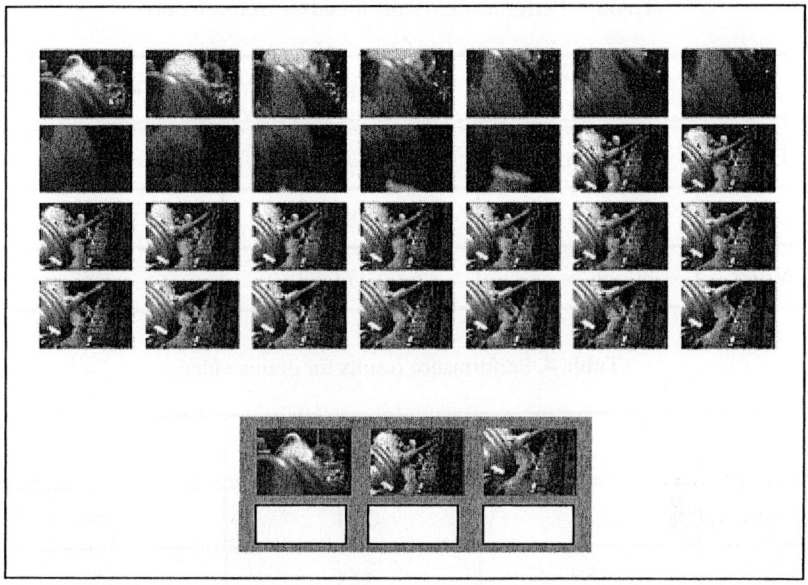

Fig. 4. Format of evaluation survey used in the experiment

Table 2. Performance results for news video

	Nagasaka's method	Tewfik's mehtod	Proposed method
Best	824	891	1022
Medium	506	504	539
Worst	334	269	103

key frames, students decide the satisfaction level among the three. Fig. 4 shows the format of evaluation survey used in the experiment. Experimental results for various test sequences are shown in table 2 – 6.

Fig. 5 and Fig. 6 show the number of key frames selected as the best and the worst, respectively. Experiments show that the proposed algorithm has achieved 4 – 67% improvement in the case of the best satisfaction and has achieved 33 – 77% improvement in the case of the worst satisfaction, compared to the existing algorithms. The overall performance of our algorithm has been improved by 13 – 50% over the existing ones.

Table 3. Performance results for advertisement video

	Nagasaka's method	Tewfik's mehtod	Proposed method
Best	596	776	979
Medium	514	489	459
Worst	426	271	98

Table 4. Performance results for drama video

	Nagasaka's method	Tewfik's mehtod	Proposed method
Best	523	791	954
Medium	489	484	455
Worst	428	165	31

Table 5. Performance results for movie video

	Nagasaka's method	Tewfik's mehtod	Proposed method
Best	577	706	928
Medium	428	415	487
Worst	595	479	185

Table 6. Performance results for animation video

	Nagasaka's method	Tewfik's mehtod	Proposed method
Best	511	827	1094
Medium	629	593	551
Worst	620	340	115

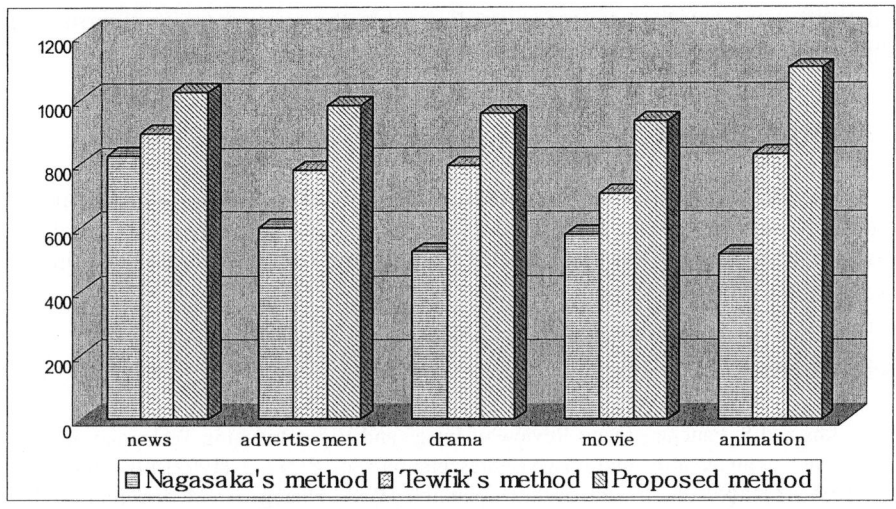

Fig. 5. The number of frames as the best satisfaction

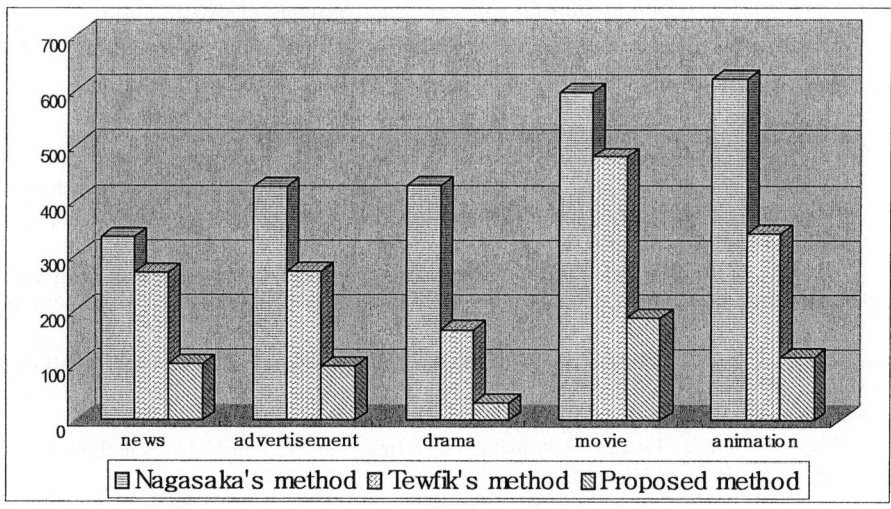

Fig. 6. The number of frames as the worst satisfaction

5 Conclusions

In this paper, we proposed a new algorithm that extracts key frames based on coverage and distortion rate. While existing methods cannot quantitatively present the fitness of the extracted key frames, our algorithm can provide a quantitative measure of fitness for the selected key frames by computing the coverage and the distortion rate to determine the key frames among candidates. In the experiments, we carried out a subjective test and verified the effectiveness of the proposed algorithm.

Acknowledgement

This research was supported by the MIC (Ministry of Information and Communication), Korea, under the ITRC (Information Technology Research Center) support program supervised by the IITA (Institute of Information Technology Assessment)

References

1. F. Idis and S. Panchanathan : Review of Image and Video Indexing Technique. Journal of Visual Communication and Image Representation, Vol. 8, No. 2, (1997) 146–166
2. M. R. Naphade, A. M. Ferman, J, Warnick, T. S. Huang, A. M. Tekalp : A High-performance Shot Boundary Detection Algorithm Using Multiple Cues. Proc. of IEEE Int. Conf. on Image Processing, Vol. 1, (1998) 884–887
3. Y. Rui. T. S. Huang, and S. Mehrotra : Exploring Video Structures beyond The Shots. Proc. of IEEE Int. Conf. Multimedia Computing and Systems, (1998) 237–240
4. P. Aigrain, H. Zhang, and D. Petkovic : Content-based Representation and Retrieval of Visual Media : A State-of-the-art Review. Multimedia Tools and Application, Vol. 3, (1996) 179–202
5. Y. Zhuang, Y. Rui, T. S. Huang, and S. Mehrotra : Adaptive Key Frame Extraction Using Unsupervised Clustering. Proc. of IEEE Int. Conf. on Image Processing, (1998) 866–870
6. P. O. Gresle and T. S. Huang : Gisting of Video Documents: A Key Frames Selection Algorithm Using Relative Activity Measure. Proc. of the second Int. Conf. on Visual Information Systems, (1997) 279–286
7. R. Brunelli, O. Mich, and C. M. Modena : A Survey on The Automatic Indexing of Video Data. Journal of Visual Communication and Image Representation. Vol. 10, (1999) 78–112
8. X. Ju, and J. Black : Summarization of Videotaped Presentations : Automatic Analysis of Motion and Gesture. IEEE Trans. on Circuits and Systems for Video Technology, Vol. 8, No. 5, (1998) 686–696
9. A. Nagasaga and Y. Tanaka : Automatic Video Indexing and Full Video Search for Object Appearances. Proc. of Visual Database Systems, (1992) 113–127
10. H. Zhang, J. Wu, D. Zhong, and S. W. Smoliar : An Integrated System for Content based Video Retrieval and Browsing. Pattern Recognition, Vol. 30, No. 4, (1997) 643–658
11. W. Wolf : Key Frame Selection by Motion Analysis. Proc. of IEEE Int. Conf. on Acoustic, Speech, and Signal Processing, (1996) 1228–1231
12. B. K. P. Horn and B. G. Schunk : Determining Optical Flow. Artificial Intelligence, Vol. 17, (1981) 185–203
13. K. J. Han and A. H. Tewfik L Eigen Image based Video Segmentation and Indexing. Proc. of IEEE Int. Conf. on Image Processing, Vol. 2, (1997) 26–29
14. T. Vlachos : Cut Detection in Video Sequences Using Phase Correlation. IEEE signal Processing Letters, Vol. 7, Issue 7, (2000) 173–175

Secret Message Location Steganalysis Based on Local Coherences of Hue[*]

Xiang-Wei Kong, Wen-Feng Liu, and Xin-Gang You

School of Electronic and Information Engineering,
Dalian University of Technology, China
{kongxw, youxg}@dlut.edu.cn, liuwf1980@163.com

Abstract. The aim of steganalysis is to uncover the concealed secret message in the multimedia carrier. Now, most steganalysis approaches focus on two issues: one is detecting whether there existed a secret message, and the other is estimating the length of the secret message. In this paper, we present a new secret message location steganalysis based on local coherences of hue (LCH) to determine the stego-bearing regions for color digital images. For the stego-image, which is sequentially embedded with messages in spatial domain, stego-bearing regions can be determined by analyzing the changes of coherence of hue. Experimental results show that the proposed LCH steganalysis has high detection accuracy.

Keywords: steganalysis, steganography, locating secret message, the coherences of hue.

1 Introduction

Steganography and steganalysis are becoming two of the important branches in the area of information security. The former mainly embeds secret messages into the redundancy parts of images, while the latter is the technique of revealing hiding data including breaking covert channels [1].

Most of the steganalysis algorithms published in current literatures focus on detecting the existence and the length of the secret message. For example, the IQM [2] algorithm by Ismail Avcıbas and wavelet detecting [3] by Hany Farid can judge whether an image contains a secret message or not by training cover-images and stego-images, while RS algorithm [4] by Fridrich and Sample pair [5] by Sorina Dumitrescu can estimate the length of the secret messages. However, as the ultimate intention of steganalysis is to extract the secret message, the location of the secret message must be determined. Unfortunately, there are only few related publications: Ian Davidson in [6] treats the hidden message location problem as outlier detection using probability/energy measurement motivated by image restoration community. It could locate the most 0.33% energized pixels, in which 87% are actually stego-bearing for color images and 61% for grayscale images. Sos S.Agaian in [7] proposed

---

[*] This paper is supported by the project of National Nature Science Foundation of China (Grant No.60372083).

an approach to localize informative regions based on pixel comparison and complexity measure to detect and remove the hidden data, which is effected by the complexity of images.

In this paper, we first analyze the changes of general color system caused by the embedded secret message, and then extract statistical features of hue in stego-images. A new secret message location steganalysis based on local coherences of hue (LCH) for color images is proposed. Experimental results show that the presented LCH steganalysis for sequentially embed messages in spatial domain could locate the stego-bearing regions with high accuracy.

The paper is organized as follows. In the next section, we analyze the variety of hue caused by embedding secret messages. LCH steganalysis method to locate the stego-bearing regions is proposed in section 3. In section 4, we give the experimental results. Section 5 is conclusion.

2 The Analysis of Coherence of Hue on General Color Systems

For BMP color image steganography, secret messages are carried on RGB color channels independently; no matter it is LSB algorithms or non-LSB algorithms such as SES [8], pixel value differencing (PVD) [9] and so on. Both of these two types introduce invisible changes to the digital images. Opposite steganalysis algorithms only detect the statistical features of pixels in the same RGB color channels, such as RS [4], sample pair [5], and so on. However, when the antagonizing part try to seek statistical features of pixels that differs when embed messages, they ignore a potential important fact, that is, the minor changes of value of the pixels in RGB channels will induce obvious statistical feature changes in other color systems. It may uncover the local distinguished changes so as to locate the hidden message.

Investigating color channels other than RGB which respectively describe color by luminance, hue and saturation, such as HIS (Hue Saturation Intensity), YUV, YIQ and YCbCr, we notice that when the values of pixels in RGB channels are altered independently, the statistical features of hue behave differently. It is generally believed that color hue varies smoothly in natural images, and can be assumed to be constant in small neighborhood [10]. When we embed messages in RGB channels independently, the local constant of hue in small neighborhood would be disturbed. Therefore, by detecting the local coherence of hue, we could judge whether a digital image has been altered.

2.1 The Relationship of General Color Systems and RGB Color System

The general color systems composed of luminance and chrominance include HIS color system, YUV color system, YIQ color system, YCbCr color system etc. The relationship of these color systems and RBG color system are as follows:

2.1.1 HIS Color System
HIS color system is one of the most frequently used color systems that aimed at color processing, in which H denotes hue, I denotes intensity and S denotes saturation. It can be transformed from RGB as follows [11]:

$$H = \arctan\left(\frac{\sqrt{3}(R-B)}{(R-G)+(R-B)}\right)$$
$$S = I - \frac{\min(R,G,B)}{R+G+B} \qquad (1)$$
$$I = 0.299R + 0.587G + 0.114B$$

2.1.2 YUV Color System and YIQ Color System

YUV is the color system adopted by European television system. Y represents luminance, U and V represent hue and saturation respectively. Likewise, YIQ is the color system adopted by North America television, Y still represents luminance, I and Q represent hue and saturation respectively. The relationship between YUV, YIQ and RGB are:

$$\begin{bmatrix} Y \\ U \\ V \end{bmatrix} = \begin{bmatrix} 0.299 & 0.587 & 0.114 \\ -0.418 & -0.289 & 0.437 \\ 0.615 & -0.515 & -0.100 \end{bmatrix} \begin{bmatrix} R \\ G \\ B \end{bmatrix} \quad \begin{bmatrix} R \\ G \\ B \end{bmatrix} = \begin{bmatrix} 1 & 0 & 1.140 \\ 1 & -0.395 & -0.581 \\ 1 & 2.032 & 0 \end{bmatrix} \begin{bmatrix} Y \\ U \\ V \end{bmatrix} \qquad (2)$$

$$\begin{bmatrix} Y \\ I \\ Q \end{bmatrix} = \begin{bmatrix} 0.299 & 0.587 & 0.114 \\ 0.596 & -0.274 & -0.322 \\ 0.211 & -0.523 & 0.312 \end{bmatrix} \begin{bmatrix} R \\ G \\ B \end{bmatrix} \quad \begin{bmatrix} R \\ G \\ B \end{bmatrix} = \begin{bmatrix} 1 & 0.956 & 0.621 \\ 1 & -0.272 & -0.647 \\ 1 & -1.106 & -1.703 \end{bmatrix} \begin{bmatrix} Y \\ I \\ Q \end{bmatrix} \qquad (3)$$

2.1.3 YCbCr Color System

YCbCr is the color system adopted by JPEG image format, which is derived from YUV color system and is more suitable for compression. In this color system, Y stands for luminance, while Cb and Cr stand for hue and saturation. Its relationship with RGB is:

$$\begin{bmatrix} Y \\ Cb \\ Cr \end{bmatrix} = \begin{bmatrix} 0.2990 & 0.5870 & 0.1140 \\ -0.1687 & -0.3313 & 0.5000 \\ 0.5000 & -0.4187 & -0.0813 \end{bmatrix} \begin{bmatrix} R \\ G \\ B \end{bmatrix} \quad \begin{bmatrix} R \\ G \\ B \end{bmatrix} = \begin{bmatrix} 1 & 0 & 1.40200 \\ 1 & -0.34414 & -0.71414 \\ 1 & 1.77200 & 0 \end{bmatrix} \begin{bmatrix} Y \\ Cb \\ Cr \end{bmatrix} \qquad (4)$$

From the relationship of general color systems and RGB color system, it is not difficult to draw the conclusion that a minor change in RGB color system will also make changes in other color systems.

2.2 The Statistical Features of Hue of Stego-Images

Now we will take HIS color system for example to illustrate the influence to the statistical features of hue for stego-images. Similar results will be gotten in the other color systems described above.

First, let's take a look at how H will be modified when we embed messages in RGB channels. S will have a similar modification.

0.86759	0.86759	0.87917	0.87917	0.89196	0.88637	0.86759	0.86759	0.87225	0.87225
0.86759	0.86759	0.87225	0.87917	0.88637	0.87917	0.86759	0.8612	0.87225	0.87225
0.8592	0.8592	0.86816	0.87517	0.87517	0.86816	0.85706	0.84887	0.85706	0.85706
0.8592	0.8592	0.86816	0.86816	0.87517	0.86816	0.85706	0.84887	0.85706	0.85706
0.8592	0.8592	0.86816	0.86816	0.87517	0.87517	0.8592	0.85706	0.85706	0.85706
0.85706	0.85706	0.85706	0.8592	0.87517	0.86816	0.8592	0.85706	0.85706	0.85706
0.83729	0.83729	0.84298	0.84887	0.8592	0.8592	0.85706	0.85706	0.85706	0.84887
0.82867	0.83397	0.83729	0.84298	0.85706	0.8592	0.85706	0.85706	0.84887	0.84887
0.82575	0.82575	0.83284	0.83857	0.84038	0.84844	0.85486	0.84844	0.84038	0.83857
0.83284	0.83284	0.83857	0.83857	0.84844	0.84844	0.85486	0.84844	0.83857	0.83857

Fig. 1. The values of H of a region in a digital photograph taken by Kodak-DC290 camera

0.86336	0.8612	0.87719	0.87023	0.88912	0.88637	0.86956	0.85759	0.86989	0.872
0.87225	0.86759	0.87686	0.88111	0.88828	0.87225	0.86787	0.85915	0.88558	0.874
0.85706	0.8592	0.8658	0.87978	0.87719	0.86787	0.8613	0.85295	0.85067	0.857
0.86352	0.86352	0.8658	0.86352	0.87776	0.8658	0.85706	0.85083	0.85492	0.86
0.85706	0.86352	0.86141	0.86818	0.87776	0.86246	0.86338	0.8592	0.88558	0.86
0.85083	0.8592	0.85706	0.86352	0.87517	0.86141	0.86352	0.86558	0.85706	0.869
0.83509	0.83509	0.8368	0.84696	0.86558	0.85273	0.85284	0.85067	0.8613	0.846
0.82067	0.83179	0.84119	0.8408	0.8613	0.85706	0.86352	0.8613	0.84482	0.852
0.828	0.82424	0.83054	0.84262	0.84038	0.85067	0.8548	0.8505	0.84671	0.833
0.83454	0.8289	0.83223	0.83902	0.84844	0.85273	0.85486	0.85067	0.8406	0.83

Fig. 2. The values of H of the corresponding region of the image after fully embedded by stash777 [12] (which only modify the least significant bit)

Comparing the marked regions of the two figures, we will notice that in the cover image, there exits local coherence. However, in the stego-image, this local coherence is destroyed. For the purpose of convenience, we only mark parts of the regions that have the same value in cover image but have different values in stego-image. There are many other similar regions that we haven't marked. Now we will analysis why this happens via the mechanism of embedding.

For pixels A (R_0, G_0, B_0) and B (R_1, G_1, B_1), if they have the same value of H before embedding messages, it is satisfied that

$$\arctan \frac{\sqrt{3}(R_0 - B_0)}{(R_0 - B_0) + (R_0 - G_0)} = \arctan \frac{\sqrt{3}(R_1 - B_1)}{(R_1 - B_1) + (R_1 - G_1)} \tag{5}$$

Combined with the character of trigonometric function, equation (5) becomes:

$$\frac{R_0 - G_0}{R_0 - B_0} = \frac{R_1 - G_1}{R_1 - B_1} \tag{6}$$

After embedding messages, pixels A and B turn to A (R_0', G_0', B_0') and B (R_1', G_1', B_1'), and now the H of these two pixels are:

$$H(R_0', G_0', B_0') = \arctan \frac{\sqrt{3}(R_0' - B_0')}{(R_0' - B_0') + (R_0' - G_0')} \tag{7}$$

$$H(R_1', G_1', B_1') = \arctan \frac{\sqrt{3}(R_1' - B_1')}{(R_1' - B_1') + (R_1' - G_1')} \tag{8}$$

If these two pixels still have the same value of H, they must satisfy:

$$\frac{R_0' - G_0'}{R_0' - B_0'} = \frac{R_1' - G_1'}{R_1' - B_1'} \tag{9}$$

Suppose that the two pixels have the same value of H before embedding, for the common embedding algorithms of LSB, only in one of the following conditions that the value of H will still equal after embedding:

1. $\Delta R_0 = \Delta R_1 = \Delta G_0 = \Delta G_1 = \Delta B_0 = \Delta B_1$. This means that the values of R G B in these two pixels are modified in the same way, which can be subdivided into three cases: (1) all the six values keep the same, in which case the probability is $(\frac{1}{2})^6$; (2) all the six values are modified by adding 1, the probability of which is $(\frac{1}{4})^6$; (3) all the six values are modified by minuses 1, whose probability is also $(\frac{1}{4})^6$. The probability in all is:

$$(\frac{1}{2})^6 + (\frac{1}{4})^6 + (\frac{1}{4})^6 = 0.0161 \tag{10}$$

2. If $R_0, G_0, B_0, R_1, G_1, B_1$ have some given initial values, H will still keep the same, even if they are not modified in the same way. Although the probability of this condition is impossible to calculate, we can imagine that the probability is very low.

From above it can be seen that after embedding with LSB algorithm, there is few chance that the H of pixels A and B still keep the same. In most cases, they become different with each other.

As for the non-LSB algorithms, which usually modifies the R G B values of pixels by $\pm k$ (k =1,2....) according to the initial values and the message bits to be embedded. In this case, the probability that H keeps the same will be much lower than that of LSB algorithm.

So, we could come to the conclusion that after embedding in RGB channels, the local coherence of H will be destroyed with high probability. Hence, we could check the local coherence of H to tell whether the image has been embedded with secret messages.

3 A Location Steganalysis Based on Local Coherence of Hue

We have analyzed the difference of the statistical characteristics of hue in digital images before and after embedding secret messages, and now we sum them up as follows:

1. To digital photographs, the hue takes on local coherence in most of the image blocks;
2. After fully embedded with secret messages, the local coherence of hue is destroyed with high probability.
3. We could check the coherence of hue in a small region without evaluate the entire digital image.

These three characters determine that the local coherence of hue could be used as a distinguishing statistic to check the sequential steganography in spatial domain for color images. Moreover, it could also locate the stego-bearing regions.

If we divide the image into blocks, then for most of the blocks, it is the matter of fully embedded or not embedded at all, which will enhance the detecting accuracy. Besides, our work is a blind steganalysis approach since we assume no knowledge of the hiding algorithm. Therefore it has a large range of application.

3.1 Classify Stego-Bearing Regions and Innocent Regions

The main idea of our approach is to divide the image into image-blocks, and check the coherence of hue for each block independently. If the ratio of the pixels that have different hues with its surroundings and the total pixels is larger than a given threshold, we judge that this block is stego-bearing; otherwise, we judge it innocent.

The detailed approach is as follows:

For the image that is to be analyzed, suppose its size is M×N, we divide it into blocks with M1×N1 pixels from the upper left corner right down to the lower right corner. The blocks maybe overlapped or not depending on the accuracy that demanded. We detect each block to see if it is stego-bearing. For each block A, we first calculate its luminance A_y and hue A_c, then for each pixel $A_{i,j}$ in block A, determine its neighborhood R (exclude $A_{i,j}$). The following example will illustrate how to choose R. According to the distributing characteristic of hue in nature images, the neighborhood R with rank 3 has the following three choices:

$$\begin{bmatrix} A_{i-1,j-1} & A_{i-1,j} & A_{i-1,j+1} \\ A_{i,j-1} & & A_{i,j+1} \\ A_{i+1,j-1} & A_{i+1,j} & A_{i+1,j+1} \end{bmatrix} \begin{bmatrix} A_{i-1,j-1} & & A_{i-1,j+1} \\ & & \\ A_{i+1,j-1} & & A_{i+1,j+1} \end{bmatrix} \begin{bmatrix} & A_{i-1,j} & \\ A_{i,j-1} & & A_{i,j+1} \\ & A_{i+1,j} & \end{bmatrix}$$
$$(1) \qquad\qquad\qquad (2) \qquad\qquad\qquad (3)$$

Fig. 3. The three choices of neighborhood R

The neighborhood R with rank n ($n = 2k+1, k = 1, 2, \hbar$) will be created by the same rule. Then calculate the maximal difference between the luminance and the hue of $A_{i,j}$ and those of the pixels in the neighborhoods R of $A_{i,j}$, denote as max_y and max_c respectively:

max_$y = \max(|A\_y_{i,j} - A\_y_{i+m,j+n}|)$, where $A\_y_{i,j}$ is the luminance of pixel $A_{i,j}$, m and n take values depending on the choice of R and $m \neq 0, n \neq 0$.

max_$c = \max(|A\_c_{i,j} - A\_c_{i+m,j+n}|)$, where $A\_c_{i,j}$ is the hue of pixel $A_{i,j}$, m and n take values depending on the choice of R, and $m \neq 0, n \neq 0$.

We introduce two sets X and Y to distinguish the pixels. If it is satisfied that max_$y < y_0$ and max_$c < c_0$ at the same time, where y_0 and c_0 are two thresholds, then we judge that $A_{i,j}$ belongs to set Y. By doing this, we effectively avoid the influence of different complexity. If $A_{i,j}$ belongs to set Y, then check whether there exists any pixel in R that has the same hue with $A_{i,j}$, if none, judge that $A_{i,j}$ belongs to set X meanwhile. If $A_{i,j}$ does not belong to set Y, then begin to detect the next pixel. After all the pixels in block A have been detected (the pixels at the borderline are excluded), we count the number of pixels in set X and set Y respectively, denote as $\|X\|$ and $\|Y\|$, then calculate the feature α:

$$\alpha = \frac{\|X\|}{\|Y\|} \tag{11}$$

Given a threshold α_0, if $\alpha > \alpha_0$, we judge that block A is stego-bearing, otherwise it is innocent. If there are no pixels in set Y, then this method is ineffective, we don't make any judgment in this condition.

3.2 Calibrate the Feature

It was experimentally shown that every stego-bearing block has a lager α than its innocent counterpart. However, as the feature α of the innocent block may varies extensively, it is difficult to find a fixed α_0 as threshold. We solve this problem by constructing a calibrate image, which is obtained by resaving the suspicious image in JPEG format with the quality of 100. Experimental results show that the feature α of the calibrate image (denote as α') is close to that of the innocent counterpart. This can be interpreted as that when we resave the image with JPEG format, one value of luminance is saved for every pixel and only one value of hue is saved for every 2×2 pixels. As a result, it could eliminate the non-coherence of hue caused by imbedding messages. Therefore, as to α, resave the suspicious image in JPEG format is a good choice to estimate the calibrate image. Then, we could calculate $\Delta\alpha = \alpha - \alpha'$ as the distinguishing statistic, which is immune to the variety of α in innocent blocks.

Now we can summarize our method as follows: denote j_1 as the suspicious image block and j_2 as the calibrate image block, F is a function as described above in which the input is the image block and the output is the feature α. Applied function F to j_1 and j_2 respectively, then the final distinguishing statistic f is obtained as their difference:

$$f = F(j_1) - F(j_2) \tag{12}$$

For a given threshold f_0, if $f > f_0$, we judge that this block is stego-bearing; otherwise, it is innocent.

4 Experimental Results

The images in our experiments come from camera Kodak DC290, NIKON E5700 and Sony CYBERSHOT. In all, there are about 1000 digital photos in JPEG format. We transformed them to BMP format with ACDSEE7.0. We have purposely chosen natural images, as they are conductive to hide message.

The steganographic method we mainly employed is the common sequential LSB we code by ourselves. In order to detect the adaptability of our approach, we also employ some existed steganographic software to detect the first 70 images of all kinds of the above images, containing stsah777 [12], which embed with sequential LSB; info stego [13] which sequentially embed in the last two LSBs; and pixel value differencing (PVD)[9] which sequentially embed with non-LSB. And we get the similar results.

It is experimentally shown that when the block is larger the detecting accuracy is higher. However, if the image is not fully embedded, the block that is half embedded would be detected as either innocent or stego-bearing. In this case, if the block is larger, then there will be more pixels that are wrongly detected. As a result, when we choose the block size, we should split the difference. As our method is to divide the image into image blocks and detect whether each block is innocent or stego-bearing independently, then most blocks are innocent or fully embedded. For the sake of simplicity, in our experiments, the image is fully embedded or not embedded at all. Table 1 is the detecting results of the cover image blocks and the corresponding stego- images blocks embedded by common LSB. In order to detect the universality of our method, we also detect stego-images embedded (not fully) by some existed steganographic software, including stash777, infostego and PVD. Figure4 to Figure 6 are examples of the detecting results. The embedding methods include the steganography of LSB (Figure 5), the last two LSBs (Figure 4) and non-LSB (Figure 6). And the embedded manners include sequentially embedded from the upper left corner (Figure 5), from the lower left corner (Figure 4) and from the middle of the image (Figure 6). Experimental results imply that our approach is robust and capable of identifying the stego-bearing regions with high accuracy.

Table 1. Detecting results of cover image blocks and stego-image-blocks fully embedded with common LSB, each block in our experiment contains about 30,000 pixels (notice: the false negative rates and false posotive rates are the rate of the blocks, not the pixels)

Image Source		Detecting Results		False Negative Rate	False Positive Rate
Camera Type	Raw Image Format	Raw Image Size	Block Number		
KODAK DC290	JPEG	1200×1792	14200	0.08%	0.17%
	JPEG	720×480	4020	0.075%	1.11%
NIKON E5700	JPEG	1280×960	8200	0.56%	0.58%
SONY CYBERSHOT	JPEG	1280×960	8200	0.34%	0.57%

Fig. 4. One of the cover images of 1200×1792 after embedded 49.03% secret message with info stego, the region in the rectangle of the left picture is the region that actually embedded messages, and the black region in the right picture is the region which is detected to have been embedded secret message in, which is 51.39% of the full image

Fig. 5. One of the cover images of 1200×1792 after embedded 31.83% secret message with stash777, the region in the rectangle of the left picture is the region that actually embedded messages, and the black region in the right picture is the region which is detected to have been embedded secret message in, which is 29.17% of the full image

Fig. 6. One of the cover images of 1200×1792 after embedded secret message in line 475 to 815 with PVD (28.42%), the region in the rectangle of the left picture is the region that actually embedded messages, and the black region in the right picture is the region which is detected to have been embedded secret message in, which is 29.17% of the full image

From above, we could also come to the conclusion that it is not enough to preserve the first and higher order statistical features of the images when we design new steganographic methods. In addition, the statistical features of pixels in other domains, for example in color channels other than R G B, should also take into account.

5 Conclusions and Future Work

In this paper, we first analyze the influence to the color weight of hue when embedding messages in RGB color channels, then present a blind steganalysis approach LCH, which could locate the stego-bearing regions for those sequential steganographic methods in spatial domain. It is experimentally shown that our approach is robust and capable of identifying the stego-bearing regions with high accuracy. However, we must acknowledge that we could only judge the image blocks to be innocent or stego-bearing, and the image blocks should not be very small. Besides, our approach could be defeated if the steganographic algorithm have knowledge of our LCH detection and the message is carefully embedded to keep the coherence of the hue. However, by doing this the capacity would be greatly reduced. The future work would be on seeking other statistical features to make judgment for smaller blocks while keeping the high detecting accuracy. Besides, it is relatively straightforward to locate the stego-bearing regions with sequentially embedding algorithms and we would try to locate stego-bearing pixels with random embedding algorithms and the algorithms that embed messages in frequency domain.

References

1. Xiangwei Kong, Ting Zhang, Xingang You, and Deli Yang: A New Steganalysis Approach Based on Both Complexity Estimate and Statistical Filter. IEEE Pacifica Rim Conference on Multimedia (2002) 434-441
2. Ismail Avcıbas, Nasir Memon, and Bülent Sankur: Steganalysis Using Image Quality Metrics. IEEE transactions on image processing, VOL. 12, NO. 2 February (2003)
3. S. Lyu and H. Farid: Detecting hidden messages using higher-order statistics and support vector machines. In 5th International Workshop on Information Hiding (2002)
4. J. Fridrich, M. Goljan, and R. Du: Reliable detection of LSB steganography in color and grayscale images. ACM Workshop Multimedia Security (2001) pp. 27–30
5. Sorina Dumitrescu, Xiaolin Wu, and Zhe Wang: Detection of LSB Steganography via Sample Pair Analysis. IEEE, JULY (2003)
6. Ian Davidson Goutam Paul: Locating Secret Messages in Images, ACM (2004)
7. Sos S. Agaian, Benjamin M. Rodriguez, Glenn Dietrich: steganlysis using modified pixel comparison and complexity measure, SPIE (2004)
8. Jeong-Jae Yu, Jae-won Han, Kwang-su Lee, Dae-hyun Ryu_ and Sang-jin Lee: SES(Steganography Evading Statistical analyses) (2003)
9. Wu, D.C., Tsai, W.H.: A steganographic method for images by pixel-value differencing. Pattern Recognition Lett. 24, 1613–1626 (2003)
10. Hany Farid: Statistical Tools for Digital Image Forensics. http://www.cs.dartmouth.edu/~farid/publications (2005)
11. Alex Leykin and Florin Cutzu: difference of edge properties in photographs and paintings IEEE (2003)
12. stash-it, http://www.smalleranimals.com/stash.htm
13. Info stego v3.0, http://www.antiy.net/infostego/index.htm

Feature-Based Image Watermarking Method Using Scale-Invariant Keypoints

Hae-Yeoun Lee[1], Choong-hoon Lee[1], Heung-Kyu Lee[1], and Jeho Nam[2]

[1] Department of EECS, Korea Advanced Institute of Science and Technology,
Guseong-dong, Yuseong-gu, Daejeon, Korea (Republic of)
hytoiy@casaturn.kaist.ac.kr
[2] Broadcasting Media Research Group, Electronics and
Telecommunications Research Institute, Gaejeong-dong,
Yuseong-gu, Daejeon, Korea (Republic of)

Abstract. This paper addresses feature-based image watermarking methods for digital contents. Most previous watermarking algorithms suffer from geometric distortion attacks that desynchronize the location of the inserted watermark. In order to synchronize the watermark location, watermark synchronization should be performed. One solution for watermark synchronization is to use image features. This paper describes a feature-based watermarking method based on scale-invariant keypoints. We extract feature points from the scale-invariant keypoint extractor and then decompose feature points into a set of disjoint triangles. These triangles are watermarked by an additive spread-spectrum method on the spatial domain. We perform an intensive simulation in comparison with other feature-based watermarking methods using 100 test images. Results show that the proposed method is considerably robust against both geometric distortion attacks and signal processing attacks listed in Stirmark 3.1.

1 Introduction

Digital technologies have grown over the last decades, wherein all multimedia have been digitalized. However, digital multimedia can be copied, manipulated, and reproduced illegally, without quality degradation and protection. Digital watermarking is an efficient solution for copyright protection. Copyright information, *the watermark*, is inserted into the contents themselves. This information is used as evidence of the ownership. Many watermarking researches have been conducted and performed well against signal processing attacks. Nevertheless, in blind watermarking in particular, these researches exhibit severe weakness to geometric distortion attacks, which desynchronize the location of the inserted watermark.

Geometric distortion desynchronizes the location of the watermark and hence causes incorrect watermark detection. In such cases, watermark synchronization process is required to calculate the watermark location before watermark insertion and detection. In what follows, we refer to the location for watermark insertion and detection as *the patch*. A significant amount of research related to watermark synchronization has been conducted. The use of periodical sequences [1], the insertion of templates [2], and the use of invariant transforms [3-6] have been reported. The use of image features is a solution to synchronize the watermark location. Image features represent an invariant reference for geometric distortions so that referring to features can solve the problems of watermark synchronization. We review feature-based watermarking methods in Section 2.

In watermark synchronization by reference to image features, feature extraction is important for archiving the robustness of the watermark. This paper describes a new feature-based watermarking method using scale-invariant keypoints. We extract feature points using the scale-invariant keypoint extractor and then decompose feature points into a set of disjoint triangles. These triangles are watermarked by an additive way on the spatial domain. Using 100 images randomly collected, we perform an intensive simulation in comparison with other feature-based watermarking methods. Results show that our method is considerably robust against geometric distortion attacks as well as signal processing attacks listed in Stirmark 3.1.

The following section reviews representative feature-based watermarking methods. Section 3 describes the scale-invariant keypoint extractor. In Section 4, we describe the watermarking method using scale-invariant keypoints. Simulation results are shown in Section 5. Section 6 concludes.

2 Feature-Based Watermarking Methods

Kutter *et al.* [7] describe a feature-based watermarking method, where they extract feature points by Mexican Hat wavelet scale interaction and segment the image relatively to these points using a Voronoi diagram. The spread-spectrum watermark is inserted into each segment separately. This method is robust against most attacks, but fails to synchronize the watermark location in scaling attacks because the feature points from the scale interaction method are sensitive to the scale change of images.

Bas *et al.* [8] extract salient feature points by applying the Harris corner detector and then decompose these points into a set of disjoint triangles by Delaunay tessellation. These triangles are watermarked by an additive spread-spectrum method on the spatial domain. The drawback of this method is that the extracted feature points from the original image and attacked images are not matched. Therefore, the set of triangles generated during watermark insertion and detection are different and the resulting patches do not correspond.

Nikolaidis and Pitas [9] consider an image-segmentation based watermarking method. By applying an adaptive k-mean clustering technique, they segment images and select several largest regions. The bounding rectangles of these regions are watermarked on the spatial domain. The problem with this method is that image segmentation depends on image contents, so that image distortions affect the segmentation result. Also, it is difficult to select regions when images are complexly textured.

Tang and Hang [10] extract feature points using Mexican Hat wavelet scale interaction and the disks of fixed radius R centered at each feature point are normalized to achieve geometric distortion invariance. These normalized disks are watermarked on the frequency domain. Although this method works well in response to most attacks, it shows severe weakness to scaling attacks, because radius of the disks are fixed in such a manner that different contents are used for normalization.

3 Scale-Invariant Keypoint Extractor

Affine-invariant features in object recognition and image retrieval applications have recently been studied [11-13]. These features are highly distinctive and matched with high probability against large image distortions. For robust watermarking, we adopt scale-invariant keypoints, which was proposed by Lowe [11] and has been proved to be invariant to image rotation, scaling, translation, partly illumination changes, and projective transform.

The basic idea of the scale-invariant keypoint extractor is to extract features through a staged filtering that identifies stable points in the scale-space. In order to extract candidate locations for features, the scale-space is computed using Difference of Gaussian function, where an image is filtered by Gaussian function of different scales and then difference images are calculated. In this scale-space, they retrieve all local maximums and minimums by checking the eight closest neighborhoods in the same scale and nine neighborhoods in the scale above and below (see Fig. 1). These extrema determine the location and the scale of the features and invariant to the scale and orientation change of images.

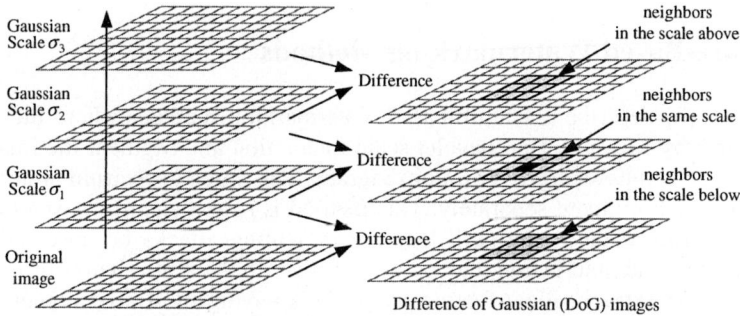

Fig. 1. Scale-space from DoG function and the closest neighborhoods of a pixel

After candidate locations have been found, the locations that have a low contrast or are poorly localized along edges are removed by measuring the stability of each feature using a 2 by 2 Hessian matrix H as Eq. (1):

$$Stability = \frac{(D_{xx}+D_{yy})^2}{D_{xx}D_{yy}-D_{xy}^2} < \frac{(r+1)^2}{r}, \quad H = \begin{bmatrix} D_{xx} & D_{xy} \\ D_{xy} & D_{yy} \end{bmatrix}. \qquad (1)$$

The r value is ratio between the largest and smallest eigen values and used to control stability. D represents the derivative of the scale-space image in x- and y-axis.

In order to achieve invariance to image rotation, they assign a consistent orientation to each feature. In the Gaussian smoothed image with the scale of the extracted features, they calculate gradient orientation of all sample points within the circular window of a feature location and form an orientation histogram. The peak in this histogram corresponds to the dominant direction of that feature. Scale-invariant keypoints obtained through this process are invariant to the rotation, scaling, translation, and partly illumination changes of images and useful to design robust watermarking.

4 Our Watermarking Method Using Scale-Invariant Keypoints

Watermarking algorithms are divided into two processes: watermark insertion and detection. Watermark insertion is a process for inserting the watermark into contents imperceptibly. Watermark detection is a process for detecting the inserted watermark from contents to prove ownership. We first describe the watermark synchronization procedure to calculate the patches and then explain watermark insertion and detection.

4.1 Watermark Synchronization

As mentioned in Section 3, we extract feature points using the scale-invariant keypoint extractor. Feature points should be relatively related to calculate the watermark location, *the patches*. We decompose the feature points into a set of disjoint triangles by Delaunay tessellation commonly used. Given a set of feature points, Delaunay tessellation is the straight-line dual of the corresponding Voronoi diagram partitioning an image into segments such that all points in one segment are closer to the location of the feature points. This tessellation is independent of image rotation, scaling and translation. Moreover, computational cost is low.

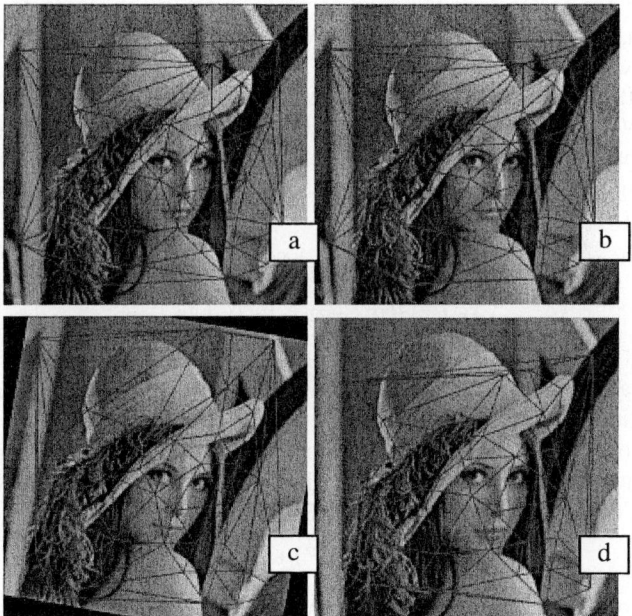

Fig. 2. Patches for watermarking against attacks: (a) original image, (b) image with additive uniform noise, (c) image with rotation 10°, and (d) image with scaling 1.1x

The distribution of feature points is related to the performance of the watermarking systems [8]. In other words, the distance between adjacent features must be determined carefully. If the distance is too small, the distribution of feature points is concentrated on textured areas. Furthermore, the inserted watermark must be sampled, because the patch size is also small. If the distance is too large, feature points become isolated. In order to obtain the homogeneous distribution of feature points, we apply a circular neighborhood constraint, in which feature points whose strength is the largest are selected [8]. The distance D between adjacent features depends on the dimensions of the image and is quantized by the r value as Eq. (2):

$$D = \frac{w+h}{r}. \quad (2)$$

The width and height of the image are denoted by w and h, respectively. The r value is a constant to control the distance between adjacent features.

Fig. 2 shows the extracted patches for watermark insertion and detection against additive uniform noise, rotation 10°, and scaling 1.1x of the image. Although signal processing attacks and geometric distortion attacks result in a different tessellation by modifying the relative location of feature points, several patches match. Therefore, we can synchronize successfully the watermark location.

4.2 Watermark Insertion

The first step for watermark insertion is to analyze image contents to extract the patches. Then, the watermark is inserted repeatedly into all patches. Our watermark insertion process is shown in Fig. 3.

To extract the patches, we apply the watermark synchronization process explained in Section 4.1. We use the watermark whose shape is a right-angled triangle. Because the shape of the patch and the watermark different, we should warp the triangular watermark according to the shape of the patches. This warping is modeled as affine transformation as Eq. (3):

$$\begin{pmatrix} x_n \\ y_n \end{pmatrix} = \begin{pmatrix} a_{11} & a_{12} \\ a_{21} & a_{22} \end{pmatrix} \begin{pmatrix} x_o \\ y_o \end{pmatrix} + \begin{pmatrix} s_1 \\ s_2 \end{pmatrix}. \quad (3)$$

(x_o, y_o) and (x_n, y_n) are the coordinates of original points and warped points respectively. This transform is composed of 6 unknown parameters $(a_{11}, a_{12}, a_{21}, a_{22}, s_1, s_2)$ and mathematically calculated using three corner points of a triangle.

The insertion of the watermark must not affect the perceptual quality of images. This constraint refines the insertion strength of the watermark. We apply the perceptual mask of Voloshynovskiy et al. [14] as Eq. (4):

$$\Lambda = \alpha \cdot (1 - NVF) + \beta \cdot NVF. \quad (4)$$

α is the lower bound of visibility in smooth regions. β is the upper bound in highly textured regions. The noise visibility function is calculated as following Eq. (5):

$$NVF(i,j) = \frac{1}{1 + \theta \cdot \sigma_x^2(i,j)}, \quad \theta = \frac{D}{\sigma_{x_{max}}^2}. \quad (5)$$

$\sigma_x^2(i,j)$ and $\sigma_{x_{max}}^2$ denote local variance and maximum of neighboring pixels. D is a scaling constant.

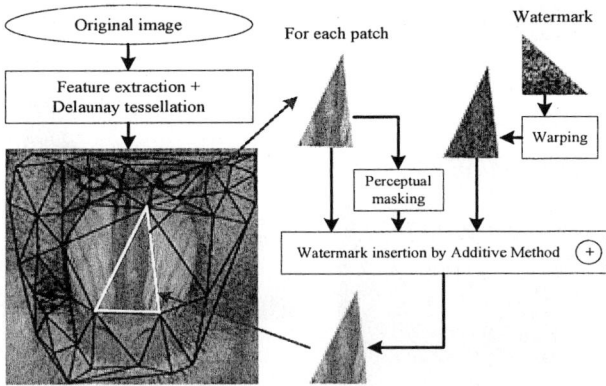

Fig. 3. Watermark insertion process

Finally, we insert the watermark additively into the patches on the spatial domain. The insertion of the watermark is represented as the spatial addition between the pixels of image and the pixels of the warped watermark as Eq. (6):

$$\hat{v}_i = v_i + \Lambda_i wc_i \quad \text{where} \quad wc_i \approx N(0,1). \tag{6}$$

v_i and wc_i denote the pixels of the image and the watermark, respectively. Λ represents the perceptual mask that controls the insertion strength of the watermark.

4.3 Watermark Detection

Similarly to watermark insertion, the first step for watermark detection is analyzing contents to extract patches. The watermark is then detected from the patches. If the watermark is correctly detected from at least one patch, we can prove ownership successfully. Our watermark detection process is shown in Fig. 4.

To extract the patches, we apply the watermark synchronization process explained in Section 4.1. There are several patches in an image and we try to detect the watermark from all patches. The additive watermarking method on the spatial domain inserts the watermark into image contents as noise. Therefore, we apply a Wiener filter to calculate this noise and regard it as the retrieved watermark. We can compensate for the modification by perceptual masks, but such compensation does not have a great affect the performance of watermark detection.

To measure similarity between the reference watermark generated during watermark insertion and the retrieved watermark, the retrieved watermark should be converted into the shape of the reference watermark (a right-angled triangle) by applying affine transformation as watermark insertion.

We apply normalized correlation to the reference watermark and the retrieved watermark. The degree of similarity between the two is represented as Eq. (7):

$$nc = \frac{w(m,n) \cdot w^*(m,n)}{\sqrt{w(m,n) \cdot w(m,n)}}. \tag{7}$$

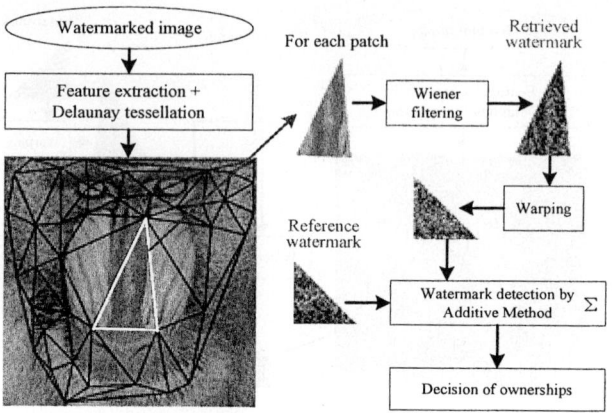

Fig. 4. Watermark detection process

w is the reference watermark and w^* is the retrieved watermark. The range of similarity is from −1 to 1. If the similarity exceeds a pre-defined threshold, we can be satisfied that the reference watermark has been inserted. The way to determine the threshold will be described in the following section.

The fact that we insert the watermark into several patches, rather than just one, makes it highly likely that the described method will detect the watermark, even after image attacks.

4.4 Error Probability Analysis

Since ownership is verified by deciding whether or not the similarity exceeds a pre-defined threshold, the probability that our watermark detector will generate errors depends on what threshold is selected. In practice, it is difficult to analyze the probability that the watermark detector fails to retrieve the watermark from the watermarked image because of the wide variety of possible attacks. We commonly select the threshold based on the probability that the watermark is detected correctly when images are not watermarked.

In most cases, the simplest way to estimate the error probability is to assume that the distribution of detection values follows a Gaussian distribution [15] as Eq. (8):

$$f(x;\mu,\sigma) = \frac{1}{\sqrt{2\pi}\sigma} e^{-(x-\mu)^2/(2\sigma^2)}. \tag{8}$$

x is a continuous random variable. μ and σ satisfy $-\infty < \mu < \infty$ and $0 < \sigma$ respectively. In order to estimate the error probability of our watermark detector, we attempted to retrieve 20 random watermarks from 100 randomly collected images. 40,000 patches were processed to detect the watermark, because each image contained several patches. The x- and y-size of the triangular watermark was 48 by 48 pixels. Based on the results, the mean and variance of the detector value x

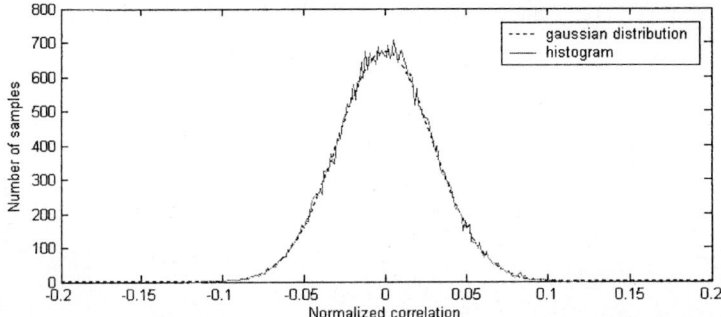

Fig. 5. Histogram of normalized correlation values and its Gaussian distribution

Table 1. Error probability of our watermark detector and its threshold

Error probability	Thresholds
10^{-4}	0.1099
10^{-5}	0.1261
10^{-6}	0.1405
10^{-7}	0.1537

were -5.147e-004 and 0.029. The histogram of similarity values and its Gaussian distribution are shown in Fig. 5. Table 1 shows the probability of our watermark detector generating an error based on the chosen threshold.

5 Simulation Results

This section evaluates three feature-based watermarking methods: Kutter method [1], Bas method [8], and Our method. Kutter method extracted feature points using Mexican Hat wavelet scale interaction and decomposed these points into a set of triangles by Delaunay tessellation. Bas method extracted feature points using the Harris corner detector and decomposed these points into a set of triangles by Delaunay tessellation. The triangles were watermarked additively on the spatial domain.

We tested 100 randomly collected 512x512 images from the Internet that included commonly used images in image-processing applications. Some images are shown in Fig. 6. The size of the triangular watermark was 48 by 48 pixels and the weighting factors α and β of the noise visibility function were set at 5.0 and 1.0, respectively. We achieved a 10^{-6} error probability by setting the threshold at 0.1405.

The PSNR values between the original images and the watermarked images are summarized in Table 2. In the highly-textured images, such as Baboon, Bridge, and Pentagon images, PSNR values were relatively low because we inserted the watermark strongly due to the fact that noise was imperceptible.

We applied signal processing attacks (median filter, Gaussian filter, additive uniform noise, and JPEG compression) and geometric distortion attacks (cropping, linear

Fig. 6. Test images: Baboon, Boat, Lake, Bridge, Couple, Pepper, Lena, Indian, Plane, and Pentagon

Table 2. Peak Signal to Noise Ratio (PSNR)

	Kutter method	Bas method	Our method
PSNR	38.34	38.68	39.12

geometric transformation, random bending, row-column removal, shearing, rotation + cropping, and scaling + cropping) listed in Stirmark 3.1. Tables 3 and 4 show the number of images where the watermark was detected correctly, i.e. whose similarity values exceeded the chosen threshold.

In aspect of feature extraction, the inserted watermark itself works as a kind of attacks and hence feature extraction methods were affected without attacks. Although the Harris corner detector is known as robust to image noise, the set of feature points was sensitive to image noise. In other words, some feature points were

Table 3. Number of images where the watermark is detected correctly under signal processing attacks and their similarity values

	Kutter method		Bas method		Our method	
	# of images	Similarity	# of images	Similarity	# of images	Similarity
No attack	100	0.78	99	0.60	100	0.70
Median 2×2	100	0.62	91	0.41	97	0.47
Median 3×3	99	0.59	93	0.39	99	0.45
Median 4×4	96	0.48	83	0.32	85	0.36
Gaussian filter	99	0.64	96	0.39	98	0.50
Additive uniform noise	100	0.45	91	0.28	95	0.33
JPEG compress. 50	99	0.41	78	0.26	83	0.30
JPEG compress. 70	100	0.57	92	0.34	99	0.43
JPEG compress. 90	100	0.73	99	0.51	100	0.62

appeared or disappeared because the Harris corner detector considered differential features of images. Therefore, Bas method showed lower performance than others in signal processing attacks and in particular worked poorly in Baboon or Pentagon images whose texture was complex. However, Bas method outperformed in scaling attacks, because differential features were well preserved in the scale change of images.

Because Mexican Hat wavelet scale interaction consider image intensity distributed to the wide area, small distortions do not affect performance so that the patches is able to be generated robustly in signal processing attacks. Therefore, Kutter method outperformed than others in signal processing attacks. However, this method showed severe weakness in scaling attacks because Mexican Hat wavelet scale interaction was sensitive to the scale change of images.

In signal processing attacks, our method showed relatively higher performance than Bas method. Against most geometric distortion attacks except scaling attacks,

Table 4. Number of images where the watermark is detected correctly under geometric distortion attacks and their similarity values

	Kutter method		Bas method		Our method	
	# of images	Similarity	# of images	Similarity	# of images	Similarity
Crop 5%	99	0.59	99	0.54	100	0.62
Crop 10%	99	0.55	100	0.52	100	0.59
Crop 15%	99	0.50	97	0.51	100	0.53
Crop 25%	96	0.40	94	0.46	95	0.46
Linear trans. 1.008	98	0.52	99	0.48	100	0.51
Linear trans. 1.011	98	0.51	98	0.49	97	0.52
Linear trans. 1.012	99	0.51	96	0.48	99	0.51
Random bending	99	0.52	99	0.49	99	0.50
Row/Col Removal 1 1	100	0.72	99	0.57	100	0.62
Row/Col Removal 1 5	99	0.63	99	0.54	100	0.55
Row/Col Removal 5 1	99	0.63	99	0.54	99	0.57
Row/Col Removal 5 17	96	0.40	97	0.47	98	0.45
Row/Col Removal 17 5	96	0.40	97	0.48	97	0.44
Shearing x 0 y 5	98	0.51	99	0.51	100	0.52
Shearing x 5 y 0	97	0.53	99	0.52	99	0.54
Shearing x 1 y 1	99	0.57	100	0.51	100	0.51
Shearing x 5 y 5	90	0.32	96	0.44	95	0.38
Rotation 0.5°+Crop	100	0.66	99	0.49	99	0.54
Rotation 1.0°+Crop	100	0.63	99	0.48	99	0.51
Rotation 5.0°+Crop	98	0.58	98	0.47	98	0.48
Rotation 10.0°+Crop	95	0.54	99	0.46	97	0.46
Rotation 15.0°+Crop	97	0.50	95	0.46	99	0.43
Rotation 30.0°+Crop	96	0.42	96	0.43	97	0.39
Scaling 0.8×	0	0.00	74	0.34	61	0.24
Scaling 0.9×	13	0.19	96	0.41	95	0.31
Scaling 1.1×+Crop	32	0.22	97	0.47	94	0.38
Scaling 1.2×+Crop	2	0.15	93	0.41	84	0.28

our method performed better than others, although the performance difference was small to be ignorable. Overall performance of our method was acceptable because we could prove ownership successfully if the watermark was detected from at least one patch. These results support the contention that the method using scale-invariant keypoints is robust against geometric distortion attacks as well as signal processing attacks. In fact, the probability to redetect the patches against image attacks was much higher. However, it is unlikely that the additive watermarking method can detect the watermark correctly when images contain complex texture or are distorted by noise.

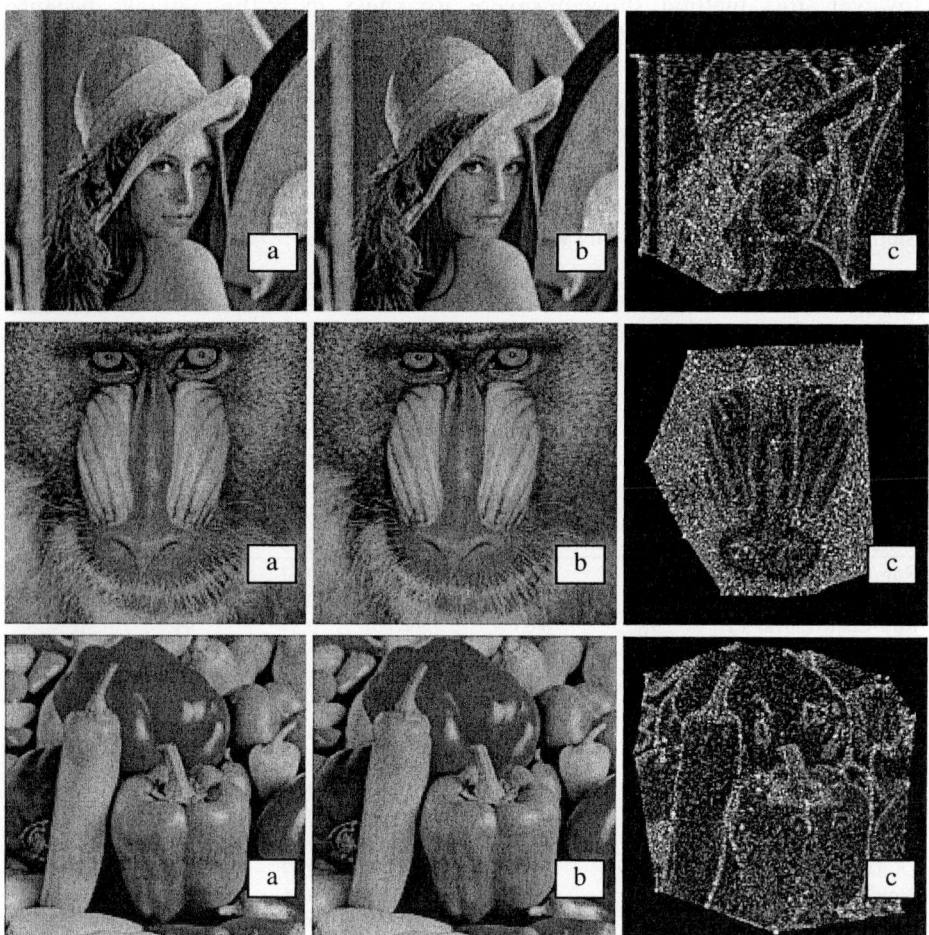

Fig. 7. (a) original image, (b) watermarked image, and (c) residual image in the Lena, Baboon, and Pepper images

6 Discussions and Conclusions

Fig. 7 shows original images, watermarked images, and residual images between the original and watermarked images. We modified the histogram of residual images for convenience. As may be seen in watermarked images, we inserted the watermark into images by modifying partly not to be visible to the naked eye. Residual images show the patch locations and how we insert the watermark on the spatial domain. When the image is well-textured, the patches are scattered all over the images, which allows the watermark to be inserted over the whole image. However, if the texture of the image is simple, the watermark is concentrated on the area near to objects.

In most watermarking methods, the performance in scaling attacks was relatively lower than other attacks. In general, scaling attacks require interpolation, which distorts or attenuates the inserted watermark severely without quality degradation. Our method cannot be directly used in real-time applications due to the computation time for scale-invariant keypoints. Our future work will focus on solving these problems.

It is important to synchronize the watermark location to design robust watermarking. One solution for watermark synchronization is to use image features where features should be selected carefully to achieve the robustness of the watermarking systems. This paper described a feature-based watermarking method based on scale-invariant keypoints. We first extracted feature points using the scale-invariant keypoint extractor and then decomposed these points into a set of disjoint triangles. The triangles (patches) were watermarked by an additive way on the spatial domain. The proposed method is robust because the patches are invariant to geometric distortion attacks. We performed an intensive simulation to evaluate the method in comparison with Kutter method and Bas method. Results support the contention that considering scale invariant keypoints is robust against various attacks listed in Stirmark 3.1 and useful to design robust watermarking algorithms.

References

1. Kutter, M.: Watermarking resisting to translation, rotation and scaling. in *Multimedia Systems and Applications*, Proc. SPIE 3528 (1998) 423-431
2. Pereira, S., Pun, T.: Robust template matching for affine resistant image watermark. IEEE T. Image Process. 9 (2000) 1123-1129
3. Ruanaidh, J.J.K.O., Pun, T.: Rotation, scale and translation invariant spread spectrum digital image watermarking. Signal Process. 66 (1998) 303-317
4. Lin, C., Cox, I.J.: Rotation, scale and translation resilient watermarking for images. IEEE T. Image Process. 10 (2001) 767-782
5. Simitopoulos, D., Koutsonanos, D.E., Strintzis, M.G.: Robust image watermarking based on generalized radon transformation. IEEE T. Circ. Syst. Vid. 13 (2003) 732-745
6. Arghoniemy, M., Twefik, A.H.: Geometric invariance in image watermarking. IEEE T. Image Process. 13 (2004) 145-153
7. Kutter, M., Bhattacharjee, S.K., Ebrahimi, T.: Towards second generation watermarking schemes. in *Proceedings of IEEE Conference on Image Processing* (1999) 320-323
8. Bas, P., Chassery, J-M., Macq, B.: Geometrically invariant watermarking using feature points. IEEE T. Image Process. 11 (2002) 1014-1028

9. Nikolaidis, A., Pitas, I.: Region-based image watermarking. IEEE T. Image Process. 10 (2001) 1726-1740
10. Tang, C.W., Hang, H-M.: A feature-based robust digital image watermarking scheme. IEEE T. Signal Process. 51 (2003) 950-959
11. Lowe, D.G.: Distinctive image features from scale-invariant keypoints. Int. J. Comput. Vision 60 (2004) 91-110
12. Mikolajczyk, K., Schmid, C.: Scale and affine invariant interest point detectors. Int. J. Comput. Vision 60 (2004) 63-86
13. Tuytelaars, T., Gool, L.V.: Matching widely separated views based on affine invariant regions. Int. J. Comput. Vision 59 (2004) 61-85
14. Voloshynovskiy, S., Herrigel, A., Pun, T.: A stochastic approach to content adaptive digital image watermarking. in Proceedings of International Workshop on Information Hiding (1999) 212-236
15. Cox, I.J., Miller, M.L., Bloom, J.A.: Digital Watermarking. Morgan Kaufmann Publishers San Francisco CA (2002)

Watermarking NURBS Surfaces

Zhigeng Pan, Shusen Sun,
Mingmin Zhang, and Daxing Zhang

State Key Lab of CAD&CG,
Zhejiang University, Hangzhou 310027, China
{zgpan, sss, zmm, dxzhang}@cad.zju.edu.cn
http://www.cad.zju.edu.cn/vrmm/index.htm

Abstract. The popularity of the worldwide web and the easy availability of the digital content has brought the security issues to the forefront. NURBS is widely used in computer-aided geometry design and computer graphics for its strong representative properties. In this paper, we present a blind watermarking algorithm for NURBS surfaces. First the points sampled from the NURBS surface are watermarked in DCT domain, then the watermarked NURBS surface is obtained by fitting the watermarked points iteratively. In watermark detection stage, the sign correlation detector is used, which is a blind detector and accordingly the original NURBS surface is not required for detection. The experimental results show that the algorithm preserves the shape of the NURBS surface. The proposed algorithm is robust against attacks such as knot insertion, knot removal, reparameterization, order elevation, order reduction, additive white Gaussian noise, rotation, translation, scaling, multi-watermark attacks, etc.

1 Introduction

Non-uniform rational B-splines (NURBS), as a *de facto* industry-standard, is proverbially used in computer-aided design and manufacturing (CAD/CAM), computer-aided geometric design (CAGD) and computer graphics because of their powerful representation ability of free form shapes as well as commonly used analytic shapes. Many models in industry and 3D games are represented in NURBS. The easy availability of these models via world wide web brings the intellectual property problem of NURBS data to the forefront.

As a copyright protection technology, digital watermarking draws a lot of attention from scientists, enterprises and governments. Although digital watermarking for image, audio and video has been studied deeply, watermarking for 3D models does not attract researchers' interests before 19997.In 1997, Ohbuchi first proposed the concept of 3D model watermarking in [1] and several watermarking algorithms including Triangle Similarity Quadrupple (TSQ), Tetrahedral Volume Ratio (TVR), Triangle Strip Peeling Sequence (TSPS)and Macro Density Pattern (MDP) etc are presented in same paper. Benedens presented several watermarking algorithms resilient to affine transforms [2, 3]. Praun proposed a robust 3D mesh watermarking algorithm using spread spectrum techniques based on constructing a set of scalar basis functions [4]. More information about 3D polygonal mesh watermarking can be found in [5, 6].

In comparison with 3D mesh watermarking, until 1999 the first paper on NURBS watermarking come forth [7]. In this paper, Ohbuchi embeds watermarks to NURBS with rational linear reparametrization. In [8], Ohbuchi et. al treats 3D geometric CAD data as one multimedia data type and presents another NURBS watermarking algorithm which embeds messages through knot insertion. The merits of these two algorithms are that both of them preserve the shape of NURBS models strictly and the former one does not change the size of the model file. However, for both algorithms, a slight change of knots or control points can make it impossible to detect watermark information. Lee's watermarking method [9, 10] is different from Ohbuchi's. The watermark is embedded into 2D virtual images extracted by parameter sampling of the 3D NURBS graphic data. Mitrea et al [11, 12] embed the watermark, which is preprocessed with spread spectrum technique, into the DCT coefficients of the NURBS surfaces' control points, which are regarded as virtual images too. For Mitrea's method, it must concatenate the coefficients of many small NURBS patch to satisfy the requirement of spread spectrum for enough control points because many NURBS patches only have a small quantity of control points.

The proposed algorithm in this paper embeds the watermark by means of modifying the points sampled from NURBS surface. Then the watermarked points are fitted iteratively using the method proposed by Lin et al [13]. The different precision can be achieved on demand by tuning iteration times. The error between watermarked surface and original surface is measured with Hausdorff distance. Sign correlation detector is used to detect watermark. The original non-watermarked NURBS surface is not required for detection. Therefore the proposed algorithm is blind and suitable for practical applications.

This paper is organized as follows. In Section 2 the concept and terminologies of NURBS curves and surfaces are introduced briefly. The details of sampling process and how to fit the watermarked points are described in Section 3. The watermark embedding and detection will be described in detail in Section 4, followed by Section 5, which is the experimental results and related analysis. Finally, the conclusions are drawn in last section.

2 NURBS Curves and Surfaces

Nowadays, NURBS may be considered as a *de facto* industry-standard for CAD, data representation and exchanging. It provide a common mathematical form for representing different shapes including analytic forms shapes and free forms entities. Here let's recall the related notations simply. The details are explained in [14].

2.1 NURBS Curves

A pth-degree (order $p+1$) NURBS curves $C(u)$ is defined as

$$C(u) = \frac{\sum_{i=0}^{n} N_i^p(u) \omega_i P_i}{\sum_{i=0}^{n} N_i^p(u) \omega_i} \qquad (1)$$

where the P_i are control points, the ω_i are weights and the $N_i^p(u)$ are the ith B-spline basis functions of degree p, which can be defined recursively as

$$\begin{cases} N_i^p(u) = \begin{cases} 1 & \text{if } u_i \leq u < u_{i+1} \\ 0 & \text{otherwise} \end{cases} \\ N_i^p(u) = \dfrac{u - u_i}{u_{i+p} - u_i} N_i^{p-1}(u) \\ \qquad + \dfrac{u_{i+p+1} - u}{u_{i+p+1} - u_{i+1}} N_{i+1}^{p-1}(u) \\ 0/0 = 0 \end{cases} \qquad (2)$$

on non-periodic knot vector

$$U = \{\underbrace{u_0, \cdots, u_p}_{p+1}, u_{p+1}, \cdots, u_{r-p-1}, \underbrace{u_{r-p}, \cdots, u_r}_{p+1}\} \qquad (3)$$

where $\{u_i\}$ satisfy $a = u_0 = \cdots = u_p \leq u_{p+1} \leq \cdots \leq u_{r-p-1} \leq u_{r-p} = \cdots = u_r = b$, and $r = n + p + 1$. The weights ω_i are assumed to be greater than zero for all i.

2.2 NURBS Surfaces

A NURBS surface of pth degree in u direction and qth degree in v direction are determined by a bidirectional net of control points $P_{i,j}$, their weights $\omega_{i,j}$ and two knots vectors. It can defined as

$$S(u,v) = \frac{\sum_{i=0}^{n} \sum_{j=0}^{m} N_i^p(u) N_j^q(v) \omega_{i,j} P_{i,j}}{\sum_{i=0}^{n} \sum_{j=0}^{m} N_i^p(u) N_j^q(v) \omega_{i,j}} \qquad (4)$$

where $N_i^p(u)$ and $N_j^q(v)$ are the ith B-spline basis function of degree p and jth one of degree q (see Eq. 2). Knot vector U is same as shown in Eq. 3. Knot vector V can be expressed similarly as

$$V = \{\underbrace{v_0, \cdots, u_q}_{q+1}, v_{q+1}, \cdots, v_{s-q-1}, \underbrace{v_{s-q}, \cdots, v_s}_{q+1}\} \qquad (5)$$

where $\{v_i\}$ satisfy $c = v_0 = \cdots = v_q \leq u_{q+1} \leq \cdots \leq v_{s-q-1} \leq v_{s-q} = \cdots = v_s = d$, and $s = m + q + 1$.

3 Sampling and Fitting

For a NURBS surface, a NURBS curve can be obtained by fixing knot value u or v. Lee uses iso-chord length to sample NURBS surface [10]. Though the iso-chord length based sampling has its advantages in NURBS surface reconstruction from watermarked points, it is not unique for a given curve, as shown in Fig. 1, $|ab| = |bc| = |cd|$ and $|ae| = |ef| = |fd|$. Therefore iso-chord length based sampling is not stable. Here we use iso-arc length to sample a NURBS surface. The sampling procedure can be done in following steps:

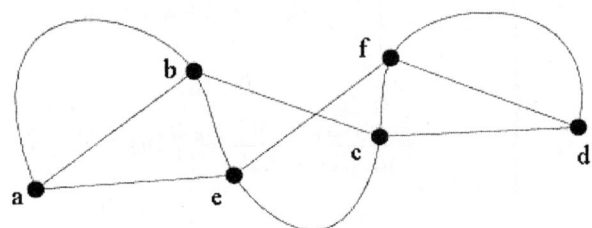

Fig. 1. The non-uniqueness of iso-chord length sampling

Step 1: Generate an iso-parametric curve $C_{u_*}(v) \equiv S(u,v)|_{u=u^*}$ which goes through u^*. There are many ways to select u^*. One simple and stable method is that let $u^* = u_0 = a$. The method that let $u^* = arg\ max \int_c^d \|\ C'_u(v)\ \|_2 dv$ is efficient but not stable.

Step 2: Divide the curve $C_{u_*}(v)$ into h sections according to arc length. That is to say:

$$L = \int_c^d \|\ C'_{u_*}(v)\ \|_2 dv \qquad (6)$$

We select $h - 1$ internal knot values $\{v_i\}_{i=1}^{h-1}$ which satisfy following conditions.

$$c = v_0 < v_1 < \cdots < v_{h-1} < v_h = d \qquad (7)$$

and

$$\int_{v_i}^{v_{i+1}} \|\ C'_{u_*}(v)\ \|_2 dv = \frac{L}{h} \pm \epsilon, \quad i = 0, \cdots, h-1 \qquad (8)$$

where ϵ is error limit.

Step 3: Generate h iso-parametric curves $C_{v_i}(u) \equiv S(u,v)|_{v=v_i}$, which goes through v_i achieved in Step 2 respectively, $i = 0, \cdots, h-1$.

Step 4: Each curve $C_{v_i}(u)$ is divided into w parts using the same way in Step 2.

Thus we obtain a u, v matrix $\{u_i, v_j\}_{i=0\ j=0}^{w-1\ h-1}$. For each pair of $\{u_i, v_j\}$, there is a point d_{ij} on the surface $S(u,v)$ corresponding to it.

Step 5: Once the sample points obtained, they can be watermarked as usual images. The details will be described in next section.

Step 6: The fitting algorithm proposed by Lin [13] is used to reconstruct the NURBS surface from the watermarked sample points.

Given an ordered point set $\{P_{ij}\}_{i=1}^{m}{}_{j=1}^{n} \in R^3$, they can be fitted by the following iterative NURBS surfaces. The non-uniform B-splines bases $B_i^3(u)$ and $B_i^3(v)$ are defined on the knot-vectors $\{u_i\}_{i=1}^{m+5}$ and $\{v_i\}_{j=1}^{n+5}$, here

$$\begin{cases} u_i = u_{i-1} + \frac{1}{n}\sum_{j=1}^{n} \| P_{i-2,j} - P_{i-3,j} \|, \\ \quad i = 4, 5, \cdots, m+2 \\ u_0 = u_1 = u_2 = u_3 = 0, \\ u_{m+2} = u_{m+3} = u_{m+4} = u_{m+5} \end{cases} \quad (9)$$

$$\begin{cases} v_j = v_{j-1} + \frac{1}{m}\sum_{i=1}^{m} \| P_{i,j-2} - P_{i,j-3} \|, \\ \quad j = 4, 5, \cdots, n+2 \\ v_0 = v_1 = v_2 = v_3 = 0, \\ v_{n+2} = v_{n+3} = v_{n+4} = v_{n+5} \end{cases} \quad (10)$$

At the beginning of the iteration, let

$$\begin{cases} \{P_{ij}^0 = P_{ij}\}_{i=1\,j=1}^{m\ \ n}, \\ \{P_{0j}^0 = P_{1j}^0, \ P_{m+1,j}^0 = P_{m,j}^0\}_{j=1}^{n}, \\ \{P_{i0}^0 = P_{i1}^0, \ P_{i,n+1}^0 = P_{i,n}^0\}_{i=1}^{m}, \\ P_{00}^0 = P_{11}^0, \ P_{0,n+1}^0 = P_{1,n}^0, \\ P_{m+1,0}^0 = P_{m,1}^0, \ P_{m+1,n+1}^0 = P_{m,n}^0 \end{cases} \quad (11)$$

Thus, taking $\{P_{ij}^0\}_{i=0\,j=0}^{m+1\,n+1}$ as control point set, a NURBS surface $r^k(u,v), k = 0$ can be obtained.

$$r^k(u,v) = \sum_{i=0}^{m+1}\sum_{j=0}^{n+1} P_{ij}^k N_i^3(u) N_j^3(v), \quad (12)$$
$$k = 0, 1, \cdots; \quad (u,v) \in [u_3, u_{m+2}] \times [v_3, v_{n+2}]$$

The control point set $\{P_{ij}^k\}_{i=0\,j=0}^{m+1\,n+1}, k = 1, 2, \cdots$, is updated according to following equation:

$$\{P_{ij}^k = P_{ij}^{k-1} + \Delta_{ij}^{k-1}\}_{i=0\,j=0}^{m+1\,n+1}, k = 1, 2, \cdots \quad (13)$$

where Δ are defined by

$$\begin{cases} \Delta_{ij}^k = P_{ij}^k - r^k(u_{i+2}, v_{j+2}), \\ \{\Delta_{h,0}^k = \Delta_{h,1}^k\}_{h=1}^{m}, \ \{\Delta_{0,l}^k = \Delta_{1,l}^k\}_{l=1}^{n}, \\ \Delta_{00}^k = \Delta_{m+1,0}^k = \Delta_{0,n+1}^k = \Delta_{m+1,n+1}^k = 0 \end{cases} \quad (14)$$

where $k = 0, 1, \cdots, i = 1, \cdots, m, j = 1, \cdots, n$.

It is proved that Δ_{ij}^k is convergent. i.e. the iterative surface r_{ij}^k interpolates the control point set $\{P_{ij}\}$. For details of proving procedure, please refer to [13].

4 Watermarking Process

In previous section, we introduced how to do sampling and how to fit the watermarked sample points with iterative NURBS surfaces. In this section, the details of embedding watermarks on the sample points and watermark detection will be described.

4.1 Watermark Embedding

The watermarking embedding procedure can be done in following steps:

Step 1: The sampling method introduced in section 3 are used to generate sample points $\{d_{ij}\}$. The watermark sequence will be embedded to these points.

Step 2: In order to make the watermarking algorithm resistant to rotation and translation transforms. The coordinates of the sample points can not be used to embed watermark directly. What is used to embed watermark is the length of the vectors defined by $I_{ij} = d_{ij} - d_{0,0}$. It is obvious that I_{ij} are constant of translation and rotation does not change their length $\{|I_{ij}|\}$. Then the full frame discrete cosine transform (DCT) is done to $\{|I_{ij}|\}$.

$$D_{ij} = \mathcal{DCT}(|I_{ij}|) \tag{15}$$

where $|\cdot|$ denotes the length of the vector.

Step 3: Without loss of generality, we embed the watermark information w_{ij} into the medium frequency part of the DCT coefficients as that in [15].

$$\hat{D}_{ij} = \begin{cases} D_{ij} + \alpha w_{ij} & \text{medium frequency} \\ D_{ij} & \text{else} \end{cases} \tag{16}$$

where α is the scaling parameter. Watermark $W = \{w_{ij}\}$ is a pseudo-random sequence, each elements of which obeys the normal distribution with mean zero, variance one and standard deviation one. It can be generated with a key K as seed. i.e.

$$W = rand(K); \tag{17}$$

Step 4: Reconstruct watermarked NURBS surface with iterative fitting method mentioned above. It is trivial to achieve the watermarked sample points from the watermarked DCT coefficients and the direction of vectors $\{I_{ij}\}$. Then the watermarked surface is achieved through iterative fitting mentioned in previous section.

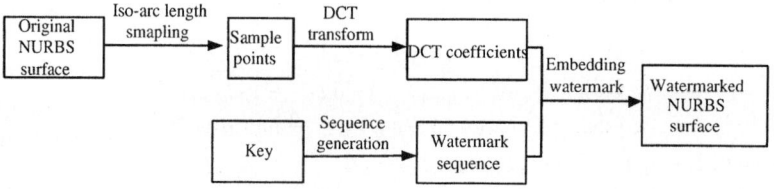

Fig. 2. Block diagram of watermark embedding

4.2 Watermark Detection

The detection process is simple in comparison with watermark embedding. For most of 3D watermarking methods, the original non-watermarked object or other other assistant information related to original object are required to detect watermark. In our watermarking scheme, the sign correlation detector proposed by Bo [16] is used to check watermark presence or not in a suspect surface. Both original non-watermarked surface and sampling positions are not required for detecting watermarks. Therefore the proposed algorithm is a blind solution. The detection procedure can be done in following steps:

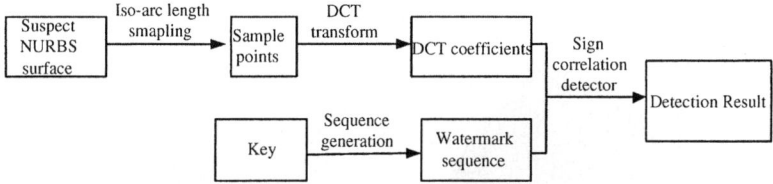

Fig. 3. Block diagram of watermark detection

Step 1: The first step is to sample the suspect NURBS surface. There is no any difference with the sampling process in watermarking embedding stage.

Step 2: In this step, DCT transform is done in the same way as in watermark embedding process.

Step 3: For our algorithm, the original watermark is not supplied at all because it can be generated again in watermark detection stage. What is required is the key K used in watermark embedding. It will be used as seed to generate same watermark sequence as the one embedded previously.

Step 4: After sampling the watermarked NURBS surface and discrete cosine transform, the response of the sign correlation detector to watermark sequences can be calculated with following equation.

$$T = \sum_{i=1}^{n} w_{ij} sgn(\tilde{D}_{ij}) \tag{18}$$

where $sgn(\cdot)$ is sign function. $\tilde{D}_{ij}$ is the medium part of DCT coefficients calculated from the sample points from the NURBS surface to be detected with the same way used in watermark embedding. Whether the surface is watermarked or not is decided by $T > T_g$ or not. T_g is the threshold.

Considering the condition that the watermarked surface maybe transposed, this scenario can solved by transposing the suspect model first, and then watermark detection process are done again. That is to say, both suspect model and transposed suspect model are tried to detect wether there exist the watermark.

5 Experimental Results and Analysis

In order to test our algorithm, some models such as pumpkin, duck are used in our experiment. The original pumpkin model and its sample points, the watermarked model and its sample points are shown in Fig. 4.

Table 1. The numbers of control points original watermarked model

Model name	Original	watermarked
Pumpkin	9 × 22	32 × 32
Duck	14 × 13	32 × 32

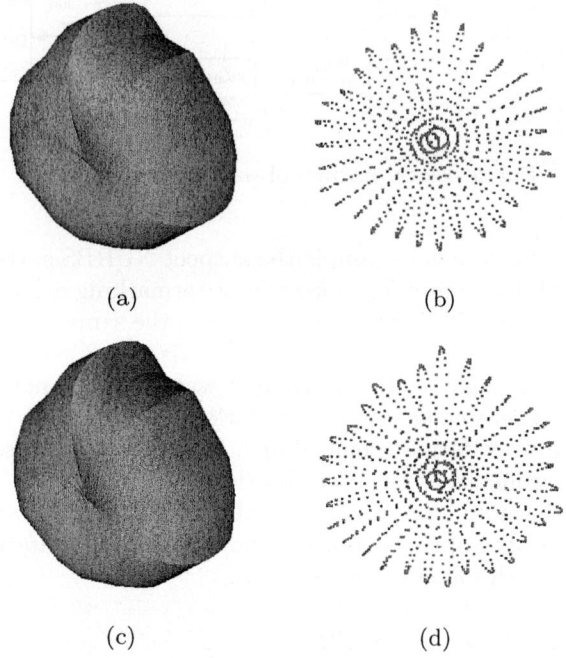

(a) (b)

(c) (d)

Fig. 4. (a) and (c) are original model and watermarked model respectively. (b)and (d) are points sampled from original model and watermarked model respectively.

The sampling rate is 32 by 32 in u and v directions respectively, i.e $h = 32$, $w = 32$ at Step 2 and 4 in section 3. We add the watermark to the 400 median DCT coefficients. The watermark is a normal distributed pseudo-random sequence of 400 elements with mean zero, variance one and standard deviation one. 1000 this kind of random sequences are generated randomly with different keys. Among them, only the 500th is the embedded one (One exception is Fig. 6 (f) , in which the 250th is the second embedded watermark).

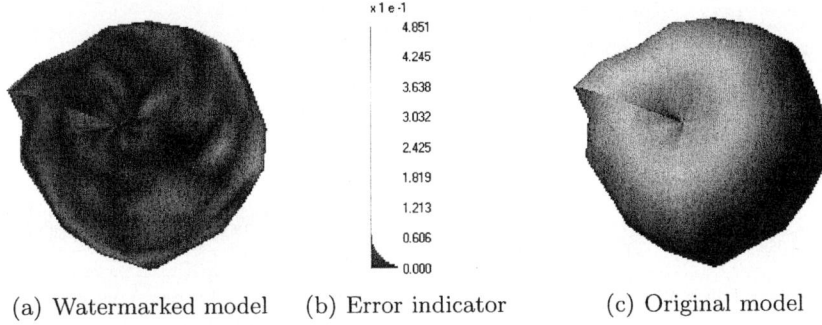

(a) Watermarked model (b) Error indicator (c) Original model

Fig. 5. The error between original model and watermarked one

5.1 Visual Quality Evaluation

To measure error between original model and watermarked model, we use Hausdorff distance to evaluate their difference. The original and watermarked NURBS surfaces are tesselated first. Then the Hausdorff distance between the two tesselated triangle meshes is calculated with a software named MESH, which can be download from http://mesh.berlios.de. The detail of the Hausdorff distance and how to calculate the it between surfaces can be found in [17]. The result is shown in Fig. 5. The following conclusion can be drawn that the error is very small.

5.2 Robustness

In order to evaluate the robustness of our watermarking scheme. We test our algorithm under condition of different attacks. The responses of the detector to the 1000 random watermarks for different models is shown in Fig.6. Fig.6(a) is the detection result of non-attacked watermarked model. Fig.6 (b)-(e) are the results of models attacked by rotation, scaling, translation and noise addition. It is obvious that the algorithm is robust against these attacks. Here we do not care scaling which inputs big distortions in scale or shape. In fact, serious distorted model can be seen as another model other than original one.

In addition, the proposed algorithm is flexible against multi-watermark attack too, as shown in Fig.6 (f). It is obvious that the responses to the first and second watermarks (the 500th and 250th one) are larger than that to other random sequences.

For reparameterization, knot insertion, order elevation, and weight-related attacks, the detection result is not affected at all since the sampling process is only related to the u, v values instead of x, y, z coordinates and reparameterization, knot insertion, order elevation and weight-related attacks keep the shape of the NURBS surface unchanged strictly. And the errors imported by knot removal and order reduction usually are very little, their effect on the sampling process is limited. Therefore, our algorithm is robust to NURBS parameters related operations.

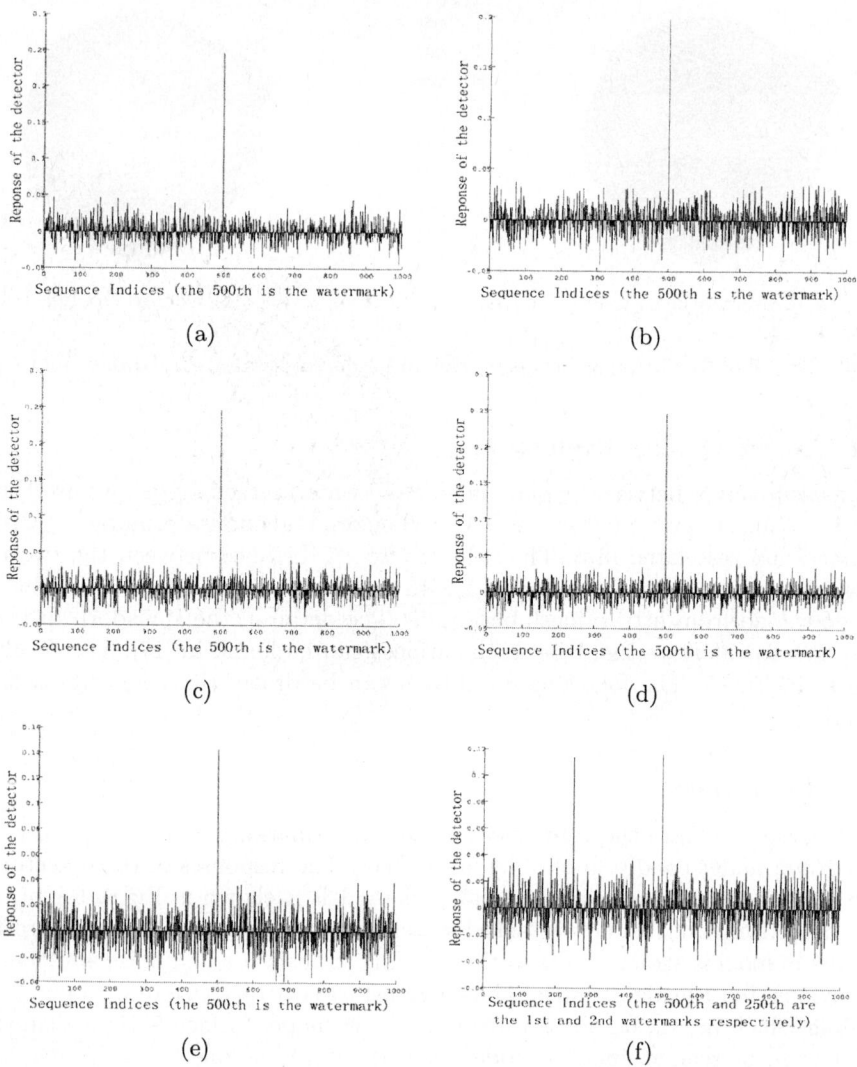

Fig. 6. Experimental results. Each figure is the response of the watermark detector to 1000 sequences including random generated sequences and the watermark extracted from different suspect models (a) non-attacked watermarked model, (b) rotation-attacked watermarked model (c) scaling-attacked watermarked model (d) translation-attacked watermarked model (e)noise-addition-attacked watermarked model and (f) multi-watermarked model

The watermarking method proposed in this paper is by no means perfect. One disadvantage of this algorithm is that the watermarked NURBS surfaces fitted from watermarked sample points have more control points than the original one. But some redundant control points can be removed to some extent via knot removal if error limits are allowed. The evaluation of visual quality and the methods of error measurement of watermarked NURBS surface can be improved in future.

6 Conclusion and Future Work

This paper proposed a new blind NURBS watermarking algorithm. The algorithm has no strict requirement for the number of NURBS control points because the watermark information is embedded to the points sampled from the NURBS surface rather than to control points directly. The precision of the watermarked NURBS surface can satisfy different error limits by increasing the iteration times of fitting. The experimental results show that the algorithm is robust against many common manipulations such as knot insertion, knot removal, weight related attacks, reparameterizaion, translation, scaling etc.

The results presented in this paper is by no means perfect. There are still some space for improvement. For example, how to keep the number of control points unchanged before and after watermark embedding. In addition, it is very useful to develop the algorithm that embeds readable watermark on NURBS surfaces and does not require original surface to extract watermark and be robust against common attacks.

Acknowledgment

We would like to appreciate Hongwei Lin, Guoxian Zheng, Hongwei Wang and Xianyong Fang for their constructive advices and very helpful discussions during the development of these ideas.

This research is supported by the National Natural Science Foundation of China (No. 60473111) and the Excellent Young Teacher Program of MOE, China.

References

1. Ohbuchi, R., Masuda, H., Aono, M.: Watermarking three-dimensional polygonal models. In: Proceedings of the ACM International Conference on Multimedia '97, Seattle, USA (1997) 261–272
2. Benedens, O.: Geometry-based watermarking of 3d models. IEEE Computer Graphics and Applications **19** (1999) 46–55
3. Benedens, O., Busch, C.: Towards blind detection of robust watermarks in polygonal models. In: Proceeding of EUROGRAPHICS 2000, Computer Graphics Forum. Volume 19., Blackwell (2000) C199–C208
4. Praun, E., Hoppe, H., Finkelstein, A.: Robust mesh watermarking. In: Proceeding of SIGGRAPH 1999. (1999) 69–76
5. Corsini, M., Barni, M., Bartolini, F., Caldelli, R., Piva, A.: Towards 3D watermarking technology. In: Proc. EUROCON 2003, Ljubljana, Solvenia (2003) 393–396
6. Zhang, X., Peng, W., Zhang, S., Ye, Z.: Review of watermarking techniques for 3D polygonal models. Journal of Computer-aided Design and Computer Graphics **15** (2003) 913–820 (In Chinese).

7. Ohbuchi, R., Masuda, H., Aono, M.: A shape-preserving data embedding algorithm for nurbs curves and surfaces. In: Computer Graphics International 1999 (CGI'99), Canmore, Canada (1999) 1–8
8. Ohbuchi, R., Masuda, H.: Managing CAD data as a multimedia data type using digital watermarking. In: the proceedings of the Fourth International Workshop on Knowledge Intensive CAD (KIC-4), Parma, Italy (2000) 113–125
9. Lee, J., Cho, N., Nam, J.: Watermarking for 3D NURBS graphic data. In: IEEE International Workshop on MMSP. (2002) 304–307
10. Lee, J.J., Cho, N.I., Lee, S.U.: Watermarking algorithms for 3D NURBS graphic data. EURASIP journal on applied signal processing **2004** (2004) 2142–2152
11. Mitrea, M., Zaharia, T., Preteux, F.: Spread spectrum robust watermarking for NURBS surfaces. WSEAS Transactions on Communications **3** (2004) 734–710
12. Mitrea, M.: Toward robust spread spectrum watermarking of 3D data. Technical report, Institut National des Tlcommunications - ARTEMIS Project Unit (2004)
13. Lin, H., Wang, G., Dong, C.: Constructing iterative non-uniform B-spline curve and surface to fit data points. Science in China (Series F Information Science) **47** (2004) 315–331
14. Piegl, L., Tiller, W.: The NURBS Book. Springer-Verlag (1997)
15. Cox, J., Killian, J., Leighton, T., Shamoon, T.: Secure spread spectrum watermarking for multimedia. IEEE Transactions on Image Processing **6** (1997) 1673–1687
16. Bo, X., Shen, L., Chang, W.: Sign correlation detector for blind image watermarking in the DCT domain. LNCS **2195** (2001) 780–787
17. Aspert, N., Santa-Cruz, D., Ebrahimi, T.: Mesh: Measuring errors between surfaces using the hausdorff distance. In: Proceedings of the IEEE International Conference on Multimedia and Expo. Volume I. (2002) 705 – 708 http://mesh.epfl.ch.

Digital Watermarking Based on Three-Dimensional Wavelet Transform for Video Data

Seung-Jin Kim[1], Tae-Su Kim[1], Ki-Ryong Kwon[2], Sang-Ho Ahn[3], and Kuhn-Il Lee[1]

[1] School of Electrical Engineering and Computer Science,
Kyungpook National University,
1370, Sankyug-Dong, Buk-Gu, Daegu, 702-701, Korea
{starksjin, kts1101, kilee}@ee.knu.ac.kr

[2] Department of Electronic Engineering, Pusan University of Foreign Studies,
55-1, Uam-Dong, Nam-Gu, Pusan, 608-738, Korea
krkwon@pufs.ac.kr

[3] School of Electronic Telecommunication Engineering, Inje University,
607, Obang-Dong, Kimhae, Kyungnam, 621-749, Korea
elecash@inje.ac.kr

Abstract. With the increment of digital media, multimedia technology and copyright protection have been the important issue. In this paper, an effective watermarking algorithm is proposed to protect copyright of video data. In the watermark embedding step, a three-dimensional discrete wavelet transform (3D DWT) is used to decompose original video data, because a pirate can easily extract the watermark by statistically comparing successive frames in case that the watermark is embedded in spatial doamin. The binary image is used as the watermark. It is changed into the video watermark by a two-dimensional (2D) pseudorandom permutation and the spread spectrum technique. The video watermark is embedded into the 3D DWT coefficients of the selected subbands. In the watermark extracting step, the embedded video watermark is detected by the similarity of the unit of subband and the final watermark image is extracted by a watermark decision rule and a reverse permutation. Experimental results show that the watermarked frames are subjectively indistinguishable from the original frames, plus the proposed video watermarking algorithm is sufficiently robust against various attacks.

1 Introduction

Due to the rapid growth in network distributions and multimedia system, digital media such as images and video data have been distributed on the internet and via CD-ROM and DVD easier and faster. In this process, a number of original digital media can be copied and forged easily. As a result, creators and distributors of digital media have become increasingly interested in protecting their property. Digital watermarking has been attracting attention as an effective method to protect copyright and ownership.

Digital watermarking is a concept of embedding copyright information, that is a watermark, into digital data in secret and inconspicuous way. Basic requirements of digital watermarking are invisibility, robustness, and capacity. Invisibility is a degree that an embedded watermark remains unnoticeable when a user views watermarked digital media. Robustness is the resilience of an embedded watermark against being removed by incidental and intended attacks. Capacity is the amount of information that can reliably be hidden when the scheme provides the ability to change digital data. The relative importance of each property is dependent on the requirement of the applications and the role of the watermark [1]-[4]. As the protection of intellectual property has become an important issue in the digital world, a variety of watermarking algorithms for digital contents have been proposed in order to address this issue. As the research area of image watermarking becomes mature and video data have been increased in recent years, researchers have begun to gradually focus on video watermarking [1], [5]-[9].

In several methods about the video watermarking, Hsu et al. [6] use a discrete cosine transform (DCT) and the relationship between neighboring blocks. The binary watermark is embedded into both the intraframe and the interframe with different residual masks. A preprocessed watermark is embedded into middle frequency coefficients using the polarity modification between the corresponding pixels in a neighboring block. This method takes advantage of the DCT that is used in the video coding standards. Since DCT coefficients, however, are changed in order to maintain polarity, an error is accumulated during the watermark embedding procedure. Niu et al. [7] use a 3D DWT and a gray-level watermark image, where the watermark is preprocessed using a multi-resolution hierarchical structure and a hamming code. Then, a 3D DWT is performed as a unit of 64 frames. Since this method, however, uses error correction coding to correct error bits, the side information is large. Thus, in the procedure to embed bit planes of the gray watermark and error correction bits, a complex structure is required. The bit error of the most significant pixel also affects the extracted gray watermark image. Li et al. [8] use a 3D DWT and the spread spectrum technique. The preprocessed watermark is embedded into a baseband after performing a 3D DWT. Therefore, while this method is robust to various attacks, it is perceptually visible. Also, since a one-dimensional (1D) DWT of the three levels is performed along the temporal axis, a selected video shot always must consist of the number of frames that can be decomposited by a 3D DWT.

Accordingly, an effective video watermarking algorithm using a 3D DWT and the spread spectrum technique is proposed. After the visible binary watermark image is preprocessed by the 2D pseudorandom permutation, it is changed to the video watermark by the spread spectrum technique. Thereafter, a 3D DWT is performed for the video shots that are divided from the video sequence. The generated video watermark is embedded in the subbands that are determined considering robustness and invisibility. The embedded watermark is extracted by comparing similarity between the original video watermark and the detected video watermark. Finally, the watermark image is determined by a watermark decision rule and a reverse permutation. Although the visible binary watermark image is used, the use of two spread spectrum sequences allows for different watermarks to be embedded into each video frame, making it robust against various attacks. Also, it increases the precision of watermark extraction. As such, the proposed algorithm produces watermarked frames that are subjectively not different from the original frames and robust against such various attacks as low pass filtering (LPF), dropping, clopping, averaging, and MPEG coding about frames.

This paper is organized as follows. The procedures of preprocessing the watermark, embedding the watermark, and extracting the watermark are described in Section 2. Experimental results and performance comparison of different algorithms are shown in Section 3. Section 4 offers conclusion remarks.

2 Proposed Video Watermarking Algorithm

2.1 Watermark Preprocessing

In daily life, one claims a document or a creative work by signing one's signature, using a personal seal, or an organization's logo. When using such kinds of binary images to prove identity, the viewer can subjectively compare the original watermark with the extracted watermark. Therefore, a binary image is more visually effective than a sequence which is made up of random numbers and it is used as the watermark in our method. During image manipulation, usually some part of the image can be cropped. It would be easy for a pirate to remove the watermark. Accordingly, the binary watermark image is preprocessed by a 2D pseudorandom permutation [2], [10], as it is without the appropriate adjustment for the spatial relationship of the watermark. The binary watermark $w_P(i',j')$, that is permuted by the 2D pseudorandom number traversing method is

$$W_\mathrm{p} = P(W)$$
$$w_\mathrm{p}(i,j) = P(w(i',j'))$$
$$\text{where} \quad 0 \leq i, i' \leq M \quad \text{and} \quad 0 \leq j, j' \leq N \quad (1)$$

where $P(\cdot)$ is the 2D pseudorandom permutation function and $w(i',j')$ is the original watermark image. Also, the pixel (i',j') is permuted to the pixel (i,j) in pseudorandom order and $M \times N$ is the size of the watermark image.

The watermark consist of a binary bit after performing the 2D pseudorandom permutation. When the watermark, however, is embedded, it is no longer a binary bit but a real value that is selected in two independent spread spectrum sequences [4], [8], [11], which can be defined as the secret key and it is necessary in the watermark extracting step. Two spectrum sequences, **P** and **Q**, are

$$\mathbf{P} = \{p_1, p_1, \cdots, p_f, \cdots, p_F\}$$
$$\mathbf{Q} = \{q_1, q_1, \cdots, q_f, \cdots, q_F\} \quad (2)$$

where F is the length of the spread spectrum sequence. Two spread spectrum sequences are repeatedly used in every frame shot. This method is sufficiently

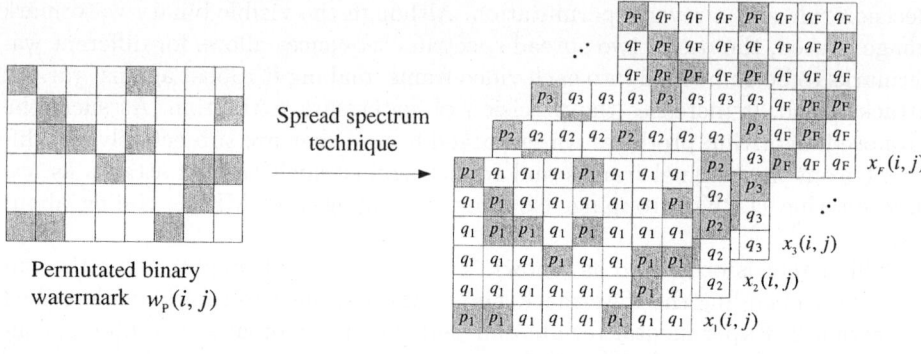

Fig. 1. An example of the method that changes the permutated watermark into a video watermark by the spread spectrum technique

robust against various attacks such as frame dropping, frame average, and MPEG coding. Different spread spectrum sequences, however, can be used in every frame shot for robust scheme against estimation attacks.

The spread spectrum technique is that the spread spectrum sequence, **P** and **Q**, are used according as bit 0 or 1 of the binary watermark image. The real watermark $x_f(i,j)$, embedded in the fth frame is

$$x_f(i,j) = \begin{cases} p_f & if \quad w_p(i,j) = 1 \\ q_f & if \quad w_p(i,j) = 0 \end{cases} \quad (3)$$

where $0 \leq f \leq F$ and $w_p(i,j)$ is the preprocessed watermark. Also, the video watermark $\mathbf{X}_{i,j}$ generated by the spread spectrum technique is

$$\mathbf{X}_{i,j} = \{x_1(i,j), x_2(i,j), \cdots, x_F(i,j)\} \quad (4)$$

Therefore, the embedded watermark is not the binary image but a real value which is determined by two spread spectrum sequences. An example of the method that changes the permutated watermark into the video watermark by the spread spectrum technique is shown in Fig. 1.

2.2 Watermark Embedding

In considering a video watermarking scheme as a direct extension of image watermarking by treating each frame as an individual still image, this is ineffective for two reasons. First, a pirate can easily extract the watermark by statistically comparing or averaging successive video frames. Second, if different watermarks are embedded into each frame, the watermark amount is large. Thus, to prevent pirate attacks on the watermark and to reduce a watermark amount, the proposed method uses a 3D DWT that is computed by applying separate one-dimensional (1D) transform along the temporal axis of the video frames transformed by a 2D DWT [5], [12], [13].

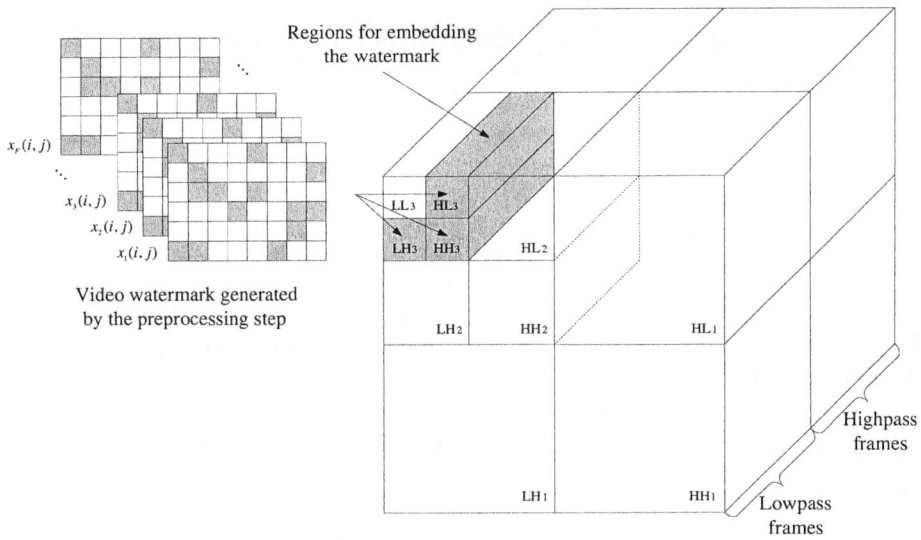

Fig. 2. Structure of 3D DWT used for the proposed watermark method and regions of embedding the video mark generated by the preprocessing step

The 3D DWT, that is used in the proposed video watermarking method, is a powerful tool that decomposes signals at multiple resolutions in space and time domain. It, however, is based on a group of frames (GOF) concept. Therefore, the video sequence is first divided into video shots to enhance the efficiency of the 3D DWT. In this process, a spatial different metric (SDM) [14] is used to determine the dissimilarity between an adjoining frame pair. Although the efficiency of the SDM is lower than other methods, the algorithm is simple. Second, both a spatial 2D DWT of three levels and a temporal 1D DWT of one level are performed about the selected video shots.

In the resulting 3D DWT coefficients, the video watermark is embedded into the HL subband, LH subband, and HH subband of the three-level (HL_3, LH_3, and HH_3) about the spatial axis and the lowpass frames about the temporal axis. As human eyes are more sensitive to low frequency components, low frequency subbands are excluded to satisfy invisibility. As the energy of most images is concentrated on low frequency subbands and high frequency components are discarded by a quantization of lossy compression, high frequency subbands are excluded to satisfy robustness. The 3D DWT structure and regions that are selected to embed the video watermark are shown in Fig. 2. The size of the watermark image is the same size as a three-level subband. The video watermark $x_f(i,j)$, on the frame number f, is embedded using the following relationship [1], [9], [15].

$$v'_f(i,j) = v_f(i,j) \times (1 + \alpha \times \beta \times x_f(i,j))$$
$$where \quad \beta = \begin{cases} \sqrt{2} & if \quad v_f(i,j) \in HH_3 \\ 1 & otherwise \end{cases} \tag{5}$$

where $v'_f(i,j)$ and $v_f(i,j)$ denote the 3D DWT coefficient of HL_3, LH_3, and HH_3 in the watermarked frame and the original frame, respectively. Also, α is the scaling parameter that reflects the degree to embed the watermark. In addition, β is the scaling parameter determined by the human visual system that is more insensitive to noises of the diagonal subband.

2.3 Watermark Extracting

The watermark extraction process is the inverse procedure of the watermark embedding process. Similarity and a watermark decision rule are used to extract the embedded watermark image. A block diagram of the watermark extracting procedure is shown in Fig. 3.

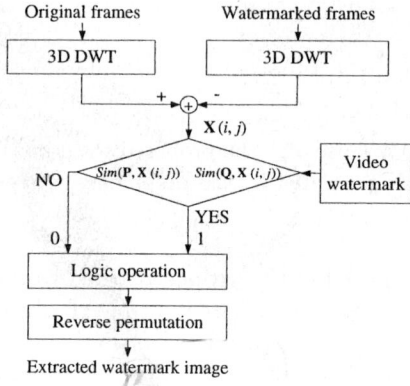

Fig. 3. A block diagram of the proposed watermarking algorithm to extract the embedded watermark

The proposed watermarking algorithm requires a original video sequence and two spread spectrum sequences. Although we get different values between wavelet coefficients of the original frame and the watermarked frame, these values are not of the extracted binary watermark images, they are of the detected spread spectrum sequences which are modified by attacks, namely, the detected video watermark. Accordingly, Similarity between two spread spectrum sequences and the detected video watermark is calculated in order to extract the binary watermark. The binary watermark $\tilde{w}_b(l,j)$ is extracted using the following relationship in HL_3, LH_3, and HH_3, respectively.

$$\tilde{w}_b(i,j) = \begin{cases} 1 & if \quad Sim(\mathbf{P}, \mathbf{X}'_{i,j}) \geq Sim(\mathbf{Q}, \mathbf{X}'_{i,j}) \\ 0 & otherwise \end{cases} \quad (6)$$

where b represents the HL_3, LH_3, and HH_3, respectively and $\mathbf{X}'_{i,j}$ is the detected video watermark. The similarity is defined as the following equation.

$$Sim(\mathbf{P}, \mathbf{X}'_{i,j}) = \frac{\sum_{f=0}^{F} p_f \cdot x'_f(i,j)}{\sum_{f=0}^{F} p_f^2} \quad (7)$$

KSJ

Fig. 4. Watermark image with visually recognizable binary patterns

The binary watermark image $\tilde{w}'(i,j)$ is determined by the following equation regarding the binary watermark $\tilde{w}_{HL_3}(i,j)$, $\tilde{w}_{LH_3}(i,j)$, and $\tilde{w}_{HH_3}(i,j)$ that are extracted from HL_3, LH_3, and HH_3, respectively. If the sum of the binary value is more than two in the same position of the binary watermark images, the binary bit 1 exists in at least two binary watermark images. Namely,

$$\tilde{w}'(i,j) = \begin{cases} 1 & if \quad (\tilde{w}_{HL_3}(i,j) + \tilde{w}_{LH_3}(i,j) + \tilde{w}_{HH_3}(i,j)) \geq 2 \\ 0 & otherwise \end{cases} \quad (8)$$

A 2D reverse pseudorandom permutation is performed and the embedded binary watermark image is finally extracted. Since the resulting watermark is a binary image, the viewer can subjectively compare the extracted watermark with the original watermark.

3 Experimental Results

Computer simulations were carried out to demonstrate the performance of the proposed watermarking method with conventional watermarking methods. FOOTBALL and TABLE TENNIS were used as the test video sequences. The size of each frame is 352 × 240. The watermark is a binary image with 44 × 30 sized, as shown in Fig. 4. The watermark images were enlarged in this paper. The video sequence was divided into video shots by the SDM. The total frame number of the video shots, however, is an odd number that is to carry out a temporal 1D DWT of one level after a spatial 2D DWT. The peak signal-to-noise ratio (PSNR) was used as an objective measure of invisibility, while the bit-error rate (BER), which is the number of total watermark bits to error bits ratio was used to measure robustness.

The 17th original frame and the 17th frame watermarked by the proposed method of the FOOTBALL and the TABLE TENNIS video sequences are shown in Fig. 5 and Fig. 6, respectively. The PSNR of the watermarked frames is 33.23 dB and 34.58 dB, respectively. The proposed algorithm produced a hardly detectable subjective difference between the original frame and the watermarked frame. The PSNR for the FOOTBALL 64 frames, which is watermarked by the proposed method and conventional methods, is shown in Fig. 7. The proposed algorithm produced a higher PSNR than that of the conventional methods. Therefore, the propose method produces frames that are good in subjective and objective quality.

In order to measure robustness, various attacks were used, such as clopping, spatial LPF, frame dropping, frame average, and MPEG coding. For clopping

Fig. 5. (a) 17th original frame and (b) 17th watermarked frame of the FOOTBALL video sequence

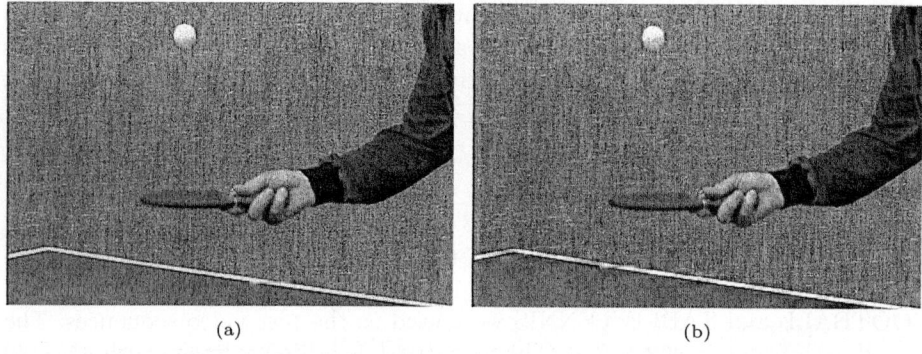

Fig. 6. (a) 17th original frame and (b) 17th watermarked frame of the TABLE TENNIS video sequence

attack, all frames of the video shot were clopped as shown in Fig. 8. As described in Section 2, the 2D pseudorandom permutation is performed against the clopping attack. Therefore, the extracted watermark image, with a permutation procedure, reveals spatial information which is sufficient in proving the ownership as shown in Fig. 8. For frame dropping and interpolation attack, the odd index frames were dropped and the missing frames are replaced with the average of the two neighboring frames. For frame average attack, each frame was averaged with neighbor frames. For MPEG coding attack, video frames coded at 1.5 Mbps were used. The watermark images, which are extracted in test sequences after various attacks, are shown in Fig. 9 and Fig. 10. The BER of the extracted watermark images that are shown in Fig. 9 was 7.4%, 30.2%, 8.9%, and 17.5%, respectively. The BER of the extracted watermark images that is shown in Fig. 10 was 18.9%, 21.7%, 4.8%, and 19.9%, respectively. The quality of the extracted watermark images was sufficient to claim copyright and ownership of the digital video sequence.

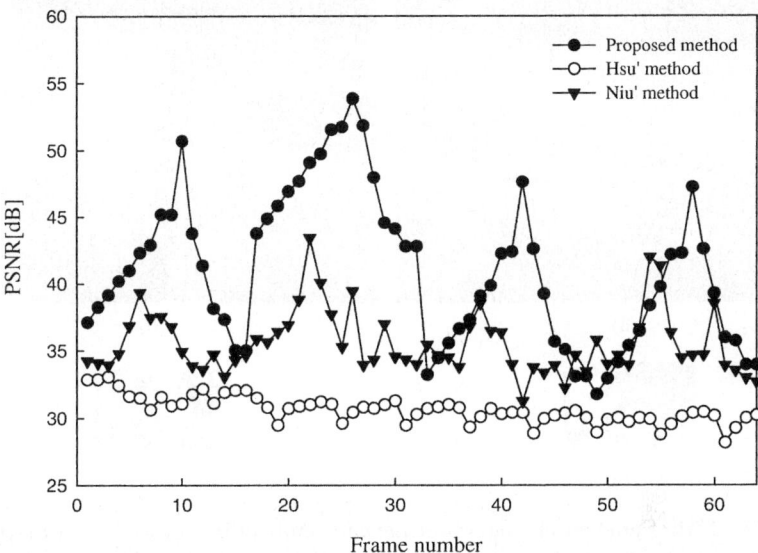

Fig. 7. PSNR for the FOOTBALL 64 frames watermarked by the proposed method and the conventional methods

Table 1. The average BER of the watermark images extracted from the test video sequence after various attacks.

Sequences	Methods / Attacks	BER [%]		
		Hsu's method	Niu's method	Proposed method
FOOTBALL	Spatial LPF	59.0	35.4	9.2
	Frame Dropping	38.6	38.4	32.2
	Frame Average	51.8	24.6	9.8
	MPEG Coding	49.0	33.0	17.8
TABLE TENNIS	Spatial LPF	48.6	37.3	18.1
	Frame Dropping	40.2	39.0	29.7
	Frame Average	53.8	16.9	10.2
	MPEG Coding	49.7	32.7	21.3

The experimental results, after various attacks, were summarized in Table I. The watermark image that was extracted by the proposed method had a lower BER than those that was extracted by conventional methods. As shown the results, the proposed algorithm was sufficiently robust against all the attacks listed above.

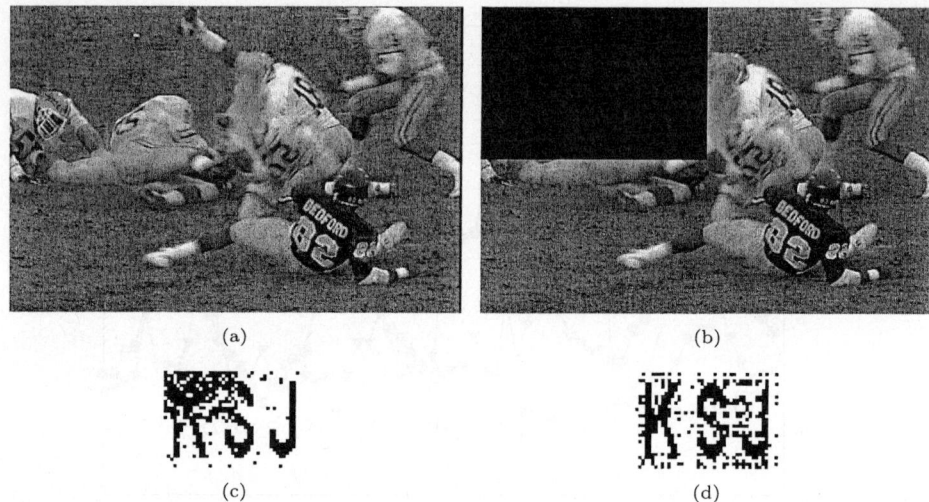

Fig. 8. (a) 17th frame after the watermarking embedding procedure and (b) 17th frame after a clopping attack that discards a quarter of a watermarked frame. the binary watermark image that is extracted (c) without a permutation procedure and (d) with a permutation procedure.

Fig. 9. Watermark images extracted from the FOOTBALL video sequence after various attacks such as (a) spatial LPF, (b) frame dropping, (c) frame average, and (d) MPEG coding

Fig. 10. Watermark images extracted from the TABLE TENNIS video sequence after various attacks such as (a) spatial LPF, (b) frame dropping, (c) frame average, and (d) MPEG coding

4 Conclusions

A new video watermarking algorithm was proposed using a 3D DWT and a spread spectrum technique. The watermark is a visible binary image that is preprocessed by the 2D pseudorandom permutation. It is changed into the video watermark by the spread spectrum technique. The video sequence is then divided into video shots and a 3D DWT is performed about the video shots. The generated video watermark is embedded into specific subbands in a 3D DWT domain, based on considering robustness and invisibility. The binary watermark is extracted by comparing similarity between the original video watermark and the detected video watermark. The final watermark is determined by a watermark decision rule and a reverse permutation. The 3D DWT, which is a powerful tool that decomposes signals at multiple resolutions in space and time domain, is used in the proposed video watermarking method. Although we use visible binary images as the watermark, the proposed algorithm actually embeds different watermarks into each video frame due to use the two spread spectrum sequences. Therefore, the proposed algorithm produces watermarked frames that are subjectively not different from the original frames and are sufficiently robust against various attacks.

Our current work is focusing on other kinds of attacks, such as rotation and scaling. The goal of our future work is to improve the proposed watermarking algorithm for the blind watermarking scheme.

Acknowledgements. This research was supported by the Program for the Training Graduate Students in Regional Innovation which was conducted by the Ministry of Commerce, Industry and Energy of the Korea Government.

References

1. R. B. Wolfgang, C. I. Pdilchuk, and E. J. Delp: Perceptual watermarks for digital images and video. Proc. of the IEEE, Vol. 87, No. 7, (1999) 1108-1126
2. C. T. Hsu and J. L. Wu: Hidden digital watermarks in images. IEEE Trans. Image Processing, Vol. 8, No. 1, (1999) 58-68
3. A. P. Fabien and Petitcolas: Watermarking schemes evaluation. IEEE Signal Proc. Magazine. Vol. 17, Issue 5, (2000) 58-64
4. F. Hartung and B. Girod: Watermarking o uncompressed and compressed video. Signal Proc., Vol. 66, No. 3, (1998) 283-301
5. M. D. Swanson, B. Zhu, and A. H. Tewfik: Multiresolution scene-based video watermarking using perceptual models. IEEE Journal Selected Areas in Communication, Vol. 16, No. 4, (1998) 540-550
6. C. T. Hsu and J. L. Wu: Dct-based watermarking for video. IEEE Trans. Consumer Electronics, Vol. 44, No. 1, (1998) 206-216
7. X. Niu, S. Sun, and W. Xiang: Multiresolution watermarking for video based on gray-level digital watermark. IEEE Trans. Consumer Electronics, Vol. 46, No. 2, (2000) 375-384
8. Y. Li and X. Gao: A 3D wavelet based spatial-temporal approach for video watermarking, ICCIMA 2003 Proc., (2003) 260-265
9. I. J. Cox, I. Kilian, T. Leighton, and T. Shamoon: Secure spread spectrum watermarking for multimedia. IEEE Trans. Image Proc., Vol. 6, No. 12, (1997) 1673-1687
10. B. Sklar: Digital communications. Prentice-Hall (1988)

11. J. J. K. O Ruanaidh and G. Csurka: A bayesian approach to spread spectrum watermark detection and secure copyright protection of digital Image libraries. IEEE Conf. Computer Vision and Pattern Recognition, Vol. 1, (1999) 23-25
12. M. Antonini, M. Barlaud, P. Mathieu, and I. Daubechies: Image coding using wavelet transform, IEEE Trans. on Image Processing, Vol. 1, No. 2, (1992) 205-220
13. C. I. Podilchuk, N. S. Jayant, and N. Farvardin: Three-dimensional subband coding of video. IEEE Trans. Image Processing, Vol. 4, No. 2, (1995) 125-139
14. X. Gao and X. Tang: Unsupervised video-shot segmentation and model-free anchor-person detection for news video story parsing. IEEE Trans. Circuits and Systems for Video Tech., Vol. 12, No. 9, (2002) 765-776
15. C. I. Podilchuk and E. J. Delp: Digital watermarking: algorithms and applications. IEEE Signal Proc. Magazine. Vol. 18, Issue 4, (2001) 33-46

Using Space-Time Coding for Watermarking of Three-Dimensional Triangle Mesh

Mohsen Ashourian and Keyvan Mohebbi

Islamic Azad University of Iran,
Mobarakeh Branch, P.O.Box 84815-119, Isfahan, Iran
mohsena@ieee.org

Abstract. In this paper, we propose a new scheme for digital watermarking of three-dimensional (3-D) triangle meshes. In order to insert and extract watermark signals, we generate triangle strips by traversing the 3-D mesh model. We split the strips into two groups. For the first groups we embed the watermark signal into vertex positions of the 3-D model in the DCT domain, and for the second group, we embed the watermark in the vertex positions in the spherical coordinates. We use space-time coding for watermark data before embedding in the mesh. The information of the two generated bitstream of space-time coder are embedded in DCT and spherical coordinate of the mesh. At the receiver, the space-time decoder combines the information of each bitstream to reconstruct the watermark data. In both cases, we apply masking operation for the watermark signal according to the variation of the host data along the traversed strips so that we can change the embedding strength adaptively, and reduce the visibility distortion of the data embedding. We test robustness of the watermarking scheme by embedding a random binary sequence and applying different attacks, such as additive random noise, compression by MPEG-4 SNHC, and affine transform.

1 Introduction

Triangle meshes are a general representation of a 3-D visual object that very well suited to communication systems. Over the past few years, three-dimensional (3-D) hardware has become much more affordable than ever, allowing the widespread use of 3-D meshes from CAM/CAD industry into video games and other end-user applications. Triangle meshes are a general representation of a 3-D visual object that very well suited to communication systems. Even if the visualization process uses a different representation or if the object is acquired in a specific representation, it is possible to derive a triangulated representation in any cases. The 3-D meshes offer many possibilities for data hiding through modifications of their elementary features, vertices (geometry), and connectivity (topology). However; due to non-regular structure of vertex positions in the space, it is not possible to easily use the various watermarking methods of digital audio, images and video for them.

The data embedding in the polygonal model could be in the spatial or frequency domain. While data embedding in the spatial domain is more robust to geometrical attacks, such as cropping and simplification, data embedding in the frequency domain usually has more robustness to signal processing attacks such as addition of noise and compression [1], [2]. Also it should be noted that all major frequency domain data embedding methods for the triangle meshes have high complexity computation [1], [3], [4], [5], [6] . In this paper, we combine the watermarking schemes in [7], [8] to develop a joint data embedding in the spatial and DCT domain. The data embedding in two domains makes the watermarking scheme robust to both types of signal processing and geometric attacks.

In order to further increase system robustness to various types of attacks, we use space-time coding for watermark data. Watermarking a multimedia signal can be modelled as transmission of a message (watermark signal) through a communication channel (the multimedia signal). With this view, many of the methods used in digital communication system can be extended for watermarking problem. Based on this analogy, we propose a space-time block coding system for data embedding in a mesh. Space-time coding is popularly used for communication system with deep fading. If we consider host mesh as the communication channel for the watermark data, fading could be happened due to cropping the mesh, or its filtering and smoothing. Alamouti pioneered a remarkable space-time block coding scheme over two transmit antennas [9]. This scheme support simple decoding complexity based on linear processing at the receiver. The code provides diversity with half of the maxi-mum possible transmission rate. Fig.1 shows an overview of the space-time coder. In Alamouti's scheme the transmitter send out data in groups of 2 symbols (s_0 and s_1). The scheme uses two transmit antennas and one receive antenna. At the receiver, we can decode only one channel, when data on the other channel is highly corrupted; otherwise we can combine the received information from both channels.

In the following sections at first we explain how we used space-time coding in the proposed watermarking system in Section 2. Section 3 explains the watermark insertion, and the watermark extraction operations. Finally in Section 4 we present experimental results of the proposed scheme and make conclusions in Section 5.

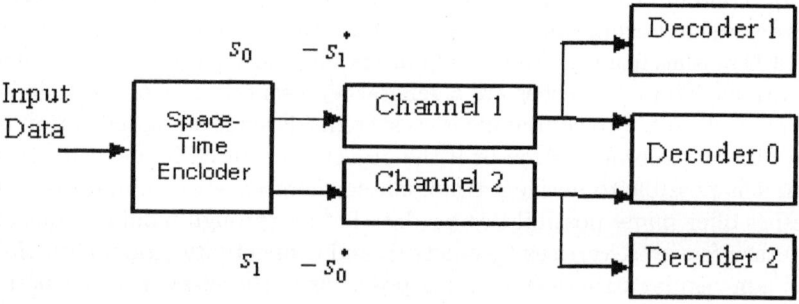

Fig. 1. Alamouti's detection scheme using channel estimation

2 Overview of the Proposed Scheme

Fig. 2 shows the overall structure of the proposed scheme for data embedding based on space-time coding. We encode the embedded data by a space time coder which generates two output sequences. The two portions of the host mesh are analogous to two communication channels for transmission of the two descriptors. One sequence is embedded in spatial domain and the other in the DCT domain. The proposed watermarking consists of two main function blocks, as shown in Fig. 2: creating triangle strips, splitting the strips into two groups, changing the traversed vertex coordinate to DCT domain and spherical coordinate in each group, and watermark insertion, which are explained in the following sub-sections.

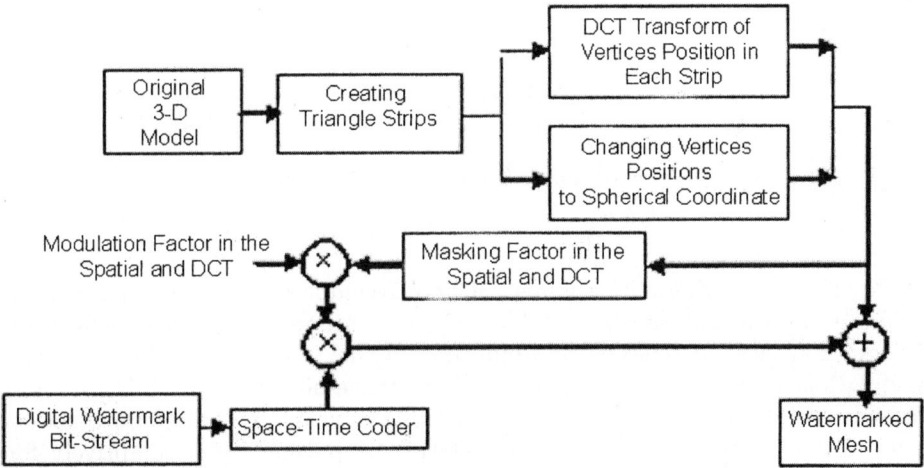

Fig. 2. Data embedding in the mesh

2.1 Rendering the Mesh

Efficient rendering of triangle-based meshes often requires that we pack them into triangle strips. Strips provide interesting advantage: the mesh is stored in a more compact way because of wasting less memory space and we can save bandwidth when we send it to our favorite rendering API (application program interface). In order to create triangle strips from a triangle mesh, we use the algorithm described in [8]. The algorithm extends the strip in the chosen direction until it reaches a triangle with no forward connections and then reverses the strip and extends it in the opposite direction.

2.2 The Watermark Insertion

The watermark signal can be a company logo, some meaningful string, or random values. In this paper, a string of five characters is used as a watermark. The string provided by the user is converted into the ASCII code a as

$$a_j = (a_1, ..., a_m), \quad a_m \in 0, 1 \tag{1}$$

In order to spread the digit signal into a wide bandwidth, each bit a_j is duplicated by the chip rate c.

$$b_i = a_j, \quad j.c \leq i \leq j.(c+1) \tag{2}$$

The chip rate c plays an important role of increment of robustness against an additive random noise. If b_i is zero, it is changed to the negative sign by

$$b'_i = 2b_i - 1 \tag{3}$$

For the first series of strips, we insert the watermark signal into the mid-frequency band of AC coefficients. New DCT coefficients are derived from the current DCT coefficients by D_1

$$\hat{W}_{x,j} = W_{x,j} + \alpha_{x_i}.b'_i.p_i \tag{4}$$

$$\hat{W}_{y,j} = W_{y,j} + \alpha_{y_i}.b'_i.p_i \tag{5}$$

$$\hat{W}_{z,j} = W_{z,j} + \alpha_{z_i}.b'_i.p_i \tag{6}$$

where b'_i is the watermark signals, p_i is a pseudo-random number sequence generated by the watermark key, $(\alpha_{x_i}, \alpha_{y_i}, \alpha_{z_i})$ are masking factors which are derived from a fixed modulation amplitude in the DCT domain α_{DCT}. The modulation amplitude factors play a role of trade-off between robustness and imperceptibility. In fact, we can have some kind of visual masking for our watermarking scheme by changing the modulation amplitude factor adaptively for each vertex on the traversed strip. It is possible to embed watermark with stronger amplitude in those area of a strip where the vertex coordinates have higher variations. At first for each strip we calculate D_i the summation of the $2N_B$ middle DCT coefficients of strip i

$$D_i = \sum_{j=i-N_B}^{j=i+N_B-1} |W_{x,j}| + \sum_{j=i-N_B}^{j=i+N_B-1} |W_{y,j}| + \sum_{j=i-N_B}^{j=i+N_B-1} |W_{z,j}| \tag{7}$$

Then we derive each modulation factor from the modulation amplitude in the DCT domain α_{DCT}, using the Eq. (8), (9) and (10).

$$\alpha_{x,i} = \alpha_{DCT}.\frac{\sum_{j=i-N_B}^{j=i+N_B-1} |W_{x,j}|}{D_i} \tag{8}$$

$$\alpha_{y,i} = \alpha_{DCT}.\frac{\sum_{j=i-N_B}^{j=i+N_B-1} |W_{y,j}|}{D_i} \tag{9}$$

$$\alpha_{z,i} = \alpha_{DCT}.\frac{\sum_{j=i-N_B}^{j=i+N_B-1} |W_{z,j}|}{D_i} \tag{10}$$

Similarly we derive α_{y_i} and α_{z_i}. For the second series of strips we insert the watermark signal in the spherical coordinate of mesh vertices. The spherical coordinates (r, θ, ϕ) are derived from the Cartesian (x, y, z) coordinates. New vertex position values $(\hat{r}_i, \hat{\theta}_i, \hat{\phi}_i)$ are derived from the current values, (r_i, θ_i, ϕ_i), by Eq.(11), (12) and (13).

$$\hat{r}_i = r_i + b'_i . \alpha_{r,i} \qquad (11)$$

$$\hat{\theta}_i = r_i + c'_i . \alpha_{\theta,i} \qquad (12)$$

$$\hat{\phi}_i = \phi_i + b'_i . \alpha_{\phi,i} \qquad (13)$$

where (b'_i, c'_i, d'_i) are the watermark signals, and $(\alpha_{r,i}, \alpha_{\theta,i}, \alpha_{\phi,i})$ are the spatial domain modulation amplitude factors for each coordinate of the vertex i. Similarly we use a masking scheme for spatial domain watermarking. We define D_i as the summation of the spherical coordinate variations in the $2N_B$ vertices in the neighborhood of the vertex i.

$$D_i = \sum_{j=i-N_B}^{j=i+N_B-1} |r_{j+1} - r_j| + \sum_{j=i-N_B}^{j=i+N_B-1} |\theta_{j+1} - \theta_j| + \sum_{j=i-N_B}^{j=i+N_B-1} |\phi_{j+1} - \phi_j| \qquad (14)$$

Then we derive the three embedding amplitude $(\alpha_r, \alpha_\theta, \alpha_\phi)$ from the main modulation amplitude in the spatial domain, α_{SP}. It means we have.

$$\alpha_{r,i} = \alpha_{SP} . \frac{\sum_{j=i-N_B}^{j=i+N_B-1} |r_{j+1} - r_j|}{D_i} \qquad (15)$$

$$\alpha_{\theta,i} = \alpha_{SP} . \frac{\sum_{j=i-N_B}^{j=i+N_B-1} |\theta_{j+1} - \theta_j|}{D_i} \qquad (16)$$

$$\alpha_{\phi,i} = \alpha_{SP} . \frac{\sum_{j=i-N_B}^{j=i+N_B-1} |\phi_{j+1} - \phi_j|}{D_i} \qquad (17)$$

2.3 The Watermark Extraction

The watermark extraction operation in the proposed private watermarking algorithm needs the original and the watermarked 3-D models. The process is similar in both spatial and DCT domains. We do registration between original mesh and watermarked one. In the next step we calculate the spatial and DCT coefficients and finally we subtract the coefficients to extract the embedded data. Equ.(18) shows this process for DCT coefficient in the x-coordinate.

$$b'_i = sign(\hat{W}_{x,i} - W_{x,i}) \qquad (18)$$

The extracted b'_i is changed to b_i by Eq. (3) and is converted to a_i by Eq. (2). After is converted to a string by the ASCII code, we can assert the ownership by the extracted string.

3 Experimental Results and Analysis

In order to evaluate the perceptual invisibility between the original and the watermarked models and resiliency against various attacks, such as additive random noise, mesh compression, affine transformation, and multiple watermarking, we perform computer simulations on 3-D mesh models: Beethoven model with 2521 vertices and 5030 faces, Horse model with 2620 vertices and 5200 faces, and Bunny model with 3116 vertices and 6100 faces.Figure 3 shows sample of these meshes. Watermarking parameters are selected as follow:

Modulation amplitude. The two modulation amplitude $\alpha_{SP}, \alpha_{DCT}$ are selected by the user in such a way that they are small enough to preserve appearance of the model, while large enough to withstand from attacks.

Perceptual invisibility. Asper et al. reported a method to estimate the distance between discrete 3-D surfaces [10]. We employ their method to measure the distortion of watermarked 3-D models. The MESH (measuring error between surfaces using the Hausdorff distance) tool [10] indicates the degree deformed by watermarks or attacks. The MESH tool evaluates on a variety of 3-D mesh models with the root-mean-square (RMS) distance as a function of the sampling step, which plays an important role in the precision of the measured distance. Among various methods to calculate RMS distances, we use one with the symmetric distance.Simulation results for the RMS distance between the original and the watermarked models are shown in Table 1.

Fig. 3. Beethoven Mesh Model

Fig. 4. Beethoven MSE Error

Fig. 5. Horse Mesh Model

Fig. 6. Horse MSE Model

Fig. 7. Bunny Mesh Model

Fig. 8. Bunny MSE Model

Watermark lengths, chip rate. In this paper, the watermark string is "WATER" with 35 bits, and the chip rate is one. As we mentioned, even if the chip rate plays an important role for strengthening robustness of watermarks, we use one as the parameter value because watermarks are repeatedly inserted into the spatial and frequency domain of multiple triangle strips.

3.1 Resiliency Against Various Attacks

We test watermark detections for attacked Beethoven, Horse, and Bunny models. Three sets of modulation amplitudes are selected and the models are attacked by additive random noise, geometry compression by the MPEG-4 SNHC coding standard, affine transform, and multiple watermarking.

As the additive random noise attack, we add noises to vertex coordinates of the watermarked model with a uniform random noise. The percentage of the additive random noise represents the ratio between the largest displacement and the largest side of the watermarked model [3]. As shown in Table 1, for example, our algorithm extracts the full string "WATER" of seventeen, twenty, and twenty four numbers, respectively, when 0.6, 0.4, and 0.2 percent random noises are uniformly added to the watermarked Beethoven model.

For the compression attack, we apply the geometry compression by the MPEG-4 SNHC standard. Generally, the x-, y-, z-vertex coordinates of the 3-D polygonal model are stored by the floating-point variable of 32 bits per each coordinate. Each of the first row elements in Table 2 is the bit number compressed by the MPEG-4 standard compression algorithm, and each of the second row elements in Table 2 represents the number of completely recovered strings.

For the affine transformation, we translate, scale, rotate, and shear the watermarked model. The results are shown in Table 3. The multiple watermarking attacks have two different types. The first type is a consecutive attack to the first

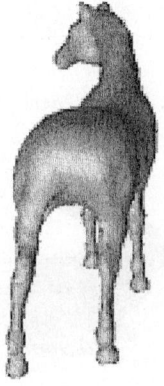

Fig. 9. 0.5 percent noise

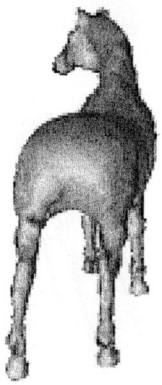

Fig. 10. Compression (12.6 bits)

Fig. 11. Affine Transform

column of multiple watermarking in Table 4. For example, C+N attack of the Beethoven model adds random noise to the watermarked model after geometry compression. The second type is all attack, which applies the affine transformation to the Beethoven model after the first type attack.

In order to evaluate performance of the proposed algorithm, we do not use the bit error rate (BER), which is the ratio of the numbers of the inserted and extracted watermarks because the owner can clearly assert the ownership of the 3-D model through perfect reconstruction of at least one of the inserted watermark string. As results in Table 1, 2 and 3 shows the inserted watermark can survive various attacks, such as additive random noise, geometry compression by the MPEG-4 SNHC standard, affine transformation, and multiple watermarking. If we compare the results with similar results in [8], [7], we notice that there is around 20 to 30 percent higher chance in recovery of the key.

Fig. 12. All attacks (0.7 percent+Aff.+18.9 bits)

Table 1. Resiliency against additive random noise attack

Models (Number of inserted string)	α_{DCT}	α_{SP}	RMS	Additive Random Noise Number of Recovered Key		
Beethoven(21)	3.05	1.034	0.055	$\frac{0.6}{20}$	$\frac{0.4}{21}$	$\frac{0.2}{21}$
Horse(24)	0.0005	0.0032	0.065	$\frac{0.6}{20}$	$\frac{0.4}{21}$	$\frac{0.2}{23}$
Bunny(23)	0.0006	0.0021	0.075	$\frac{0.6}{20}$	$\frac{0.4}{21}$	$\frac{0.2}{22}$

Table 2. Resiliency against affine transform attacks

Models (Number of inserted string)	α_{DCT}	α_{SP}	RMS	Number of Recovered Key		
Beethoven(21)	3.05	1.034	0.055	$\frac{15.8}{19}$	$\frac{18.8}{21}$	$\frac{0.2}{21}$
Horse(24)	0.0005	0.0032	0.065	$\frac{12.3}{21}$	$\frac{15.3}{19}$	$\frac{18.3}{23}$
Bunny(23)	0.0006	0.0021	0.075	$\frac{11.9}{7}$	$\frac{14.6}{6}$	$\frac{17.5}{21}$

Table 3. Resiliency against multiple attacks; (C: Geometry Compression, N: Additive Random Noise)

Models (Number of inserted string)	α_{DCT}	α_{SP}	RMS	Number of Recovered Key	
Beethoven(21)	3.05	1.034	0.055	$\frac{C+N}{3}$	$\frac{All}{2}$
Horse(24)	0.0005	0.0032	0.065	$\frac{N+A}{9}$	$\frac{All}{7}$
Bunny(23)	0.0006	0.0021	0.075	$\frac{C+N}{13}$	$\frac{All}{9}$

4 Conclusions

In this paper, we have developed a new scheme for watermarking of 3-D triangle meshes jointly in the DCT and spatial domain. We use proper masking method in each domain that adapts the strength of data embedding according to coefficient amplitude. Since we use space-time coding, we are able to recover the watermark information when the model faces serious attack in spatial or DCT domain. The composite watermarking makes the system robust to various types of geometrical and signal processing attacks, and increases the possibility of recovering at least one key.

References

1. Praun, E., Hoppe, H., and Finkelstein, A.: Robust Mesh Watermarking. SIGGRAPH Proceedings,(**1999**)49-56.
2. Yin, K. et.al.: Robust Mesh Watermarking Based on Multiresolution. Proc. of Computer and Graphics, Vol. 25,(**2001**)409-420.
3. Obuchi, R., et. al. : A Frequency-Domain Approach to Watermarking 3D Shapes. Computer Graphics Forum, Vol. 21, No. 3,(**2002**)373-382.
4. Benedens O.: Watermarking of 3D polygon based models with robustness against mesh simplification, Proc. SPIE: Security Watermarking Multimedia Contents,(**1999**) 329-340
5. Benedens O. and Busch C. :Toward blind detection of robust watermarks in polygonal models, Proc. EUROGRAPHICS, 19(C), (**2000**)199-208.
6. Wagner M. G.:Robust watermarking of polygonal meshes, Proc. Geometric Modeling, Hong Kong, (**2001**)201-208.
7. Jeon J., Lee S.K., and Ho Y.S.: A DCT-Domain Watermarking Algorithm for Three-Dimensional Triangle Meshes. Lecture Notes in Computer Science, Springer-Verlog, Vol. 2939, (**2004**)508-517.
8. Ashourian, M., Jeon, J., and R. Ershadi. :Digital Watermarking of Three-dimensional Polygonal Models in the Spherical Coordinate System. International Conference on Computer Graphics, Greece,(**2004**).
9. Alamouti, S.: A simple transmitter diversity scheme for wireless communication. IEEE Journal of Selected Areas in Communication, vol 17, Oct. 1998,(**1998**)1451-1458.
10. Aspert, N., Santa-Cruz, D., and Ebrahimi, T. :MESH: Measuring Errors between Surfaces using the Hausdroff Distance. Proceedings of the IEEE Int. Conf. in Multimedia and Expo 2002, vol. 1, (**2002**).
11. Hsueh Y. L., Hongyuan M. L., Chunshien L. and Jachen L.: Fragile Watermarking for Authenticating 3D Polygonal Meshes, Proc. 16th IPPR Conf on CVGIP, (**2003**) 298-304

Perceptually Tuned Auto-correlation Based Video Watermarking Using Independent Component Analysis

Seong-Whan Kim and Hyun-Sung Sung

Department of Computer Science, University of Seoul,
Jeon-Nong-Dong, Seoul, Korea
{swkim7, wigman}@uos.ac.kr

Abstract. Video watermarking hides information (e.g. ownership, recipient information, etc) into video contents. Video watermarking research is classified into (1) extension of still image watermarking, (2) use of the temporal domain features, and (3) use of video compression formats. In this paper, we propose a watermarking scheme to resist geometric attack (rotation, scaling, translation, and mixed) for H.264 (MPEG-4 Part 10 Advanced Video Coding) compressed video contents. Our scheme is based on auto-correlation method for geometric attack, a video perceptual model for maximal watermark capacity, and watermark detection based on natural image statistics. We experiment with the standard images and video sequences and the result shows that our video watermarking scheme is robust against H.264 video compression (average PSNR = 31 dB) and geometric attacks (rotation with 0-90 degree, scaling with 75-200%, and 50%~75% cropping).

1 Introduction

A digital watermark or watermark in short, is an invisible mark inserted in digital media such as digital images, audio and video so that it can later be detected and used as evidence of copyright infringement. However, insertion of such invisible mark should not alter the perceived quality of the digital media (it is the transparency requirement) while being extremely robust to attack (it is a robust requirement) and being impossible to insert another watermarks for rightful ownership (it is a maximal capacity requirement). Watermark attacks are classified into (1) intentional attacks, and (2) unintentional attacks. Basic requirements for video watermarking are geometric attack robustness (intentional attacks) and H.264 video compression (unintentional attacks). There are four major researches for geometric attack robustness, (1) invariant transform, (2) template based, (3) feature point based, and (4) auto-correlation based [1]. Invariant transform approach is to embed the watermark in an invariant domain, like Fourier-Mellin transform [2], whereby geometric transform is still a linear operation. Template approach is to identify the transformation by retrieving artificially embedded references [3]. Feature point based approach is an embedding and detection scheme, where the mark is bound with a content descriptor defined by salient points [1]. Finally, Auto-correlation approach is to insert the mark periodically during the embedding process, and use auto-correlation during the detection process [4, 5].

We designed an auto-correlation based watermark detection scheme for geometric attack robustness, and present a video watermarking scheme, which is robust on geometric attack (scaling, cropping, rotation, and mixed) and H.264 video compression. In autocorrelation based approaches, separation of Gaussian noise components from raw and watermarked images is a crucial function for watermark performance. To improve performance, we applied Gaussian noise filtering method based on statistical model of natural images. The statistic model is based on ICA (independent component analysis) which models image as factorial distribution of super-Gaussian distribution. Since this model is more relevant for natural image than Gaussian distribution model, ICA based de-noising method shows superior performance for filtering (or de-noising) Gaussian noise. We implemented a new watermark insertion and detection scheme based on this method and evaluated performance advantages over conventional Wiener filter approach. Result shows that new watermark scheme is more robust and reliable than Wiener filters approach. Lastly our method considers human perception model for video to achieve maximal watermark capacity. Using this perceptual model we can insure the quality of watermarked videos while achieving maximum watermark robustness.

2 Watermark Embedding and Detection Scheme

H.264 is a widely used video compression standard, in which it uses different coding techniques for INTRA (reference) and INTER (motion predicted) frames. We embed the auto-correlated watermark for geometric synchronization in H.264 reference (INTRA) frames, because INTRA frames are used for reference frames of motion predicted (INTER) frames, and they are usually less compressed than INTER frames.

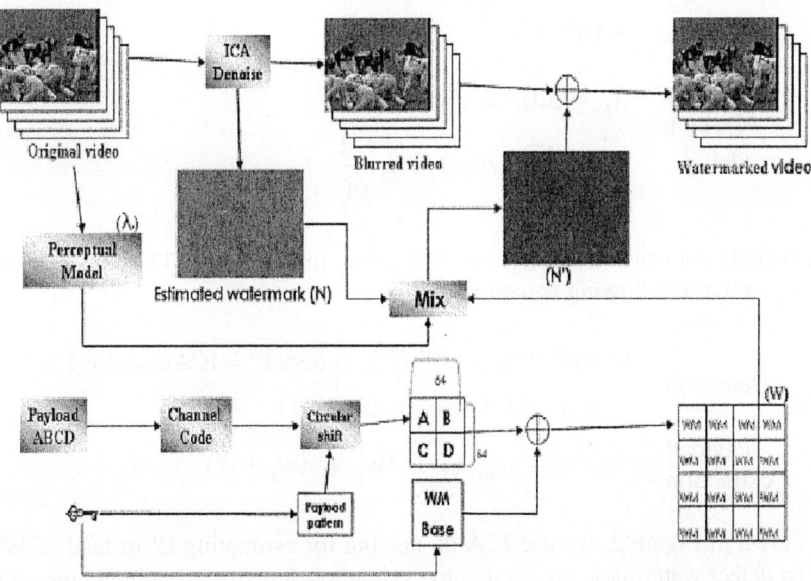

Fig. 1. Watermark embedding for H.264 INTRA frames

In case of geometric attacks for video frames, we can use the watermark in INTRA frames to restore the synchronization misses. Figure 1 shows the auto-correlation based watermark embedding scheme for INTRA coded frames. We changed the auto-correlation based watermark embedding approach as in [6] with different JND (just noticeable difference) model and different watermark estimation scheme, and also changed the Wiener filter to ICA de-noising based approach. As shown in Figure 1, we embedded the 64*64 block-wise watermarks repeatedly over whole image, thereby we can restore watermark even from 128x128 cropped image blocks.

Watermark embedding for H.264 INTRA frames can be summarized in (1) and (2). In this equation, I' is watermarked frame, E is ICA de-noised frame, N is the ICA estimated noise, λ is perceptual mask as specified in the previous equation, w_p is payload watermark, and w_s is synchronization watermark.

Previous research uses the Wiener filter to compute E and N. For each 64x64 blocks, we adjusted the watermark strength as image complexity using a mixed perceptual model of NVF (noise visibility function) and entropy masking [7, 8, 9, 10]. We experimentally set the multiplication factor of entropy model as 3.0. Also the A and B values are set to 5.0 and 1.0.

Embedding $\quad I' = I + \lambda N(w_p + w_s)$, where $\quad$ (1)
$\quad\quad\quad\quad\quad$, $N = I - E$, and $E = \text{ICADenoise}(I)$

Watermark strength $\quad \lambda = \max(\lambda_N, \lambda_E)$ $\quad$ (2)

NVF model λ_N $\quad \lambda_N = (1 - NVF) * A + NVF * B$, where

$$NVF = \frac{1}{1+\sigma^2}$$

Entropy Masking model λ_E $\quad \lambda_E = 3.0 * E$, where

$$E = \sum_{x \in N(X)} p(x) \cdot \log \frac{1}{p(x)}$$

Watermark detection and payload extraction for H.264 INTRA frames can be summarized in the following equations.

Detection $\quad \begin{aligned} w_s \cdot w' &= w_s \cdot (I' - E'), \text{ where } E' = \text{ICADenoise}(I') \\ &= w_s \cdot (I + \lambda w_p + \lambda w_s + \delta) \end{aligned}$ $\quad$ (3)

Payload extraction $\quad w_p \cdot w' = w_p \cdot (I + \lambda w_p + \lambda w_s + \delta)$ $\quad$ (4)

As shown in Figure 2, we use ICA de-noising for estimating E' instead of Wiener filter. To detect watermark, we used auto-correlation function to estimate the geometric transform, and used ICA de-noising (modification of Wiener filter box) to estimate the watermark in blind manner. We improved the auto-correlation based watermark detection approach as [6], using ICA de-noising for better watermark estimation than Wiener filter approach. Moreover, to improve the payload detection performance, we used a different payload coding techniques and smaller auto-correlation block size 64x64 than 128x128 [11]. Decreasing auto-correlation block size makes multiple auto-correlated blocks to be folded, and it increases the watermark robustness.

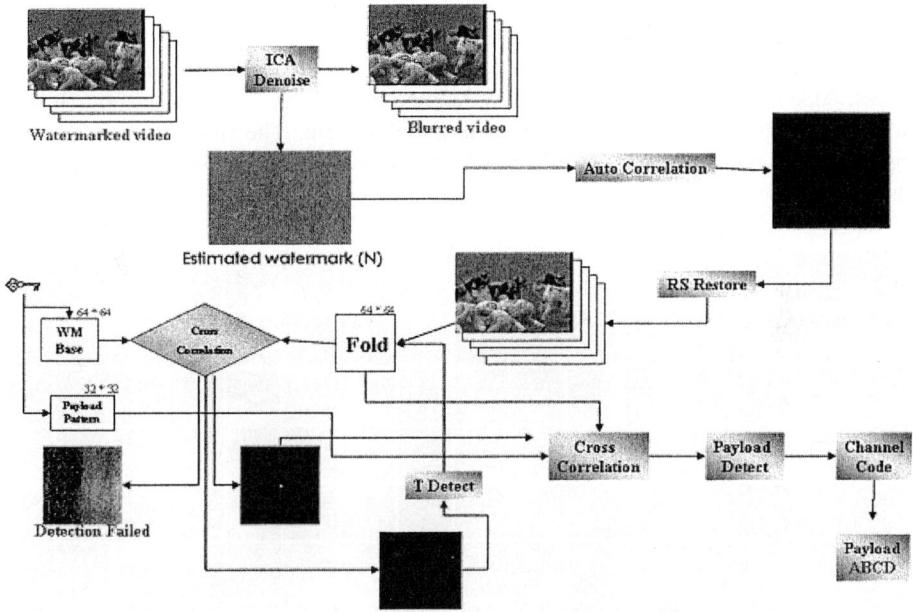

Fig. 2. Watermark detection for H/264 INTRA frames

3 Watermark Estimation Using ICA De-noising

We applied Independent Component Analysis (ICA) based Gaussian noise filtering (de-noising) instead of Wiener filter. From the Bayesian viewpoint Wiener filter is an inference method which computes Maximum Likely (ML) estimates of image signal given the noise variance. Wiener filter assumes Gaussian distribution for both original image and noise. But real image statistics are much different from Gaussian distribution and are better modeled by the ICA model. If the ICA model provides better approximation of real image signals, then it can dramatically enhance noise filtering step in Watermark insertion and detection. ICA is an unsupervised learning method which has found wide range of applications in image processing [15]. ICA finds a linear transform W that maps high dimensional data X into maximally independent source signals S. The source signal S is modeled by a factorial probability density function which is usually super-Gaussian distributions like Laplacian distribution.

Super-Gaussian distribution is a distribution which has higher peak at 0 and longer trails than Gaussian distribution.

$$S = WX, \quad X = AS \quad (A = W^{-1})$$
$$P(S) = \prod_{i}^{M} P(s_i)$$

In [16], it is reported that natural image statistics are well described by such ICA model. Also the linear transform filter W learned by ICA algorithm shows much similarity to simple cell filters [17] in human visual system. The filters learned by ICA algorithm are similar to Gabor filters which are multi-orientation, multi-scale edge filters as shown in Figure 3.

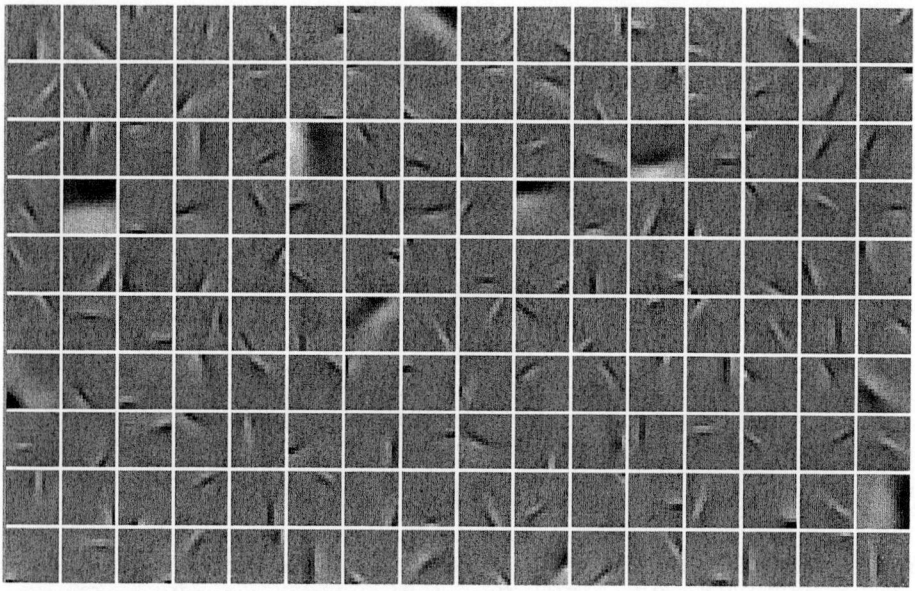

Fig. 3. ICA driven basis images

ICA models complex statistics of natural image well by factorized independent source distributions. Such independent source distributions are usually modeled as generalized Laplacian distribution which is super-Gaussian and symmetric. This simple PDF can be learned from image data and can be used for Bayesian de-noising of images [18].

Let's assume image patch X that follows ICA model (X=AS) and an independent Gaussian noise n with 0 mean and known variance σ. We assume that ICA source signal S has unit variance. Then we can define noisy image Y as follows.

$$Y = AS + n$$

In Bayesian de-noising the goal is to find $\hat{S}$ s.t.

$$\hat{S} = \underset{S}{argmax} \log P(S|Y)$$
$$= \underset{S}{argmax} \left[\log P(Y|S) + \log P(S)\right]$$
$$= \underset{S}{argmax} \left[\log N(Y - AS; \sigma) + \log P(S)\right]$$
$$= \underset{S}{argmax} \left[-\frac{|Y - AS|^2}{2\sigma^2} - \sum_{i}^{M} \log P(s_i)\right]$$

If we assume unit Laplacian distribution for S and Gaussian noise with signal s, then those equations can be written as.

$$\hat{S} = \underset{S}{argmax} \left[-\frac{|Y - AS|^2}{2\sigma^2} - \sum_{i}^{M} |s_i|\right]$$

The objective function of above equation can be further simplified if we assume orthogonal W s.t. $W^T = W^{-1} = A$.

$$-\frac{|Y - AS|^2}{2\sigma^2} - \sum_{i}|s_i| = -\frac{1}{2\sigma^2}(Y - AS)^T(Y - AS) - \sum_{i}|s_i|$$
$$= -\frac{1}{2\sigma^2}(Y - AS)^T(W^T W)(Y - AS) - \sum_{i}|s_i|$$
$$= -\frac{1}{2\sigma^2}(WY - WAS)^T(WY - WAS) - \sum_{i}|s_i|$$
$$= -\frac{1}{2\sigma^2}(WY - S)^T(WY - S) - \sum_{i}|s_i|$$
$$= -\frac{1}{2\sigma^2}|WY - S|^2 - \sum_{i}|s_i| = -\frac{1}{2\sigma_n^2}|S' - S|^2 - \sum_{i}|s_i|$$
$$= -\sum_{i}\left(\frac{1}{2\sigma^2}(s'_i - s_i)^2 + |s_i|\right)$$

As shown, the objective function can be expressed as sum of independent and positive 1D objective functions. So the minimization of the entire objective function is equivalent to minimization of individual source dimensions. The solution to this 1D optimization problem is summarized in [4]. Then using the estimated $\hat{S}$, we can compute de-noised image $\hat{X} = A\hat{S}$ as well as the Gaussian noise $n = Y - \hat{X}$.

Figure 4 compares Wiener filter and ICA de-noising for separating Gaussian noise N. ICA de-noising result shows the strong edge-like features, whereas Wiener filtered result shows rather weak edge-like features.

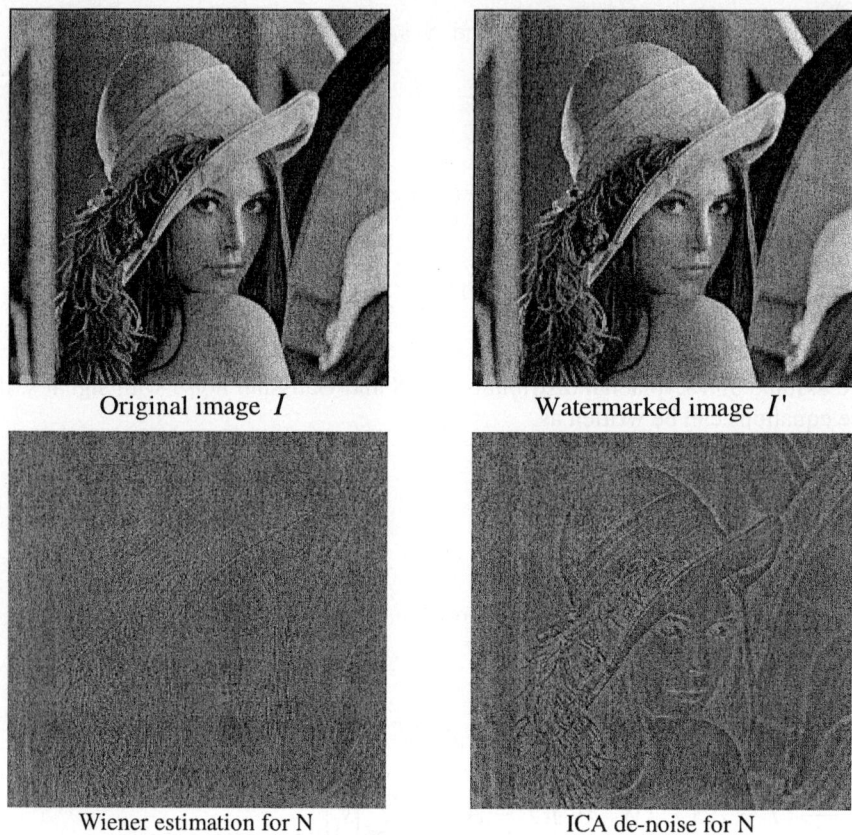

Fig. 4. Noise estimation comparison between Wiener filter and ICA de-noising

4 Simulation Results

We experimented with the standard test images, and Table 1 shows that we improve the watermark detection performance (increase both correlation value and threshold value) using ICA de-noising based approach over Wiener approach. Threshold value depends on the local characteristics of the resulting auto-correlation image. ICA de-noising increases the threshold more than Wiener filter and it can filter many noisy auto-correlation peaks, whereby we can make more accurate detection performance. We tested our approach over 20 standard test images, and showed that superior detection performance.

We experimented with the standard test image sequence from VQEG (Video Quality Expert Group) as shown in Figure 5 [13]. After INTRA frame watermark embedding, the watermarked images show good subjective quality. For the original and watermarked frames of Mobile&Calendar and Football test sequences, the average PSNR for two test sequence's INTRA frames are 32.03 and 31.80, respectively.

Table 1. ICA driven watermark detection improvements over Wiener

	Using Wiener		Using ICA	
	Correlation value	Threshold	Correlation value	Threshold
aerial.bmp	0.252816	0.074945	0.418893	0.246213
airplane.bmp	0.230755	0.046858	0.353133	0.172529
airport.bmp	0.198668	0.037124	0.411544	0.214705
baboon.bmp	0.192640	0.041524	0.362268	0.204293
barbara.bmp	0.203092	0.036492	0.321886	0.154950
boat.bmp	0.236444	0.041021	0.362430	0.158109
couple.bmp	0.230765	0.041714	0.380771	0.171419
elaine.bmp	0.253149	0.044271	0.350184	0.139988
girl.bmp	0.255930	0.052973	0.388574	0.177383
girls.bmp	0.243981	0.038508	0.346012	0.154674
goldhill.bmp	0.228562	0.039083	0.328786	0.144241
house.bmp	0.219754	0.046751	0.328289	0.161131
lake.bmp	0.213744	0.034296	0.302019	0.138336
lena.bmp	0.236769	0.039555	0.352069	0.156090
man.bmp	0.216027	0.035835	0.326558	0.138451
pepper.bmp	0.254798	0.044070	0.361369	0.157697
splash.bmp	0.250747	0.045205	0.351555	0.166243
stream and bridge.bmp	0.186301	0.037753	0.293211	0.159628
toys.bmp	0.222101	0.058213	0.236835	0.160865

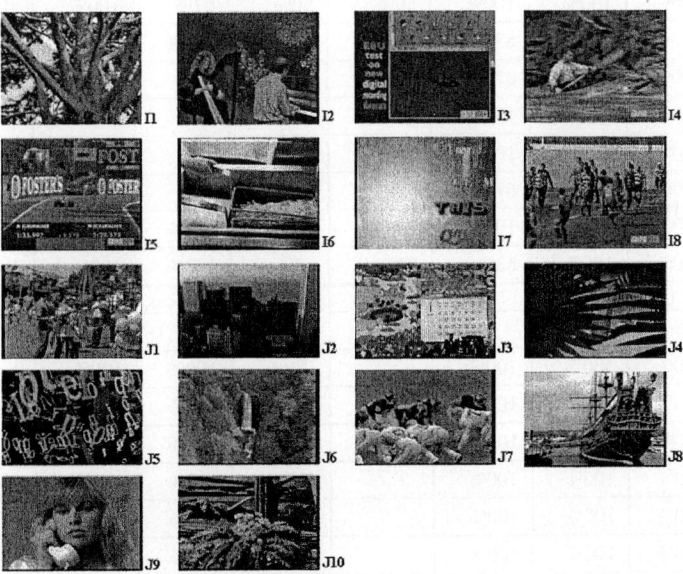

Fig. 5. VQEG Test Sequences

To experiment the geometric attack, we used Stirmark 4.0 [14] geometric attack packages for various geometric attacks (rotation with 0-90 degrees, scaling with 75-200%, cropping with 50-75%, and mixed). We experimented with five cases: (case 1) rotation with 1, 2, and 5 degree clockwise; (case 2) case 1 rotation and scaling to fit original image size; (case 3) cropping with 50% and 75%; (case 4) scaling with 50%, 75%, 150%, and 200%; and (case 5) median, Gaussian, and sharpening filter attacks.

Table 2 shows robustness result for the various geometric attacks on INTRA frames, and shows successful payload detection results in most geometric attack cases, and shows some misses under combined attack of rotation and scaling.

Table 2. Payload detection after geometric attack (only for INTRA frames)

	Case 1: Rotation			Case 2: Rotation + Scaling			Case 3: Cropping	
	1	2	5	1	2	5	50	75
I1	100%	100%	67%	50%	34%	50%	100%	100%
I2	100%	100%	100%	67%	83%	67%	100%	100%
I3	100%	100%	67%	50%	50%	67%	100%	100%
I4	100%	100%	50%	100%	100%	100%	100%	100%
I5	100%	100%	83%	100%	100%	83%	100%	100%
I6	100%	100%	100%	67%	100%	50%	100%	100%
I7	100%	100%	100%	50%	83%	50%	100%	100%
I8	100%	100%	83%	67%	83%	50%	100%	100%
J1	100%	100%	67%	67%	67%	100%	100%	100%
J2	100%	100%	100%	67%	100%	100%	100%	100%
J3	100%	100%	100%	50%	50%	67%	100%	100%
J4	100%	100%	83%	34%	67%	100%	100%	100%
J5	100%	100%	67%	34%	50%	83%	100%	83%
J6	100%	100%	100%	100%	83%	100%	100%	100%
J7	100%	100%	100%	100%	83%	83%	100%	100%
J8	100%	100%	67%	67%	83%	83%	100%	100%
J9	100%	100%	100%	100%	100%	100%	100%	100%
J10	100%	100%	83%	83%	67%	100%	100%	100%
	Case 4: Scaling				Case 5: Median, Gaussian, Sharpening			
	50	75	150		M	G	S	
I1	100%	100%	100%		100%	100%	100%	
I2	100%	100%	100%		100%	100%	100%	
I3	100%	100%	100%		100%	100%	100%	
I4	100%	100%	100%		100%	100%	100%	
I5	100%	100%	100%		100%	100%	100%	
I6	100%	100%	100%		100%	100%	100%	
I7	100%	100%	100%		100%	100%	100%	

Table 2. *(Continued)*

I8	100%	100%	100%		100%	100%	100%	
J1	100%	100%	100%		100%	100%	100%	
J2	100%	100%	100%		100%	100%	100%	
J3	100%	100%	100%		100%	100%	100%	
J4	100%	100%	100%		100%	100%	100%	
J5	100%	100%	100%		100%	100%	100%	
J6	100%	100%	100%		100%	100%	100%	
J7	100%	100%	100%		100%	100%	100%	
J8	100%	100%	100%		100%	100%	100%	
J9	100%	100%	100%		100%	100%	100%	
J10	100%	100%	100%		100%	100%	100%	

5 Conclusions

In this paper, we presented a robust video watermarking scheme, which uses auto-correlation based scheme for geometric attack recovery, and uses human visual system characteristics for H.264 compression. For watermark insertion and detection our method uses ICA-based filtering method which better utilizes natural image statistics than conventional Wiener filter. Result shows that the proposed scheme enhances robustness while keeping watermark invisible. Our video watermarking scheme is robust against H.264 video compression (average PSNR = 31 dB) and geometric attacks (rotation with 0-90 degree, scaling with 75-200%, and 50%~75% cropping).

References

1. Bas, P., Chassery, JM, and Macq, B.: Geometrically invariant watermarking using feature points. IEEE Trans. Image Proc., vol. 11, no. 9, Sept. (2002) 1014–1028
2. O'Ruanaidh, J.J., Pun, T.: Rotation, scale and translation invariant digital image watermarking. Proc. IEEE Int. Conf. Image Proc. (1997) 536 -539
3. Pereira, S., Pun, T.: Robust template matching for affine resistant image watermarks. IEEE Trans. Image Proc., vol. 9, no. 6, June (2000)
4. Kutter, M.,: Watermarking resisting to translation, rotation, and scaling. Proc. of SPIE Int. Conf. on Multimedia Systems and Applications, vol. 3528, (1998) 423-431.
5. Su, P.-C., Kuo, C.-C. J.: Synchronized detection of the block-based watermark with invisible grid embedding. Proc. SPIE Electronic imaging (Security and Watermarking of Multimedia Contents III) (2001)
6. Lee, C. H., Lee, H. K., Suh, Y. H.,: Autocorrelation Function-based Watermarking with Side Information. IS&T/SPIE, 15th Annual Symposium Electronic Imaging Science and Technology : Security and Watermarking of Multimedia Contents, San Jose, USA, January (2003) 20-24
7. Voloshynovskiy, S. Herrige, A., Baumgaertner, N., Pun, T.: A stochastic approach to content adaptive digital image watermarking. Lecture Notes in Computer Science: 3rd Int. Workshop on Information Hiding, vol. 1768, Sept. (1999) 211-236

8. Watson, A. B., Borthwick, R., Taylor, M.: Image quality and entropy masking. Proc. SPIE Conf. Human Vision, Visual Processing, and Digital Display VI (1997)
9. Podilchuk, C., Zeng, W.: Image adaptive watermarking using visual models. IEEE J. Selected Areas in Communications, vol. 16, no. 4, May (1998)
10. Kim, S.W., Suthaharan, S., Lee, H.K., Rao, K.R.: An image watermarking scheme using visual model and BN distribution. IEE Elect. Letter, vol. 35 (3), Feb. (1999)
11. Sung, H.S., Kim, S.W.: A robust video watermarking scheme for geometric attack and H.264 compression. ICIP submitted.
12. Barni, M., Bartolini, F., Cappellini, V., Lippi, A., Piva, A.: A DWT based technique for spatio frequency masking of digital signatures. Proc. IS&T/SPIE Conf. Security and watermarking of multimedia contents, vol. 3657, Jan. (1999) 31-39
13. http://www.its.bldrdoc.gov/vqeg/
14. http://www.petitcolas.net/fabien/watermarking/stirmark/
15. Hinton, G. E., Sejnowski, T. J.: Unsupervised learning: foundations of neural computation (edited), MIT Press, Cambridge, Massachusetts (1999)
16. Bell, A. J., Sejnowski, T. J.: The 'independent components' of natural scenes are edge filters. Vision Research, 37(23) (1997) 3327–3338
17. van Hateren, J. H., A_ van der Schaaf : Independent component filters of natural images comared with simple cells in primary visual cortex. Proc. Royal Soc. Lond. B. (1998) 265:359-336
18. Hyvarinen, A., Sparse Code Shrinkage: De-noising of non-gaussian data by maximum likelihood estimation. Neural Computation, 11(7) (1999) 1739-1768

Invertible Watermarking Scheme for Authentication and Integrity

Kil-Sang Yoo, Mi-Ae Kim, and Won-Hyung Lee

Chung-Ang University, Department of Image Engineering,
Graduate School of Advanced Imaging Science and Multimedia and Film,
221 Hukseok-Dong, Dongjak-Gu, Seoul, Korea
lucky@ms.cau.ac.kr, kimma@dreamwiz.com, whlee@cau.ac.kr

Abstract. In this paper, we propose a new method for authentication, integrity and invertibility of digital images using invertible watermarking. While all watermarking schemes introduce some small amount of non-invertible distortion in the image, the new method is invertible in the sense that, if the image is deemed authentic, the distortion on the extraction procedure can be removed to obtain the original image data. Authentication data is produced from XOR operation between watermark signal and binary bits obtained from a hash function of one block image. If the unmodified watermarked image is used, the extraction process will return the correct watermark signal and exact original image The techniques provide new assurance tools for integrity protection of sensitive imagery such as medical images

Keywords: Watermarking, Invertible, Authentication, Watermark, tamper detection, image integrity.

1 Introduction

Due to the rapid and extensive growth of multimedia network system, data can be distributed much faster and easier than before. The protection and enforcement of intellectual property rights for digital media have become an important issue, and many watermarking techniques have been developed. On the other hand, thanks to powerful editing programs, it is very easy even for an amateur to maliciously modify digital media and create 'perfect' forgeries. It is usually much more complicated to tamper with analog tapes and images. Invertible watermarking schemes that help us establish the authenticity and integrity of digital media are thus essential and can prove when questions are raised about the origin of an image and its integrity in the courts.

Watermarking is a technique to embed additional data or signal into multimedia data. Most image watermarking methods [1] introduce distortions to the original content. Fragile watermarking has the same principle, embedding watermark to a digital data, except that the watermark is likely to become undetectable if the data is modified in any way. An example of earliest fragile watermarking techniques is embedding watermark to the LSB (least significant bit) of the image that does not cause visual artifacts to the image. But such LSB manipulation is not secure against malicious attacks, because it is possible to alter an image without changing the LSB value. Yeung-Mintzer [2] proposed an authentication method using key-dependent binary-valued function (lookup-table) to modify the pixels value in order to embed a watermark, and deployed error diffusion method to maintain proper average color. Although this technique can detect any changes in pixel values, it does not resist to impersonation attack if the same lookup table and watermark are used for multiple watermarked images [3]. Wong-Memon [4] proposed a secret and public-key image watermarking scheme for image authentication. They used cryptographic hash function such as MD5, which makes the implementation of this scheme integrity.It is clear that these techniques authenticate modified signal rather than the original one.

In many applications, the loss of fidelity is not prohibitive as long as original and watermarked signals are perceptually equivalent. Often, the embedding distortion is irreversible, i.e. it cannot be removed to recover the original host signal. But some other authentication applications such as medical imagery and military image, prohibit the permanent loss of image fidelity during watermarking. It is often desirable to embed a watermark in a reversible way so that the loss of signal fidelity can be remedied by the use of Lossless Authentication techniques.

1.1 Our Contribution

In this paper, we propose a invertible watermarking scheme for authentication, integrity and invertiblity. The authentication data is produced from XOR operation between the binary Pseudo Noise sequences and invertible information obtained from the hash function value of the image. Using modular arithmetic as in [5], binary bits are generated from the singular value of one image block. The localization property is obtained by dividing the original image into same size $m \times n$ blocks, and embedding the authentication data to LSB plane for each block. The security of this scheme, have a key used in the embedding process and extracting process. The key, which consists of 128 bits, is used to replace the LSB of each image block before calculating the hash function value. If wrong key is used in the extraction process, it will return signal, which resembles noise, not the watermark sequential.

This paper is organized as follows. Section 2 discusses the principles and shortcomings of previous work on invertible watermarking. The watermark embedding and extracting approach are described in Section 3. In Section 4, the experimental results are shown. The conclusions of our study are stated in Section 5.

2 Invertible Watermarking

Until recently, almost all data embedding techniques, especially high-capacity data embedding techniques, introduced some amount of distortion into the original image and the distortion was permanent and not reversible. As an example, we can take the simple Least Significant Bit (LSB) embedding in which the LSB plane is irreversibly replaced with the message bits. In this paper, we present a solution to the problem of how to embed a large payload in digital images in a invertible manner so that after the payload bits are extracted, the image can be restored to its original form before the embedding started. Even though the distortion is completely invertible, we pay close attention to minimizing the amount of the distortion after embedding. We note that in this paper, the expressions "distortion-free", "invertible", and "lossless" are used as synonyms[6].

In some require integrity applications, it is vital for a legitimate user to be able to verify the integrity of the image before using it. The following are some examples:

X-ray images of medical are used for disease diagnosis. Thus small changes in such images might lead to erroneous conclusions about a patient's health. Satellite images are used to locate military strategic targets or to produce weather forecasts. Manipulation might lead to wrong interpretation of the real situation in the photographed area. In this kind of applications integrity are crucial. Therefore, removing the watermark from an image must be allows the original version of that part to be recovered and its integrity to be verified. expert owner can completely invert the watermarking process so as to obtain the original image in an authenticated way.

A basic approach of reversible watermarking is to select an embedding area in an image, and embed both the payload and the original values in this area (needed for exact recovery of the original image) into such area. As the amount of information needed to be embedded (payload and original values in the embedding area) is larger than that of the embedding area, most reversible watermarking techniques [7] [8] [9] rely on lossless data compression on the original values in the embedding area, and the space saved from compression will be used for embedding the payload.

Fridrich et al. [6] introduced the concept of optimal parity assignment for the color palette. The optimal parity is independent of the image histogram and depends only on the image palette. To embedding messages to the image, an embedding while dithering technique is designed for palette images obtained from true color images using color quantization and dithering.

As shown in figure 1, Fridrich et al. approach to lossless data embedding is also based on the presence of subsets with specific properties in X. The sample sets S(x) and S(y) form a compressible bitstream (under some scan of X). For example, for a digital image, S(123) is the set of all pixels with the grayscale value equal to 123. This approach can again be used for all image formats, but it is especially suitable for palette images.

Yang et al. [10] developed an invertible watermarking scheme exclusively for authentication of electronic clinical brain atlas. The scheme segments the brain atlas based on the region outline, then embedding the messages into the region by considering the parity of the number of points in scanned outline row. If the parity is inconsistent with the watermarked bit, the leftmost point of the outline is replaced with the neighbor color, otherwise, no modification is applied.To authenticate the watermarked image, the watermark is extracted from the outline of the image and checked.

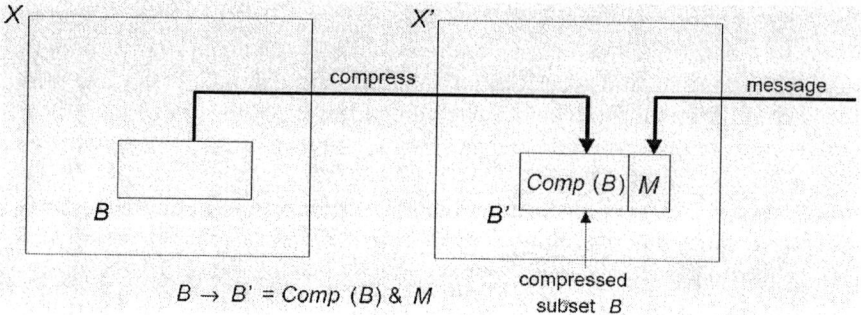

Fig. 1. Diagram for lossless data embedding using lossless compression

3 Proposed Invertible Watermarking Scheme

Invertible Watermarking scheme embeds invisible watermark into a digital content in a invertible fashion. As a basic requirement, the quality degradation on the digital content after data embedding should be low. A intriguing feature of invertible data is the reversibility, that is, when the digital content has been authenticated, one can remove the embedded data to restore the original content.

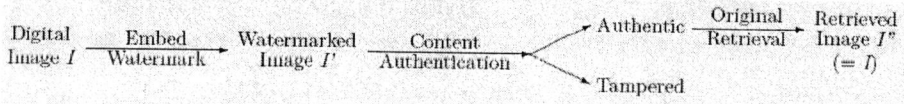

Fig. 2. A Block diagram of Invertible watermarking

As shown in figure 2, we embed a watermark signal in a digital image I by modifying its pixel values, and obtain the embedded image I'. The quality degradation of I' from I should be low. Before sending it to the content authenticator, the image I might or might not have been tampered by some intentional or unintentional manipulations. if the authenticator finds that no tampering happened in I', i.e, I' is authentic, then the authenticator can remove the watermark signal from I' and restore the original image, which results in a new image I''. By definition of invertible watermark embedding, the restored image I'' will be clearly the same as the original image I. The motivation of invertible data embedding is distortion-free data embedding [11]. Invertible watermark embedding will provide the original, raw data when the digital content is authenticated.

3.1 Watermark Embedding Procedure

In this section we describe the details of our invertible authentication watermarking scheme that embed Message Authentication Code (MAC) in gray images in an invertible way so that anyone who possesses the authentication key can revert to the exact copy of the original image before authentication occurred. For color images, the same scheme can be applied independently to the color planes of the image, either in the RGB color space or in any other color space such as YUV.

Consider a grayscale image B of size $m \times n$ pixels as the original image, and PN(pseudo noise) sequences W used as the watermark, which has the same size as B. The embedding scheme is detailed as follows and the watermark embedding procedure for each image block is shown in figure 3.

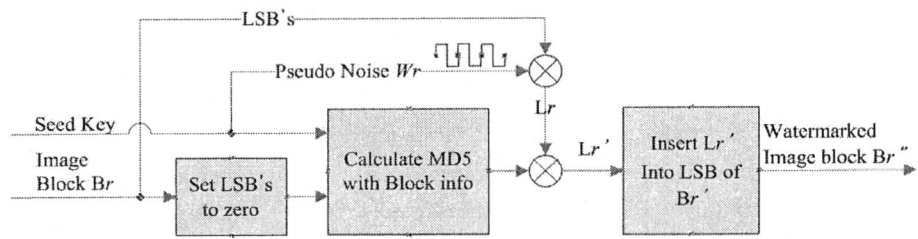

Fig. 3. Block diagram of watermark embedding process

First, we divide the original image B and the watermark PN sequence W into $m \times n$ square blocks. Let us assume the original image size to be 512×512 pixels, and it is divided into 128 image blocks. Denote B_r to be the image block and W_r as the watermark block where $r = 1, 2, \ldots, 128$. Note that r is the index block in the image. Then, a 128-bits Key is generated, which has the same size as the numbers of pixels in each image block B_r. For each block B_r, do the following process:

Step 1. Replace all the LSBs of B_r to 0

Step 2. Generate PN sequence $W_r \in \{0,1\}$ with Seed key which is owner's security key. A secret key is used to disable any attempt to remove or replace the message. It is closed in the sense that only authorized persons possess this key and can access the watermark to check integrity.

Step 3. Compute the MD5 [12] with block information of B_r. A cryptographic hash function has the property that given an input bit string S and its corresponding output $\sigma_1, \sigma_2, \ldots, \sigma_r$.

$$H(S) = (\sigma_1, \sigma_2, \ldots, \sigma_r) \qquad (1)$$

The hashing function such as the popular MD5 is classically used to provide strict integrity control. In the system shown in figure 3, the hash value of the image (or part of the image) generates the message that is embedded into the original image. The algorithm of step 3 for image authentication, i.e. for verification of image integrity.

Step 4. Apply XOR operation between the PN sequences W_r and the image block B_r to get the invertible data L_r

$$L_r = W_r \oplus B_r \tag{2}$$

Step 5. Apply XOR operation between the L_r and the output of hash value σr to get the authentication data L'_r

$$L'_r = L_r \oplus \sigma_r \tag{3}$$

Step 6. Finally we embed the authentication data L'_r into the least significant bit of the image block B_r to form the output watermarked image block B'_r. This procedure is repeated for each block of data and all the output blocks B'_r are assembled together to form the watermarked image B^w_r.

3.2 Watermark Extraction Procedure

The extraction process is almost the same as insertion process except that the last XOR operation is done between the scrambled binary bits B_r and the LSB value of watermarked image in block r. The detailed process is as follow: first,

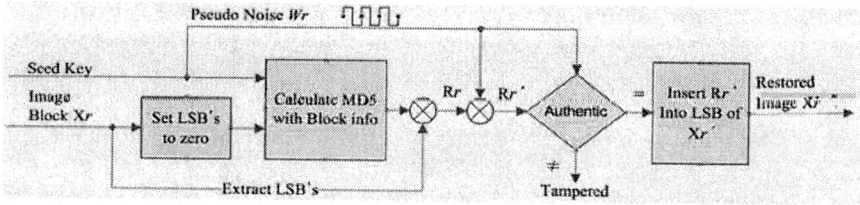

Fig. 4. Block diagram of watermark extraction process

divide the possibly tampered watermarked image we want to check into the 8 × 8 block size, as in embedding process. For each block, do the following steps:

Step 1. Extract the LSB of watermarked image block B'_r (we call it X_r).

Step 2. Replace all the LSBs of X_r to 0

Step 3. Generate PN sequence W_r with Seed key which is owner's security key used in the embedding process.

Step 4. Calculate MD5 with image block information such as image size, key and image block r.

Step 5. Apply XOR operation between the extracted LSB's from image block X_r and the output of hash value σr to get R_r.

Step 6. Apply XOR operation between the PN sequences W_r and the image block R_r to get the invertible data R'_r.

Step 7. compare W_r and R'_r to decision authentic. If the X_r, is authentic, then the authenticator can inserting original LSB's pixel value R'_r into LSB of X_r and restore the original image, which results in a new image X_r^W. By definition of invertible data embedding, the restored image X_r^W will be exactly the same as the original image X_r, pixel by pixel, bit by bit. if the image X_r have been tampered by some intentional manipulations, tempered locations will displayed.

Note that the index w is used to indicate that the image block processed is the possibly watermarked image. By doing this process to whole block of watermarked image, we will get the extracted watermark image which from it we can tell whether the image is tampered or not. If the image is not tampered and the right keys are used, the result will be the right watermark image, clear without noise.

4 Experimental Results

As basic requirements, the quality degradation on the digital content after data embedding should be low. Figure 5 shows original 512 × 512 Lena image, and its watermarked image(right) by modifying LSBs pixel values. No degradation in quality or any noticeable distortion. The watermarked image quality is measured using PSNR (Peak Signal to Noise Ratio) by the equation (4) where MSE is the mean-square error between a watermarked image and original image [13]. The PSNR is 54.16 dB.

$$PSNR = 10\log_{10}\frac{255^2}{MSE} = 10\log_{10}\frac{255^2}{\sum(f(x)-f(x)')^2} \qquad (4)$$

Fig. 5. Original image (Left) and watermarked image (Right)

Figure 6(Left) shows the watermark distributed PN-sequence where in original image which is used in the experiment, and figure 6(Right) is the extracted watermark Pick, retrieved from the untampered watermarked image, where the

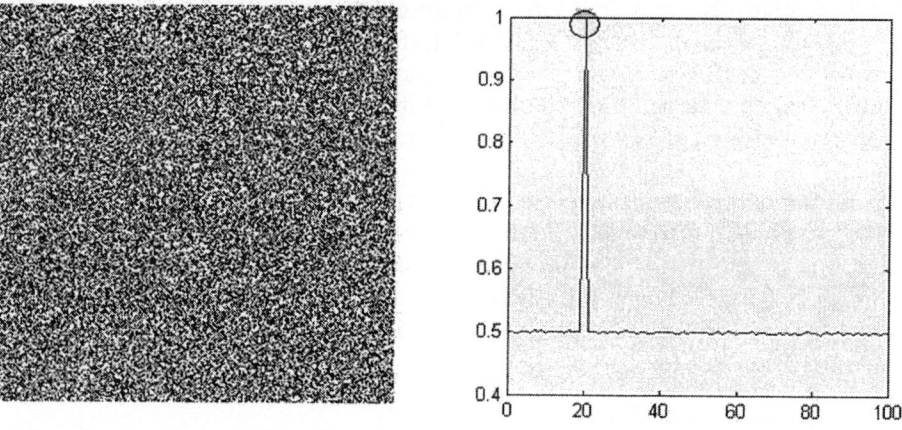

Fig. 6. (Left) embedded watermark PN-sequence, (Right) Extracted watermark sequence when no tamper occurred

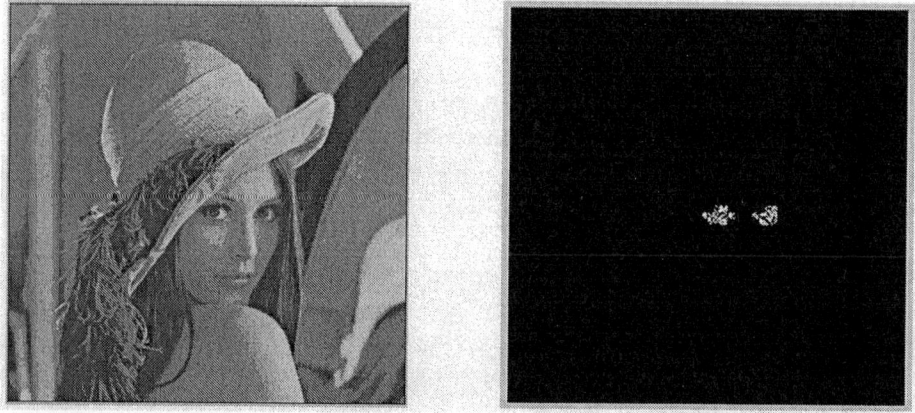

Fig. 7. (Left) Tampered Lena image, (Right) Localization

correct keys were used in the extraction process. Watermark detector response to 100 randomly generated watermarks. Only one watermark (the one to which the detector was set to respond) matches.

Below is the experimental result for gray image using classic image 'Lena'. The tampered version of Lena image is shown in figure 7 where the Lena eyes was changed. From the extracted watermark image, we can tell that tampered has occurred and its location.

Finally, as shown in figure 8 we can clearly recover the image from watermarked image When it is verified to be authentic, one can remove the embedded data to restore the original image exactly. The Normalized Correlation result is 1 between watermarked image and recovered image.

Fig. 8. (Left)Original Lena Image, (Right) Recovered Lena image

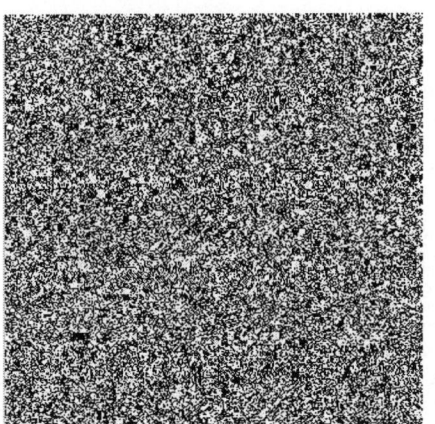 

Fig. 9. (Left)Original Watermark Signal, (Right)Extracted watermark signal if the wrong key were used

If the wrong keys were used, the extracted watermark sequence will not matched compare to other sequences, which resembles noise as shown in figure 9. if the extracted signal and original signal was changed, the NC(normalized correlation) value is close to 0. We also conducted a series of experiment for other image processing such as compression, scaling, and filtering, and the extracted watermark also resembled noise. Only unmodified watermarked image produce the right watermark and the image can be regarded as authentic.

5 Conclusion

Fragile digital watermarking schemes have drawn lots of interest recently. It serves for the purposes of both self authentication and integrity. While virtually all previous authentication watermarking schemes introduced some small amount of non-invertible distortion in the image, the new method is invertible in the sense that, if the image is deemed authentic, the distortion due to authentication can be completely removed to obtain the original image data.

In this paper, we propose an invertible watermarking scheme for the purposes of image authentication, integrity and invertibility. The authentication is based on the decoded authentication hash. The original content restoration information, an authentication hash, and additional watermark data will all be embedded into the LSBs. In the extraction process, if the image is deemed authentic, the distortion due to authentication can be removed to obtain the original image data. Being invertible, the original digital content can be completely restored after authentication.

This scheme also can detect location where the changes occurred and provide new information assurance tools for integrity of sensitive imagery, such as medical images.

Acknowledgement

The research was supported by Chung-Ang University Research Grants in 2005.

References

1. Cox, I.J., Kilian, J., Leighton, T., Shamoon, T.: Secure Spread Spectrum Watermarking for Multimedia, IEEE Trans. on Image Processing, Vol. 6, No. 12 (1997) 1673-1687
2. Yeung, M., Mintzer, F.: An Invisible Watermarking Technique for Image Verification. Proc. ICIP, vol. 2. Santa Barbara, CA (1997) 680-683
3. Memon, N., Shende, S., Wong, P.: On the Security of the Yeung-Mintzer Authentication Watermark. Proc. Of the IS and TPICS Symposium, Savannah, Georgia (2000)
4. Wong, P., Memon, N.: Secret and Public Key Image Watermarking Schemes for Image Authentication and Ownership Verification. IEEE Trans. on Image Processing, vol. 10 (2001) 1593-1601
5. Byun, S., Lee, S., Tewfik, A., Ahn, B.: A SVD-Based Fragile Watermarking Scheme for Image Authentication. International Workshop on Digital Watermarking. Lecture Notes in Computer Science vol. 2613 (2002) 170-178
6. Fridrich, J., Goljan, M., Rui, D.: Lossless Data Embedding For All Image Formats, SPIE Photonics West, Security and Watermarking of Multimedia Contents (2002) 572-583
7. J. M. Barton.: Method and apparatus for embedding authentication information within digital data. United States Patent, (1997) 5,646,997
8. M. U. Celik, G. Sharma, A. M. Tekalp, and E. Saber.: Reversible data hiding. In Proc. of International Conference on Image Processing, volume II, Sept.(2002) 157-160
9. J. Fridrich, M. Goljan, and R. Du. :Lossless data embedding - new paradigm in digital watermarking. EURASIP Journal on Applied Signal Processing, Feb. (2002) 185-196

10. Yang,Y., Bao, F.: An Invertible Watermarking Schemes for Authentication of Electronic Clinical Brain Atlas, ICASSP (2003)
11. Miroslav Goljan , Jessica J. Fridrich , Rui Du,: Distortion-Free Data Embedding for Images, Proceedings of the 4th International Workshop on Information Hiding, April (2001) 27-41
12. R.L.Rivest,:The MD5 message digest algorithm, Tech.Rep.,(1992)
13. Stefan Katzenbeisser, Fabien A. P, Petttcolas.: Information hiding techniques for steg-anography and digital watermarking. Artech House, Boston London (2000) 128-129

Adaptive Congestion Control Scheme Based on DCCP for Wireless/Mobile Access Networks*

Si-Yong Park, Sung-Min Kim, Tae-Hoon Lee, and Ki-Dong Chung

Dept. of Computer Science, Pusan National University,
Kumjeong-Ku, Busan 609-735, Korea
{sypark, morethannow, withsoul, kdchung}@melon.cs.pusan.ac.kr

Abstract. In this paper, we propose an adaptive congestion control scheme to control congestion caused in wireless/mobile access networks of ubiquitous computing environment. Significantly, this scheme includes a new reverse congestion avoidance phase, which can classify packet loss due to bit error or network congestion. Also, it includes a new slow stop phase which can minimize an wasted bandwidth due to previous congestion control schemes. And, this scheme controls network congestion more adaptive than previous congestion control schemes by a new method of congestion measurement and various phases in the adaptive congestion control scheme. The new method of congestion measurement classifies degree of congestion by a relation of the number of loss packets and increment size of a congestion window. This scheme is designed based on DCCP(Datagram Congestion Control Protocol) being proposed by IETF(Internet Engineering Task Force). In our simulation, this scheme provides a good bandwidth throughput not in wireless/mobile access networks but also in wired networks.

1 Introduction

All IT devices must always be connected wired/wireless access network to get a Internet service in anywhere and at anytime on ubiquitous computing environment. Representative examples of ubiquitous computing are wearable computing, pervasive computing, which attaches computer to anything, and nomadic computing, which makes it possible to use computers in anywhere.

Heterogenous networks and various kind of devices will coexist in ubiquitous computing environment. Especially, many wireless access networks and mobile access networks will be included to maximize mobility in ubiquitous computing environment. To support such mobility, devices will be done lightweight. And, we must consider such lightweight devices to transmit effectively multimedia data or logistic data, which is continuous and large. Lightweight devices to support mobility will be limited H/W resource unlike existing wired network devices.

---

* This work was supported by the Regional Research Centers Program(Research Center for Logistics Information Technology), granted by the Korean Ministry of Education & Human Resources Development.

BSD based TCP in the OS Kernel is a heavy protocol stack to support many functions i.e, congestion control, flow control, re-transmission, etc. UDP is a lightweight protocol stack without functions like TCP and does not guarantee reliability. To guarantee reliability to UDP, application layer based congestion control schemes have been researched. But, In case such congestion control schemes is used on application layer, all application softwares for multimedia streaming must have congestion control function and it is difficult to adapt in fast bandwidth change. To solve such problem, IETF is standardizing DCCP which provides congestion control function in a transport network layer without reliability[3,4,5,6,7,8].

To serve effectively multimedia data or logistic data on ubiquitous computing environment, we consider few problems, which are mobility of devices and mobility of services. Such mobility makes it hard to guarantee QoS. Also, we should consider keeping seamless multimedia service among heterogenous networks and various devices with such mobility problem.

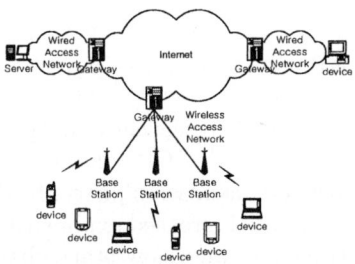

Fig. 1. Ubiquitous network coexisted wired and wireless networks

In this paper, we define a new concept of congestion cause mobility on wireless/mobile access network and propose a new congestion control scheme to control such congestion . First, we consider ubiquitous network like figure 1. In figure 1, ubiquitous network is divided into two regions, which are Internet and access network, by a gateway, which have functions like a protocol transfer and so on. And, access network is classified wireless access network and wired access network by access media of a device.

Mobility of devices can cause congestion in each access network or access point. For example, if many mobile devices move into a cell at the same time and request transmitting of packets over capacity of a basestation in the cell, the basestation can not transmit all requested packets. In case of mobility of services, services can move freely between devices and it causes fast change of network traffic and congestion. These are clear difference with congestion on wired network. Congestion in wired network is happened due to heavy traffic in a router but that in wireless/mobile access network is happened by moving of devices.

In previous congestion control schemes for wired network, delay is an important factor because packets pass many router on Internet not one router. But, delay in wireless/mobile access network is not an important factor than that in wired network because packets pass only one hop which is between a gateway and a device in figure 1. Preferably, classifying packet loss due to congestion or bit error is more important factor than delay.

In his paper, we propose an adaptive congestion control scheme based on DCCP for wireless/mobile access network. The proposed scheme can adaptively control congestion of wireless/mobile access network by two new phases and a new method of congestion measurement. Also, this scheme provides all devices in wireless or mobile access network with the fair bandwidth utilization rate because of being controlled congestion by a gateway.

The rest of this paper is organized as follows. Section 2 reviews the related works about previous congestion control schemes, transport layer protocol and DCCP being background of this paper. Section 3 proposes the adaptive congestion control scheme for wireless/mobile access network. In section 4, we show the results of simulation of our scheme. In the conclusion, we present a summary of our research.

2 Related Works

In this section, we present previous researches and papers related with our research. A congestion control scheme of TCP consists of slow start phase, congestion avoidance phase and fast retransmission phase. In slow start phase, if packet does not loss, congestion window is increased exponentially until congestion window reaches a slow start threshold and slow start phase changes to congestion avoidance phase. In the congestion avoidance phase, congestion window is increased by a size of one packet per RTT(Round Trip Time) to avoid congestion. If one more packets are lost due to time out in congestion avoidance phase, congestion window becomes a size of one packet and slow start threshold sets a half of current congestion window. And, the last phase is fast retransmission phase to improve throughput of slow start phase[1,2]. In fast retransmission phase, if three duplicated acks is received to a sender, lost packet is fast retransmitted.

TCP-friendly congestion control scheme was proposed to control congestion which causes by multimedia data[2,4,7,10]. Specially, [2,4] proposed TFRC(TCP-friendly Rate Control), which can fairly divide bandwidth with TCP sessions and UDP sessions by using a rate control equality modeled throughput of TCP. RAP(Rate Adaption Protocol) controls a throughput by TCP-friendly based on packet loss. RAP uses AIMD(Additive Increase Multiplicative Decrease) algorithm controlled by IPG(Inter Packet Gap)[10]. LDA(Loss-Delay based Adjustment algorithm) defines congestion with a throughput of TCP and packet loss[4].

DCCP being proposed by IETF is protocol which replaces application layer congestion control based on UDP by congestion control of transport layer. DCCP providers two congestion control schemes, which are CCID 2(TCP-like) and CCID 3(TCP-friendly). DCCP can dynamically change congestion control scheme according to network traffic.

DCCP is an unreliable protocol similar to UDP but includes a connection establish step and a connection destruction step. And, it controls congestion window when packet has been received or send. CCID 2 is a TCP-like congestion control mechanism similar to that of TCP but reduces the number of acks by using ack vector[5]. The ack vector denotes whether packets were received or not to a receiver. CCID 3 is a TFRC mechanism which controls congestion window by using a method similar to rate control mechanism of TCP. This shares fairly network bandwidth with competing other TCP traffics. And, CCID 3 estimates transmission bandwidth of TCP by using an average loss rate and delay[6].

3 Adaptive Congestion Control for Wireless Access Network

We propose an adaptive congestion control scheme based on DCCP for wireless/mobile access network to access ubiquitous computing environments i.e, EPC global network. In wireless/mobile access network, we assume that there is just one hop or little hops between a device and a gateway like figure 1 and all sessions are connected to Internet through the gateway in figure 1.

Congestion control schemes for TCP and DCCP designed for wired network. So, we can not expect a good performance in wireless/mobile access network. Especially, congestion control schemes for DCCP determine congestion window according to packet loss rate and delay time to control sending rate like that of TCP.

In wireless/mobile access network, all devices connect to the gateway by one hop or little hops. Therefore, packet loss on immediate nodes(routers) can be ignored and congestion can be control based on the gateway. The gateway maintains information of all session to control congestion. Our adaptive congestion control scheme considers not only packet loss but also congestion window of all sessions in the gateway and an available transmission window of the gateway.

3.1 Issues of the Adaptive Congestion Control Scheme

Issues to design the adaptive congestion control scheme are as follows.

- Classifying packet loss due to bit error or congestion. Congestion control scheme for wireless/mobile access network must not regard packet loss due to bit error and packet loss due to congestion as same case.
- Improvement wasted bandwidth due to AIMD. In previous congestion control scheme, if congestion is happened, each congestion window of sessions are reduced by half of the current congestion window. In this case, if congestion is slight and many sessions reduce their congestion windows as half, it causes reducing so many bandwidth more bandwidth to solve congestion.
- Preventing packet loss due to mobility of devices. In wireless/mobile access network, packet loss is happened due to a basestation which connected so many devices over the maximum capability of the basestation. Therefore, congestion control scheme for wireless/mobile access network needs to consider such congestion.

– Controlling a congestion window by the gateway. Because all basestations are connected the gateway, the gateway can maintain each congestion window of all sessions and an available transmission window of the gateway. This information is used for the adaptive congestion control scheme.

3.2 Adaptive Congestion Control Scheme

The proposed adaptive congestion control scheme consists of five phases, which include a new slow stop phase and a new reverse congestion avoidance phase and a new constant phase with previous two phase of TCP. In the reverse congestion avoidance phase, when the number of packet loss is smaller than a threshold, all phases change to the reverse congestion avoidance phase to determine whether the packet loss is caused by congestion or bit error. The slow stop phase reduces a congestion window exponentially to improve network bandwidth throughput in slight congestion.

In the adaptive congestion control scheme, when a new session is initialized, the adaptive congestion control scheme becomes a slow start phase like that of TCP. And, depending on degree of congestion, the slow start phase changes to a slow stop phase, the initialized slow start phase or a reverse congestion avoidance phase. If packet loss is not happened and a congestion window of the new session becomes a slow start threshold, the slow start phase changes to a congestion avoidance phase like that of TCP. In the congestion avoidance phase, if packet loss is not happened, congestion window is increased by the size of one packet per one round trip time. But, if one more packet is lost, the congestion avoidance phase changes to one phase of the reverse congestion avoidance phase, the slow stop phase or the slow start phase according to degree of congestion. When congestion window becomes a maximum transmission threshold, the congestion avoidance phase changes to the a constant phase which does not increase congestion window. This phase is same to the congestion avoidance phase exception no longer increasing congestion window. Figure 2 shows transitions among five phase in the adaptive congestion control scheme.

In figure 2, SS is the slow start phase, CA is the congestion avoidance phase, C is the constant phase, ST is the slow stop phase, and RCA is the reverse congestion avoidance phase. Transition between each phase is classified by (1).

$$i_B^A -> C \qquad (1)$$

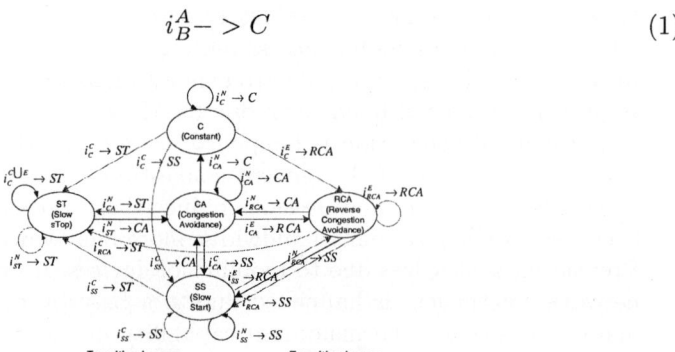

Fig. 2. Transition diagram among five phases in the adaptive congestion control scheme

In (1), A is an argument to denote state of packet. If a current packet is lost and the packet loss is caused by congestion, A is denoted by C and if the packet loss is caused by bit error, A is denoted by E. And, if A is N, it means that the current packet is not lost. $B->C$ denotes a transition from the B phase to the C phase. For example, $i_{CA}^{C}->ST$ means that the congestion avoidance phase changes to the slow stop phase due to congestion. In the congestion control scheme of TCP, thresholds to control congestion window are a slow start threshold and a maximum transmission threshold. In an initialization state of TCP, the slow start threshold is a half of the maximum transmission threshold and whenever one more packets are lost, the slow start threshold will become half of the current congestion window. In proposed the adaptive congestion control scheme, the slow start threshold and the maximum transmission threshold are similar to those of TCP in aspect of functionality. But, the two thresholds in this paper are calculated by the number of sessions connected the gateway. Table 1 defines symbols which will be used in this paper.

First, the maximum transmission threshold(T_{max}^i) is defined by (2).

$$T_{max}^i = min(W_{max}^G/N, W_{recv}^i) \qquad (2)$$

In (2), the maximum transmission threshold is minimum value of a receive window size of session i and a maximum window size which can be allocated by the gateway. And, whenever a new session is initialized or ongoing session is closed, T_{max}^i is recalculated by (2).

$$T_{SS}^i = \begin{cases} T_{max}^i & , \sum_{i=1}^{N} T_{max}^i < W_{maxG} \\ (1 - \frac{1}{N+1}) \times T_{max}^i & , \sum_{i=1}^{N} T_{max}^i \geq W_{maxG} \end{cases} \qquad (3)$$

(3) denotes the slow start threshold. In (3), if an available transmission window of the gateway is larger than required transmission window size of new session, T_{SS}^i is T_{max}^i. Otherwise, T_{SS}^i is $(1 - \frac{1}{N+1}) \times T_{max}^i$ to prevent congestion by already considering bandwidth for future a session. And, whenever the number

Table 1. Symbol definition

Symbol	Means
i	An index of session
N	The number of sessions connected a gateway
T_{max}^i	The maximum transmission threshold of a session i
W_{max}^G	An available maximum window size of a gateway
W_i^{recv}	A receive window size of a session i
T_i^{SS}	A slow start threshold of a session i
P_i^{loss}	The number of lost packets of session i
W_i^{inc}	The increased congestion window size of session i
AV_i^{loss}	The number of lost packets in a ack vector
W_i^{prev}	The Previous congestion window size of session i

of sessions connected the gateway changes, T^i_{SS} is recalculated by (3). If packets are lost by congestion, T^i_{SS} is recalculated by (4).

$$T^i_{SS} = \frac{T^i_{max}}{2} \quad (4)$$

1) Classification of congestion degree

In this paper, to classify a degree of congestion, we use a difference of the number of loss packet and increment size of a congestion window during a cycle.

$$P^i_{loss} = W^i_{inc} - AV^i_{loss} \quad (5)$$

In figure 3, the number of transmission packets in I region is m. If the m packets send to a client and are not lost, an ack packet including an ack vector be send to the gateway. All bits of the ack vector are 1. And, in $I+1$ region, $m+n$ packets increased n packets are send to the client but k packets are lost. Because m packets of packets were safely send to client in I region, packet loss in $I+1$ region may be happen due to the increased n packets. Therefore the degree of congestion is defined by (5). (5) in figure 3 is $n - k$ that is a difference of the number of loss packet(k) and increment size of the congestion window(n).

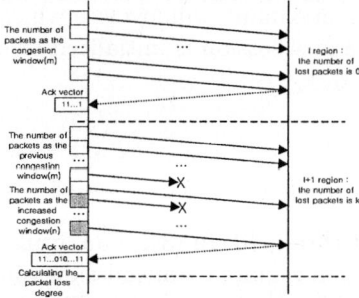

Fig. 3. Classifying of congestion degree

2) Adaptive congestion control

Next phase of each five phase is determined by degree of congestion(P^i_{loss}). First, the next phase of the slow start phase shows in figure 4.

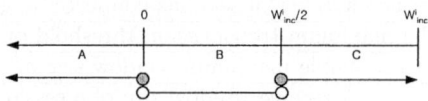

Fig. 4. Congestion control for the slow start phase

If P^i_{loss} is belonged to the region A, it means that more packets than increased packets by no pack loss in previous congestion window are lost. Therefore, because congestion is happened in a basestation belonged to the session i, the slow start phase is restarted after the size of congestion window is reduced a size of one packet. If P_{loss}^i is in the region B, the slow start phase changes to the slow stop phase because the number of loss packet is smaller than that in the region A and it means slight congestion. Because the slow stop phase decreases the congestion window exponentially, though recovery of congestion is slower than that in the slow start phase, throughput of bandwidth is improved. If P_{loss}^i belongs to the region C, little packets are lost. In this case, the adaptive congestion control scheme decides whether current packet loss is happened by congestion or bit error by using the reverse congestion control state. In figure 4, we use $W_{inc}^i/2$ to classify the region B and the region C because congestion window in the slow start phase increases exponentially. If a congestion window becomes the slow start threshold, the slow start phase changes to the congestion avoidance phase. In the congestion avoidance phase, the next phase is decided according

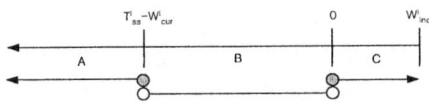

Fig. 5. Congestion control in the congestion avoidance phase

to the degree of congestion. Figure 5 shows congestion control for the congestion avoidance phase. Region A, B and C in the figure 5 are regions to determine the degree of congestion. If the degree of congestion is in the region A, it means that the number of transmitted packets is smaller than the slow start threshold due to many loss packets. And, in this case, the congestion avoidance phase changes to the slow start phase for strong recovery of congestion. Region B is the region, which is larger than the slow start threshold and smaller than previous congestion window. This region is difference of the maximum congestion window in the slow start phase and the previous congestion window in the congestion avoidance phase. Because congestion control in this region is required the recovery of congestion to improve throughput of bandwidth, the congestion avoidance phase changes to the slow stop phase. Region C in the figure 5 is similar to the region C in the figure 4 but a size of C is a size of one packet because the congestion window in the congestion avoidance phase increases linearly. And, if the number of loss packet is belonged to the region C, the congestion avoidance phase changes to the reverse congestion avoidance phase for classifying packet loss due to congestion or bit error.

When a congestion window becomes the maximum transmission threshold, the congestion avoidance phase changes to the constant phase and congestion window is not increased. But, if the number of sessions through the gateway changes, the maximum transmission threshold is changed and this phase changes to the congestion avoidance phase or the slow stop phase. If the maximum transmission threshold is increased, a next phase is the congestion avoidance phase, otherwise the next phase is the slow stop phase. Congestion control according to packet loss in the constant phase is similar to that in the congestion avoidance phase like figure 5. The reason is that the constant phase is same the congestion avoidance phase except no increasing congestion window. So, because we assume that the constant phase is the congestion avoidance phase series, congestion control in the constant phase follows as that in the congestion avoidance phase. In the wireless network, bit error happens frequently due to features of

```
A : the number of loss packets in the current RCA phase
B : the number of loss packets before the current RCA phase

If (A = 0)
    Processing a phase before the current RCA phase
Else if (A = 1)
    Processing still the current RCA phase
Else if ((A > B) OR (A = B))
    Processing the slow start phase
Else
    Processing the slow start phase

RCA : the Reverse Congestion Avoidance phase
```

Fig. 6. Congestion control in the reverse congestion avoidance phase

radio wave. Packet loss due to such bit error makes confusedly congestion control scheme. Therefore, when little packet loss is happened, it needs a phase to classify whether a packet is lost due to congestion or bit error.

The reverse congestion avoidance phase decreases a congestion window by a size of one packet and determines whether the packet loss is due to congestion or bit error according to the number of next loss packet. If this packet loss is due to congestion, the number of next loss packet may grow, otherwise the number of next loss packet is little or none. Therefore, we examine the cause of the packet loss by passing the reverse congestion avoidance phase. Figure 6 shows an algorithm of the reverse congestion avoidance phase.

The congestion control scheme of TCP does not classify degree of congestion. And, this causes fast falling throughput of bandwidth though congestion is slight. But, the proposed slow stop phase does not reduce the congestion window as a size of one packet and decreases a congestion window exponentially contrary to the slow start phase. This can prevent from fast falling throughput of bandwidth in slight congestion. Figure 7 shows congestion control in the

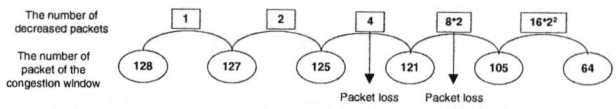

Fig. 7. Congestion control in the slow stop phase

slow stop phase. In figure 7, when a congestion window is a size of 128 packets, packet loss is happened. The congestion window is decreased exponentially until the congestion window reaches a size of 64 packets. When the congestion widow is a size of 125 packets, if packet loss is not happened, the congestion window will be decreased by a size of 8 packets that is double of a previous decreased size(a size of 4 packets). But, if packet loss happens in this time, the congestion window will be decreased by a size of 16 packets that is four times of a previous decreased size(a size of 8 packets).

4 Performance Evaluation and Analysis

We evaluate a performance of the adaptive congestion control scheme proposed in this paper. Table 2 shows environment and parameters for simulation. Wireless access network for simulation is consisted of one gateway, three basestations and many devices as like figure 1. Figure 8 shows a performance in a case of 10^{-3} BER(Bit Error Rate). In our simulation, BER=10^{-3} is a case that bit error rate is small relatively. In figure 8, using bandwidth of the basestation 2 gets into maximum. So, we can see that congestion is happening continuously in the basestation 2. In this case, performance of our scheme is superior to that of TCP-like. Such reason is because our scheme controls congestion efficiently without loss of bandwidth by added the slow stop phase and the reverse congestion avoidance phase newly.

Figure 9 shows a performance in a case of 10^{-2} BER(Bit Error Rate). In this case, we can see that basestation 2, which should be congestion and other basestations is almost congestion-free. This is due to the fact that congestion could not occur because of the higher BER. So, all nodes in high BER could not be with satisfactory in their services. But, also in this case, the proposed scheme is superior to TCP-like congestion control scheme in terms of throughput

Table 2. Simulation environment

Gateway	Capability(Window Size)	2000
Basestation 1	Capability(Window Size)	1000
	Nodes	10
Basestation 2	Capability(Window Size)	300
	Nodes	25
Basestation 3	Capability(Window Size)	700
	Nodes	10

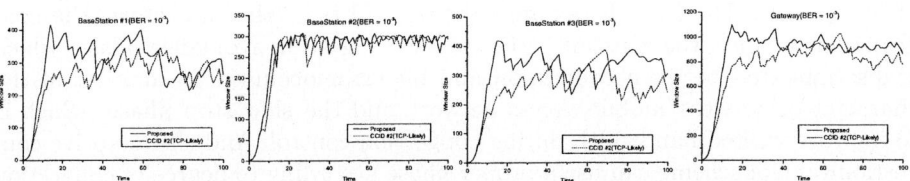

Fig. 8. Throughput comparison with TCP-like(BER=10^{-3})

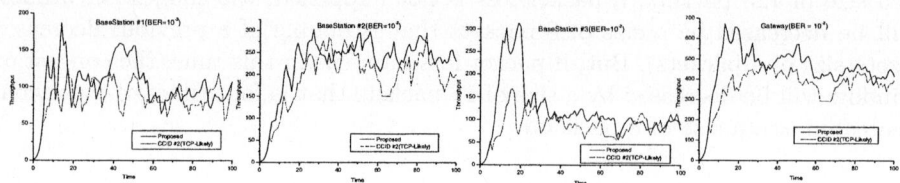

Fig. 9. Throughput comparison with TCP-like(BER=10^{-2})

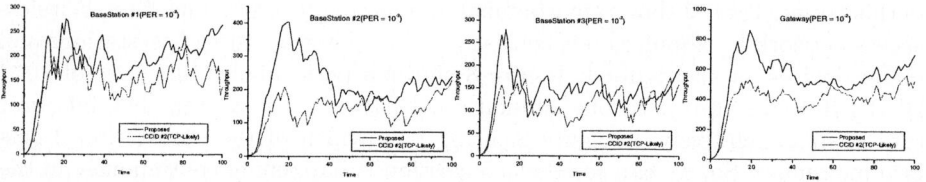

Fig. 10. Throughput comparison with TCP-like(PER=10^{-2})

by the reverse congestion avoidance phase and the slow stop phase. Thus, the proposed scheme is more intelligent than TCP-like in congestion control. In this paper, although we propose congestion control in wireless/mobile access network, we also concern integrated network including wired network. If the adaptive congestion control scheme shows a good performance in wired network, we don't need protocol translation in gateway. Figure 10 assumes packet loss, which is occurred by routing delay like wired networks. We set packet error rate to 10^{-2}. In this simulation, the result shows that the adaptive congestion control scheme is well applied to wired network. After this, we could develop the congestion control of integrated networks.

5 Conclusions

In this paper, we proposed the transportation layer congestion control scheme adapted ubiquitous environment. And, this scheme guaranteed mobility of devices and service. This congestion control scheme is based on DCCP, the transport layer protocol drafted by IETF. This congestion control scheme consists of five phases. The five phases are existing 3 phases (the slow start, the congestion avoidance, the constant), the reverse congestion avoidance phase, which is discriminated between congestion and bit error occurred on account of the character of wireless/mobile access network and the slow stop phase, which is to improve wasted bandwidth during congestion control. And the adaptive congestion control scheme can use a proper phase according to degree of congestion degree, which is calculated by a difference of the number of loss packets and increment size of a congestion window.

Our scheme is send-based congestion control. So, all the congestion control is performed on the gateway. Each device only transmits the ack vector to sender. This can be a lightweight protocol stack for ubiquitous devices. There are two future works. In the first, we are going to add a receiver-based congestion control policy to our adaptive congestion control scheme. In the second, we will research about various algorithms to provide reliability.

References

[1] W. Richard Stevens, "TCP/IP Illustrated, Volume1, The Protocols," Addision-Wesley.
[2] W. Richard Stevens, "TCP Slow Start, Congestion Avoidance, Fast Retransmit, and Fast Recovery Algorithms," RFC 2001, January 1997.
[3] Sally Floyd, Eddie Kohler, "Profile for DCCP Congestion Control ID 2: TCP-like Congestion Control," Internet-Draft draft-ietf-dccp-ccid2-08.txt , November 2004.
[4] D. Sisalem and A. Wolisz, "LDA+ TCP-friendly adaptation: A measurements and comparison study," Proc. International Workshop on Network and Operating systems Support for Digital Audio and Video , NOSSDAV'99, June 2000.
[5] Eddie Kohler, Mark Handley, Sally Floyd, "Datagram Congestion Control Protocol (DCCP)," Internet-Draft draft-ietf-dccp-spec-09.txt, November 2004.
[6] Sally Floyd, Eddie Kohler, Jitendra Padhye, "Profile for DCCP Congestion Control ID 3: TFRC Congestion Control," Internet-Draft draft-ietf-dccp-ccid3-09.txt, December 2004.
[7] T. Phelan, "Datagram Congestion Control Protocol (DCCP) User Guide," Internet-Draft draft-ietf-dccp-user-guide-02.txt, July 2004.
[8] S. Floyd, M. Handley, J. Padhye, J. Widmer, "Equation-Based Congestion Control for Unicast Applications," Proc SIGCOMM 2000, August 2000.
[9] S. Floyd, M. Handley, J. Padhye, and J. Widmer, "TCP Friendly Rate Control (TFRC): Protocol Specification," Internet-Draft draft-ietf-tsvwg-tfrc-02.txt, October 2002.
[10] R. Rejaie, M. Handley, and D. Estin, "Rap: An end-to-end rate-based congestion control mechanism for realtime streams in the internet," Proc. IEEE Infocom, March 1999.

SARS : A Linear Source Model Based Adaptive Rate-Control Scheme for TCP-Friendly Real-Time MPEG-4 Video Streaming

Eric Hsiao-Kuang Wu, Ming-I Hsieh, and Chung-Yuan Knight Chang

Department of Computer Science and Information Engineering,
National Central University, Chung-Li, Taiwan, R.O.C
hsiao@csie.ncu.edu.tw, {mihs, tnnd}@wmlab.csie.ncu.edu.tw

Abstract. The increasing demand for streaming video applications on the Internet motivates the problem of building an adaptive rate control scheme for the time-varying network condition. The time-varying available bandwidth and latency make the real-time streaming applications difficult to achieve high bandwidth utilization and video quality at receivers. MPEG-4 is a widely-used streaming protocol and a MPEG-4 video streaming system should be able to provide an adaptive rate control mechanism to satisfy these changing conditions.

In this paper we analyze the problem of transmitting MPEG-4 video streaming over IP network with some well-known TCP-friendly rate control protocols. This paper is focused on solving the challenging issues in application layer, compression layer to reduce the frame dropping rate. With this aim, we provide a solution called "SARS" (Smoothed and Adaptive Rate-control Scheme) in compression layer and application layer for an MPEG-4 video streaming system and discuss the characteristics of its components. Furthermore, we assess the effects of SARS by simulation with the well-known solution for MPEG-4 transmission.

1 Introduction

As fast-growing of broadband network access, the real-time video streaming, such as Internet television, unicast video conferences, IP telephony, distance learning, and video-on-demand, are feasible[4] and may change the user behaviors on Internet and their amusements. However, since the network resources are shared and competed with various Internet flows, the quality of a video streaming flow might only be effects by packet-loss, bandwidth variation and fluctuating end-to-end latency. In addition, current Internet Service Provider does not provide quality of service (QoS) guarantee for real-time video streaming applications and raises three challenges for real-time video streaming applications.

1) The first challenge is to satisfy the bandwidth requirement. A minimum bandwidth is required for real-time video streaming applications to maintain an acceptable perceptual quality. Additionally, the unsteady bandwidth of the Internet[5] will affect the transmission of the real-time video streams and the quality of video presentation. 2) The second challenge is to satisfy the packet-loss

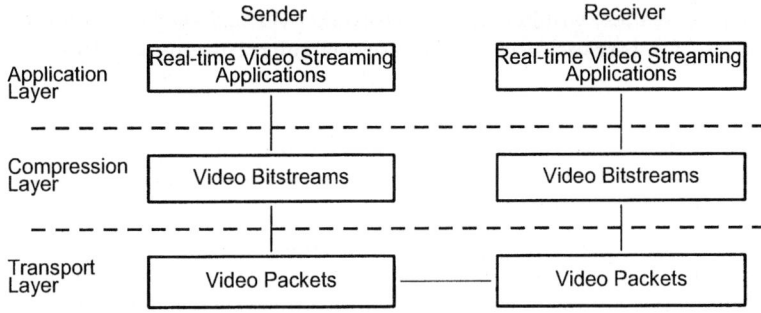

Fig. 1. Layer structure of an end-to-end real time video streaming system

requirement. Because of packet-loss and fragment requirements for large video frame, the receiver may get a lot of incomplete frame and get a poor quality of video. 3) The final challenge is to satisfy the end-to-end latency requirement. Because Internet is a packet-switch network, the transmission delay for a packet is unsteady and may be large. If the transmission delay for a video frame is longer than the acceptable latency, this video frame will be considered useless and the application will be "starvation" because of delay of the video frame. Thus, a feasible end-to-end video streaming protocol should consider those three challenges and provide feasible solutions to solve those challenges.

An general end-to-end real-time video streaming system which employs control techniques can then be illustrated in Fig. 1 as a layer-structure system[17].

The system consists of application layer, compression layer and transport layer.

Application layer defines the maximum end-to-end latency and the acceptable visual quality in this layer. The real-time video streaming applications are subject to different end-to-end latency constraints.

Compression layer is the video encoder that provides a wide range of coding bit rate and encodes the live video based on adaptive rate control algorithm.

Transport layer is required to estimate the bandwidth and control the throughput not to exceed the available bandwidth.

In this architecture, the challenges of bandwidth, end-to-end latency and packet-loss consist in *Compression Layer* and *Transport Layer*. Later, we discuss the known approaches for *Transport Layer* and *Compression Layer*.

a) Transport Layer Approach: A feasible transport layer protocol should be introduced 1) to react to network congestion; 2) to adjust sending rate to avoid congestion collapse; and 3) to keep high network utilization and low packet-loss ratio. In traditional rate control mechanism, there are two major types, window-based and rate-based. However, the window based schemes lead the longer propagation delay out. Thus, the rate based schemes are more attractive for real-time streaming applications.

For handling lost packets, there are usually two major types of methods to handle errors caused by packet-loss, namely packet retransmission[6] and Forward Error Correction (FEC)[7]. The idea of the FEC is to generate redundant packets at the sender, which can be used to recover lost packets in an acceptable lost ratio. As for retransmission-based error control method, ARQ (Automatic Repeat reQuest), the sender attempts to retransmit the lost packets upon receiving the packet retransmission responses. It is only feasible to recover burst loss with minimum cost of network bandwidth if round trip delay is low[8].

b) Compression Layer Approaches: State-of-the-art video coding standards, such as H.263, H.263+, H.264, and MPEG-4, are designed for video transmission on Internet. H.263 is a provisional ITU-T standard codec for video conferences. It was designed for low bitrate communication, early draft specified coding bit rate less than 64Kbits/s, however the limitation has now been removed. H.263 was later extended to H.263+ (version 2) and H.263++ (version 3).

MPEG-4 video coding standard, unlike previous standards from the Motion Pictures Experts Group Consortium (MPEG-1 and MPEG-2), is gaining increasing acceptance and offers the digital video community an open standard in the face of the dominant, yet proprietary, digital video formats from RealNetworks and Microsoft[9][10][11][12]. It provides a wide range of coding bit rate and resolution to perform adaptive encoding.

However, a video encoder with error control techniques is still not enough for solving the challenges in this layer. An adaptive rate control schemes or a scalable coding mode is needed to combat these problems. The adaptive rate control schemes allocate the target bit rate to each frame for video encoding, control the bit rate generated and adapts to the time-varying available bandwidth. Thus, the frame can be transmitted, received, played out at receiver on time if no packet-loss occurs. It is typically known as layered coding and intended for progressive transmission. H.263+ and H.263++ coding standard support the scalable coding mode. In MPEG-4 coding standard, it provides Fine Granularity Scalability (FGS).[13]

This paper is organized as following. In Section II, we briefly review recent researches on the end-to-end congestion control mechanisms and rate control schemes in the video codec. The proposed scheme, *SARS*, is described in Section III. The performance comparison of *SARS* and the rate control scheme in [1] under CBR and VBR and over several rate based congestion control protocols are evaluated in Section IV. At the end of this paper, we summarize our study and point out the future works in Section V.

2 Related Work

2.1 MPEG-4 Video Rate Control

A conventional rate control scheme for a video encoder is a technique to determine the target bit rate R of each encoded frame, maintain a good visual quality and minimize the distortion measure D under a limited bandwidth constraint[14]. The distortion D means that the difference between the original source picture and the reconstructed picture after it has been decoded. In typical transform coding, both the bit rate R and the distortion D are controlled by the quantization parameter. The rate control scheme allocates the bit budget to each group of pictures (GOP), individual picture and/or macroblock in a video sequence and derive the quantization parameter from a wide range of quantization parameter sets. The conventional rate control scheme embedded in the video encoder generally has two components.

- Rate Control : It consists of the rate allocation and the skipping frame mechanisms. In rate allocation, it estimates the number of bits available to encode the frames in the video sequence. Video delivery over the Internet meet the constraints imposed by the changing network conditions. The allocated bit rate has to adapt to the time-varying available bandwidth. In order to keep the below the pre-defined threshold of end-to-end latency, the skipping frame mechanism is initiated.
- Source Model : The source model is used to help the video encoder to produce the output bit rate closer to its target.

We briefly review current researches related to these two components in the following sections.

Researches on Source Model for Video Coding. A source model, aka rate-quantization model, for video coding is the most important part of a rate control scheme. The rate-quantization model defines the relationship between the coding bit rate and quantization parameter. A suitable quantization parameter used for encoding a frame or a macroblock to achieve the target bit rate is derived from the rate-quantization model.

Researches on Rate Control for Video Coding. A rate control algorithm generally includes three steps. A fixed size of buffer based on the maximum acceptable latency is determined in the first step. The second step is to estimate the target bit rate according to the buffer occupancy, remaining bits in this video sequence and available bandwidth. The allocated bit budget can then be applied on the source models to derive the quantization parameter. The final step is to control the buffer occupancy and start the frame skipping mechanism if buffer overflow occurs.

Many researches focus on the MPEG-4 Q2 rate control algorithm which is based on the quadratic rate-distortion model[15] [20][17][21].

However, the MPEG-4 Q2 rate control schemes[15] [17][22] are heuristic and are designed for CBR applications which are not suitable for real-time streaming video on Internet. In [1], Li adopted the fluid-flow traffic model and the linear tracking theory to calculate the target bit rate and the quantization parameter for P-frames corresponding to time-varying available bandwidth. However, there is a problem with such an adjustment. If target buffer level is low and current buffer level is high, the first target bit rate is possible to be negative. But the final adjustment with remaining bits will make the target bit rate positive. The buffer level thus remains increasing and is unable to meet the target buffer level. If the rate decreases suddenly, the buffer overflow will occur. Furthermore, there is also a problem with the skipping frame control. It is possible to cause frames to be skipped continuously even some frames had already been skipped.

3 SARS: Smoothed and Adaptive Rate-Control Scheme

3.1 Overview of System Architecture

There are two objectives in this system. The first objective is that the system has to regulate the output bit rate that adapts to the time-varying available bandwidth. The second objective is coding bit rate allocation and coding bit rate adjustment for the MPEG-4 video encoder. The bit budget will be allocated before encoding and controlled during the encoding process. The four main components of the system are presented: the *TCP-friendly Rate Control*, the *TFRS Module*, the *LD Module*, and the *RSF Module*, whose functions are described in the following sections.

3.2 Bandwidth Adaptation: TCP-Friendly Rate Control

Internet conditions change with time; as a result, real-time application should tailor their transmission rate in a manner that achieves high utilization while sharing bandwidth appropriately with competing traffic (e.g., Email, web traffic, etc.). Additionally, the quality of the received video should react to the available bandwidth, so that users receive the highest possible quality video for their available bandwidth.

A rate based congestion control protocol provides an estimated tcp-friendly sending rate calculated either from receiver or at sender. Every time an estimated rate report is received from receiver or calculated at sender, the sender reacts with the report of rate to adjust its sending rate with the new one. We denote the $T_{rate}(n)$ as the nth estimated tcp-friendly sending rate. The event of changing rate and the information of $T_{rate}(n)$ are then passed to the *Rate Smoother* component. The transmission of packets will be scheduled using an transmitting packet interval.

3.3 TFRS Module: A TCP Friendly Rate Smoother with Memory Wiper

In multimedia streaming applications, the users can not tolerate rapidly change of quality. We may not vary the rate for video encoding so frequently. The *TFRS Module* is to smooth the rate for video encoding and It has three main functions. The TFRS module is based on the EWMA filter to get a smoother rate.

$$T_{rate_{smoothed}}(n) = (1-\gamma) \times T_{rate_{smoothed}}(n-1) + \gamma \times T_{rate}(n) \qquad (1)$$

where N_c is current number of coded frames, γ is the weighting parameter whose default value is 0.5, *n* and *n-1* are the time that n^{th} and $n-1^{th}$ rate-change events occurred, respectively.

In the process of the *TFRS Module*, the available bandwidth variations can be regulated by the weighting parameter γ. If the value of γ is larger, the system is more responsible to the available bandwidth estimated by rate based congestion control protocols. In contrast, The rate may fluctuate much and the system becomes unstable. Afterwards, the smoothed rate $T_{rate_{smoothed}}$ is passed to the *RSF Module*.

3.4 LD Module: A Linear Source Model for MPEG-4 Video Coding

The ratio of non-zero DCT and quantized coefficients NZ_{ratio} is defined as follow:

$$NZ_{ratio} = NZ_{DCT_Q}/NZ_{DCT} \qquad (2)$$

Construction of Linear Source Model. As mentioned above, we observe that there is a linear relationship between the coding bit rate R and non-zero ratio of transformed and quantized DCT coefficients NZ_{ratio}. We can see that the coding bit rate R could be a linear function of NZ_{ratio}. Therefore, based on these observations, the linear relationship between R and NZ_{ratio} can be characterized by the following expression:

$$R = \kappa \times NZ_{ratio} \qquad (3)$$

where κ is the model parameter and it is the slope of the approximation line and R is the coding bit rate represented by bits per pixel.

The linear source model is an augmentation of the source model proposed in [2][3] and there is still only one model parameter. The number of non-zero quantized coefficients can be easily derived from (3). But the slope κ is also a key role in the linear source model, we provide an adaptive estimation method for slope κ.

Adaptive Estimation of The Model Parameter κ. Let NZ_{DCT_m} and NZ_{Q_m} be the number of non-zero DCT coefficients and non-zero quantized coefficients in m^{th} macroblock, respectively. Let R_m be the actual coding bit rate in m^{th} macroblock. Let M be the number of encoded macroblocks. Note that in a macroblock, there are total 384 coefficients. The model parameter κ can be estimated using the following expression:

$$\kappa = \frac{\sum_{m=1}^{M} R_m}{384 \times M} \times \frac{\sum_{m=1}^{M} NZ_{DCT_m}}{\sum_{m=1}^{M} NZ_{Q_m}} \qquad (4)$$

The initial value of κ is set to 7.6438.

3.5 RSF Module: A Reduced Skipped Frames and Adaptive Rate-Control Scheme.

The *RSF Module* is summarized and depicted in Fig. 2.

Initialization. Let $D_{latency}$ denote the maximum acceptable latency during the transmission. For a given tcp-friendly rate $T_{rate_{smoothed}}$, the size of the virtual buffer model B_s is computed as follows:

$$B_s(0,0) = T_{rate_{smoothed}} \times D_{latency} \qquad (5)$$

The size of the virtual buffer model is not fixed during the real-time video streaming, it will be adjusted if the rate $T_{rate_{smoothed}}$ is changed. The use of such a virtual buffer model is to assure that the video data in the buffer could be transmitted out under the acceptable delay constraints.

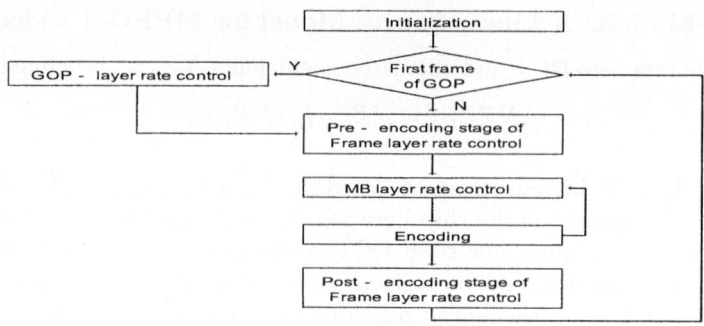

Fig. 2. RSF Module

GOP-Layer Rate Control. Before allocating the target bit rate for each frame, we first estimate a rough bit budget for an entire GOP at the beginning of each GOP. We thus estimate it from the predicted available bandwidth $T_{rate_{smoothed}}$, frame rate and the total number of frames in a GOP. Let N_{GOP} denote the number of frames in the GOP and there are one I-frame and N_{GOP} - 1 P-frames.

The rough bit budget for i^{th} GOP is calculated as follows:

$$R_{GOP}(i,1) = \frac{T_{rate_{smoothed}}(n)}{F_r} \times N_{GOP} - B_l(i,1) \qquad (6)$$

where $R_{GOP}(i,1)$ is the total number of bits for i^{th} GOP, F_r is the frame rate, and $B_l(i,1)$ is buffer level at the beginning of ith GOP.

Pre-Encoding Stage of Frame-Layer Rate Control. The most important processes in the pre-encoding stage are to calculate the target bit rate for a frame. Therefore, we can calculate the target bit rate for a frame based on the available bandwidth and the encoding frame rate in the video encoder. The draining rate d at each frame interval is also the same as the target bit rate for a frame. The calculation is expressed as follows:

$$R'_f(i,j) = d(i,j) = \frac{T_{rate_{smoothed}}(n)}{F_r} \qquad (7)$$

where $R'_f(i,j)$ and $d(i,j)$ are the target bit rate and draining rate of jth frame in i^{th} GOP respectively, $T_{rate_{smoothed}}(n)$ is the newest estimated rate, and F_r is frame rate.

We define the target virtual buffer level as a function of the frame position in a GOP and compute it for each P-frame in a GOP as follows:

$$TB_l(i,j) = TB_l(i,j-1) - \Delta_p \qquad (8)$$

$$TB_l(i,1) = B_l(i,1) \qquad (9)$$

$$\Delta_p = \frac{TB_l(i,1)}{N_{GOP}-1} \tag{10}$$

We now have the target virtual buffer level for each P-frame in i^{th} GOP. The target bit rate for j^{th} frame in i^{th} GOP can be calculated based on the target virtual buffer level $TB_l(i,j)$, current virtual buffer level $B_l(i,j)$, encoding frame rate F_r, and the available bandwidth $T_{rate_{smoothed}}(n)$. We divide the allocation of target bit rate for j^{th} frame in i^{th} GOP into two steps :

Step 1: Allocation of target bit rate for j^{th} frame

$$R_f(i,j) = \frac{T_{rate_{smoothed}}(n)}{F_r} + (TB_l(i,j) - B_l(i,j)) \tag{11}$$

where $R_f(i,j)$ is the target bit rate for j^{th} frame in i^{th} GOP, $TB_l(i,j)$ is the target virtual buffer level, and $B_l(i,j)$ is the current virtual buffer level.

Post-Encoding Stage of Frame Layer Rate Control. If the sampling time-out occurs, the $T_{rate_{smoothed}}$ is re-calculated by using (1). The remaining bit budget of ith GOP is adjusted by the new $T_{rate_{smoothed}}$. The adjustment of remaining bit budget of ith GOP is expressed as follows:

$$R_{GOP}(i,j) = R_{GOP}(i,j-1) + \Delta_{GOP} - A(i,j-1) \tag{12}$$

$$\Delta_{GOP} = \frac{T_{rate_{smoothed}}(n) - T_{rate_{smoothed}}(n-1)}{F_r} \times N_{r_{GOP}}(i) \tag{13}$$

where $N_{r_{GOP}}(i)$ is the remaining frames to be encoded in the ith GOP and $A(i,j-1)$ is the actual coding bit rate of $j-1^{th}$ frame.

The virtual buffer level is increased by adding the actual bits produced by the jth frame in the ith GOP and decreased by draining the bits from the virtual buffer using (14). If the virtual buffer level is too high, we start the frame-skipping control mechanism. The frames will be skipped until the virtual buffer level is under a safe level. The buffer condition is expressed as follows:

$$B_l(i,j) < \rho \times B_s(i,j) \tag{14}$$

where ρ is a constant and its typical value is 0.8.

Also, if buffer overflow occurs, the target buffer level $TB_l(i,j)$ will be recalculated using the following equation:

$$TB_l(i,j) = B_l(i,j-N_{skipped}) - \frac{T_{rate_{smoothed}}}{F_r} \times N_{skipped} \tag{15}$$

where $N_{skipped}$ is the number of skipped frames after the frame-skipping control is started.

4 Simulation

Numerical experiments have been conducted to evaluate the performance of our proposed rate control algorithm in this section. We implement the proposed rate control algorithm in a MPEG-4 video encoder. Then, we compare the rate control scheme proposed by [1] and SARS. In our simulation results, SARS controls the coding bit rate more accurately and keep the buffer level closer to its target. Also, the perceptual quality is improved using *SARS*.

4.1 Performance Evaluation of SARS Under CBR and VBR

In this simulation, we consider a video sequence "Mobile" in this scenario. The size of the video sequence is CIF(352x288). The frame rate is 30 fps. This video sequence is coded by the unit of GOP. The length of a GOP is 60. The predefined quantization parameter for I-frame is 15. The experimental results are discussed in the following subsections.

CBR-256kbps. Because of page limits, we only show the PSNR results here. In fig. 3, we show the PSNR results of each frame and each GOP. It can be seen clearly that the frames are started to be skipped in the first GOP and the skipping frame can't be stopped by using Li's scheme. It is noted that by using Li's scheme, there are 38 frames skipped, while there are 15 frames skipped by using *SARS*. The overall performance of *SARS* is still better than Li's scheme.

VBR-256kbps. In VBR scenario, we experiment the *SARS* over tcp-friendly congestion control protocols. The target coding bit rate of the test video sequence are given in fig. 4. The frame rate is 30 and the GOP length is 60. The experimental results are shown in fig. 5.

It can be seen clearly that, for Li's scheme, the average PSNR of GOP is much lower than that in *SARS* due to more skipped frames in Li's scheme. It is noted that by using Li's scheme, there are 17 frames skipped, while there are 9 frames skipped by using *SARS*. It can be seen clearly that, for Li's scheme, the average PSNR of third GOP is higher than that in *SARS* due to the high control error of coding bit rate at 130th frame. However, the overall performance of *SARS* is still better than Li's scheme.

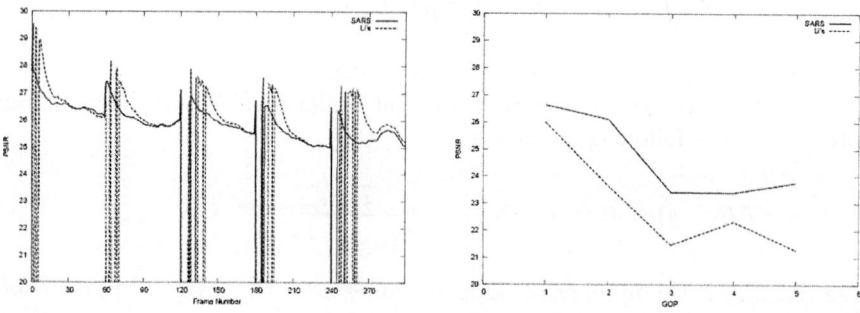

Fig. 3. PSNR results of each frame and each GOP for video sequence Mobile" in CBR scenario

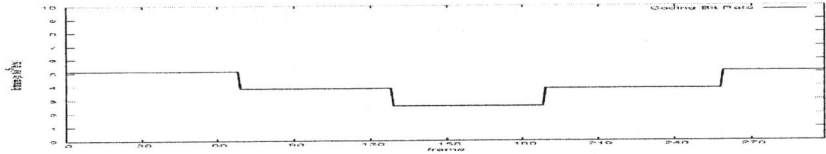

Fig. 4. Target bit rate for encoding

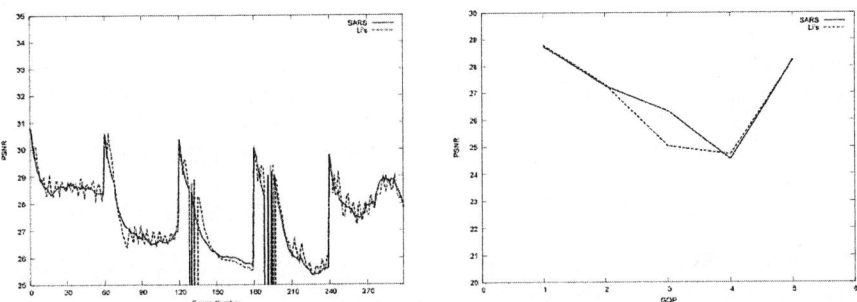

Fig. 5. PSNR results of each frame and each GOP for video sequence Mobile" in VBR scenario

5 Conclusion

In this paper, we propose a novel protocol for MPEG-4 video streaming system, called SARS. In our simulations, we have shown the performance of SARS is better than Li's solution either in CBR or in VBR. And, the transmission delay is shorter and smoother than Li's solution, the PSNR is also better than Li's solution.

Although our solution is successful to reduce the frame-dropping rate and obtain the better performance, there is still some problems when a real-time video streaming over a lossy link. As mentioned in Section I and Section II, over a lossy link, the error control schemes are required to reduce the effects of packet losses and then to incrase the quality of video streaming. The continuous efforts will address the issue.

References

1. Z. G. Li, C. Zhu, N. Ling, X. K. Yang, G. N. Feng, S. Wu, and F. Pan, "A Unified Architecture for Real-Time Video-Coding Systems", IEEE Trans. Circuits Syst. Video Technol., vol 13, pp. 472-487, June 2003.
2. Z. He, Y.-K. Kim, and Sanjit K. Mitra, "Low-Delay Rate Control for DCT Video Coding via ρ-Doamin Source Modeling", IEEE Trans. Circuits Syst. Video Technol., vol 11, pp. 928-940, Aug. 2001.
3. Z. He and Sanjit K. Mitra, "A Linear Source Model and a Unified Rate Control Algorithm for DCT Video Coding", IEEE Trans. Circuits Syst. Video Technol., vol 12, pp. 970-982, Nov. 2002.

4. H. Shojania and B. Li, "Experiences with MPEG-4 Multimedia Streaming", ACM Multimedia, pp. 492-494, 2001.
5. B. Braden, D. Clark, J. Crowcroft, B. Davie, S. Deering, D. Estrin, S. Floyd, V. Jacobson, G. Minshall, C. Partridge, L. Peterson, K. Ramakrishnan, S. Shenker, J. Wroclawski, and L. Zhang, "Recommendations on Queue Management and Congestion Avoidance in the Internet", RFC 2309, Informational, Apr. 1998.
6. G. Carle and E. W. Biersack, "Survey of Error Recovery Techniques for IP-based Audio-Visual Multicast Applications", IEEE Networks, vol. 11, no. 6, pp. 24-36, Nov. 1997.
7. U. Horn, K. Stuhlmüller, M. Link, and B. Girod, "Robust Internet Video Transmission Based on Scalable Coding And Unequal Error Protection", Signal Processing: Image Communication, vol.15, no. 1-2, pp. 77-94, Sept. 1999.
8. C.-H. Wang, R.-I Chang, J.-M. Ho, S.-C. Hsu, "Rate-Sensitive ARQ for Real-time Video Streaming", in Proc. GLOBECOM'03, San Francisco, USA, Dec. 2003.
9. L. Chiariglione, "MPEG-4 FAQs", Technical report, ISO/IEQ JTC1/SC29/WG11, July 1997.
10. ISO/IEC JTC1/SC29/WG11, "Overview of the MPEG-4 Standard", N4668, Mar. 2002.
11. ISO/IEC JTC1/SC29/WG11, "Information Technology - Coding of Audiovisual Objects - Part 2: Visual", N2502, FDIS 14496-2.
12. MPEG Homepage, http://www.cselt.it/mpeg/.
13. ISO/IEC, "MPEG-4 Video, Proposed Draft Amendment (PDAM), FGS v.4.0", 14496-2, Mar. 2000.
14. D. T. Hoang and J. S. Vitter, "Efficient Algorithm for MPEG Video Compression", Wiley-Interscience Inc. Sep. 2001.
15. T. Chiang and Y.-Q. Zhang, "A New Rate Control Scheme Using Quadratic Rate Distortion Model", IEEE Trans. Circuits Syst. Video Technol., vol 7, pp. 246-250, Feb. 1997.
16. Jordi Ribas-Corbera and Shawmin Lei, "Rate Control in DCT Video Coding for Low-Delay Communications", IEEE Trans. Circuits Syst. Video Technol., vol. 9, pp. 172-185, Feb. 1999.
17. H.-J. Lee, T. Chiang, and Y.-Q. Zhang, "Scalable Rate Control for MPEG-4 Video", IEEE Trans. Circuits Syst. Video Technol., vol. 10, pp. 878-894, Sept. 2000.
18. Z. Lei and N. D. Georganas, "Rate Adaptaion Transcoding for Precoded Video Streams", in Proc. ACM Multimedia'02, Juan-les-Pins, France, Dec. 2002.
19. Z.G. Li, N. Ling, G. N. Feng, F. Pan, K. P. Lim, and S. Wu, "Adaptive Rate Control For Real Time Video Coding Process", in Proc. DCV'02, Clearwater, Florida, Nov. 2002.
20. A. Vetro, H. Sun, and Y. Wang, "MPEG-4 Rate Control for Multiple Video Objects", IEEE Trans. Circuits Syst. Video Technol., vol. 9, pp. 186-199, Feb. 1999.
21. ISO/IEC JTC1/SC29/WG11, "MPEG-4 Video Verification Model Version 18.0", N4350, July 2001.
22. F. Pan, Z. Li, K. Lim, and G. Feng, "A Study of MPEG-4 Rate Control Scheme and Its Improvements", IEEE Trans. Circuits Syst. Video Technol., vol 13, pp. 440-446, May 2003.

Evaluation of a Crossover Router Based QoS Mechanism in Fast Mobile IPv6 Networks*

Zheng Wan, Zhengyou Wang, Zhijun Fang, Weiming Zeng, and Shiqian Wu

College of Information Management, Jiangxi University of Finance and Economics,
Nanchang, P.R. China, 330013
zhengwan66@yahoo.com.cn

Abstract. A "Crossover Router" (CR) based QoS provisioning mechanism under an enhanced "Fast Handovers for Mobile IPv6" (FMIPv6) architecture has been proposed to provide better performance for multimedia applications in Mobile IPv6 (MIPv6) networks. In the proposal we extend the FBU and HI messages to notify the QoS requirement of "Mobile Node" (MN). Advance reservations along the possible future-forwarding paths are performed only between CR and MN to reduce reservation hops and signaling delays. In this paper we present the detailed performance evaluation results of this scheme compared with "Mobile RSVP" (MRSVP) protocol, using the network simulator (NS-2). In the simulations RSVP signaling cost, total bandwidth requirements, RSVP signaling and data packet delay in different scenarios of both schemes were considered. Results show that the proposed scheme for QoS guarantee has lower RSVP signaling cost and delay, as well as less bandwidth requirements in comparison with MRSVP. Furthermore, fluctuation and peak values of data packet delays in different scenarios are much lower.

1 Introduction

Mobile IPv6 (MIPv6) protocol [1] was proposed to manage mobility and maintain network connectivity in the next generation Internet. However, the handover latency and packet loss in basic MIPv6 protocol are not ideal, which raises the need for a fast and smooth handover mechanism. A number of ways of introducing hierarchy into MIPv6 networks, and realizing the advanced configuration have been proposed in the last few years [2-4]. On the other hand, QoS requirements should be satisfied for multimedia applications, such as bandwidth and delay requirements.

We have proposed a scheme [5] for QoS provisioning in an enhanced *"Fast Handovers for Mobile IPv6"* (FMIPv6) architecture [2]. We introduce the *Crossover Router* (CR) to reduce tunnel distance between the Previous Access Router (PAR) and the New Access Router (NAR). CR is the first common router of the old path and the new forwarding path. As for QoS guarantee, we define extended FBU and HI messages to inform the NAR of the MN's QoS requirement. Upon receiving the

---

* This work was supported by Jiangxi University of Finance & Economics Innovation Fund.

information, the NAR initiates an advance reservation process along the possible future-forwarding path before the MN arrives the NAR's link. Again the CR is used to reduce the length of reservation path.

In this paper we present detailed simulation results based on the *Network Simulator* (NS-2) [11]. Experiments were designed to achieve evaluation results in RSVP signaling cost and delay, required bandwidth, and data packets delay in different scenarios, compared with *Mobile Resource reSerVation Protocol* (MRSVP) [6].

The rest of the paper is organized as follows. Section 2 discusses some wireless QoS techniques. Next we describe the novel QoS provisioning scheme. Simulation configuration and numerical results are presented in section 4 and section 5 respectively. And Section 6 concludes the paper and presents future work.

2 Wireless QoS Techniques

Due to host mobility and characteristics of wireless networks, there are several problems in applying RSVP to mobile wireless networks. In the past several years many RSVP extensions were proposed to solve the problems. Talukdar et al. [6] proposed the MRSVP protocol in which resource reservations are pre-established in the neighboring ARs to reduce the timing delay for QoS re-establishment. However, too many advance reservations may use up network resources.

Chaskar et al. [7] proposed a solution to perform QoS signaling during the binding registration process. This mechanism defines the structure of *"QoS OBJECT"* which contains the QoS requirement of MN's packet stream. One or more QoS OBJECTs are carried in a new IPv6 option called *"QoS OBJECT OPTION"* (QoS-OP), which may be included in the hop-by-hop extension header of binding update and acknowledgement messages.

Moon et al. [8] explained the concept of CR, which is the beginning router of the common path. And the common path is the overlapped part of the new path and previous path. Fig. 1 presents an example of the common path and the CR. Shen et al. [9] presented an interoperation framework for RSVP and MIPv6 based on the "Flow Transparency" concept, which made use of common path by determining the "Nearest Common Router" (just like CR). In both schemes the CR ensures that reservation will not be re-established in the routers along common path. Thus the QoS signaling overheads and delays as well as data packet delays and losses during handover can be significantly reduced.

3 Proposed Architecture

3.1 Enhancement for FMIPv6

First let's define some abbreviations: CN denotes *"Correspondent Node"*, PAR denotes *"Previous Access Router"*, and NAR denotes *"New Access Router"*. Assuming that we have determined the location of CR, data forwarding path using the bi-directional tunnel of FMIPv6 would be CN-CR-PAR-CR-NAR. Obviously we can

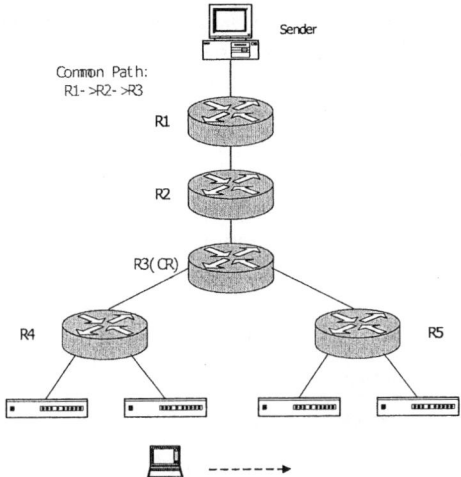

Fig. 1. Common Path and Crossover Router (CR)

shorten the path to CN-CR-NAR. Though the bi-directional tunnel is eliminated, a unidirectional tunnel from PAR to NAR is still included. When tunneling process begins, the PAR sends a TUN_BEGIN message which enables the CR to intercept the packets destined to the MN's PCoA and forward them to the NAR. In the opposite direction, the NAR directly sends packets with the CN's address filled in the destination address field. With the binding of PCoA and NCoA the CR intercepts these packets, sets the source address field to the MN's PCoA and forwards them to the CN. A further modification to the basic FMIPv6 is the elimination of DAD procedure. We adopt the method of "Address Pool based Stateful NCoA Configuration" [10]. The NCoA pools are established at NAR or PAR. Each NCoA pool maintains a list of NCoAs already confirmed by the corresponding NAR. Thus the NCoA assigned to the MN at each handover event is already confirmed so that the DAD procedure can be ignored.

3.2 Mechanisms for QoS Guarantee

Now come to the part of QoS guarantee. As we know in FMIPv6 architecture, the NCoA is pre-established. Thus we can set up reservation along several possible future-forwarding paths (one or more NARs may be detected in FMIPv6) in advance when the MN still locates in the PAR's link. Just like MRSVP, *active* and *passive* Path/Resv messages and reservations are defined in our proposal. The NAR, which makes advance reservation and maintains soft state on behalf of the MN, acts as *remote mobile proxy*. To inform the NAR of the MN's QoS requirements, we extend the FBU and HI messages with QoS-OP [7] in the hop-by-hop extension header.

Then we can initiate advance reservation along possible future path. Since there may be more than one NARs detected by the MN, all the possible future-forwarding paths must perform advance reservation. If the MN is a receiver, the CR issues the *passive Path* message to the NAR on behalf of the CN and the NAR in turn sends the *passive Resv* message to the CR. If the MN is a sender, the NAR issues the passive

Path message. Upon receiving Path message, the CR immediately replies with a passive Resv message to the NAR. By performing these operations, the passive RSVP messages are restricted within the truly new part of the possible future path, which results in decreased RSVP signaling overheads and delays.

When the MN attaches to certain NAR's link, the packets sent from or destined to it can acquire QoS guarantee without any delay. At the same time advance reservations in other NARs' link must be released immediately. The modified FMIPv6 handover and resource reservation procedures when the MN acts as a receiver are depicted in Fig. 2.

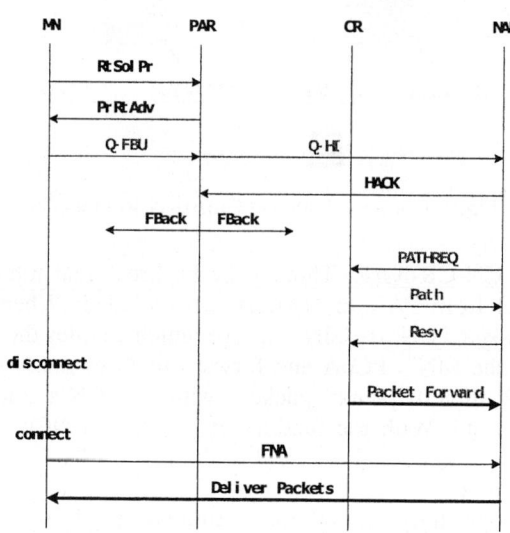

Fig. 2. Handover and Reservation Procedures of a Mobile Receiver

3.3 Determination of CR

The mechanism to decide if a RSVP router is CR is similar to that of reference [9]. When MN acts as the sender, a binding of PCoA and NCoA is also included in a hop-by-hop extension header of the passive Path message issued by NAR. A RSVP router compares the home address, the NCoA and the previous RSVP hop carried in the passive Path message against the same information stored in the Path State. If there is a Path state related to the home address of passive Path message, and for the same home address both the CoA and the previous RSVP hop have been changed, then the router decides it is the CR.

If MN is a receiver, the NAR will send a PATHREQ message which has the CN's address as destination address (thus the CR can intercept this message) to request passive Path message. The PATHREQ message, which contains MN's home address and new CoA as introduced in [9], is extended to include the binding of PCoA and NCoA. A RSVP router decides if it is the CR by searching the home address in

PATHREQ against the same field in PATH state on the downlink direction. If there is a match of the home address in the Path State in the downlink direction, then the router decides it is the CR.

3.4 Detailed Operations

First of all, we assume that the MN moves into the boundary of the PAR so that the fast handover procedure launches. The procedures of proposed fast handover and resource reservation are as follows:

1) The MN discovers available APs using link-layer specific mechanisms and then sends a *Router Solicitation for Proxy* (RtSolPr) message including the identifiers of the APs to the PAR.
2) After the reception of the RtSolPr message, the PAR resolves the access point identifiers to subnet router(s) (i.e. the [AP-ID, AR-Info] tuples). Though several NARs may be discovered, the following description will just focus on the operations of certain NAR. Using the *"PAR-based stateful NCoA configuration"* proposed in [10], the PAR obtains a confirmed NCoA and responds the NCoA as well as the [AP-ID, AR-Info] tuple (via PrRtAdv) to MN.
3) In response to the PrRtAdv message, the MN sends a *Q-FBU* message to the PAR before its disconnection from the PAR's link. The Q-FBU message includes a QoS-OP (contains one or more QoS OBJECTs) in the hop-by-hop extension header. The QoS OBJECT may contain RSVP objects such as FLOW_SPEC, SENDER_TSPEC and FILTER_SPEC.
4) On reception of the Q-FBU message, the PAR again includes the MN's QoS requirement in the *Q-HI* message and sends it to the NAR. The Q-HI message should also contain the CN address corresponding to each QoS OBJECT, which will be used as the destination address of the *PATHREQ* message when the MN acts as a receiver.

Case 1. When the MN acts as a sender,

5a) The NAR directly issues the passive Path message. Mechanism mentioned in the last section is used to locate a CR. The CR does not forward the Path message further to the CN, but immediately replies with a passive Resv message to the NAR. By performing these operations, the RSVP states in the routers along the common path will not change. Fig. 3a describes the advance reservation process when the MN acts as the sender.

Case 2. Otherwise, the MN acts as a receiver,

5b) The NAR sends a PATHREQ message to the CN's address. When a RSVP router detects that it is the CR, it then issues the passive Path message to the NAR on behalf of the CN because the path between the CR and the CN is the common path and needn't any change. Finally the NAR will issue the passive Resv message towards the CR. Fig. 3b depicts the advance reservation process when the MN acts as the receiver.

6) At the same time as advance reservation process initiates, the NAR replies with a HACK message to the PAR, which may in turn issue the FBack message. The PAR may ignore sending this message because the NCoA is already confirmed.
7) When packet tunneling launches, the PAR will send a *TUN_BEGIN* message which has the CN's address as destination address. Upon receiving this message the CR begins to intercept packets destined to the PCoA and forward them to the NAR. Reversely, the NAR directly sends packets with the CN's address filled in the destination address field. The CR intercepts these packets, sets the source address field to the MN's PCoA and forwards them to the CN.
8) As soon as the MN attaches to the NAR, it sends the FNA message to the NAR. As a response, the NAR forwards buffered packets to the MN.

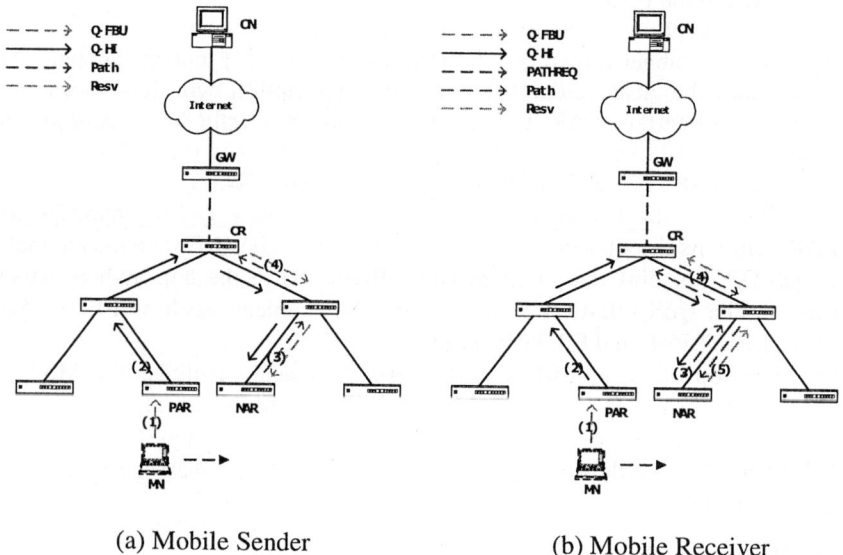

(a) Mobile Sender   (b) Mobile Receiver

Fig. 3. Procedures of Advance Resource Reservation

Finally, the MN will send a binding update to HA and CN. After it completes binding update, the CR stops intercepting packets sent from or destined to the MN. The packets will be forwarded with QoS guarantee along the new RSVP path.

4 Simulation Configuration

In this section we compare our CR-based handover and QoS provisioning scheme (abbreviated as C-FMIPv6) with basic FMIPv6 using MRSVP as resource reservation mechanism (abbreviated as M-FMIPv6). We present a little modification to MRSVP to adopt it in FMIPv6. The process of advance reservation will be launched after the MN have received PrRtAdv message and only be performed along the possible future-forwarding paths. Thus MRSVP can make use of advantages achieved from handover procedures of FMIPv6. We focus on the case when MN acts as a receiver.

The simulation is based on ns-2 version 2.27 [11]. The handover code used for the experiments was designed on top of INRIA/Motorola MIPv6 for ns-2.27 [12]. We have extended it with C-FMIPv6 implementation. And we implemented procedures of advance reservation on the basis of "RSVP/ns for ns-2.27" [13], both for M-FMIPv6 and our C-FMIPv6.

Fig. 4 shows the studied network topology. Eight wireless micro-cellular based Local Area Networks are connected by a two-level hierarchy of intermediate routers to the CN. Each cell represents a different IP subnet and has a base station (acts as AR). As for wireless medium, ns-2 provides the 2Mbps Wireless LAN 802.11 standard. The transmission range of the base stations is 250 meters. All these nodes are deployed in an area of approximately 1600×1600 square meters. The MN moves directly from the coverage area of cell 1 to that of cell 8 at 1s. It performs handover every 3 seconds. We choose such a small handover interval in order to obtain a clear figure of data packet delay (Fig. 8).

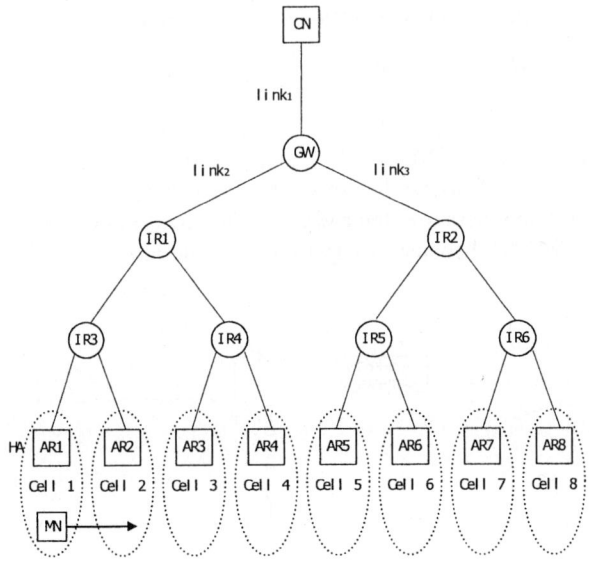

Fig. 4. Network Topology of Simulation

When the simulation starts, the CN generates eight best-effort background flows, each to a randomly selected base station. These flows are exponential On/Off flows with an average of 1s and 0.5s for the burst time and idle time respectively. The packet size is 500 bytes and the peak rate is 500kbps. These flows are used for congestion generation with certain limited bandwidths provision. The real-time traffic flow is a 500kbps UDP/CBR flow with packet size of 500 bytes, from the CN to the MN.

5 Numerical Results

Fig. 5 shows the comparison of registration cost. From the figure we can find that registration cost in C-FMIPv6 is mainly determined by the location of CR. The gateway router (GW) acts as the CR when the MN performs handover from cell 4 to cell 5 at 19s. QoS related messages travel the longest distance in this case. Signaling messages for resource reservation include Q-FBU, Q-HI, PATHREQ, Path and Resv messages. Let s_a denote the average size of these messages. The RSVP signaling cost can be computed as follows.

$$C_{C-FMIPv6} = s_a \times (d_{MN\_PAR} + d_{PAR\_NAR} + 3 \times d_{NAR\_CR}) \times N_n \quad (1)$$

where N_n is the number of possible NARs in FMIPv6, and d_{x_y} is the number of hops between x and y.

In M-FMIPv6, Spec, MSpec, Path, active Resv and passive Resv message are the signaling messages. In this paper we consider the scenario that the sender acts as the *receiver_anchor* node [6]. All messages of MRSVP except *Spec* message are always forwarded between the CN and AR, which causes larger cost than C-FMIPv6 and slight difference of registration cost among different handovers.

$$C_{M-FMIPv6} = s_a \times (d_{PAR\_NAR} \times N_n + d_{PAR\_CN} + 2d_{NAR\_CN} \times (N_n + 1)) \quad (2)$$

Fig. 6 shows required bandwidth of advance reservation. Since the duration of advance reservations of C-FMIPv6 is much shorter than that of M-FMIPv6 as described in section 2, C-FMIPv6 has lower bandwidth requirement. Furthermore, the results of different handovers are determined by the location of CR in C-FMIPv6 and are similar in M-FMIPv6 because reservation is made along the whole path between CN and NAR.

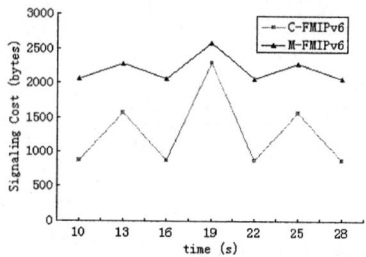 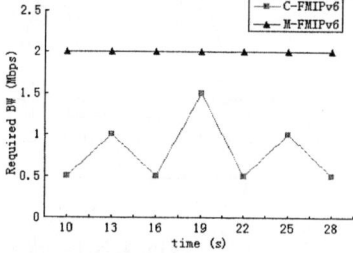

Fig. 5. RSVP Signaling Cost   **Fig. 6.** Required Bandwidth

Then we compare the *RSVP signaling delay* of both schemes. The "Internet" link between the CN and the GW ($link_1$) is given a delay of 30ms to model an Internet connection. All other links are given a delay of 5ms. We introduce four scenarios to model non-congestion and three congestion environments.

Scenario I. Both parts of the networks have sufficient bandwidth so that no traffic congestion happens. In this scenario all other links are given 10Mbps bandwidth.

Scenario II. The edge network has sufficient bandwidth and traffic congestion happens at the core network, i.e. $link_1$. In this scenario, $link_1$ is given 2Mbps and all other links 10Mbps bandwidth.

Scenario III. The core network has sufficient bandwidth and traffic congestion happens at the edge network. In this scenario $link_1$ is given 10Mbps and all other links 1Mbps bandwidth.

Scenario IV. Traffic congestion happens at both parts of the networks. In this scenario link1 is given 2Mbps and all other links 1Mbps bandwidth.

Fig. 7 (a) shows the comparison of RSVP signaling delay without congestion in any link. In C-FMIPv6 passive Path and Resv messages only traverse between CR and AR. However, messages of M-FMIPv6 must travel from the CN to AR through the Internet link—$link_1$. Thus delays of our C-FMIPv6 are relatively lower than that of M-FMIPv6. In Scenario II, $link_1$ is congestion link and the place where Path message must traverse. The Path message delay incurred in $link_1$ can be approximated as follows:

$$d_{path(link_1)} = \frac{s_{Path}}{bw_{RSVP}} \quad (3)$$

where bw_{RSVP} is the bandwidth reserved for RSVP messages to prevent them from getting lost in case of congestion and is set to 2000bps in our simulation.

Fig. 7 (c) depicts the situation that congestion happens at $link_2$ and $link_3$. We find that only handover at 19s incurs large delay in C-FMIPv6 for that passive Path message is sent from GW to AR5 through $link_3$. In other cases Path message will not travel the congestion link. However, Path message has to traverse $link_2$ or $link_3$ during each handover operation in M-FMIPv6. Thus RSVP signaling delay is significantly larger.

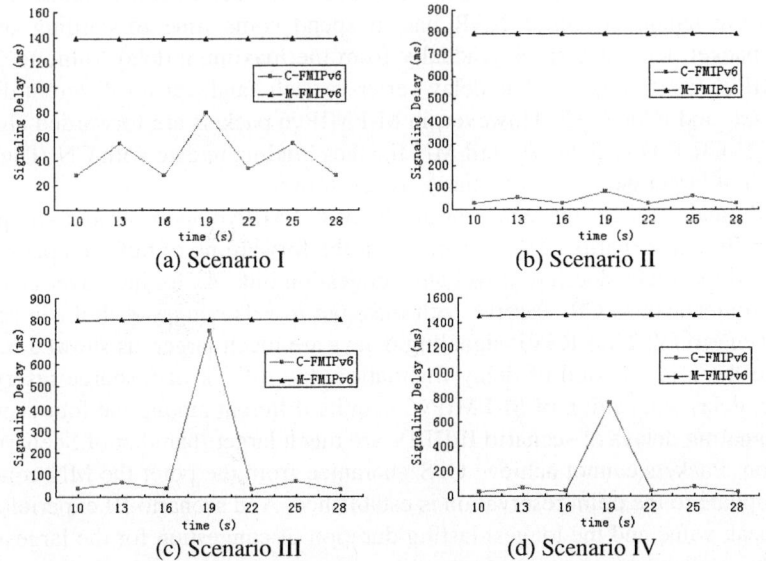

Fig. 7. RSVP Signaling Delay in Different Scenarios

Delays of M-FMIPv6 in Fig. 7 (d) are approximately twice than those in Fig. 7 (c) because both $link_1$ and $link_2$/$link_3$ are congestion links. However, delays of C-FMIPv6 in scenario IV are approximately equal to those in scenario III.

Table 1 shows the percentage reduction of RSVP signaling delay obtained by our C-FMIPv6. From the table we find that the percentage reduction of the reservation signaling delay of C-FMIPv6 over M-FMIPv6 ranges from 42.7% to 79.6% when no congestion occurs. When congestion happens only at the Internet link, percentage reduction range from 90.0% to 96.4%. In Scenario III and IV, the value range from 91.4% to 97.8% except for handover at 19s.

Table 1. Reduction in RSVP Signaling Delay

	Scenario I	Scenario II	Scenario III	Scenario IV
10s	79.6%	96.4%	95.2%	97.7%
13s	61.3%	93.2%	92.1%	95.7%
16s	79.7%	96.4%	95.2%	97.2%
19s	42.7%	90.0%	6.4%	48.2%
22s	75.4%	96.4%	95.9%	97.4%
25s	61.3%	92.5%	91.4%	95.3%
28s	79.6%	96.4%	96.0%	97.8%

Fig. 8 presents comparison result of data packet delay. According to simulation configuration, data packet delays without handover operations in four scenarios are approximately 51.6ms, 59.2ms, 66.4ms, and 74ms respectively. We notice that difference among four scenarios is little in C-FMIPv6 while simulation results vary in M-FMIPv6. In Scenario I, buffering at NAR until MN arrives causes relatively large delay during handover. Since NAR has to spend some time forwarding buffered packets, packet delay decreases gradually from the maximum delay value to 51.6ms in C-FMIPv6, as (b) depicts. The delay varies in each handover for different distance between CR and PAR/NAR. However, in M-FMIPv6 packets are forwarded along the path of CN-CR-PAR-CR-NAR until MN finishes binding update with CN. Thus there is a period of larger delay (than 51.6ms), as (a) shows.

All the handovers except handover at 19s of C-FMIPv6 show similar sharp delay pulse in different scenarios. The reason is that the forwarding of buffered packets and QoS related messages does not travel any congestion link. As for handover at 19s, the gateway router acts as CR. Passive path message travels congested $link_3$ in scenario III and scenario IV. Thus RSVP signaling delays are much larger, as showed in Fig.8. Therefore there is a period of delay fluctuation due to lack of resource reservation. However, delay fluctuation of M-FMIPv6 is quite different among the four scenarios. RSVP signaling delays of scenario II/III/IV are much larger than that of Scenario I for congestion. Packets cannot achieve QoS guarantee from the point the MN completes binding update to the point reservation is established. And scenario III experiences the highest peak value and the longest lasting duration of congestion for the largest delay of RSVP signaling.

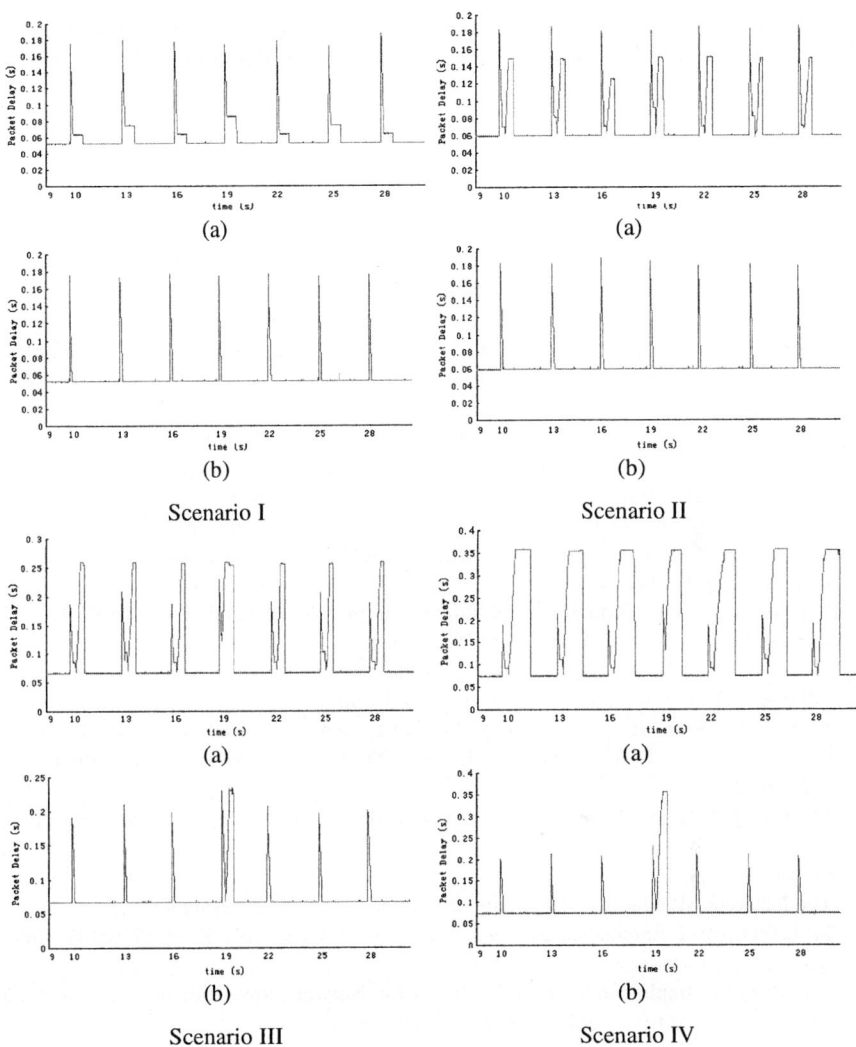

Fig. 8. Packet Delay in Different Scenarios for (a) M-FMIPv6; (b) C-FMIPv6

6 Conclusion

This paper presents performance evaluation of a novel crossover router based QoS guarantee scheme in an enhanced FMIPv6 architecture. Simulations are performed in network simulator (NS-2). Results show that the novel scheme has better performance over the simple combination of MRSVP and FMIPv6 in RSVP signaling cost and delay, bandwidth requirement, and data packets delay of four different scenarios.

When and how to release passive reservations on other NARs' link after the MN attaches to certain NAR's link, should be considered. And we are trying to establish a testbed in which more experiments under various environments could be performed.

References

1. D. Johnson, C. Perkins, J. Arkko, "Mobility support in IPv6", IETF RFC 3775, June 2004.
2. R. Koodli (Ed.), "Fast Handovers for Mobile IPv6", Internet Draft, IETF, draft-ietf-mipshop-fast-mipv6-03.txt, October 2004.
3. H. Soliman, C. Castelluccia, K. El-Malki, L. Bellier, "Hierarchical Mobile IPv6 mobility management", Internet Draft, IETF, draft-ietf-mipshop-hmipv6-03.txt, October, 2004.
4. H.Y Jung, S.J. Koh, H. Soliman, K. El-Malki, "Fast Handover for Hierarchical MIPv6 (F-HMIPv6)", Internet Draft, draft-jungmobileip-fastho-hmipv6-04.txt, June 2004.
5. Z. Wan, X.Z. Pan, L.D. Ping, "QoS Provisioning in an Enhanced FMIPv6 Architecture", International Conference on Computational Science and its Applications (ICCSA'05), Lecture Notes in Computer Science, vol.3481, pp.704-713, May 2005.
6. A.K. Talukdar, B.R. Badrinath and A. Acharya, "MRSVP: A resource reservation protocol for an integrated services network with mobile hosts", Journal of Wireless Networks, vol.7, iss.1, pp.5-19 (2001).
7. H. Chaskar, and R. Koodli, "QoS support in mobile IP version 6", IEEE Broadband Wireless Summit (Networld+Interop), May 2001.
8. B. Moon and A.H. Aghvami, "Quality of service mechanisms in all-IP wireless access networks", IEEE Journal on Selected Areas in Communications, June 2004.
9. Q. Shen, W. Seah, A. Lo, H. Zheng, M. Greis, "An interoperation framework for using RSVP in mobile IPv6 networks", Internet Draft, draft-shen-rsvp-mobileipv6-interop-00.txt, July 2001.
10. Hee Young Jung, Seok Joo Koh, Dae Young Kim, "Address Pool based Stateful NCoA Configuration for FMIPv6", Internet Draft, draft-jung-mipshop-stateful-fmipv6-00.txt, August 2003.
11. "The Network Simulator - NS (version 2)", http://www.isi.edu/nsnam/ns/
12. "MobiWan: ns-2 Extensions to Study Mobility in Wide-Area IPv6 Networks (for ns-2 2.27)", http://www.ti-wmc.nl/mobiwan2/
13. "RSVP/ns: An Implementation of RSVP for the Network Simulator ns-2 (for ns-2 2.27)", http://www.cc.jyu.fi/~sayenko/pages/en/projects.htm

Adaptive and QoS Downlink Multimedia Packet Scheduling for Broadband Wireless Systems

Seungwan Ryu[1,2], Byunghan Ryu[2], and Hyunhwa Seo[2]

[1] Deaprtment of Information Systems, Chung-Ang University,
72-3 Naeri, Ansung, Kyungki-Do, 456-756, Korea
rush2384@cau.ac.kr
[2] Broadband Mobile MAC team, ETRI, 61 Gajong-Dong,
Yusung-Gu, Taejon 305-350, Korea

Abstract. In this paper, we propose an adaptive urgency and efficiency based packet scheduling (A-UEPS) algorithm that is to designed to maximize throughput of non-real-time (NRT) traffics as long as QoS requirements of real-time (RT) traffics such as the packet delay and the loss rate requirements are satisfied. In addition, the A-UEPS algorithm provides trade-off between performance objectives of RT and NRT traffics adaptively by adjusting scheduling precedence of packets of RT and NRT traffics in accordance with the time-varying traffic situations such as the offered traffic load and traffic mix. Simulation study shows that A-UEPS algorithm results in efficient and adaptive scheduling performance under various traffic situations.

1 Introduction

Challenges on delivering quality of service (QoS) to users in packet based wireless networks have been watched with keen interest. The packet scheduler operates at the medium access control (MAC) layer is considered as the key component for QoS provisioning to users as well as in maximizing utilization of the limited radio resources. There are many existing packet scheduling algorithms designed to support data traffics in the third generation partnership project (3GPP) and 3GPP2 wireless systems. For the 3GPP2 system, Proportional Fair (PF) [1] and Modified-Largest weighted delay first (M-LWDF) [2] algorithms are designed mainly to support NRT data services in CDMA-1x-EVDO (HDR) system. In the 3GPP wideband-CDMA (WCDMA) system, only NRT data traffic classes such as the streaming, the interactive and the background traffic classes are subjects of scheduling, and transmitted on the common channel or the shared channel [3]. On the other hand, the conversational traffic class such as voice telephony and voice over IP (VoIP) traffic is transmitted on the dedicated channel (DCH) without scheduling.

In general, QoS requirements of RT and NRT traffics are different each other. RT traffics such as the voice and the video streaming traffics require a low and bounded delay but can tolerate some information loss. Thus, it is imperative for RT traffics to meet delay and loss requirements. In contrast, NRT data traffics require low information loss but less stringent delay requirements compared to the RT traffics. In addition, since the amount of NRT data traffics to be transmitted is much larger than that of RT traffic data, throughput maximization is the main performance measure for NRT data traffic. As a result, performance objectives of RT and NRT traffics to be achieved within a scheduler are conflicting each other.

In this paper, we propose *an adaptive urgency and efficiency based packet scheduling (A-UEPS)* algorithm that is designed to achieve two conflict objectives of RT and NRT traffics at the same time. The idea behind A-UEPS algorithm is to maximize throughput of NRT traffics as long as QoS requirements of RT traffics such as the packet delay and the loss rate requirements are satisfied. A-UEPS algorithm uses two scheduling factors, the *urgency* of scheduling and the *efficiency* of radio resource usage, to take the time-variant wireless channel condition and QoS requirements of each traffic into account for. In this approach, the time-utility function is used to represent the urgency of scheduling while the channel state is used to indicate efficiency of usage of the radio resource. Then, to make A-UEPS schedule packets of different traffic types adaptively to the dynamically changing traffic situations, the concept of the marginal scheduling time interval (MSTI) is introduced for RT traffics. As a result, A-UEPS algorithm is designed to be capable of supporting packets of RT and NRT traffics at the same time with giving adaptive trade-off between conflict performance objectives of RT and NRT traffics to the time-varying traffic situations.

This paper is organized as follows. In the next section, we introduce the OFDMA wireless system model and the structure of the UEPS algorithm. In section 3, we discuss scheduling approaches with time constraints including urgency of scheduling and the efficiency of radio resource usage. In section 4, we proposed the A-UEPS algorithm. In section 5, we evaluate performance of the A-UEPS algorithm via simulation study. Finally, we summarize this study.

2 System Model

We consider an OFDMA system with 20MHz of bandwidth. It is assumed that there are 1,536 subcarriers, and all subcarriers are shared by all users in a cell in terms of sub-channels, a subset of the subcarriers. We assume that there are 12 sub-channels and each sub-channel is a group of 128 subcarriers. It is also assumed that all subcarriers are used for data transmission for simplification, and subcarriers in each sub-channel are selected by a pre-determined random pattern. The modulation and coding scheme is determined by the prescribed adaptive modulation code (AMC) table based on the instantaneous signal-interference-ratio (SIR) of each sub-channel. A summary of system parameters is shown in Table 1.

The proposed packet scheduling system in a base station (BS) consists of three blocks: a packet classifier (PC), a buffer management block (BMB), and a packet scheduler (PS). The packet classifier classifies incoming packets according to their types (or userID) and QoS profiles, and sends them to buffers in BMB. The BMB maintains QoS statistics such as the arrival time and the

Table 1. A summary of OFDMA system parameters

Parameters	Value
Downlink channel bandwidth	20 MHz
OFDM symbol duration	100 μs
Total number of subcarriers	1536
Number of subcarriers per subchannel	128
Number of subchannels	12
frame/slit period	12 ms / 1 ms

delay deadline of each packet, the number of packets, and the head-of-line (HOL) delay in each buffer. Finally, the PS transmits packets to users according to the scheduling priority obtained using channel status reported by user equipments and QoS statistics maintained in BMB.

3 Scheduling with Timing Constraints

3.1 The Urgency of Scheduling

A time-utility function (TUF) of a delay-sensitive RT traffic can be expressed as a hard time-utility as shown in figure 1. On the other hand, TUF of an NRT traffic is a continuously decreasing function in delay, in that utility of an NRT traffic decreases slowly as delay increases. Among NRT traffics some has a (soft) deadline like WWW traffics as described in the righthand side of figure 1. On the other hand, some NRT traffics such as email and FTP traffics have much longer deadline or no deadline.

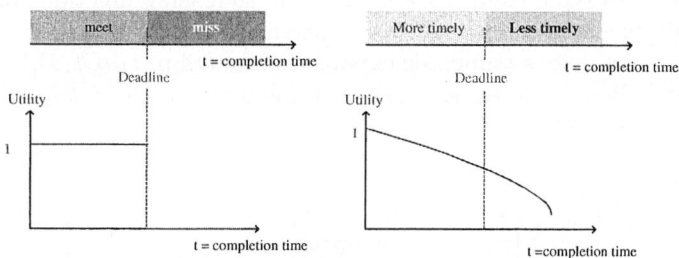

Fig. 1. Concepts of a hard and a soft deadlines and related time-utility functions

The unit change of TUF value at any time instant indicates the urgency of scheduling of packets as time passes by. Let $U_i(t)$ be the TUF of a HOL packet of traffic i at time t. Then the unit change of TUF value of the packet at time t is the absolute value of the first derivative of $U_i(t)$, i.e., $|U'_i(t)|$, at time t. A possible packet scheduling rule is to select a packet among HOL packets based on $|U'_i(t)|, \forall i \in I$.

Since the downlink between a BS and UEs is the last link to users, the end-to-end delay can be met as long as packets are delivered to UEs within the deadline. Hence the time interval of an RT traffic packet from its arrival time to its deadline, $[a_i, D_i] = [a_i, a_i + d_i]$, can be divided into two sub-intervals, $[a_i, D_i - j_i)$ and $[D_i - j_i, D_i]$ (so called *the marginal scheduling time interval (MSTI)*), by introducing a negative jitter from its deadline, where a_i, D_i, d_i and $0 \leq j_i < d_i$ are the arrival time, the delay deadline, the maximum allowable delay margin of the packet of an RT traffic i, and the delay jitter respectively. Then, packet of an RT traffic i is transmitted only during the time interval $[D_i - j_i, D_i]$, and NRT packets are transmitted during the remaining time interval, $[a_i, D_i - j_i)$.

To schedule the RT traffic packet during MSTI, a non-zero value is assigned to $|U'_i(t)|$ for this time interval and 0 for the remaining time interval. However, since the TUF of an RT traffic is a hard and discontinuous function in delay, the unit change of the utility, $|U'_i(t)|$, can not be obtained directly at its delay deadline. To address this problem, the TUF of an RT traffic can be relaxed into a continuous *z-shaped* function which has properties similar to the original hard discontinuous function. A z-shaped function relaxation of the TUF of an RT traffic can be easily obtained analytically using an s-shaped function having close relation with z-shaped function. For example, a z-shaped function can be obtained using the s-shaped sigmoid function, $f_{Sigmoid}(t, a, c) = 1/(1+e^{-a(t-c)})$, where a and c are parameters that determine slope and location of the inflection point of the function. Then, the relaxed z-shaped TUF function is $U_{RT}(t) = 1 - f_{Sigmoid}(t, a, c) = e^{-a(t-c)}/(1 + e^{-a(t-c)})$, and the unit change of utility of a RT traffic at the inflection point ($t = c$) is $|U'_{RT}(t = c)| = a/4$. This value is assigned as the urgency factor of an RT traffic packet during MSTI. Figure 2 describes examples of a generic hard TUF of an RT traffic and its z-shaped function relaxation. Then, we can obtain a non-zero $|U'_i(t)|$ value for MSTI from the relaxed TUF.

Since TUFs of NRT traffics are monotonic decreasing functions in time (delay), an analytic model can be easily obtained using related monotonic increasing functions. For example, a truncated exponential function, $f(a_i, t, D_i) = exp(a_i t)$, can be used, where a_i is an arbitrary parameter and $D_i \geq t \geq 0$ is the de-

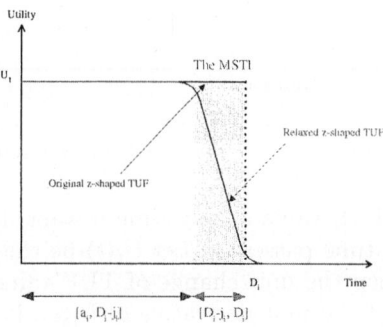

Fig. 2. An example of z-shaped function relaxation of a TUF of an RT traffic

lay deadline of an NRT traffic i. Then a possible TUF of an NRT traffic i is $f_{NRT_i}(t) = 1 - f(a_i, t, D_i) = 1 - exp(a_i t)/exp(D_i)^1$, and the urgency is $|U'_{NRT_i}(t)| = a_i exp(a_i t)/exp(D_i)$.

The urgency factor, $|U'_i(t)|$, of each traffic type is used to determine scheduling precedence among HOL packets, and choice of these values for each traffic type is dependent on designer's preference. A rule of thumb is to give RT traffics a higher scheduling precedence over NRT traffics. In this paper, we set the urgency factors of all traffic types in the order of RT voice, RT video, NRT traffics by setting urgency factors as follow.

$$|U'_{RT-Voice}(t)| > |U'_{RT-Video}(t)| > |U'_{NRT-Data1}(t)| > |U'_{NRT-Data2}(t)| \quad (1)$$

3.2 Efficiency of Radio Resource Usage

Efficiency in wireless communications is related to usage of the limited radio resources, i.e., the limited number of radio channels or limited bandwidth. Thus the channel state of available radio channels can be used as an efficiency indicator. For example, the current channel state ($R_i(t)$), the average channel state ($\overline{R_i}(t)$) or the ratio of the current channel state to the average ($R_i(t)/\overline{R_i}(t)$) can be used as an efficiency indicator. In this study, a moving average of the channel state of each user $i \in M$ in past W timeslots, $\overline{R_i}(t) = (1-1/W)\overline{R_i}+(1/W)R_i(t)$, is used for the average channel state, where W is the time window used in calculation of the moving average of the channel state. Note that $\overline{R_i}(t)$ used in our paper is different from the average throughput of user i, $T_i(t)$, in past t_c timeslots used in PF algorithm [1]. Therefore the higher the user's instantaneous channel quality relative to its average value, the higher the chance of a user to transmit data with a rate near to its peak value.

4 The Adaptive Urgency and Efficiency Based Packet Scheduling (A-UEPS) Algorithm

We propose *adaptive urgency and efficiency based packet scheduling (A-UEPS)* algorithm designed to address problems stemming from three characteristics of the packet based next generation wireless networks: 1) QoS requirements of each traffic class, 2) the time-variant nature of wireless channel condition, and 3) the dynamically changing traffic situation over time. A static-UEPS (S-UEPS) algorithm with fixed lengths of MSTI for RT traffics was proposed in [6] by using two factors, the urgency of scheduling and the efficiency of radio resource usage, to solve problems related with the first two characteristics. However, S-UEPS algorithm was not able to address problems caused by the time-varying traffic situations.

Since the traffic situations such as traffic load level of each traffic class and different traffic mix between RT and NRT traffics are varying dynamically with

---

[1] It is normalized by the maximum time, D_i, so that it can have smoother slope.

respect to time, it is necessary for a scheduler to response adaptively to the traffic situations. The A-UEPS algorithm adjusts lengths of MSTI of RT traffics adaptively to time-varying traffic situation, and thus it can give adaptive trade-off between two conflict performance objectives of RT and NRT traffics as a result. In detail, lengths of MSTI of RT traffics are adjusted adaptively to the changing RT traffic load to maintain QoS requirements of RT traffics such as delay and loss requirements within allowable ranges at the expense of throughput reduction of NRT traffics.

4.1 Update of the Length of MSTI

The A-UEPS algorithm updates lengths of MSTI of RT traffics periodically to the changing traffic situation. Changes on RT traffic load is monitored by observing changes on delay and loss rate. Then lengths of MSTI values are adjusted periodically to maintain the delay and the loss rate within desired ranges, $[Min_{delay}, Max_{delay}]$ and $[Min_{loss}, Max_{loss}]$, to meet QoS requirements of RT traffics, where $Min_{delay} \geq 0$, $Min_{loss} \geq 0$, Max_{delay} and Max_{loss} are lower and upper bounds of the desired ranges respectively. Lengths of MSTI values are updated at every T ms as follow

- When the delay (or loss rate) of an RT traffic, $delay_{RT}$ (or $loss_{RT}$), is increased above Max_{delay} (or Max_{loss}), this means that the traffic load of the RT traffic is increasing, and there is a high possibility of violating the delay (or loss) requirement. Then, the length of MSTI is increased by a certain amount, Δn.
- When $delay_{RT}$ (or $loss_{RT}$) is decreased below Min_{delay} (or Min_{loss}), this means that the traffic load of the RT traffic is decreasing, and the delay (or loss) of an RT traffic can be maintained with smaller MSTI value. Then, the length of MSTI is decreased by a certain amount, Δn.
- When $delay_{RT}$ (or $loss_{RT}$) is maintained between two threshold values of the desired range, i.e., $Min_{delay} < delay_{RT} < Max_{delay}$ (or $Min_{loss} < loss{RT} < Max_{loss}$), this means that the delay (or loss) requirement of an RT traffic can be maintained within its requirement with the current MSTI value.

4.2 The A-UEPS Algorithm

The A-UEPS algorithm operates at a BS in three steps; STEP 0 for packet arrival events, STEP 1 for scheduling priority of each user and STEP 2 for scheduling and transmission of packets.

- In **STEP 0**, the arrived packet is sent to a user's buffer by the packet classifier based on its userID. QoS profiles of the arrived packet such as the arrival time, the deadline, the packet type, and the packet size are maintained in BMB.
- In **STEP 1**, at each scheduling instant the urgency factor of HOL packets of each buffer, $|U'_i(t)|$, is calculated for representing the urgency factor of

user i, i.e., $|U'_i(t)|$. In addition, the efficiency factor of the user i, $\bar{R}_i(t) = \bar{R}_i(t-1)(1-1/W) + R_i(t)/W$, is obtained. Finally, the scheduling priority value of the user i is $p_i(t) = |U'_i(t)| * (R_i(t)/\bar{R}_i(t))$.
- In **STEP 2**, at each scheduling time instant, multiple users are selected based on their scheduling priority value obtained as follow

$$i^* = \arg\ \max_{i \in I} |U'_i(t)| \frac{R_i(t)}{\bar{R}_i(t)} \qquad (2)$$

Then, a sub-channel is allocated to each selected user i^*. The capacity of each allocated sub-channel is determined from the AMC option. Finally, the scheduler loads user i^*'s packets on the sub-channel as much as possible when there is room.

5 Performance Evaluation

5.1 Simulation Model and Traffic Environments

In the simulation study, it is assumed that there are four different traffic types, and each user generates one of four traffics. *RT voice* is assumed to be the voice on IP (VoIP) that periodically generate packets of fixed size. Assuming that silence suppression is used, voice traffic is modeled by a 2-state Markov (ON/OFF) model. The length of the ON and OFF periods follow the exponential distribution with mean of one second and 1.35 seconds respectively. *RT video* is assumed to be the RT video steaming service that periodically generate packets of variable sizes. We uses 3GPP streaming video traffic for this type of traffic [7]. Characteristics of an RT video traffic are shown in table 2.

We use WWW model for *NRT data service type 1* which requires wide bandwidth and variable sized bursty data. The WWW model was proposed to have a session consisting of several web pages which contains multiple packets or datagrams. Characteristics of WWW traffic model are summarized in table 3. Best effort such as emailing traffic is assumed to be the *NRT data type 2* with assuming that messages arrival to the mailboxes is modelled by Poisson process.

Table 2. A summary of characteristics of a real-time video traffic model

Characteristics	Distribution
Inter-arrival time between frames	Deterministic: 100ms
Number of packets/frame	Deterministic: 8
Packet size	Truncated Pareto Mean:50, Max.:125 (bytes)
Inter-arrival time between packets	Truncated Pareto Mean:6, Max:12.5 (ms)

Table 3. A summary of characteristics of WWW traffic model

Component	Distribution
Main Object size	Truncated Normal: μ:11Kbytes, σ: 25Kbytes Min.:100 bytes, Max: 2Mbytes
Embedded Object size	Truncated Normal: μ:8 Kbytes, σ:12Kbytes Min.:50 bytes, Max: 2Mbytes
Number of embedded objects	Truncated Pareto: μ: 5.64, σ: 53
Reading time	Exponential: μ=30 sec.
Parsing time	Exponential: μ=0.13 sec.

Table 4. A summary of simulation parameters for system model

Parameters	Value
User distribution	Uniform
Number of cells/layout	7/hexagonal
Beam pattern	Omni-directional
Radius of a cell	1km
Velocity of a MS	Uniform: 3 ~ 100 km/second
Path loss model[2]	$L = 128.1 + 37.6 log_{10} R$
BS total Tx power	12 W

We consider a hexagonal cell structure consisting of a reference cell and 6 surrounding cells with 1 km of radius. We assume that all cells use omni-directional antenna. UEs are uniformly distributed in a cell, and move with velocity of uniform distribution in a random direction. The BS transmission power is 12W which is evenly distributed to all 12 sub-channels. A summary of simulation parameters for system model is shown in Table 4.

5.2 Performance Metrics and Traffic Environments

Performance Metrics. In this study, we evaluate performance of A-UEPS, S-UEPS and M-LWDF algorithms in terms of several performance metrics, the packet loss rate and the average packet delay for RT traffics, and the transmission success probability (TSP) for NRT traffics, via simulation study. In order to examine performance of these algorithms under time-varying traffic situations, three different traffic load levels are generated within the same simulation run.

For NRT traffics, throughput is mainly used to evaluate performance in general. However, since transmission of NRT traffics under time-varying traffic situations is greatly dependent on lengths of MSTI of RT voice and video traffics, we evaluate performance of NRT traffics in terms of the transmission success probability (TSP) instead of throughput.

For RT traffics, the average packet delay is mainly used to evaluate performance. Although the RT traffic is tolerant to packet loss, it has maximum allowable packet loss rate. Therefore, performance of RT traffics is also evaluated in terms of the packet loss rate. QoS requirements of the RT voice and the video traffics [8] are

– RT Voice: delay < 40ms, loss rate < 3%
– RT Video: delay <150 ms, loss rate < 1%

QoS Parameters. To update of the MSTI of RT traffics, values of several parameters such as the length of update (T), threshold values of the delay (Max_{delay} and Min_{delay}) and loss rate (Max_{delay} and Min_{delay}) should be determined. In general, these values are determined by the designer's preference. We set T twice the length of the frame period, i.e., 24ms, and threshold values for delay and loss rate as follow.

– Delay: Voice: Max_{delay}=30ms, Min_{delay}=10ms,   Video: Max_{delay}=120ms, Min_{delay}=60ms,
– Loss rate: Voice: $Max_{loss} = 2.5\%$, $Min_{loss} = 1.0\%$,   Video: $Max_{loss} = 0.8\%$, $Min_{loss} = 0.2\%$,

Traffic Environments. Performance and adaptability of the A-UEPS algorithm has been examined extensively under various traffic situations from the light to the heavy traffic load situations via simulation study. In this paper, because of page limitation, we show adaptability of A-UEPS algorithm under the worst case traffic scenario where the offered traffic load is always higher than the scheduling capacity and varies abruptly with respect to time. In particular, we aim to show how the A-UEPS algorithm is successful in supporting QoS requirements of RT and NRT traffics with giving performance trade-off between two conflict objectives adaptively even under the worst traffic situation.

Since the scheduler selects 12 users at each timeslot, the number of users arrived in each timeslot is used as the offered traffic load (λ). Packets of four different traffic types are generated evenly from different users at the same time, but the traffic load varies with respect to time. The experiment begins with 12 arriving packets in average consisting of 3 RT voice, 3 RT video streaming, 3 WWW traffic, and 3 email packets in average. Thus, the initial offered traffic load is λ=1.0. Then, from time 2.0 sec., the traffic load becomes λ=2.0 consisting of 6 RT voice, 6 RT video streaming, 6 WWW traffic, and 6 email packets in average. Finally, at time 3.0 sec. the traffic load decreases to λ=1.5 consisting of 4 RT voice, 4 RT video streaming, 4 WWW traffic, and 4 email packets in average.

5.3 Performance Evaluation

Performance of RT traffics. Figure 3 shows the mean delay (left) and the packet loss rate (right) of voice traffic and the corresponding MSTI value in A-UEPS algorithm. When $\lambda = 1.0$, MSTI value is increased from 20 to 23 to maintain the mean delay and the packet loss rate within the desired ranges,

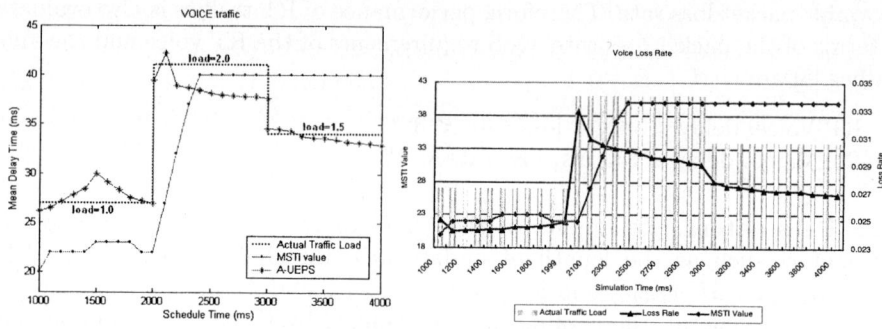

Fig. 3. Mean delay and loss rate of voice traffic with A-UEPS algorithm

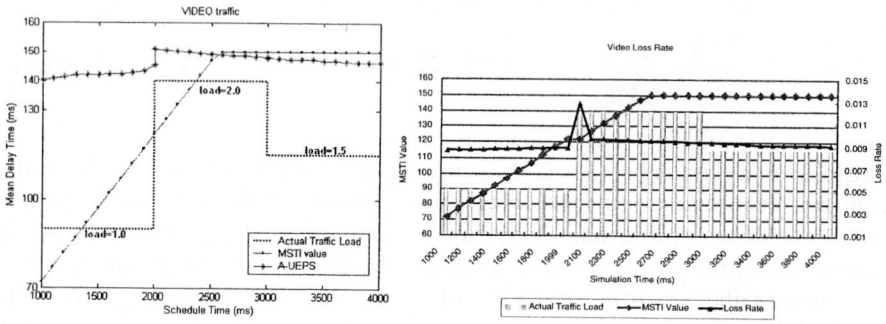

Fig. 4. Mean delay and loss rate of video traffic with A-UEPS algorithm

[10, 30]ms and [1.0, 2.5]%. During time interval [2.0, 3.0] second ($\lambda = 2.0$), MSTI value is increased rapidly and reaches its maximum value (40) at 2.4 sec. From this time, the mean delay is still maintained lower than 40ms although it is higher than Max_{delay} =30ms. On the other hand, the packet loss rate falls below 3%. After the traffic load is decreased to $\lambda = 1.5$ at time 3.0 sec., the mean delay and the loss rate are still maintained lower 40ms and 3%, although they are higher than Max_{delay} =30 ms and $Max_{loss} = 2.5\%$, respectively. However, the MSTI value remains at its maximum value (40) because it is designed to decrease by Δn only when the mean delay or the loss rate falls below the lower bound (10ms or 1%) of the desired range. In summary, the QoS requirements of the voice traffic such as the delay and the packet loss rate requirements are satisfied under the worst case traffic scenario.

Figure 4 shows the mean delay (left) and the loss rate (right) of video traffic and corresponding MSTI value in A-UEPS algorithm. When $\lambda = 1.0$, the mean delay and the packet loss rate are maintained within desired ranges, [60, 120]ms and [0.2, 0.8]% by increasing MSTI value. During time interval [2.0, 3.0] second($\lambda = 2.0$), MSTI value increases continuously and reaches its maximum value (150) at time 2.6 sec. From this time, the means delay is still maintained lower than the maximum value (150ms), but higher than $Max_{delay}=120$ ms. However, the packet loss rate stays slightly above the maximum allowable value, 1%. Therefore, the mean delay and the packet loss requirements of video traffics are almost satisfied during this worst case traffic situation. From time 3.0 sec. ($\lambda = 1.5$), the packet loss rate and the delay requirements are maintained blow 1% and 150ms respectively.

Performance of NRT traffics. Figure 5 shows TSPs of WWW (left) and email (right) traffics with A-UEPS, S-UEPS and M-LWDF algorithms under the same traffic situation. The TSP of WWW traffic with A-UEPS is shown to be much higher than those with S-UEPS and M-LWDF algorithms under all traffic loads. MSTI of voice and video traffics in A-UEPS algorithm are adjusted when the offered traffic load is changed, and tends to converge a value. As a result, the TSP of WWW traffic tends to increasing in accordance with the converging tendency of MSTI values of RT traffics. In case with S-UEPS, since lengths of MSTI of RT traffics are fixed and the offered traffic load is larger than 1.0, i.e., $\lambda > 1.0$, the number of urgent packets of RT voice and video traffic waiting in their BMB tends to increase. As a result, the TSP of WWW traffic with S-UEPS shows a decreasing tendency as time elapses under all subperiods.

In case of email traffic, tendency of the TSP is similar to the case of WWW traffic under all subperiods. However, since the scheduling priority of email traffic is set to be lower than that of WWW traffic in A-UEPS and S-UEPS algorithms, TSPs with A-UEPS and S-UEPS is lower than that with M-LWDF at the beginning of each subperiods. However, as time elapses, TSP of email traffic tends to increase with A-UEPS, but decrease with S-UEPS because of the same reason for WWW traffics as explained before. Furthermore, TSP of email traffic with A-UEPS becomes higher than that with M-LWDF in the middle of each subperiod.

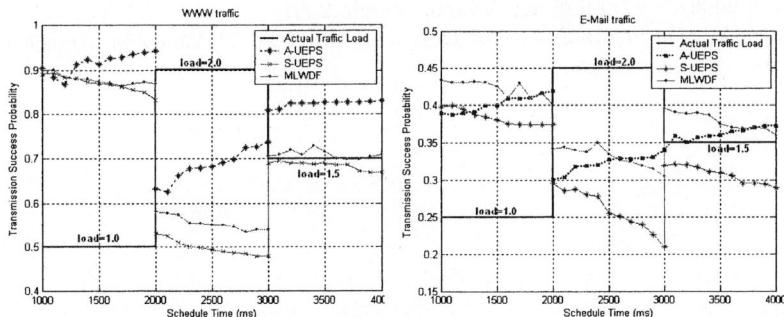

Fig. 5. Transmission success probabilities of WWW and email traffics under time-varying traffic situation

6 Conclusion

In this paper, we deigned an efficient wireless downlink packet scheduling algorithm, *A-UEPS algorithm*, that is able to schedule RT and NRT traffics simultaneously and adaptively to the time-varying traffic situation. However, in this paper, because of page limitation, we give limited performance evaluation results to emphasize how good is the A-UEPS algorithm in supporting support QoS requirements of RT and NRT traffics and in giving performance trade-off between two conflict objectives adaptively even under the worst traffic situation.

Acknowledgement

This study was partially supported by Chung-Ang University Research Grant in 2005.

References

1. A. Jalali, et al.: "Data Throughput of CDMA HDR a High Efficiency-High Data Rate Personal Communication Wireless System," *Proc. of VTC2000-Spring* ,2000, pp1854–1858.
2. M. Andrews, et al.: "Providing Quality of Service over a Shared Wireless Link," *IEEE Communicaions Magazine*, 39(2), pp. 150–154, Feb., 2001.
3. H. Holma, and A. Toskala: *WCDMA for UMTS*, John Wiley and Sons, Ltd., Second edition, 2002.
4. T. Schwarzfisher: "Quality and Utility-Towards a Generalization of Deadline and Anytime Scheduling," *Proc. of 13th ICAPS*, June, 2003.
5. E. Jensen,: "Real-time Systems," `http://www.real-time.org/realtime.htm`.
6. S. Ryu, H. Ryu, and H. Seo: "Urgency and Efficiency based Packet Scheduling Algorithm for OFDMA wireless System," *Proc. of ICC2005*, May, 2005.
7. 3GPP: "Physical Layer Aspects of UTRA High Speed Downlink Packet Access (Release 2000)," 3G TR25.848 V4.0.0, March, 2001.
8. T. Janevski: *Traffic Analysis and Design of Wireless IP Networks*, Artech House, MA, Artech House, 2003.

A Practical Multicast Transmission Control Method for Multi-channel HDTV IP Broadcasting System

Kazuhiro Kamimura[1], Teruyuki Hasegawa[2], Haruo Hoshino[1], Shigehiro Ano[2], and Toru Hasegawa[2]

[1] Japan Broadcasting Corporation (NHK), Science & Technical Research Laboratories,
1-10-11 Kinuta, Setagaya-ku, Tokyo 157-8510, Japan
kamimura.k-he@nhk.or.jp
[2] KDDI R&D Laboratories Inc., 2-1-15 Ohara, Kamifukuoka-shi, Saitama 356-8502, Japan
teru@kddilabs.jp

Abstract. According to deployment of broadband access networks like FTTH (Fiber-To-The-Home), many Internet Service Providers in Japan start providing video broadcasting services via IP multicast. As the service develops into higher quality and more diverse, a broadcasting system capable of handling high bit-rate contents will be required. However, typical implementation of broadcasting server may have problems because of poor packet timing control precision. In this paper, we present a new transmission control method for IP multicast that is synchronized with TCP flow control, which can be applied to QoS-guaranteed networks. We evaluate its validity using an experimental system with HDTV (High Definition TV) streams. We are able to demonstrate that the system can simultaneously distribute eight-channel HDTV streams.

1 Introduction

Since the middle of 2003, Internet Service Providers (ISPs) in Japan have been providing commercial video broadcasting services via IP multicast. On these services, ISPs lend Set-Top-Boxes (STBs) to their customers to watch video programs with TV sets (not with PCs) and distribute SDTV (Standard Definition TV) streams to the customers through their closed Contents Delivery Network (CDN)[1].

In order to distribute high quality video streams via IP multicast, ISPs optimize their service infrastructure for multicast traffic[2]. For example, ISPs:

- construct well-provisioned CDN with QoS (Quality-of-Service) function to differentiate real-time broadcasting traffic from the other best effort traffic,
- use packet-based FEC (Forward Error Correction) to compensate for continuous packet loss in periods of several 10 milliseconds or less caused by unexpected congestion among prioritized traffic (e.g. streaming and VoIP) or link layer protection mechanisms, and
- adopt redundant network topology with no single points of failure between server and client sides edge routers.

Therefore, the CDN can be regarded as nearly lossless and bandwidth-guaranteed communication channel as for the video streaming traffic.

However, even if the CDN can be treated as an almost ideal network, some problems with control of packet transmission still remain. On video streaming systems via IP multicast, packet transmission rates must be adjusted to the decoding rate of their content, otherwise the client receiving buffers might be either overrun or underrun. IP broadcasting systems, which are made up of only a few servers and many clients, must use multicast with UDP protocol. The transmission application on the server must therefore adjust the transmission rate. In actual operation, the transmission application must maintain a constant precise time interval between packets and adjust the long-term transmission rate to the decoding rate, based on interval timer functions provided by the server's operating system such as *usleep()* and *nanosleep()* (timer functions for short). However, as the video streaming services will handle higher bit-rate contents, this operation may encounter the following problem.

The problem is the accuracy of the control provided by timer functions, which is especially significant in the case of high bit-rate contents. For example, HDTV contents broadcasted by satellite in Japan are encoded in MPEG-2 TS whose information rate is approximately 24Mbps. In the case of distributing the HDTV contents with Ethernet frames of a 1500-byte long payload, the transmission application must maintain a precise frame time interval of 500 microseconds. On the other hand, general operating systems commonly used in multi-purpose servers, such as UNIX and its clones, have only 10 milliseconds resolution of their timer functions in default due to their process scheduling algorithm[3]. In consequence, a cluster of packets is frequently transmitted close together in a short period of time, that is burst transmission. This causes the packets to be discarded at intermediate routers and switches in the CDN, and the clients are affected by such packet losses, however the streaming traffic is QoS-guaranteed nevertheless.

There are some solutions to address these problems, for example, implementing the server on real-time operating systems to improve accuracy[4] or adjusting the transmission rate by supplemental protocols based on feedback from clients and its aggregation on intermediate routers[5]. However, because the commercial system takes high precedence over initial costs to deploy the system and facility to replace failed components, the infrastructure is preferably constructed with commodity hardware and the application software are preferably implemented with basic protocols in general OSes.

In this paper, we present a new transmission control method for IP multicast that is independent of timer functions. Our method consists of long-term rate adjustment of multicast traffic synchronized with TCP flow control and short-term burst suppression by means of bandwidth limiting function built in to a commodity layer-2 switch. Using this method, practical IP broadcasting systems can be constructed easily using commodity hardware and application software implemented only with standard TCP and UDP protocols.

2 Proposed Transmission Control Method

2.1 Long-Term Rate Adjustment

Figure 1 shows an overview of our packet transmission control method. There is a broadcasting server communicating with many clients through a QoS-guaranteed CDN. All clients join in the same multicast group G and receive multicast packets from the server. Besides these general clients, we provide a representative client close to the server and which communicates with the server by TCP protocol. This TCP client controls its unicast data flow according to its play-out speed. Except for the transport protocols, there is no difference in architecture and functions between the TCP client and the other multicast clients.

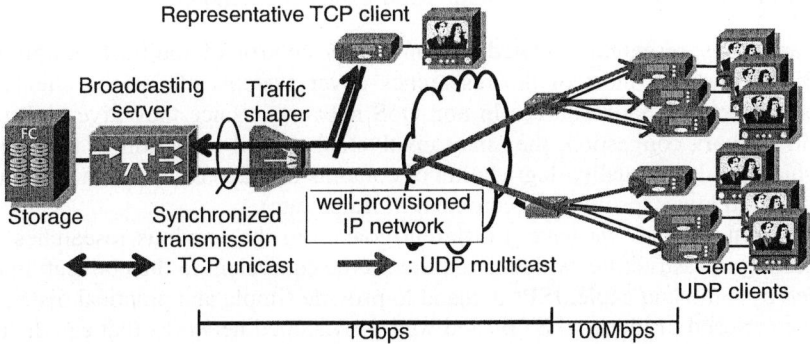

Fig. 1. Schematic diagram of proposed transmission control method

The transmission application on the server repeats the following operations.

1. Reading fixed-length data to transmit from storage.
2. Writing data to TCP socket connected with the representative client in blocking I/O mode.
3. Writing the same data to UDP socket bound to the multicast group G, immediately after completion of operation 2.

Because the packet transmission to the representative client is adjusted by TCP flow control, the buffer on the client is neither overrun nor underrun. So, if the transmission of multicast packet is kept synchronized with TCP flow control, then we can adjust the long-term transmission rate of the multicast stream.

Note that the server is not dependent on the content format because the server simply repeats the *"file data read and write"* operation and never uses any timer functions.

2.2 Short-Term Burst Suppression

In view of the bandwidth requirement for multi-channel HDTV broadcasting, the network should possess at least 1Gbps capacity except for client access links. In other words, while the server can generate short-term traffic burst whose peak rate is 1Gbps, client access links tend to be bandwidth bottleneck where packets are dropped due to the burst traffic. It is therefore important to suppress burst transmission in broadcasting traffic. To suppress burst transmissions, we apply traffic shapers for each the TCP unicast and multicast traffic. At first, in order to suppress bursts in TCP traffic to the representative client, the shaper is configured to shape the traffic into approximately the same bandwidth as the content decoding rate. The shaper is also configured to shape the multicast traffic into an appropriate bandwidth preventing packet losses on the bottleneck switches. Although the transmission rate of multicast traffic is adjusted by the TCP traffic, the multicast traffic may still contain some bursts since the application controls the transmission merely through the sockets in user-layer and its actual timing is scheduled by protocol stacks in kernel-layer.

2.3 Difference from Related Transmission Control Methods

There are many researches related to congestion control of multicast communication[5][6]. However, most of the researches cover systems of various clients with different computational resources in non-QoS networks. Since they give high priory to avoid network congestion, they may involve substantial reduction of transmission rate, which results in quality degradation of contents in video distribution system (e.g. transcoding to lower resolution, decrement of frame rate).

On the other hand, we have a different goal from the previous researches. As a broadcasting infrastructure, which is required to be equivalent to the conventional one provided by radio and cable, ISPs demand to provide simple and practical distribution system composed of identical STBs and well-provisioned networks that can distribute Constant-Bit-Rate (CBR) contents to their customers without any quality degradation. In such systems, we have an interest in simple implementation of flow control to avoid overrunning buffers on clients. With the presented method, we can implement server and client software without any implementation of supplemental protocols and any modification of kernel-layer IP stack. Because the system does not need additional protocol implementation on network nodes and intermediate routers, the practical system can be build easily and cost-effectively using commodity devices.

Note that there is a similar approach that use a representative client to control transmission rate[6]. However, dynamic selection scheme of the representative client in [6] requires additional protocol implementation and may cause unexpected side effect, e.g. too frequent change of the representative client. Therefore, we believe our simpler approach using standard TCP and UDP protocols is quite effective for practical IP broadcasting systems.

3 Configuring the Experimental System

We implemented an experimental system to evaluate our proposed method for multi-channel HDTV IP broadcasting. Figure 2 and Table 1 show the configuration and its component devices in the experimental system. The configuration consists of four multicast routers in which OSPF[7] for unicast and PIM-SM[8] for multicast routing processes are running. There is no traffic interference other than the IP broadcasting traffic.

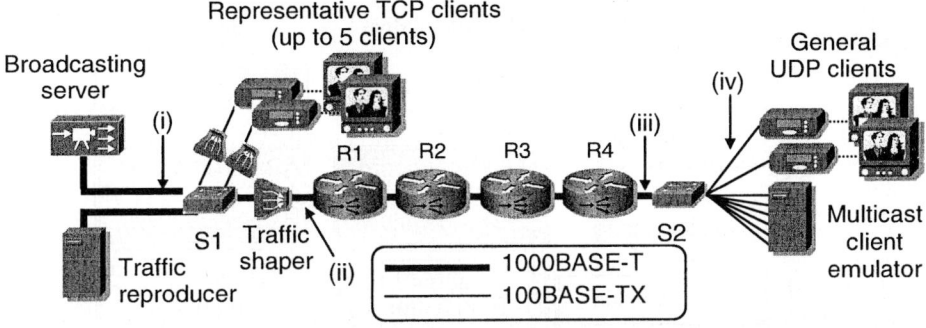

Fig. 2. Overview of experimental system

Table 1. Component devices in the experimental system

Broadcasting server	Xeon 2GHz x 2/Linux 2.4.18 (tick=10ms)
Traffic reproducer	Xeon 2GHz x 2/FreeBSD 5.2 (tick=100us)
TCP and UDP clients	Celeron 2.5GHz/Linux 2.4.22
Traffic shaper	Catalyst 3750/IOS 12.1(19)EA1d
R1-R3	Catalyst 3550/IOS 12.2(25)SEA
R4	Catalyst 4503/IOS 12.2(20)EWA
S1	Catalyst 3750/IOS 12.1(19)EA1d
S2	Catalyst 2940/IOS 12.1(22)EA1

In multi-channel evaluation, different multicast groups are assigned to each channel. The representative clients for each channel are also arranged. We also utilize a traffic reproducer[9] and a multicast client emulator as needed. The reproducer can generate the same traffic as that captured in advance. The emulator can simultaneously join in any multicast group and detect loss of packets by monitoring the sequence number field in the received packets. They virtually act as broadcasting servers and multicast clients and distribute multi-channel HDTV streams to stress intermediate nodes in the network, in particular the shaper and the bottleneck switch.

3.1 Implementation of Server and Clients

Figure 3 illustrates implementation of the server and clients. The receivers consist of a MPEG-2 decoder that can handle HDTV streams and a client PC as the network adopter of the decoder. The receiving application on the clients consists of a ring-buffer and two threads. One thread is *packet receiver thread* ("Rx thread" in the figure) which unpacks the PDU and stores TS packets in the ring-buffer and the other is *TS writer thread* ("Tx thread") which retrieves the TS packets from the ring-buffer and sends them to the MPEG-2 output board. The MPEG-2 board driver monitors PCRs in TS and controls its output rate to the decoder. If packets arrive faster than the output rate, the TS packets are queued in the board driver's buffer, the ring-buffer and then the socket buffer. When each buffer are filled up, the TS writer thread and the packet receiver thread are blocked, and then the transmission application on the server is blocked in the *write()* system call to the TCP socket. The buffer size of the

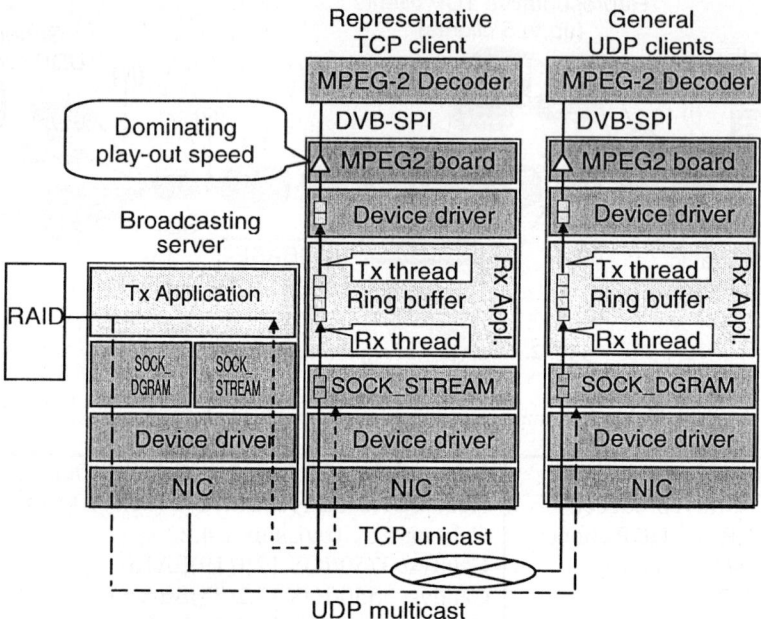

Fig. 3. Overview of implementation of server and clients

receiving socket is configured to 8KB for TCP clients and 256KB for multicast clients. In the case of multi-channel evaluation, transmission processes corresponding to each channel are run simultaneously on the broadcasting server.

3.2 HDTV Streams and Their Packetizing Format

The Japan Broadcasting Corporation (NHK) provides a digital broadcasting service by satellite with High-Definition TV contents encoded as MPEG-2 TS whose information rate is 23.91Mbps[10][11]. In this evaluation, we used MPEG-2 TS streams that conform to HDTV broadcasting service standards in Japan. The server application reads the 204-bytes TS packets from storage and packs them into 1224-byte PDU (Protocol Data Unit), which consists of one 204-byte header including its sequence number and five TS packets.

In addition, because of unexpected breaks of packet forwarding when the routers change their incoming port of multicast traffic, the server generates horizontal XOR-parity packets to compensate for continuous 500 packet losses with a 20% additional bandwidth[12]. The total transmission rate per HDTV stream therefore becomes about 38.75Mbps. In this evaluation, the transmission rate is fixed.

3.3 Traffic Shaping

In this experimental system, we realized traffic shapers with a commodity layer-2 switch enabling bandwidth limitation of its links[13]. Our proposed method does not essentially require highly accurate traffic shaping, since long-term transmission rate is adjusted in synchronization with TCP flow control. So that shapers implemented by software, such as dummynet[14], are also applicable. However, since IP broadcasting systems must remain in service for many days, we prefer implementing the shaper with inexpensive hardware components. In this evaluation, the shaper is configured to limit both TCP and multicast traffic of a HDTV channel to 50Mbps respectively. In multicast traffic on the multi-channel evaluation, the shaper are configured as shown in Figure 4, to separate the multi-channel streams to different switch ports by static assignment in the IGMP snooping table and shape each traffic by limiting the bandwidth at each individual port.

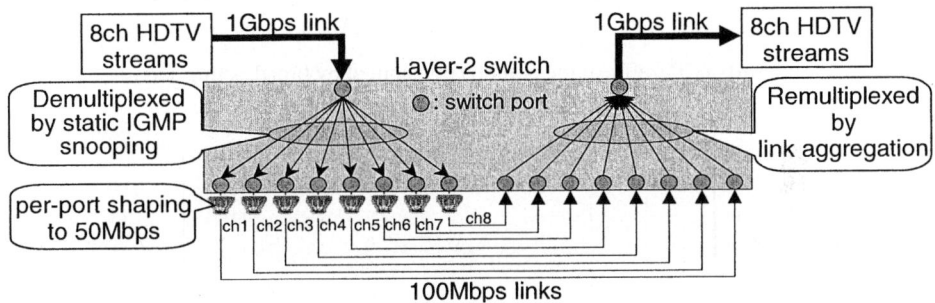

Fig. 4. Schematic diagram of layer-2 switch configuration as a shaper

4 Results and Discussions

Using the experimental systems described in Section 3, we evaluated our multicast transmission control method for multi-channel HDTV IP broadcasting. We measured traffic at certain points in the system denoted by roman numerals in Figure 2, using a traffic monitor[15] capable of capturing packets with 1 microsecond accuracy.

4.1 Evaluating the Proposed Transmission Control Method

We first evaluated our proposed method by distributing a single-channel HDTV stream in the experimental system. We simultaneously measured TCP traffic and multicast traffic at the point (i) that the broadcasting server transmits and multicast traffic through the shaper at the point (ii). Figure 5 shows the results. The vertical axis denotes the number of packets per millisecond (ppms).

Figure 5(a) shows that TCP traffic reaches 4.1ppms, as the server transmits the 1518-bytes long TCP frame to the 50Mbps link. The server was observed to stop transmitting packets for 100 milliseconds. Since the link capacity is slightly faster than the content decoding rate, the client buffer is filled up and the client advertises TCP ACK with Zero Window. On the other hand, Figure 5(b) shows that multicast traffic from the server is synchronized with the TCP traffic. The multicast traffic is expected to reach 5.1ppms since the server transmits the same amount of data as the TCP carried by UDP packets with a 1224-byte long payload. However, the traffic fluctuates quickly and contains some bursts which reaches a maximum of 17ppms.

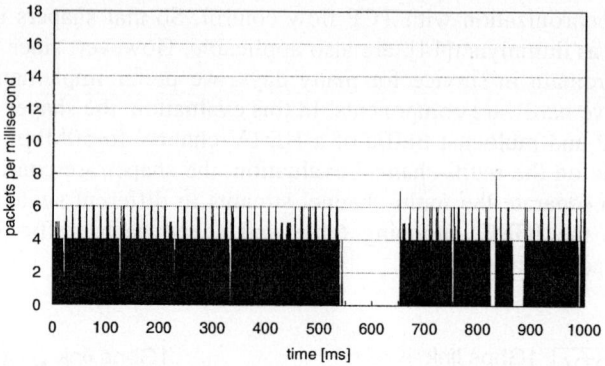

Fig. 5(a). TCP traffic at the point (i) transmitted by broadcasting server

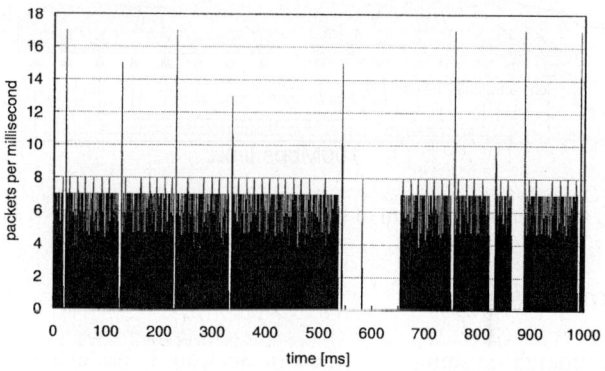

Fig. 5(b). Multicast traffic at the point (i) transmitted by broadcasting server

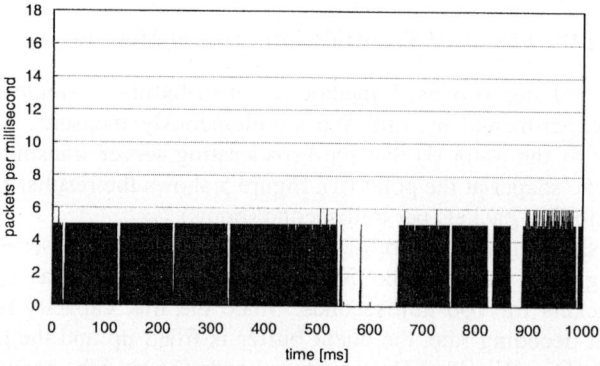

Fig. 5(c). Multicast traffic at the point (ii) through the shaper

This bursty traffic is smoothly shaped to less than 6ppms by the shaper as shown in Figure 5(c). We consequently confirmed that general UDP clients detected no packet loss and the receiver can continue to decode the HDTV content without problems.

4.2 Multi-channel HDTV IP Broadcasting

We next evaluated the validity of our system for multi-channel HDTV IP broadcasting, focusing switching capability of the shaper and the client-side edge switch. In this evaluation, the broadcasting server transmits two HDTV streams and the traffic reproducer emulates six HDTV streams. The reproducer is configured to replay multicast traffic that was captured at the point (i) in advance.

Figure 6(a) shows all incoming multicast traffic to client-side edge switch (S2) at the point (iii). The traffic does not exceed 45ppms or 440Mbps. The traffic fluctuation is caused by overlapping pause periods in the packet transmission shown in Figure 5(c). This result shows that the shaper has capability enough to shape eight-channel

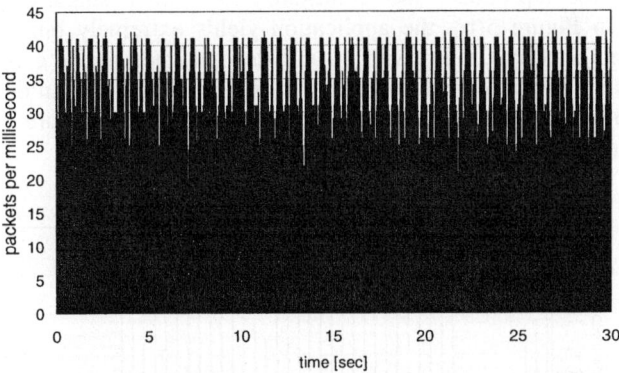

Fig. 6(a). All incoming multicast traffic to client-side edge switch at the point (iii)

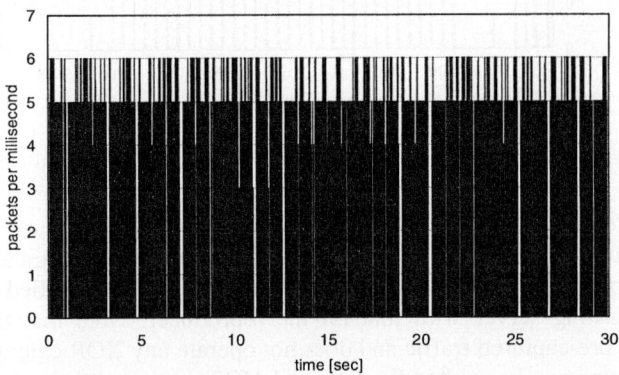

Fig. 6(b). Incoming multicast traffic of group G0 to a UDP client at the point (iv)

HDTV streams. Figure 6(b) shows the multicast traffic at the point (iv) to clients which have joined in a group G0. Traffic is constantly maintained within 6ppms and no burst transmissions were observed. For all of these results, we conclude that our experimental system can smoothly distribute eight-channel HDTV streams to clients preventing burst transmissions. Finally, we continued to distribute eight-channel HDTV streams for many hours and confirmed that the client observed no loss of packet throughout for more than 48 hours.

4.3 Comparison with the Typical Transmission Control Method

To discuss the advantages of our proposed method, we compared it with a server application using a typical transmission control method. As one example of such typical applications, we evaluated the traffic reproducer[9]. The traffic reproducer controls its packet transmission by *nanosleep()* system call, whose accuracy is affected by a *tick*, in other word, a clock interrupt period of OS.

Figure 7 shows multicast traffic that the reproducer transmits with a 10 millisecond tick. Although the reproducer was configured to emulate single-channel multicast traffic shown in Figure 5(b), the application yields extremely bursty traffic which exceeds 60ppms at a maximum with 20 millisecond intervals. We confirmed that a reproducer with a 1 millisecond tick also yields a 30ppms burst. In order to suppress these bursts to under 20ppms as the same level as shown in Figure 5(b), we had to customize the reproducer with a 200 microseconds tick.

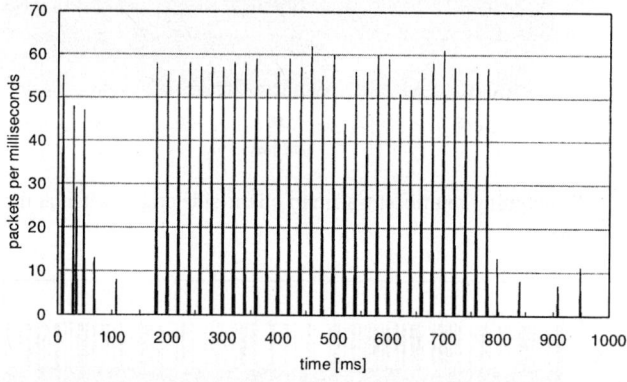

Fig. 7. Multicast traffic transmitted by server based on the typical method

Compared to a typical transmission control method, a server using our method must transmit twice the number of packets. In other words, it must transmit both TCP and multicast packets for each HDTV stream. In this way, we verified the CPU load on our broadcasting server with that on the reproducer. Note that the reproducer merely replays pre-captured traffic and does not operate any XOR calculation.

Figure 8 shows results with a five-channel HDTV streaming load on the server. Our server consumes almost twice CPU resources as that of the reproducer. It is understandable that our server requires more system CPU resources because the server

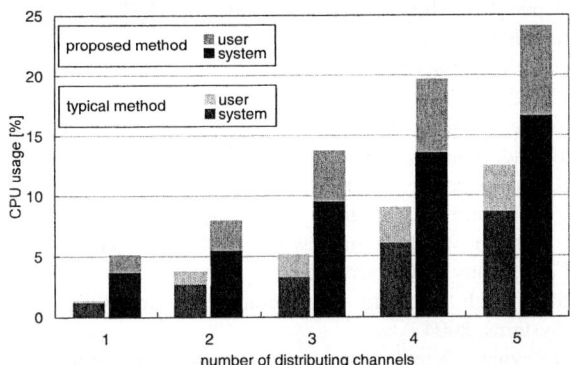

Fig. 8. Broadcasting server loads in both transmission control methods

must process kernel-layer operations in TCP socket in addition to UDP socket. As for user-layer operations, it is possible to reduce the load of our server by generating XOR parity packets in advance or off-line. We confirmed that the server disabling the XOR operations reduced 3% load at the five-channel streaming.

5 Conclusions

This paper presents a novel multicast transmission control method applicable to practical HDTV IP broadcasting and evaluates the validity of the method. The proposed method is based on long-term rate adjustment synchronized with TCP flow control and short-term burst suppression by a commodity layer-2 switch. We also implement an experimental system and demonstrate that this system can handle simultaneous eight-channel HDTV streams. Evaluation results showed that there was no loss of packet due to burst transmission in multicast traffic throughout for more than 48 hours. We believe our method is very effective as a practical means to implement multi-channel IP broadcasting system with high bit-rate contents.

References

[1] http://www.kddi.com/english/corporate/news_release/2003/1212a/index.html
[2] T. Hasegawa and T. Hasegawa, "A Gateway Approach for Providing Non-Stop IP Broadcasting Service Infrastructure," IEEE ICACT2005, Feb. 2005.
[3] M. K. McKusick, B. Bostic, M. J. Karels and J. S. Quaterman, "The Design and Implementation of the 4.4BSD Operating System," Addison-Wesley, MA (1996)
[4] D. L. Moal, T. Takeuchi and T. Bandoh, "Cost-effective streaming sever implementation using Hi-tactix," ACM Multimedia, Dec. 2002
[5] I. Rhee, N. Balaguru and G. N. Rousakas, "MTCP: Scalable TCP-like Congestion Control For Reliable Multicast," IEEE INFOCOM 1999, Mar. 1999
[6] L. Rizzo, "pgmcc: A TCP-friendly single rate multicast congestion control scheme," ACM SIGCOMM 2000, Aug. 2000.
[7] "OSPF Version 2," RFC2328, April 1998.

[8] "Protocol Independent Multicast-Sparse Mode (PIM-SM) Protocol Specification, " RFC2362, June 1998.
[9] http://tcpreplay.sourceforge.net/
[10] Association of Radio Industries and Businesses (ARIB), "Transmission System for Digital Satellite Broadcasting," ARIB STD-B20, May 2001 (in Japanese).
[11] Association of Radio Industries and Buisinesses (ARIB), "Operational Guidelines for Digital Satellite Broadcasting," ARIB TR-B15, Feb. 2004 (in Japanese).
[12] T. Hasegawa, K. Kamimura, H. Hoshino, S. Ano and T. Hasegawa, "IP-based HDTV Broadcasting System Architecture with Non-stop Service Availability," IEEE GLOBECOM 2005, Nov. 2005 (accepted)
[13] "Catalyst 3750 Switch Software Configuration Guide, Rel. 12.1(19)EA1, February 2004," Cisco Systems, 2004
[14] L. Rizzo, "Dummynet: a simple approach to the evaluation of network protocols," ACM Computing Communication Review, Jan. 1997.
[15] T. Hasegawa, T. Ohgishi and T. Hasegawa, "A Framework for Gigabit-rate Packet Header Collection to Realize Cost-effective Internet Monitoring System," IPSJ Journal, Vol.42 no. 12, Dec. 2001.

MEET : Multicast Debugging Toolkit with End-to-End Packet Trace

Jinyong Jo, Jaiseung Kwak, and Okhwan Byeon

High Performance Research Networking Dep.,
Korea Institute of Science and Technology Information (KISTI), Daejeon, Korea
{jiny92, jskwak, ohbyeon}@kisti.re.kr

Abstract. The Access Grid (AG) for collaborative environment exploits IP multicast, which is quite a promising technology for sharing network bandwidth. IP multicast however, faces lots of challenges such as unreliable data transport and immature network infrastructure. As a step to improve reliability and stability in IP multicast, it is essential to properly monitor and debug multicast networks. In this paper we introduce MEET (Multicast debugging toolkit with End-to-End packet Trace), an user-oriented multicast debugging toolkit for AG. MEET provides proactive ways of debugging multicast reachablility and measuring end-to-end delivery statistics. We are sure that MEET supports multicast users with a simple yet extensive view of end-to-end multicast reachability and delivery statistics.

1 Introduction

Growing demands for the support of collaborative works in cyberspace have brought an advent of Access Grid (AG) [1] technology. AG is a kind of video conferencing toolkit which exploits IP multicast to efficiently exchange audio and video data on IP networks. As AG broadens the scope of application areas even to the medical science, the demands for high quality video and audio presentations are accordingly increasing now. Multicast infrastructures however are not so stabilized that we could hardly expect to disseminate data to a multicast group seamlessly. We have been using the IP multicast for AG since in 2002 and frequently experiencing communication failures caused by the immaturity of IP multicast infrastructure including the use of private IP, mis-configuration in routers or host systems, multicast enability at the access network, and so forth. At this moment, monitoring and debugging IP multicast with end-to-end perspective becomes important so as to stabilize multicast networks and to achieve advanced streaming features (e.g., high density video) in AG toolkit.

Based on our experience of running AG, we make a summary of user demands on what a multicast monitoring toolkit has to have as follows. First, the toolkit has to check multicast problems, particularly occurred in the network layer, and have an easy interface which describes the problems intutively. Since multicast packets are normally traversing across inter-domain networks, it is very helpful for AG or NOC (Network operating center) operators to get bi-directional monitoring information (e.g, QoS statistics and path traces). Second, we have to expand the monitoring scopes from transport networks to all possible things which make trobules in communications (e.g., firewall). For example, NAT (Network address translator) is one of the representative trouble-makers which disturbs seamless transmission over the Internet. Restricted connectivity in the network comes to a very common issue due to the proliferation of using NAT and firewalls. Finally, a toolkit must provide easy-to-manage, easy-to-use, and easy-to-access monitoring framework.

In this paper, we introduce MEET, Multicast debugging toolkit with End-to-End packet Trace, which is a near real-time multicast reachability and quality monitoring framework with a web-based graphical user interface. MEET is able to 1) do proactive multicast diagnosis. The diagnosing features include multicast ping, uni-/bi-directional path trace, multicast enability, NAT (Network Address Translator) detection, and end-to-end packet delivery statistics. It 2) offers easy accessibility to multicast users. The users can trigger all measurement events from our web-based user interface. It also provides a global view of session reachabilities as well as the process of uni-/bi-directional path QoS probings.

The rest of this paper is organized as follows. We will first review related works for monitoring a multicast session in Section 2. Section 3 introduces Multicast debugging toolkit with End-to-End packet Trace and explains core components of our monitoring frameworks. We summarize the paper in Section 4.

2 Related Works

We briefly describe existing efforts to implement multicast monitoring tools. Note that there are a number of other existing tools but we just select only a few approaches which are the most comparable to our work.

Multicast beacon [2] consists of distributed clients and a central server. Clients exchange RTP packet streams with session participants. A server then acquires the delivery statistics from the clients with unicast connections and presents a QoS matrix to a web-based user interface. The QoS matrix includes the statistics of loss, delay, jitter, out-of-sequence, and the number of duplicated packets. The beacon provides ease access to use (i.e., web-based interface). It however has no facilities to check multicast problems in network layer and is unable to detect private networks. Also, uncontrolled RTP streaming for quality measurements can negatively impact on the network even if the sending rate is low.

For multicast reachability, the work in [3] introduces the multicast reachability monitor (MRM), which has been implemented on some Cisco^{TM} routers. MRM is a protocol which provides an integrated framework for multicast monitoring. It consists of test senders (TS), test receivers (TR), and central manager. The manager performs measurement tasks. It also specifies several requests such that how to collect or report reception statistics in TR, and to schedule a stream of packets sent by TS. Allowing central management enables MRM to mitigate negative impacts on the operation of the networks. Another reachablity montoring framework is the multicast quality monitor (MQM [4]). MQM inherits the working ideas of MRM but has differences in the distinctions in reachability and quality measurements, and the sort of communications for inter-probing.

MEET also adopts main ideas from MRM and MQM. In comparison with MQM, MEET has differences in 1) the robust ways of diagnosing multicast problems. While MQM only deals with reachablity and delivery statistics in application layer, MEET additionally gathers diagnostic information both from network and system level. MEET 2) distinguishes a control/data plane from a debugging plane, and restricts the measurement domain to a pair of agents. Splitting the control/data plane is very effective to detect isolated agents in multicast networks, and to collect measured results under the souce-specific multicast (SSM) environment. We are able to prevent excessive packet injection to multicast networks by restricting the measurement domain. Finally, MEET 3) provides a web-based user interface, which improves the accessability to the monitoring framework.

3 Multicast Diagnosing Framework

MEET toolkit comprises three core components as shown in Fig. 1: a management server, agents, and a web-based user interface.

The roles of the management server, denoted as MEET Server, are to relay messages, to handle a local database, and to manage a monitoring session. The server delivers `command` messages to each designate agent, or `return` messages to each command originator (i.e., users). On receiving the `return` messages at the server, the database handler logs them into the local storage, which contains information about each agent, and end-to-end measurement results between a pair of the agents. The server helps get agents to maintain a toolkit consistency

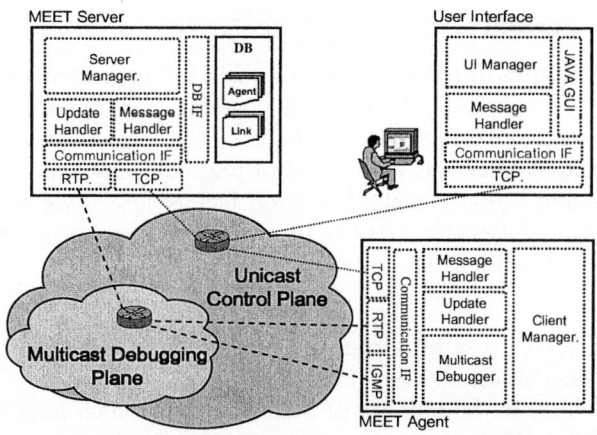

Fig. 1. MEET core components

with the other agents. Note that each client conveys its toolkit version to the server by means of a `heartbeat` message. The `heartbeat` message is also used to detect the agents isolated from IP multicast. Session manager periodically injects multicast probing packets to the monitoring session. It is to make agents check its multicast enability.

Agents perform a local debugging module based on the types in the server-relayed `command` messages. The `command` messages include JOIN, PING, BURST, and TRACE. Agents determine its multicast enability if they receive the JOIN message. The server and session members are periodically disseminating the JOIN message for the purpose. On receiving the PING mesage, the agent starts sending multicast ping packets to the session. The agent should play roles of both a ping generator and a pong replier. We use the BURST message to order an agent to generate a large number of packets or to receive the packets and gather the delivery statistics. An agent receiving the TRACE message runs `mtrace` to a designate agent. Two agents simultaneously participate in the measurement when they receive the PING or the BURST message while making an independent measurement when they get the TRACE `command`. Note that a user originates a `command` message and assigns a pair of agents, and that the management server relays the messeage to the designate agents.

We split the communication domain into a control/data plane and a debug plane. The control/data plane uses a unicast communication to exchange relevant messages among the core components. In the debug plane, each agent injects RTP (Real-time Transport Protocol [5]) packets or IGMP (Internet Group Management Protocol [6]) packets to the monitoring session[1]. The reason why we spilt the communication domain is to let the server easily detect the agents isolated from IP multicast. The split also can provide a novel method to collect session information from other agents exploiting the source specific multicast (SSM). Note that bi-directional multicast communication is impossible in the SSM environment.

3.1 Message Format

We designed two types of message formats : MEET unicast packet header and multicast packet header. Each header is dependent of the underlying communication domain (i.e., control and degug plane).

A MEET unicast packet is comprised of packet header and descriptions as shown in Fig. 2 and Table 1 each. The fixed header size is set to 16 bytes and can attach additional $4 \times n$ ($n \leq 16$) bytes of IP addresses if necessary. n is the number of designate agents. The role of each fields in the MEET unicast packet is as follows.

- Protocol version (V, 1 byte), extension (X, 1 bit) indicates whether the packet contains a description message.
- Count (C, 4 bits) is the number of MEET agents which have to participate in measurement ($C = n$).

---

[1] At this stage, we do not implement RTCP (RTP Control Protocol) mechanisms.

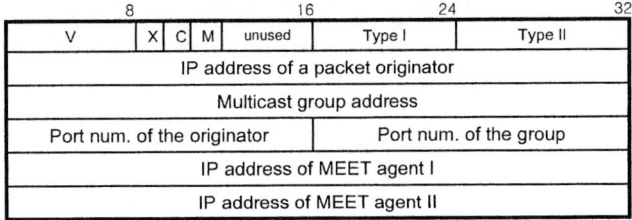

Fig. 2. MEET unicast common header format

- Mode (M, 1 bit) presents a type of a relay message. If it is set to 1, the direction of command message is orignated from a user to MEET agents. Otherwise, the direction goes toward a requestor from a MEET agent. The mananagement server reads this bit to determine the command type of a packet to be relayed.
- Type I (1 byte) contains a type of primary commands such as RELAY, ORDER, and RETURN. The type II (1 byte) includes a sort of secondary command such as JOIN, PING, BURST, TRACE, and so forth [2].
- IP address of the packet originator (4 bytes). The server must not be a packet originator even though it modifies relay packets.
- IP address of MEET agent. It plays important roles in two folds. First, it confines a measurement domain to the limited number of agents listed in the field. It is of help to prevent feedback implosion, which puts heavy burdens on an active sender in case of performing multicast ping. Second, a heartbeat message issued by an agent exploits this field to report a bundle of IP addresses proved to have multicast reachability from the agent.
- For NAT detection, we currently use unicast <address of an originator, port num. of the originator> information.

For an instance, if the management server receives a MEET unicast packet with the <RELAY, PING> and $M = 1$, it alters the <type I, type II> to <ORDER, PING>. Based on the type, the server adaptively allocates the subsequent bytes (i.e., 'IP addresses of MEET agent') and forwards the packet to designate agents. Note that the management server never changes the 'IP address of the packet originator' if the type I is set to RELAY mode.

If the extension bit (X) is set to 1, a MEET unicast packet has a description message like Table 1. The description message can be structured into three parts: agent, timing, and result description. Detail explanations are as follows.

- Agent version ('v='), ownership ('o='), whether the agent uses private IP or not ('p=') and its multicast enability status ('e=').
- Timing description ('t=') specifies the time at the meaurement is performed.
- Result description ('r=') contains the address of a peer agent, if necessary, and a set of results.

---

[2] We intentionally leave out explaining the types since the implementation is going on progress.

Table 1. Description message

v=0
o=meet@localhost
p=true/false
e=true/false
t=2873493469
r=<peer, results> (or r=results)

We also design another header format to compensate for the shortcomings of RTP packets, wich do not provide any tight facilities to calculate a round trip time. Fig. 3 shows the MEET multicast header format. Note that the MEET multicast header is encapulated in a IP/UDP/RTP packet (i.e., each agent obtains packet delivery statistics by analyzing RTP packets and MEET multicast header). The fixed MEET multicast header size is 16 bytes.

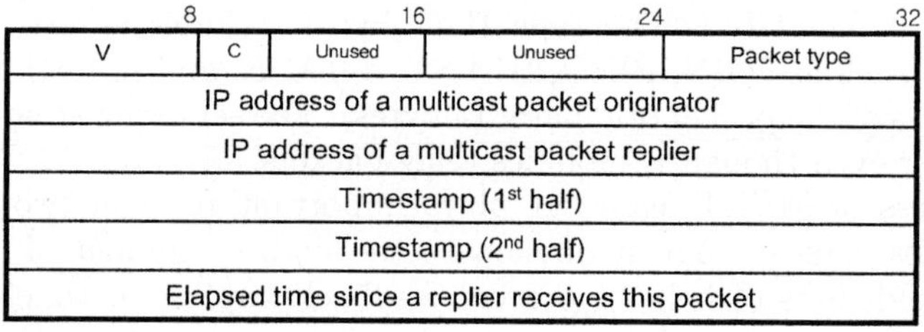

8	16	24	32
V C	Unused	Unused	Packet type
IP address of a multicast packet originator			
IP address of a multicast packet replier			
Timestamp (1st half)			
Timestamp (2nd half)			
Elapsed time since a replier receives this packet			

Fig. 3. MEET multicast common header format

The MEET multicast header is used to measure the round trip time from multicast ping and to get the other QoS parameters such as loss, delay jitter, and so forth. MEET Agents exclusively make use of the MEET multicast packet header. The count (C, 4 bits) field presents the number of multicast packet repliers. Note that the maximum number of measurement participants is fixed to two agents at this stage, so it is of no use to attach additional bytes to the MEET multicast header. The timestamp (8 bytes) records the time at the packet is injected to the monitoring session. The 8-byte timestamp accommodates microseconds. The elapsed time (4 bytes) is the amount of time between the arrival of a ping packet, and the departure of a pong packet at a agent.

3.2 Multicast Enability and IP Analysis

Knowing what if the multicast is enabled at the access network is the very first step to diagnose multicast problems. To check the multicat enability, all MEET agents keep listening to packet arrivals from the monitoring session. The management server transmits a probing packet (i.e., JOIN message) to the session once in every 5 seconds. All MEET agents also asynchronously inject the probing packets to the session with 30 second interval. Consideration on the packet spacing should be carefully taken not to make the prune message interval expired by the routers and the agent removed from the multicast tree. Each agent keeps track of whether it receives the probing packets, and from where they are initiated. The ingatherings are reported to the management server via a `heartbeat` message.

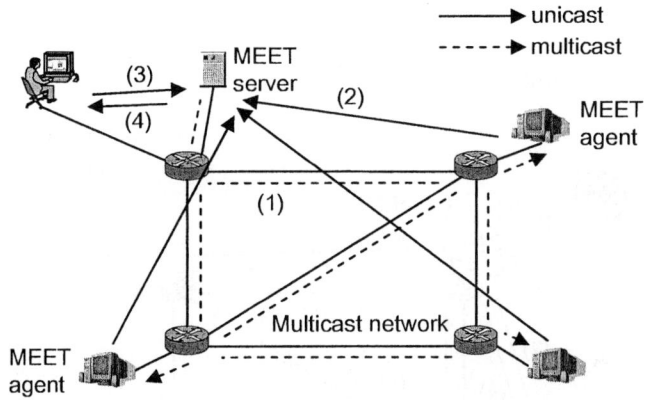

Fig. 4. Check multicast enability at MEET agents

MEET agents and the management server exchange `heartbeat` messages to 1) monitor agent faults, and maintain toolkit consistency between the agents and the server, and to 2) check what if the agent is behind a private network. To achieve 1), each MEET agent unicasts `heartbeat` messages to the server. The `heartbeat` packet includes toolkit version, an apparent IP address of the agent, and what if the client is using a private IP and whether the agent can receive multicast packets (i.e., multicast enability). If the server does not get any `heartbeat` messages from an agent within predefined time interval, it considers the agent went down due to internal faults. The server then removes the faulty agent from its state table keeping tracks of active agents in the session. For 2), a MEET agent first checks its apparent IP address whether it uses a private IP, and record the IP to a MEET unicast packet. Whenever receives a `heartbeat` message, the management server compares the apparent IP address/port reported by the agent and the IP address/port observed at the server. If the server detects a difference between the the two, it then assumes that the agent is behind a network address translator (NAT). You need to make sure that using a NAT can disturb the seamless communications in regard to providing multimedia over IP services.

3.3 QoS Measurement

We first define the QoS parameters for AG, a real-time audio/video conferencing toolkit. Basically, real-time applications are strongly impacted by end-to-end delay and packet loss. Since MEET agents do not use globally synchronized timestamp, it is implausible to directly use the end-to-end delay measured but for calculating jitters. Delay jitter is another factor degrading perceptual quality in real-time multimedia applications even though we can adaptively compensate for it. Additionally, out-of-ordered packet arrivals, and packet duplications also deteriorate the media quality. To measure such QoS parameters in a multicast session, we select RTP for transport protocol. A RTP packet encapsulates the MEET multicast common header, which informs agents about a packet originator, a replier, and so forth. RTP header offers information about timestamps and the sequence number of the packet.

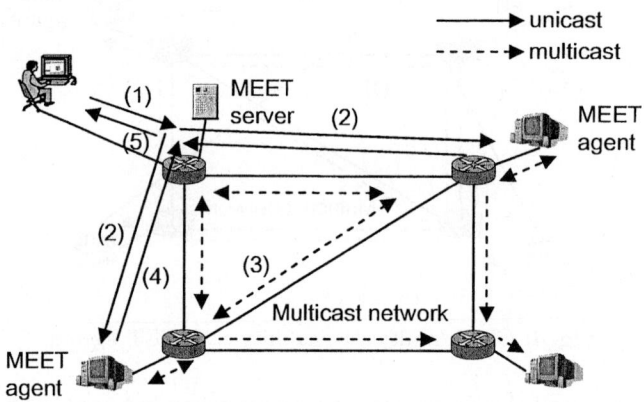

Fig. 5. QoS measurement with burst test

Fig. 5 illustrates how MEET agents measure the QoS parameters in a multicast session. First, (1) a user designates two MEET agents to have them participate in the measurement. On receiving a (2) server-relayed BURST message, the designate agents (3) start transmitting RTP packets to the monitoring session. The two agents assigned to a sender and a replier concurrently join the QoS measurement while the others in the session are just listening to the session. We set the multicast packet size to 64 bytes including IP and UDP header, and interpacket spacing at the sender is fixed to 10 ms. The measurement is lasting for 30 seconds, unless otherwise mentioned. The gathered result is (5) fed back to the originator of the `command` message after (4) being logged into a local database in the server. Note that there is no direct connections between a web-based user interface and MEET agents.

3.4 Reachability Measurement

In order to check multicast reachablility, we make use of multicast ping and `mtrace`. To get the results from multicast ping, we follow the same steps as in the QoS measurement except that the agents receiving ping packets are the only agents which have to response to the multicast ping. Since multicast ping packets are transmitted to all session participants, restricting the number of repliers can mitigate packet floodings with pong in the multicast session. The following pseudocode shows the multicast ping-pong mechanism.

Require: valid message
 1: **if** COMMAND == PING **then**
 2:   get current time, T_c
 3:   **if** host address == packet replier **then**
 4:     ...
 5:     get elapsed time, T_e since it received a PING
 6:     make a PONG packet
 7:     send the PONG to the multicast group
 8:   **else if** host address == packet originator **then**
 9:     ...
10:     get sending time from the PONG packet, T_s
11:     get elapsed time from the PONG packet, T_e
12:     return T_c-T_s-T_e
13:   **end if**
14: **end if**

All are undertaken based on header information in a MEET multicast packet. If an agent gets a valid multicast packet, it first checks whether the agent itself becomes a packet originator or a replier. In case of picking it up as an originator, the agent keeps the record of round-trip time. The round trip time is calculated as T_c-T_s-T_e. Otherwise, the replier fills out the T_e field and injects a corresponding pong packet to the multicast session. The interpacket spacing at the sender is fixed to 250 ms.

The mtrace provides a robust way to debugging multicast reachability. It is widely used in the time of the occurrence of multicast failures since the tool is very handy to diagnose multicast problems. We can obtain full information about a reverse routing path and a per-hop loss rate from a source to a receiver as we throw a mtrace query. On receiving the TRACE command from the management

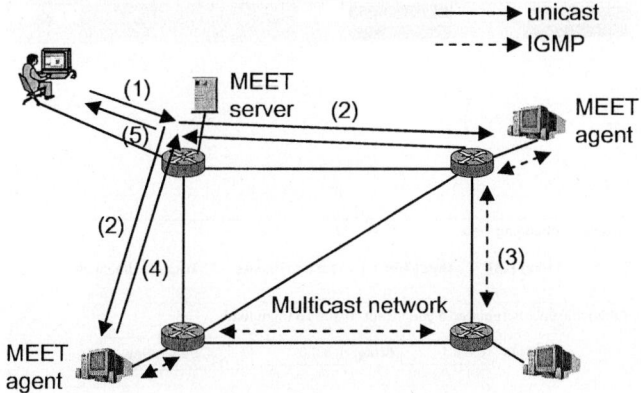

Fig. 6. Reachability measurement with mtrace

server, a pair of designate agents simultaneously traces the reverse routing path. Note that each MEET agent has the capability of tracing multicast reachability from itself to an unknown host (i.e., the host which is not a member of MEET agents). The `mtrace` is used to not only check multicast reachability but also go through problems occurred in the network layer.

3.5 Features

We have been implementing the framework using JAVA language. Currently, MEET supports platforms such as $Windows^{TM}$ 2000/NT/XP and Linux.

Fig. 7 shows the web-based user interface of our framework. The interface fetches multicast session information (i.e., group address, group port, server address, and server port) and the list of all active agents from the management server. An agent information includes its IP address, ownership, whether it is behind in the private network, and its multicast enability status. We use different color codes based on the measurement results to increase user perception (e.g., if multicast is enabled, the corresponding cell to the agent, `enable`, is colorized to green). A user selects an agent or a pair of agents (i.e., `target`) at the interface. They are the only agents that have to participate in an active measurement and the others should play a role of passive listeners.

Our framework provides four types of active measurements including multicast ping (`ping test`), `burst test`, `mtrace` between a pair of agents (`trace to agents`), and `mtrace` to an end host (`trace to unknown`). We need the address of the end host (destination) and a multicast group address (group) to trace a reverse routing path from an agent to the end host. The user interface offers a facility to set the <destination, group> to perform `trace to unknown`.

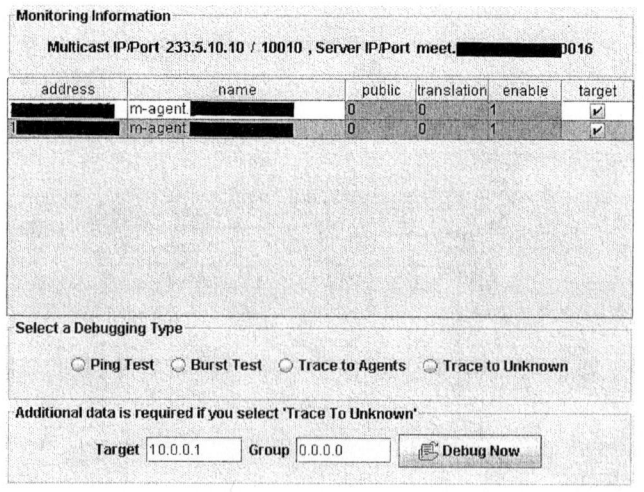

Fig. 7. MEET web-based user interface

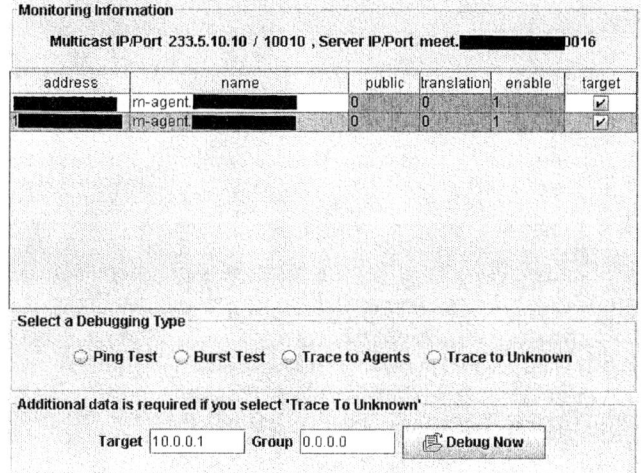

Fig. 8. Result view

Table 2. Sort of tests and QoS parameters

Test	QoS parameters	command
Heartbeat	private network	HEART
Enability	multicast enability	JOIN
Ping	round trip time	PING
Burst	latency, loss, jitter, out-of-order, duplication	BURST
Trace	reverse path, loss	TRACE

Fig. 8 shows the measurement results of the burst test. The result view reports packet delivery statistics between the designate agents. All measurable QoS parameters with our framework are listed in the Table 2. At this stage, MEET performs 5 sorts of measurements and retrieves more than 10 QoS parameters from the tests.

4 Conclusions and Future Works

In this paper we introduced an end-to-end multicast diagnosing toolkit, MEET, which debugs multicast networks as well as the address spaces of the agents. MEET allows Access Grid users to easily access the toolkit and efficiently assess the end-to-end delivery statistics by adopting proactive ways of bi-directional measurement. We are sure that MEET contributes to the stabilization of multicast network and the prevalence of the AG even though the implementation is now in progress.

Considering on the toolkit management, 1) the server has to have a job scheduling mechanism to alleviate system loads in itself and agents. And, 2) the toolkit needs more fine-tuing about the internally fixed values to loosen the traffic loads in a multicast session.

References

1. Childers, L., Disz, T., Olson, R., Papka, M., Stevens, R., Udeshi, T.: Access Grid: Immersive group-to-group collaborative visualization, in Proc. 4th International Immersive Projection Technology Workshop, 2000.
2. Kutzko, M., Rimovsky, T.: Multicast Beacon v0.9, http://dast.nlanr.net/projects/beacon/, Nov. 2003.
3. Almeroth, K., Sarac, K., Wei, L.: Supporting multicast management using the multicast reachability monitor (MRM) protocol, Tech. Rep., UCSB, May 2000.
4. Dressler, F.: An approach for QoS measurements in IP multicast networks - MQM Multicast Quality Monitor, in Proc. Third International Network Conference (INC2002), Plymouth, UK, July 2002.
5. Schulzrinne, H., Casner, S., Frederick, R., Jacobson, V.: RTP: A transport protocol for real-time applications, RFC 3550, July 2003.
6. Fenner, W.: Internet group management protocol, version 2, RFC 2236, Nov. 1997.

Traffic Management for Video Streaming Service over Diff-Serv

Sang-Hyun Park[1], Jeong-Sik Park[2], and Jae-Young Pyun[3]

[1] Sunchon National University, Sunchon, Korea
Tel: +82-61-750-3833, Fax: +82-61-750-3830
shark@sunchon.ac.kr
[2] Sungkonghoe University, Seoul, Korea
jspark@mail.skhu.ac.kr
[3] Chosun University, Gwangju, Korea
jypyun@chosun.ac.kr

Abstract. The Internet Engineering Task Force (IETF) has proposed the Diff-Serv model with firm delay and bandwidth guarantees. In the Diff-Serv model, it is essential that the traffic management algorithm be carefully designed to guarantee the QoS requirements of real-time applications such as video services. In this paper, we propose a new traffic management scheme for the video service over the Diff-Serv network. In the proposed scheme, when a new video flow is requested, the bandwidth broker decides if the Diff-Serv network can provide the video flow with its negotiated QoS without violating the QoS guarantees of existing flows in the network by calculating the loss probability of the aggregate video traffic. Experimental results show that the proposed method can determine the number of acceptable flows more precisely and efficiently than other existing methods.

1 Introduction

Current IP network elements treat all traffic equally without any mechanism for providing priority to the packets carrying delay-sensitive real-time video. However, within the next few years, an exponential growth of real-time applications such as video and multimedia over the Internet is expected. The IETF proposed the IntServe framework to provide QoS guarantee to real-time applications. Nevertheless, to date, the deployment of the IntServ has been limited for its lack of scalability. In order to address the problems of IntServ, the IETF decided to look for a more scalable alternative and developed the Diff-Serv architecture. In the Diff-Serv model, individual flows map their QoS requirements to a specific service class at the edge router. Thus, different flows choosing the same service class are aggregated at the edge router and forwarded according to the assigned differentiated service code point (DSCP) at the core router. That is, the Diff-Serv handles traffic aggregates instead of individual flows [1, 2].

In Diff-Serv model, traffic management is a key component for QoS guarantee because it determines the extent to which network resources are utilized.

Namely, traffic management is used as a protection against oversubscription of the available resources. In this paper, we propose a new traffic management scheme with admission control for real-time MPEG video service over the Diff-Serv where QoS guarantees are only provided at the aggregate level. Admission control usually employs comparison between the QoS requirements and the resources available and then decides to accept or reject the service request [1]. In the proposed scheme, when a new real-time video service is requested, a bandwidth broker decides if network resources can provide the new request with its QoS requirements without violating the QoS guarantees of existing flows.

The rest of this paper is organized as follows. Sect. 2 describes the Diff-Serv architecture in brief and introduces related works. The proposed traffic management scheme is presented in Sect. 3. Sect. 4 presents and discusses the experimental results. Finally, our conclusions are given in Sect. 5.

2 Background and Related Work

In this section, we introduce the Diff-Serv model architecture and summarize some related works upon the traffic management scheme with admission control.

2.1 Diff-Serv Architecture

The Diff-Serv working group has put forth a number of specifications outlining the general architecture of the Diff-Serv approach. Fig. 1 illustrates a typical architecture of the Diff-Serv network which consists of multiple Diff-Serv domains (DS's) that can be viewed as autonomous systems [1]. Within the DS, a bandwidth broker (BB) must be in charge of controlling network resources. When a new flow requests the Diff-Serv service, the BB must sequentially perform the following steps: 1) it determines the path of the flow through the domains; 2) it computes the end-to-end QoS parameters and check if they are compliant with the request QoS; 3) it admits the flow only if the computed results meet the request QoS in all DS's. The BB's communicate with each other in order to establish end-to-end services and maintain the necessary state information. The BB can use RSVP with the POLICY-DATA object for signaling and admission control with end-users.

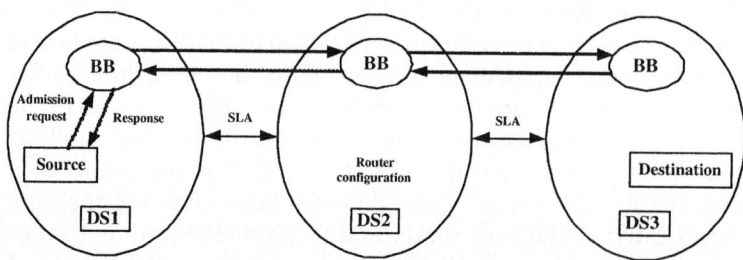

Fig. 1. Diff-Serv model architecture

2.2 Traffic Management for Video Service in Diff-Serv

The current Diff-Serv model simply provides a coarse end-to-end QoS granularity, which may result in low resource utilization. Thus, various researches on how to accommodate various types of traffic with fine end-to-end QoS granularity while maintaining current Diff-Serv scalability are in progress [2]. Under the fine QoS granularity environment, a specific service class can be assigned to video streams with similar QoS parameters. That is, similar video streams are multiplexed in the same buffer at the edge router.

The important QoS parameters of real-time video services are delay and jitter constraints and low packet loss. In Diff-Serv model, when multiple video flows are multiplexed, delay and jitter constraints can be determined according to the method proposed in the RFC 3246. Given a known error value of E_p, a delay bound is given by

$$D = B/R + E_p \tag{1}$$

where R is the configured service rate on the output interface. The total offered load entering the buffer from all interfaces and destined for a single outgoing interface is bounded by a token bucket of rate $r <= R$ and burstsize B. That is, given delay and jitter bounds, the token bucket parameters can be determined by (1). Then, using the token bucket parameters, the BB determines to accept or reject the new flow by computing the loss probability of the aggregate traffic [1, 3].

3 Proposed Traffic Management Scheme

In this section, we describe how the BB calculates the loss probability of the aggregate video traffic to determine if it admits a new real-time video service request or not.

3.1 Traffic Model for Multiplexed MPEG Videos

In the MPEG video, three frame types (I-, P-, and B-frames) appear periodically according to the GOP structure. The GOP structure is specified by two parameters $(\bar{N}, \bar{M})$, where $\bar{N}$ is the distance between two successive I-frames and $\bar{M}$ is the distance between I- and subsequent P-frames or two successive P-frames. To model the subsequence of each frame type, we use the arrival rate histogram model [4], where the arrival rate is the number of bytes generated for one frame divided by the frame duration which is a reciprocal of the frame rate. Since the MPEG video is a sequence of three frame types, it is modeled by a sequence of arrival rate histograms of three frame types according to its GOP structure. Fig. 2 shows a single source model which is a sequence with the three arrival rate histograms, where λ_k is the arrival rate of the kth histogram bin of the I-, P-, or B-frame type.

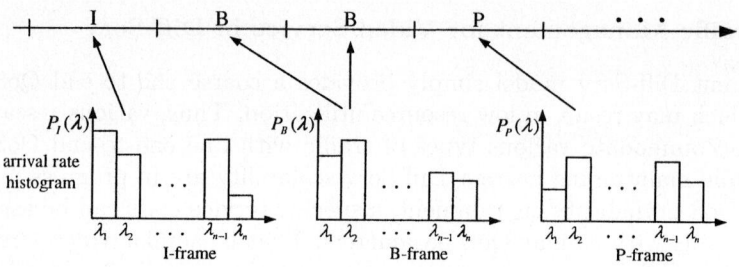

Fig. 2. Single MPEG source model composed of three arrival rate histograms of I-, P-, and B-frames and the GOP structure

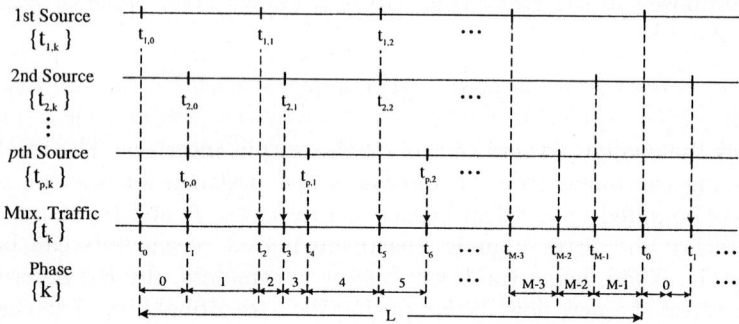

Fig. 3. Multiplexed traffic with heterogeneous p MPEG video sources

The traffic model of the multiplexed MPEG videos is obtained from the individual MPEG video source models as follows: Fig. 3 shows an example where heterogeneous p MPEG video sources are multiplexed. It is obvious that the multiplexed traffic of the periodic sources is also periodic. The period of the multiplexed traffic is $L = LCM(L_1, L_2, \cdots, L_p)$, where LCM represents the least common multiple and L_k denotes the period of the GOP of the kth source. The number of histograms of the multiplexed traffic depends on the arrangement of the I-frames and the GOP structures of individual sources. Let $t_{k,m}$ be the starting time of the mth frame of the kth source.

The nth phase is defined as the nth interval when the $t_{k,m}$'s are arranged in time within L. If the number of phases is M, the multiplexed traffic can be modeled by M different arrival rate histograms. Let the random variables $X_{k,m}$ and X_n represent the arrival rate of the kth source for $[t_{k,m}, t_{k,m+1})$ and the arrival rate of the multiplexed traffic for $[t_n, t_{n+1})$, respectively, where t_n is the starting time of the nth phase. Since the arrival rate of the multiplexed traffic is the sum of the arrival rates of individual sources, X_n is given by

$$X_n = \sum_{\{(k,m)|t_{k,m} \leq t_n, t_{k,m+1} \geq t_{n+1}\}} X_{k,m}. \qquad (2)$$

Therefore, the histogram of X_n can be directly calculated by convolving the histograms of $X_{k,m}$'s.

3.2 Loss Calculation

Given a token bucket of rate $r <= R$ and burst size K, the loss probability of the token bucket can be determined by calculating the loss probability of the queue with service rate R and buffer size K [5]. It is also well-known that there are typically two main regions, the uncorrelated region and the correlated region in which increasing the buffer size reduces the loss [4, 6]. In the uncorrelated region where the buffer size is small, the loss depends only on the first order statistics of the MEPG frame sequence. However, in the correlated region where the buffer size is large, correlations of GOP's play their role and affect the loss.

Our method of adopting different approximation for the two regions consists of three steps: In the first step, the loss in the uncorrelated region is calculated using the proposed arrival rate histogram model. In the second step, the loss in the burst region is obtained using the Markov Modulated Fluid (MMF) model [6] for GOP-layer traffic. In the third step, the loss is finally determined using results of the first and second steps.

Step 1: Determining the loss in the uncorrelated region. In order to determine the loss in the uncorrelated region, we use the arrival rate histogram model proposed in Section 3.1 which accurately describes the periodic pattern and the first order statistics of the multiplexed MPEG video traffic. For each frame, states of the queueing system employed are defined in terms of the quantities (b_n, s_n), where b_n and s_n, respectively, are the histogram bin number and the phase number at the nth frame. Note that the stochastic process $\{b_n, s_n\}$ is a Markov chain with state space $\{(i,j) : 1 \leq i \leq B, \ 0 \leq j \leq M-1\}$, where (i,j) represents that the arrival rate is the ith histogram bin of X_j. The probability that the Markov chain $\{b_n, s_n\}$ moves from state (i,j) to state (i',j') is defined as $p(i,j,i',j')$, and is determined by,

$$p(i,j,i',j') = \begin{cases} p_{i,i'}^{j+1}, & \text{if } j' = j+1 \\ 0, & \text{otherwise} \end{cases}$$

where $p_{i,i'}^j$ is the conditional probability which is determined by

$$p_{i,i'}^j = Pr(X_j = \lambda_{i',j} | X_{j-1} = \lambda_{i,j-1}) \qquad (3)$$
$$= \frac{Pr(X_{j-1} = \lambda_{i,j-1}, X_j = \lambda_{i',j})}{Pr(X_{j-1} = \lambda_{i,j-1})}.$$

When the probability $p(i,j,i',j')$ is mapped into 2-dimensional space through the mapping,

$$l = i + Bj \quad \text{and} \quad l' = i' + Bj',$$

the resulting transition matrix, P, which is of order MB with elements $p(l, l')$, takes the form

$$P = \begin{bmatrix} 0 & P_1 & 0 & 0 & \cdots & 0 \\ 0 & 0 & P_2 & 0 & \cdots & 0 \\ \vdots & \vdots & \vdots & \vdots & \ddots & \vdots \\ 0 & 0 & 0 & 0 & \cdots & P_{M-1} \\ P_0 & 0 & 0 & 0 & \cdots & 0 \end{bmatrix}, \qquad (4)$$

where P_j is the submatrix whose i, i'th element is $p_{i,i'}^j$.

In addition, the bit rate matrix that identifies the bit rate at state (i, j) is defined by Λ, so the overall transition behavior of the multiplexed MPEG video sequence can be fully described by the set of matrices $\{P, \Lambda\}$.

$$\Lambda = diag(\lambda'_{1,0}, \lambda'_{2,0}, \cdots, \lambda'_{B-1,M-1}, \lambda'_{B,M-1}) \qquad (5)$$

with

$$\lambda'_{i,j} = (t_{j+1} - t_j)\tau \lambda_{i,j}$$

where τ is the phase rate (phases/sec) of the multiplexed MPEG video sources.

The state transition matrix (4) is a discrete time Markov chain that determines the next transition at every phase time. In order to more easily solve queueing problems, we approximate the system with a continuous time chain.

$$Q = \tau(P - I). \qquad (6)$$

where I is the identity matrix of size $\{MB \times MB\}$. Let $K(t)$ be the virtual fluid content of the buffer; let $B(t)$ be the histogram bin number; let $S(t)$ be the phase number at time t. Let $F_i^j(t, x)$, $t \geq 0$, $x \geq 0$, be the probability that at given time t, the histogram bin number is i, the phase number is j, and the buffer content does not exceed x as

$$F_i^j(t, x) = Pr\{K(t) \leq x, B(t) = i, S(t) = j\} \qquad (7)$$
$$(i \in \{1, 2, \cdots, B\}, j \in \{0, 1, \cdots, M-1\}).$$

The forward transition equation from time t to $t + \Delta t$ is written as

$$F_i^j(t + \Delta t, x) - F_i^j\{t, x - (\lambda_{i,j} - R)\Delta t\} \qquad (8)$$
$$= \sum_{k=0, k \neq j}^{M-1} \sum_{l=1}^{B} q_{l,i}^{k,j} F_l^k(t, x) \Delta t + q_{i,i}^{j,j} \Delta t F_i^j(t, x),$$

where $q_{i,l}^{j,k}$ is the i,lth element of $Q_{j,k}$ and R is the output service rate. In the steady state, it is

$$(\lambda_{i,j} - R)\frac{\partial}{\partial x} F_i^j(t, x) = \sum_{k=0}^{M-1} \sum_{l=1}^{B} q_{l,i}^{k,j} F_l^k(t, x). \qquad (9)$$

Let us define the $F(x)$ and D matrices as

$$F(x) = [F_1^0(x), F_2^0(x), F_3^0, \cdots, F_{B-1}^{M-1}, F_B^{M-1}] \tag{10}$$

$$\text{and } D = \Lambda - RI. \tag{11}$$

Then, (9) becomes a unified form

$$\frac{\partial}{\partial x} F(x) D = F(x) Q. \tag{12}$$

It is also well-known by [7] that the solution (12) is given by

$$F(x) = \sum_{\{k|Re(z_k)<0\}} a_k \phi_k e^{z_k x} \tag{13}$$

where $\{z_k, \phi_k\}$ are respectively the eigenvalue and eigenvector pair of the eigenvalue problem given by $z_k \phi_k D = \phi_k Q$.

In (13), $\{a_k\}$ can be calculated by the following boundary condition.

$$F_i^j(0) = 0 = \sum_k a_k \phi_k \quad if \ \lambda_{i,j} > R \tag{14}$$

Finally, for a given buffer size K, the probability of buffer overflow is given by

$$P_D(K) = Pr(k > K) = 1 - <F(K), 1> \tag{15}$$

where the symbol $<\cdot,\cdot>$ denotes the inner product of the vectors.

Step 2: Determining the loss in the correlated region. As the buffer size increased, the burstiness by the I-frame is absorbed and the loss is mainly caused by the successive GOP's whose sizes exceed the multiplication of the output service rate by the GOP duration. Thus, the loss in the correlated region can be determined by the GOP-layer traffic model [8]. In the VBR MPEG video, the statistical characteristics of a GOP sequence are similar to those of non-MPEG-type VBR video traffic. In this step, we use MMF model [9] for the GOP-layer

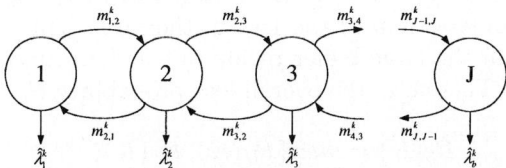

Fig. 4. A Markov Modulated Fluid (MMF) model having J states for the kth MPEG GOP sequence

MPEG traffic, as shown in Fig. 4 where $\hat{\lambda}_i^k$ and $m_{i,j}^k$ are, respectively, the arrival rate of the ith state and the transition rate from state i to state j of the kth source. In the MMF model, traffic parameters, $\hat{\lambda}_i^k$, $m_{i,j}^k$, and the number of states, J, can be easily determined by the values of the mean, the variance, and the correlation coefficient of the kth source (See [5]).

The loss probability of the MMF model as a function of the buffer size K is of the form of a negative exponential as

$$P_C(K) = P_C(0)e^{\delta K} \quad (16)$$

where $P_C(0)$ is the loss probability when the buffer size is zero [5, 6]. To obtain $P_C(0)$, we determine the arrival rate of the aggregated source $\{\hat{\lambda}_i, p_i\}$ which can be directly calculated by convolving the arrival rate of each source $\{\hat{\lambda}_i^k, p_i^k\}$. Here, $\hat{\lambda}_i$ is the arrival rate of the ith state of the aggregate source, and p_i and p_i^k are, respectively, the stationary probability of state i of the aggregate source and of the kth source. Then, the loss probability with no buffer is given by

$$P_C(0) = \frac{1}{E(\hat{\lambda}_i)} \sum_{i:\hat{\lambda}_i > R} \hat{\lambda}_i p_i \left(1 - \frac{R}{\hat{\lambda}_i}\right) \quad (17)$$

Next, we determine the slope of the loss probability, δ, in (16). Suppose that there are p sources characterized by $(M^k, \boldsymbol{\lambda}^k)$ where $M^k = [m_{i,j}^k]$ and $\boldsymbol{\lambda}^k$ is the vector whose ith element is $\hat{\lambda}_i^k$. Let $\Lambda^k = diag(\boldsymbol{\lambda}^k)$. It can then be shown that δ can be found by solving for the root of the equation,

$$g_1(\delta) + g_2(\delta) + \cdots + g_p(\delta) = R \quad (18)$$

where $g_k(\delta)$, the eigenvalue with the greatest real part, is found by solving the inverse eigenvalue problem [6]

$$g_k(\delta)\phi^k(\delta) = \phi^k(\delta)(\Lambda^k - M^k/\delta). \quad (19)$$

We can solve for (18) by using standard iterative root-finding techniques (such as the Newton's method), which have been found to work very efficiently [6].

Step 3: Determining the loss. Next, we determine the overall loss using the results of the previous steps. $P_U(K)$ accurately estimates the loss in the small buffer region but underestimates the loss in the large buffer region. However, $P_C(K)$ is accurate in the large buffer region but underestimates the loss in the small buffer region. Therefore, the overall loss probability P_L is given by

$$P_L(K) = max\{P_U(K), P_C(K)\} \quad (20)$$

For a given loss requirement, the acceptance criterion is as follows: That is, if $P_L(K)$ is smaller than the loss requirement, the BB accepts the new video service request, otherwise, the BB rejects the new request.

4 Experimental Results

For experiments, we use the MPEG coded video sequences obtained from [10]. Table 1 shows main statistics of the used sequences. The GOP parameters $(\bar{N}, \bar{M})$ of all the video sequences are (12,3) and the picture rates are 25 frames/s.

For the analysis of the proposed method, each MPEG video source is modeled by the three arrival rate histograms for I-, P-, and B-frames. In the arrival rate histogram model, the number of bins of the arrival rate histogram affects the performance accuracy as well as the computational complexity. Through extensive simulations, we have found that eight bins are sufficient to model each picture type of MPEG video. Further increasing the number of bins does not result in a significant change in the I-frame arrangement. For the multiplexed traffic, we have also found that 20 bins are sufficient to model each phase.

When several MPEG videos are multiplexed, the arrangement of I-pictures may significantly affect the loss probability of the multiplexed traffic [11]. To investigate the relationship between the I-frame arrangement and the loss, q sources out of p sources are arranged to have the same I-frame starting time, and $p - q$ sources are evenly distributed over the period L. Fig. 5 shows the loss characteristics with $\rho = 0.7$ and $\rho = 0.9$. It is seen that the loss probability with $q = 3$ is greater than that with $q = 1$, as expected. Note that for the low traffic intensity ($\rho = 0.7$), the loss probability rapidly decreases as the buffer size increases. In this case, the I-frame arrangement plays an important role in the loss characteristics. On the other hand, for the high traffic intensity ($\rho = 0.9$), as the buffer size increases, the loss characteristics become more independent of the I-frame arrangement since the variability by the I-frame arrangement is absorbed by the large buffer. It is also seen that the results of the proposed loss calculation method are very similar to simulation results.

Next, we present the number of acceptable sources that can be accommodated into the network by admission control using the *Star Wars* sequence. The constraint on each flow is a maximum loss probability of 10^{-4} and the buffer size of 5K bytes. We compare the proposed admission control method with the admission control methods using the PD-EB model [11] and PD-PCR model [12]. In the PD-EB model and the PD-PCR model, each frame type is modeled by the effective bandwidth (EB) and the peak cell rate (PCR), respectively. Although the PD-EB and the PD-PCR can represent the arrangement of

Table 1. Main statistics of sequences used in experiments

Sequence	Frames		GOPs	
	Mean [bytes]	Peak/Mean	Mean [bytes]	Peak/Mean
Starwars	1237	13.18	14844	3.96
Dino	1728	9.03	20728	3.96
Asterix	2933	6.54	35212	4.00
Atp	2875	8.66	34496	2.98

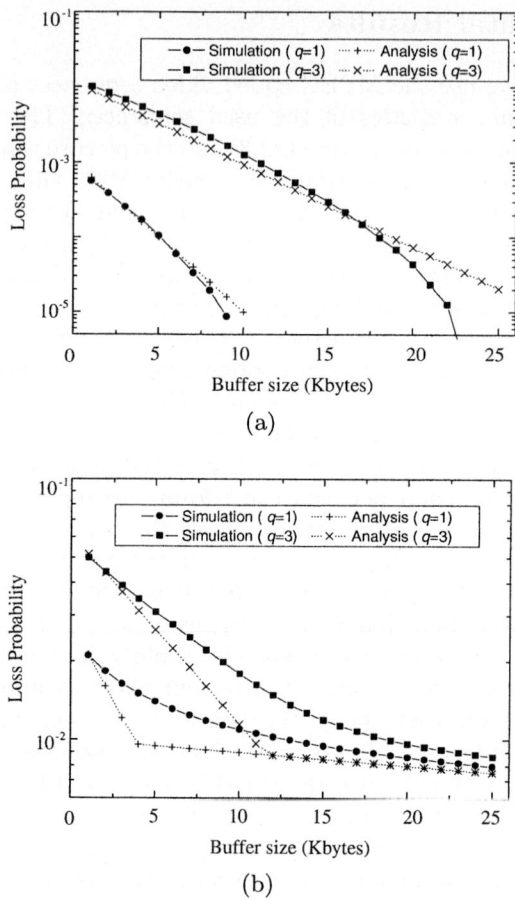

Fig. 5. Periodic peak position effect when 12 sources are multiplexed: (a) $\rho = 0.7$ and (b) $\rho = 0.9$

the I-frame starting times of the multiplexed MPEG videos, it cannot reflect the statistical multiplexing gain since the EB and PCR of the multiplexed traffic are simply identical to the sum of the EB's and PCR's of individual sources, respectively. Fig. 6 shows the number of acceptable sources as a function of the output service rate. It is seen that the results of the proposed admission control is very similar to the simulation results, while the results of the other admission control methods (PD-EB and PD-PCR) are somewhat different from those of the computer simulation.

5 Conclusion

In this paper, we have proposed a new traffic management scheme with admission control which can be effectively used for real-time MPEG video service over the Diff-Serv. For traffic management, we have proposed the traffic model for the

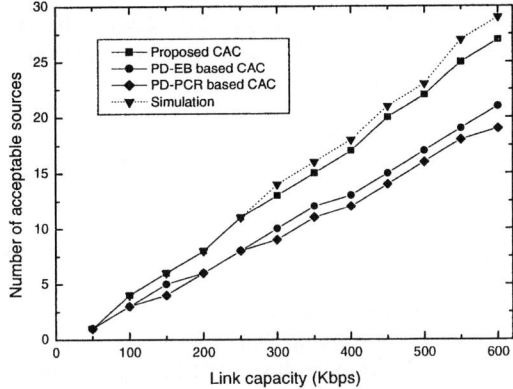

Fig. 6. Number of acceptable MPEG videos for different admission control methods with the buffer size of 5K bytes and the desired loss probability of 10^{-4}

multiplexed MPEG videos. Using the proposed traffic model, the loss probability was determined to decide if Diff-Serv network can provide the new flow with its request QoS.

Experimental results showed that the proposed method accurately determines the loss probability of the multiplexed traffic. Moreover, it was shown that the number of acceptable sources that can be accommodated into the Diff-Serv network can be precisely estimated by the proposed scheme.

Acknowledgements. This work is financially supported by the Ministry of Education and Human Resources Development(MOE) and the Ministry of Commerce, Industry and Energy(MOCIE) through the fostering project of the Industrial-Academic Cooperation Centered University.

References

1. M. A. El-Gendy, A. Bose, and K. G. Shin, "Evolution of the Internet QoS and Support for Soft Real-Time Applications," *Proc. IEEE*, vol. 91, pp. 1086–1104, July 2003.
2. J. Yang, J. Ye, and S. Papavassiliou, "Enhancing end-to-end QoS granularity in DiffServ networks via service vector and explicit endpoint admission control," *IEE Proc. Commun.*, vol. 151, p. 7781, Feb. 2004.
3. Y. Xu and R. Guerin, "Individual QoS versus aggregate QoS: A loss performance study," in *INFOCOM'02*, pp. 634–643, June 2002.
4. P. Skelly, M. Schwartz, and S. Dixit, "A histogram-based model for video traffic behavior in an ATM multiplexer," *IEEE/ACM Trans. Networking*, vol. 1, pp. 446–459, Aug. 1993.
5. M. Schwartz, *Broadband Integrated Networks*. New Jersey: Prentice Hall PTR, 1996.
6. N. Shroff and M. Schwartz, "Improved Loss Calculation at an ATM Multiplexer," *IEEE/ACM Trans. Networking*, vol. 6, pp. 411–421, Aug. 1998.

7. D. Anick, D. Mitra, and M. M. Dondhi, "Stochastic theory of a data-handling system with multiple sources," *Bell Syst. Technical Journal*, vol. 61, pp. 1871–1894, Aug. 1982.
8. N. Blefari-Melazzi, "Study of Statistical Characteristics and Queueing Performance of MEPG1 and MPEG2 video Sources," in *Proceedings of the IEEE GLOBECOM'95*, pp. 488–493, 1995.
9. A. I. Elwalid, D. Heyman, T. Lakshman, D. Mitra, and A. Weiss, "A new approach for allocating buffers and bandwidth to heterogeneous regulated traffic in an ATM node," *IEEE Journal on Selected Areas in Communications*, vol. 13, pp. 1017–1027, Aug. 1995.
10. http://nero.informatik.uni-wuerzburg.de/MPEG/.
11. B. H. Roh and J. K. Kim, "Starting Time Selection and Scheduling Methods for Minimum Cell Loss Ratio of Superposed VBR MPEG Video Traffic," *IEEE Trans. Circuits Syst. Video Tech.*, vol. 9, pp. 920–928, Sept. 1999.
12. M. Krunz, "Bandwidth Allocation Strategies for Transporting Variable-Bit-Rate Video Traffic," *IEEE Commun. Mag.*, vol. 37, pp. 40–46, Jan. 1999.

Scalable and Adaptive QoS Mapping Control Framework for Packet Video Delivery

Gooyoun Hwang[1], Jitae Shin[2], and JongWon Kim[1]

[1] Networked Media Lab., Department of Information and Communications,
Gwangju Institute of Science and Technology (GIST), Gwangju, 500-712, Korea
{gyhwang, jongwon}@netmedia.gist.ac.kr

[2] School of Information and Communication Engineering,
Sungkyunkwan Univ., Suwon, 440-746, Korea
{jtshin@ece.skku.ac.kr}

Abstract. With the exploding volume of traffic and expanding Quality of Service (QoS) requirements from emerging multimedia applications, many research efforts have been carried out to establish multi-class network service model in next-generation Internet. To successfully support multiple classes of service, network resources must be managed effectively to ensure end-to-end QoS while simultaneously sustaining stable network QoS. First, we present a scalable and adaptive QoS mapping control (SAQM) framework over the differentiated services network focusing reactive edge-to-edge QoS control in class-based. Secondly, under SAQM framework, end-to-end QoS control for per-flow service guarantee is proposed through incorporating relative priority index (RPI)-based video streaming and a special access node called media gateway (MG) at network edge. The SAQM framework is composed of the functionalities of proactive and reactive QoS mapping controls to provide reliable and consistent service guarantee. In our framework, edge-to-edge active monitoring is utilized to obtain measures reflecting each class performance and then measurement-based reactive mapping control for relative network QoS provisioning is performed at MG located in the ingress edges. Simulation results demonstrate the feasibility of an edge-based QoS control and show how to enhance the QoS performance of video streaming in proposed SAQM framework.

1 Introduction

The explosively increased capacity of packet switched networks makes it feasible to support new applications, such as IP telephony, video-conferencing, and online TV broadcast. Meanwhile, the volume of traditional Best Effort (BE) data traffic continues to grow with web applications and I/O-intensive scientific applications. To meet these diverse application needs, the Internet is evolving from a network that provides a single BE service to a network that supports multiple classes of services. Tremendous effort has been devoted to defining new service models that deliver better end-to-end Quality of Service (QoS) than current BE service can deliver. The differentiated services (DiffServ, or DS) model [1] has been proposed as a scalable and manageable architecture for network QoS provisioning. There are two basic types of service differentiation approaches: premium service (PS) [2] and assured service (AS) [3]. Especially, the assured service provides a relative service differentiation among DS classes, in the sense that high-priority classes receives a better or at least not worse service than low-priority ones. In this context, applications do not get an absolute service quality assurance. So, it is up to the applications to select appropriate QoS levels that best meet their requirements, cost, and device constraints. Since most of recent multimedia applications have become more and more resilient to occasional packet loss and delay fluctuation, the AS of DS networks seems a more attractive choice due to its simplicity and flexibility.

However, unstable network service situations caused by instantaneous class load fluctuations still occur even though the resource provisioning policy of underlying network is strictly managed. The unstable situations obstruct multimedia applications to achieve their desired service requirements persistently. Since the end-to-end QoS perceived by the applications mainly depend on the current network load condition, the applications should response to this fluctuation in a proper way. Accordingly, an adaptive QoS mapping[1] mechanism considering the network situation is required to support the end-to-end QoS guarantee dynamically to end systems and to improve the network utilization. From this point of view, we present a scalable and adaptive QoS mapping control (shortly, SAQM) framework, which consists of proactive QoS mapping control and reactive QoS mapping control in network class/flow-based granularity, over the DS domain even for packet video delivery. In the SAQM framework, edge to edge active monitoring is utilized to obtain measures reflecting each class behavior and then measurement-based reactive mapping control for relative network QoS provisioning is performed at the ingress edges of the network.

Finally, we propose a reactive end-to-end QoS mapping control to enhance service differentiation-aware video streaming. With the help of network feedback, the end-host video application can recognize the status of network classes and can now react in advance. By leveraging the end-to-end feedback (i.e., in tie with the required congestion control), the feedback is relayed to the sender in a similar way as the explicit congestion notification (ECN) [4]. The network feedback-based QoS control triggers the QoS mapping adjustment at the boundary node of an access domain. The network simulation based on NS-2 is performed to demonstrate the enhanced performance of the proposed QoS mapping control framework (i.e., more efficient and adaptive to network variation).

The remainder of this paper is organized as follows. Section 2 presents overview of the scalable and adaptive QoS mapping framework with video delivery scenario. In section 3, we propose a reactive edge-to-edge QoS mapping control for stable class-based service differentiation and a reactive end-to-end

---

[1] The issue of *QoS mapping* occurs when we map prioritized and classified groups of some applications(or users or flows) based on their importance into different DS levels or network classes.

QoS control to enhance relative differentiation-aware video streaming. Various sets of performance evaluation through computer simulations are presented in section 4. Finally, section 5 concludes this paper.

2 The SAQM Framework

2.1 Overview of the SAQM Framework

As stated in section 1, the network QoS of a DS domain may be time-varying due to instantaneous class load fluctuation. It is clear that this QoS variation results in network service violation and also exerts bad influence on the end-to-end QoS guarantee. To ensure the overall QoS, we present a scalable and adaptive QoS mapping control framework in the DiffServ network. The SAQM framework can be divided into three QoS controls : 1) proactive QoS control for initially managing traffic aggregates at the entrance of the network, 2) reactive edge-to-edge QoS control based class-based active monitoring for stable network service provisioning, and 3) reactive end-to-end QoS control for flow-based service guarantee.

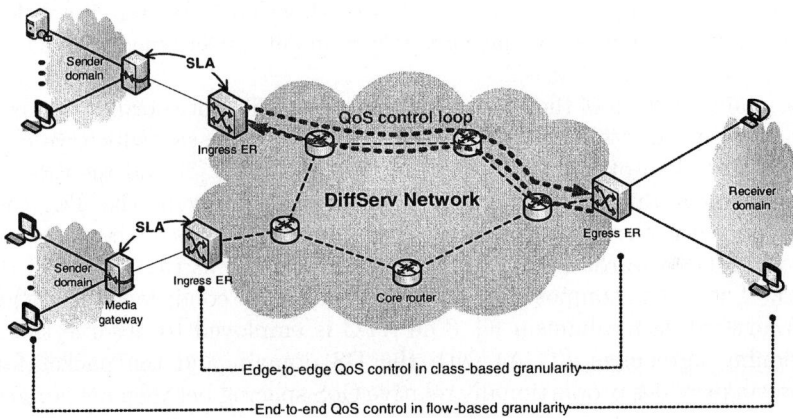

Fig. 1. The scalable and adaptive QoS mapping framework

As shown in Fig. 1, we assume that there is several ingress points and only one egress point in the DiffServ network. For class-based QoS monitoring between ingress-egress pair, we insert probe packets into the data stream of each class periodically at an ingress edge router (ER). The egress ER is responsible for classifying the probe packets and measuring the QoS metrics of each class, such as edge-to-edge delay and packet loss rate. Then the egress ER notifies the measured information to the corresponding ingress ER. Based on the feedback analysis, the ingress ER decides whether to perform a reactive QoS mapping adjustment or not. This reactive edge-to-edge QoS control (shortly, EG2EG control) process can build a control loop between ingress-egress pair. The detailed description of the EG2EG control will be presented in section 3.1. Finally, a proper network-aware feedback control (i.e., reactive end-to-end QoS control), which can give the applications a guidance of network status, enables the fine-tuned refinement on top of coarse edge-to-edge QoS control. For this, a network-adaptive QoS control for packet video streaming will be presented in section 3.2.

2.2 Video Delivery Scenario Under the SAQM Framework

For the end-to-end video streaming, sources within the access network send videos to the corresponding clients. The access network subscribes to DS services, and traffic is delivered to the clients through the DS domain. The access network has SLAs [1] with the DS domain. In this framework, the video applications at the source assign a relative priority-based index (RPI) to each packet in terms of loss probability and delay as studied in [5] so that each packet can reflect its influence to the end-to-end video quality. The source then furnishes each packet with this prioritization information for a special boundary node called media gateway (MG) as shown in Fig. 2. Thus, the video streams from the sources are merged at the MG. In order to prevent the sources from violating their SLAs and protect resources from a selfish source, the MG exercises the traffic shaping on a per-flow basis through the token buckets (TBs) assigned for individual flows, as seen in Fig. 2. The packets violating this agreement are assigned with the lowest DS class (i.e., best-effort class).

The main function of the MG is to make a cost-efficient coordination between the prioritized packets (or flows) and the DS service classes, which we call *QoS mapping*. For the optimal QoS mapping, we just refer [5] and mention briefly due to page limitation. That is, for packets conforming to the TB, the MG assigns to each packet a DS codepoint (DSCP) on the basis of the packet's RPI. Then, the MG forwards the packet streams to the ER at the ingress of the DS network. The ER is composed of an aggregate traffic conditioner (ATC) and a packet forwarding mechanism [6]. The ATC is employed to observe the traffic conditioning agreement (TCA) with the DS domain and the packet forward mechanism provides proportionally relative QoS spacing between network service

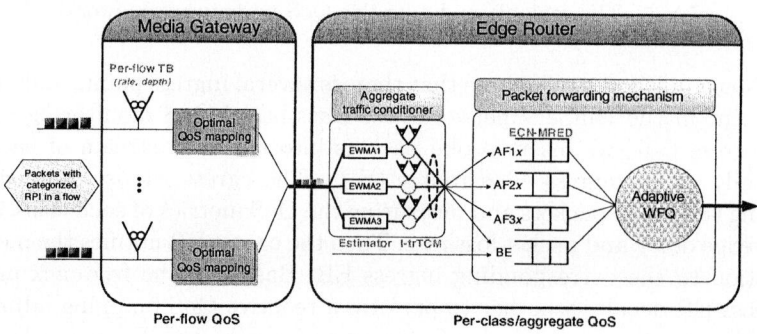

Fig. 2. Overall structures of media gateway and edge router

classes by using a multiple random early detection (MRED) queue and adaptive WFQ. In order to support the relative service differentiation, the DS domain provides three assured forwarding (AF) classes and each class queue has three drop precedences [3]. That is, the order of DS level, or DSCP, from high to low is $\{AF_{11}, AF_{12}, AF_{13}; AF_{21}, AF_{22}, AF_{23}; AF_{31}, AF_{32}, AF_{33}; BE\}$. Hence, the proactive QoS control is realized as discussed.

3 Reactive QoS Controls in the SAQM Framework

This section presents two types of reactive QoS mapping controls in the SAQM framework. One is an edge-based QoS control (i.e., the EG2EG control) proceeded inside the DS network domain and another is a flow-based QoS control performed at the boundary node, i.e., the MG, of an access domain. The latter is specialized for source-marked video streaming and is activated by user's request.

3.1 The EG2EG Control

The EG2EG control relies on class-based QoS monitoring to obtain adequate information of each class behavior and performance so that a reactive QoS mapping adjustment can be performed. In our framework, the monitoring scheme measures delay and packet loss on per-class basis and then compares these measurements to the predefined values in the SLA. The combined monitoring of delay and packet loss information can be used for reliable estimation of network condition. Note that delay is defined as the edge-to-edge latency and packet loss rate is defined as the ratio of total number of packets dropped from the aggregated flows mapped into a class in the domain to the total number of packets belonged to the same class entering into the domain [7].

Function blocks of the EG2EG control between ingress-egress pair are illustrated in Fig. 3. The probe packet generation and insertion module encodes the following states into probe packet inserted in the network:

[Ingress ID; Class ID; Sequence number; Timestamp]

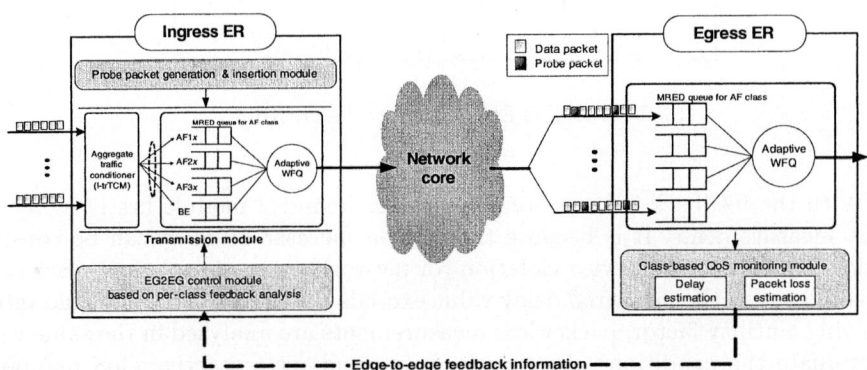

Fig. 3. Building blocks of the EG2EG control

The ingress and class identifier will allow the EG2EG control on a per-path, per-class (i.e., ingress-egress pair) basis. The sequence number is used to identify loss on the path at the egress ER. To measure delay, the probe packets should also contain their current timestamps. Assume that all router clocks in a domain are synchronized fairly accurately. The probing frequency is important because it determines the overhead of the monitoring process. In our simulations, we found that the overhead of about 10% of the total bandwidth is adequate to monitor the network resources. The class-based QoS monitoring module at the egress ER classifies the probe packets as belonging to a class i of an ingress ER j, and then measures delay $\tilde{D}^i_j$ and packet loss $\tilde{L}^i_j$ at time t using an exponentially weighted moving average (EWMA) according to the following equations respectively:

$$\tilde{D}^i_j(t) = (1-\alpha) * \tilde{D}^i_j(t-1) + \alpha * D^i_j(t), \qquad (1)$$

$$\tilde{L}^i_j(t) = (1-\beta) * \tilde{L}^i_j(t-1) + \beta * L^i_j(t), \qquad (2)$$

where $0 < \alpha < 1$ and $0 < \beta < 1$ are smoothing factors. Then the monitoring module feeds the measurements back to the edge-to-edge QoS control module at the corresponding ingress ER.

Parameter Definition:
  $\hat{D}^i$: the delay guarantee of class i;
  $\hat{L}^i$: the packet loss guarantee of class i;
  γ, δ, κ, φ: utility factors;
  DP^i: downgrading probability in the ATC;

Reactive Edge-to-edge QoS Control algorithm:
  if ($\tilde{D}^i > \gamma * \hat{D}^i$) then
    if ($\tilde{L}^i > \delta * \hat{L}^i$) then
      $DP^i \leftarrow DP^i + \kappa * (1 - \frac{\hat{L}^i}{\tilde{L}^i})$
    else
      $DP^i \leftarrow DP^i + \varphi * (1 - \frac{\hat{D}^i}{\tilde{D}^i})$
  else BREAK;

Fig. 4. The EG2EG control algorithm

With the feedback information, the EG2EG control module firstly analyzes delay measurements. It is because the sudden increase of delay can be considered as a precursor of service violation (or network congestion) before occurring packet losses. If the measured delay value exceeds the predefined delay guarantee applying a utility factor, packet loss measurements are analyzed in the same way to evaluate the conditions of network classes and set a reactive QoS mapping adjustment in a per-class basis. For the QoS mapping adjustment, the incoming packets entering into the corresponding class queue are randomly re-directed by the ATC to a lower class queue with an updated downgrading probability. When a packet is re-directed to a lower AF class, the drop precedence is set to the highest priority in that lower class. By doing so, we believe that the EG2EG control can help to maintain the quality spacing between network classes independent of the class load variations. The EG2EG control algorithm is described in Fig. 4.

The operation of the algorithm is affected by the above utility factors. The determination of the factors is difficult due to their trade-off properties and mainly depends on network environment. The specific factor values for a specific network environment can be obtained through a number of simulations. For this sensitivity study, we have performed a number of simulations but we do not present in this paper due to page limitation. Usually, the factors must be relatively insensitive to minor changes in network characteristics.

3.2 Network-Adaptive QoS Control for Video Streaming

A proper combination of congestion signalling from network and source reaction will be an effective solution to the instantaneous network fluctuation in the Internet. The major idea behind our end-to-end feedback control is employing ECN mechanism in conjunction with the proactive QoS control at the MG. It is possible that not only the congestion status of network class is notified to the end-host video applications but also a reactive flow-based QoS mapping control is triggered in a faster manner.

Fig. 5 shows the outline of the proposed network-adaptive QoS control under the SAQM framework. When a DS class queue of ECN-MRED router exceeds an predefined threshold, the router sets the CE bit of the packets to indicate the onset of congestion to the end nodes [4]. An ECN-aware receiver monitors the CE bit on each packet arrival i of a flow and calculates the received average cost of the flow $\overline{C}_{recv}^f$ using the following equation:

$$\overline{C}_{recv}^f = \frac{\sum_{i=1}^{N^f} C_{q(i)}}{N^f}, \qquad (3)$$

where N^f and C_q are total received packet numbers of the flow f and unit cost of DS level q specified in the SLA, respectively. This observed value is considered as a barometer to interpret the degree of service degradation which the receiver experiences. Upon the receipt of an ECN-marked packet, the receiver immediately sends a 2-tuple $\{\tilde{q}, \overline{C}_{recv}^f\}$ feedback report to the MG through the corresponding sender. Based on this feedback information, the MG regards $\tilde{q}$ as a congested class and compares $\overline{C}_{recv}^f$ with the requested average payment $\overline{C}_{send}^f$[2]. The MG adjusts the initial mapping of source category k to DS level q based on the comparison. That is, k involved in the reported congestion class $\tilde{q}$ is

---

[2] $\overline{C}_{send}^f$ is computed by the Eq. (3) in case that video packets of a flow are initially sent.

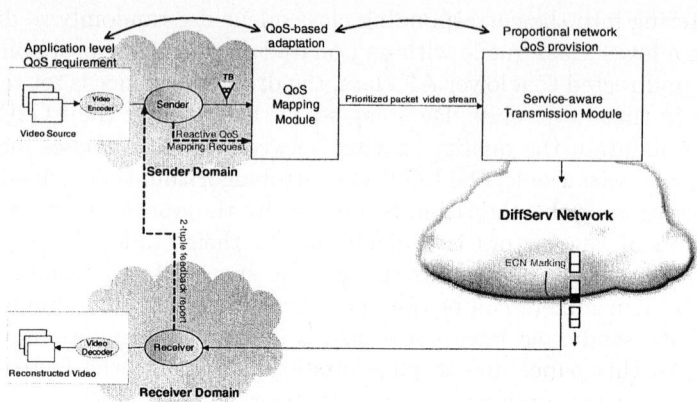

Fig. 5. The network-adaptive QoS control

re-mapped to higher non-congested classes, for $\overline{C}_{recv}^{f} \leq \overline{C}_{send}^{f}$. Otherwise, k is re-mapped to lower non-congested ones. The reactive QoS mapping is summarized as follows:

- DS level: Let q be a DS level, where $1 \leq q \leq Q$ with the increasing order of network service quality and Q is the total number of DS levels.
- RPI partitioning: Let $R_q^k(i)$ be a partition i among the RPI k categories and be assigned into DS level q. Each k category has equal number of packets initially and is sorted in an increasing order, that is, $1 \leq k \leq K$, where K is the category with highest RPI values. Generally, the packets within the same k could be assigned into different q levels.
- Proactive mapping: Each packet, whose RPI is k ($k \in R_q$), is mapped to q in an optimal way while satifying the requested $\overline{C}_{send}^{f}$.
- Reactive mapping: When a congestion feedback, i.e., ECN, from a class $\tilde{q}$ is received, $R_q^k(i)$ is distributed into $S_q(t)$ subset, where $S_q(t)$ is the number of non-congested DS levels at time t and $1 \leq j \leq S_q(t)$, which are higher levels than the level q for $\overline{C}_{recv}^{f} \leq \overline{C}_{send}^{f}$. Then, the packets belonged to $R_q^k(i)$ are re-mapped to DS level j.

This reactive control is operated in time of $[t_{ACK}, t_{ACK} + \Delta]$, where t_{ACK} and Δ denote the time of receiving feedback packet and a certain time interval, respectively. The arrivals of the subsequent feedbacks with the same $\tilde{q}$ are ignored during Δ. After expiration of $t_{ACK} + \Delta$, the MG returns back to the normal state.

4 Simulation Results

In this section, we investigate the feasibility of the proposed EG2EG control by comparison with the proactive approach (PQ-only) having no reactive QoS mapping mechanism. Next, we evaluate the effectiveness of our network feedback-based QoS control (PQ-NBF) in the end-to-end video streaming.

4.1 Simulation Specification

The simulation topology model is shown in Fig. 6, which is used to generate underlying network dynamics. Each source connected with ER1 and ER2 generates a mix of CBR and On/Off UDP flows. The sending rates of the flows are varied according to the desired network load level. One test video source is also connected to the DS network through the MG and communicates with one destination nodes. The link capacities and delays between the routers are shown in the links of Fig. 6. As described in section 2.2, the ER implements three major components for managing traffic aggregates: the interconnected trTCM[3], the MRED, and adaptive WFQ. For our simulations, the ER uses the MRED with the values of [50, 70, 0.01] for AF_{x1}, [30, 50, 0.02] for AF_{x2}, and [10, 30, 0.1] for AF_{x3} [8]. The weighting factors of the WFQ for class queues are set as $AF1 : AF2 : AF3 : BE = 4 : 3 : 2 : 1$. We also set the trTCM's peak rate to be equal to the bandwidth assigned by the WFQ.

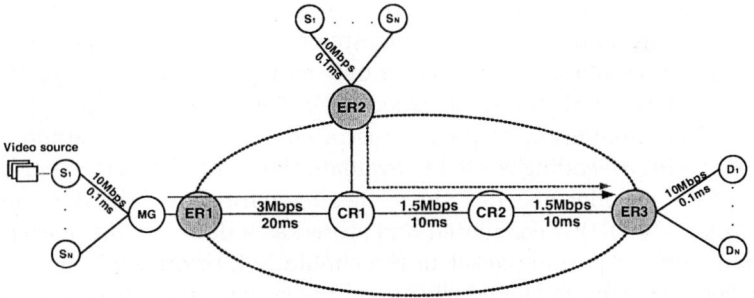

Fig. 6. Simulation topology model

4.2 Feasibility of the EG2EG Control

To show the impact of the EG2EG control in the framework, an unbalanced input load is considered. Three input load levels are allocated to the AF classes: $AF1 : AF2 : AF3 = 120\% : 110\% : 103\%$. For all the flows assigned with the AF class, the drop precedence is set to AF_{x1}. To accurately evaluate the QoS performance of the classes between ingress-egress pair, we observe all data packets traversing on the path. The performance results in Table 1 show that the EG2EG control can detect network condition in per-class basis and keep inter-class service order. That is, the EG2EG control is valuable for providing stable class-based differentiation compared to PQ-only. As discussed in section 3.1, the efficiency of the EG2EG control depends on the utility factor values. For instance, if κ and η are set to relatively high value, the class remapping process is occurred frequently. It results in overall system instability. Accordingly, careful choice of the factor values should be required. The sensitivity analysis of the factors is under our further investigation. In the simulation, we select the following values for the EG2EG control: $\{\gamma, \delta, \kappa, \eta\} = \{0.70, 0.85, 0.45, 0.30\}$.

---

[3] Please refer [6] for the detailed description of the inter-connected trTCM.

Table 1. Performance evaluation of the EG2EG QoS control

	PQ-only			EG2EG		
	Throughput (kbps)	Packet loss (%)	Delay (msec)	Throughput (kbps)	Packet loss (%)	Delay (msec)
AF_1	936.1	22.68	85.4	1049.3	3.67	57.1
AF_2	817.4	17.71	74.2	955.2	6.53	64.3
AF_3	586	3.60	91.7	441.5	27.38	87.6
BE	131	6.41	110.9	75.1	64.78	118.0

4.3 Performance Evaluation of the NBF Control for Video Delviery

In this section, the main objective of the experiments is to investigate the effectiveness of PQ-NBF. To make a congestion period, the sending rates of AF_{2x} sources and AF_{3x} sources are adjusted in runtime from 10 to 17 (sec) and from 17 to 20 (sec) alternately so that it corresponds to total provision level of 120%. For the sake of simplicity, the range of unit cost per packet in PQ-NBF is 9 to 0 and is associated with the same order of DS level.

The overall simulation setup is illustrated in Fig. 7. The standard-based H.263+ encoding/decoding is used to evaluate the end-to-end video performance. While H.263+ encoder encodes video, mean-square-error (MSE) value of each group of block (GOB) is calculated and stored as a data file. Since each GOB is packetized into a separate packet in the simulation, priority will be assigned to each packet according to the relative loss importance of payload. Error patterns generated from results by the NS-2 simulations are used to decide whether the packet is lost or not. Then, at the receiver side, encoded bitstream is decoded with the error pattern file. Consequently, peak signal to noise ratio (PSNR) between original and reconstructed video is calculated to quantify how much video quality is degraded by the packet loss during transmission.

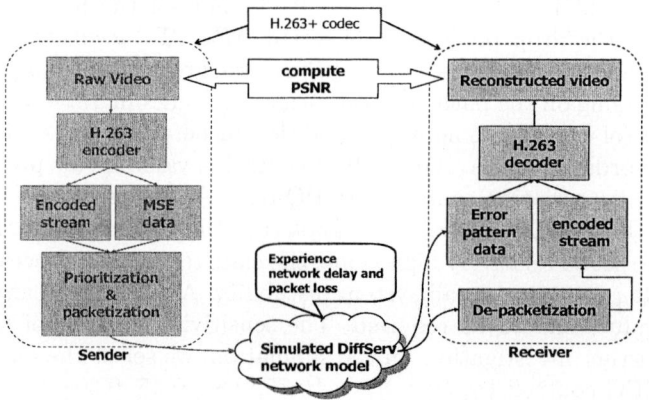

Fig. 7. Simulation diagram for H.263+ streaming video over a simulated DS network

Table 2. Performance evaluation of PQ-NBF

	End-to-end QoS Parameters			
	Throughput (kbps)	Packet loss (%)	Delay (msec)	PSNR (dB)
PQ-only	391.446	7.672	73.608	29.797
PQ-NBF	406.518	1.387	61.727	33.378

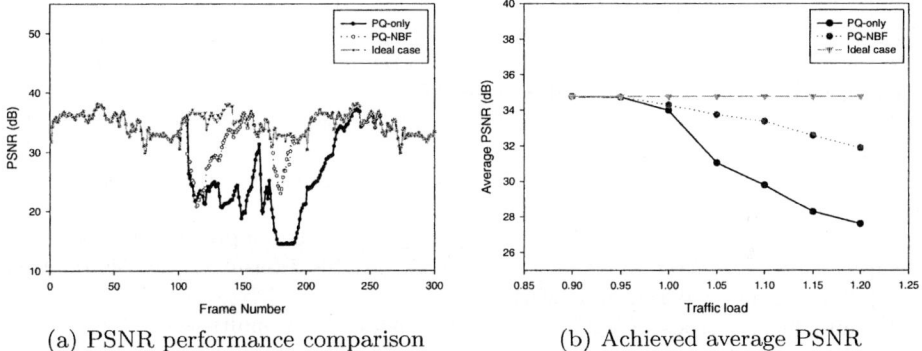

(a) PSNR performance comparison (b) Achieved average PSNR

Fig. 8. PSNR performance comparison and achieved average PSNR at different traffic loads

Table 2 presents the end-to-end performance results of PQ-only and PQ-NBF. It represents that the proposed feedback control effectively responses to the network congestion and has competitive advantage for video streaming. To examine the perceptual quality of the H.263+ video, we play out the decoded video sequence at the receiver and measure the PSNR as an objective quality metric. Note that the average original PSNR for the video trace is about 34.76 dB (i.e., ideal case). In the simulations, we do not differently use the reference QoS mapping between categorized packets and DS levels in order to get a fair comparison. Fig. 8(a) and Fig. 8(b) present PSNR performance comparison of different QoS controls and achieved average PNSR at different traffic loads. The objective PSNR quality measure of PQ-NBF is better than that of PQ-only over various under-provisioned situations.

5 Conclusion

In this paper, we introduced the scalable and adaptive QoS mapping control (SAQM) framework. On this framework, we proposed two types of reactive QoS controls: an edge-based QoS control for stable class-based service differentiation and a reactive end-to-end QoS control to enhance relative differentiation-aware video streaming. Simulation results verified the validity of the QoS controls. Further work would include the refinement of our framework and take care of the end-to-end video streaming over multiple DS domains.

Acknowledgement

This work was supported in part by the BK21 Program and in part by the Korea Institute of Industrial Technology Evaluation and Planning (ITEP) through the Incheon IT Promotion Agency.

References

1. S. Blake, D. Black, M. Carlson, E. Davies, Z. Wang, and W. Weiss, "An architecture for differentiated services,", IETF RFC 2475, Dec. 1998.
2. K. Nichols, V. Jacobson, and L. Zhang, "A two-bit differentiated servicesarchitecture for the Internet,", IETF RFC 2638, July 1999.
3. J. Heinanen, F. Baker, W. Weiss, and J. Wroclawski, "Assured forwarding PHB group,", IETF RFC 2597, June 1999.
4. K. K. Ramakrishnan and S. Floyd, "A proposal to add explicit congestion notification (ECN) to IP,", IETF RFC 2481, Jan. 1999.
5. J. Shin, J. Kim, and C.-C. J. Kuo, "Quality-of-Service mapping mechanism for packet video in differentiated services network," *IEEE Transaction on Multimedia*, vol. 3, no. 2, pp. 219-231, June 2001.
6. J. Shin, "An analysis of aggregated traffic marking for multi-service networks," *IEICE Transactions on communications*, vol. E86-B, no.2, pp. 682-689, Feb. 2003.
7. A. Habib, M. Khan, and B. Bhargava, "Edge-to-edge measurement-based distributed network monitoring," *Computer Communicatons* vol. 44, pp. 211-233, Aug. 2004.
8. S. Floyd and V. Jacobson, "Random early detection gateway for congestion avoidance," *IEEE/ACM Transactions on Networking*, vol. 1, no. 4, pp. 397-413, Aug. 1999.

A Frame-Layer Rate Control Algorithm for H.264 Using Rate-Dependent Mode Selection

Jun-Yup Kim, Seung-Hwan Kim, and Yo-Sung Ho

Gwangju Institute of Science and Technology (GIST),
1 Oryong-dong Buk-gu, Gwangju, 500-712, Korea
{jykim77, kshkim, hoyo}@gist.ac.kr

Abstract. Since the H.264 video coding standard becomes quite popular for transmission of diverse multimedia data due to its high coding efficiency, bit allocation and buffer management schemes are required for various applications. In this paper, we propose a new bit rate control algorithm for H.264 based on an accurate bit allocation strategy, where we introduce a reference quantization parameter (QP) table for the intra frame. For the inter frame, we propose a new bit allocation scheme by adjusting QP considering overhead bits and rate-dependent mode selection. Experimental results demonstrate that the number of the actual coding bits and the number of estimated bits match well such that we can avoid severe degradation of picture quality at the end of the group of pictures (GOP). Moreover, we have improved coding efficiency and average PSNR by up to 0.25dB.

Keywords: H.264 video coding, Rate control, Rate-dependent mode selection.

1 Introduction

Although rate control schemes are generally not included in the normative parts of video coding standards, they play important roles in video coding algorithms. Rate control is thus the necessary part of the encoder, and has been widely studied in several video coding standards, such as MPEG-2, MPEG-4, and H.263 [1], [2], [3], [4], [5]. However, since the quantization parameter (QP) should be determined before the rate distortion optimization (RDO) operation is applied in H.264, the study of rate control for H.264 is more difficult than those of previous standards.

Ma [6] proposed a rate control scheme based on the TM5 model of MPEG-2, assuming a linear relationship between rate and distortion. A rate control algorithm based on VM8 for MPEG-4 has been proposed and adopted by the H.264 test model [7]. The test model for H.264 employs the linear model for predicting the distortion of the current basic unit. In this scheme, the target bit is estimated based only on the buffer fullness, regardless of the current frame complexity. This may lead to drastic drops in PSNR values, especially in the case of high motion scenes or scene changes. In order to improve the video quality at scene changes, Jiang [8] introduced an MAD ratio as a measure of motion complexity. In his approach, a bit budget was allocated to each frame according to the MAD ratio of the current frame.

Generally, the rate control algorithm consists of three parts. The first part is to allocate an appropriate number of coding bits to each picture. The bit allocation process is constrained by the test model defined in the video coding standard. The second part is to adjust QP for each coding unit (e.g. the macroblock or the frame) in order to achieve the target bit rate constraint. In other words, the key point is to find the relation between the rate and QP. The final part is to update the coding parameters.

However, the rate control scheme for H.264 has some problems. The first problem is the selection of the initial QP. H.264 includes a different framework for motion estimation and motion compensation (ME/MC) using multiple reference frames and various coding modes. Hence, errors caused by an inappropriate initial QP are largely propagated in the whole frames of the group of pictures (GOP). The second problem is the abrupt change in PSNR values due to unsuitable bit allocation. The improper bit allocation results in a large fluctuation of PSNR values that degrades the subjective video quality significantly.

In this paper, we propose solutions to overcome those problems. In order to solve the initial QP problem, we have done extensive experiments, and have obtained the best QP range that depends on both the target bit rate and the image size. In order to avoid the abrupt fluctuation of PSNR values, we take an adaptive buffer control strategy by which we adjust the target buffer level using the distance from the intra frame. We select the rate-dependent optimum mode to reduce the bit consumption for the inter frame when the number of actual coding bits is greater than that of threshold bits.

This paper is organized as follows. After we describe the rate control scheme for estimating the target bits in Section 2, we propose a new bit allocation scheme for intra frame and inter frame in Section 3. Then, experimental results are presented in Section 4, and we conclude this paper in Section 5.

2 Target Bit Estimation for H.264

Before we discuss the rate control scheme, we need to determine the initial QP. In order to select the initial QP for H.264, we calculate

$$bpp = \frac{1.0 \times bit\_rate}{frame\_rate \times image\_width \times image\_height} \quad (1)$$

where *bpp* represents bit per pixel. The initial QP is then selected from 10, 20, 25 and 35 using the *bpp* value of Eq. (1). Figure 1 illustrates the decision of the initial QP according to *bpp*. However, the above specific initial QP is not adaptive and the range between the initial QPs is much large. In Section 3, we propose a new method for the initial QP selection.

Generally, the frame-layer rate control scheme for H.264 consists of two stages: pre-encoding and post-encoding. The objective of the pre-encoding stage is to determine QP for all frames and it has two sub-steps: (a) determine a target bit for each P-frame and (b) compute QP using a quadratic rate-distortion (R-D) model and perform RDO. In the post-encoding stages, we update the model parameters continually and control frame-skipping.

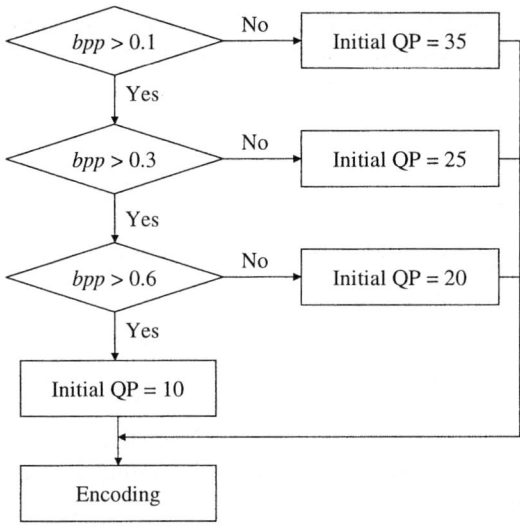

Fig. 1. Flow Chart for Selection of the Initial QP

In order to estimate target bits for the current frame, we employ a fluid traffic model based on the linear tracking theory [9]. For explaining simply, we assume one GOP consisting of first I-frame and subsequent P-frames. Let N denote the total number of frames in a GOP, n_j $(j=1,2,...,N)$ denote the jth frame, and $B_c(n_j)$ denote the occupancy of the virtual buffer after coding the jth frame. The fluid traffic model is described by

$$B_c(n_{j+1}) = \min\{\max\{0, B_c(n_j) + A(n_j) - \frac{u(n_j)}{F_r}\}, B_s\} \quad (2)$$

$$B_c(n_1) = \frac{B_s}{8}$$

where $A(n_j)$ is the number of bits generated by the jth frame, $u(n_j)$ is the available channel bandwidth, F_r is the predefined frame rate, and B_s is the buffer size. In order to determine the target bits for the current P-frame, we take the following two steps.

STEP 1: Allocate the bit budget among pictures. Since the QP of the first P frame is given at the GOP layer in this scheme, the initial target buffer level $Tbl(n_2)$ is set by

$$Tbl(n_2) = B_c(n_2) \quad (3)$$

Then the target buffer levels of other P-frames in the GOP are predefined by

$$Tbl(n_{j+1}) = Tbl(n_j) - \frac{Tbl(n_2) - B_s/8}{N_p - 1} \quad (4)$$

where N_p is the total number of P-frames in the GOP.

STEP 2: Calculate the target bit rate. Using the linear tracking theory, we can determine the number of target bits allocated for the jth frame based on the target buffer level, the frame rate, the available channel bandwidth, and the actual buffer occupancy

$$T_{buf}(n_j) = \frac{u(n_j)}{F_r} + \gamma(Tbl(n_j) - B_c(n_j)) \quad (5)$$

where γ is a constant and its typical value is 0.75. Meanwhile, the average value of remaining bits is also computed by

$$T_r = \frac{R_r}{N_r} \quad (6)$$

where R_r is the number of bits remaining for encoding, and N_r is the number of P frames remaining for encoding. Therefore, the estimated target bit $T_{estimated}$ is a weighted combination of T_{buf} and T_r

$$T_{estimated}(n_j) = \beta \times T_r(n_j) + (1-\beta) \times T_{buf}(n_j) \quad (7)$$

3 New Frame-Layer Rate Control

3.1 Bit Allocation for Intra Frame

Like the rate control of MPEG video coding standards, the frame-layer rate control for H.264 can be used to encode the video sequence by the unit of GOP. Each GOP consists of at least one intra frame and other frames which are motion compensated from the intra frame directly or indirectly. Hence, the quality of the intra frame determines coding efficiency of all other frames in the same GOP through motion compensation. Especially, since H.264 includes good ME/MC processes, the quality of the intra frame is more important than that of the previous video coding standards. In other words, if we encode the intra frame with high quality, we have improved the picture quality of succeeding frames in the same GOP by allocating lower bits.

Figure 2 shows the importance of selecting the initial QP value for the intra frame. As shown in Fig. 2, we have improved coding performance by up to 0.91dB with the optimal initial QP.

In order to choose the optimal initial QP, *bpp* is calculated with the I-frame and the initial P-frame because the I-frame and the first P-frame deal with still images.

$$bpp_{mod} = \frac{a \times bit\_rate}{b \times image\_width \times image\_height} \quad (8)$$

where a is a constant and the typical value is 0.4, and b is $1+\varepsilon$ ($0<\varepsilon\leq 1$) which represents the sum of weighting factors for the I-frame and the initial P-frame.

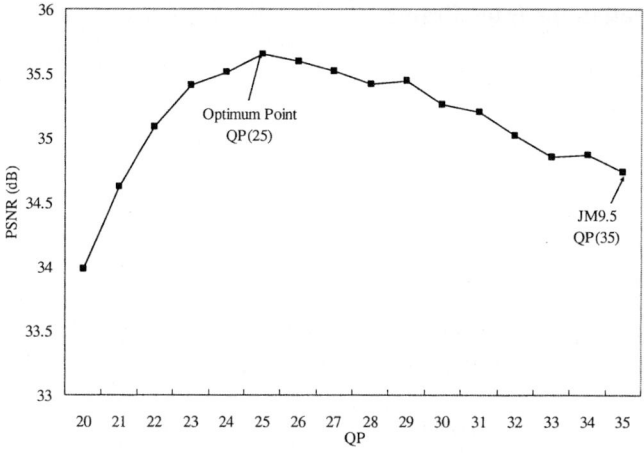

Fig. 2. Initial QP and Average PSNR Value for NEWS Sequence in 64kbps

Table 1. Initial QP and bpp_{mod} Value

Initial QP	bpp_{mod}	Initial QP	bpp_{mod}
10	2.7548927	23	0.7803819
11	2.5195049	24	0.7021517
12	2.2879709	25	0.6440709
13	2.1126631	26	0.5706939
14	1.9089462	27	0.5178741
15	1.7430161	28	0.4701441
16	1.6042719	29	0.4167456
17	1.4442603	30	0.3821154
18	1.3093566	31	0.3501026
19	1.2066104	32	0.3106850
20	1.0757050	33	0.2785275
21	0.9686448	34	0.2536564
22	0.8777515	35	0.2247080

In order to decide the initial QP based on bpp_{mod}, we introduce a reference table that is derived from extensive experiments with various test sequences. For simplicity, we set the b to two which represents that the weighting factor ε for the initial P-frame is one. Table 1 lists the relationship between the QP and bpp_{mod}.

From Table 1, we can choose the initial QP adaptively and improve coding efficiency by allocating a proper number of bits for the I-frame and the initial P-frame. In Table 1, we limit the range of the initial QP from 10 to 35 because the other range is not appropriate for practical applications.

3.2 Bit Allocation for Inter Frame

3.2.1 Improved Buffer Control

In Eq. (4), the target buffer level is controlled by the uniform allocation. However, each frame has a different weighting value according to the temporal distance from the reference I-frame. In other words, since early P-frames are used as references by many subsequent P-frames in the same GOP, P-frames that are closer to the reference I-frame should be allocated with more target bits than other P-frames.

In order to control the buffer adaptively for H.264, we employ the linear weighting function [10] for the target buffer level. Let n_j be the distance between P-frame and its reference I-frame, N_p be the GOP length, and σ be an adjustable parameter. Then, improved target buffer control is defined by.

$$Tbl(n_{j+1}) = Tbl(n_j) - \frac{Tbl(n_2) - B_s/8}{N_p - 1} + \Delta Tbl(n_j) \tag{9}$$

$$\Delta Tbl(n_j) = \sigma \frac{N_p - 2n_j}{N_p - 2}, \qquad n = 1, \cdots, N_p - 1 \tag{10}$$

where σ is equal to one third of the average target buffer level.

3.2.2 Optimal Bit Allocation for Inter Frame

The rate control scheme for H.264 has a problem that the difference value between the estimated coding bits and the actual coding bits is not reflected efficiently when QP is determined for the inter frame.

Figure 3 shows that the estimated coding bits and the actual coding bits do not match well in the AKIYO sequence when the GOP size is 30. This problem causes that all the target bits are abruptly consumed and picture quality of remaining frames is seriously degraded.

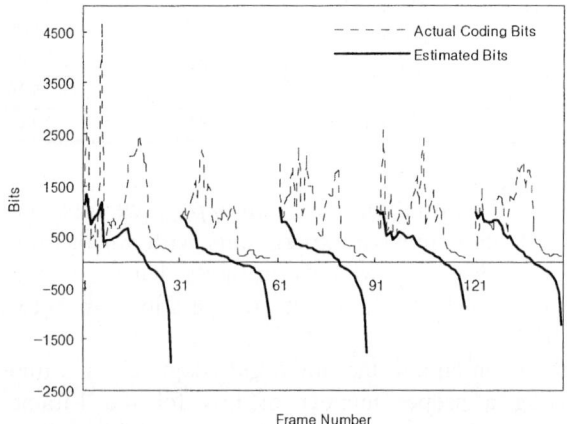

Fig. 3. Estimated Bits and Actual Coding Bits for Akiyo (48kbps)

Our rate control algorithm consists of two steps for this mismatch problem.

STEP 1: Consider the overhead bits when determining QP. The size of the overhead bits for mode and motion information is abruptly changed in H.264 depending on various coding modes. Therefore, the estimated target bits need to reflect the change of both the texture bits and the overhead bits efficiently.

Let $T_{overhead}(j\text{-}1)$ denote the bits used for motion and header information of previous frame, and $T_{texure}(j\text{-}1)$ denote the number of bits for texture(i.e., residual) coding of previous frame. Then, we distribute estimated target bits $T_{estimated}(j)$ to $T_{overhead}(j)$ and $T_{texutre}(j)$, effectively

$$T_{estimated}(j) = T_{texture}(j) + T_{overhead}(j) \tag{11}$$

If we assume $T_{overhead}(j) = T_{overhead}(j\text{-}1)$, the quantization step $Q_{step}(j)$ of the current frame is computed based on a quadratic R-D model

$$\begin{aligned} T_{texture}(j) &= T_{estimated}(j) - T_{overhead}(j-1) \\ &= X_1 \frac{MAD}{Q_{step}(j)} + X_2 \frac{MAD}{Q_{step}^2(j)} \end{aligned} \tag{12}$$

where X_1 and X_2 are the first-order and second-order model parameters respectively, and MAD is calculated by a linear model.

In the proposed scheme, we adjust $QP(j)$ simply by adding 2 when $T_{estimated}(j)$ is smaller than $T_{overhead}(j\text{-}1)$. In other case, $QP(j)$ is calculated to the corresponding quantization step $Q_{step}(j)$ with the method provided by H.264.

$$QP(j) = \begin{cases} QP(j-1)+2, & T_{estimated}(j) < T_{overhead}(j-1) \\ round(6\log_2 Q_{step}(j))+4, & otherwise \end{cases} \tag{13}$$

In order to maintain the smoothness of visual quality among successive frames, we restrict the $QP(j)$ as follows

$$\begin{aligned} QP(j) &= Max\{QP(j-1) - \Delta QP, \ QP(j)\} \\ QP(j) &= Max\{QP(j-1) + \Delta QP, \ QP(j)\} \end{aligned} \tag{14}$$

where ΔQP is the varying range of QP and its typical value is 2.

STEP 2: Adjust the fine-granular QP with the rate-dependent mode selection. In the RDO process, we examine all coding modes for every macroblock and calculate the rate (R) and the distortion (D) for every mode. Hence, the mode with the minimum cost (J) is selected as the optimum mode for every macroblock. However, we control the rate for each macroblock by selecting other modes before actual encoding. We propose a rate-dependent mode selection, where we select the mode by considering the remaining bits

$$J = D + \lambda \times R \tag{15}$$

where the Lagrangian multiplier (λ) is

$$\lambda = 0.85 \times 2^{\frac{QP-12}{3}} \tag{16}$$

In the rate-dependent mode selection, we do not select the optimum mode when the actual coding bits exceed the threshold value composed of estimated bits and the weighting factor. In other words, if the number of actual coding bits for the optimum mode is larger than the threshold value, we select the second optimum mode that has minimum J among the restricted modes whose rates are less than rates of the optimum mode.

Figure 4 shows the flow diagram of the proposed algorithm with two steps. In the proposed scheme, k represents a weighting factor and its typical value is 1.2.

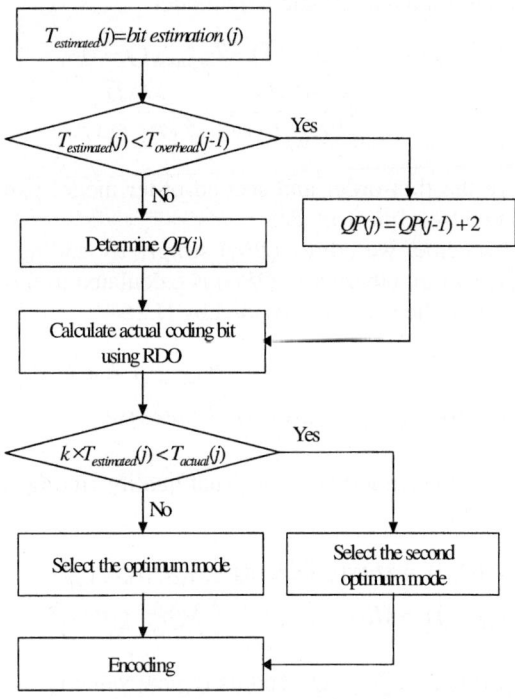

Fig. 4. Flow Diagram of the Proposed Algorithm

4 Experimental Results and Analysis

In order to evaluate performance of the proposed scheme, we have implemented the proposed rate control scheme on the JM9.5 test model software and have compared it with the original JM9.5. The initial QP is set as shown in Table 1, and we experiment 150 frames. Test conditions are given in Table 2.

Table 2. Test Conditions

MV Resolution	1/4
Hadamard	ON
RD Optimization	ON
Search Range	±16
Restrict Search Range	2
Reference Frames	5
Symbol Mode	CAVLC
GOP Structure	IPPP
Intra Period	30
Image Format	QCIF (176×144) CIF (352×288)

Figure 5 depicts the estimated bits and the actual coding bits for the AKIYO sequence. The actual coding bits are well matched to the target bits in the proposed algorithm, and the target bits are efficiently distributed in the whole frames of GOP.

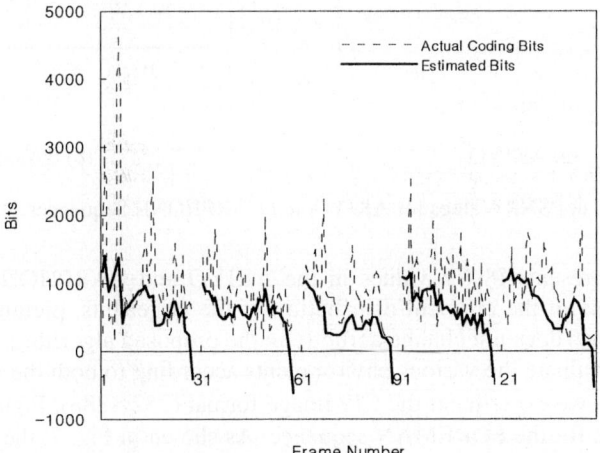

Fig. 5. Estimated Bits and Actual Coding Bits for Akiyo in the Proposed Scheme (48kbps)

Table 3 compares the average PSNR values with JM9.5. As shown in Table 3, we have improved coding efficiency and average PSNR by up to 0.25dB. It also shows the both algorithms can achieve accurate target bit rates.

Table 3. Comparison of the proposed Algorithm with JM9.5

Sequences	Frame Rate	Average PSNR(dB)			Bit Rate(kbps)	
		JM9.5	Proposed	Gain	JM9.5	Proposed
AKIYO	30	36.76	37.21	+0.45	32.78	32.57
SILENT	30	32.88	33.11	+0.23	48.19	48.23
NEWS	30	33.64	33.74	+0.10	48.33	48.41
CARPHONE	30	33.82	34.09	+0.27	48.31	48.39
FOREMAN	30	32.52	32.72	+0.20	64.75	64.64

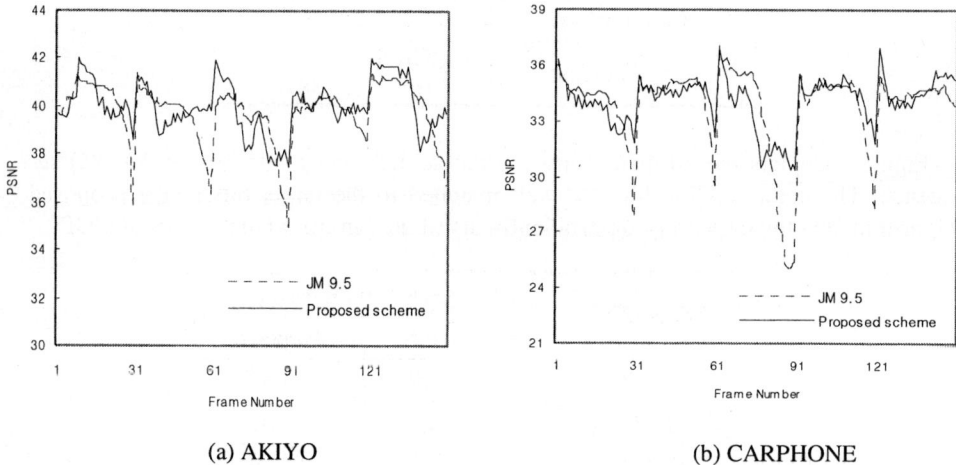

(a) AKIYO (b) CARPHONE

Fig. 6. PSNR Values for AKIYO and CARPHONE Sequences (48kbps)

Figure 6 represents PNSR values in the AKIYO and CARPHONE sequences in 48kbps. Because of the efficient distribution of the target bits, picture quality of the successive frames does not change abruptly in the proposed algorithm.

In order to evaluate the various environments according to both the variable bit rate and image size, we experiment the CIF image format (352×288). Figure 7 shows rate distortion curve for the FOREMAN sequence. As shown in Fig. 7, the proposed algorithm outperforms the JM9.5 in the all the bit rate. Especially, we have improved better coding efficiency and PSNR value at the low bit rate.

Table 4 compares the standard deviation of PSNR values with JM9.5. In order to evaluate the effect on the human visual system, we employ the standard deviation for PSNR values. As shown in Table 4, the proposed scheme has a smaller variance which is better effect on the human visual system in comparison with JM9.5. Especially, video sequences, such as CARPHONE and FOREMAN, which have low temporal correlation and high complexity between frames, have better visual quality.

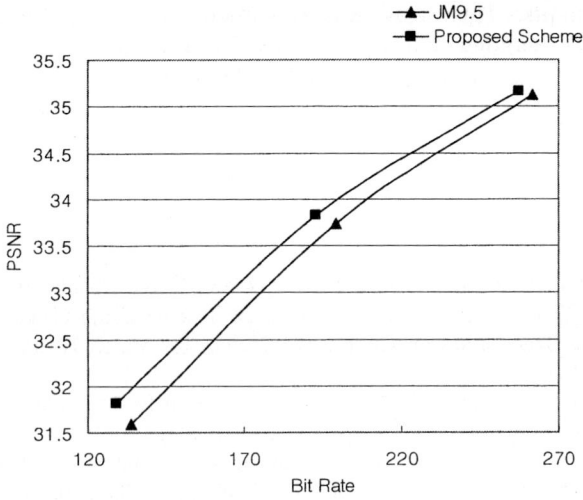

Fig. 7. PSNR Values for AKIYO and CARPHONE Sequences (48kbps)

Table 4. Comparison of the Proposed Algorithm with JM9.5

Sequences	Standard Deviation	
	JM9.5	Proposed
AKIYO	1.439	1.082
SILENT	1.702	1.099
NEWS	1.633	1.289
CARPHONE	2.371	1.293
FOREMAN	2.513	1.844

5 Conclusions

In this paper, we proposed a new rate control algorithm based on accurate bit allocation for H.264 video coding. In the proposed scheme, we introduced the reference table for the intra frame and proposed an optimal bit allocation by adjusting QP such that the number of actual coding bits is as close as possible to the target number of bits, while maintaining the uniform picture quality. In order to determine QP, we consider the overhead bits and control the actual coding bits with the rate-dependent mode selection. Since the number of target bits and the number of actual coding bits for a picture match well in our proposed algorithm, severe degradation of picture quality can be avoided at the end of GOP.

Acknowledgements. This work was supported in part by Gwangju Institute of Science and Technology (GIST), in part by the Ministry of Information and Communication (MIC) through the Realistic Broadcasting Research Center (RBRC), and in part by the Ministry of Education (MOE) through the Brain Korea 21 (BK21) project.

References

1. ISO/IEC JTC1/SC29/WG11 MPEG/N0400: MPEG-2 Test Model5 (1993)
2. Chiang, T., Zhang, Y.Q.: A New Rate Control Scheme Using Quadratic Rate Distortion Model. IEEE Transaction on Circuit and System for Video Technology, Vol. 7, No 1 (1997) 246-250
3. Vetro, A., Sun, H., Wang, Y.: MPEG-4 Rate Control for Multiple Video Objects. IEEE Transaction on Circuit and System for Video Technology, Vol. 9, No 1 (1999) 172-185
4. Lee, H.J., Chiang, T.H., Zhang, Y.Q.: Scalable Rate Control for MPEG-4 Video. IEEE Transaction on Circuit and System for Video Technology, Vol. 10, No 6 (2000) 878-894
5. Corbera, J., Lei, S.: Rate Control for Low-delay Video Communications. ITU Study Group 16. Video Coding Experts Group Documents Q15-A-20 (1997)
6. Ma, S., Gao, W., Wu, F., Lu, Y.: Rate Control for AVC Coding scheme with HRD Considerations. Proceedings of International Conference on Image Processing (2003) 14-17
7. ISO/IEC TC JTC1/SC29 MPEG/N5821: Draft ISO/IEC 14496-5:2002 /PDAM6. (2003)
8. Jiang, M.Q., Yi, X.Q., Ling, N.: Improved Frame-Layer Rate Control for H.264 Using MAD Ratio. Proceedings of IEEE International Symposium on Circuits and Systems, Vol. 3 (2004) 813-816
9. Li, Z.G., Xiao, L., Zhu, C., Pan, F.: A Novel Rate Control Scheme for Video Over the Internet. Proceedings of International Conference on Acoustics, Speech, and Signal Processing, Vol. 2, (2002) 2065-2068
10. Pan, F., Li, Z.G., Lim, K., Feng, G.: A Study of MPEG-4 Rate Control Scheme and Its Implementations. IEEE Transaction on Circuit and System for Video Technology, Vol. 13, No. 5 (2003) 440-446

TCP-Friendly Congestion Control over Heterogeneous Wired/Wireless IP Network

Jae-Young Pyun[1], Jong An Park[1], Seung Jo Han[1],
Yoon Kim[2], and Sang-Hyun Park[3]

[1] Department of Information Communication Engineering,
Chosun University, Gwangju, 501-759, Korea
{jypyun, japark, sjbhan}@chosun.ac.kr
[2] Department of Electrical and Computer Engineering,
Kangwon National University, Chunchon, 200-701, Korea
yooni@kangwon.ac.kr
[3] Department of Multimedia Engineering,
Sunchon National University, Sunchon, 540-742, Korea
shark@sunchon.ac.kr

Abstract. TCP-friendly congestion controls are widely accepted for video streaming over wired network, but not applicable to wireless networks. For streaming video over wireless network where packets can be corrupted by wireless channel errors at the physical layer, conventional TCP-friendly congestion control should be revised. In this paper, wireless measurement based TCP-friendly rate control is introduced, which employs a new loss differentiation algorithm using packet loss statistics. Experimental results show that this method produces the TCP-friendly rates while sharing the backbone bandwidth with TCP flows because of eliminating the effect of wireless losses in flow control. As a result, the abrupt quality degradation of the video streaming over the unreliable wireless link status could be substantially reduced.

1 Introduction

Wireless media streaming is envisioned to become an important service over packet-switched 3G and 4G wireless networks. With rapid growth of emerging demand and deployment of wireless LAN, much of IP traffic including multimedia traffic is forced to travel through wireless networks [1]. Such a change in networking environments brings us a necessity to refine conventional rate control schemes [2]. In general, the quality of networked multimedia applications is more sensitive to packet delay and delay jitter than to packet loss because interruption in playback due to packet delay annoys users more seriously than degradation of picture quality due to packet loss. Therefore, most of multimedia applications use UDP as its transport layer protocol because UDP incurs no retransmission delay and jitter. However, UDP itself provides no flow control mechanism so that sources cannot adapt its transmission rate to time-varying available bandwidth which depends on network loading. Therefore, it is necessary to have an application-layer flow control scheme for the adaptive transmission of multimedia over UDP. The TCP-friendly rate-adaptation behavior for multimedia flows has become an important IETF requirement [3]. In order to facilitate this necessity, the receiver communicates the packet loss information back to the sender, which adapts its transmission rate to the degree of congestion estimated from the loss rate [3, 4].

Packet losses in the heterogeneous wired/wireless network can be caused by not only network congestion but also unreliable error-prone wireless links. Therefore, TCP-friendly end-to-end congestion control schemes which use end-to-end packet loss information as a congestion measure can not be directly applicable to a wireless network because there is no way to distinguish congestion losses from wireless losses. The congestion control needs end-to-end loss differentiation algorithm (LDA) for use with congestion-sensitive video transport protocols for heterogeneous wired/wireless network [6, 7, 8]. Video transport protocols can take advantage of loss differentiation in two key ways. The first one is that wireless losses do not restrict the sending rate. The second is to provide useful feedback to the video encoder. For example, if wireless losses are dominating, the encoder can transmit the video streaming under a lossy environment in cooperation with the error-resilience coding methods [5, 10].

Some previous researches show that congestion and wireless losses are differentiated by using proxy server on access point (AP) or explicit congestion notification (ECN) mechanism. The proxy-based TCP-friendly streaming method uses a *snoop* protocol running on a proxy agent that is implemented in the AP [6]. *Snoop* protocol intercepts streaming packets, analyzes them, and retransmits them to a client if necessary. Thus, the protocol improves the performance of communication over wireless links. The disadvantages are as follows. First, per-packet processing overhead and memory usage may become significant. Second, *snoop* module does not work when the forward route is different from the reverse route. This is because *snoop* can not block ACK packets sent from the receiver to the sender causing to reduce the sending rate unnecessarily when doing local retransmission. Third, this *snoop* based TCP-friendly streaming method is only applicable to the case of last-hop wireless network. On the other hand, ECN-based TFRC calculates TCP-friendly rate by using ECN-marked packet loss ratio (PLR) instead of end-to-end PLR including the packet losses occurred in the wireless link [7]. An ECN-capable random early detection (RED) router marks ECN-bit in incoming packets' IP header in a probabilistic manner when it detects congestion. The loss information of ECN-marked packets is collected in a client and transmitted to the sender by real time control protocol (RTCP) packets [13]. Therefore, the effect of wireless losses in TCP-friendly rate control is effectively eliminated, irrespective of the location of the wireless hop in the end-to-end transmission path. However, ECN-based

TFRC approach has shortcomings. It assumes that all routers in the transmission path should be ECN-capable and equipped with RED queue management scheme.

In this paper, we assume that wireless channel exists at the first-hop link as the access channel of streaming server and/or the last-hop link as the access channel of streaming client. A new LDA is presented to recover the shortcomings of the previous LDA methods over heterogeneous wired/wireless network. The proposed LDA reduces memory usages and computation overhead of *snoop* by eliminating packet retransmission process and transferring packet arrival statistics on AP(s) into the streaming server and/or client. That is, the proposed method uses two kinds of feedback messages which convey the channel information of both wireless and end-to-end link. By using a local transport protocol over the wireless network, congestion related PLR is obtained and utilized for the decision of TCP-friendly rate. Therefore, the encoded bit rates are only restricted by the network congestion. The proposed method does work even though the forward route is different from the reverse route, because it does not have to block ACK messages sent from the receiver to the sender. Also, the proposed method does not have to modify all routers in the transmission path.

This paper is organized as follows. TCP-friendly congestion control methods are briefly described in Sect. 2. Sect. 3 presents the proposed wireless measurement based TCP friendly rate control system. Experimental results and conclusions are followed.

2 Overview of TCP-Friendly Rate Control

2.1 TCP-Friendly Rate Control (TFRC)

Existing TCP-friendly end-to-end congestion control schemes for Internet video proposed to date can be classified into two categories. One is to mimic the TCP congestion control mechanism directly by adopting the additive increase & multiplicative decrease (AIMD) rule [11]. The other one is to utilize the TCP throughput equation. The sender estimates the current TCP's throughput and sends its data bounded by this throughput value [3, 4]. The significant difference between them is how to translate the congestion signal and how to behave to congestion. The first approach suffers from unnecessary rate fluctuation, since the AIMD rule is sensitive to the short-term network status. The second approach such as TCP-friendly rate control (TFRC) proposed by S. Floyd et al [3] can prevent this unnecessary rate fluctuation by considering time-average of network status and transmitting in average TCP throughput sense. In addition to the smoothness property, TFRC also ensures fairness when TFRC-flows are competing for bandwidth with other TCP flows. TFRC sender relies on feedback messages from TFRC receiver in order to adjust its sender rate. The receiver measures the PLR and receives updates of the round-trip time (RTT) from the sender. These PLR and RTT information transferred from the receiver is utilized for the calculation of TCP friendly rates.

2.2 TFRC over Wireless Link

Notice that packet losses in a heterogeneous wired/wireless network can be caused by not only network congestion but unreliable error-prone wireless links. Fig. 1 shows the network topology to evaluate the TFRC flows traveling through the wireless link. It is implemented onto ns-2 simulator [9]. In this simulation, 8 TFRC flows, 4 omniscient TCP flows, and 4 TCP flows share the 100 ms-long, 1.5 Mbps bottleneck link, where the term omniscient TCP is referred to an ideal TCP user having precise knowledge of the cause of every packet loss. Therefore, the omniscient TCP protocol does not decrease its sending rates owing to the packet losses occurred in the wireless link [12]. However, the conventional TFRC flows reduce the sending rates in response to the packet losses occurred in the wireless link. These losses are generated by a two-state Markov chain model with the average PLR of 0.05 and average burst length of 1.5. If all flows fairly share the backbone capacity, each flow will have average 93.75 Kbps (1.5 Mbps/16 flows) of the overall available bandwidth because 16 flows share the bottleneck link. From experimental results, we note that the TFRC flows produce the low and unfair throughput performance, since the TFRC flows reduce their sending rates according to the end-to-end packet loss statistics received from the streaming clients. Fig. 7 illustrates the average throughput of TCP and TFRC flows. In this figure, TCP throughput is calculated by averaging the throughput of both 4 TCP flows and 4 omniscient TCP flows. It is observed that the throughput of TFRC flows is degraded whenever packet losses are generated in the wireless link. That is, TFRC scheme can not be directly applicable to a wireless network because there is no way to distinguish congestion losses from wireless losses.

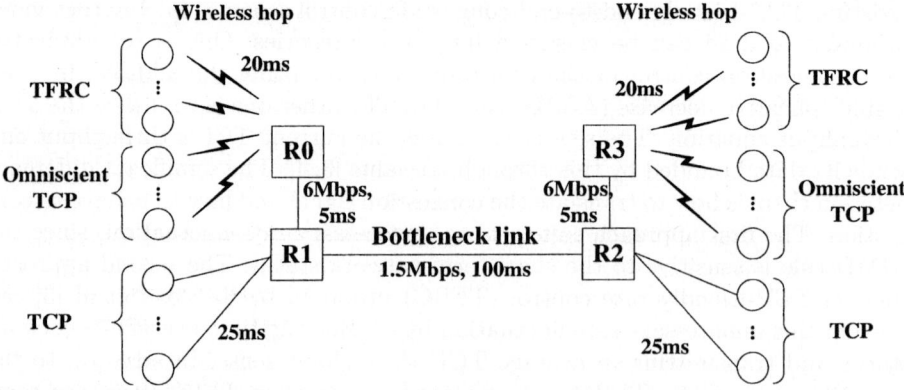

Fig. 1. Network scenario for the study of traditional TFRC and proposed TFRC models over wireless link

3 Proposed Wireless Measurement Based TFRC (WM-TFRC) System

Fig. 2 shows that the proposed wireless measurement based TFRC streaming system, called WM-TFRC, transmits video streams to the streaming clients for the integration service which enables transfer of data between a station on an IEEE 802.11 LAN and a station on an integrated IEEE 802.x LAN. RTS/CTS signaling messages in IEEE 802.11 wireless LAN are commonly used to reduce the collision caused by the hidden node problem [1]. Thus, the collisions of video packets are rarely occurred in the infrastructure networks. We assume that the packet losses in the first-hop and/or last-hop wireless network are caused by the unreliable wireless channel status. In this video streaming system, the streaming server, client, and AP(s) have an additional module, so called the wireless adaptation layer (WAL) that can be seen as an OSI 2.5 layer. This layer is used for service provisioning at the link layer. The WAL monitors the incoming traffics of all video sessions and sends the feedback messages including the packet loss statistics back to senders periodically. To request these packet loss statistics to the WAL module on AP, both the streaming server and client should know if they are connected to wireless channel link. The case of the first-hop wireless channel is firstly described. Then, the case of the last-hop wireless channel is presented. To collect each wireless channel information, the streaming server and client has a respective PLR acquisition process using WAL packets. After obtaining both end-to-end PLR and wireless PLR information by using RTCP and WAL, congestion related PLR is calculated and utilized to generate TCP-friendly rates on the streaming server.

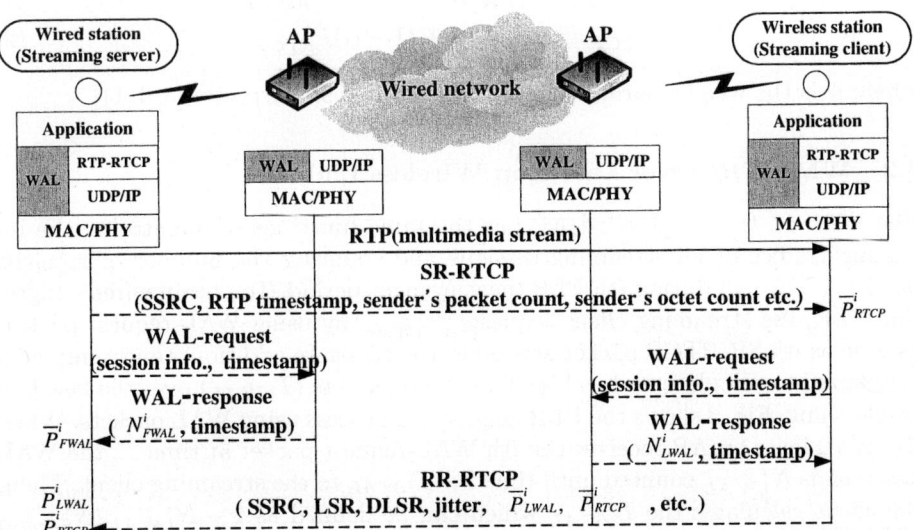

Fig. 2. Proposed wireless video streaming system implemented over IEEE 802.11 wireless LAN

3.1 WM-TFRC over First-Hop Wireless Link

As shown in Fig. 2, the streaming server transmits real time protocol (RTP)-based video streams through wireless and wired channel to the streaming client [13]. In the general RTP/UDP/IP transmission environments, the channel information is reported to the sender by RTCP. At the streaming server side, RTCP and WAL-request packets are transferred successively every periodic time δ. The WAL layer on AP adjacent streaming server counts the number of received packets (N^i_{FWAL}) during ith PLR measurement period. To obtain wireless PLR ($\bar{P}^i_{FWAL}$) in the first-hop wireless link, the streaming server requests N^i_{FWAL} by using WAL-request packet which is immediately transmitted after ith sender report RTCP (SR-RTCP) packet [13]. The WAL-request packet consists of session fields such as IP addresses and port numbers of both server and client to identify each streaming session. When the WAL layer on AP receives the ith WAL-request packet, the WAL immediately sends N^i_{FWAL} to the streaming server. Then, the server calculates the $\bar{P}^i_{FWAL}$ which can be defined as $1 - N^i_{FWAL}/N^i_{Server}$, where N^i_{Server} is the number of all RTP packets sent from the streaming server during ith PLR measurement period. Then, the wireless streaming server calculates the smoothed current wireless PLR $\widetilde{P}^i_{FWAL}$ occurred in the first-hop wireless link. On the other hand, the other packet loss information $\widetilde{P}^i_{RTCP}$ is obtained from the returned ith receiver-report RTCP (RR-RTCP) packets [13]. $\widetilde{P}^i_{RTCP}$ is end-to-end PLR caused by both unreliable error-prone wireless channel and traffic congestion in the wired network. In this work, the RTCP transmission period δ is set to 1 sec by default [7]. When WAL and RTCP feedback packets are received, two PLRs are smoothed by

$$\widetilde{P}^i_{FWAL} = \alpha \widetilde{P}^i_{FWAL} + (1-\alpha)\bar{P}^i_{FWAL} \tag{1}$$

$$\widetilde{P}^i_{RTCP} = \alpha \widetilde{P}^i_{RTCP} + (1-\alpha)\bar{P}^i_{RTCP}, \tag{2}$$

where α is the weight parameter which is set to 0.95 currently [3, 4, 11].

3.2 WM-TFRC over Last-Hop Wireless Link

The WAL on the client-sided AP has the same functions of monitoring the incoming traffics of all streaming sessions and counting the number of received packets (N^i_{LWAL}) during ith PLR measurement period. To obtain wired congestion PLR, the streaming client requests N^i_{LWAL} by using WAL-request packet, as soon as ith SR-RTCP packet arrived at the client. In addition, timestamp field is required to calculate an local RTT of WAL packets (T_{LWAL}) over the last-hop wireless link. Fig. 3 shows the PLR acquisition process using WAL packets. When the WAL layer on AP receives the ith WAL-request packet at time T, the WAL layer sends N^i_{LWAL} counted until time $T-T_{LWAL}$ to the streaming client. Then, the client calculates the $\bar{P}^i_{LWAL}$ which can be defined as $1 - N^i_{LWAL}/N^i_{Server}$, where N^i_{Server} is simply obtained by using a value of *sender's packet count* field of SR-RTCP packet [13]. Therefore, $\bar{P}^i_{LWAL}$ implies the PLR occurred at between the streaming server and AP adjacent to the streaming client. As a result, the

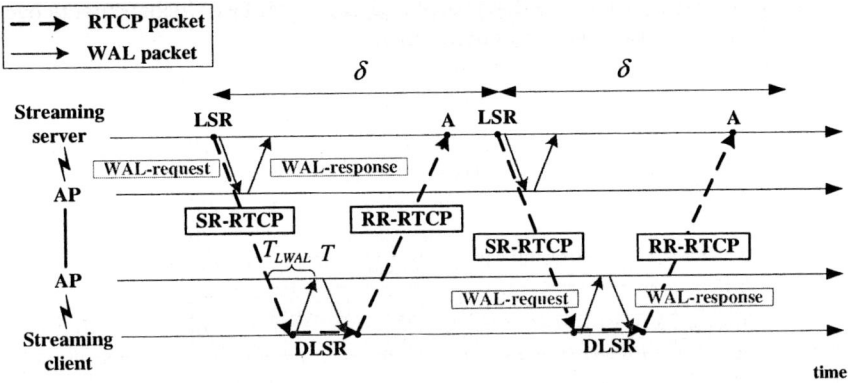

Fig. 3. Network measurement method based on the echoed RTCP and WAL messages which convey the packet loss statistics and round trip time information

streaming client can collect both $\bar{P}^i_{LWAL}$ and end-to-end PLR $\bar{P}^i_{RTCP}$ calculated at the RTP level of the client. These two PLRs are transferred into streaming server by using RR-RTCP packet. When $\bar{P}^i_{WAL}$ is gathered, it is smoothed by

$$\widetilde{P}^i_{LWAL} = \alpha \widetilde{P}^i_{LWAL} + (1-\alpha)\bar{P}^i_{LWAL}. \tag{3}$$

Now, the streaming server has three smoothed PLR information, i.e., $\widetilde{P}^i_{FWAL}$, $\widetilde{P}^i_{RTCP}$, and $\widetilde{P}^i_{LWAL}$. As mentioned earlier, we assumed that wireless channel(s) exist only first-hop and/or last-hop link. When both the first-hop and last-hop are wireless channels, the congestion PLR is determined by

$$\widetilde{P}^i_{WAL} = max(\widetilde{P}^i_{LWAL} - \widetilde{P}^i_{FWAL}, 0).$$

In addition, if the only wireless channel exists on the first-hop or last-hop, the congestion PLR is respectively determined by

$$\widetilde{P}^i_{WAL} = max(\widetilde{P}^i_{RTCP} - \widetilde{P}^i_{BWAL}, 0)$$
$$\text{or} \quad \widetilde{P}^i_{WAL} = max(\widetilde{P}^i_{RTCP} - \widetilde{P}^i_{FWAL}, 0). \tag{4}$$

As a result, TCP-friendly rate T_{rate} using TCP throughput equation is defined as

$$T_{rate} = \frac{MTU}{RTT\sqrt{\frac{2\widetilde{P}^i_{WAL}}{3}} + T_o\sqrt{\frac{27}{8}\widetilde{P}^i_{WAL}}(1+32(\widetilde{P}^i_{WAL})^2)}. \tag{5}$$

This gives an upper bound on the sending rate T_{rate} in bytes/sec, where MTU is the maximum transmission unit (packet size), T_o is the retransmission time out, and RTT is the round trip time obtained from RR-RTCP packets sent from the client. That is to say, the target rate T_{rate} can be calculated by using $\widetilde{P}^i_{LWAL}$ regardless of the wireless losses [3]. Fig. 3 shows RTT computation

Table 1. Simulation parameters for traditional and WM-TFRC experiments over the wired/wireless integration network environment

Experiment condition	parameter	value
TFRC	Packet size	1024 bytes
	History factor in EWMA	0.75
	Decay factor in RTT	0.95
TCP	Packet size	1024 bytes
	Window size	20
Router (R1,R2)	Buffering management	RED
	Buffer size	50

process expressed as $RTT = A - LSR - DLSR$, where A is the arrival time of RR-RTCP packet at the server, LSR is the transmission starting time of the last SR-RTCP packet from the server, and $DLSR$ is the delay time between receiving the last SR-RTCP from server and sending the RR-RTCP [13]. $DLSR$ includes the elapsed time to exchange WAL packets over the wireless local network.

Now, the multimedia streaming traffics generated with the transmission rate of T_{rate} can share fairly the bottleneck link with TCP traffics. This scheme does not only make wireless losses transparent to the sender, but also provide the opportunity for the sender to explicitly react at the application level to wireless losses (e.g., source coding and channel coding) [5]. The wireless PLR which can be defined as $\widetilde{P}^i_{wireless} = max(\widetilde{P}^i_{RTCP} - \widetilde{P}^i_{WAL}, 0)$.

4 Experimental Results

In Sect. 2, the simulation network topology of ns-2 has been introduced to evaluate the throughput performance of TFRC traveling through the wireless link with the packet loss distribution shown in Fig. 4. In this network topology, 8 TFRC flows are replaced by 8 flows of the proposed WM-TFRC. For the simulation of omniscient and background TCP flows, the parameters are set as in

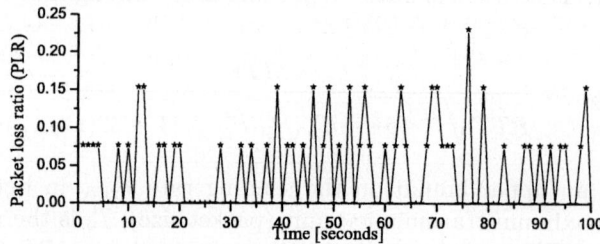

Fig. 4. Packet loss ratio generated by a two-state Markov chain model with the average PLR of 0.05 and average burst length of 1.5

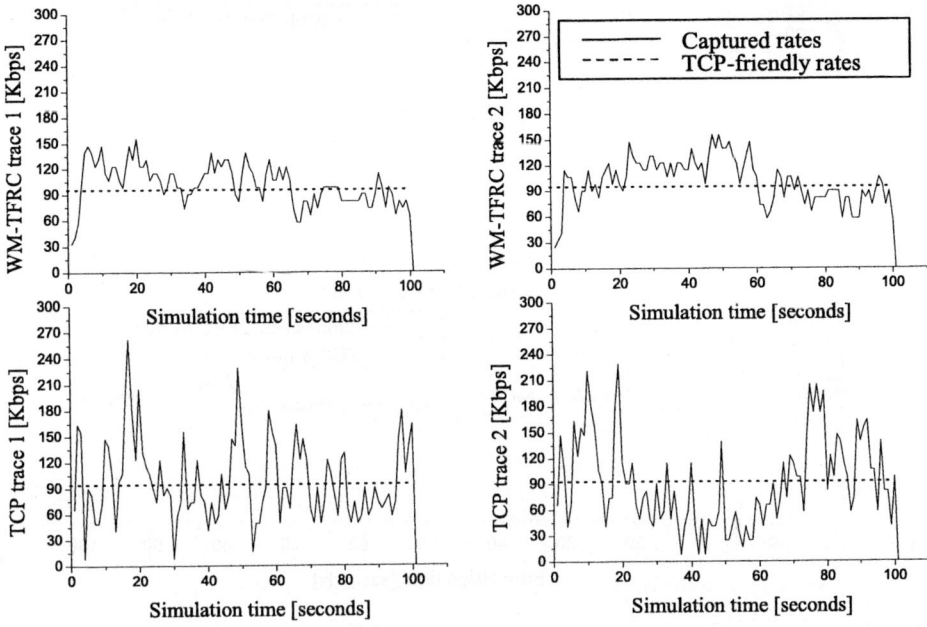

Fig. 5. Throughput traces of WM-TFRC and TCP sample flows traveling through the wireless link

Table 1. Thus, the WM-TFRC flows share the backbone link with the omniscient TCP and background TCP traffics and travel through the wireless link.

Fig. 5 illustrates the throughput traces of WM-TFRC and TCP sample flows traveling through the wireless link. The WM-TFRC flows equally share the bottleneck bandwidth with TCP flows. That is, WM-TFRC flows are almost TCP-friendly with the rate of 93.75 Kbps, while the throughput of the original TFRC flows are significantly reduced by the packet losses in the wireless link. It is clear that WM-TFRC can observe the wireless and wired packet loss information and properly measure the packet losses occurred by the network congestion at the bottleneck link. Also, it is observed that WM-TFRC's rate fluctuation is lower than TCP flow, making it more appropriate for streaming applications which require constant video quality. Fig. 8 depicts the average throughput results of 8 WM-TFRC flows and 8 TCP flows. As compared with the original TFRC flows shown in Fig. 7, throughput of WM-TFRC flows are almost equal to that of TCP flows with more than 93% equivalence ratio ER in a long-term average sense. ER is expressed by $min(R_{tfrc}/R_{tcp}, R_{tcp}/R_{tfrc})$, where R_{tfrc} and R_{tcp} are the average throughput of TFRC and TCP flows, respectively [4].

Another simulation result is depicted to compare the fairness performance with the other LDA methods. For this experiment, 4 omniscient TFRC flows are transferred instead of 4 proposed TFRC flows on the simulation network topology shown in Fig. 1. These omniscient TFRC flows do not decrease their sending

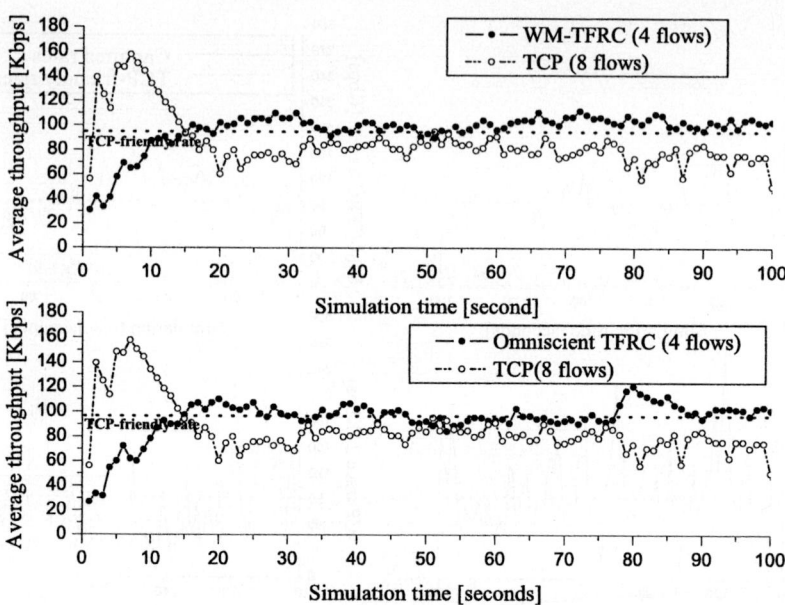

Fig. 6. Average throughput traces of 8 WM-TFRC and 8 omniscient TFRC flows traveling through the wireless link

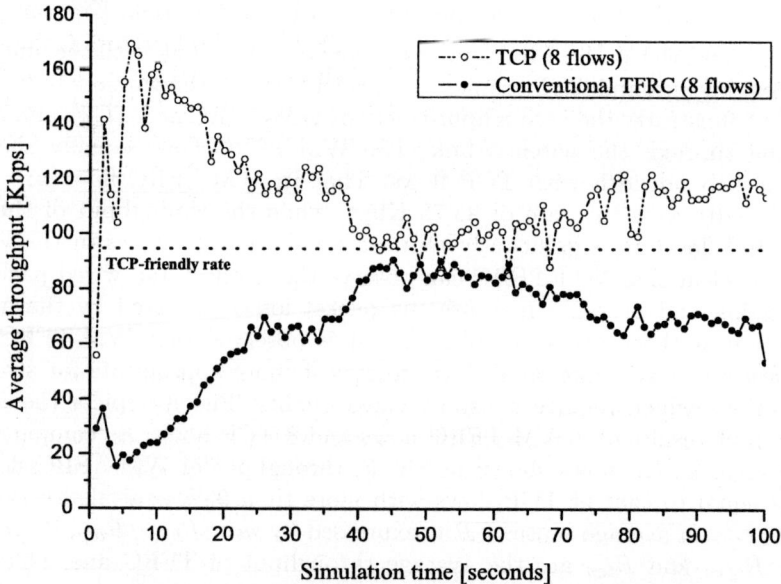

Fig. 7. Average throughput of 8 TFRC and 8 TCP flows traveling through the wireless link

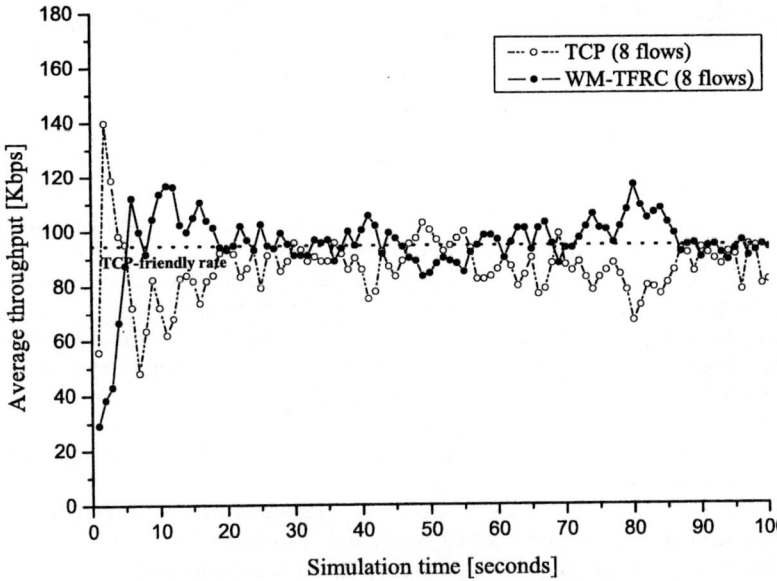

Fig. 8. Average throughput of 8 WM-TFRC and 8 TCP flows traveling through the wireless link

rates owing to the packet losses occurred in the wireless link. The omniscient TFRC can represent the ideal ECN based TFRC method. Figure 6 shows that the proposed TFRC and omniscient TFRC share the bottleneck link fairly with TCP flows. The average throughput of both proposed WM-TFRC and omniscient TFRC flows is almost equal to that of TCP flows with more than 93% equivalence ratio ER in a long-term average sense. Thus, we can conclude that the proposed WM-TFRC using WAL packets produces the TCP-friendly rate by effectively eliminating the effect of wireless losses.

5 Conclusions

In this paper, it is shown that the proposed TFRC called WM-TFRC can distinguish congestion losses from wireless losses by obtaining two types of packet losses from AP and streaming client. Thus, WM-TFRC streaming system can share fairly the bottleneck link with TCP flows over heterogeneous wired/wireless networks. Moreover, in the time-varying error prone wireless link, the quality degradation of video streaming is expected to be significantly reduced when the proposed TCP-friendly rate-adaptation mechanism is incorporated with the error-resilient video coding methods. With the growing popularity of hand-held devices and wireless LANs, proving good network service guarantees for real-time video traffic will be more significant, and TCP-friendly flow control over the heterogeneous wired/wireless IP network could be a step towards that goal.

References

1. B. P. Crow, I. Widjaja, J. G. Kim, and P. T. Sakai,: IEEE 802.11 wireless local area networks. IEEE Commun. Mag., (1997) 116–126
2. H. J. Song and K. M. Lee,: Adaptive rate control algorithms for low-bit-rate video under the networks supporting band-width renegotiation. Signal Process.:Image Commun., Vol. 17, No. 10, (2002) 759–779
3. M. handley, S. Floyd, J. Padhye, and J. Widmer,: TCP friendly rate control (TFRC): protocol specification. RFC 3448, (2003)
4. S. Floyd, M. Handley, J. Padhye, and J. Widmer,: Equation-based congestion control for unicast applications. in Proc. SIGCOMM, (2000)
5. W. T. Tan and A. Zakhor,: Real-time Internet video using error resilient scalable compression and TCP-friendly transport protocol. IEEE Trans. Multimedia, Vol. 1, No. 2, (1999) 172–186
6. L. Huang, U. Horn, F. Hartung, and M. Kampmann,: Proxy-based TCP-friendly streaming over mobile networks. in Proc. ACM Workshop on Wireless and Mobile Multimedia (WOWMOM02), (2002)
7. S.-J. Bae and S. Chong,: TCP-Friendly Wireless Multimedia Flow Control Using ECN Marking. in Proc. GLOBECOM02, Vol. 2 (2002) 1794–1799
8. S. Cen, P. C. Cosman, and G. M. Voelker,: End-to-end differentiation of congestion and wireless losses. in Proc. Multimedia Computing and Networking, (2002) 1–15
9. The Network Simulator-ns-2, http://www.isi.edu/nsnam/ns/
10. Y. G. Kim, J. Kim, and C. C. Jay Kuo,: Network-Aware error control using smooth and fast rate adaptation mechanism for TCP-friendly Internet video. in Proc. Int. Conf. Computer Communications and Networks, (2000) 320–325
11. D. Wu, Y. T. Hou, W. Zhu, H. J. Lee, T. Chiang, Y. Q. Zhang, and H. J. Chao,: On end-to-end architecture for transporting MPEG-4 video over the Internet. IEEE Trans. Circuits Syst. Video Technol., Vol.10, No.6, (2000) 923–941
12. R. Ramani and A. Karandikar,: Explicit congestion notification (ECN) in TCP over wireless network. in Proc. Int. Conf. Personal Wireless Communications, (2000) 495–499
13. H. Schulzrinne, S. Casner, R. Frederick, V. Jacobson,:RTP: A Transport Protocol for Real-Time Applications. RFC 3550, 2003

A Balanced Revenue-Based Resource Sharing Scheme for Advance and Immediate Reservations

Dong-Hoon Yi and JongWon Kim

Networked Media Lab., Department of Info. and Comm.
Gwangju Institute of Science and Technology (GIST), Gwangju, 500-712, Korea
{dhyi, jongwon}@netmedia.gist.ac.kr

Abstract. In order to provide the QoS (Quality of Service) effectively to the network-based media applications consuming large bandwidth (e.g., video conferencing), the service providers of QoS-provisioned networks should allow customers to reserve their resources in advance. The service provider, however, should also provide conventional reservations (generally known as immediate reservations) that do not specify session duration. To adaptively control the amount of sharable resources between resource partitions for the respective immediate and advance reservations, in this paper, we propose a balanced revenue-based resource sharing scheme that maintains expected revenue within a pre-defined range while minimizing the management overhead. By analyzing the relationship between the revenue and the amount of resources under conflict (i.e., immediately reserved flows should be preempted to make room for advance reservation flows), we control the trade-off. That is, a resource boundary between two types of reservations is dynamically adjusted by a weighting parameter that represents the sharing modes for the expected revenue: aggressive and conservative. Network simulation results show that the proposed scheme exhibits enhanced performance (i.e., stabilized revenue and low management overhead) in comparison to alternative schemes, especially when the demand for two types of reservations varies.

Keywords: Resource sharing, advance and immediate reservation, indefinite session duration, service revenue, and QoS provisioning.

1 Introduction

To guarantee the QoS (Quality of Service) of the deployed applications in a resource-sharing environment like the Internet, resources should be reserved prior to the actual use. Traditionally, resource reservation has been handled by a resource manager whose well-known function is an admission control. Moreover, majority of reservations have been *immediate*. That is, the request to reserve resources is made immediately before it needs to use the resources. We denote this type of reservation as IR (immediate reservation). Another type of reservations that books resources ahead is denoted as AR (advance reservation). Usually, to secure the required resources, the QoS-stringent applications need to reserve resources in advance [1]. These AR requests generally notify not only the required amount of resources but also the detailed session information (i.e., actual start time and duration) to the resource manager. For example, this kind of advance reservation is commonly observed in pre-scheduled multi-party video conferences [2].

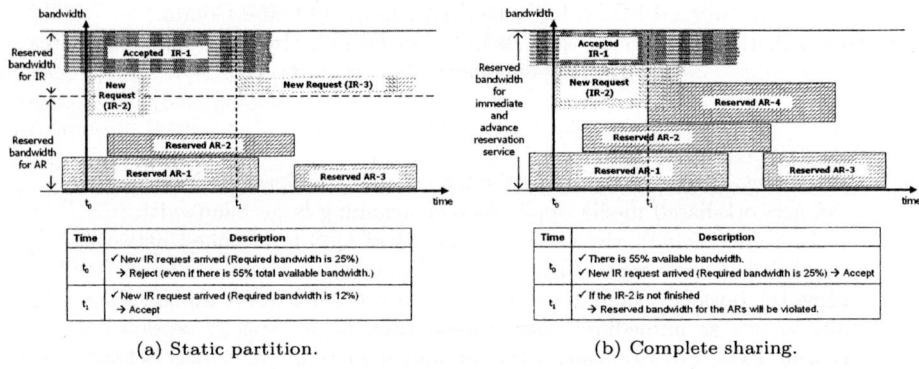

(a) Static partition. (b) Complete sharing.

Fig. 1. Problems of the resource management with two types of reservations

To handle both types of reservations, the resource manager has now been facing several challenges. One of them caused by the indefinite session duration of the IR requests. Most previous researches on the admission control have not considered the session duration of the IR requests. How to check weather it could be accepted with the requested resources at the moment that the request is invoked has been the focus of IR-only admission control [3]. Thus, so far, the studies on the resource management with AR requests have been proposing several ways. The simple choice is to statically partition the whole resource pool for each type of reservations, which is denoted as SP (static partitioning) scheme. It, however, leads to under-utilized resources, since the reservation request is rejected even when the other resource partition stays idle (Figure 1(a)). Another extreme choice is to completely share the resource pool. This CS (complete sharing) scheme allows sharing at the possible cost of so-called *conflict*, which means the overlap caused by the indefinite session duration of IR requests (Figure 1(b)). This conflict degrades the QoS of application, even through the resource utilization may be improved nominally. Of course, if the resource manager can avoid the conflicts completely, the CS scheme becomes ideal (if we can ignore the management overhead of the resource manager). In this way, there is a trade-off between resource utilization and QoS guarantee (or management overhead) [16,4].

As a compromise, in this paper, we propose a resource sharing scheme that attempts to balance the trade-off based on the expected revenue. The revenue is defined in this paper as the total amount of money that is earned by the service provider after excluding the provisioning cost for the resources. It essentially depends on the pricing policy and should include the amount of resource experienced the QoS degradations (i.e., conflicted) as well as served well. To make balanced resource sharing, the resource manager dynamically changes the sharing mode by using a resource boundary. For example, when the achievable revenue is smaller than the expected, it becomes aggressive and the sharing mode shifts toward the CS scheme in order to increase the revenue. If the expected revenue is set reasonably, this shift is a proper methodology because the resource manager may create extra revenue by promoting the sharing of under-utilized resources. In this paper, we intend to keep the revenue higher than a pre-defined threshold by controlling the resource boundary. On the contrary, the proposed scheme can shift toward conservative sharing (i.e., SP scheme), since the excessive sharing may cause negative impact on the revenue as well as introducing extra management overhead. To guide this in an effective manner, we define a simple function that dynamically changes the resource boundary according to the chosen weighting parameter. Network simulation results show that the proposed scheme exhibits enhanced performance (i,e, stabilized revenue and low management overhead) in comparison to alternative schemes, especially when the demands for two types of reservations varies.

This paper is organized as follows. In Section 2, we review relevant works on the resource management with the AR request. We then consider the service revenue after reviewing the underlying assumptions in Section 3. The proposed resource management scheme is presented in Section 4 and the simulation results follow in Section 5. Finally, we conclude this paper in Section 6.

2 Related Work

Early works on the resource management with the AR request have been concentrating on the prerequisites to support such mechanisms as an admission control [4], while others have proposed and implemented architectures based on an agent (e.g., bandwidth broker) to verify feasibility [5, 6]. Regarding the agent implementation, many other works extend existing signaling protocols (e.g., RSVP [7], ST-II [8]) to provide reservation functionality over the Internet. The impact of AR requests on the dynamic routing in a network is also discussed in [9]. Note that early works in this area have been concerned with the static routing infrastructure. The AR proposals running on MPLS-aware core network have recently appeared to address an effective traffic engineering [10]. To store the reservation status, an array scheme is examined and compared with a tree-based scheme in [12]. The results verify that the array scheme is better in terms of computation time and memory efficiency.

While the above works have been focusing on the implementation-side issues of the AR mechanism, other approaches consider the aspects such as resource utilization, user utility, and revenue. In [10,11], flexible reservation requests are defined to dynamically modify the reservation parameters (i.e., start and end time of the session, and required bandwidth) when a link capacity is insufficient to accept the request. However, there has been no discussion on the QoS degradation due to modified reservation requests, even though the flexible reservation requests enhance overall resource utilization and acceptance rate. The degradation of QoS and the interruption of accepted requests are studied in [13,14]. The authors commonly define utility functions reflecting the type of applications and propose a heuristic resource allocation scheme that maximizes the overall served utility (as in [13]) and user satisfaction (as in [14]). In comparison, in this paper, we consider the benefit of service provider by introducing the notion of revenue to support the AR requests. The proposed scheme dynamically switches resource sharing mode according to the expected revenue of the service provider. For this, we analyze a quantitative relationship between price and cost of the resources.

In [15], the analysis on the problems that can be introduced due to indefinite session duration of IR requests is performed. The authors proposes an admission control through a mathematical modelling, which approximates the probability of interruption of IR requests (similar to the notion of conflict). To avoid the conflict between reservation requests, a safety margin is used along with time axis [16,17]. Similar to this, in [5], the authors use the lookahead time to show that the overall resource utilization is affected by difference in ranges of the lookahead. However, they lack to discuss about determining proper range of lookahead with varying demand. On the contrary, in this paper, we define a dynamic resource boundary that sets the resource margin representing the amount of sharable resource. In [18,19], we can find several resource allocation algorithms that determine the resource boundary based on the demand. In this paper, we use a simplified version of equation in [19] so as to decide the dynamic resource boundary presented.

3 Advance Reservation Model

3.1 Environmental Assumptions

We start the discussion of the proposed resource sharing scheme by noting several environmental assumptions. The main focus of this paper is how to effectively handle both types of reservation requests with fixed amount of given resources. We, firstly, assume that there is a resource manager (or a bandwidth broker) assigning bandwidth to the reservation requests along with static routing path within its management domain. We also assume that each reservation request has strict QoS requirements. Hence, the modification of reservation parameters is not allowed and reserved resource is fully utilized by the request. For the sake of simplicity, the priority policy used is that the AR requests have higher priority than IR ones when the conflict happens. The IR requests can be interrupted and they can undergo QoS degradations. Note that the priority of the AR request is set to reflect that the AR helps the resource manager to schedule the resource pool. In this paper, we define non-bookable duration (Δ) [1] as a minimum time gap between present and actual start time of the AR request.

---

[1] In [5], it is mentioned as 'bookahead time'.

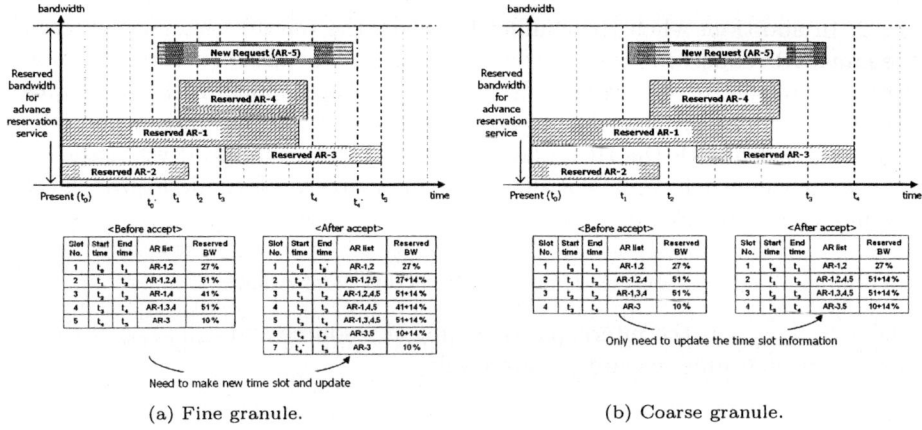

(a) Fine granule. (b) Coarse granule.

Fig. 2. Time slot table with different time granule

To provide and manage the AR requests, the resource manager has to know their session information. Using this information, the resource manager schedules and allocates the resources with time slot table. The time slot table (based on the array proposed in [12]) stores the status of reserved resources in advance. In this process, the resource manager has to determine proper time granule for the time slot table in order to consider the management overhead and memory efficiency. Figure 2 shows the effect on the management overhead (e.g., number of slots) according to the difference in time granules. However, in this paper, we simply assume that the time granule is 1 second to concentrate our focus. In addition, we assume that the Δ is 30 seconds.

3.2 Revenue for Reservation Service

To the service provider, the main purpose of reservation service is to earn the revenue. For this, the service provider has to determine the amount of resources that has to be provisioned and the prices of those resources. A simple formula for the revenue ($\Re$) is

$$\Re = B_{avg} \cdot p - B_{provision} \cdot c_{provision}. \quad (1)$$

where $B_{provision}$ is the provisioned link capacity, B_{avg} is the averaged amount of utilized link capacity, p is the resource price per unit resource, and $c_{provision}$ is the provisioning cost per unit resource, respectively. If we assume that $B_{provision}$ is statically determined and B_{avg} is λ % of the $B_{provision}$, the relationship between p and $c_{provision}$ should satisfy Eq. 2 for a positive revenue.

$$p \geq (B_{provision} \cdot c_{provision})/(B_{avg}),$$
$$\geq c_{provision} \cdot (\frac{\lambda}{100})^{-1}. \quad (2)$$

In this paper, we assume that the service provider expects their utilization rate of the provisioned resources as λ % and determines a price policy satisfying

Eq. 2. In addition, when the conflict happens, the resource manager interrupts the latest IR request in order to guarantee the QoS of AR requests. The resource dedicated to the IR request is returned to the resource pool for the AR requests. Hence the service provider has to consider a penalty for the reservation failure, which is related with the IR request forced to be eliminated. If we consider the penalty as the provisioning cost for wasted resources, a formula for the effective revenue can be written as

$$\Re_{effective} = \Re - (B_{interrupt} \cdot c_{interrupt}). \tag{3}$$

where $B_{interrupt}$ is the interrupted amount of resource and $c_{interrupt}$ is the cost per interrupted unit resource, respectively.

4 Admission Control with Revenue-Based Resource Sharing

As already discussed, the AR requests have to notify their session information as well as the required amount of resources ($AR_i = \{t_i^s, t_i^e, b_i\}$). This information is stored in the time slot table after the admission. By referring to this time slot table, the resource manager can easily check the resource availability at given time instance. However, in case of IR requests, it is difficult to confirm the resource availability in advance since the IR requests only notify the amount of required bandwidth ($IR_j = \{b_j\}$).

To avoid the conflict as much as possible, the resource manager restrictively shares the resources using the dynamic resource boundary. By settling down (i.e., fixing) the resource allocation for AR requests, it is possible to check the resource availability within Δ [2]. Now, the possible cause of conflict is the IR requests only. To control the potential risk of conflict, the proposed scheme adaptively changes (every Δ) the resource boundary according to the expected revenue guideline. Figure 3 describes the proposed admission control algorithm, where C_{imm} and C_{adv} are the initially-provisioned link capacities for IR and AR requests, respectively. Also, B_{imm} and B_{adv} are the available bandwidths to check the admissibility of IR and AR requests, respectively. B_{sha} is the sharable bandwidth from the AR resource pool and $R(t)$ represents the actually reserved bandwidth for AR requests. $\bar{R}(t)$ presents the virtual envelop of $R(t)$ and it is called as resource boundary. ζ is the weighting parameter used in controlling the dynamic resource boundary.

4.1 Resource Boundary for the Sharable Resource

To separate the resource pool for each reservation type and adaptively adjust the separation, we utilize a simple function generating decision threshold value as in Eq. 4. By using this, the resource manager can determine a resource boundary,

---

[2] Requests made Δ(sec) earlier than their start time are regarded as advance reservations.

```
INITIAL STAGE:
    Set Parameters.
        B_adv := C_adv;
        B_imm := C_imm;
        B_sha := 0;
    Call Resource Boundary Decision Function at t_0;

Resource Boundary Decision(R(t), ζ):
    Every Δ do
        find R̄(t) that minimize the D_th;
    UPDATE R̄(t);

Admission for Imm request(b_j):
    UPDATE B_sha = B_adv - R̄(t);
    if b_j ≤ B_imm then
        UPDATE B_imm = B_imm - b_j;
        ACCEPT request;
        BREAK;
    else if b_j ≤ B_imm + B_sha then
        UPDATE B_imm = B_imm - b_j;
        ACCEPT & INSERT request to preemption list;
        BREAK;
    else REJECT request;

Admission for Adv request(t_i^s, t_i^e, b_i):
    if t_i^s ≤ t_p+Δ then
        REJECT request;
        BREAK;
    else if b_i ≤ min {B_adv-R(t)}, where t ∈ [t_i^s, t_i^e] then
        UPDATE time slot table; (Add b_i within t ∈ [t_i^s, t_i^e])
        ACCEPT request;
        BREAK;
    else REJECT request;
```

Fig. 3. The proposed admission control algorithm with dynamic resource boundary

($\bar{R}(t)$), that minimizes decision threshold (D_{th}) by comparing with the status of the actual reservation, ($R(t)$), using time slot information within Δ.

$$D_{th}(R(t), \zeta) = \zeta \times n_{\bar{R}(t)} + (1-\zeta) \times \int_{t_p}^{t_p+\Delta} [\bar{R}(t) - R(t)]dt,$$

where t_p is the present time. The D_{th} is determined by considering two issues: the variation number of resource boundary ($n_{\bar{R}(t)}$) and the difference amount between resource boundary and actually reserved resource ($\bar{R}(t) - R(t)$). The decision threshold is calculated with the weighting parameter (ζ). As ζ increases, resource boundary tends to be static (i.e., conservative). In contrast, when ζ decreases, resource boundary tends to change aggressively. Figure 4 shows the sample traces of the resource boundary determined according to ζ.

4.2 Resource Sharing with Dynamic Resource Boundary

The proposed resource sharing scheme sets the resource boundary based on the status of resource allocation (stored in the time slot table) and the weighting

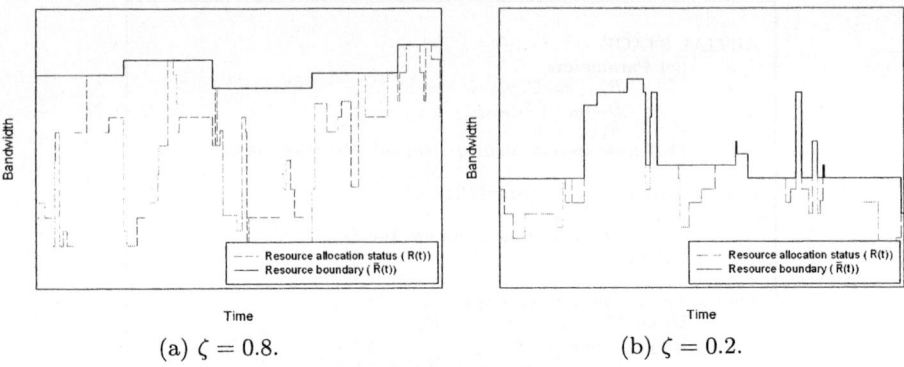

(a) $\zeta = 0.8$. (b) $\zeta = 0.2$.

Fig. 4. Sample traces of the resource boundary according to the weighting parameter

parameter. Determined resource boundary provides guideline about available resources for the IR requests through sharing, since remaining resource within Δ could not be utilized by the AR requests.

As presented in Figure 3, when the resource manager receives an IR request, it checks for the resource availability at that time instance. If the available resource from its own pool is not sufficient, it once more checks resources that can be shared without rejecting the request. If the IR request is acceptable through the resource sharing, then the information about the IR request is stored with an order index. Later when the conflict occurs, the IR request is interrupted with the indexed order and allocated resources are returned to the resource pool. Hence the interruption rate of the IR requests is directly related to the management overhead of the resource manager.

The proposed scheme periodically checks the average reserved resources for the AR requests (B_{AR}) within Δ and determines the resource boundary. If B_{AR} is greater than λ % of the provisioned link capacity, the resource manager determines flat resource boundary by setting the weighting parameter as $\zeta = 1.0$. In this case, because the service provider already achieves a positive revenue within Δ, there is no need to set the dynamic resource boundary to share the remaining resources for the IR requests with the risk of possible conflict. When the B_{AR} is smaller than λ % of the provisioned link capacity, however, the resource manager sets the dynamic resource boundary to make more revenue by setting the weight parameter according to Eq. 4.

$$\zeta = \begin{cases} B_{AR} \cdot \lambda^{-1} & 0 \leq B_{AR} \leq \lambda, \\ 1.0 & \lambda < B_{AR} \leq 100. \end{cases} \quad (4)$$

As the average resource utilization for the AR requests is low, the risk of conflict becomes relatively low. Hence the proposed scheme can achieve an effective resource sharing with low rate of conflict. Note that we assume that the returned resources from interrupted IR requests have no contribution to the revenue.

5 Simulation

We evaluate the performance of the proposed scheme with simulation parameters shown in Table 1. Simulation results are compared using several evaluation metrics like resource utilization and management overhead incurred by the resource manager. In addition, to verify the feasible aspect, we compare the packet loss rate under assumption that the resource manager has no capability to check the conflicts and interrupt the IR requests.

Table 1. Simulation parameters

	AR requests	IR requests
Traffic source	UDP/CBR	
Session time[sec]	Exponential distribution	
Arrival rate[requests/sec]	0.34	0.17
Mean bandwidth[kpbs]	450	300
Link capacity[Mbps]	2.0	1.5
Simulation time	100000 seconds	

5.1 Resource Utilization

To make a reasonable evaluation, we use the effective service revenue rate(Θ) as in Eq. 5 instead of using resource utilization directly. For the sake of simplicity, in this simulation, we assume that p is equal to the right-hand side of Eq. 2 and $c_{interrupt}$ is double of p. We also set the expected average utilization rate of resources (λ) as 50 % in the simulations.

$$\Theta(\%) = \frac{\Re_{effective}}{BW_{provision} \times (p - c_{provision})} \times 100. \quad (5)$$

In the first simulation summarized in Figure 5(a), we set the mean session duration of IR requests (d_{IR}) as 5 seconds. The simulation results compare the proposed scheme to alternative schemes such as SP, CS, and lookahead with two fixed ranges (10, 40 sec) [3]. The comparison is made over mean-varying session duration of AR requests from 5 to 55 sec. Since the mean session duration of IR requests is relatively short, we can expect that the conflict rate becomes relatively low. It means that, comparing with other schemes, the CS scheme makes more revenue through resource sharing. However, in case of the SP scheme, the expected revenue of IR requests is limited in its resource partition and the simulation result shows that it has the lowest revenue as we expected. In case of the lookahead scheme, we can observe that the lookahead with short range has better performance than long range one under light demand.

To confirm on what merits the proposed scheme has, we set the mean session duration of IR requests (d_{IR}) as 55 seconds in the second simulation

---

[3] The CS scheme can be regarded as a lookahead scheme with zero range and the SP scheme can be regarded as a lookahead scheme with infinite range.

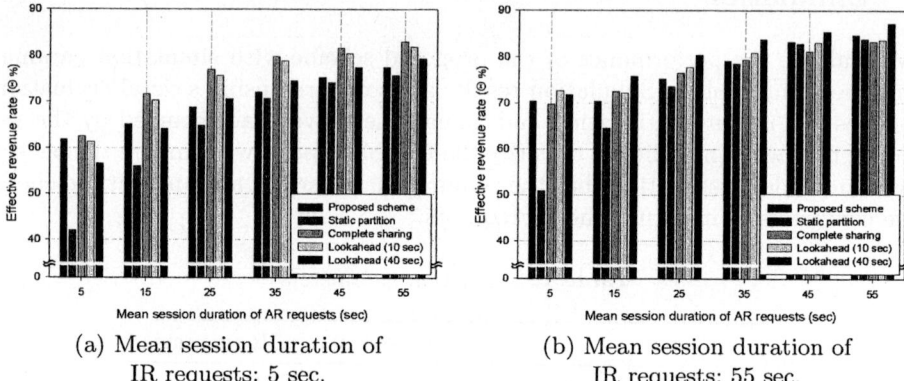

Fig. 5. Effective revenue rate (Θ %)

(Figure 5(b)). In this case, because the mean session duration is relatively long, the conflict rate becomes higher than in the former case. It means that most of allocated resource to the IR requests may be interrupted, and hence the CS scheme has relatively lower effective revenue rate than the former one. On the contrary, the SP scheme gets more revenue with higher resource utilization of IR requests since it originally prohibits the resource sharing. One among interesting results is that the performance of lookahead scheme is reversed under heavy demand comparing to the former case. With the proposed resource sharing scheme, however, we can confirm that it provides relatively stabilized effective revenue comparing to other schemes even though the demand of resources is varied. Note that, since the resource utilization is directly related to the revenue of the service provider, the stabilized utilization is meaningful. Consequently, we can assert that the proposed scheme has relatively good performance in the resource sharing, especially with the advance reservation support.

5.2 Management Overhead and Feasibility

The interruption of IR requests is closely related to the management overhead of the resource manager that is responsible to guarantee the QoS (i.e., to guarantee the reserved resource). In this sense, the SP scheme actually has no management overhead, since it fundamentally prohibits the resource sharing. However, the CS scheme suffers form the management overhead as the overall demand of resource reservations increases. As shown in Table 2, the proposed resource sharing scheme achieves lower interruption rate for IR requests than the CS scheme. It means that the proposed scheme effectively shares the resource pool with low management overhead. Note that the lookahead schemes has relative large variations according to the mean session duration of the IR requests and it has no capability to adapt to those variations.

Table 3 shows packet loss rate under assumption that the resource manager has no capability to check the conflict and interrupt the request (i.e., the resource

Table 2. Mean interruption rate(%) of accepted IR requests

	$d_{IR} = 5$ sec	$d_{IR} = 55$ sec
Proposed scheme	0.46	11.71
SP scheme	0.00	0.00
CS scheme	3.44	34.13
Look-ahead (10 sec)	3.70	28.89
Look-ahead (40 sec)	0.05	0.94

Table 3. Mean packet loss rate(%) with no interruption

	$d_{IR} = 5$ sec	$d_{IR} = 55$ sec
Proposed scheme	0.02	2.17
SP scheme	0.00	0.00
CS scheme	0.11	8.71
Look-ahead (10 sec)	3.99	29.74
Look-ahead (40 sec)	0.09	0.32

manager has no management overhead in a sense of the conflicts). The proposed scheme has much lower packet loss rate comparing to alternative schemes, even thought there is no handling for the conflicts. While the lookahead scheme with long range has also good performance, it has no adaptation capability for the varying demand as we discussed. From this, we can verify the feasible aspect of the proposed resource sharing scheme in practice.

6 Conclusion

In this paper, we have proposed the balanced revenue-based resource sharing scheme to support both types of reservation request: advance and immediate. To handle the potential conflict caused by sharing, we use the dynamic resource boundary that controls the trade-off. By analyzing the revenue notion of service provider, the proposed scheme adaptively changes its resource boundary to sustain the expected revenue within a preset margin. The simulation results verify that the proposed scheme provides not only relatively stabilized resource utilization but also low management overhead. Further analysis, related with user utility and prioritized reservation requests, will be pursued in future works.

Acknowledgments

This research was supported in part by University IT Research Center Project and in part by GIST.

References

1. W. Smith, I. Foster and V. Taylor, "Scheduling with advanced reservation," in *Proc. IEEE 14th International Parallel and Distributed Processing Symposium (IPDPS'00)*, pp. 127-132, May 2000.
2. A. Gupta, "Advance reservation in real-time communication services," in *Proc. IEEE 22nd Annual Conference on Local Computer Networks (LCN '97)*, 1997.
3. S. Sargento and R. Valadas, "Call admission control in IP networks with QoS support," in *Proc. IEEE INFOCOM'00*, Mar. 2000.
4. L. C. Wolf, L. Delgrosii, R. Steinmetz, S. Schaller, and H. Wittig, "Issues of reserving resource in advance," in *Proc. International Workshop on Network and Operating System Support for Digital Audio and Video (NOSSDAV'95)*, 1995.
5. O. Schelen and S. Pink, "Sharing resources through advance reservation agents," in *Proc. IFIP Fifth International Workshop on Quality of Service (IWQoS'97)*, May 1997.
6. I. Khalil and T. Braun, "Implementation of a bandwidth broker for dynamic end-to-end resource reservation in outsourced virtual private networks," in *Proc. IEEE 25th Annual Conference on Local Computer Networks (LCN'00)*, pp. 511-519, Nov. 2000.
7. A. Schill, F. Brejter, and S. Kühn, "Design and evaluation of an advance reservation protocol on top of RSVP," in *Proc. 4th International Conference on Broadband Communications*, pp. 430-442, Apr. 1998.
8. W. Reinhardt, "Advance resource reservation and its impact on reservation protocol," in *Proc. Broadband Islands'95*, Sept. 1995.
9. R.A. Guerin, and A. Orda, "Networks with advance reservations: the routing Perspective," in *Proc. IEEE INFOCOM'00*, pp. 118-127, Mar. 2000.
10. L.-O. Burchard, "On the performance of computer networks with advance reservation mechanisms," in *Proc. 11th IEEE International Conference on Networks*, Sept. 2003.
11. F. Sallabi, and A. Karmouch, "Resource reservation admission control algorithm with user interactions," in *Proc. IEEE GLOBECOM'99*, vol. 4, pp. 2086-2090, Dec. 1999.
12. L.-O. Burchard and H.-U. Heiss, "Performance evaluation of data structures for admission control in bandwidth brokers," in *Proc. International Symposium on Performance Evaluation of Computer and Telecommunication Systems*, Jul. 2002.
13. P. Dharwadkar, H. J. Siegel, and E. K. P. Chong, "A heuristic for dynamic bandwidth allocation with preemption and degradation for prioritized requests," in *Proc. 21st International Conference on Distributed Computing Systems*, Apr. 2001.
14. V. Stanisic and M. Devetsikiotis, "Dynamic utility-based bandwidth allocation policies: The case of overloaded network," in *Proc. IEEE International Conference on Communications*, Jun. 2004.
15. A.G. Greenberg, R. Srikant, and W. Whitt, "Resource sharing for book-ahead and instantaneous-request calls," *IEEE/ACM Transactions on Networking*, vol. 7, pp. 10-22, Feb. 1999.
16. M. Degermark, T. Kohler, S. Pink, and O. Schelen, "Advance reservations for predictive service in the Internet," *ACM/Springer Journal of Multimedia Systems*, vol. 5, pp. 177-186, May 1997.

17. S. Kim, and P. K. Varshney, "An adaptive advance reservation algorithm for QoS sensitive multimedia networks," in *Proc. SPIE Int. Soc. Opt. Eng. Digital Wireless Communications VI*, Apr. 2004.
18. A. Bar-Noy, Y. Mansour, and B. Schieber, "Competitive dynamic bandwidth allocation," in *Proc. 17th Annual ACM symposium on Principles of Distributed Computing*, Jun. 1998.
19. J. Schmitt, O. Heckmann, M. Karsten, and R. Steinmetz, "Decoupling different time scales of network QoS systems," in *Proc. International Symposium on Performance Evaluation of Computer and Telecommunication Systems*, Jul. 2001.

Sequential Mesh Coding Using Wave Partitioning

Tae-Wan Kim[1], Kyoung Won Min[1], Byeong Ho Choi[1], and Yo-Sung Ho[2]

[1] Korea Electronics Technology Institute (KETI),
#68, Yatap-dong, Pundang-gu, Sungnam-Si, Kyunggi-do, 463-816, Korea
{kimtw, minkw, bhchoi}@keti.re.kr
[2] Gwangju Institute of Science and Technology (GIST),
1 Oryong-dong, Buk-gu, Gwangju, 500-712, Korea
hoyo@gist.ac.kr

Abstract. Recently, various three-dimensional(3-D) mesh coding schemes have been proposed to improve compression efficiency or error resilience. However, we need to consider both coding efficiency and error resilience when we send 3-D mesh data over bandwidth-limited transmission channels. In this paper, we propose a sequential mesh coding algorithm using the vertex pedigree based on the wave partitioning. After a 3-D mesh model is partitioned into several small processing blocks (SPB) using wave partitioning, we obtain vertices for each SPB along circumferences defined by outer edges of the attached triangles. Once all the vertices within each circumference are arranged into one line, we can encode the mesh model. Computer simulations show that the proposed algorithm provides both higher error resilience and improved coding efficiency.

1 Introduction

In recent days, three-dimensional (3-D) synthetic VRML models have been used in various applications, such as computer animation, computer vision, and studio graphic design. However, such mesh representation has a problem that 3-D objects with fine details have an excessive amount of data. Therefore, compression of mesh models is necessary to transmit them efficiently over a bandwidth-limited transmission channels.

Hoppe proposed a progressive mesh coding algorithm using mesh optimization to represent a 3-D model by a base mesh and vertex split variables; thus, the model can be shown in a progressive way using mesh simplification [1]. Taubin and Rossignac proposed a topological surgery method using vertex and triangle spanning trees to encode the connectivity and geometry data [2]. Touma and Gotsman improved coding efficiency of triangle mesh compression through traversal ordering using vertex degrees [3]. These schemes have focused on mesh compression and mesh simplification. If any bit errors occur during the transmission of 3-D model data, the reconstructed model can be severely damaged. Yan et al. suggested a robust coding scheme for 3-D graphic models using mesh segmentation and data partitioning, where the mesh model is partitioned and each partitioned mesh is encoded and transmitted in the packet to enhance error resilience. However, they did not consider coding efficiency seriously [4][5][6].

In this paper, we propose a sequential mesh coding scheme using wave partitioning, aiming at both coding efficiency and error resilience [10][11]. After we partition a 3-D mesh model into several pieces, we define a mother vertex and its son vertices based on their topological relationship. We describe this relationship in detail in Chapter 3. Then, we encode the 3-D mesh model based on the index difference of each mother vertex of the current vertex and the next vertex with additional parameters, which is described in Chapter 4.

2 Wave Partitioning

In general, mesh partitioning and mesh segmentation techniques are used to divide the 3-D model into a set of small independent parts. Even though errors occur in one part, they will not affect the decoding of other parts in the model because the errors are limited to one part rather than the whole model. Therefore, when the channel error rate is high, mesh partitioning and mesh segmentation schemes are very effective. In the proposed algorithm, after the 3-D input model is partitioned, each partitioned unit is separated to several small processing block units. Encoding and decoding operations are performed on these small processing block units.

2.1 Basic Principle

The wave partitioning is simply based on the natural wave phenomenon that one drop of water is dropped on the water surface and spreads out, making circles in the lake.

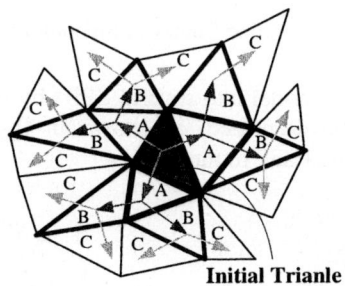

Fig. 1. SPB Formation Using Wave Partitioning

In the wave partitioning, an initial triangle is chosen and a number of triangles are attached to the initial triangle along the arrow direction. As shown in Fig. 1, triangles A which are sharing edges of the initial triangle, triangles B which are sharing edges of the triangles A, triangles C which are sharing edges of the triangles B, are attached to the initial triangle consecutively. Some attached triangles from the initial triangle consist of one partitioned part of the model.

This partitioned part of the model is called as SPB(Small Processing Block). In order to obtain a uniform size of SPB, we place two initial triangles on both ends of the model. After the whole model is divided into half, each part can be partitioned into several SPBs recursively. If we place one initial triangle on the model, the model is not partitioned into several pieces.

2.2 Modified Boundary Smoothing (MBS)

In order to reduce the boundary length and the processing complexity as much as possible, we apply a boundary smoothing algorithm [4]. As illustrated in Fig. 2, holes in one separate SPB can be filled up by projected triangles from its adjacent SPB. If there are N vertices on the SPB boundary and the model is partitioned into A SPB and B SPB in Fig. 2, choose one of these N vertices (v_i) in SPB A and v_k on the boundary except v_{i-1} and v_{i+1}. Check whether there exist the edge (v_i, v_k) and the path ($v_i \rightarrow v_{i-1} \rightarrow v_k$) in SPB A. If there are (v_i, v_k) and ($v_i \rightarrow v_{i-1} \rightarrow v_k$) in SPB A, we regard that there exists a hole in SPB B. By removing the path ($v_i \rightarrow v_{i-1} \rightarrow v_k$) from the boundary in SPB A and adding the edge (v_i, v_k) into the boundary in SPB B, holes in SPB B are filled up by triangles in SPB A.

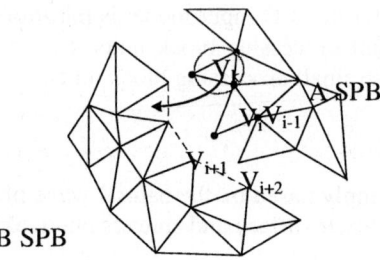

Fig. 2. Modified Boundary Smoothing Scheme

When we partition a mesh model into several SPBs by using the wave partitioning, the partitioned SPB can be described, as shown in Fig. 3(a). The bold lines in Fig. 3(a)(b) are defined as the Rank in the SPB.

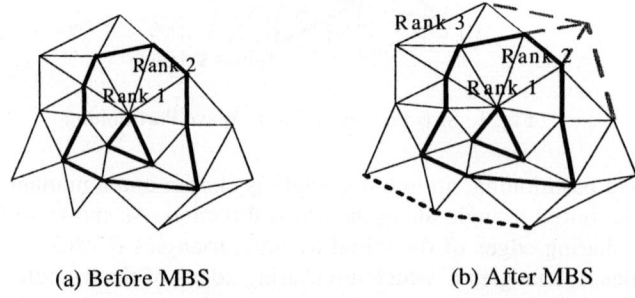

(a) Before MBS (b) After MBS

Fig. 3. Modified Boundary Smoothing Scheme

If we apply the boundary smoothing scheme [4] to the partitioned SPB, small dotted triangles are attached to the partitioned SPB, as shown in Fig. 3(b). However, the outer line does not construct the rank. We add the long dotted triangles to the partitioned SPB which are already applied by the boundary smoothing scheme, as shown in Fig. 3(b). Then, *Rank 3* is constructed. This scheme is defined as modified boundary scheme (MBS). Figure 4 shows the procedure in which one model is partitioned into two SPBs and two SPBs are partitioned into four SPBs again. MBS followed by wave partitioning is also applied.

Fig. 4. Object Applied with MBS & Wave Partitioning Scheme

3 Two Types of SPBs

SPBs are classified into circular or semi-circular types based on the location of the initial triangle. In the case that the initial triangle is located on the inner space of the mesh, these SPBs are called as a circular SPB. On the contrary, if the initial triangle is placed on the boundary of the mesh, these SPBs are called as a semi-circular SPB.

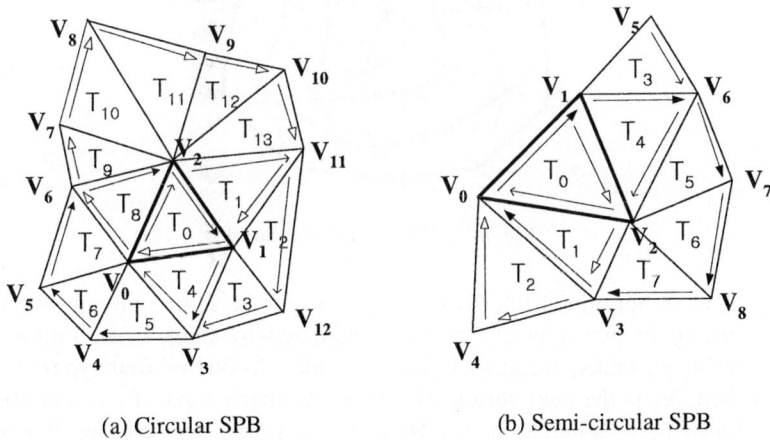

(a) Circular SPB (b) Semi-circular SPB

Fig. 5. Two Types of SPB

Figure 5(a) shows an example of the circular SPB. The closed thick line in Fig. 5(a) that is composed of v_0, v_1 and v_2 is defined as *Rank 1*. The path composed of vertices $v_3 \rightarrow v_4 \rightarrow v_5 \rightarrow v_6 \rightarrow v_7 \rightarrow v_8 \rightarrow v_9 \rightarrow v_{10} \rightarrow v_{11} \rightarrow v_{12}$ surrounding *Rank 1* is defined as *Rank 2* consecutively. Vertices surrounding a particular vertex, except for those vertices that are already included in the inner rank, are defined as son vertices(Sv) of the particular vertex, which is called as the mother vertex(Mv) of its surrounding son vertices. In Fig. 5(a), v_0 is surrounded with vertices $v_1 \rightarrow v_3 \rightarrow v_4 \rightarrow v_5 \rightarrow v_6 \rightarrow v_2$. Because v_1 and v_2 are already included in the *Rank 1*, v_0 is a Mv of $v_3 \sim v_6$ except v_1 and v_2. v_1 is surrounded with vertices $v_0 \rightarrow v_2 \rightarrow v_{11} \rightarrow v_{12} \rightarrow v_3$. As v_1 and v_2 are already included in the *Rank 1* and v_3 is a Sv of v_0, v_1 is a Mv of $v_{11} \sim v_{12}$. In the same way, v_2 becomes a Mv of $v_7 \sim v_{10}$.

Figure 5(b) shows an example of the semi-circular SPB. Compared to a circular SPB, the left part of path $v_4 \rightarrow v_1 \rightarrow v_2 \rightarrow v_5$ is not included in the semi-circular SPB and the rank does not consist of the closed loop. However, the principle of making ranks and relations between a Mv and a Sv is the same as that of the circular SPB. Therefore, v_0 is a Mv of $v_3 \sim v_4$, v_1 is a Mv of $v_5 \sim v_6$ and v_2 is a Mv of $v_7 \sim v_8$.

3.1 Circular SPB

Figure 6 shows a partitioned circular SPB by wave partitioning and MBS. The thick lines in Fig. 6 indicate ranks in a SPB. Vertices of the initial triangle, $v_0 \sim v_2$, consist of *Rank 1* and the path composed of $v_3 \rightarrow v_4 \rightarrow v_5 \rightarrow v_6 \rightarrow v_7 \rightarrow v_8 \rightarrow v_9 \rightarrow v_{10} \rightarrow v_{11}$ becomes *Rank 2*. When we arrange all the vertices included in each rank in Fig. 6 into a row on the plane, we can form a map of the vertices, as shown in Fig. 7.

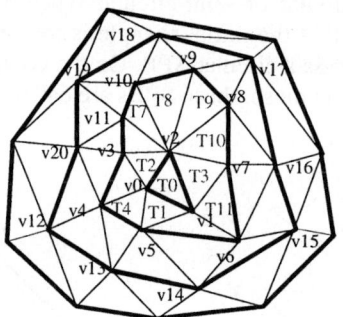

Fig. 6. A Partitioned Circular SPB

In Fig. 7, each horizontal line lists the vertices of the same rank and the mother-son relationship in two adjacent ranks is indicated by thick lines. Following the vertex ordering in ranks, we classify each vertex into one of four types: Cv is the current vertex, Nv is the next vertex, Mv_1 is the mother vertex of Cv, and Mv_2 is the mother vertex of Nv. Whereas v_0 is a Mv of $v_3 \sim v_5$, v_1 is a Mv of $v_6 \sim v_7$. If v_5 is a Cv, v_6 is a Nv, v_0 is a Mv_1 and v_1 is a Mv_2. Since each rank forms a closed loop in the circular SPB, the first vertex in each rank reappears at the last position of the rank in Fig. 7. In order to represent the topological information of the vertices, we define the index of each vertex by its distance from the first vertex in the same rank and express the mother-son relationship by encoding the indices of their mother vertices differentially.

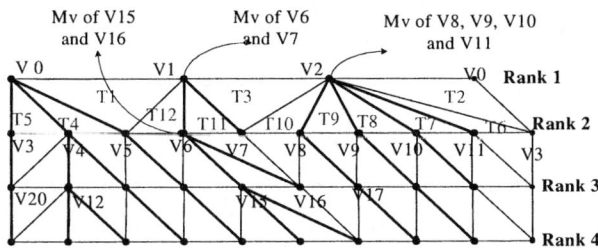

Fig. 7. Vertex Arrangement of the Circular SPB

In Fig. 7, v_6 in *Rank 2* is the mother vertex of v_{16}. Since v_6 is the third vertex from v_3, its index is 3. Similarly, v_8 in *Rank 2* is the mother vertex of v_{17} and its index is 5. Thus, we can represent the topological relationship of v_{16} and v_{17} by the index difference of their mother vertices, v_6 and v_8, i.e., $5 - 3 = 2$.

3.2 Semi-circular SPB

Figure 8 shows an example of the semi-circular SPB. As in the circular SPB, we can define the rank: *Rank 1* includes v_0~v_2 and *Rank 2* includes v_3~v_8. In Fig. 8, we indicate all ranks in the semi-circular SPB by thick lines. As shown in Fig. 8, each rank, except for the first rank, forms the semi-circular shape since there is no connecting edge between v_4 and v_5, or between v_{11} and v_{12}.

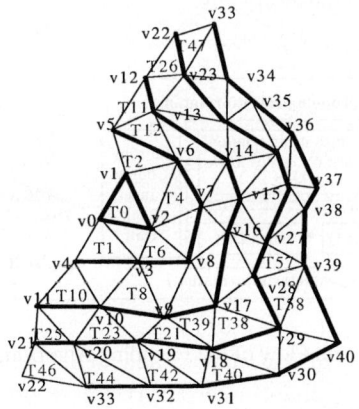

Fig. 8. A Partitioned Semi-Circular SPB

When we arrange all the vertices included in each rank in Fig. 8 into a row on the plane, we can form the map of the vertices, as shown in Fig. 9.

Since there is no connecting edge between v_4 and v_5 or between v_{11} and v_{12} in Fig. 8, we do not have a triangle containing v_4 and v_5 or v_{11} and v_{12} in Fig. 9. To make *Rank 2*, *Sv*'s of v_0 are found at first. Then, v_3 becomes the first vertex of *Rank 2* and shown in the last position in *Rank 2* again in Fig. 9.

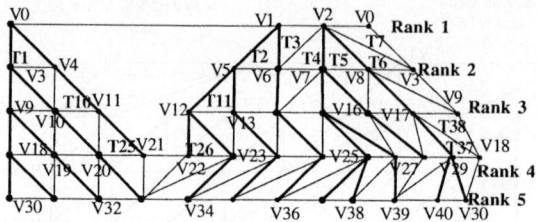

Fig. 9. Vertex Arrangement of a Semi-circular SPB

4 Sequential Encoding and Decoding

In the proposed algorithm, a mesh model is encoded and decoded in a SPB unit independently. Therefore, the model is partitioned into several SPBs and we obtain the map of the vertices, as shown in Fig. 7 and Fig. 9. Then, the encoding processes of Block A and Block B in Fig. 10 are applied to topological information and geometry information, respectively. In the case of topological information, as shown in Section 3.1, index differences which indicate the position from the first vertex in each rank, are acquired and encoded with the numbers of vertex in each rank. Both topological information and geometry information are coded in a rank unit to enhance error resilience. These processes are continued repeatedly until all SPBs will be encoded. Specially, we add the decoder and the comparator at the end of the encoder to transmit topological information that is not coded by our proposed algorithm. However, this data is very rare in most 3-D mesh models.

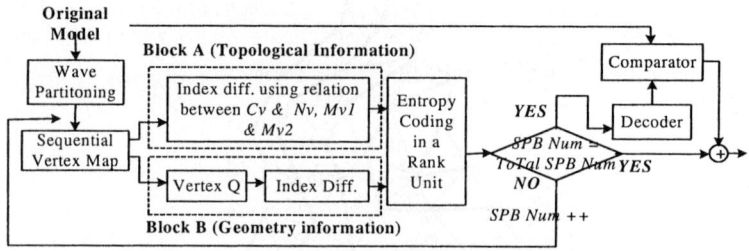

Fig. 10. Flow of the Encoding Algorithm

4.1 Topological Information

For the topological information, we transmit the numbers of vertices in each rank and $|Mv_1 - Mv_2|$ for each vertex at the encoder. The order of encoding is from left to right in a rank unit. Based on the value of $|Mv_1 - Mv_2|$, the proposed algorithm is classified into 4 types.

For the case of $|Mv_1 - Mv_2| = 0$, the triangle (Cv, Nv, Mv_1) is reconstructed at the decoder. In Fig. 7, when Cv is v_3, Nv is v_4, Mv_1 is v_0 and Mv_2 is v_0, $|Mv_1 - Mv_2| = |0 - 0| = 0$ and triangle (v_3, v_4, v_0) is reconstructed.

In the case of $|Mv_1 - Mv_2| = 1$, two triangles (Cv, Nv, Mv_2) and (Mv_1, Mv_2, Cv) are at the decoder. In Fig. 7, when Cv is v_7, Nv is v_8, Mv_1 is v_1 and Mv_2 is v_2, $|Mv_1 - Mv_2| = |1 - 2| = 1$. Triangles ($v_7$, v_2, v_1) and (v_7, v_8, v_2) are reconstructed.

In the case of $|Mv_1 - Mv_2| = 2$, we can consider 28 patterns, as shown in Fig. 11.

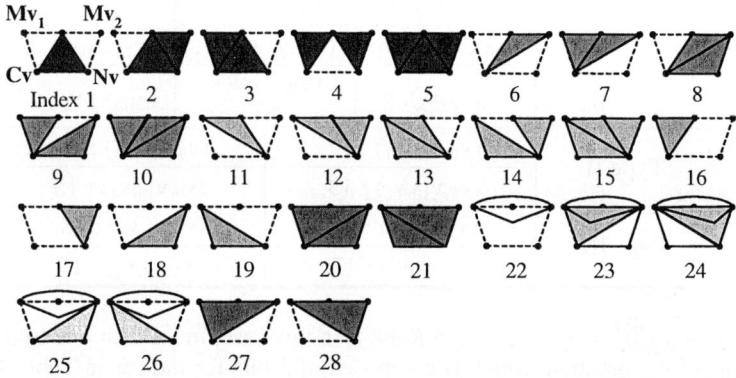

Fig. 11. Twenty-eight Patterns and Its Indices when $|Mv_1 - Mv_2| = 2$

At the decoder, one of 28 patterns is decoded based on the received index. So, in addition to the value of $|Mv_1 - Mv_2|$, 1 byte, which is composed of 5 index bits and 3 reserved bits, for a pattern index is also added to the bit-stream. Triangles that are composed of dotted edges are not real triangles. The cone shape in the $22^{nd} \sim 26^{th}$ patterns represents the triangle that is composed of Mv_1, Mv_2 and one vertex between Mv_1 and Mv_2. In Fig. 7, when Cv is v_{16}, Nv is v_{17}, Mv_1 is v_6 and Mv_2 is v_8, $|Mv_1 - Mv_2| = |3 - 5| = 2$. This case corresponds to the 10th pattern in Fig. 11. Index 10 is transmitted at the encoder and the 10th pattern is reconstructed at the decoder.

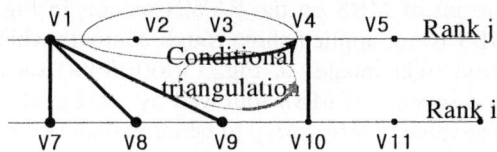

Fig. 12. Conditional Triangulation

If $|Mv_1 - Mv_2| > 2$, triangles are made conditionally, as shown in Fig. 12. According to the locations of vertices, triangles can be classified into three types. Table 1 indicates the types and indices for the conditional triangulation of Fig. 12. In Fig. 12, when v_9 in the *Rank i* is regarded as Cv, v_{10} is regarded as Nv, v_1 as Mv_1 and v_4 as Mv_2. Then $|Mv_1 - Mv_2|$ equals to 3 and triangles indicated in Table 1 will be made. Type I indicates triangles composed of v_9 or v_{10} in *Rank i* and two of $v_1 \sim v_4$ *Rank j*. Type II indicates triangles composed of v_9 and v_{10} in *Rank i* and one of $v_1 \sim v_4$ in *Rank j*. Type III indicates

Table 1. Vertex Types and Indices for Conditional Triangulation

	Indices of each triangle		
Type I	(v_9,v_1,v_2): 0,	(v_9,v_1,v_3): 1,	(v_9,v_1,v_4): 2,
	(v_9,v_2,v_3): 3,	(v_9,v_2,v_4): 4,	(v_9,v_3,v_4): 5,
	(v_{10},v_4,v_3): 6	(v_{10},v_4,v_2): 7,	(v_{10},v_4,v_1): 8,
	(v_{10},v_3,v_2): 9,	(v_{10},v_3,v_1): 10,	(v_{10},v_2,v_1): 11
Type II	(v_9,v_{10},v_1) : 12,		(v_9,v_{10},v_3) : 14,
	(v_9,v_{10},v_2) : 13,		(v_9,v_{10},v_4) : 15
Type III	(v_1,v_2,v_3) : 16,		(v_2,v_3,v_4) : 18,
	(v_1,v_2,v_4) : 17,		(v_1,v_3,v_4) : 19

triangles composed of 3 of $v_1 \sim v_4$ in *Rank j*. In this case, more than one triangle can be made. Therefore, one byte which is composed of 5 bits for indices in Table 1 and three bits for the number of triangles is encoded for each vertex in the encoder.

4.2 Geometry Information

For geometry information, the difference between Cv and Nv in the same rank quantized and entropy coded. Then, their indices are transmitted. As the geometry information is encoded in the same order as the topological information, models can be decoded using the values of $|Mv_1 - Mv_2|$ for the topological information and geometry information.

5 Experimental Results

Fig. 13 shows the result of MBS on the PAWN model. In Fig. 13 (a)(b)(c)(d), left images to which MBS is not applied show rough contours which cannot construct a rank. On the contrary, right images in Fig. 13(a)(b)(c)(d) show the result of wave partitioning and MBS scheme. If MBS followed by wave partitioning is not applied, the probability for the value of $|Mv_1 - Mv_2|$ to be more than two becomes higher. Then, additional indices must be added and coding efficiency can be lower. Besides, in some cases, the amount of residual data which is acquired by comparing the comparator with the decoder in Fig. 10 can be increased.

In order to evaluate the performance of the proposed scheme, we run computer simulations on several VRML mesh models and compare the results with those of the MPEG-4 SNHC standard which is based on the topological surgery.

Figure 14 demonstrates the test models that are decoded sequentially by the rank unit. As we put one initial seed triangle on the test models, test models are not partitioned into two or three pieces though we scan triangles to be encoded in the way of wave partitioning. While the topological information in each model is decoded losslessly, the geometrical information has been encoded by a 256-level quantizer and the arithmetic encoder. The coding efficiency is summarized in Table 2. We have improved coding efficiency for the topological information by about 1bit/vertex relative to the MPEG-4 SNHC standard. For geometrical information, even if coding efficiency depends on the mesh model, we get lower coding efficiency than that of the MPEG-4 SNHC algorithm by about less than 1 bit/vertex because we consider only one adjacent vertex to encode the current vertex in each rank.

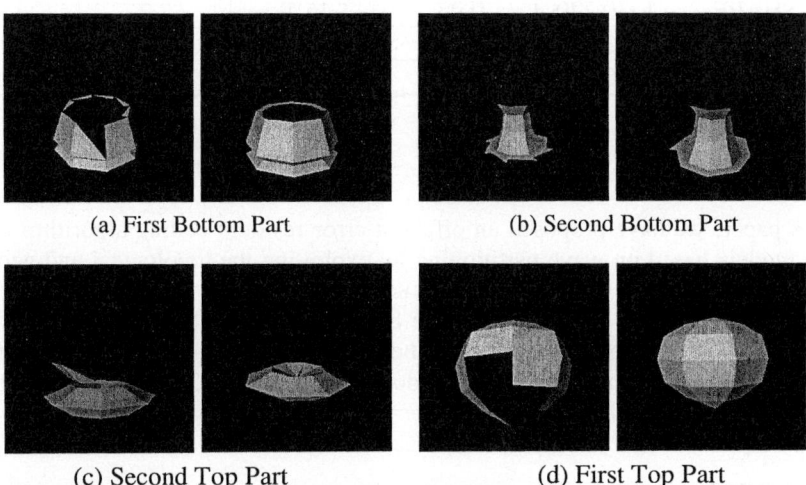

(a) First Bottom Part   (b) Second Bottom Part

(c) Second Top Part   (d) First Top Part

Fig. 13. Partitioned Pawn Model Applied with MBS

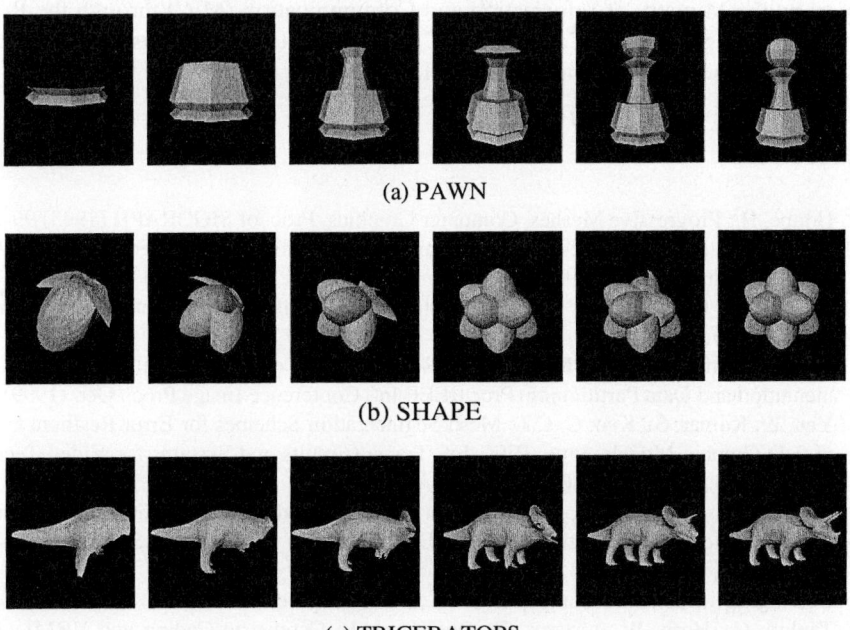

(a) PAWN

(b) SHAPE

(c) TRICERATOPS

Fig. 14. Sequential Decoding Results

Table 2. Coding Efficiency of Topological Information

	Model (Bytes)	Coding Efficiency (bits/vertex)			
		Proposed Algorithm		MPEG-4 SNHC	
		Topology	Geometry	Topology	Geometry
SHAPE	30,720	0.95	15.1	2.2	14.3
TRICERATOPS	33,960	3.31	11.2	4.3	10.4
BEETHOVEN	30,168	3.32	14.3	4.8	15

6 Conclusions

In this paper, we have proposed an efficient error resilient coding algorithm for 3-D mesh models based on wave partitioning by exploiting the topological and geometrical information. Since all the processing is executed rank by rank independently, the proposed algorithm is error resilient. We have also improved coding efficiency over the MPEG-4 SNHC coding scheme by about 1bit/vertex for the topological information. We have obtained reasonably good reconstructed 3-D models at 0.2~0.3 bit/vertex.

Acknowledgements

This work was supported in part by Korea Electronics Technology Institute (KETI), in part by the Ministry of Information and Communication (MIC) through the Realistic Broadcasting Research Center (RBRC), and in part by the Ministry of Education (MOE) through the Brain Korea 21 (BK21) project.

References

1. Hoppe, H.: Progressive Meshes. Computer Graphics, Proc. of SIGGRAPH (1993) 99-26
2. Taubin, G., Rossignac, J.: Geometry Compression through Topological Surgery. ACM Trans. Graphics, Vol. 17 (1998)
3. Touma, C., Gotsman, C.: Triangle Mesh Compression. Graphics Interface Conference Proc. (1998) 26-34
4. Yan, Z., Kumar, S., Li, J., Kuo, C.-C.J.: Robust Coding of 3D Graphic Models Mesh Segmentation and Data Partitioning. Proc. IEEE Int. Conference Image Proc., Oct. (1999)
5. Yan, Z., Kumar, S., Kuo, C.-C.J.: Mesh Segmentation Schemes for Error Resilient Coding of 3-D Graphic Models. Proc. IEEE Int. Trans. Circuits and Systems for Video Technology, Vol. 15, No. 1, Jan. (2005)
6. Yan, Z., Kumar, S., Kuo, C.-C.J.: Error-Resilient Coding of 3-D Graphic Models via Adaptive Mesh Segmentation. Proc. IEEE Int. Trans. Circuits and Systems for Video Technology, Vol. 11, No. 7, Jan. (2001)
7. Deering, M.: Geometric Compression. Computer Graphics Proc. (1995) 13-20
8. Taubin, G., Horn, W., Lazarus, F., Rossignac, J.: Geometric Coding and VRML. Proc. IEEE, Vol. 86 (1988)

9. Schroeder, W.J., Zarge, J.A.: Decimation of Triangle Meshes, Computer Graphics. Proc. of SIGGRAPH (1992) 65-70
10. Witten, I., Neal, Cleary, J.: Arithmetic Coding for Data Compression. Commun. ACM, Vol. 30, June (1987) 520-540
11. Bajaj, C.L., Pascucci, V., Zhuang, G.: Progressive Compression and Transmission of Arbitrary Triangular Meshes. Visualization '99, Proceedings, Oct. (1999) 307-537

Dimension-Reduction Technique for MPEG-7 Audio Descriptors*

Jui-Yu Lee[1] and Shingchern D. You[2]

[1] InterVideo Inc., Taiwan branch, Taipei, Taiwan
[2] Department of Computer Science and Information Engineering,
National Taipei University of Technology,
1, Sec. 3, Chung-Hsiao East Rd., Taipei 106, Taiwan
you@csie.ntut.edu.tw

Abstract. The MPEG-7 audio signature descriptors can be used to identify whether one piece of sound track is the same as another one in the database. This technique, known as music identification, can be applied to broadcast monitoring and copyright control. However, a practical database usually has a lot of sound tracks, therefore it requires too much time to directly compare the descriptors in the database with the unknown ones. In this paper, we propose an averaging method to reduce the dimensionality of the descriptors to a much lower degree. Our experiments show that the dimension-reduced descriptors still have a high discrimination capability. Using these descriptors, an efficient dual-resolution search method can be implemented for music identification.

1 Introduction

Traditionally people use texts as the key to search information in a database. With the advances of technology, multimedia information is getting more and more popular. Then, it becomes inconvenient if pure texts are used to represent the multimedia information. For example, it is almost impossible to use texts as the key to describe the melody of a song when retrieving it from a database. On the other hand, a query-by-humming [1] method is much more nature in this case. Thus, a content-based query is a fundamental capability of a multimedia database.

When a musical database is to be queried by contents, one may use "query by humming" or "query by descriptors" [2, 3, 4, 5, 6]. The first method uses the melody of a song as a comparison basis. Therefore, if two persons sing (hum) the same melody as queries to the multimedia database, they will retrieve the same song. On the other hand, the second method uses descriptors (or features), derived from a segment of the music waveform, as queries to the database. The multimedia information will be retrieved only if the database contains the same

---

* JYL performed the work while she was with the Department of Computer Science and Information Engineering, National Taipei University of Technology, Taipei, Taiwan.

segment of the waveform. Thus, if two persons sing the same song for recording, their recorded files (sound tracks) will be treated as different ones because their waveforms (and then descriptors) are different. Since the second method uses the descriptors as the basis of the database search, this technique is also known as music identification.

There are several potential applications of the music identification technique, such as to identify the title and the performer of the unknown sound track, to screen copyrighted materials, and to provide the broadcast monitoring [3, 5]. In these applications, the same song (melody) sang by a well-known performer and by an amateur should be treated as different ones. Therefore, the query-by-descriptors cannot be substituted by the query-by-humming method, as their applications are different.

For the music identification problem, the most straightforward solution is to compare the PCM samples (raw data) of the unknown music with the samples stored in the database. However, this approach is computationally too intensive to be practically used. For example, a typical musical CD has about 600M bytes of PCM samples from about ten songs. If a database contains 10,000 different songs, then the PCM samples occupy about 600G bytes of space. A piece of unknown music with duration of ten seconds has about 880k bytes of data. It is obvious that sequentially comparing the 880k bytes of data with the 600G bytes of data in the database requires too much computation. Therefore, a dimension-reduction technique must be employed for lower computation. The dimension-reduced representations of the original sources are known as descriptors or features.

2 MPEG-7 Audio

In the past, each company had its own proprietary descriptors, and the associated dimension-reduction techniques, for multimedia contents [5]. For the reason of interoperability, standardized features have been developed by ISO for multimedia content description [8, 9, 10, 11, 12]. The part 4 of the MPEG-7 standard provides procedures to calculate low-level and high-level descriptors.

2.1 Low-Level Descriptors of the MPEG-7 Audio

There are 17 low-level audio descriptors defined in the standard. All of these low-level descriptors are derived from the waveform of the music. They can be divided into six different categories, as listed below:

1. Basic: containing AudioWaveform descriptors and AudioPower descriptors.
2. Basic spectral: containing AudioSpectrumEnvelop descriptors, AudiospectrumCentroid descriptors, and AudioSpectrumFlatness descriptors.
3. Signal parameter: containing AudioFundamentalFrequency descriptors, and AudioHarmonicity descriptors.
4. Timbral temporal: containing LogAttackTime descriptors and Temporal descriptors.

5. Timbral spectral: containing SpectrumCentroid descriptors, HarmonicSpectrumCentroid descriptors, HarmonicSpectralDeviation descriptors, and HarmonicSpectralVariation descriptors.
6. Spectral basis representation: containing AudioSpectrumBasis descriptors and AudioSpectrumProjection descriptors.

2.2 High-Level Descriptors of the MPEG-7 Audio

The standard also defines high-level tools in the standard. They use low-level descriptors as the basis for higher level of information processing. The tools are listed in the following:

1. Audio signature description: this tool is mainly used for audio identification. We use this tool in this paper.
2. Instrument timbre description: generally two different musical instruments playing with the same pitch and loudness will sound different. This tool provides the features for describing different sounds of different instruments.
3. General sound recognition and indexing description: this tool is for classification of different types of music (e.g., rock, vocal, or classical).
4. Spoken content description: this tool can be used for speech recognition.
5. Melody description: this tool provides the high-level information of the musical melody so that matching of melodic similarity can be efficiently performed.

Using MPEG-7 audio descriptors to identify music has been studied [4, 6, 13, 14]. The conclusions of these studies indicate that the AudioSignature descriptors provide higher discrimination capability than the MPEG-7 low-level descriptors. Therefore, we use the AudioSignature descriptors as the basic features in our study. Although the AudioSignature descriptors have fewer dimensions than the raw data, the search for a piece of ten-second music from the database with, say, 10,000 different songs still require a lot of computation (comparison). Therefore, it is beneficial to further reduce the dimensionality of the AudioSignature descriptors to attain a shorter search time.

3 The MPEG-7 AudioSignature Descriptors

In this section, we shall briefly describe the calculation procedure for obtaining the AudioSignature descriptors. The descriptors are the mean values and variance values of a series of the AudioSpectrumFlatness descriptors. Then, We shall discuss the issue of the comptational complexity when the descriptors are used for music identification.

3.1 Calculation of MPEG-7 AudioSignature

The following is the procedure to calculate the MPEG-7 AudioSignature descriptors:

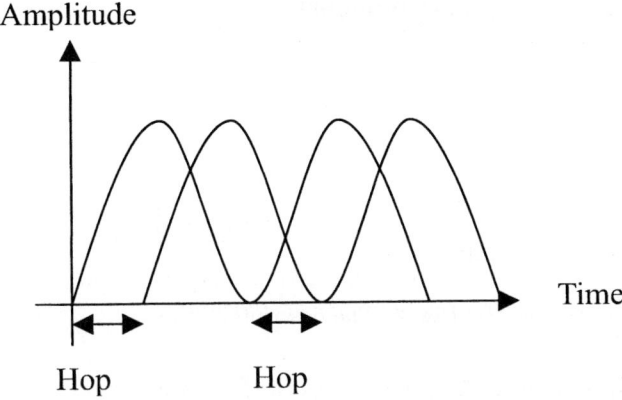

Fig. 1. The hop size

Table 1. Frequency range of various subbands with and without overlapping

Nominal	Actual (Overlapped)
250.0 - 297.3 Hz	237.5 - 312.2 Hz
297.3 - 353.6 Hz	282.4 - 371.2 Hz
353.6 - 420.4 Hz	335.9 - 441.5 Hz

1. Analyze the audio signal. This step converts the signal from time domain to frequency domain using the AudioSpectrumEnvelope descriptors, whose calculation steps are listed below:
   - Obtain the hop length. The hop size, with a default value of 30 ms, specifies the time difference between two consecutive windows, as shown in Fig. 1. The hop length is defined as the hop size times the sampling rate.
   - Define the window length lw. The window length is three times the hop length. The window used is the Hamming window.
   - Determine the length of FFT, denoted as $NFFT$. This value is the smallest power-of-2 number which is equal to or larger than lw. For example, if $lw = 3969$, then $NFFT = 4096$. All the sample points after the lw should set to zero.
   - Perform the FFT of the windowed samples.
2. Determine the values of loEdge and hiEdge and use these values to divide the spectrum of the signal into several subbands, with each subband having a bandwidth of one-fourth of an octave. The loEdge is fixed at 250 Hz and the default value of hiEdge is 4 kHz. The values of loEdge and hiEdge must satisfy the following constraint:

$$\text{Edge} = 2^{0.25m} \times 1 \text{ kHz, where } m \in Z$$

In addition, two consecutive subbands should overlap each other by 10 % in frequency span. That is, the calculated loEdge must be multiplied by 0.95

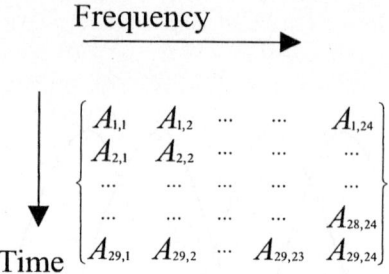

Fig. 2. The descriptor array

and the hiEdge by 1.05. Table 1 lists the frequency ranges of some subbands before and after the frequency overlapping.

3. Find the flatness measure of each subband. The flatness measure SFM of subband b is calculated as follows:

$$SFM_b = \frac{\sqrt[ih(b)-il(b)+1]{\prod_{i=il(b)}^{ih(b)} c(i)}}{\frac{1}{ih(b)-il(b)+1} \sum_{i=il(b)}^{ih(b)} c(i)}$$

In the equation, $c(i)$ is the coefficients of the power spectrum, b is the subband number, $ih(b)$ and $il(b)$ are the highest and lowest indices "i", respectively, of the $c(i)$ within subband b.

4. Use the scaling ratio, default value to be 32, to find the mean and variance of a subband in a certain number, specified by the scaling ratio, of successive FFT windows.
5. The series of mean and variance values are the AudioSignature descriptors.

As a brief example, we consider the number of AudioSignature descriptors in a piece of music with a duration of 15 second. The scaling ratio is set to 16 and the loEdge and the hiEdge are set to 250 Hz and 16 kHz, respectively. Recall that one subband consists of one-fourth of an octave and there are six octaves from 250 Hz to 16 kHz. Therefore, there are totally 24 subbands in the frequency domain. In the time domain, about $(15-0.09)/0.03 = 497$ windows must be used to cover the 15-second signal given that the hop size is 30 ms. Due to the scaling ratio of 16, the time-domain features reduce to $497/16 \simeq 31$ per subband. Thus, the descriptors representing the 15-second signal have $24 \times 31 = 744$ distinct mean values and another 744 distinct variance values. These descriptors can be arranged in the matrix form, as shown in Fig. 2. The horizontal direction of the matrix represents different frequency components at a time. The $A_{x,1}$ is the lowest frequency component and the $A_{x,24}$ is the highest frequency one. In addition, $A_{x,1}$ to $A_{x,4}$ are the representations of frequencies from 250 Hz to 500 Hz, and the next four from 500 Hz to 1000 Hz, and so on. Similarly, the vertical direction represents different time instances in a fixed frequency band. Since the hop size is 30 ms and the scaling ratio is 16, the time difference between $A_{1,x}$ and $A_{2,x}$ is about 0.485 second. The representation of descriptors, given in Fig. 2, will be used in the following of the paper. Also note that the descriptors derived from the mean values and those from the variance values should be separately compared. For brevity, we shall only mention how to process and compare descriptors for the mean values. It will be understood that the same procedure should be applied to the variance descriptors.

3.2 Complexity of Search by Using the AudioSignature Descriptors

We now consider the complexity of searching the database using the AudioSignature descriptors. Suppose that a database contains 1,000 audio files, with each one having a duration of 30 seconds, and the music to be identified has a duration of 15 seconds. Since the unknown music may not be excerpted from the very beginning of an audio file, the comparison of the unknown with an audio file should be carried out with all possible starting points to to find the best match, as shown in Fig. 3. Recall that for a time instance there are 24 descriptors associated with different subbands. Thus one needs to compare $744/24 + 1 = 32$ segments of data for one file. In terms of arithmetic operations, there are $1,488 \times 32 \times 1,000 = 47,616,000$ subtractions if the Euclidean distance is to be used. This number is still very large for practical applications, therefore a more efficient search algorithm is highly desirable.

Conceptually, a multi-resolution (pyramid) search algorithm can be applied to this problem with higher efficiency. In the multi-resolution algorithm, descriptors with lower dimensions, possibly derived from full-dimensional ones, are firstly used to find possible candidates among the entire database. Due to the use of low-dimensional descriptors, this step does not demand too much computation. After that, descriptors with full dimensions are then applied to find the best match from the candidates. Since the full-dimensional descriptors are

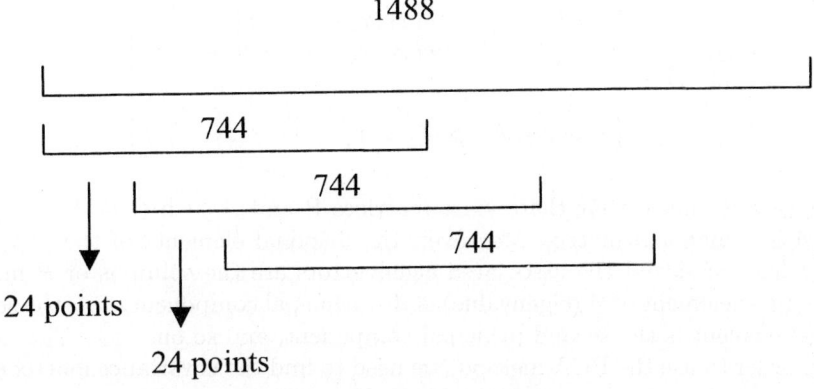

Fig. 3. The sliding comparison

used to compare with only a small group of possible candidates, this step can be accomplished with a much lower computational complexity. Therefore, the multi-resolution approach can greatly reduce the overall computation. However, the effectiveness of the multi-resolution method relies heavily on the high discrimination capability of the low-dimensional descriptors. In this paper, we only concentrate on the process of obtaining low-dimensional features with good discrimination capability.

4 The Proposed Approach

The dimension-reduction technique for MPEG-7 audio signature descriptors has been studied previously [4, 6]. However, one paper [6] provides a reduction ratio of about only 16, which is not large enough. The method used in another one [4] is promising, but it requires to store descriptors derived from coded audio, say through MP-3 compression and then de-compression, if a coded audio is to be used as the query. Therefore, we decide to use some "obvious" methods to check if these methods work. The first one is to use the Principal Component Analysis (PCA) [15] for reducing the dimensions of the descriptors because the PCA method has been applied to the pattern recognition field for years. The second method is simply averaging some descriptors for dimension reduction.

4.1 Principal Component Analysis

In the following, we briefly describe the Principal Component Analysis (PCA) method and how to use it to our problem. Suppose that

$$\boldsymbol{x} = [x_1, x_2, ... x_N]^T$$

is a column matrix with $x_1, ..., x_N$ to be random variables. The covariance of random variables x_i and x_j is $cov(x_i, x_j) = E[(x_i - \bar{x}_i) \cdot (x_j - \bar{x}_j)]$ where $\bar{x}_i$ is the mean of the random variable x_i. The covariance matrix A of $\boldsymbol{x}$ is defined as follows:

$$A = \begin{bmatrix} cov(x_1, x_1) & cov(x_1, x_2) & \cdots & cov(x_1, x_N) \\ cov(x_2, x_1) & cov(x_2, x_2) & \cdots & cov(x_2, x_N) \\ \vdots & \vdots & \vdots & \vdots \\ cov(x_N, x_1) & cov(x_N, x_2) & \cdots & cov(x_N, x_N) \end{bmatrix}$$

It can be shown that there exist matrices P and Λ such that $\Lambda = P^{-1}AP$ and Λ is a diagonal matrix. Moreover, the diagonal elements of the Λ are the eigenvalues of A and the associated eigenvectors are the columns of P matrix. The largest element of Λ (eigenvalue) is the principal component of A, the second largest element is the second principal component, and so on.

In order to use the PCA method, we need to find the covariance matrix of the descriptors. However, in general we do not know the distribution of the collected data. Therefore, we need to use the sample mean and sample covariance as the

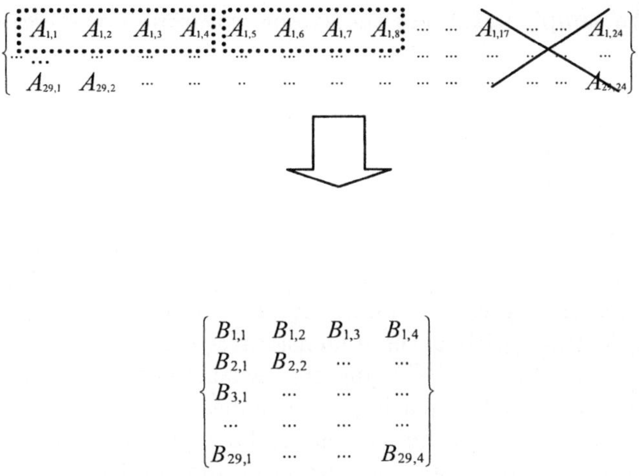

$$\begin{Bmatrix} A_{1,1} & A_{1,2} & A_{1,3} & A_{1,4} & A_{1,5} & A_{1,6} & A_{1,7} & A_{1,8} & \cdots & \cdots & A_{1,17} & \cdots & \cdots & A_{1,24} \\ A_{29,1} & A_{29,2} & \cdots & & & & & & & & & & & A_{29,24} \end{Bmatrix}$$

$$\Downarrow$$

$$\begin{Bmatrix} B_{1,1} & B_{1,2} & B_{1,3} & B_{1,4} \\ B_{2,1} & B_{2,2} & \cdots & \cdots \\ B_{3,1} & \cdots & \cdots & \cdots \\ \cdots & \cdots & \cdots & \cdots \\ B_{29,1} & \cdots & \cdots & B_{29,4} \end{Bmatrix}$$

Fig. 4. The dimension reduction technique, step 1

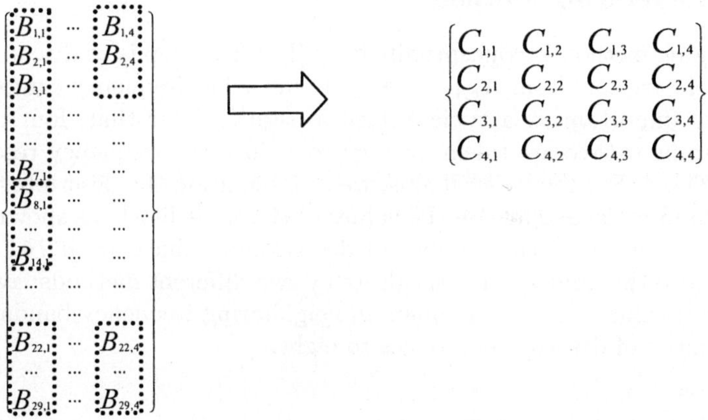

$$\Longrightarrow \quad \begin{Bmatrix} C_{1,1} & C_{1,2} & C_{1,3} & C_{1,4} \\ C_{2,1} & C_{2,2} & C_{2,3} & C_{2,4} \\ C_{3,1} & C_{3,2} & C_{3,3} & C_{3,4} \\ C_{4,1} & C_{4,2} & C_{4,3} & C_{4,4} \end{Bmatrix}$$

Fig. 5. The dimension reduction technique, step 2

estimates. Specifically, let $x^{(1)}, \ldots, x^{(M)}$ be the collected data arranged in the column-matrix form from a random experiment, then we can find the sample mean of the random variable x_k as

$$\bar{X}_k = \frac{1}{M} \sum_{j=1}^{M} x_k^{(j)}$$

The sample covariance can be obtained using the following equation:

$$COV(x_i, x_j) = \frac{1}{M-1} \sum_{j=1}^{M} (x_i^{(i)} - \bar{X}_i) \cdot (x_j^{(j)} - \bar{X}_j)$$

Having the sample mean and the sample covariance, the corresponding covariance matrix can then be constructed. Consequently, the eigenvalues and eigenvectors can be obtained.

It requires some thoughts to apply the concept of the PCA to reduce the dimensionality of the MPEG-7 descriptors. The problem is that the descriptors have 744 values. If we treat these values as elements of a vector, then the obtained covariance matrix has a dimension of 744 by 744. Thus, it would take very long time to find the eigenvalues of such a huge matrix. Considering this difficulty, we decide not to put them in a 744-element column matrix for PCA calculation. In stead, the matrix representation of Fig. 2 is to be used. The transformation for obtaining features with lower dimensions is conducted in two steps. The first step is to calculate the PCA and the associated transformation matrix in the horizontal direction by treating the original descriptors in one matrix as many row matrices. The second step is similar to the first step, but this time the matrices obtained from step one are used and the PCA is obtained in the vertical direction.

4.2 The Averaging Method

The averaging method is conceptually easy. The first step is to discard the high-frequency descriptors from $A_{x,17}$ to $A_{x,24}$ because low frequency components are much more important in a typical musical signal. After that, four descriptors from the same octave are taken average to reduce the frequency resolution, as shown in Fig. 4. For the vertical axis, we also partition the descriptors into four subblocks and make average on the values of the same block, as shown in Fig. 5. With these operations, the number of descriptors reduces from 744 to 16. We further reduce the number of descriptors by two different methods: averaging or choose the maximum of two numbers in neighboring frequency bands. By doing so, the number of descriptors reduces to eight.

5 Experiments and Results

Before conducting the experiments, we collected 39 different CD titles with a total of 400 different sound tracks. From them, 500 audio files are obtained, with each one having a duration of 30 seconds. To simulate songs of similar melodies inside the database, some of the sound tracks individually contribute two audio files, one from the beginning of the sound track and the other one from the middle part.

Experiment I was conducted to verify the discrimination capability of the MPEG-7 audio signature descriptors. To do so, test files with a duration of 15 seconds from each of the (30-second) audio files were extracted. These test files and the original audio files were then applied to the MPEG-7 reference program to obtain the descriptors. To check whether the descriptors can be used to identify distorted music, the test files were encoded and then decoded with the MP-3 coder. The encoding bitrates were 192 kbps, 128 kbps, and 96 kbps,

Table 2. Results of experiment I in terms of percentage of accuracy

Music length	Original	96 kbps MP-3	128 kbps MP-3	192 kbps MP-3
15 sec	100.0 %	99.8 %	100.0 %	100.0 %
7 sec	99.8 %	99.8 %	99.8 %	99.8 %

Table 3. Results of experiment II

	Avg 8p	Max 8p	PCA 8p
Lossless	Top 5	Top 4	Top 4
192 kbps MP-3	Top 8	Top 6	More than 20
96 kbps MP-3	Top 20	Top 9	More than 20

Table 4. Results of experiment III

	Avg 4p	max 4p
Lossless	Top 17	More than 20
96 kbps MP-3	More than 20	More than 20

respectively. Note that the descriptors stored in the database were obtained from the audio files without distortion. A simple Euclidean distance was used as the classifier. The same experiment was also repeated for the test files with a duration of 7 seconds. The experimental results are listed in Table 2. It can be seen that the performance of the AudioSignature descriptors is very good even if they are used to identify distorted samples.

Experiment II was conducted using the same procedure as in Experiment I, except that the dimension-reduced descriptors are used this time. The results are listed in Table 3. The results reveal that a simple averaging method yields satisfactory results with the Euclidean distance. On the other hand, the PCA approach has a good discrimination capability for distortion-less signals, but yields relatively poor results for distorted ones. Probably due to this situation, Crysandt [4] uses a different similarity measurement, the Mahalanobis distance, in the paper. However, the Mahalanobis distance has a much higher computational complexity than the Euclidean one. One way to cope with this problem, as suggested by Crysandt, is to store descriptors after a linear transform in the database. However, the problem associated with this approach is the need to store multiple copies of descriptors for the same music with different types (degrees) of distortion, which is a waste of the database space.

To put the averaging method to the extreme, we tried to use only 4 descriptors (for mean) in the comparison. The results, shown in Table 4, are not very good as the correct one distributes over a range of more than top 20. We are now performing more experiments to find the suitable number of descriptors for efficient comparison. As mentioned previously, using the low-resolution (dimension) descriptors in the first-run enables us to use the high-resolution descriptors to search only among the possible candidates for finding the best one.

Viewing from this point, a good approach for finding low-dimensional features with high discrimination capability is essential to the multi-resolution identification system.

6 Conclusions

In this paper, we demonstrate that a simple averaging approach can be effective in reducing the dimensionality of the MPEG-7 AudioSignature descriptors. The dimension-reduced descriptors can be used in the coarse search in a database. The candidates in the top list are then verified using full-resolution descriptors. The experimental results also show that the PCA features are more susceptible to distortion, and thus a simple Euclidean distance cannot be applied. Considering all the factors, we conclude that the averaging approach is a better one for obtaining low-dimensional features due to its simplicity.

Acknowledgement

This project was partially supported by the National Science Concil, Taiwan through contract no. NSC 94-2213-E-027-042, which is gratefully acknowledged.

References

1. Jang J.-S. R. Jang, Jang Y.-S.: On the Implementation of Melody Recognition on 8-bit And 16-bit Microcontrollers. The Fourth IEEE Pacific-Rim Conference on Multimedia, Singapore, (2003).
2. Hellmuth O., et al.: Content-based Identification of Audio Material Using MPEG-7 Low Level Description. Available at
http://ismir2001.ismir.net/pdf/allamanche.pdf.
3. Hellmuth O., et al.: Using MPEG-7 Audio Fingerprinting in Real-world Application. 115th AES Convention, (2003) Convention Paper 5961.
4. Crysandt H.: Music Identification with MPEG-7. 115th AES Convention, (2003) Convention Paper 5967.
5. Haistma J. A.: A New Technology To Identify Music. Nat. Lab. Unclassified Report 2002/824, Koninklijke Philips, Electronics N.V. (2002).
6. Herre J., Hellmuth O., Cremer M.: Scalable Robust Audio Fingerprinting Using MPEG-7 Content Description. Proceedings of IEEE Workshop on Multimedia Signal Processing, (2002) 165-168.
7. Casey M. A.: MPEG-7 Sound Recognition Tools. IEEE Trans. Circuits and Systems for Video Tech. 11 (2001) 737-747.
8. ISO/IEC: Information Technology V Multimedia Content Description Interface - Part 4: Audio. IS 15938-4 (2002).
9. ISO/IEC: Overview of the MPEG-7 Standard (version 9). JTC1/SC29/WG11 N5525 (2003).
10. Nack F., Lindsay A. T.: Everything You Wanted to Know about MPEG-7, Part I. IEEE Mutimedia Magazine 6/3 (1999) 65-77.

11. Nack F., Lindsay A. T.: Everything You Wanted to Know about MPEG-7, Part II. IEEE Mutimedia Magazine 6/4 (1999) 64-73.
12. Quackenbush S., Lindsay A.: Overview of MPEG-7 Audio. IEEE Trans. on Circuits and Systems for Video Tech. 11 (2001) 725-729.
13. Luksiak J., et al.: An Examination of Practical Information Manipulation Using the MPEG-7 Low Level Audio Descriptors. Available at http://www.elec.uow.edu.au/staff/wysocki/WITSP_02_PDF/Lukasik.pdf.
14. Lukasiak J. et al.:, Performance of MPEG-7 Low Level Audio Descriptors with Compressed Data. Proceedings of IEEE Multimedia and Expo, (2003) III-237-6.
15. Hunteman G. H.: Principal Component Analysis. Newbury Park Sage Publications (1989).

Design of an Asynchronous Switch Based on Butterfly Fat-Tree for Network-on-Chip Applications

Min-Chang Kang[1], Eun-Gu Jung[2], and Dong-Soo Har[2]

[1] SoC Design Group, SIC R&D Center, System IC Division,
LG Electronics, Republic of Korea
mindow@lge.com
[2] Department of Information and Communications,
Gwangju Institute of Science and Technology, Republic of Korea
{egjung, hardon}@gist.ac.kr

Abstract. The future System-on-Chip (*SoC*) design will integrate a variety of intellectual properties (IPs). The clocked bus architectures to interconnect the IPs under the deep submicron technology suffer from problems related with the clock distribution, the synchronization of all IPs, the long arbitration delay and the limited bandwidth. These problems can be resolved by adopting new interconnection architecture such as Network-on-Chip (*NoC*) or the asynchronous design method. In this paper, a design methodology for an asynchronous switch based on butterfly fat-tree topology is proposed. The wormhole switching technique is adopted to reduce the latency and the buffer size. The source-based routing mechanism and the output buffering strategy are used to reduce the switch design cost and increase the performance.

1 Introduction

The complexity of the future System-on-Chip (*SoC*) significantly depends on the communication architecture, rather than the computation architecture according to ITRS2001[1]. Most of the current interconnection architectures are designed as clocked systems. However, the clock distribution across a large die and dataflow processes at the same clock rate makes it difficult to synchronize of all the IPs on a single chip.

As a result, communication architectures likely shift to asynchronous design paradigm. In Globally Asynchronous and Locally Synchronous (*GALS*) systems, all the synchronous IPs communicate each other through the asynchronous interconnection architecture.

To accommodate the interconnections of the IPs, the on-chip bus, *OCB*, has been used. On-chip bus architecture, however, has limitations such as the long arbitration delay, the limited bandwidth and the non-scalability. In the bus architecture, several bus masters compete to use the shared medium. Therefore, the arbiter delay grows as the number of bus masters increases. Because the single arbiter should process all the arbitration requests from the bus masters, the arbiter for many bus masters has a high complexity. Also, the slow slave IPs can decrease the overall performance of the bus. As the bus is non-scalable and shared by all units, the bandwidth of the bus is limited, and therefore it becomes the bottleneck of the system.

To address the aforementioned problems, a new paradigm for *SoC* design has been suggested to replace the bus with the network-centric architecture. The arbitration operations of the *NoC* are distributed over network switches, so that the delay of the arbitration time can be reduced substantially. Unlike the shared bus, the network is scalable and the overall throughput will increase as the number of IPs grows.

To reduce the design cost and the complexity without sacrificing the performance, the architecture level approaches originated from the parallel computing scheme are suggested. The design issues strongly affect the resulting system complexity and the consequential performance of the communication architecture. In this paper, four design issues topology, switching technique, routing mechanism and buffering scheme are considered within the asynchronous design methodology to achieve low design cost and high performance. In our approach, we assume that the architecture is targeted on connecting the multi-processors.

Regarding the application area of the network on chip, no architecture satisfies the general requirements that interconnection network should provide. In our approach, we assume that the architecture is targeted on connecting the multi-processors.

The design options such as the switching technique (Section 2), the routing mechanism (Section 3), the buffering scheme (Section 4) and the topology (Section 5) are discussed in this paper. In Section 6, the internal architecture of the self-timed switch, including the operations of individual modules, is considered. In Section 7, the performance of *NoC* is measured, and in Section 8 concluding remarks are presented.

2 Switching Technique

The switching technique determines when and how internal switches are set to connect router inputs to outputs and the time at which message components may be transferred along these paths.

In a circuit switching, a physical path from the source to the destination is established by a header and reserved until the last message reaches the destination. This header information is sent toward the destination reserving physical links. When the header reaches the destination, a complete path has been set up. Circuit switching is advantageous when messages are long and infrequent[6]. However, between many IPs as in *NoCs*, the size of messages is small and communications are frequent.

The path from the source to the destination for small messages can be determined by the network situation. The whole message is broken into the packets. This packet switching is good for short and frequent messages. Each packet contains the routing information and data. At each switch in the network, a received packet is stripped to find the desired output port. The need to buffer complete packets within a switch, however, can make it difficult to construct compact and fast switches.

In a wormhole switching, the message packets are partitioned into the fixed length flow control unit, flits. The first flit, header, contains the addresses of the source and destination and the routing information to reserve the path for transmitting the remaining flits to the destination. The remaining data flits simply follow the path established by the header flit. The message divided into flits is typically larger than the size of the buffers within a single switch. Thus, when a header flit is blocked by the other flits, the blocked flits occupy buffers in several switches through the network. This is called a cascaded contention.

The wormhole switching technique allows simple, small, cheap, and fast switch designs because the buffer requirements within the switches are substantially reduced over the requirements for the packet switching.

3 Routing Mechanism

To identify the output channels for the packets to be transmitted, a routing mechanism is required. The routing mechanism can be categorized into a dimension-order routing, a table-driven approach and a source-based routing. The dimension-order routing mechanism needs the testing logic to determine the relative addresses. In a table-driven routing, the routing table should be implemented in each switch to decide the desired output ports.

However, the source-based routing simply strips off the routing information in the header and sends the message to the specified channel. This allows a very simple switch with little control state and without even arithmetic units to support complex routing functions. Therefore the source-based routing involves minimal processing delay at each switch.

An interconnection network for *NoCs* must satisfy a very strict timing constraint, namely, low processing delay. This requires a simple switch implementation with little control state to achieve. Source-based routing algorithm is better for achieving of simple implementation of switches.

4 Buffering Strategy

The organization of a buffer position in the individual switches strongly impacts on the performance of the switch and network.

In the input buffering strategy, each FIFO buffer is placed between input ports and the crossbar. A single packet at the head of the FIFO can be transmitted at a time. The input buffering suffers from the Head Of Line (*HOL*) problem. The packet at the head of the queue can be blocked when packets from different input buffers are propagated to the same output. In this case, all packets behind the blocked FIFO have to be blocked wherever their destinations are. Some schemes can handle the *HOL* problem. However, the cost is prohibitive.

Centralized or shared buffering utilizes the buffer resources supremely but the control logic for the shared buffer management is more complicated than those of the input buffering and output buffering.

In the output buffering, the frequency of contention at any output buffer is lower than that at a centralized buffer because flits are distributed over different output buffers. The output buffering is thus the one least likely to involve contention among three buffering strategies. This scheme does not suffer from the *HOL* problem like the input buffering and the control logic for the output buffering management is much simpler than the shared buffering scheme.

5 Topology

The proposed butterfly fat-tree architecture of the asynchronous interconnections for the IPs is illustrated in Figure 1. The processors are located at the leaves and the switches are placed at the vertices. In the butterfly fat-tree architecture, the switch depth is determined according to the number of IPs. If the number of IPs are N, the depth is calculated as $log_4 N$.

The switches over the butterfly fat-tree network are identical and the top level switch does not have the up channels and doesn't depend on the speed of the IPs on the leaves because of the asynchronous characteristics. The switches at each level do not require the additional information of their positions which is used in routing the flits. The only information required for routing is the output ports at each switch. These identical switch configurations provide the flexibility and simplicity in designing a *NoC*. The implemented network topology is shown in Figure 2.

The number of switches in the butterfly fat-tree converges to a constant, which is independent of the number of tree levels in the network[2]. Consider the number of switches N. The number of switches in the first level is $N/4$ and the number of switches in the next level is half of the number in the previous level. Accordingly, the total number of switches is calculated as follows[2].

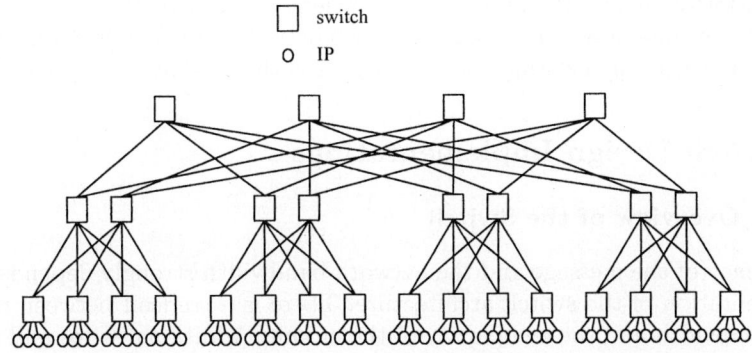

Fig. 1. Butterfly fat-tree architecture interconnecting 64 IPs

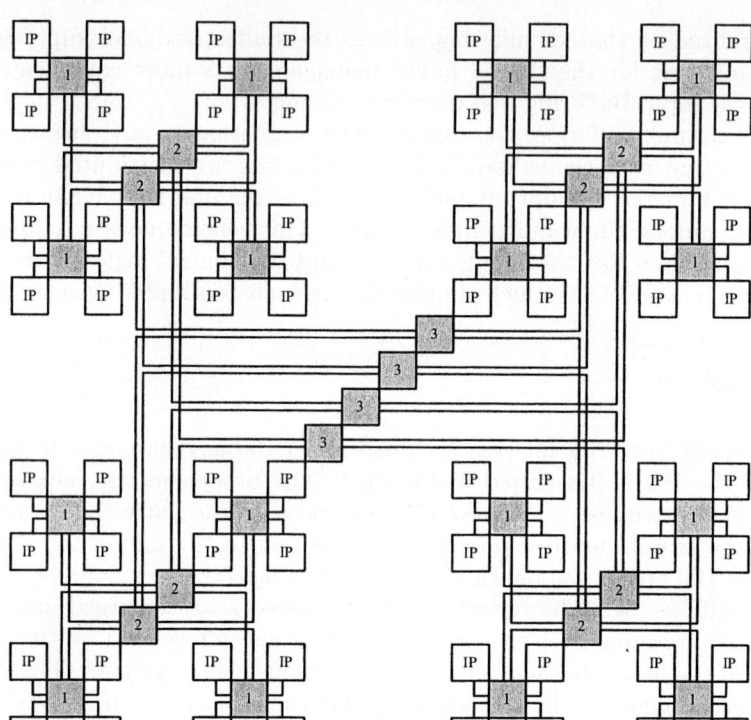

Fig. 2. The Implemented Topology of Butterfly Fat-Tree Architecture

$$N_{switches} = \frac{N}{4} + \frac{1}{2}(\frac{N}{4}) + \frac{1}{4}(\frac{N}{4}) + \cdots \leq \frac{N}{2}$$

Of the merits of the butterfly fat-tree architecture, the wire structure is predictable and the wire length from a switch to each end node is uniform[2, 3, 4]. Butterfly fat-tree is the most cost-efficient in VLSI realization[5] and non-blocking, because any input port can be connected to any free output port without affecting the existing connections, as is the case of the crossbar.

6 Switch Design Implementations

6.1 A Overview of the Switch

The latency of the message and the network bandwidth strongly depends on the implementation of the switch architecture. There is a tradeoff between the network bandwidth and the complexity of the circuit. Additional wires and storage elements are required to accommodate the increased bandwidth which could reduce the performance of the switch. In packet or flit based network, as it is ad-

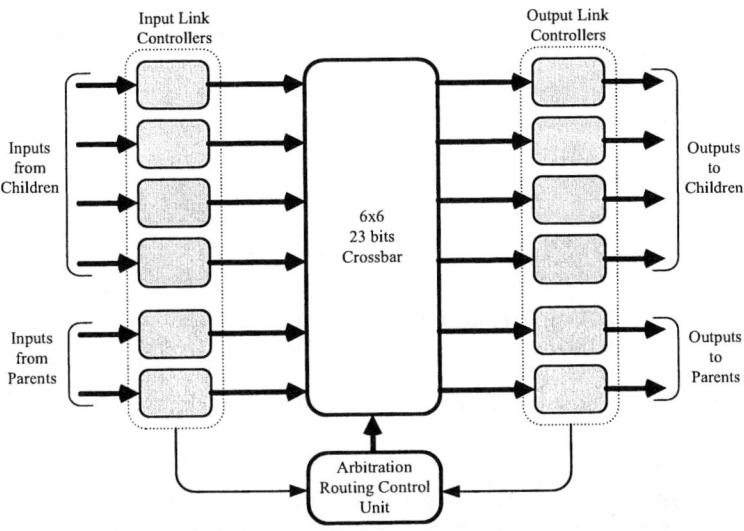

Fig. 3. The overview of the proposed switch

vantageous when the messages are frequent and short, we suggest the minimum packet size and bandwidth to reduce the complexity of the switch implementation.

The architecture of the proposed switch is shown is Figure 3. Link Controllers are responsible for the flow of messages across the physical channel between adjacent switches. The Link controllers communicate each other with an asynchronous protocol to transmit the units of the flow control. In the output link controllers, 2-stage FIFO is implemented for buffering the flits going to the output port. The crossbar component implements the interconnection of switch inputs and switch output buffers. The arbitration and routing control unit is in charge of arbitrating the concurrent input requests from the input link controllers to the same output ports and establishing the path to the desired outputs. Also, it supports the wormhole switching technique to hold the path until the last payload is transmitted to the requested output.

6.2 Packet Format

The proposed packet structure is comprised of header flit and payload flits shown in Figure 4. The header flit contains the Type field (2 bits), Source Address field (6 bits) and Routing Information field (15 bits). There are three kinds of type field; '00' denotes header, '10' implies payload and '11' notifies the last payload.

The flit length is constant but the total number of flits in a packet can vary, i.e. this Type filed supports various length packet sizes. The routing information field contains 5 sub-fields which can be used in each switch to identify the output path respectively. In butterfly fat-tree architecture suggested in this paper, the maximum number of switches that a message passes through is 5 and in each switch, there are 6 inputs and 6 outputs so that total 15 bits can be used to identify the

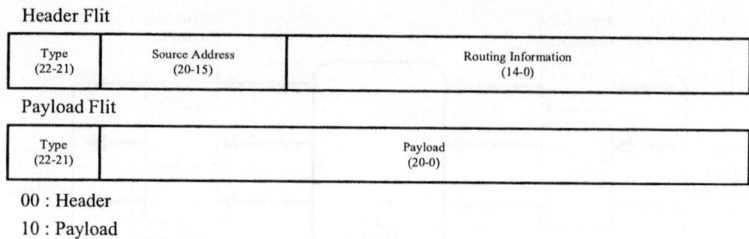

00 : Header
10 : Payload
11 : Last Payload

Fig. 4. The flit format of header and payload

path from a sending IP to a receiving counterpart. The payload flit consists of two fields, Type (2 bits) and Data (21 bits). Therefore, the minimum size of the flit in the butterfly fat-tree architecture consisting of 64 IPs is 23 bits.

The flit format strongly depends on the routing algorithm. In our suggested approach, it is remarkable that there is no need of destination address field in the header flit. The switch can transfer the message to the intended destinations using the routing information bits. The responsibility of deciding the path is on the IP interface circuits. This can reduce the flit length significantly. As shown from the above, the size of the header flit determines the one flit size to minimize the datapath and the complexity.

6.3 Input and Output Link Controller

The input link controller consists of the input controller and the input data path as shown in Figure 5. The input controller handles the input requests and, in case of the header flit, sends the arbitration requests to the arbiter.

If receiving a grant signal from the arbiter, the input controller communicates with output link controller and send flits through the crossbar. If the flit is the last of the packet, the input controller notifies to the arbiter, and then the arbiter cuts off the established path. The input controller is synthesized by the *Petrify 4.0* to support asynchronous control circuits. The *Petrify* is Signal Transition Graph (*STG*) based methodology to implement a speed-independent circuit based on the pure delay model, in which a circuit can delay the propagation of a waveform but does not otherwise alter it.

The input data path consists of processing logic circuits and latches. When the header flit arrives, which is recognized by the first field of flit, the header processing logic extracts the routing information bits, 3 bits each, from the least significant bit and shifts the remaining routing information bits of the header flit to the least significant bit positions. After extracting the routing bits, which will not be used later, 0 is inserted into the most significant bit position of the routing information field to reconstruct the routing information bits of the header flit.

The output link controller is implemented as a 2-stage FIFOs, which is handled by the semi-decoupled 4-phase latch controller. To reduce the processing cycle time, the decoupling between input and output sides of latch is realized in this FIFO [7].

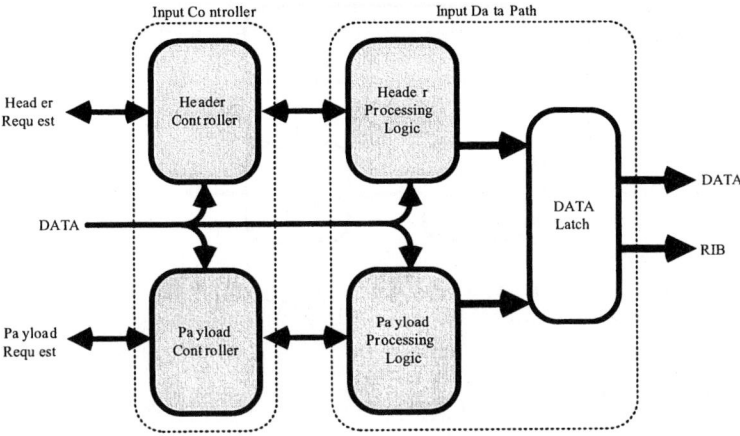

Fig. 5. The input link controller

The buffering strategy incorporated in the butterfly fat-tree network switch implementation is the output buffering scheme. To buffer the header and payload flits, 2-stage FIFO is used. The asynchronous design methodology provides the elegant scheme such as modularity which means the easy adaptation of provided components. That is, in the output link controller, no other control logic for connecting the output port to the next input port isn't needed.

6.4 Crossbar

The basic methods to implement a crossbar are a multiplexer based crossbar and a crosspoint based crossbar. In the multiplexer based method, a multiplexer at each output port selects data from the input ports. However, the cost of implementations is not effective. A crosspoint based method provides a possibility to build large switch in a cost-effective manner. The crosspoint based method is implemented using a transmission gates.

6.5 Arbitration and Routing Unit

As shown in Figure 6, the arbitration and routing control unit is responsible for the arbitrating of simultaneous input requests, the controlling of the wormhole routing and the handling of establishing the path of crossbar from input to output. The wormhole supporting unit could be located in the input control logic. Such a case, however, the input control circuit should have more states, so that it could make a circuit more complex and the performance slow. To move the processing logic to this unit can eliminate the required control states and hide the processing time because the time to process flit and release the crossbar path is overlapped. This scheme reduces the processing time of the input control logic significantly. In Figure 7, the implemented core is presented.

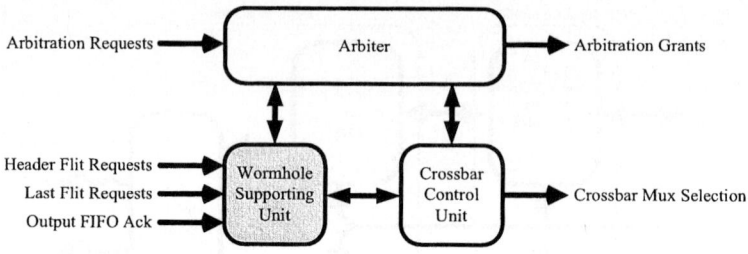

Fig. 6. The arbitration and routing unit

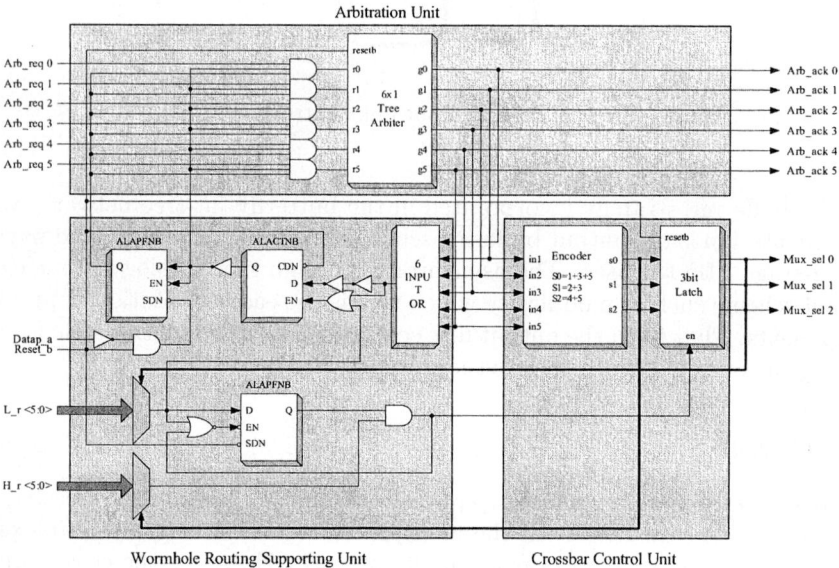

Fig. 7. The implementation of arbitration and routing unit core

7 Design Costs and Performance Evaluation

The individual switches are evaluated in terms of the transmission time for header and payload. The transmission time of a single flit consists of the processing delay, the arbitration delay, the propagation delay through the crossbar and the buffering delay. The processing delay occurs in the input link controller and is the time from receiving data to requesting the arbitration to the arbiter unit. The header flit takes more time to process because it should set the path to transmit itself and the following payload flits. The arbitration delay only corresponds to the header flit and last payload flit deliveries. Once the path is set by the header flit, the path is preserved until the last payload passes through the crossbar. The crossbar delay is fixed by the amount of transmission gate. The buffering delay is the 2 stage FIFO

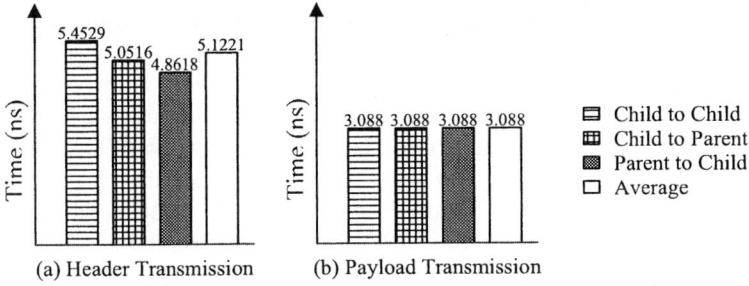

Fig. 8. The latency of flit transmission

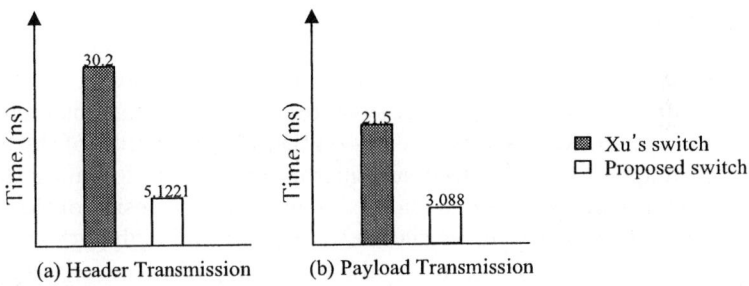

Fig. 9. The comparisons of latency

delay to pass the input data to the output channel. The suggested switch design is compared with the switch which is designed in the Jun Xu's Ph.D. thesis [8].

The simulation environment of the nMOS and pMOS transistors are *width (w)=1.78um, length (l)=0.24um* and *w=0.58um, l=0.24m*. Xu's simulation is based on the *0.5um* submicron process, with *w=2.5um* and *l=0.5um* for nMOS transistors, *w=10um* and *l=0.5um* for pMOS transistors.

The latency of the header and payload flit of the proposed switch is measured by the amount of time the flit travels from the input port to the output port.

In Figure 8, Child to Child means the input request comes from the child port and the output request goes out to the child port. Similarly, Child to Parent (Parent to Child) represent the input request from child (parent) port and the output request to parent (child) port. According to Figure 8, the transmission time of header through the parent ports is less than that through the child ports. The flits from the child ports can be transmitted both child and parent ports, however, the flits from the parent ports can be delivered only to the child port. Therefore, the circuit handling the parent port is simpler than that of the child port. The header flit transmission takes more time than the payload flit delivery because the header processing involves more states to handle the settings of crossbar path.

In Figure 9, Xu's switch and the proposed switch is compared in terms of the latency. The main difference of two switches' latency is due to i) the complexity of the control circuit in the input link controller design and ii) the different design options. Xu's switch design used different architectural approaches such as butterfly topology and virtual cut through switching method, which is based on the flow control unit of a packet. The switch used in the butterfly topology has two input ports and two output ports. However, the proposed switch has 6 input and 6 output ports. The difference of the bandwidth of two switches becomes also significant. All of the design options affect the performance and cost of the switch.

Considering a 2 input NAND gate for a gate in gate counting, the gate counts of Xu's switch except the datapath are 223.5 (input control logic) plus 28 (output control logic). The gate counts of the proposed switch are 112.5 (input control logic) plus 54 (output control logic). Total gate counts of the control logic of the proposed switch are about 50 percent of that for the Xu's switch.

8 Conclusion

We have presented the design options and the characteristics of the proposed switch, a globally asynchronous, locally synchronous interconnection architecture for future SoC system. We have also discussed the basic principles of the network, which can be mapped into the deep sub micron circuits. In designing the interconnection architecture, we have to choose the appropriate design options for the desired target. In our approach, we choose to low cost and high performance.

A novel asynchronous switch based on butterfly fat-tree topology is proposed for NoC design. Design issues for low cost and high performance NoC are discussed, including proposed packet structure. Performance of the proposed switch is evaluated and compared with Xu's switch[8]. The latency of the proposed switches is 1/5.89 for header transmission and 1/6.69 for payload transmission. Moreover, the gate counts of the control logic for switch is reduced to 50 percent of that for Xu's switch. The authors believe that the asynchronous design methodology provide an elegant way for NoC design.

Acknowledgements

This work has been supported in part by the Center for Distributed Sensor Network (CDSN) at GIST, in part by IC Design Education Center (IDEC), in part by the KAIST/GIST IT-21 Initiative in BK21 of Ministry of Education, and in part by the GIST Technology Initiative (GTI).

References

1. International Technology Roadmap For Semiconductors 2001 edition, http://public.itrs.net/Files/2001ITRS/Home.htm.
2. Dehon, A.: Compact, Multilayer Layout for Butterfly Fat-Tree. Twelfth Annual ACM Symposium on Parallel Algorithms and Architectures (SPAA 2000, July 9-12, 2000), pp. 206-215
3. Guerrier, P., Greiner, A.: A generic architecture for on-chip packet-switched interconnections. In Proceedings of Design Automation and Test Conference in Europe, pages 250-256, 2000.

4. Greenberg, R.I., Guan, L.: An improved analytical model for wormhole routed networks with application to butterfly fat-trees. Proceedings of the 1997 International Conference on Parallel Processing, pp. 44-48.
5. Leiserson, C.E.: Fat Trees: Universal networks for hardware efficient supercomputing. IEEE Transactions on Computers, C-34 (10): pp. 892-901. Oct. 1985.
6. Duato, J., Yalamanchile, S.: Interconnection Networks: An Engineering Approach. pp. 43-78. IEEE Computer Society, Los Alamitos, CA, 1997.
7. Stephen B. Furber, Paul Day.: Four-Phase Micropipeline Latch Control Circuits. IEEE Transactions on Very Large Scale Integration (VLSI) Systems, VOL. 4, No. 2, JUNE 1996
8. Jun Xu.: Asynchronous interconnection and interfacing of intellectual property cores in the design of systems-on-chip. Ph.D. thesis, South Bank University, July, 2002.

Adaptive Deinterlacing for Real-Time Applications

Qian Huang[1,2], Wen Gao[1,2], Debin Zhao[1], and Huifang Sun[3]

[1] Institute of Computing Technology, Chinese Academy of Sciences,
Beijing 100080, China
[2] Graduate University of the Chinese Academy of Sciences,
Beijing 100039, China
{qhuang, wgao, dbzhao}@jdl.ac.cn
[3] Mitsubishi Electric Research Laboratories,
Massachusetts 02139, USA
hsun@merl.com

Abstract. In general, motion compensated (MC) deinterlacing algorithms can outperform non-MC (NMC) ones. However, we often prefer to choose the latter due to the considerations of error propagation and computational complexity, especially in real-time applications such as video compression and transcoding [1]. How to get a compromised solution between performance and complexity is a challenging problem, which will be addressed in this paper. We first propose a directional adaptive algorithm for motion detection, and then introduce a reasonable and applicable adaptive MC/NMC deinterlacing mechanism to meet the requirements of real-time applications. The proposed adaptive deinterlacing scheme is proved efficient by both subjective visual sensation and objective experimental results. Feasibility of real-time applications is given as well as the coding efficiency tested by the Audio Video coding Standard (AVS) of China. For further improvement, a block-based local modal is brought forward aiming at perfect effects on unconventional motion.

1 Introduction

Interlaced scanning with well-known artifacts [2] was chosen in television industry for many historical reasons [3]. Nowadays, with the progress in technologies, we have at least four reasons to embrace the progressive format. Firstly, artifacts of interlacing that can be eliminated by progressive scanning become more and more obvious [3]. Secondly, there are a number of applications where interlaced scanning is unacceptable [4]. Thirdly, interlaced scanning makes video coding less efficient and more complex [5], while the spatio-temporal increased correlations within and between frames have the possibility to simplify the video codec and improve the coding efficiency, as will be shown in this paper. Fourthly, nearly all the modern cameras and displays are progressive, whereas most of the video scan formats approved by the ATSC [6] in actual use are interlaced. Hence the demand for conversion from interlaced videos to progressive ones grows day by day since people have piled up hundreds of thousands of valuable interlaced videos during the past decades and it is unadvisable for us to throw them away. The AVS standard of China [7], which targets at higher coding efficiency and lower complexity than existing standards for high definition (HD) video coding, also endows this conversion with great significance and far-ranging applications.

With regard to converting an interlaced video at 50/60 fields per second to progressive format, we usually have to make a choice of the outcome between 25/30 frames and 50/60 frames per second first. To be concise, we call the former the same frame rate conversion (SFRC) and the latter the double frame rate conversion (DFRC). DFRC is selected out of the following four considerations. Firstly, the process of interlacing can be viewed as a form of spatio-temporal down-sampling from a progressive video as many researchers do [4, 8-16]. Hence we shall intuitively choose the up-sampling conversion DFRC. Secondly, the result of SFRC bears an analogy to movies at 24 frames per second, each frame of which should be displayed twice in the movie theater so as to get rid of flicking. Since the display refresh rate shouldn't be lower than 50 times per second in order to achieve continuous flicker-free motion [17], SFRC is not favorable. Thirdly, DFRC maintains all the original information of the interlaced video such that a lossless re-interlacing can easily be performed while SFRC takes the risk of changing all the original interlaced fields. Lastly, seen from the video compression aspect, although the video codec is burdened with additional pixels introduced by DFRC, experiments in this paper will show the possibility of more efficient coding due to higher spatio-temporal correlations.

Academically and industrially, DFRC is what is called deinterlacing, which can generally be classified into motion compensated (MC) ones and non-MC (NMC) ones. Although MC methods generate better results, they are threatened by latent error propagations; and it is not always the case that we have the necessity to afford their time-delay, additional storage, and the required expensive hardware equipments. Therefore, we need to bring in NMC means as a compromise sometimes, especially in real-time applications where the consideration of space-time cost and additional hardware/software spending might be of greater importance than the requirement for pleasant visual impression to some extent.

Based on the MTI scores provided in [11], line averaging (LA) or its improved version edge-based LA (ELA) [18] is the best NMC approach, whose weakness of being poor in still images can be compensated by field insertion or median filtering; and spatio-temporal filtering acts best for horizontal motion among all the NMC methods. Hence we may have intuitively sufficient reasons to form a MC deinterlacing approach that adaptively takes in NMC techniques.

In this paper, we bring forward an adaptive way of directional motion detection, whose memory requirement is optimized for real-time processing. There are four possible output states (stationary, horizontal moving, vertical moving, undirectional) of our motion detection at present, which will be enriched by a block-based local model for unconventional motion in the future. Chroma rectification is provided for the undirectional state and each of the other three states correlates to a certain NMC method adaptively, namely field insertion (replaced by median filtering for better subjective visual sensation), spatio-temporal filtering, and LA, respectively. An efficient adaptive deinterlacing mechanism verified by the AVS standard is also introduced for the purpose of real-time applications.

The rest of this paper is organized as follows. Section 2 presents a directional adaptive motion detection (DAMD) algorithm. Section 3 describes the adaptive deinterlacing mechanism in detail. Section 4 presents and discusses the experimental results. Finally, we draw our conclusion in Section 5.

2 Proposed Directional Adaptive Motion Detection

Motion detection, whose output will be used to control the switch among various processing branches in the next section, can be implemented by either hardware [19] or software [8-16]. Taking our low-complexity real-time environment into account, the number of fields stored for motion detection is restricted to no more than two. Since pure two-field case may act no better than pure one-field case except for stationary scenarios [20], and both fields of one interlaced frame are needed to theoretically ensure the quality while deinterlacing each field of the frame [9], we use a bidirectional motion estimation (ME) for top fields and a unidirectional ME for bottom fields. The proposed deinterlacing flowchart is depicted in Fig. 1, where the two kinds of ME share the same Forward Motion Estimation (FME) module and have only one difference that the sum of absolute difference (SAD) is calculated between blocks in current and forward fields for unidirectional ME while among blocks in current, forward, and backward fields for bidirectional ME.

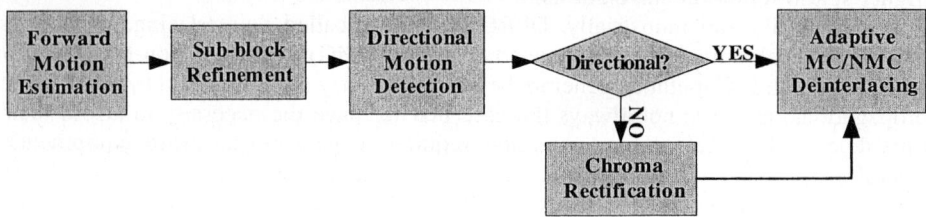

Fig. 1. Proposed Deinterlacing Flowchart

The FME is based on motion estimation blocks (MEB) sized 8 by 8. Each MEB can be partitioned into four motion compensated blocks (MCB) sized 4 by 4. Thus a sub-block refinement (SBR) necessary for accurate motion information is available.

The FME and SBR used here are implemented according to [21]. Unidirectional ME is ignored until the end of this section to simplify our discussions.

2.1 MCB-Based Directional Motion Detection

Blocks used for our MCB-based motion detection are sized 4 by 2 since only the existing pixels are used for the field-based FME, as illustrated in Fig. 2.

If the average of SAD_3 and SAD_4 is not less than that of SAD_1 and SAD_2, which indicates that the similarity between current and referenced blocks is smaller than that between current and co-located blocks, it is reasonable for us to doubt the validity of the previous ME. Out of regard for the fact that large SAD doesn't necessarily lead to small similarity due to brightness change as shown in Fig. 3, the standard deviation (SD) of current block is also taken into account to rationalize our criterion.

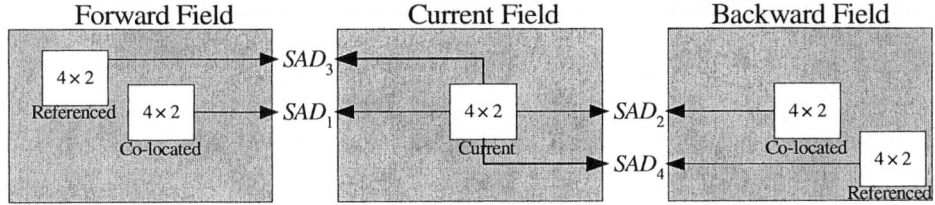

Fig. 2. Blocks Used For Motion Detection

255	255	255	255	253	253	253	253
255	255	255	255	253	253	253	253
255	255	255	255	253	253	253	253
255	255	255	255	253	253	253	253

Fig. 3. Small Brightness Change Makes Large SAD

Let (x, y), f_{n-1}, f_n and f_{n+1} denote horizontal/vertical pixel coordinates of current MCB, forward, current and backward fields, respectively. The output state of our proposed motion detection is determined by the following criterion:

$$\text{motionDirection} = \begin{cases} 0 \ (stationary), & \text{if } SAD_1+SAD_2 \le SAD_3+SAD_4 \ \&\& \ \dfrac{SAD_1+SAD_2}{2} \le SD \\ 1 \ (horizontal), & \text{else if } MV_x \ge \text{Threshold}_1 \times MV_y \\ 2 \ (vertical), & \text{else if } MV_y \ge \text{Threshold}_2 \times MV_x \\ 3 \ (undirectional), & \text{otherwise} \end{cases} \quad (1)$$

with MV_x and MV_y the absolute values of the current horizontal and vertical motion vector (MV) components, respectively. Threshold$_1$ and Threshold$_2$ are experientially set to 5. SAD_i (i=1, 2, 3, 4) can be formalized as follows.

$$SAD_i = \sum_x \sum_y \left\{ \left[0.5 - (-1)^n (y\%2 - 0.5) \right] \left| f_n(x,y) - f_{n+(-1)^i}(x+g_i, y+h_i) \right| \right\}, \quad (2)$$

where g_i and h_i are defined as:

$$g_i = \begin{cases} 0, & i=1, 2 \\ (7-2i)MV_x, & i=3, 4 \end{cases} \qquad h_i = \begin{cases} 1, & i=1, 2 \\ (7-2i)MV_y, & i=3, 4 \end{cases} \quad (3)$$

SD used in (1) is actually N times the value of the standard deviation of MCB, where N is half the number of pixels in a MCB, that is, 8.

$$SD=\sqrt{\left[0.5-(-1)^n(y\%2-0.5)\right]\left[N\sum_x\sum_y f_n^2(x,y)-(\sum_x\sum_y f_n(x,y))^2\right]}. \quad (4)$$

In Section 3, median filtering, linear spatio-temporal filtering (LSTF) and LA will be used if NMC method is selected for the stationary state, the horizontal moving state, and the vertical moving state, respectively.

2.2 Chroma Rectification

Most of the deinterlacing methods as well as the to be proposed mechanism lay stress on luminance processing since the number of rod cells for black/white vision is much more than that of cone cells for color vision in the vertebrate retina and rod vision is much more sensitive than cone vision [22]. But chroma information is also very useful for better results as experiments show.

The criterion used above is a bit too strict and we may mistake the stationary state for one of the moving states, especially the undirectional state. Hence chroma information is used to rectify the output state. Our rectification strategy is that if the average of SAD_3 and SAD_4 is greater than or equal to SD, the output state should be changed to stationary. Note that the SAD_3, SAD_4 and SD mentioned here are for chroma components and are a little different from that defined in (2) and (4).

For bottom fields, SAD_2 and SAD_4 are assumed to be equal to SAD_1 and SAD_3, respectively, similarly hereinafter. In this way all the above discussions on DAMD is applicable to unidirectional ME.

3 Proposed Adaptive MC/NMC Deinterlacing Mechanism

The idea of combining MC and NMC deinterlacing was brought forward more than ten years ago. Unfortunately, existing implementations are either adopting weighted averaging methods [23, 24] that introduce blurring or hard to achieve optimal results. Our adaptive mechanism based on DAMD makes local optimal choice for each MCB and avoids the above problems. For clarity, the deinterlacing means for the stationary state and moving states are discussed separately.

3.1 Deinterlacing for the Stationary State

For top fields, a five-tap median filter being able to effectively eliminate interpolation errors caused by incorrect MV [13] is used for the stationary state, as formulated below.

$$F_o(\vec{x},n) = \begin{cases} F(\vec{x},n), & y\%2 = n\%2 \\ F_i(\vec{x},n) = Median(A,B,C,D,\frac{(C+D)}{2}), & otherwise \end{cases}, \quad (5)$$

where $\vec{x} = (x,y)^T$ designates the spatial position while $F_o(\vec{x},n)$, $F_i(\vec{x},n)$ and $F(\vec{x},n)$ denote the output, interpolated and original pixel values of field f_n, respectively. *A, B, C* and *D* represent the values of the spatially above, spatially below, forward referenced and backward referenced pixels, respectively.

For bottom fields where unidirectional ME is used, *D* is not available. The median filter for the stationary state should be:

$$F_o(\vec{x},n) = \begin{cases} F(\vec{x},n), & y\%2 = n\%2 \\ F_i(\vec{x},n) = Median(A,B,C,\frac{(A+B)}{2},\frac{(3A+3B+2C)}{8}), & otherwise \end{cases} \quad (6)$$

3.2 Adaptive MC/NMC Switching for Moving States

LA and LSTF are selected as NMC candidates for our adaptive mechanism while adaptive recursive (AR) and edge-based median filtering (EMF) methods are chosen as MC ones. Note that the ELA method proposed in [18] is not chosen since its performance depends on the implementation to a great extent.

The LSTF and AR methods proposed in [10] are chosen based on the experimental results from [11]. The EMF method is given below.

$$F_o(\vec{x},n) = \begin{cases} F(\vec{x},n), & y\%2 = n\%2 \\ F_i(\vec{x},n) = Median(A_i,B_i,C,D,\frac{(C+D)}{2}), & else\ if\ top\ fields \\ F_i(\vec{x},n) = Median(A_i,B_i,C,C,\frac{(A_i+B_i+2C)}{4}), & otherwise \end{cases} \quad (7)$$

where A_i and B_i (i=1, 2, 3, 4, 5) are the edge-based spatially above and below pixels, respectively, such that the absolute difference between A_i and B_i is the smallest, as shown in Fig. 4.

In our adaptive mechanism, MC deinterlacing is applied when the average of SAD_3 and SAD_4 is less than that of SAD_1 and SAD_2 for the horizontal moving state or less than *SD* defined in (4) for the vertical moving state, as shown in Fig. 2. As for the unidirectional output state that is in the majority seen from (1), Canny edge detection [25] is simplified for performance and practicability purposes before the same MC/NMC switching for the vertical moving state is applied.

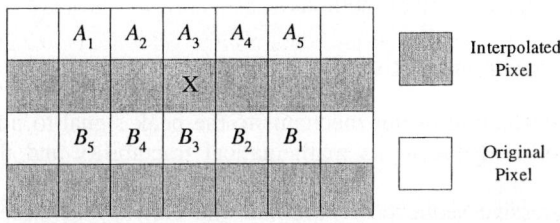

Fig. 4. Edge-based Median Filtering Method

The simplified Canny edge detection (SCED) is actually based on motion compensated blocks sized 4 by 2, that is, half the size of MCB. Considering the computational complexity, we make use of the motion and texture information and do not perform edge detection unless necessary. Concretely speaking, the edge intensities of forward frames calculated by SCED can be reused if no acute motion exists. The same NMC deinterlacing with the vertical moving state is selected if there is no rich texture. Here an acute motion is detected if the MV magnitude exceeds a certain threshold tied to the video resolution.

3.3 Adaptive Deinterlacing for Moving States

For MC deinterlacing, if the to be processed MCB has acute motion, AR is simply used; otherwise AR is used iff the processed pixel is detected as edge and the correlated MCB has no rich detail. In other cases we select the EMF method.

NMC deinterlacing is trivial. But the five-tap median filter supplied below is needed to rule out flickers caused by LSTF.

$$F_o(\vec{x},n) = \begin{cases} F(\vec{x},n), & y\%2 = n\%2 \\ F_i(\vec{x},n) = Median(A_i, B_i, C, D, ST), & \text{else if top fields} \\ F_i(\vec{x},n) = Median(A_i, B_i, C, C, ST), & \text{otherwise} \end{cases} \quad (8)$$

where ST is the result of LSTF.

4 Experimental Results and Discussions

4.1 Subjective Visual Sensation

The proposed deinterlacing algorithm provides perfect performance, especially, in the areas with continuous motions where the most of flickers and serrations have been eliminated. For most of the standard definition sequences (Basketball, Flower Garden, Horse Riding, Interview, etc.) except Mobile Calendar, the proposed deinterlacing produces much better visual effects than conventional approaches, as shown in Fig. 5.

Our deinterlacing also outperforms AR, which is one of the best methods nowadays. But it is hard to see their differences subjectively in a discrete frame whose resolution should be reduced here. Hence an objective evaluation is also indispensable to show our advantage over other methods.

4.2 Objective Experimental Results

For an objective evaluation of our mechanism, the peak signal to noise ratio (PSNR) in decibel (dB) is used due to its mathematical tractability and the lack of better alternatives [27].

Two CIF progressive sequences (Foreman and News) and three HD progressive sequences (Crew, Night, and Spin Calendar) are selected to generate interlaced sequences for objective evaluation of our adaptive deinterlacing mechanism. Table 1 shows the PSNR (dB) comparisons between original progressive sequences and deinterlaced sequences.

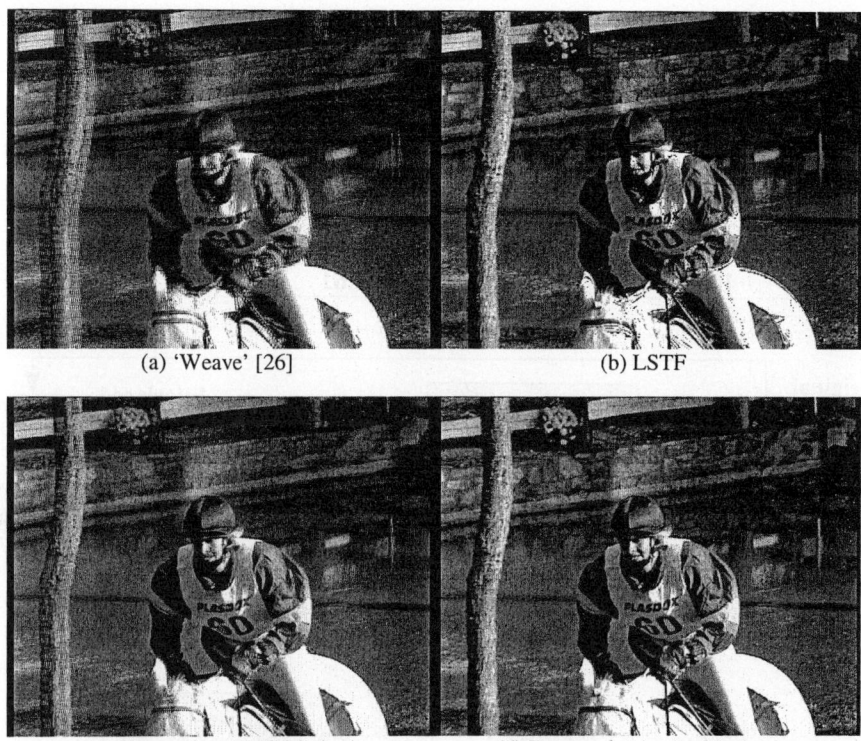

Fig. 5. Deinterlacing Effect on Standard Definition Sequence "Horse Riding"

Table 1. PSNR (dB) Between Original Progressive And Deinterlaced Sequences

Sequence Algorithm	Foreman	News	Crew	Night	Spin Calendar
LA	32.64	34.15	38.52	32.04	29.25
LSTF	31.58	27.60	39.79	34.33	26.68
AR	33.43	43.00	40.19	35.73	29.63
EMF	36.80	41.91	38.14	33.72	26.65
Proposed	37.02	43.03	40.64	36.78	29.78

4.3 Feasibility of Real-Time Applications

In Table 2, an AVS encoder is employed to illustrate the coding efficiency before and after deinterlacing, where $PSNR_{int}$ and $PSNR_{reint}$ are computed as Fig. 6 depicts. Coding experiments also show that the bit-rate increment is less than 50% although the frame rate is doubled, thus satisfactory bit-rate and coding performance can be acquired by involving proper bit-rate control and real-time deinterlacing techniques in the encoder.

Table 2. PSNR (dB) For Interlaced Coding And Corresponding Deinterlaced Coding

Sequence QP	Basketball		Flower Garden	
	$PSNR_{int}$(dB)	$PSNR_{reint}$(dB)	$PSNR_{int}$(dB)	$PSNR_{reint}$(dB)
28	37.43	37.84	39.03	39.39
32	35.12	35.70	36.46	36.97
36	33.06	33.77	34.24	34.88
40	30.76	31.61	31.81	32.61

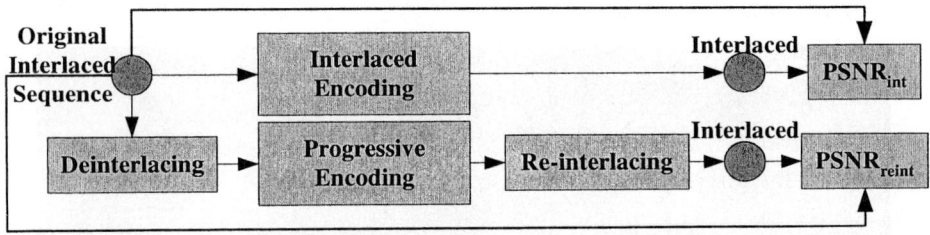

Fig. 6. Computation of $PSNR_{int}$ and $PSNR_{reint}$

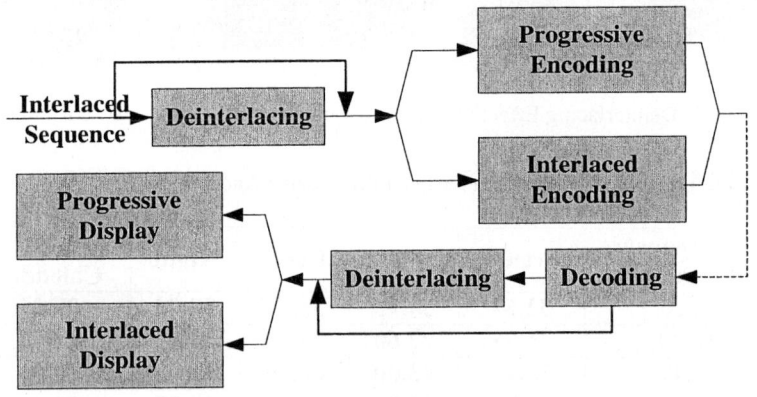

Fig. 7. Interlaced Video Sequence Flowchart

Fig. 7 describes the usual flowchart of an interlaced video sequence. Most of the time, we use deinterlacing either before video encoders or after video decoders.

Note that in order not to burden the network, signals are usually encoded before transmission and decoded in the video displays. This makes it possible for the decoder to access motion vectors from the encoder. Hence a real-time MC deinterlacing without ME can be involved in the decoder. It is particularly true that the proposed adaptive deinterlacing mechanism is applicable for low-complexity real-time decoding and transcoding since unidirectional ME is used for bottom fields.

5 Concluding Remarks and Further Work

In this paper, we propose an adaptive MC/NMC deinterlacing algorithm to address real-time applications based on DAMD. Subjective visual sensation and objective experimental results show the validity of the proposed adaptive mechanism and the feasibility of real-time applications.

Taking one with another, the proposed deinterlacing mechanism is satisfactory. But we get poor results when unconventional motion occurs (e.g. Mobile Calendar and Spin Calendar), although we could also get slightly better results than other ones. Hence DAMD should be enriched into more rational modal adaptive motion detection (MAMD), where there are more MCB-based states, e.g. stationary, translational (horizontal, vertical), zoom, rotational (in plane, out of plane) and others (occlusive, exposed, etc.).

Based on the experiments and discussions in Section 4, deinterlacing involved in the video codec will be studied in the next step.

Acknowledgement

This work is partially supported by the National Hi-Tech Development 863 Program of China under grant No. 2004AA119010, the National Natural Science Foundation of China under grant No. 60333020, the Natural Science Foundation of Beijing under grant No. 4041003, and the Hundred Talents Program of the Chinese Academy of Sciences. The authors would like to thank Dr. Cliff Reader, Dr. Qingming Huang, Longshe Huo, Peng Zhang, Jianguo Du and Songnan Li for their valuable comments and support.

References

1. Vetro, A., Christopoulos, C., Sun, H.: Video Transcoding Architectures and Techniques: An Overview. IEEE Signal Processing Magazine, Vol. 20, No. 2, pp. 18-29, March 2003
2. Glenn, W.E.: Interlace and Progressive Scan Comparisons Based on Visual Perception Data. SMPTE Journal, pp. 114–117, February 1999
3. Pigeon, S., Guillotel, P.: Advantages and Drawbacks of Interlaced and Progressive Scanning Formats. CEC RACE/HAMLET Deliverable R2110/WP2/DS/R/004/b1, June 1995
4. Heng, B.: Application of Deinterlacing for the Improvement of Surveillance Video. MS Thesis, Massachusetts Institute of Technology, June 2001
5. Vandendorpe, L., Cuvelier L.: Statistical Properties of Coded Interlaced and Progressive Image Sequences. IEEE Transactions on Image Processing, Vol. 8, No. 6, pp. 749-761, June 1999
6. Advanced Television Systems Committee: http://www.atsc.org
7. Audio Video coding Standard Working Group of China: http://www.avs.org.cn/en
8. Kwon, S., Seo, K., Kim, J., Kim, Y.: A Motion-Adaptive De-interlacing Method. IEEE Transactions on Consumer Electronics, Vol. 38, No. 3, pp. 145-150, August 1992
9. Delogne, P., Cuvelier, L., Maison, B., Caillie, B.V., Vandendorpe, L.: Improved Interpolation, Motion Estimation and Compensation for Interlaced Pictures. IEEE Transactions on Image Processing, Vol. 3, No. 5, pp. 482–491, September 1994

10. De Haan, G., Bellers, E.B.: Deinterlacing of Video Data. IEEE Transactions on Consumer Electronics, Vol. 43, No. 3, pp. 819-825, August 1997
11. De Haan, G., Bellers, E.B.: Deinterlacing—An Overview. Proceedings of the IEEE, Vol. 86, No. 9, pp. 1839–1857, September 1998
12. Sugiyama K., Nakamura, H.: A Method of De-interlacing with Motion Compensated Interpolation. IEEE Transactions on Consumer Electronics, Vol. 45, No. 3, pp. 611-616, August 1999
13. Jung, Y., Choi, B., Park, Y., Ko, S.: An Effective Deinterlacing Technique Using Motion Compensated Interpolation. IEEE Transactions on Consumer Electronics, Vol. 46, No. 3, pp. 460–466, August 2000
14. Kwon, O., Sohn, K., Lee, C.: Deinterlacing Using Directional Interpolation and Motion Compensation. IEEE Transactions on Consumer Electronics, Vol. 49, No. 1, pp. 198–203, February 2003
15. Lee, S., Lee, D.: A Motion-Adaptive De-interlacing Method Using an Efficient Spatial and Temporal Interpolation. IEEE Transactions on Consumer Electronics, Vol. 49, No. 4, pp. 1266–1271, November 2003
16. Yang, S., Jung, Y., Lee, Y.H., Park, R.: Motion Compensated Assisted Motion Adaptive Interlaced-to-Progressive Conversion. IEEE Transactions on Circuits and Systems for Video Technology, Vol. 14, No. 9, pp. 1138–1148, September 2004
17. Steinmetz, R., Nahrstedt, K.: Multimedia: Computing, Communications and Applications. Prentice Hall, 1995
18. Lee, H.Y., Park, J.W., Bae, T.M., Choi, S.U., Ha, Y.H.: Adaptive Scan Rate Up-Conversion System Based on Human Visual Characteristics. IEEE Transactions on Consumer Electronics, Vol. 46, No. 4, pp. 999-1006, November 2000
19. Filliman, P.D., Christopher, T.J., Keen, R.T.: Interlace to Progressive Scan Converter for IDTV. IEEE Transactions on Consumer Electronics, Vol. 38, No. 3, pp. 135-144, August 1992
20. Koivunen, T.: Motion Detection of an Interlaced Video Signal. IEEE Transactions on Consumer Electronics, Vol. 40, No. 3, pp. 753–760, August 1994
21. De Haan, G., Biezen, P.W.A.C., Huijgen, H., Ojo, O.A.: True-Motion Estimation with 3-D Recursive Search Block Matching. IEEE Transactions on Circuits and Systems for Video Technology, Vol. 3, No. 5, pp. 368–379, October 1993
22. Lee, D.: Extending Human Vision. Victoria Centre of the national Royal Astronomical Society of Canada, 2003, available from internet: http://victoria.rasc.ca
23. Nguyen, A., Dubois, E.: Spatio-Temporal Adaptive Interlaced-to-Progressive Conversion. In Signal Processing of HDTV IV, E. Dubois and L. Chiariglione, Eds. Amsterdam, The Netherlands: Elsevier, pp. 749–756, 1993
24. Kovacevic, J., Safranek, R.J., Yeh, E.M.: Deinterlacing by Successive Approximation. IEEE Transactions on Image Processing, Vol. 6, No. 2, pp. 339–344, February 1997
25. Canny, J.: A Computational Approach to Edge Detection. IEEE Transactions on Pattern Analysis and Machine Intelligence, Vol. 8, No. 6, pp. 679–698, November 1986
26. Microsoft Corporation: Broadcast-Enabled Computer Hardware Requirements. Broadcast Technologies White Paper, pp. 11-12, 1997
27. Wang, Y., Ostermann, J., Zhang, Y.-Q.: Video Processing and Communications. Pearson Education, 2003

Adaptive MAP High-Resolution Image Reconstruction Algorithm Using Local Statistics

Kyung-Ho Kim, Yoan Shin, and Min-Cheol Hong

School of Electronic Engineering, Soongsil University, Korea
rokmcops821@vipl.ssu.ac.kr, {yashin, mhong}@e.ssu.ac.kr

Abstract. In this paper, we propose an adaptive MAP (Maximum A Posteriori) high-resolution image reconstruction algorithm using local statistics. In order to preserve an edge information of an original high-resolution image, a visibility function defined by local statistics of the low-resolution image is incorporated into MAP estimation process, so that the local smoothness is adaptively controlled. The weighted non-quadratic convex functional is defined to obtain the optimal solution that is as close as possible to the original high-resolution image. An iterative algorithm is utilized for obtaining the solution. The smoothing parameter is updated at each iteration step from the partially reconstructed high-resolution image, and therfore no knowledge about of the original high-resolution image is required. Experimental results demonstrate the capability of the proposed algorithm.

1 Introduction

The high resolution restoration is very important in the area of image analysis, conversion of image dimension and video zooming [1,2,3,4]. For example, when the precise maps of Earth's weather are acquired from a satellite, weather forecasters need to expand the map of small regions to forecast the weather in more detail. The high resolution restoration can be applied to medical imaging to search for anomalies from low resolution X-ray, the dimensional conversion in high definition television (HDTV), multimedia image, and video printing.

The high resolution problem can be classified into two distinct processes: (1) interpolation and (2) enhancement. The image expansion has been extensively studied in the past years [3,4,5]. Simple approaches are bilinear interpolation, zero-order hold expansion and cubic-spline interpolation. Zero-order hold expansion results in blockiness image, which gives annoying effects to viewer. Both the bilinear interpolation and the cubic spline approaches result in blurred version of an original image. Other approaches such as emphasizing edges and incorporating a hybrid local edges used statistics of local edge direction and mapping low resolution image into a best fit continuous space.

High-resolution reconstruction and expansion are ill-posed inverse problems [4,5,6]. It means that there is an infinite set of enhanced and expanded images corresponding to an original high-resolution image. In order to obtain a unique and stable solution from the observed data, an ill-posed problem must be replaced by well-posed problem. A regularization method replaces an ill-posed problem by a well posed one whose solution is an acceptable approximation to the solution of the given ill-posed problem.

There have been reported results in improving the resolution of image sequences. In [7], a projection onto convex set (POCS) algorithm was used to improve image quality. For motion blur, they assumed that velocities are constant over the aperture time. Nakazawa et. al. [8] proposed an algorithm based on image segmentation. Also, there have been reported results in improving the resolution of image sequences. In Ref. [9], total least squares (TLS) approach was used to obtain better conditioned formation. It has been shown that the motion estimation and compensation is very useful to improve the resolution from the low resolution video sequence [12,13,14,15]. However, motion estimation errors between the current frame and the reference frames are not adaptively handled to obtain the high resolution video sequences. Also, they require very expensive computational cost to obtain a high-resolution frame from multiple low-resolution frames.

Maximum A Posteriori (MAP) estimation has been widely used in image restoration and high-resolution reconstruction [11]. However, local statistics is not reflected into enhancement process, resulting in over-smoothness of edge information in the reconstructed image. Therefore, it is promising to incorporate the local information into MAP estimation process, so that the degree of local smoothness is adjustably controlled.

This paper is organized as follows. In Section 2, the background of MAP estimation is briefly reviewed. Section 3 describes the proposed algorithm. The weighted nonquadratic convex functional using visibility function is addressed and analyzed. Finally, experimental results and conclusions are discussed in Sections 4 and 5.

2 Problem formulation

Let us assume that z and y represent the original high-resolution image and the corresponding low-resolution image by a factor of q. Then the relation between the images can be written as

$$y(i,j) = \frac{1}{q^2} \sum_{k=qi}^{q(i+1)-1} \sum_{l=qj}^{q(j+1)-1} z(k,l), \tag{1}$$

where (i,j) and (k,l) denote pixel's positions of the high-resolution image and the low-resolution image, respectively.

When the original high-resolution image is degraded by contaminating noise, for an $N_1 \times N_2$ dimensional low-resolution image, the relationship between the low-resolution image and high-resolution image can be described by

$$y = Dz + n, \tag{2}$$

where y, z, and n represent the lexicographically ordered low-resolution, original high-resolution, and additive noise, respectively. The matrix D represents the point spread function (PSF) caused by low-resolution imaging system. Then, the problem at hand is to obtain an estimated high-resolution image that is as close as possible to the original high-resolution image. MAP estimation has been widely used in image restoration and reconstruction problems [4,11]. According to it, the estimation can be computed as

$$\hat{z} = \arg\max[log \Pr(y|z) + log \Pr(z)]. \qquad (3)$$

It was shown that Markov Random Field (MRF) model with the Gibbs density function for the original high-resolution image and Gaussian density function for the contaminating noise in Eq. (3) work well for obtaining the high-resolution image. They can be described as

$$Pr(z) = \frac{1}{Z} exp[-\frac{1}{\lambda}\sum_{c \in C} V_c(z)], \qquad (4)$$

and

$$Pr(y|z) = \frac{1}{(2\pi\sigma^2)^{\frac{N_1 N_2}{2}}} exp(\frac{-||y - Dz||^2}{2\sigma^2}). \qquad (5)$$

In Eq. (4), Z and λ denote a normalizing constant and the "temperature" parameter of the density, $V_c(.)$ that is a function of a local group c called clique. Then, Eq. (3) becomes

$$\hat{z} = \arg\min(\frac{||y - Dz||^2}{2\sigma^2} + \frac{1}{\lambda}\sum_{c \in C} V_c(z)). \qquad (6)$$

3 Adaptive MAP Expansion Algorithm

MAP estimation described in Sec. 2 outperforms the previous image expansion method such as zero-order interpolation, linear interpolation, and cubic B-spline

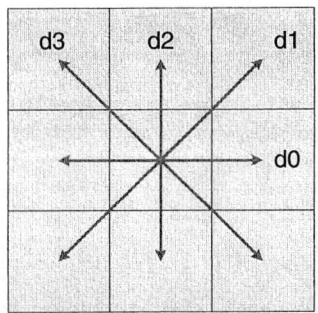

Fig. 1. Weighted clique function

expansion. However, there still exist edge-smoothness problem since local statistics is not incorporated into the estimation process. Therefore, it is necessary to define a local activity function. In this work, we use the local mean and variance to represent the function. Local mean and variance are defined as

$$m_z(k,l) = \frac{1}{(2P+1)(2Q+1)} \sum_{m=k-P}^{k+P} \sum_{n=l-Q}^{l+Q} z(m,n) \qquad (7)$$

and

$$\sigma^2(k,l) = \frac{1}{(2P+1)(2Q+1)} \sum_{m=k-P}^{k+P} \sum_{n=l-Q}^{l+Q} (z(m,n) - m_z(k,l))^2, \qquad (8)$$

where $(2P+1)(2Q+1)$ is the extent of the analysis window. Then, the local activity is defined as

$$w(k,l) = \frac{1}{\sqrt{\sigma^2(k,l)+1}}. \qquad (9)$$

The local activity takes the value between 0 and 1. The value goes to zero for spatially high activity areas, while it goes to one for flat areas. Then, the nonquadratic weighted convex functional is defined by the local activity and Huber function described in Ref. [11], It is

$$M_\lambda[Wz,T] = \Omega[Wz,T] + \frac{\lambda}{2\sigma^2}\|y - Dz\|^2, \qquad (10)$$

Table 1. PSNR comparisons

Image	Method	PSNR (dB)	
		q=2	q=4
Lena	Zero-order hold interpolation	26.67	25.13
	Blinear interpolation	26.54	24.83
	MAP estimation	28.68	25.53
	proposed algorithm	29.68	25.92
Bird	Zero-order hold interpolation	33.51	27.99
	Blinear interpolation	33.45	27.88
	MAP estimation	34.15	28.89
	proposed algorithm	35.83	29.04
Cameraman	Zero-order hold interpolation	24.42	23.26
	Bilinear interpolation	24.23	23.13
	MAP estimation	26.34	23.53
	proposed algorithm	26.76	23.84
Airfield	Zero-order hold interpolation	25.36	22.37
	Bilinear interpolation	25.11	22.26
	MAP estimation	26.50	22.53
	proposed algorithm	26.88	22.90

where T represents the threshold of the Huber function [11]. Also, $\Omega[Wz,T]$ represents the symbol for the sum of clique functions and it is described as

$$\Omega[Wz,T] = \sum_{c\in C} V_c(Wz) = \sum_{k=0}^{qN_1-1}\sum_{l=0}^{qN_2-1}\sum_{m=0}^{3} \rho_T(d^t(k,l,m)Wz), \quad (11)$$

where the clique functions are shown in Figure 1 and defined as

$$d^t(k,l,0)Wz = [w(k,l+1)z(k,l+1) - 2w(k,l)z(k,l) + w(k,l-1)z(k,l-1)]$$
$$d^t(k,l,1)Wz = \frac{1}{2}[w(k-1,l+1)z(k-1,l+1) - 2w(k,l)z(k,l) + $$
$$\quad w(k+1,l-1)z(k+1,l-1)]$$
$$d^t(k,l,2)Wz = w(k-1,l)z(k-1,l) - 2w(k-1,l)z(k,l) + w(k+1,l)z(k+1,l)$$
$$d^t(k,l,3)Wz = \frac{1}{2}[w(k-1,l-1)z(k-1,l-1) - 2w(k-1,l-1)z(k,l) + $$
$$\quad w(k+1,l+1)z(k+1,l+1)]. \quad (12)$$

We propose to use a gradient descent algorithm to obtain a solution to the minimization problem. The image gradient becomes

$$g_{(n)} = \nabla\Omega[Wz,T] + \frac{\lambda}{2\sigma^2}(2D^tDz_{(n)} - 2D^ty), \quad (13)$$

Fig. 2. 128×128 dimensional low-resolution test images: (a) Lena, (b) Airfield, (c) Bird, (d) Cameraman

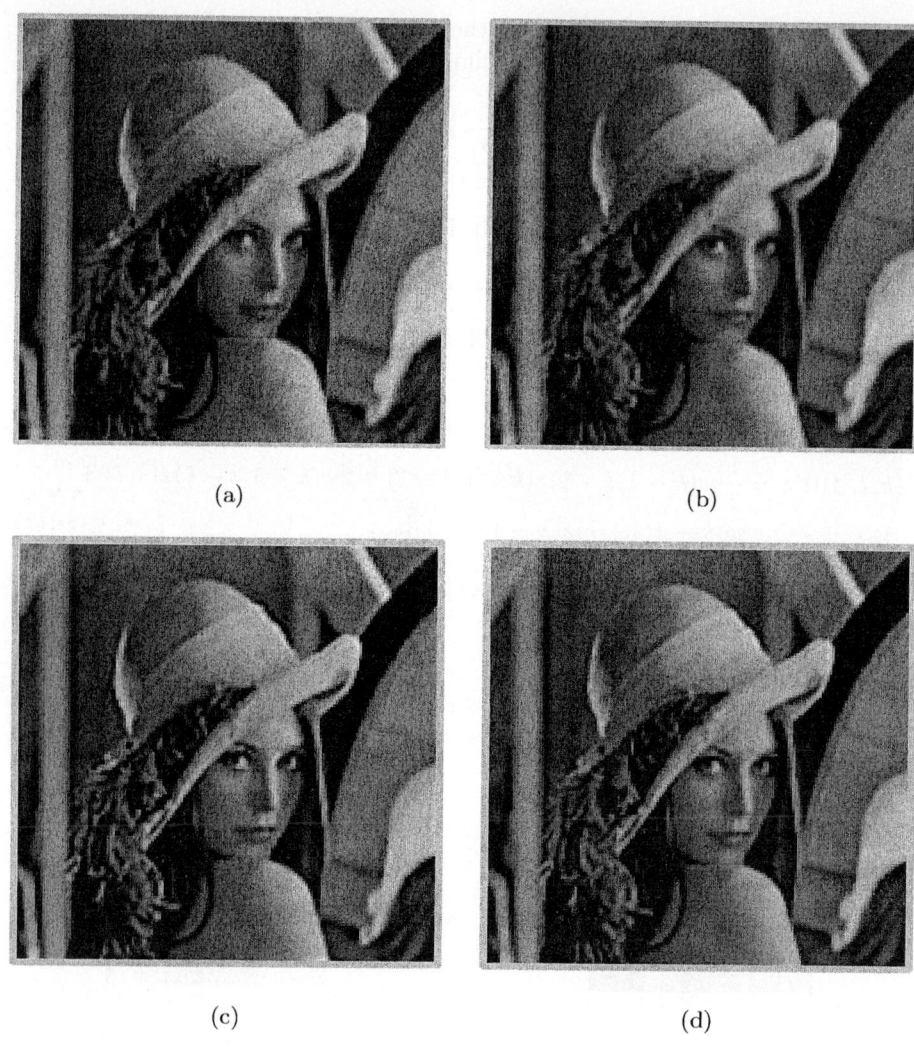

Fig. 3. 256×256 dimensional reconstructed high-resolution results of Fig. 2-a: (a) Zero-order hold interpolation, (b) bilinear interpolation, (c) MAP estimation, (d) proposed algorithm

and the direction of descent for the minimization can be written as

$$d_{(n)} = -[I - D^t(DD^t)^{-1}D]g_{(n)}, \qquad (14)$$

where ∇ is the gradient operation and I represent the identity matrix. Then, the successive iteration approximation becomes

$$z_{(n+1)} = z_{(n)} + \alpha_{(n)}d_{(n)}, \qquad (15)$$

where $z_{(n+1)}$ represents the updated value of z after $n + 1$-th iteration, and $\alpha_{(n)}$ denotes the relaxation parameter that controls the convergence rate of the iteration. In Eq. (15), the maximum decrease of $d_{(n)}$ is chosen by minimizing the functional along $d_{(n)}$. It is

$$\alpha_{(n)} = \arg\min \Omega[z_{(n)} + \alpha_{(n)}d(n), T]. \tag{16}$$

Taking the derivative with respect to $\alpha_{(n)}$, the step size for the n-th iteration is given by

$$\alpha_{(n)} = \frac{-\nabla M_\lambda[(Wz)_{(n)}, T]^t d_{(n)}}{d_{(n)}^t \nabla^2 M_\lambda[(Wz)_{(n)}, T] d_{(n)}}. \tag{17}$$

4 Experimental Results

The proposed adaptive MAP high-resolution image enhancement algorithm was tested with various images at a number of resolution. In the set of such experiments, the 128 × 128-pixel "Lena", "Airfield", "Bird", and "Cameraman" low-resolution images shown in Figure 2 were used. PSNR (Peak Signal to Noise Ratio) was used to evaluate the performance of the algorithm. For $qN_1 \times qN_2$

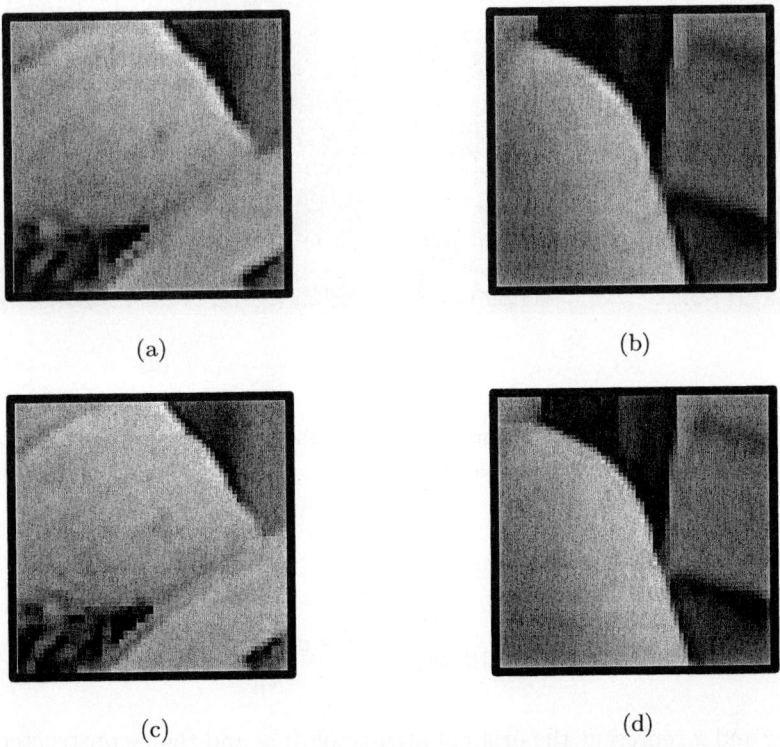

(a)   (b)

(c)   (d)

Fig. 4. Visual quality comparison of reconstructed high-resolution Lena images: (a) MAP estimation, (b) MAP estimation, (c) proposed algorithm, (d) proposed algorithm

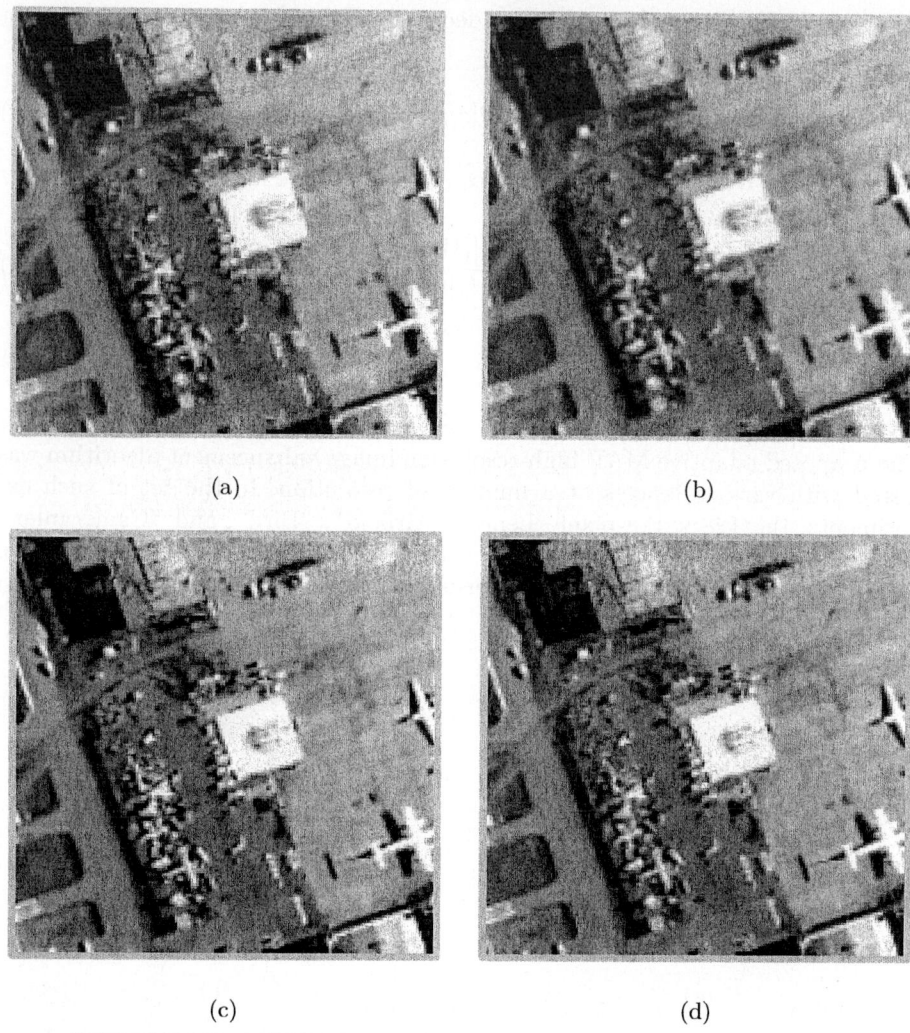

Fig. 5. 256×256 dimensional reconstructed high-resolution results of Fig. 2-b: (a) Zero-order hold interpolation, (b) bilinear interpolation, (c) MAP estimation, (d) proposed algorithm

size high-resolution image, it is defined as

$$PSNR = 10\log_{10}\frac{255^2 \times qN_1 \times qN_2}{||z - \hat{z}||^2}, \qquad (18)$$

where z and $\hat{z}$ represent the original high-resolution and the reconstructed high-resolution images. Also, $T = 4$ is used for the threshold of the Huber function, and $q = 2$ and $q = 4$ are used to obtain high-resolution image.

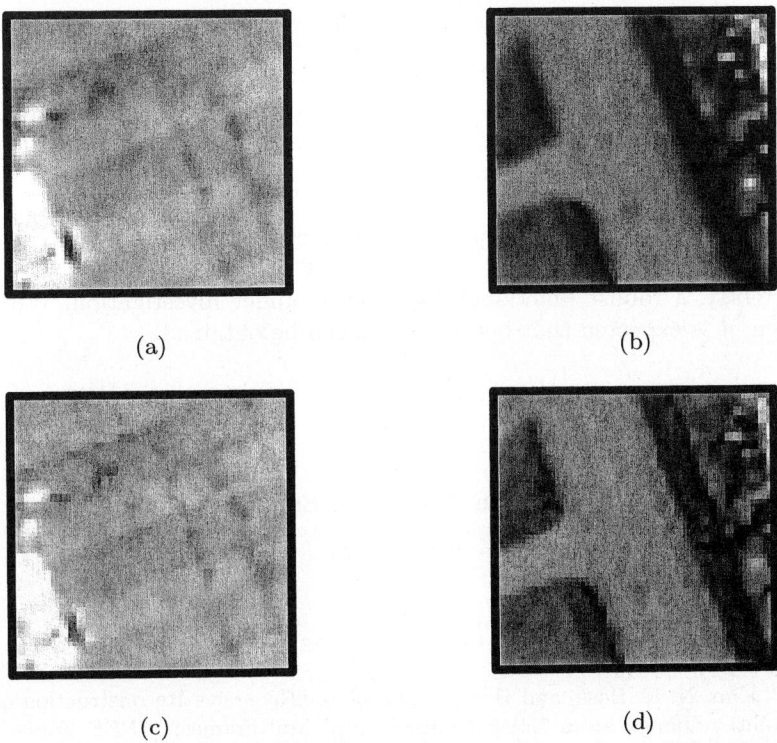

Fig. 6. Visual quality comparison of reconstructed high-resolution Airfield images: (a) MAP estimation, (b) MAP estimation, (c) proposed algorithm, (d) proposed algorithm

The proposed algorithm is compared with zero-order hold interpolation, bilinear interpolation, and MAP estimation approach. In Table 1, comparative results are shown for MAP high-resolution approach in Ref. [11]. From the table, it is verified that the proposed algorithm outperforms other methods. However, the gain is lowered as q is higher since the low-resolution image has very limited information to obtain the high-resolution image.

The reconstructed high-resolution images of Figure 2-(a) by zero-order hold interpolation, bilinear interpolation, MAP estimation, and the proposed algorithm are shown in Figure 3. The reconstructed images by zero-order hold interpolation and bilinear interpolation result in over-smoothness at edge areas such as "hat" and shoulder. On the other hand, the reconstructed images with MAP estimation and proposed algorithm reduce the smoothness. The visual quality difference between MAP estimation and proposed algorithm is clearly shown in Figure 4. Important information such as edge regions and objects is effectively reconstructed by proposed algorithm. Also, Figure 5 show the corresponding reconstructed high-resolution images of Figure 2-(b). "road" and "small" objects are consistently well-reconstructed by the proposed algorithm. Enlarged parts of Figure 5 are shown in Figure 6.

5 Conclusions

In this paper, we presented an adaptive MAP high-resolution image enhancement algorithm. Local statistics is used to determine the local activity that is used to adaptively control the degree of local smoothness. The weighted nonquadratic convex functional is defined to obtain the optimal solution that is as close as possible to the original high-resolution image. The experimental results show that the proposed algorithm outperforms MAP estimation with respect to PSNR and visual quality.

Currently, a robust functional approach is under investigation. With such approach, it is expected that better results can be obtained.

Acknowledgement

This work was supported by grant No. R01-2005-000-10540-0 from the Basic Research Program of the Korean Science and Engineering Foundation

References

1. T. S. Huang Ed., *Advances in Computer Vision and Image Processing*, JAI Press, 1984.
2. S. P. Kim, N. K. Bose, and H. M. Valenzuela, "Recursive Reconstruction of High Resolution Image From Noisy Undersampled Multiframes," *IEEE Trans. Signal Processing*, vol. 38, pp. 1013-1027, June 1990.
3. A. K. Jain, *Fundamentals of Digital Image Processing*, New York: Prentice-Hall, 1989.
4. S. C. Park, M. K. Park, and M. G. Kang, "Super-resolution image reconstruction: A Technical Overview," *IEEE Signal Processing Magazine*, vol. 20, no. 3, pp. 21-36, May 2003.
5. A. N. Tikhonov and A. V. Gonchrsky, eds., *Ill-Posed Problems in the Natural Science*, MIP Pub., 1987.
6. M. Bertero, T. A. Poggio, and V. Torre, "Ill-posed problems in early vision," *IEEE Proceeding*, vol. 76, no. 8, pp. 869-889, Aug. 1988.
7. A. J. Patti, M. I. Sezan, and A. M. Tekalp, "High-Resolution Image Reconstruction from A Low-Resolution Image Sequence in the Presence of Time-Varying Motion Blur," *IEEE Proceeding of International Conference on Image Processing*, pp. 343-347, Nov. 1994.
8. Y. Nakazawa, T. Saito, T. Komatsu, T. Skimori, and K. Aizawa, "Two Approaches for Image Processing Based on High Resolution Image Acquisition," *IEEE Proceeding of International Conference on Image Processing*, pp. 147-151, Nov. 1994.
9. N. K. Bose, H. C. Kim, and N. Bose, "Constrained total least squares computations for high resolution image reconstruction with multisensors," *Int. J. Imaging Syst. Tech.*, vol. 12, pp. 35-42, 2002.
10. Michael Unser, Akram Aldroubi, and Murray Eden, "B-Spline Signal Processing: Part I-Theory," *IEEE Tras. ASSP*, vol.41, no 2. pp. 821-833, Feb. 1993.
11. R. R. Schultz and R. L. Stevenson, "A Baysian Approach to Image Expansion for Improved Definition," *IEEE Trans. Image Processing*, vol. 3, no. 3, pp. 996-1011, May 1994.

12. B. C. Tom and A. K. Katsaggelos, "Reconstruction of a high-resolution image by simultaneously registration, restoration, and interpolation of low-resolution images," *in Proc. IEEE Int. Conf. Image Processing,* vol. 2, pp. 539-542, Oct. 1995.
13. M. C. Hong, M. G. Kang, and A. K. Katsaggelos, "An iterative regularized weighted regularized algorithm for improving the resolution of video sequences," *in Proc. IEEE Int. Conf. Image Processing,* vol. 2, pp. 474-477, Oct. 1997.
14. P. E. Eren, M. I. Sezan, and A. M. Tekalp, "Robust object-based high-resolution image reconstruction from low-resolution video," *IEEE Trans. Image Processing,* vol. 6, no. 10, pp. 1446-1451, Oct. 1997.
15. N. R. Shah and A. Zakhor, "Multiframe Spatial Resolution Enhancement of Color Video," *in Pro. IEEE Int. Conf. on Image Processing,* pp. 985-988, Sep. 1995.

Energy-Efficient Cooperative Image Processing in Video Sensor Networks[*]

Dan Tao[1], Huadong Ma[1], and Yonghe Liu[2]

[1] Beijing Key Laboratory of Intelligent Telecommunications Software and Multimedia,
School of Computer Science & Technology,
Beijing University of Posts and Telecommunications, Beijing 100876, China
tdfxy@vip.sina.com, mhd@bupt.edu.cn
[2] Department of Computer Science and Engineering,
The University of Texas at Arlington, Arlington, TX 76019, USA
Yonghe@cse.uta.edu

Abstract. Different from conventional sensor networks, video sensor networks are distinctly characterized by their immense information and directional sensing models. In this paper, we propose an innovative, systematic method for image processing in video sensor networks in order to reduce the workload for individual sensors. Given the severe resource constraints on individual sensor nodes, our approach is to employ the redundancy among sensor nodes by partitioning the sensing task among highly correlated sensors. For an object of interest, each sensor only needs to capture and deliver a fraction of the scene of interests and these partial images can be fused at the sink to reconstruct a composite image. In particular, we detail how the sensing task can be partitioned among the sensors and propose an image fusion algorithms based on epipolar line constraint to fuse the received partial images at the sink. The experimental results show that our approach can achieve satisfactory results and we give detailed discussions on the effects of different system parameters.

1 Introduction

Recently sensor networks have attracted tremendous research interests due to its vast potential applications [1,2]. Although conventional sensor networks are capable of collecting and fusing immense data, information is specialized for a particular purpose constrained by severe resource limitations on a single sensor node. In this paper we investigate video sensor networks that are characterized by information-intensive visual streams, which doubtlessly can benefit a plethora of data hungry applications such as environment monitoring in civil applications.

With no exception from conventional sensor networks, video sensor networks are composed of a large amount of deeply embedded nodes equipped with optical sensing capability, connected via multi-hop wireless links, and aimed at harnessing the immense amount of information gathered therein. However, video sensor networks

---

[*] This work reported in this paper is supported by the NSFC under Grant 60242002, and the NCET program of MOE, China.

are also distinctly characterized by their relatively immense data and directional sensing range. The rich content contained in visual streams demands much more sophisticated processes for sensing, processing, transmitting, securing, and analyzing. These advanced requirements, when coupled with the severe resource constraints imposed on individual sensor nodes, dictate innovative solutions for energy conservation in every aspect of the system.

In this paper we propose an energy efficient, cooperative solution for task partitioning and image fusion in video sensor networks. Our key idea is to explore the redundancy among multiple sensors [3,4,5]. By partitioning the same sensing task among multiple related sensors and allowing each sensor to capture only a partial image, redundant processing in sensing and transmitting in network can be significantly reduced and hence network life can be prolonged. At the same time, scenes of interest can be fully reconstructed at the sink by fusing the corresponding partial images together. In particular, we develop an effective image fusion algorithm specifically for this scheme based on epipolar line constraint. As long as the parameters of source video sensors are given, we show that a fused image at a virtual viewpoint can be effectively constructed.

While conventional visual surveillance systems have been the subject of extensive research, the front end is composed of powerful nodes with high resolution cameras and computation power which are connected to central servers via readily available high bandwidth backhaul networks. Therefore, energy and bandwidth limitations are essentially of no concern, which dictates that the problems and solutions are in spirit different from the one addressed by this paper.

At the same time, conventional sensor networks have excelled largely thanks to its concept of a vast amount of deeply embedded, distributed, and coordinated sensor nodes. However, the information gathered therein is often of simple scalar format exemplified by temperature or humidity. On the contrary, video information possesses two significantly different characteristics: video streams are of much greater data and of more complex, vectorial format. While the first characteristic demands in-network information fusion in order to reduce load over band-limited networks and to save networks resource; the second one dictates in-network image fusion itself is a new challenge never seen before in the context of sensor networks.

Extensive work has indeed investigated the problem of image fusion, which can generally be categorized into three classes: (1) image synthesis of multiple reference images taken from more than one viewpoint. (2) fusion of images taken from different instruments. (3) fusion of two images taken at the same viewpoint but with different fuzzy parts. All classes of fusion require the presence of multiple images with full resolution. On the contrary, our method is to reconstruct a composite image based on partial images from multiple sensors, in order to reduce the workload of individual sensors and extend their lifetime. A few pioneer papers have addressed the problem of scarce resources faced by video sensor networks [6,7,8], their approaches mainly focus on power efficient techniques for individual components. Our solution is a system level approach with focus on reduction of data amount through cooperative image processing.

While assumption of omni-directional sensing area has facilitated elegant properties of conventional sensor networks [10,11], video sensor is characterized by its directional sensing range. This characteristic introduces different properties in terms of network coverage and information correlation targeted by this paper.

The reminder of this paper is organized as follows. In Section 2, we outline cooperative video processing in video sensor networks based on the correlation among individual nodes, including the video sensing model, video capturing, and video transmission. In Section 3 we detail our video fusion algorithm based on epipolar line followed by experimental studies in Section 4. Finally, we conclude and outline our future work in Section 5.

2 Cooperative Video Processing Based on Correlation Among Multiple Sensors

If an object of interest is covered by multiple sensors, they can cooperatively capture the scene and independently deliver partial information to the sink where composite scene can then be constructed. Intuitively we can divide the sensing area into multiple parts, each sensor will be responsible for capturing one part resulting in video streams with only a fraction of the original size.

Our approach of grouping sensors into cooperative teams is based on the correlation matrix obtained from our previous paper [9]. If sensors are highly correlated, redundancy will be high among their captured images and hence partitioning the sensing task across multiple sensors can most effectively reduce individual sensor's workload. Using a two-cooperative-sensor example we will detail the video processing based on correlation in this section. The case for multiple sensors will be a trivial extension which is omitted in this paper.

2.1 Video Sensing Model and Correlation Degree

Conventional sensing models share one thing in common: sensing ability is isotropic and attenuates with distance. However as far as video sensors are concerned, their sensing model is directional. The directional video sensors are constrained by the field of view. Although omni-cameras are available, they are only suitable for captured moving objects with a short distance.

Here we consider a 2D model as proposed in our previous work [9]. A video sensor N is a sector denoted by 5-tuple $<X,Y,R,V,\alpha>$. Here X,Y are the 2D position coordinates of the video sensor, R is the sensing radius. V is the center line of sight of the camera's field of view which will be termed *sensing direction*, and α is the offset angle of the field of view on both sides of V. Without otherwise specified, $V=(V_x,V_y)$ is of unit length, where V_x and V_y are the components along x-Axis and y-Axis respectively. The sensing model of video sensor is illustrated in Fig. 1.

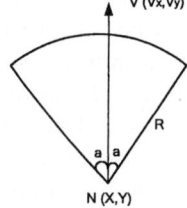

Fig. 1. Video sensing model

As in our previous work, we define the correlation degree between two video sensors based on the overlapping area of their sensing ranges. Two sensors are correlated if their sensing areas overlap with each other. Based on their relative positions, correlation between two sensors can be roughly classified into four cases as depicted in Fig. 2.

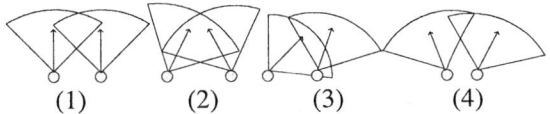

Fig. 2. Relative positions of two video sensors

From Fig. 2 we observe that even if two sensors possess physical proximity, as illustrated in Fig.2 (4), the overlapping area and hence correlation among them can be rather small. On the contrary, in Fig. 2(1)-(3), shorter distance between sensors indeed indicates higher correlation. Naturally, larger overlapping sensing areas will lead to higher correlation degrees. We will proceed with our discussion for cooperative processing based on the case depicted in Fig. 2(2). Other cases can be addressed in similar ways and are omitted due to space limitation.

2.2 Allocating the Sensing Task

Assume that we have found the two video sensors, denoted by N_1 and N_2, with strong correlation regarding the target of interests. Let (X_1, Y_1) and (X_2, Y_2) denote their 2D position coordinates; $V_1=(V_{1,x}, V_{1,y})$ and $V_2=(V_{2,x}, V_{2,y})$ denote their respective sensing directions. Their relative sensing areas are depicted in Figure 4(a).

In order to efficiently divide the sensing task between N_1 and N_2, we first need to determine respective sensing areas for them to cover. Our objective is to obtain a fused image as if it was captured by a virtual camera located at the middle point N_v between N_1 and N_2. $V_v=(V_{v,x}, V_{v,y})$ is the sensing direction of the virtual camera. As illustrated in Fig. 3(a). Assume that segment A_1A_2 is the scan line for the virtual camera in the image plane and A_m is the middle point of A_1A_2. If the images delivered by N_1 and N_2 can be utilized to restore A_1A_m and A_mA_2 respectively, they can then be fused together to construct the virtual image.

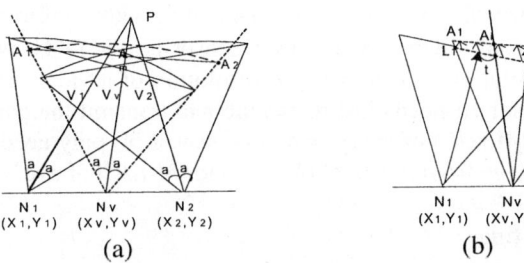

Fig. 3. Video processing based on correlation

The task now is to determine the exact partial image $[L_l, L_m]$ and $[R_m, R_2]$ that should be captured and transmitted by N_1 and N_2 respectively. As shown in Fig. 3(b), A_1A_m

which is the left half of the virtual image can be generated by corresponding L_1L_m from N_1. The solution to generate the right half of the virtual image is similar. The distance between the location and the image plane for all sensors are the same and denoted by $F=n*f$, where f is the focal length of video sensor and n is an adjustable factor. The scan line A_1A_m can be represented as

$$A_1A_m: \begin{cases} x = X_v + FV_{v,x} - tV_{v,y} \\ y = Y_v + FV_{v,y} + tV_{v,x} \end{cases} \qquad (1)$$

Notice that distance between left end point A_1 and middle point A_m is $tan\alpha F$, therefore the 2D position coordinate of A_1 is $(X_v + FV_{v,x} - tan\alpha FV_{v,y}, Y_v + FV_{v,y} + tan\alpha FV_{v,x})$. For sensor N_1, located at (X_1, Y_1) and with the sensing direction $V_1=(V_{1,x}, V_{1,y})$, the middle point of its scan line is $(X_1 + FV_{1,x}, Y_1 + FV_{1,y})$ and hence the scan line L_1L_m can be represented as

$$L_1L_m: \begin{cases} x = X_1 + FV_{1,x} - tV_{1,y} \\ y = Y_1 + FV_{1,y} + tV_{1,x} \end{cases} \qquad (2)$$

For the virtual camera located at (X_v, Y_v) and sensing direction V_v, assume that M number of pixels shall cover segment $[A_1, A_m]$. According to Equation (1) and (2), points A_1 and A_m in the image plane will be mapped to $(M-t_1/C)$ and $(M-t_m/C)$ respectively in N_1's image plane, where $C=tan\alpha F$ and t_1, t_m can be obtained by replacing (X_i, Y_i) in Equation (3) with the coordinates of A_1 and A_m.

$$t = \frac{(X_1+FV_{1,x}-X_i)(Y_v-Y_i)-(Y_1+FV_{1,y}-Y_i)(X_v-X_i)}{V_{1,x}(X_v-X_i)+V_{1,y}(Y_v-Y_i)} \qquad (3)$$

Scan line of sensor N_2 can be represented similarly. According to the same approach we can also determine the mapping from R_mR_2 to A_mA_2.

2.3 Video Capturing

Once the relation between the two sensors' overage is determined, we can employ this information to empower the network with cooperative video information capturing. Assume the resolution of video captured by a sensor is $(2M) \times N$, where 2M and N are the horizontal resolution and the vertical resolution of a video frame. In order to achieve this goal, sensor N_1 needs just to capture and transmit the partial image from the pixel $(M-t_1/C)$ to $(M-t_m/C)$ of every scan line; sensor N_2 only needs to capture and transmit the partial image from the pixel $(M-t_m/C)$ to $(M-t_2/C)$ of every scan line.

2.4 Video Transmitting

Once the images are captured and tailored accordingly, the partial video streams will be sent to the sink independently by N_1 and N_2 via different routes to balance the network load. To find the route from the sensor to the sink, we can adopt existing sensor-initiated routing algorithms such as SPIN [12]. Notice that in SPIN, a two-step routing strategy is employed. In the first step, the sensor broadcasts a probe packet that describes the sensor data that will locate a QoS-guaranteed route by negotiation and resource adaptation. Once the route is determined, in the second step, the whole video stream is transmitted.

3 Image Fusion Based on Epipolar Line Constraint

Once the images are transmitted to the sink, they will be fused together to construct the composite image from the two sensors. Instead of merging the two partial images directly in our previous work [9], we employ the properties of epipolar line constraint to transform the two partial images before merging them, which will result in higher visual quality of the fused image than before.

Evidently, respective projective positions of a 3D point in the two image planes are different with the change of viewpoints. The key challenge is then to determine the corresponding relations of pixel points between different image planes. Toward this end, epipolar line constraint commonly used in computer vision provides us an effective solution. However, conventional methods for obtaining these relations are to correspond the six (at least) 3D points to their exact 2D position coordinates in the image plane and thus establish a group of multidimensional equations in order to derive a projective matrix $M_{3\times 4}$ with twelve coefficients. Unfortunately, this method cannot be directly adopted for image fusion in video sensor networks.

In this section, utilizing the properties of epipolar line constraint, we propose a method for obtaining the corresponding relation of pixel points between different image planes, which in turn will provide the basis for image fusion.

3.1 Epipolar Line Constraint

As illustrated in Fig. 4(a) and (b), we define two image planes I_1 and I_2 corresponding to video sensors N_1 and N_2, respectively. Before detailing our algorithm, we first provide some preliminaries.

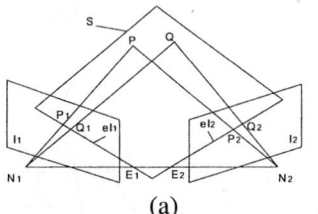 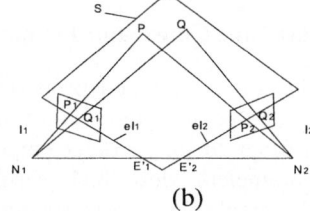

(a)   (b)

Fig. 4. Inner /Outer epipolar line

Assume that a 3D point P is projected onto I_1 and I_2 and its corresponding projective points are P_1 in I_1 and P_2 in I_2 respectively. P_1 and P_2 are termed *corresponding point* of each other. Given point P_1 and P_2 are corresponding points of P, we call the plane outlined by points P, P_1, P_2 as an *epipolar plane* and denote it by S. The intersection line $el_1(el_2)$ between the epipolar plane S and the image plane I_1

(I_2) where point P_1 (P_2) is located is termed as inner (outer) epipolar line. And el_1 and el_2 are called corresponding epipolar line each other.

The intersection point, E_1 (E_2), of all the inner epipolar lines in the image plane I_1 (I_2) is called inner epipole. Similarly, the intersection point, E'_1 (E'_2), of all the outer epipolar lines in the image plane I_1 (I_2) is called outer epipole. Given the above definitions, we have the following properties.

Property 1 On-one-line constraint. The four points N_1, E_1, E_2, N_2 are on the same line, and so do points N_1, E'_1, E'_2, N_2.

Property 2 Continuity constraint. If point P_1 and Q_1 are located on the inner epipolar el_1 in I_1, their respective corresponding points P_2 and Q_2 are located on the inner epipolar el_2 in I_2. Furthermore, the imaging location relation of P_2, Q_2 in I_2 accords with that of P_1, Q_1 in I_1. If the depth information of P, Q is the same, the distance between P and Q in the same image plane is the same as well.

Property 3 Similarity constraint. If a 3D point P corresponds P_1 in I_1 and P_2 in I_2, color information of P_1 and P_2 and their neighboring points have great similarity.

Property 4 Uniqueness constraint Except for certain special cases, any point in I_1 corresponds to only one point in I_2.

Among the above four properties, Property 1 is the computational foundation of our fusion algorithm. By establishing epipolar line constraint formula based on it, the 2D position coordinates of outer epipole can be located. Other properties provide the possibility of holistic epipolar lines matching, which is further explained below.

If el_1 and el_2 are corresponding epipolar lines, pixel points p_i on el_1 and p_j on el_2 ($i,j=1,2,3,..., M$) are corresponding when i is equal to j. In our case, el_1, el_v are corresponding epipolar lines on I_1 from N_1 and I_v from N_v respectively. The pixel point p_j on el_v can be generated by the pixel point p_i on el_1, as long as i equals to j. Based on this property, we can determine each pair of corresponding epipolar lines between I_1 and I_v. Compared to pixel-by-pixel matching, holistic epipolar line matching simplifies the process of searching the corresponding pixel points.

3.2 Epipolar Line Constraint Formula

Based on the aforementioned properties, we define epipolar line constraint formulas in order to locate outer epipole and the parameters described earlier. Subsequently, pixel points' corresponding relations between the two partial image planes can be established. In order to perform this, we first illustrate the concept of sensing angle.

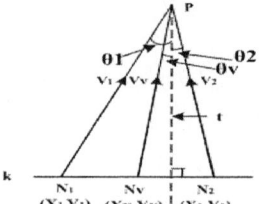

Fig. 5. Sensing angle

As shown in Fig. 5, assume three video sensors N_1, N_v and N_2 are located on the same line k and their sensing directions denoted by V_1, V_v and V_2 intersect at P. Draw a vertical line t perpendicular to line k via P. The angle between the sensing direction and the vertical line t is termed *sensing angle*. Obviously, the value of sensing angle θ of a sensor is determined by its sensing direction $V=(V_x, V_y)$. If $V_x=0$, θ equals to zero; otherwise, θ equals to $arctan(V_y/V_x)$. When $V_y/V_x>0$, $θ>0$; otherwise, $θ<0$.

Now let us examine our focused case in this paper as depicted in Fig. 3(a) with the outer epipolar line illustrated in Fig. 4(b). Using sensor N_1 as an example, based on Property 1, we know that N_1 and outer epipole E'_1 are on the same line as shown in Fig. 6. Based on exact sensing angle $θ_1$ and sensing direction V_1, we know that the location of the outer epipole E'_1 is in the extended image plane I_1, which is to the right of video sensor N_1.

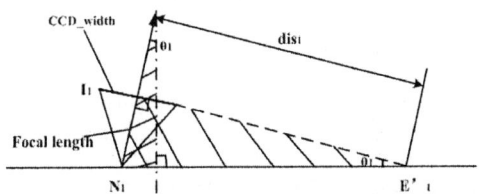

Fig. 6. Computing position of outer epipole

From the two hatched triangles that are similar, we can conclude that $dis_1 =f*ctanθ_1$, where dis_1 denotes the perpendicular distance from outer epipole E'_1 to the sensing direction V_1. Based on this, we obtain the outer epipolar line constraint equation depicted in Fig. 7(a). The matching process of the two groups of epipolar lines in I_1 and I_v is as follows: (1) Compute the values of dis given by $dis =f*ctanθ$. (2) Establish epipolar line constraint equations through connecting the leftmost (rightmost) pixels of each row with the outer epipole. (3) Match each corresponding epipolar line between the two images pixel-by-pixel, from top to bottom and from left to right.

Matching of the epipolar lines in I_v and I_2 can be processed similarly, which are shown in Fig. 7(b) and (c). Notice that the outer epipole of N_2 is on its left side, which is determined by the relevant positions of V_1 and V_2. Since we assume the sensing angle of video sensor N_2 is opposite to those of N_1 and N_v, the position of the outer epipole is also opposite to those of N_1 and N_v.

From Fig. 7, we observe that as dis decreases, the maximal slope value of the corresponding outer epipolar lines increases. The smaller the difference between

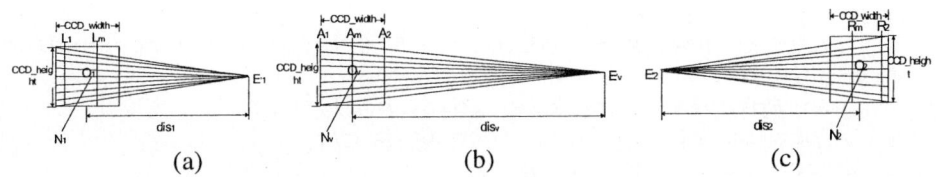

Fig. 7. Computing outer epipolar line constraint equation N_1, N_v, N_2, respectively

two distances from outer epipole to the sensing direction is, the smaller the difference between their maximal slopes is. Notice that the maximal slope value reflects the maximal distortion between the source image and the virtual image. So, if a 3D point P corresponds projective points P_1 in I_1 and P_2 in I_2 respectively, its 2D position coordinates change between projective points P_1 in I_1 and P_2 in I_2 is small when both the distance between the two sensors and the difference between the sensing directions of the two sensors are small. And the position coordinates change relation satisfies approximately certain linear transformation. Thus, our approach of utilizing pixel points of the source image to generate corresponding pixel points of the virtual image will result in good quality fusion if certain conditions are satisfied. The video processing algorithm is summarized in Table 1.

Table 1. Fusion algorithm

```
Fusion(Gv, G', G1)
/* Take example for the half of Gv, which is the fused
image; G' is the temporary image;G1 is the partial image
from video sensor N1;*/
{//Initialize;
(X,Y):=A1;C1:=Ftanα/M;
for i=1 to M do
  {//find current the value of parameter t in G1;
  t=mapping(x,y,G1);
  //find the current pixel index corresponding to t;
  l=M-t/ C1;
  for j=1 to N do
    {//put pxiel G1(l,j) into G' (i,j);
    Putpxiel(G1,l, G',i,j); }
  X:=X+ C1Vv,y;Y:=Y- C1Vv,x;}
/*match the corresponding pairs of epipolar lines
between G' and Gv.*/
//get the values of dis1 and disv;
dis1=f*ctanθ1;disv=f*ctanθv;
/*establish corresponding epipolar line constraint
equations for G' and Gv , find the pixels in G' in order
to generate corresponding pixels in Gv.*/
For q=1 to N do
  For p=1 to M do
    {//find the Y-coordinate of Gv(p,q)'s corresponding
pixel in G';
    y'= Epipolar_line(dis1 ,disv,p,q);
    //put pxiel G'(p,y') into Gv(p,q);
    Putpxiel(G', y', Gv,p,q);}
Output(Gv);}
```

4 Experimental Results and Performance Analysis

We have performed a set of experiments to verify the feasibility and efficiency of our approach. In our experiments, we employ two video sensors and use our algorithms to allocate the sensing task between them and perform image fusion. Both sensors possess the same inner parameters and their sensing angles are set to be 30 degrees apart. Table 2 summarizes the parameters.

Table 2. Parameters Setting

Parameter	Parameter Setting (unit)
Sensing angle θ_1/θ_2	15°/-15°
Focal length f	10mm
Offset angle α	25°
Image size	320pixel*240pixel
CCD chip size	8.8mm*6.6mm

Fig. 8 shows a typical set of experimental results. Two images taken by two different sensors N_1 and N_2 for the same scene from different viewpoints are shown in Fig. 8(1) and Fig. 8(2), respectively. Fig. 8(3) and Fig. 8(4) are the partial images shown at a virtual viewpoint N_v which have been transformed by the epipolar line constraint formula. They are used to obtain the fused images depicted in Fig. 8(5) based on our proposed approach. The experimental results show that our image fusion method obtains satisfactory results.

Through our experiments, we also notice that the results are heavily dependent on three parameters, namely the distance between the two video sensor nodes denoted by

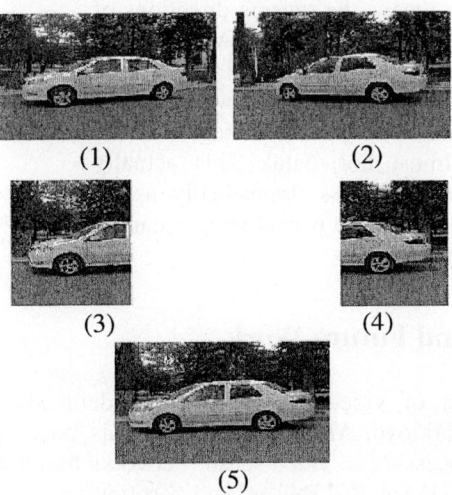

Fig. 8. Some experimental results

D, the absolute angle difference between the two sensing directions denoted by |Δθ|, and the distance from the detected target to image plane or object distance denoted by F. Our conclusion is that the quality of image fusion is proportional to the object distance F, and inverse proportional to the distance between the two video sensor nodes D and the absolute angle difference between the two sensing directions |Δθ|. The reasons are described below.

As depicted in Fig. 9, construct an *isoceles triangle model* to represent the relationship among F, D and |Δθ|. This model indicates the restrictions of the three key parameters. Moreover, *equilateral triangle model* as a special case of isoceles triangle model restricts the boundary values of the three parameters. The angle of the equilateral triangle is the upper boundary of |Δθ|. And the edge relationship of the equilateral triangle defines the basic relationship between F and D. In other words, F must be equal or more than D. The relationship among these three parameters can be further examined based on this model as follows.

First we assume that D is fixed and examine the effect of F. Fig. 9 shows the relationship between F and |Δθ|. The greater F is, the smaller |Δθ| becomes. Intuitively, this denotes that the more visual information is shared among the two images for fusion, the better the image fusion effect is.

Next we assume that F is fixed and we examine the effect of D. As shown in Fig. 10, |Δθ| will decrease with the decreasing of D. The smaller |Δθ| is, the better the fusion effect becomes. Intuitively smaller |Δθ| denotes more similar viewing angles of the two sensors and hence better fusion quality.

We also observe that the fusion algorithm is applicable if and only if $F>D$ and $|Δθ| \in [0°, 60°]$. When $F>D$ and $|Δθ| \in [0°, 30°]$, the fusion effect is fairly good. Notice that when $F>>D$, |Δθ| essentially approaches zero. This means the sensing directions of two video sensor nodes become parallel. According to $dis = f*ctan\theta$, when θ is zero, $ctan\theta$ approaches infinite and *dis* approaches infinite as well. In this case, the epiploar lines on the source image and the virtual image are almost horizontal. This actually simplifies the matching process dramatically as no matching is needed and the two partial images can be directly combined together.

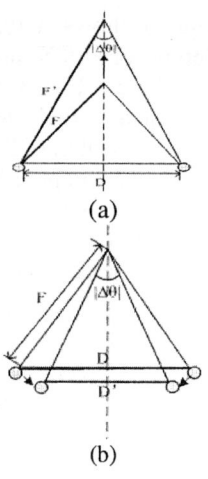

Fig. 9. The effect of the parameters F and D, respectively

5 Conclusions and Future Work

Immense information of video sensor networks demands efficient methods for reducing sensor's workload. Motivated by this, this paper proposes a systematic method for video processing in video sensor networks based on sensors' correlation. By teaming up highly correlated sensors and partitioning sensing areas among them, individual sensor's processing load is significantly reduced. In particular, we propose a simple and yet effective image fusion algorithm for fusing partial images delivered by multiple sensors. The algorithm is based on epipolar line constraint and proved to be effective through our experimental study. Furthermore, based on the isoceles triangle model, we analyze the effects of key parameters of the sensors in determining the quality of the resultant images.

Our method still has its limitation. Although it has considered that a 3D point's projective pixel is different in different image planes, it is still not a pure 3D model. The fusion algorithm is mainly based on correlation between multiple video sensors. With the increase of the angle between multiple video sensors' sensing directions, the quality of fusion will decrease dramatically. In our ongoing work, we are investigating image fusion algorithms based on true 3D models in order to further improve the quality of fusion.

References

1. I.F. Akyildiz, W. Su, Y. Sankarasubramaniam, and E. Cayirci, "Wireless sensor networks: a survey," *Computer Networks*, vol.38, pp.393-422, 2002.
2. M. Vieira, C. Coelho, "Survey on wireless sensor network devices," in *Proceedings IEEE ETFA'03*, vol.1, pp.16-19,Sept. 2003.
3. Moigne, A. Cole-Rhodes, R.Eastman, T. El- Ghazawi, K. Johnson, "Multiple sensor image registration, image fusion and dimension reduction of earth science imagery," in *Proceedings of the Fifth International Conference on Information Fusion*,vol.2, pp.8-11,July. 2002.
4. Y. Gao, K. Wu, and F. Li, "Analysis on the redundancy of wireless sensor networks," in *Proceedings of ACM WSNA'03*, San Diego, pp.108-114, Sep. 2003.
5. V Chandramohan and K. Christensen, "A first look at wired sensor networks for video surveillance systems," in *Proceedings of the High Speed Local Networks Workshop at the IEEE Conference in Local Computer Networks*, Tampa, FL, pp.728-729, Nov. 2002.
6. G. Foresti and L. Snidaro, "A distributed sensor network for video surveillance of outdoor environments," in *Proceedings of IEEE International Conference On Image Processing*, New York, NY, pp.525-528, 2002.
7. C.-K. Chang and J. Huang, "Video surveillance for Hazardous Conditions Using Sensor Networks," in *Proceedings of the 2004 IEEE International Conference on Networking, Sensing & Control*, pp.1008-1013, Mar. 2004.
8. W. Feng, J. Walpole, W. Feng and C. Pu, "Moving towards massively scalable video-based sensor networks," in *Proceedings of the Workshop on New Visions for LargeScale Networks: Research and Applications*, Washington, DC, Mar. 2001.
9. H. Ma and Y. Liu. "Correlation Based Video Processing in Video Sensor Networks," in *Proceedings of IEEE WirelessCom 2005*, Maui, HI, June. 2005.
10. D. Tian and N. Georganas, "A coverage-preserving node scheduling scheme for large wireless sensor networks," in *Proceeding of ACM WSNA*, Atlanta, GA, pp.32-41, 2002.
11. X. Wang, G. Xing, Y. Zhang, C. Lu, R. Pless and C. Gill, "Integrated coverage and connectivity configuration in wireless sensor networks," in *Proceeding of ACM Sensys*, Los Angeles, CA, pp.28-39, Nov. 2003.
12. W. Heinzelman, J. Kulik and H. Balakrishnan, "Adaptive protocol for information dissemination in wireless sensor networks," in *Proceedings of ACM Mobicom*,Seattle,WA, pp.178-185, 1999.

Mathematical PSNR Prediction Model Between Compressed Normal Maps and Rendered 3D Images

Toshihiko Yamasaki, Kazuya Hayase, and Kiyoharu Aizawa

Department of Frontier Informatics, Graduate School of Frontier Sciences,
The University of Tokyo, 5-1-5 Kashiwano-ha,
Kashiwa, Chiba, 277-8561, Japan
{yamasaki, hayase, aizawa}@hal.k.u-tokyo.ac.jp

Abstract. Normal mapping is an essential rendering technique in 3D computer graphics to express detailed wrincleness and bumpy texture of the surface. As the normal mapping is increasingly utilized, compression of normal maps is becoming a significant issue. The problem is there is no quality evaluation model for lossy compressed normal maps. Therefore, in this paper, we have developed a mathematical model to analyze the characteristics between lossy compressed normal maps and 3D images rendered with them. By calculating averages of the parameters which cannot be defined uniquely and by introducing some assumptions, the model has been expressed in a simple form. The validity and generality of our model have been demonstrated by experiments. The model proposed in this paper will be helpful for deciding normal map compression strategy considering the target quality of the rendered 3D images.

1 Introduction

As more realism and visual complexity of scenes are required in 3D computer graphics, expressing 3D objects only by polygons has become problematic in terms of data storage and computational cost. In this regard, a number of elaborated texture mapping techniques have been developed such as bump mapping [1], displacement mapping [2], reflection mapping [3][4], relief mapping [5], and so forth.

Bump mapping, which is nowadays extended to normal mapping [6] to express more detailed and complicated texture, is especially a key technology to enhance the roughness and wrinkles of the surface with small amount of polygon data. For this purpose, hardware acceleration chips have been developed [7][8], and algorithms to achieve hardware accelerated normal mapping using standard texture-mapping processors have been discussed [9]. In addition, the development of software that can automatically generate normal maps from high resolution polygon models as well as normal map extraction techniques from images and 3D scan data [10]-[12] contributed to the increasing popularity of normal mapping. As a result, normal mapping is now supported by major 3D graphic API libraries such as OpenGL [13] and DirectX [14] by default.

On the other hand, generating and using high resolution normal maps for every surface of the whole of 3D objects cause a lack of video memory resources and a storage problem. In this regard, some of the general-purpose texture compression algorithms have been applied to normal map compression [17]. In addition, a dedicated compression algorithm called 3Dc has been developed [18] and implemented onto off-the-shelf Graphics Processing Units (GPU's). We have also been developing efficient normal map compression algorithms using standard 2D image compression techniques such as JPEG and JPEG2000, as well [15][16]. However, the problem we need to point out is that there is no mathematical quality evaluation model between the lossy compressed normal maps and the images rendered with them so far. Therefore, the quality of the rendered images are evaluated by PSNR between the original normal maps and the compressed ones, which is not accurate, or by PSNR between the rendered images, which is computationally expensive.

The purpose of this study is to analyze the relationships between the quality of compressed normal maps and that of rendered images, and to propose a peak signal-to-noise ratio (PSNR) model of the 3D images rendered with lossy compressed normal maps. In 3D image rendering, there are some parameters which cannot be defined uniquely such as kinds and positions of light sources, shape of objects, color texture, reflectance factors, and so on. Therefore, we have introduced some assumptions and averaging operations to some parameters for simplicity. Nevertheless, experimental results have demonstrated that our simple PSNR model is fairly accurate for estimating the quality of the rendered images. As a result, compression quality factors of normal maps can be decided effectively considering the target quality of the final rendered images.

2 Normal Maps

Normal maps are the maps of three-dimensional vectors which represent directions of normal vectors of 3D object surfaces. Therefore, normal maps can be simply expressed as RGB bitmaps, in which the [-1, 1] range of normal vectors is mapped to [0, 255] based on the equation as described in the following (therefore, xyz values are discrete):

$$(x, y, z) = \frac{2}{255}(R, G, B) - 1 \qquad (1)$$

where (x, y, z) and (R, G, B) represent element values of each pixel in a normal map and their corresponding full color pixel values, respectively.

In addition, the length of normal vectors is fixed at one in order to simplify the weight factor calculation of color and luminance into the inner product operation between the normal vector and the luminance vector as will be demonstrated in Eq. (4):

$$x^2 + y^2 + z^2 = 1 \qquad (2)$$

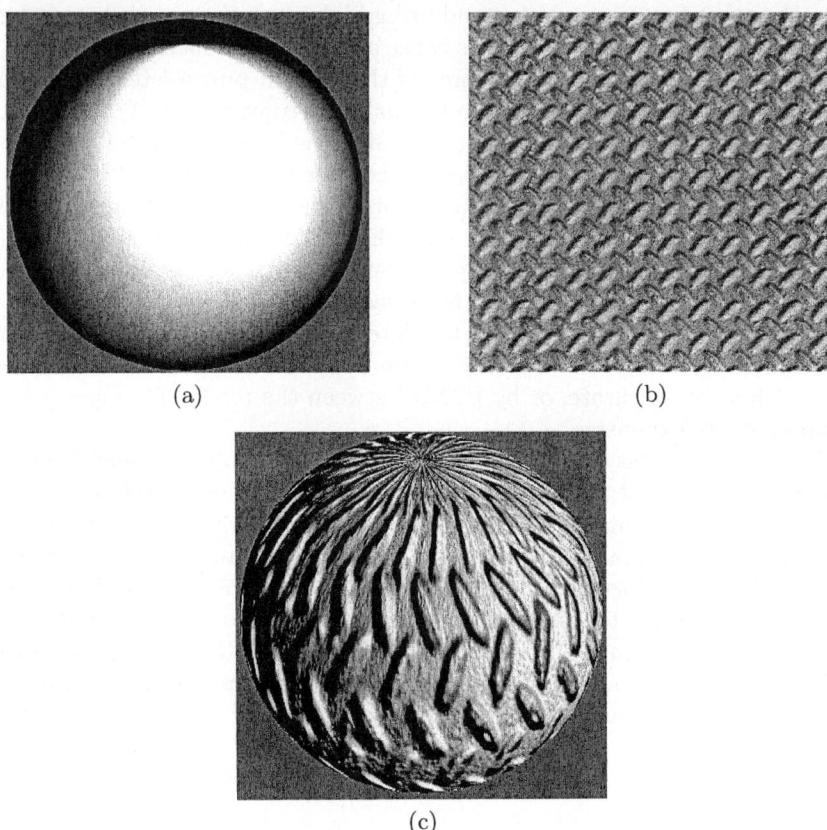

Fig. 1. Example of normal mapping: (a) 3D image with smooth surface; (b) normal map of metal grill texture (512 x 512); (c) rendered 3D image using normal map. Detailed grill texture is expressed without complicated polygons.

Here, the z component is always equal to or greater than 0 because the normal vectors are in the direction of outer side of the surface:

$$-1 \leq x \leq +1, \ -1 \leq y \leq +1, \ 0 \leq z \leq +1 \qquad (3)$$

An example of normal map and the rendering result on a smooth sphere is shown in Fig. 1. It is observed that the complicated metal grill texture is expressed on the 3D object sphere only by the simple shape data and the normal map. Since color and shading are calculated on-line according to the normal map data, highlits and shadows on the surface can be rendered depending on where the lights in the scene are located, resulting in more realistic expression.

3 PSNR Model of Rendered 3D Images

In 3D image rendering, there are some parameters which cannot be defined uniquely such as kinds and positions of light sources, color texture, reflection models, and so on. In our model, one of the simplest but fundamental lighting models is assumed where there is no ambient light, light emission, attenuation/spotlight effects, nor specular. In addition, it is assumed that there is a diffuse point light source in the infinite distance in the scene. Since the light source is located in the infinite distance, our PSNR model is independent of the shape of the object as will be demonstrated in the experimental results. In such a simple model, lighting equation for each pixel is described as in the following:

$$\mathbf{I} = max(\mathbf{L} \cdot \mathbf{N}, 0) \cdot \mathbf{D} \tag{4}$$

where $\mathbf{I}$, $\mathbf{L}$, and $\mathbf{N}$ represent the brightness, the light source vector, and the original normal vector, respectively. Besides, $\mathbf{D}$ is the color which is the product of the light's diffuse color and the material's diffuse color. In the same manner, the brightness ($\mathbf{I'}$) rendered with the lossy compressed normal vector ($\mathbf{N'}$) is expressed as in the following:

$$\mathbf{I'} = max(\mathbf{L} \cdot \mathbf{N'}, 0) \cdot \mathbf{D} \tag{5}$$

Although $\mathbf{L} \cdot \mathbf{N}$ and $\mathbf{L} \cdot \mathbf{N'}$ are scene dependent due to the maximum condition in Eqs. (4) and (5), we simplified the equations for simplicity as shown below:

$$\mathbf{I} = (\mathbf{L} \cdot \mathbf{N}) \cdot \mathbf{D} \tag{6}$$
$$\mathbf{I'} = (\mathbf{L} \cdot \mathbf{N'}) \cdot \mathbf{D} \tag{7}$$

Here, let us define new PSNR for color images by averaging errors of R, G, and B:

$$PSNR = 10 \cdot log_{10} \frac{255^2}{\frac{1}{3}(MSE_R + MSE_G + MSE_B)} \tag{8}$$

where MSE_R, MSE_G, and MSE_B represent the mean square errors (MSE's) of the red, green, and blue color spaces, respectively. From Eqs. (6) and (7), the PSNR for the rendered image is calculated as in the following equation:

$$\begin{aligned} PSNR_{rendered} &= 10 \cdot log_{10} \frac{255^2}{\frac{1}{3} \cdot \frac{1}{M} \sum(\sum_{j=R,G,B}((\mathbf{L} \cdot \mathbf{N}) \cdot \mathbf{D}_j - (\mathbf{L} \cdot \mathbf{N'}) \cdot \mathbf{D}_j)^2)} \\ &= 10 \cdot log_{10} \frac{255^2}{\frac{1}{3} \cdot \frac{1}{M} \sum(D_R^2 + D_G^2 + D_B^2) \cdot (\mathbf{L} \cdot \mathbf{N} - \mathbf{L} \cdot \mathbf{N'})^2} \end{aligned} \tag{9}$$

where M represents the total number of pixels. And, D_R, D_G, and D_B stand for red, green, blue elements of $\mathbf{D}$, respectively. Then, we define $\mathbf{L}$, $\mathbf{N}$, and $\mathbf{N'}$ as in the following equation (see Fig. 2):

$$\mathbf{N} = (x, y, z) \tag{10}$$
$$\mathbf{N'} = (x', y', z') \tag{11}$$
$$\mathbf{L} = (sin\theta cos\phi, sin\theta sin\phi, cos\theta), \ (0 \leq \theta \leq \frac{\pi}{2}, 0 \leq \phi \leq 2\pi) \tag{12}$$

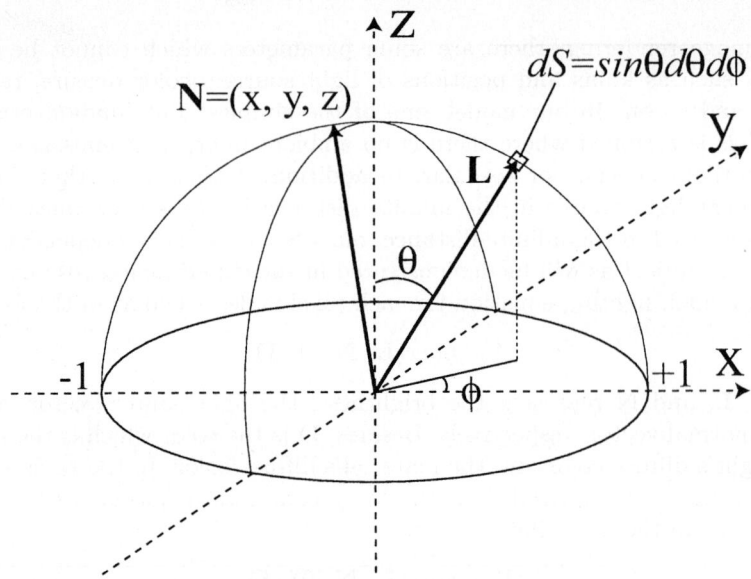

Fig. 2. Definition of **N** and **L**. **L** is expressed by the spherical polar coordinates.

where **L** is expressed by the spherical polar coordinates. From Eqs. (10)-(12), the square error between $\mathbf{L} \cdot \mathbf{N}$ and $\mathbf{L} \cdot \mathbf{N'}$ is expressed as in Eq. (13):

$$E(\theta, \phi)^2 \equiv (\mathbf{L} \cdot \mathbf{N} - \mathbf{L} \cdot \mathbf{N'})^2$$
$$= ((\Delta x \cdot cos\phi + \Delta y \cdot sin\phi)sin\theta + \Delta z \cdot cos\theta)^2 \quad (13)$$

where Δx, Δy, and Δz represent $(x-x')$, $(y-y')$, and $(z-z')$, respectively. In order to define $PSNR_{rendered}$ uniquely independent of the light source position, the mean value of Eq. (13) for the whole range of the hemisphere (see Fig. 2) is calculated by taking the double integrals as shown in Eq. (14):

$$\overline{E(\theta,\phi)^2} = \frac{1}{2\pi} \int\!\!\int_S E(\theta,\phi)^2 dS$$
$$= \frac{1}{2\pi} \int_0^{\frac{\pi}{2}} \left(\int_0^{2\pi} E(\theta,\phi)^2 d\phi \right) sin\theta d\theta$$
$$= \frac{2}{\pi} \int_0^{\frac{\pi}{2}} \left(\frac{1}{2}((\Delta x)^2 + (\Delta y)^2) \cdot sin^3\theta + (\Delta z)^2 \cdot cos^2\theta sin\theta \right) d\theta$$
$$= \frac{1}{3} \left((\Delta x)^2 + (\Delta y)^2 + (\Delta z)^2 \right) \quad (14)$$

Finally, $PSNR_{renderd}$ is described as

$$PSNR_{rendered} = 10 \cdot log_{10} \frac{255^2 \cdot 3 \cdot M}{\sum (D_R^2 + D_G^2 + D_B^2) \cdot \frac{1}{3}((\Delta x)^2 + (\Delta y)^2 + (\Delta z)^2)} \quad (15)$$

On the other hand, the PSNR of a normal map, which is employed in the conventional approach, is calculated as shown in the following equation:

$$\begin{aligned}PSNR_{normal} &= 10 \cdot \log_{10} \frac{255^2 \cdot 3 \cdot M}{\sum((R-R')^2 + (G-G')^2 + (B-B')^2)} \\ &= 10 \cdot \log_{10} \frac{255^2 \cdot 3 \cdot M}{(\frac{255}{2})^2 \cdot \sum((x-x')^2 + (y-y')^2 + (z-z')^2)} \\ &= 10 \cdot \log_{10} \frac{255^2 \cdot 3 \cdot M}{(\frac{255\sqrt{3}}{2})^2 \cdot \sum \frac{1}{3}((\Delta x)^2 + (\Delta y)^2 + (\Delta z)^2)}\end{aligned} \quad (16)$$

By comparing Eqs. (15) and (16), it is observed Eq. (16) would overestimate the quality of the rendered images in most cases since the color texture of the surface is not considered properly. Although the normal maps have three dimensional data of x, y, and z, the normal maps have only two degrees of freedom due to the unity condition as described in Eqs. (2) and (3). Therefore, Eq. (16) can be re-written by using only x and y component values as in the following if needed:

$$PSNR_{normal} = \\ 10 \cdot \log_{10} \frac{255^2 \cdot 3 \cdot M}{(\frac{255\sqrt{3}}{2})^2 \cdot \sum \frac{1}{3}\left((\Delta x)^2 + (\Delta y)^2 + (\sqrt{1-x^2-y^2} - \sqrt{1-x'^2-y'^2})^2\right)} \quad (17)$$

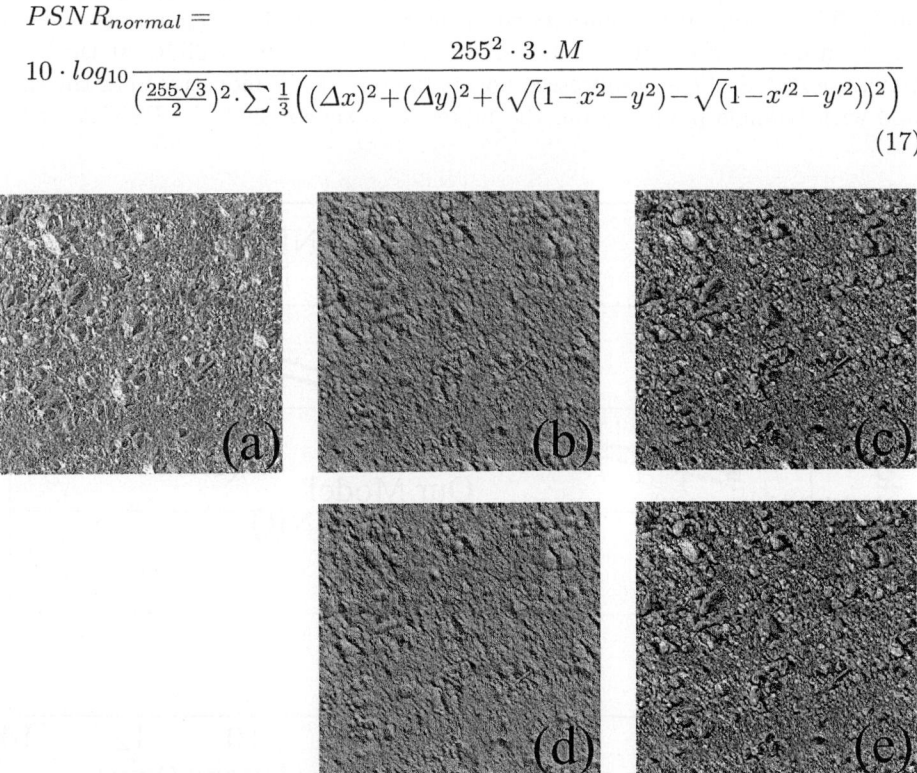

Fig. 3. Rocky texture and its normal map: (a) color texture; (b) original normal map; (c) original rendered image at $\theta = 30$, $\phi = 45$; (d) compressed normal map (3bpp); (e) renderd image using (d) at $\theta = 30$, $\phi = 45$. Texture and normal map is attached to flat board.

4 Experimental Results and Discussions

The experiments were carried out using normal maps in "Bump Texture Library [19]" provided by Computer Graphics Systems Development Corporation. The normal maps were compressed into JPEG format with several quality factors. Important to note here is that our model is independent of compression algorithms. Therefore, the PSNR model presented in this paper is applicable to normal maps with any compression algorithm. The color texture data, which were also included in the library, were uncompressed.

An example of the rendered image of the rock texture using compressed and uncompressed normal maps is shown in Fig. 3. In the experiments, the normal map was attached to a flat square board and the other conditions were same as those introduced in Section 3. ϕ was changed from 0 to 2π while keeping θ at 0, 30, and 60.

The PSNR's of the rendered images shown in Fig. 3 are demonstrated in Fig. 4. Since the white point light source in infinite distance is assumed, (R, G, B) data of the color texture data were directly used for (D_R, D_G, D_B) (see Eq. (15)). The dotted line represents the PSNR's predicted by our model whereas the solid line with square points correspond to the actual PSNR. At the same time, the PSNR of the compressed normal map is also demonstrated as the solid line with triangle points. From the figure, it is shown that the PSNR's of the

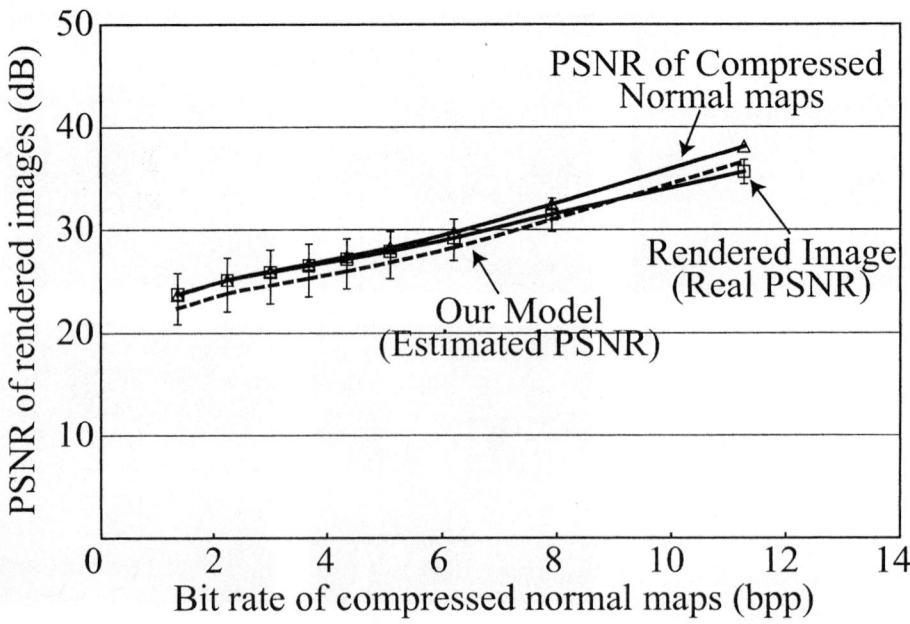

Fig. 4. PSNR as a function of bit rate of compressed normal maps where our model is plotted by dotted lines

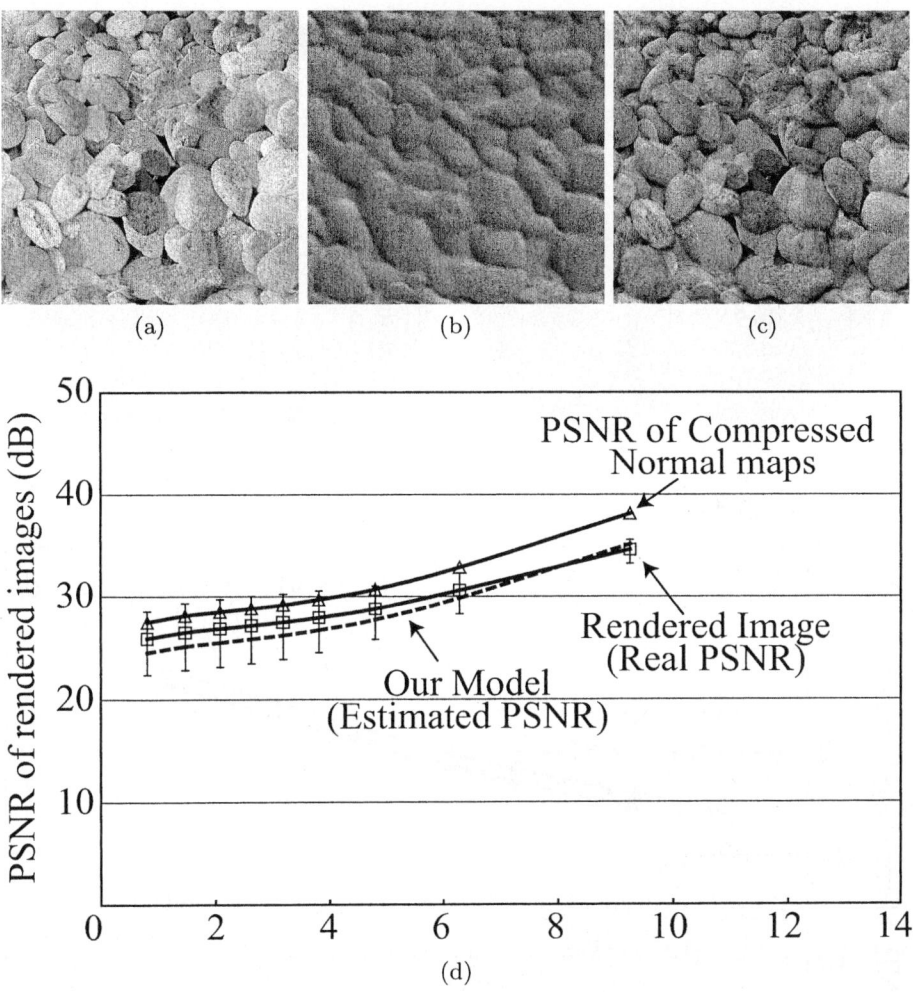

Fig. 5. Results using stone texture: (a) color texture; (b) normal map; (c) rendered image at $\theta=30$ and $\phi=45$; (d) PSNR

rendered images coincide with our model fairly well. The PSNR estimated by our model is within error bars for all the range of bit rate. When the bit rate of the compressed normal map is low, our model tends to underpredict the quality. This is due to the model simplification introduced in Eqs. (6) and (7). On the other hand, PSNR of the normal map begins to overpredict when the bit rate of the compressed normal map is large. In practice, the PSNR of the rendered image is 30dB or higher to maintain the image quality. Therefore, our PSNR model coincide with the actual PSNR better than the conventional approach in practical situation.

Another example of the experimental results is shown in Fig. 5. Again, our model estimates the PSNR of the rendered 3D image better than that of com-

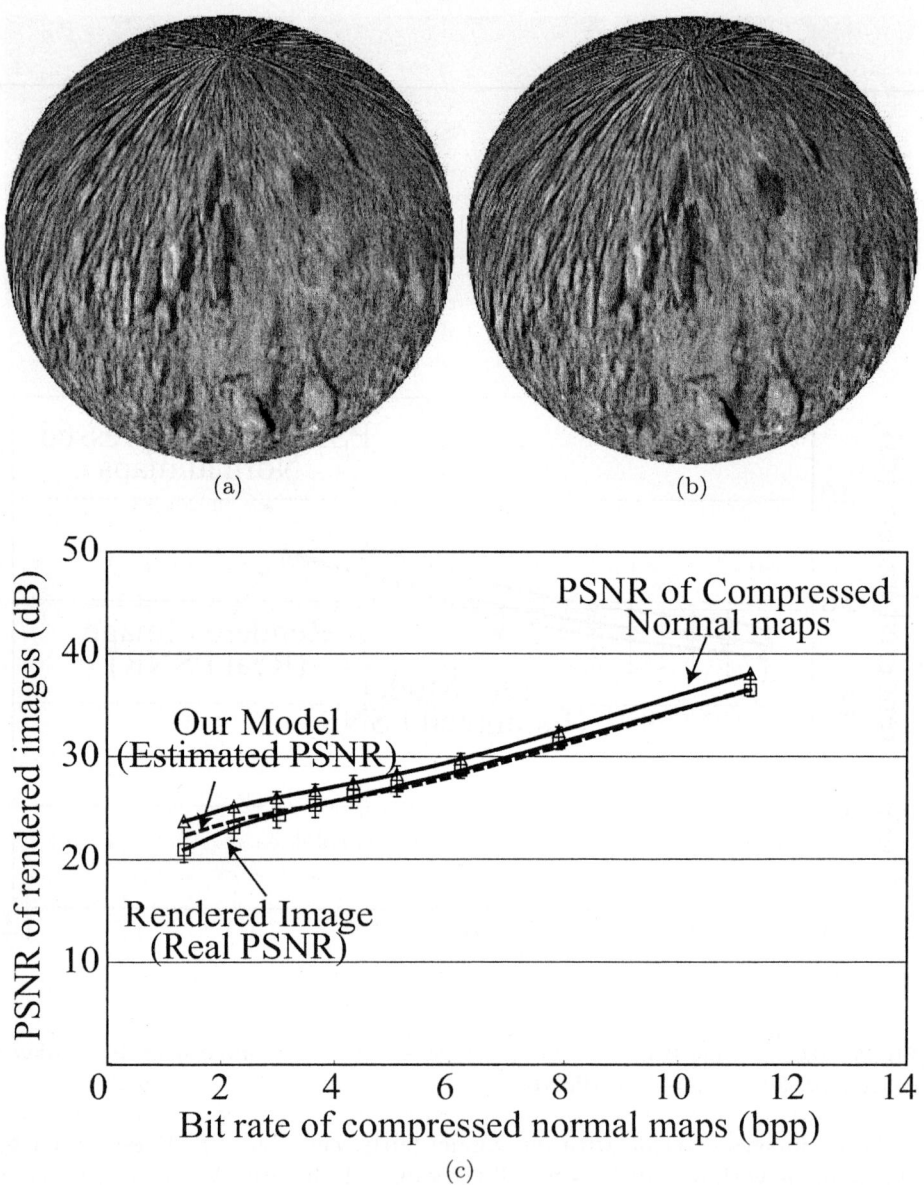

Fig. 6. Experimental results when normal map was rendered on sphere: (a) rendered image at $\theta=30$ and $\phi=45$; (b) rendered image at $\theta=30$ and $\phi=45$ with normal map compressed at 3bpp; (c) PSNR. Txture and normal map of Fig. 3 was used.

pressed normal maps. In particular, the prediction accuracy is pretty good in practical PSNR region.

The PSNR when the normal map of the rocky texture (see Fig. 3) was attached to a sphere is illustrated in Fig. 6. Since the rim of the sphere is almost black and does not contribute to the quality degradation, 20% of the area on the rim was not included in PSNR calculation. It is demonstrated that our PSNR model is robust to the variation of the shapes of 3D objects and predicts the actual PSNR properly in spite of its simple form of equation.

In case detailed quality evaluation under more complicated scene where our simple assumption does not hold any more is required, the parameters such as kinds and positions of light sources, shape of objects, color texture, reflectance factors, and so on need to be involved in Eqs. (4) and (5). It is the trade-off between the computational cost and acurracy of quality evaluation.

5 Conclusions

We have developed a mathematical model between the error of lossy compressed normal maps and its influence on the 3D images. By assuming some simple conditions and taking averages of the parameters that cannot be defined uniquely, the model has been made simple. The generality and robustness of our PSNR model for rendered 3D images have been demonstrated by experiments. As a result, it has been made possible to decide compression ratios of normal maps considering the target quality of final rendered images.

Acknowledgements

A part of this work is financially supported by Ministry of Education, Culture, Sports, Science and Technology under the "Development of fundamental software technologies for digital archives" project. The authors would like to thank Mr. Jianfeng Xu, Mr. SeungRyong Han, and Mr. Ryuji Nakamura for their insightful discussions.

References

1. J.F. Blinn, "Simulation of wrinkled surfaces," Proc. the 5th annual conference on Computer graphics and interactive techniques, vol. 12, no. 3, pp.286-292, 1978.
2. J.D. Foley, A. Dam, S.K. Feiner, and J.F. Hughes, "Computer Graphics PRINCIPLES AND PRACTICE, 2nd Edition," Addison-Wesley Publishing Company, 1996.
3. J.F. Blinn, "Texture and Reflection in Computer Generated Images," Comm. ACM, vol. 19, no. 10, Oct. 1976, pp. 542-547.
4. G.S. Miller and C.R. Hoffman, "Illumination and Reflection Maps: Simulated Objects in Simulated and Real Environments," Proc. Siggraph 84, Course Notes for Advanced Computer Graphics Animation, ACM Press, New York, 1984.
5. M. M. Oliveira, G. Bishop, and D. McAllister, "Relief texture mapping," Pros. Siggraph2000, Computer Graphics Proceedings, pp. 359-368, 2000.
6. M. J. Kilgard, "A practical and robust bump-mapping technique for today's GPUs," Game Developers Conference, Advanced OpenGL Game Development, 2000.

7. M. Peercy, A. Airey, and B. Cabral, "Efficient Bump Mapping Hardware," Proceedings of SIGGRAPH 97, August 3-8, pp 303-306. 1997.
8. T. Ikedo and E. Ohbuchi, "A Realtime Rough Surface Renderer," Proc. of Computer Graphics International 2001 (CGI2001), pp. 355-358, 2001.
9. G. Miller, M. Halstead, and M. Clifton, "On-the-Fly Texture Computation for Real-Time Surface Shading," IEEE Computer Graphics and Applications, vol. 18, no. 2, March-April 1998.
10. J.M. Dischler, D. Ghazanfarpour, "A survey of 3D texturing," Computer & Graphics 25, pp. 135-151, 2001.
11. M.L. Smith, T. Hill, G. smith, "Surface texture analysis based upon the visually acquired perturbation of surface normals," Image and Vision Computing 15, pp. 949-955, 1997.
12. S.T. Oh and K.H. Lee, "Bump map generation from 3D scan data," Proceedings of the 2003 International Conference on Geometric Modeling and Graphics, pp. 180-185, 2003.
13. http://www.opengl.org/
14. http://www.microsoft.com/windows/directx/default.aspx
15. T. Yamasaki, K. Hayase, and K. Aizawa, "Mathematical Error Analysis of Normal Map Compression Based on Unity Condition," Proceedings of 2005 IEEE International Conference on Image Processing (ICIP2005), Sep 11-14 2005 (accepted).
16. R. Nakamura, T. Yamasaki, and K. Aizawa, "JPEG Optimization for Efficient Bump Map Compression," Proc. of the 2005 IEICE General Conf., D-11-17, March, 2005 [In Japanese].
17. S. Green, "Bump Map Compression Whitepaper," http://download.nvidia.com/developer/Papers/2004/Bump_Map_Compression/Bump_Map_Compression.pdf, Oct. 2004.
18. "ATI RADEON X800 3Dc white paper," http://www.ati.com/products/radeonx800/3DcWhitePaper.pdf.
19. "Bump Texture Library," Computer Graphics Systems Development Corporation, http://cgsd.com/.

Fast Adaptive Skin Detection in JPEG Images

Qing-Fang Zheng[1,2] and Wen Gao[1,2]

[1] Institute of Computing Technology, Chinese Academy of Sciences,
No.6 Kexueyuan South Road, Zhongguancun,
Haidian District, Beijing, China, 100080
[2] Graduate School of Chinese Academy of Sciences,
Beijing, China, 100039
qfzheng@jdl.ac.cn, wgao@jdl.ac.cn

Abstract. Skin region detection plays an important role in a variety of applications such as face detection, adult image filtering and gesture recognition. To improve the accuracy and speed of skin detection, in this paper, we describe a fast adaptive skin detection approach that works on DCT domain of JPEG image and classifies each image block according to its color and texture properties. Main contributions of our skin detector are: 1) It jointly takes into consideration the color and texture characteristics of human skin for classification and can adaptively control the detection threshold according to image content; 2) It requires no full decompression of JPEG compressed images and directly derives color and texture features of each image block from DCT coefficients. Comparisons with other existing skin detection techniques demonstrate that our algorithm can compute very fast and achieve good accuracy.

1 Introduction

Color is an obviously distinguishing feature of an object. Pattern recognition methods based on color can be invariant to object rotation, translation and deformation. Specifically, skin color can provide a useful and robust cue for human-related image analysis, such as face detection and pornographic image filtering. Numerous techniques have been propose to detect human skin color regions in still images, for example, [1, 2, 3, 4, 5, 6, 7], to name just a few. These techniques can be generally summarized as pixel-based detection with static skin color models: a static skin color model is learned off-line and each input image pixel is checked according to the learned skin color model. If a pixel's color value satisfies the model, it is marked as skin pixel, otherwise, it is marked as non-skin pixel.

Despite the enormous research efforts that have been devoted, two requirements for skin detection still remain challenging: accuracy and efficiency. As for accuracy requirement, we mean that skin detection should be robust to imaging conditions and not biased by human race. Skin color varies among different human races and can change greatly under different illumination conditions. Therefore, skin detection methods that use static skin color models can not function properly in unconstrained conditions. To alleviate the limitations of static methods and to improve the accuracy of skin detection, adaptive techniques have been introduced [8, 9, 10]. However, these techniques need full decompression of JPEG images to pixels domain and iterative operations to select the most appropriate skin model, such as iterative region segmentation in Phung's method [8], iterative thresholding on Gaussian mixture model in Quan's method [9] and iterative update of thresholding-box on H-S color component in Cho's method [10].

Both full decompression of JPEG image and iterative operations bring about the problem of computational burden. Sacrificing efficiency for accuracy may be tolerated in some applications, but not in some other applications. For example, in adult images filtering systems [1, 3], skin detection is a preliminary step to identify benign images with few skin pixels and pass images with sufficiently large skin regions for further examination. The computation cost of skin detection can significantly affect the efficiency of the overall system. To improve the accuracy and efficiency of skin detection, we propose an adaptive block-based skin detection approach in this paper. Our approach works on compressed domain and determines each image block according to its color and texture properties. We focus our effort on JPEG images because these type of images are mostly used in web and the work reported here is part of our current project to develop a system to block pornographic web images. Skin detection in JPEG compressed domain has been previously introduced in [11], our approach differs from [11] in feature extraction method and classification method. Two main contributions of our approach are:

1. Our skin detector jointly takes into consideration the color and texture characteristics of human skin for classification and can adaptively control the detection threshold according to image content;
2. Our skin detector is very fast. It requires no full decompression of JPEG compressed images and directly derives color and texture features of each image block from DCT coefficients.

The rest of the paper is organized as follows: Section 2 gives an overview of our approach followed by detailed descriptions in Section 3. Section 4 presents our empirical study and Section 5 concludes the paper.

2 Overview

The basic to-be-process image unit in our algorithm is 4×4 image block, we note here that we have tried different block sizes including 8×8 and 2×2 and we found 4×4 block size yields the best result, so far as accuracy and speed are jointly concerned. First, compressed JPEG image data are Huffman decoded and de-quantized to get the DCT coefficients of each 8×8 image block. Since JPEG image data are compressed using 8×8 block, we need to decompose each 8×8 block to four 4×4 sub-blocks and we then directly extracted color and textural features of each sub-block from their DCT coefficients. Each block is classified into skin and non-skin block using an initial threshold, adjacent skin blocks forms

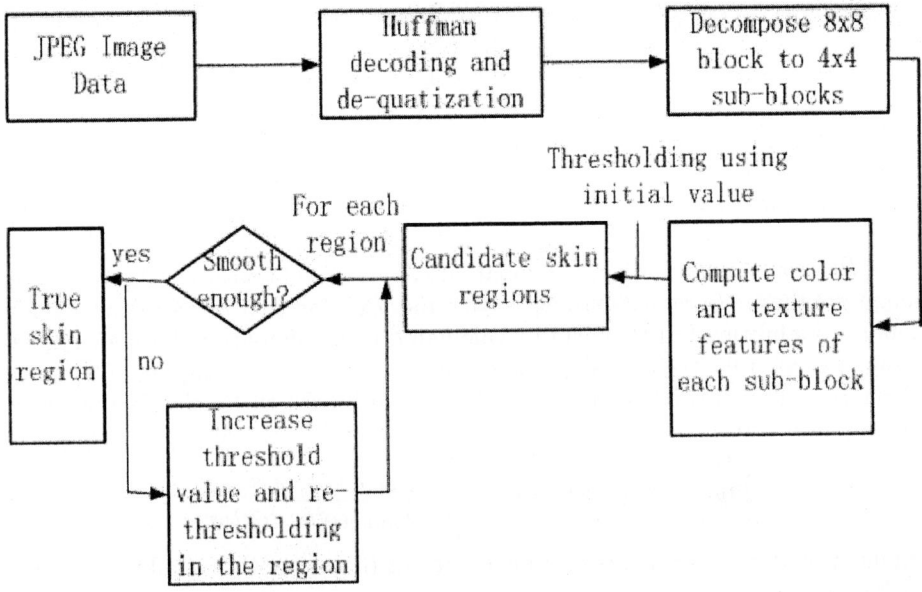

Fig. 1. Schematic description of our skin detection algorithm

a candidate skin region. For each candidate skin region, we examine whether it is smooth enough. If candidate skin region is smooth enough, it is decided as true a skin region, else, we increase the threshold and use the updated threshold to remove noise blocks in the candidate region. This process iterates until each skin region is smooth. The outline of our algorithm is schematically shown in Fig.1. Although iterative operations are still needed to find the optimal threshold value, our algorithm works on compressed image domain and thus can compute on the fly. Details of computational complexity analysis is presented in section 4.1.

3 Details

This section provides detailed description of three core components of our approach: skin classifier, adaptive threshold selection and feature extraction in JPEG compressed domain.

3.1 Skin Classifier

The task of skin detection is to classify each image block (or pixel) into skin or non-skin categories. Although there exist many sophisticated classifiers, we opt for Bayesian classifier because its effectiveness in skin detection has been shown previously [1]. For an image block with color feature *color* and textural feature *texture*, its posterior probability of being human skin region can be calculated as:

$$P(skin|color, texture) = P(color, texture|skin) \times \frac{P(skin)}{P(color, texture)} \quad (1)$$

Its posterior probability of being non-skin can be calculated as:

$$P(\neg skin|color, texture) = P(color, texture|\neg skin) \times \frac{P(\neg skin)}{P(color, texture)} \quad (2)$$

Here, $P(color, texutre)$ are joint probability of color and texture in the domain of image database. $P(color, texture|\neg skin)$ and $P(color, texture|skin)$ are conditional probabilities and they can be calculated using histogram method. For example, we can use a training skin image dataset to obtain a histogram $H_{skin}(x, y)$ where $H_{skin}(color, texutre)$ is the count of skin blocks with color feature $color$ and textural feature $texture$, then we can get the conditional probability as:

$$P(color, texture|skin) = \frac{H_{skin}(color, texture)}{\sum H_{skin}(color, texture)} \quad (3)$$

Similarly, we can use a non-skin image dataset to get another conditional probability as:

$$P(color, texture|\neg skin) = \frac{H_{\neg skin}(color, texture)}{\sum H_{\neg skin}(color, texture)} \quad (4)$$

To avoid the computation of joint probability $P(color, texture)$, we dived (1) by (2) and have:

$$\frac{P(skin|color, texture)}{P(\neg skin|color, texture)} = \frac{P(color, texture|skin)}{P(color, texture|\neg skin)} \times \frac{P(skin)}{P(\neg skin)} \quad (5)$$

When (5) is larger than a predefined threshold, the image block is classified as skin region. Since the class prior $P(skin)$ and $P(\neg skin)$ are unknown constants, we can fold them into the threshold, so our skin classifier is:

$$F(color, texture) = \frac{P(color, texture|skin)}{P(color, texture|\neg skin)} > \tau \quad (6)$$

Two major aspects distinguish our classifier from [1]. Firstly, [1] is pixel-based and only the pixel's color feature can be used for classification. As a comparison, ours is block-based and, besides color features, additional textural feature can make classification more robust. Secondly, [1] use a fixed threshold obtained by trial-and-error, while our threshold is automatically controlled according to image content, which will be described in section 2.2.

3.2 Adaptive Thresholding

The threshold value τ is crucially important for accurate classification. If the threshold is too low, many non-skin regions will be mistaken as true skin regions. On the other hand, if the threshold is too high, many true skin regions will be wrongly classified as non-skin regions. Traditional selection of threshold value τ is through trial-and-error and the final decision is a "global optimal" one that strikes balance between precision and recall on the validation dataset, which, however, may not be suitable for each image. An alternative is to find optimum thresholds for each image according to its content. We observe that human skin region in image usually cover a certain area that are larger than 4×4 pixels (more than one skin block), and skin region are usually homogeneous in texture property. This observation inspires us with an adaptive threshold selection mechanism. We can initially set the threshold with a relatively small one and image blocks that satisfy equation (6) are marked as skin blocks. Adjacent skin blocks forms a candidate skin regions, which may not miss true skin region but may include non-skin regions. True skin regions and non-skin regions together will make the candidate skin regions exhibit dis-homogeneous texture property. Then we increase the threshold, say, $\tau = \alpha\tau(1 < \alpha)$, and skin blocks who no longer satisfy (6) are removed from candidate skin regions. The process repeats until candidate skin region become homogeneous and then marked as true skin region. Actually, we adopt a coarse-to-fine selection, which is in spirit similar to [8].

3.3 Feature Extraction

In JPEG compression scheme, color images use YCbCr color space and each individual color component is compressed separately. Image data are compressed in 8×8 block called data unit and Discrete Cosine Transform (DCT) is employed to convert the data unit values into a sum of cosine functions. Conventional skin detection approaches need to decode the images to the pixel domain first and require inverse DCT (IDCT). Our feature extraction directly works on DCT domain and bypasses the IDCT, which is computationally expensive. We adopt YCbCr color space to describe image block's color feature: $color = [y, cb, cr]$. The reason for this adoption is twofold: First, it is consistent with JPEG compression scheme and avoid the computation for color space conversion. Second, previous work has demonstrate YCbCr is more valid than other color spaces for skin detection [5]. The reason for us to choose block as basic processing unit is as follows:

- It's also consistent with JPEG compression scheme, and color and texture features can be directly extracted.
- It can speed up the detection (see section 4.1 for analysis).
- Besides color feature, additional available texture feature can make our skin detection more robust (see section 4.2 for comparison).

To describe block's texture feature, we adopt intensity variance in Y color component: $texture = \sigma^2(y)$. The more homogeneous a region is, the smaller its $texture$ is. We denotes DCT coefficients of an 4×4 image block to be $F^X_{(u,v)}$, where X denotes color component, and u and v represents frequency indices.

According to the definition of 2D DCT:

$$F_{(u,v)} = \frac{1}{2}C(u)C(v)\sum_{i=0}^{3}\sum_{j=0}^{3} f_{(i,j)} \cos\frac{(2i+1)u\pi}{8} \cos\frac{(2j+1)v\pi}{8} \tag{7}$$

The corresponding inverse DCT is:

$$f_{(i,j)} = \frac{1}{2}\sum_{u=0}^{3}\sum_{v=0}^{3} C(u)C(v) F_{(u,v)} \cos\frac{(2i+1)u\pi}{8} \cos\frac{(2j+1)v\pi}{8} \tag{8}$$

where

$$C(u) = \begin{cases} \frac{1}{\sqrt{2}}, & u=0 \\ 1, & others \end{cases} \tag{9}$$

So the mean value of the block is:

$$\mu_{block} = \frac{1}{16}\sum_{i=0}^{3}\sum_{j=0}^{3} f_{(i,j)}$$

$$= \frac{1}{32}\sum_{u=0}^{3}\sum_{v=0}^{3} C(u)C(v) \times \sum_{i=0}^{3}\cos\frac{(2i+1)u\pi}{8}\sum_{j=0}^{3}\cos\frac{(2j+1)v\pi}{8} \tag{10}$$

Since

$$\sum_{i=0}^{3}\cos\frac{(2i+1)u\pi}{8} = \begin{cases} 4, & u=0 \\ 0, & others \end{cases} \tag{11}$$

We get:

$$\mu_{block} = \frac{1}{4}F_{(0,0)} \tag{12}$$

So we can compute block's color feature as:

$$color = [\frac{1}{4}F^{Y}_{(0,0)}, \frac{1}{4}F^{Cb}_{(0,0)}, \frac{1}{4}F^{Cr}_{(0,0)}] \tag{13}$$

The block's texture property is computed as:

$$texture_{block} = \sigma^2_{block} = \frac{1}{16}[\sum_{i=0}^{3}\sum_{j=0}^{3} f^2_{(i,j)}] - \mu^2_{block} \tag{14}$$

According to Parseval's theorem:

$$\sum_{i=0}^{3}\sum_{j=0}^{3} f^2_{(i,j)} = \sum_{u=0}^{3}\sum_{v=0}^{3} F^2_{(u,v)} \tag{15}$$

Equation (14) can be reformulated as:

$$texture_{block} = \frac{1}{16}[\sum_{u=0}^{3}\sum_{v=0}^{3} (F^Y_{(u,v)})^2 - (F^Y_{(0,0)})^2]$$

$$= \frac{1}{16}\sum_{u=0}^{3}\sum_{v=0}^{3} (F^Y_{(u,v)})^2, (u,v) \neq (0,0) \tag{16}$$

For an image region containing N adjacent blocks, texture property can be similarly computed as:

$$texture_{region} = \sigma^2_{region}$$

$$= \frac{1}{16N}\sum_{k=1}^{N}\sum_{i=0}^{3}\sum_{j=0}^{3}[F_k^Y(i,j)]^2 - [\frac{1}{4N}\sum_{k=1}^{N}F_k^Y(0,0)]^2 \qquad (17)$$

$$= \frac{1}{N}[\sum_{k=1}^{N}texture_{block} + \frac{1}{16}\sum_{k=1}^{N}(F_k^Y(0,0)))^2] - [\frac{1}{4N}\sum_{k=1}^{N}F_k^Y(0,0)]^2$$

Since natural block size in JPEG is 8×8, we have to decompose each block to four sub-blocks. Let F_{88} denote DCT coefficient of a 8×8 block, and let $F_{44}^i, (i = 0, 1, 2, 3)$ denote the coefficients of corresponding 4×4 sub-blocks. We can have:

$$\begin{bmatrix} F_{44}^0 & F_{44}^1 \\ F_{44}^2 & F_{44}^3 \end{bmatrix} = 2CF_{88}C^T \qquad (18)$$

where C is the transcoding matrix, and readers are referred to [12] for more details.

4 Experiment

Our experiments are designed to answer the following questions:

1. What is the performance (accuracy and speed) of our skin detector?
2. What is the gain of using both color and texture feature over using only color feature?

4.1 Experiment A

To evaluate the accuracy and efficiency of our adaptive block-based skin detection algorithm, we compare our method with the adaptive methods proposed by Phung [8] and non-adaptive method proposed by Jones [1]. We study true positive (TP) and false positive (FP) of each method. True positive is defined as the ratio of the number of ground truth skin pixels identified to the total number of skin pixels. False positive is defined as the ratio of the number of non-skin pixels misclassified as skin pixels, to the total number of non-skin pixels. The more accurate an algorithm is, the higher TP and lower FP it will have. As for efficiency, we calculate the time (in milliseconds) used to detect all the images in test set by each method. Each algorithm is implemented using C++ programming language and we run each algorithm five times to get the average time. The experiments are done on a 1GHz Pentium IV PC running Microsoft Windows 2000 operation system.

The dataset used in this experiment includes 3000 face images and 300 adult images. Face images are from ECU face database [8]. Adult images are downloaded from Internet and for offensive reason, we don't present adult images in

Table 1. Comparison results of three skin detectors

	Ours	Jones's[1]	Phung's[8]
TP	85.24%	82.27%	85.09%
FP	4.60%	4.61%	5.14%
Time(ms)	85,744	166,667	472,110
Average Speed (fram/second)	12.82	6.60	2.33

this paper. We use 2200 images for training and 1100 images for test. All skin detectors are trained on the same training data and tested on the same testing data. Testing data contains 53,412,219 skin pixels and 235,305,733 non-skin pixels. Skin and non-skin pixels are manually labelled.

Table 1 lists the comparison of accuracy and efficiency of three skin detectors. As can be seen from the table, our skin detector outperforms two counterparts in both accuracy and speed. In terms of accuracy, our detector surpasses two others with higher TPs and lower FPs. Compared with Jones's non-adaptive method, our method gains 2.97% in TP while their FPs are almost identical. Compared with Phung's adaptive method, our method increases 0.15% in TP and decreases 0.54% in FP. The superiority of our detector lies in the fact that we jointly take human skin's color and texture property into account and

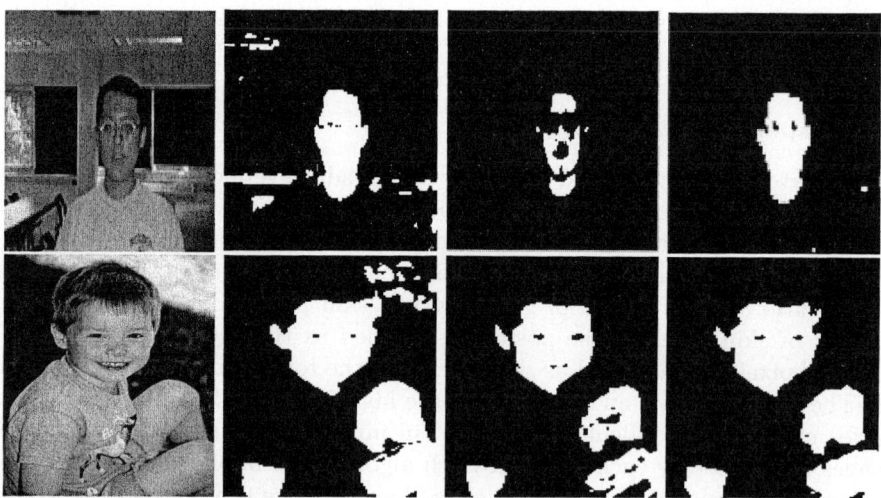

Fig. 2. Some example images. The first column is original image, the second column is the detection result using a small threshold, the third column is the detection result using a high threshold and the fourth cloumn is detection result by our adaptive threshold. The white regions denotes the detected skin regions.

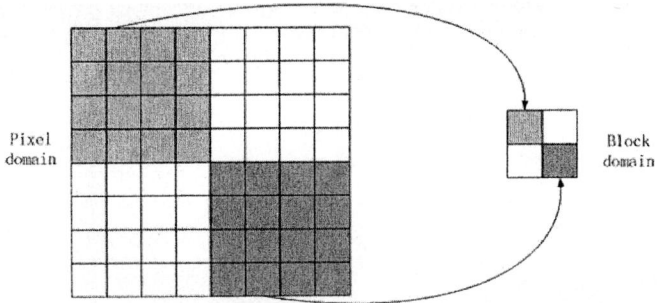

Fig. 3. Each block contains 16 pixels. If we consider each block as a "pixel" in "block domain image", the block domain image's size is only $\frac{1}{16}$ to that of original image.

adaptively select the most appropriate threshold for each image. Although both our detector and Phung's use similar adaptive methods, the difference of their accuracy are mainly due to the features they used, which we further explore in experiment B. We give two skin detection results in Fig. 2, which also clearly demonstrated the effectiveness of the adaptive threshold selection mechanism. In terms of computational speed, the average speed of ours is nearly doubled compared with Jones's method and is almost 6 times as fast as that of Phung's method. The gain of speed can be attributed to three facts. First, our approach works on compressed domain and avoids the time-consuming IDCT. Second, our method derives color and texture features directly from DCT coefficients. Each block (16 pixels) needs only 3 multiplication to compute color value and 15 multiplications and additions to compute texture feature. For further computation of texture feature of a region consisting of N block, only another $N + 5$ multiplication and $3N + 1$ additions are required. Third, each 4×4 block is considered as a whole and as a basic processing unit. Iterative segmentation is performed on block domain as if on an image whose size is only $\frac{1}{16}$ of original image (see Fig. 3).

4.2 Experiment B

This experiment demonstrates the advantage of using both color and texture features in our skin detector. The dataset used here including 100 images containing no human skin regions but lion, food, dessert, plant and so on. These objects share similar color with human skin but differ in texture property. We compare our skin detection method with Phung's [8], because these two method adopt similar adaptive mechanism but different features: Phung's method only consider the color feature of each pixel while ours takes into account both color and texture of each image block. Fig. 4 lists some detection results. These examples clearly shows jointly consideration of color and texture property can significantly decease FP in these images. We note here this is very important

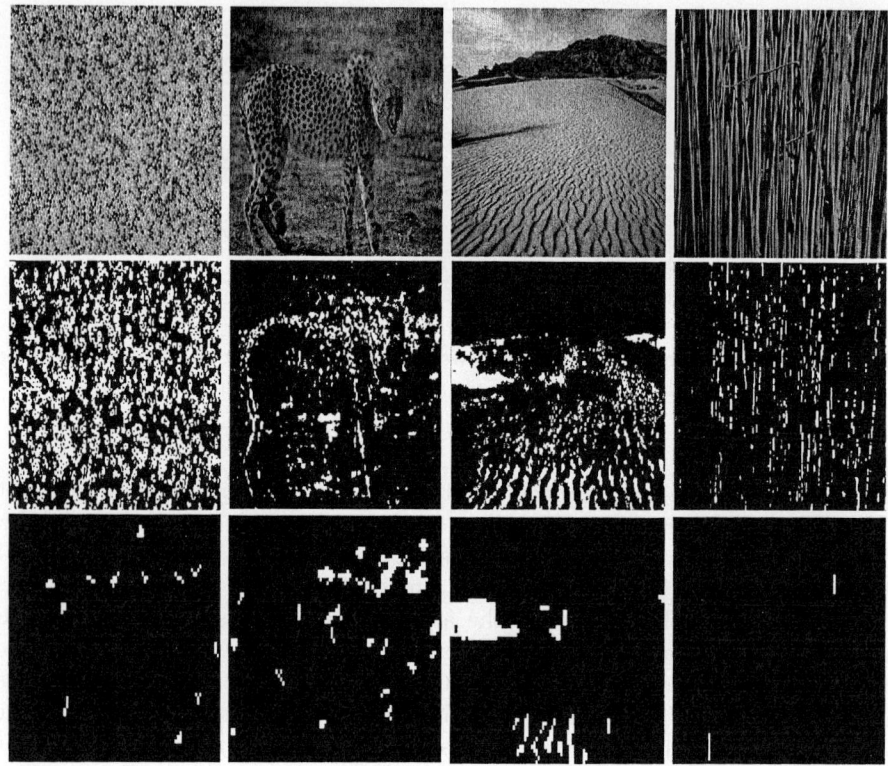

Fig. 4. Skin detection results. Images in the top row are original images, images in middle row are detection results by Phung's method, and images in bottom row are our results. The white regions denotes the detected skin regions.

for our adult web image filtering application, because when these images are detected as containing large skin regions they will more likely be classified as adult images.

5 Conclusion and Future Works

In this paper, we focus on improving the accuracy and speed of skin detection in JPEG compressed images. To speed up detection, our skin detector works on JPEG compressed domain and directly derives color and texture features from DCT coefficients, thus circumvents the computational expensive inverse Discrete Cosine Transform operation. To improve accuracy, we jointly consider texture and color property of human skin region and use an adaptive threshold selection method the find the optimal threshold for detection. We report experimental results to demonstrate the high accuracy and low computational complexity of our approach. In future work, we will integrate the skin detection algorithm with other techniques to develop a robust content-based adult web image filtering system.

Acknowledgements

This work has been financed by the National Hi-Tech R&D Program (the 863 Pro-gram) under contract No.2003AA142140.

References

1. Jones, M.J. and Rehg, J.M.: Statistical Color Models with Application to Skin Detection, IJCV(46), No. 1, January 2002, pp. 81-96.
2. Hsu, R.L, Abdel-Mottaleb, M. and Jain, A.K.: Face Detection in Color Images, IEEE Trans. Pattern Analysis and Machine Intelligence, Vol 24, Issue 5, May 2002, pp.696-706.
3. Fleck, M.M , Forsyth, D.A, and Bregler, C.: Finding naked people ECCV 1996, pp: 593-602.
4. Greenspan, H., Goldberger, J., and Eshet, I.: Mixture Model for Face Color Modeling and Segmentation, Pattern Recognition Letters, vol.22, September 2001, pp.1525-1536.
5. Phung, S.L., Bouzerdoum A., Chai D.: A Novel Skin Color Model in YCbCr Color Space and Its Application to Human Face Detection. International Conference on Image Processing, vol. 1, pp.289-292. 2002
6. Phung, S.L., Bouzerdoum, Chai, D.: Skin Segmentation Using Color Pixel Classification: Analysis and Comparison. IEEE Trans. On Pattern Analysis and Machine Intelligence. vol.27, No.1,pp.148-154, 2005
7. Yang, J., Tan, T., Hu, W.: Skin color detection using multiple cues, International Conference on Pattern Recognition, vol.1, pp.632-635, August. 2004
8. Phung, S.L., Chai, D., and Bouzerdoum, A.: Adaptive Skin Segmentation in Color Images, IEEE International Conference on Acoustics, Speech and Signal Processing - Proceedings, vol 3, 2003, pp. 353-356.
9. Quan,H.T, Meguro, M. and Kaneko, M.: Skin-Color Extraction in Images with Complex Background and Varying Illumination, Sixth IEEE Workshop on Applications of Computer Vision (WACV02), 2002, pp.280-285.
10. Cho, K.M., Jang, J.H. and Hong, K.S.: Adaptive Skin-Color Filter, Pattern Recognition, Volume 34, Issue 5, May, 2001, pp 1067-1073.
11. Butler, D., Sridharan, S., Chandran, V.: Chromatic Colour Spaces For Skin Detection Using GMMs, ICASSP'02, 2002.
12. Jiang, J., Armstrong, A.J. and Feng, G.C.: Direct Content Access and Extraction From JPEG Compressed Images, Pattern Recognition, Vol.35, 2002, pp.2511-2519.

Effective Blocking Artifact Reduction Using Classification of Block Boundary Area

Jung-Youp Suk, Gun-Woo Lee, and Kuhn-Il Lee

School of Electrical Engineering and Computer Science, Kyungpook National University,
1370 Sankyuk-dong, Puk-gu, Daegu 702-701, South Korea
youbi75@naver.com, teiler@lycos.co.kr, kilee@knu.ac.kr

Abstract. This paper proposes a new blocking artifact reduction algorithm using an adaptive filter based on classifying the block boundary area. Generally, block-based coding, such as JPEG and MPEG, introduces blocking and ringing artifacts to an image, where the blocking artifact consists of grid noise, staircase noise, and corner outliers. In the proposed method, a 1D low-pass filter reduces staircase noise and corner outliers. Next, the block boundaries are divided into two classes based on the gradient of the pixel intensity in the boundary region. For each class, an adaptive filter is applied so that the grid noise is reduced in the block boundary regions. Thereafter, for those blocks with an edge component, the ringing artifact is removed by applying an adaptive filter around the edge. Finally, high frequency components are added to those block boundaries where the natural characteristics have been lost due to the adaptive filter. The computer simulation results confirmed a better performance by the proposed method in both the subjective and objective image qualities.

1 Introduction

When using JPEG [1], H.261, H.263, and MPEG [6] as block-based image and video coding standards, inter- and intra-block degradation of the image quality can occur. As such, blocking and ringing artifacts are two of the main phenomena caused by these block-based coding algorithms. Moreover, the discontinuity effect between adjacent blocks in decompressed images is more serious for highly compressed image. Consequently, an efficient blocking artifacts reduction scheme is essential for preserving the visual quality of compressed images.

The blocking artifact consists of the grid noise, staircase noise, and corner outlier. Grid noise appears as a slight change of image intensity along a block boundary in a monotone area. Staircase noise represents the discontinuation of a continuous edge located among blocks. A corner outlier is visible at the corner point of a block, where the corner point is either much larger or much smaller than the neighboring pixels. Plus, improper truncations of high frequency components introduce a pseudo-edge called the ringing artifact.

The iterative POCS-based recovery algorithm has been proposed [7]. But, this algorithm has the drawback of the computational complexity. It has been proposed a filtering algorithm in wavelet transform that used for the characterization of edges and singularity in multiscales [8]. This algorithm needs to accurately classify quantization errors in multiscales.

A spatial LPF (low pass filter) is widely used to eliminate the blocking artifact. Ramamurthi et al [2] classify an image into monotone and edge blocks. Then a 2-D LPF is applied to remove any grid noise in the monotone block and a 1-D LPF is applied to remove the staircase noise in the edge block parallel to the edge block, respectively. However, the classifier used in this algorithm is inaccurate, therefore, the edge block can be blurred if it is classified as a monotone block.

H. C. Kim et al [3] proposed an algorithm using an SAF (signal adaptive filter) based on global, local, and contour edge maps obtained using a sobel operator plus the mean and variance of the pixel gradient in the block. A 2-D SAF is applied to all the blocks based on the global and local edge maps, whereas a 1-D LPF is applied along the edge using the contour edge map. The corner outlier is replaced with the mean value of the weighted corner-point pixels. This algorithm produces a better image quality than the algorithm proposed by Ramamurthi et al [2] and works well in eliminating grid noise yet not staircase noise.

The algorithm proposed by S. D. Kim et al [4] classifies an image into smooth region and default modes using the pixel difference in the block boundary. A 1-D LPF is applied to the smooth region mode, then, according to the frequency components in the block boundary, an LPF is applied to the default mode. Although this algorithm can conserve the complex region, it does not eliminate the blocking artifact in the edge region.

Chung J. Kuo et al [5] classifies blocks with visible blocking effects according to the visibility, and then detects edge in the visible blocks. A space-variant lowpass filter is employed to smooth the pixels at block boundary of the visible blocks and edge neighborhood in those blocks. As this algorithm employ the filters per block, it may be blurred the pixels except the edges in the visible blocks. It must be needed the detailed filtering.

Accordingly, this paper proposes a blocking artifact reduction algorithm using an adaptive filter based on the classification of the block boundary area. A 1-D 3-tap filter is applied in the entire block boundary to eliminate the staircase noise and corner outlier. Next, the bloc k boundary representing the blocking artifact is classified into monotone and smooth edge regions. A 1-D 5-tap SAF and 2-D 3-tap SAF are then applied to the monotone and smooth edge region, respectively, and a 2-D 3-tap SAF is applied to the edge block to eliminate the ringing artifact. When an SAF is applied to the block boundary and edge block, an edge map is used to conserve the characteristic of the edge.

However, since an LPF is applied to the block boundary in which the blocking artifact occurs, high frequency components around the block boundary are improperly eliminated. Therefore, to obtain a more natural image, dithering is applied in the filtered block boundary.

To test the proposed algorithm, experiments were performed on images coded using baseline JPEG [1] and MPEG TM5 [6]. The experimental results confirmed that the proposed algorithm is superior to the conventional algorithm due to the adaptive filter and dithering.

2 Proposed Blocking Artifacts Reduction Algorithm

A blocking artifact reduction algorithm is proposed using an adaptive filter based on classifying the block boundary area. An SAF is applied to the entire block boundary to eliminate the staircase noise and corner outlier. Then an SAF is applied to the edge block and block boundary with the blocking artifact. Finally, high frequency noise is embedded in the filtered block boundary to produce a natural image.

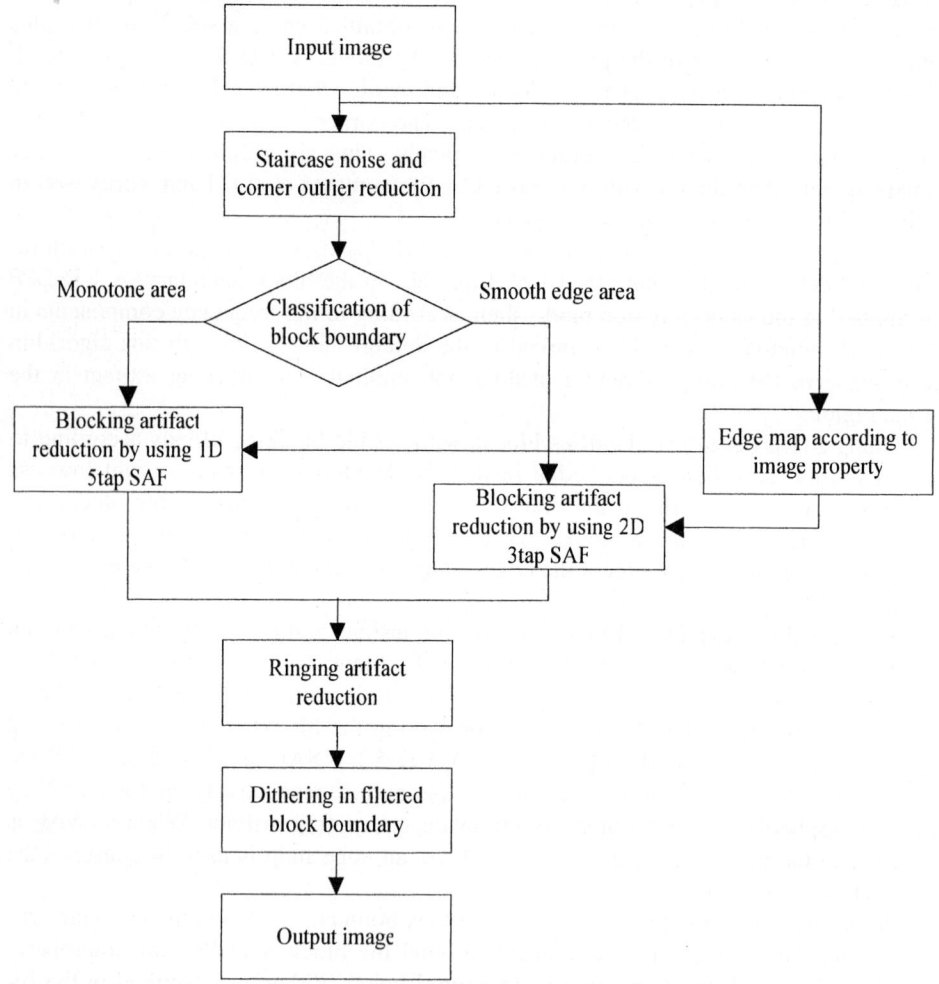

Fig. 1. Block diagram of the proposed method

2.1 Reduction of the Staircase Noise and Corner Outlier

At all the horizontal and vertical of block boundaries, a 1-D 3-tap pre-filter is performed to reduce the staircase noise and corner outlier, as shown in Fig. 2.

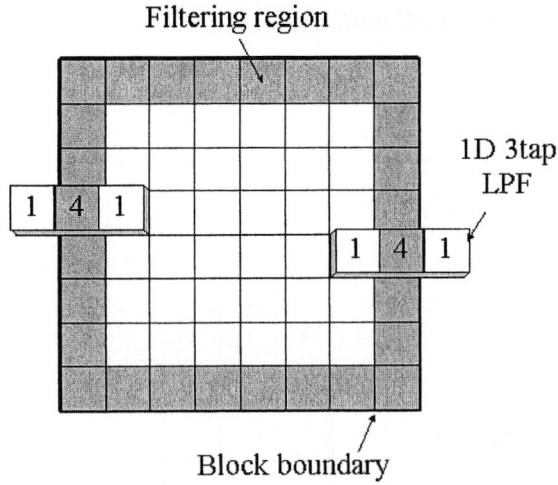

Fig. 2. 1-D 3-tap filtering at block boundary

2.2 Determination of Blocking Artifacts and Classification of Block Boundary

The existence of blocking artifacts is determined using the intensity change rate of the 6 pixels within a block boundary, as shown in Fig. 3. If blocking artifacts are found to exist, the block boundary is classified into one of two regions. First, the intensity difference between two neighboring pixels, D_n is calculated as follows:

$$D_n = |x_{n+1} - x_n|, \qquad n = 0, 1, \cdots, 4 \qquad (1)$$

If D_n is larger than any other intensity difference, the blocking artifact is decided to exist within the block boundary. Within the block boundary, if $D_0 = D_1 = D_3 = D_4 = 0$ and $D_2 > 0$ then it is classified as a monotone area, whereas if $D_1 > 0$, $D_3 > 0$ and $D_2 > D_1$, $D_2 > D_3$, then it is classified as a smooth edge area.

2.3 Edge Map According to Image Property

The SAF applied in the proposed method requires an edge map to preserve an edge. This edge map is created by comparing a threshold value, T_n with an absolute gradient value calculated by a sobel operator. T_n is calculated as follows:

$$T_n = T_g - \sigma_n \qquad (2)$$

where σ_n is the standard deviation of each block, and T_g is the global threshold value.

$$T_g = \alpha Q_f - \beta \qquad (3)$$

Where Q_f is the quantization factor, and α and β are experimentally determined.

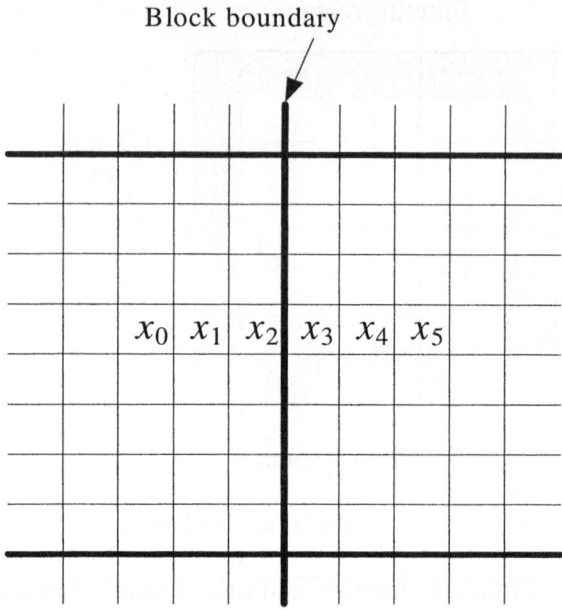

x_i: pixel value

Fig. 3. 6 pixels for classification within block boundary area

2.4 Adaptive SAF According to the Classification of Block Boundary

To reduce any staircase noise still remaining after the 1-D LPF in section 2.1, an SAF is performed on the two classified regions. If there is an edge in the filtering mask, the pixels at that location as well as the direction of the edge are not included in the filtering. That is, the weighting values of the filtering mask are set to zero at that location, as shown in Fig. 4. A 1-D 5-tap SAF is performed to smooth the block boundary within a monotone area, whereas a 2-D 3-tap SAF is performed within a smooth edge area, as shown in Figs. 4 and 5.

2.5 Reduction of Ringing Artifact

To reduce the ringing artifact appearing as a pseudo-edge in the neighborhood of the original edge, a 2-D SAF is performed on the edge blocks as shown in Fig. 5. Every block is tested as to whether it contains an edge as follows:

$$\sigma_n \geq \sigma_m \tag{4}$$

where σ_n is the standard deviation of the current block, and σ_m is the mean value of the standard deviation in all blocks. If σ_n is larger than σ_m, the block is determined as an edge block.

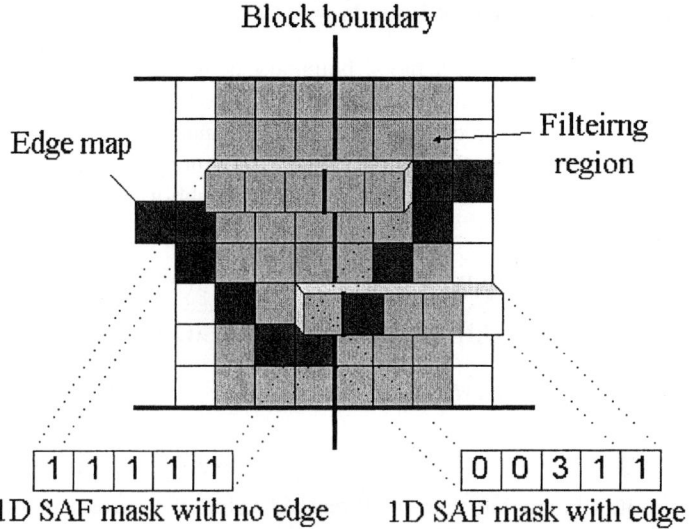

Fig. 4. 1-D 5-tap SAF within monotone area

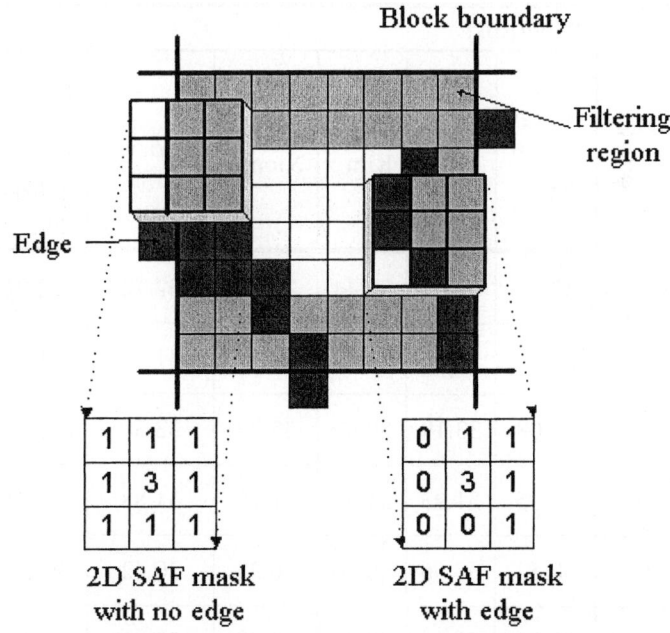

Fig. 5. 2-D 3-tap SAF within smooth edge area

2.6. Dithering in Filtered Block Boundary

When an LPF is performed on a block boundary determined as having a blocking artifact, the high frequency in the neighboring block boundary can be illegally removed, as a result, the filtered image will appear unnatural. Accordingly, dithering is performed in the filtered block boundary to obtain a more natural image. The intensity differences between a current pixel and its 4-neighboring pixels are calculated as follows:

$$t_1 = |x(1,1) - x(0,1)|, \quad t_2 = |x(1,1) - x(2,1)|$$
$$t_3 = |x(1,1) - x(1,0)|, \quad t_4 = |x(1,1) - x(1,2)| \quad (5)$$
$$max(t_1, t_2, t_3, t_4) < T_n / 6$$

where $x(1,1)$ is the current pixel, and T_n is the threshold value. If the maximum value among these values is smaller than the threshold value, the current pixel is added to uniform random noise within a 3% limit.

Table 1. PSNR of the proposed method and conventional methods on still images

Test image	Qf	PSNR[dB]						
		JPEG decoding	H. C. Kim	S. D. Kim	Z. Xiong	Y. Yang	Proposed method	
							Before dithering	After dithering
LENA	2	32.53	32.67	32.44	32.71	32.72	32.91	32.69
	3	31.31	31.68	31.36	31.72	31.58	31.89	31.69
BOAT	2	33.08	33.19	32.93	33.24	33.30	33.59	33.39
	3	31.55	31.93	31.56	31.95	31.88	32.21	32.04
BANK	2	30.52	30.66	30.50	30.33	30.42	30.73	30.61
	3	29.21	29.54	29.26	29.28	29.21	29.62	29.52

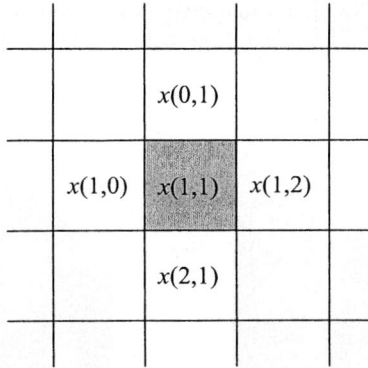

Fig. 6. The pixel to be dithered and four neighbor pixels

Table 2. PSNR of the proposed method and conventional methods on FOOTBALL sequences

Bit rate	Average PSNR[dB]				
	MPEG decoding	H. C. Kim	S. D. Kim	Proposed method	
				Before dithering	After dithering
TM5 1Mbps	28.23	28.27	27.96	28.37	28.33
TM5 1.5Mbps	30.26	30.16	29.35	29.93	29.84

3 Experimental Results

Computer simulations were carried out to demonstrate the effect of the proposed method on reducing the blocking artifact in JPEG and MPEG decoded images.

The proposed method was applied to test images decoded using baseline JPEG [1], such as LENA, BOAT, and BANK with a size of 512×512, and test sequences decoded using MPEG TM5 [6], such as FOOTBALL with a size of 352×288, using 30 frames. Its sequence was compressed at the condition that GOP is 12, I/P frame distance is 3, 25 frame/sec, and progressive scan method at 1 Mbps and 1.5 Mbps. Although the PSNR is not always a good objective measure of image quality, it is still one of the most popular criteria and, therefore, used as the objective measure in the current experiments. The parameters used in Eq. (3), α and β, were experimentally determined as 45 and 35, respectively.

The PSNR results for the post-processed images using JPEG decoding with quantization factors of 2 and 3 are summarized in Table 1. The proposed method produced a 0.07~0.4 dB higher PSNR than the conventional methods. Fig. 7 shows a magnified portion of LENA using JPEG decoding with a quantization factor 3 and the post-processed image.

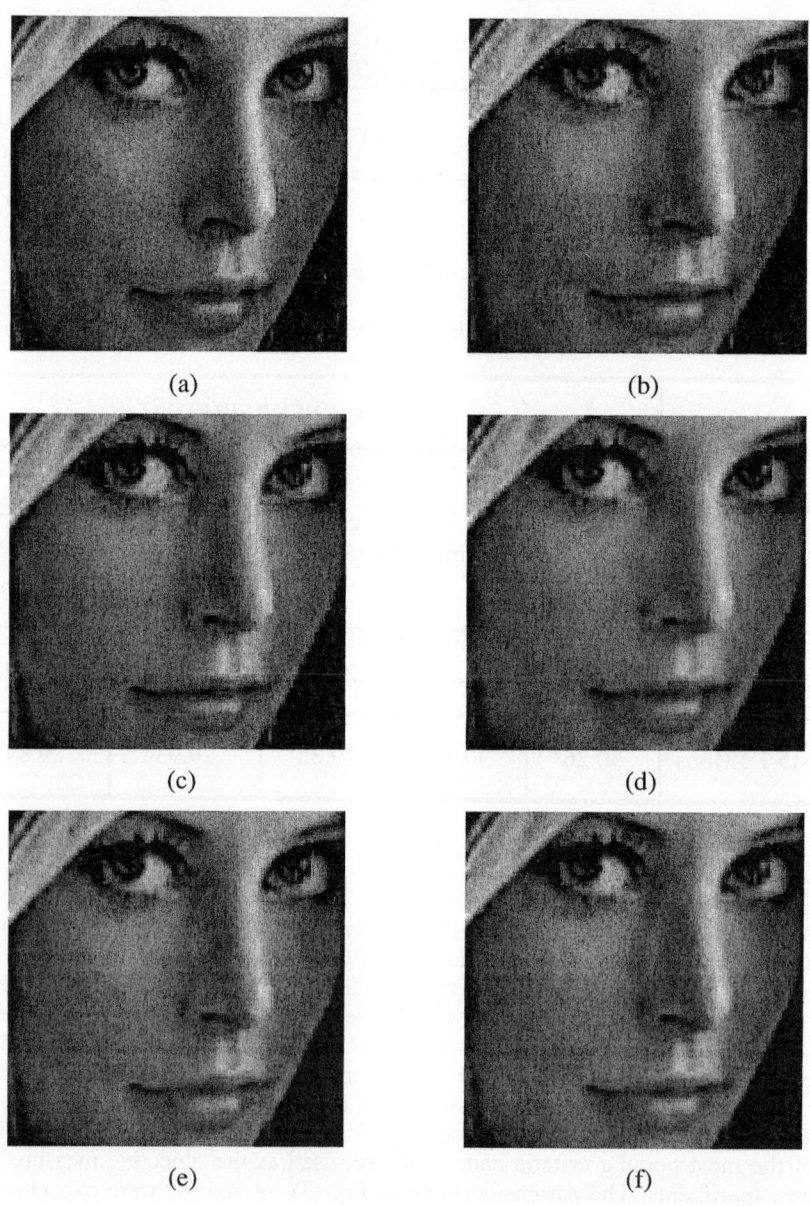

Fig. 7. (a) Original LENA image, (b) JPEG decoded image, (c) S. D. Kim method, (d) H. C. Kim method

Table 2 is shown that the average PSNR of the proposed algorithm is about 0.5 dB higher than that of MPEG sequences. Fig. 8 shows FOOTBALL using MPEG decoding and the post-processed image. The image processed by the proposed method appeared to reduce the blocking artifacts.

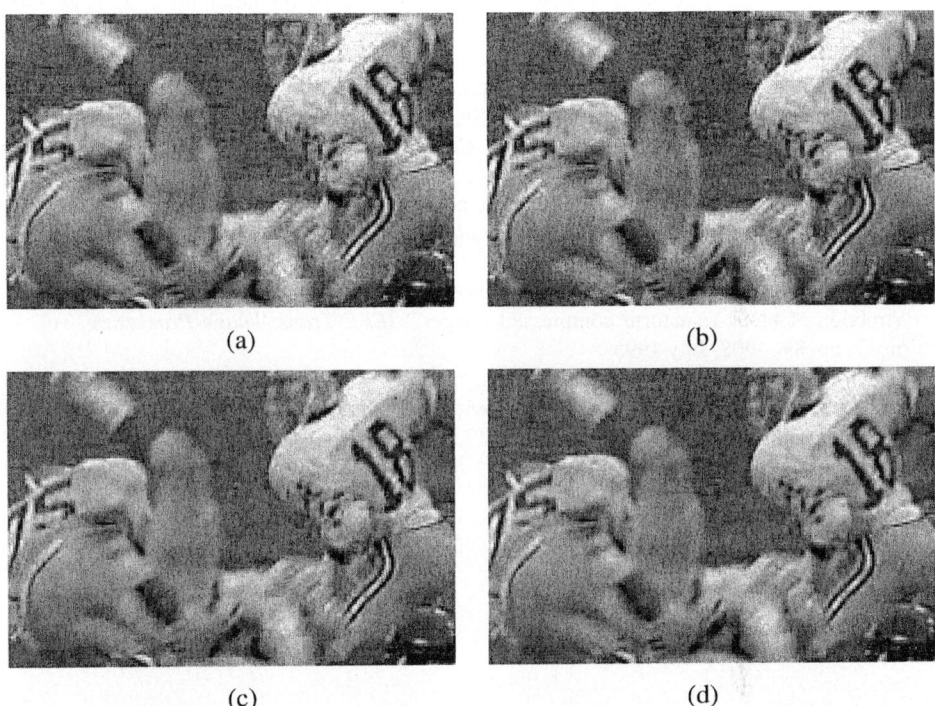

Fig. 8. (a) 1Mbps MPEG decoded image and post-processed images by (b) S. D. Kim method, (c) H. C. Kim method, and (d) proposed method (after dithering)

4 Conclusions

A blocking artifact reduction algorithm was proposed using an adaptive filter based on classifying the block boundary area. A 1-D 3-tap filter is applied to the entire block boundary to eliminate the staircase noise and corner outlier. Next, the block boundaries representing blocking artifacts are classified into monotone and smooth edge regions. A 1-D 5-tap SAF and 2-D 3-tap SAF are applied to the monotone and smooth edge regions respectively, and a 2-D 3-tap SAF is applied to the edge block to eliminate the ringing artifact. When the SAF is applied to the block boundary and edge block, an edge map is used to conserve the characteristic of the edge. To obtain more natural image high frequency noise is embedded in the filtered block boundary. In the experiments of JPEG and MPEG at various images, the performance of the proposed algorithm could be confirmed that was better than that of the conventional algorithm in viewpoint of PSNR and subjective image quality.

References

1. G. K. Wallace, "The JPEG still picture compression standard," *IEEE Trans. Consumer Electronics*, vol. 38, no. 1, pp. 108-124, Feb. 1992.
2. B. Ramamurthi and A. Gersho, "Nonlinear space variant postprocessing of block coded images," *IEEE Trans. Acoustics, Speech, Signal Processing*, vol. 34, no. 5, pp. 1258-1268, Oct. 1986.
3. H. C. Kim and H. W. Park, "Signal adaptive postprocessing for blocking effects reduction in JPEG image," *Proc. ICIP*, vol. 2, no. 1, pp. 41-44. Sep. 1996.
4. S. D. Kim, J. Y. Yi, H. M. Kim, and J. B. Ra, "A deblocking filter with two separate modes in block-based video coding," *IEEE Trans. Circuits and Systems for Video Technology*, vol. 9, no. 1, pp. 156-160, Feb. 1999.
5. Chung J. Kuo and Ruey J. Hsieh, "Adaptive postprocessor for block encoded images," *IEEE Trans. Circuits and System for Video Technology,* vol. 5, pp. 298-304, Aug. 1995.
6. *ISO/IEC JTC1/SC29/WG11/602,* "MPEG test model 5 draft revision 2,", Nov. 1993.
7. Y. Yang, N. Galatsanos, and A. Katsaggelos, "Projection-based spatially adaptive reconstruction of block-transform compressed images," *IEEE Trans. Image Processing*, vol. 4, no. 7, pp. 896~908, July 1995.
8. Z. Xiong, M. T. Orchard, and Y. Q. Zhang, "A deblocking algorithm for JPEG compressed images using overcomplete wavelet representations," *IEEE Trans. Circuits and Systems for Video Technology*, vol. 7, no. 2, pp. 433~437, Apr. 1997.

Adaptive Rate-Distortion Optimization for H.264

Kwan-Jung Oh and Yo-Sung Ho

Gwangju Institute of Science and Technology (GIST),
1 Oryong-dong Buk-gu, Gwangju, 500-712, Korea
{kjoh81,hoyo}@gist.ac.kr

Abstract. In video coding standards, such as MPEG-4 and H.263, one important question is how to determine motion vectors for motion compensation in the INTER mode. Usually the sum of absolute differences (SAD) or the sum of squared differences (SSD) is employed as a matching criterion. Although these criteria are related to the distortion, they do not consider the bit rate appropriately. If we want to consider both the rate and the distortion, a Lagrangian technique targeting for rate-distortion optimization (RDO) is a good alternative. Even if H.264 used the RDO scheme to decide the best macroblock mode among several candidates, H.264 employs only one RDO model for all macroblocks. Since the characteristics of each macroblock is different, each macroblock should have its own RDO model. In this paper, we propose an adaptive rate-distortion optimization algorithm for H.264. We regulate the Lagrangian multiplier according to the picture type and characteristics of each macroblock.

Keywords: Adaptive RDO, Lagrangian Multiplier, H.264.

1 Introduction

Motion-compensated transform video coding, also called as hybrid video coding, provides a good combination of data compression tools. In various video coding standards, motion vectors are determined by the sum of absolute differences (SAD) or the sum of squared differences (SSD), related to the distortion of the motion prediction. However, these criteria do not consider the bit rate. Thus, different matching criteria have been proposed to consider both the distortion and the bit rate [1].

A common way of formulating such a criterion is the Lagrangian optimization, which is adopted in H.264 for selecting the best macroblock mode. Usually, the Lagrangian multiplier λ is only defined as a function of the quantization parameter (QP). However, the optimal choice of λ should depend on the characteristics of each macroblock as well as QP [2].

The current rate-distortion optimization (RDO) model used in H.264 is applied to each macroblock, but it does not provide the optimization of the whole sequence. However, this problem can be improved by using an adaptive RDO model. There have been previous efforts that incorporate perceptual characteristics into video coding. However, they have focused on the perceptual distortion which is related to the human visual system (HVS). Despite of slightly improved performance with respect to HVS, they cannot provide good performance in terms of the rate and distortion [2].

In this paper, we propose an adaptive rate-distortion optimization algorithm for H.264. After we find a Lagrangian multiplier for each picture through several experiments, we regulate the Lagrangian multiplier for each macroblock considering characteristics of each macroblock. We take the distortion variance as the characteristics of each macroblock.

The distortion variance is obtained after the motion estimation process. During motion estimation, we calculate distortions for several different modes. We get the distortion variance from the distortions of 16×16, 16×8, and 8×16 modes. The distortion variance reflects the characteristics of each macroblock. If the distortion variance is small, this macroblock belongs to a flat area. While we give more weights to the rate part of the RDO model when the macroblock belongs to a flat area, we give more weights to the distortion part of the RDO model when the macroblock belongs to a complex area. In this manner, we can optimize the rate and the distortion for the whole sequence more efficiently.

This paper is organized as follows. After the Lagrangian optimization in hybrid video coding is explained in Section 2, we propose an adaptive RDO algorithm in Section 3. In Section 4, experimental results show effectiveness of the proposed algorithm, and we conclude this paper in Section 5.

2 Lagrangian Optimization

2.1 Optimization Using Lagrangian Techniques

Consider K source samples that are collected from the set $S = (S_1, \cdots, S_k)$. Each source sample S_k can be quantized using several possible coding options that are indicated by an index out of the set $O_k = (O_{k1}, \cdots, O_k)$. Let $I_k \in O_k$ be the selected index for a code S_k.

The coding options assigned to the elements in S are given by the components in the set $I = (I_1, \cdots, I_k)$. The problem of finding the combination of coding options that minimizes the distortion subject to a given rate constraint R_C can be formulated as

$$\min_I D(S, I)$$
$$\text{subject to } R(S, I) \le R_C \tag{1}$$

where $D(S, I)$ and $R(S, I)$ represent the total distortion and bit rate, respectively. These parameters result from the quantization of S with a particular combination of coding options I. In practice, rather than solving the constrained problem in Eq. (1), an unconstrained formulation is employed, that is

$$I^* = \arg\min_I J(S, I \mid \lambda)$$
$$\text{with } J(S, I \mid \lambda) = D(S, I) + \lambda \cdot R(S, I) \tag{2}$$

and $\lambda \ge 0$ being Lagrange parameter. I^* in Eq. (2) is optimal in the sense that if a rate constraint R_C corresponds to λ. The total distortion $D(S, I^*)$ is minimum for all combinations of coding options with bit rate less or equal to R_C [3].

Assume that the additive distortion and rate measures only depend on the choice of the parameter corresponding to each sample. Then, a simplified Lagrangian cost function can be computed by using

$$J(S_k, I \mid \lambda) = J(S_k, I_k \mid \lambda) \tag{3}$$

In this case, the optimization problem reduces to

$$\min_I \sum_{k=1}^{K} J(S_k, I \mid \lambda) = \sum_{k=1}^{K} \min_{I_k} J(S_k, I_k \mid \lambda) \tag{4}$$

and can be easily solved by independently selecting the coding option for each $S_k \in S$. For this particular scenario, the problem formulation is equivalent to the bit-allocation problem for an arbitrary set of quantizers, proposed by Shoham and Gersho [4].

2.2 Lagrangian Optimization in Hybrid Video Coding

The Lagrangian technique can be used for the motion estimation. The motion estimation is so heavy process that we do not employ the Lagrangian technique for the motion estimation. However, the efficiency of the macroblock mode decision can be improved by Lagrangian technique. In previous video coding standards, the macroblock mode is determined by using the previously coded macroblock [5]. However, the coding mode for each macroblock should be determined using the Lagrangian cost function. Assume that Lagrangian parameter λ_{MODE} and the quantizer value Q were given. The Lagrangian mode decision for a macroblock S_k proceeds by minimizing

$$J_{MODE}(S_k, I_k \mid Q, \lambda_{MODE}) = D_{REC}(S_k, I_k \mid Q) + \lambda_{MODE} R_{REC}(S_k, I_k \mid Q) \tag{5}$$

where the macroblock mode I_k varies as the sets of possible macroblock modes for the various standards.

MPEG-2: SKIP, 16×16, INTRA
H.263/MPEG-4: SKIP, 16×16, 8×8, INTRA
H.264: SKIP, 16×16, 16×8, 8×16, P8×8, I16×16, I4×4

H.264 additionally provides the following sets of sub-macroblock types for P8×8:

8×8, 8×4, 4×8, 4×4

The distortion $D_{REC}(S_k, I_k|Q)$ and the rate $R_{REC}(S_k, I_k|Q)$ for the various modes are computed as follows: For INTRA modes, the corresponding 4×4 blocks (H.264) or 8×8 blocks (MPEG-2, H.263/MPEG-4) of the macroblock S_k are processed by transformation and subsequent quantization. The distortion $D_{REC}(S_k, \text{INTRA}|Q)$ is measured by calculating SSD between the reconstructed (s') and the original (s) macroblock pixels

$$SSD = \sum_{(x,y) \in A} |s[x, y, t] - s'[x, y, t]|^2 \tag{6}$$

where A is the subject macroblock. The rate $R_{REC}(S_k, \text{INTRA}|Q)$ is the rate that results after entropy coding.

For SKIP mode, the distortion $D_{REC}(S_k, INTRA|Q)$ and the rate $R_{REC}(S_k, INTRA|Q)$ do not depend on the current quantizer value. The distortion is determined by SSD between the current picture and the value of the inferred INTER prediction.

The computation of the Lagrangian costs for INTER modes is much more demanding than for INTRA and SKIP modes. This is because of the block motion estimation step. Given the Lagrangian parameter λ_{MOTION} and the decoded reference picture s', the rate-constrained motion estimation for a block S_i is performed by minimizing the Lagrangian cost function

$$m_i = \arg\min_{m \in M}\{D_{DFD}(S_i, m) + \lambda_{MOTION} R_{MOTION}(S_i, m)\} \tag{7}$$

where m is the set of possible coding modes. Eq. (7) has the distortion term given by

$$D_{DFD}(S_i, m) = \sum_{(x,y) \in A_i} |s[x, y, t] - s'[x - m_x, y - m_y, t - m_t]|^P \tag{8}$$

with $p=1$ for SAD and $p=2$ for SSD. $R_{MOTION}(S_i, m)$ is the number of bits used to transmit all the components of the motion vector (m_x, m_y), and m_t when multiple reference frames are used. The search range M is ±32 integer pixel positions horizontally and vertically and either one or more previously decoded pictures are referenced. Depending on SSD or SAD, the Lagrangian parameter λ_{MOTION} has to be adjusted.

The Lagrangian parameter λ_{MODE} for H.263/MPEG-4 is obtained by the following equation:

$$\lambda_{MODE} = 0.85 \cdot Q^2_{H.263} \tag{9}$$

The corresponding λ_{MOTION} for SAD or SSD is as follows, respectively:
For SAD

$$\lambda_{MOTION} = \sqrt{\lambda_{MODE}} \tag{10}$$

In case of SSD,

$$\lambda_{MOTION} = \lambda_{MODE} \tag{11}$$

By conducting the same experiment that leads to the relationship in Eq. (8) again for H.264, λ_{MODE} is obtained as follows:

$$\lambda_{MODE} = 0.85 \cdot 2^{(Q_{H.264} - 12)/3} \tag{12}$$

The corresponding λ_{MOTION} for H.264 is calculated by Eq. (10) and Eq. (11).
Following equation is the cost function which is used in H.264

$$J_{MODE}(s, r, MODE | \lambda_{MODE}) = \\ SSD(s, r, MODE) + \lambda_{MODE} \cdot R(s, r, MODE) \tag{13}$$

where s and r represent the current block and the reference block, respectively. *MODE* represents the various macroblock modes [6].

3 Adaptive Rate-Distortion Optimization

Since H.264 encoder employs many sophisticated schemes in the coding procedure, the H.264 video coding standard achieves much higher coding efficiency than the previous video coding standards such as H.263 and MPEG-4. One important scheme is variable block size motion estimation and mode decision. Generally, the motion estimation is performed on the macroblock level, thus each macroblock needs one motion vector which can lead to a minimum block matching error.

However, when the macroblock contains multiple objects and every object moves in different directions or when the macroblock lies on the boundary of a moving object, only one motion vector will not be enough to represent real motions. It will result in serious prediction error. In order to improve the prediction accuracy, H.264 uses seven different modes which are SKIP, 16×16, 16×8, 8×16, P8×8, I16×16, and I4×4. Using these various macroblock modes, the efficiency of the motion estimation and the motion compensation of H.264 is improved. Figure 1 shows these modes.

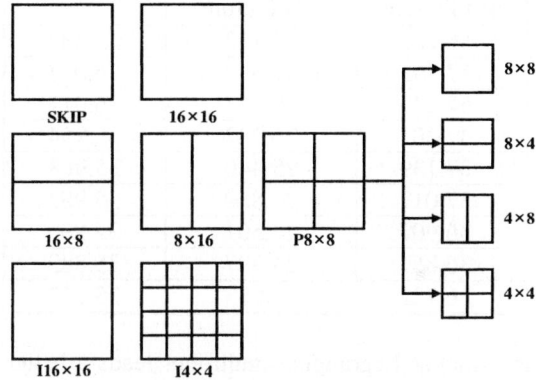

Fig. 1. Various Macroblock Modes

A problem of the mode selection is how to select the best macroblock mode among several modes. The Lagrangian cost function in Eq. (13) provides the solution for this problem. During the encoding process, all macroblock modes are examined and the resulting rate and the distortions are calculated. The mode that has the minimum Lagrangian cost is selected as the best mode for the macroblock [7].

However, as we can see from the Lagrangian function in Eq. (13), there is no parameter which reflects characteristics of a given macroblock. H.264 uses only one RDO model for all macroblocks for whole sequence. Although the current RDO model provides the best result for each macroblock, it does not lead to the optimization of whole sequence. Since the each picture type and characteristics of each macroblock are different, RDO model need to be changed to the adaptive RDO model considering picture type and characteristics of macroblock. After we find the proper Lagrangian multiplier for each picture, we expand it into macroblock level.

3.1 Adaptive Lagrangian Multiplier for Each Picture

In hybrid video coding, the structure of GOP (group of picture) influences the whole coding efficiency. GOP is consists of the one I picture and several other kinds of pictures. IPPP··· and IBBP··· are good examples of the GOP structures. Picture types also influence the coding efficiency. Among them, I picture is most important since it used as a reference picture for P picture. So, it is not too much to say that I picture runs the coding efficiency of the given GOP. In order to evaluate the influencing power of I picture, we employ the first 90 frames from the FOREMAN sequence in QCIF format 176×144 and QP is 28. GOP structure is IPPP... and intra period is 30. Search range is ±32. Table 1 shows the simulation results. We yield the results for whole sequence by changing the Lagrangian multiplier from 0.1 to 0.8 for I picture.

Table 1. Influencing Power of I Picture for FOREMAN

Lagrangian Multiplier	PSNR (dB) of I Picture	Bit Rate (bits) of I Picture	PSNR (dB)	Bit Rate (kbits/s)
Original (0.85)	36.763	24,112	35.837	116.69
0.1	37.893	31,632	36.067	122.69
0.2	37.579	28,387	36.011	119.60
0.3	37.302	26,232	35.954	117.58
0.4	37.139	25,440	35.968	118.13
0.5	37.017	24,880	35.903	116.87
0.6	36.907	24,501	35.900	116.91
0.7	36.861	24,397	35.889	116.71
0.8	36.722	24,083	35.852	116.17

As we can see, the smaller Lagrangian multiplier leads a better quality but needs larger bits. We have done extensive experiments to obtain the proper Lagrangian multiplier for I and P picture. We yield the results by changing the Lagrangian multiplier from 0.2 to 0.4 for I picture and from 0.9 to 1.1 for P picture.

Table 2. Lagrangian Multiplier and Its Coding Efficiency for FOREMAN

Lagrangian Multiplier	PSNR (dB)	Bit Rate (kbits/s)	ΔPSNR (dB)	ΔBit Rate (kbits/s)
Original (0.85, 0.85)	35.837	116.69	0	0
0.2, 0.9	35.941	118.16	0.104	1.47
0.2, 1.0	35.804	114.63	-0.033	-2.06
0.2, 1.1	35.750	112.99	-0.087	-3.70
0.3, 0.9	35.878	116.02	0.041	-0.67
0.3, 1.0	35.762	113.11	-0.075	-3.58
0.3, 1.1	35.654	110.46	-0.183	-6.23
0.4, 0.9	35.867	115.57	-0.030	-1.12
0.4, 1.0	35.737	112.17	-0.100	-4.52
0.4, 1.1	35.640	110.60	-0.197	-6.09

As we can see, if we well select the Lagrangian multiplier for each picture, we can get a better coding efficiency. A better coding efficiency means that we can get better quality in spite of using less bits. Through the extensive experiments, we set the Lagrangian multiplier which shows the best coding efficiency for several test sequences.

To derive the general Lagrangian multiplier for picture, we investigate the best Lagrangian multiplier for eight QCIF sequences. Table 3 shows the proposed Lagrangian multiplier and comparison of coding efficiency between H.264 and proposed algorithm. We use the first 90 frames from the eight test video sequences in QCIF format and QP = 28. Other test conditions are same with the test conditions of previous experiments.

Table 3. Proposed Lagrangian Multiplier and Its Coding Efficiency

Test Sequences	Lagrangian Multiplier (I, P Picture)	H.264 PSNR (dB)	Proposed PSNR (dB)	H.264 Bit Rate (kbits/s)	Proposed Bit Rate (kbits/s)
AKIYO	0.3, 1.0	38.725	38.873	38.85	38.64
CARPHONE	0.3, 0.9	37.486	37.538	100.88	100.76
CONTAINER	0.3, 1.1	36.461	36.545	49.37	48.31
FOREMAN	0.4, 0.9	37.837	35.867	116.69	115.57
MOBILE	0.2, 0.9	33.607	33.633	421.89	418.03
MOTHER & DAUGHTER	0.2, 1.0	36.599	36.626	92.54	91.78
NEWS	0.3, 1.0	37.063	37.293	83.74	83.57
SALESMAN	0.3, 1.1	35.825	36.045	74.57	74.37
Average	0.2875, 0.975				

From Table 3 we can know most Lagrangian multipliers are similar and most results show better coding efficiency than H.264 coding efficiency. The PSNR values are increased and bit rates are decreased. From the results of previous experiments, we can get the general Lagrangian multiplier for I picture and P picture in case of QP=28. The values are 0.2875 and 0.9875. However these values are adaptively changed by QP. If QP is increased Lagrangian multiplier for I picture should be increased and Lagrangian multiplier for P picture should be decreased. In this manner, we experiment for several QP and we can obtain following equation from these results.

$$\text{Lagrangian multiplier for I Picture}$$
$$\lambda_{MODE} = \frac{QP}{\alpha} \cdot 2^{(Q_{H.264}-12)/3}$$
$$\text{Lagrangian multiplier for P Picture} \quad (14)$$
$$\lambda_{MODE} = \left(1.2 - \frac{QP}{\beta}\right) \cdot 2^{(Q_{H.264}-12)/3}$$

where, α is 97 and β is 132. Since I picture use more bits than original I picture, we give more weights to the rate part of the RDO model for P pictures.

3.2 Adaptive Lagrangian Multiplier for Each Macroblock

In the previous section, we proposed the adaptive Lagrangian multiplier for picture. Even though we proposed adaptive RDO model for each picture, the macroblocks in same picture still use a same RDO model. Now, we derive the adaptive RDO model for each macroblock considering the characteristics of each macroblock.

We change the previous RDO model as follows:

$$J_{MODE}(s,r,MODE \mid \lambda_{MODE}) = \\ SSD(s,r,MODE) + \chi \cdot \lambda_{MODE} \cdot R(s,r,MODE) \tag{15}$$

where χ is the new parameter, which reflects the characteristics of the macroblock. To derive the χ, firstly we introduce a parameter which is called log-scaled standard deviation (LSD). LSD is calculated for 16×16, 16×8, and 8×16 modes.

$$LSD = \log\left(\sqrt{\frac{1}{3}\sum_{MODE=0}^{2}(M_{distortion} - D_{MODE})^2}\right) \tag{16}$$

where $M_{distortion}$ is the mean value of the distortion corresponding to each mode, and D_{MODE} is the distortion of a given mode. By using LSD, χ is calculated by

$$\begin{aligned} &if\ (LSD_{cur} < LSD_{mean}) \\ &\quad \chi = 1 - \frac{|LSD_{mean} - LSD_{cur}|}{20\delta} \\ &else \\ &\quad \chi = 1 + \frac{|LSD_{mean} - LSD_{cur}|}{20\delta} \end{aligned} \tag{17}$$

where LSD_{cur} represents the LSD value for current macroblock and LSD_{mean} is the mean value of the LSD until the previous macroblock. Through this procedure, we obtain χ which is around 1. Since the rate is more sensitive with respect to RDO than the distortion, we use different denominator. δ reflects the characteristics of the given sequence. δ is derived by

$$\delta = \frac{I_{bitrate}}{V \times H} + \sqrt{\frac{255^2}{10^{\frac{PSNR}{10}}}} \tag{18}$$

where $I_{bitrate}$ is the number of coded bits for first I-frame. V and H represent vertical size and horizontal size of the given image, respectively. So the first term of the right-hand side of Eq. (18) is the average value of the bit per pixel for I-frame and the second term is the square-rooted MSE. The reason why δ is defined as Eq. (18) is because each sequence has different characteristics. If motional characteristics of a sequence is monotonous, δ is small or otherwise, δ shall be large.

In this section, we propose the adaptive rate-distortion optimization algorithm for each macroblock. The proposed RDO model depends on χ as well as on the previous parameters such as QP, distortion, and bit rate. In this way, we can save the bits in the flat area and can assign more bits to the complex area. In the latter case, although the proposed algorithm needs more bits, it can be compensated in next frames through the motion compensation. Smaller amount of distortion leads to better motion estimation and better motion estimation leads to the bit saving. Figure 2 shows the flow diagram of the proposed algorithm.

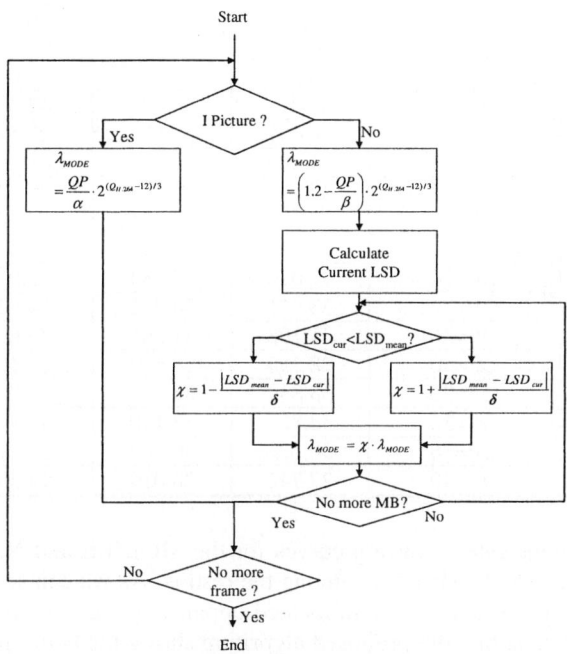

Fig. 2. Flow Diagram of the Proposed Algorithm

4 Experimental Results and Analysis

In order to evaluate the performance of the proposed algorithm, we use the first 120 frames from the five test video sequences (AKIYO, FOREMAN, MOBILE, NEWS, and SALESMAN) in QCIF format 176×144. JM 9.5 is used to conduct the experiments [8]. The Hadamard transform, CABAC, and reconstruction filter are enabled. In the motion estimation, five reference frames are enabled with the maximum search range ±32 and the motion vector resolution is 1/4 pixel. The frame rate is 30 fps and the frame coding structure is IPPP···P. Intra period is 30. The experiments are performed for four quantization parameters QP=28, 32, 36, and 40. We perform the two experiments. At first, we experiment about the efficiency of the adaptive RDO model for each picture. Then we combine this scheme with the adaptive RDO model for each macroblock.

The PSNR value and bit rate comparison between the H.264 and the proposed algorithm for the adaptive RDO model for each picture are tabulated in Table 5. As we can see, most results of the proposed algorithm show better performance compared with H.264 standard.

Table 5. Comparison for PSNR Values and Bit Rates

Test Sequences	Quantization Parameter	PSNR (dB) H.264	PSNR (dB) Proposed	Bit Rate (kbits/s) H.264	Bit Rate (kbits/s) Proposed
AKIYO	QP=28	38.690	38.872	38.02	38.09
	QP=32	35.781	36.049	23.45	24.03
	QP=36	33.209	33.423	15.35	15.70
	QP=40	30.634	30.993	10.54	10.88
FOREMAN	QP=28	35.929	35.879	121.99	119.45
	QP=32	33.386	33.363	69.02	68.23
	QP=36	31.013	31.035	42.38	41.83
	QP=40	28.651	28.694	27.54	27.23
MOBILE	QP=28	33.580	33.493	434.02	422.47
	QP=32	30.179	30.199	221.52	217.10
	QP=36	27.231	27.321	119.39	118.24
	QP=40	24.124	24.407	72.43	71.56
NEWS	QP=28	37.076	37.284	88.01	88.27
	QP=32	33.971	34.222	54.62	54.90
	QP=36	31.108	31.305	33.69	33.99
	QP=40	28.358	28.606	20.45	20.66
SALESMAN	QP=28	35.839	36.177	75.70	77.13
	QP=32	32.821	33.110	43.91	45.24
	QP=36	30.192	30.462	25.39	26.09
	QP=40	27.742	28.019	14.30	14.62

Figure 3 shows the rate distortion curves for the MOBILE and NEWS. Left is the worst case and right is the best case among the results. As we can see, the rate distortion curves of the proposed algorithm located upper than the rate distortion curves of the H.264. This means that the proposed algorithm shows the better performance with respect to PSNR value and the bit rate.

The PSNR value and bit rate comparison between the H.264 and the proposed algorithm for CIF format 352×288 are tabulated in Table 6. We use the first 120 frames

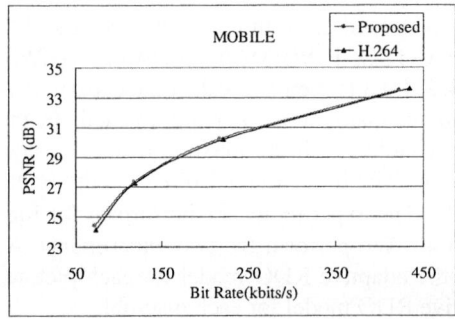
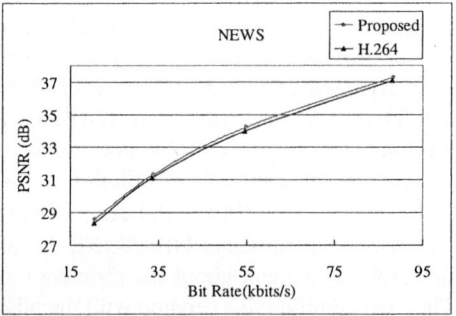

Fig. 3. Rate Distortion Curves for MOBILE and NEWS

Table 6. Comparison for PSNR Values and Bit Rates

Test Sequences	Quantization Parameter	PSNR (dB)		Bit Rate (kbits/s)	
		H.264	Proposed	H.264	Proposed
AKIYO	QP=28	40.109	40.225	107.61	106.81
	QP=32	37.555	37.764	62.32	62.69
	QP=36	35.130	35.424	38.69	39.28
	QP=40	32.573	32.877	24.61	25.23
FOREMAN	QP=28	37.076	37.040	362.77	355.89
	QP=32	34.689	34.683	210.78	207.03
	QP=36	32.462	32.480	129.04	127.85
	QP=40	30.277	30.346	83.07	82.91
MOBILE	QP=28	34.381	34.321	1718.54	1701.66
	QP=32	31.064	31.023	884.26	873.67
	QP=36	28.159	28.193	504.13	491.55
	QP=40	24.955	25.045	260.48	255.29
NEWS	QP=28	38.469	38.566	237.96	237.46
	QP=32	35.660	35.833	145.80	146.40
	QP=36	32.990	33.205	89.92	90.20
	QP=40	30.274	30.543	54.47	55.12
SALESMAN	QP=28	36.160	36.340	239.16	242.53
	QP=32	33.660	33.877	129.61	132.11
	QP=36	31.265	31.536	74.16	76.50
	QP=40	28.912	29.159	42.28	43.32

from the same five test video sequences. As we can see, the proposed algorithm shows better performance compared to H.264 standard.

Figure 4 shows the rate distortion curves for the FOREMAN and AKIYO. Left is the worst case and right is the best case among the results. As we can see, the rate distortion curves of the proposed algorithm located upper than the rate distortion curves of the H.264. Also the proposed algorithm shows the better performance in case of CIF.

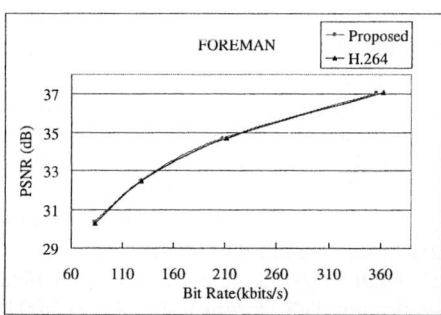
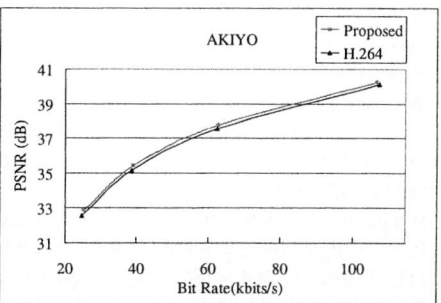

Fig. 4. Rate Distortion Curves for FOREMAN and AKIYO

5 Conclusions

In this paper, we have proposed an adaptive rate-distortion optimization algorithm for H.264. The proposed algorithm added the weighting factor to the previous RDO model. This weighting factor is changed according to the picture type and the standard deviation of the distortion for the current macroblock mode. In the picture level, we give more weights to the distortion part for I picture and we give more weight to the rate part of the RDO model for P picture. In the macroblock level, we give more weights to the rate part of the RDO model when the macroblock belongs to a flat area, and we give more weights to the distortion part of the RDO model when the macroblock belongs to a complex area. Experimental results show that the proposed algorithm achieves the better result compared to H.264. We obtain higher PSNR values though we use less or similar bit rate.

Acknowledgements

This work was supported in part by Gwangju Institute of Science and Technology (GIST), in part by the Ministry of Information and Communication (MIC) through the Realistic Broadcasting Research Center (RBRC), and in part by the Ministry of Education (MOE) through the Brain Korea 21 (BK21) project.

References

1. Pekka, S., Janne, H., Olli, S.: Selection of the Lagrange Multiplier for Block-Based Motion Estimation Criteria. Proceeding of International Conference on Acoustics, Speech, and Signal Processing, Vol. 3 (2004) 325-328
2. Tsai, C.J., Tang, C.W., Chen, C.H., Yu, Y.H.: Adaptive Rate-Distortion Optimization using Perceptual Hints. Proceeding of International Congress on Mathematical Education (2004) 667-670
3. Sullivan, G.J., Baker, R.L.: Rate-Distortion Optimized Motion Compensation for Compression Using Fixed or Variable Size Blocks. Global Telecommunications Conference, Vol. 1 (1991) 85-90
4. Shoham, Y., Gersho, A.: Efficient Bit Allocation for an Arbitrary Set of Quantizers. IEEE Transaction on Speech and Signal Processing, Vol. 36, No. 9 (1988) 1445-1453
5. Wiegand, T., Lightstone, M., Mukherjee, D., Campbell, T.G., Mitra, S.K.: Rate-Distortion Optimized Mode Selection for Very Low Bit Rate Video Coding and the Emerging H.263 Standard. IEEE Transaction on Circuit and System for Video Technology, Vol. 6, No. 2 (1996) 182-190
6. Wiegand, T., Girod, B.: Lagrangian Multiplier Selection in Hybrid Video Coder Control. Proceeding of International Conference on Image Processing (2001) 542-545
7. ITU-T Rec. H.264 I ISO/IEC 14496-10 AVC: Draft ITU-T Recommendation and Final Draft International Standard of Joint Video Specification. JVT Document JVT G050 (2003)
8. JVT Reference Software Version 9.5: http://iphome.hhi.de/suehring/tml/download/jm_old

Directional Lifting-Based Wavelet Transform for Multiple Description Image Coding with Quincunx Segmentation

Nan Zhang[1,*], Yan Lu[2], Feng Wu[2], and Baocai Yin[1]

[1] Multimedia and Intelligent Software Technology, Beijing Municipal Key Laboratory,
College of Computer Science Technology, Beijing University of Technology,
100022 Beijing, China
{duan, yinbc}@emails.bjut.edu.cn
http://www.bjut.edu.cn
[2] Microsoft Research Asia,
100080 Beijing, China
{yanlu, fengwu}@microsoft.com

Abstract. In this paper, a new multiple description image coding scheme using directional lifting transform is proposed. The basic idea is to divide an image into two descriptions with quincunx segmentation. The traditional spatial domain multiple description image coding techniques usually result in the very low coding efficiency. To tackle this problem, we propose a directional lifting technique to extensively exploit the correlations among neighboring pixels. The lifting directions are selected and organized based on the quadtree partition. In addition, a novel interpolation scheme is employed in the side decoder to reconstruct one description with full resolution. As for the central decoder operated on the two descriptions, data fusion algorithm is employed to reconstruct the whole image. Thus, the visual quality from the central decoder can be further improved.

1 Introduction

For a typical image distribution system, the images are first compressed and then stored in the local storage or transmitted to the end users through networks. At the compression stage, the coding efficiency is usually the most important consideration in the design. While the compressed images are transmitted through error-prone networks, the error robustness becomes an important issue. Therefore, in an image distribution scenario, it is a very challenging problem about how to obtain the best Quality of Services (QoS). Multiple Description Coding (MDC) is a well-known error resilience coding technique, which can achieve the improved QoS. A typical multiple description image coding scheme usually divides an image into several descriptions, and then compresses each description individually. These coded image descriptions can be decoded either jointly or separately based on the availabilities. One of the

---

* This work has been done while the author is an intern at Microsoft Research Asia. Part of this work has been sponsored by NSFC Grant 60375007 and NSFC Grant 60572104."

novel features of MDC is that it can reconstruct a visually acceptable image when any one or several descriptions are received. Therefore, it presents many advantages over scalable coding, in that the layered bit-streams generated from scalable coding usually have dependencies.

In the past two decades, a number of MDC techniques have been developed. The early algorithms were focused on the spatial-domain processing, e.g. the down-sampling method [1]. The main shortcoming of these techniques lies in the decreased absolute coding efficiency. Later, the techniques focused on transform-domain processing were developed, including the correlation transformation method[2][3], the scalar and the vector quantization method [4], and so on. Particularly, the multiple description scalar quantization (MDSQ) [4] and the multiple description correlation transformation code (MDTC) [2] are two classical types of schemes. However, these techniques have the limitation that they are usually not compatible with the existing image coding standards. And also, the overall coding performance is not as good as expected after balancing the coding efficiency of side and central descriptions. Recently, the temporal-domain processing techniques have been developed for multiple description video coding, e.g. the motion compensation method [5][6].

In this paper, we propose a new multiple description image coding scheme using the quincunx segmentation in spatial domain. The reasons to select spatial-domain processing are twofold. On the one hand, the spatial domain processing is usually very simple and can be easily extended for standard-compatible multiple description image coding; and on the other hand, the spatial domain processing offers the opportunity to further improve the subjective visual quality from one side description. Nevertheless, the main shortcoming is still the overall coding performance. To tackle this problem, we proposed a directional lifting-based wavelet transform to further remove the correlation among neighboring pixels, and hence improve the overall coding performance. The selection of lifting direction is content adaptive in the sense of rate-distortion optimization (RDO). JPEG2000 codec is employed in the proposed algorithm except for the lifting-based transform. In addition, the interpolation and data fusion techniques have been developed to reconstruct image from side or central descriptions.

The rest of this paper is organized as follows. Section 2 presents the proposed algorithm architecture. Section 3 presents the proposed directional lifting-based wavelet transform in detail. Section 4 and Section 5 present the encoding and decoding issues, respectively. The experimental results are given in Section 6. Finally, Section 7 concludes this paper.

2 Algorithm Framework

In this paper, we only discuss the multiple description image coding technique with two descriptions. The basic idea of the proposed algorithm is to generate the two descriptions based on the spatial-domain quincunx segmentation. Fig. 1 shows the architecture of the proposed scheme. As shown in Fig. 1, the input image I is first divided into two sub-images I_{sd1} and I_{sd2} using the quincunx segmentation. Then, each sub-image or description is individually processed with directional lifting-based wavelet transform, followed by the traditional JPEG2000 codec. The coded sub-images can be transmitted to the end users over the different channels. When only one description is received, it is individually decoded with the side decoder, and the decoded sub-image is interpolated to reconstruct the whole image. When both descriptions are received, they are jointly decoded to reconstruct the whole image, and meanwhile each description can be individually decoded and interpolated to further improve the quality of the whole image using the data-fusion algorithm.

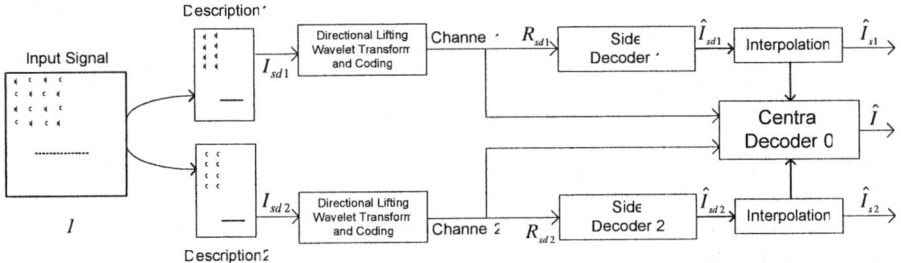

Fig. 1. Algorithm framework

3 Directional Lifting-Based Wavelet Transform

3.1 Problem Analysis

The lifting technique is an efficient implementation of wavelet transform with low memory and computational complexity. First of all, we briefly review the conventional lifting technique proposed by Daubechies et al [7]. Let $x(m, n)_{m,n \in Z}$ be a 2D image. It is well-know that the 2D wavelet transform can be separated into two 1D wavelet transforms. Without losing the generality, we only discuss the 1D wavelet transform on the vertical direction. According to the technique proposed in [7], the 1D wavelet transform can be performed with one or multiple lifting stages. A typical lifting stage consists of three steps: split, predict and update. Firstly, all samples are split into two sub-sets: the even sample set and the odd sample set, i.e.

$$\begin{cases} x_e(m,n) = x(m,2n); \\ x_o(m,n) = x(m,2n+1). \end{cases} \quad (1)$$

Then, the sample at the odd rows is predicted from the samples at the neighboring even rows. The high-pass coefficient $h(m, n)$ is calculated with

$$h(m,n) = x_o(m,n) - P_e(m,n). \quad (2)$$

where $P_e(m,n)$ is the predicting value.

Finally, the sample at the even row is updated with the updating value $U_h(m,n)$ to produce the low-pass coefficient $l(m,n)$, i.e.

$$l(m,n) = x_e(m,n) + U_h(m,n). \quad (3)$$

The above lifting steps can be easily applied on a regular image. However, due to the pixel-misalignment between the even and odd rows in each description from the quincunx segmentation, as shown in Fig. (2), it is not efficient to directly use the conventional prediction and updating lifting operations. Fig. 3(a) and Fig. 3(b) show the low-pass and high-pass subbands derived from the conventional lifting technique, respectively. Obviously, the high-pass subband is still with relatively larger energy, in that the correlation between neighboring pixels has not been fully exploited. Actually, the true locations of pixels at the even and odd rows are shown in Fig. 2(b). The intuitive solution of tackling the pixel-misalignment problem is to predict $x_{m,n+1}$ from the interpolation values between $x_{m,n}$ and $x_{m+1,n}$ and between $x_{m,n+2}$ and $x_{m+1,n+2}$. In other words, the prediction direction should be considered in the lifting steps. The similar problem exists in the updating step. Therefore, in this paper, we introduce the interpolation operations into the lifting steps. Actually, more lifting directions are employed to further improve the performance. Fig. 3(c) and Fig. 3(d) show the low-pass and high-pass subbands derived from the proposed lifting technique, respectively. Obviously, the high-pass subband only has small energy. The proposed directional lifting transform are described in detail in the next subsection.

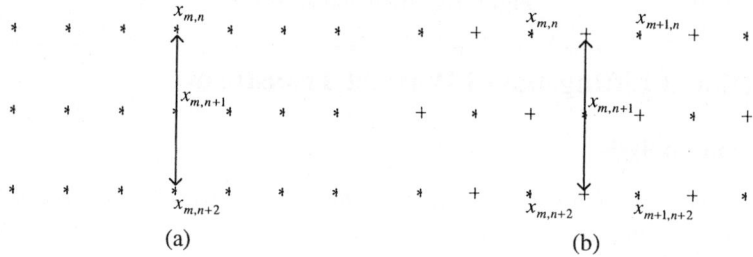

Fig. 2. (a) Misalignment between even and odd rows, and (b) true pixel locations of even and odd rows

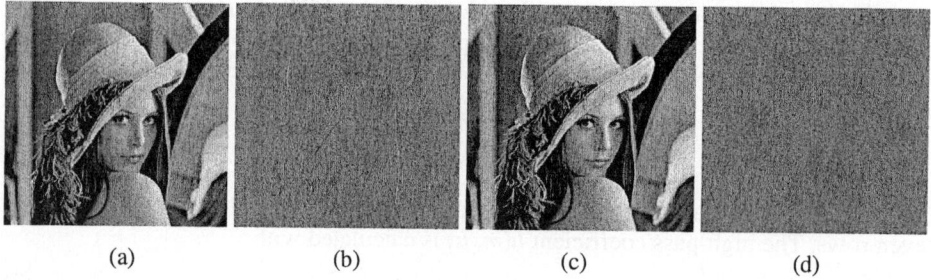

Fig. 3. First level lifting-based decomposition results. (a) Low-pass subband and (b) high-pass subband from the traditional lifting technique; and (c) low-pass subband and (d) high-pass subband from the proposed lifting technique.

3.2 Directional Lifting Structure

The proposed directional lifting techniques aims at extensively exploiting the spatial correlation among neighboring pixels in a description. Briefly, the proposed algorithm first analyzes the spatial correlation in all directions for a pixel, and then selects the direction with the smallest prediction errors for the lifting operations. The problem arises from the unavailability of some pixels in some directions in a description. Therefore, the missed pixels have to be interpolated. In this paper, the classical image interpolation algorithm using sinc function is employed. The interpolation is performed up to quarter pixel. Thus, instead of always predicting along horizontal or vertical direction, the proposed algorithm analyzes the local spatial correlations in all directions, and then chooses a direction with the minimum prediction errors. Fig. 4 shows all prediction directions. The prediction value $P_e(m,n)$ of pixel $x(m,2n+1)$ is taken as a linear combination of the samples at even rows indicated with the arrows. Specially,

$$P_e(m,n) = \begin{cases} \sum_i p_i x_e(m + \frac{2+(-1)^{i-1}(dir-2)}{4}, n+i) & dir = 0,1,2,3,4 \\ \sum_i p_i x_e(m+i, n+\frac{2+(-1)^i(dir-6)}{4}) & dir = 5,6,7 \end{cases} \quad (4)$$

where the weights p_i are given by the filter taps, dir denotes the prediction direction, and x_e, which is in half-pixel or quarter-pixel precision, is interpolated using adjacent integer pixels by sinc function.

The corresponding finite impulse response function is

$$P(z_1, z_2) = \begin{cases} \sum_{i=a}^{b} p_i z_1^{\frac{2+(-1)^{i-1}(dir-2)}{4}} z_2^i & dir = 0,1,2,3,4 \\ \sum_{i=a}^{b} p_i z_1^i z_2^{\frac{2+(-1)^i(dir-6)}{4}} & dir = 5,6,7 \end{cases} \quad (5)$$

where a and b delimit the finite support of the FIR wavelet filter. Since the prediction is still calculated from the samples at even rows, if the prediction direction is known, the proposed lifting can still perfectly reconstruct the samples at odd rows with Eq (2).

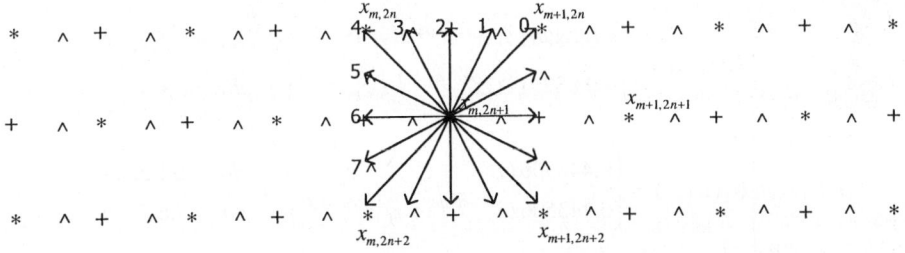

Fig. 4. The directions in the proposed lifting-based decomposition

The updating step is carried out in the same direction as that in the prediction step. Note that the proposed framework is very general, and it does not have any restriction on the update direction. We keep the prediction and updating direction the same to save the bits to code the side information of direction. Actually, the optimal updating direction should also be consistent with the prediction direction in most cases. Consequently, after the updating step, the samples at even rows are updated as

$$U_h(m,n) = \begin{cases} \sum_j u_j h(m + \frac{2+(-1)^j(dir-2)}{4}, n+j) & dir = 0,1,2,3,4 \\ \sum_j u_j h(m+j, n + \frac{2+(-1)^{j-1}(dir-6)}{4}) & dir = 5,6,7 \end{cases} \tag{6}$$

where the weights u_j are given by the filter taps.

The corresponding finite impulse response function is

$$U(z_1, z_2) = \begin{cases} \sum_{j=c}^{d} u_j z_1^{\frac{2+(-1)^j(dir-2)}{4}} z_2^j & dir = 0,1,2,3,4 \\ \sum_{j=c}^{d} u_j z_1^j z_2^{\frac{2+(-1)^{j-1}(dir-6)}{4}} & dir = 5,6,7 \end{cases} \tag{7}$$

where c and d specify the kernel of the FIR wavelet filter.

Fig. 5 shows the diagram of the proposed directional lifting-based wavelet transform to a description. In particularly, the proposed FIR function of 9/7 filters is given below.

$$9/7 : \begin{cases} P_0(z_1, z_2) = \begin{cases} 1.586134\,(z_1^{(4-dir)/4} + z_1^{dir/4} z_2) & dir = 0,1,2,3,4 \\ 1.586134\,(z_2^{(dir-4)/4} + z_1 z_2^{(8-dir)/4}) & dir = 5,6,7 \end{cases} \\[1em] U_0(z_1, z_2) = \begin{cases} -0.05298\,(z_1^{dir/4} + z_1^{(4-dir)/4} z_2^{-1}) & dir = 0,1,2,3,4 \\ -0.05298\,(z_2^{(8-dir)/4} + z_1^{-1} z_2^{(dir-4)/4}) & dir = 5,6,7 \end{cases} \\[1em] P_1(z_1, z_2) = \begin{cases} -0.882911\,(z_1^{(4-dir)/4} + z_1^{dir/4} z_2) & dir = 0,1,2,3,4 \\ -0.882911\,(z_2^{(dir-4)/4} + z_1 z_2^{(8-dir)/4}) & dir = 5,6,7 \end{cases} \\[1em] U_1(z_1, z_2) = \begin{cases} 0.443506\,(z_1^{dir/4} + z_1^{(4-dir)/4} z_2^{-1}) & dir = 0,1,2,3,4 \\ 0.443506\,(z_2^{(8-dir)/4} + z_1^{-1} z_2^{(dir-4)/4}) & dir = 5,6,7 \end{cases} \\[1em] s_0 = 1.230174; \quad s_1 = 1/s_0 \end{cases} \tag{8}$$

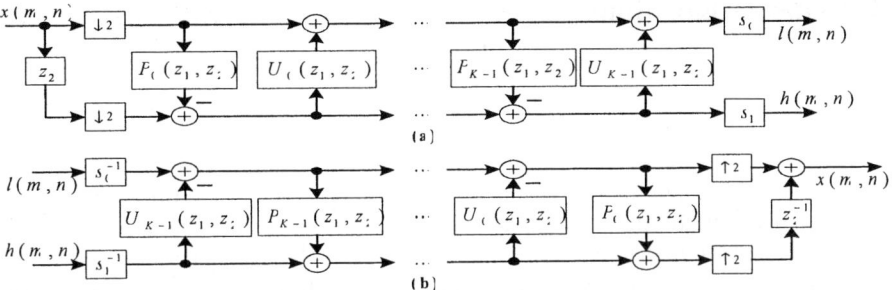

Fig. 5. The generic 1D directional lifting wavelet transform of sub-description. (a) Analysis side, and (b) Synthesis side.

3.3 Multi-level Decomposition Structure

As we know, in wavelet-based image coding techniques, the multi-level decomposition structure is always used. The above directional lifting structure can be applied for the first level decomposition. Afterwards, a low-pass subband and a high-pass subband are produced, and both are pixel aligned. The remained decompositions can follow two ways. The first one is to further decompose the high-pass subband, as shown in Fig. 6(a), which results in the Mallat decomposition tree of the current description. However, since the high-pass subband is equivalent to be down-sampled, the horizontal correlation is not as strong as expected. Therefore, in this paper, we employ the decomposition structure of Fig. 6(b) for multi-level wavelet transform.

The lifting directions of the first level decomposition ranges from 0° from 360°, as shown in Fig. 4. As for the other level decompositions, the directional lifting technique is also employed. Since in this case the subband image to be decomposed is pixel-aligned, the new candidate lifting directions are defined. Specially, the lifting directions range from -135° to -45° and from 45° to 135°, as shown in Fig. 7. The integer pixels are marked by "*", the half pixels are marked by "+", and the quarter pixels by "^". Thus, totally nine lifting directions are defined.

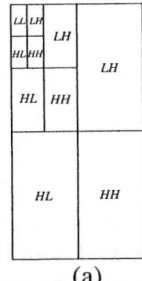
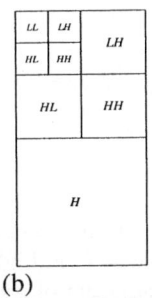
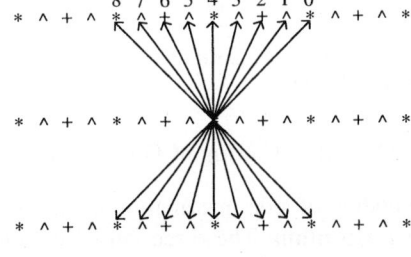

Fig. 6. The three levels spatial decomposition tree for sub-description. (a)Mallat decomposition, and (b)Proposed decomposition.

Fig. 7. Directions of the others levels lifting wavelet transform

4 Encoding Algorithms

4.1 Quadtree Partition for Directional Lifting

One of the key problems of the directional lifting technique is how to decide and organize the lifting directions. With the adaptability of lifting-based transform to the texture orientation, a natural step to enhance the performance of the proposed scheme is adaptive spatial partition of an image into regions of uniform gradients. The image is recursively partitioned into blocks of variable sizes by quadtree. All pixels in a quadtree block will be subject to the same directional lifting-based wavelet transform. The finer the partition, the greater degree of gradient uniformity in the resulting blocks, the better fit of the proposed lifting to image signal, and hence the lower the distortion. However, the improved signal approximation is achieved at the expense of increased side information to description the partition tree and the lifting directions of individual blocks. To find the quadtree of optimal balance between the cost of coding the tree and the quality of partition, we apply the well-known BFOS algorithm for optimal pruning tree. Fig. 8 shows the partitioning results of Lena. Obviously, the division becomes finer with the rate increases.

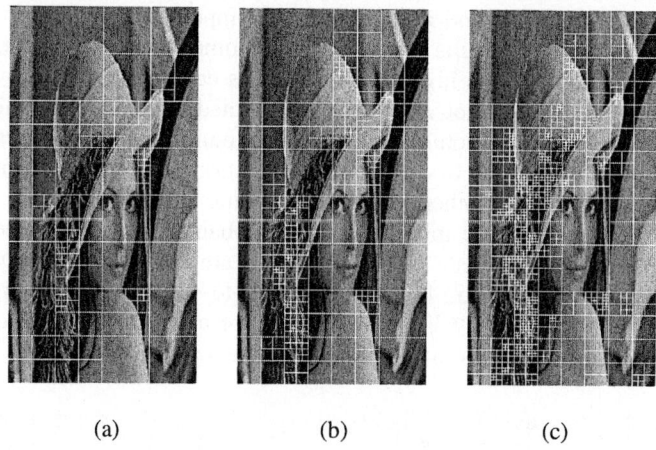

(a) (b) (c)

Fig. 8. The quadtree partition of Lena at different rate. (a) Rate = 0.5bpss, (b) Rate = 1bpss, and (c) Rate = 2bpss.

4.2 Direction Coding of One Description

The coding of side information of lifting direction is also an essential part in the proposed algorithm. The direction of the current block C is highly correlated with the direction of the up adjacent block U and the left adjacent block L. Therefore, it can be predictive coded. If one of the blocks U or L is outside or not in the image, the prediction direction is equal to 2 or 4, i.e.

$$\begin{cases} C_{pred} = 2 & \text{if the level is first level;} \\ C_{pred} = 4 & \text{if the level is other levels.} \end{cases} \quad (9)$$

Otherwise, we use the following criterion to select predicted direction:

$$C_{pred} = \min(U_{dir}, L_{dir}). \tag{10}$$

To signal direction number C_{dir} for a block, the parameter $flag_{dir\_pred}$ is transmitted, which is represented by 1 bit with value 0 or 1:

$$\begin{cases} flag_{dir\_pred} = 1 & C_{dir} = C_{pred}; \\ flag_{dir\_pred} = 0 & \text{Otherwise.} \end{cases} \tag{11}$$

Then, the additional parameter $C_{dircode}$, which can take value from 0 to 7 and be sent as 3 bit codeword:

$$\begin{cases} C_{dircode} = C_{dir} & C_{dir} < C_{pred}; \\ C_{dircode} = C_{dir} - 1 & \text{Otherwise.} \end{cases} \tag{12}$$

Thus, the current direction C_{dir} is coded with prediction.

5 Decoding Algorithms

5.1 Side Decoding and Image Interpolation

In this subsection, we discuss how to decode a single description. Suppose only one description is available at the decoder, from which it is easy to decode a sub-image. However, the decoded sub-image is not the image with full resolution. Thus, the key problem is how to reconstruct the whole image from the decoded sub-image. In other words, we have to use some interpolation or image restoring methods. Thanks to the quincunx distribution of the pixels in one description, the interpolation of the missed pixels is somewhat easier. In this paper, we employ the method proposed in [8]. Briefly, we first analyze the texture in the sub-image with the Gabor filter and find the local structure, and then perform the interpolation along the texture direction based on the extracted information.

5.2 Central Decoding and Data Fusion

When two descriptions are simultaneously available at the decoder, the straightforward method of central decoding is to decode the sub-images from the two descriptions respectively and then merge them together. However, based on the above side decoding scheme, it can also reconstruct a whole image with some interpolated pixels. In other words, one pixel in the image corresponds to two reconstructed values, i.e. one is from the directly decoded pixel in the current description, and the other one is from the interpolated pixel in the other description. Therefore, some data fusion algorithm can be employed to achieve the better quality rather than the simply merging. In this paper, we use the simple linear fusion scheme. Suppose $\hat{I}_{s1}$ and $\hat{I}_{s2}$ denote the reconstructed images from description $\hat{I}_{sd1}$ and description $\hat{I}_{sd2}$, respectively. Then, the final reconstruction value is calculated as:

$$\hat{I}(n,m) = \begin{cases} \alpha_1 \times \hat{I}_{s1}(n,m) + (1-\alpha_1) \times \hat{I}_{s2}(n,m) & (n,m) \in \hat{I}_{sd1}; \\ \beta_1 \times \hat{I}_{s1}(n,m) + (1-\beta_1) \times \hat{I}_{s2}(n,m) & (n,m) \in \hat{I}_{sd2}. \end{cases} \qquad (13)$$

where α_1 and β_1 are the weighing factors, which can be trained at the encoder and encoded into the bitstream.

6 Experiments

The proposed multiple description image coding method is implemented based on the JPEG2000 reference software VM9.0. We take Lena of dimension 512×512 as an example to show the experimental results. In these experiments, we employ the 9/7 filter and do five-level decomposition for wavelet transform. For the first level lifting-based transform, the 8 directions range from 0° from 360° with the quarter-pixel precision. The directions of the other levels range from -135° to -45° and from 45° to 135°. There are totally 9 different directions. Following the same testing method in [9], we select the redundancy rate to be 25%. Thus, we can have the results of single description coding (SDC) and duplicated SDC (2SDC). Both are from the original VM9.0. And also, we can have the expected results, which mean that the bitrate is 25% more than SDC at the same distortion.

The performance comparison is shown in Fig. 9. The method proposed in [9] works very close to the expected results. As shown in Fig. 9, the proposed side decoder can achieve better rate-distortion performance at the same central performance rather than the expected results at moderate and low bit rates. However, the result of the proposed algorithm is somewhat lower at high bitrate. Some more efficient data fusion algorithm may be helpful to tackle this problem, which remains the future work. Fig. 10 shows the results of central PSNR versus the side PSNR at the 0.5bpss (bits per source symbol) and the 1bpss, respectively. Besides the proposed algorithm, the results of MDUSQ [10], PTSQ [11] and the algorithm in [9] (denoted as Reference) are also illustrated. The problem of the proposed algorithm is that it has only one testing point, because the central PSNR and side PSNR in the proposed algorithm cannot be adaptively adjusted. However, at this point, the proposed algorithm outperforms any other schemes. The reconstructed images from the side decoder are shown in Fig. 11.

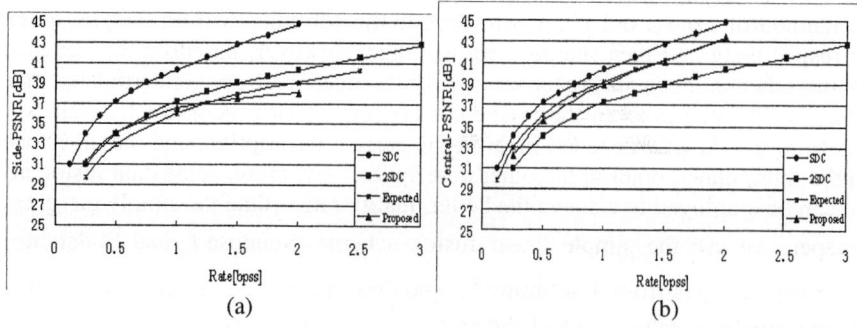

Fig. 9. Result of Lena. (a) Side PSNR (dB), and (b) Central PSNR (dB).

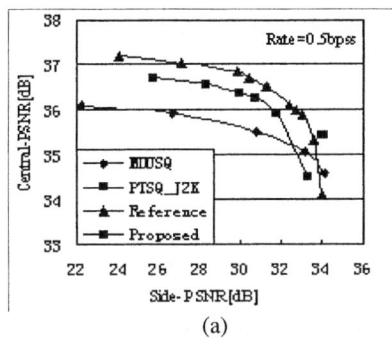 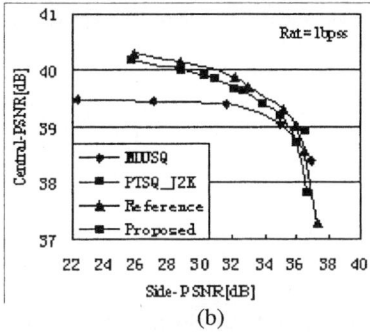

Fig. 10. Central PSNR versus Side PSNR at (a) 0.5bpss, and (b) 1bpss, respectively

(a)   (b)

Fig. 11. Reconstructed images from one description. (a) Rate = 0.5bpss, and (b) Rate = 1bpss

7 Conclusions

In this paper, we have proposed a new multiple description image coding scheme based on quincunx segmentation. The directional lifting-based wavelet transform, which complies with the inherent feature of quincunx distortion of pixels in one description, is developed to further improve the coding performance. The proposed algorithm can not only remove the redundancy among the neighboring pixels very well, but also enhance the performance of the central decoder when two descriptions are available simultaneously. Since the proposed algorithm does not consider the correlation between two descriptions during encoding, it is difficult to balance the distortions between the side decoder and central decoder. Therefore, how to utilize the correlations between two descriptions remains a future work.

References

1. Tom, A.S., Yeh, C.L., Chu, F.: Packet Video for Cell Loss Protection Using Deinterleaving and Scrambling. In Proc. IEEE. Int. Con on Acoust., Speech, Signal Processing, (1991) 2857-2860
2. Wang, Y., Orchard, M.T., Vaishampayan, V., Reibman, A.R.: Multiple Description Coding Using Pairwise Correlating Transforms. IEEE Transactions on Image Processing, Vol. 10(3) (2001) 351-366

3. Goyal, V.K., Kovacevic, J.: Generalized Multiple Description Coding with Correlating Transforms. IEEE Transactions on Information Theory, Vol. 47(6) (2001) 2199-2224
4. Vaishampayan, V.A.: Design of Multiple Description Scalar Quantizers. IEEE Transactions on Information Theory, Vol. 39(5) (1993) 821-834
5. Kim, C.-S., Lee, S.-U.: Multiple Description Coding of Motion Fields for Robust Video Technology. IEEE Transactions on Circuits and Systems for Video Technology, Vol. 11(9) (2001) 999-1010
6. Wang, Y., Lin, S.-N.: Error-Resilient Video Coding Using Multiple Description Motion Compensation. IEEE Transactions on Circuits and Systems for Video Technology, Vol. 12(6) (2002) 438-452
7. Daubechies, I., Sweldens, W.: Factoring Wavelet Transforms into Lifting Steps. Journal of Fourier Analysis and Application, Vol. 4(3) (1998) 245-267
8. Zhang, X.J., Wu, X.L.: Image Interpolation Using Texture Orientation Map and Kernel Fisher Discriminant. International Conference on Image Processing, (2005) Accepted
9. Tillo, T., Olmo, G.: A Novel Multiple Description Coding Scheme Compatible With the JPEG2000 Decoder. IEEE Signal Processing Letters, Vol. 11(11) (2004) 908-911
10. Guionnet, T., Guillemot, C., Pateux, S.: Embedded Multiple Description Coding for Progressive Image Transmission over Unreliable Channels. In Proc. Int. Conf. Image Processing, Vol. 1 (2001) 94-97
11. Jiang, W., Ortega, A.: Multiple Description Coding via Polyphase Transform and Quantization Selection. Proc. SPIE Intl. Conference on Visual Communication and Image Processing, (1999) 998-1008

Non-periodic Frame Refreshment Based on the Uncertainty Models of the Reference Frames

Yong Tae Kim[1], Youngil Yoo[1], Dong Wook Kang[1], Kyeong Hoon Jung[1], Ki-Doo Kim[1], and Seung-Jun Lee[2]

[1] School of Electrical Engineering, Kookmin University,
861-1, Chongnung-Dong, Songbuk-Gu, Seoul, 136-702 Korea
{ytkim, young0125, dwkang, khjung, kdk}@kookmin.ac.kr
[2] Mcubeworks, Inc. 942-1 8th fl. Miraewasaram Bd., 942-1, Daechi-dong,
Kangnam-Gu, Seoul, 135-280 Korea
jun@mcubeworks.com

Abstract. Intra-frame insertion, conventionally periodic, is inevitable to provide the decoders with the capability of random access for the streamed videos. In this paper, we propose a new non-periodic intra-frame insertion method which encodes a frame as I-picture when the propagated and accumulated uncertainties of the reference frame are greater than a threshold and show that it can be used for the purpose of the error resilient video encoding. The uncertainties of the reference frame reflect the drift noise resulting from the transmission errors. Simulation results over 3GPP/3GPP2 show that the transmission error resiliency of the proposed algorithm is superior to that of the conventional periodic intra-frame- insertion methods with the same encoding efficiency.

1 Introduction

1.1 A Video Communication in the Error Environment

It is important to devise video encoding and decoding schemes that can make the compressed bit stream resilient to transmission errors in real-time video communications over unreliable networks. But, it is very difficult to make an error resilient bitstream, because the errors arise from lots of the causes. Furthermore, it is not easy task to find the optimal ways to applicable to the error-environment, especially, when the error-resiliency is jointly considered with the coding efficiency.

1.2 The Error Resilient and Concealment Techniques

The purpose to adopt the error resilient encoding methods is that the missing or erroneous bits in a compressed stream will not cause the serious degradation in the reconstructed video quality. Error concealment techniques are a sort of the techniques used at the decoder side, which replace the missing image samples due to transmission errors with the artificially computed values based on the surrounding received samples. They make use of inherent correlation among spatially and temporally adjacent samples. Basically, the purpose to maintain the reconstructed video quality against the transmission errors can be more effectively accomplished by utilizing the error-resilient encoding tools at the encoder side. There have been many tools devised for improving the error resiliency, such as robust entropy coding, error resilient prediction, layered coding with unequal error protection, multiple descriptions coding etc[2].

Focusing on the error resiliency, we can find that the temporal prediction causes propagation of errors. Namely, once an error occurs so that a reconstructed frame at the decoder differs from that assumed at the encoder, the reference frames used at the decoder from there onwards will differ from those used at the encoder, and consequently all subsequent reconstructed frames will be in error. To overcome this error propagation problem, an *intra*-refreshment has been used.

When a corruption occurs during streaming of encoded video signals the frames reconstructed by a remote decoder may differ from the corresponding frames reconstructed by the local decoder residing in the encoder. We call this kind of difference as the drift noise. As we said again, in the Fig. 1, we can define the drift noises as follows [1]:

$$d_n = y_n - \hat{f}_n \qquad (1)$$

where $\hat{f}_n$ and y_n are the reference pixel values for motion compensation in the local decoder and the remote decoder, respectively. The drift noise will increase the end-to-end distortion level of the reconstructed pictures at the remote decoder drastically; an *intra*-refreshment may reduce the drift noise and consequently get over the effect of the transmission errors. However, it may decrease the coding efficiency [2]. Hence, it is very important to find optimum tradeoff between error resiliency and coding efficiency.

1.3 The Intra-refreshment

One can accomplish the *intra*-refreshment by inserting intra-coded frame (frame refreshment), group of blocks (GOB refreshment) or macroblock (MB refreshment). In all cases, you can make use of *intra*-refreshment algorithms periodically or non-periodically. But, you must keep the fact in mind that forced-intra refreshment may result in decreasing the coding efficiency. In other words, if you use *intra*-refreshments too much, it will cause severe decrease of coding efficiency. Therefore, you have to utilize intra-refreshments in the proper manner and at the proper time. Generally speaking, non-periodic intra-refreshments yields better performance than periodic intra-refreshments in the sense of joint-optimization of error resiliency and coding efficiency. However, it is not easy to recognize the proper time to use the *intra*-refreshment.

In this paper, we propose a new non-periodic frame-refreshment method which encodes a frame as I-picture when the propagated and accumulated drift noises or the uncertainties of the reference frame are greater than a threshold. With simulation results, we will show the error resiliency of the proposed non-periodic frame-refreshment algorithm is superior to the conventional periodic frame-refreshment methods with the same encoding efficiency.

2 Various Models for Error-Prone Environments

2.1 Introduction

To compromise the coding efficiency and error resiliency better, many researchers have devised the high-complexity mode decision algorithms, in which they implement mode decision-incorporated *intra* refreshment algorithms [3-7]. When those algorithms estimate the end-to-end distortion of a macroblock according to the encoding mode, *intra* or *inter*, they consider the amount of to-be-propagated drift noise as the additional distortion of the *inter*-mode and add it to the rate-distortion cost computation, which generate more the *intra*-mode MB than usual. To compute the drift noise, the encoder either estimates the inherited distortion using propagation model of the drift noise [3-6] or emulate the distortion from the statistical average of distortions obtained from a number of local decoders affected by the assumed random partial loss of bitstream [7]. However, almost all of them incorporate the *intra*-refreshment with time-consuming RD-optimization procedure.

Recently, in [1] Kang has introduced the propagation model for the uncertainty of reference pixels. With the newly introduced model for the uncertainty propagation, we can implement the frame refreshing algorithms for the low-complexity mode decision method as well as for the high-complexity mode decision method.

2.2 High Complexity Mode Decision for Error-Prone Environment in H.263 [3]

This model uses a high complexity algorithm for error-prone environments. In this model, independently for every macroblock, the encoder selects the coding mode that minimizes the following cost:

$$J = \begin{cases} (1-p)D_q + pD_2 + \lambda_{MODE}R, & \text{intra-mode} \\ (1-p)pD_2(v,n-1) + (1-p)D_q + pD_2 + \lambda_{MODE}R & \text{inter-mode} \end{cases} \quad (2)$$

Where λ_{mode} is the Lagrangian coefficient, $\lambda_{mode} = 0.85*QP^2$, p means the lost probability of the given MB during transmission, R denotes the rate to encode the target MB including all control parameters, $D_2(v,n-1)$ represents the concealment distortion of the motion compensated MB in the *n-1*th frame, D_q is the quantization distortion, v is the motion-vector. Because D_2 is defined as the sum squared difference (SSD) between the reconstructed pixels values of the coded MB and the concealed pixel values, D_2 depends on the error concealment method employed and is constant for all coding modes considered. Also, based on this algorithm, D_2 is computed independently in every frame. Besides, if the encoded MB, including transmission error, is in the quasi-stationary area, it causes the qualities of that to dip sharply. This algorithm try to select more the *intra* mode than the *inter* mode as the probability of p.

2.3 Error Propagation Model in H.264 [4]

This model uses the frame-to-frame error propagation of the concealment distortion. In this error resilient method, the power of the drift noise called as D_3 is used. The way to decide the mode in this algorithm is to choose the minimum value of the cost function using D_{total} which is added D_3 to D_q. This error propagation model is expressed as follows,

$$D_3 = \begin{cases} p[D_2 + D_3(0, n-1)], & \text{intra-mode} \\ (1-p)D_3(v, n-1) + p[D_2 + D_3(0, n-1)], & \text{inter-mode} \end{cases} \quad (3)$$

Where p denotes the probability of covered packet loss, D_2 is the same meaning, as above mentioned in Eq. (2), and $D_3(v, n-1)$ represents the motion compensated drift noise with v, motion vector. Also, $D_3(0, n-1)$ is the drift noise in the previous frame. This model updates the drift noise by D_2 in every frame. Though the drift noise power propagation model yields better performance compared with the error model in TMN11, it still have a defect in quasi-stationary area.

2.4 Weighting of Consecutively Propagated Drift Noise by $e^{p(n-n_0)}$ [5](WIAMIS)

This model appears to surmount weak points that spend a long time on the forced intra update of the MB in quasi-stationary area. On the other words, this algorithm improves an effect to obstruct the transmission error propagation in quasi-stationary area after scene change. Intra refreshment is performed during the mode decision procedure: the mode is selected in view of minimization of the cost defined as,

$$D_3 = \begin{cases} p[D_2 + D_3(0, n-1)], & \text{intra-mode} \\ \{(1-p)D_3(v, n-1) + p[D_2 + D_3(0, n-1)]\}e^{p(n-n_0)}, & \text{inter-mode} \end{cases} \quad (4)$$

A marked characteristic in comparison with the presented model above, for *inter*-mode, is that the drift noise power have a mechanism with weighting by $e^{p(n-n_0)}$ according to $p(n-n_0)$. So, it makes frequently the encoding-mode to select *intra*-mode to shorten the time when corresponding MB is in the quasi-stationary area.

2.5 Propagation Model for the Uncertainties in the Reference Pixel [1] (RTI)

This uncertainty model has distinguished features compared with the other algorithms. It offers the low complexity mode decision and has a little more error resilient improvement. This model is founded on an uncertainty in the reference pixel by using the conceptual reference pixels for computing the RD cost in substitute for the pixels reconstructed by the local decoder. The uncertainty in the reference pixel means, quite simply, a random variable reflected on the estimated and compensated drift noise in the error-prone environment, which is defined as follows,

$$u_n(i) = \tilde{f}_n(i) - \hat{f}_n(i) \quad (5)$$

where $\tilde{f}_n(i)$ means a random variable representing statistically the pixel reconstructed by the remote decoders and $\hat{f}_n(i)$ is the pixel reconstructed error-freely by the local decoder. You can know the exact meaning of $\tilde{f}_n(i)$ and $\hat{f}_n(i)$ in the Fig. 1.

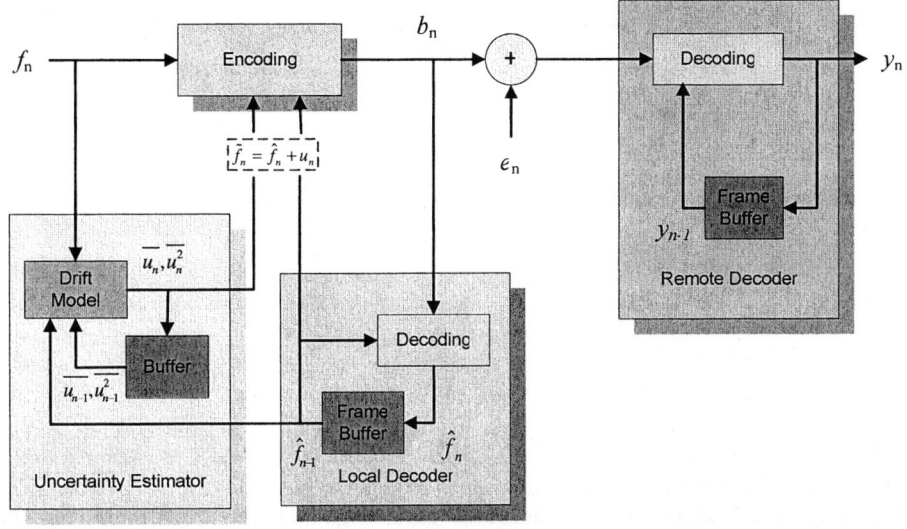

Fig. 1. Principle of the error-resilient encoding scheme in the error-prone environment: The newly introduced uncertainty estimator estimates the first and second moments of the drift noises based on the propagation model of the uncertainties in the reference pixels [1]

The uncertainty in the reference pixel is updated as follows:

For *intra* and *inter*-mode, supposing that remote decoders approximate the pixels with probability of p, the uncertainty in the reference pixel is also updated as follows,

$$u_n(i) = \begin{cases} 0 & \text{with } 1-p \\ (1-p)\left[u_{n-1}(i) + \hat{f}_{n-1}(i)\right] + p \cdot 128 - \hat{f}_n(i) & \text{with } p \end{cases}, \text{ intra-mode} \quad (6)$$

$$u_n(i) = \begin{cases} u_{n-k}(i+v) & \text{with } 1-p \\ (1-p)\left[u_{n-1}(i) + \hat{f}_{n-1}(i)\right] + p \cdot 128 - \hat{f}_n(i) & \text{with } p \end{cases}, \text{ inter-mode} \quad (7)$$

where $u_{n-1}(i)$ and $u_n(i)$ mean the *n-1*-th and *n*-th frame uncertainty in the reference pixel, p is the probability resulting from the partial loss of bitstream, k is the frame index offset can be one out of K values when motion compensation uses K reference frames. $u_{n-k}(i+v)$ is the motion compensated previously decoded uncertainty in the reference pixel at the local decoder. $\hat{f}_{n-1}(i)$ and $\hat{f}_n(i)$ are *i*-th reconstructed error-freely pixel of *n-1*-th and *n*-th frame by the local decoder.

In the meantime, the propagation model of the first and second moments of the uncertainty in the reference pixel of the *intra*-mode is expressed as follows,

$$m_n^I(i) = E[u_n(i)] \\ = p\left((1-p)\left[m_{n-1}(i) + \hat{f}_{n-1}(i)\right] + p \cdot 128 - \hat{f}_n(i)\right) \quad (8)$$

$$M_n^I(i) = E\left[u_n^2(i)\right]$$
$$= p(1-p)^2 \left(M_{n-1}(i) - m_{n-1}^2(i)\right) \qquad (9)$$
$$+ p\left((1-p)\left[m_{n-1}(i) + \hat{f}_{n-1}(i)\right] + p \cdot 128 - \hat{f}_n(i)\right)^2$$

For *inter*-mode, the first and second moments of the uncertainty in the reference pixel is as follows,

$$m_n^P(i) = E\left[u_n(i)\right]$$
$$= (1-p)m_{n-k}(i+v) + m_n^I(i) \qquad (10)$$

$$M_n^P(i) = E\left[u_n^2(i)\right]$$
$$= (1-p)M_{n-k}(i+v) + M_n^I(i) \qquad (11)$$

Using the reference pixels, we can express the end-to-end distortion. Utilizing the above-mentioned uncertainty model and assuming that the uncertainty in the reference pixel is uncorrelated with the zero-mean quantization noise, we can conclude that the end-to-end distortion will be

$$D_n(i) = E\left[\left(f_n(i) - \tilde{f}_n(i)\right)^2\right]$$
$$= q_n^2(i) + M_n(i) \qquad (12)$$

In Eq. (12), $q_n(i) = f_n(i) - \hat{f}_n(i)$ means the quantization noise. And $M_n(i)$ is the second moment of the uncertainty in the reference pixel shown as Eq's. (9) and (11) when the encoding mode is *intra* and *inter*, respectively. In addition, we can present two types of *intra* refreshment methods based on the end-to-end distortions expressed in Eq. (12); one for the RD-optimizing high-complexity mode decision and the other for the sum absolute differences (SAD)-based low-complexity mode decision [1].

For an RD-optimizing high-complexity mode decision and an SAD-based low-complexity mode decision, we can represent the cost functions as

$$J_{HC}(m) = \sum_{i \in I_m} D_n(i) + \lambda_{RD-Opt} R_m \qquad (13)$$

$$J_{LC}(m) = \sum_{i \in I_m} \tilde{D}_n(i) + \lambda_{SAD} \tilde{R}_m(v) \qquad (14)$$

where each $D_n(i)$ and $\tilde{D}_n(i)$ denotes the end-to-end distortion summation each MB given in Eq. (12), but $\tilde{D}_n(i)$ means the end-to-end distortion's estimated value by the SAD between original and predicted pixels, λ_{RD-Opt} and λ_{SAD} are the Lagrangian coefficient, $\lambda_{SAD} = \sqrt{\lambda_{RD-Opt}}$, Moreover each R_m and $\tilde{R}_m(v)$ represents the number of bits used to encode and expected to be used to encode the corresponding MB information which is estimated by the motion vector, v, Finally I_m is the set of pixels comprising the *m*-th macroblock[1].

Actually, the distortion in Eq. (13) computed as follows,

$$D_n(i) = \begin{cases} q_n^2(i) + M_n^I(i), & \text{intra-mode} \\ q_n^2(i) + M_n^I(i) + (1-p)M_{n-k}(i+v), & \text{inter-mode} \end{cases} \quad (15)$$

where $n-k$ means the index of reference frame for motion compensated prediction. Also, in Eq. (14), $\tilde{D}_n(i)$ is defined as follows,

$$\tilde{D}_n(i) = \begin{cases} |f_n(i) - f_n^I(i)|, & \text{intra-mode} \\ |f_n(i) - \hat{f}_{n-k}(i+v)| \\ \quad + (1-p)\left[m_{n-k}(i+v) + \sqrt{M_{n-k}(i+v) - m_{n-k}^2(i+v)}\right], & \text{inter-mode} \end{cases} \quad (16)$$

where $f_n^I(i)$ denotes the values constructed by the intra-prediction, $n-k$ means the index of reference frame for motion compensated prediction, and $m_{n-k}(i+v)$ and $M_{n-k}(i+v)$ are the first and second moments of the uncertainty in the motion compensated reference pixel [1].

4 Proposed Intra-refreshment Method

We propose the frame-refreshment, using the above-introduced uncertainty model. We can apply to an *intra*-refreshment by expanding its criterion (or threshold) as the unit of the MB in the reference pixel with that as the unit of frame in order to apply to the *intra*-refreshment by a frame. In order to do that, preferentially, we first should calculate the amount of the amount of the drift noise grounded on this model. It is as follows, for the RD-optimizing high-complexity mode decision,

$$U_{tot}(n) = \begin{cases} \sum_{j \in J_n} \sum_{i \in I_j} M_n(i) & \text{high-complexity} \\ \sum_{j \in J_n} \sum_{i \in I_j} m_{n-k}(i+v) + \sqrt{M_{n-k}(i+v) - m_{n-k}^2(i+v)} & \text{low-complexity} \end{cases} \quad (17)$$

where $U_{tot}(n)$ denotes the total of drift noise of n-th frame, J_n is the set of MBs comprising the n-th frame, $m_n(i)$ and $M_n(i)$ are the first and second moments of the uncertainty.

By the way, we should determine a *intra*-refreshment's threshold compared to Eq. (17). As for this matter, we can think many ways to decide the threshold for the *intra*-refreshments in the encoding algorithm. For example, we can have any decisions about the threshold, associated with the cost function, the drift noise or the whole distortion, including the quantization noise. Though it leaves some room for deliberation, we should keep on discussing and experimenting how to determine the threshold. Even if we should solve this problem after due consideration, we attempt to take a simple approach to decide a threshold. We regard a threshold as the entire quantization. So, if $U_{tot}(n)$ is greater than that, the local encoder encodes a frame as I-picture. Also, in the video streaming service, with estimating the drift noise, we can make a video stream to be a little robust and some more sensitive to a channel error.

In the sequel, we can know the proper time when an *intra*-refreshment method conducts because this model reflects well on the channel error, in comparison with the other error propagation models. And this offers the environment to make occasional frame-refreshment possible. Even more, by carrying out non-periodic frame-refreshment, contrary to the existing and conventional *intra*-refreshments, we can obtain the more efficient video stream. Needless to say, if *intra*-refreshments are executed frequently, the coding efficiency will go down. Therefore, we must use that on the condition not to reduce the coding efficiency and not to consume the bitrates.

5 Simulation Results

Using the above-mentioned various error propagation models, we carried out experiments on the performance of the proposed non-periodic frame refreshment algorithm compared with periodic *intra*-refreshment. Table 1 shows simulation conditions. The reference system encodes frames as I-slices periodically for random access capability. The period of 2 seconds is tested. The tested sequences are 3 sequences of QVGA format and 2 sequences of CIF format. The sequences are encoded with four different bit rates of 256, 320, 384, and 448 kbps. We use the bit error patterns acquired by a 50kmph vehicular receiver over 3GPP/3GPP2 [8], the bit error rate of which is 2×10^{-4}. We perform 10 channel simulations and evaluate the overall average quality of the decoded pictures.

Table 1. Simulation conditions for comparison of the PSNR performances from constant bitrate (CBR) encoding

Sequence	QVGA : News, Drama, Sport CIF : Mobile, Tempete
Frame rate(Hz)	15
Total frames	150
Codec	JM8.6, Baseline profile w/o DP, RS, FMO
Coding options	1 slice/frame MV search range of 16 1 reference frame
Bitrate(kbps)	256, 320, 384, 448

With CIF format, we compute the PSNR defined as

$$PSNR = 10 \cdot \log_{10} \left(\frac{255^2 (150)(352 \times 288)(10)}{\sum_{n=1}^{150} \sum_{i=1}^{352 \times 288} \sum_{j=1}^{10} \left(f_n(i) - \hat{r}_{n,j}(i) \right)^2} \right) \quad (18)$$

where $f_n(i)$ represents the i-th pixel in the n-th original frame and $\hat{r}_{n,j}(i)$ means the i-th pixel in the n-th frame reconstructed by the j-th remote decoder. If the input sequence is QVGA(320×240), the corresponding values in Eq. (18) will readjust to QVGA format.

Table 2 and 3 shows the performances of the *intra*-refreshment algorithms according to the mode decision. For the low-complexity mode decision, the uncertainty model in [1] is tested, and for the high-complexity mode decision, all the above-mentioned models are tested. It verifies that the uncertainty model-based non-periodic *intra*-frame refreshment algorithm yields the average PSNR improvement of 1.55 and 1.30 dB according to mode decision. All the other non-periodic intra-frame refreshment algorithms with each drift noise model incorporated with the high-complexity mode decision also yield better performance than the conventional periodic intra-frame refreshment by from 0.95 to 1.32 dB.

Figure 2 and 3 compare the PSNR performances of the frame refreshment algorithms applied to encoding *Drama* and *Mobile & Calendar*, respectively, where *Drama* is a sequence of QVGA format and *Mobile & Calendar* is a sequence of CIF format. They show vividly that the non-periodic frame refreshment improves the PSNR performance much more as the bit rate of the encoded bitstream increases.

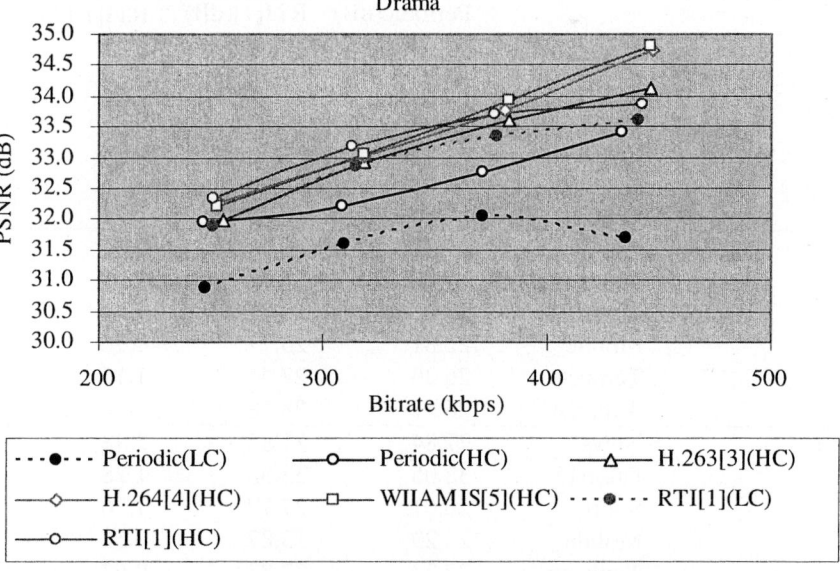

Fig. 2. The rate-distortion performances of the frame refreshment algorithms with a QVGA sequence

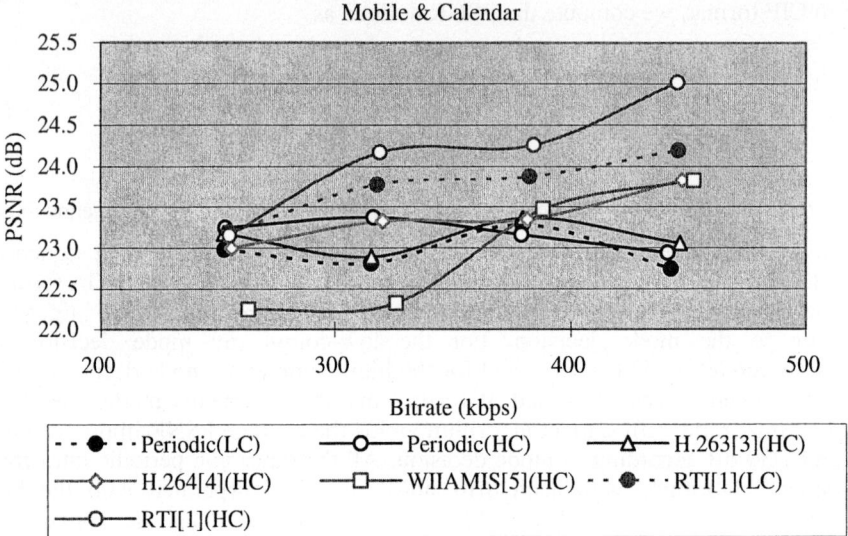

Fig. 3. The rate-distortion performances of the frame refreshment algorithms with a CIF sequence

Table 2. PSNR performance of *intra*-frame refreshment algorithms on low-complexity

Bitrate(kbps)	Sequence	Frame Refreshment (propagation Model)		
		Periodic(dB)	RTI[1](dB)	RTI[1](Δ)
256	News	28.55	28.97	0.42
	Drama	30.87	31.88	1.01
	Sport	25.34	26.29	0.95
	Mobile	22.98	23.19	0.21
	Tempete	26.50	26.83	0.33
	Average	26.85	27.43	0.58
320	News	27.19	30.44	3.26
	Drama	31.60	32.87	1.27
	Sport	25.45	26.89	1.44
	Mobile	22.81	23.77	0.96
	Tempete	26.29	27.44	1.15
	Average	26.67	28.28	1.61
384	News	27.84	31.82	3.98
	Drama	32.05	33.33	1.28
	Sport	26.01	27.77	1.76
	Mobile	23.29	23.87	0.58
	Tempete	27.20	27.83	0.63
	Average	27.28	28.93	1.65

Table 2. *(Continued.)*

448	News	27.77	33.00	5.24
	MV1	31.70	33.59	1.89
	Baseball	26.35	28.03	1.69
	Mobile	22.74	24.19	1.45
	Tempete	26.98	28.43	1.45
	Average	27.11	29.45	2.34
Overall average		26.98	28.52	1.55

Table 3. PSNR performance of *intra*-frame refreshment algorithms on high-complexity

Bitrate (kbps)	Sequence	Frame Refreshment (propagation Model)					
		Periodic (dB)	H.263[3] (dB)	H.264[4] (dB)	WIAMIS[5] (dB)	RTI[1] (dB)	RTI[1] (Δ)
256	News	28.78	29.16	29.67	29.56	29.18	0.40
	Drama	31.93	31.97	32.29	32.22	32.34	0.40
	Sport	25.67	26.52	26.66	26.51	26.51	0.84
	Mobile	23.25	23.18	23.00	22.25	23.15	-0.10
	Tempete	26.61	27.30	27.01	26.88	27.24	0.63
	Average	27.25	27.63	27.72	27.48	27.68	0.44
320	News	27.42	30.32	30.72	30.69	30.44	3.02
	Drama	32.21	32.92	33.03	33.04	33.17	0.96
	Sport	26.00	27.03	26.93	27.33	26.87	0.87
	Mobile	23.37	22.89	23.33	22.32	24.17	0.80
	Tempete	26.46	26.47	26.98	27.21	26.87	0.41
	Average	27.09	27.93	28.20	28.12	28.30	1.21
384	News	28.04	30.96	31.71	31.78	31.80	3.76
	Drama	32.77	33.60	33.77	33.94	33.72	0.95
	Sport	26.49	28.18	28.63	28.57	27.70	1.21
	Mobile	23.16	23.36	23.35	23.47	24.26	1.10
	Tempete	27.21	27.43	27.87	27.90	27.83	0.62
	Average	27.53	28.71	29.07	29.13	29.06	1.53
448	News	28.13	31.84	32.69	32.68	32.82	4.70
	MV1	33.39	34.12	34.73	34.82	33.86	0.47
	Baseball	26.64	28.28	29.27	29.22	28.35	1.71
	Mobile	22.94	23.06	23.83	23.82	25.02	2.08
	Tempete	26.86	27.80	28.34	27.94	28.14	1.27
	Average	27.59	29.02	29.77	29.70	29.64	2.05
Overall average		27.37	28.32	28.69	28.61	28.67	1.30

6 Conclusions

It is important to devise video encoding and decoding schemes in the error-prone channel environments for the streaming service. We have presented that intra-frame refreshment which has been used for the random access capability can be a very effective tool to improve the error resiliency. Based on propagation models for the drift noise or the uncertainty in the reference pixels, we could make it possible to accomplish efficient non-periodic *intra*-frame refreshment. With the uncertainty propagation model, especially, we could implement non-periodic intra-frame refreshment in both the low-complexity (SAD-based fast) mode decision scheme and the high-complexity (RD-optimizing) mode decision schemes. We claim that the non-periodic intra-frame refreshment algorithms can reveal superior error-resiliency performance to the conventional periodic *intra*-refreshment algorithms with the same encoding efficiency. We simulated with QVGA and CIF 15 frames/s video signals for the terrestrial-digital multimedia broadcasting (T-DMB) service, and the simulation results verified it. The proposed non-periodic *intra*-refreshment algorithm based on the uncertainty model yields the average PSNR improvement of 1.55 dB in the low-complexity mode and 1.30 dB in the high-complexity mode.

References

1. Dong Wook Kang et al., "Forced intra refreshment method based on the propagation model of uncertainties in the reference pixels for H.264 streaming service," will appear in *Real Time Imaging*.
2. Y. Wang, S. Wenger, W. Jiantao, A. K. Katsaggelos, "Error resilient video coding techniques," IEEE Signal Processing Magazine (2000) pp. 61-82.
3. Stephan Wenger, Guy Côté, Michael Gallant, Faouzi Kossentini, H.263 Test Model Number 11 (TMN-11) rev. 3 (1999).
4. Chul-Woo Kim, Dong Wook Kang, In-Seong Hwang, "High complexity mode decision for error prone channel," ITU-T SG16/Q6 Contribution: JVT-C101 (2002).
5. Dong Wook Kang et al., "Propagation Model for Uncertainty of Reference Pixels and Model-Based Intra Refreshment for H.264 BitStreams," WIAMIS (2004).
6. M. Zhonguha, Y. Songyu, Z. Zhaoping, "Error resilient intra refresh scheme H.26L stream," Electronics Letters 38 (2002) pp. 1153-1154.
7. Gisle Bjontegaard, H.26L Test Model Long Term Number 8 (TML-8) draft 0, 2001.
8. Viktor Varsa, Marta Karczewicz, Göran Roth, Rickard Sjöberg, Thomas Stockhammer, Günther Liebl, "Common Test Conditions for RTP/IP over 3GPP/3GPP2," ITU-T SG16/Q6 Contribution: VCEG-M77 (2001).

Color Quantization of Digital Images

Xin Zhang[1], Zuman Song[2], Yunli Wang[1], and Hui Wang[1]

[1] Multimedia Research & Development Center, National Univ. of Defense Tech., Changsha, Hunan Province, 410073, P.R.C
ijunzhang@hotmail.com
[2] School of Computer Science, National Univ. of Defense Tech., Changsha, Hunan Province, 410073, P.R.C

Abstract. A two-stage color quantization method is proposed in this paper. At the first stage, a palette selection scheme suitable to the quantization level requirement is chosen and an initial palette is selected. At the second stage, a fast LBG algorithm is adopted to iteratively refine the palette. Experimental results show that this approach is superior to most of the prevalent methods in terms of quantization distortion measured by the MSE metric.

1 Introduction

$2^{24} (=16777216)$ colors can be displayed in a 24-bit true color image at best. But, due to the constraint of image size, factually, total number of colors occurring in a true color image always ranges from 10^4 to a little more than 10^6. That is even too many to be distinguished by the HVS (Human Visual System). Furthermore, 3-dimensional color vectors increase both temporal and spatial cost of processing and analyzing of images, such as texture analysis and image segmentation, etc. An effective approach to circumvent these problems is to convert the 24-bit true color image to an indexed one with at most hundreds of palette colors and visually acceptable distortions, or rather, to perform color quantization. Generally, *color quantization is defined as the process of reducing the number of colors in a digital image by replacing them with the "closest" representative colors* [1], [2]. Since it is a lossy process, it inevitably introduces distortions. The challenge is just how to minimize the distortions perceived by an average human observer.

Let I be an input 24-bit true color image, and it contain N colors $\{c_1, c_2, ..., c_N\}$ inside, each of which has an occurrence frequency $f_i (i = 1, ..N)$. f_i is defined as the total of pixels having the same color vector c_i. The task of color quantization is to convert I into an indexed image I_Q^K in only K colors with least visual distortion, where $K \ll N$ and generally $K \leq 255$. K is always called the *Quantization Level*.

Obviously, how to model the visual distortion of color quantization is the first problem we should consider. Mean squared error (MSE) [1], [2], [5], [6] or (peak) signal to noise ratio (PSNR/SNR) [7] is always employed as an objective metric for color quantization distortion. Despite the common use, these measures have defects, especial the contradiction with visual quality human perceived. A criticism of them can be found in [8]. Tremeau et al [8] proposed a new error metric in terms of perceived image quality. Puzicha et al. generalized MSE to a psychophysically motivated error metric for simultaneous quantization and halftoning. All these extensions can be viewed as weighed forms of the original MSE metric. Allowing for this and the popularity of MSE, this paper still adopts it as the minimizing target of color quantization. Assuming that there are m rows and n columns in I, the quantization distortion measured by MSE can be calculated as

$$D_Q = \frac{1}{m \times n} \sum_{x=0}^{m-1} \sum_{y=0}^{n-1} \left\| I(x,y) - I_Q^K(x,y) \right\|^2, \quad (1)$$

in which $I(x, y)$ and $I_Q^K(x, y)$ represent the color vector of pixel (x, y) on the image plane before and after quantization respectively, $\|\bullet\|$ depicts the difference between these two color vectors. According to psycho-visual principles, Euclidean distance in some perceptual uniform color space, such as CIE L*a*b, CIE L*u*v, etc., is the best metric to estimate visual difference between colors [4].

Formula (1) has other transforms. Let $P = \{c_1^p, c_2^p, ..., c_K^p\}$ be the selected palette colors set, and C_i be the set of colors mapped to c_i^p $(i = 1, 2, ... K)$. Then in each set C_i, quantization distortion measured by MSE is

$$D_Q^i = \sum_{c \in C_i} f(c) \left\| c - c_i^p \right\|^2 \quad (2)$$

As a result, the total MSE, used as the quantization distortion metric, between the quantized and original image is

$$D_Q = \sum_{i=1}^{K} D_Q^i \quad (3)$$

Since these two formulas are derived from a clustering view, MSE computed through (2) and (3) is sometimes called K-means quantization error.

It is known that the problem of seeking an optimum palette color set to minimize D_Q (when K is given) is NP-complete [5]. Therefore, researchers focus their attentions on how to introduce some heuristics to find out the suboptimal solutions. Existing methods can be categorized into two classes: splitting and clustering ones. Splitting approaches operate in a top-down mode. They regard all color vectors in the input image as a whole set, and partition it into K subsets in some recursive way and use the centroid as the representative color of each subset. Typical splitting schemes include median-cut [10], center-cut [11], variance-based [12], the *octree* splitting [13], RWM-cut [14], cut along a selected line [7], etc. In contrast, clustering methods work in a bottom-up mode. They choose K representative colors as the initial palette elements and then group color vectors in the input image into K clusters according to their distance from the representatives. K-means and fuzzy K-means clustering are the classical algorithms belonging to this class. Some other clustering methods include the famous popularity algorithm [10], pairwise clustering [15], agglomerative clustering algorithm proposed by Xiang et al. [16], etc.

Generally speaking, splitting methods are always more time-consuming while more suboptimality guaranteed; clustering ones are comparatively simple in order to keep the algorithms efficient, but the results are greatly influenced by the scanning order and initial palette selection.

To overcome the drawbacks of clustering approaches and acquire more satisfactory quantization results, this paper proposes a two-stage quantization method. At the first stage, a merging or popularity scheme is adopted to select an initial palette. And at the second stage, a fast LBG algorithm is exploited to refine the palette. Experimental results show the proposed approach to be better than most of the methods mentioned above in terms of quantized image quality measured by MSE.

The rest of this paper is organized as follows. Section 2 describes the proposed quantization approach in detail. Then the experimental results are shown in section 3. Finally, discussions of the results and the concluding remarks are given in section 4.

2 The Proposed Quantization Method

Back to (2), let the cardinality of C_i be M ($|C_i|=M$,), $\overline{c_M}$ be the centroid of cluster C_i. For any $c_0 \in R^3$, we have

$$D(C_i,c_0) = \sum_{j=1}^{M} f_j \|c_j - c_0\|^2 = \sum_{j=1}^{M} f_j \|c_j - \overline{c_M}\|^2 + \|c_0 - \overline{c_M}\|^2 \cdot \sum_{j=1}^{M} f_j . \quad (4)$$

in which $D(C_i,c_0)$ denotes the sum-of-squared error (SSE)[1] introduced by mapping colors in C_i to c_0, and f_j is the occurrence frequency of color vector c_j. The centroid $\overline{c_M}$ can be calculated as

$$\overline{c_M} = \sum_{j=1}^{M} f_j c_j \bigg/ \sum_{j=1}^{M} f_j . \quad (5)$$

It is evident by (4) that $D(C_i,c_0)$ will get smaller when c_0 goes closer to the centroid $\overline{c_M}$ of C_i, and that $D(C_i,c_0)$ will reach the minimum when $c_0 = \overline{c_M}$.

Furthermore, given an initial palette $P_0 = \{c_0^1, c_0^2, ..., c_0^K\}$, each color in the input image can be mapped to one of these palette colors according to some mapping criterion. This mapping process produces an initial clustering, or rather, an initial quantization of the image colors. Because $c_0^i (i=1,...,K)$ is not always the centroid

---

[1] Because MSE is proportional to SSE of the same image (region), we use SSE instead for the convenience of mathematical deduction.

of its corresponding cluster C_i, the quantization error calculated according to formula (2) and (3) will surely be reduced if we replace the selected palette colors with the centroids of formerly resulted clusters. This replacement causes alterations to the palette, thus re-clustering is need... Repeating this palette replacement and re-clustering processes until all palette colors are centroids of the corresponding clusters, we can at least get a local minimum of the mean squared quantization error. These thoughts motivated us to introduce LGB algorithm [17] to our color quantization method.

What criterion should be adopted to perform color mapping? It is natural that a color should be mapped to the palette one that is most visually similar to it. As mentioned above, Euclidean distance between color vectors in some uniform color space can be used to depict color differences. Thus, a color vector should be mapped to the palette one that is nearest to it. In some literatures (such as [18]), this is called *the nearest neighbor rule*.

In short, the proposed color quantization approach is a two-stage method. At the first stage, some heuristics are introduced to select an initial palette. At the second stage, a fast LGB algorithm is exploited to iteratively refine the palette and quantize the image.

2.1 Initial Palette Selection Schemes

As an iterative clustering process, the final quantization results depend greatly on initial palette selection. From above reasoning, it is intuitive that initial palette can be selected by partitioning color set of the input image into K subsets and taking centroid (or point near the centroid) of each subset as the representative ones.

This partitioning should according to the distribution of color vectors in the color space. It is known to us that color histograms can be used to obtain that distribution information. However, direct computation of 3-dimensional color histogram is both time and space consuming. Viewing of this, we adopt a down-sampled color histogram in our implementation. For the convenience of computation, integer power of 2 is always taken as the down-sampling factor for each color component. Let the factor be 2^k. Too small k will not save computation time effectively, while too large k will bring unacceptable approximation errors. Based on comparative experiments, we choose $2^5 = 32$ as the down-sampling factor for all three color components, namely, the color space is split into a set of 32^3 sub-cubes. Rarely, the number of bins in the 32 down-sampled color histogram is smaller than the quantization level K. Then the down-sampling factor should be decrease to $2^4 = 16$.

The resulted color histogram provides total occurrence frequency of colors in each sub-cube and gives the approximate distribution of colors in the input image. Assuming there be h bins in the histogram, it is obvious that $h \geq K$. Therefore, color subsets bounded by those sub-cubes need some merging process to produce K clusters. Choosing a representative for color subset encompassed by each sub-cube, the most intuitive merging criterion is according to the distance between these representatives. But intuitive ones are not always the best ones. Let's consider the error introduced by merging two clusters. If cluster C_i and C_j are merged into one cluster C_{merge}, denoting their centroids respectively as $\overline{c_i}$, $\overline{c_j}$ and $\overline{c_{merge}}$, it is obvious that the sum-of-squared error in C_{merge} can be calculated by

$$\sum_{c_k \in C_{merge}} f_k \left\| c_k - \overline{c_{merge}} \right\|^2 = \sum_{c_m \in C_i} f_m \left\| c_m - \overline{c_{merge}} \right\|^2 + \sum_{c_n \in C_{merge}} f_n \left\| c_n - \overline{c_{merge}} \right\|^2$$

$$= D(C_i, \overline{c_{merge}}) + D(C_j, \overline{c_{merge}}). \tag{6}$$

According to formula (4), the increment of sum-of-squared error caused by merging can be formulated as

$$\Delta SSE = SSE_{merge} - SSE_i - SSE_j = |C_i| \cdot \left\| \overline{c_i} - \overline{c_{merge}} \right\|^2 + |C_j| \cdot \left\| \overline{c_j} - \overline{c_{merge}} \right\|^2. \tag{7}$$

where $|\bullet|$ denotes the cardinal of a set, SSE_i, SSE_j and SSE_{merge} represent the sum-of-squared error of C_i, C_j and C_{merge} respectively. In (7), $\overline{c_{merge}}$ can be computed by

$$\overline{c_{merge}} = \frac{|C_i| \cdot \overline{c_i} + |C_j| \cdot \overline{c_j}}{|C_i| + |C_j|}. \tag{8}$$

Self-evidently, it is more reasonable to merge the pair of clusters corresponds to the minimal ΔSSE. The initial palette selection through merging, called *the merging scheme*, can be summarized as: take centroid of subset bounded by each sub-cube as the representative, and iteratively merge the pair of current subsets who have the minimal ΔSSE given in formula (7) until only K subsets left.

Above merging scheme is theoretically sound but computational intensive for initial palette selection. Another simpler scheme we proposed is motivated by the principles of Heckbert's popularity algorithm. We call it *the popularity scheme*, in which all bins in the down-sampled color histogram are sorted according to their occurrence frequency, the K most frequent ones are selected, and the centroids of their corresponding sub-cube encompassed clusters are taken as the initial palette colors.

2.2 Iterative Palette Refinement

After selection of the initial palette, we borrow LBG algorithm to refine it. As mentioned above, this refinement is an iterative process of repeating palette updating and color re-clustering. In each loop, palette updating is a simple operation, thus, speeding up color re-clustering (i.e., color mapping) is critical to reduce temporal complexity of the refinement process. Our acceleration scheme is similar to the Equal-Average Equal-Norm Nearest Neighbor searching method proposed in [19]. And the refinement iteration is stopped when the difference of MSE values computed in two consecutive loops is zero.

Color re-clustering is fulfilled by searching a nearest palette color for each pixel in the input image. Let c_i be the current color vector to be mapped (i.e., clustered) and $P_t = \{c_1^{p(t)}, c_2^{p(t)}, ..., c_K^{p(t)}\}$ be the palette colors set in the t-th loop (which is computed in the $(t-1)$-th loop and $t \geq 0$). Then the problem is to find out a palette color $c_m^{p(t)}$ for c_i which satisfies

$$c_m^{p(t)} = \arg \min_{c_j^{p(t)}} \{\|c_i - c_j^{p(t)}\|^2\}. \tag{9}$$

Full search in the palette is intuitive but time consuming. Some heuristics should be introduced to speeding up this process.

Let us denote the current minimum of $\|c_i - c_j^{p(t)}\|^2$ with $d_{min}^{(t)}(c_i)$. According to the Cauchy-Schwarz inequation, we can get

$$\|c_i - c_j^{p(t)}\|^2 \geq \|c_i\|^2 + \|c_j^{p(t)}\|^2 - 2\|c_i\|\|c_j^{p(t)}\| = (\|c_i\| - \|c_j^{p(t)}\|)^2. \tag{10}$$

Obviously, palette colors $c_j^{p(t)}$ should not be searching candidates if they satisfy

$$(\|c_i\| - \|c_j^{p(t)}\|)^2 > d_{min}^{(t)}(c_i) \Leftrightarrow$$

$$\|c_j^{p(t)}\| > \|c_i\| + \sqrt{d_{min}^{(t)}(c_i)} \text{ or } \|c_j^{p(t)}\| < \|c_i\| - \sqrt{d_{min}^{(t)}(c_i)}. \tag{11}$$

Therefore, to accelerate the color re-clustering process, we firstly sort $P^t = \{c_1^{p(t)}, c_2^{p(t)}, ..., c_K^{p(t)}\}$ by norm of each palette color, then remove those colors satisfying formula (11) from the palette and take the remained ones as searching candidates.

A problem still left is how to determine $d_{min}^{(t)}(c_i)$ for each loop. Denoting the minima acquired from (9) for c_i in two consecutive loops with $\min_i^{(t-1)}$ and $\min_i^{(t)}$ respectively, it is evident that there must be

$$\min_i^{(t)} \leq \min_i^{(t-1)}. \tag{12}$$

Thus, for any $t > 0$, we can set

$$d_{min}^{(t)}(c_i) = \min_i^{(t-1)}. \tag{13}$$

And, in the first loop, we choose a color from the initial palette P_0 whose norm is closest to $\|c_i\|$, and take $d_{min}^{(0)}(c_i)$ as the distance between that color and c_i.

The most remarkable difference between our heuristic searching method and that proposed in [19] is the determination scheme of $d_{min}^{(t)}(c_i)$. We take minimum computed in the previous loop as the threshold of the current loop. In contrast, their selection of $d_{min}^{(t)}$ only allows for the closeness of norms and averages of vectors.

3 Experimental Results and Analysis

To verify the proposed approach, we implement our algorithms with Visual C++ and perform quantization experiments on a lot of 24-bit true color images. For the convenience of comparison, we give the quantization distortions of six images used in

[18], which are measured with MSE. These images are "Baboon", "Lena", "Peppers", "Airplane", "House" and "Sailboat". The quantization results of some other commonly used images in image processing are also given, which include the original images, the quantized images and corresponding MSE values. Experiments are conducted mainly in two aspects as following.

Table 1. MSE of quantization by direct using the two initial palette selection schems without palette refinement

K / Scheme		Baboon	Lena	Peppers	Airplane	House	Sailboat
16	Merging	588	294	553	1043	518	452
	Popularity	864	393	604	382	837	824
32	Merging	379	167	315	892	300	300
	Popularity	458	178	332	169	610	352
64	Merging	254	113	196	286	181	160
	Popularity	231	112	178	100	173	154
128	Merging	161	63	137	86	130	127
	Popularity	152	65	135	85	126	123

Table 2. MSE of quantization with palette refinement and total loops needed. In each data grid of this table, the left is MSE value, and the right is total loops needed (i.e. in a form as MSE / Total_loops).

K / Scheme		Baboon	Lena	Peppers	Airplane	House	Sailboat
16	Merging	532/9	238/11	412/11	237/34	455/18	309/20
	Popularity	587/12	274/11	400/11	197/12	451/11	318/17
32	Merging	311/11	135/9	242/12	167/33	245/11	202/20
	Popularity	324/16	132/8	248/10	111/13	246/9	199/10
64	Merging	186/13	82/7	149/12	111/17	153/7	131/9
	Popularity	186/10	83/7	148/8	73/7	145/9	128/7
128	Merging	121/12	54/5	99/10	51/8	91/11	88/10
	Popularity	120/8	53/6	100/8	52/8	89/10	84/10

Table 3. MSE of quantization by the proposed method, the SAU and SOM algorithm and respectively on identical test images. Results of the latter two algorithms are quoted directly from [18].

K / algorithm		Baboon	Lena	Peppers	Airplane	House	Sailboat
16	Proposed	532	238	412	237	455	309
	SAU	731	273	482	192	481	354
	SOM	667	272	479	214	511	365
32	Proposed	324	132	248	111	246	199
	SAU	424	140	298	127	288	235
	SOM	414	136	261	109	241	245
64	Proposed	186	83	148	73	145	128
	SAU	265	82	199	72	171	166
	SOM	256	83	154	54	146	157
128	Proposed	120	53	100	52	89	84
	SAU	169	53	129	34	105	112
	SOM	156	47	86	26	78	88

3.1 Which Initial Palette Selection Scheme Is Better?

MSE values caused by mapping colors in each image to the initial palette ones selected by both merging and popularity schemes at various quantization levels are given in Table 1. Table 2 gives the final MSE values after refinement iteration stops and the corresponding total loops needed.

From Table 1, we can find out that, in most cases, both schemes alone (without later refinement) can produce an acceptable quantization when compared with some algorithms mentioned in [18], such as center-cut, median-cut and *octree* algorithm. And the merging scheme is superior to the popularity one especially when quantization level $K < 32$.

From Table 2, we can conclude that poorer initial palette needs more loops for the algorithm to converge. However, better initial palette does not always bring about better final results in terms of MSE.

Based on all these findings, we suggest taking merging process as the initial palette scheme when $K < 32$ and taking its counterpart when $K \geq 32$.

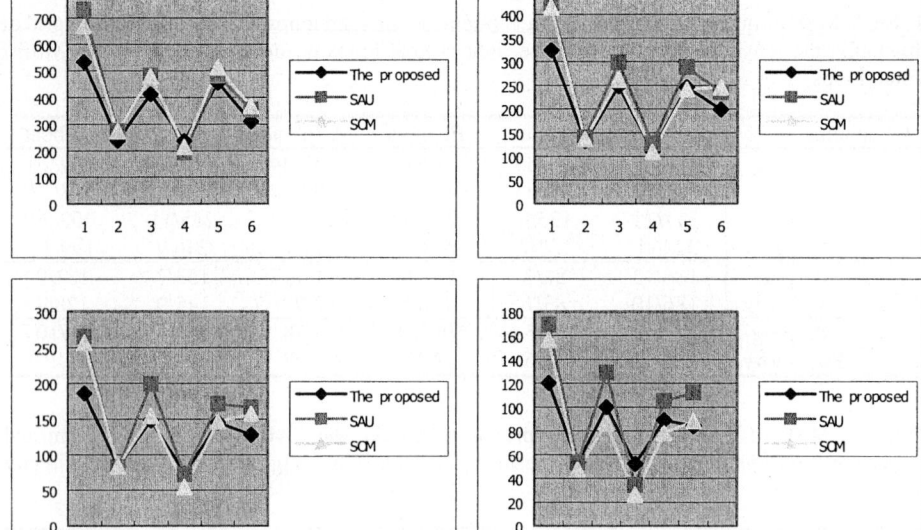

Fig. 1. The proposed approach is fairly good in terms of MSE when comparing with the SAU and SOM algorithm. This shows the MSE values of each algorithm on the same input images (six forementioned images). Form left to right and top to bottom are diagrams correspond to quantization level K=16, K=32, K=64, and K=128 respectively.

3.2 Comparison with Other Prevalent Algorithms

[18] gives the quantization results of several algorithms on forementioned six images at various quantization levels. These algorithms include the popularity algorithm, the center-cut algorithm, the median-cut algorithm, the variance-based algorithm, the

octree algorithm, the Dekker's algorithm using SOM (sampling factor=1), and the algorithm proposed in [18] (a splitting approach we called the SAU algorithm, SAU is the union of first characters of three author's name). According to those experimental results, the SAU and SOM algorithm are the best.

In Table 3, we quote the experimental results of the SAU and SOM algorithm from [18], and put them together with our results. For the convenience of comparisons, we also depict their relative superiority in Fig. 1. In each diagram, the abscissa is No. of above mentioned test images and the ordinate is MSE caused by quantization.

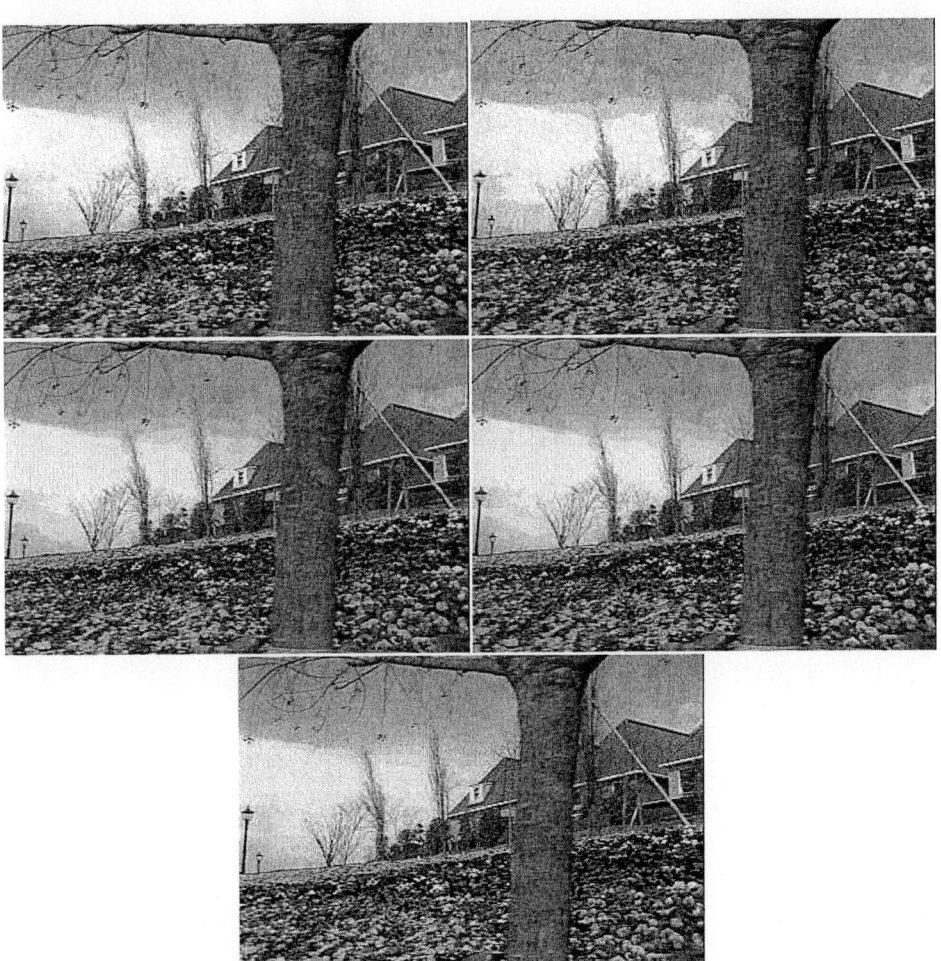

Fig. 2. Quantization results on the image "Garden" are given here. Form left to right and top to bottom are the original input image and the quantized ones correspond to quantization level $K=16$, $K=32$, $K=64$, and $K=128$ respectively. The MSE values are 457, 263, 151, 94.

Two examples of quantization results of some other images are given in Fig. 2 and Fig. 3, which include the original input image and its quantized map for $K=16$, $K=32$, $K=64$, $K=128$ respectively.

Fig. 3. Quantization results on the first frame of the popular sequence "Akiyo" are given here. Form left to right and top to bottom are the original input image and the quantized ones correspond to quantization level $K=16$, $K=32$, $K=64$, and $K=128$ respectively. The MSE values are 231, 125, 62, 34.

4 Conclusions

A two-stage color quantization method is proposed in this paper. At the first stage, a compound initial palette selection scheme is designed to select an initial palette. We proposed two schemes for this stage. The merging scheme is more suitable when quantization level $K < 32$, however, the popularity scheme is more preferable when $K \geq 32$. At the second stage, a fast LBG algorithm is adopted to iteratively refine the palette. Experimental results prove it to be superior to most of the prevalent approaches in terms of quantization distortion measured by the MSE metric.

References

1. Larabi M.C., Richard N., Fernandez C.: A Fast Color Quantization Using a Matrix of Local Pallets. Proc. of Applied Imagery Pattern Recognition Workshop (2000), 136-140
2. Uysal M., Yarman-Vural F.T.: A Fast Color Quantization Algorithm Using a Set of One Dimensional Color Intervals. Proc. of ICIP'98, 1(1998), 191-195
3. Orchard, M.T., Bouman, C.A.: Color Quantization of Images, IEEE Trans. on Signal Processing. 39(12)(1991), 2677-2690
4. Sharma, G., Trussell, H.J.: Digital Color Imaging. IEEE Trans. on Image Processing, 6(7) (1997) 901-932
5. Gervautz, M., Purgathofer, W.: A simple method for color quantization: Octree quantization. *Graphics Gems,* New York: Academic, 1990.
6. Braquelaire J.P., Brun, L.: Comparison and Optimization of Methods of Color Image Quantization. IEEE trans. on Image Processing. 6(7)(1997) 1048-1052
7. S.C. Cheng, C.K. Yang: A fast and novel technique for color quantization using reduction of color space dimensionality. Pattern Recognition Letters 22 (2001) 845-856
8. Tremeau, A., Calonnier, M.: Color quantization error in terms of perceived image quality. Proc. of ICASSP-94 5(1994) 93-96
9. Puzicha, J., Held, M., Ketterer, J., Buhmann, J.M.: On Spatial Quantization of Color Images. IEEE trans. on Image Processing 9 (2000) 666-682
10. Heckbert, P.: Color image quantization for frame buffer display. ACM Trans. Computer Graphics (SIGGRAPH) 16(3) (1982), 297-307
11. Joy, G., Xiang, Z.: Center-cut for color-image quantization. Visual Comput. 10 (1993), 62-66
12. Wan, S.J., Wong, S.K.M., Prusinkiewicz, P.: An algorithm for multidimensional data clustering. ACM Trans. on Math. Software 14 (1988), 153-162.
13. Gonzalez, A.I., Grana, M.: Competitive neural networks as adaptive algorithms for non-stationary clustering: Experimental results on the color quantization of image sequences. Proc. of Internat. Conf. on Neural Networks 3 (1997) 1602-1607
14. Yang, C.Y., Lin, J.C.: Color quantization by RWM-cut. Proc. of the Internat. Conf. on Document Analysis and Recognition. 1995. 669-672
15. Velho, L., Gomes, J., Sobreiro, M.V.R.: Color image quantization by pairwise clustering. Proc. of X Brazilian Symp. of Computer Graphics and Image, Los Alamitos, CA, (1997) 203-210
16. Xiang, Z., Joy, G.: Color image quantization by agglomerative clustering. IEEE Comput. Graph Appl. 14(1994), 44-48

17. Linde, Y., Buzo, A., Gray, R.: An algorithm for vector quantizer design. IEEE Trans. on Comm. 28 (1) (1980), 84–95
18. Sirisathitkul, Y., Auwatanamongkol, S., Uyyanonvara, B.: Color image quantization using distances between adjacent colors along the color axis with highest color variance. Pattern Recognition Letters 25 (2004) 1025–1043
19. Liu, C.H., Lu, Z.M., Sun, S.H.: An Equal-Average Equal-Norm Nearest Neighbor Codeword Search Algorithm for Vector Quantization. Acta Electronica Sinica (Published in China), 31 (10) (2003) 1558-1561

Directional Feature Detection and Correspondence

Wen-Hao Wang[1], Fu-Jen Hsiao[1], and Tsuhan Chen[2]

[1] Industrial Technology Research Institute, Taiwan
{devin, hsiaofujen}@itri.org.tw
[2] Carnegie Mellon University, US
tsuhan@andrew.cmu.edu

Abstract. A method is proposed to detect useful directional feature points other than corner points considering that the number of corner points may not be sufficient in a scene. This is achieved by directional analysis of properties of image points by virtue of the proposed gradient operators with different direction topologies. A matching criterion is also proposed to find the initial correspondence by using the feature vectors that are acquired from the results of directional analysis. For the purpose of improving the final correspondence, four constraints are employed in the system to seek and refine the correspondence.

1 Introduction

Feature detection is a fundamental task in computer vision, *e.g.* rigid registration for 3D reconstruction. In addition, robust correspondence is an important factor to the success of video-based 3D reconstruction. With robust feature points, the subsequent tasks can then be accomplished. Thus, a 3D model can be easily created by video-based 3D method rather than the complicated and time-consuming model-building process. The model can then be further used in virtual reality or augmented reality applications, like a virtual museum tour, on-line shopping exhibition, or 3D video games.

In conventional approaches, corner detection methods are mostly used. The assessing and evaluation methods for corner detection can be found in [1][2][3]. However, in some situations, number of corners may not be sufficient; thus, other useful features must be also detected. Based on this consideration, a directional feature point detection algorithm and matching procedure are proposed in this paper.

Regarding the study of directional analysis, a steerable method was introduced in [4] (wedge detector) by choosing an optimal template from a family of steerable functions based on the modification of Canny's criterion. Prior to choosing an appropriate template for an unknown orientation, analytical optimization must be performed. However, in practical applications of correspondence, orientation between two consecutive frames is usually not significant. In the proposed method, only three directions are used for evaluating similarity metric. The directional method can also be found in [5]; an eight strip shaped filters were designed for detecting the line direction. The candidates in the search area with similar directions are chosen for matching. Apart from that, affine changes between two frames can be estimated to track the features and monitor the quality of the features during tracking [6] [7].

Matching or correspondence can be accomplished by three stages [8]: (1) feature detection, (2) similarity metrics, and (3) search strategies. In the proposed method, the feature detection is based on directional analysis of image pixels in order to extract points other than corners [9]. As for the second stage, eigen values of feature points are used as feature arrays which will be employed in similarity metrics. The search strategies are also discussed in this paper; the correspondence is achieved by means of four constraints: "feature constraint," "F constraint," "Order constraint," and "Epipolar constraint."

The paper is organized as follows: The proposed directional feature detection is described in Sec. 2. The system of feature detection and correspondence is presented in Sec. 3. The constraints used for refining correspondence are elucidated in Sec. 4. Sec. 5 demonstrates the experimental results. Finally, a brief conclusion is given in Sec. 6.

2 Directional Feature Points Detection

Fig. 1 illustrates the six direction topologies used for evaluating the gradient along the specific directions. The six direction topologies are denoted as $d_1,...,d_6$. d_1 and d_2 used to analyze the directions of integer multiples of 90 degrees. $d_3,...,d_6$ are used to analyze the directions of integer multiples of 135 degrees.

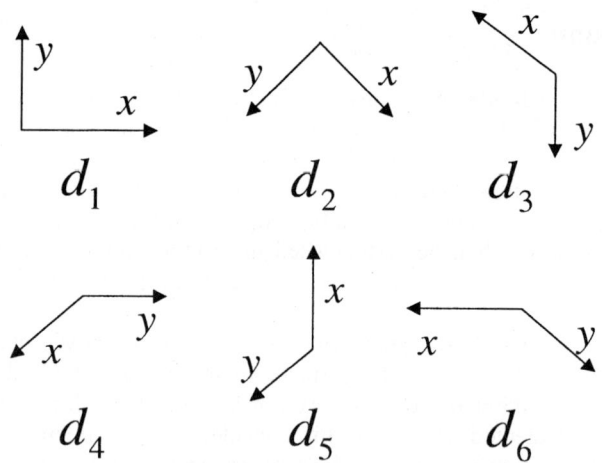

Fig. 1. Six direction topologies

Let I_x and I_y denote the partial derivative with respect to x and y, respectively. A symmetric matrix [9] can be formed as

$$\Psi = \begin{bmatrix} G \otimes I_x^2 & G \otimes I_x I_y \\ G \otimes I_x I_y & G \otimes I_y^2 \end{bmatrix} \quad (1)$$

where G is a zero mean Gaussian kernel of variance σ^2 and $\otimes$ is a convolution operator. Two eigen values can be evaluated from the matrix Ψ. Harris [9] detects corners by inspecting the value of the product of the two eigen values. Thus, only corners can be detected; however, other useful features (*e.g.* directional features) cannot be found.

For direction topology d_i ($i = 1,...,6$), we have eigen values ($\lambda_{i1}, \lambda_{i2}$) for a point in image I_1 and eigen values ($\lambda'_{i1}, \lambda'_{i2}$) for a point in Image I_2. The candidate mask M_{1i} of feature point locations for direction topology d_i in I_1 is determined by the criteria:

$$[(\lambda_{i1} > \tau_u) \text{ and } (\lambda_{i2} < \tau_l)] \text{ or } [(\lambda_{i1} < \tau_l) \text{ and } (\lambda_{i2} > \tau_u)] \quad (2)$$

where τ_l is the lower threshold and τ_u is the upper threshold. If a point $I_1(x, y)$ satisfies the above criteria, $M_{1i}(x, y) = 1$ denotes that the point (x,y) is a feature point candidate with the direction topology d_i. Let M_1 denote the mask contains all potential candidates:

$$M_1 = \bigcup M_{1i}, i = 1,...,6 \quad (3)$$

By using the same principle, we have the candidate mask in image I_2:

$$M_2 = \bigcup M_{2i}, i = 1,...,6. \quad (4)$$

In addition to finding the candidate points, which satisfy the above directional criteria, each point in the candidate area has to be evaluated according to their feature strength in a local area. The difference of the two eigen values in direction d_i is evaluated as

$$\delta_i = |\lambda_{i1} - \lambda_{i2}|. \quad (5)$$

The maximum of all differences is

$$\hat{\delta} = \max_{i=1,...,6}\{\delta_i\}. \quad (6)$$

Therefore, the following evaluation is used as directional feature:

$$\Omega_1 = \hat{\delta} - \Gamma(\delta_i) \quad (7)$$

where $\Gamma(\delta_i)$ is the average operation of the set of eigen value differences excluding the maximum. Large value of Ω_1 reveals prominent candidate of directional feature. Let $\hat{\Omega}_1$ denote the non-maximum suppression result of Ω_1. The potential candidate of feature points in image I_1 is obtained as

$$\Pi_1 = \bigcap \{\hat{\Omega}_1, M_1\}. \quad (8)$$

In addition, the potential candidate of feature points in I_2 can be obtained as Π_2. Suppose that there are J feature points in I_1. Each feature point $p_1(j), j = 1,...,J$ can be represented by a homogeneous coordinate designated by the mask Π_1. Let S_1 be the feature points set:

$$S_1 = \{(p_1(j), f_1(j)) \mid j = 1,...,J\} \tag{9}$$

where $p_1(j)$ is characterized by the feature array:

$$f_1(j) = (\lambda_{11}(j), \lambda_{12}(j),...\lambda_{61}(j), \lambda_{62}(j)). \tag{10}$$

A feature points $p_2(k)$ in image I_2 can be characterized by the feature array:

$$f_2(k) = (\lambda'_{11}(k), \lambda'_{12}(k),...\lambda'_{61}(k), \lambda'_{62}(k)). \tag{11}$$

The feature points set for I_2 (K points) is

$$S_2 = \{(p_2(k), f_2(k)) \mid k = 1,...,K\}. \tag{12}$$

3 System of Detection and Correspondence

Fig. 2 illustrates the proposed algorithm for feature point detection and correspondence. These techniques are developed based on uncalibrated camera.

I_1 and I_2 represent two input images. They are captured with the same camera in difference view angle (not a wide baseline problem). For the purpose of extracting directional feature points, firstly, the images are analyzed with six directional gradient operators (described in Sec. 2) in the block "Directional Feature Detection" of Fig. 1. S_1 and S_2 are the point sets containing potential candidates of feature points for I_1 and I_2, respectively. Each point of which is characterized by the feature array of twelve eigen values.

In the proposed algorithm, four constraints are used for correspondence. The first constraint is feature constraint based on the eigen feature arrays f_1 and f_2. In the initial matching (block "Matching with Feature Constraint"), only these directional features are employed to find the preliminary matching pairs { P_1, P_2 } where P_1 is a point set (homogeneous coordinate) whose elements correspond to the elements in P_2.

The other three constraints will be applied after the approximate epipolar geometry is estimated by using the paired point set P_1 and P_2 (correspondence results). Finally, the correspondence of feature points in I_1 and feature points in I_2 can then be acquired by means of all constraints. The detail procedure of correspondence will be elucidated in Sec. 4.

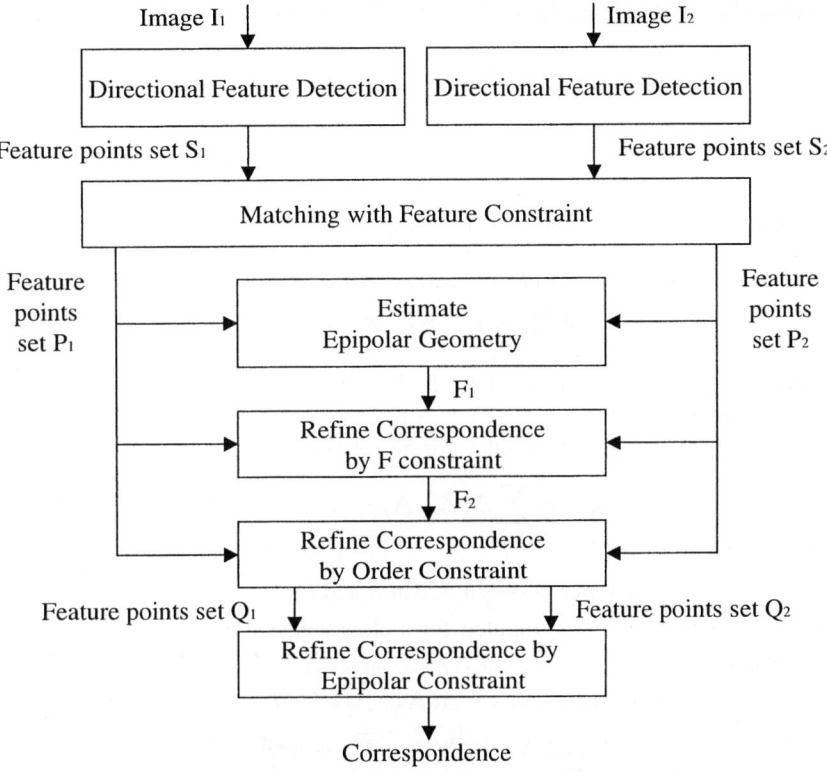

Fig. 2. Diagram of the algorithm

4 Correspondence of Feature Points by Constraints

The correspondence problem is described in this section. Four constraints are employed to find and refine the correspondence: "Directional feature constraint," "F constraint," "Order constraint," and general "Epipolar lines constraint." The first constraint is used to find the preliminary correspondence of S_1 and S_2. The matching results lead to two point sets P_1 and P_2. These two point sets are then used to estimate epipolar geometry with which correspondence can be refined.

4.1 Directional Feature Constraint

Given a point $p_1(j)$ in S_1, it is desired to find a match with a unique point in a point set $s2$ which is a subset of S_2:

$$s2 = \{p_2(k) \mid p_2(k) \in \Theta\} \tag{13}$$

where Θ is the search area centered at $p_1(j)$. The feature arrays of the two points are described as follows:

$$f_1(j) = (\lambda_{11}(j), \lambda_{12}(j), ... \lambda_{61}(j), \lambda_{62}(j)) \tag{14}$$

and

$$f_2(k) = (\lambda'_{11}(k), \lambda'_{12}(k), ... \lambda'_{61}(k), \lambda'_{62}(k)). \tag{15}$$

For convenience of description of matching, let

$$f_1 = \{\Lambda_i \mid i = 1,...,6\}, \ \Lambda_i = (\lambda_{i1}, \lambda_{i2}), \tag{16}$$
$$f_2 = \{\Lambda'_i \mid i = 1,...,6\}, \ \Lambda'_i = (\lambda'_{i1}, \lambda'_{i2}). \tag{17}$$

On account that some rotation might lie between the two images; thus, it is necessary to evaluate the similarity of the two feature arrays in three neighboring directions. The first correlation is computed for no rotation:

$$\zeta_1 = \sum_{i=1,...,6} \Delta(\Lambda_i, \Lambda'_i) \tag{18}$$

where $\Delta(a,b)$ is the distance between vector a and b.

The second correlation is computed for a clockwise rotation (45 degrees) between the two images:

$$\zeta_2 = \Delta(\Lambda_1, \Lambda'_2) + \Delta(\Lambda_2, \overline{\Lambda'_1}) + \Delta(\Lambda_3, \Lambda'_5) + \\ \Delta(\Lambda_4, \Lambda'_6) + \Delta(\Lambda_5, \overline{\Lambda'_4}) + \Delta(\Lambda_6, \Lambda'_3). \tag{19}$$

The first item means that I_1 is analyzed at direction d_1 and I_2 is analyzed at direction d_2 (as shown in Fig. 1). The second item denotes that I_1 is analyzed at direction d_2 and I_2 is analyzed at a direction opposite to d_1 whose eigen values are equivalent to reverse of eigen values of d_1; i.e.

$$\overline{\Lambda'_i} = (\lambda'_{i2}, \lambda'_{i1}). \tag{20}$$

The third correlation is computed for a counter-clockwise rotation:

$$\zeta_3 = \Delta(\Lambda_1, \overline{\Lambda'_2}) + \Delta(\Lambda_2, \Lambda'_1) + \Delta(\Lambda_3, \Lambda'_6) + \Delta(\Lambda_4, \Lambda'_5) + \\ + \Delta(\Lambda_5, \Lambda'_3) + \Delta(\Lambda_6, \Lambda'_4). \tag{21}$$

The first item means that I_2 is analyzed at the direction opposite to d_2; hence its corresponding eigen values is $\overline{\Lambda'_2}$. The minimum of the three distances is determined as the distance between the two feature points $p_1(j)$ and $p_2(k)$. By means of the above computation and comparison, $p_1(j)$ can find its best match point in s_2.

Therefore, two point sets P_1 and P_2 can then be obtained. This is accomplished in the stage "Matching with Feature Constraint" as shown in Fig. 1. By means of RANSAC [10] algorithm on the point sets P_1 and P_2, a fundamental matrix F_1 can be estimated.

The pairing number of this subset must be at least eight pairs because computation of fundamental matrix needs at least 8 correspondence pairs. In conventional corner detection methods, RANSAC may not be employed in case of insufficient number of corners.

4.2 F Constraint

According to the principle of epipolar geometry, all points $P_1(j)$ of P_1 and point $P_2(j)$ in P_2 must satisfy the formula

$$P_2(j)^T F_1 P_1(j) = 0 \qquad (22)$$

where $P_1(j)$ and $P_2(j)$ are represented by homogeneous coordinate.

On considering that the selected point pairs by RANSAC can approximate the real epipolar geometry, all points pairs in P_1 and P_2 are all verified by using the fundamental matrix [11] F_1. Let

$$\rho(j) = P_2(j)^T F_1 P_1(j). \qquad (23)$$

If $\rho(j)$ is smaller than a threshold, the (j)th pair is approved; otherwise, the (j)th pair must be removed in order to avoid potential error of the epipolar geometry.

4.3 Order Constraint

All epipolar lines must appear in the same order both in image I_1 and image I_2. For example, image I_1 and I_2 have the point pair {1 2 3 4 5 6 7 8 9}. Each feature point and the epipole can construct an epipolar line. After sorting the slopes of all epipolar lines in descending order, the point pairs are listed in order as

$$P_1' = \{1\ 4\ 2\ 3\ 8\ 5\ 6\ 9\ 7\} \qquad (24)$$

for I_1. Due to possible rotation, the sorted point pairs in I_2 may be listed as

$$P_2' = \{9\ 7\ 1\ 4\ 2\ 3\ 5\ 8\ 6\} \qquad (25)$$

which is a shifted version of P_1'.

By shifting the sorted point set P_2', the best match can be found as illustrated in Fig. 3. In such a match, the pairs 5 and 8 do not appear in order, which will imply high possibility of erroneous correspondence. After removing the two outliers, the final point sets of correspondence for I_1 and I_2 are

$$Q_1 = \{1\ 4\ 2\ 3\ 6\ 9\ 7\}, \qquad (26)$$

and

$$Q_2 = \{9\ 7\ 1\ 4\ 2\ 3\ 6\}, \qquad (27)$$

respectively.

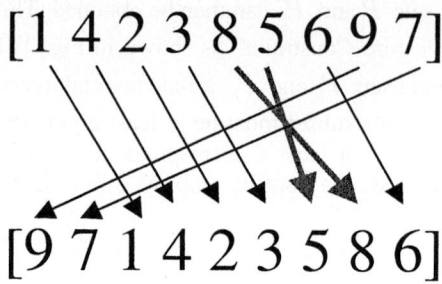

Fig. 3. Pairs 5 and 8 violates "order constraint"

4.4 Epipolar Lines Constraint

By means of the above three constraints, the correctness of the correspondence can be improved step by step. Based on the current estimated epipolar lines and pairs of correspondence, all paired feature points can be further refined by using the general epipolar line constraint: i.e. find the better matching along the epipolar lines instead of the conventional block search area. The related methods can be found in literatures.

In the example of the case of this paper, for each feature point in Q_1, a better correspondence in I_2 can be found along the epipolar line of its correspondence point q in Q_2.

5 Experimental Results

Directional features are useful for those images, which have few corners. In this case, all useful features other than corners must be detected such that the number of feature points will be sufficient for seeking satisfactory correspondence.

Fig. 4 (a) shows the detection results of I_1 by means of Harris corner detector. Each feature point is marked by a cross '+'. The number of the detected corners is insufficient to complete the whole procedure required for refining correspondence. Fig. 4(b) shows the features points of I_1 detected by means of the proposed "directional feature detection" method described in Sec. 2 (the first stage of Fig. 2). It is obvious that more feature points can be found when compared with corner detection. Therefore, more features can be employed to find robust correspondence in case of the scenes that have less corner features. Feature points of I_1 and I_2 is represented by S_1 and S_2 as shown in Fig. 2, respectively.

The proposed matching method (constraint 1: Directional Feature Constraint) outperforms conventional block matching method. In case of no noise corruption, block matching can detect 51 points in I1 and result in 32 correct correspondences. The correct ratio (CR) is 62.7%. The proposed constraint 1 can lead to CR = 76.2%. In case of Gaussian noises (0, 0.005), block matching can only obtain CR=18.8%; while the proposed constraint 1 can lead to CR=54.2%. In case of Gaussian noises (0.0, 0.01), the block matching can only obtain one correspondence; however, the proposed "Directional Feature Constraint" can achieve 11 correspondences.

Fig. 5 shows the initial correspondence for I_1 (left) and I_2 (right). The point sets are represented by P_1 and P_2, respectively.

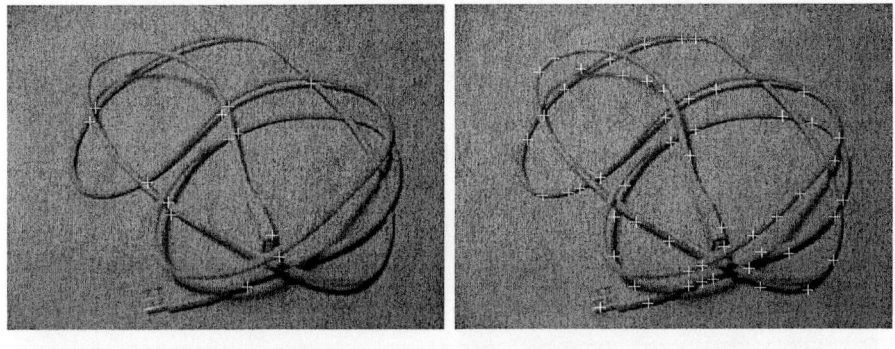

Fig. 4. (a) Harris corners   (b) Feature detected by proposed method

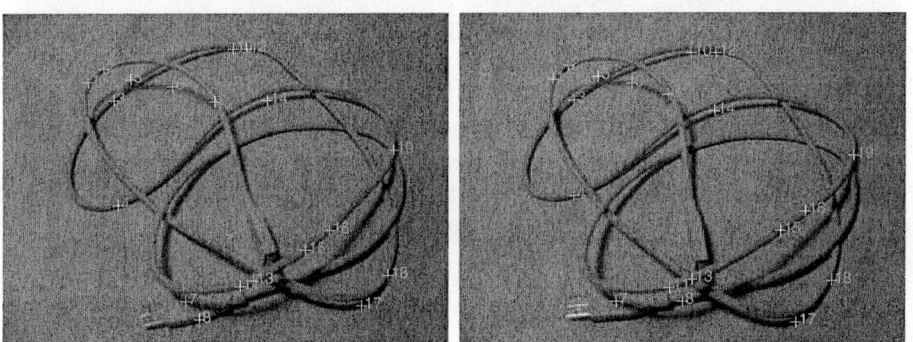

Fig. 5. Correspondence results using the "directional feature constraint"

The correspondence sets P_1 and P_2 are used for estimating epipolar geometry. By means of RANSAC algorithm, 17 pairs are selected to estimate the epipolar geometry. Fig. 6 shows the epipolar lines along each selected feature points.

As shown in Fig. 2, the stage "Refine Correspondence by F constraint" will be used to refine the epipolar geometry (Fig. 6). All feature points in P_1 and P_2 will be verified again by using the estimated fundamental matrix F1 that is obtained in the previous stage.

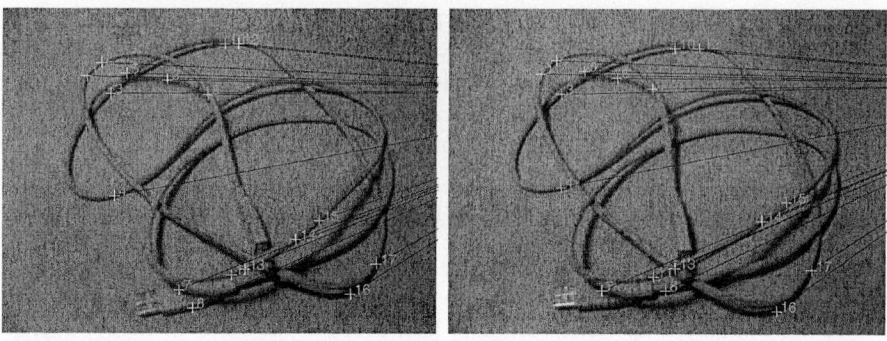

Fig. 6. Estimated epipolar geometry

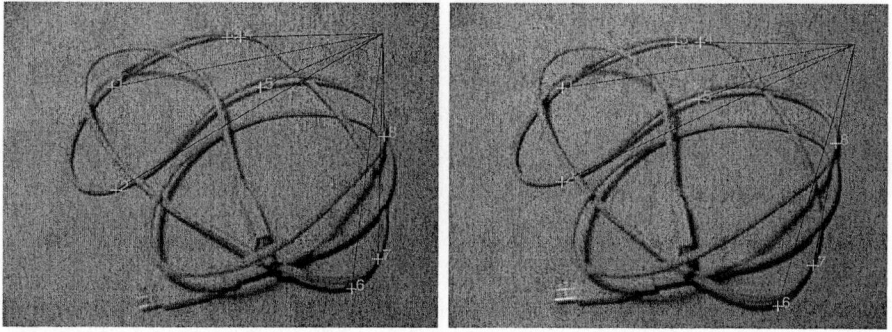

Fig. 7. Refined results by constraints 2 and 3

Fig. 7 shows the epipolar lines of all corresponding points by using the constraints 2 and 3. As shown in this figure, the correctness of correspondence and the number of correspondence are all satisfactory such that further refinement can be achieved along the epipolar lines.

6 Conclusions

An algorithm of directional feature point detection and correspondence is proposed in this paper. The features other than corners can be successfully found by means of the method. The correspondence is accomplished based on four constraints. The initial correspondence is established by using the first major constraint, which employs eigen values as feature vectors. The matching is useful for small amount of rotation between two images. Furthermore, three other constraints are used for refining the correspondence with improving epipolar geometry. As a result, outliers can be successfully removed and a satisfactory correspondence can then be obtained.

References

1. Rockett, P.I.: Performance Assessment of Feature Detection Algorithms: A Methodology and Case Study on Corner Detectors. IEEE Trans. Image Processing, Vol. 12, No. 12 (2003) 1668-1676
2. Tissainayagam, P., Suter, D.: Assessing the Performance of Corner Detectors for Point Feature Tracking Applications. Image and Vision Computing, Vol. 22, No. 8 (2004) 663-679
3. Schmid, C., Mohr, R., Bauckhage, C.: Evaluation of Interest Detectors. International Journal of Computer Vision, Vol. 37, No. 2 (2000) 151-172
4. Jacob, M., Unser, M.: Design of Steerable Filters for Feature Detection Using Canny-Like Criteria. IEEE Trans. PAMI, Vol. 26, No. 8 (2004) 1007-1019
5. Kutka, R., Stier, S.: Extraction of Line Properties Based on Direction Fields. IEEE Trans. Medical Imaging, Vol. 15, No. 1 (1996) 51-58
6. Shi, J., Tomasi, C.: Good Features to Track. IEEE Conf. on Computer Vision and Pattern Recognition (1994)
7. Lacroix, S., Jung, I.-K.: A Robust Interest Points Matching Algorithm. ICCV2001 Proceedings, Vol. II (2001) 538-543
8. Seeger, S., Laboureux, X.: Feature Extraction and Registration – An Overview. University of Erlangen-Nuremberg.
9. Harris, C., Stephens, M.: A Combined Corner and Edge Detector. Proc. 4th Alvey Vision Conf. Manchester, U.K. (1988) 147-151
10. Fischler, M., Bolles, R.: Random Sample Consensus: a Paradigm for Model Fitting with Application to Image Analysis and Automated Cartography. Communications of the ACM, Vol. 24 (1981) 381-95
11. Hartley, R.I.: In Defense of the Eight-Point Algorithm. IEEE Trans. PAMI, Vol. 19, No. 6 (1997) 580-593

An Improvement of Dead Reckoning Algorithm Using Kalman Filter for Minimizing Network Traffic of 3D On-Line Games

Hyon-Gook Kim and Seong-Whan Kim

Department of Computer Science, Univ. of Seoul, Jeon-Nong-Dong, Seoul, Korea
Tel: +82-2-2210-5316, fax: +82-2-2210-5275
seraph90@venus.uos.ac.kr, swkim7@uos.ac.kr

Abstract. Online 3D games require efficient and fast user interaction support over network, and the networking support is usually implemented using network game engine. The network game engine should minimize the network delay and mitigate the network traffic congestion. To minimize the network traffic between game users, a client-based prediction (dead reckoning algorithm) is used. Each game entity uses the algorithm to estimates its own movement (also other entities' movement), and when the estimation error is over threshold, the entity sends the UPDATE (including position, velocity, etc) packet to other entities. As the estimation accuracy is increased, each entity can minimize the transmission of the UPDATE packet. To improve the prediction accuracy of dead reckoning algorithm, we propose the Kalman filter based dead reckoning approach. To show real demonstration, we use a popular network game (BZFlag), and improve the game optimized dead reckoning algorithm using Kalman filter. We improve the prediction accuracy and reduce the network traffic by 12 percents.

1 Introduction

Online 3D games require efficient user interaction support over network, and the networking support is usually implemented using network game engine. The network game engine should minimize the network delay and mitigate the network traffic congestion. To minimize the network traffic between networking game users, dead reckoning technique is used [1]. Each game entity uses the algorithm to estimates its movement and other entities' movement, thereby, each entity can minimize the transmission of its information (position, velocity, etc) to other entities. R. Gossweiler and R. J. Laferriere introduced the dead reckoning algorithm for the multi-user game [2], and S. Aggarwal and H. Banavar proposed the use of globally synchronized clocks among the participating players and a time-stamp augmented dead reckoning vector that enables the receiver to render the entity accurately [3]. In addition, W. Cai and F. B.S. Lee proposed a multi-level threshold scheme that adaptively adjusted, based on the relative distance between entities to reduce the rate of transmitting UPDATE packets [4].

To improve the prediction accuracy of dead reckoning algorithm, we propose the Kalman filter based approach. We improve the dead reckoning of a popular networking game (BZFlag) using Kalman filter, and showed that prediction accuracy is improved and network traffic minimized.

In section 2, we review the networking techniques for 3D online Role Playing Game (RPG), for dead reckoning, and for Kalman filter. In Section 3, we propose a Kalman filter based dead reckoning algorithm. In Section 4, we apply our Kalman approach on BZFLAG games; show the experimental results with minimized UPDATE packets between game players. We conclude in section 5.

2 Related Works

RPG game players accomplish the given mission by co-operating other players in their game space. A game character grows by experience in RPG games. B. Trubshaw in England at 1980 introduced MUD (multi user dimension, multi user dungeon, or multi user dialog) game, which is the first online PRG game. MUD game is a genre that the multi-user plays the textual game by connecting with network. According to improve the graphic techniques, MUD game developed into MUG (multi user graphic or multi user game). Recently, 3D online RPG games called MMORPG (massively multiplayer online role-playing game) gets popular, and thousands of players or more players play the RPG game. In this section, we introduce the basic technique for network engine in online RPG game, dead reckoning algorithm, and Kalman filter.

The networking server technique can be implemented using three methods: (1) peer to peer, (2) client server architecture, and (3) distributed server architecture. In peer to peer, each game player transmits the occurred information to each other. It is

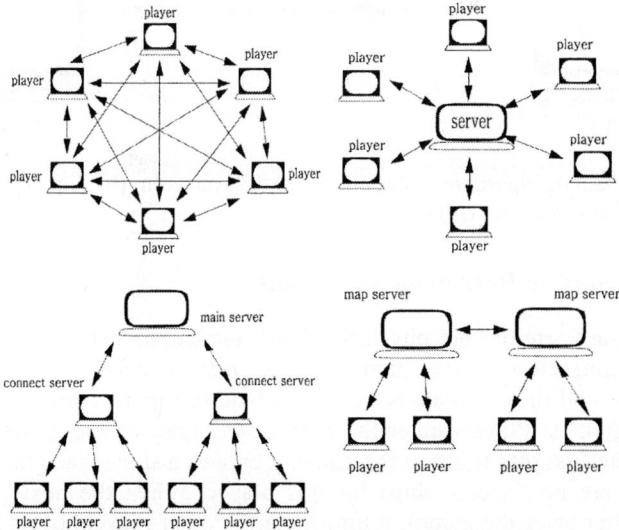

Fig. 1. Server architecture: (a) peer to peer, (b) client server architecture, (c) load distribution method, (d) map server method

suitable for the small-scale games like Starcraft. In client server (CS) architecture, the server collects all of the data from the clients, stores the changes in some data, and then sends the results to each participating client. For large-scale games, we need distributed server architecture as shown in Figure 1. To distribute server, we can use load distribution method or map server method. In the load distribution, the client connects with each server, but the main server operates the game logic. The on-line game should minimize (1) network bandwidth and (2) network delay. The bandwidth represent the game's scalability and the delay represent the game's responding ability. If many players connect the server, then the network traffic increases. As the result, the network delay increases. There is a dead reckoning (DR) technique to reduce the network traffic.

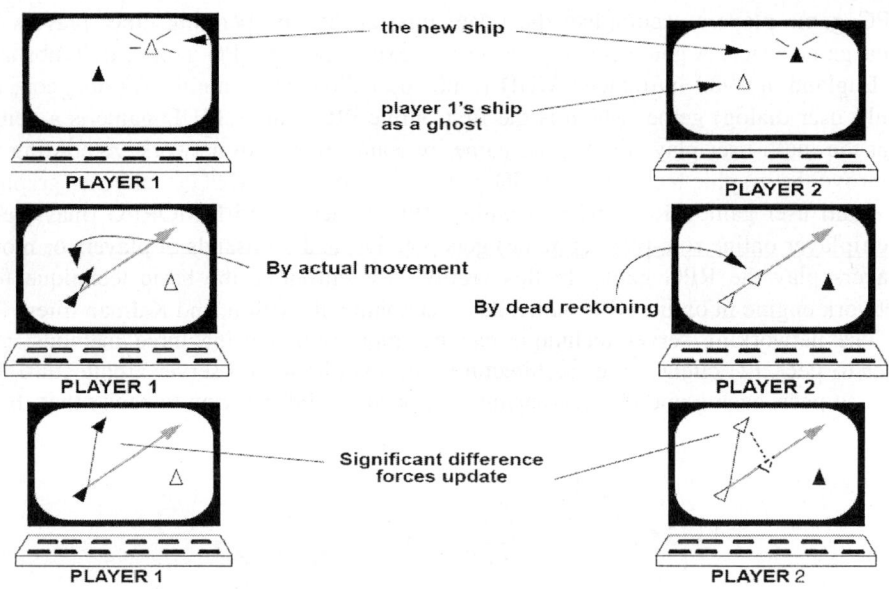

Fig. 2. Dead reckoning algorithm snapshot: (a) next Player(s) In, (b) ship position on different screens, (c) ship position after UPDATE [2]

2.1 Reviews on Dead Reckoning Algorithms

Since on-line game entities are physically distributed, updating states (e.g. each game players' position, etc) of the game entities may generate a large amount of communication and thus saturate network bandwidth. Figure 2 provides snapshots as the game progresses. Players enter the game, participate in the game and leave the game. When the first player enters the game, it creates a ship. Since there are no other players, there are no "ghost" ships for this player. When the next player (and all players thereafter enter the game), it informing the other players of its birth in Figure 2(a). With several players in the game, Figure 2(b) shows how different players' screens appear when a ship moves. When a player moves its own ship, if the movement does not deviate much from the dead reckoning, then we do not send any messages. The ship still moves on all screens as the result of the dead reckoning algorithm. If the ship does deviate significantly from the dead reckoning path like Figure 2(c), then the player informs all of the other players to update their ghost ships with the new correct ship position and velocity [2].

To reduce the amount of communication, DR technique was developed [4]. One of the important aspects in on-line games is the ability of each game player to represent accurately in real-time the state of all game entities, including both local and remote, participating in the same game. To reduce the number of state UPDATE packets, the DR technique is used. In addition to the high fidelity model that maintains the accurate position about its own game entities, each game entity also has a dead reckoning model that estimates the position of all game entities (both local and remote). Therefore, instead of transmitting state UPDATE packets, the estimated position of a remote game entity can be readily available through a simple and localized computation [4]. The game entity compares real position with DR position. If the difference between real position and DR position is greater than a threshold, the game entity informs others remote entities to update their ghost objects' position [2]. Following program is a pseudo code for the dead reckoning algorithm.

```
Algorithm : Dead Reckoning
for every received packet of remote entity do
   switch received packet type {
      case UPDATE
         fix ghost position of remote entity
         break;
      case PLAYER_QUITING
         remove remote entity
         break;
   }

[Extrapolation] Extrapolate all ghost position based on
the past state information;

if (local entity's true position - local entity's
extrapolated position) > Threshold {
   Broadcast an UPDATE packet to the group
}
Draw all ghost
```

2.2 Kalman Filter

A Kalman filter is a recursive procedure to estimate the states s_k of a discrete-time controlled process governed by the linear stochastic difference equation, from a set of measured observations t_k. The mathematical model is in (1) and (2).

$$s_k = As_{k-1} + w_{k-1} \tag{1}$$

$$t_k = Hs_k + r_k \tag{2}$$

The NxN matrix A represents an state transition matrix, w_k is an Nx1 process noise vector with $N(0, \sigma_w^2)$, t_k is Mx1 measurement vector, H is MxM measurement matrix, and r_k is Mx1 measurement noise vector with $N(0, \sigma_r^2)$. To estimate the process, Kalman filter uses a form of feedback control as shown in Figure 3 [5]. We define $\hat{s}_k^-$, $\hat{s}_k$, p_k^- and p_k as the priori state estimate, posteriori state estimate, priori estimate error covariance, and posteriori estimate error covariance, respectively. K is the Kalman gain.

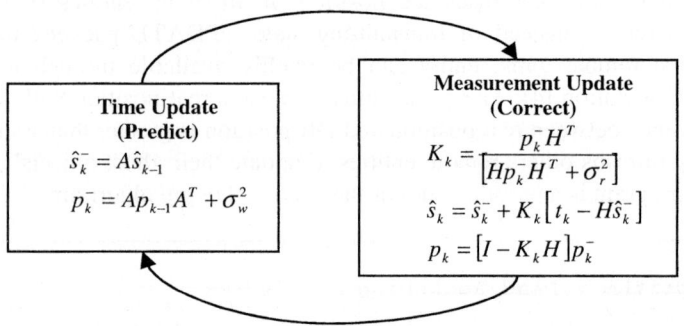

Fig. 3. Kalman filter cycle [5]

3 Kalman Filter Based Dead Reckoning Algorithm

In a distributed multi-player game, players are geographically distributed. In such games, the players are part of the game and in addition, they may control entities that make up the game. During the course of the game, the players and the entities move within the game space. A technique referred to as dead reckoning (DR) is commonly used to exchange information about player/entity movement among the players [6, 7, 8]. Each game entity sends information about its movement as well as the movement of the entities it controls to the other players using a dead reckoning vector (DRV). A DRV typically contains information about the current position of the entity in terms of x, y and z coordinates (at the time the DRV sent) as well as the trajectory of the entity in terms of the velocity component in each of the dimensions [3].

In this paper, we present a Kalman filter based dead reckoning. To evaluate our scheme, we used simple dead reckoning scenarios (scheme 1) and optimized dead reckoning algorithm for game logic (scheme 3) for comparison. For scheme 1 and scheme 3, we use Kalman filter approach (scheme 2 and scheme 4) to improve the prediction performance of scheme 1 and scheme 3 as shown in Figure 4. As shown in Figure 4, scheme 1 and scheme 2 use DRV, which includes only position and velocity information of each game entity. The details of scheme 1 and scheme 2 are as follows.

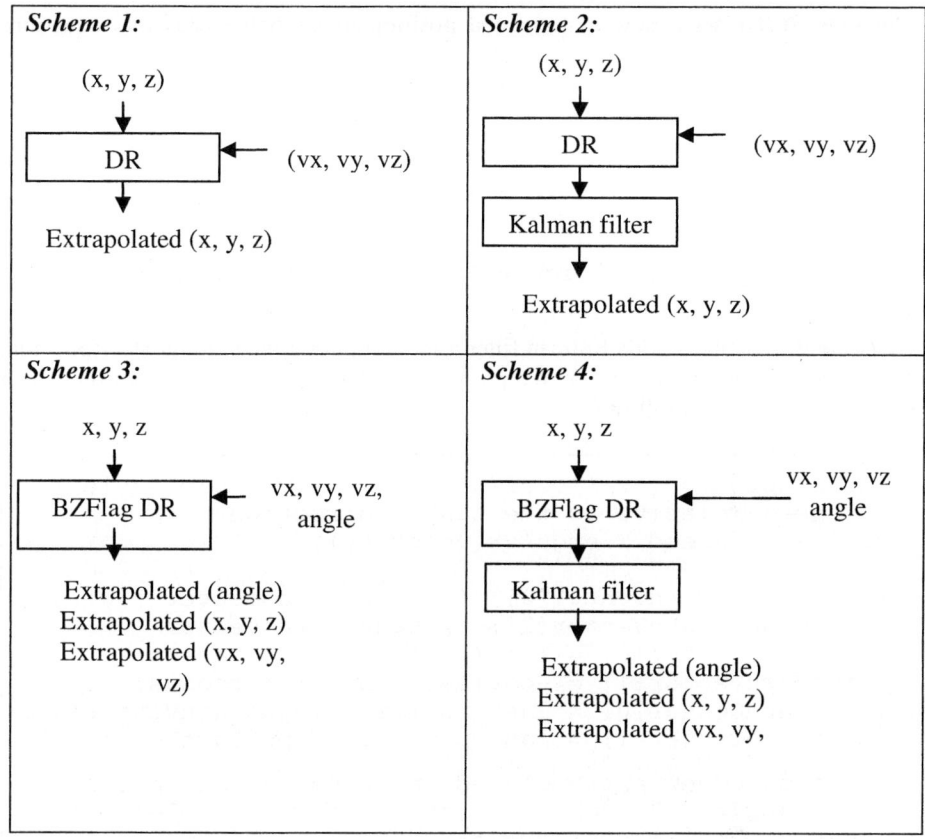

Fig. 4. Kalman filter approach for dead reckoning algorithm

Scheme 1: We compute the extrapolated position using last position, last velocity, and time step as follows. We performed the extrapolation until the difference between the extrapolated position and the true position is under threshold.

```
extrapolated position = last position + last velocity *
time step;
```

Scheme 2: Scheme 2 uses Kalman filter after computing the extrapolated position as scheme 1. We performed the extrapolation until the difference between the extrapolated position and the true position is under threshold.

```
extrapolated position = Kalman Filter (last position +
last velocity * time step);
```

In scheme 3 and scheme 4, we added the angle which is a direction of game entity for prediction improvements, and the DRV is (x, y, z, vx, vy, vz, angle, t). Scheme 3 is real dead reckoning algorithm, which optimizes BZFlag game logic. The details of scheme 3 and scheme 4 are as follows.

Scheme 3: To get a new extrapolated position, the scheme uses two equations depending on the game entity's motion type as follows. We performed the extrapolation until the difference between the extrapolated position and the true position is under threshold.

```
if (linear motion) {
  extrapolated position = last position + last velocity
* time step;
} else {
  extrapolated position = BZFlag function(angle);
}
```

Scheme 4: Scheme 4 adds Kalman filter after computing the extraploated (position, velocity, and angle) as scheme 3. We present the modified non-linear motion's dead reckoning algorithm as follows.

```
float speed = (vx * cosf(angle)) + (vy * sin(angle));
// speed relative to the tank's direction
radius = (speed / angular_velocity);

float inputTurnCenter[2]; // tank turn center
float inputTurnVector[2]; // tank turn vector
inputTurnVector[0] = +sin(last_angle) * radius;
inputTurnVector[1] = -cos(last_angle) * radius;
inputTurnCenter[0] = last_position-inputTurnVector[0];
inputTurnCenter[1] = last_position-inputTurnVector[1];

// compute new extrapolated angle using Kalman filter
float **angle** = Kalman (time step * angular_velocity);
float cos_val = cosf(**angle**);
float sin_val = sinf(**angle**);

// compute new extrapolated position
const float* tc = inputTurnCenter;
const float* tv = inputTurnVector;
new_x = tc[0]+((tv[0] * cos_val) - (tv[1] * sin_val));
new_y = tc[1]+((tv[1] * cos_val) + (tv[0] * sin_val));
new_z = last_position + (vz * time step);

// compute new extrapolated velocity
float **vx** = Kalman ((vx * cos_val) - (vy * sin_val));
float **vy** = Kalman ((vy * cos_val) + (vx * sin_val));
float **vz** = Kalman (vz);
```

4 Experimental Results with BZFlag Games

To demonstrate the real experimental results of our proposed dead reckoning algorithm, we use the popular network game BZFlag. BZFlag (Battle Zone Flag) as shown in Figure 5 is a first-person shooter game where the players in teams drive tanks and move within a battlefield. The aim of the players is to navigate and capture

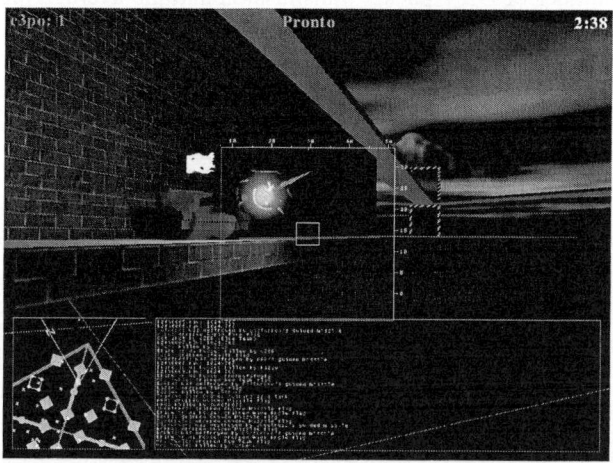

Fig. 5. BZFlag game [9]

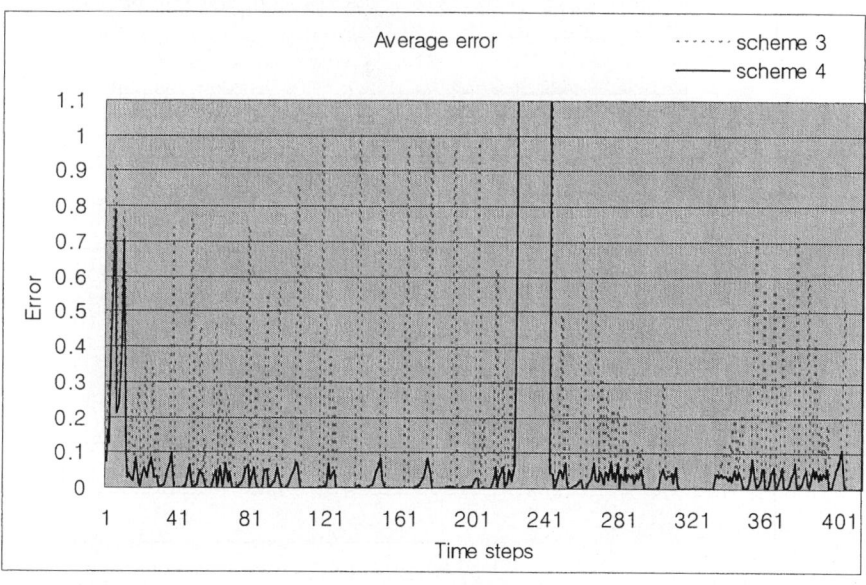

Fig. 6. Comparison of prediction accuracy for 8301 time step duration

flags belonging to the other team and bring them back to their own area. The players shoot each other's tanks using "shooting bullets" The movements of the tanks (players) as well as that of the shots (entities) exchanged among the players using DR vectors [3, 9].

For our experimentation, we gathered the dead reckoning packets, and each packet is composed of the position and velocity vales while real game users play BZFlag. We used 8301 samples for our experimentation, and set the threshold to 0.09. We compared the number of DRV packet transmission and the average prediction error E as shown in (3). In the equation, (x, y, z) represent the true position, (newx, newy, newz) represent the extrapolated position, and (n) represent the number of data.

$$E = \frac{\sum_{i=1}^{n=8301} \sqrt{(x_i - newx_i)^2 + (y_i - newy_i)^2 + (z_i - newz_i)^2}}{n} \quad (3)$$

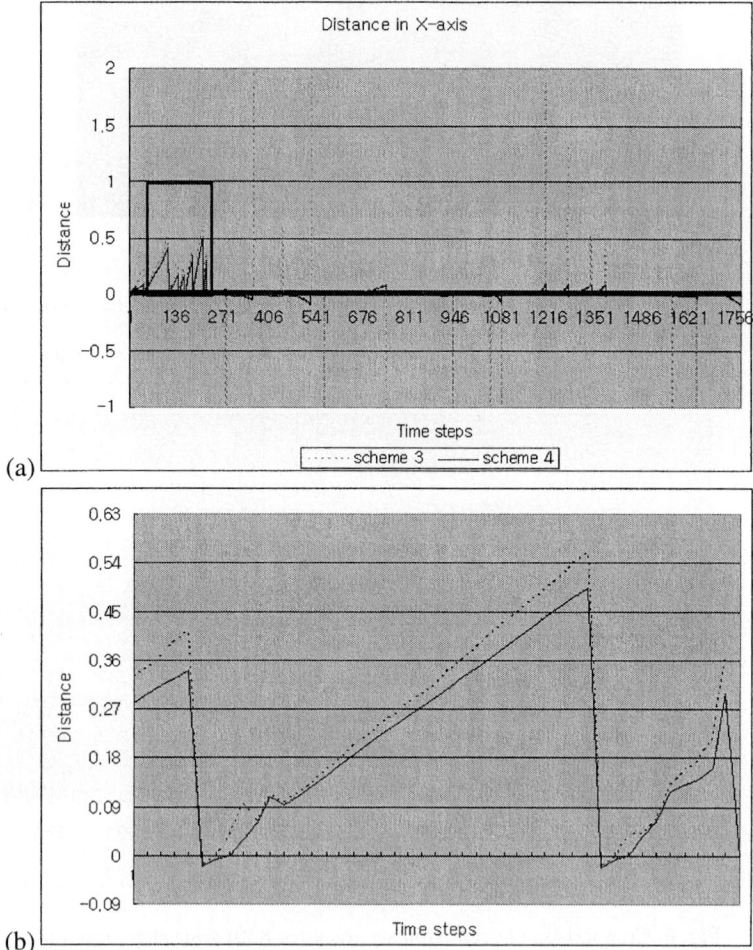

Fig. 7. Error in X prediction: (a) errors in X direction, (b) enlarged for box in (a)

Table 1 shows the experimental result. It shows that the number of DRV transmission of scheme 2 and scheme 4 (use of Kalman prediction) is smaller than that of scheme 1 and scheme 3 (no use of Kalman prediction), respectively.

Table 1. Comparision of DRV packet transmissions and prediction error E

	Scheme 1	Scheme 2	Scheme 3	Scheme 4
# of DRV transmission	4657	3965	703	611
E	4.511	2.563	0.4745	0.4048

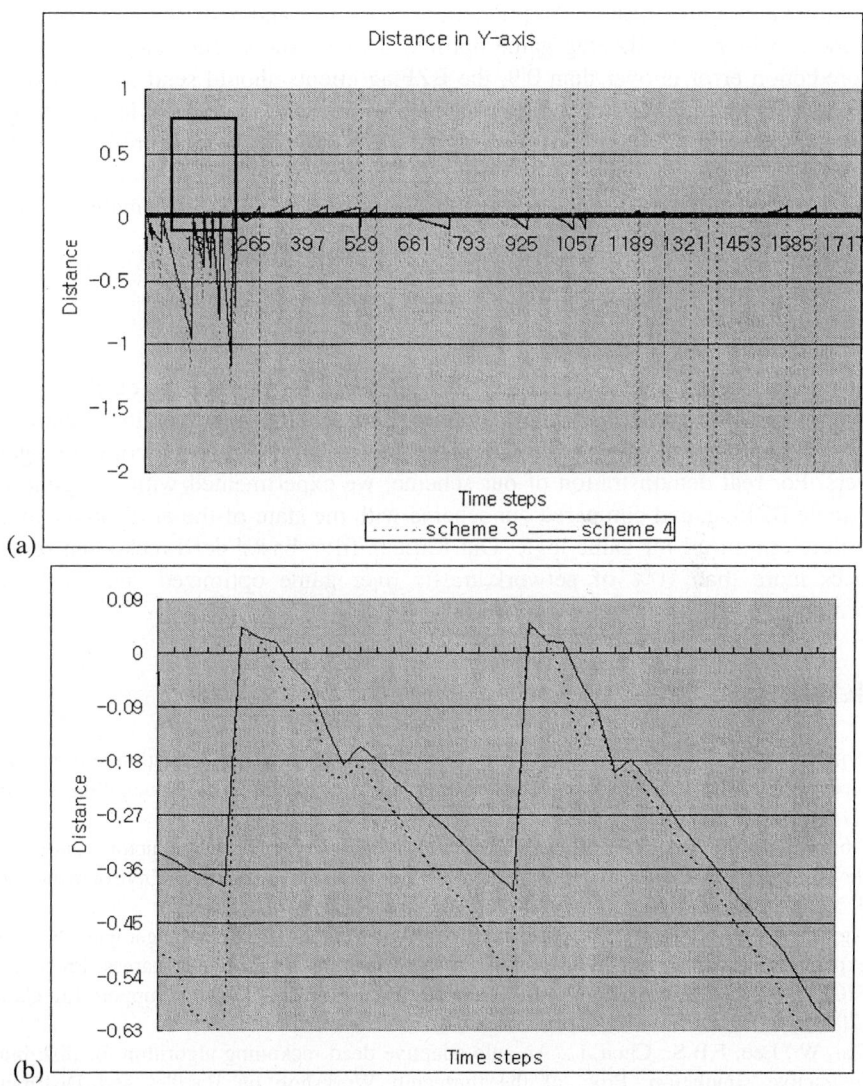

Fig. 8. Error in Y prediction: (a) errors in Y direction, (b) enlarged for box in (a)

Usually, network games use their own optimization for increased performance. BZFlag game also uses the game optimized dead reckoning algorithm, which means that it considers the two more vectors (orientation and angle) to predict the position more accurately. Scheme 3 improves the simple dead reckoning approaches: scheme 1 and scheme 2. In scheme 4, we used Kalman filter prediction on velocity and angle. Figure 6 compares the scheme 3 and scheme 4 over 8000 time steps. For better comparison, we computed moving average for each 20 samples. *The dotted line* and *the solid line* show the result of scheme 3 and scheme 4, respectively.

Figure 7 and Figure 8 show the prediction errors in X and Y direction, respectively. Scheme 3, which uses BZFlag game optimized logic, shows fluctuations, and when the prediction error is over than 0.9, the BZFlag clients should send dead reckoning packets. Minimizing dead reckoning packets also minimized network latency and the game responses time. Figure 7 (a) and Figure 8 (a) show the overall prediction errors, and Figure 7 (b) and Figure 8 (b) show the detailed view on the prediction errors. Even in the detailed view, the prediction errors of scheme 4 are smaller than the prediction errors of scheme 3.

5 Conclusions

In this paper, we propose the Kalman filter approach to improve the dead reckoning algorithm for distributed multi-player games. Our scheme improves the accuracy of dead reckoning prediction, and minimizes the network traffic among the game players. For real demonstration of our scheme, we experimented with a popular on-line game BZFlag, and compared our scheme with the state-of-the-art dead reckoning algorithm optimized for game logic. Out Kalman filter based dead reckoning scheme reduces more than 10% of network traffic over game optimized dead reckoning algorithms.

References

1. The Korean Intellectual Property Office: New technology trend investigation report – game technology. The Korean Intellectual Property Office Computer Examination Division (2004) 70-85
2. Gossweiler, R., Laferriere, R.J., Keller, M.L., Pausch, R.: An introductory tutorial for developing multi-user virtual environments. Tele-operators and Virtual Environments, Vol. 3. No. 4 (1994) 255-264
3. Aggarwal, S., Banavar, H., Khandelwal, A., Mukherjee, S., Rangarajan, S.: User experience: accuracy in dead-reckoning based distributed multi-player games. Proc. ACM SIGCOMM 2004 Workshops on Net-Games. Network and System Support for Games (2004)
4. Cai, W., Lee, F.B.S., Chen, L.: An auto-adaptive dead reckoning algorithm for distributed interactive simulation. Proc. of the thirteenth Workshop on Parallel and Distributed Simulation (1999)
5. Welch, G., Bishop, G.: An introduction to the Kalman filters. available in http://www.cs.unc.edu/~welch/Kalman/index.html

6. Gautier, L., Diot, C.: Design and Evaluation of MiMaze, a Multiplayer Game on the Internet. Proc. of IEEE Multimedia. ICMCS (1998)
7. Mauve, M.: Consistency in Replicated Continuous Interactive Media. Proc. of the ACM Conference on Computer Supported Cooperative Work (2000) 181–190
8. Singhal, S.K., Cheriton, D.R.: Exploiting Position History for Efficient Remote Rendering in Networked Virtual Reality. Tele-operators and Virtual Environments. Vol. 4. No. 2 (1995) 169-193
9. Schoeneman, C., Riker, T.: BZFlag (Battle Zone capture Flag). available in http://www.bzflag.org

IRED Gun: Infrared LED Tracking System for Game Interface

SeongHo Baek, TaeYong Kim, JongSu Kim, ChaSeop Im, and Chan Lim

Department of Image Engineering, Graduate School of Advanced Imaging Science,
Multimedia, and Film, Chung-Ang University, 221 Huksuk-dong Dongjak-ku 156-756,
Seoul, South Korea
{Shbaek, imcs}@gametech.cau.ac.kr, kimty@cau.ac.kr,
hermes@imagelab.cau.ac.kr, mj23cb@wm.cau.ac.kr

Abstract. In this paper, we propose an infrared LED tracking system called *IRED Gun*, which is designed for the game gun interface. The conventional systems are practically restricted by physical environment and have a lot of problems. We suggest the *IRED Gun* system to solve these problems. Unlike conventional systems, our tracking system uses three infrared LED lights attached on a monitor, and enables a user to interact with a game. In addition, our system calibrates reliable aim coordinates along the target position of a user by an error correction method based on an aim correction model. Therefore, our infrared LED tracking method allows users freely move in front of a monitor.

1 Introduction

A game gun is a control device for arcade and video games. The game gun is typically modeled on a ballistic weapon (usually a pistol or bazooka) and is used for targeting objects on a video screen. The two routes to conventional gun control are light guns and positional guns. Light guns are the most common for video game systems of any type. They work optically with screen and do not keep track of location on the screen until the gun is fired. When the gun is fired, the screen blanks for a moment, and the optics in the gun register where on the screen the gun is aimed. That information is sent to the computer, which registers the shot. Fig. 1 shows technique of light guns. Positional guns are mounted stationary on the arcade cabinet with the ability to aim left/right and up/down. They function much like joysticks, which maintain a known location on screen at all times and register the current location when fired. These two routes to gun control are practically restricted by physical environment and have a lot of problems. For example, a light gun designed for a VGA CRT monitor cannot be used with a LCD monitor or TV, and a TV-based light gun cannot be used with a non-TV monitor. There is no positional gun for PC on the market. The only way to go this route is to convert an arcade positional gun for use with cabinet [1].

To solve these problems, a new control method out of the conventional methods is needed. In this paper, we propose a new gun system called *IRED Gun* which uses infrared LED tracking in order to implement game interface (see Fig. 2). Beside, our system calibrates reliable coordinates by solving errors according to the changes of user's aim position (a distance and an angle).

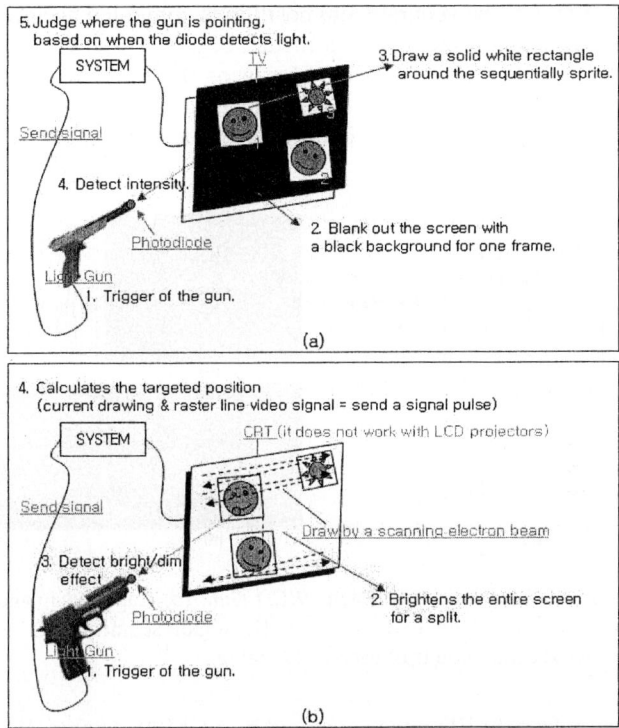

Fig. 1. Two versions of light gun technique. (a) First detection method. (b) Second detection method.

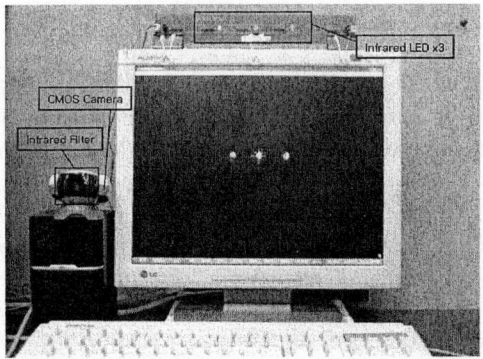

Fig. 2. The infrared LED tracking system *IRED Gun*

2 Detection of Aim Position

The developed infrared LED tracking system, *IRED Gun*, detects aim position by two processes. First, the center position of infrared LED region is detected from the captured image. Second, the accurate aim position is computed according to the position of a user based on an aim correction model. Fig. 3-(a) shows the entire structure of infrared LED tracking system. When a user using the camera aims a neighborhood infrared LED attached on monitor, the system calculates the aim position and converts the calculated aim position with the coordinate value corresponded to ICS (Image Coordinate System).

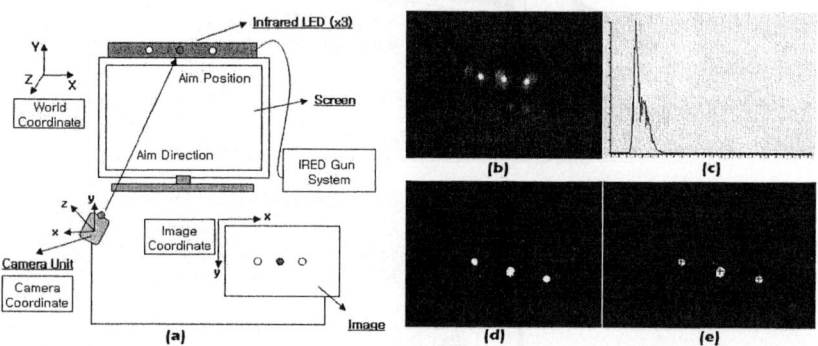

Fig. 3. (a) The infrared LED tracking system *IRED Gun*. (b) Captured image of the infrared LED. (c) The histogram of the captured image. (d) The region segmentation by region growing algorithm. (e) Extracted center points of each LED region.

Fig. 3-(b) is an infrared LED image captured by a CMOS camera. For the reflection of a camera lens and influence of surrounding illumination, low chroma level regions are included in image [2, 3]. Therefore, the exact infrared LED lights in the image are extracted through the following step-by-step image processing.

Step 1. Binarize an infrared LED image

Since infrared filter is attached in front of camera, the captured infrared LED light and background in the image have the contrast of very high brightness. Therefore, even though the suitable threshold value is set up with a constant threshold, we can get sufficiently accurate segment result. However, if the size of infrared LED light which influenced by environment of neighborhood illumination is small size segmented and the position of camera is changed according to user's position (distance or angle), the instable coordinate value will be calculated. Therefore, to make segmentation more robust, the threshold should be automatically selected by the system [4]. Hence, we have to calculate the accurate threshold value by referring the histogram of input image as shown in Fig. 3-(c) using the P-tile method [5]. Given a histogram and the percentage of black pixels desired, determine the number of black pixels by multiplying the percentage by the total number of pixels. Then simply count the pixels in histogram bins, starting at bin 0, until the count is greater than or equal to the desired number of black pixels. The threshold is the grey level associated with last bin counted.

Step 2. Label the regions form the binarized image

Segment each infrared LED regions from the binarization image using the region growing algorithm of Eq. (1) (see Fig. 3-(d)) [6].

$$P\left(R_i^{(k)} \cup \{x\}\right) = \begin{cases} TRUE \text{ if } x>T \\ FALSE \text{ otherwise} \end{cases}, \text{ for } i=1,2,...N, \quad (1)$$

where p is a logical predicate of the form $p(R,x,T)$, (k) is each stage, x is a feature vector associated with an image pixel, and T is a threshold. Each region R is segmented by using the region growing algorithm.

Step 3. Evaluate the infrared LED region by geometric property

The verification for the geometric circularity of extracted LED region enables us to decide whether exterior form is circle or not. In case of an ideal circle, since the radius from region center position to outside boundary is constant, the variance value of radius is almost zero. But the variance value of radius of fluorescent lamp is not usually zero, since the radius is not constant. The regions of big variance values are eliminated by checking geometric circularity of infrared LED region.

Step 4. Extract the center positions of infrared LED regions

Finally, calculate the center position by using the image coordinates of height and width composition pixel of each labeled infrared LED region (see Fig. 3-(e)) [7, 8].

3 Correct the Error of Aim Coordinates

The *IRED Gun* using the calculated center position of infrared LED region directly to use the aim coordinate value. However, due to the distortion of camera lens by the variety of user's aim position, its aim coordinate value is include error values [9]. For example, when a user in front aims the center point p of infrared LED board on the WCS (World Coordinate System) in Fig. 4, the coordinate value Q is correspondent with that on ICS. But when the distance and the angle is changed, if a user aims point p' (same as p), the coordinate value Q' is correspondent with that on ICS. Therefore, the correction for the coordinate value of aim position is needed. We propose the aim correction model for this purpose.

From the step 4, calculated aim coordinate value is corrected based on an aim correction model. Fig. 4 is overview the aim correction model.

However, before correction process, as depicted in the right figure of Fig. 4, the position of infrared LED is rotated by $\pm\theta$ in ICS if an aim position of a camera in CCS (Camera Coordinate System) turns to the right side or the left side (Eq. 2) [10, 11].

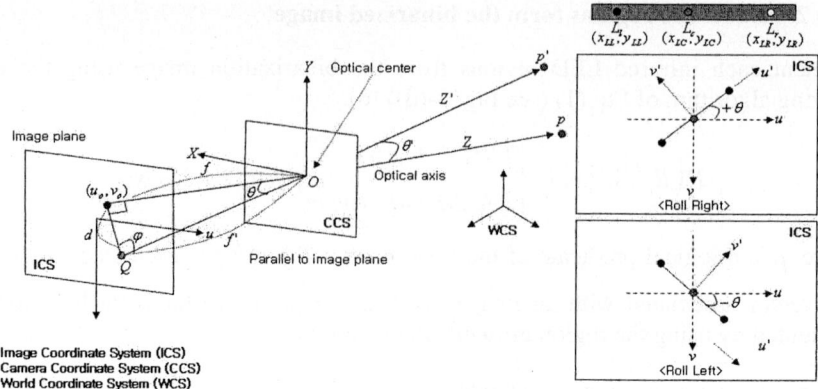

Fig. 4. The aim correction model to correct the error of aim coordinates due to the position of a user

$$\begin{pmatrix} x_{new} \\ y_{new} \end{pmatrix} = \begin{pmatrix} \cos\theta & -\sin\theta \\ \sin\theta & \cos\theta \end{pmatrix} \begin{pmatrix} x_{org} + c_x \\ y_{org} + c_y \end{pmatrix} + \begin{pmatrix} c_x \\ c_y \end{pmatrix}, \quad (2)$$

where x_{org}, y_{org} is coordinates value of left/right LED region before a rotation, x_{new}, y_{new} is coordinates value of left/right LED region after a rotation, c_x, c_y is coordinates value of middle LED region.

In this paper, to find the range of mean error values, we measured the coordinate value of the aim position with the aim point as the point p of WCS for each range (a distance 300 mm ~ 1000 mm, an angle 30° ~ 60°) in as shown in Fig. 4. As shown in Fig. 5-(a) and (b), user's distance is getting closer to the monitor, the mean error value by user's position becomes increased within the area of left/right 30° but it regularizes regardless of user's distance from left/right 30° to left/right 45°. Also, user's distance is getting further, it becomes decreased from left/right 45° to left/right 60°. That results from error value due to the change for the total length of infrared LED (interval from left LED to right LED) according to user's distance and angle as shown in Fig. 5-(c) and (d).

In this paper, we present distance estimation model table (see Table.1) and error correction table (see Table. 2) based on aim correction model with measured data. The error value from each range is corrected by linear approximation by use of these tables.

Here, we describe a method to correct the error value based on the aim correction model. There are three steps to correct the error value.

Step 1. Calculate the distance between infrared LED on the monitor and a user

The Z' (distance between infrared LED on the monitor and a user) is determined. Given the total length of infrared LED $\overline{L_l L_r}$ (interval from left LED to right LED), measured average LED interval length $\overline{|L_L'L_R|}$ based on real distance β mm in the Table. 1 is calculated by Eq. (3).

$$Z' = \beta + ((\overline{|L_L'L_R|} - \overline{|L_LL_R|}) / \gamma) \times 10, \text{ if } \overline{|L_LL_R|} \subset \overline{|L_L'L_R|}, \quad (3)$$

where γ is pixel spacing value this of ICS per 10 mm in the β range section that is a camera and a distance of infrared LED in actual WCS.

Step 2. Calculate the aim angle of a user

If the infrared LED interval ratio $\overline{L_LL_C} : \overline{L_RL_C}$ from the center to the left LED and right LED is non-uniform, it denotes that the angle of a user is varied. Thus, the correction of aim coordinate value is needed and the angle (θ) should be calculated by Eq. (4).

$$\sin\theta \approx \overline{|d|} \times 10 \times \frac{100}{Z \times \overline{|L_LL_R|}}, \text{ if } \overline{L_LL_C} \neq \overline{L_RL_C}, \quad (4)$$

where d distance between the aim positions is coordinates value and the middle coordinates value of ICS.

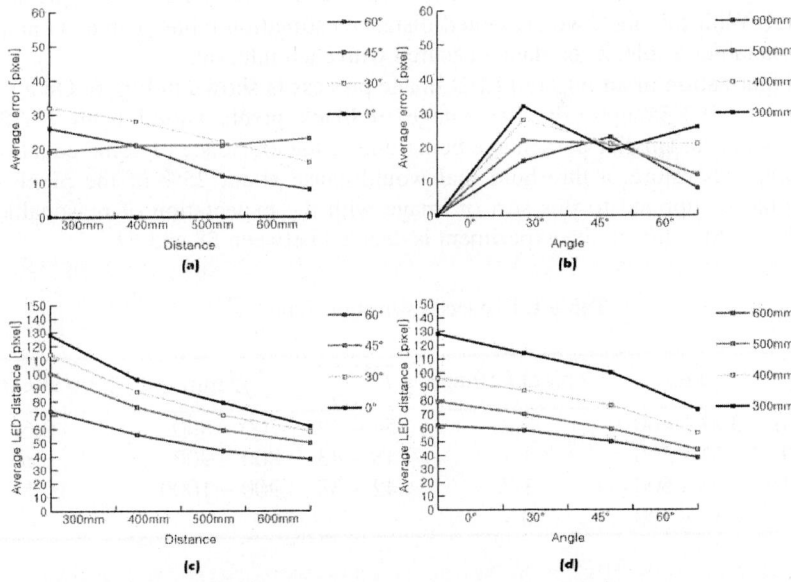

Fig. 5. Measured average error value and LED interval length. (a) Average error value by distance base on an angle. (b) Average error value by angle base on a distance. (c) Average LED interval by distance base on an angle. (d) Average LED interval by angle base on a distance.

Step 3. Calculate the correction value

Calculate ω value which will be corrected when θ is included in the range normalized by Table. 2. And as, presented in Eq. (5), correct the error value of user's aim coordinate in the range.

$$Q' = Q' - (\omega, 0)^T, if\ 30° < \theta < 60° \tag{5}$$

4 Experimental Results

The infrared LED tracking system was controlled by a Pentium IV 2.66 GHz standard PC. The image sequences were acquired using a commercial USB camera that had 24 bit RGB or 12 bit YUV2 colors and a 320×240 resolution with 30 fps (frames per seconds). Infrared filter was attached on the lens of camera. Three infrared LED (SI5313-H) with 6 mm diameter are arranged on LED board with 45 mm interval and attached to LED board on a 17 inch LCD monitor.

We conduct experiments to evaluate the accuracy of the infrared tracking system. In the experiments, LED regions apart from standard positions (distance 300 mm ~ 1000 mm, and angle 30° ~ 60°) were eliminated from relevant range because the geometrical distribution was too large or too small. Beside, the 100 mm in the point where distance between camera and infrared LED is about 384 mm in the WCS is projected as 100 pixel. With this fact, we presented distance estimation table (Table. 1) and error correction table (Table. 2) on data measured with each interval.

The binarization of an infrared LED image process is shown in Fig. 6. On a sample of infrared LED images, the percentage of black pixels varied from 13.72% to 25.09%, with the smaller percentage being due to the existence of some equations on that image. Therefore, a threshold that would cause about 25% of the pixels to be black could be applied to this sort of image with the expectation of reasonable success. Threshold value on the experiment is decided between 58 and 64.

Table 1. Distance Estimation Table(Z')

$\overline{L_L'L_R'}$	β mm	γ pixel / 10mm	$\overline{L_L'L_R'}$	β mm	γ pixel / 10mm
128 ~ 96	300 ~ 400	3.2	54 ~ 49	700 ~ 800	0.6
95 ~ 79	400 ~ 500	1.7	48 ~ 43	800 ~ 900	0.6
78 ~ 62	500 ~ 600	1.7	42 ~ 38	900 ~ 1000	0.5
61 ~ 55	600 ~ 700	0.7			

Table 2. Error Correction Table

θ	Correction pixel range (pixel)	ω
0.2 ~ 0.9	8 ~ 32	θ / 0.029

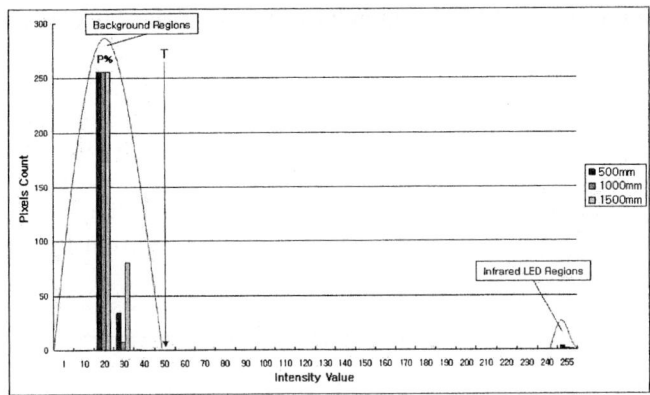

Fig. 6. The left areas in the histogram represent p percent of the image area. The threshold is selected so that p percent of histogram is assigned to the object.

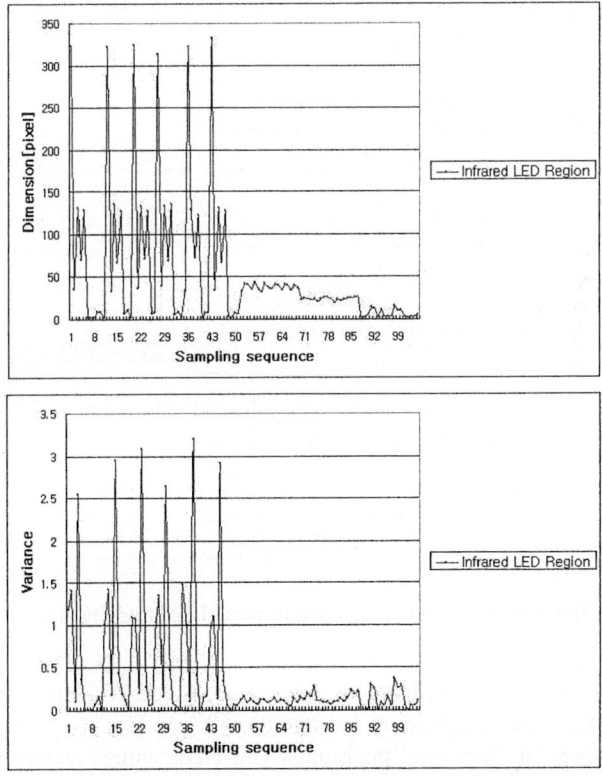

Fig. 7. The dimension and variance of infrared LED regions before filtering

In evaluate the infrared LED region by geometric property process, the dimension and variance of infrared LED regions before filtering is shown Fig. 7. The regions are too small or large dimension and variance value. After filtering, the extracted region is too small or large (the pixels of the region are 18 or over 50) was excluded, the value of circular variance filter is given as 0.3. Therefore, the fluorescent lamp light by reflection of camera lens and the noise region by surrounding illumination were removed by filtering since they have big circular variance value and they don't meet the need of the condition for circularity (see Fig. 8).

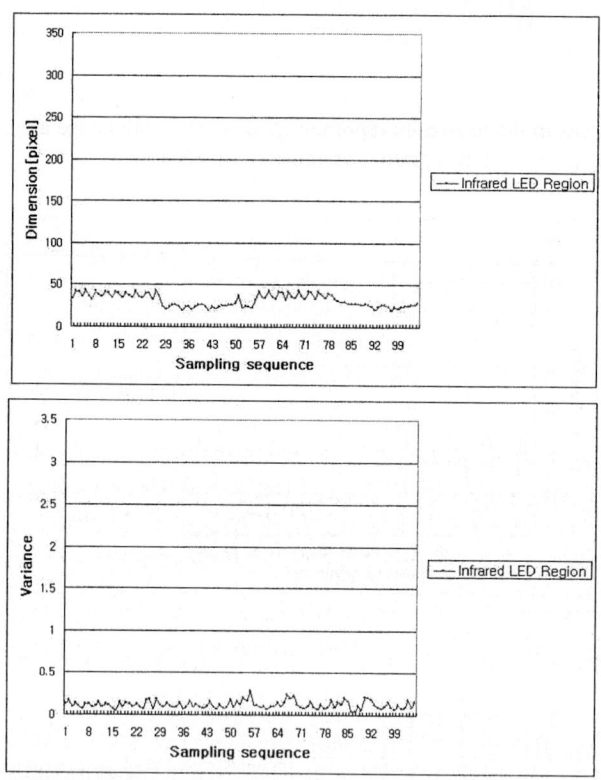

Fig. 8. The dimension and variance of infrared LED regions after filtering

In the correct the error of aim coordinates process, our system corrects errors of aim coordinates by a user position on average 8 ~ 32 (see Fig. 9).

Fig. 10 describes for each final position where error values according to the position of a user were corrected after being calculated the position of each LED region from infrared LED image.

We tested this system under worst case conditions, by points on a horizontal or a vertical line and obtaining the corresponding s_x horizontal or s_y vertical coordinates. In the experiment results, our system as shown in Fig. 11, the linearity is acceptable. Therefore, *IRED Gun* is enough for accurate aim detection, and linearity of the system is good. In addition, the system works on the interface of games performance of over 30 fps.

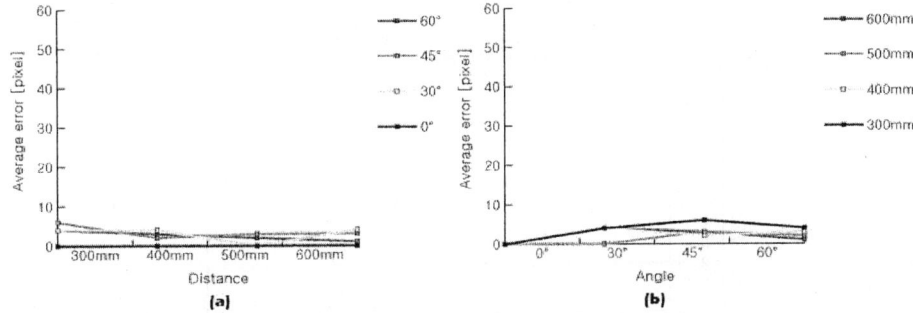

Fig. 9. The correction of aim coordinates errors according to the position of a user. (a) Aim coordinates errors by distance based on angle after correction. (b) Aim coordinates errors by angle based on distance after correction.

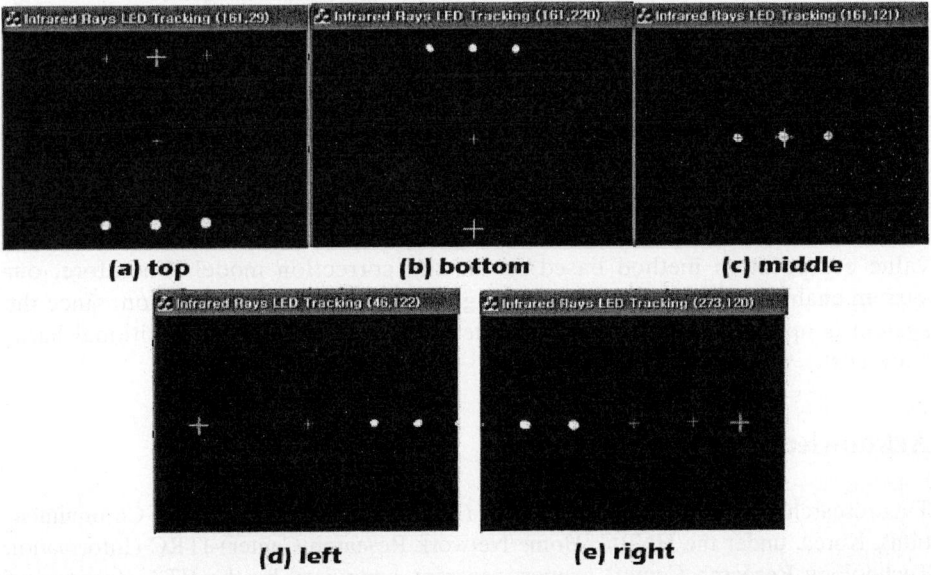

Fig. 10. Coordinates value measurement along a camera position. (a) Top. (b) Bottom. (c) Middle. (d) Left. (d) Right.

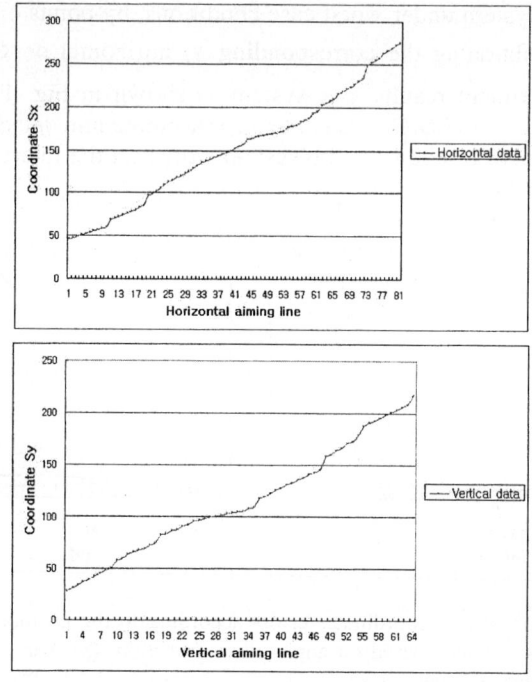

Fig. 11. The linearity of the horizontal and vertical aiming line

5 Conclusions

A real-time infrared LED tracking system was proposed for the game gun interface. The most considerable point is that the tracking method makes allows users freely move in front of a monitor. The new gun system *IRED Gun* uses a robust infrared LED image detection technique and an accurate aim coordinate value computation method based on an aim correction model. Therefore, our system enables a user move freely in a game environment. In addition, since the system is operated on personal computer, it is enough without additional hardware cost.

Acknowledgement

This research was supported by the MIC (Ministry of Information and Communication), Korea, under the HNRC (Home Network Research Center)-ITRC (Information Technology Research Center) support program supervised by the IITA (Institute of Information Technology Assessment).

References

1. J.S. Clair: Project Arcade Build Your Own Arcade Machine. WILEY, pp. 125, 2004.
2. K. Tarabanis and R.Y. Tasi: Computing Viewpoints that Satisfy Optical Constraint. IEEE Computer Society Conference on Computer Vision and Pattern Recognition, pp. 152-158, 1991.
3. P. Xu, P. Abshire: Threshold detection of intensity flashes in the blowfly photoreceptor by an ideal observer. Neurocomputing, Vol. 65-66, pp. 229-236, 2005.
4. H. Gao, W. C. Siu, and C. H. Hou: Improved Techniques for Automatic Image Segmentation. IEEE Trans, Circuits and Systems for Video Technology, Vol. 11, No. 12, pp. 1273-1280, 2001.
5. Yasuno. M, Yasuda. N, Aoki. M: Pedestrian Detection and Tracking in Far Infrared Images. Computer Vision and Pattern Recognition Workshop, Vol. 08, No. 8, pp. 125, 2004.
6. P. J. Besl, R. C. Jain: Segmentation through variable-order surface fitting. Pattern Analysis and Machine Intelligence. IEEE Trans, Vol. 10, No. 2, pp. 167-192, 1988.
7. A.K. Jain: Fundamentals of Digital Image Processing. Prentice Hall, pp. 409, 1989.
8. R. Jain, R. Kasturi, B. G. Schunck: MACHINE VISION. McGraw-Hill, pp. 6-10, 1995.
9. R.Y. Tasi: A Versatile Camera Calibration Technique for High-Accuracy 3D Machine Vision Metrology Using Off-the-Shelf TV Cameras and Lenses. IEEE Journal of Robotics and Automation, Vol. 3, No. 4, pp. 323-344, 1987.
10. R.K. Lenz, R.Y. Tasi: Techniques for Calibration of the Scale Factor and Image Center for High Accuracy 3-D Maching Vision Metrology. Pattern Analysis and Machine Intelligence, IEEE Transactions on, Vol. 10, No. 5, pp. 713-720, 1998.
11. S.W. Shih, Y.P. Hung and W.S Lin: Accuracy Analysis on the Estimation of Camera Parameters for Active Vision Systems. Proceedings of the 13th International Conference on Pattern Recognition, Vol. 1, pp. 930-935, 1996.

On the Implementation of Gentle Phone's Function Based on PSOLA Algorithm

JongKuk Kim and MyungJin Bae

Department of Information & Telecommunication Engineering, Soongsil University,
Sangdo 5-dong, Dongjak-gu, Seoul, 156-743, Korea
Kokjk91@ssu.ac.kr

Abstract. This paper is about a method to improve our everyday telephone which takes a big part of our daily life by making better changes in telephone ability. This paper is about a method to improve our everyday telephone which takes a big part of our daily life by making better changes in telephone ability. There are times when the receivers get displeased by hearing callers• usage of abusive language, dialect and impatient voices. Times like this soft-sound phone is necessary, if the receiver press the soft-sound key bottom which is attached to the phone, the receiver would be able to hear soft voice with in the range of the caller's voice. Soft-sound phone analysis the caller's voice through the phone and keep the meaning of the conversation and adjust the accent which indicates the caller's personality so the caller's voice sounds soft and generous as if the voice tone is not over the specific limit. Consequently, it is affective to change a blunt society to bright and calmed better telephonic mannered society.

1 Introduction

Speech synthesis, automatic generation of speech waveforms, has been under development for several decades[11]. Recent progress in speech synthesis has produced synthesizers with very high intelligibility but the sound quality and naturalness still remain a major problem. This paper is a new communication method to make better changes classifying utterance conversion technique in speech communication or audio signal process, using tele-communication networks like cell-phone, common telephone and internet. Such methods of communication, has disadvantage where, feelings or voice tones resulted from it of a person carried through and characteristic passes on to the receiver and may feel the unpleasantness and lot of stress.

Therefore, this paper is there to improve disadvantages like this. so we suggest a new communication method, soft-sound without strong intonation, by applying digital utterance process technique to the caller's voice. Human voice made when air from lungs vibrates the vocal cords and when this vibration comes out of the vocal cords, resonant occurs. Vibration of the vocal cords periodicity or utterance habit shows the speakers personality, resonant of voice level is often appear phoneme information to pass on to the meaning of the message. Like this, resonant characteristics of vocal track which shows the meaning of message is preserved and show speakers personality as it is and adjusting necessary information of the intonation, apply the principal of tele-communication makes voice sound soft and friendly.

2 Speech Synthesis

2.1 Voice Conversion

Voice conversion technology enables a user to transform one person's speech pattern into another pattern with distinct characteristics, giving it a new identity, while preserving the original meaning. Voice conversion is a fertile field for speech research as the problems of concern are related to almost all of the primary topics in speech processing. First, the analysis stage of voice conversion is related to developing appropriate models that capture speaker specific information and estimating the model parameters which are closely related to acoustical modeling, speech coding, and psychoacoustics. Next, the relation between the source and target models must be determined and generalized to unobserved data. The learning and generalization processes relate voice conversion with speech/pattern recognition, and machine learning.

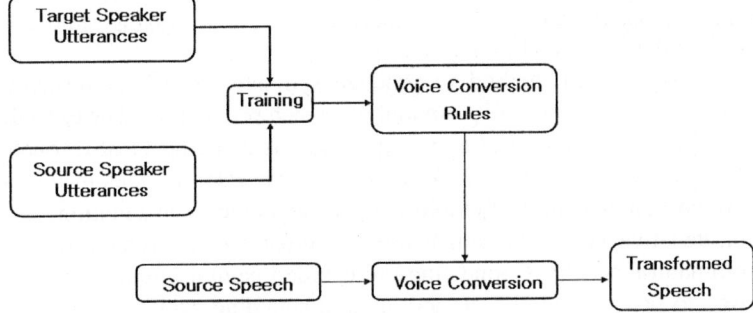

Fig. 1. General framework for voice conversion

Finally, convenient methods must be employed for processing the source signal with minimized distortion and maximized resemblence of the output to the target speaker. These methods are also addressed in speech synthesis and coding applications. Robustness is perhaps the most important point of concern in voice conversion as the aim is to develop methods that perform well for a wide variety of source-target speaker pairs[12]. Voice conversion systems typically use features that correlate with the aspects of the vocal system that are critical to voice quality. In order to modify the voice, some method of analysis and synthesis is required. First, the analysis portion provides an alternative presentation of the acoustic waveform. And second, once this analysis has been performed, the parameters can be used to synthesize a new waveform. Altering the parameters and then listening to the synthesized results allows one to correlate specific physical characteristics with changes in voice color. These parameters are modified using various mapping techniques, which modify the spectral excitation and filter response as well as the prosody characteristics of the speech signal[3]. It is hard to determine an optimal method for voice conversion that can achieve success for all possible speaker characteristics and combinations. A general framework for voice conversion with basic building blocks is shown in Figure 1.

2.2 Techniques

Recent progress in speech synthesis has produced synthesizers with very high intelligibility but the sound quality and naturalness still remain a major problem. However, the quality of present products has reached an adequate level for several applications, such as multimedia and telecommunications. Synthesized speech can be produced by several different methods.

First, Articulatory synthesis tries to model the human vocal organs as perfectly as possible, so it is potentially the most satisfying method to produce high-quality synthetic speech. On the other hand, it is also one of the most difficult methods to implement and the computational load is also considerably higher than with other common methods. Thus, it has received less attention than other synthesis methods and has not yet achieved the same level of success. Advantages of articulatory synthesis are that the vocal tract models allow accurate modeling of transients due to abrupt area changes, whereas formant synthesis models only spectral behavior. The articulatory synthesis is quite rarely used in present systems, but since the analysis methods are developing fast and the computational resources are increasing rapidly, it might be a potential synthesis method in the future[6][11].

Another widely used method to produce synthetic speech is formant synthesis which is based on the source-filter-model of speech production. The excitation is then gained and filtered with a vocal tract filter which is constructed of resonators similar to the formants of natural speech. Formant synthesis also provides infinite number of sounds which makes it more flexible than for example concatenation methods. The last, Concatenative synthesis, which uses different length prerecorded samples derived from natural speech. Connecting prerecorded natural utterances is probably the easiest way to produce intelligible and natural sounding synthetic speech[7]. One of the most important aspects in concatenative synthesis is to find correct unit length. The selection is usually a trade-off between longer and shorter units. With longer units high naturalness, less concatenation points and good control of coarticulation are achieved, but the amount of required units and memory is increased. With shorter units, less memory is needed, but the sample collecting and labeling procedures become more difficult and complex.

In present systems units used are usually words, syllables, demisyllables, phonemes, diphones, and sometimes even triphones. However, concatenative synthesizers are usually limited to one speaker and one voice and usually require more memory capacity than other method[8]. In conclusion, the formant and concatenative methods are the most commonly used in present synthesis systems. The formant synthesis was dominant for long time, but today the concatenative method is becoming more and more popular. The articulatory method is still too complicated for high quality implementations, but may arise as a potential method in the future[11].

2.3 Prosody

Finding correct intonation, stress, and duration from written text is probably the most challenging problem for years to come. These features together are called prosodic or suprasegmental features and may be considered as the melody, rhythm, and emphasis of the speech at the perceptual level. The intonation means how the pitch pattern or fundamental frequency changes during speech. The prosody of continuous speech depends on many separate aspects, such as the meaning of the sentence and the speaker characteristics and emotions[11]. Prosodic features consist of pitch, duration, and stress over the time. With good controlling of these gender, age, emotions, and other features in speech can be well modeled. However, almost everything seems to have effect on prosodic features of natural speech which makes accurate modeling very difficult.

The pitch or fundamental frequency over an intonation in natural speech is a combination of many factors. The pitch contour is affected by gender, physical and emotional state, and attitude of the speaker. Also the duration or time characteristics can also be investigated at several levels from phoneme durations to sentence level timing, speaking rate, and rhythm. With some methods to control duration or pitch, such as the PSOLA methods[4], the manipulation of one feature affects to another. Together the intensity of a voiced sound goes up in proportion to fundamental frequency. The speaker's feelings and emotional state affect speech in many ways and the proper implementation of these features in synthesized speech may increase the quality considerably. Prosodic components is shown in Figure 2.

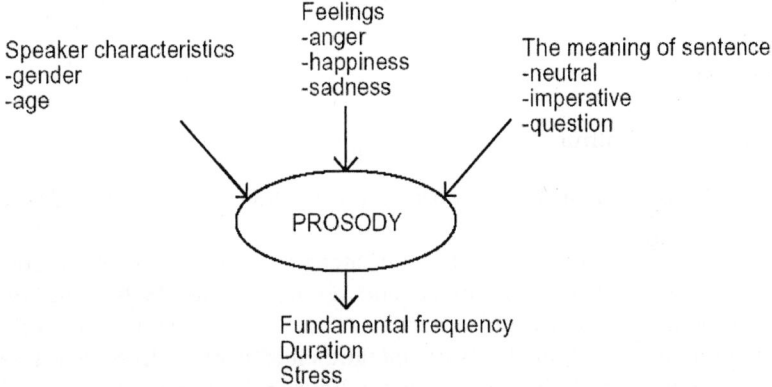

Fig. 2. Prosody

3 Hardware Equipments Organization

Figure 3 represents the equipment that receives the analog-shaped voice signal from microphone, and it changes pitch and synthesis voices. The voices that recorded as shape of analog is amplified at an amplifier, and going through the Low Pass Filter to remove aliasing effect. Also it passes through analog-digital converter to achieve quantization and coding, then the voices changed into PCM shaped digital signal. Last process is occurred in software or firmware at CPU or DSP.

During digital treatment process, the computer manager could use the other equipment that constructed outside, and it could use outside memory to save management result or input digital signal. The multiple voice synthesized digital signal by altering pitch software in CPU would be converted into analog shaped signal which is sampled. If you pass this signal through Low Pass Filter, it would be the analog signal without quantization noises. Also if you amplify that signal with right rates, it would be analog signal that could be listened through speaker[9][10].

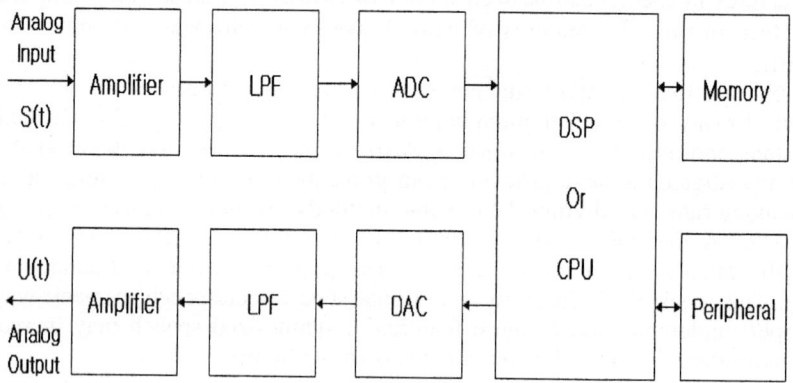

Fig. 3. Organization of multiple-speech synthesizer hardware

4 Procedure

4.1 POSOLA Algorithm

The PSOLA(Pitch Synchronous Overlap Add) method was originally developed at France Telecom(CNET). It is actually not a synthesis method itself but allows prerecorded speech samples smoothly concatenated and provides good controlling for pitch and duration[7]. There are several versions of the PSOLA algorithm and all of them work in essence the same way. Time-domain version, TD-PSOLA, is the most commonly used due to its computational efficiency. In time scale modification, We know from the properties of the Fourier Transform that expanding the time scale of a signal causes a compression in the frequency domain so the output is a pitch scale compressed version of the original signal. On the other hand, when the time scale is compressed -i.e. when the signal is played back faster, the pitch will be higher.

The aim of time scale modification is to prevent these inherent modifications in the signal spectrum while modifying the time axis and obtain an output that has similar spectra as the original signal. Frequency is achieved by changing the time intervals between pitch markers. The modification of duration is achieved by either repeating or omitting speech segments. In principle, modification of fundamental frequency also implies a modification of duration. In pitch modification, the aim is to modify the short-time spectral content of the signal without modifying its temporal characteristics. The spectral envelope must also remain constant but rather the locations of the pitch harmonics must be modified because modifying the vocal tract will severely effect the perceived speaker identity[12]. It is also clear that pitch scale modification results in the modificiation of the time-scale. Since this is not desired, compensating time-scale modification must be employed. In synthesis by overlap-add, the output signal is constructed using overlap-add method with windowing.

The second method to be considered for prosodic modifications is FD-PSOLA that operates in the frequency domain. FD-PSOLA and the Linear-Predictive PSOLA(LP-PSOLA), are theoretically more appropriate approaches for pitch-scale modifications because they provide independent control over the spectral envelope of the synthesis signal[1]. FD-PSOLA is used only for pitch-scale modifications and LP-PSOLA is used with residual excited vocoders. Some drawbacks with PSOLA method exists. The pitch can be determined only for voiced sounds and applied to unvoiced signal parts it might generate a tonal noise[11].The POSOLA algorithm shows in Equation 4.1 and Figure 4.

$$x[n] = \sum_{j=-\infty}^{\infty} x_i[n - t_a[i]]$$

$$x_i[n] = w_i[n]x[n]$$

$$\sum_{i=-\infty}^{\infty} w_i[n - t_a[i]] = 1$$ (4.1)

$$y[n] = \sum_{j=-\infty}^{\infty} y_j[n - t_s[j]]$$

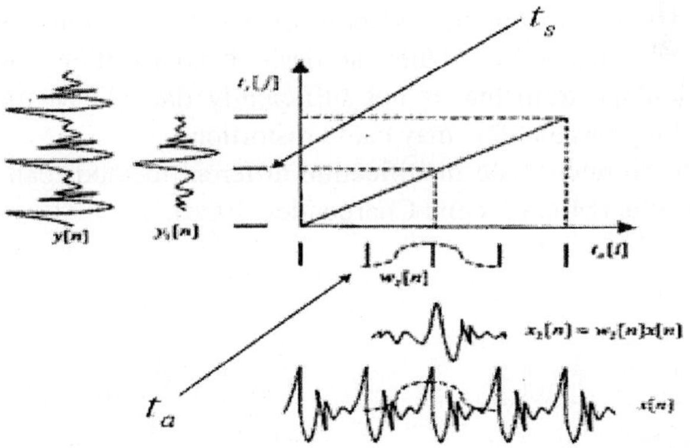

Fig. 4. PSOLA algorithm

4.1.1 TD-PSOLA Algorithm

TD-PSOLA is a simple and effective method for performing prosodic modifications on speech signals. It is well suited for real-time applications. The idea is to process the speech signal on a short-time basis where the segments are obtained pitch synchronously. These segments are concatenated in an appropriate manner to obtain the desired modification. Time and pitch scale modifications are performed as described in Figure 5 and Figure 6. The overall process is as follows:

- The start and end instants of pitch periods over the voiced regions are determined by pitch marking. The algorithm described in (Gold and Rabiner, 1969) can be used. Pitch detection methods are not suitable for this purpose as the exact instants where the pitch period starts and ends are required.
- Pitch synchronous speech segments are extracted by covering 2 to 5 pitch periods per frame. Windowing is applied.
- Time and pitch scale modifications are performed as described later on and the output is reconstructed using overlap-add synthesis by windowing.

4.1.2 FD-PSOLA Algorithm

The second method to be considered for prosodic modifications is FD-PSOLA that operates in the frequency domain. The algorithm is composed of the following step:

- The short term spectrum of the signal is estimated pitch-synchronously. 2-5 pitch periods are used as the window size. It is possible to use pitch marks as in TD-PSOLA but FD-PSOLA performs considerably well without the pitch marks. However, a robust pitch detection algorithm is required.
- The spectral envelope is estimated. Although it is common to employ linear prediction techniques, any spectral envelope estimation method can be used. It is important to obtain a smooth excitation spectrum. As the excitation spectrum is warped to obtain the desired modifications, any region of the excitation spectrum that is not sufficiently flat will be translated to other spectral regions and this may cause distortion.
- To perform pitch-scale modification different methods can be employed as described in (Moulines and Charpentier, 1990).

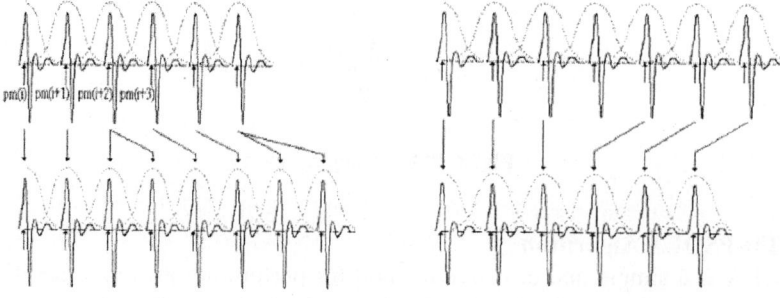

Fig. 5. Time scale expansion (left) and compression (right)

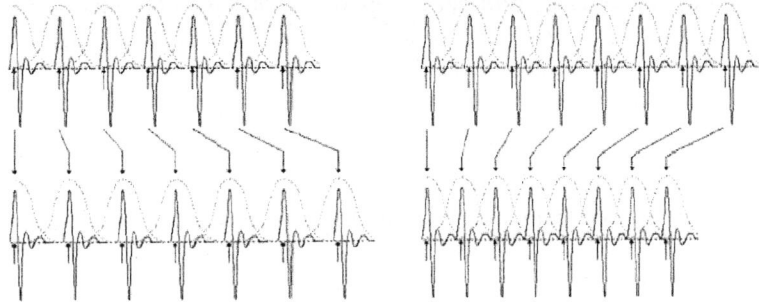

Fig. 6. Pitch scale expansion (left) and compression (right)

4.2 LPC Analysis

Linear predictive methods are originally designed for speech coding systems, but may be also used in speech synthesis. Like formant synthesis, the basic LPC is based on the source-filter-model of speech production model[5]. The basis of linear prediction is that the current speech sample y(n) can be approximated or predicted from a finite number of previous p samples y(n-1) to y(n-k) by a linear combination with small error term e(n) called residual signal. Thus,

$$y(n) = e(n) + \sum_{k=1}^{p} a(k)y(n-k)$$

$$e(n) = y(n) - \sum_{k=1}^{p} a(k)y(n-k) = y(n) - \tilde{y}(n)$$

(4.2)

Where y(n) is a predicted value, p is the linear predictor order, and a(k) are the linear prediction coefficients which are found by minimizing the sum of the squared errors over a frame. The autocorrelation method is commonly used to calculate these coefficients[5]. The autocorrelation method shows in Equation 4.3.

$$r(m) = \sum_{n=0}^{N-1-m} \hat{x}_l(n) x_l(n+m), m = 0,1,...,p$$

(4.3)

Two methods, the covariance method and the autocorrelation method, are commonly used to calculate these coefficients. Only with the autocorrelation method the filter is guaranteed to be stable. In synthesis phase the used excitation is approximated by a train of impulses for voiced sounds and by random noise for unvoiced. The excitation signal is then gained and filtered with a digital filter for which the coefficients are a(k). The filter order is typically between 10 and 12 at 8 kHz sampling rate, but for higher quality at 22 kHz sampling rate. The main deficiency of the ordinary LP method is that it represents an all-pole model, which means that phonemes that contain antiformants such as nasals and nasalized vowels are poorly modeled. The quality is also poor with short plosives because the time-scale events may be shorter than the frame size used for analysis. With these deficiencies the speech synthesis quality with standard LPC method is generally considered poor, but with some modifications and extensions for the basic model the quality may be increased[11].

Several other variations of linear prediction have been developed to increase the quality of the basic method. With these methods the used excitation signal is different from ordinary LP method and the source and filter are no longer separated. These kind of variations are for example multi-pulse linear prediction(MLPC) where the complex excitation is constructed from a set of several pulses, residual excited linear prediction

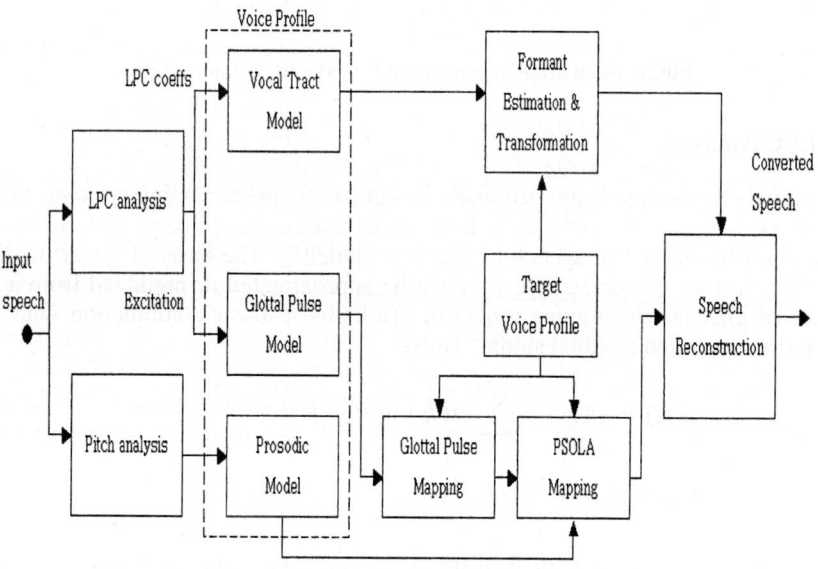

Fig. 7. Overall block diagram

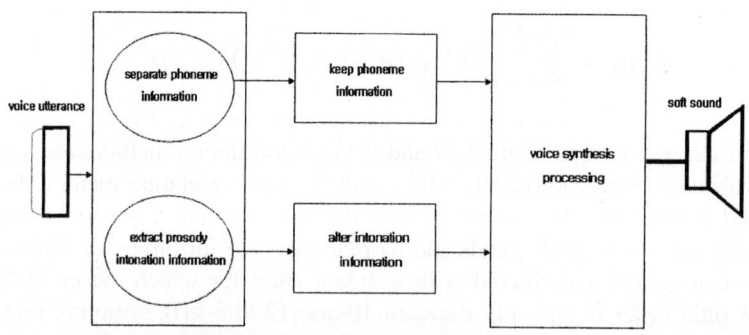

Fig. 8. Analysis and synthesis of voice

(RELP) where the error signal or residual is used as an excitation signal and the speech signal can be reconstructed exactly, and code excited linear prediction(CELP) where a finite number of excitations used are stored in a finite codebook[11]. Following the Figure 7 shows the overall block diagram proposed in this paper.

4.3 Implementation

Soft-sound phone is a phone with established phone technical and soft-sound technical added. Get to hear other person's sound when the call is been answered, if you hear other persons sound too fast and unclearly, press soft-sound key button. Soft-sound key adjust intonation of the other person's voice on the phone and make the sound softer and friendlier when soft-sound key is pressed. On the other side, other person's voice converts to natural intonation if the soft-sound key is pressed once more. Soft sound phone is equal to the Figure 8. The main point of Soft-sound phone is that prosodic information which shows phoneme information and characteristic of one's voice is classified automatically preserving speaker's characteristic and meaning information is the main point of Soft-sound phone, increased soft voice characteristic.

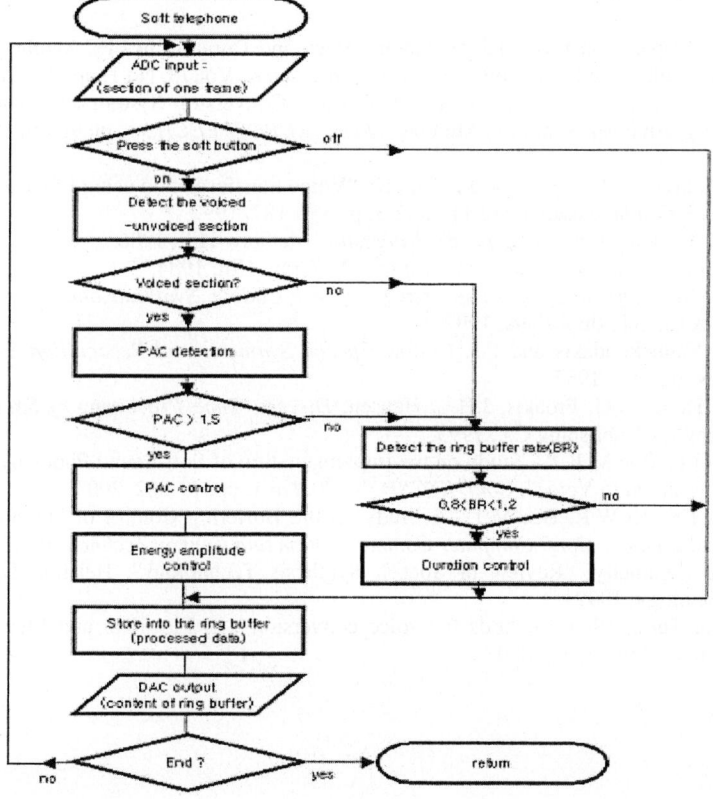

Fig. 9. Flow diagram implemented Gentle phone

6 Conclusions

In this paper, we proposed one of the technologies of the step to human's five senses. When people grow old, their sensation technology gets old as well, and they start to dislike the sound of big intonation change. The soft-sound telephone has a unique way of changing the big intonation change sounds to a complementary sound. Therefore, it is unique to apply a welfare society service communication techniques which is offered to old or disability people. This sound-soft telephone is essential to our society as it brings the friendliness function. Moreover, the soft-sound telephone has a technology of recording the conversation and also a shorthand writer the supplementary system. For these above reasons, this soft-sound telephone can be used in our daily life in various ways with a big effect to our world.

Acknowledgement. This work was supported by the Korean Science and Engineering Foundation, grant no. R01-2002-000-00278-0.

References

[1] B.E. Caspers and B.S. Atal, "Changing Pitch and Duration in LPC Synthesised Speech using Multipulse Excitation", *J. Acoust. Soc. Amer.*, Vol.73, No.1, pp.55, 1983.
[2] T. Takagi, E. Miyasaka, "A Speech Prosody Conversion System with a high Quality Speech Analysis-Synthesis Method", *Proc. EUROSPEECH'93*, pp.995-998, September 1993.
[3] H.Valbret, E.Moulines, and J.P.Tubach, "Voice transformation using PSOLA technique", *Speech Communication*, vol.11, no.2-3, pp.175-187, 1992.
[4] T.W. Parsons, *Voice and Speech Processing*, McGraw-Hill, 1986.
[5] G. Bristow, *Electronic Speech Synthesis*, McGraw-Hill, 1984.
[6] A.N. Ince, *Digital Speech Processing - Speech Coding, Synthesis and Recognition*, Kluwer Academic Publishers, 1992.
[7] E.J. Yannakoudakis and P.J. Hutton, *Speech Synthesis and Recognition Systems*, Ellis Horwood Ltd., 1987.
[8] J.R. Deller, J.G. Proakis, J.H.L. Hansen, *Discrete-Time Processing of Speech Signals*, Macmillan Publishing Co., 1993.
[9] Kim J.K, Bae M.J , "A Study on the Implementation of Soft-Sound Phone by the Control of Intonation in Voice", *Conf. KSCSP* Vol.20, No.1, pp379-382, 2003.
[10] Kim J.K, Jo W.R, Bae M.J, "A Study on the Buffering Control of Duration for Soft-Sound Phone", *Conf. Computer Communication and Control Technologies,* Vol 4, 2003.
[11] Sami Lemmetty, "Review of Speech Synthesis Technology", Helsinki University of Technology, 1999.
[12] Oytun Türk, "New Methods for voice conversion", in Electrical and Electronics Eng. Boðaziçi University, 2000.

A Novel Blind Equalizer Based on Dual-Mode MCMA and DD Algorithm*

Seokho Yoon[1], Sang Won Choi[2], Jumi Lee[2],
Hyoungmoon Kwon[2], and Iickho Song[2],**

[1] School of Information and Communication Engineering,
Sungkyunkwan University, 300 Cheoncheon Dong,
Jangan Gu, Suwon 440-746, Korea
syoon@ece.skku.ac.kr
[2] Department of Electrical Engineering and Computer Science,
Korea Advanced Institute of Science and Technology,
373-1 Guseong Dong, Yuseong Gu, Daejeon 305-701, Korea
{swchoi, jmlee, kwon}@Sejong.kaist.ac.kr, i.song@ieee.org

Abstract. We address a new blind equalizer incorporating both the good initial convergence characteristic of the dual-mode modified constant modulus algorithm (MCMA) and the low residual error characteristic after convergence of the decision-directed (DD) algorithm. In the proposed scheme, a convergence detector is employed to help switching from the dual-mode MCMA to the DD algorithm. We have observed that the proposed scheme exhibits a good overall performance in comparison with the CMA, MCMA, and dual-mode MCMA.

1 Introduction

In many modern communication systems including digital mobile and digital TV systems, data is often transmitted through unknown channels and is thus subject to intersymbol interference (ISI), mostly due to the channel dispersion characterized by the non-ideal nature of the channel. The ISI is a primary cause degrading the performance of digital communication systems. Thus minimizing ISI in digital communication channel is crucial for the improvement of system performance at high speed transmission rate.

Being an efficient tool to extract the transmitted symbol sequence by counteracting the effects of ISI, an equalizer increases the probability of correct symbol detection. Data-aided algorithms initialize and adjust equalizer coefficients with a known training sequence from the transmitter before information-bearing data

---

* This research was supported by the Ministry of Science and Technology (MOST) under the National Research Laboratory (NRL) Program of Korea Science and Engineering Foundation (KOSEF), for which the authors would like to express their thanks.
** Corresponding author.

transmission. Use of a training sequence, however, reduces the bandwidth efficiency and may become impractical when updating of the coefficients should be performed frequently at the receiver end.

It is therefore desirable to equalize a channel without the aid of a training sequence, resulting in the self-recovering, blind, or non-data aided equalization [1]–[3]. Among the major advantages of blind equalization techniques is that no training sequence is necessary to start-up or restart the equalization system when the communication breaks down unpredictably. Blind equalization methods also offer potential improvement in system capacity by eliminating the training overhead.

Numerous studies on blind equalization can be found in the literature. For example, normalized sliding-window constant-modulus and decision-directed (DD) algorithms have been proposed in [4], establishing a link between blind equalization and classical adaptive filtering. A minimum-disturbance technique was proposed in [5] to avoid the gradient noise amplification problem and achieve improved stability and robustness with low computational complexity. The multimodulus algorithm (MMA) introduced in [6] takes advantage of the symbol statistics of such signal constellations as nonsquare and very dense constellations.

Among the various adaptive blind equalization algorithms, the Godard algorithm [1] is one of the best known and simplest adaptive blind equalization algorithms. This algorithm was also developed independently and extended as the constant modulus algorithm (CMA) in [2]. Since the CMA is phase-blind, the equalizer output has an arbitrary phase rotation after convergence. Some performance improvement of DD algorithm has also been achieved in [7] by controlling the step size parameter according to the regions in which the equalized output lies in a constellation.

A particular problem of the CMA and modified CMA (MCMA) is that the residual mean square error (MSE) in the steady state is sometimes not sufficiently small for the system to exhibit adequate performance. Minimizing the residual MSE and/or speeding up the convergence rate, the dual-mode algorithms such as those considered in [8] are possibly a plausible solution to improving the overall performance. The dual-mode algorithms possess a faster convergence rate and lower residual MSE than the CMA and MCMA at a small additional complexity to detect the convergence and/or an open eye pattern. The concurrent CMA and soft DD adaptation proposed in [9] has lower computational requirements than the concurrent CMA and DD algorithm.

In this paper, we propose a new blind equalization algorithm employing the dual-mode MCMA with modified parameters in the blind mode to improve the convergence rate and the DD algorithm in the steady state mode to reduce the residual MSE.

2 The Channel and Equalizer Models

Assume that the transmitted data $\{a_n\}$ are an independent and identically distributed (i.i.d.) zero-mean sequence with independent real and imaginary parts derived from a quadrature amplitude modulation (QAM) constellation. Let the causal and linear time-invariant channel has coefficients $\{h(0), h(1), \cdots, h(L-1)\}$ with L the length of the channel impulse response, channel memory, or channel order. Then, the received signal at time index n is

$$x_n = \sum_{k=0}^{L-1} h^*(k) a_{n-k} + v_n, \qquad (1)$$

where v_n is an i.i.d. additive white Gaussian noise (AWGN) and $*$ denotes complex conjugate.

To recover $\{a_n\}$, the received signals $\{x_n\}$ are passed through an equalizer modelled as an N-tap FIR filter with coefficients $\{w(0), w(1), \cdots, w(N-1)\}$. The output is then

$$y_n = \mathbf{W}_n^H \mathbf{X}_n, \qquad (2)$$

where $\mathbf{X}_n = [x_n, x_{n-1}, \cdots, x_{n-N+1}]^T$ is the vector of the received signals, $\mathbf{W}_n = [w(0), w(1), \cdots, w(N-1)]^T$ is the vector of the equalizer tap weights (coefficients), and the superscript H denotes the complex conjugate transpose.

3 A Novel Scheme for Blind Equalization

3.1 Dual-Mode MCMA

Let the error signal of the dual-mode MCMA be

$$e_n = \gamma_n \cdot e_n^{\text{MCMA}} + \beta_n \cdot e_n^{\text{DD}}, \qquad (3)$$

where γ_n and β_n are adaptive parameters,

$$e_n^{\text{MCMA}} = y_{n,R}(y_{n,R}^2 - R_{2,R}) + i y_{n,I}(y_{n,I}^2 - R_{2,I}), \qquad (4)$$

and

$$e_n^{\text{DD}} = y_n - \hat{a}_n \qquad (5)$$

with $i = \sqrt{-1}$. Here, $y_{n,R}$ and $y_{n,I}$ are the real and imaginary parts of the equalizer output y_n, respectively, and the hard decision output $\hat{a}_n$ of y_n is an estimate of a_n. The real quantities $R_{2,R}$ and $R_{2,I}$ in (4) are obtained as

$$R_{2,R} = \frac{E[a_{n,R}^4]}{E[a_{n,R}^2]} \qquad (6)$$

and

$$R_{2,I} = \frac{E[a_{n,I}^4]}{E[a_{n,I}^2]} \qquad (7)$$

by setting the derivative of a non-convex cost function with respect to the equalizer tap weights to be zero to minimize the cost function.

Using a stochastic gradient algorithm as the updating rule, the vector $\mathbf{W}_n$ is adapted by

$$\mathbf{W}_{n+1} = \mathbf{W}_n - \mu \cdot e_n^* \mathbf{X}_n, \tag{8}$$

where μ is the step size. The dual-mode MCMA is known to have good performance in terms of the convergence rate and residual MSE when it uses a sigmoid function in the construction of the relation between γ_n and β_n. Note that the sigmoid function (11) is the cumulative distribution function (cdf) of the logistic pdf [10], one of the well-known heavy-tailed pdf's.

To illustrate simply and clearly a drawback of the dual-mode MCMA, let us consider the adaptive parameters

$$\gamma_n^{\text{sigmoid}} = g(|e_n^{\text{DD}}|) \tag{9}$$

and

$$\beta_n^{\text{sigmoid}} = \frac{|e_n^{\text{MCMA}}|}{|e_n^{\text{DD}}|} \{1 - g(|e_n^{\text{DD}}|)\} \tag{10}$$

of the dual-mode MCMA with the sigmoid function

$$g(x) = \frac{1}{1 + e^{-a(x-0.5)}}, \quad a > 0. \tag{11}$$

From (3), (9), and (11), it is obvious that the component $\gamma_n^{\text{sigmoid}} e_n^{\text{MCMA}}$ of the error signal (3) will not be zero in the steady state since $\gamma_n^{\text{sigmoid}}$ is not zero even when the channel is perfectly equalized. This results in a large output error level (relative to the case where $e_n = \beta_n^{\text{sigmoid}} e_n^{\text{DD}}$) in the steady state after the equalizer has converged completely. In addition, the parameter a in (11) has some restriction on its range due to a tradeoff relationship that a large value of a increases the convergence rate but results in a large error signal in the steady state, and vice versa.

3.2 The Proposed Algorithm for Blind Equalization

To overcome the drawback of the dual-mode MCMA, we propose a method in which only the DD algorithm operates in the steady state thereby improving the residual MSE performance of the dual-mode MCMA in the steady state. The proposed equalization algorithm consists of the dual-mode MCMA, DD algorithm, and a convergence detector as shown in Figure 1. The combination proposed in Figure 1 basically attempts to utilize the advantages of the dual-mode MCMA and DD algorithm, thereby improving both the convergence rate and the residual MSE in the steady state.

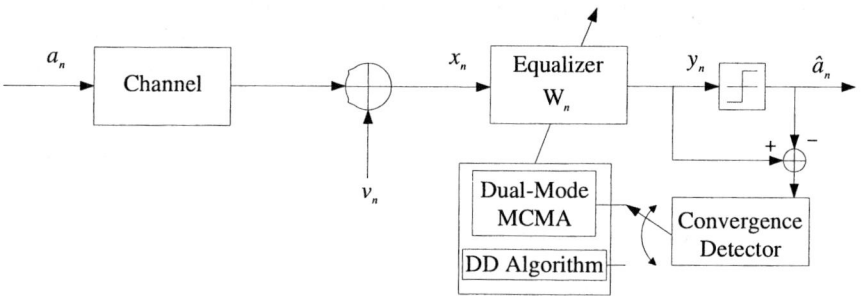

Fig. 1. A block diagram of the proposed system

Blind Mode: At the beginning of the equalization process, the blind mode error e_n^{DD} will tend to be large. Thus, based on the simplification $\frac{1}{1+\exp(-x)} \approx 1 - \exp(-x)$ for x sufficiently large in (9) and (10), we propose to use

$$\gamma_n^{\text{prop}} = 1 - e^{-\alpha_1 |\eta_n'|} \tag{12}$$

and

$$\beta_n^{\text{prop}} = \frac{|e_n^{\text{MCMA}}|}{|e_n^{\text{DD}}|} \cdot e^{-\alpha_2 |\eta_n'|}, \tag{13}$$

where α_1 and α_2 are positive numbers,

$$\eta_n' = \eta_n - \eta_{n-1}, \tag{14}$$

and

$$\eta_n = (1-\psi)\eta_{n-1} + \psi |e_n^{\text{DD}}|^2, \qquad 0 < \psi < 1 \tag{15}$$

with $\eta_0 = 0$.

When the present output error level (represented approximately by η_n) has a larger value with respect to the previous output error level (represented approximately by η_{n-1}), γ_n^{prop} has a large value while β_n^{prop} is small, and vice versa. Since we consider only the convergence rate but not the residual MSE in the blind mode, we have more flexibility at the expense of some more complexity for the tuning of the parameters α_1, ψ, and α_2. Because of this advantage, we can use larger values of both γ_n^{prop} and β_n^{prop} in the blind mode. Consequently, the convergence is expected to be faster in the proposed method than in the dual-mode MCMA using (9) and (10).

Steady State Mode: In our context, the steady state means a state after an initial convergence has been attained during the training period with the dual mode MCMA. Once the proposed equalizer begins to converge, the dual-mode MCMA is switched into the DD algorithm by a convergence detector. The convergence rate after the shift from the dual-mode MCMA to the DD algorithm gets lower and lower while the residual MSE gets smaller and smaller. Since only the DD algorithm is employed in the steady state mode, the residual MSE is expected to be reduced more compared with the dual-mode MCMA.

Let the error signal of the proposed algorithm in the steady state mode be

$$e_n^{\text{prop}} = \lambda_n \cdot (y_n - \hat{a}_n), \tag{16}$$

where the adaptive gain λ_n is given by

$$\lambda_n = |e_n^{\text{MCMA}}|. \tag{17}$$

Note that $e_n^{\text{prop}} = |e_n^{\text{MCMA}}| \cdot e_n^{\text{DD}}$. Normally a larger λ_n results in a faster convergence at the cost of less residual MSE reduction, and vice versa; the ubiquitous tradeoff between the convergence rate and residual MSE reduction. We are to select λ_n considering this tradeoff between the convergence rate and residual MSE reduction. The choice (17) of λ_n essentially allows us to change smoothly from the dual-mode MCMA to the DD algorithm and has been found to cope effectively with variant SNR and channels in simulations also.

Convergence Detector: If the DD algorithm is triggered too early before the proposed scheme converges, the convergence will be slow, and if it starts too late after the convergence, the equalizer may converge to a different state. It is therefore highly important to adequately determine the instant of the switching to the DD algorithm.

To derive a measure for the detection of convergence, let us consider Figure 2, where S_t denotes a time interval of length C and

$$d_t = \frac{1}{C}\left\{\sum_{S_t}|e^{\text{DD}}| - \sum_{S_{t-1}}|e^{\text{DD}}|\right\}$$
$$= \frac{1}{C}\sum_{l=1}^{C}\left(|e^{\text{DD}}_{C*(t-1)+l}| - |e^{\text{DD}}_{C*(t-2)+l}|\right), \quad t = 2, 3, \cdots. \tag{18}$$

We assume $d_1 = 1$ and the superscripts 'before' and 'after' refer to before and after the convergence, respectively. Since the time interval S_t^{before} would be located on the steep slope and S_t^{after} on the convergence floor, we can find the (approximate) time instant of the convergence by computing the value of d_t and comparing it with a reference value.

It is clear that d_t is small also at the beginning of the blind mode where the output error level is large. If we judge the convergence solely on the basis of the value of d_t, we might therefore end up with an undesirable result. In [8], by noting that an open eye condition can be expressed as $|e^{\text{DD}}| = |y_n - \hat{a}_n| < \frac{D'}{2}$, a detection scheme $|e^{\text{DD}}| < \frac{D'}{4}$ is proposed, where D' is the minimum distance between the symbols in the constellation. To detect the convergence more correctly by smoothing the effects of the fluctuation of the errors $\{|e^{\text{DD}}|\}$

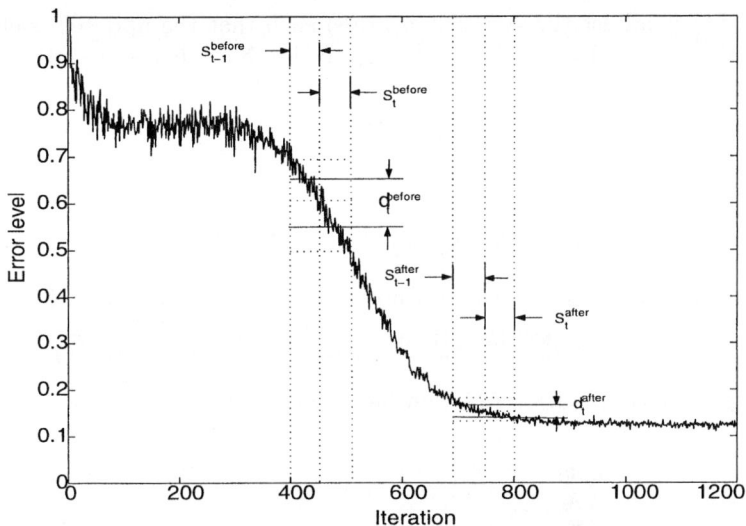

Fig. 2. A graph for the detection algorithm

and consequently making the detector less dependent on the problem, we propose to use the average

$$E_t = \frac{1}{C} \sum_{S_t} |e^{\mathrm{DD}}| \qquad (19)$$

of the output errors in S_t in addition to d_t in the decision of the convergence.

In summary, the steps of the detection algorithm are as follows:

i) Let $t = 2$.
ii) Check if $|d_t| < d$ and $E_t < \frac{D'}{4}$, where d is a positive constant.
iii) If the results in ii) are both positive, the convergence detector switches dual-mode MCMA into DD algorithm at $50 * t + 1$. Otherwise, we repeat ii) and iii) with $t = 3, 4, \cdots$.

The DD algorithm is known [4], [8] to converge surely when an initial convergence has already been obtained during a training period, which occur for example when the eye pattern of the signal is initially open. By using (19) with the threshold guaranteeing the eye to open (i.e., $\frac{D'}{4} < \frac{D'}{2}$) except for a severe distortion case, the convergence detector can be used to switch from the dual MCMA to DD algorithm.

Step Size of the Proposed Algorithm: Using the methods similar to the normalized least mean square (NLMS) algorithm [11], we can derive the stability criterion for the proposed algorithm. The NLMS adjusts the step size μ such that the updated filter coefficients would produce zero error with the current data vector.

First, let us adjust the step size μ in (8) such that the updated coefficients would achieve the desired modulus when applied to $\mathbf{X}_n$. That is, we select μ_n^{MCMA} such that

$$\mathbf{W}_{n+1}^H \mathbf{X}_n = \sqrt{R_{2,R}} + i\sqrt{R_{2,I}}. \tag{20}$$

From (8), we have

$$\mathbf{W}_{n+1}^H \mathbf{X}_n = \mathbf{W}_n^H \mathbf{X}_n - \mu_n^{\text{MCMA}} \cdot e_n^{\text{MCMA}} \cdot ||\mathbf{X}_n||^2 \tag{21}$$

after some algebraic manipulations. Substituting (2) and (20) into (21) gives

$$y_{n,R} + iy_{n,I} - \mu_n^{\text{MCMA}} \cdot e_n^{\text{MCMA}} \cdot ||\mathbf{X}_n||^2 = \sqrt{R_{2,R}} + i\sqrt{R_{2,I}}. \tag{22}$$

The solution to the equation (22) can be shown to be

$$\mu_{n,R}^{\text{MCMA}} = \frac{1}{y_{n,R}(y_{n,R} + \sqrt{R_{2,R}}) \cdot ||\mathbf{X}_n||^2} \tag{23}$$

and

$$\mu_{n,I}^{\text{MCMA}} = \frac{1}{y_{n,I}(y_{n,I} + \sqrt{R_{2,I}}) \cdot ||\mathbf{X}_n||^2} \tag{24}$$

for the real and imaginary parts of μ_n^{MCMA}, respectively.

Similarly, the step size for the DD algorithm is obtained to be

$$\mu_n^{\text{DD}} = \frac{1}{||\mathbf{X}_n||^2} \tag{25}$$

from

$$\mathbf{W}_{n+1}^H \mathbf{X}_n = \hat{a}_n \tag{26}$$

and

$$y_{n,R} + iy_{n,I} - \mu_n^{\text{DD}} \cdot e_n^{\text{DD}} \cdot ||\mathbf{X}_n||^2 = \hat{a}_n. \tag{27}$$

Finally, let us derive the step size of the proposed algorithm using the results (23)–(25). Multiplying both sides of (22) by $\gamma_n^{\text{prop}} \cdot \mu_n^{\text{DD}}$ and both sides of (27) by $\beta_n^{\text{prop}} \cdot \mu_n^{\text{MCMA}}$, and then adding the results, we get

$$y_{n,R} + iy_{n,I} - \frac{1}{\frac{\gamma_n^{\text{prop}}}{\mu_n^{\text{MCMA}}} + \frac{\beta_n^{\text{prop}}}{\mu_n^{\text{DD}}}} \cdot e_n^{\text{prop}} \cdot ||\mathbf{X}_n||^2$$

$$= \frac{\gamma_n^{\text{prop}} \cdot \mu_n^{\text{DD}} \cdot (\sqrt{R_{2,R}} + i\sqrt{R_{2,I}}) + \beta_n^{\text{prop}} \cdot \mu_n^{\text{MCMA}} \cdot \hat{a}_n}{\gamma_n^{\text{prop}} \cdot \mu_n^{\text{DD}} + \beta_n^{\text{prop}} \cdot \mu_n^{\text{MCMA}}} \tag{28}$$

after some algebraic manipulations using (3). Comparing (22), (27), and (28), it looks reasonable at the first glance to choose the step size as

$$\tilde{\mu}_n = \frac{1}{\frac{\gamma_n^{\text{prop}}}{\mu_n^{\text{MCMA}}} + \frac{\beta_n^{\text{prop}}}{\mu_n^{\text{DD}}}}. \tag{29}$$

Unfortunately, we have observed in preliminary simulations that the step size (29) is sometimes too large and the algorithm may fail to converge when $||\mathbf{X}_n||^2$ is too small. One simple solution is clearly to use the modified step size

$$\mu_n^{\text{prop}} = \frac{1}{\sigma + \frac{\gamma_n^{\text{prop}}}{\mu_n^{\text{MCMA}}} + \frac{\beta_n^{\text{prop}}}{\mu_n^{\text{DD}}}}, \qquad (30)$$

where σ is a small positive number. The proposed algorithm converges in the mean-square sense if the step size μ satisfies the condition

$$0 < \mu < \min(\mu_n^{\text{prop}}). \qquad (31)$$

4 Simulation Results

In all the simulations herein, we have assumed that the clock of the received signal is perfectly recovered and a carrier phase offset does not affect the equalizer. A simple 16-QAM constellation has been chosen and the signal to noise ratio

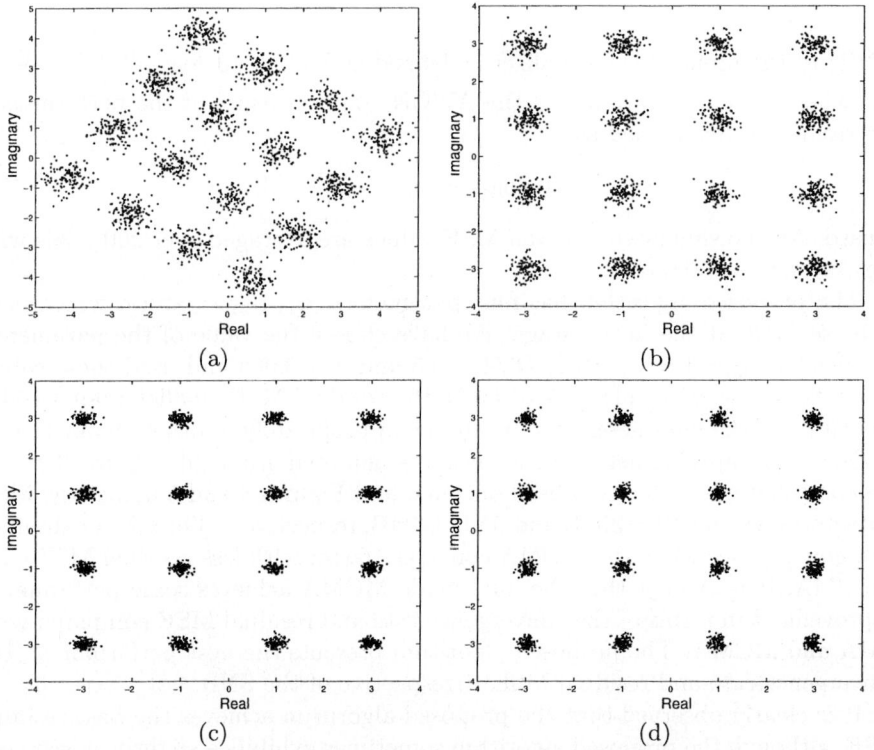

Fig. 3. The constellations of the equalized 16-QAM signals when SNR=30dB. (a) CMA, (b) MCMA, (c) dual-mode MCMA, (d) proposed algorithm.

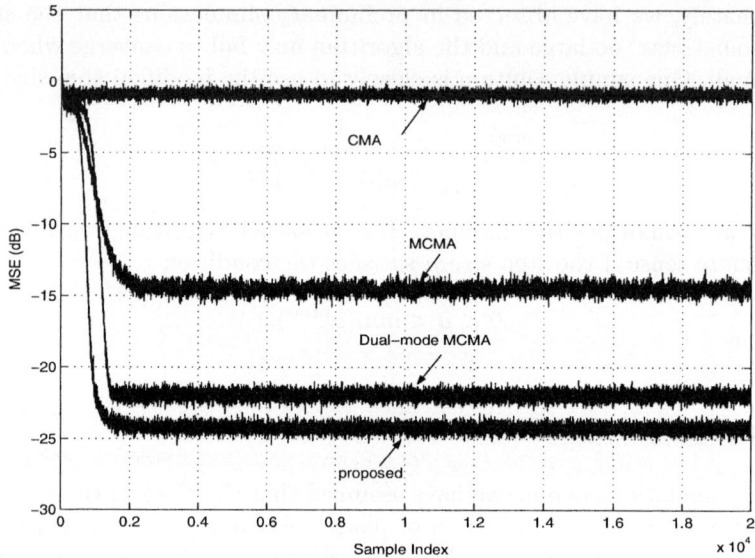

Fig. 4. The MSE of various schemes when SNR=40dB

(SNR) at the input of the equalizer is defined as SNR $= 10 \ \log_{10} \frac{E[|a_n * h(n)|^2]}{\sigma_n^2}$ in dB, where σ_n^2 is the variance of the AWGN. As a measure of the performance, the residual MSE defined as

$$\text{MSE} = 10 \ \log_{10} E[|y_n - \hat{a}_n|^2] \quad [\text{dB}] \tag{32}$$

is used. All the simulated residual MSE values are averaged over 200 trials with the step size $\mu = 0.00008$.

The proposed algorithm has four parameters, α_1, α_2, ψ, and d which need to be set only at the initial stage. We have chosen the value of the parameters as $\alpha_1 = 20$, $\alpha_2 = 1.5$, $\psi = 0.9$, $D'/4 = 0.5$ and $d = 0.008$ and used these values in all the following simulations to make the residual MSE smaller than -10dB: the values of the parameters can be chosen appropriately in other channels also.

For a 22-tap channel impulse response adopted from [9], Figure 3 shows the constellations of the equalized outputs, and Figures 4 and 5 depict the MSE trajectories when SNR=30dB and SNR=40dB, respectively. The CMA exhibits a slow convergence while the MCMA converges faster with less residual MSE than the CMA. It is evident that the dual-mode MCMA achieves some performance improvement in terms of the convergence rate and residual MSE compared with CMA and MCMA. The proposed algorithm presents the best performance (the convergence rate and residual MSE) irrespective of the SNR.

It is clearly observed that the proposed algorithm achieves the best residual MSE, although the proposed algorithm sometimes exhibits a slightly slower convergence than the dual-mode MCMA. This is due to the inherent characteristics of the DD algorithm which, after the convergence, reduces the residual MSE

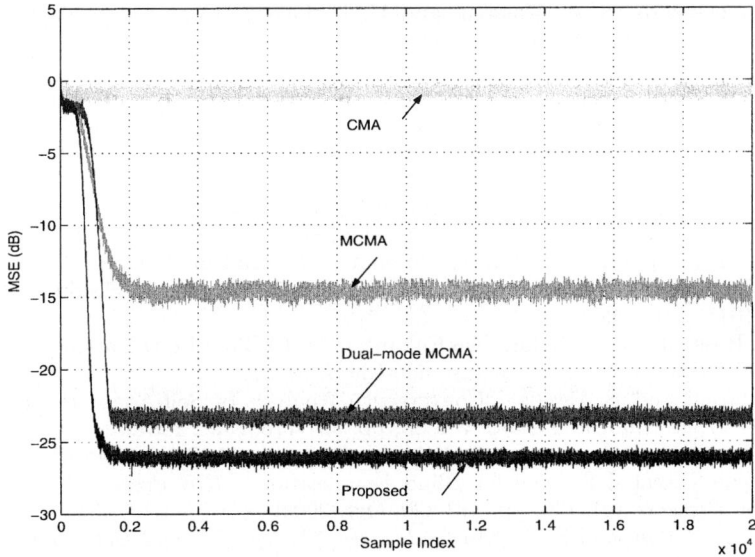

Fig. 5. The MSE of various schemes when SNR=50dB.

more while converges slowly with a very small adaptive gain when the SNR is high. The proposed algorithm always has a lower residual MSE than the dual-mode MCMA and the difference of convergence rate between the two algorithms in the blind mode is negligible.

5 Conclusion

In this paper, we have proposed a new blind equalizer allowing reduced residual error level and faster convergence compared with the CMA, MCMA, and dual-mode MCMA. The proposed algorithm makes use of both the good initial convergence characteristic of the dual-mode MCMA and the low residual error characteristic of the DD algorithm after convergence. The proposed algorithm, in exchange for a slightly higher complexity when compared to other conventional algorithms, offers improved equalization performance. Simulation results have supported the performance advantages of the proposed algorithm in general.

References

1. D. N. Godard, "Self-Recovering Equalization and Carrier Tracking in Two-Dimensional Data Communication Systems," *IEEE Trans. Comm.*, vol. 28, pp. 1867-1875, Nov. 1980.
2. J. R. Treichler and B. G. Agee, "A New Approach to Multipath Correction of Constant Modulus Signals," *IEEE Trans. Acoust., Speech, Signal Process.*, vol. 31, pp. 456-472, Apr. 1983.

3. V. Weerackody, S. A. Kassam, and K. R. Laker, "Convergence Analysis of an Algorithm for Blind Equalization," *IEEE Trans. Comm.*, vol. 39, pp. 856-865, June 1991.
4. C. B. Papadias and D. T. M. Slock, "Normalized Sliding-Window Constant-Modulus and Decision-Directed Algorithms: A Link between Blind Equalization and Classical Adaptive Filtering," *IEEE Trans. Signal Process.*, vol. 45, pp. 231-235, Jan. 1997.
5. J. C. Lin, "Blind Equalisation Technique Based on an Improved Constant Modulus Adaptive Algorithm," *IEE Proc. – Comm.*, vol. 149, pp. 45-50, Feb. 2002.
6. J. Yang, J. -J. Werner, and G. A. Dumont, "The Multimodulus Blind Equalization and Its Generalized Algorithms," *IEEE Journ. Selected Areas Comm.*, vol. 20, pp. 997-1015, June 2002.
7. F. J. Ross and D. P. Taylor, "An Enhancement to Blind Equalization Algorithms," *IEEE Trans. Comm.*, vol. 39, pp. 636-639, May 1991.
8. O. Macchi and E. Eweda, "Convergence Analysis of Self-Adaptive Equalizers," *IEEE Trans. Inform. Theory*, vol. 30, pp. 161-176, Mar. 1984.
9. S. Chen, "Low Complexity Concurrent Constant Modulus Algorithm and Soft Decision Directed Scheme for Blind Equalisation," *IEE Proc. – Vision, Image, Signal Process.*, vol. 150, pp. 312-320, Oct. 2003.
10. I. Song, J. Bae, and S. Y. Kim, *Advanced Theory of Signal Detection*, Springer-Verlag, 2002.
11. M. H. Hayes, *Statistical Digital Signal Processing and Modeling*, John Wiley and Sons, 1996.
12. G. Picchi and G. Prati, "Blind Equalization and Carrier Recovery Using a 'Stop-and-Go' Decision-Directed Algorithm," *IEEE Trans. Comm.*, vol. 35, pp. 877-887, Sep. 1987.

Robust Secret Key Based Authentication Scheme Using Smart Cards

Eun-Jun Yoon and Kee-Young Yoo*

Department of Computer Engineering,
Kyungpook National University, Daegu 702-701, South Korea
ejyoon@infosec.knu.ac.kr, yook@knu.ac.kr
Tel.: +82-53-950-5553, Fax:+82-53-957-4846

Abstract. User authentication is an important part of security, along with confidentiality and integrity, for systems that allow remote access over untrustworthy networks, like the Internet. Recently, Chen et al. proposed an improvement on the SAS-like password authentication schemes to make not only keep the original advantages but also highlight a feature, mutual authentication between a user and a remote server. However, we find that their schemes are vulnerable to a denial-of-service attack and an insider attack. In addition, their schemes is not easily reparable. Accordingly, the current paper presents a secret-key-based authentication scheme using smart cards. Based on low-cost smart cards that support only simple hashing operations, the proposed scheme has a highly efficient and is designed to resist existing known attacks.

Keywords: Cryptography, secret key, authentication, smart card.

1 Introduction

ISO 10202 standards have been established for the security architecture of financial transaction systems using integrated circuit cards (IC cards or smart cards). A smart card originates from an IC memory card used in industry about 10 years ago [1][2]. The main characteristics of a smart card are small size and low-power consumption. Generally speaking, a smart card contains a microprocessor which can quickly manipulate logical and mathematical operations, a RAM which is used as a data or instruction buffer, and a ROM which stores the user's secret key and the necessary public parameters and algorithmic descriptions of executing programs. The merits of a smart card for password authentication are its high simplicity and efficiency of the login and authentication processes.

User authentication is an important part of security, along with confidentiality and integrity, for systems that allow remote access over untrustworthy networks, like the Internet. Password-based authentication is one of the most popular methods because of its simplicity and effectiveness. As such, a remote password authentication scheme authenticates the legitimacy of users over an insecure channel, where the password is often regarded as a secret shared between

---

* Corresponding author.

the remote system and the user. Based on knowledge of the password, the user can use it to create and send a valid login message to a remote system to gain the right to access. Meanwhile, the remote system also uses the shared password to check the validity of the login message and authenticate the user.

In 2000, Sandirigama et al. [3] proposed a simple and secure password authentication scheme, the so-called SAS. Because of the advantages of lower storage, processing, and transmission overheads, the SAS-like schemes are widely concerned in the researches for user authentication. Therefore, there are several articles [4][5][6][7] proposed to continuously enhance SAS-like protocols. Unfortunately, those enhancements still have security flaws. In 2001, Lin et al. [4] proposed an optimal strong-password authentication scheme, called OSPA, to enhance the security of SAS which is suffering from the replay attack and the denial-of-service attack. Subsequently, the OSPA scheme has been shown vulnerable to the stolen-verifier attack [5] and the impersonation attack [6]. In 2003, Lin et al. [7] proposed an other SAS-like version for OSPA to withstand the stolen-verifier attack. Thereafter, in 2004, Chen et al. [8] pointed out that the Lin et al.'s scheme suffers from the denial-of-service attack and further proposed an improvement on the SAS-like password authentication scheme to make not only keep the original advantages but also highlight a feature, mutual authentication between a user and a remote server. However, we find that their schemes are vulnerable to a denial-of-service attack [9] and an insider attack [11]. In addition, their schemes is not easily reparable [11][12][13]. Accordingly, the current paper shows the weaknesses of Chen et al.'s scheme, and then presents a secret-key-based authentication scheme using smart cards with better security strength. Based on low-cost smart cards that support only simple hashing operations, the proposed scheme has a highly efficient and is designed to resist existing known attacks while generating a session key agreed by the user and the server.

This paper is organized as follows: In Section 2, we define the security properties. In Section 3, we briefly review Chen et al.'s password authentication schemes. In Section 4, we argue the problems of the Chen et al.'s schemes. In Section 5, we propose a secret-key-based authentication scheme. In Section 6, we discuss the security of the proposed scheme. Finally, conclusion is given in Section 7.

2 Security Properties

The following security properties of the authentication schemes should be considered [9][10][14].

(1) **Guessing attack:** A guessing attack involves an adversary (randomly or systematically) trying long-term private keys (e.g. user password or server secret key), one at a time, in the hope of finding the correct private key. Ensuring long-term private keys chosen from a sufficiently large space can reduce exhaustive searches. Most users, however, select passwords from a small subset of the full password space. Such weak passwords with low entropy are easily guessed by using the so-called dictionary attack.

(2) **Replay attack:** A replay attack is an offensive action in which an adversary impersonates or deceives another legitimate participant through the reuse of information obtained in a protocol.
(3) **Stolen-verifier attack:** In most applications, the server stores verifiers of users' passwords (e.g. hashed passwords) instead of the clear text of passwords. The stolen-verifier attack means that an adversary who steals the password-verifier from the server can use it *directly* to masquerade as a legitimate user in a user authentication execution.
(4) **Denial-of-service attack:** The denial of service attack prevents or inhibits the normal use or management of communications facilities. This attack may act on a specific user. For example, an adversary may perform this attack to cause the server to reject the login of a specific user.

In addition, the following security properties of session key agreement schemes should be considered since they are often desirable in some environments [10][14].

(1) **Implicit key authentication:** Implicit key authentication is the property obtained when identifying a party based on a shared session key, which assures that no other entity than the specifically identified entity can gain access to the session key.
(2) **Explicit key authentication:** Explicit key authentication is the property obtained when both implicit key authentication and key confirmation hold.
(3) **Mutual authentication:** Mutual authentication means that both the client and server are authenticated to each other within the same protocol.
(4) **Session key security:** Session key security means that at the end of the key exchange, the session key is not known by anyone but user and server.
(5) **Perfect forward secrecy:** Perfect forward secrecy means that if a long-term private key (e.g. user password or server private key) is compromised, this does not compromise any earlier session keys.

3 Review of Chen et al.'s Authentication Schemes

In this section, we briefly review Chen et al.'s two password authentication schemes [8] that are unilateral authentication scheme and mutual authentication scheme. Some of the notations used in this paper are defined as follows:

- U_i, S, E: a user, remote server and attacker, respectively.
- ID_i, PW_i: U_i's identity and password, respectively.
- N, r, r': random nonces.
- x: S's strong secret key.
- $h(\cdot)$: a strong one-way hash function.
- $\oplus$: bit-wise XOR operation.
- $||$: concatenation operation.

3.1 Chen et al.'s Unilateral Authentication Scheme

Chen et al.'s unilateral authentication scheme is composed of two phases, which are the registration phase and the authentication phase.

Registration Phase: The registration phase is shown as follows:

(R.1) $U_i \to S$: $ID_i, h^2(PW_i \oplus N), N$

A user U_i with his identity ID_i chooses password PW_i freely and computes $h^2(PW_i \oplus N)$, where N is a random nonce. Then, U_i sends ID_i, $h^2(PW_i \oplus N)$ and N to S.

(R.2) $S \to U_i$: a smart card $\{N, h(x||ID_i)\}$

Upon receiving ID_i, $h^2(PW_i \oplus N)$, S stores $h^2(PW_i \oplus N)$ into the verification table. S computes $h(x||ID_i)$ and writes $\{N, h(x||ID_i)\}$ into U_i's smart card and releases it to U_i, where x is the secret key of S.

Authentication Phase: The authentication phase is shown as follows:

(A.1) $U_i \to S$: $ID_i, r \oplus h(x||ID_i), h(r), c_1, c_2, c_3$

U_i inserts his smart card into a login device and enters his identity ID_i and password PW_i. The smart card calculates c_1, c_2 and c_3 as follows:
$c_1 = h(PW_i \oplus N) \oplus h(h^2(PW_i \oplus N) \oplus r)$,
$c_2 = h^2(PW_i \oplus \overline{N}) \oplus h(PW_i \oplus N)$,
$c_3 = h^3(PW_i \oplus \overline{N})$,
where r is a random nonce and $\overline{N}$ is a new random nonce. The smart card computes $r \oplus h(x||ID_i)$ and $h(r)$, and then sends $\{ID_i, r \oplus h(x||ID_i), h(r), c_1, c_2, c_3\}$ to S as a login request.

(A.2) $S \to U_i$: Access grant/ reject

Upon receiving the login request, S checks the format of ID_i, calculates $h(x||ID_i)$ to extract r from $r \oplus h(x||ID_i)$ and verifies the validity of r by $h(r)$. Then S hashes $h^2(PW_i \oplus N) \oplus r$ to extract $h(PW_i \oplus N)$ from c_1, and uses $h(PW_i \oplus N)$ to extract $h^2(PW_i \oplus \overline{N})$ from c_2, respectively. S checks if the hash value of the extracted $h(PW_i \oplus N)$ is equal to that of the stored $h^2(PW_i \oplus N)$. If equivalent, U_i is authenticated; otherwise, this login request is rejected. Finally, S checks if the hash value of the extracted $h^2(PW_i \oplus \overline{N})$ is equal to the received c_3. If it holds, S updates the verification table by replacing $h^2(PW_i \oplus N)$ with $h^2(PW_i \oplus \overline{N})$.

3.2 Chen et al.'s Mutual Authentication Scheme

Chen et al.'s mutual authentication scheme is also composed of two phases, which are the registration phase and the authentication phase. The registration phase is the same as that of unilateral authentication scheme.

Authentication Phase: The authentication phase is shown as follows:

(A.1) $U_i \to S$: ID_i, r'

U_i inserts his smart card into a login device and enters the identity ID_i and password PW_i to enable the card. Then the identity ID_i and a random nonce r' used to identify this transaction uniquely are sent to S.

(A.2) $S \to U_i$: $r \oplus h(x||ID_i), h(r||r')$

After checking the format of ID_i, S generates a new random nonce r and returns $r \oplus h(x||ID_i)$ and $h(r||r')$ to assure this client U_i that its correspondent is a regular server S.

(A.3) $U_i \to S$: c_1, c_2, c_3

Upon receiving $\{r \oplus h(x||ID_i), h(r||r')\}$, U_i's smart card extracts r from $r \oplus h(x||ID_i)$. Then, with r, U_i verifies $h(r||r')$ contains r' to authenticate S. The smart card computes c_1, c_2, and c_3 as follows:
$c_1 = h(PW_i \oplus N) \oplus h(h^2(PW_i \oplus N) \oplus r)$,
$c_2 = h^2(PW_i \oplus \overline{N}) \oplus h(PW_i \oplus N)$,
$c_3 = h^3(PW_i \oplus \overline{N})$,
where $\overline{N}$ is a new random nonce. The smart card send $\{c_1, c_2, c_3\}$ to S as a login request.

(A.4) $S \to U_i$: Access grant/ reject

Upon receiving the login request, S hashes $h^2(PW_i \oplus N) \oplus r$ to extract $h(PW_i \oplus N)$ from c_1, and uses $h(PW_i \oplus N)$ to extract $h^2(PW_i \oplus \overline{N})$ from c_2, respectively. S checks if the hash value of the extracted $h(PW_i \oplus N)$ is equal to that of the stored $h^2(PW_i \oplus N)$. If equivalent, U_i is authenticated; otherwise, this login request is rejected. Finally, S checks if the hash value of the extracted $h^2(PW_i \oplus \overline{N})$ is equal to the received c_3. If it holds, the server updates the verification table by replacing $h^2(PW_i \oplus N)$ with $h^2(PW_i \oplus \overline{N})$.

4 Weaknesses of Chen et al.'s Schemes

In this section, we will show that Chen et al.'s schemes are vulnerable to a denial-of-service attack and an insider attack, and are not easily reparable [11][12][13].

4.1 Denial-of-Service Attack

The denial-of-service attack, where the server is cheated by an attacker to update the false verification information for the next login phase, is found in the Chen et al.'s schemes so that the server will reject all subsequent login requests of the legal user.

In Chen et al.'s unilateral authentication scheme, to cheat the user U_i and the server S, the attacker E intercept user's login request message $\{ID_i, r \oplus h(x||ID_i), h(r), c_1, c_2, c_3\}$ in authentication phase, and then E impersonate S and send 'access rejected' to U_i's login request. Then, U_i will be fooled into believing that U_i's own login request message $\{c_1, c_2, c_3\}$ has the matter. After cheat U_i, E send intercepting message $\{ID_i, r \oplus h(x||ID_i), h(r), c_1, c_2, c_3\}$ to S, then S update the verification table by replacing $h^2(PW_i \oplus N)$ with $h^2(PW_i \oplus \overline{N})$. Therefore, this makes the server be fooled to store the false verifier and reject all subsequent login requests of the legal user U_i.

In Chen et al.'s mutual authentication scheme, to cheat U_i and S, E intercept user's login request message $\{c_1, c_2, c_3\}$ in authentication phase, and then E impersonate S and send 'access rejected' to U_i's login request. Then, U_i will be fooled into believing that U_i's own login request message $\{c_1, c_2, c_3\}$ has the matter. After cheat U_i, E send intercepting message $\{c_1, c_2, c_3\}$ to S, then S update the verification table by replacing $h^2(PW_i \oplus N)$ with $h^2(PW_i \oplus \overline{N})$. From now on, U_i's succeeding requests for either accessing the resources or changing password will be denied by S. Hence, the attacker can easily lock the account of any client without using cryptographic techniques.

Since this attack does not require password guessing, Chen et al.'s scheme is vulnerable to the denial-of-service attack regardless of whether password is strong or weak.

4.2 Insider Attack

In the registration phase, user U_i's password PW_i will be revealed to remote server S after Step (R.1). The insider of S guesses a candidate password PW_i^* and computes $h^2(PW_i^* \oplus N)$ using received N. If $h^2(PW_i^* \oplus N)$ equals the received $h^2(PW_i \oplus N)$, the insider of S has correctly guessed $PW_i^* = PW_i$. Otherwise, the insider of S tries another candidate password. If U_i uses PW_i to access several servers for his convenience, the insider of S can impersonate U_i to access other servers.

4.3 Poor Reparability

In general, the tamper resistance of smart cards is widely assumed in most smart card based schemes. However, such an assumption may be problematic in practice. In 1998, Kocher et al. [12] stated that all existing smart cards were vulnerable in that the secret keys stored in the smart card could be extracted by monitoring the power consumption. In 2002, Messerges et al. [13] showed that the secrets stored in a smart card may be breached by analyzing the leaked information. Next, we will show that once the attacker E has obtained the $h(x||ID_i)$ stored in U_i's smart card, E can perform an impersonating server attack at the authentication phase in Chen et al.'s mutual authentication scheme.

In Chen et al.'s mutual authentication scheme, if an attacker E wants to impersonate the remote server S successfully, E sends $r \oplus h(x||ID_i)$, $h(r||r')$ to U_i (see Step (A.2) in Chen et al.'s mutual authentication scheme). Then, U_i will extract r from $r \oplus h(x||ID_i)$ and verify the validity of r by using $h(r||r')$ and r'. With r, the smart card computes c_1, c_2, and c_3. Upon receiving the login request, E drop intercepted the messages c_1, c_2, c_3 and accepts U_i's login request. Then impersonating server attack is therefore possible. However, since x is commonly used for all users rather than specifically used for only user, it is unreasonable and inefficient if x should be changed to recover the security for user only. Additionally, it is also impractical to change ID, which should be tied to user uniquely in most application systems. Hence, Chen et al.'s scheme is not easily repairable [11].

5 A Secret-Key-Based Authentication Scheme

This section proposes a secret-key-based authentication scheme. In fact, Chen et al.'s SAS-like password authentication schemes make no sense in the development of password-based schemes. In general, password-based schemes are suitable for the environment of no additional device to store secret information. Therefore, the ability to achieve authentication is only based on the user's password which is easy to memory by the user. In Chen et al.'s SAS-like schemes, they assume each user has a smart card with him. If the assumption holds, it does not need use password-based schemes. Instead, secret-key-based schemes, which are more secure and cost-efficient than those password-based schemes, are sufficient. The proposed authentication scheme is composed of two phases, which are the registration phase and the authentication phase.

5.1 Registration Phase

The registration phase is illustrated in Fig. 1 and goes as follows:

(R.1) $U_i \to S$: $ID_i, h(PW_i \oplus N)$
U_i selects ID_i, PW_i and N freely and computes $h(PW_i \oplus N)$. Then, U_i sends ID_i and $h(PW_i \oplus N)$ to S.

(R.2) $S \to U_i$: a smart card $\{K, R, h(\cdot)\}$
If it is U_i's initial registration, S creates an entry for U_i in the account database and stores $n = 0$ in this entry. Otherwise, S sets $n = n + 1$ in the existing entry for U_i. Next, S computes $K = h(x||SID_i)$ and $R = h(x||SID_i) \oplus h(PW_i \oplus N)$, where $SID_i = (ID_i||n)$, and then writes $\{K, R, h(\cdot)\}$ into U_i's smart card and releases it to U_i. U_i enters N into his smart card.

Note that U_i's smart card contains K, R, N and $h(\cdot)$, and U_i does not need to remember N after finishing Step (R.2). All data on the smart card are highly protected. Others cannot read the sensitive and confidential information even when someone loses the card.

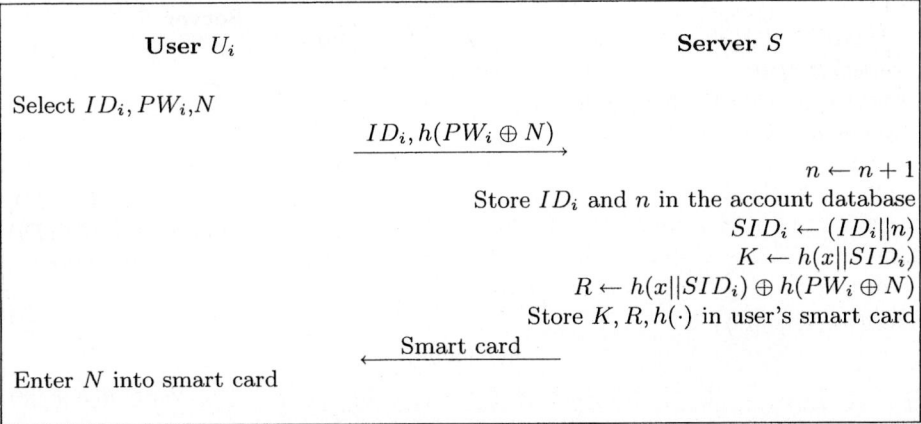

Fig. 1. n-*th* Registration Phase

5.2 Authentication Phase

The authentication phase is illustrated in Fig. 2 and goes as follows:

(A.1) $U_i \to S$: ID_i, r

U_i inserts his smart card into a login device and enters ID_i and PW_i to enable the card. Then the card computes $h(x||SID_i) = R \oplus h(PW_i \oplus N)$ and verifies whether $h(x||SID_i)$ equals to the stored K. If they are equal, the card chooses a random nonce r and sends it with ID_i to S as a login request.

(A.2) $S \to U_i$: $r', h(K||r||r')$

Upon receiving the login request, S checks the format of ID_i and computes $K = h(x||SID_i)$. Then, S chooses a random nonce r' and computes $h(K||r||r')$. Finally, S sends r' and $h(K||r||r')$ to U_i.

(A.3) $U_i \to S$: $h(K||r'||r)$

Upon receiving r' and $h(K||r||r')$, U_i's smart card verifies that $h(K||r||r')$ contains K to authenticate S. If the result is positive, U_i can ensure S is legal. Finally, with r', U_i computes $h(K||r'||r)$ as U_i's authentication token and sends $h(K||r'||r)$ to S.

(A.4) $S \to U_i$: Access grant/ reject

Upon receiving $h(K||r'||r)$, S verifies $h(K||r'||r)$ contains K to authenticate U_i. If the result is positive, S can ensure that U_i is legal.

After mutual authentication between U_i and S, $SK = h(ID_i||K||r||r')$ is used as the session key.

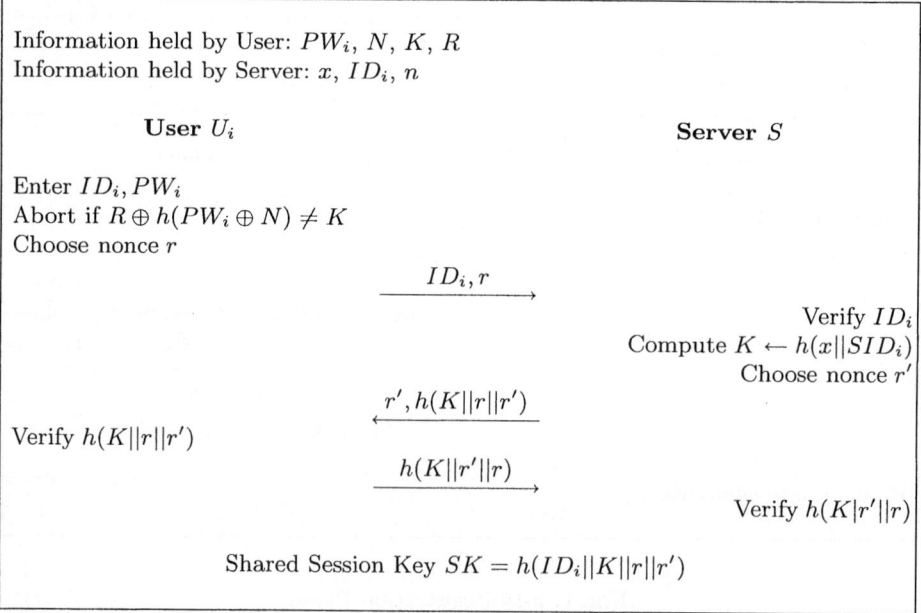

Fig. 2. Authentication Phase

6 Security Analysis

This section analyzes the security of the proposed authentication scheme. At first, we define the security terms needed for the analysis of the proposed authentication scheme.

Definition 1. *A weak secret key (password PW_i) is a value of low entropy $W(k)$, which can be guessed in polynomial time.*

Definition 2. *A strong secret key (x) is a value of high entropy $H(k)$, which cannot be guessed in polynomial time.*

Definition 3. *A secure one-way hash function $y = h(x)$ is one where given x it is easy to compute y and where given y it is hard to compute x.*

Definition 4. *The discrete logarithm problem (DLP) is explained by the following: Given a prime p, a generator g of Z_p^*, and an element $\beta \in Z_p^*$, find the integer α, $0 \leq \alpha \leq p-2$, such that $g^\alpha \equiv \beta \pmod p$.*

Definition 5. *The Diffie-Hellman problem (DHP) is explained by the following: Given a prime p, a generator g of Z_p^*, and elements $g^c \pmod p$ and $g^s \pmod p$, find $g^{cs} \pmod p$.*

Here, security properties: guessing attack, replay attack, impersonation attack, stolen-verifier attack, denial-of-service attack, insider attack, reparable, mutual authentication, session key security, and perfect forward secrecy, would be considered for the proposed authentication scheme. Under the above definitions, the following theorems are used to analyze the security properties in the proposed protocol.

Theorem 1. *The proposed scheme can resist the guessing attacks.*

Proof. Due to the fact that a one-way hash function is computationally difficult to invert, it is extremely hard for any attacker to derive x from $h(x||SID_i)$. Assume that E intercepts U_i's login request message $\{ID_i, r\}$ and S's response message $\{r', h(K||r||r')\}$ over a public network. However, due to the one-way property of a secure one-way hash function, E cannot derive $K = h(x||SID_i)$ from $h(K||r||r')$.

Theorem 2. *The proposed scheme can resist the replay attacks.*

Proof. If E intercepts $\{ID_i, r\}$ sent by U_i in Step (A.1) and uses it to impersonate U_i when sending the next login message. However, for a random challenge, the nonce r separately generated by U_i is different every time. As a result, the replay of U_i's old login message in Steps (1) and (3) is detected by server S because attacker E has no K to compute a correct $h(K||r'||r)$.

Theorem 3. *The proposed scheme can resist the impersonation attack.*

Proof. E can attempt to modify a message $\{ID_i, r\}$ into $\{ID_i, r^*\}$ and send it to S, where r^* is a random nonce selected by E. However, such a modification will fail in Step (A.3) of the authentication phase, because E has no way of obtaining the values K to compute the valid parameters $h(K||r'||r^*)$. If a masqueraded server tries to cheat the requesting U_i, it has to prepare a valid message $\{r', h(K||r||r')\}$. However, this is infeasible, as there is no way to derive the value $K = h(x||SID_i)$ to compute the value $\{h(K||r||r')\}$, due to the one-way property of a secure one-way hash function. Therefore, E has no chance to login by launching the impersonation attack.

Theorem 4. *The proposed scheme can resist the stolen-verifier attack and the denial-of-service attack.*

Proof. Servers are always the target of attacks. An attacker may try to steal or modify the verification table stored in the server. If the verification table is stolen by an attacker, the attacker may masquerade as a legitimate user. If the verification table is modified, a legitimate user cannot successfully login to the server. This results in a denial-of-service attack. The proposed scheme is a nonce-based authentication scheme, but it does not require a verification table in the server S. Even though, E gets ID_i and n in U_i's account database from S, due to the one-way property of a secure one-way hash function, E cannot compute a shared secret key $K = h(x||SID_i)$. Obviously, the proposed scheme can prevent the stolen-verifier attack and the denial-of-service attack.

Theorem 5. *The proposed scheme can resist the insider attack.*

Proof. Since U_i registers to S by presenting $\{ID_i, h(PW_i \oplus N)\}$ instead of $\{ID_i, h(PW_i \oplus N), N\}$, the insider of S cannot directly obtain PW_i without knowing of random nonce N.

Theorem 6. *The proposed scheme is easily reparable.*

Proof. If U_i finds or suspects that his $h(x||SID_i)$ has been compromised, he can select a new random number N' and new password PW'_i, and then compute $h(PW_i \oplus N')$. Next, U_i can re-register to S by using $h(PW_i \oplus N')$. Upon receiving U_i's re-registration request, S will set $n' = n+1$ and compute $h(x||SID'_i)$, where $SID'_i = (ID_i||n')$. Next, S stores $h(x||SID'_i)$ in U_i's new smart card. After receiving the new smart card from S through a secure channel, U_i enters N' into it. From now on, U_i can securely login S by using his new smart card and new password PW'_i. In the meanwhile, the compromised $h(x||SID_i)$ has been revoked automatically, i.e., the login request of the adversary who has obtained $h(x||SID_i)$ will be rejected. Therefore, the proposed scheme is easily reparable.

Theorem 7. *The proposed scheme provides mutual authentication.*

Proof. The proposed scheme uses the session key exchange algorithm to provide mutual authentication, then the key is explicitly authenticated by a mutual confirmation values $h(K||r||r')$ and $h(K||r'||r)$, respectively.

Theorem 8. *The proposed scheme provides session key security.*

Proof. The session key $SK = h(ID_i||K||r||r')$ is known to nobody but U_i and S since the session key SK is protected by K and the secure one-way hash function.

Theorem 9. *The proposed scheme provides perfect forward secrecy.*

Proof. If E can get some used random values r and r' and the shared long-term secret key $h(x||SID_i)$ or x, he can compute the used session key SK. For remedying this problem, the Diffie-Hellman key exchange algorithm can be used for computing the session key. In this approach, we let $r = g^a$ and $r' = g^b$, where a and b are random exponents chosen by U_i and S separately, and $SK = h(ID_i||K||g^{ab})$. Obviously, the proposed scheme provides perfect forward secrecy.

7 Conclusion

The current paper demonstrated that Chen et al.'s SAS-like password authentication schemes are insecure against some attacks. To defeat those attacks, we presented a secret-key-based authentication scheme using smart cards. Based on low-cost smart cards that support only simple hashing operations, the proposed scheme has a highly efficient and is resistance to existing known attacks. Thus, the proposed secret-key-based authentication scheme is designed to secure and cost-efficient.

Acknowledgements

This research was supported by the MIC (Ministry of Information and Communication), Korea, under the ITRC (Information Technology Research Center) support program supervised by the IITA (Institute of Information Technology Assessment).

References

1. P. Peyret, G. Lisimaque, T.Y. Chua, "Smart cards provide very high security and flexibility in subscribers management," IEEE Trans. on Consumer Electronics, vol.36, no.3, pp.744–752, 1990.
2. D. Sternglass, "The future is in the PC cards," IEEE Spectrum, vol.29, no.6, pp.46–50, 1992.
3. M. Sandirigama, A. Shimizu, M.T. Noda, "Simple and secure password authentication protocol (SAS)," IEICE Trans. on Communications, vol.E83-B, no.6, pp.1363–1365, 2000.
4. C.L. Lin, H.M. Sun, T. Hwang, "Attacks and solutions on strong-password authentication," IEICE Trans. on Communications,vo.E84-B, no.9, pp.2622–2627, 2001.
5. C.M. Chen, W.C. Ku, "Stolen-verifier attack on two new strong-password authentication protocols," IEICE Trans. on Communications, vol.E85-B, no.11, pp.2519–2521, 2002.
6. T. Tsuji, A. Shimizu, "An impersonation attack on one-time password authentication protocol OSPA," IEICE Trans. on Communications, vol.E86-B, no.7, pp.2182–2185, 2003.

7. C.W. Lin, J.J. Shen, M.S. Hwang, "Security enhancement for optimal strong-password authentication protocol," ACM SIGOPS Operating Systems Review, vol.37, no.2, pp.7–12, 2003.
8. T.H. Chen, W.B. Lee, G. Hornga, "Secure SAS-like password authentication schemes," Computer Standards and Interfaces, vol.27, no.1, pp.25–31, 2004.
9. C.L. Lin, T. Hwang, "A password authentication scheme with secure password updating," Computer & Security, vol.22, no.1, pp.68–72, 2003.
10. E.J. Yoon, W.H. Kim, K.Y. Yoo, "Robust and simple authentication protocol for secure communication on the web," LNCS, ICWE 2005, vol.3579, pp.352–362, 2005.
11. W.C. Ku, S.M. Chen, "Weaknesses and improvements of an efficient password based remote user authentication scheme using smart cards," IEEE Trans. on Consumer Electronics, vol.50, no.1, pp.204–207, 2004.
12. P. Kocher, J. Jaffe, B. Jun, "Differential power analysis," Proc. Advances in Cryptology (CRYPTO'99), pp.388–397, 1999.
13. T.S. Messerges, E.A. Dabbish, R.H. Sloan, "Examining smartcard security under the threat of power analysis attacks," IEEE Trans. on Computers, vol.51, no.5, pp.541–552, 2002.
14. A.J. Menezes, P.C. Oorschot, S.A. Vanstone, "Handbook of applied cryptograph," CRC Press, New York, 1997.

A Dynamically Configurable Multimedia Middleware

Hendry and Munchurl Kim

Laboratory for Multimedia Computing, Communications, and Broadcasting,
School of Engineering, Information and Communications University (ICU),
119 Munji Street, Yuseong-Gu, Daejeon, 305-714, Korea
{hendry, mkim}@icu.ac.kr
http://mccb.icu.ac.kr

Abstract. Multimedia applications become more dependent on software than hardware. However this dependency reduces the executability of multimedia applications over a various software platforms. Therefore, it is required that a multimedia middleware provides a generic software platform on which necessary set of required Services can be dynamically configured on-the-fly for a given multimedia application. This dynamic configuration can be possible by signaling to the middleware a metadata which contains information about Services for the given multimedia application on a standardized multimedia middleware, which is called MPEG Multimedia Middleware (M3W). In this paper, an open, flexible, and resource-efficient multimedia middleware is designed with a hierarchical model of multimedia Services and metadata schema for supporting a dynamic configuration of the middleware Services so that the necessary set of Services is dynamically configurable in the middleware.

1 Introduction

As the end-user's demand for content consumption is increasing, various kinds of multimedia applications have been and/or being developed for variety of multimedia environments from the end-user applications such as games, DVD player, mp3 player, and digital television to the enterprise applications such as video teleconference, e-learning, etc. However, the advance of information technology has offered multimedia consumption markets with various multimedia environments. There are many devices with various kinds of operating systems (OS). There are also many application development environments. As a result, it has been difficult for application developers to create and maintain multimedia applications that can be deployed over a variety of different software platforms [1]. This means that one single application needs be developed in different but customized ways for their respective software platforms, which is not only inefficient but also costly for multimedia applications.

To cope with these difficulties, portable and interoperable multimedia applications should be possible to be executed on different platforms with the minimum modification. This can be achieved by having a generic middleware in which a set of standard API's provides common functionalities to the applications.

In this paper, we propose a dynamically configurable middleware architecture which provides a generic service-based middleware to multimedia applications.

The architecture of the middleware is designed to have entities to handle the Service's life-cycle. Since the Services can be independently deployed/un-deployed to/from the middleware, the middleware can dynamically be configured to meet the necessity of the applications upon request. Moreover, each Service and its interaction are modeled by metadata in XML form so that the configuration description becomes simpler.

This paper is organized as follow. In section 2, we will briefly describe the concept of M3W which can be realized by our proposed middleware architecture; In Section 3, the proposed middleware is introduced. It will cover the architecture and entities that build the middleware, the concept of a hierarchical Service structure, and metadata schema for describing the Service and its container (Component); In Section 4, we show an interesting use-case scenario that uses our proposed middleware; In Section 5, the implementation of the proposed middleware is presented; In Section 6 we present two other related work and compare them analytically to our work; and Finally, Section 7 concludes our works.

2 MPEG Multimedia Middleware (M3W)

To ensure that a middleware is interoperable for various platforms and devices, it must be standardized. Therefore, MPEG has started an activity of standardizing the middleware for multimedia applications, which is called MPEG Multimedia Middleware (M3W) [1][3]. The M3W will standardize the followings:

- Multimedia APIs. They are intended to give the requesting application access to multimedia functionalities provided by the middleware components.
- Management APIs. They are intended to allow the handling and management of the middleware components, procedures are requiring to deal with processes like Service validation, downloading, instantiation, etc.
- In-Operation APIs. They are intended to take extra functionalities into account that are essential for the sound execution of the application that request the Services from the middleware.
- Other APIs. It is intended to accommodate ideas/concepts brought by he submitted technologies that are not stated in detail yet.

We design and implement our middleware with the guideline from M3W's management APIs, in-operation APIs, and/or other APIs.

3 A Dynamically Configurable Multimedia Middleware

A dynamically configurable multimedia middleware is designed to provide an infrastructure to host and manage Services as well as access to them. The Service will be the implementation of the multimedia APIs which will be standardized by M3W [1][3].

3.1 Middleware Design Objectives

The middleware is designed to be open to host and manage any compliant implementations of the Service. Services can be implemented by any third parties as long as the implementation fulfils two requirements: First, it can be described by the proposed metadata so that it can be recognized in the middleware. Second, it implements a set of APIs for managing its life-cycles of Service components.

The Services which are hosted and managed in the middleware should be flexible and efficient in their implementation. To achieve this, we introduce a concept of hierarchical model for the Service in which the implementation of more complex Service can be hierarchically configured by the functions provided by other Services. In this way, each Service can be implemented efficiently in a modular manner. If a required function has been instantiated in the middleware already, there should not be duplication by instantiating the same functionality from other Services. The Service should be flexibly linked to the already activated Service.

The middleware should have a mechanism to configure the available Service. It provides a mechanism to instantiate the Services required by a client application. The application can signal its required functionality it needed to the middleware and based on that the middleware will accordingly configure its state by instantiating the best possible Services that meet the required functions and also by de-instantiating unused Services. Such automatic configuration of the required Services for the application is enabled signaling to the middleware the metadata that completely describes information about the Services and their functionalities from the applications and/or application providers.

Finally, the middleware should operate in a resource efficient manner. It should use the resource from the terminal efficiently. The middleware will instantiate any Service only if its functionality is requested and will de-instantiate it when the application does not need it anymore. Therefore, this prevents the middleware from wasting terminal resources (memory, processing power, etc) for any Service that is not necessary for the applications during execution.

3.2 Middleware Architecture

Fig 1 shows the middleware architecture which contains the following entities:

- *Service Manager.* The Service Manager is a singleton entity which provides a Service to manage Services along with their containers (component) that are available in the middleware. The Service Manager shall have the responsibilities such as:
  - Register/un-register a Service. Recording the information about the Service and its Component (packager) so that when the Service Manager receives a request for a certain Service, it can tell whether the Service is available or not.
  - Load/unload an instance of Service to/from the middleware environment.
  - Response to the applications' request for a Service from an application, and give the handler/pointer of Service instance to the requestor.
- *Service.* Provides a certain function to the applications. Each Service offers/implements M3W multimedia interface(s). M3W multimedia interface is a collection of APIs that provide access to multimedia Services.

o   *Component.* The Component is the container for carrying Services. It is also the trading unit which is delivered by the third party (the Service implementer) to the end-user to be installed to the middleware.

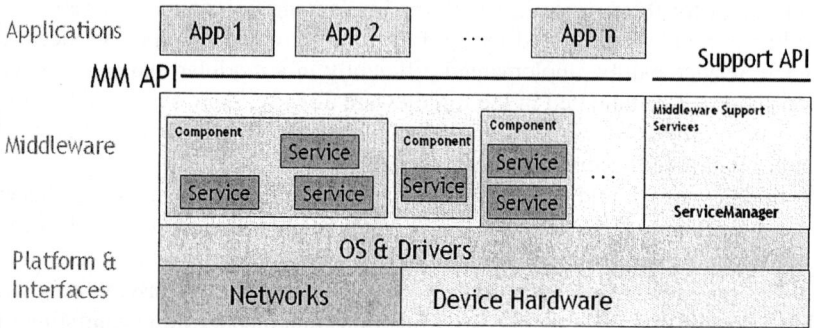

Fig. 1. A conceptual diagram of the proposed middleware architecture

3.3   A Hierarchical Model of Service

A Service is designed to be flexible, modular, and efficient in its implementation. It can be achieved by letting an implementation of a Service with the interfaces exposed to other Service.

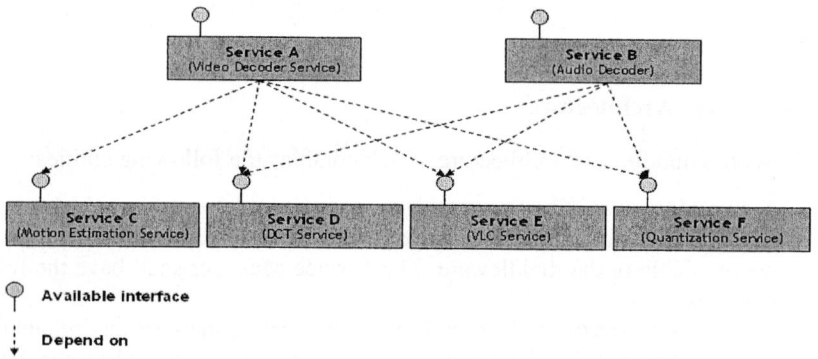

Fig. 2. A Service composition examples

Fig 2 illustrates the implementation of a Service that efficiently uses the functionality from other Services. In Fig 2, the Video Decoder Service, for example, may consist of several independent functions such as a variable length coding (VLC) function, discrete cosine transform (DCT) function, quantization function, motion estimation/compensation function, etc. The Video Decoder Service can be implemented in a modular way by using other implementations that offers the required functionalities. Hence, in its implementation, the implementer needs to code the execution flow of those sub Services.

In other cases, suppose that, in the same middleware, the Audio Decoder Service also requires for the application at the same time. With the hierarchical concept of the Service implementation, it may not be necessary to have two DCT, VLC, and Quantization Services. The same Services that are used for the Video Decoder Service (Service A) can also be used to serve the Audio Decoder Service (Service B) as well so that the middleware can be configured efficiently in the sense that there is no duplication in the offered function.

The binding between a Service and its dependencies is mediated by the Service Manager. During its initialization, a Service can request to the Service Manager to provide its dependent Service(s). The Service Manager gives the best possible Service by using the knowledge from the available metadata of Services.

3.4 Metadata for Component and Service Description and Signaling

In this middleware design, the metadata serves as a "Model". It provides a representation or description for middleware Component and Service. It is a deployment unit which is delivered to the Service Manager to be stored.

The metadata is defined by using XML Schema [6]. We design the metadata to carry the information such as:

o   Component identification information such as globally unique identification (GUID), title, creator, abstract/synopsis of the component.
o   The content of the component.
   o   List of offered interfaces for multimedia APIs.
   o   List of Services that implement those offered interfaces.
o   List of the target platforms (if the implementation can be deployed into several platforms).
o   The license information that governs the usage of the component/Services.
o   Required usage environment for the best usage of the component.
o   Signature information to guarantee the integrity of the carried information.

Fig 3 shows the structure of the information conceived in the metadata. By using the metadata, the Service Manager can determine whether a request for a certain function (Service) can be fulfilled or not. Another important capability is that the Service Manager can decide which the Service is the most appropriate one to be instantiated when there is more than one Service are available for the requested functionality. The selection policy depends on the implementation of the Service Manager.

The Service Manager's selection policy can be designed in different ways according to its objectives. For example, if the Service Manager can be designed to select:

o   The component that its Service (that implements the requested interface) required the smallest number of dependent interfaces.
o   The component that its description is signed by it providing vendor so that the Service Manager can trust it integrity.
o   The component that its Service's process run its process is run at (from most preferred to the least preferred):

- In-process. The Service's process runs in the same space as the caller application's space.
- Cross-process. The Service's process runs at the same machine but different space from the caller application's space.
- Remote. The Service's process runs at different machine.
o The component that does not required a strict usage environment.

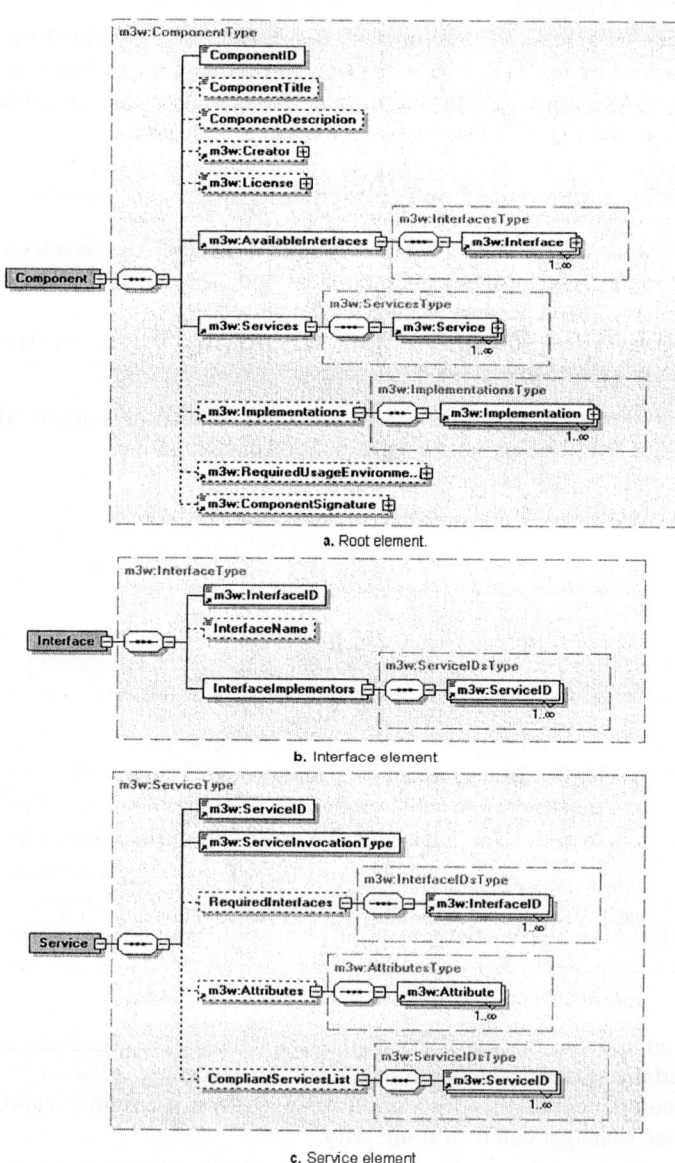

Fig. 3. Metadata for component & Service description

We introduce a use case scenario in which a multimedia application can signal the information in the metadata with interfaces and/or environment properties to the peer application as well as to the middleware. For such a signaling purpose, we design an element that can carry such information.

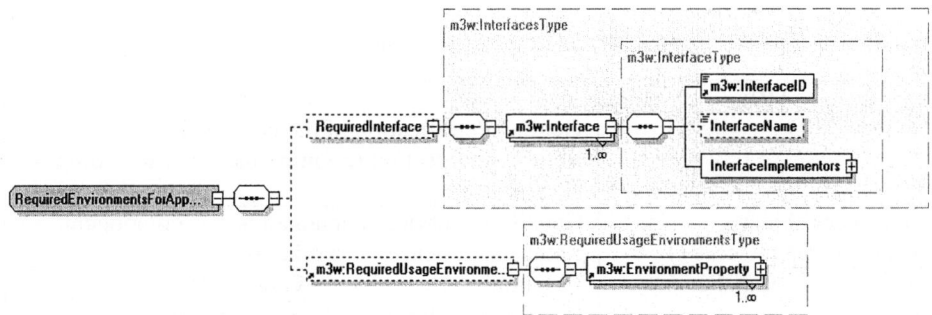

Fig. 4. Metadata for interface & environment properties signaling

Fig 4 shows the structure of the element for signaling the required interfaces and environment properties. The elements that describe the interface and required usage environment are taken from the Component and Service descriptions.

3.5 Basic APIs for Middleware's Entities

We specify a set of APIs for which all the implementations of their entities reside in the middleware. These APIs are defined for the interaction amongst all the stakeholder entities of the middleware, both internal interaction (Service Manager –

Table 1. APIs for Service

APIs	Description
object getID ()	Get the identification of the Service. Return an object representing the ID of the Service.
boolean initialize ()	Initialize the Service instance. During initialization, the implementation may request the Service Manager to provide some other Service instance. Return a Boolean indicating whether it is success of not.
sequence<object> getImplementedInterfaces ()	Get all the multimedia interface(s) that this Service implements. Return a sequence of interface ID.
void startProcess ()	Start the process of this Service.
void stopProcess ()	Stop the process of this Service.
void releaseResources ()	Release all the resources used by this Service during its execution. The resource can be other Service instance it uses and/or platform's resources

Component – Service) and external interaction (applications – Service Manager – Service). The interfaces are specified by using the Interface Definition Language (IDL) defined by the Object Management Group (OMG). The syntax and semantics of all required APIs for Service, Component, and Service Manager are shown in the Table 1, Table 2, and Table 3, respectively.

Table 2. APIs for component

APIs	Description
object getID ()	Get the identification of the component. Return an object representing the ID of the component.
sequence<object> getAvailableServices ()	Get all the Services contained in this component. Return a sequence of Service ID
Service instantiateService (object guid)	Instantiate a Service by giving its ID. Input: guid - the ID of the Service to be instantiated. Return a pointer to the instantiated Service. Null if fail.

Table 3. APIs for Service Manager

APIs	Description
boolean isServiceAvailable (object interfaceID)	Check whether there is a Service that provides a certain function. Input: interfaceID – the ID of the standard interface for certain functionality. Return a boolean indicating whether the Service is available or not.
Service getService (object interfaceID)	Get an instance of a Service. Input: interfaceID – the ID of the standard interface for certain functionality. Return a pointer to the Service instance. Null if fail.
boolean releaseService (object ServiceID)	Release the Service after using it. Input: ServiceID – the ID of the Service to be released. Return a boolean indicating whether releasing process is success of not.
boolean register (object metadata)	Register a component and all its Services. Input: metadata – the metadata of the component. Return a boolean indicating whether registration process is success or not.
boolean unregister (object componentID)	Un-register a component and all its Services. Input: componentID – the ID of the component to be un-registered. Return a boolean indicating whether un-registration process is success or not.

4 A Use Case: Configuring the Middleware

A use-case scenario is described to show the efficiency of the middleware in Section 3. The scenario involves a server application which provides content, a multimedia application (client application) that runs on the client terminal, and middleware that provide the multimedia functionality on the client application.

When the client application requests a specific content to the server, the server sends the list of the required Services for consuming the content instead of sending the content first. The format of the list follows the metadata for signaling the required interface and environment properties as described in Section 3.4. The client application needs to make sure that all required Services are available in the middleware.

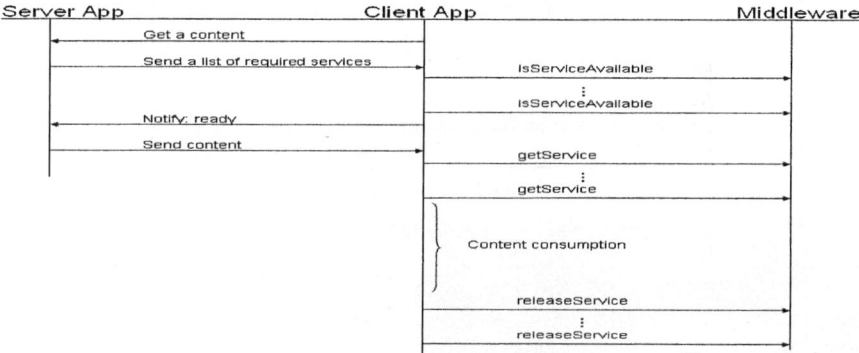

Fig. 5. A use-case sequence diagram

Fig 5 shows a brief sequence diagram of this scenario. There is a missing Service in the middleware, the client application may need to get the missing Service implementation (probably provided by the server as well) and register it to the middleware. The middleware will only instantiate the Service that is requested by the application so that, at a snapshot of time, only the in-used Service instances are active in the middleware.

5 Middleware Implementation and Experimental Results

We have implemented our proposed middleware and an application that demonstrates the use-case described in Section 3. The middleware infrastructure is implemented by using Java^{TM} programming language. The communication protocol for middleware's stakeholder is implemented by the Remote Method Invocation (RMI). Our implementation has been tested whether it also performs properly on a PC with the Microsoft Windows XP^{TM} as its operating system.

Fig 6 shows the graphical user interface (GUI) of the implementation. The middleware observer displays the status information of the middleware, starting from the registering Services, loading Services, and events from all entities of the middleware. As shown in Fig 6.a, the middleware does not have any loaded Service when there is no application in execution.

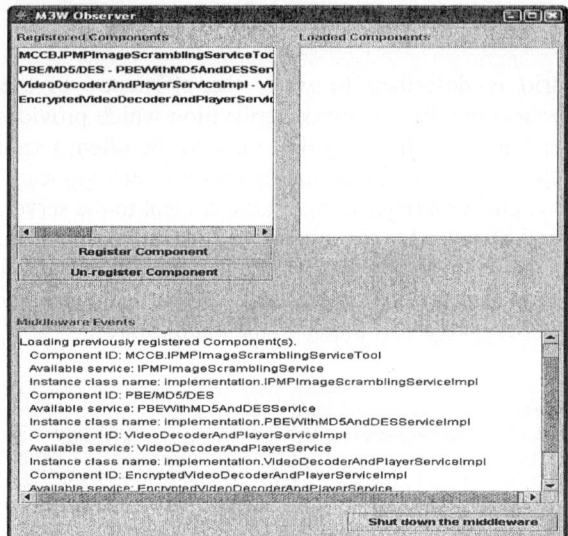

a. Middleware observer GUI

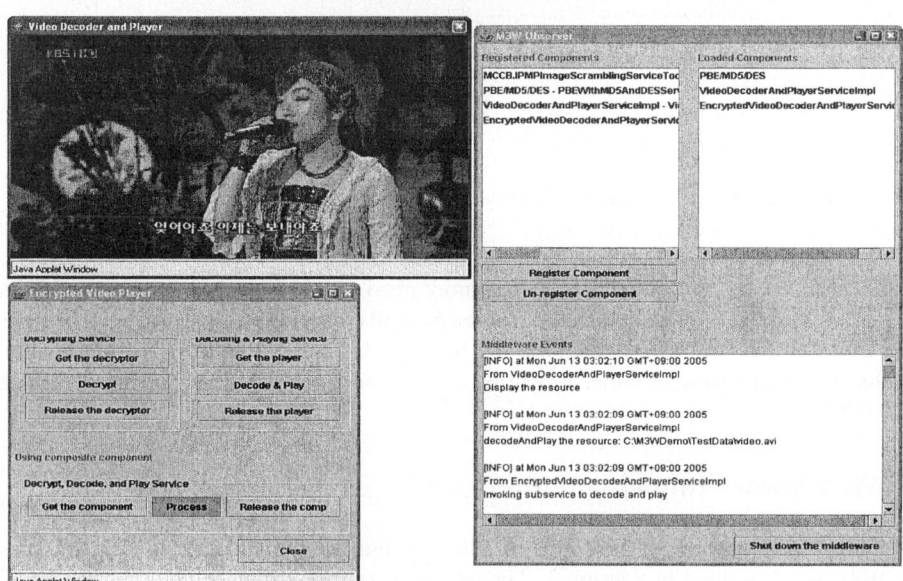

b. Middleware with Encrypted Video Player is running

Fig. 6. An implementation of the middleware

The client application as shown in Fig 6.b is an secured video player. It plays a DES-encrypted MPEG-2 video content. For content-consumption process, the application requests the middleware to instantiate the required Services such as a DES decryption Service, and an MPEG-2 decoder and player Service. All the events that happen in the middleware are displayed as shown in Fig 6.b.

6 Related Work

Two recent works in the multimedia middleware and component-based framework for multimedia application are most related to our work for which some concepts and/or objectives are similar. So those two related works might be used for comparison analytically. Layaida and Hagimont develop a component-based framework for building self-adaptive multimedia applications, so called PLASMA [5]. PLASMA uses the component-based concept in which every function of the multimedia application is realized. The application in the PLASMA framework is made up of the combination of PLASMA components. The PLASMA components can be configured automatically according to the condition of its execution environment. Compared to our work, PLASMA has major differences as follow:

o   The components are implemented in the application itself as there is no clear separation concept between the application and the middleware layer. Hence, the application is not independent of the middleware since it has to know how the implementation is made in detail. On the other hand, our work has a clear separation between the application and the middleware layer. Any application can access its required functionalities offered by the middleware (in the form of Service) via defined a set of standard APIs only.
o   Although both our work and PLASMA uses the component-based (Service-based in our case) and hierarchical model, the component sharing in PLASMA is only intra application while in our work since the Services are reside in the middleware layer that serve many applications, the sharing can be done inter applications. Hence in the case that terminal hosts several concurrent applications, our proposed middleware shall be more efficient regarding the resource consumption.
o   We use metadata for describing the Component and Services so that they can be controlled in a higher level compared to the PLASMA framework control its Components.

A more popular work is Oscar (open source implementation of OSGi) middleware developed by OSGi (Open Services Gateway initiative) alliance (see http://www.osgi.org). In Oscar, the applications are considered the bundles or components that will be installed onto the middleware. The middleware itself then provides a common platform to handle the life cycle of the application such as executing, stopping, pausing, removing it from the middleware, etc. So the application itself is part of the middleware. However in our work, the object that is installed onto the middleware is the Service, not the application.

7 Conclusion

In this paper we present a dynamically configurable multimedia middleware. With the combination of Service-based architecture, metadata schema, and a hierarchical model of the Service, our proposed middleware has four advantages:

- o It is open to any third party for their own implementation as long as it is compliant to the defined metadata and APIs for managing the life-cycle of Services in the middleware.
- o The implementation of the Service is flexible and efficient since the hierarchical model of Services allows a Service implementation to make use of any required functionality provided by other Services.
- o The middleware is dynamically configurable to provide functionalities for the multimedia applications by instantiating and/or de-instantiating the necessary Services.
- o The middleware is also resource-efficient since, at a snapshot of time, only the instances of Services that are used by the application become active.

The proposed middleware has been submitted as a contribution to the standardization of M3W. The concept of the metadata based middleware configuration has been accepted as a basis for further development of the M3W. Our future work will pursue to enhance this middleware as the M3W activity towards an international standard of a multimedia middleware.

References

1. MPEG Requirements/Systems/MDS Group. MPEG Multimedia Middleware: Context and Objective. ISO/IEC TC JTCI/SC29/WG11/N6335. Munchen, Germany. March 2004
2. MPEG. Call for Proposals on Multimedia Middleware (M3W). ISO/IEC TC JTCI/SC29/WG11/N6981. Hong Kong, China. January 2005
3. MPEG Requirements/Systems Group. MPEG Multimedia Middleware Requirements v.2.0. ISO/IEC TC JTCI/SC29/WG11/N6835. Palma de Mallorca, Spain. October 2004
4. MPEG MDS Group. MPEG-21 Vision, Technology, and Strategy. ISO/IEC TC JTCI/SC29/WG11/N6269. Hawaii, USA. December 2003
5. Layaida, Oussama and Hagimont, Daniel. PLASMA: A Component-based Framework for Building Self-Adaptive Multimedia Applications. In the proceeding of IS&T/SPIE 17th Annual Symposium - Electronic Imaging: Science and Technology. San Jose, USA. January 2005
6. Duckett, Jon., Griffin, Oliver., Mohr, Stephen., Norton, Francis., Stokes-Rees, Ian., Williams, Kevin., Cagle, Kurt., Ozu, Nikola., and Tennison, Jeni. Professional XML Schemas. Wrox Press Ltd. 2001

Adaptive VoIP Smoothing of Pareto Traffic Based on Optimal E-Model Quality

Shyh-Fang Huang[1], Eric Hsiao-Kuang Wu[2], and Pao-Chi Chang[3]

[1] Department of Electrical Engineering, National Central University, Taiwan
hsf@vaplab.ee.ncu.edu.tw
[2] Department of Computer Science & Information Engineering,
National Central University, Taiwan
hsiao@csie.ncu.edu.tw
[3] Department of Communication Engineering,
National Central University, Taiwan
pcchang@ce.ncu.edu.tw

Abstract. Perceived voice quality is a key metric for VoIP applications. It is mainly affected by IP network impairments such as delay, jitter and packet loss. Adaptive smoothing algorithms are capable of adjusting dynamically the smoothing size by introducing a variable delay based on the network delay and loss parameters to archive the best voice quality. This work formulates an online loss model which incorporates buffer sizes and introduces an efficient and feasible perceived quality method for buffer optimization. Distinct from the other optimal smoothers, the proposed optimal smoother suitable for most of codecs carries the lowest complexity. Since the adaptive smoothing scheme introduces variable playback delays, the buffer re-synchronization between the capture and the playback becomes essential. This work also presents a buffer re-synchronization algorithm to prevent unacceptable increase in the buffer overflow. Simulation experiments validate that the proposed adaptive smoother archives significant improvement in the voice quality.

1 Introduction

The rapid progress of the development of IP-base network has enabled numerous applications that deliver not only traditional data but also multimedia information in real time. The next generation network, like an ALL-IP network, is a future trend to integrate all heterogeneous wired and wireless networks and provide seamless worldwide mobility. In an All-IP network, one revolution of the new generation Internet applications will realize VoIP services that people can talk freely around through the mobile-phones, the desktops and VoIP telephones at any time and place. Unfortunately, the IP-based networks do not guarantee the available bandwidth and assure the constant delay jitters (i.e., the delay variance) for real time applications. In other words, individual transmission delays for a given flow of packets in a network may be continuing to change caused by varying traffic load and differing routing paths due to congestions, so that the packet network delays for a continuous series of intervals (i.e. talkspursts) at the receiver may not be the same (i.e. constant) as the sender. In addition, a packet delay may introduce by the signal hand-out or the difference of bandwidth transportation in wireless/fixed networks.

For delay sensitive applications, a dominating portion of packet losses might be likely due to delay constraint. A late packet that arrives after a delay threshold determined by playback time is treated as a lost packet. A tight delay threshold not only degrades the quality of playback but also reduces the effective bandwidth because a large fraction of delivered packets are dropped. In fact, delay and loss are normally not independent of each other. In order to reduce the loss impact, a number of applications utilize an adaptive smoothing technique in which buffers are adopted to reduce the quality damage caused by loss packets. However, a large buffer will introduce excessive end-to-end delay and deteriorate the multimedia quality in interactive real-time applications. Therefore, a tradeoff is required between increased packet loss and buffer delay to achieve satisfactory results for playout buffer algorithms.

In the past, the works on the degradation of the voice quality consider the effect of packet loss, but not that of packet delay. Within literature on predicting delays, the use of neural network models to learn traffic behaviors [1] requires relatively high complexity or a long learning period. Therefore, we consider the smoothers [2]-[8] which employ statistical network parameters related with the voice characteristic, i.e. loss, delay and talk-spurt that have significant influence to the voice quality. They detect delay spike in traffic and quickly calculate the required buffer size to keep the quality as good as possible.

The E-model is a computational model, standardized by ITU-T in G.107, G.109 and G.113 which uses the various transmission parameters to predict the subjective quality of packetized voice. Unfortunately, the E-model is complex to analyze in the optimization process. An alternative study is to apply a simplified E-model, first proposed by R. Cole and J. Rosenbluth [9], based upon observed transport measurements in the VoIP gateways and the transport paths. Authors indicated the simplified E-model method requires more pattern cases for traces to enhance the validation. Atzori and Lobina [10], and L. Sun and E. Ifeachor [11] proposed to utilize a simplified E-model that considers the loss and delay together to set a dijitter time, which is the optimal playout delay derived by a dynamic programming-based solution. However, the usability and the accuracy of a simplified E-model will be limited by non-typical traffic patterns.

For perceptual-based buffer optimization schemes for VoIP, voice quality is evaluated as a key metric since it represents user's perceived QoS. However, it requires an efficient and accurate objective way to optimize perceived voice quality. To consider the well-defined delay and loss impairments of the E-model, we employ a complete E-model for the quality optimization to obtain optimal perceived voice quality.

In a packet switching network, without a resynchronization scheme, a playback clock with a minor frequency error will eventually cause a buffer overflow or an underflow at the receiving end. The overflow packets are usually discarded due to the finite buffer size and the real-time requirement. This discontinuity caused by discarded packets might create an unpleasant effect to the playback quality because the lost packets could be the important part of the signals. This effect is more serious for audio signals than video signals because human ears are more sensitive to the continuity of sounds than human eyes.

The contributions of this paper are three-fold: (i) A new method optimizing voice quality for VoIP is easily applied to codecs which were well-defined in the ITU-T E-model. (ii) Different from the other optimal smoothers, our optimal smoother has the lowest complexity with $O(n)$. (iii) A feasible scheme is introduced to solve the buffer re-synchronization problem.

2 Related Work

The performances of the proposed playout approach are compared with the other approach. In particular, for non-dynamic programming-based solutions, i.e. the linear filter, Spike Detection (SD) algorithm [2]-[11] was referred by most people. A delay spike is defined as a sudden and significant increase of network delay in a short period often less than one round-trip. This algorithm adjusts the smoothing size, i.e. playback delay, at the beginning of each talk-spurt. The results of this algorithm are therefore compared to the results obtained herein.

The SD Algorithm in [2] estimates the playout time p_i of the first packet in a talk-spurt from the mean network delay d_i and the variance v_i for packet i as

$$p_i = t_i + d_i + \gamma v_i \quad (1)$$

where t_i represents the time at which packet i is generated at the sending host and γ is a constant factor used to set the playout time to be "far enough" beyond the delay estimate such that only a small fraction of the arriving packets could be lost due to late arrival. The value of $\gamma = 4$ is used in simulations [3]. The estimates are recomputed each time a packet arrives, but only applied when a new talk-spurt is initiated.

The mean network delay d_i and variance v_i are calculated based on a linear recursive filter characterized by the factors α and β.

$$\begin{cases} \text{If } n_i > d_{i-1} \Rightarrow \begin{cases} d_i = \beta d_{i-1} + (1-\beta)n_i \\ v_i = \beta v_{i-1} + (1-\beta)|d_{i-1} - n_i| \end{cases} & (SPIKE\_MODE) \\ \text{If } n_i \leq d_{i-1} \Rightarrow \begin{cases} d_i = \alpha d_{i-1} + (1-\alpha)n_i \\ v_i = \alpha v_{i-1} + (1-\alpha)|d_{i-1} - n_i| \end{cases} \end{cases} \quad (2)$$

Where n_i is the total "delay" introduced by the network and typical values of α and β are 0.998002 and 0.75 [3], respectively.

The decision to select α or β is based on the current delay condition. The condition $n_i > d_{i-1}$ represents network congestion (SPIKE_MODE) and the weight β is used to emphasize the current network delay. On the other hand, $n_i \leq d_{i-1}$ represents network traffic is stable, and α is used to emphasize the long-term average.

In estimating the delay and variance, the SD Algorithm uses only two values α and β that are simple but may not be adequate, particularly when the traffic is unstable. For example, an under-estimated problem is when a network becomes spiked, but the delay n_i is just below the d_{i-1}, the SD Algorithm will judge the network to be stable and will not enter the *SIPKE_MODE*.

3 Adaptive Smoother with Optimal Delay-Loss Trade off

The proposed optimal smoother is derived using the E-model to trade off the delay and loss. This method involves, first, building the traffic delay model and the loss model. Second, the delay and loss impairments of the E-model are calculated according to the delay and the loss models. Third, the E-model rank R is maximized and thus the delay and loss optimized solution is obtained.

In this study, voice packets are assumed to be generated at a constant packet rate. Current voice codecs used in standard VOIP (H.323 or SIP) systems, e.g., G.711, G.723.1 and G.729, generally fit this assumption although the packet size may be different when the voice is inactive.

3.1 E-Model Description

In the E-model, a rating factor R represents voice quality and considers relevant transmission parameters for the considered connection. It is defined in [12] as:

$$R = Ro - Is - Id - Ie\_eff + A \qquad (3)$$

Ro denotes the basic signal-to-noise ratio, which is derived from the sum of different noise sources which contain circuit noise and room noise, send and receive loudness ratings. *Is* denotes the sum of all impairments associated with the voice signal, which is derived from the incorrect loudness level, non-optimum sidetone and quantizing distortion. Id represents the impairments due to delay of voice signals, that is the sum of Talker Echo delay (*Idte*), Listener Echo delay (*Idle*) and end-to-end delay (*Idd*). *Ie_eff* denotes the equipment impairments, depending on the low bit rate codecs (*Ie*, *Bpl*) and packet loss (*Ppl*) levels. Finally, the advantage factor A is no relation to all other transmission parameters. The use of factor A in a specific application is left to the designer's decision.

3.2 The Delay and Loss Models in E-Model

For perceived buffer design, it is critical to understand the delay distribution modeling as it is directly related to buffer loss. The multimedia characteristics of packet transmission delay over Internet can be suggested by statistical models which follow a Pareto distribution for Internet packets (for an UDP traffic) has been shown to consistent with a Pareto distribution [13][14]. In order to derive an online loss model, the packet end-to-end delay is assumed as a Pareto distribution with parameter a and k at the receiving end for a multimedia traffic. The CDF of the delay distribution $F(t)$ can also be represented by [13][15]

$$F(t) = 1 - \left(\frac{k}{t}\right)^a, \text{ for } t \geq k$$

where $k = \min_i x_i$ and $a = n\left[\sum_{i=1}^{n} \log\left(\frac{x_i}{k}\right)\right]^{-1}$ (4)

and the PDF of the delay distribution $f(t)$ is

$$f(t) = \frac{dF(t)}{dt} = \frac{a \cdot k^a}{t^{a+1}}, \text{ for } t \geq k \quad (5)$$

In a real-time application, a packet loss that is solely caused by extra delay can be derived from the delay model $f(t)$. Figure 1 plots the delay function $f(t)$, which shows that when the packet delay exceeds the smoothing time; the delayed packet is regarded as a lost packet. The loss function $l(t_b)$ can be derived from Fig. 1 as

$$l(t_b) = \int_{t_b}^{\infty} f(t)dt = \left.\left(\frac{a \cdot k^a}{t^{a+1}}\right)\right|_{t_b}^{\infty} = \left(\frac{k}{t_b}\right)^a \quad (6)$$

From Eqs. (5) and (6), we obtain the delay and loss functions that will be used in delay and loss impairments of the E-model.

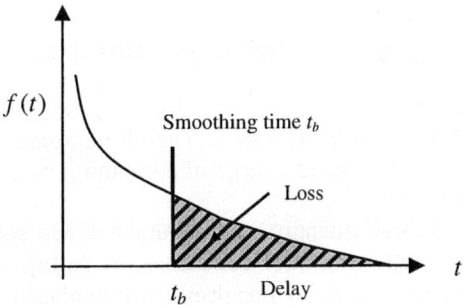

Fig. 1. The relation of smoothing delay and loss

3.3 Optimization on E-Model

The delay and loss factors over transmission have greater impacts to the voice quality than the environments or equipments. To simplify the optimization complexity, we make assumptions in a communication connection as the following: (i). The circuit noise, room noise and terminate signals will not change. (*Ro* and *Is* are fixed). (ii). An echo delay in the Sender/Receiver will not change. (*Idte* and *Idle* are fixed). (iii). A codec will not change (*Ie* is fixed). In [12], R is rewritten as Eq. (7)

$$R = (Ro - Is - Idte - Idle + A) - Idd - Ie\_eff \quad (7)$$

where Idd is approximated by

$$Idd = 25\left\{\left(1+X^6\right)^{1/6} - 3\left(1+\left[\frac{X}{3}\right]^6\right)^{1/6} + 2\right\}, \quad X = \frac{\ln\left(\frac{T_a}{100}\right)}{\ln(2)}, \quad (8)$$

when $T_a > 100$ ms and $Idd = 0$ when $T_a \leq 100$,

and

$$Ie\_eff = Ie + (95 - Ie) \cdot \frac{Ppl}{Ppl + Bpl} \quad (9)$$

Factors Ie and Bpl are defined in [16] and T_a is one-way absolute delay for echo-free connections.

Due to the three assumptions above, the optimization process can be concentrated on the parameters of Idd and Ie_eff. Eq. (7) is derived to yield Eq. (10)

$$R = Cons\tan t - 25\left\{\left(1+X^6\right)^{1/6} - 3\left(1+\left[\frac{X}{3}\right]^6\right)^{1/6} + 2\right\} - (95 - Ie) \cdot \frac{Ppl}{Ppl + Bpl}, \quad (10)$$

when $t > 100$ ms

According to Eq. (6), the loss probability of a smoothing time t is $Ppl = \left(\frac{k}{t}\right)^a$, so the solutions for t are difficult to get directly from Eq. (10) since it contains the complex polynomial and exponential function. Therefore, some researches employ dynamic programming tools that need a large of computing procedures, like MATLAB, to calculate an optimal solution.

Owing to simplify a large quantity of computations and solve the best smoothing time t, we consider the following three conditions. (i). In Eq. (8), when the smoothing time $t \leq 100$ ms, Idd is zero (no delay impairment). It implies a smoother should set the minimum smoothing delay to 100 ms to prevent the most packet loss. (ii). The maximum end-to-end delay of 250 ms is acceptable for most user applications to prevent serious voice quality destruction. (iii). For a common low bit rate codec, like G.723.1 and G.729, the frame rate is fixed. Based on a fixed frame rate of various codec i, denodes as fr_i, we can analyze some cases, $t_1 = (100 + fr_i)$ ms, $t_2 = (100 + fr_i \cdot 2)$ ms, ..., $t_n = (100 + fr_i \cdot n)$ ms, and t_n should less than the maximum acceptable delay 250 ms to calculate the correspondence, R_1, R_2, ..., R_n, by the numerical analysis in Eq. (10) and an error is less than 0.001. Here we can find a maximum $R_m \in \{R_1, R_2, \cdots, R_n\}$ by computing the $n = \left\lfloor \frac{250-100}{fr_i} \right\rfloor$ times to obtain the optimal smoothing buffer size. The optimal smoothing buffer size will be calculated as $100 + m \cdot fr_i$ ms to keep the optimal voice quality.

4 Buffer Re-synchronization

A necessary condition that a smoother can work correctly is the synchronization between the capture and the playback. This section proposes a buffer re-synchronization machine (BRM) to help synchronization and the clock drift analysis of re-synchronization to validate the effectiveness.

4.1 Buffer Re-synchronization Machine

This work proposes a synchronization scheme that segments audio signals by detecting silences. The mismatch between the capture and the playback clocks is solved by skipping silences at the receiving end. The duration of the silent period may be shortened negligibly degrading the quality of playback. An active packet contains voice-compressed data, whereas a silent packet does not. Skipping some silent packets will not significantly degrade the quality of the voice, but can efficiently prevent the buffer from overflowing. Notably, k (could be adjusted) continuous silent packets could be utilized to separate different talkspurts.

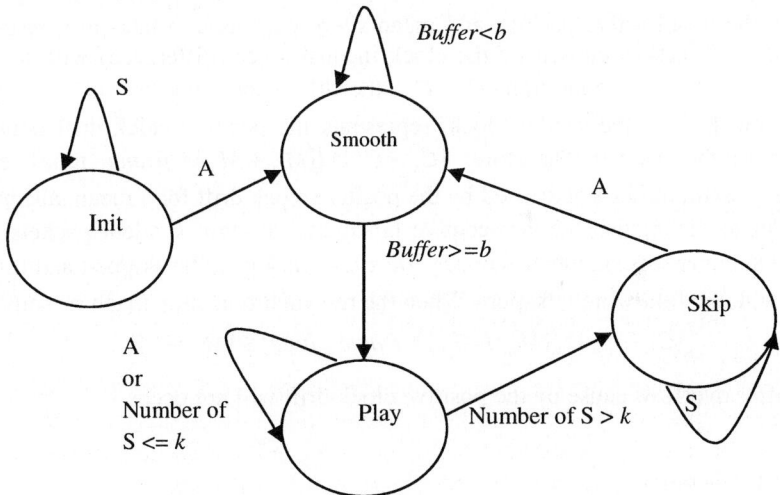

Fig. 2. Buffer Re-synchronization Machine

Figure 2 depicts the buffer re-synchronization algorithm. Init-state, Smooth-state, Play-state and Skip-state are used to represent the voice conference initialing, the buffer smoothing, the buffer playing out, and the silent packets skipping, respectively, and "A" and "S" represents an active packet and a silent packet, respectively.

In the Init-state the buffer waits for the first arriving packets to initialize a voice conference. If Init-state receives an "S", it stays in Init-state; otherwise when an "A" is received, the Smooth-state is activated to smooth the packets. In the Smooth-state, the smoothing time b is computed by applying the optimal adaptive smoother algorithm dynamically. When the buffer smoothing time is over b, the Play-state is activated; otherwise it stays in Smooth-state for smoothing. In the Play-State the packet is fetched from the buffer and played out. In fetching process, when it encounters three consecutive S packets, implying that the talk-spurt can be ended, the buffer re-synchronization procedure then switches to the Skip-state. In the Skip-state, if "A" is fetched from buffer, it means the new talk-spurt has begun, and then it skips remained silent packets in the buffer, and switches to the Smooth-state to smooth the next talk-spurt. Otherwise, if "S" is fetched from buffer, it implies current talk-spurt is not ended and will be decoded to play out at the same state.

With the above four-state machine, the smoother can smooth the packets at the beginning of the talkspurt to avoid buffer underflow in the Smooth-state and skip the silent packets at the end of the talkspurt to prevent the overflow in the Skip-state.

4.2 Effectiveness of Re-synchronization

To demonstrate the effectiveness of re-synchronization machine for buffer overflow, we analyze the clock inconsistence constraint as the following. C_s and C_r represent the sender clock (frame/sec) and the receiver clock, respectively, and M_a and M_s denote the mean active packets and mean silent packets in a talkspurt, respectively. The buffer overflow caused by the clock inconsistence (difference) will occur when C_s is large than C_r condition. $C_s - C_r$, the difference value by subtracting the receiver clock from the sender clock, represents the positive clock drift between the sender and the receiver. Therefore, $(C_s - C_r) * ((M_a + M_s) * frame\_time)$ represents the mean extra buffer size caused by the positive clock drift for a mean talkspurt time. In order to distinguish the consecutive talkspurts, at lease k silent packets are utilized. Therefore, the smoother has $M_s - k$ silent packets to be skipped and resynchronizes with the following talkspurt. When the re-synchronization machine satisfies

$$(C_s - C_r) * ((M_a + M_s) * frame\_time) \leq (M_s - k), \tag{12}$$

the buffer overflow cause by the positive clock drift will not occur.

5 Simulation

5.1 Simulation Configuration

A set of simulation experiments are performed to evaluate the effectiveness of the proposed adaptive smoothing scheme. The OPNET simulation tools are adopted to trace the voice traffic transported between two different LANs for a VoIP environment. Ninety personal computers with G.729 traffics are deployed in each LAN. The duration and frequency of the connection time of the personal computers follow Poisson distributions. A six-hour simulation was run to probe the backbone network delay patterns, which were used to trace the adaptive smoothers and compare the effects of the original with the adapted voice quality.

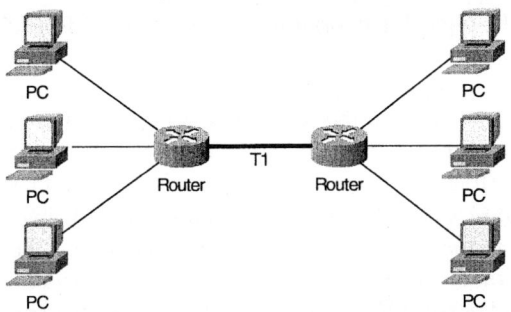

Fig. 3. The simulation environment of VoIP

Table 1. Simulation parameters

Attribute	Value
Numbers of PC in one LAN	90 PCs
Codec	G.729
Backbone	T1 (1.544 Mps)
LAN	100 Mbps
Propagation delay	Constant
Router buffer	Infinite
Packet size	50 bytes

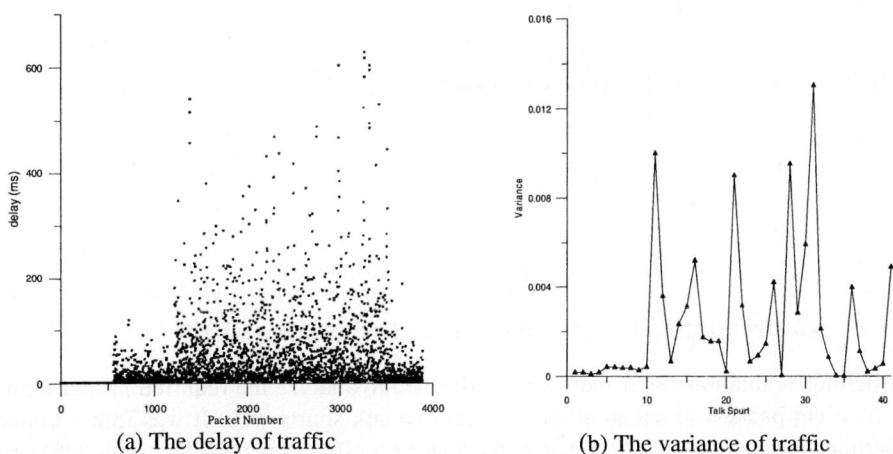

(a) The delay of traffic   (b) The variance of traffic

Fig. 4. VoIP traffic pattern

Figure 3 shows the typical network topology in which a T1 (1.544 Mbps) backbone connects two LANs, and 100 Mbps lines are connected within each LAN. The propagation delay of all links is assumed to be a constant value and will be ignored (the derivative value will be zero) in the optimization process. The buffer size of the bottlenecked router is assumed to be infinite since the packet loss in router buffer is not considered in the performance comparison of adaptive smoothers. The network end-to-end delay for the G.729 traffic with data frame size (10 bytes) and RTP/UDP/IP headers (40 bytes) is measured for six hours by employing the OPNET simulation network. Table 1 summarizes the simulation parameters. Figure 4(a) and 4(b) plot the end-to-end traffic delay patterns and the corresponding delay variances for VoIP traffic observed at a given receiver. The results validate that individual transmission delays for a given G.729 flow of packets in a network are continuing to change caused by varying traffic load; therefore, the arrival packet rates for a continuous series of intervals (i.e. talkspursts) at the receiver are not constant any more as the sender.

5.2 Voice Quality in Smoothers

The test sequence is sampled at 8 kHz, 23.44 seconds long, and includes English and Mandarin sentences spoken by male and female. Fig. 5 lists the E-mode score R of the voice quality. It shows that the optimal method has the significant improvement in the voice quality over SD smoother, because our proposed optimal smoother truly optimizes with the delay and loss impairments in a transmission planning of the E-model.

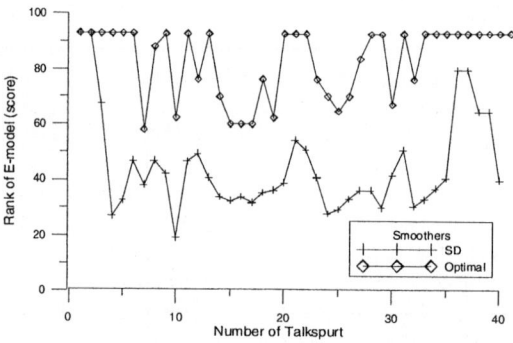

Fig. 5. The quality scores of smoothers

5.3 Re-synchronization Effectiveness for the Positive Clock Drift

A listening evaluation experiment was performed to analyze the required proper number of silent packets to segment the consecutive talk-spurts well. It was found in our experiments that at least three silent packets (e.q. 10 ms per packet in G.729) are required to separate talkspurts.

We analyze the G.729 voice sources used in our experiments and find the percentage of the mean active and mean silent segment length in a talkspurt are 0.51 and 0.49 respectively, and the maximum talkspurt length is 257 packets. $k=3$ is adopted to segment the consecutive talkspurt. From the Eq. (12), we can calculate the effective clock drift between the sender and the receiver $C_s - C_r$ should be less than or equal to $(257*0.49-3)/((257)*10*10^{-3}) = 47.8$ (frame/sec). Normally, the clock drift will not be over 47.8 (frame/sec) when a sender of G.729 transmits 100 (frame/sec) to the networks. Consequently, the smoother can avoid the buffer overflow well in our case.

6 Conclusion

This article proposes an adaptive smoothing algorithm that utilizes the complete E-model to optimize the smoothing size to obtain the best voice quality. The buffer re-synchronization algorithm is also proposed to prevent buffer overflow by skipping some silent packets of the tail of talk-spurts. It can efficiently solve the mismatch between the capture and the playback clocks. Numerical results have shown that our proposed method can get significant improvements in the voice quality which balances the target delay and loss.

References

[1] Tien P. L., Yuang M. C.: Intelligent voice smoother for silence-suppressed voice over internet. IEEE JSAC, Vol. 17, No. 1. (1999) 29-41
[2] Ramjee R., Kurise J., Towsley D., Schulzrinne H.: Adaptive playout mechanisms for packetized audio applications in wide-area networks. Proc. IEEE INFOCOM. (1994) 680-686
[3] Jeske D. R., Matragi W., Samadi B.: Adaptive play-out algorithms for voice packets. Proc. IEEE Conf. on Commun., Vol. 3. (2001) 775-779
[4] Pinto J., Christensen K. J.: An algorithm for playout of packet voice based on adaptive adjustment of talkspurt silence periods. Proc. IEEE Conf. on Local Computer Networks. (1999) 224-231
[5] Liang Y. J., Farber N., Girod B.,: Adaptive playout scheduling using time-scale modification in packet voice communications. Proc. IEEE Conf. on Acoustics, Speech, and Signal Processing, Vol. 3. (2001) 1445-1448
[6] Kansal A., Karandikar A.: Adaptive delay estimation for low jitter audio over Internet. IEEE GLOBECOM, Vol. 4. (2001) 2591-2595
[7] Anandakumar A. K., McCree A., Paksoy E.: An adaptive voice playout method for VOP applications. IEEE GLOBECOM, Vol. 3. (2001) 1637-1640
[8] DeLeon P., Sreenan C. J.: An Adaptive predictor for media playout buffering. Proc. IEEE Conf. on Acoustics, Speech, and Signal Processing, Vol. 6. (1999) 3097-3100
[9] Cole R., Rosenbluth J.: Voice over IP performance monitoring, Journal on Computer Commun. Review, Vol. 31. (2001)
[10] Atzori L., Lobina M.: Speech playout buffering based on a simplified version of the ITU-T E-model. IEEE Signal Processing Letters, Vol. 11 , Iss 3. (2004) 382-385
[11] Sun L., Ifeachor E.: New models for perceived voice quality prediction and their applications in playout buffer optimization for VoIP networks. Proc. ICC. (2004)
[12] ITU-T Recommendation G.107,: The E-model, a Computational Model for use in Transmission Planning. (2003)

[13] Huebner F., Liu D., Fernandez J. M.: Queueing Performance Comparsion of Traffic Models for Internet Traffic. GLOBECOM 98, Vol. 1. (1998) 471–476
[14] Fujimoto K., Ata S., Murata M.: Statistical Analysis of Packet Delays in the Internet and its Application to Playout Control for Streaming Applications. IEICE Trans. Commun., Vol. E84-B, No. 6. (2001) 1504-1512
[15] Brazauskas V., Serfling R.: Robust and efficient estimation of the tail index of a one-parameter pareto distribution. North American Actuarial Journal available at http://www.utdallas.edu/~serfling. (2000).
[16] ITU-T SG12 D.106: Estimates of Ie and Bpl for a range of Codecs. (2003)

Indoor Scene Reconstruction Using a Projection-Based Registration Technique of Multi-view Depth Images[*]

Sehwan Kim and Woontack Woo

GIST U-VR Lab, Gwangju 500-712, S. Korea
{skim, wwoo}@gist.ac.kr

Abstract. A novel registration method is presented for 3D point clouds, acquired from a multi-view camera, for scene reconstruction. In general, conventional registration methods require a high computational complexity, and are not robust for 3D point clouds with a low precision. To remedy these drawbacks, a projection-based registration is proposed. Firstly, depth images are refined based on temporal property by excluding 3D points with large variations, and spatial property by filling holes referring to neighboring 3D points. Secondly, 3D point clouds are projected to find correspondences and fine registration is conducted through minimizing errors. Finally, final colors are evaluated using colors of correspondences, and a 3D virtual environment is reconstructed by applying the above procedure to several views. The proposed method not only reduces computational complexity by searching for correspondences on an image plane, but also enables an effective registration even for 3D points with a low precision. The generated model can be adopted for interaction with a virtual environment as well as navigation in it.

1 Introduction

Image-based reconstruction of a real environment plays a key role in providing visual realism while allowing a user to navigate in and interact with a Virtual Environment (VE). The visual realism of reconstructed models encourages a user to interact with the VE proactively. Furthermore, the generated VE allows the user to manipulate augmented objects while walking around the VE by removing/augmenting virtual objects from the viewpoint of Mediated Reality (MR) [1]. Unlike the methods using modeling tools or ones based on active range sensors, image-based modeling methods not only preserve realism but also provide a simple modeling process. Especially, off-the-shelf multi-view cameras enable to generate models more easily. Thus, a delicate registration is required to register 3D point clouds to reconstruct models. Note that unlike 2D registration, 3D registration may generate interactive image-based models.

Until now, various registration methods have been proposed. ICP (Iterative Closest Point) has been widely used, and Color ICP was proposed by Johnson [2][3]. Another approach is to project data sets onto an image plane and to pair points [4][5]. Color or intensity image was used to improve matches by using the intensity gradients on the projection plane, and back-projecting to get a 3D point pair [6]. Especially, Pulli

---

[*] This work was supported in part by MIC through RBRC at GIST, and in part by CTRC at GIST.

adopted a projective registration method employing planar perspective warping, and Bernardini et al. searched the neighborhood and paired locations that maximize the cross-correlations [7][8]. Sharp et al. defined invariant features to improve ICP, and Fisher applied projective ICP to Augmented Reality [9][10]. On the other hand, Nishino et al. presented an optimization method based on M-estimator [11]. However, most methods rely on accurate equipments and require much time for modeling. If 3D points have large error variations, results are not reliable. Stereo cameras are usually exploited for an object modeling instead of an indoor scene reconstruction.

To address these weaknesses, a projection-based registration is proposed. Firstly, a depth image is refined based on the spatio-temporal property of 3D point clouds using adaptive uncertainty region. Secondly, correspondences are searched for through the modified KLT feature tracker for projected 3D point clouds. Then, 3D point clouds are fine-registered by minimizing errors. Finally, each 3D point is evaluated referring to correspondences, and a new color is assigned. Thus, we reconstruct an indoor environment by applying the above procedure to several views. The proposed method is carried out effectively even if the precision of 3D point cloud is relatively low by using the correlation of features with the neighborhood. Thanks to 2D-based registration, computational complexity is also low. Also, the proposed method makes 3D reconstruction easy just by placing a multi-view camera at several positions.

The paper is organized as follows. In Chapter 2, 3D reconstruction of an indoor scene is explained. After experimental results are analyzed in Chapter 3, conclusions and future work are presented in Chapter 4.

2 3D Reconstruction of an Indoor Scene

2.1 Depth Image Refinement

In general, passive techniques use images generated by the light reflected by objects. However, disparity estimation results in inherent stereo mismatching errors, usually at depth discontinuities and on homogeneous areas. These errors cause poor registration results. Thus, unreliable areas should be eliminated before registration. In this regard, a depth image is refined by spatio-temporal property. In the first step, erroneous 3D points are removed using the temporal property that the erroneous 3D points change dramatically in 3D space with time. In the second step, holes are filled by means of the spatial property that there is a spatial correlation among neighboring pixels. Fig. 1 shows a flow diagram for 3D reconstruction. Overall procedure and its projection-based registration part are described in Fig. 1(a) and Fig. 1(b), respectively.

In the depth map of a static scene, depth variation of each pixel is modeled as a Gaussian distribution. After investigating the depth value of each pixel, we get rid of the pixels whose depth variation is larger than the threshold value, Th_i, for the ith pixel.

$$\sigma_i > \alpha Th_i(x_c, y_c, z_c) \tag{1}$$

where σ_i represents a standard deviation for the ith pixel and α denotes a scale factor. $(x_c\ y_c\ z_c)^T$ is a translation vector from the optical center of a camera to the center of uncertainty region.

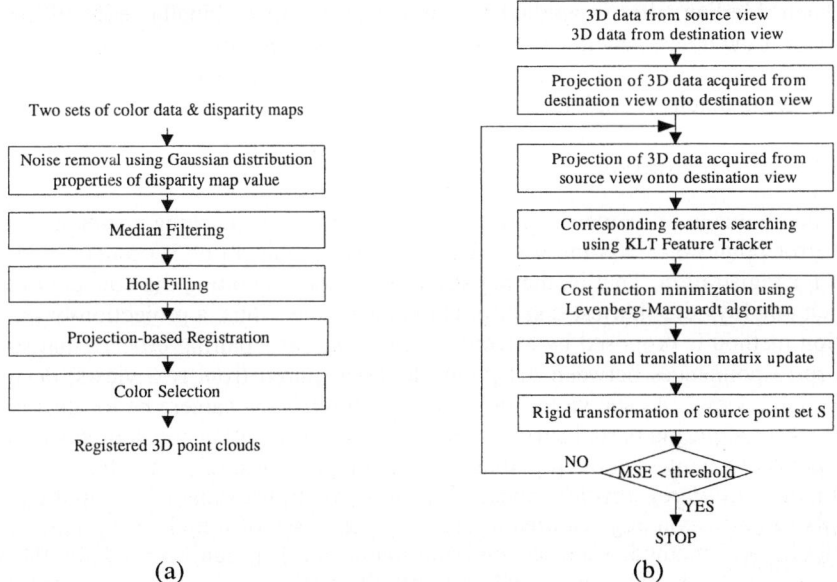

Fig. 1. Flow diagram for 3D reconstruction (a) overall procedure (b) projection-based registration part of (a)

The adaptively changing error bound appears to be ellipsoidal in a 3D space, and we call it as *Adaptive Uncertainty Region (AUR)*. The AURs are determined based on the error tolerance of each axis [12]. Its uncertainty distance, for each axis, is modeled as a Gaussian distribution. The Gaussian distributions increase linearly with the distance along x or y axis, and increase monotonically with the distance along z axis, respectively. The ellipsoid is also rotated with respect to the optical center reflecting the direction of ray that originates at the camera center and passes though each pixel.

$$\frac{x^2}{(\Delta x)^2} + \frac{y^2}{(\Delta y)^2} + \frac{z^2}{(\Delta z)^2} = 1 \quad (2)$$

$$\begin{pmatrix} x' \\ y' \\ z' \end{pmatrix} = R_1 R_2 \begin{pmatrix} x \\ y \\ z \end{pmatrix} + \begin{pmatrix} x_c \\ y_c \\ z_c \end{pmatrix} \quad (3)$$

$$R_1 = \begin{pmatrix} 1 & 0 & 0 \\ 0 & z_c/d & y_c/d \\ 0 & -y_c/d & z_c/d \end{pmatrix} \quad R_2 = \begin{pmatrix} d & 0 & x_c \\ 0 & 1 & 0 \\ -x_c & 0 & d \end{pmatrix} \quad d = \sqrt{y_c^2 + z_c^2}$$

where $(x'\ y'\ z')^T$ is a final uncertainty region in terms of 3D coordinates of a scene with respect to the optical center. Δx, Δy and Δz represent uncertainty distances along each axis.

Then, Median filter is applied to remove spot noises. Finally, hole filling is required for the holes, generated during the above step, and homogeneous areas. That is, spatial property for a current 3D point, i.e. spatial correlation among 3D points of neighboring pixels, is exploited.

2.2 Initial Registration

The depth image refinement removes inherent stereo mismatching errors, and reduces the error bound of 3D point cloud. However, the precision of 3D point cloud is still low for registration. That is, the registration method exploiting the conventional ICP, which employs the shortest distance, is inappropriate. Thus, a projection-based registration method is proposed by effectively carrying out a pairing process that searches for correspondences between 3D point clouds acquired from two views, destination and source views. As shown in Fig. 6, we let a multi-view camera be located around a wall while acquiring partial surfaces successively. Destination and source views mean the views of a camera at the previous and current positions, respectively.

In the *initial registration* phase, a rigid-body transformation is applied to 3D points of corresponding features to estimate the poses of a multi-view camera [13]. Actually, any method, such as semi-automatic one [7], can be used for the initial registration. Thus, 3D point clouds are initially registered. Fig. 2 shows the projection of each 3D point cloud acquired from destination and source views onto the destination view after the initial registration. Fig. 2(a) and Fig. 2(b) are projection results of 3D point clouds, which are acquired from the destination and source views, onto the destination view. A constant value is assigned to unprojected pixels to differentiate them from projected ones. It should be noted that the projection of 3D point cloud acquired from the source view causes self-occlusion. This is eliminated based on the rays that originate at the camera center and pass though each pixel. Theoretically, Fig. 2(b) should be a subset of Fig. 2(a). However, discrepancies exist due to the errors in disparity estimation, camera calibration, etc. Therefore, an accurate geometric relationship between two views is found by minimizing distance errors between correspondences. Thus, *fine registration* should be employed to compensate the errors.

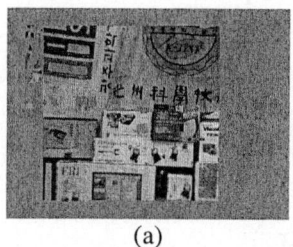 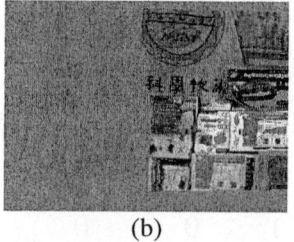

(a)　　　　　　　　　　　　　　(b)

Fig. 2. Projected images (a) projection of 3D point cloud of destination view onto its own view (b) projection of 3D point cloud of source view onto destination view

In general, projection of 3D point cloud acquired from the source view onto the destination view results in floating-point numbers. Thus, there occur unprojected pixels. These generate false alarms when corresponding features are searched for through a modified KLT [14]. In this case, linear interpolation is useless since it makes the object boundaries smoothed. On the other hand, bi-linear interpolation cannot be used since the relation of two images is unknown.

Not only to preserve an original image but also to remove unprojected pixels, a two-step integer mapping is presented as shown in Fig. 3. Firstly, a search range is set to −0.5~0.5 along x and y axes for a grid point. The color of grid point is decided by relative distances with neighboring pixels. Secondly, the search range is expanded to −1.0~1.0 and a similar procedure is conducted for grid points which do not include any projected point at the first step. Fig. 4 shows the results. Fig. 4(a) is an enlarged part of Fig. 2(b), and Fig. 4(b) is the result after applying the mapping.

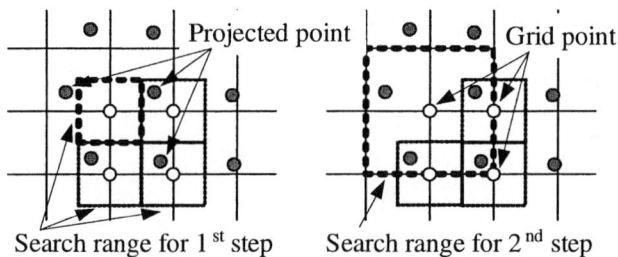

Fig. 3. Two-step integer mapping

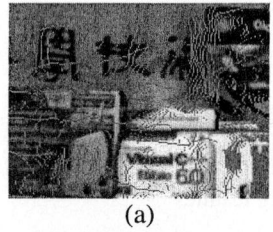
(a)

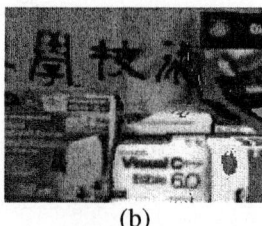
(b)

Fig. 4. Two-step integer mapping results (a) before (b) after

2.3 Projection-Based Registration for Partial 3D Point Clouds

Correct pairing plays a key role in accurate registration to compensate the errors induced by the disparity estimation, camera calibration, etc. In *fine registration phase*, corresponding features, on 2D image plane instead of 3D space, are employed. That is, a feature-based approach is proposed by exploiting corresponding features within the overlapping area.

Let us consider two textured surfaces that are already in the initial alignment. If you render the acquired 3D surfaces, as they would be seen from an arbitrary viewpoint, the resulting 2D color images are also in alignment. Each point on the source surface projects to the same pixel as its corresponding point on the destination surface. If we could move the partial surface of source view such that its projected image aligns well with the image of the other surface, we could be confident that visible surface points projecting to the same pixel correspond to the same point on the object surface. We can then find good point pairs by pairing points that project to the same pixel.

We apply our registration method to align two partial surfaces by iteratively adjusting extrinsic calibration parameters of source view with respect to destination view. In other words, we apply a Euclidean transformation T: $\Re^3 \rightarrow \Re^3$ to the source surface. The destination surface, S_{Dst}, is projected onto its own image plane and features, f_{Dst}, are extracted in the projected image plane. On the other hand, at each iteration, the source surface, S_{Src}, is projected onto the destination image plane and corresponding features, f_{Src}', are searched for. This is illustrated in Fig. 5.

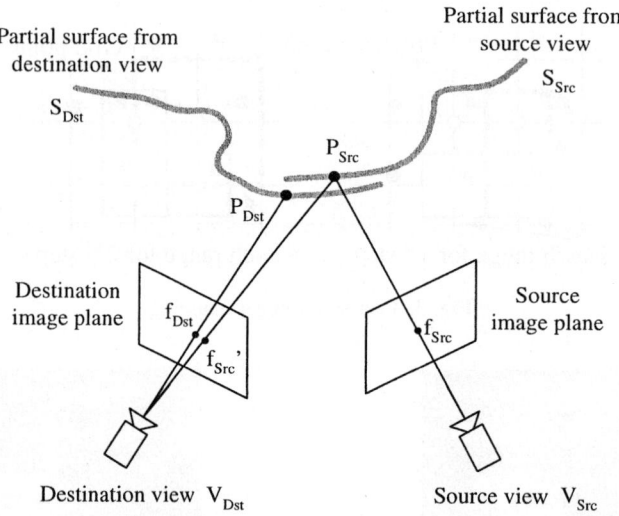

Fig. 5. Selection of corresponding features

For each feature f_{Dst} of the destination image, the corresponding feature f_{Src}' of the source image is found in the neighborhood of the same position as f_{Dst} using the modified KLT feature tracker. P_{Dst} and P_{Src} are 3D points of f_{Dst} and f_{Src}, respectively. And c_{Dst} and c_{Src} are RGB color components of f_{Dst} and f_{Src}, respectively.

Firstly, features are extracted over the overlapping area, Ω, in the destination image. The modified KLT feature tracker is adopted to extract feature corners that are robust to noise and can be tracked well. For this, local autocorrelation and eigenvalues are computed. After features are extracted, S_{Src} is projected onto the destination image plane using the same calibration parameters as the projection of S_{Dst}. Then, correspondences are searched for in the projected source image using cross-correlation in sub-pixel unit. However, there may occur some mismatches that should be filtered out. In order to guarantee correct paring, RANSAC is applied at each iteration [15]. By exploiting RANSAC, we can eliminate outliners and obtain only correct pairs between source and destination views.

Projecting S_{Src} onto the destination image plane produces an image I_{Src}'. Then, we can define a cost function measuring the mismatch between I_{Src}' and destination image I_{Dst}.

$$L = \sum_{i=0}^{N-1} \kappa_1 \left\{ \left(1 - \frac{\|f_{Dst,i} - f_{Src,i}\|}{Dist_{max}}\right) \|f_{Dst,i} - f_{Src,i}\|^2 + \kappa_2 \|c_{Dst,i} - c_{Src,i}\|^2 \right\} \quad (4)$$

where κ_1 is described as follows to exclude the pair whose distance in 3D space exceeds a preset threshold Th. In other words, the pair, whose depth difference is large, is not included.

$$\kappa_1 = \begin{cases} 1 & if \; \|P_{Dst} - P_{Src}\| < Th \\ 0 & o/w \end{cases} \quad (5)$$

κ_2 is a weighting factor for color information and N denotes the number of features. And $\|.\|$ and $Dist_{max}$ represent the norm and a maximum distance between f_{Dst} and f_{Src}', respectively.

In summary, we search for correspondences and use them to define a total cost function within the overlapping area. By minimizing the cost function, a final pose of the source view is estimated. That is, we can estimate the pose of source view $\{R_{Src}, T_{Src}\}$, with respect to the pose of destination view $\{R_{Dst}, T_{Dst}\}$ through minimizing the errors on N feature points as follows.

Given two sets of corresponding points,

Find $\{R_{Src}, T_{Src}\}$ *w.r.t* $\{R_{Dst}, T_{Dst}\}$ \quad (6)

such that $\arg\min_{\{R_{Src}, T_{Src}\}} L$

The total error is minimized through Levenberg-Marquardt non-linear optimization algorithm.

By employing the proposed method, the correspondences between destination and projected source images can be found. Therefore, correspondences between destination and original source images can be established after applying RANSAC. Usually, it is hard to find correspondences between two views with a wide baseline. However, if depth image and initial camera pose are available, corresponding features can be extracted effectively.

2.4 Surface Reconstruction of Registered 3D Point Clouds

After pose estimation, trimming and color selection are required. We obtain the correspondences through a registration process. Then, final 3D coordinates are calculated by a linear triangulation method [16].

Color adjustment is also required to consider changes in lighting conditions depending on the camera position.

$$\begin{bmatrix} R' \\ G' \\ B' \end{bmatrix} = \left(v \times \begin{bmatrix} R_{Dst} \\ G_{Dst} \\ B_{Dst} \end{bmatrix} + u \times \begin{bmatrix} R_{Src} \\ G_{Src} \\ B_{Src} \end{bmatrix} \right) / (u+v) \quad (7)$$

where u and v are distances from left and right borders of the overlapping area to the current pixel, respectively. R_{Dst} (or G_{Dst}, B_{Dst}) and R_{Src} (or G_{Src}, B_{Src}) are red (or green, blue) of a current pixel for both images. On the other hand, R' (or G', B') means final colors within the overlapping area.

To reconstruct a final surface, after placing a multi-view camera at several positions and acquiring images and 3D point clouds, we apply the above procedure to them. Fig. 6 shows a conceptual diagram.

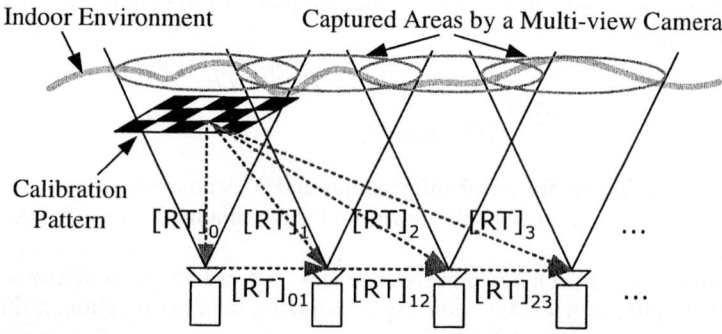

Fig. 6. Indoor scene reconstruction

We first place a pattern whose relative position is already known. Then, we estimate intrinsic/extrinsic parameters with respect to the world coordinate. A camera pose with respect to a specific point of the pattern, $[R\ T]_0$, is evaluated by exploiting Intra-/Inter-calibration and structural information of the multi-view camera [13][17]. After moving the camera to other positions, through the above-mentioned procedure, we can get a relative pose $[R\ T]_i$ at each position, and carry out surface reconstruction.

3 Experimental Results and Analysis

The experiments were carried out under a normal illumination condition of general indoor environment. We used Digiclops which is a multi-view camera for image acquisition [18]. It calculates 3D coordinates through disparity estimation. We employed a planar pattern with 7×5 grid points. Distance between two consecutive points is 10.6 cm. For depth image refinement, 30 frames are used to get mean and standard deviation.

Fig. 7 demonstrates the results of minimizing distance errors between correspondences. Enlarged areas are shown in Fig. 7(a) and Fig. 7(b) at the initial and final steps. Red and white markers represent features of source and destination views, respectively, on the destination view. We can see that the distances between correspondences are effectively minimized.

Fig. 7. Distance error minimization (a) before (b) after

Fig. 8 illustrates registration results. Fig. 8(a) is a combined 3D point cloud and Fig. 8(b) is the results after registration. We can see that the registration works well by observing the boundary of a circle, Chinese or English characters in Fig. 8(c) to Fig. 8 (f). Furthermore, the navigation, from left to right view within the VE as shown in Fig. 8(g) to Fig. 8(i), proves the depth information of the model and some motion parallax.

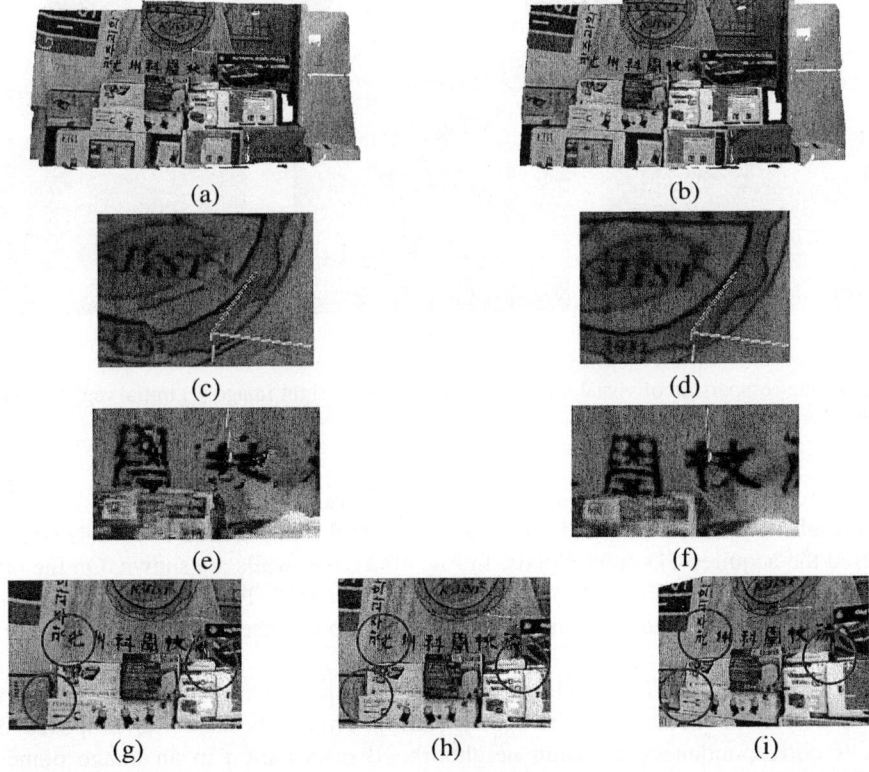

Fig. 8. Registration results (a) combined 3D point cloud (b) registered 3D point cloud (c) enlarged area I in (a) (d) enlarged area I in (b) (e) enlarged area II in (a) (f) enlarged area II in (b) (g) left view (h) front view (i) right view

The registration results for another scene are shown in Fig. 9, which explain that the visual quality of the proposed method is better than that of ICP. Fig. 9(a) and Fig. 9(b) show left and right images, respectively. After initial registration, we can obtain the results as shown in Fig. 9(c). Note that heart shape, face part of bear and some letters are smeared. In Fig. 9(d) and Fig. 9(e), we can see the final registration results of ICP and the proposed method, respectively. Actually, total error is larger than the conventional ICP in terms of the closest distance. However, we observed that the visual quality of the proposed method is much better than that of the conventional ICP. The reason is that the conventional ICP only considers the closest distance instead of data themselves.

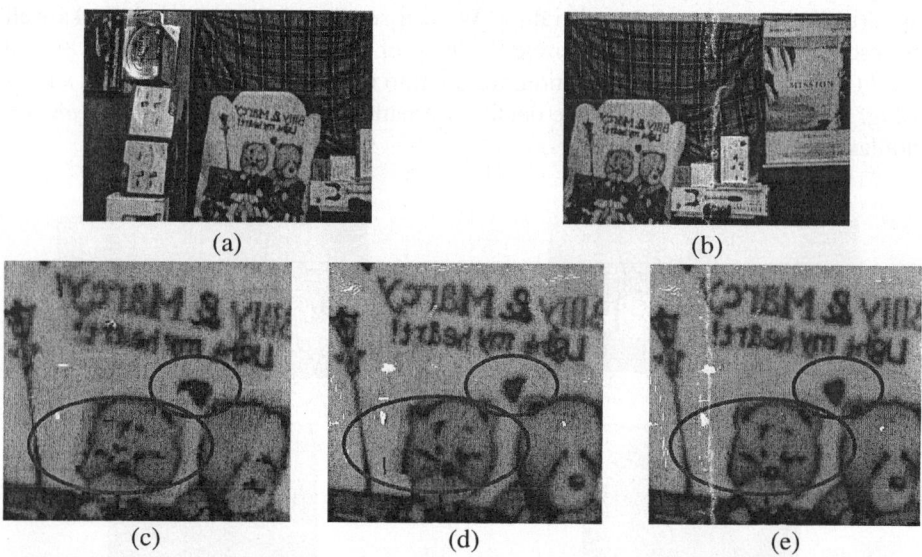

Fig. 9. The comparison of visual quality (a) left image (b) right image (c) initial registration (d) ICP (e) proposed method

The registration and modeling results for two walls are shown in Fig. 10. To get this result, we moved the multi-view camera several times around two walls and registered the acquired 3D point clouds. In Fig. 10(a), two walls are shown. On the other hand, Fig. 10(b) and Fig. 10(c) are scenes for each wall. By applying the proposed method to several sets of 3D point clouds, we can do a dense 3D reconstruction for an indoor environment.

As shown in Fig. 11, the proposed method is superior to ICP or color ICP in the sense of PSNR (Peak Signal to Noise Ratio). This is because the proposed one tracks correspondences by using neighborhood information in an image plane as well as geometric information. The convergence rate of the proposed one is also faster than that of color/texture-based method ($\alpha=7.0$, $N_B=192$). The reason is that ICP or color ICP takes longer to search for correspondences than does the proposed method.

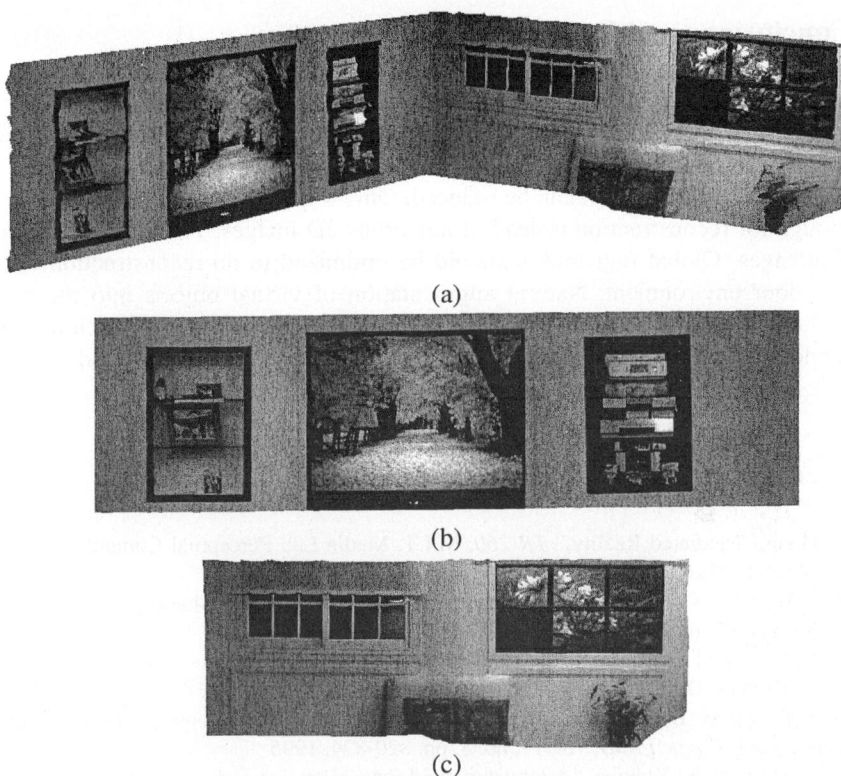

Fig. 10. Indoor Scene reconstruction (a) two walls (b) left wall (c) right wall

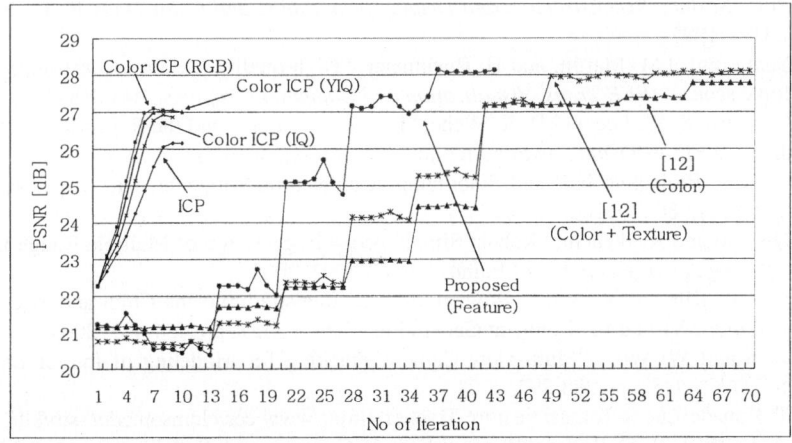

Fig. 11. Performance comparison

4 Conclusions and Future Work

We proposed a novel registration method for 3D point clouds to carry out 3D reconstruction for an indoor environment. We proved that even though the error of depth information is relatively large, effective registration is possible. Furthermore, the required time for registration can be reduced. Only a few views of a real environment are enough for reconstruction instead of numerous 2D images. There are still remaining challenges. Global registration should be optimized to do reconstruction for the entire indoor environment. Natural augmentation of virtual objects into the reconstructed environment requires light source estimation and analysis to match illumination condition of the VE. Finally, dense disparity estimation is required to obtain better results.

References

1. S. Mann, "Mediated Reality," *TR 260*, M.I.T. Media Lab Perceptual Computing Section, Cambridge, Massachusetts, 1994.
2. P. J. Besl and N. D. McKay, "A Method for Registration of 3-D Shapes," *IEEE Trans. on PAMI*, vol. 14, no. 2, pp. 239-256, 1992.
3. A. Johnson and S. Kang, "Registration and Integration of Textured 3-D Data," Tech. report CRL96/4, Digital Equipment Corp., Cambridge Research Lab, Oct., 1996.
4. G. Blais and M. D. Levine, "Registering multiview range data to create 3-D computer objects," *IEEE Trans. PAMI*, vol. 17, no. 8, pp. 820-824, 1995.
5. T. Masuda and N. Yokoya. "A robust method for registration and segmentation of multiple range images," *Computer Vision and Image Understanding*, 61(3):295–307, May 1995.
6. S. Weik. "Registration of 3-d partial surface models using luminance and depth information," *Proc. of 3-D Digital Imaging and Modeling*, pp. 93-100, 1997.
7. K. Pulli, *Surface Reconstruction and Display from Range and Color Data*, Ph.D. dissertation, UW, 1997.
8. F. Bernardini, I.M. Martin, and H. Rushmeier, "High-quality texture reconstruction from multiple scans," *IEEE Trans. Visualization and Computer Graphics*, 7(4):318–332, 2001.
9. G. C. Sharp, S. W. Lee and D. K. Wehe, "Invariant Features and the Registration of Rigid Bodies," *IEEE Int'l Conf., on Robotics and Automation*, pp. 932-937, 1999.
10. R. Fisher, "Projective ICP and Stabilizing Architectural Augmented Reality Overlays," *VAA01*, pp 69-80, 2001.
11. K. Nishino and K. Ikeuchi, "Robust Simultaneous Registration of Multiple Range Images Comprising A Large Number of Points," *ACCV2002*, 2002.
12. S. Kim, K. Kim and W. Woo, "Projection-based Registration using Color and Texture Information for Virtual Environment Generation," *LNCS 3331*, pp. 434-443, 2004.
13. K. Kim and W. Woo, "Multi-view Camera Tracking for Modeling of Indoor Environment," *LNCS 3331*, pp.288-297, 2004.
14. KLT: Kanade-Lucas-Tomasi Feature Tracker, http://www.ces.clemson.edu/~stb/klt/, 2005.
15. M. A. Fischler, R. C. Bolles, "Random Sample Consensus: A Paradigm for Model Fitting with Applications to Image Analysis and Automated Cartography," *Comm. of ACM*, Vol 24, pp 381-395, 1981.

16. R. Hartley and A. Zisserman, *Multiple View Geometry in Computer Vision*, Cambridge University Press, 2004.
17. R. Tsai, "A versatile camera calibration technique for high-accuracy 3d machine vision metrology using off-the-shelf tv cameras and lenses," *IEEE Journal of Robotics and Automation*, vol. 3, no. 4, pp. 323-344, 1987.
18. Point Grey Research Inc., http://www.ptgrey.com, 2002.

Image-Based Relighting in Dynamic Scenes

Yong-Ho Hwang[1], Hyun-Ki Hong[1], and Jun-Sik Kwon[2]

[1] Dept. of Image Eng., Graduate School of Advanced Imaging Science,
Multimedia and Film, Chung-Ang Univ., 221 Huksuk-dong, Dongjak-ku,
Seoul, 156-756, Korea
hwangyh@wm.cau.ac.kr, honghk@cau.ac.kr
[2] Dept. of Electrical Eng., Se-Myung Univ.,
San 22-1 Shinwol-dong, Jechon-shi, Chungbuk, 390-711, Korea
jskwon@semyung.ac.kr

Abstract. Image-based lighting (IBL) is the process of illuminating scenes and objects with images of light from the real world. To generate a high quality synthesized image, consistency of geometry and illumination has to be taken into account. In general, lighting design for realistically rendering synthetic objects into a real-world scene, is labor intensive process and not always successful. Though many researches on IBL have been presented up to now, most of them assumed static situations that light sources and the objects were not moved. This paper presents a novel algorithm that integrates synthetic objects in the real photographs by using the global illumination model and HDR (High Dynamic Range) radiance map. We identify the camera positions and the light types, and then construct 3D illumination environment of the scene. The proposed method makes it possible to handle dynamic scenes and generate photo-realistic images.

1 Introduction

The seamless integration of synthetic objects with real photographs or video images has long been one of the central topics in computer vision and computer graphics [1~7]. Generating a high quality synthesized image requires first matching the geometric characteristics of both the synthetic and real cameras, and then shading the synthetic objects so that they appear to be illuminated by the same lights as the other objects in the background image.

In general, lighting design for solving the problem of illuminating the synthetic objects in a realistic and believable way is labor intensive process and not always successful due to the enormous complexities of real-world illumination, which includes both direct and indirect illumination from complex light-sources, shadows, and glossy reflections and refractions. Although many rendering tools that help in automating the synthesis process have been proposed, most of them is restricted to static situations that light sources and the objects are not moved. Since various types of light sources such as spot and area lights are located from place to place in a real scene, their radiant distributions are dependent on the position of the camera to capture lights. However, there were few methods to render animations where the synthetic objects move between scenes with different illumination environments.

This paper presents a novel method for identifying the positions and characteristics of the lights in the real image on dynamic situations to illuminate the computer generated images. First, we capture illumination from all directions by using omni-directional images taken by a digital camera with a fisheye lens. Second, the positions and types of the light sources in the scene are identified and classified automatically from the correspondences between images. In final, we can construct 3D illumination environment and render efficiently scenes illuminated by distant natural illumination given in an environment map. Experimental results show that the proposed method makes it possible to render dynamic scenes with different radiant distributions and generate photo-realistic images. It is expected that animators and lighting experts for the film industry would benefit highly from it.

The remainder of this paper is structured as follows: Sec. 2 reviews previous researches for rendering synthetic objects into real scenes, and the proposed algorithm and the experimental results are presented on Sec. 3. The conclusion is described in Sec. 4.

2 Previous Studies

Many Image-Based Lighting (IBL) researches for illuminating scenes and objects with images of light from the real world have been proposed up to now. Table 1 shows previous studies may be classified according to three viewpoints: how to construct a geometric model of the scene, how to capture illuminations of the scene, and how to render the synthetic scene.

Table 1. Previous researches for image-based lighting

Work	Geometry	Capturing illumination	Rendering
1	user's specification for 3D construction of the scene	photographs	radiosity
2	light-based model: distant and local scene, synthetic objects	HDRI of scene reflections on a spherical mirror	RADIANCE system
3	omni-directional stereo algorithm	HDR omni-directional images by fish-eye lens	ray casting
4	user's specification	HDRI by sphere mapping	OpenGL

In table 1, Founier et al cannot consider illumination from outside of the input image without user's specification owing to using 2D photographs[1]. Debevec's, which is one of the most representative works, constructs light-based model by mapping reflections on a spherical mirror onto a geometric model of the scene. Therefore, a degree of realism of the rendering image depends on selecting viewpoints for observing the mirror so that the reflections on the mirror can cover the entire geometric model of the scene[2]. Sato et al simplified user's direct specification of a geometric model of the scene by using an omni-directional stereo algorithm, and measured the radiance distribution. However, because of using the omni-directional stereo, it is required a prior camera calibration including positions and internal parameters, which is complex and difficult process[3]. In addition, Gibson et al proposed integration algorithms at interactive rates for augmented reality applications by using a single graphics pipeline[4].

IBL (Image-based Lighting) algorithms in table 1 did not take into account dynamic situations where the synthetic objects move between scenes with different illumination environments. This paper addresses the issue of automatic identification of light positions and types to generate animated sequences.

3 Proposed Algorithm

In this section, we describe how to identify the positions and characteristics of the lights in the real image on dynamic situations to illuminate scenes and objects. The proposed algorithm consists of three steps: identifying the light-capturing positions to determine 3D coordinates of the lights, classifying the characteristic of lights to render moving objects in the scene more photo-realistically, and constructing 3D illumination environment. A block diagram (Fig. 1) shows the workflow of the proposed algorithm.

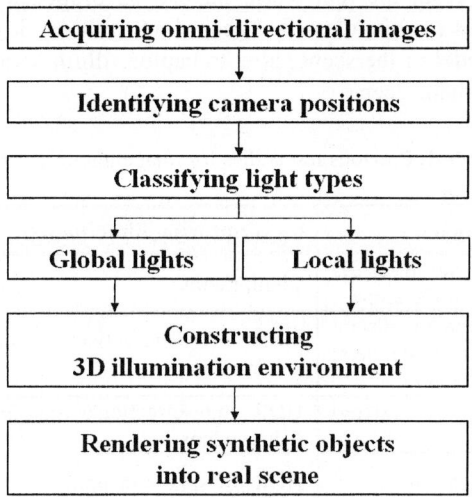

Fig. 1. Block diagram for the proposed method

3.1 Identifying Camera Positions

A digital camera with a fisheye lens takes omni-directional images of the real scene[5]. Due to the limited dynamic range of a digital camera, pixel values of an image taken with one shutter speed cannot measure radiance in the scene accurately. To avoid this problem, multiple images taken with different shutter speeds are combined to produce each omni-directional image with a high dynamic range[6].

The environment map is generally used to generate scenes illuminated by distant natural lights. More specifically, by sampling bright regions of the environment map, we can obtain an illumination distribution of the scene. In real-world, the radiant distribution captured at the fixed position may not represent all of light sources in the scene. Even though all lights contribute radiant distribution of the scene in global illumination, some of lights due to their locality may not be found on the environment map.

In this paper, the cameras are placed at specific locations in the scene to capture some local lights from different locations. The imaging system used in our method is illustrated in Fig. 2. C_i (i = 1, 2, 3, ..., n) are the camera projection centers at each of the locations. We assume that all cameras are not rotated about their vertical axes and the real scene has cube-like space as Fig. 2.

Latitude-longitude (L-L) environment maps are generated by panoramic transformations from two (front and back) hemi-sphere images taken at each camera position. Then the directional vectors of the lights can be extracted at each location by using the structured importance sampling[7]. In order to determine coordinates of 3D points of the lights from each L-L image, we should identify the light-capturing positions C_i.

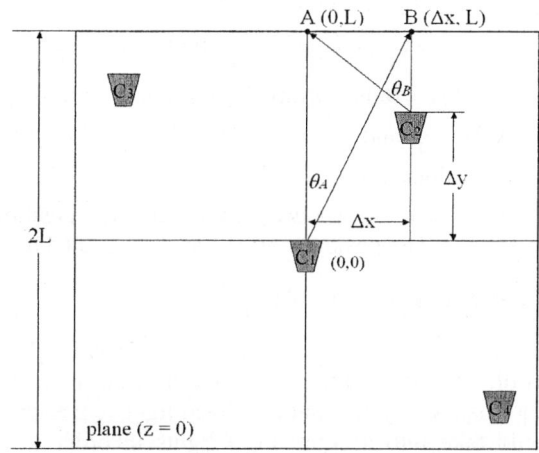

Fig. 2. Top view of the light-capturing system

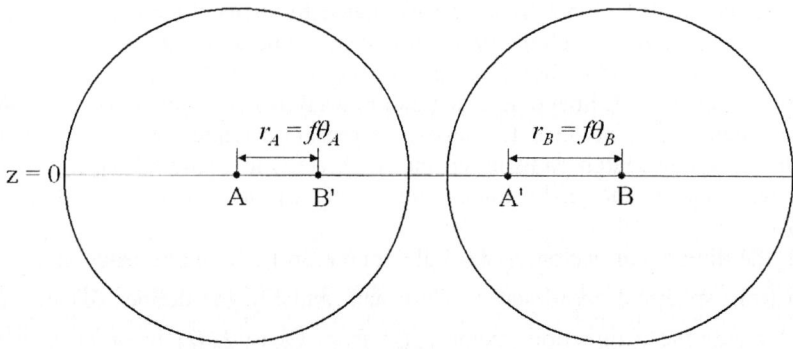

Fig. 3. Front hemi-sphere images at C_1 and C_2

First, C_1 is defined as an origin of the world coordinate system, and then relative displacements between C_1 and other positions (C_2, C_3, ..., C_n) are calculated. In the case of C_2, we can define the coordinates of the center points A and B in two front hemi-sphere images as (0, L) and (Δx, L), respectively. Fig. 3 represents two hemisphere images at C_1 and C_2.

As shown in Fig. 3, the projected center points A´ and B´ can be extracted by using the feature extraction algorithm[8]. Then we calculate the angles θ_A ($\angle AC_1B$) and θ_B ($\angle C_1BC_2$) as follows:

$$\theta_A = r_A / f, \quad \theta_B = r_B / f, \tag{1}$$

where f is the focal length of the lens, r_A and r_B are the distances between the image centers and the projections of B and A, respectively.

After calculating θ_A and θ_B, we define the directional vectors and lines as following:

$$v_1 = [\sin\theta_A, \cos\theta_A], \quad v_2 = [\sin\theta_B, \cos\theta_B], \tag{2}$$
$$L_1(t) = C_1 + tv_1, \quad L_2(s) = A - sv_2, \tag{3}$$

where, $L_1(t)$ is the line that extends from C_1 through B, and $L_2(s)$ is that from A through C_2, respectively. v_1 and $-v_2$ are the directional vectors of $L_1(t)$ and $L_2(s)$ with t and s scalar values, respectively.

Finally, we can find Δx and Δy when $L_1(t)$ intersects the position (y=L) and $L_2(s)$ meets at the position (x=Δx). The positions of C_n can be identified by the same method.

3.2 Classifying Light Types

This paper classifies the captured light sources into two groups: global lights and local lights. Global lights directly illuminate all regions in the scene and they are found on most of environment images. On the contrary, local lights cover the specific region in the scene. We should take into account local lights in order to render animations where the synthetic objects move in the real scenes.

3.2.1 Global Lights

3D coordinates of the global lights are estimated by using the correspondences between L-L images. We search the projection of the camera position C_1 on the position (x=L) and its corresponding point on other images at C_i (i = 2, 3, 4, ..., n). Because of the distortion of the L-L image, it is difficult to establish correspondences. In order to find corresponding points in L-L images, we present a feature extraction algorithm, which has adaptive search paths based on the directional vector of the lights. In this paper, we denote the L-L image taken at C_1 as LLI_1, and that at C_2 as LLI_2.

First, the directional vector v_L of a light source on LLI_1 can be calculated by conversion from spherical coordinate to Cartesian, and Eq. (4) defines 3D line $L_L(t)$. Second, we define a direction vector $v_C(t)$ from C_2 to $L_L(t)$ in order to define a search range for correspondence on LLI_2 by Eq. (5) and $v_C(t)$ is depends on t as in Fig. 4.

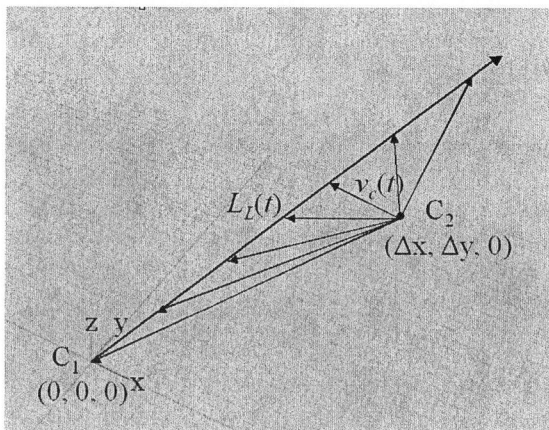

Fig. 4. Directional vector in Cartesian coordinate

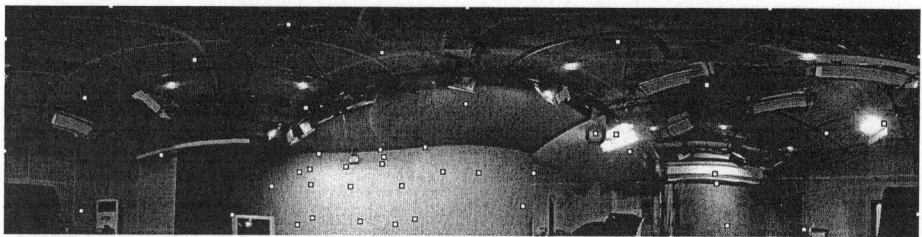
(a) Sampled light position on LLI_1

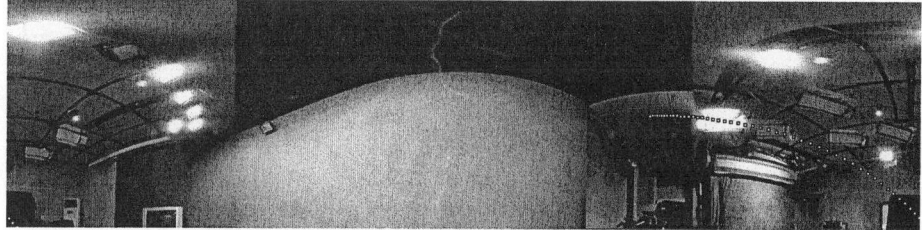
(b) Search path for corresponding point on LLI_2

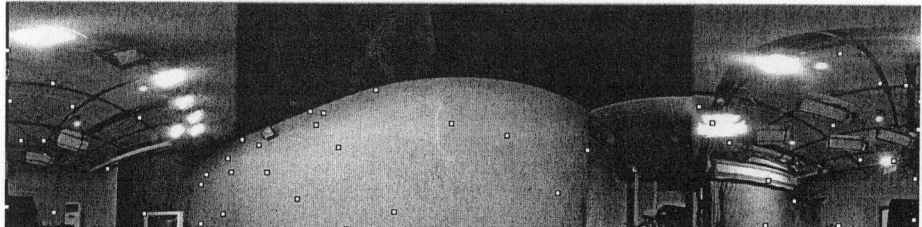
(c) corresponding points in LLI_2

Fig. 5. Sampled light position and search paths

$$L_L(t) = C_1 + tv_L .\qquad(4)$$

$$v_C(t) = L_L(t) - \overrightarrow{C_1 C_2} .\qquad(5)$$

At the next step, we can find a locus of $v_C(t)$ into the LLI_2 by conversion from Cartesian coordinate to spherical as Fig. 5(b). Stereo matching mask to establish correspondence is translated along the computed search paths (white points). More consideration of various matching algorithms can achieve better performances. Fig. 5(c) shows the corresponding points in LLI_2. Note that many points on the blue screen may be regarded as light sources because light sources on the ceiling emitted the radiant energy toward these points and most of the incoming energy was strongly reflected.

3.2.2 Local Lights

The sampled lights in LLI_2, which is the image captured at C_2, include not only local lights but also global lights. For generating more realistic animation where the synthetic objects move from C_1 to C_2, we should take into account local lights at C_2, which are presented at only the LLI_2. To extract the local lights, we use strata S_i that partition an arbitrary set of pixels in the environment map into k disjoint partitions, where k is the number of light samples[7].

Fig. 6 and 7 represent pseudo-code for the local light information including the position and the intensity, and corresponding points and strata S_i in LLI_2, respectively.

```
// Cp is the corresponding point
// n is the number of Cp

For i=1,2,3...,k
    For j=1,2,3...,n
        if Cpj ∈ Si then false
        else true
    Loop j
    If true then Si is the stratum of local light
Loop i
```

Fig. 6. Pseudo-code for extracting local lights in LLI_2

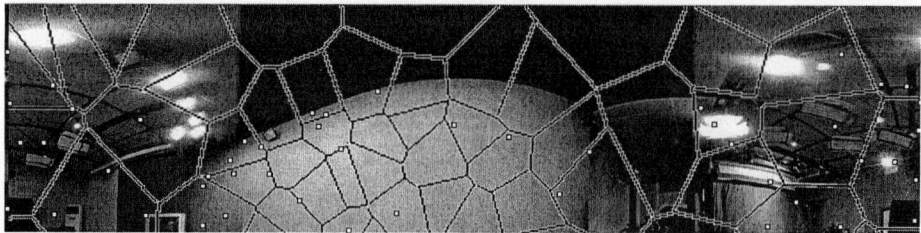

Fig. 7. Superimposed image of corresponding points and strata S_i in LLI_2

3.3 Constructing 3D Illumination Environment

After identifying camera positions and classifying light types, we construct 3D illumination environment. 3D coordinates of global lights are determined by using stereo algorithm[9]. 2D point in L-L image is converted to 3D directional vectors v as following:

$$v = [\sin\theta\cos\phi, \sin\theta\sin\phi, \cos\theta], \qquad (6)$$

By using Eq. 6, we obtain directional vectors v_{1i} and v_{2i} of the sampled lights in LLI_1 and the corresponding points in LLI_2, respectively. Then, two 3D line $L_{1i}(t)$ and $L_{2i}(s)$ are given as:

$$L_{1i}(t) = C_1 + tv_{1i}, \quad L_{2i}(s) = C_2 + sv_{2i}, \; (i = 1, 2, 3, ..., n) \qquad (7)$$

where n is the number of global lights. Each pair of the lines $L_{1i}(t)$ and $L_{2i}(s)$ intersect at 3D points that is the coordinate of global lights.

However, due to various kinds of errors, the two lines may not intersect. Therefore, we consider that the two lines intersect if the distance between the two lines is sufficiently short. The distance between the two 3D lines is given by substituting t and s from the following equations[10]:

$$t = \frac{Det\{(C_2 - C_1), v_{2i}, v_{1i} \times v_{2i}\}}{|v_{1i} \times v_{2i}|^2}, \; s = \frac{Det\{(C_2 - C_1), v_{1i}, v_{1i} \times v_{2i}\}}{|v_{1i} \times v_{2i}|^2} \qquad (8)$$

Local lights are positioned with their direction vectors and intersecting points on the scene cube specified by the user. Since 3D points of global lights are known, we may construct mesh for illumination environment of the scene by using more dense correspondences of L-L images.

3.4 Experimental Results

We have experimented on integration of synthetic objects into the real scene. In order to evaluate performance of the proposed algorithm, we rendered virtual objects that are moved from arbitrary positions C_1 to C_2 in the scene. In the constructed illumination environment, positions of lights and some regions illuminated by local lights are identified.

Fig. 8 represents animation results of three cases: (a) objects are rendered at C_1, (b) only the global lights are considered at C_2, and (c) both global and local lights are simulated at C_2. Since there are only the global lights at C_1, the rendering results of two methods are the same each other. However, as objects are moved toward C_2, consideration of the locality of lights makes it to generate more photo-realistic image. More specifically, Fig. 5(a) shows that there are many lights on the blue screen. Therefore, when the synthetic objects: sphere, torus, table, etc. are translated to C_2 where is closer to the blue screen than C_1, these received much more illuminations from both global and local lights as Fig. 8(c).

(a) Rendering result of synthetic objects at C_1

(b) Rendering with global lights at C_2 c) Rendering with global and local lights at C_2

Fig. 8. Comparison of the rendering images

4 Conclusion

We have presented a novel algorithm that integrates synthetic objects in the real photographs by using the global illumination model and HDR radiance map. The proposed algorithm consists of three steps: identifying the camera positions, classifying the light types into global and local lights, and constructing 3D illumination environment. The proposed method makes it possible to handle multiple environment maps and generates photo-realistic images. Future work will include omni-direction image acquisition system that allows local cameras to rotate for arbitrary angle, and 3D scene reconstruction model to represent more accurate light environments.

Acknowledgements

This work was supported by Korea Research Foundation Grant(KRF-2004-041-D00620).

References

1. A. Fournier, A. Gunawan, and C. Romanzin, "Common illumination between real and computer generated scenes," Proc. of Graphics Interface, (1993) 254-262
2. P. Debevec, "Rendering synthetic objects into real scenes: Bridging traditional and image-based graphics with global illumination and high dynamic range photography," Siggraph (1998) 189-198

3. I. Sato, Y. Sato, and K. Ikeuchi, "Acquiring a radiance distribution to superimpose virtual objects onto a real scene," IEEE Trans. on Visualization and Computer Graphics, vol. 5, no. 1, (1999) 1-12
4. S. Gibson and A. Murta, "Interactive rendering with real-world illumination," Proc. of the 11th Eurographics Workshop on Rendering, (2000) 365-376
5. M. Bajura, H. Fuchs, and R. Ohbuchi, "Merging virtual objects with the real world: seeing ultrasound imagery within the patient," *proc. SIGGRAPH 92*, (1992) 203-210
6. P. Debevec and J. Malik, "Recovering high dynamic range radiance maps from photographs," "*proc. SIGGRAPH 97* (1997) 369-378
7. S. Agarwal, R. Ramamoorthi, S. Belongie, and H. Jensen. "Structured importance sampling of environment maps," *ACM Trans. on Graphics 22*, 3 (July), (2003) 605-612
8. C. Tomasi and T. Kanade, "Shape and Motion from Image Streams under Orthography: a Factorization Method," *Int'l J. Computer Vision*, vol. 9, no.2, (1992) 137-154
9. O. Faugeras, *Three-Dimensional Computer Vision: A Geometric Viewpoint*, MIT Press, Cambridge, (1993) MA.
10. A. S. Glassner, *Graphics Gems*, AP Professional, Cambridge, MA. (1990)

Stippling Technique Based on Color Analysis

Seok Jang and Hyun-Ki Hong

Dept. of Image Eng., Graduate School of Advanced Imaging Science, Multimedia and Film,
Chung-Ang Univ., 221 Huksuk-dong, Dongjak-ku, Seoul, 156-756, Korea
seokj@wm.cau.ac.kr, honghk@cau.ac.kr

Abstract. This paper presents a new stippling technique that effectively represents color images similar to the stippling works of artists. First, the proposed method creates a reference image from combining a smoothed image and with an edge image of the source. The color density function, defined by analyzing the information from the HSV color model of the reference image, is applied to the automatic computation of the number, size, and position of the points. Then, we use the weighted Penrose-based importance sampling to make points to be distributed randomly but almost evenly spaced in accordance with the color density within few seconds. In addition, our color jittering can generate efficiently stippling drawings having various colors. For more artistic representation, the points are transformed into the oval-shaped ones and their orientations are defined according to the direction field of color image. Our application areas include animation, digital art, and video processing.

1 Introduction

Neo-impressionists in the late 1800s introduced a very interesting artistic technique that represents objects with numerous points. Since 1990s, there has been consistent research of stippling techniques using computers in Non-Photorealistic Rendering (NPR).

Early stippling research was about a technique that consistently distributed unicolored points under the user's control using Voronoi Diagram [1], which shortened the work time and simplified the process of completing a single stippling piece of art by an artist. After this, various stippling techniques were proposed, such as the method of automatic distribution of points according to the tone of gray image using weighted CVD (Centroidal Voronoi Diagrams) [2,3], using points with orientations and various shapes instead of simply circle-shaped points [4], applying stippling on volume rendering [5], representing the material or shading of objects by applying stippling to the surface of 3D model [6], etc. However, most previous stippling techniques represented gray images or objects with tones of gray levels, using unicolored points. The stippling technique, which represents images similar to the stippling works of neo-impressionists using points of various colors, has hardly ever been researched. This paper presents a color-based stippling technique for artistic drawing that makes the points to be distributed randomly but almost evenly spaced. By analyzing color information from HSV color model of color images such as pictures or photos, we define color density function, which automatically computes the numbers, sizes, and distribution of points. The colors of points, computed by color jittering, represent color-based stippling effectively. In addition, PIS (Penrose-based Importance

Sampling) [7] is applied instead of CVD generally used in distributing points, which guarantees speedy processing time. This paper presents the easy and speedy computer generated color-based stippling technique that effectively represents color images similar to the stippling works of artists in Fig. 1.

(a) (b)

Fig. 1. (a) The Seine at Le Grande Jatte, 1888, (b) The Seine at Courbevoie, 1885

2 Related Work

The stippling technique introduced by G. Seurat [8,9] is different from the general painting techniques in several ways. First, the stippling represents the image not by brush strokes but by numerous pure color points distributed on a canvas. At this point, points are distributed randomly and evenly not to make any patterns. Secondly, the stippling is different in the way that colors are mixed. In contrast to the general painting techniques that make the colors by mixing them on palette or canvas, the stippling technique uses various pure colors which are mixed in the human retinas. However, Seurat's painting technique is not applicable to computers. The visual mixture of colors is quite difficult on the RGB-based display device to which additive color model is applied, not alike on the CMY-based painting or printing device to which subtractive color model is applied. In other words, the mixture of numerous red and green points can never be perceived as brown color on the monitors but as yellow color or red and green colors respectively. Ultimately, the size, number, distribution, color and shape of points need to be effectively computed according to color images in order to generate color stippling by computer similar to the traditional stippling arts.

In most color images, color information is stored in the form of RGB model in order to make it fit for display device such as monitor. Though this kind of quality makes it simple to design the computer graphics system and the display device, it is very difficult to intuitively categorize and express colors because the correlation of RGB values is too big [10, 11]. For an easy analysis of color information, the RGB model needs to be converted to other color model [12]. This paper analyzes and redefines the distribution of colors by changing the color information of images stored in the form of RGB model into HSV model which is similar to the human perception of colors [13].

It is important to distribute points randomly and evenly in stippling. Most 2D stippling techniques use CVD [2] in distributing points. Though CVD is effective in the random and even distribution of points, the processing time is dependent on the image resolution and the number of points. This paper has applied PIS [7] for the effective and speedy distribution of points. PIS is an application of the principles of Penrose tiling [14]. The method shortens the processing time due to raster scan, and distributes numerous points randomly and evenly in a nearly real-time. Though PIS is suitable for the distribution of points in stippling, there may be happened the unwanted tiling pattern. Based on the color density of the image, our method determines the point distribution by PIS to remove the unwanted patterns.

3 Color Stippling System

We first create a reference image by smoothing the source image and abstracting edge, before color stippling process. Smoothing is performed by color median filter [10], because the median filter not only reduces noise but also keeps the specific edge, unlike other low-pass filters. Edges are abstracted by Canny edge detector [15] and we define the color of edges as lowering the *Lightness* (*Value* in HSV) value of the edge region on the input image by 20% in order to emphasize the outlines (Fig. 2 (b)).

3.1 Color Density Function

For color-based stippling, points should be distributed according to the colors of the image and we need to compute the proper size and the number of points. Though most color images are stored in RGB model, they are transformed into HSV model suitable for color analysis [12]. Our method defines an importance value $I_h(x,y)$ and a color density function $\rho_c(x,y)$ for computing the number, size, and position of the points according to the color information of the image. An importance value $I_h(x,y)$ is defined by *Saturation* $S(x,y)$ and *Value* $V(x,y)$ at (x,y) as follows:

$$I_h(x,y) = V(x,y) \cdot (1 - k \cdot S(x,y)), \quad \rho_c(x,y) = 1 - I_h(x,y) \tag{1}$$

where k (= 0.896) is a constant for $I_h(x,y)$ to reflect the difference of luminance from pure color with *Saturation* 1 to black color. More specifically, when *Saturation* is 1, k enables $1-k \cdot S(x,y)$ not to be zero. Since the blue luminance L_b having the darkest value among all colors is 0.114, k can make $I_h(x,y)$ distinguishable between the pure color including the blue and the black. Therefore, in case *Saturation* is 1, the importance value can represent a difference of brightness within the same colors. Color density ρ_c becomes 0 in white color and 1 in black color according to *Saturation* and *Value* of each *Hue*. Fig. 2 (d) is the color density image represented by 256 gray levels, and finally color density ρ_c is applied with the value from 0 to 255.

Like above, the reason for defining color density function $\rho_c(x,y)$ is that it is difficult to generate proper color stippling when only the luminance of gray level is taken into consideration. In order to express sufficient color information, we should compute ρ_c for every *Hue* (pure color). For example, a yellow color with a high luminance should have high ρ_c values, which guarantee enough color points to represent a pure yellow.

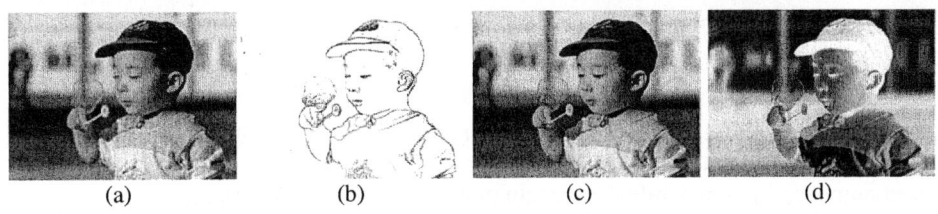

Fig. 2. (a) Source image, (b) Edge image, (c) Reference image, (d) Color density image

3.2 Distribution of Points with PIS

The distribution of points is very important in stippling. Especially in computer generated stippling, image and processing time depend on the way to distribute points. Even though CVD in the previous 2D stippling techniques distributes points randomly and evenly, it takes long processing time as the number of points and the size of source image. On the contrary, color points are distributed applying the weighted PIS with the color density ρ_c of the reference image. This method shortens the processing time of raster scan and guarantees highly speedy process (Section 5). The process of distribution of points by PIS is summarized as follows:

- Cover the region of interest with a pair of tiles of type `e' and `f', as in Fig. 3 (a).
- Apply the recursive subdivision process according to the production rules, as in Fig. 3 (b)).
- Stop subdividing when the required local subdivision level k is reached.
- Draw point on the center of the `a' and `b' type tiles, if the local importance is greater than the decimal value of the F-code of the current tile. as in Fig. 3 (c).

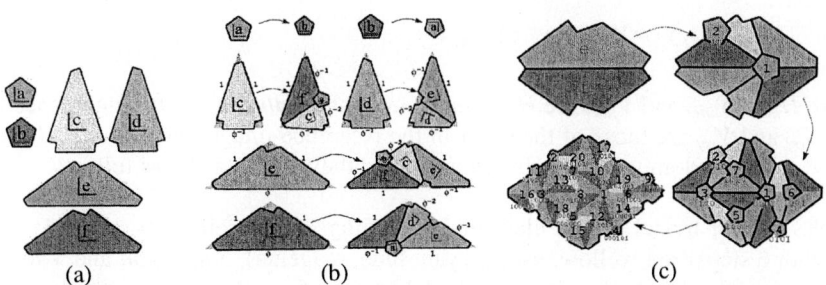

Fig. 3. (a) Six initial tile, (b) Subdivision process according to the production rules, (c) Three subdivisions according to the production rules in PIS.

The local level of subdivision k is calculated by (2).

$$k = \log_{\phi^2} \max_{tile}(mag \cdot \rho_c(x, y)) \qquad (2)$$

where $\phi = (1+\sqrt{5}) \div 2$ is the *Golden Ratio*, and *mag* is a magnitude factor to determine the number of `e' and `f' tiles in the image. When distributing points by weighted PIS with color density ρ_c, it is difficult to generate points distribution as much as desired. Therefore, *mag* should be controlled properly for the distribution of the desired number of points. We automatically determine *mag* by Eq. (3), which distributes the desired number of points while the margin of error is 1% (Section 5).

$$mag = N_p \cdot \left(\frac{R_{aspect} \cdot Sd_{max}}{Cd_{level} \cdot Cd_{mean}} \right) \qquad (3)$$

where N_p and R_{aspect} are the desired number of points and the aspect ratio of reference image. Sd_{max}, Cd_{level} and Cd_{mean} are the maximum subdivision level, the color density level, and the average of color density of the reference image, respectively. In this paper, we fix that $Sd_{max} = 10$ and $Cd_{level} = 255$.

3.3 Color Jittering

In the stippling works of neo-impressionists, the colors of points are selected so that the combination of pure colors of points can be seen as the referred color in distance [1,2]. This representation is possible only in the device using colors or ink to which subtractive color model is applied. In computer generated color-based stippling, a new method is needed which can generate images similar to the traditional stippling works on additive color model. This paper decides the color points with the values of each jittered *Hue*, *Saturation*, and *Value* in HSV color model on the basis of the colors on the position of points of the reference image. Color jittering is randomly jittered for each *Hue H*, *Saturation S*, *Value V* as follows:

$$H_{jitter}(x, y) = H_{ref}(x, y) \pm H_{rand}, \quad S_{jitter}(x, y) = S_{ref}(x, y) \pm S_{rand},$$
$$V_{jitter}(x, y) = V_{ref}(x, y) \pm V_{rand}, \qquad (4)$$

where H_{jitter}, S_{jitter} and V_{jitter} are *Hue*, *Saturation*, and *Value* after jittering, respectively. H_{ref}, S_{ref} and V_{ref} are those of the color in the reference image, respectively H_{rand}, S_{rand} and V_{rand} are random variations by jittering, and they are obtained as follows:

- HSV color model [16] is classified according to Munsell color model [17]: *Hue* with 6 steps (red, yellow, green, cyan, blue, magenta), *Saturation* and *Value* have 5 steps in which each unit equals to 0.2 ranging from 0 to 1, respectively.
- Above minimum unit to discriminate colors on Munsell model are used as the maximum range of jittering in representing the referred colors. Therefore, the jittering variations, j_h, j_s, and j_v (Eq. (5)) for *Hue*, *Saturation* and *Value* on HSV model are $-30° \le j_h \le 30°$, $-0.2 \le j_s \le 0.2$, and $-0.2 \le j_v \le 0.2$ respectively.
- The basic steps of *Hue*, *Saturation*, and *Value*, divided into 10 steps for each unit, are classified into 60 steps for *Hue* and 50 steps for *Saturation* and *Value*. Jittering values j_h, j_s, j_v are determined randomly as arbitrary values in the jittering range.

- H_{rand}, S_{rand} and V_{rand} are computed from the jittering variations j_h, j_s, j_v as follows:

$$L_h = 0.299 \cdot R + 0.587 \cdot G + 0.114 \cdot B \qquad (5)$$

$$H_{rand} = \frac{2 \cdot Rand(j_h) \cdot L_h + 3 \cdot Rand(j_h)}{5}, \quad S_{rand} = \frac{2 \cdot Rand(j_s) \cdot L_h + 3 \cdot Rand(j_s)}{5},$$

$$V_{rand} = \frac{2 \cdot Rand(j_v) \cdot L_h + 3 \cdot Rand(j_v)}{5}, \qquad (6)$$

where $Rand(\cdot)$ is the function which generates random values, and L_h is the luminance value of the *Hue*. L_h is applied in Eq. (5) in order to make a difference in jittering ranges from the colors of high luminance such as yellow to those of low luminance like blue and black. The reason for including the luminance in Eq. (6) is that the jittering range should depend on the luminance for the point. For example, the higher color of high luminance such as yellow, the narrower range for jittering should be selected. Otherwise, jittered colors may look like noise.

The point colors by color jittering represent various colors instead of using only pure colors, and describe effectively the referred color. Our color selection can achieve artistic representation on additive model similar to the stippling works of neo-impressionists.

4 Point Variations

Points in stippling have different variables: size, number and shape. Even in traditional stippling arts, these variables are determined according to the artist's intention. This section describes analysis of the point variables and an automatic method to compute these for an effective stippling representation.

4.1 Shape

Fig. 4 shows that the shape of points is much changed. This paper defines the point shape as being oval as in Fig. 4 (b) for the representation similar to the stippling arts with points touched by brush. This is because most points are represented as being oval and not circular in the stippling works of artists in Fig. 4 (a). Moreover, it allows easy and different representations of points varying from circle to line by controlling the ratio, the length (r_x) of x axis of the oval, and the length (r_y) of y. The next subsection presents a method for the orientation of the oval points.

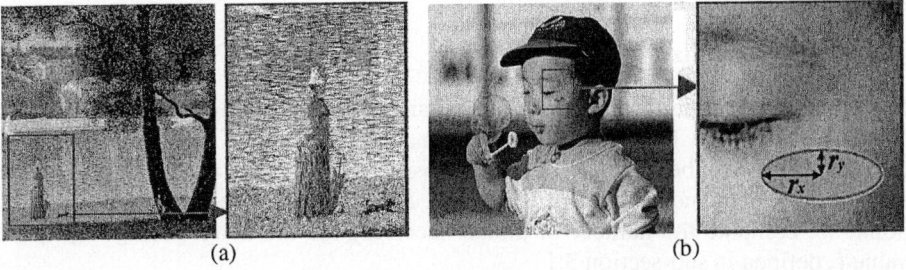

Fig. 4. (a) The shape of point in the stippling works of artist (G. Seurat), (b) The example of the oval point in our method

4.2 Direction

Our stippling method gives orientations to the oval points to represent strokes by brush, which clearly shows the outlines of objects and has greater artistic effect (Fig. 8). First, the directions (d_r, d_g, and d_b) of RGB channel are obtained by Canny edge detector used to extract edge in section 3. $d_r(x,y)$, $d_g(x,y)$ and $d_b(x,y)$ on (x,y) are represented from 0° to 180° angle for the edge, and become maximum at 90°, and minimum at 0° and 180°. After combining each direction, we obtain the direction field d_{field} as follows:

$$D_r = \sin(d_r(x, y)), \quad D_g = \sin(d_g(x, y)), \quad D_b = \sin(d_b(x, y)),$$

$$D_{\max} = Max(D_r, D_g, D_b),$$

$$d_{field}(x, y) = \begin{cases} d_r(x, y), & if\ D_{\max} = D_r \\ d_g(x, y), & if\ D_{\max} = D_g \\ d_b(x, y), & if\ D_{\max} = D_b \end{cases}, \tag{7}$$

where D_r, D_g and D_b are the values by sine function ranging from 0 to 1, and $D_{\max}$ is the value having the strongest direction in RGB channel. $Max(\cdot)$ is the function that selects the maximum value among different variables. Fig. 5 (b) shows the image with 256 gray level of the direction field. The orientation of the oval point is given according to the direction information of the reference image.

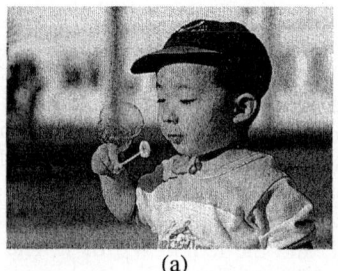 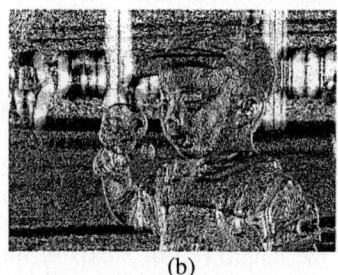

(a) (b)

Fig. 5. (a) Reference image, (b) Direction field image

4.3 Number and Size

In computer generated stippling, the size and number of points according to the source image greatly influences the output image. Especially in color-based stippling, the appropriate number and size of points have to be decided in order to clearly represent all the colors and outlines of the image. After deciding the minimum size of the point, we compute the number of points necessary for the image, using importance value I_h defined in sub-section 3.1.

First, the minimum size of the oval point as in Fig. 4 (b) is decided. Then, the number of points necessary for representing the reference image is computed as follows:

$$S_{p\min} = r_{x\min} \cdot r_{y\min} \cdot \pi,$$

$$N_p = \int_0^{height} \int_0^{width} \frac{1}{S_{p\min} \cdot (1 + \alpha \cdot I_h(x,y))} dxdy \qquad (8)$$

where S_{pmin} and N_p are the minimum area of points and the number of points, respectively. α is the amplification factor of the point size according to I_h of the reference image, and $\alpha = 1$ in the proposed method because it is proper that the maximum size of points is twice the minimum size of points in changing sizes of points [3].

After deciding the number of necessary points, points are distributed as in subsection 3.2, and the point size $S_p(x,y)$ is computed by Eq. (9) according to the reference image.

$$S_p(x,y) = S_{p\min} \cdot (1 + \alpha \cdot I_h(x,y)) \qquad (9)$$

Finally, we compute the size of the point by using $S_p=1.2\times S_p$ to minimize an empty space among points and to effectively represent the colored areas in the image. Overlapping by this enables points to fully cover the colored areas, and generate an effective representation.

5 Results

The color image of 24bit bitmap file format was used as the source image for testing color-based stippling. The experiment was performed under system environment composed of Pentium 4 2.53GHz CPU, 512MB RAM, and nVidia GeForce 2 Ti 64MB graphic card. The stippling should use a real number framing for the random and even distribution of points, and we programmed application using OpenGL library based on a real number framing.

In the experiment of distributing the equal number of points in the equal-sized areas (600×600) to compare the processing times of CVD with PIS used in distributing points, Table 1 shows the processing time by PIS improved to be near real-time. The processing time of PIS is about 15,000 times faster than that of CVD.

Table 1. The processing time comparison between CVD and PIS (Fig. 6)

Method	Number of points	Processing time (sec.)
CVD	4188	2145.43
PIS	4188	0.14

When points were distributed by PIS, a pattern was generated which was not seen in the method of using CVD of (a) as in figure 6 (b). However, this pattern can be removed by applying the weighted PIS with the color density and overlapping oval points in color-based stippling.

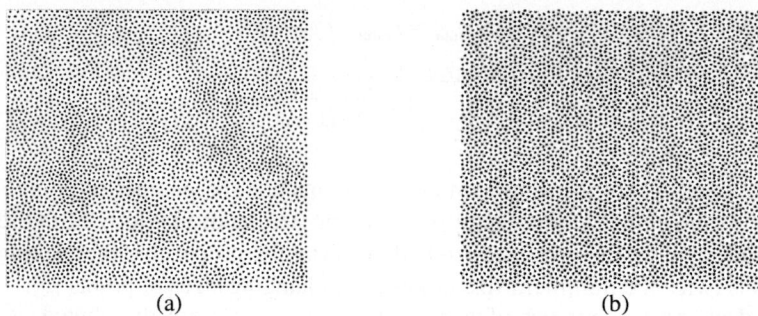

Fig. 6. The result of points distribution comparison between (a) CVD with (b) PIS

Table 2 shows the result of comparing the case (B) in which each image is automatically and accordingly controlled by Eq. (2) and (3), with the case (A) in which each one is not. The desired number of points and the number of distributed points greatly varied depending on images. In the results our method can generate the desired number of points with the margin of error being 1%.

Table 2. The comparing the number of points by *mag* (Fig. 7)

Image	N_{input}	N_{output} (error ratio, %)			
		Case A		Case B	
White Image	1,888	932	(50.6)	1,899	(0.6)
Black Image	7,407	18,963	(156.0)	7,395	(0.2)
Color Image 1	11,588	12,517	(8.0)	11,547	(0.4)
Color Image 2	10,643	19,800	(86.0)	10,639	(0.03)

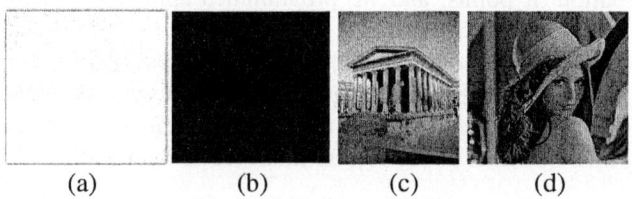

(a)   (b)   (c)   (d)

Fig. 7. The source image for comparing the number of points by *mag*; (a) White image (252 gray level), (b) Black image, (c) Color image 1, (d) Color image 2

Fig. 8 shows the result of comparing the case in which oval points are given orientations and edge is reflected (b) and the case in which circular points are used and edge is not reflected (a). The former shows more clear outlines of objects and more artistic representation in which strokes of brush are well described.

Fig. 9 presents the result of changing the minimum size of points. The result showed that the number of necessary points was automatically computed only by the input of the minimum size. Therefore, it is effective to decide the minimum size according to the size of the image. It is difficult to see the outlines of the image clearly

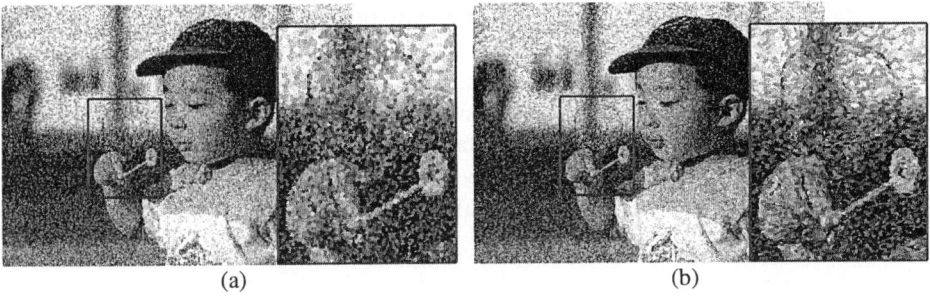

Fig. 8. The result of comparing the circular points with the oval-shaped points (*kid*, 1024×768 size); (a) Using the circular points and no edge (S_{pmin}=1.50×1.50 π), (b) Using the oval-shaped points and edge (S_{pmin}=2.40×0.96 π)

Fig. 9. The result of changing the size of points (*window*, 800×600 size); (a) N_p=87,819, S_{pmin}=1.50×0.90 π, t=3.75 sec, (b) N_p=27,164, S_{pmin}=2.70×1.62 π, t=2.34 sec, (c) N_p=8,552, S_{pmin}=4.80×2.88 π, t=1.93 sec

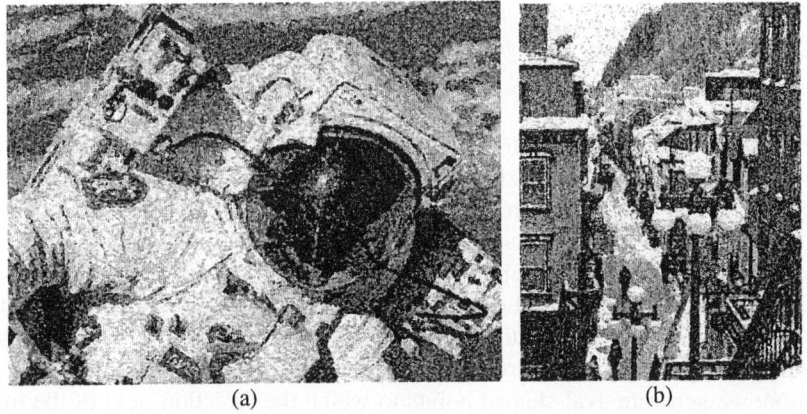

Fig. 10. The rendered color stippling works of various images; (a) *space*, 1024×794 size (N_p=45,293, S_{pmin}=2.40×1.44 π, t=4.21 sec), (b) *street*, 600×800 size (N_p=51,527, S_{pmin}=1.80×1.08 π, t=3.30 sec)

when the point size is too large in spite of its artistic effect. Meanwhile, the stippling effect lessens when the size of point is too small, though it shows the outlines clearly.

Fig. 10 and 11 depicts the rendered stippling works of various images such as people, objects, and landscape. These results show that the method is applicable to most color images, enabling the representation similar to the stippling works of neo-impressionists within a few seconds. Especially, Fig. 11 shows the result of changing the point shape. They are the oval-shaped points (a) and the line-shaped points (b).

(a)   (b)

Fig. 11. The result of changing the shape of points (*people*1, 600×800); (a) N_p=54,410, S_{pmin}=1.80×1.08 π , t=3.33 sec, (b) N_p=40,735, S_{pmin}=3.60×0.72 π , t=2.53 sec.

6 Conclusion

This paper has presented a new stippling technique for representation similar to the traditional stippling arts. We introduced a color density function and a color jittering which are defined by analyzing the color information from the HSV model of the source image. The color density function was used for computing the number, size, and position of the points according to the color distribution in the image, and the color jittering was used to represent the color points similar to the ones in artistic stippling works. Our method guarantees very speedy processing time by distributing points with PIS. In the stippling, the points have generally oval-like shape since they are generated with artist's brush stroke. In order to more artistic representation, we generate oval-shaped points to which the direction field of the image was given. The proposed color-based stippling is expected to be applied to many areas such as animation, interactive digital art and video processing. In the future works, we will make further consideration including artist's drawing process and real-time visualization.

Acknowledgments

This research was supported by the Ministry of Education, Korea, and under the BK21 project.

References

1. O. Deussen, S. Hiller, K. van Overveld, T. Strothotte, "Floating Points: A Method for Computing Stipple Drawings", *Proc. of Eurographics 2000* (2000) 40-51
2. Q. Du, V. Faber, M. Gunzburger, "Centroidal Voronoi Tessellations", *Siam Review*, vol. 41 (1999) 637-676
3. A. Secord, "Weighted Voronoi Stippling", *Proc. of 2nd International Symposium on Non-Realistic Animation and Rendering* (2002) 37-43
4. S. Hiller, H. Hellwig, O. Deussen, "Beyond Stippling: Method for Distributing Objects on The Plane", *Proc. of Eurographics 2003*, vol. 22 (2003) 515-522
5. A. Lu, C. Morris, D. Ebert, P. Rheingans, P. Hansen, "Non-Photorealistic Volume Rendering using Stippling Techniques", *Proc. of IEEE Visualization 2002* (2002) 211-218
6. A. Lu, C. Morris, J. Taylor, D. Ebert, C. Hansen, P. Rheingans, M. Hartner, "Illustrative Interactive Stipple Rendering", *IEEE Transactions on Visualization and Computer Graphics*, vol. 9 (2003) 127-138
7. V. Ostromoukhov, C. Donohue, P. Jodoin, "Fast Hierarchical Importance Sampling with Blue Noise Properties", *Proc. of SIGGRAPH 2004* (2004) 488-495
8. M. Schapiro, *Modern Art: Nineteenth and Twentieth Centuries*, George Braziller (1982)
9. A. Distel, *Georges Seurat (1859-1891)*, Metropolitan Museum of Art (1991)
10. R. Crane, *A Simplified Approach to Image Processing: Classical and Modern Techniques in C*, Prentice Hall PTR (1996)
11. R.C. Gonzalez, R. E. Woods, *Digital Image Processing 2nd edition*, Prentice Hall (2002)
12. M. Schwarz, W. Cowan, J. Beatty, "An Experimental comparison of RGB, YIQ, LAB, HSV, and Opponent Color Models", *ACM Transactions on Graphics*, vol. 6 (1987) 123-158
13. F. A. Baqai, J. H. Lee, A. U. Agar, J. P. Allebach, "Digital Color Halftoning - Problems, Algorithms, and Recent Trends", *IEEE Signal Processing Magazine*, vol. 22 (2005) 87-96
14. A. Glassner, "Andrew Glassner's Notebook: Penrose Tiling", *IEEE Computer Graphics and Applications*, vol. 18 (1998) 78-86
15. J. Canny, "A Computational Approach to Edge Detection", *IEEE Transactions On Pattern Analysis And Machine Inteligence*, vol.PAMI-8 (1986)
16. A. R. Smith, "Color Gamut Transform Pairs", *Proc. of SIGGRAPH 1978*, vol. 12 (1978) 12-19
17. A. H. Munsell, *A Color Notation*, Munsell color company (1939)
18. A. Hertzmann, "Painterly Rendering with Curved Brush Strokes of Multiple Sizes", *Proc. of ACM SIGGRAPH 98* (1998) 453-460
19. A. Hausner, "Simulating Decorative Mosaics", *Proc. of ACM SIGGRAPH 2001*, (2001) 573-580

Photometry Data Coding for Three-Dimensional Mesh Models Using Connectivity and Geometry Information

Young-Suk Yoon[1], Sung-Yeol Kim[2], and Yo-Sung Ho[2]

[1] Electronics and Telecommunications Research Institute (ETRI),
161 Gajeong-dong, Yuseong-gu, Deajeon, 305-350, Korea
ys.yoon@etri.re.kr
[2] Gwangju Institute of Science and Technology (GIST),
1 Oryong-dong, Buk-gu, Gwangju, 500-712, Korea
{sykim75, hoyo}@gist.ac.kr

Abstract. In this paper, we propose new predictive coding schemes for photometry data of three-dimensional (3-D) mesh models as per-vertex binding. We exploit geometry and connectivity information to enhance coding efficiency of the color and normal vector data. For color coding, we predict the color of the current vertex by a weighted sum of colors of adjacent vertices considering angles between the current vertex and the adjacent vertices. For normal vector coding, we generate an optimal plane using distance equalization to predict the normal vector of the current vertex. Experimental results show that the proposed coding schemes provide improved coding performance over previous works for various 3-D mesh models.

Keywords: Color coding, normal vector coding, photometry coding, 3-D mesh compression.

1 Introduction

As applications of three-dimensional (3-D) computer graphics become more popular, we handle a large number of 3-D objects that are created by many digital contents providers. In order to keep and deliver 3-D objects more efficiently in the multimedia processing system being able to include digital contents distribution structure [1], we need to compress 3-D objects to reduce the number of bits for storage and transmission.

The 3-D mesh model is one of the standard methods to represent 3-D objects, where the 3-D surface is covered by polygons. In general, a 3-D mesh model can be constructed by combining three major information: connectivity, geometry, and photometry data [2]. While geometry data specify vertex locations in the 3-D space, connectivity data describe the incidence relationship among vertices. Photometry data, which are colors, surface normal vectors, and texture coordinates, are required to paint and shade 3-D mesh models. In this paper, we focus on photometry data coding of the 3-D mesh model as per-vertex binding.

Bajaj et al. [3] developed a 3-D mesh compression method for the photometry information using vertices and triangle layers. They employed a second-order predictor to compress geometry information and color data. In order to predict the normal vector of current vertex, they calculated the average of normal vectors for incident faces. However, they did not exploit the coded information for the photometry data coding. Especially, their color coding method was identical to the geometry coding algorithm.

Ahn et al. [4] employed a mapping table for color coding, when the target compression ratio was not high. Otherwise, they adopted the MPEG-4 3-D mesh coding (3DMC) method [2]. However, their method is not suitable for 3-D mesh models of high quality when the number of colors is large. They also developed a compression scheme for normal vectors using the average prediction and the 6-4 subdivision [4]. Although their work produces good results for even meshes, there are some rooms for improvement for uneven meshes.

In this paper, we try to utilize photometry data of adjacent vertices and reflect characteristics of 3-D mesh models. We have proposed new predictors for colors and normal vectors using geometry and connectivity information of the 3-D mesh model. This paper is organized as follows. At first, we talk about several types of vertex in Section 2. Section 3 explains our proposed color coding scheme, and Section 4 describes the proposed normal vector coding method. After providing experimental results in Section 5, we conclude in Section 6.

2 Vertex Classification

In order to explain the proposed coding schemes for photometry data, we need to define a current vertex (CV), a previous vertex (PV), a nearest vertex (NV), and adjacent vertices (AVs) [5]. CV is a vertex to be coded directly along the order of vertex traversal, but PV is a vertex which have already coded. NV is closest to CV, and AVs are the set of vertices connected to CV.

In general, previous works employed only the PV to predict the photometry data of CV. However, since either NV or AVs have very similar photometry data for CV, it is inefficient to use only the PV as the photometry data coding. When we examined the case that the photometry data of NV was analogous to those of AV, the probability was about 99%. Also, the probability was approximately 18% when a vertex that was both one of AVs and PVs contained the same photometry data as CV. Moreover, the probability was around 82% while CV possessed the similar photometry data to not PV but one of AVs. With considering the simple tests mentioned above, we can conclude that we should consider the photometry data of AVs as well as PV as the photometry data coding.

3 Color Coding

3.1 Color Coder

Since angles between CV and AVs influence on the color data of CV, we can develop an angle prediction method for color coding of the 3-D mesh model.

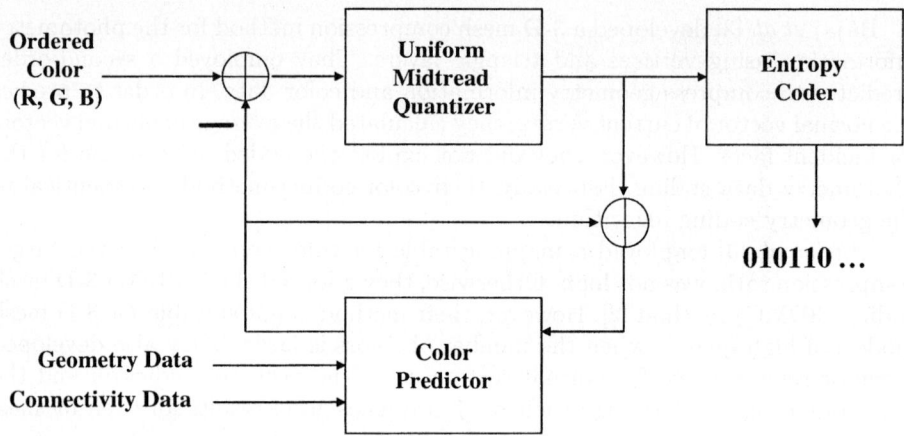

Fig. 1. Block diagram of the proposed color encoder

Figure 1 shows the block diagram of the proposed color coder. First, we use a color predictor characterized by the angle prediction to calculate the predicted color. Then, the difference between the original and the predicted colors goes into the an uniform midtread quantizer. Finally, the quantized residual error is coded by the entropy coder.

In the proposed color coder, we predict the color of CV by a weighted sum of colors of AVs, i.e.,

$$color_p(CV) = \sum_{i=1}^{n(AVs)} w_i \times color(AVs_i) \qquad (1)$$

where $color_p(CV)$ is the predicted color of CV, $n(AVs)$ represents the number of AVs, w_i depicts the weighting factor of the ith vertex of AVs, and $color(AVs_i)$ denotes the reconstructed color of the ith vertex of AVs. In Eq. 1, the sum of the weighting factors should be equal to 1.

$$\sum_i^{n(AVs)} w_i = 1 \qquad (2)$$

3.2 Angle Prediction

Most image compression algorithms are based on the inspection that for any randomly chosen pixel in the 2-D image, its near neighboring pixels tend to have the very similar value to the pixel. A context-based image compression technique universalize this inspection. It is founded by the intuition that the context of a pixel can be used to estimate the probability of the pixel. Thus the context-based coding technique which is generally used in image compression supports very good coding performance. It predicts a pixel value exploiting coded values of

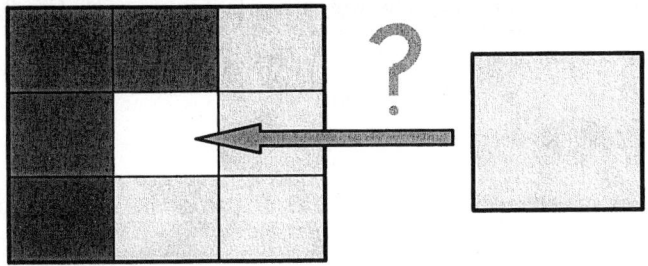

Fig. 2. Simple example of context-based coding method

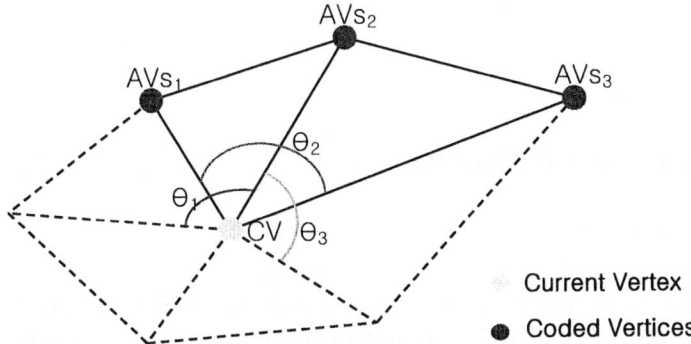

Fig. 3. Example of angle prediction

neighboring pixels [6][7][8]. Figure 2 depicts the uncomplicated case of context-based coding technique which reckons coding pixel value as the most occurring coded value of adjacent pixels.

We should consider two essential respects for employing traditional context-based coding technique in the 2-D space as compressing 3-D mesh models. First, vertices of a 3-D mesh model exist any place on the 3-D space, unlike pixels of 2-D image. Second, pixels always have eight neighboring pixels except for boundary pixels but vertices do not possess the fixed number of AVs. Moreover the mesh topology is so various. Hence, it is very difficult to find the context for color coding from AVs in the 3-D space. In this paper, considering angles between CV and AVs, we can predict the color value of CV by a weighted sum of colors of AVs. This is called an *angle prediction*:

$$color_p(CV) \propto \theta_i \tag{3}$$

where we define θ_i as the sum of angles affected by the color data of AVs_i.

Figure 3 illustrates an example of the angle prediction. CV is the current vertex and AVs_i is one of AVs. As shown in Fig. 3, we can represent θ_i as

$$\theta_i = \angle AVs_{(i-1)\%n(AVs)}CVAVs_i + \angle AVs_iCVAVs_{(i+1)\%n(AVs)} \tag{4}$$

where % denote the modulo operation.

First of all, we can produce the weighting factor w_i with Eq. 2, Eq. 3, and Eq. 4:

$$w_i = \frac{\theta_i}{\sum_{j=1}^{n(AVs)} \theta_j}. \tag{5}$$

Finally, we can predict the color data of CV using the angle prediction from Eq. 1 and Eq. 5:

$$color_p(CV) = \frac{\sum_{i=1}^{n(AVs)} \theta_i \times color(AVs_i)}{\sum_{j=1}^{n(AVs)} \theta_j}. \tag{6}$$

4 Normal Vector Coding

4.1 Normal Vector Encoder

Since previous works [2][3][4] do not consider the normal vector of the opposite side and simply use the normal vectors of non-AVs which are not highly correlated with CV, they fail to obtain a good prediction of the original normal vector. However, our proposed scheme for normal vector coding exploits all the available geometry and connectivity information of the 3-D mesh model. The main idea of our normal vector coding scheme is to generate an optimal plane using distance equalization for normal vector prediction [5].

Figure 4 shows the block diagram of the normal vector coder with an normal vector predictor. Then, we transform the Cartesian coordinate system into the

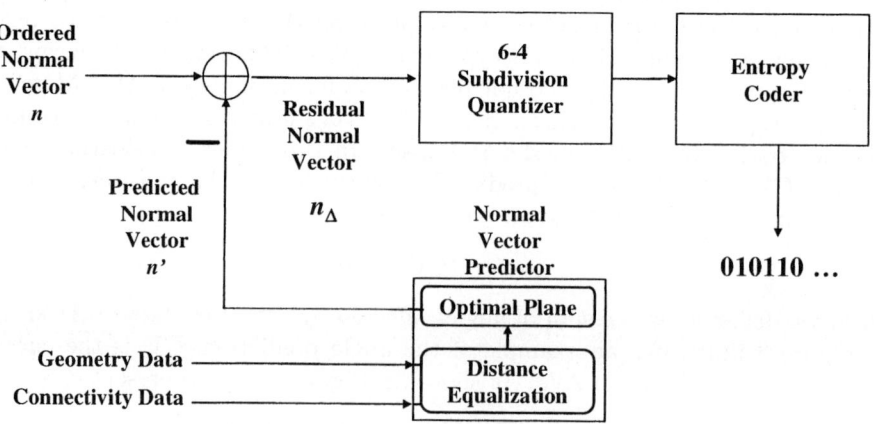

Fig. 4. Block diagram of the proposed normal vector encoder

spherical coordinate system with the unit radius, we can obtain the predicted normal vector and the residual normal vector. Then, we use the 6-4 subdivision quantizer to quantize the residual normal vector and encode the quantizer index by the QM coder [4].

4.2 Optimal Plane Using Distance Equalization

Optimal Plane. In order to predict the normal vector of CV, we generate an optimal plane with the minimum square error from AVs. The optimal plane for CV is obtained from AVs using the least squares approximation (LSA) method [9].

Figure 5 describes the generation of the optimal plane for CV. Figure 5(a) represents the plane view of optimal plane and Figure 5(b) depicts the side view of optimal plane. As shown in Fig. 5, the optimal plane of CV may not include the all of the AVs for CV.

When the optimal plane has the shortest average distance from AVs, the equation of the optimal plane can be expressed by

$$ax + by + cz + d = 0 \tag{7}$$

where the normal vector of the optimal plane, $\boldsymbol{n}_{op} = (a, b, c)$ and $\|\boldsymbol{n}_{op}\| = 1$. If $a \neq 0$, Eq. 7 can be rewritten as

$$\frac{b}{a}y + \frac{c}{a}z + \frac{d}{a} = -x, a \neq 0. \tag{8}$$

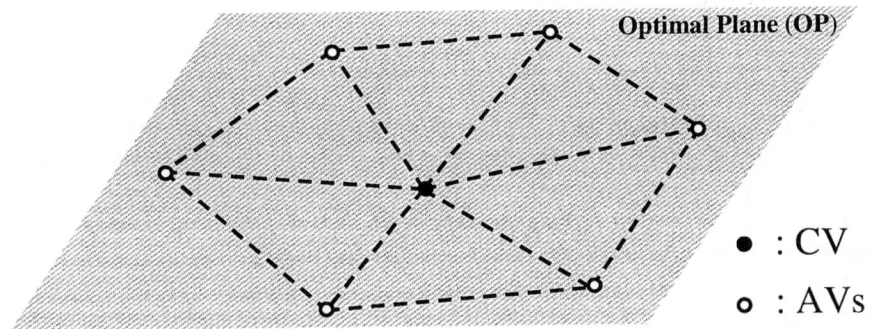

(a) Plane view of optimal plane

(b) Lateral view of optimal plane

Fig. 5. Optimal plane

Moreover, the coordinate of the ith AV can be represented by (x_i, y_i, z_i). We can write down the equations which would hold if the optimal plane could go through all AVs:

$$\begin{bmatrix} 1 & y_1 & z_1 \\ \vdots & \vdots & \vdots \\ 1 & y_{n(AVs)} & z_{n(AVs)} \end{bmatrix} \begin{bmatrix} \dfrac{d}{a} \\ \dfrac{b}{a} \\ \dfrac{c}{a} \end{bmatrix} = \begin{bmatrix} x_1 \\ \vdots \\ x_{n(AVs)} \end{bmatrix} \wedge Ax = b \qquad (9)$$

When Eq. 9 has a solution, there would be no minimum square error and AVs would be on the optimal plane. However, since the number of AVs is generally greater than 3, the matrix A is $n(AVs) \times 3$ and we can obtain $\boldsymbol{n}_{op}$ by the least squares approximation.

Let $\bar{x}$ be a solution to Eq. 9; thus $A\bar{x}$ is the closest point to b. In this case, the difference $A\bar{x} - b$ must be a vector orthogonal to the column space of A. This means that $A\bar{x} - b$ is perpendicular to each of the columns of A, and hence $A^T(A\bar{x} - b) = 0$. Multiplying and separating terms gives an equation

$$A^T A \bar{x} = A^T b. \qquad (10)$$

Although A is not of full rank, this set of equations should have a solution, since both the columns of A are linearly independent and $A^T b$ lies in the column space of $A^T A$. The matrix $A^T A$ is invertible, and so $\bar{x}$ may be found by

$$\bar{x} = (A^T A)^{-1} A^T b. \qquad (11)$$

Thus we can obtain $\boldsymbol{n}_{op}$ with Eq. 11 and $\|\boldsymbol{n}_{op}\| = 1$.

Distance Equalization. If a 3-D mesh model is regular and even, the optimal plane provides a good prediction for the normal vector. However, there are some rooms for improvement in other cases. In order to obtain a better prediction for the normal vector, we propose a distance equalization technique that adjusts the distance between CV and each of the AVs be the same.

Figure 6 describes the difference between the method adopting only the optimal plane and the approach employing optimal plane applied to distance equalization technique. Figure 6(a) shows a simple example of the 3-D mesh model that has similar dihedral angles, i.e., $\theta_i \cong \theta_j$. As a result, the predicted normal vector of CV is equal to the normal vector of the optimal plane. Figure 6(b) illustrates a general case having different dihedral angles, i.e., $\theta_i \neq \theta_j$. In this case, we have an error when substituting the normal vector of CV by the normal vector of the optimal plane. We apply the distance equalization to AVs to reduce the prediction error of the normal vector of CV. With distance equalization, we obtain very similar dihedral angles, i.e., $\theta'_i \cong \theta'_j$. Since distance equalization is intrinsic to the characteristics of an isosceles triangle, we can obtain accurate predicted normal vectors.

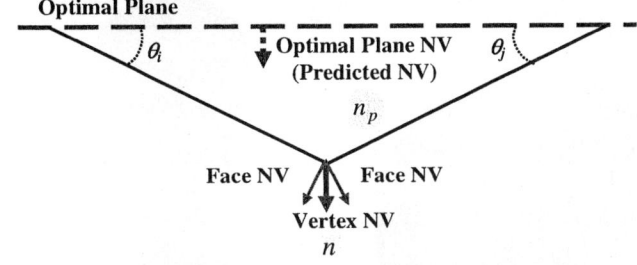

(a) Normal vector of the optimal plane

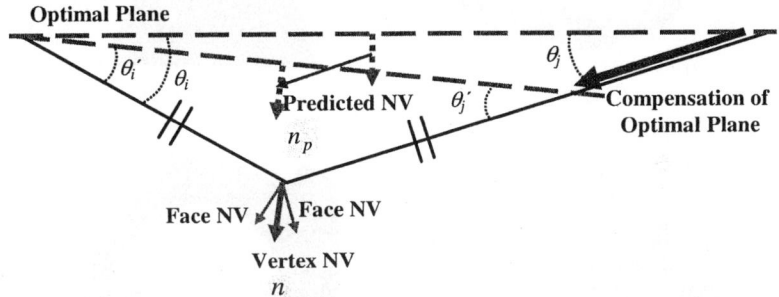

(b) Normal vector of the optimal plane using distance equalization

Fig. 6. Distance equalization

5 Experimental Results

In order to evaluate the performance of the proposed methods, we compare experimental results of the our schemes with those of the existing algorithms.

5.1 Results of Color Coding

Figure 7 shows 3-D mesh models used for performance evaluation of color coding. Table 1 lists properties of test models for color coding. We define that $n(F)$ be the number of the set of faces F, $n(C)$ denotes the number of the set of colors C, and $n'(C)$ indicates the number of the colors without duplication. Since we employ a coding scheme for color data as per-vertex binding, $n(V)$ is equal to $n(C)$.

Table 1. Test models for color coding

	GLOBE	NERFERTITI	SPHERE	TAL
$n(V)$	36,866	10,013	41,369	30,737
$n(F)$	73,728	20,022	82,734	61,470
$n(C)$	36,866	10,013	41,369	30,737
$n'(C)$	5,562	7,943	337	8,412

Fig. 7. Test models with color data

Table 2. Performance comparison of color coding

	GLOBE	NEFERTITI	SPHERE	TAL
MPEG-4 3DMC	9.80	15.63	18.98	14.09
Angle Prediction	9.79	14.21	17.83	13.18

In Table 2, we compare coding performances of the proposed algorithm with those of the MPEG-4 3DMC algorithm [2] when they have the similar color distortion. The coding performances represent compressed sizes for color data of 3-D test models when the quantization level is 24 bits per color (bpc). As shown in Table 2, the proposed scheme outperforms the MPEG-4 3DMC algorithm. Hence, we note that the proposed angle prediction is efficient for color coding.

5.2 Results of Normal Vector Coding

Figure 8 shows 3-D mesh models used for comparison on coding efficiency of normal vector. In this simulation, we included the 'CROCODILE' and 'HORSE' models instead of using the 'GLOBE' and 'NEFERTITI' models so as to check the coding performance with respect to uneven mesh models.

Table 3 shows properties of test models for normal vector coding. We define $n(N)$ as the number of normal vectors N. Owing to per-vertex binding, $n(V)$ is equal to $n(C)$. Furthermore, the amount of uncompressed normal vectors is equal to the amount of uncompressed colors and the amount of uncompressed geometry information.

A proper measure for distance between two normal vectors is the angular distortion that is defined by

$$d_{normal} = \frac{1}{n(V)} \sum_{i=1}^{n(V)} \arccos(n_i \cdot n'_i) \qquad (12)$$

where n_i and n'_i represent the source and reconstructed normal vectors of the ith vertex, respectively.

Table 4 compares coding performances of the proposed scheme employing the optimal plane using distance equalization to previous works when the quantization level is 15 bits per normal vector. From Table 4, we can conclude that the proposed scheme produces less angular distortion than the existing algorithms.

(a) CROCODILE (b) HORSE

Fig. 8. Test models with normal vector data

Table 3. Test models for normal vector coding

	CROCODILE	HORSE	SPHERE	TAL
$n(V)$	17,332	19,851	41,369	30,737
$n(F)$	34,404	39,698	82,734	61,470
$n(N)$	17,332	19,851	41,369	30,737

Table 4. Comparison of coding efficiency for normal vectors

	CROCODILE	HORSE	SPHERE	TAL
MPEG-4 3DMC	0.88	0.36	0.05	0.26
Average Prediction	0.82	0.30	0.03	0.24
Proposed scheme	0.38	0.06	0.004	0.06

Thus, the proposed scheme employing the optimal plane using distance equalization contributes to efficient coding of normal vectors for uneven mesh models as well as even mesh models.

6 Conclusions

In this paper, we have proposed new coding schemes of photometry data using geometry and connectivity information of the 3-D mesh model. With considering the spatial correlation among those information, we can develop improved predictive coding schemes for colors and normal vectors. For color coding, we have developed a new prediction algorithm for the color of the current vertex by considering the angles between the current vertex and adjacent vertices. For normal vector coding, we proposed to form an optimal plane using distance equalization. Experimental results have demonstrated that the proposed coding methods outperform previous works for various test models.

Acknowledgements. This work was supported in part by Electronics and Telecommunications Research Institute (ETRI), in part by the Ministry of Information and Communication (MIC) through the Realistic Broadcasting Research Center (RBRC) at Gwangju Institute of Science and Technology (GIST), and in part by the Ministry of Education (MOE) through the Brain Korea 21 (BK21) project.

References

1. Lee, J.S., Hwang, S.O., Jeong, S.W., Yoon, K.S., Park, C.S., and Ryou, J.C. : A DRM Framework for Distributing Digital Contents through the Internet. ETRI Journal (2003) 423-436
2. ISO/IEC JTC1/SC29/WG11 MPEG/M3325 : Description of core experiments on 3D model coding (1998)
3. Bajaj, V., Pascucci, V., and Zhuang, G. : Single Resolution Compression of Arbitrary Triangular Meshes with Properties. Proceedings of the Data Compression Conference (1999) 167-186
4. Ahn, J.H., Kim, C.S., and Ho, Y.S. : An Efficient Coding Algorithm for Color and Normal Data of Three-dimensional Mesh Models. Proceedings of International Conference on Image Processing (2003) 789-792

5. Yoon, Y.S., Kim, S.Y., and Ho, Y.S. : Predictive Coding of Photometry Information of Three-dimensional Meshes Using Geometry and Connectivity Information. Proceedings of International Workshop on Advanced Image Technology (2005) 7-12
6. Sayood, K. : Introduction of Data Compression, Morgan Kaufmann (2000)
7. Salomon, D. : Data Compression : The Complete Reference. Springer Verlag (2004)
8. Jain, A.K. : Fundamentals of Digital Image Processing. Prentice-Hall (1989)
9. Strang, G. : Linear Algebra and Its Applications. Tomson Learning (1986)

Adaptation of MPEG-4 BIFS Scenes into MPEG-4 LASeR Scenes in MPEG-21 DIA Framework

Qonita M. Shahab and Munchurl Kim

Laboratory for Multimedia Computing, Communications and Broadcasting,
Information and Communications University,
119 Munji-ro, Yuseong-gu, Daejeon 305-732, Korea
{niet, mkim}@icu.ac.kr

Abstract. Description and adaptation of digital items can be performed in either binary levels or metadata levels, which are the abilities of MPEG-21 Digital Item Adaptation (DIA) tools. BIFS and LASeR are parts of MPEG-4 standard for describing multimedia scenes, which can be written in XML format and then be encoded into binary format for the consumption of MPEG-4 terminals. BIFS is a stable standard, but LASeR is an emerging standard that is newly developed for lightweight applications in constrained terminals. We present a method for automatic adaptation of scenes constructed on BIFS into those constructed on LASeR. We focus on automatic adaptation of real objects' sizes and other conversion rules by employing MPEG-21 DIA tools. The motivation of this paper is to enable a real-time transcoding from BIFS to LASeR so that MPEG-4 content authors can distribute their existing contents to mobile devices without the need of reauthoring according to the new standard, LASeR.

1 Introduction

A scene description is constituted of text, graphics, animation, and interactivity with information about spatial and temporal layouts. In MPEG-4 Systems standard, scene description is used to incorporate media (such as images, videos, audios, font data etc) into a multimedia presentation. Multimedia content authors employ scene description schemes in order to create multimedia presentations to be sent to consumer devices. At certain times, they may need to reproduce multimedia presentations for different devices. A multimedia presentation originally made for high-powered devices should be easily reproduced into a format suitable for low-powered devices. This practice enables content authors to distribute their existing contents to low-powered devices such as mobile phones and other mobile or embedded systems.

BIFS (Binary Format for Scene) and LASeR (Lightweight Application Scene Representation) are binary scene description schemes based on textual language. Like BIFS, LASeR is a binary format for encoding scenes and updates of the scenes in MPEG-4 Systems. The main goal of LASeR is to provide a representation of scene data that is well suited for resource-constrained environments, such as mobile devices. Therefore, unlike the complex BIFS, LASeR has only a limited description for representing scenes [1].

According to the current version of the LASeR Requirements Document [3], a lightweight scene representation should allow easy conversion from other graphics formats. Since both BIFS and LASeR represent MPEG-4 multimedia presentation, content authors may want to create one type of contents and then reproduce them for the consumption of mobile devices without the need of reauthoring or learning a new standard. Therefore, the need of an easy conversion from BIFS to LASeR is inevitable.

In an MPEG-4 system, a scene consists of visual and audio components, which are structured hierarchically into a tree of scene nodes [2]. While BIFS nodes are adopted from VRML (Virtual Reality Markup Language) nodes, LASeR nodes are adopted from SVG (Scalable Vector Graphics) nodes. In addition, while BIFS scenes can be either 3D or 2D, LASeR scenes are only 2D due to the way of its rendering process. It is made so, because LASeR is supposed to be lightweight and consumed by resource-constrained devices. Therefore, we considered only 2D BIFS scenes to be converted into LASeR scenes.

MPEG-4 Systems specification [4] defines profiles for terminal capabilities in playing MPEG-4 multimedia files (usually with .mp4 extension). An MPEG-4 terminal may support a profile to which it can render the presentation accordingly. This profile information is not sufficient to provide a full characterization of an end terminal's capabilities and the resources needed for a presentation. In MPEG-21 framework, Digital Item Adaptation (DIA) tools can be used in order to provide a full characterization of an end terminal's capabilities [5]. This is suitable to the aim of MPEG-21 framework, which is "to enable transparent and augmented use of multimedia resources across a wide range of networks and devices" [6]. With the addition of information on user characteristics and network characteristics, adaptation of the BIFS scenes into LASeR scenes can be performed more completely and automatically, so that such a transcoding mechanism of BIFS scenes into LASeR scenes can be performed in real time.

This paper is organized as follows: Section 2 explains the conversion process of BIFS scenes into LASeR scenes; Section 3 explains the MPEG-21 DIA in order to show the tools and describes the details of the adaptation rules; Section 4 describes the system implementation, and the results are presented in section 5; Finally, Section 6 brings out the conclusion of this research.

2 Conversion of BIFS Scenes into LASeR Scenes

There are several aspects to be noted during the conversion of BIFS scenes into LASeR scenes. The difference between BIFS and LASeR scene descriptions lies in the node tree structures and physical sizes including the sizes of real media objects embedded in the scenes.

2.1 Scene Nodes Mapping

The whole structure of the scene node tree consists of header, body, and commands. Header tells many aspects of the rendering process such as how many elementary streams (ES) pointing to real media objects included in the scene. The body contains the descriptions of how the scene looks like and behaves. The commands contain scene updates information. The mapping procedure for the node is a many-to-one mapping, by the fact that there are a lot more of BIFS nodes than LASeR ones. Also, the mapping procedure is not straightforward. Summary of the nodes mapping can be seen in Table 1.

Table 1. Summary of mapping of BIFS nodes into LASeR nodes

BIFS Nodes	LASeR Nodes
Geometry nodes such as `Rectangle`, `Curve2D` together with their parent `Shape` node and `Appearance` attribute node	Geometry nodes such as `svg:rect`, `svg:path`
`Text` and `FontStyle` nodes	`svg:text` and `svg:tspan` nodes
Hyperlinking nodes such as `Anchor` and `Inline`	`svg:a` and `svg:foreignObject` nodes
Grouping nodes such as `Transform2D`	`svg:g` node
Top level nodes such as `OrderedGroup` and `Layer2D`	`svg:svg` node
`WorldInfo` node	`svg:desc` and `svg:title` nodes
`ImageTexture` and `PixelTexture` nodes, and `MovieTexture` nodes	`svg:image` and `svg:video` nodes
`Interpolator` type nodes and `Routes` combined with `TimeSensor` nodes	`svg:animate` type nodes
Only `TouchSensor` nodes among the `Sensor` type nodes	`lsr:trigger` node
`Conditional` node	`lsr:script` node
Only `AudioClip` and `AudioSource` among the `Audio` nodes	`svg:audio` nodes
`Switch` node	`svg:g` node with `choice` attribute
`Valuator` node	unmapped (no counterpart nodes)
`PointSet2D`, `CompositeTexture2D`, and `TextureCoordinate` nodes	unmapped (no counterpart nodes)
`TermCap` and `QuantizationParameter`	unmapped (not applicable)

2.2 Physical Mapping

Scaling and translation of origin coordinates are to be carefully considered in mapping BIFS to LASeR scenes. The BIFS coordinate system has the x-axis positive to the right and y-axis positive to the top of the scene, while the LASeR coordinate system has the same x-axis rule but y-axis positive to the bottom of the scene. Moreover, the BIFS origin coordinate starts from the center of the scene, while the LASeR origin coordinate starts from the top-left of the scene.

Scaling is also applied to the whole scene sizes. While a high-powered device playing BIFS scenes can display objects of large sizes in spatial resolution, a low-powered device can only display objects of small sizes according to its screen size limit.

The scaling attribute is according to the ratio of LASeR scene to the original BIFS scene. Translation is needed to interpret all BIFS geometrical description correctly into LASeR one. This includes motion paths, polygon coordinates, and any other things involved in geometry transformations and object animations.

A scene may also contain real audiovisual objects such as images, audios, and videos which are transported through ES. While high-powered devices can present audiovisual objects of high quality to users, low-powered devices can only present low quality audiovisual objects due to its limited computing capability, storage and memory. Therefore, an object transcoder is needed for converting real objects of large spatial and/or temporal resolutions into lower quality ones.

3 The Adaptation in the MPEG-21 Framework

The multimedia content delivery value chain includes creation, transaction, delivery and consumption of digital items. Based on this fact, MPEG-21 multimedia framework aims at universally accessible and uniquely consumable environment for multimedia under various conditions. MPEG-21 provides such a framework to include all the members of a multimedia content delivery value chain. In the framework, there is no difference between multimedia creators and consumers or any other members of the value chain. Any entity that makes use or interacts with a Digital Item (DI) is called User.

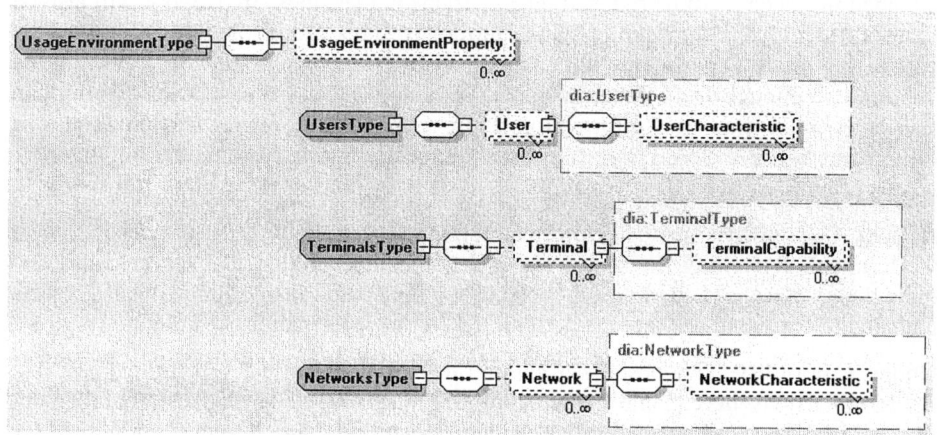

Fig. 1. The XML Schema of Usage Environment Tools

In order to provide such an integrated multimedia framework between al related Users, MPEG-21 defines a set of normative specifications divided into 17 parts. The Part 7 of MPEG-21 Multimedia Framework, called MPEG-21 DIA, specifies the syntax and semantics of defined tools needed for universally accessible and uniquely consumable multimedia environments. The DIA tools enable various ways of adapting multimedia contents [5], whether it is in binary level or metadata level.

The DIA tools are described in structured textual or binary XML files. These XML files can be used as an input to a transcoding process by the MPEG-21 DIA engine.

This means that the DIA descriptors (XML) are transferred to related parties during the delivery and usage of the MPEG-4 scenes. Since BIFS and LASeR are both metadata, the DIA Engine [5] performs adaptation on the metadata contained in the scene description schemes.

The DIA tools are employed for adapting the DI according to the environment during the delivery and usage of the DI. Therefore, Usage Environment Description tools are employed for the purpose of transcoding BIFS scenes into LASeR scenes. They include the descriptions for the user characteristics, terminal capabilities, network characteristics and natural characteristics, as showed in Fig. 1.

3.1 Adaptation Based on Terminal Capability

Terminal Capabilities include various descriptors for describing many aspects related to terminals, such as device class, codec capabilities, screen resolution, available storage, available memory, CPU power, etc. In the following, the choice of descriptors included in our implementation is explained. We used a set of descriptors to give information about Codec Capability, Display, and Device Class of the terminal.

Device Class. This descriptor can tell the server about what kind of terminal is going to consume the resource about to be sent by the server. By telling the server about the device class, first of all, the server can decide which scene (BIFS or LASeR?) should be sent to terminal. Then between PDA and Mobile Phone device class, the server can decide on various aspects. If the terminal is a PDA, frame rate of any video objects included in a scene will be reduced into 24 frame per seconds (fps), and it will also be reduced into 15 fps for Mobile Phone terminals. This reduction rule is decided by conducting some experiments with human vision, whether a specific frame rate is comfortable enough for a specific spatial resolution. The use of LASeR profile can also be decided using this information. PDA terminals can render LASeR scenes of full profile, while Mobile Phone terminals are mostly restricted to render only LASeR scenes of mini profile.

Display Capability. This descriptor can tell the server about the screen resolution of the terminal. By telling the server about the screen resolution, the server can determine the resolution of the LASeR scene. Then the spatial resolution of visual objects included in the scene can then be determined by this information.

Codec Capability. This descriptor can tell the server about the specific formats that the terminal may be capable of decoding and encoding. The Codec Capability descriptor includes Audio Capabilities, Video Capabilities, and Image Capabilities. By telling the server about the decoding codec capability, the server can determine the new format of real media objects possible to be rendered by the terminal.

Codec Capability Extension. The Codec Capability descriptors are only limited to describing the media codec available in the terminal. A set of descriptors for describing terminal capability of rendering specific file formats is also needed, because the Codec Capability is not complete enough for representing various types of codec embodied in each file formats. The File Format descriptors can be used as a complement or supplement to the Codec Capability descriptors. The descriptors for File Format are taken from MPEG-7 technology part 5 (Multimedia Description Schemes) [7].

3.2 Adaptation Based on Network Characteristic

The Network Capability descriptor is used for describing information on the available bandwidth for the server to send MPEG-4 scenes to the requesting client. By telling the server the amount of maximum and average of available bandwidth, the server can convert the bit rate of temporal-dependent media files included in the scene (audio and video) and the size of temporal-independent media files (image) so that all related files sum up to a size appropriate for delivery.

3.3 Adaptation Based on User Characteristic

The Presentation Priority Preference used for describing information on the Modality Priorities descriptor is used for indicating what type of real media files preferred by the user to have the closest quality to the original ones. This descriptor is needed by the server after bandwidth information is received. With the Modality Priorities descriptor, the server can preserve the quality of the most preferred media modality of the user. For example, if a user always wants to hear a good quality audio, then the first priority is given to any audio files included in the MPEG-4 scene. If the bandwidth is limited, the other files such as images and videos will be transcoded into smaller size according to the limit of the bandwidth.

4 Implementation

4.1 The BIFS-to-LASeR Transcoding

We implement a script using XSLT (Extensible Stylesheet Language Transformation) for the purpose of mapping from one XML format (BIFS XMT-A format [2], [4]) into another (LASeR XML format [1]). An XSLT processor is executed in order to read the XSLT file as the input of mapping rules for transforming BIFS textual description into LASeR textual description. A Content Object Transcoder is applied in order to convert real files included in BIFS scenes. This system is called a BIFS-to-LASeR Transcoding Engine as shown in Fig. 2.

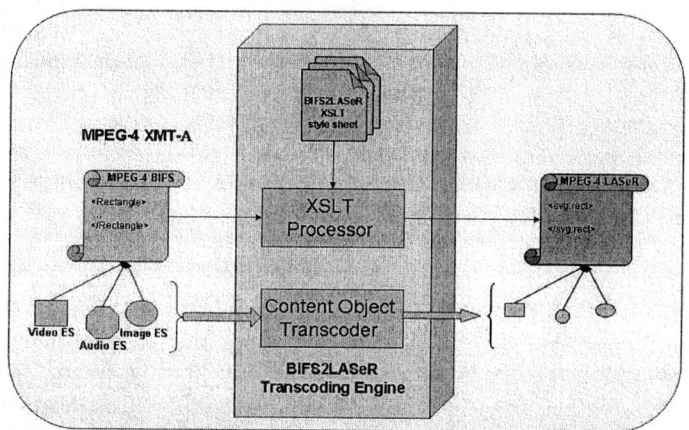

Fig. 2. The BIFS-to-LASeR Transcoding Engine for text to text conversion

We implement a BIFS-to-LASeR Transcoding Engine with the concatenation of a BIFS Decoder [8] and a LASeR Encoder [9] in order to enable the binary to binary conversion. When a mobile client requests a multimedia presentation in MP4 (containing binary BIFS) format, the BIFS Decoder firstly decodes the binary MP4 input into XMT-A (textual BIFS) format. Then, the BIFS-to-LASeR Transcoding Engine converts the XMT-A file into the LASeR XML format and transcodes its associated audiovisual objects accordingly. The LASeR Encoder is then executed in order to create LSR (binary LASeR) file to be sent to the mobile client. The technical details of this implementation are explained in our previous publication [10].

4.2 The MPEG-21 Framework

We include a DIA parser as an engine for processing all information contained in the DIA descriptors both from the server and from clients. The DIA parser then sends information to the XSLT processor and Content Object Transcoder in order to convert the scene description files (XML files) and transcoding the related audiovisual objects.

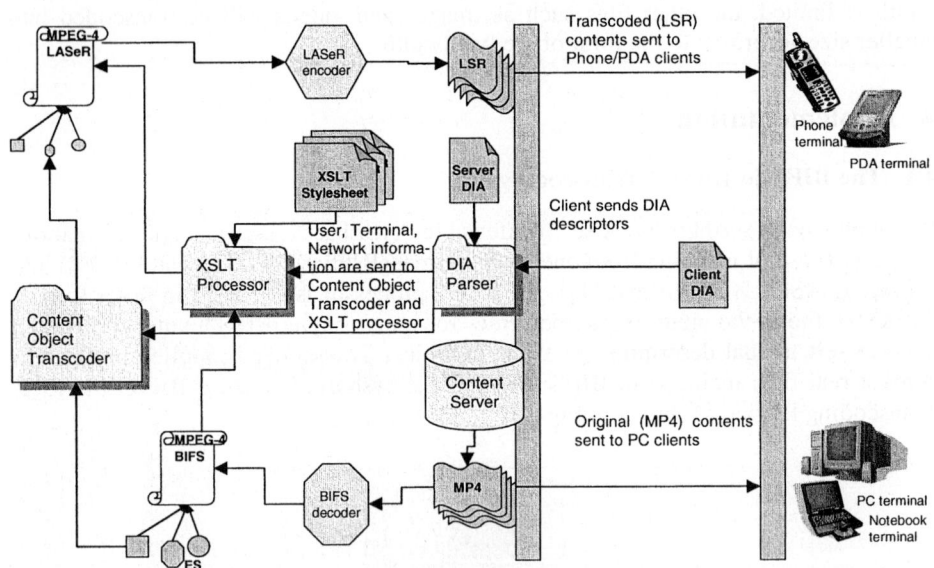

Fig. 3. Request, transcoding, and delivery of MPEG-4 Scenes over MPEG-21 Framework

As shown in Fig. 3, at first a client sends a request to the server for delivering an MPEG-4 scene by also sending a file containing DIA descriptors. The default MPEG-4 scenes are written in BIFS and stored in MP4 file format. If the client is a PC or Notebook terminal, then the server will send the original (MP4) files to the client. If the client is a PDA or Mobile Phone, the server will gather all information contained in the DIA descriptors so that the BIFS-to-LASeR Transcoding Engine will be able to convert the XML and the audiovisual media files according to the usage environment. Before calling the BIFS-to-LASeR Transcoding Engine, the server calls the BIFS Decoder so that the MP4 files are converted into XMT files. After the execution of the BIFS-to-LASeR Transcoding Engine, the server then calls the LASeR encoder so that the resulting XML files and adapted media files are encoded into one binary LSR file. Lastly, the server sends the adapted MPEG-4 scene to the client to be consumed.

5 Experimental Results

We present a test case with several visual objects in order to show our results. The first object is a set of JPEG images displayed in small sizes, and the second object is a video display of MPEG-4 visual format with a spatial resolution of 320x240 pixels, bitrate 1177600 bps, and frame rate 30 fps, placed in the middle of the scene.

The test case is a channel browser where a user can view the thumbnail for each program in the channel. The user can click the thumbnail in order to see the corresponding video content. Each thumbnail size is 80x60 pixels. The BIFS version of the scene has a size of 480x360 pixels as shown in Fig. 4. The figure on the left part shows the first display of the scene, and then the user can click on the thumbnail in order to see the video content, as shown by the figure on the right part.

The Device Class information for this test case is a Mobile Phone, as seen in Fig. 5. With this information, the server automatically decides that the MP4 file should be converted into LSR file, and a LASeR Mini Profile is used. The frame rate of the video files is converted into 15 fps.

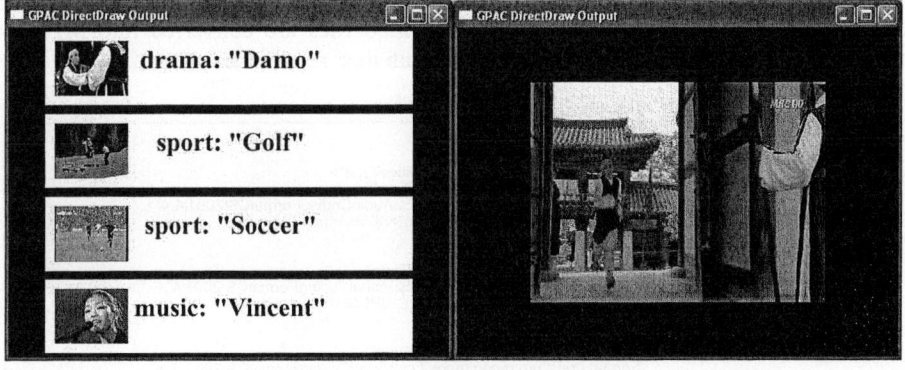

Fig. 4. The playing of binary (MP4) format of the test case on PC application

```
<UsageEnvironmentProperty xsi:type="TerminalsType">
    <Terminal>
        <TerminalCapability xsi:type="DeviceClassType">
            <DeviceClass href="urn:mpeg:mpeg21:2003:01-DIA-DeviceClassCS-NS:5">
                <mpeg7:Name xml:lang="en">Mobile Phone</mpeg7:Name>
            </DeviceClass>
        </TerminalCapability>
    </Terminal>
</UsageEnvironmentProperty>
```

Fig. 5. The Device Class descriptor

The Display Capability information for this test case is a screen resolution of 192x144, as seen in Fig. 6. With this information, the server automatically decides the conversion of spatial resolution of the images in the scene. For the thumbnail images, the spatial resolution is reduced according to a scaling factor of 192/480 = 0.4 and the width and height of the rectangle object. Therefore, the new size of the thumbnail images will be 80*0.4 x 60*0.4 = 32x24 pixels, and the new spatial resolution of the videos will be 320*0.4 x 240*0.4 = 128x96 pixels. We employ third-party image [11] and video [12] transcoding tools for this purpose.

```
<UsageEnvironmentProperty xsi:type="TerminalsType">
    <Terminal>
        <TerminalCapability xsi:type="DisplaysType">
            <Display>
                <DisplayCapability xsi:type="DisplayCapabilityType">
                    <Mode>
                        <Resolution horizontal="192" vertical="144"/>
                    </Mode>
                </DisplayCapability>
            </Display>
        </TerminalCapability>
    </Terminal>
</UsageEnvironmentProperty>
```

Fig. 6. The Display Capability (Resolution) descriptor

The Codec Capability information for this test case is file formats of MP3 for audio, JPEG for images, and MPEG-4 for video. The video file format is further specified as avi file format. The descriptor can be seen in Fig. 7. With this information, any images will be converted into JPEG format. Since the BIFS scene already contains images in JPEG format, no conversion is needed. The video files are converted into MPEG-4 format with avi extension so that the terminal can then render the content.

```
<UsageEnvironmentProperty xsi:type="TerminalsType">
    <Terminal>
        <TerminalCapability xsi:type="CodecCapabilitiesType">
            <Decoding xsi:type="AudioCapabilitiesType">
                <Format href="urn:mpeg:mpeg7:cs:AudioCodingFormatCS:2001:4.4">
                    <mpeg7:Name xml:lang="en">MP3</mpeg7:Name>
                </Format>
            </Decoding>
            <Decoding xsi:type="ImageCapabilitiesType">
                <Format href="urn:mpeg:mpeg7:cs:VisualCodingFormatCS:2001:4">
                    <mpeg7:Name xml:lang="en">JPEG</mpeg7:Name>
                </Format>
            </Decoding>
            <Decoding xsi:type="VideoCapabilitiesType">
                <Format href="urn:mpeg:mpeg7:cs:VisualCodingFormatCS:2001:3">
                    <mpeg7:Name xml:lang="en">MPEG-4 Visual</mpeg7:Name>
                </Format>
                <Format href="urn:mpeg:mpeg7:cs:FileFormatCS:2001:7">
                    <mpeg7:Name xml:lang="en">avi</mpeg7:Name>
                </Format>
            </Decoding>
        </TerminalCapability>
    </Terminal>
</UsageEnvironmentProperty>
```

Fig. 7. The Codec Capabilities descriptor

The bandwidth information of the network can be seen from the Network Condition descriptor in Fig. 8, which shows that the average bandwidth is 256 kbps and the maximum bandwidth is 512 kbps. The modality preference descriptor is

```
<UsageEnvironmentProperty xsi:type="NetworksType">
    <Network>
        <NetworkCharacteristic xsi:type="NetworkConditionType">
            <AvailableBandwidth maximum="512000" average="256000"/>
        </NetworkCharacteristic>
    </Network>
</UsageEnvironmentProperty>
```

Fig. 8. The Network Characteristics (Available Bandwidth) descriptor

```
<UsageEnvironmentProperty xsi:type="UsersType">
    <User>
        <UserCharacteristic xsi:type="PresentationPriorityPreferenceType">
            <GeneralResourcePriorities>
                <ModalityPriorities>
                    <Modality priorityLevel="1" href="urn:mpeg:mpeg7:cs:ContentCS:2001:1">
                        <mpeg7:Name>Audio</mpeg7:Name>
                    </Modality>
                    <Modality priorityLevel="2" href="urn:mpeg:mpeg7:cs:ContentCS:2001:4.2">
                        <mpeg7:Name>Video</mpeg7:Name>
                    </Modality>
                    <Modality priorityLevel="3" href="urn:mpeg:mpeg7:cs:ContentCS:2001:4.1">
                        <mpeg7:Name>Image</mpeg7:Name>
                    </Modality>
                </ModalityPriorities>
            </GeneralResourcePriorities>
        </UserCharacteristic>
    </User>
</UsageEnvironmentProperty>
```

Fig. 9. The Modality Priorities descriptor

Fig. 10. The playing of the binary (LSR) file on Mobile Phone emulator

shown in Fig. 9. There is no audio content in the scene so that the first preference does not apply. The video bitrate exceeds the bandwidth limit, so that the bitrate of the video should be reduced into average bandwidth (256,000 bps). Therefore, the remaining available bandwidth is 256,000 bps. For the images, the total size is 50,265 bytes = 402,120 bits. In the presence of remaining maximum bandwidth limit, we decided a 2 second maximum limit for the images to be transferred. Since the time transfer for the images is 402,120/256,000 = 1.57 seconds, there is no conversion needed to further reduce the file size of the images.

After the transcoding process, the client receives a LASeR scene. The scene with the size of 192x144 pixels including the transcoded images and videos can be seen in Fig. 10. The left part shows the first display of the scene, and the right part shows one of the videos being played.

6 Conclusion

We have implemented an adaptation engine for the purpose of transcoding BIFS scenes into their corresponding LASeR scenes. The adaptation engine can automatically decide the conversion rules and audiovisual object reduction formats contained in the MPEG-21 DIA descriptors. The terminal capabilities and user and network characteristics are considered for determining the adaptation decisions.

The MPEG-21 DIA descriptors contain a set of rules that is sent to BIFS-to-LASeR Transcoding Engine, which includes a BIFS-to-LASeR transcoding scheme with an XSLT stylesheet for automatic conversion of BIFS XMT-A files into LASeR XML files. This implementation enables content authors to reproduce existing scenes described textually in BIFS format into their identical scenes described textually in LASeR format. Finally, together with BIFS decoder and LASeR encoder, content providers are allowed to convert BIFS binary files into LASeR binary files for direct consumption by low-powered devices.

This research can contribute to interactive MPEG-4 content providers, because the number of low-powered consumer devices is increasing these days. The whole system enables content authors to create one type of contents, and then reproduce and distribute them in real-time without the need of reauthoring or learning a new standard for the consumption of mobile devices.

References

1. MPEG Systems Group: MPEG-4 Lightweight Application Scene Representation (LASeR) Final Committee Draft (FCD) Study, ISO/IEC JTC1/SC29/WG11/N7239, April 2005, Busan, Korea.
2. Fernando Pereira and Touradj Ebrahimi (editors): The MPEG-4 Book, Prentice Hall, 2003.
3. MPEG Requirements Group: LASeR Requirements Document, ISO/IEC JTC1/SC29/WG11/N7061, April 2005, Busan, Korea.
4. MPEG Systems Group: MPEG-4 Systems, ISO/IEC JTC1/SC29/WG11/N3850, February 2001, Pisa, Italy.
5. MPEG MDS Group: MPEG-21 Digital Item Adaptation Final Draft for International Standard (FDIS), ISO/IEC JTC1/SC29/WG11/N6168, December 2003, Hawaii, USA.
6. MPEG MDS Group: MPEG-21 Vision, Technology, and Strategy, ISO/IEC JTC1/SC29/WG11/N6269, December 2003, Hawaii, USA.
7. MPEG MDS Group: MPEG-7 Part 5: Multimedia Description Schemes, ISO/IEC JTC1/SC29/WG11/N4242, July 2001, Sydney, Australia.
8. GPAC Project, http://gpac.sourceforge.net/.

9. Jean-Claude Dufourd: WD3.0 of ISO/IEC 14496-20 Reference Software, ISO/IEC JTC1/SC29/WG11/N6968, January 2005, Hong Kong, China.
10. Qonita Shahab and Munchurl Kim: Transcoding of MPEG-4 BIFS into MPEG-4 LASeR, Visual Communications and Image Processing (VCIP), Beijing, China, 12-15 July 2005
11. ImageMagick, http://www.imagemagick.com/.
12. FFMPEG project, http://ffmpeg.sourceforge.net/.

Performance Evaluation of H.264 Mapping Strategies over IEEE 802.11e WLAN for Robust Video Streaming

Umar Iqbal Choudhry and JongWon Kim

Networked Media Laboratory, Department of Information and Communications,
Gwangju Institute of Science and Technology,
1 Oryong–dong, Buk–gu, Gwangju, 500-712, Republic of Korea
{umar, jongwon}@netmedia.gist.ac.kr

Abstract. In this paper we propose several mapping schemes for streaming video generated by state–of–the–art H.264 codec over IEEE 802.11e enabled wireless LANs. The schemes take advantage of both 802.11e's QoS mechanism and some novel features of the H.264 codec, so as to protect the most important information in terms of visual quality and reduce distortion under network congestion. The proposed methods are evaluated by means of the H.264 reference software codec, network simulation, and objective video quality measurements. Results show that the proposed methods achieve a robust and error resilient H.264 video streaming over wireless LANs than traditional best–effort streaming.

1 Introduction

Video streaming is one of the most promising applications of the next–generation wireless LANs. Thanks to major advances in both video coding and networking technologies, services such as live broadcasting and video–on–demand over wireless networks are becoming feasible. Recently, a new video codec has been standardized by the ITU–T under the name of H.264/AVC (Advanced Video Coding) [1]. This new codec offers several powerful features that make it especially attractive for streaming applications. These features include, an improved coding efficiency, network "friendliness", i.e., a better adaptation to the underlying network, and error resiliency.

These features can be complemented by network quality of service (QoS) techniques, so that the combined effect of application– and network–level mechanisms limits the visual distortion brought about by the inherent jitter, loss, and bandwidth dynamics of wireless networks.

1.1 QoS–Aware Video Streaming and Mapping

The term QoS–aware video streaming is used here to describe a type of streaming system characterized by the integration of two main components; a QoS–enabled wireless network, and a QoS–aware video streaming application.

The general idea behind this concept is that the performance may be improved if applications are "aware"—i.e., *make use*—of the service differentiation provided by the IEEE 802.11e QoS architecture. Thus, a QoS–aware video application marks the outgoing packets with some priority, taking into account the type of video information they carry, in order for them to take advantage of the service differentiation offered by the network. This approach is called application–driven (or application–controlled) *mapping*, and is different from the typical router–based marking which is done by edge routers based on rate–metering or flow identification. This way, the differentiated treatment inside the network yields a better visual quality by assuring a particular rate, limiting delay and jitter, and discarding first *less important packets* when congestion arises. This type of mapping has also been called *semantic mapping*. Note that when we speak of QoS–aware streaming, we refer to methods in which a video stream is somehow separated in "segments" (layers, frame types, partitions, etc.) to which unequal priorities are mapped and then these segments are forwarded using the differentiation mechanism of IEEE 802.11e.

In this paper, we propose and evaluate several mapping schemes to adapt the QoS–aware video streaming concept to the state–of–the–art H.264 video codec. The service differentiation approach of IEEE 802.11e can best leverage the network adaptation and error resilience techniques of H.264.

1.2 Related Work

The idea of applying differentiated forwarding to different segments of coded video streams is not new. Such approaches can usually be classified in three categories. The first category consists of a straightforward mapping between frame types in the coded video stream and discard priorities. In this case, the video stream is coded as a single–layer and forwarding is done in a single queue with prioritized discard. In the second category, mapping is done so that each layer is assigned to a specific IEEE 802.11e access category (AC) [2]. Some proposals isolate layers in different queues serviced by a scheduler. Others use a mixture of isolation/scheduling and prioritized discard [3]. Finally in the third classification mapping is applied based on a distortion estimation. In [4], a classification scheme for H.263+ streams is defined, in which each packet gets a score that represents the impact its loss would have on quality. Afterwards, a DiffServ mapping is applied based on this pricing model. Mapping is then an optimization problem where the objective is to minimize distortion (based on the loss index of the packets and the loss rates of the DiffServ classes) under a budget constraint.

1.3 Outline of the Paper

The remainder of this paper is organized as follows. Section 2 presents an overview of the main characteristics of both the H.264 video codec and IEEE 802.11e QoS mechanism. Our proposals of mapping strategies for H.264 video using IEEE 802.11e service differentiation are introduced in Section 3. Section 4 describes the performance evaluation carried out to study some of our proposals, followed by the conclusions and perspectives in Section 5.

2 H.264 Video Coding Standard and IEEE 802.11e QoS Mechanism

2.1 Overview of the H.264 Video Coding Standard

As stated earlier, H.264 [1] offers an improved compression efficiency [5]. In addition to an improved coding efficiency, a very important feature of H.264 is that it is specifically designed for the transportation of coded video over a variety of existing and future network transport technologies. The design of H.264 addresses this need for flexibility and customizability by means of separating the coded information into two layers: the Video Coding Layer (VCL) and the *Network Adaptation Layer* (NAL) [6]. VCL represents the coded video information in the most efficient manner possible, while NAL formats the VCL data and organizes it in elements with the appropriate headers for its transport or storage.

Regarding error robustness, H.264 includes several advanced features that are closely related to the concept of NAL [7]. First, the key syntax elements of the H.264 structure are flexible-sized slices. Each slice is conveyed in a single logical data packet (called NAL-unit). H.264 also includes the concepts of Flexible Macroblock Ordering (FMO) and Data Partitioning (DP). Section 3 discusses these concepts in more detail.

2.2 Overview of the IEEE 802.11e QoS Mechanism

IEEE 802.11e [8] aims to support QoS by providing differentiated classes of service in the medium access control (MAC) layer and to enhance the ability of all the physical layers so that they can deliver time-critical multimedia traffic, in addition to traditional data packets.

IEEE 802.11e uses enhanced distributed channel access (EDCA), a contention based channel access function, to support multimedia applications such as voice and video over the wireless medium [8][9][10]. EDCA is based on differentiating priorities at which traffic is to be delivered, and it works with four ACs (access categories), where each AC achieves differentiated channel access. This differentiation is achieved through varying the amount of time a station would sense the channel as idle and the length of the contention window during a backoff. For a given station, traffics of different ACs are buffered in different queues. Each AC within a station behaves like a virtual station. When a collision occurs among different ACs within the same station, the higher priority AC is granted the opportunity for physical transmission, while the lower priority AC suffers from a virtual collision, which is similar to a real collision outside the station [8].

EDCA supports eight different priorities, which are further mapped to the four ACs, with AC3 having the highest priority while AC0 has the lowest priority [8]. AC3 is for voice transmissions; AC2 and AC1 are for video transmissions; while AC0 is for best-effort data transmissions. Each frame arriving at the MAC with a priority is mapped into an AC as shown in Table 1 [8].

Table 1. Priority to access category mappings in IEEE 802.11e EDCA

Priority	Access Category (AC)	Designation (Informative)
1	0	Best–effort
2	0	Best–effort
0	0	Best–effort
3	1	Video Probe
4	2	Video
5	2	Video
6	3	Voice
7	3	Voice

3 Mapping Strategies for H.264 Video Using IEEE 802.11e Service Differentiation

Following an analysis of the existing proposals described in Section 1.2, we decided to adopt an approach of straightforward mapping between coarse syntax elements (like frames or slices) to IEEE 802.11e ACs, as in this case the information required for mapping is directly available in the stream's headers and no complex parsing operations are required for this purpose. This approach is particularly suitable for streaming applications, which are time–sensitive in nature and hence cannot sustain time consuming complex parsing operations. Remark that, even if we have focused on streaming, the differentiated forwarding concept of IEEE 802.11e can also be applied to interactive and real–time conversational video services.

Several possible mapping strategies can therefore be envisaged for implementing a QoS–aware H.264 streaming system, based on the following syntactic elements or features of the H.264 standard: slices, FMO, and DP. Next, we describe our proposals for performing such a mapping, assuming an IEEE 802.11e based wireless network scenario with ACs reserved for video streaming. Here it is important to note that such a mapping is purely static in nature where the arriving packets are differentiated solely on the basis of their pre–marked priorities and hence their associations to different access categories with different priorities. In other words, the underlying admission control mechanism is also assumed to be static in nature.

3.1 Mapping Strategy Based on Slices

Each video frame can be divided in several parts of the same type called slices, which are the main syntax element of the H.264 NAL and whose size is decided at encoding time. Each slice contains a certain number of macroblocks in contiguous positions, except for FMO (see Section 3.2). Slices are intended to be directly converted into network packets, and can be decoded independently from each other: this way, if each slice is transported in a single packet, the loss of a packet—that is, a slice—shouldn't break the decoding process [11].

An H.264–coded video sequence is composed of Intra (I), Predicted (P), and Bi–directional predicted (B) slices. In addition, B frames can also be used as a reference for other B frames. Moreover, H.264 does not include a picture or frame syntax element; it's the slice header that carries the information on the type (I, P, or B) of frame it belongs to.

Hence a mapping strategy can be based on slices. It consists of assigning highest priority to I slices, medium priority to P slices, and lowest priority to B slices. Thus I slices will be mapped to AC3, P slices to AC2, and B slices to AC1, as presented in Table 2. Alternative strategies may be envisioned if, for instance, there are only two access categories available for video data. For example, one can map I and P slices to AC3 (highest priority) and B slices to AC2 (lower priority).

3.2 Mapping Strategy Based on Flexible Macroblock Ordering (FMO)

FMO is one of the novel error resilience and concealment features available in H.264. In general, a slice contains contiguous macroblocks (in scan order). FMO permits to create slices with non–contiguous macroblocks and assign these slices to different groups. This way, error concealment algorithms can take advantage of interleaved or scattered layouts [12].

Several mapping strategies based on FMO seem worthwhile exploring. To begin with, the different groups of slices may be assigned to the different ACs. Moreover, the way in which groups of slices are created might take into account explicit error concealment for hiding visual impairments. For instance, the center of an image may arguably be more relevant to the viewer than its edges; therefore, in order to achieve a good subjective quality, one may imagine that macroblocks at the center of a frame are assigned to a slice group which is forwarded with the highest priority and, conversely, those at the edges are transported by lower priority packets.

Thus for FMO resulting in two slice groups, the highest priority slice group will be mapped to AC3, while the lower priority slice group will be mapped to AC2, as shown in Table 2.

3.3 Mapping Strategy Based on Data Partitioning (DP)

DP is an error resilience feature that relies on the hierarchical separation of coded video data in different elements at a very low level. Normally, all symbols of a macroblock are coded together in a single bit string that forms a slice. Data partitioning, however, creates more than one bit strings (called partitions) per slice, and allocates all symbols that have a close semantic relationship with each other into an individual partition [11]. There are three hierarchically ordered levels of partitions: A (headers, macroblock types, quantization parameters and motion vectors), B (intra coefficients), and C (inter coefficients). A–type is the most important partition. B–type partitions require the availability of the corresponding A–type partitions. C–type partitions are the least important ones and they require A–type but not B–type partitions.

Table 2. Main mapping strategies for H.264 video

Codec Feature	Mapping Strategy
Slices	I slices → AC3 P slices → AC2 B slices → AC1
FMO	Slice group 1 (High Priority) → AC3 Slice group 2 (Low Priority) → AC2
DP	A–type partitions → AC3 B–type partitions → AC2 C–type partitions → AC1

DP is also a natural candidate for IEEE 802.11e AC mapping. It offers a very granular semantic separation of the coded video, and this separation is done in three hierarchical levels, which can be directly mapped to the three ACs, as depicted in Table 2.

4 Performance Evaluation

An evaluation procedure is carried out using two of our proposed mapping strategies, namely slice–based and FMO–based, with the goal of verifying whether the syntax element–based QoS–aware H.264 streaming over IEEE 802.11e enabled WLAN yields a better visual quality than the regular best–effort WLAN streaming under different levels of congestion and channel degradation. We consider an IEEE 802.11e enabled wireless LAN scenario where video flows are transported over UDP and generate heavy congestion in a particular bottleneck link.

4.1 Overview of the Simulation Methodology

The evaluation is done following the simulation–based process depicted in Fig. 1. The point of departure is a raw YUV digital video sequence. The sequence is processed by an encoder that generates the H.264 bitstream. The second block is a parser/packetizer that analyzes the bitstream, identifies the syntax elements (NAL units), applies a particular mapping strategy and generates a trace file for the network simulator. The parser embodies our proposals for QoS–aware semantic mapping of H.264 video.

The third block is the simulation, which is performed by the ns–2 network simulator [13]. The simulator uses an input trace file as a traffic generator while a simulation script defines the network topology, the background traffic, and so on. The result of the simulation is an output trace file which is used by the error insertion block to detect lost packets and erase them from the original H.264 bitstream. Then, the distorted bitstream is decoded to a raw video file for visualization and quality evaluation. Quality evaluation is an important issue regarding multimedia networking applications. In this paper, we have chosen PSNR as the objective quality evaluation method to evaluate the perceptual QoS maintenance performance.

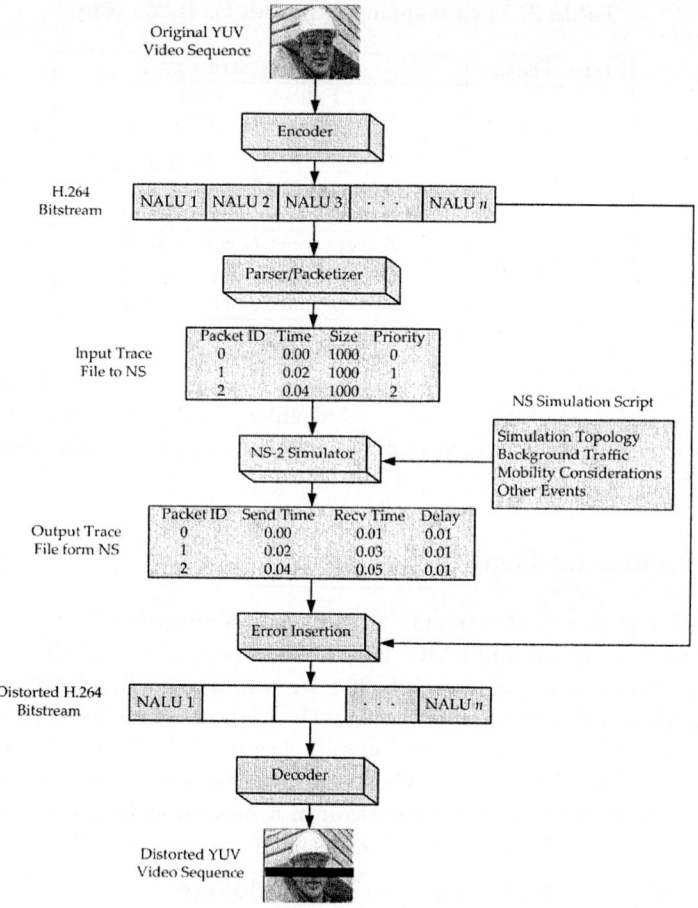

Fig. 1. H.264 evaluation process

This process requires the integration of several components, of which we developed the parser, the ns–2 extensions and the error insertion module. At both ends of the process we find the H.264 codec, as the key component. In addition to its coding features, error robustness in the decoder is mandatory. We work with version 9.6 of the codec [14], which is, to the best of our knowledge, the most recent version with documented error–robustness. Nevertheless, robustness features in this version are somewhat limited. As a consequence, the reference code for the codec is modified to make it error resilient enough in order to enable it to decode the resulting distorted bitstream. This is one of the key accomplishments of this work.

4.2 Procedures for Video Coding, Mapping, and Error Insertion

As seen in Section 3, the proposed mapping strategies are defined in terms of coding options. For this evaluation and according to the error robustness features

Table 3. H.264 encoder configuration parameters

Parameter/Option	Value
Frequency for encoded bitstream	15
Hadamard transform	Used
Image format	352 × 288
Error robustness	On
Search range	16
Total number of references	5
References for P slices	5
Sequence type	I–B–P–B–P
Quantization parameter for I slices	28
Quantization parameter for P slices	28
Quantization parameter for B slices	30
Entropy coding method	CABAC
Profile/Level IDC	100/40
Search range restrictions	None
RD–optimized mode decision	Used
Data partitioning (DP) mode	1 partition
Output file format	H.264 bitstream file format
Residue color transform	Not used

available in the codec, we focused on two of our proposed mapping strategies, i.e., the mapping of slice types, and slice groups (using FMO, based on "interleaved" mapping, resulting in two slice groups) to IEEE 802.11e ACs.

We select a video sequence called 'Foreman' in CIF format (352 × 288 pixels). The sequence is encoded at 15 fps with a target rate of 451 kbit/s. The output format is chosen as Annex B NAL units and fixed–size slicing mode is selected, with a target size of 1000 bytes per slice. Table 3 summarizes the various configuration parameters used in generating the H.264 bitstream.

The parsing module reads the NAL units from the bitstream, identifies the different slice types/groups and generates a trace line per packet with the following information: emission time, size, and priority. The emission time is set in function of the target frame rate (15 fps). For the final packet size, the parser adds 28 bytes to the original NAL unit size (20 bytes from the IP header and 8 bytes from the UDP header). Precedence is set according to the slice and FMO based mapping schemes shown in Table 2, following the guidelines described in Section 3.

The error insertion module erases from the original coded stream those packets that were lost during the simulation due only to forced or early discard in the bottleneck link. No losses related to excessive delay or jitter are considered in this evaluation (i.e., playout buffers are not taken into account).

4.3 Results

The proposed schemes are evaluated using a video streaming scenario over wireless LAN. By comparing our proposed mapping based streaming approaches,

Table 4. Average PSNR of received Foreman video sequence

Method	Datarate	Average PSNR (dB)	
		Slice–based	FMO–based
Best–effort	High	31.59	32.04
	Medium	32.78	33.26
	Low	34.13	34.69
	Average	32.83	33.33
Proposed	High	35.87	36.17
	Medium	36.79	37.11
	Low	38.06	38.35
	Average	36.91	37.21

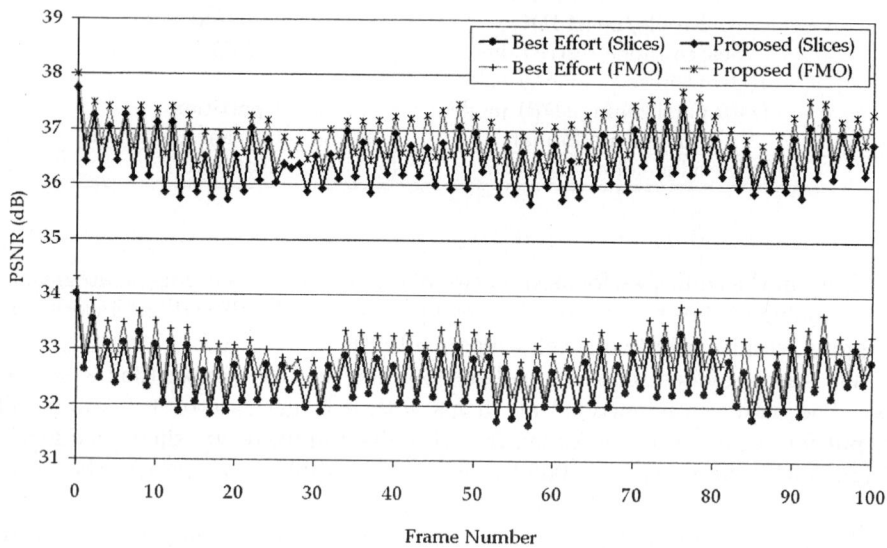

Fig. 2. PSNR values for the received Foreman sequence

employing IEEE 802.11e service differentiation mechanism, with the regular best–effort streaming, we strive to show the enhanced performance achieved.

To simulate an IEEE 802.11e based wireless streaming environment a QoS Basic Service Set (QBSS) infrastructure is considered. First of all, the QBSS is fully loaded by injecting an 8 Mbps best–effort traffic into the simulation environment. Then, after 5 seconds, the H.264 video flows are injected into the network. To apply congestion control to the best–effort flow, a simple rate control scheme is applied which locks AC0 to limit it to further congesting the network. In order to simulate the effects of wireless channel degradation, we successively deteriorate the link quality between QAP (QoS access point) and QSTAs (QoS

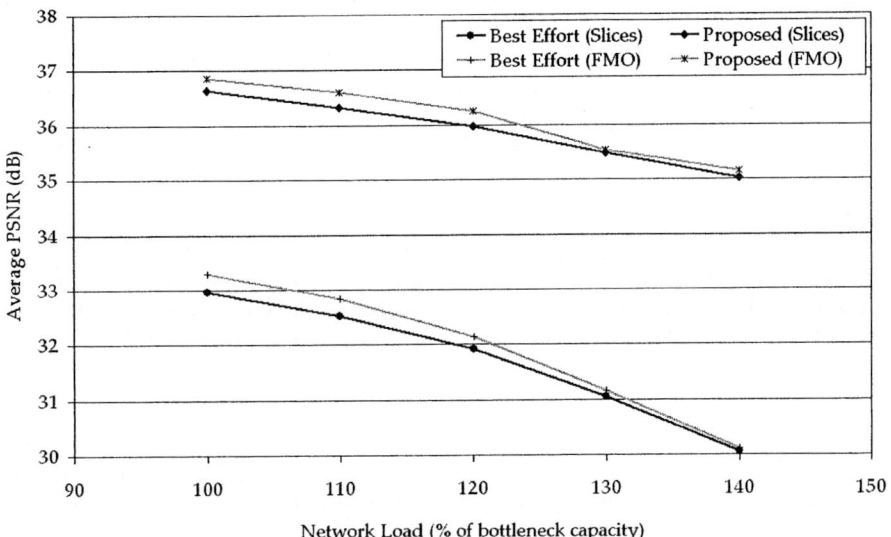

Fig. 3. Average PSNR

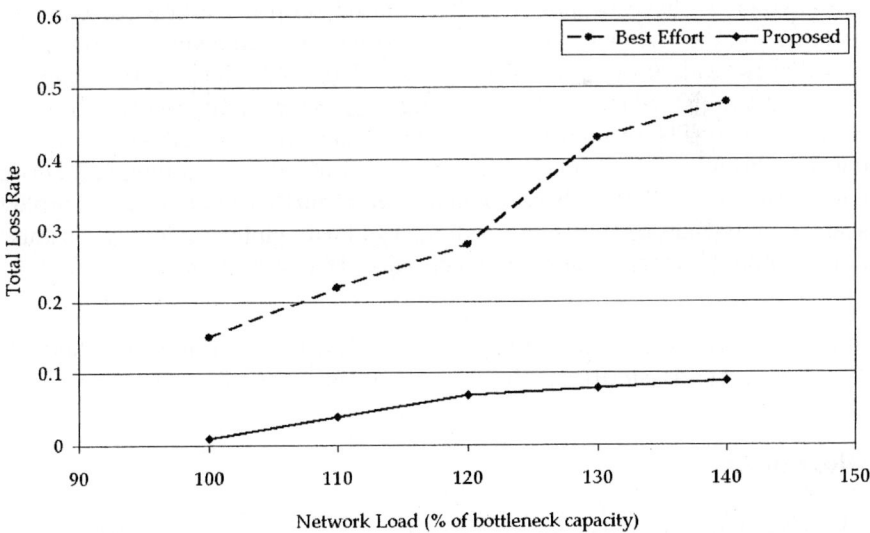

Fig. 4. Total loss rate

stations) which in turn reduces the data rate of the corresponding link and thus limits the total available bandwidth. As a result, for example in the slice–based mapping case, the QoS–demanding video flows of I and P slices suffer a shortage of available bandwidth during that period. Thus in order to achieve the target bitrates of I and P slices, QAP drops the packets belonging to B slices.

Table 4 shows the receiver–side video quality in terms of average PSNR of the 'Foreman (CIF)' video sequence in deteriorating channel conditions for both the proposed and the best–effort streaming scenarios. High values of average PSNR for the proposed streaming schemes, clearly demonstrate the effectiveness of our streaming solutions. Not only the resulting stream is error resilient, it also adapts well to the changing network environment due to varying channel condition. Fig. 2 shows the plots of PSNR values for the proposed as well as the best–effort streaming scenarios. These plots clearly show that the proposed streaming schemes have outperformed the best–effort ones, with FMO–based mapping strategy giving slightly better performance than the slice–based mapping strategy.

The plots in Fig. 3 and 4 show the results of quality evaluation for all simulation scenarios. The plots reveal that as the network load is increased beyond its bottleneck capacity, not only our proposed streaming schemes perform better than the best–effort streaming methods, but these also offer very low loss rates compared to the best–effort ones.

5 Conclusions and Future Work

In this paper we have proposed and evaluated several methods of QoS–aware streaming for the H.264 video codec over IEEE 802.11e enabled wireless LAN. According to evaluation results, the proposed methods help in reducing visual impairments in deteriorating channel conditions when compared to a best–effort network service. The evaluation methodology and tools described in Section 4.1 allow for a broad range of specific studies for a variety of streaming and networking scenarios. In addition, these schemes can be further enhanced by employing a scalable extension of the H.264 coding standard, while employing various dynamic mapping strategies not implemented in the current work.

Acknowledgements. This research was supported by grant R05–2004–000–10987–0 from the Basic Research Program of the Korea Research Foundation.

References

1. ITU–T: Advanced video coding for generic audiovisual services. ITU–T Recommendation H.264. (2003)
2. Yoon, H., Kim, J.: Dynamic admission control for differentiated quality of video in IEEE 802.11e wireless LANs. In: Proc. SPIE ITCOM 2004: Internet Multimedia Management Systems V, Philadelphia, PA USA (2004)
3. Ahmed, T., Mehaoua, A., Buridant, G.: Implementing MPEG–4 video on demand over IP differentiated services. In: IEEE Globecom 2001, San Antonio, Texas, USA (2001) 2489–2493

4. Shin, J., Kim, J., Kuo, C.: Quality-of-service mapping mechanism for packet video in differentiated services network. IEEE Transactions on Multimedia (2001) 219–231
5. Kamaci, N., Altunbasak, Y.: Performance comparison of the emerging H.264 video coding standard with the existing standards. In: Proceedings of the IEEE International Conference on Multimedia and Expo ICME 2003. Number 6–9, Baltimore (2003)
6. Wiegand, T., Sullivan, G., Bjontegaard, G., Luthra, A.: Overview of the H.264/AVC video coding standard. IEEE Transactions on Circuits and Systems for Video Technology (2003)
7. Richardson, I.E.G.: H.264 and MPEG-4 Video Compression: Video Coding for Next-generation Multimedia. Wiley (2003)
8. IEEE: Wireless medium access control (MAC) and physical layer (PHY) specifications: Medium access control (MAC) enhancements for quality of service (QoS), IEEE Std. 802.11e/Draft 5.0. (2003)
9. Choi, S., Prado, J.D., Shankar, S., Mangold, S.: IEEE 802.11e contention-based channel access (EDCF) performance evaluation. In: Proc. IEEE ICC03. Volume 2. (2003) 1151–1156
10. Mangold, S., Choi, S., May, P., Klein, O., Hiertz, G., Stibor, L.: IEEE 802.11e wireless LAN for quality of service. In: Proc. Eur. Wireless 2002. Volume 1. (2002) 32–39
11. Wenger, S.: H.264/AVC over IP. IEEE Transactions on Circuits and Systems for Video Technology (2003) 645–656
12. Wenger, S., Horowitz, M.: Flexible macroblock ordering; a new error resilience tool for IP based video. In: Tyrrhenian International Workshop on Digital Communications – IWDC 2002, Capri, Italy (2002)
13. McCanne, S., Floyd, S.: ns Network Simulator, (http://www.isi.edu/nsnam/ns/)
14. HHI: H.264/AVC Software Coordination, (http://iphome.hhi.de/suehring/tml/)

Reducing Spatial Resolution for MPEG-2 to H.264/AVC Transcoding

Bo Hu, Peng Zhang, Qingming Huang, and Wen Gao

Institute of Computing Technology, Chinese Academy of Sciences, Beijing, 100080, China
Graduate School of Chinese Academy of Sciences, Beijing, 100039, China
{bhu, peng.zhang, qmhuang, wgao}@jdl.ac.cn

Abstract. Transcoding is an important technique for reducing the bit rate or spatial resolution to meet the constrained transmission bandwidths and terminal capabilities. In this paper, we propose a spatial downscaling transcoding method to convert an MPEG-2 bitstream into an H.264/AVC bitstream. A novel feature of the proposed method is to focus on the fast mode decision that fully exploits the advantages of variable block-size motion compensation feature in H.264/AVC. In the transcoder, types and motion vectors of pre-encoded macroblocks are considered together to decide the new encoding block type. While maintaining a reasonable image quality, the proposed method significantly reduces the computational complexity and facilitates the video servers to provide multimedia service in real time for heterogeneous clients. Experimental results show that our method is very effective.

1 Introduction

Over the past several years, the Internet has witnessed a tremendous growth in the use of video streaming. As the number of terminal devices and multimedia compress formats increase, interoperability between different systems and different networks becomes more and more important. Therefore, devices such as gateways, multipoint control units, and servers must be developed to provide a seamless interaction between content creation and consumption [1]. Transcoding is an important technology for solving this problem. Specially, during the transcoding the feature of spatial resolution reduction should be included to adapt for the various terminal devices.

H.264/AVC is the up-to-date video compression standard, which employs variable block-size motion compensation for inter coding and directional spatial prediction for intra coding to achieve high coding efficiency [2]. But currently most multimedia resources are based on MPEG-2, so a flexible transcoding method from MPEG-2 bit stream to H.264/AVC bit stream is highly desirable.

In the literatures, several transcoding methods have been proposed and most of them focus on motion vectors mapping, motion vector refinement and error resilience etc. [3-10]. Spatial resolution transcoding is mainly focused on mode decision, motion vectors mapping, re-estimation and refinement [3-6]. In [3], the problems associated with mapping motion vectors and MB-level data were addressed. Macroblock mode decision by reusing the pre-encoded information was discussed in [3] and [4]. The primary contribution of the work in [5] and [6] was on motion vector scaling techniques. However they are all designed for fixed-size block-based motion estimation. Therefore they are not suitable for the MPEG-2 to H.264/AVC transcoding system because of the variable block-size motion estimation feature adopted in H.264/AVC.

In this paper, we propose a new method to convert an MPEG-2 stream into an H.264/AVC stream with half the spatial resolution. While enhancing the coding efficiency for H.264/AVC compression standard, multiple modes decision and motion estimation consume most encoding time. So reducing the complexity of mode decision and motion estimation is one key technique for transcoding. Our proposed method is such a solution to simplify this procedure. Compared with the methods listed above, in our method, the feature of variable block-size motion estimation is fully exploited to obtain an adaptive transcoding method suitable for the H.264/AVC standard. We consider all the modes supported by H.264/AVC such as Inter16x16, 16x8, 8x16, 8x8, 8x4, 4x8, 4x4. While re-encoding a frame, we mainly focus on how to get the proper encoding mode fast by reusing the MB-level data extracted from the MPEG-2 bitstream. And then get new adaptive motion vectors for the new macroblock of the downscaled sequence. Furthermore, we could do a motion vector refinement to obtain a better result. Additionally, motion estimation based on block sizes smaller than 8x8 is enabled in the H.264/AVC standard and it can make identifiable coding gain at high bit rates [13]. We will apply it on some areas with complex motion to further improve the performance.

The rest of this paper is organized as follows. In Section 2, we will propose our transcoding architecture. Then we will describe our algorithm in detail in Section 3. In this section, mode decision and motion vector re-estimation will be discussed. Finally, experiment results are presented in Section 4 and Section 5 concludes this paper.

2 Transcoding Architecture

Two major transcoding architectures are popular: the cascaded pixel domain transcoder (CPDT) [10] and the DCT domain transcoder (DDT) [11]. CPDT is such a straightforward way which decodes the video bit stream and fully re-encodes the

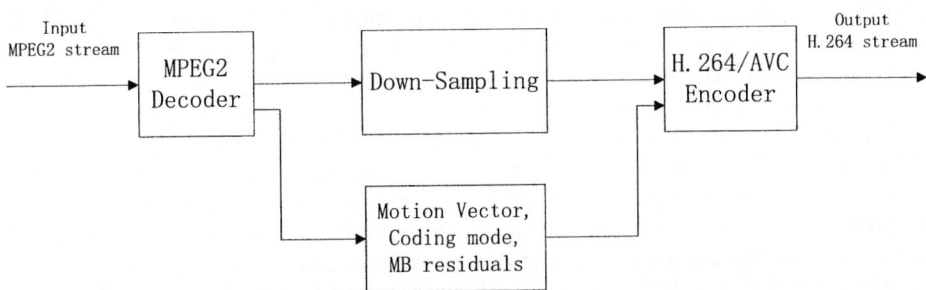

Fig. 1. CPDT transcoder architecture with spatial resolution reduction

reconstructed images at the new rate. As its decoder-loop and encoder-loop can be totally independent, CPDT is flexible and drift-free. DDT directly processes the DCT coefficients and it is difficult to handle spatial resolution changes without causing considerable drift. So for MPEG-2 to H.264/AVC transcoding, as the different transform methods used in two standards, we would prefer to CPDT architecture. As shown in Fig.1, it is flexible for the architecture to reuse the pre-encoded information in the H.264/AVC encoder. And we could mainly focus on the mode decision algorithm independently.

In our transcoding scheme, we mainly focus on how to simplify the process of mode selection, so as to reduce the computational complexity in the re-encoding greatly and make the real-time transcoding into reality.

Consider a downscale-by-two spatial reduction. As shown in Fig.2, four original macroblocks generate one output macroblock. Each of the original macroblocks and its reference blocks are downscaled to an individual block (8x8) and the corresponding motion vectors are related to each 8x8 block.

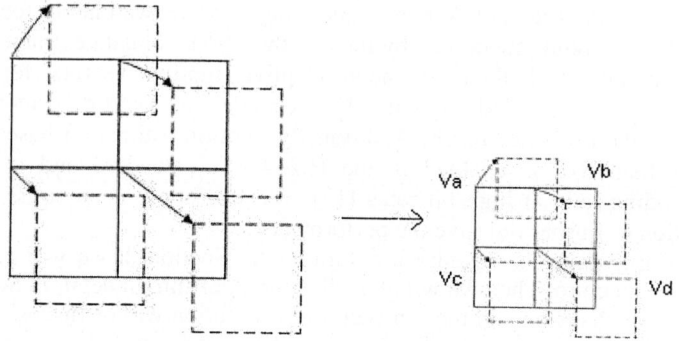

Fig. 2. downscaled motion vector by two

A straightforward approach is to average the four motion vectors available and employ inter_16x16 mode for encoding. This can be well used in transcoding for the old compression standards. It would not introduce any problem if all the four motion vectors of the four original macroblocks are equal. However, when the four motion vectors are not well aligned, such a scheme will yield a poor result. To improve the algorithm, AMVR architecture [5] and AME method [6] are proposed to obtain an adaptive motion vector for the new 16x16 macroblock. But all these methods are not well suitable for the H.264/AVC transcoding because of the variable block-size motion estimation and compensation. To address this problem, we propose a new hybrid algorithm for downscaled transcoding from MPEG-2 to H.264/AVC.

In this hybrid system, firstly, we fully decode the MPEG-2 bitstream and record the coding type, motion vectors and residuals of every pre-encoded macroblock. After downscaling by factor 2, four pre-encoded macroblocks turn into four 8x8 blocks and each 8x8 block has a motion vector. Based on the four 8x8 blocks, we perform merge or split operation and fully make use of the feature of multiple modes in motion estimation in the H.264/AVC standard. Inter_16x16, inter16x8, inter8x16 and inter8x8 are used in this hybrid architecture. Furthermore, if the inter_8x8 is selected, all the sub-block modes such as 8x4, 4x8 and 4x4, are considered. The explicit algorithm will be introduced in the next section. Fig.3 shows the architecture of this hybrid transcoding.

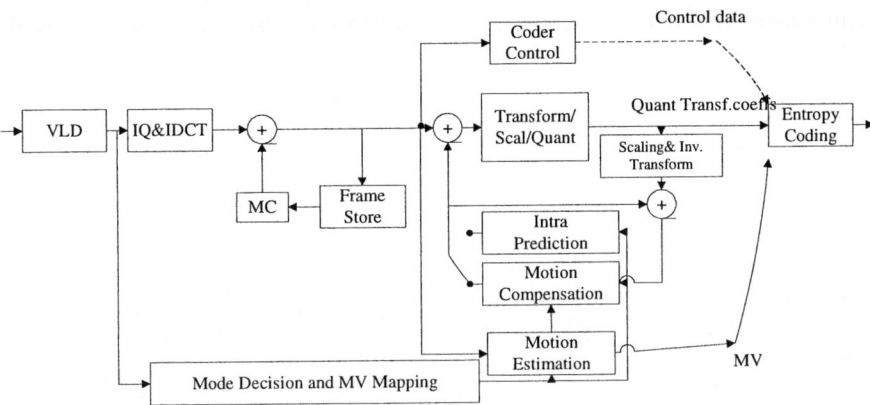

Fig. 3. Transcoding architecture with mode decision and MV mapping

3 Proposed Algorithm

We mainly focus on I and P frames. (B frames can be processed as P frames similarly) In MPEG-2 to H.264/AVC transcoding, after down sampling, every four pre-encoded 16x16 macroblocks are downscaled to four new 8x8 blocks in one macroblock. As shown in Fig.2, four 8x8 blocks have four motion vectors (for intra macroblocks, we set the motion vectors equal to 0 temporarily). If one or more pre-encoded macroblocks of the four, but not all the four, are intra coded, we will select a motion vector for the intra from the other inter macroblocks in these four by:

$$t = \arg\min_i SAD(mv_i) \qquad i=a, b, c, d$$
$$mv_{intra} = mv_t \qquad (1)$$

where $SAD(mv_i)$ means the sum of absolute differences of the intra macroblock by using motion vector mv_i. And we set the mv_{intra} as the motion vector of the intra macroblock.

The re-encoding technique is described as following:

1. For I frame: After fully decoded from MPEG-2 bit stream and downsampled, the frame is fully re-encoded as intra frame in H.264/AVC formant.
2. For P frame: After fully decoding and downsampling, we use the info extracted from the MPEG-2 bit stream to decide the re-encoding mode. Then do the motion vector mapping and refinement to obtain the adaptive motion vector.

In the following two sub-section, we will mainly discuss how to re-encode an inter frame.

3.1 Blocks Merge or Partition Procedure

As H.264/AVC supports variable block-size motion estimation, it will allow us to use the original information to select the best encoding mode for the current macroblock in transcoding. We could merge some 8x8 blocks into larger ones or separate them into smaller ones. Fig.4 illustrates the flow:

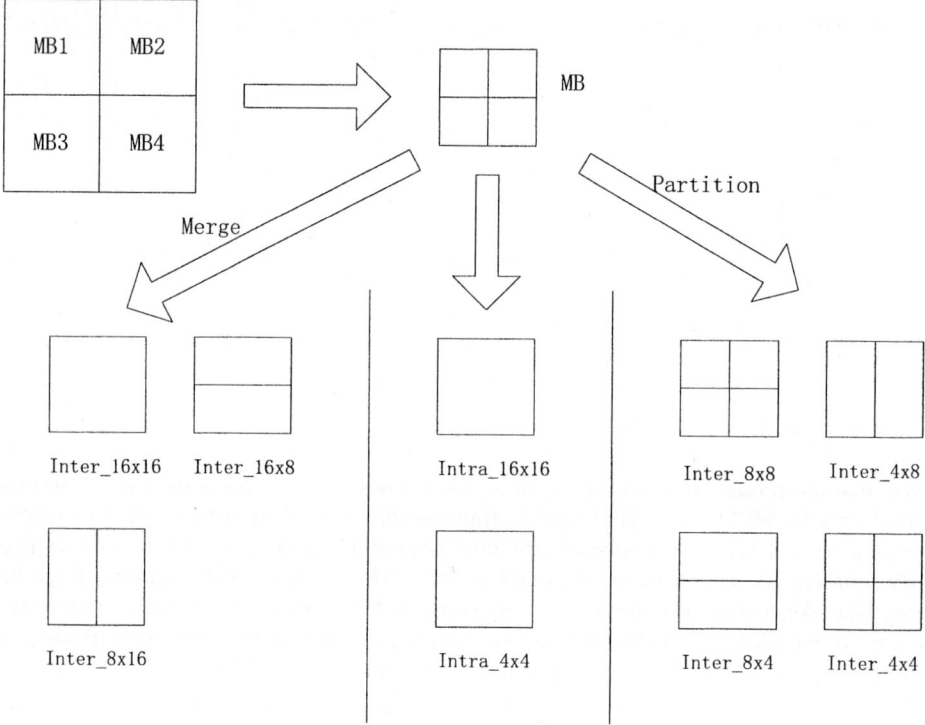

Fig. 4. Merge and partition

As known, although small block-size motion compensation, such as inter_8x4, inter_4x8, inter_4x4, can produce less residuals, but it consumes more bits for motion vectors. And sometimes it does not represent the real motion. On the other hand, big block motion estimation produce more residuals with less bits on motion vector. Generally speaking, for a larger homogeneous area, large block-size may give better overall performance. And for an area with detailed textures or edges, small blocks may be more suitable [12]. In our transcoding scheme, with little computational complexity increasing, all of the modes should be included to make a better performance. After down-sampling, if the motion vectors of the neighbor 8x8 blocks are similar, the blocks are predicted in the same direction and we could merge them into a larger one to save bits for motion vectors. While no merge procedure happens, it shows that the motion vectors of four 8x8 blocks are not well aligned. And if these four blocks have more details, small block-size prediction should be done to reduce the bits for residuals. Such is a merge or partition procedure in re-encoding the frame. The merge and partition are two parallel modules and they do not increase the computational complexity much.

One merging procedure is listed in [12], and our merge constraint is as follows:

$$D(V_a, V_b) = |x_1 - x_2| + |y_1 - y_2| <= TH \qquad (2)$$

where V_a and V_b are two motion vectors representing V_a (x_1, y_1), V_b(x_2, y_2), and function D is designed to represent the difference between the motion vectors. *TH* is a threshold which is selected equal to 2 in our experiments. And the *TH* can also be dynamically adjusted as explained in [12]. When the difference between the motion vectors of two neighboring 8x8 blocks a and b are not larger than *TH*, blocks a and b are merged to a larger one. The merging process can be expressed as follows:

1. *if (D(V_a, V_b)<= TH && D(V_c, V_d)<=TH)*
    inter_16x8 *mode is selected*
2. *if (D(V_a, V_c)<= TH && D(V_b, V_d)<=TH)*
    inter_8x16 *mode is selected*
3. *if 1 and 2 are both true*
    inter_16x16 *mode is selected*
   else if 1 and 2 are both false
   inter_8x8 *mode is selected.*

If four 8x8 blocks are merged into a 16x16 block or two 16x8 blocks, the motion vector MV_{16x16} can be obtained by the AMVR [5] or the AME [6] method. Other scheme such as align-to-best (ABW) and align-to-worst (AWW) [5] can also be used to produce the motion vector MV_{16x16}. Here we would choose ABW method to do the mv mapping.

If inter_8x8 mode is selected, we will partition the 8x8 block into small ones in some conditions. For some macroblock with more detail or not well predicted, the motion estimation based on block sizes smaller than 8x8 can achieve a coding gain. So we will do this partition for the macroblocks that have large residuals and the constraint is

$$A_i \geq \kappa \frac{W}{total\_macroblock\_number_{original}} \qquad (3)$$

Here, A_i represents the predictive residuals of the pre-encoded macroblock in the MPEG-2 sequence. W is the whole residuals of the first I frame in the same GOP. κ is an adaptive coefficient. Through our experiments, it is set to 1/4. Generally, if a video contains high motion activity, the difference between two consecutive frames will be large [14]. This means the predicted picture have more residuals or details and it will consume more bits for coding. To increase the prediction accuracy and reduce the residuals, small block-size motion estimation will be used here. So in formula 3, the efficient κ has much relation with the motion activity. In Fig.5 [14], it shows the relation between the motion activity and actual number of bits required to encode each of P-frame in a 200-frame test video segment. Therefore, we could guess the κ has a linear relation with the motion activity and we would further validate it in the future work. An adapative κ would give a better performance not only in quality but also in computational complexity.

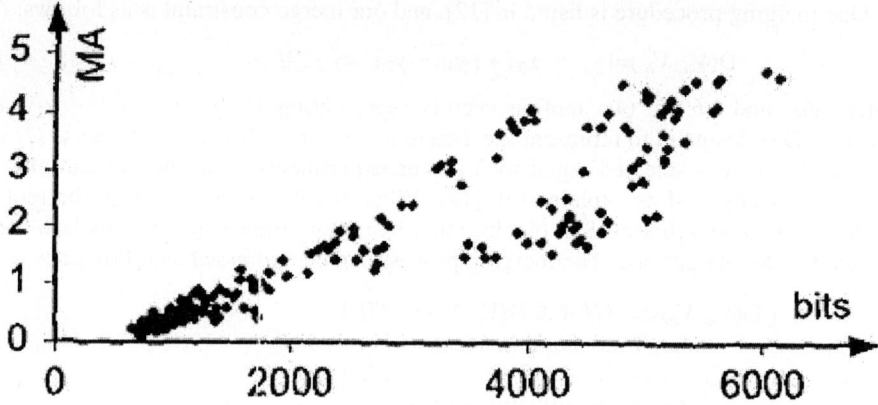

Fig. 5. The relation between motion activity and the number of bits required to encode each P-frame of a test video segment

Including small block-size inter prediction may not present the real motion, but it could prevent residuals expansion especially for those with more details.

3.2 Encoding Architecture: Mode Decision

When re-encoding, if the original frame is I frame, it is fully re-encoded as intra frame. And for P frame in the original sequence, every downscaled new macroblock coding type is processed as follow:

1. If all four original macroblocks are intra coded, the corresponding new macroblock will be coded with intra mode.
2. If one or more of the four original macroblocks, but not all four, are intra coded, we will first select motion vectors for the intra blocks and then do the merge and partition operation described in Section 3.1. After get the inter mode, the selected inter mode and the intra mode are compared to decide the final coding mode for the current macroblock.
3. If four original macroblocks are all inter coded, we will do the merge and partition procedure as described in Section 3.1. Then the coding type is selected and the corresponding motion vectors are reused and further refined.

For the inter frames encoding, all the integer-pel motion vectors are obtained directly from the MPEG-2 bitstream. The motion vectors are right shifted two bits to the get integer-pel motion for H.264/AVC. Furthermore, as H.264/AVC includes quarter-sample motion compensation, we should do a motion vector refinement by searching the surrounding positions in sub-pel accuracy after obtaining the integer-sample motion vector. This will make notable gains in quality and re-using the motion vector will reduce the time of motion estimation greatly.

4 Experimental Results

To test our proposed transcoding scheme, experiments are conducted with H.264/AVC reference software JM8.2. In our simulation, the input MPEG-2 bitstreams are of CIF resolution (352 x 288) at 2 Mbps. Each group of pictures (GOP) contains 10 frames just including I and P frames (B frames can be processed similarly as P frames). The target H.264/AVC bitstream is of QCIF resolution (176x144). We use PARIS, NEWS, FOREMAN and MOBILE as our test sequence and the results are presented. For each sequence, four transcoders are simulated which are different at the re-encoding process.

- Full mode: Encode with all the supported modes in H.264/AVC and do an exhaustive search for motion estimation
- Only inter_16x16: Besides the intra and skipped type in H.264/AVC, only inter_16x16 mode is selected for encoding the inter frame. Also do an exhaustive search for motion estimation.
- Only inter_8x8: Besides the intra and skipped type in H.264/AVC, only inter_8x8 mode is selected for encoding the inter frame. Also do an exhaustive search for motion estimation.
- Proposed method: Our proposed transcoding architecture.

In the simulation, the AMVR architecture and the AME method are not simulated. This is because they are for fixed-block-size transcoding, and its performance would not be better than that of our second simulation method in which only inter_16x16 is selected. The four sequences have variable motion activities and we could compare the simulation convictively.

Fig.6 shows the R-D performance of the four sequences. It can be seen from the four figures that our proposed method has a steady performance not only at low bit rate but also at high bit rate. Our proposed method has almost the same performance as the full mode transcoding especially for the News and Mobile sequence. Although full mode transcoding obtains the best performance, it has the biggest computational complexity. Our proposed method performs not as well as the full mode, but it is better than the ones with only inter16x16 and only inter_8x8 applied, although the two transcoders do the exhaustive search for the best motion vector.

So we can conclude that, for some sequences with less motion such as News and Paris, the merge procedure will take effect. While maintaining the same image quality, lots of bits are saved from motion vectors when re-encoding. On the other hand, for some sequences with large motion activity such as Mobile sequence, the partition procedure will work and make a more accurate prediction with small block-size. How to balance the big block-size prediction and small block-size prediction is an important factor to affect the coding quality. And it is a further topic we will focus.

In the meantime, our proposed method has a very low computational complexity and it is more practical for real-time transcoding. As shown in Fig.7, the relative computational complexity of our proposed transcoding method is about 21.4% of the full-mode ME re-encoding method. To further reducing the re-encoding time, we will focus on the transcoding technologies in frequency domain with close loop architecture. There are some difficulties because of the variable block-size motion compensation with small block sizes and we will do it in the future research work.

The following figures are the experiment results:

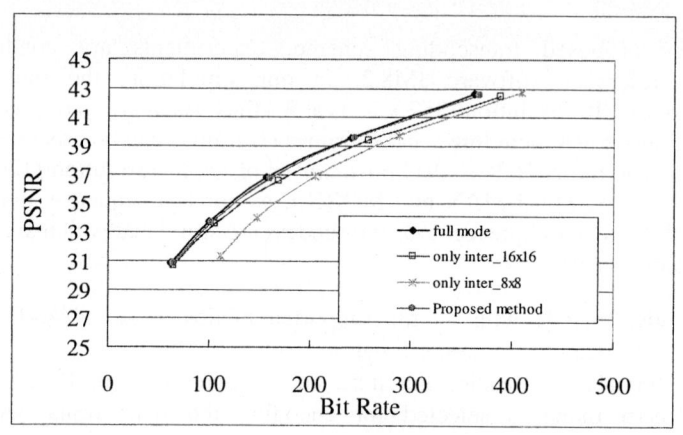

(a) News

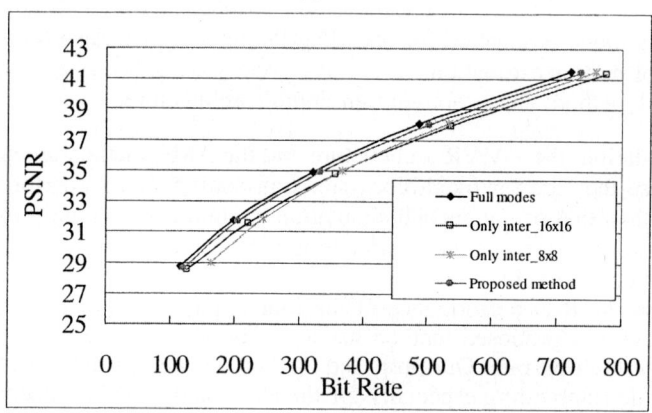

(b) Paris

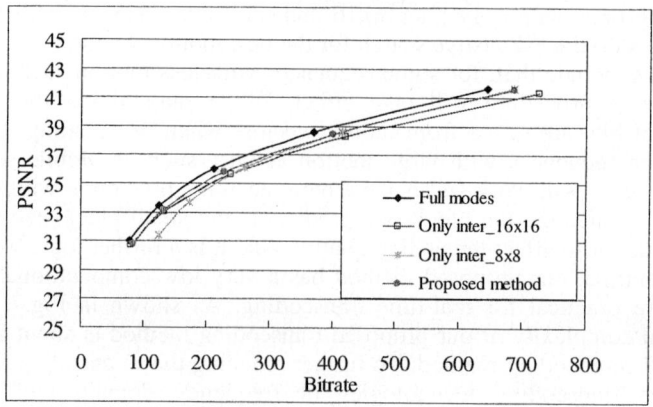

(c) Foreman

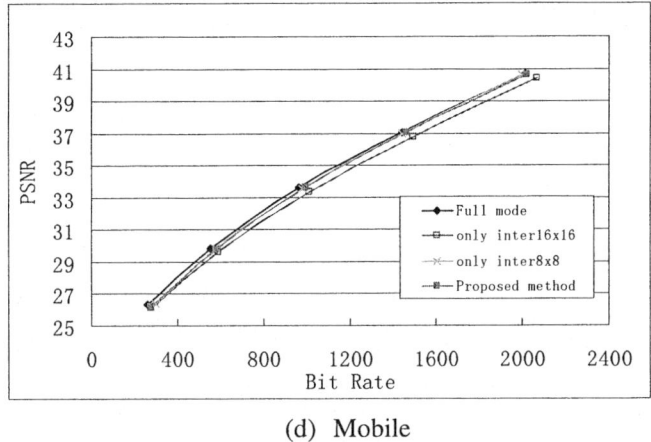

(d) Mobile

Fig. 6. RD curves of different transcoding methods

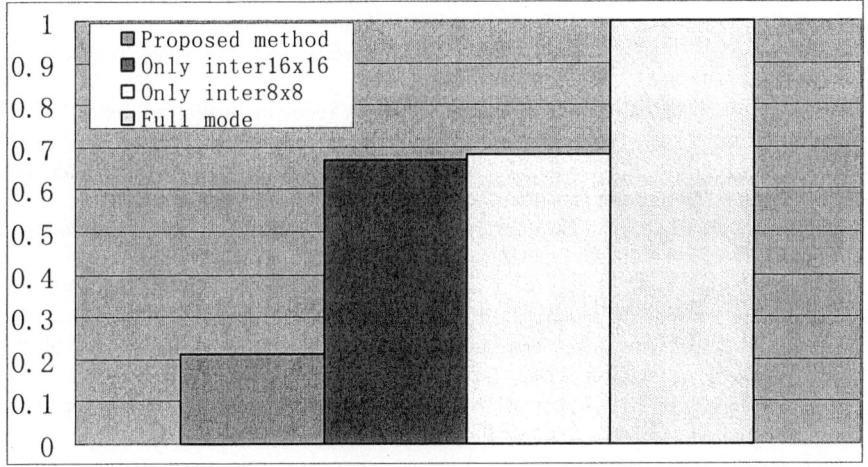

Fig. 7. Average computation complexity

5 Conclusions

In this paper, we have proposed a novel approach to convert an MPEG-2 bitstream into an H.264/AVC bitstream with only half spatial resolution of the original. Unlike the traditional methods, we make a good use of the new feature of H.264/AVC, variable block-size motion compensation with small block sizes. Our proposed method combines the MPEG-2 decoder and H.264/AVC encoder closely in the downscaled transcoding. While maintaining the reasonable image quality, we reduce the computational complexity greatly. This method, combined with temporal resolution reduction methods, will produce a more applicable future in the mobile multimedia access. To perfect our method, a further research will focus on adaptive κ coefficient and DCT-domain transcoding in H.264/AVC.

Acknowledgement

This work was supported in part by the National Science Foundation of China (60333020), by the National Hi-Tech Research and Development Program (863) of China (2004AA119010), by the Beijing Science Foundation (4041003) and Science 100 Project of CAS.

References

1. A. Vetro, C. Christopoulos, and H. Sun, "Video Transcoding Architectures and Techniques: An Overview," IEEE Signal Processing magazine, Mar. 2003
2. T.Wiegand, G.J.Sullivan, G. Bjntegaard, A.Luthra, " Overview of the H.264/AVC Video Coding Standar," IEEE Trans.Circuits Syst. for Video Technol., Vol.13, No.7, July 2003
3. N.Bjork and C.Christopoulos, "Transcoder architectures for video coding," IEEE Trans. Consumer Electron., vol.44, no.1, pp.191-199, Feb.1998.
4. T.Shanableh and M.Ghanbari, "Heterogeneous video transcoding to lower spatio-temporal resolutions and different encoding formats," IEEE Trans. Multimedia, vol.2, pp.101-110, June 2000.
5. B. Shen, I. K. Sethi and B. Vasudev, "Adaptive Motion-Vector Resampling for compressed Video Downscaling," IEEE Trans. Circuits Syst. for video Technol., Vol.9, No.6, Sept. 1999
6. P. Yin, M. Wu, and B. Liu, "Video transcoding by reducing spatial resolution," in Proc. IEEE Int. Conf. Image Processing, Vol. 1, pp.972-975, Oct.2000
7. J. Xin, M. T. Sun, B. S. Choi, and K. W. Chun, "An HDTV-to-SDTV spatial Transcoder," IEEE Trans. Circuits Syst. for Video Technol., Vol.12, No.11, Nov. 2002
8. H.Y. Shu, L.P. Chau, "A fast arbitrary downsizing algorithm for video transcoding," in Proc. IEEE Int. Conf. Image Processing, Vol. 1, pp.I - 201-4, Sept.2003
9. P. Zhang, Y. Lu, Q.M. Huang, W. Gao, "Mode mapping method for H.264/AVC spatial downscaling transcoding," in Proc. IEEE Int. Conf. Image Processing, 2004.
10. H. Sun, W. Kwok, and J. W. Zdepski, "Architectures for MPEG compressed bitstream scaling," IEEE Trans. Circuits Syst. for Video Technol., Vol.6, No.2, April 1996
11. P.A.A. Assuncao and M. Ghanbari, "A frequency-domain video transcoder for dynamic bitrate reduction of MPEG-2 bit streams," IEEE Trans.Circuits Syst. for Video Technol., Vol.8, pp.953-967, Dec. 1998.
12. Y. K. Tu, J.F. Yang, Y. N. Shen, M.T. Sun, "Fast variable-size block motion estimation using merging procedure with an adaptive threshold," Proc. 2003 International Conf. on Multimedia and Expo. pp.II - 789-92 vol.2 July 2003
13. A.Joch, F.Kossentini, and P.Nasiopoulos, "A performance analysis of the ITU-T draft h.26L video coding standard", 12th International Packetvideo workshop, April 2002.
14. Y.Q. Liang, Y.P. Tan, "A New Content-Based Hybrid Video Transcoding Method", in Proc. IEEE Int. Conf. Image Processing, Vol. 1, pp. 429 - 432, Oct.2001

Low-Bitrate Video Quality Enhancement by Frame Rate Up-Conversion and Adaptive Frame Encoding

Ya-Ting Yang[1], Yi-Shin Tung[2], Ja-Ling Wu[1,2], and Chung-Yi Weng[1]

[1] Department of Computer Science and Information Engineering,
National Taiwan University
[2] The Graduate Institute of Networking and Multimedia, National Taiwan University
{ytyang, tung, wjl, chunye}@cmlab.csie.ntu.edu.tw

Abstract. Frame rate up-conversion (FRUC) is a useful technique for a lot of practical applications, such as display format conversion, low bitrate video coding and slow motion playback. Unlike traditional approaches, such as frame repetition or linear frame interpolation, motion-compensated frame interpolation (MCFI) technique which takes block motion into account is regarded as a more efficient scheme. By considering the deficiencies in previous works, new criteria and coding schemes for enhancing motion derivation and interpolation processes are suggested. We then integrate the proposed MCFI scheme into the decoding process of the latest coding standard, H.264/AVC. In addition, adaptive frame skip is fulfilled at the encoder side to maximize the power of MCFI in video coding applications. As a result, the encoder can adopt the MCFI dynamically and can decide whether the input frame should be coded or dropped then interpolated. Experimental results show that our proposal indeed enhances the overall quality, both subjectively and objectively, especially for the low bitrate video coding.

Keywords: Frame Rate Up-Conversion, Motion Compensated Frame Interpolation, Adaptive Frame Skip.

1 Introduction

The popularity of advanced television and multimedia information systems has caused a rapid increase in the number of video sources and variety of display formats. This has resulted in a demand for converting between various formats efficiently. In contrast with super-resolution video reconstruction [1], frame rate up conversion (FRUC), as implied by the name, is a process to convert the video frame rate from a lower number to a higher one. When a video sequence is encoded to a certain compression ratio, frame interpolation technique (FIT) is always used as a post-processing tool to reconstruct the skipped frames. FIT reduces the temporal jerkiness by representing video at any desired frame rate (even to the full frame rate) on the basis of interpolation techniques.

The development of FRUC potentiates a lot of video applications. The most practical one, probably, is to enhance the reconstructed quality of a low bitrate coded video. For example, in the video conferencing applications, it is inevitable for an encoder to have a number of frames skipped. A temporal interpolation is then helpful to smooth over those discontinuities. Besides these applications, FRUC can also benefit slow-motion playback by synthesizing those inexistent intermediate frames for smoothing slow motion playback. Other well-known applications include PAL-NTSC conversion and the video editing. FRUC may also impact on the rate allocation policy of a scalable video coding scheme.

Conventional FRUC approaches (such as frame repetition and linear frame interpolation) did not take motion information into account. As long as the video sequence has large or complex motion, those approaches may fail, and annoying artifacts such as motion jerkiness or image blur may appear. In recent researches [2-10], the motion-compensated frame interpolation (MCFI) scheme is widely adopted. MCFI enhances the reconstruction video quality by exploring block motions of interpolated frames.

Although MCFI is a post-processing tool at the decoder end, it still has something to do with the encoder. Since the activity of the object movement often varies from time to time, adaptive frame skip is performed to overcome the shortage that the video quality of FRUC is seriously constrained by the information provided by the encoder. When the object motion is slower and more linear-like, we may skip more frames between two coded frames. Otherwise, the number of skipped frames should be kept small. Adaptive frame skip (AFS) scheme was also presented in [10], where a suitable skipping number is selected from a pre-defined set. Inspired by [10] and observed from our simulation results, we found that there is still large room for enhancing the performance of FRUC with the aid of AFS.

The remainder of this paper is organized as follows. Section 2 gives an overview of MCFI. A system framework of the adopted MCFI process is presented in Section 3. Next, in Section 4 our implementation of AFS in the encoder end is addressed. Experimental results and discussions are given in Section 5. Finally, Section 6 concludes this write-up.

2 An Overview of Motion Compensated Frame Interpolation (MCFI)

Video sequences usually contain a huge amount of temporal redundancy that can be exploited for coding and processing purposes. Motion estimation and motion compensation are powerful means for exploiting such redundancy and are used in most advanced video coding standards. Although the concept of MCFI is similar to the bidirectional prediction mode of B-frame in all prevalent coding standards, the application of MCFI is different from that of the bidirectional prediction since the motion fields of the interpolated frame are not estimated at the encoder and transmitted to the decoder. The success of MCFI depends on how well the real motion vector can be obtained since there is no residual information favoring the reconstruction of those skipped frames. Once the motion vectors are incorrect, block artifacts will be introduced thereafter. Therefore, it is crucial 1) to correctly evaluate the reliability of the motion vectors no matter the motion vectors are derived from block-based motion fields within the bitstream or obtained from the re-estimation process, and 2) to estimate *true* motion vectors efficiently if the motion description is not available or not appropriate.

The main assumption of MCFI is that: there is a linear object translation within a short time period. In the case of 1:2 up conversion, the motion of the interpolated frame is $V/2$ to the previous frame and $-V/2$ to the current frame, where V is the motion from the current frame to the previous one. A bidirectional interpolation is introduced to synthesize the in-between frame, and therefore, each pixel in the interpolated frame is generated by combining the corresponding pixels in the forward and the backward reference frames. In other words, the values of the interpolated pixels should be:

$$f(x, t-\frac{1}{2}) = \frac{f(x+\frac{v}{2}, t-1) + f(x-\frac{v}{2}, t)}{2}, \qquad (1)$$

where $f(x,t)$ denotes the pixel value at location x and in time t.

In addition, Fig. 1 reveals the general framework to cooperate FRUC with the MPEG decoding process. It fulfills interpolation independently of the encoder except for the use of block motion vectors provided by the encoder. By utilizing the embedded motion information and the reconstructed frames in the MPEG decoding process, MCFI can be done efficiently due to the significant decrease of computation of motion estimation. Finally, the decoded frames and interpolated frames are multiplexed to form an up-converted video. However, the precision of the available motion vectors limit the quality of interpolation, so it is essential to identify unreliable motion vectors and fine-tune them further.

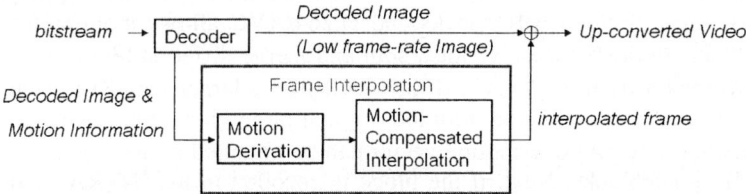

Fig. 1. A generic flowchart to integrate FRUC with the MPEG decoding process

3 System Framework of MCFI

The major components of our frame interpolator include *motion derivation* and *motion-compensated interpolation*, as shown in Fig. 2. The purpose of motion derivation is to obtain accurate motion vectors such that motion-compensated interpolation can perform well since the performance of MCFI depends significantly on the motion vector accuracy. In the motion derivation process, motion vectors embedded in the bitstream are extracted and then classified adaptively into a bad or good category first. If the motion vector is not available or has been categorized into the bad group, overlapped block bi-directional motion estimation (OBME) is performed. A median filter to eliminate the discontinuities and to smooth the motion fields in the neighboring blocks is then applied. Finally, motion vectors of all blocks are generated, and adaptive OBMC is employed to obtain the to-be-interpolated frames.

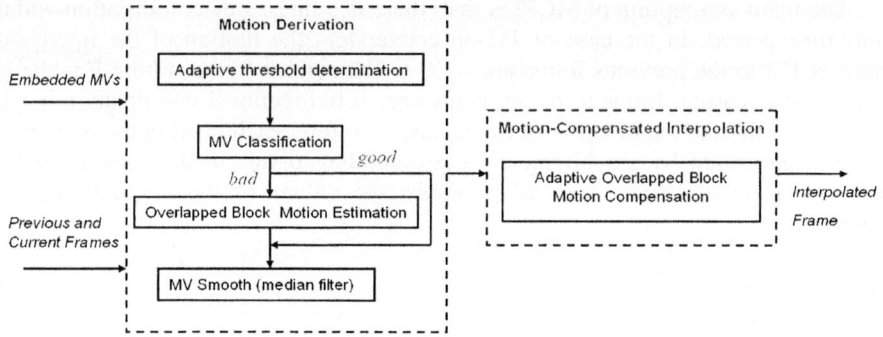

Fig. 2. The flowchart of the proposed MCFI approach

3.1 Obtaining Motion Vectors of the Interpolated Frame

Before realizing the process of MCFI, we first determine some basic characteristics, e.g. the resolution of a motion vector and the block size, of the interpolated frame. Clearly, small block sizes aim to minimize the residual energy, while large block sizes intend to get more true motion vectors. Under these considerations, 8×8 block size is selected as the basic processing unit to trade off the energy reduction of residual images and the correctness of obtained motion vectors. Further, state-of-the-art video coding standards support variable block sizes, e.g. MPEG-4 Visual supports motions for individual 8×8 and 16×16 blocks and H.264/AVC allows motions from 4×4 to 16×16 blocks. In those cases, we must split and merge different block sizes to form a motion vector for each 8×8 block. If the block size is larger than 8×8, each 8×8 sub-block derives its motion vector from the original large block. Otherwise, if the block size is smaller than 8×8, the motion vector can be obtained by averaging motion vectors of all its subblocks. Next, if the block is encoded in the INTRA mode, motion estimation has to be performed in a later stage. In our implementation, for retaining the motion vector resolution and utilizing its effectiveness, a 6-tapped quarter-pel filter and an eighth-pel bilinear filter are adopted for luminance and chrominance interpolations, respectively. As far as the motion vector accuracy and fractional sample interpolation are concerned, our realization compliantly follows the specification of the adopted coding standard (H.264/AVC in our case), so as to preserve the coding efficiency and the prediction accuracy of received motion vectors.

3.2 Motion Vector Classification

It is the fact that the block motion vectors generated in the encoder are for compression purpose but not for obtaining the real motion of objects. As a result, even motion vectors are available at the decoder side, not all of them are really close to the true motions and a re-estimation for those blocks with unreliable motion vectors is of necessity. To eliminate the unnecessary computation, a reliable classification for all available motion vectors becomes critical. It is well known that the sum of absolute difference (SAD) can be used to measure the signal similarity between two blocks in their supporting regions (8×8 in our case) and the boundary absolute difference

(BAD) can be used to measure the connecting smoothness between the interior and the exterior of block boundaries. So we consider SAD as well as BAD simultaneously and compare them with some content-adaptive thresholds, which will be addressed later.

For a block, e.g. B_1, in the interpolated frame, we first find the co-located block, B_4, in the current frame (frame t) and employ its motion, mv_{B4}, to obtain the blocks B_2 and B_3 respectively in the previous (frame $t-1$) and the current frames with the same motion trajectory, as shown in Fig. 3. For example, if the interpolated frame is right in the middle of the previous and the current frames, the motion vectors pointing to B_2 and B_3 are $mv_{B4}/2$ and $-mv_{B4}/2$, respectively. Then, we calculate SAD_{B1} and BAD_{B1}, i.e. the SAD and the BAD between B_2 and B_3, as follows:

$$SAD_{B1} = \sum_{i=0}^{7}\sum_{j=0}^{7} |f_{n-1}(m_{B_2}+i, n_{B_2}+j) - f_n(m_{B_3}+i, n_{B_3}+j)|$$

$$BAD_{B1} = \sum_{j=0}^{7}(|f_{n-1}(m_{B_2}, n_{B_2}+j) - f_n(m_{B_3}-1, n_{B_3}+j)| + |f_{n-1}(m_{B_2}+7, n_{B_2}+j) - f_n(m_{B_3}+8, n_{B_3}+j)|$$

$$\sum_{i=0}^{7}(|f_{n-1}(m_{B_2}+i, n_{B_2}) - f_n(m_{B_3}+i, n_{B_3}-1)| + |f_{n-1}(m_{B_2}+i, n_{B_2}+7) - f_n(m_{B_3}+i, n_{B_3}+8)|),$$

(2)

where $f_n(x, y)$ represents the intensity of the image pixel at location (x, y) in the time instance n, (i,j) is the spatial domain index of pixels in a block, and (m,n) is the coordinate for an 8×8 block which is denoted by a subscript.

After obtaining SAD_{B1} and BAD_{B1}, we compare them with their corresponding thresholds, T_{SAD} and T_{BAD}, which are determined by the SAD and the BAD between blocks B_4 and B_5, which mv_{B4} points to. It is observed that there is usually a high spatial correlation between B_3 and B_4 so the thresholds determined by blocks B_4 and B_5 are rational. However, mv_{B4} may be incorrect and leads to ineffective thresholds. Thus, if T_{SAD} is excessively large, the motion vector mv_{B4} is regarded as unreliable and then T_{SAD} as well as T_{BAD} are determined by using zero motion, instead. The idea is based on the fact that zero motion vector is the most commonly used vector in video coding. Finally, when either SAD_{B1} or BAD_{B1} exceeds their corresponding thresholds, the motion vector is classified into the bad category and motion re-estimation will be applied to this block.

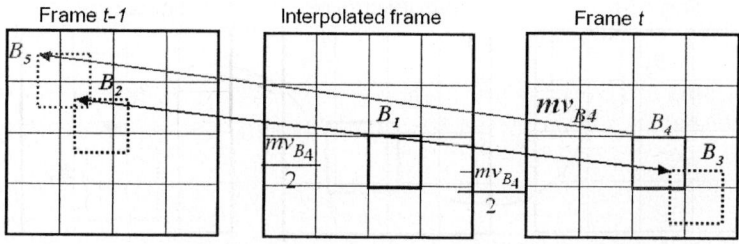

Fig. 3. Motion derivation for the interpolated frame

3.3 Overlapped Block Bi-directional Motion Estimation

More correct motion trajectory can be obtained when performing motion estimation with large blocks because the estimated motion vector may fall into a local minimum if the block is not large enough. To meet the requirement, overlapped block motion estimation is adopted. In addition, since we use bi-directional motion compensation, the more similarity between two directional predictors is, the more accuracy of the to-be-interpolated block can be derived. For this purpose, as shown in Fig. 4, deriving motion vectors from the to-be-interpolated block to the previous and current reference blocks for minimizing the difference between the bi-directional predictors is desired. The use of motion vectors pointing from the interpolated frame to the reference frame also releases the deficiencies of overlapped pixels and holes in the interpolated frames, which are unavoidable in conventional MCFI approaches [2-4]. Instead of applying bi-directional OBME directly, we first use uni-directional OBME to generate an initial motion vector. In our observation, directly applying bi-directional OBME will possibly lead to an undesired motion vector since there is no known pixel value of the to-be-interpolated block as the ground truth. Without using the initial motion vector, a block in the plain areas may be found, which leads to a fairly small SAD between the two directional predictors, and therefore, an erroneous motion vector is derived instead of the real object motion [12].

In our work, we use a general block matching algorithm (BMA) over a 12×12 enlarged block to get the initial motion vector for an 8×8 block by minimizing the following cost, first.

$$\sum_{j=-2}^{9}\sum_{i=-2}^{9} |I_t(x_c+i, y_c+j) - I_{t-1}(x_c+mv_x+i, y_c+mv_y+j)|, \quad (3)$$

where (mv_x, mv_y) represent the horizontal and vertical motion vector components, $I_t(x,y)$ is the luminance value in frame t at coordinates (x,y), and (x_c, y_c) is the top left point of the block to be estimated. In the refinement process, by minimizing the following cost we can obtain a pair of motion vectors from the to-be-interpolated block to the previous and the current predictors, respectively.

$$\sum_{j=-2}^{9}\sum_{i=-2}^{9} |I_t(x_c - \tfrac{mv_x}{2} - mv_{rx} + i, y_c - \tfrac{mv_y}{2} - mv_{ry} + j) - I_{t-1}(x_c + \tfrac{mv_x}{2} + mv_{rx} + i, y_c + \tfrac{mv_y}{2} + mv_{rx} + j)| \quad (4)$$

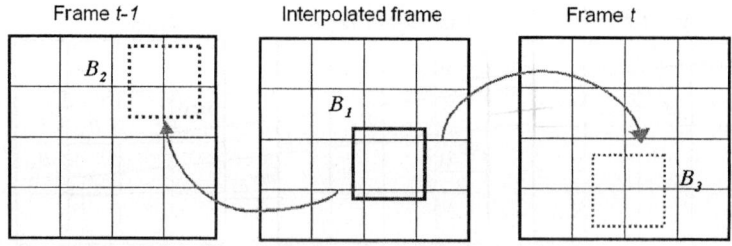

Fig. 4. Minimizing the difference between blocks B_2 and B_3 is the target of overlapped block bi-direction motion estimation

Until the current stage, we have derived the motion vectors to be ($mv_x/2+mv_{rx}$, $mv_y/2+mv_{ry}$) and ($-mv_x/2-mv_{rx}$, $-mv_y/2-mv_{ry}$) from the to-be-interpolated block to the previous and the current reference blocks, respectively. Summarily speaking, the use of forward motion estimation first and followed by bi-directional motion estimation can not only successfully reduce the probability of finding an undesired motion vector but also get a smaller SAD between two directional predictors.

3.4 Motion Vector Smoothing

Once the bi-directional motion vectors are constructed, motion-compensated interpolation is performed to reconstruct the interpolated frames. Nevertheless, it is observed that some estimated motion vectors are so inconsistent with that of its neighbors that they will cause annoying artifacts and degrade video quality significantly. Most artifacts originate from discontinuities in the motion fields, so a refinement by applying a median filter to do outlier-rejection and motion field smoothing is desired. By this process, we can identify those motion vectors which destroy the continuity of the motion fields.

Since we would like to remove an incoherent motion vector, the median motion vector among motion fields within a neighborhood will be viewed as the candidate motion vector. Besides, in our observation, majority voting should also be taken into consideration. If a certain motion vector dominates the motions in a 3×3 window of blocks, we also treat that motion vector as one candidate motion vector. For example, if there are four identical motion vectors within the 3×3 window, the motion really represents the motion trajectory in the region even though it is not the median one.

3.5 Adaptive Overlapped Block Motion Compensated Interpolation

When motion vectors of all blocks are well determined, interpolation is performed via using these motion vectors. A straightforward way to average two block-based bi-directional motion compensated predictors can be formulated as follows:

$$f_i(x) = w_f \times f_{t_1}(x+mv_f) + w_b \times f_{t_2}(x+mv_b), \tag{5}$$

where x denotes the location in the interpolated frame, and w_f and w_b are the weighs of forward and backward predictions in frames t_1 and t_2, respectively. The major drawback of the straightforward block-based scheme is the occurrence of well-known blocking artifacts. It is often introduced when motion vectors are not correct or significantly uncorrelated with that of their corresponding neighboring blocks. OBMC provides an effective way to reduce blocking artifacts in video coding. It exploits motion vectors of adjacent blocks to reduce the undesired discontinuity. However, if all blocks carry out OBMC, the whole frame may become over-blurred [5]. An effectual criterion to decide whether the block motion across the block boundary should be involved in the OBMC process is essential. We calculate the difference between the motion vector of the current block and that of its four neighboring blocks. If the difference is large, the boundary between two blocks is labeled as blockiness, and its neighboring block predictor overlapping the current block with 4×8 or 8×4 pixels will be considered, as indicated in Fig. 5(a). As a result, each pixel in an 8×8 block is combined using a weighted sum of at most three prediction values, which are obtained by using the motion vectors of the current block, the block at the left or right side and the block above or below the current block.

Figs. 5(b)–(d) give the weighting matrices for prediction generated by the motions of the current block, the top or bottom block, and the left or right block of the current block. For the matrix of the current block, the weights decrease as the location is approaching to the block boundary, while for the other two, the change of weights is opposite. This type of weighting causes smooth transitions across block boundary and less pronounced block edge because the contribution of each block varies depending on the pixel location within the block. In addition, if one or more block motions across the block boundary are decided not to be involved, their weights are added up to the matrix of the current block. For example, if the motion of the top block is not considered, the top half of the matrix in Fig. 5(c) will be merged into the weight of the current block. In the extreme, if all neighboring motions are not considered, OBMC is disabled for the current block.

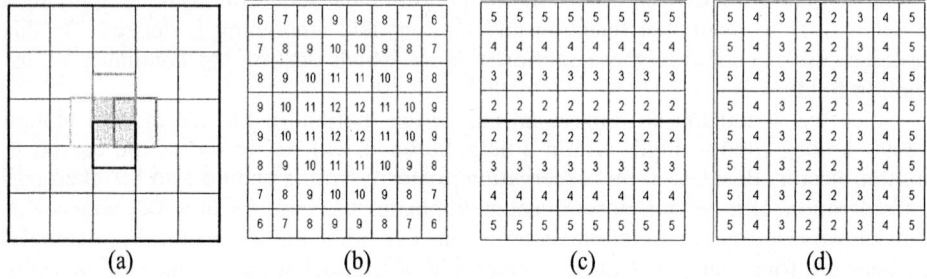

Fig. 5. (a) Four neighboring blocks are taken into account and overlapped four pixels with the current block. (b-d) Weighting matrices of the current, top and bottom, and left and right blocks, respectively.

4 Adaptive Frame Skip in the Encoder

Even though we have elaborated an effective MCFI algorithm, some interpolated frames are inevitable to have poor reconstructions. It is observed that the quality of interpolated frames relates to the information provided by the encoder; that is to say, the reconstructed quality is restricted by what is received at the decoder side. In order to enhance the quality of frame rate up-converted video sequences, in addition to improving the MCFI performance, it is essential to make an effort at the encoder side.

An intuitive solution is to adaptively skip frames according to characteristics of object motions in a short instance, e.g., from the previous coded frame to the next coded frame. Instead of regular frame skipping, an adaptive frame skipping technique can achieve a more efficient compression ratio. In our observation, the activity of object movement varies along the time axis in most video sequences. When the frame activity is low or a unified motion is detected, the motion almost coincides with the predictable trajectory and those intermediate frames are easy to be generated well at the decoder. On the contrary, the motion trajectory changes dramatically when the frame activity is very high. As a result of this characteristic, if the entire sequence is encoded with a fixed frame skip, the power of MCFI is not totally exploited. The bits used for coding low activity frames are regarded as waste if these frames can be well interpolated by two frames at a far distance. At this time, a larger frame skip number should be employed during the periods of low motion variation. Similarly, the fixed frame skip also results in poor performance for the video segment with high frame activity. In this case, a smaller frame skip number or even no skip will be better.

Fig. 6 reveals our implementation of the adaptive frame skip to determine which frames are encoded or skipped in the encoder. The *MCFI module* and *quality measurement of interpolated frames* are embedded in the encoding process as flow control units. We pre-define a maximum of frame skips between two coded frames. In each trial, starting from the largest frame skip number, we perform MCFI in the loop until a satisfactory frame skip number is found. In the flow-control feedback loop, a current reconstructed frame is sent to MCFI module together with a previous coded frame. Assuming that *n* frames are skipped, skipped frames are interpolated with motion compensation, and then evaluated by referencing the original frame. If the quality of interpolated frames is good enough, the current coded frame is taken and served as the previous frame in the next encoding. Otherwise, the current coded frame is regarded as useless, and re-encoding the immediately previous frame is employed. In other words, the module of quality measurement will give feedbacks to control the reading of the next encoding frame, the writing back of the current reconstructed frame and the permission of outputting encoding results. This iteration continues until all MCFI frames (i.e. interpolated frames) between the two coded frames are acceptable, and the worst case is that all frames should be encoded without any skip.

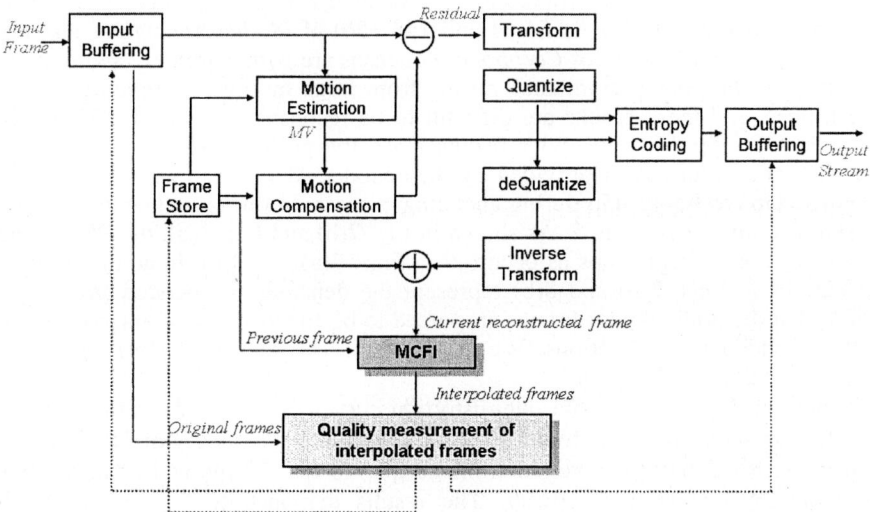

Fig. 6. Embed MCFI module and quality measurement of interpolated frames into the encoder as flow control units. The dotted lines represent control signals to notify the next loaded frame and the current write-back frame.

An interpolated frame is regarded as poor when there is a bad region in this frame. As long as an annoying region exists, human beings will feel uncomfortable even if all other parts are with good quality. Therefore, we do not assess the overall frame quality but detect the existence of any poor region. However, it is not trivial to find a suitable criterion since videos are ultimately viewed by human beings, the only "correct" method for quantifying visual quality is through subjective evaluation. Especially for those interpolated frames, the purpose of generating them is to make users feel more comfortable as compared with viewing a reduced frame rate video sequence. Precisely predicting the object location in the original missing frames is not the only criterion. Classical quality measurements, such as PSNR and mean squared error (MSE), may not represent accurate perceptual quality since they do not take the characteristics of human perception into account. Thus, the simple-computed PSNR is not a good evaluation metric to assess the performance of frame interpolation. On the other hand, subjective evaluation is usually too inconvenient, time-consuming and expensive. Therefore, we need an objective quality assessment to automatically predict perceived video quality. Here, we adopt the structural similarity (SSIM) indexing approach proposed in [11], which works under the assumption that human visual perception is highly adaptive and sensitive to the extracted structural information in a scene rather than absolute signal difference. In this way, the feedback control in the encoder is well behaved according the quality assessment of interpolated frames, which makes FRUC work more efficient at the decoder side.

5 Experimental Results

To demonstrate the effectiveness of the proposed adaptive frame skip, we integrate FRUC into the H.264/AVC reference software, Joint Model version 9.0. We first exhibit the case where certain frames are interpolated with poor quality. Figs. 7(a) and 8(a) show that intervals (frame 54-64 and 148-156) of *Mother&Daughter* and intervals (frame 4-11 and 56-58) of *Carphone* sequences are with extremely awful quality, respectively. The poor performance results from large motions of several blocks in these frames, and these blocks are difficult to be reconstructed well by MCFI. It is inevitable to suffer from the poor results since the performance of MCFI is constrained by the information provided by the encoder. We overcome the problem by applying adaptive frame skip during encoding process. In our experiments, the maximal skipped number is set to 2. As shown in Fig. 7(b) and Fig. 8(b), the PSNR traces are both without abrupt drops as occurred in Figs. 7(a) and 8(a). In addition, the dot distributions in Figs. 7(b) and 8(b) represent the densities of encoded frames. It is obvious that the original poor frames are forced to be encoded to guarantee the overall quality of video reconstructions. We attribute the satisfactory performance to the success of adaptive frame skip.

In addition, Fig. 9 shows the rate-distortion curves of the *Mother&Daughter* and the *Salesman* sequences. The four PSNR traces indicate the quality of full-frame-rate video reconstructions up-converted from 30-fps, 15-fps, 10-fps and adaptive frame rate coded bitstreams, respectively. The results demonstrate that: reconstructing frame-skipped videos by MCFI to achieve a full frame rate video communication is more effective than directly encoding videos with the full frame rate, especially for slow motion sequences. In this situation, lots of bitrate is saved while the video quality degrades slightly. Generally speaking, the improvements are 2 dB and 1 dB for low-bitrate coding and high-bitrate coding, respectively. In spite of the effectiveness of the adaptive frame skip is slightly worse than that of the regular frame skip. Nevertheless, the quality of each frame is ensured if the adaptive frame skip is adopted. Subjectively, this is an attractive merit in comparison with an abrupt quality drop in the regular frame skip mechanism.

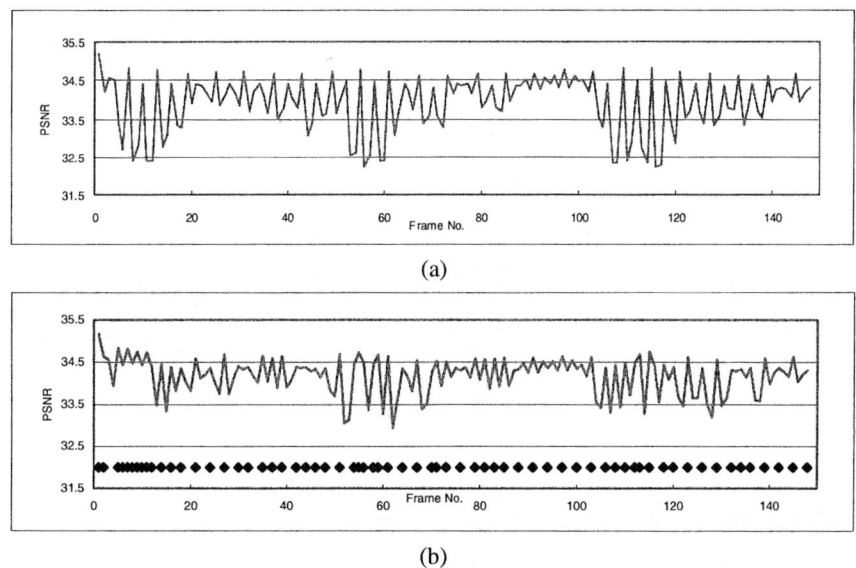

Fig. 7. PSNR traces of *Salesman* sequence: (a) regular frame skip = 2, (b) adaptive frame skip, and the occurrence of a dot means that the frame at that instance is coded. Dot distribution represents the density of encoded frames.

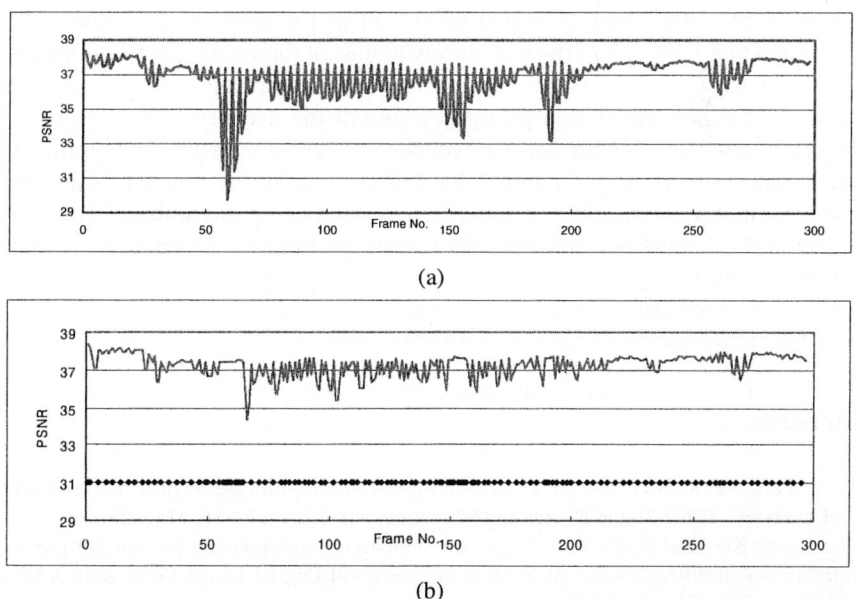

Fig. 8. PSNR traces of *Mother&Daughter* sequence: (a) regular frame skip = 2, (b) adaptive frame skip, and the occurrence of a dot means that the frame at that instance is coded. Dot distribution represents the density of encoded frames.

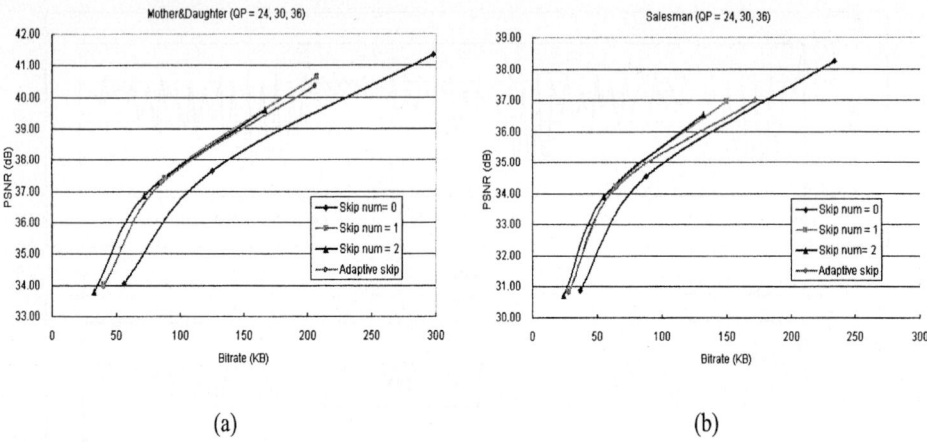

Fig. 9. The rate-distortion curves of the (a) *Mother&Daughter* and (b) *Salesman* sequences for regular frame skip number = 0, 1, 2 and adaptive frame skip

6 Conclusions

This paper presents an adaptive frame skip mechanism to overcome the restriction that interpolation performance is intrinsically constrained by the information provided by the encoder. Attempting to embed the MCFI and quality measurement modules into the encoding loop is an effective means to ensure the interpolation performance. Once we embed our MCFI module into the encoder, interpolated frames can be generated as if it is performed as a post-processing at the decoder side. Therefore, the quality of interpolated frames can be evaluated in advance, which is helpful to enhance the performance of to-be-interpolated frames, either by rejecting some unfair motion descriptions or prohibiting some frames from being interpolated. Experimental results show that the poor interpolated frames are forced to be encoded so that the overall video quality becomes much better. Besides our proposal, what the encoder can assist is to implicitly or explicitly transfer useful information to decoder for improving the reconstruction quality of interpolated frames.

References

1. S. C. Park, M. K. Park, and M. G. Kang, Super-resolution image reconstruction: a technical overview, IEEE Signal Processing Magazine, vol. 20, pp. 21-36, May 2003.
2. Tien-ying Kuo and C.-CJ Kuo, "Motion-compensated interpolation for low-bit-rate video quality enhancement," Proc. of SPIE Applications of Digital Image Processing XXI, vol. 3460, pp. 277-288, July 1998.
3. Bo-Won Jeon, Gun-Ill Lee, Sung-Hee Lee, and Rae-Hong Park, "Coarse-to-fine frame interpolation for frame rate up-conversion using pyramid structure," IEEE Trans. on Consumer Electronics, vol.49, No. 3, pp. 499-508, Aug. 2003.

4. Tieyan Liu, Kwok-Tung Lo, Jian Feng and Xudong Zhang, "Frame interpolation scheme using inertia motion interpolation", Proc. of Signal Processing:Image Communication, vol.18, pp221-229, March 2003.
5. Sung-Hee Lee, Ohjae Kwon, and Rae-Hong Park, "Weighted-adaptive motion-compensated frame rate-up conversion," IEEE Trans. on Consumer Electronics, vol.49, No. 3, pp. 485-492, Aug. 2003.
6. Taehyeun Ha, Seongjoo Lee, and Jaeseok Kim, "Motion compensated frame interpolation by new block-based motion estimation algorithm," IEEE Trans. on Consumer Electronics, vol.50, No. 2, pp. 752-759, May. 2004.
7. Yen-Kuang Chen, Anthony Vetro, Huifang Sun, and S. Y. Kung, "Frame-rate up-conversion using transmitted true motion vectors," Multimedia Signal Processing, IEEE Second Workshop on, pp. 622-627, Dec. 1998.
8. Hisao Sasai, Satoshi Kondo, and Shinya Kadono, "Frame-rate up-conversion using reliable analysis of transmitted motion information," Proc. of IEEE International Conference on Acoustics, Speech, & Signal Processing, May 2004.
9. Jiefu Zhai, Keman Yu, Jiang Li, and Shipeng Li, "A low complexity motion compensated frame interpolation method," to be appeared in Proc. of IEEE International Symposium on Circuits and Systems, 2005.
10. Tien-yung Kuo, JongWon Kim, and C.-C. Jay Kuo, "Motion-compensated frame interpolation scheme for H.263 codec," IEEE International Symposium on Circuits and Systems, vol. 4, pp 491-494, May 1999.
11. Zhou Wang, Alan Conrad Bovik, Hamid Rahim Sheikh, and Eero P. Simoncelli, "Image quality assessment: from error visibility to structural similarity," IEEE Trans. on Image Processing, vol.13, No. 4, pp. 600-612, Apr. 2004.
12. Ya-Ting Yang, Sung-Wen Wang, Yi-Shin Tung, Yi-Chin Huang, Ja-Ling Wu, "Low Bitrate and Full Frame Rate Video Communication by Motion-Compensated Frame Interpolation," to be appeared in EURASIP 2005

Face Recognition Using Neighborhood Preserving Projections

Yanwei Pang, Nenghai Yu, Houqiang Li, Rong Zhang, and Zhengkai Liu

MOE-Microsoft Key Laboratory of Multimedia Computing and Communication,
University of Science and Technology of China, Hefei 230027, China
{pyw, ynh, lihq, rongzhang, zhengkai}@ustc.edu.cn

Abstract. Subspace learning is one of the main directions for face recognition. In this paper, a novel unsupervised subspace learning method, *Neighborhood Preserving Projections* (NPP), is proposed. In contrast to traditional linear dimension reduction method, such as principal component analysis (PCA), the proposed method has good neighborhood-preserving property. The central idea is to modify the classical locally linear embedding by introducing a linear transform matrix. The transform matrix is obtained by optimizing a certain objective function. Experimental results on Yale face database and FERET face database show the effectiveness of the proposed method....

1 Introduction

Face recognition has rapidly emerged as an important area of research with many scientific and engineering disciplines. The applications of face recognition include surveillance, secure access, human/computer interface and so on. Face recognition spans several research fields such as content-based image retrieval, machine learning and computer vision.

In general, there are two main approaches to face recognition, geometric feature-based and template-based [1]. Geometric feature-based methods analyze explicit local features (such as eyes, mouth and nose) and their geometric relationships. Representative works include Hidden Markov Model (HMM) proposed by Samaria [2], elastic bunch graph matching algorithm proposed by Wiskott et al. [3], and Local Feature Analysis (LFA) proposed by Penev et al. [4]. Template-based (or appearance-based) methods match faces using the holistic features of face images. The current state-of-the art of such methods is characterized by a family of subspace methods originated by "eigenface" [5]. The underlying idea of eigenface is principal component analysis (PCA). Peter et al. switched from "eigenface" to "fisherface" [6]. The underlying idea of fisherface is linear discriminant anlaysis (LDA). To solve the small sample problem, Yu et al. proposed the "direct LDA" algorithm [21] while Wang et al. proposed the "dual-space LDA" [22]. Moghaddam et al. proposed to estimate density in high-dimensional spaces using eigenspace decomposition [7] and then derived a probabilistic similarity measure based on Bayesian analysis of image differences [8]. The underlying ideas of Moghaddam's method are probabilistic principal component analysis

(PPCA)[15] and the Bayes theory. Wang et al. further developed a unified analysis method that uses three subspace dimensions, i.e. intrinsic difference, transform difference and noise, and achieved better recognition performance than the standard subspace methods [9][23]. He et al. proposed to use Laplacianfaces for face recognition which is based on Locality Preserving Projections [10].

Generally speaking, besides the feature-based method and templated method, there is another kind of face recognition method, hybrid method. Compared with feature-based method and template-based method, the hybrid method utilize both local features and the whole face region to recognize a face [24].

Due to the large variations of face appearance caused by variations in expression, illumination and pose, the manifold of the face space is believed to be too complex to be described effectively by linear subspace learning algorithm. Though the structure of this manifold can be represented by the locally linear structure using locally linear embedding (LLE) [11], LLE cannot map a new testing point directly, which is referred to as the out-of-sample problem [20].

In this paper we propose a novel template-based face recognition method using Neighborhood Preserving Projections (NPP). NPP is an unsupervised subspace learning approach. The differences between NPP and other subspace learning approaches such as PCA and LDA lie in their different motivations and objective functions. PCA ,an unsupervised subspace learning method, seeks a projection that best represent the data in a least-squares sense. LDA, an supervised learning method, selects a transform matrix in such a way that the ratio of the between-class scatter and the within-class scatter is maximized. In contrast to PCA and LDA, NPP utilizes local neighborhood relations to learn the global structure. The central idea of NPP is to modify the classical locally linear embedding (LLE) [11] by introducing a linear transform matrix. The transform matrix is obtained by optimizing a certain objective function. Since the proposed method is a linear form of the original nonlinear LLE, NPP inherits LLE's neighborhood preserving property naturally.

The rest of this paper is organized as follows: Section 2 gives an overview of the NPP. Section 3 provides a brief description of LLE. In section 4, the motivation and justification of NPP is presented. Section 5 describes how to apply NPP for face recognition. In section 6, experiments are performed on the Yale and FERET face databases. Finally, conclusions are offered in section 6.

2 Overview of the Proposed Method: NPP

Given N points $\mathbf{X}=[\mathbf{x}_1,\mathbf{x}_2,\ldots,\mathbf{x}_N]$ in D dimensional space, dimension reduction is conducted such that these points are mapped to be new points $\mathbf{Y}=[\mathbf{y}_1,\mathbf{y}_2,\ldots,\mathbf{y}_N]$ in d dimensional space where $d << D$. A linear transformation matrix $\mathbf{A}$ is determined so that

$$\mathbf{y}_i = \mathbf{A}^T \mathbf{x}_i. \tag{1}$$

Before presenting a detailed derivation of NPP algorithm, we will give an overview of it in next subsection.

The first two steps of NPP algorithm are the same as those of LLE. Our main contribution lies in third step. The justification will be given in section 4.

Step 1. Assign neighbors to each data point $\mathbf{x}_i$ (for example by using the K nearest neighbors)

Step 2. Compute the weights W_{ij} that best linearly reconstruct $\mathbf{x}_i$ from its neighbors.

Step 3. Compute the linear transform matrix $\mathbf{A}$ by solving the generalized eigenvalue problem:

$$\mathbf{L}\mathbf{A}^T = \lambda \mathbf{C}\mathbf{A}^T. \tag{2}$$

Where

$$\mathbf{L} = \mathbf{X}\mathbf{M}\mathbf{X}^T$$
$$\mathbf{C} = \mathbf{X}\mathbf{X}^T$$
$$\mathbf{M} = (\mathbf{I} - \mathbf{W})(\mathbf{I} - \mathbf{W})^T.$$

Note that to find the solution of the equation reliably, we usually perform dimension reduction by PCA prior to NPP. we will explain step 3 in detail in section 3.

Step 4. Dimension reduction is performed simply by

$$\mathbf{Y} = \mathbf{A}^T\mathbf{X}.$$

Because the proposed method is closely related to LLE algorithm, we will give a breif introduction of LLE before the detailed derivation of NPP.

3 Locally Linear Embedding (LLE)

To begin, suppose the data consist of N real-valued vectors $\mathbf{x}_i$, each of dimensionality D, sampled from a smooth underlying manifold. Provided the manifold is well-sampled, it is expected that each data point and its neighbors lie on or close to a locally linear patch of the manifold. We characterize the local geometry of these patches by linear coefficients W_{ij} that reconstruct each data point $\mathbf{x}_i$ from its K neighbors $\mathbf{x}_j$. Choose W_{ij} to minimize a cost function of squared reconstruction errors:

$$J_1(\mathbf{W}) = \sum_{i=1}^{N} ||\mathbf{x}_i - \sum_{j=1}^{K} W_{ij}\mathbf{x}_j||^2. \tag{3}$$

The reconstruction error can be minimized analytically using a Lagrange multiplier to enforce the constraint that (see [11] for details).

A basic idea behind LLE is that the same weights W_{ij} that reconstruct the ith data in D dimensions should also reconstruct its embedded manifold coordinates in d dimensions. Hence, each high-dimensional data $\mathbf{x}_i$ can be mapped to a low-dimensional vector $\mathbf{y}_i$ by minimizing the embedding cost function:

$$J_2(\mathbf{Y}) = \sum_{i=1}^{N} ||\mathbf{y}_i - \sum_{j=1}^{K} W_{ij}\mathbf{y}_j||^2. \tag{4}$$

$$= ||\mathbf{Y}(\mathbf{I} - \mathbf{W})||^2$$
$$= trace(\mathbf{Y}(\mathbf{I} - \mathbf{W})(\mathbf{I} - \mathbf{W})^T \mathbf{Y}^T)$$
$$= trace(\mathbf{Y}\mathbf{M}\mathbf{Y}^T.$$

where
$$\mathbf{M} = (\mathbf{I} - \mathbf{W})(\mathbf{I} - \mathbf{W})^T. \tag{5}$$
$$\mathbf{W} = [\mathbf{w}_1 \ \mathbf{w}_2 \ \cdots \ \mathbf{w}_N].$$

I represents an identity matrix.

To make the optimization problem well posed, two constrains can be imposed to remove the translational and rotational degree of freedom:

$$\sum_{i=1}^{N} \mathbf{y}_i = 0 \quad or$$

$$\mathbf{Y}\mathbf{1} = 0. \tag{6}$$

$$\frac{1}{N-1} \sum_{i=1}^{N} \mathbf{y}_i \mathbf{y}_i^T = \mathbf{I} \quad or$$

$$\frac{1}{N-1} \mathbf{Y}\mathbf{Y}^T = \mathbf{I}. \tag{7}$$

where **1** stands for a summing vector: $\mathbf{1} = [1, 1, \ldots, 1]^T$.

The constrained minimization can then be done using the method of Lagrange multipliers:

$$L(\mathbf{Y}) = \mathbf{Y}\mathbf{M}\mathbf{Y}^T + \lambda((N-1)\mathbf{I} - \mathbf{Y}\mathbf{Y}^T). \tag{8}$$

Setting the gradients with respect to **Y** to zero

$$\frac{\partial L}{\partial Y} = 0 \Rightarrow$$

$$2\mathbf{M}\mathbf{Y}^T - 2\lambda \mathbf{Y}^T = 0. \tag{9}$$

leads to a symmetric eigenvalue problem:

$$\mathbf{M}\mathbf{Y}^T = \lambda \mathbf{Y}^T. \tag{10}$$

We can impose the first constraint above (for zero mean) by discarding the eigenvectors associated with eigenvalue 0 (free translation), and keeping the eigenvectors, $\mathbf{u}_i$, associated with the bottom d nonzero eigenvalues. These produce the d rows of the d-by-N output matrix **Y** [15]:

$$\mathbf{Y} = [\mathbf{y}_1 \ \mathbf{y}_2 \ \cdots \ \mathbf{y}_N]_{d \times N} = \begin{bmatrix} \mathbf{u}_1 \\ \mathbf{u}_2 \\ \vdots \\ \mathbf{u}_d \end{bmatrix}_{d \times N}. \tag{11}$$

4 The Proposed Method (NPP)

4.1 Motivation

Though LLE possesses some favorable properties [12], its computational cost is expensive than most linear dimension reduction methods. Moreover, it cannot map a new testing point directly, which is referred to as out-of-sample problem. The out-of-sample problem states that only the low dimensional embedding map of training samples can be computed but the samples out of the training set (i.e. testing samples) cannot be calculated directly, analytically or even cannot be calculated at all. This problem arises from the fact that the embedding of $\mathbf{y}_i$ is obtained in a way that does not explicitly involve the input point $\mathbf{x}_i$. The cost function J of LLE

$$J(\mathbf{Y}) = \sum_{i=1}^{N} ||\mathbf{y}_i - \sum_{j=1}^{K} W_{ij}\mathbf{y}_j||^2. \tag{12}$$

depends merely on the weights W_{ij}. To establish a bridge across this gap, we plug equation (1) into the cost function J and the resultant cost function is optimized. The process of NPP has been presented in section 2. In the next subsection its justification will be given. Because the first two steps of NPP are the same as LLE, only justification related to step 3 is presented.

4.2 Justification

Here we rewrite equation (1)

$$\mathbf{y}_i = \mathbf{A}^T \mathbf{x}_i \quad or$$

$$\mathbf{Y} = \mathbf{A}^T \mathbf{X}. \tag{13}$$

where

$$\mathbf{A} = [\mathbf{a}_0, \mathbf{a}_1, \cdots, \mathbf{a}_d].$$

We plug equation (13) into the cost function J:

$$J(\mathbf{Y}) = \sum_{i=1}^{N} ||\mathbf{y}_i - \sum_{j=1}^{K} W_{ij}\mathbf{y}_j||^2. \tag{14}$$

$$= trace(\mathbf{Y}\mathbf{M}\mathbf{Y}^T)$$

$$= trace((\mathbf{A}^T\mathbf{X})\mathbf{M}(\mathbf{A}^T\mathbf{X})^T)$$

$$= trace(\mathbf{A}^T(\mathbf{X}\mathbf{M}\mathbf{X}^T)\mathbf{A}).$$

To make the minimization problem well posed, we add a constrain:

$$\frac{1}{N-1}\mathbf{YY}^T = \mathbf{I} \Rightarrow$$

$$\frac{1}{N-1}\mathbf{A}^T\mathbf{X}(\mathbf{A}^T\mathbf{X})^T = \frac{1}{N-1}\mathbf{A}^T(\mathbf{XX}^T)\mathbf{A} = \mathbf{I}. \tag{15}$$

The constrained minimization can then be done using the method of Lagrange multipliers:

$$\mathcal{L}(\mathbf{A}) = \mathbf{A}^T(\mathbf{XMX}^T)\mathbf{A} + \lambda((N-1)\mathbf{I} - \mathbf{A}^T\mathbf{XX}^T\mathbf{A}). \tag{16}$$

Setting the gradients with respect to $\mathbf{A}$ to zero we have

$$\frac{\partial \mathcal{L}}{\partial \mathbf{A}} = 0 \Rightarrow$$

$$2(\mathbf{XMX}^T)\mathbf{A}^T - 2\lambda\mathbf{XX}^T\mathbf{A}^T = 0. \tag{17}$$

By defining

$$\mathbf{L} = \mathbf{XMX}^T \tag{18}$$

$$\mathbf{C} = \mathbf{XX}^T. \tag{19}$$

we can rewrite equation (17) in the form of a generalized eigenvalue problem:

$$\mathbf{LA}^T = \lambda \mathbf{CA}^T. \tag{20}$$

If $\mathbf{C}$ is invertible, equation (20) can be transformed to a standard eigenvlaue problem:

$$(\mathbf{C}^{-1}\mathbf{L})\mathbf{A}^T = \lambda \mathbf{A}^T. \tag{21}$$

Once $\mathbf{A}$ is obtained by solving equation (20) or (21), $\mathbf{X}$ can be mapped to a low dimensional space by

$$\mathbf{Y} = \mathbf{A}^T\mathbf{X}.$$

That is

$$\mathbf{y}_i = \mathbf{A}^T\mathbf{x}_i$$

where $i=1,2,...,N$.

5 Face Recognition Using NPP

Denote the solution of equation (21) by $\mathbf{A}_{npp}$. It should be noted that equation (21) is an ill-posed problem when the matrix $\mathbf{C}$ is singular. The size of $\mathbf{C}$ is $D*D$ while the rank of C is at most N. Thus, $\mathbf{C}$ is always singular if $D > N$, i.e. the number of training samples is less than the dimension of feature vectors. Unfortunately, this is often the case in face recognition. To deal with this problem, we propose to perform dimension reduction by PCA prior to applying NPP. In fact, this technique were also used in fisherfaces [6] and Laplacianfaces [10][14]. Let the transform matrix of PCA is $\mathbf{A}_{pca}$, then the process is

$$\mathbf{x}^* = \mathbf{A}_{pca}^T \mathbf{x}$$

$$\mathbf{y} = \mathbf{A}_{npp}^T \mathbf{x}^*.$$

where the size of $\mathbf{A}_{pca}$ is $D*(N\text{-}1)$ and the size of $\mathbf{A}_{npp}$ is $(N\text{-}1)*d$.

Equivalently, it holds

$$\mathbf{y} = \mathbf{A}^T \mathbf{x}.$$

where

$$\mathbf{A}^T = \mathbf{A}_{npp}^T * \mathbf{A}_{pca}^T. \tag{22}$$

Since fisherface method can be called PCA plus LDA (PCA+LDA), we may call the proposed method as PCA plus NPP (PCA+NPP).

6 Experimental Results

The Yale [6] and FERET [13] face databases were used to evaluate the proposed method. In addition to our proposed method, we also tested the Eigenface method and the Fisherface method, two of the most popular methods in face recognition. Nearest neighborhood classifier was employed in the experiments. The accuracy we reported is refer to as the rank one (top match) recognition rate.

6.1 Experiment with the Yale Face Database

The Yale face database consists of images from 15 different people, using 11 images from each person, for a total 165 images. The images contain variations with the following facial expressions or configurations: center-light, with glasses, happy, left-right, without glasses, normal, right-left, sad, sleepy, surprised and wink. The 11 images of one person in Yale face database are shown in

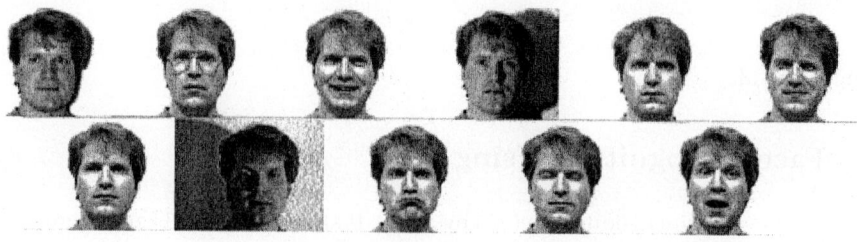

Fig. 1. Eleven images in the Yale face database

Figure 1. Six face images of each subject are randomly chosen for training, while the remaining five images are used for testing. Thus, the training sample set size is 90 and the testing set sample size is 75. In this way, we run the system 5 times and obtain 5 different training and testing sample sets. The recognition rates were found by averaging the recognition rate of eahc run.

We preprocessed these images by aligning and scaling them so that the distances between the eyes were the same for all images and also ensuring that the eyes occurred in the same coordinates of the image. The resulting image was then cropped. The final image size was 32*32.

The results for the Yale database are given in figure 2. The horizontal axis represents the dimension (feature number) of the subspace and the vertical axis stand for the recognition rate. The best results of each method are listed in table 1. As can be seen, out proposed method, NPP, outperforms both Eigenface and Fisherface methods. It is noted that when the feature number is between 50 and 80, NPP achieves its best performance. The feature number of Fisherface is at most 15-1=14.

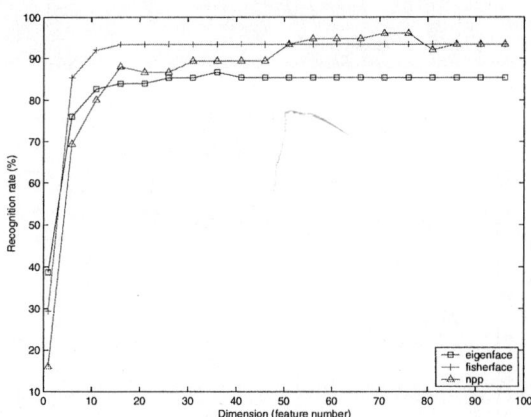

Fig. 2. The recognition rates versus the subspace dimension on Yale database

Both Eigenface and NPP are unsupervised subspace learning methods. However, NPP is superior to PCA for face recognition. Moreover, NPP is even better than LDA, a well-known supervised method which utilizes the class label information.

Table 1. Comparison of different methods on Yale database

Method	Eigenface	Fisherface	NPP
Result (%)	86.6	93.3	96.0

6.2 Experiments with the FERET Face Database

We also tested the proposed method on a subset of the FERET face database. This subset includes 420 frontal images of 70 individuals with 6 images per person. The 6 images of one person in FERET face database are shown in Figure 3. Two face images of each subject are randomly chosen for training, while the remaining four images are used for testing. Thus, the training sample set size is 140 and the testing set sample size is 280. In this way, we run the system 2 times and obtain 2 different training and testing sample sets. The recognition rates were found by averaging the recognition rate of eahc run. We preprocessed these images by aligning and scaling them so that the distances between the eyes were the same for all images and also ensuring that the eyes occurred in the same coordinates of the image. The resulting image was then cropped. The final image size was 32*32.

Fig. 3. Six images in the Feret face database

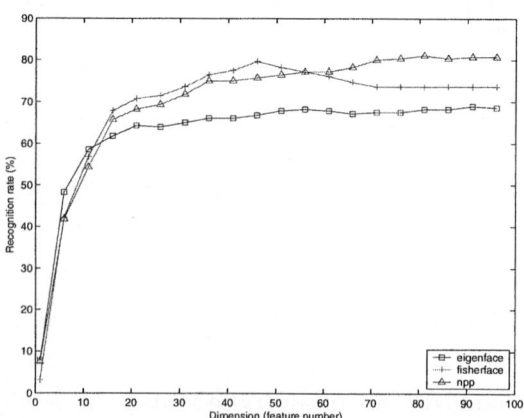

Fig. 4. The recognition rates versus the subspace dimension on FERET database

The recognition results are shown in figure 4. The meaning of the horizontal and vertical axes is the same as that in figure 2. The horizontal axis represents the dimension (feature number) of the subspace and the vertical axis stand for the recognition rate. The best results of Eigenface, Fisherface and the proposed method are listed in table 2. As can be seen, out proposed method, NPP, outperforms both Eigenface and Fisherface methods. The reason is that NPP has neighborhood preserving property while the Eigeface and Fisheface methods do not.

Table 2. Comparison of different methods on FERET face database

Method	Eigenface	Fisherface	NPP
Result (%)	68.21	79.63	81.03

7 Conclusions

A novel unsupervised face recognition algorithm is proposed where Neighborhood Preserving Projections (NPP) is employed. NPP is derived by introducing a linear transform matrix into LLE algorithm. The linear transform matrix is obtained by optimizing a certain objective function which is similar to that of LLE. Hence, NPP inherits LLE's neighborhood property naturally.

In contrast to the Eigenface (PCA) method, the proposed method has good neighborhood-preserving property. The neighborhood-preserving property leads NPP to even outperform the Fisherface (LDA) method, a well-known supervised method which utilizes the class label information.

Though NPP is similar in some sense to locality preserving projections (LPP) [14], NPP has less parameters to tune than LPP. Both in NPP and LPP algorithms, the neighborhood number should be selected beforehand. But in LPP additional parameter t should be tuned carefully, which make the algorithm not convenient to be used. The function of the parameter t is to measure the similarity between a sample concerned and its neighbor. See [14] for the details.

As for the future work, we will investigate how to modify NPP from an unsupervised subspace learning method to a supervised subspace learning method where class labels are used. Alternatively, one also develop a labelled-unlabelled learning algorithm [17] or semi-supervised learning algorithm [16] using NPP . Due to the large variations of face appearance caused by variations in expression, illumination and pose, the face space is more likely nonlinear and is difficult to described by linear subspace learning algorithms such as NPP. Therefore, we will perform NPP in a large high-dimensional space by introducing a kernel [18][19]. It is expected that the kernel NPP, which is a nonlinear learning algorithm, can outperform NPP.

Acknowledgements

The work was supported by Open Fund of MOE-Microsoft Key Laboratory under Grant No. 050718-6 and Open Fund of Image Processing and Image Communication Lab, Nanjing University of Posts and Telecommunications, under Grant No. KJS03039.

References

1. Zhao, W., Chellappa, R., Rosenfeld, A., Phillips, J.: Face recognition: A Literature Survey. ACM Computing Surveys, Vol. 12, (2003) 399-458
2. Samaria, F.S.: Face Recognition Using Hidden Markov Models. PhD thesis, University of Cambridge, 1994

3. Wiskott, L., Fellous J., Kruger, N., Malsburg, C.: Face Recognition by Elastic Bunch Graph Matching. IEEE Transactions on Pattern Analysis and Machine Intelligence, Vol. 19, No. 7, (1997) 775-779
4. Penev, P.S.: Local Feature Analysis: a General Statistical Theory for Object Repentation. Network: Computation in Neural Systems, Vol. 7, (1996) 477-500
5. Turk, M., Pentland, A.: Face Recognition Using Eigenfaces. In: IEEE Computer Society Conference on Computer Vision and Pattern Recognition, (1991) 586-591
6. Peter, N.B., Joao, P.H., David, J.K.: Eigenfaces vs. Fisherfaces: Recognition Using Class Specific Linear Projection, Vol. 19, No. 7, (1997) 711-720
7. Moghaddam, B., Pentland, A.: Probabilistc Visual Learning For Object Reprentation. IEEE Transactions on Pattern Analysis and Machine Intelligence, Vol. 19, No.7, (1997) 696-710
8. Moghaddam, B, Jebara, B., Pentland, A.: Bayesian Face Recognition. Pattern Recognition, Vol. 33, (2000) 1771-1782
9. Wang, X., Tang, X.: Unified Subspace Analysis for Face Recognition. In Proc. IEEE Conference on Computer Vision, 2003
10. He,X., S. Yan, Hu,Y., Niyogi,P., Zhang,H.J.: Face Recognition Using Laplacianfaces. IEEE Transactions on Pattern Analysis and Machine Intelligence, Vol. 27, No. 3, (2005)328-340
11. Roweis,S., Saul,L.: Nonlinear dimensionality reduction by locally linear embedding. Science, Vol. 290, No. 5500 , (2000) 2323-2326
12. Saul,L.K., Roweis,S.T.: Think Globally, Fit Locally: Unsupervised Learning of Low Dimensional Manifolds. Journal of Machine Learning Research, Vol. 4, (2003) 119-155
13. Phillips, P.J., Moon, H., Rivzi, S., and Rauss, P.: The FERET evaluation methodology for face-recognition algorithms. IEEE Transaction on Pattern Analysis and Machine Intelligence, Vol. 22, (2000) 1090-1104
14. He, X., Yan,S.,Yan,Hu, Y.,Zhang H.: Learning a locality preserving subspace for visual recognition. In: IEEE International Conference on Computer Vision. (2003)I: 385-392.
15. Tipping, M., Bishop,C.: Probabilistic principal component analysis. Journal of the Royal Statistical Society, Vol. 61, No. 3, (1999) 611-622.
16. Belkin, M., Niyogi, P.: Using manifold structure for partially labeled classification. In: Advances in Neural Information Processing System 15. (2002).
17. Blum, A., Chawla, S.: Learning from labeled and unlabeled data using graph mincuts. In: International Conference on Machine Learning. (2001) 19-26.
18. John, S.T., Nello, C.: Kernel Methods for Pattern Analysis, Cambridge University Press, 2004.
19. Scholkopf, B., Smola, A., Muller, K.: Nonlinear component analysis as a kernel eigenvale problem. Neural Computation, Vol. 10, No. 5, (1998) 1299-1319.
20. Bengio, Y., Paiemetn, J., Vincent, P.: Out-of-sample extensions for LLE, Isomap, MDS, Eigenmaps, and Spectral Clustering. In: Advances in Neural Information Processing System. (2003).
21. Yu, H., Yang, J.: A direct LDA algorithm for high dimensional data with application to face recognition. Pattern Recognition. Vol. 34. (2001) 2067-2070.
22. Wang, X., Tang, X.: Dual-space linear discriminant analysis for face recognition. In: Proceedings of IEEE International Conference on Computer Vision and Pattern Recognition. (2004) .
23. Wang, X., Tang, X.: Unified subspace analysis for face recognition. In: Proceedings of the Ninth IEEE International Conference on Computer Vision (ICCV). Vol. 1, No. 1. (2003)679-686.
24. Zhao, W., Chellappa, R., Phillips, P.J., Rosenfeld, A.: Face recogntion: a literature survey. ACM Computing. Vol. 35, No.4. (2003) 399-458.

An Efficient Virtual Aesthetic Surgery Model Based on 2D Color Photograph

Hyun Park[1], Kee Wook Rim[2], and Young Shik Moon[1]

[1] Department of Computer Science and Engineering, Hanyang University,
1271 Sa-Dong, Ansan, Kyunggi-Do 425-791, Korea
{hpark, ysmoon}@cse.hanyang.ac.kr
[2] Department of Knowledge and Industrial Engineering,
Sun Moon University, Chung-Nam, Korea
rim@sunmoon.ac.kr

Abstract. In this paper, we propose a virtual aesthetic surgery (VAS) system using a deformation technique based on a radial basis function (RBF) and blending technique that combines the deformed facial component with the original face. The proposed VAS system is composed of three main steps. First, various deformation templates are matched to facial components by a multi-resolution active appearance model (MAAM), which is trained by 2D color face images. Next, the VAS system computes the degree of deformation for lattice cells on the free-form deformation (FFD) using the proposed RBF. The deformation error is compensated for by the coefficients of the mapping function, which is recursively solved by the singular value decomposition (SVD) technique using the sum of squared error (SSE) between the deformed control points and target control points on the base curves. Finally, the deformed facial component is blended with the original face using a blending ratio that is computed by the modified Euclidean distance transform. Experimental results show that the proposed deformation and blending techniques are very efficient in terms of smoothness, accuracy, and distortion.

1 Introduction

Recently, many people have shown an interest in their facial appearance due to images propagated by the mass media. The development of modern medical technology can now satisfy an individual's needs for altering their appearance through aesthetic surgery.

Even if a face is only slightly deformed, the overall facial appearance may look more affected [1]. Thus, individuals who want to undergo aesthetic surgery need a VAS system that can realistically predict the appearance of altered features after surgery. The proposed VAS system consists of deformation template tools and various filters (double eyelid filter, skin care filter, etc.) for aesthetic effects.

Two-dimensional (2D) or three-dimensional (3D) face deformation models, which are the basic techniques of a computer-based virtual surgery system, typically fall into two main categories: (i) physically/anatomically based models and (ii) non-physically based models using morphing or special deformation [2].

Physically-based models attempt to model the structure and function of the muscles and skin of the face using a mass-spring or finite element model [1], [2]. Since physically-based models can predict the results of virtual surgery with high accuracy, these models are used for plastic reconstructive surgery systems, which can virtually correct craniofacial deformities [3], [4], [5]. However, physically-based models have some drawbacks. Typically, it is very difficult to define physical models for faces, they require a large amount of computation time, and do not properly handle facial color and textures. These models are used on a limited basis for facial surgery of some parts of faces.

Non-physically based models use generic animation techniques, such as morphing and spatial deformations, to create facial expressions or deformation. Lee et al. described a morphing technique based on a multilevel free-form deformation (MFFD). The MFFD model is controlled by a set of feature points that place positional constraints on the MFFD lattice [6], [7]. The MFFD model affects or distorts facial components other than the deformation region because it uses only a global deformation. Also, MFFD does not properly handle the facial texture distortion. Lin et al. described a deformation technique that used radial basis functions (RBFs) and the displacements of feature points for facial expression and animation [8]. This model also has drawbacks: it does not produce an accurate facial deformation and the facial components outside of the deformation region are also distorted. Noh et al. described a deformation technique for 3D facial expression. This deformation technique, after defining deformable regions on lattice cells for a particular face, computes the degree of deformation by using RBFs and the displacements of feature points [9]. Although this deformation technique has locality, it has the same drawbacks as Lin's method.

The VAS system requires four main characteristics: (i) convenience in representing virtual surgery regions and using deformation tools; (ii) smoothness and accuracy in deforming facial components (eye, nose, mouth, jaws, etc.); (iii) locality that does not affect or distort other facial components outside of the deformation region; and (iv) preservation of the facial color texture.

To satisfy these four characteristics, the proposed VAS system is composed of three main steps. First, various deformation templates are semi-automatically matched to facial components by the multi-resolution active appearance model (MAAM) that is trained by 2D color face images. As in the original AAM (active appearance model) method, this appearance model will be constructed with multiple resolutions to provide coarse-to-fine fitting. Next, the VAS system computes the degree of deformation for lattice cells on the free-form deformation (FFD) using the proposed RBF. As RBFs can compute the degree of deformation efficiently with less computing time, RBFs are typically used for facial deformations that require real time processing. The deformation error is compensated for by the coefficients of the mapping function, which is recursively solved by the singular value decomposition (SVD) technique using the sum of squared error (SSE) between the deformed control points and target control points on base curves. Finally, a blending technique is proposed to minimize the distortion of facial color textures, which are important in the VAS system. The blending technique combines the deformed facial component with the original face by using a blending ratio that is computed by the modified Euclidean distance transform.

In this paper, the proposed facial deformation framework uses a flexible framework that is proposed by Pixar Animation Studios and Princeton University [10]. Figure 1 shows the total framework of the proposed VAS system.

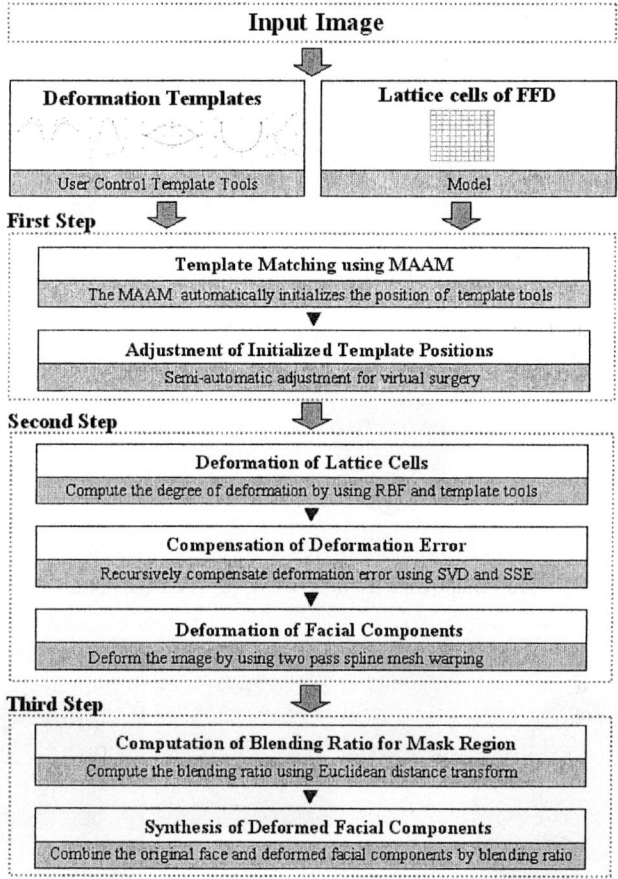

Fig. 1. Framework of the proposed VAS system

2 Search-Based Matching of Various Deformation Templates

In the VAS system, it is not easy for an operator to indicate facial components manually using a pointing device such as a mouse. Therefore, a semi-automatic matching step for deformation templates is provided to help the operator indicate the deformation regions for virtual aesthetic surgery easily and efficiently.

2.1 Training of Face Images

The data set consists of 100 still images of 100 different frontal-view human faces, all without glasses and with a neutral expression. Images are acquired in 1187 x 1190 bitmap color format. As shown in Figure 2(b), the facial structures are manually annotated using 72 total landmarks of the eyebrows, eyes, nose, mouth, and jaw. In this paper, the training method for AAM uses the Jacobian learning scheme. As in the original AAM method, these AAMs are built at each level of a scale-pyramid for coarse-to-fine fitting based on multi-resolution [11], [12].

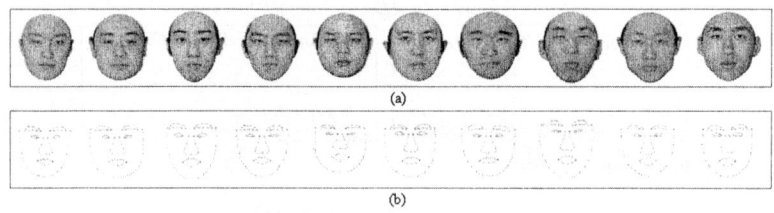

Fig. 2. Face image set for training the AAM. (a) Frontal human color texture. (b) Facial landmarks.

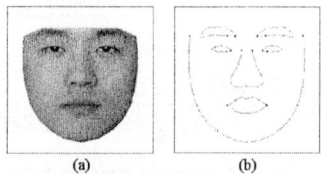

Fig. 3. Average texture and shape on a trained AAM. (a) Average texture. (b) Average shape.

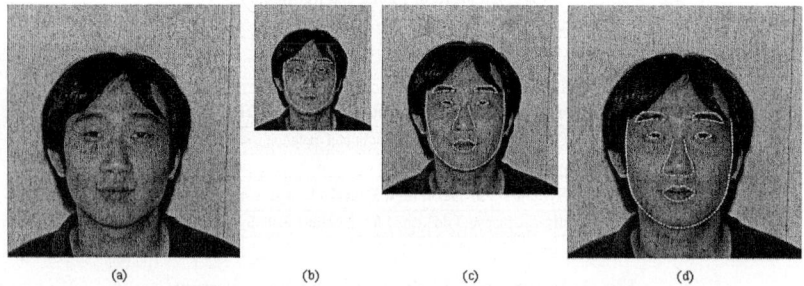

Fig. 4. Search-based initialization of deformation templates using multi-resolution AAM. (a) Original image. (b) Search result in level 2 (50 % scaled down of level 1). (c) Search result in level 1 (50 % scaled down of level 0). (d) Final search result in level 0 (not scaled down).

2.2 Template Matching by Multi-resolution Active Appearance Model

In this paper, to improve the efficiency and robustness of the matching algorithm, various deformation templates were matched by using the MAAM based on color images. This involves searching for the object in a coarse image first, then refining the location in a series of finer resolution images [13].

As shown in Figure 4, a multi-resolution pyramid is scaled into three levels. Figure 4(d) is the final search result in which parameters of the combined model for

AAM were optimized (translation, scaling, rotation, texture model parameters, and shape model parameters).

3 Proposed Deformation Technique for Virtual Aesthetic Surgery

First, we briefly describe the properties of the RBF interpolation that actually computes the degree of lattice cell deformation on the FFD. Second, after suggesting the three characteristics that are required for the deformation technique using the VAS system, we define an RBF mapping function to satisfy those characteristics. Finally, we describe the technique that compensates for deformation errors, which results in greater accuracy.

3.1 RBF Interpolation

RBFs define the interpolation functions as a linear combination of radial symmetric basis functions, each of which is centered on a particular control-point. RBFs are smooth, continuous functions that provide at least C^1 continuity [7].

The RBF mapping function can be decomposed into a global and local component, as given in equation (1). Although the two components are distinct, they can be computed almost simultaneously.

$$f_k(\vec{x}) = P_{mk}(\vec{x}) + \sum_{i=1}^{n} A_{ik} g(r_i), \quad r_i = \left\| \vec{x} - \vec{x_i} \right\| \tag{1}$$

Here k is the dimension, m is the degree of polynomial, n is the number of control points, r_i is the Euclidean norm between a point $\vec{x}$ and a source control point $\vec{x_i}$, and $P_{mk}(\vec{x})$ is the global component. If the degree of polynomial is 1, it yields the global component to an affine transformation, as in equation (2) [14].

$$P_{1k}(\vec{x}) = a_{0k} + a_{1k} x + a_{2k} y \tag{2}$$

3.2 Radial Basis Function for VAS System

In this paper, we suggest three characteristics that are required for the deformation technique of the VAS system.

[1] It should achieve the consistency of deformation regardless of the number of control points on base curves (source curve and target curve).
[2] It should maintain the visual smoothness and the accuracy of deformation according to the base curves.
[3] It should have a locality to limit the range of deformation influence so that other facial components are not affected.

Inverse multiquadric RBF has local attributes similar to a Gaussian RBF, but it is smoother than a Gaussian RBF. Therefore, we define a deformation technique that has the above three characteristics by using an inverse multiquadric RBF. As shown in equation (3), the inverse multiquadric RBF is represented by a formula with a stiffness constants s_i that regulates the local or global effects of the control points, where μ is a constant [9], [14, [15]. In this paper, we design an inverse stiffness that increases the deformation force as the control points are spread apart, and decreases the deformation force when the control points are closer to each other.

$$g(r_i) = (r_i^2 + s_i^2)^{-\mu}, \mu > 0 \qquad (3)$$

The inverse stiffness is computed by equation (4), according to the adaptive method proposed by Ruprecht and Müller [16].

$$inverse \ s_i = \max_{i \neq j} \left(\frac{\| \vec{x}_j^{source\ position} - \vec{x}_i^{source\ position} \|}{N} \right) \qquad (4)$$

Here $\vec{x}^{source\ position}$ is a control point on the base curve (source curve), and N is the number of control points on the base curve.

3.3 Compensation of Deformation Error

For facial deformation, 2(n+3) coefficients of the basis function and the polynomial are solved by the singular value decomposition (SVD) technique. The coefficients are used for a lattice cell deformation on the FFD.

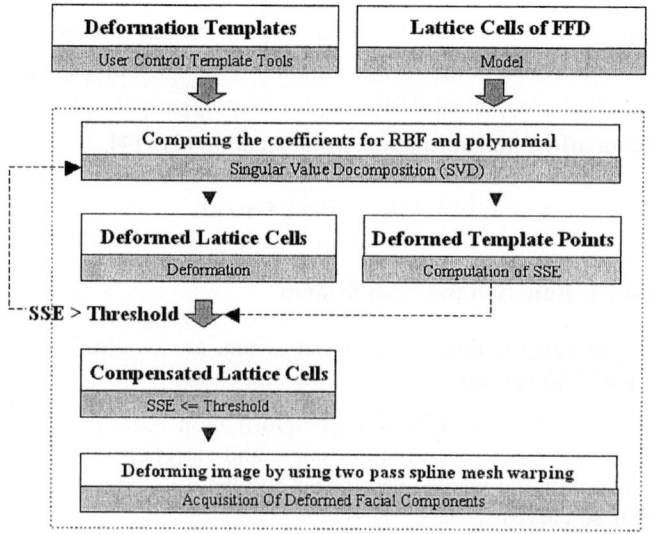

Fig. 5. Error compensation process using SSE and SVD

To compute the deformation error, we used the SSE as given in equation (5). SSE involves the computation of the distance between the target positions and the deformed positions of control points on the base curves.

$$SSE = \sum_{i=1}^{n}\varepsilon^2 = \sum_{i=1}^{m}(x^{\rightarrow deformed\ position} - x^{\rightarrow target\ position})^2 \qquad (5)$$

Here $x^{\rightarrow deformed\ position}$ is a position of deformed control points and $x^{\rightarrow target\ position}$ is a position of control points on base curve (target curve). Therefore, the deformation error of lattice cells on the FFD is compensated by the coefficients that are solved by SVD iteratively until the SSE value becomes less than a threshold value. Finally, facial components are deformed by a two-pass spline mesh warping, based on the compensated lattice cells.

4 Proposed Blending Technique for Virtual Aesthetic Surgery

The following section describes the blending technique used to minimize the distortion of facial color, texture, and the distortion of facial components in the remainder of the deformation region.

4.1 Blending Ratio Computed by Modified Euclidean Distance Transform

In our VAS system, the deformation technique does not affect or distort facial components outside of the deformation region. However, since it is difficult to define a RBF with a perfect locality, the deformation of a specific facial component may affect or distort some facial components. Generally, a global deformation makes the resulting image visually smooth, but globally distorted. On the other hand, a local deformation makes the resulting image without global distortion, but does not produce a visually smooth image. In this paper, we suggest a blending technique that has the advantages of global deformation and local deformation.

First, blending mask regions on the face are automatically computed by using deformation templates. Next, the blending ratio is computed by the modified Euclidean distance transformation (EDT) that computes the distance to the closest boundary from each point [17]. Finally, the blending technique combines the deformed facial component with the original face by using the blending ratio.

As shown in equation (6), the proposed blending technique uses the modified EDT to compute the blending ratio.

As shown in equation (6), the proposed blending technique uses the modified EDT to compute the blending ratio.

$$D_{Euclidean} = \sqrt{(x_2 - x_1)^2 + (y_2 - y_1)^2}$$
$$B_{ratio} = Scaling\ Factor * D_{Euclidean}$$
$$I_{result} = (255 - B_{ratio}) * I_{original} + B_{ratio} * I_{deformed} \qquad (6)$$
$$B_{ratio} = Scaling\ Factor * D_{Euclidean}$$

Here $D_{Euclidean}$ is the distance to the closest boundary from each point, B_{ratio} is the blending ratio on the facial mask region, $I_{original}$ is the original face, $I_{deformed}$ is the deformed facial component, I_{result} is the final result that combines the deformed facial component with the original face using the blending ratio, and the *Scaling Factor* is a ratio that varies the B_{ratio} value in the range from 0 to 255.

In Figure 6, the resulting image shows a visual smoothness without global distortion over all facial components.

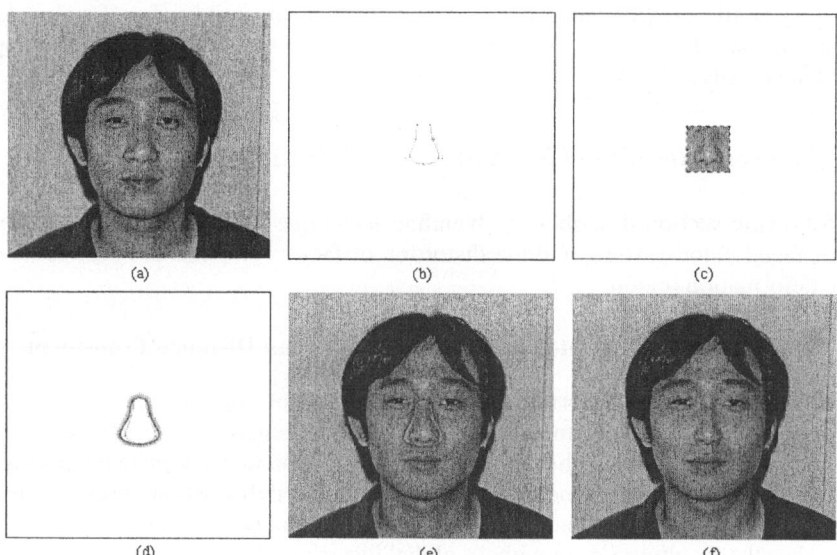

Fig. 6. Deformation using the blending technique. (a) Original image. (b) Deformation template on nose. (c) Deformation of nose. (d) Mask with blending ratio. (e) Blending of the deformed facial component and the original face. (f) Final result.

Figure 7 shows the degree of texture distortion on a face with a complex texture (pockmarks, pimples, blotches, etc.). Figure 7(b) shows that a local deformation distorts the texture around the nose region. Figure 7(c) shows that the proposed deformation and blending techniques are very efficient in terms of smoothness and distortion for color images of faces with complex textures.

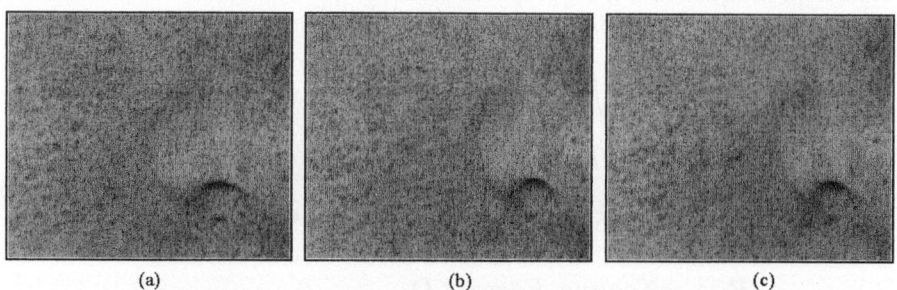

Fig. 7. Comparison of the degree of distortion for a color texture (a) Original image, (b) Local deformation, (c) Deformation using the blending technique

5 Experimental Results

In this paper, we compared the Gaussian RBF of equation (7) used in Gaussian elastic body splines (GEBS), the general Gaussian RBF of equation (8), and the proposed inverse multiquadric RBF with inverse stiffness [18]. When a Gaussian function is used as a basis function, the deviation value must be carefully chosen because the Gaussian RBF performs poorly without a good deviation value. However, it is very difficult to choose the best deviation value.

To satisfy the three characteristics that are required for the deformation technique of the proposed VAS system, the deviation value of Gaussian RBFs is calculated by an adaptive stiffness, as given in equation (9).

$$g(r) = c \frac{1}{(\sqrt{2\pi}\sigma)^3} e^{-\frac{r^2}{2\sigma^2}} \tag{7}$$

$$g(r) = e^{-\frac{r^2}{\sigma^2}} \tag{8}$$

$$\sigma_i = \min_{i \neq j} \left(\frac{\| \overrightarrow{x_j}^{source} - \overrightarrow{x_i}^{source} \|}{N} \right), \quad (j = 1, \ldots, n) \tag{9}$$

Figure 8 shows that the deformation accuracy of the proposed method is better than the Gaussian RBF of GEBS and the general Gaussian RBF. The deformation errors for these three methods are shown in Figure 8 (d), (f), and (h).

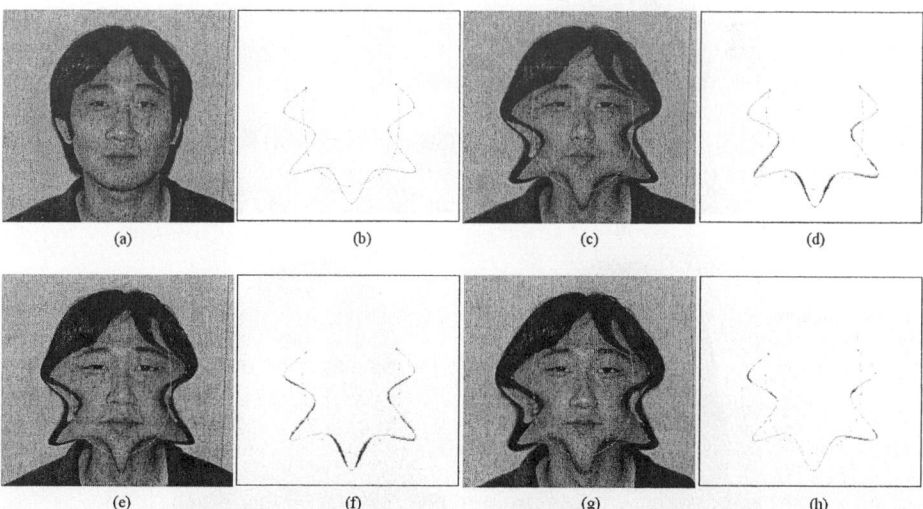

Fig. 8. Comparison of deformation results on various RBFs. (a) Original face image. (b) Deformation template. (c) Result using the Gaussian RBF of GEBS. (d) Deformation error in (c). (e) Result using the general Gaussian RBF. (f) Deformation error in (e). (g) Result using the proposed RBF. (h) Deformation error in (g).

In this paper, we estimate the deformation accuracy by using equations (10) and (11) [19].

$$CDR(Correct\ Deformation\ Ratio) = 1 - DR \qquad (10)$$

$$DR(Distortion\ Ratio) = \frac{Distortion\ Area}{Target\ Template\ Area} \qquad (11)$$

Table 1 shows that the proposed RBF is more accurate than Gaussian type RBF.

Table 1. Comparison of deformation accuracy for various RBFs

Type of RBF	CDR (correct deformation ratio)
Gaussian RBF of equation(7)	0.9619
Gaussian RBF of equation(8)	0.9608
Proposed RBF	0.9923

6 Conclusion

In this paper, we proposed a semi-automatic initialization of deformation templates, facial deformation, and blending techniques that are suitable for the VAS system. The choice of the best RBF to use depends primarily on the application objectives.

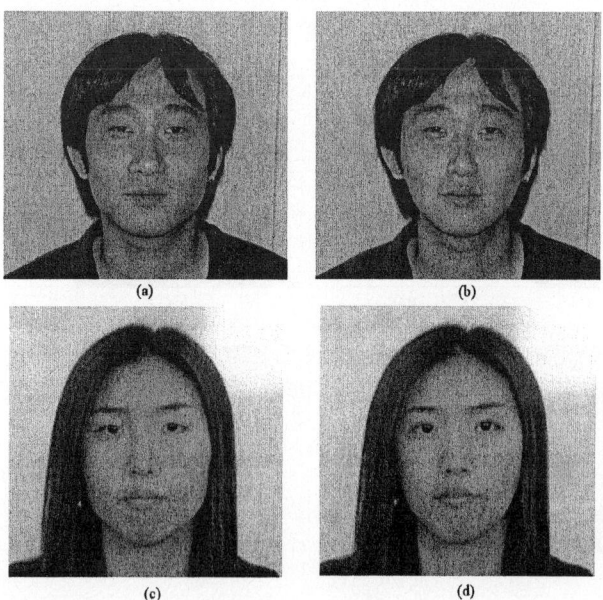

Fig. 9. Final results of the proposed deformation and blending technique. (a) Original image. (b) Result that corrects the nose and jaw. (c) Original image. (d) Aesthetic result using an eyelid filter and jaw correction.

We carried out experiments that compared various RBFs in order to develop a deformation technique for a VAS system. It has also been found that RBFs that have Gaussian function form are very difficult to control.

We have shown that the deformation technique using an inverse multiquadric RBF with inverse stiffness is suitable for a VAS system, and that the blending ratio computed by the Euclidean distance transform can be used to produce a good deformation result.

As shown in Figure 9, the proposed deformation technique achieves excellent deformation results on a face image as well as a natural image.

Acknowledgement

This research was supported by the MIC (Ministry of Information and Communication) of Korea, under the ITRC (Information Technology Research Center) support program supervised by the IITA (Institute of Information Technology Assessment).

References

1. Frakas, L.G.: Anthropometry of the Head and Face, 3rd edn. Raven Press (1994)
2. Massaro, D.: Perceiving Talking Faces: From Speech Perception to a Behavioral Principle, MIT Press (1998)
3. Keeve, E., Girod, S., Kininis, R., Girod, B.: Deformable Modeling of Facial Tissue for Craniofacial Surgery Simulation, Computer Aided Surgery, Vol. 3, March (1999) 228-238
4. Wu, Y., Beylot, P., Thalmann, N. M.: Skin Aging Estimation by Facial Simulation, Computer Animation 1999, May (1999) 210-219
5. Koch, R. M., Gross, M. H., Crals, E. R.: Simulating Facial Surgery Using Finite Element Models, SIGGRAPH 96 Conference Proceeding, August (1996) 421-428
6. Lee, S. Y., Wolberg, G., Chwa, K. Y., Shin, S. Y.: Image Metamorphosis with Scattered Feature Constraints, IEEE Transaction on Visualization and Computer Graphics, Vol. 2, No. 4, December (1996)
7. Gomes, J., Darsa, L., Costa, B., Velho, L.: Warping and Morphing of Graphical Objects, Morgan Kaufmann Publishers (1999)
8. Lin, D. T., Huang, H.: Facial Expression Morphing and Animation with Local Warping Methods, ICIAP (1999)
9. Noh, J. Y., Fidaleo, D., Neumann, U.: Animated Deformations With Radial Basis Functions, Virtual Reality Software and Technology, VRST 2000
10. Milliron, T., Jensen, R. J., Barzel, R.: A Framework for Geometric Warps and Deformations, ACM Transaction on Graphics, Vol. 21, No. 1, January (2002) 20-51
11. Cootes, T. F., Taylor, C. J., Cooper, D. H., Graham, J.: Active shape models their training and application, Computer Vision and Image Understanding, January (1995) 38-59
12. Cootes, T. F., Edwards, G. J., Taylor, C. J.: Active appearance models, In Proc. European Conf. on Computer Vision, Vol. 2, Springer-Verlag, (1998) 484-98
13. Stegmann, M. B., Ersbøll, B. K., Larsen, R: FAME – A Flexible Active Appearance Modeling Environment, IEEE Trans. Medical Imaging, Vol. 22, No. 10, Oct (2003) 1319-1331
14. Toga, A. W.: Brain Warping, Academic Press (1999)
15. Eck, M.: Interpolation Methods for Reconstruction of 3D Surfaces from Sequences of Planar Slices," CAD und Computergraphic, Vol. 13, No. 5, Feb (1991) 109-120

16. Ruprecht, D., Müller, H.: Image Warping with Scattered Data Interpolation, IEEE Computer Graphics and Applications, Vol. 15, No.2, (1995) 37-43
17. Breu, H., Gil, J., Kirkpatrick, D., Weman, M.: Linear Time Euclidean Distance Transform Algorithm, IEEE Transaction on Pattern Analysis and Machine Intelligence, Vol. 17, No. 5, May (1995) 529-533
18. Rohr, K.: Spline-Based Elastic Image Registration, In Annual Scientific Conf. GAMM' 2003, March (2003) 22-23
19. Schoepflin, T., Chalana, V., Haynor, D. R., Kim, Y. M.: Video Object Tracking With a Sequential Hierarchy of Template Deformations, IEEE Transaction on Circuits and System for Video Technology, Vol. 11, No. 11, (2001) 1171-1182

Automatic Photo Indexing Based on Person Identity

Seungji Yang[1], Kyong Sok Seo[1], Sang Kyun Kim[2], Yong Man Ro[1],
Ji-Yeon Kim[2], and Yang Suk Seo[2]

[1] Image and Video Systems Lab., Information and Communications University (ICU),
Munjiro 119, Yuseong, Daejeon, South Korea
{yangzeno, imksseo, yro}@icu.ac.kr
[2] Computing Lab., Digital Research Center, Samsung Advanced Institute of Technology
(SAIT), San 14-1, Giheung, Yongin, Kyunggi, South Korea
{skim, jikim, ysseo}@sait.samsung.co.kr

Abstract. In this paper, we propose a novel approach to automatically index digital home photos based on person identity. A person is identified by his/her face and clothes. The proposed method consists of two parts: clustering and indexing. In the clustering, a series of unlabeled photos is aligned in taken-time order, and is divided into several sub-groups by situation. The situation groups are decided by time and visual differences. In the indexing, SVMs are trained with features of pre-indexed faces to model target persons. The representative feature vector of the person group from the clustering is queried to the trained SVMs. Each SVM outputs a numeric confidence value about the query person group. The query person group is determined to the target person by the most confident SVM. The experimental results showed that the proposed method outperformed traditional person indexing method using only face feature and its performance increased to 93.56% from 72.31%.

1 Introduction

Recently, digital cameras are getting popular as providing a convenience for users to easily take a lot of photos. And it is gradually replacing traditional film camera, so the volume of digital photos is continually increased. The digitization of photos makes users easy to show their lives and experiences to their family or friends. But, people might not move their photos from digital cameras to their personal storages in PC since 'moving photos' sometimes means extra works such as manually sorting, selecting, and annotating pictures. Unless people are having enough time to do that or willing to take care of the photos for each event, they would rather leave the photos in the memory stick of digital camera.

Digital photo album [1] can be a useful tool for organizing these large amounts of digital home photos, and it basically works based on automatic clustering or indexing method. However, the traditional digital photo albums still need user's manual work in many parts. When users need to arrange the photos in the digital photo album, they often feel that it is nuisance since it is hard to browse their photos in some meaningful orders. Thus, the manual indexing is pretty time-consuming, tedious, erroneous, and inconsistent, so that it has been a big hurdle for users to use digital cameras.

Under these circumstances, person-based photo indexing is strongly needed because people are most likely to browse photos based on persons who are taken in the photos.

Traditionally, the person-based indexing has been focused on detecting face position of person and representing it efficiently as a compact feature vector. And, many researchers have been worked for this face detection and recognition. But, the main interest of the face detection and recognition technology has been focused on the security system [2 - 3], e.g., intelligent surveillance system, automatic gate control, and face search system to find criminals. Since the security camera takes pictures in a fixed place, the picture usually contains static environment. And it makes the system easy to detect or recognize face from the picture. On the contrary, general home photos contain more complex background with big illumination variation because people bring their cameras anywhere and take pictures whenever they want [4]. Thus the face detection and recognition from the general home photos must be more difficult than those for traditional security system. And, if only face information is used for the face recognition, its performance should be quite low.

To solve the recognition problem for digital home photos, we propose a novel approach for automatic person indexing. The proposed method consists of two steps: clustering and indexing. In the clustering, firstly, a sequence of unlabeled photos is divided into several subsets by situation-based clustering. The situation groups are decided by time and visual differences. So, the face and clothes features can be considered as a person identity in a situation since ones tend not to change their clothes in a certain time range. After that, using the face and clothes information, the person groups are generated by person-identity-based clustering. In the indexing process, support vector person (SVP) for each target person is modeled with support vector machine (SVM). The representative feature vector of the generated person groups in clustering process is queried to the trained SVPs. The SVPs output a confidence value representing how much the query person group is related to a target person in the database. Using the confidence value, the query person group is determined to the target person by selecting the most confident SVP.

The paper is composed of 5 sections. Section 2 covers the details regarding the person-identity-based clustering, where situation clustering is also represented. In Section 3, person-identity-based indexing is described including the clustering process. Section 4 provides the experimental results, and conclusions are drawn in Section 5.

2 Person-Identity-Based Clustering

To be an effective and accurate clustering for digital home photos, our person-identity-based clustering involves two steps. First, a sequence of photos is aligned in order of taken-time and it is divided into several sub-groups by situation clustering. In each situation group, a person is identified by his/her face and clothes. These person identity features are extracted from the photos. Second, in every situation, several person groups are generated as merging similar person identity features. Note that any similarity matching between person identity features in different situation groups would not be happened in this stage. Fig.1. illustrates the overall procedure of the person identity-based clustering.

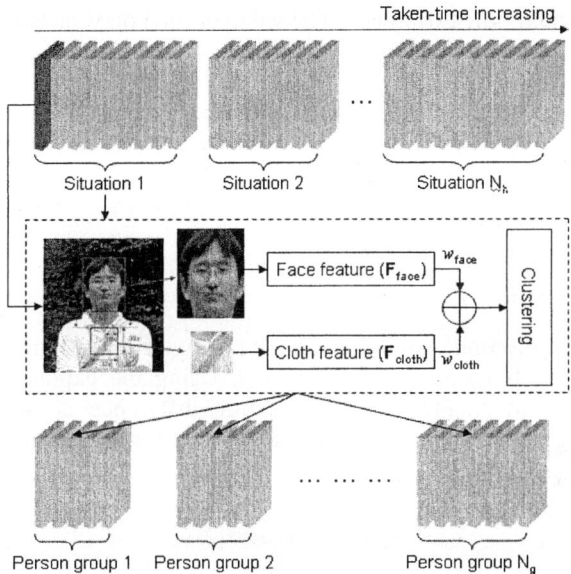

Fig. 1. Overall procedure of the person-identity-based clustering

2.1 Situation-Based Clustering

When clustering the large amounts of home photos based on human, a critical problem is that the photos are taken in a very complex background with variable illumination [4]. But, most people tend to take several pictures in the same place, and these people usually wear same clothes during a certain range of time. Then, a group of neighboring photos according to taken-time may have similar situation. Therefore, when clustering the large amount of photos, they should be divided into smaller amounts of subsets, and it is better to find the same person using helpful information in each subset. Under this observation, 'situation' is defined as the place in which photos would be taken. So, a subset of photos associated in the same situation often contains similar background. This situation can be useful as a fundamental cluster for photo clustering or indexing.

In this paper, given a sequence of photos, situation change boundary is detected by visual change and time gap between adjacent photos with time [5]. For the similarity matching to detect the situation change boundary, first, the photos are aligned in taken-time order. Then, the similarity matching is performed with two neighboring photos. The time dissimilarity (D_{time}) between the current $(i)^{th}$ photo and the previous $(i-1)^{th}$ photo are measured as follows,

$$D_{time}(i) = \frac{\log\{\mathbf{F}_{time}(i) - \mathbf{F}_{time}(i-1) + C_{time}\}}{D_{time\_max}}, \quad (1)$$

where, the taken-time feature $\mathbf{F}_{time}$ is obtained from Exif header of photo data, log(•) is a time scale function, C_{time} is a constant to avoid zero for input of the scale function.

$D_{\text{time\_max}}$ is maximum time difference. The value of time dissimilarity is scaled, so that it can be less sensitive to the large time difference. The time dissimilarity at the same situation is insensitive [5].

Using the time dissimilarity, the content-based similarity matching between the $(i)^{th}$ and $(i-1)^{th}$ photos is performed with several visual features and their importance [5]. It can be written as,

$$D_{total}(i) = \exp\left[D_{time}(i) \times \sum_{f \in F}\{w_f(i) \times D_f(i)\}\right] \quad (2)$$

where, $D_f(i)$ is the dissimilarity defined as $D_f\{\mathbf{F}_f(i) - \mathbf{F}_f(i-1)\}$ in which $D(\bullet)$ is the similarity matching function for the feature f. Using the exponential function, the dissimilarity value at smaller value of feature difference is reduced while it is enlarged at higher value. $w_f(i)$ is an importance value for the f feature. It can be adaptive to the visual semantics of photo.

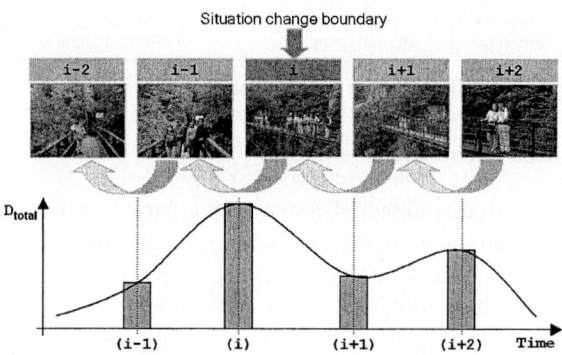

Fig. 2. Situation change detection (This is an example of situation change detection from 5 sequential photos, where the $(i)^{th}$ photo has the biggest time and visual differences from the previous photo and the difference is assumed as being over a threshold.)

To detect the change of situation between the $(i)^{th}$ photo and the $(i-1)^{th}$ photo, we compare $D_{total}(i-1)$, $D_{total}(i)$, and $D_{total}(i+1)$. If the $(i)^{th}$ photo is a situation change boundary, $D_{total}(i)$ would have a peak value among three dissimilarity values. Fig. 2 illustrates this overall situation change boundary detection in a sequence of 5 photos. Finally, the situation boundary is detected by (3).

$$D_{total}(i) > \beta \times \{\Delta D_{total}(i) + \Delta D_{total}(i+1)\}, \text{ subject to } \Delta D_{total}(i) > 0, \Delta D_{total}(i+1) < 0, \quad (3)$$

where, $\Delta D_{total}(i) = D_{total}(i) - D_{total}(i-1)$ and β is a threshold to detect situation change.

2.2 Person Identity Extraction

To extract person identity, face detection is essential, and many researches have been studied for the face detection. One of the most popular methods is the AdaBoost method with Haar-like features [7 - 8]. The AdaBoost is a boosting method that creates a strong classifier from lots of weak classifiers [9], and the Haar-like features are the inputs of AdaBoost classifier dedicated to face detection. This face detection is another big issue, so it is not considered in this paper.

As mentioned before, face and clothes information is used to identify a person in a given situation. In order to extract the person identity from a photo, the region of the face is detected first, and clothes region of corresponding face is extracted using the detected face position. The size of facial images is normalized as 46 by 56 pixels, so that the center positions of the two eyes in the facial image is located on the 24th row and the 16th and 31st column for the right and left eye, respectively. When deciding the corresponding clothes region, determining the size and position of the clothes region is difficult. There should be a trade-off, i.e., the clothes region should be not only large enough to represent individual identity, but also small enough not to be interfered with each other. Under lots of observations, a heuristic rule is discovered; the clothes location is defined by 18 lines below the face region, and the size of clothes is 32 by 32 pixels. But it is assumed that a person has no clothes information if faces are located at the margin of the photo, or two faces are too closely located, which could affect the other's body. Fig. 3 shows the detection of the face region and the corresponding clothes region.

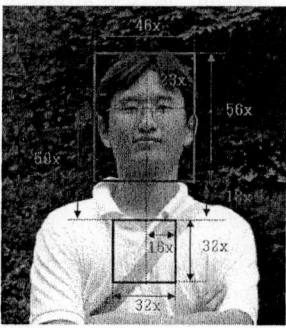

Fig. 3. Detection of face and clothes region

To describe the facial and clothes images, their visual features are extracted. When extracting features, any state-of-art technology can be applied for the face and clothes descriptions. Unlike the face feature, color and texture features seem to be effective for representing the clothes since ones would design the clothes as considering colors and shapes mostly. So the color and texture features are extracted from the defined clothes region. Furthermore, the information about people who are taken together is also helpful because people appearing in a photo means that they must be different. Using this information, a person can be more accurately recognized.

2.3 Person-Identity-Based Clustering

Person identity-based clustering merges similar person identities into a cluster so that all of person identities in a situation are clustered into several groups composed with a same person's images. First of all, feature dissimilarities of face and clothes need to be measured, which are person identities. The dissimilarity (D_{person}) between features of ith and j^{th} person identity is measured as follows,

$$D_{person}(i,j) = w_{face} \cdot \tilde{D}_{face}(i,j) + \sum_{f \in F_{clothes}} \{w_f \cdot \tilde{D}_f(i,j)\} \qquad (4)$$

where, $D_{face}(\bullet)$ is a function measuring dissimilarity of the ith and j^{th} face feature, and $D_f(\bullet)$ is a function measuring dissimilarity of the ith and j^{th} clothes features where **f** is one of the clothes feature set $\mathbf{F}_{clothes}$. w_{face} and w_f are weighting values to represent importance of the face feature and the **f** clothes features, respectively. And, '~' is the notation for the normalized dissimilarity. Since the dissimilarities might not be normally distributed, their ranges should be normalized and rescaled to have the range from 0 to 1. This normalization is calculated by (5),

$$\tilde{D}_f = \frac{\hat{D}_f - \min(\hat{D}_f)}{\max(\hat{D}_f) - \min(\hat{D}_f)}, \text{ where } \hat{D}_f = \frac{D_f - \mu_f}{\sigma_f}, \qquad (5)$$

where, μ_f and σ_f are the mean and variance of the dissimilarities of the **f** features, respectively.

After the dissimilarity measurement, person groups are generated as merging similar person identity features into a cluster so that all person identities in a situation are clustered into several groups composed with a same person's images. In this case, the revealed data is only the dissimilarity values. On this limited condition, several unsupervised clustering methods can be utilized, and one of them is Agglomerative Hierarchical clustering method [10]. This clustering method starts with all singleton clusters and forms the sequence by merging clusters. Major steps of the method are contained in the following procedures:

1. Start with all singleton clusters composed with single person identity, $C(g)$ where $g = 1, 2, ..., G$ and G is the number of the person identity clusters, in a situation.
2. Calculate the dissimilarity $D_{cluster}(a, b)$, between two clusters as follows,

$$D_{cluster}(a,b) = \frac{1}{n_{C(a)} \cdot n_{C(b)}} \cdot \sum_{i \in C(a)} \sum_{j \in C(b)} D_{person}(i,j) \qquad (6)$$

where $n_{C(a)}$ and $n_{C(b)}$ represent the number of persons in the two cluster $C(a)$ and $C(b)$, respectively.
3. Find the nearest two clusters, noted a' and b', as follows,

$$(a',b') = \underset{a,b, a \neq b}{\arg\min} D_{cluster}(a,b) \qquad (7)$$

4. Merge the two nearest clusters into one cluster as being $C(a') = C(a') \cup C(b')$ and removing $C(b')$.
5. Repeat (2), (3), (4), until specified dissimilarity has been reached.

Finally, most clusters are composed with person identities of a same person.

3 Person-Identity-Based Indexing

The proposed person-identity-based indexing uses the results of the person-identity-based clustering. The clustered person groups based on situations are automatically indexed to target people in pre-stored database. In this paper, we build a SVM model for target people, called support vector person (SVP), instead of collecting feature instances to represent a person in the database. In the database where face information is only available, the clothes information is no longer valuable.

3.1 Support Vector Person Modeling

SVM [11] is a popular learning method that uses a hypothesis space of linear functions in a high dimensional feature space. Support vectors are trained with a learning algorithm from optimization theory implementing a learning bias derived from statistical learning theory [12]. The linear function given feature instance x can be written as,

$$f_{svm}(x) = w_0 + \sum_{u=1}^{k} w_u K_u \langle x, c_u \rangle, \qquad (8)$$

where, w is the parameter vector that control the function, and K_u is a kernel function.

In this paper, we use a radial basis function (RBF) [13] as the kernel, defined as follows.

$$K_u \langle x, c \rangle = \exp\{-\gamma_u \cdot (x - c_u)^T \cdot (x - c_u)\}, \qquad (9)$$

where, the kernel K_u is a function that uses the distance between an input vector **x**, and trained the center c_u, where γ_u is a constant. This linear function is trained with labeled dataset composed with positive and negative data. To model SVP for each person, the SVPs are trained with positive and negative face features that are correctly classified by human in prior. The SVP of the person, u, is written as,

$$\mathbf{SVP}_{u \in U} = \mathbf{SVM}_u \{u^+ (\mathbf{F}_{face}), u^- (\mathbf{F}_{face})\}, \qquad (10)$$

where, **U** is a person set indexed in the database, u^+ is a set of positive face samples that belong to the person, u^+, and u^- is a set of negative face samples that belong to the others except the u.

3.2 Person-Identity-Based Indexing

Fig. 4 shows a general flow of the proposed person-identity-based indexing. As shown in the figure, from the person groups clustered in the person clustering, a representative feature vector is constructed. The representative feature vector is average of each component of the face feature vectors in the person group. It is written as,

$$\mathbf{F'}_{face}\big|_g = \{f'_{face}(1), f'_{face}(2), \cdots, f'_{face}(N_f)\}, \text{ where } f'_{face}(i) = \frac{1}{n_{C(k)}} \cdot \sum_{j=1}^{n_{C(k)}} \{f_{face}(j)\big|_i\} \qquad (11)$$

where, $\mathbf{F'}_{face}|_g$ is an average face feature representing the gth person group.

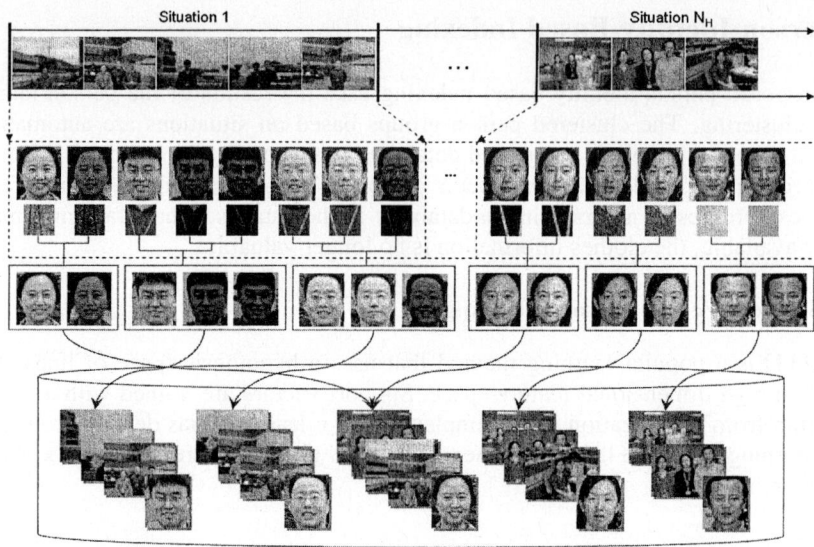

Fig. 4. A general flow of the proposed person indexing

The representative feature vector is used as input to the modeled SVPs. Then, the SVP outputs confidence values which indicates how much the face features is likely to the person. The confidence value of the gth person group for the person, u, $v_g(u)$, is obtained as follows,

$$v_g(u) = K_u\left(\mathbf{F'}_{face}\big|_g, \mathbf{SVP}_u\right), \qquad (12)$$

where, the kernel, K_u can be a distance measurement for the SVPs, and it outputs confidence value, $v_g(u)$ of the face feature $\mathbf{F'}_{face}$ of the gth person group about the SVP for the person, u.

Finally, using the confidence values from all SVPs, a target person of the person group g, g_{target}, is determined by selecting the most confident SVP, as follows,

$$g_{target} = u = \arg\max_{u \in \mathbf{U}, g \in \mathbf{G}}\{v_g(u)\}, \qquad (13)$$

4 Experiments

To verify the proposed method, experiments were performed with MPEG-7 official dataset for visual core experiment part 3 (VCE-3) [15]. This dataset contains 1385 home photos taken by general users. Using an automatic face detection tool developed by SAIT, 1819 faces were detected and proposed to the VCE-3 [16]. These 1819 facial images were extracted from 1120 photos of the dataset, and 72 people were appeared in the 1120 photos. The experiments were composed of two parts: one was for the demonstration of the usefulness of person-identity-based clustering, and the other was for the verification of the person-identity-based indexing.

4.1 Experiment 1: Person-Identity-Based Clustering

First of all, the 1819 facial images were divided into 31 situation groups by the situation-based clustering. Since the dataset is divided into many situations, every person can be appeared in any situation. To settle the truth number of clusters, we used a notation of facial image groups to represent one person's facial images in a situation. As examining all situations, total 195 facial image groups were detected. After the situation-based clustering, the person identity-based clustering got started with the 31 situations and 1819 singleton clusters. These 1819 singleton clusters would be merged into 195 facial image groups if no error was occurred.

All of the clusters are merged into smaller number of clusters based on dissimilarity values using the weighted combination of the face and clothes features. For the face description, MPEG-7 advanced face recognition descriptor (AFRD) was used, and MPEG-7 color structure descriptor (CSD) with illumination invariant color descriptor (IICD) and edge histogram descriptor (EHD) were used for the color feature and texture feature. These were combined with weight values of $w_{color} = 0.272$, $w_{texture} = 0.181$, and $w_{face} = 0.546$. As an exceptional case, $w_{face} = 1.0$ was used if the clothes features were not available.

When the clusters were being merged, evaluation method of clustering performance was needed to see how many errors are increased in each step of the proposed method. The error rate is the ratio of the number of minor facial images to the number of major facial images in the cluster. The error rate, $e(g)$, of the person group, g, is computed as changing dissimilarity threshold as follows,

$$e(g)\big|_{threshold} = \frac{n(g) - n_{major}(g)}{n(g)}, \qquad (14)$$

where, $n(g)$ is the number of facial images in the g person group, and $n_{major}(g)$ is the number of major facial images. As easily realized, the bigger dissimilarity threshold leads the smaller number of person groups but increases error rate.

In order to examine the effect using the feature combination, the proposed method was compared with the method using face features only. As Fig. 5 shows the result, 195 clusters were generated with 23.03% of error rate using the face only while 14.02% of error rate was obtained using the proposed method.

4.2 Experiment 2: Person-Identity-Based Indexing

To verify the person-identity-based indexing, some of the original data in the previous experiment was selected, which was containing facial images of 27 persons who had more than 30 facial images. Total number of facial images was 1135. These 1135 facial images were extracted from 764 photos. About 60% of them, 684 facial images were used for training data and the remainders, 451 facial images, were used for testing data. Correspondingly, the proposed SVPs were modeled for the 27 persons.

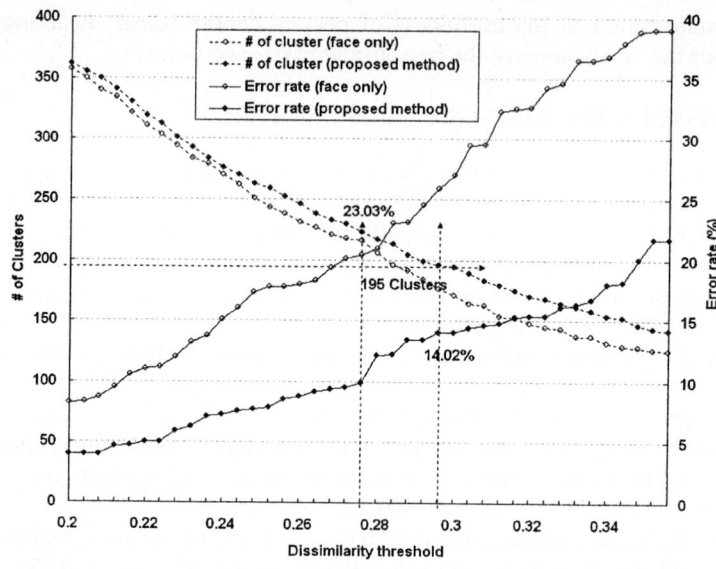

Fig. 5. Person-identity-based clustering results: with 1819 facial images

The test dataset was divided into 13 situation groups by the situation-based clustering, and the truth number of facial image groups was 36. Fig. 6 shows the person-identity-based clustering results of the test dataset. As shown in the results, the error rate was 5.987% when the person groups were merged into 36 groups.

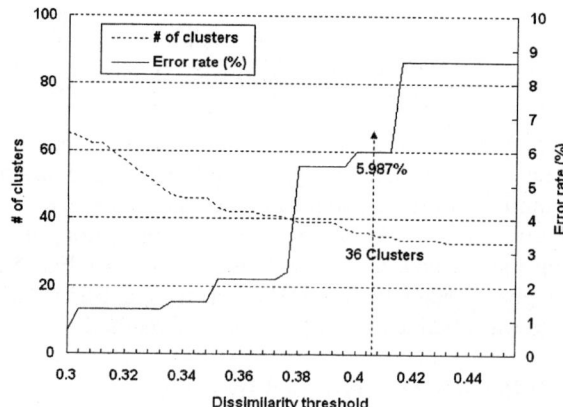

Fig. 6. Person-identity-based clustering results: with only 451 facial images

The stopping criterion for the person-identity-based clustering was heuristically determined: until the number of clusters reached to 10% of the initial number. With the criterion, the person groups were merged into 46 groups, and 1.552% of the error rate was obtained. These merged person groups were used for the next process of the person-identity-based indexing.

Recall and precision were used to evaluate indexing results. The recall is defined as G/T where G is the number of true-positive facial images and T is the number of the true facial images. The precision is defined as G/N where N is the number of positive facial images. Average performance over the all 27 persons was 93.56% (recall: 93.11% and precision: 94.01%) using the proposed method while 72.31% was obtained in the case of using only face features.

5 Conclusions

In this paper, we propose a novel approach for automatic person indexing for digital home photos. The proposed method is composed of two steps: clustering and indexing. In the clustering, a series of unlabeled photos is aligned in order of taken-time and is divided into sub-sets by situation-based clustering. The situation groups are decided by time and visual differences. In every situation group, the face and clothes features are considered as a person identity. They are used to generate the person clusters. In the indexing, pre-indexed face dataset is trained with SVMs in order to model target persons. The representative feature vector of the person clusters is queried to the trained SVMs. Each SVM outputs a numeric confidence value about the query person group. A target person for the query person cluster is determined by the most confident SVM. The experiment results showed that the proposed method outperformed the traditional indexing method using only face features and its performance increased to 93.56% from 72.31%.

References

1. Yagawa, Y., Iwai, N., Yanagi, K., Kojima, K. Matsumoto, K.: The Digital Album: a personal file-tainment system, Proc. of IEEE Intl' Conference on MCS (1996) 433-439.
2. Yang, M. H., Kriegman, D., Ahuja, N.: Detection Faces in Images: A Survey, IEEE Trans. on PAMI (2002) 34-58.
3. Zhao, W., Chellappa, R., Phillips, P.J., Rosenfeld, A.: Face Recognition: A Literature Survey, ACM Computing Surveys (2003) 399-458.
4. Ahang, L., Chen, L., Li, M., Zhang, H.: Automated Annotation of Human Faces in Family Albums, Proc. of the 11th ACM intl. conf. on Multimedia (2003) 355-358.
5. Yang, S., Kim, S.K., Seo, K.S., Ro, Y.M.: Automated Situation Clustering of Home Photos for Digital Albuming, SPIE (2005)
6. Manjunath, B. S., Salembier, P., Sikora, T.: Introduction to MPEG-7, John Wiley & Sons, LTD (2002).
7. Viola, P., Jones, M.: Rapid Object Detection using a Boosted Cascade of Simple Features, CVPR (2001) 511-518.
8. Wu, B., Ai, H., Huang, C., Lao, S.: Fast Rotation Invariant Multi-View Face Detection Based on Real Adaboost, AFGR (2004) 79-84.
9. Freund, Y., Schapire, R. E.: A decision-theoretic generalization of on-line learning and an application to boosting, Computational Learning Theory: Eurocolt '95 (1995) 23-37.
10. Duda, R.O., Hart, P.E., Stork, D.G.: Pattern Classification second ed., John Wiley & Sons, LTD, (2001)

11. Vapnik, V. N.: The Nature of Statistical Learning Theory, second ed. Springer (1999)
12. Cristianini, N., Shawe-Taylor, J.: An Introduction to Support Vector Machines and other kernel-based learning methods, Cambridge University Press (2000).
13. Moody, J., Darken, C. J.: Fast learning in networks of locally tuned processing units, Neural Computation (1989) 281-294.
14. Duda, R.O., Hart, P.E., Stork, D.G.: Pattern Classification second ed., John Wiley & Sons, LTD (2001)
15. NIST Database, /M7photo/Photo_DB/Face-CE_testset_org, MPEG-7 Visual Group, ISO/IEC JTC1/SX29/WG11 (2005)
16. Bober, M., Kim, S.K.: Description of MPEG-7 Visual Core Experiments, MPEG-7 Visual Group ISO/IEC JTC1/SC29/WG11 N6905 (2005)

Bayesian Colorization Using MRF Color Image Modeling

Hideki Noda[1], Hitoshi Korekuni[2], Nobuteru Takao[3], and Michiharu Niimi[1]

[1] Kyushu Institute of Technology, Dept. of Systems Innovation and Informatics,
680-4 Kawazu, Iizuka, 820-8502 Japan
{noda, niimi}@mip.ces.kyutech.ac.jp
[2] Kyushu Institute of Technology,
Dept. of Electrical, Electronic and Computer Engineering,
1-1 Sensui-cho, Tobata-ku, Kitakyushu, 804-8550 Japan
korekuni@know.comp.kyutech.ac.jp
[3] ASA Systems Inc., 3-3 Nakabaru-shinmachi,
Tobata-ku, Kitakyushu, 804-0003 Japan
n-takao@asasystems.co.jp

Abstract. This paper presents a colorization algorithm which produces color images from given monochrome images. Unlike previously proposed colorization methods, this paper formulates the colorization problem as the maximum a posteriori (MAP) estimation of a color image given a monochrome image. Markov random field (MRF) is used for modeling a color image which is utilized as a priori information for the MAP estimation. Under the mean field approximation, The MAP estimation problem for a whole image can be decomposed into local MAP estimation problems for each pixel. The local MAP estimation is described as a simple quadratic programming problem with constraints. Using 0.6% of whole pixels as references, the proposed method produced pretty high quality color images with 25.7 dB to 32.6 dB PSNR values for four standard images.

1 Introduction

Colorization is a process, usually a computer-aided process of adding color to monochrome images or movies. There should be considerable demands for colorization of monochrome images or movies. Colorization is now generally carried out manually using some drawing software tools. A user typically carries out segmentation of a monochrome image by giving region boundaries by hand and then assigns a color to each region. Obviously such manual work is very expensive and time-consuming.

Recently several colorization methods [1] [2] [3] have been proposed which do not require intensive manual effort. Welsh et al. proposed a semi-automatic method to colorize a monochrome image by transferring color from a reference color image [1]. The entire color "mood" of the reference image is transferred to the target monochrome image by matching luminance and texture information between the two images. This method requires an appropriate reference color image which should be prepared by a user and works well only for images where differently colored regions have distinct luminance values or distinct textures. Levin et al. have proposed an interactive method which does not require precise manual segmentation [2]. In their method, instead of manual segmentation, a user needs to give some color scribbles, and the colors are automatically propagated to produce a fully colorized image. Horiuchi [3] has proposed a method where a user gives colors for some pixels and colors for all other pixels are determined automatically by using the probabilistic relaxation [4]. One of serious problems in his method is that it is computationally very expensive; it takes almost one day to colorize one image.

Unlike previously proposed colorization methods, this paper formulates the colorization problem as Bayesian inference, i.e., the maximum a posteriori (MAP) estimation of a color image given a monochrome image. Markov random field (MRF) [5] is used for modeling a color image which is utilized as a priori information for the MAP estimation. In this paper, the MAP estimation problem for a whole image is approximately decomposed into local MAP estimation problems for each pixel, and the local MAP estimation is reduced to a simple quadratic programming problem with constraints.

The rest of this paper is organized as follows. In Section 2, after a brief introduction of MRF, color image modeling by MRF is described. In Section 3, colorization is formulated as color image estimation given a monochrome image using MAP estimation and an iterative local MAP estimation algorithm is derived. Estimation of an initial color image is also described which is required to start the iterative colorization algorithm. Experimental results are given in Section 4, and conclusions are addressed in Section 5.

2 Color Image Modeling by Markov Random Field

2.1 Markov Random Field

Let $\mathcal{L} = \{(i,j); 1 \leq i \leq N_1, 1 \leq j \leq N_2\}$ denote a finite set of sites of an $N_1 \times N_2$ rectangular lattice. Let $\eta_{ij}^X \subset \mathcal{L}$ denote the (i,j) pixel's neighborhood of a random field $X_{\mathcal{L}}$[1] defined on $\mathcal{L}$. Let $\mathcal{C}_{ij}^X$ denote the set of cliques C associated with η_{ij}^X which contains the (i,j) pixel, i.e., $(i,j) \in \mathcal{C}_{ij}^X$. For example, in the first-order neighborhood, $\eta_{ij}^X = \{(i,j+1), (i,j-1), (i+1,j), (i-1,j)\}$ and $\mathcal{C}_{ij}^X = \{\{(i,j)\}, \{(i,j),(i,j+1)\}, \{(i,j),(i,j-1)\}, \{(i,j),(i+1,j)\}, \{(i,j),(i-1,j)\}\}$ which consists of one singleton and four doubleton cliques. Let the random field $X_{\mathcal{L}} = \{X_{ij}; (i,j) \in \mathcal{L}\}$ be a Markov random field (MRF) defined on $\mathcal{L}$ with X_{ij}s taking values from a common local state space Q_X. It is well known that an MRF is completely described by a Gibbs distribution [6]

$$p(x_{\mathcal{L}}) = \frac{1}{Z_X} \exp\{-U(x_{\mathcal{L}})\}, \tag{1}$$

---

[1] In this paper, x_A and $f(x_A)$ denote the set $\{x_{a_1}, \ldots, x_{a_l}\}$ and the multivariable function $f(x_{a_1}, \ldots, x_{a_l})$ respectively, where $A = \{a_1, \ldots, a_l\}$.

where $x_\mathcal{L}$ is a realization of $X_\mathcal{L}$ from the configuration space $\Omega_X = Q_X^{N_1 \times N_2}$ and

$$U(x_\mathcal{L}) = \sum_{(i,j)\in\mathcal{L}} \sum_{C\in\mathcal{C}_{ij}^X} U(x_C) \tag{2}$$

is the global energy function whereas $U(x_C)$ is the clique energy function and

$$Z_X = \sum_{x_\mathcal{L}\in\Omega_X} \exp\{-U(x_\mathcal{L})\} \tag{3}$$

is the partition function. For details on MRFs and related concepts such as the neighborhoods and cliques, see Ref. [5].

2.2 A Color Image Model Using Gaussian MRF

A color image can be considered as a realization $\mathbf{x}_\mathcal{L} = \{\mathbf{x}_{ij}; (i,j) \in \mathcal{L}\}$ of a random field $\mathbf{X}_\mathcal{L} = \{\mathbf{X}_{ij}; (i,j) \in \mathcal{L}\}$, where $\mathbf{x}_{ij} = (r_{ij}, g_{ij}, b_{ij})^T$ is a color vector at (i,j) pixel composed of red r_{ij}, green g_{ij} and blue b_{ij} components. Color images are modeled by a Gaussian MRF characterized by the following local conditional probability density function (pdf):

$$p(\mathbf{x}_{ij} \mid \mathbf{x}_{\eta_{ij}^X}) = \frac{1}{(2\pi)^{3/2}|\Sigma_X|^{1/2}} \exp\{-\frac{1}{2}(\mathbf{x}_{ij} - \mathbf{m}_{ij})^T (\Sigma_X)^{-1}(\mathbf{x}_{ij} - \mathbf{m}_{ij})\}, \tag{4}$$

$$\mathbf{m}_{ij} = \frac{1}{|\mathcal{N}|} \sum_{\tau\in\mathcal{N}} \mathbf{x}_{ij+\tau}. \tag{5}$$

Here $\mathbf{m}_{ij}$ is the mean of neighboring pixels' color vectors $\mathbf{x}_{\eta_{ij}^X} = \{\mathbf{x}_{ij+\tau}, \tau \in \mathcal{N}\}$, where $\mathcal{N}$ denotes the neighborhood of $(0,0)$-pixel. For example, $\mathcal{N} = \{(0,1), (0,-1), (1,0), (-1,0)\}$ for the first-order neighborhood, and if $\tau = (0,1)$, $\mathbf{x}_{ij+\tau} = \mathbf{x}_{i,j+1}$. Σ_X is the covariance matrix of $\mathbf{x}_{ij} - \mathbf{m}_{ij}$.

3 Color Image Estimation

3.1 Derivation of Estimation Algorithm

We assume that a monochrome image $y_\mathcal{L} = \{y_{ij}; (i,j) \in \mathcal{L}\}$ is associated with a color image $\mathbf{x}_\mathcal{L} = \{\mathbf{x}_{ij}; (i,j) \in \mathcal{L}\}$ under the following relation:

$$y_{ij} = \mathbf{a}^T \mathbf{x}_{ij} = 0.299 r_{ij} + 0.587 g_{ij} + 0.114 b_{ij}, \quad 0 \le y_{ij}, r_{ij}, g_{ij}, b_{ij} \le 255. \tag{6}$$

Given $y_\mathcal{L}$, $\mathbf{x}_\mathcal{L}$ can be estimated by maximizing the a posteriori probability $p(\mathbf{x}_\mathcal{L} \mid y_\mathcal{L})$, i.e., by MAP estimation. The MAP estimate $\hat{\mathbf{x}}_\mathcal{L}$ is written as

$$\hat{\mathbf{x}}_\mathcal{L} = \arg \max_{\mathbf{x}_\mathcal{L}\in\Omega_X} p(\mathbf{x}_\mathcal{L} \mid y_\mathcal{L}), \tag{7}$$

where the a posteriori probability $p(\mathbf{x}_\mathcal{L} \mid y_\mathcal{L})$ is described as

$$p(\mathbf{x}_\mathcal{L} \mid y_\mathcal{L}) = \frac{p(y_\mathcal{L} \mid \mathbf{x}_\mathcal{L}) p(\mathbf{x}_\mathcal{L})}{\sum_{\mathbf{x}_\mathcal{L}\in\Omega_X} p(y_\mathcal{L} \mid \mathbf{x}_\mathcal{L}) p(\mathbf{x}_\mathcal{L})}. \tag{8}$$

Considering (6), $p(y_\mathcal{L} \mid \mathbf{x}_\mathcal{L})$ is described as

$$p(y_\mathcal{L} \mid \mathbf{x}_\mathcal{L}) = 1(\{y_{ij} = \mathbf{a}^T \mathbf{x}_{ij}, (i,j) \in \mathcal{L}\})$$
$$= \prod_{(i,j)\in\mathcal{L}} 1(y_{ij} = \mathbf{a}^T \mathbf{x}_{ij}), \qquad (9)$$

where

$$1(y_{ij} = \mathbf{a}^T \mathbf{x}_{ij}) = \begin{cases} 1 & \text{if } y_{ij} = \mathbf{a}^T \mathbf{x}_{ij} \\ 0 & \text{otherwise.} \end{cases} \qquad (10)$$

Using the mean field approximation [7], $p(\mathbf{x}_\mathcal{L})$ can be decomposed as [8]

$$p(\mathbf{x}_\mathcal{L}) \simeq \prod_{(i,j)\in\mathcal{L}} p(\mathbf{x}_{ij} \mid \langle \mathbf{x} \rangle_{\eta^x_{ij}}), \qquad (11)$$

where $\langle \mathbf{x} \rangle_{\eta^x_{ij}}$ denotes the mean fields for $\mathbf{x}_{\eta^x_{ij}}$. Substituting (9) and (11) into (8) and replacing $\sum_{\mathbf{x}_\mathcal{L} \in \Omega_X} \prod_{(i,j)\in\mathcal{L}}$ by $\prod_{(i,j)\in\mathcal{L}} \sum_{\mathbf{x}_{ij} \in Q_X}$, we obtain the following decomposition for $p(\mathbf{x}_\mathcal{L} \mid y_\mathcal{L})$:

$$p(\mathbf{x}_\mathcal{L} \mid y_\mathcal{L}) \simeq \prod_{(i,j)\in\mathcal{L}} p(\mathbf{x}_{ij} \mid y_{ij}, \langle \mathbf{x} \rangle_{\eta^x_{ij}}), \qquad (12)$$

where

$$p(\mathbf{x}_{ij} \mid y_{ij}, \langle \mathbf{x} \rangle_{\eta^x_{ij}}) = \frac{1(y_{ij} = \mathbf{a}^T \mathbf{x}_{ij}) p(\mathbf{x}_{ij} \mid \langle \mathbf{x} \rangle_{\eta^x_{ij}})}{\sum_{\mathbf{x}_{ij} \in Q_X} 1(y_{ij} = \mathbf{a}^T \mathbf{x}_{ij}) p(\mathbf{x}_{ij} \mid \langle \mathbf{x} \rangle_{\eta^x_{ij}})}. \qquad (13)$$

In the following, $\mathbf{x}_{\eta^x_{ij}}$ is simply used for $\langle \mathbf{x} \rangle_{\eta^x_{ij}}$. Then $p(\mathbf{x}_{ij} \mid y_{ij}, \mathbf{x}_{\eta^x_{ij}}) = p(\mathbf{x}_{ij} \mid y_{ij}, \langle \mathbf{x} \rangle_{\eta^x_{ij}})$ is considered as local a posteriori probability (LAP). Using these LAPs, the global optimization problem shown by Eq. (7) is approximately decomposed into the local optimization problems

$$\hat{\mathbf{x}}_{ij} = \arg\max_{\mathbf{x}_{ij} \in Q_X} p(\mathbf{x}_{ij} \mid y_{ij}, \mathbf{x}_{\eta^x_{ij}}). \qquad (14)$$

In order to solve (14) for all (i,j) pixels, their neighboring color vectors $\mathbf{x}_{\eta^x_{ij}}$ should be given. Since such a problem as shown in (14) can be solved iteratively as is popular in numerical analysis, we rewrite Eq. (14) as

$$\mathbf{x}_{ij}^{(p+1)} = \arg\max_{\mathbf{x}_{ij} \in Q_X} p(\mathbf{x}_{ij} \mid y_{ij}, \mathbf{x}_{\eta^x_{ij}}^{(p)}), \qquad (15)$$

where p represents the pth iteration. Considering (4), (5), (6) and (13), the local MAP estimation (15) is rewritten as the following constrained quadratic programming problem:

$$\text{minimize} \quad (\mathbf{x}_{ij} - \mathbf{m}_{ij})^T (\Sigma_X)^{-1} (\mathbf{x}_{ij} - \mathbf{m}_{ij}) \quad \text{with } \mathbf{m}_{ij} = \frac{1}{|\mathcal{N}|} \sum_{\tau \in \mathcal{N}} \mathbf{x}_{ij+\tau}^{(p)} \quad (16)$$

$$\text{subject to} \quad \mathbf{a}^T \mathbf{x}_{ij} = y_{ij}, \ 0 \leq r_{ij}, g_{ij}, b_{ij} \leq 255 \qquad (17)$$

3.2 Initial Color Estimation

Since the color estimation shown by Eq. (15) is carried out iteratively, an initial color image is needed to start the iterative procedure. Initial color image estimation using some reference colors is here described. Assuming that color vectors for K pixels, $\mathbf{c}_{i_k j_k}, k = 1, \ldots, K$ are given, consider how to derive an initial color image. We consider an initial color estimation procedure which consists of two steps.

(1) Selection of a reference color vector

In order to estimate an initial color image $\mathbf{x}_{\mathcal{L}}^{(0)} = \{\mathbf{x}_{ij}^{(0)}; (i,j) \in \mathcal{L}\}$, a reference color vector for each pixel is selected from given K references, $\mathbf{c}_{i_k j_k}, k = 1, \ldots, K$. The used measure to select a reference for (i,j) pixel is

$$F_{ij}(k) = w \frac{\{(i - i_k)^2 + (j - j_k)^2\}^{1/2}}{(N_1 + N_2)/2} + (1 - w) \frac{|y_{ij} - \mathbf{a}^T \mathbf{c}_{i_k j_k}|}{255}, \quad (18)$$

where w is a weighting factor, and the first term measures a spatial distance from a reference $\mathbf{c}_{i_k j_k}$ and the second term measures a difference between (i,j) pixel's brightness y_{ij} and that of $\mathbf{c}_{i_k j_k}$. The reference $\mathbf{c}_{i_k j_k}$ which minimizes $F_{ij}(k)$ is selected for the (i,j) pixel. An appropriate value of w is determined experimentally.

(2) Color estimation using a reference

Once a reference $\mathbf{c}_{i_k j_k}$ is selected for (i,j) pixel, an initial estimation $\mathbf{x}_{ij}^{(0)}$ can be determined as the closest point to $\mathbf{c}_{i_k j_k}$ within the plane $\mathbf{a}^T \mathbf{x}_{ij} = y_{ij}$. Considering that $\mathbf{c}_{i_k j_k} - \mathbf{x}_{ij}$ for such $\mathbf{x}_{ij}$ should be orthogonal to the plane, i.e., $\mathbf{x}_{ij}$ should be the projection vector of $\mathbf{c}_{i_k j_k}$ onto the plane, $\mathbf{x}_{ij}^{(0)}$ is derived as

$$\mathbf{x}_{ij}^{(0)} = \mathbf{c}_{i_k j_k} + \frac{y_{ij} - \mathbf{a}^T \mathbf{c}_{i_k j_k}}{\mathbf{a}^T \mathbf{a}} \mathbf{a}. \quad (19)$$

However the derived projection point $\mathbf{x}_{ij}^{(0)} = (r_{ij}^{(0)}, g_{ij}^{(0)}, b_{ij}^{(0)})^T$ is sometimes out of the range of $0 \leq r_{ij}, g_{ij}, b_{ij} \leq 255$. The occurrences of such cases were from about 0.5% of total $256 \times 256 = 65536$ pixels for Lena to 6% for Milkdrop among four images. In such cases, the closest point to $\mathbf{c}_{i_k j_k}$ within the color space $0 \leq r_{ij}, g_{ij}, b_{ij} \leq 255$ (color cube) should be on sides of the planar polygon which is the cross section of the color cube cut by a given brightness plane $\mathbf{a}^T \mathbf{x}_{ij} = y_{ij}$. The closest point on sides can be determined as follows.

(i) Find the closest vertex $\mathbf{x}_1$ of the planar polygon to the reference $\mathbf{c}_{i_k j_k}$.

(ii) Find two vertices ($\mathbf{x}_2$ and $\mathbf{x}_3$) adjacent to $\mathbf{x}_1$. The closest point should be on one of two sides, i.e., the side $\mathbf{x}_1 \mathbf{x}_2$ or the side $\mathbf{x}_1 \mathbf{x}_3$.

(iii) If the closest point is on the side $\mathbf{x}_1 \mathbf{x}_2$, it can be derived as follows. Let $\mathbf{x} = t\mathbf{x}_1 + (1-t)\mathbf{x}_2, 0 \leq t \leq 1$ be a point on the side. The distance $D_{12}(t)$ between $\mathbf{x}$ on the side $\mathbf{x}_1 \mathbf{x}_2$ and $\mathbf{c}_{i_k j_k}$ is written as

$$\begin{aligned} D_{12}(t) &= (\mathbf{x} - \mathbf{c}_{i_k j_k})^T (\mathbf{x} - \mathbf{c}_{i_k j_k}) \\ &= t^2 \|\mathbf{x}_1 - \mathbf{x}_2\|^2 + 2t(\mathbf{x}_2 - \mathbf{c}_{i_k j_k})^T (\mathbf{x}_1 - \mathbf{x}_2) + \|\mathbf{x}_2 - \mathbf{c}_{i_k j_k}\|^2 \quad (20) \end{aligned}$$

The closest point is derived as $t\mathbf{x}_1 + (1-t)\mathbf{x}_2$ with $t = (\mathbf{c}_{i_k j_k} - \mathbf{x}_2)^T(\mathbf{x}_1 - \mathbf{x}_2)/\|\mathbf{x}_1 - \mathbf{x}_2\|^2$ which minimizes $D_{12}(t)$.

(iv) Let t_{12} and t_{13} be t values which minimize $D_{12}(t)$ and $D_{13}(t)$, respectively, for $-\infty < t < \infty$, where the closest point is considered on the extrapolated line including the side. Considering that $t_{12}, t_{13} > 0.5$ since $\mathbf{x}_1$ is the closest vertex to $\mathbf{c}_{i_k j_k}$, there are four cases: case 1 is $0.5 < t_{12}, t_{13} < 1$, case 2 is $0.5 < t_{12} < 1, t_{13} \geq 1$, case 3 is $0.5 < t_{13} < 1, t_{12} \geq 1$, case 4 is $t_{12}, t_{13} \geq 1$. In case 1, the closest one among the two closest points on the two sides should be selected. In cases 2 and 3, the closest point on the side $\mathbf{x}_1\mathbf{x}_2$ and one on the side $\mathbf{x}_1\mathbf{x}_3$, respectively, should be selected. In case 4, $\mathbf{x}_1$ should be the closest point.

4 Experimental Results

In order to evaluate the performance of the proposed colorization method, experiments were carried out using four standard color images (Lena, Milkdrop, Peppers, Mandrill). These images are 256 × 256 pixels in size and 24 bit per pixel (bpp) full color images. Their monochrome images were produced by the transform shown in (6) from the original color images and used for colorization experiments.

Table 1. Colorization performance (PSNR(dB)) for four images

♯ references		Lena	Milkdrop	Peppers	Mandrill
3 × 3	initial	24.0	21.7	19.8	15.1
	final (♯ iterations)	25.6 (5)	22.1 (4)	21.1 (7)	16.9 (11)
5 × 5	initial	25.4	24.5	22.1	17.1
	final (♯ iterations)	26.9 (4)	24.9 (5)	23.8 (7)	19.9 (9)
10 × 10	initial	27.8	24.7	23.1	20.7
	final (♯ iterations)	29.5 (4)	25.0 (4)	25.1 (6)	23.0 (8)
20 × 20	initial	30.4	27.1	25.5	23.1
	final (♯ iterations)	32.6 (3)	27.8 (5)	27.4 (5)	25.7 (7)

For initial color estimation, several fixed numbers of reference color vectors were given from each original image, which were evenly spaced on its image lattice for the sake of simplicity. The weight value w in (18) was set as follows. After optimal weight values, which depend on the number of references as well as image, were determined experimentally, the average of optimal weight values for four images was used as w.

The local MAP estimation problem, i.e., the constrained quadratic programming problem in (16) and (17), was here directly solved using a quadratic programming solver [9]. In the calculation of $\mathbf{m}_{ij}$ in (16), the third-order neighborhood [2] was used and $\mathbf{x}^{(p)}_{ij+\tau}$ whose luminance value $y_{ij+\tau}$ is far from y_{ij} was

---

[2] For the third-order neighborhood, $\mathcal{N} = \{(0,1), (0,-1), (1,0), (-1,0), (1,1), (-1,-1), (1,-1), (-1,1), (0,2), (0,-2), (2,0), (-2,0)\}$.

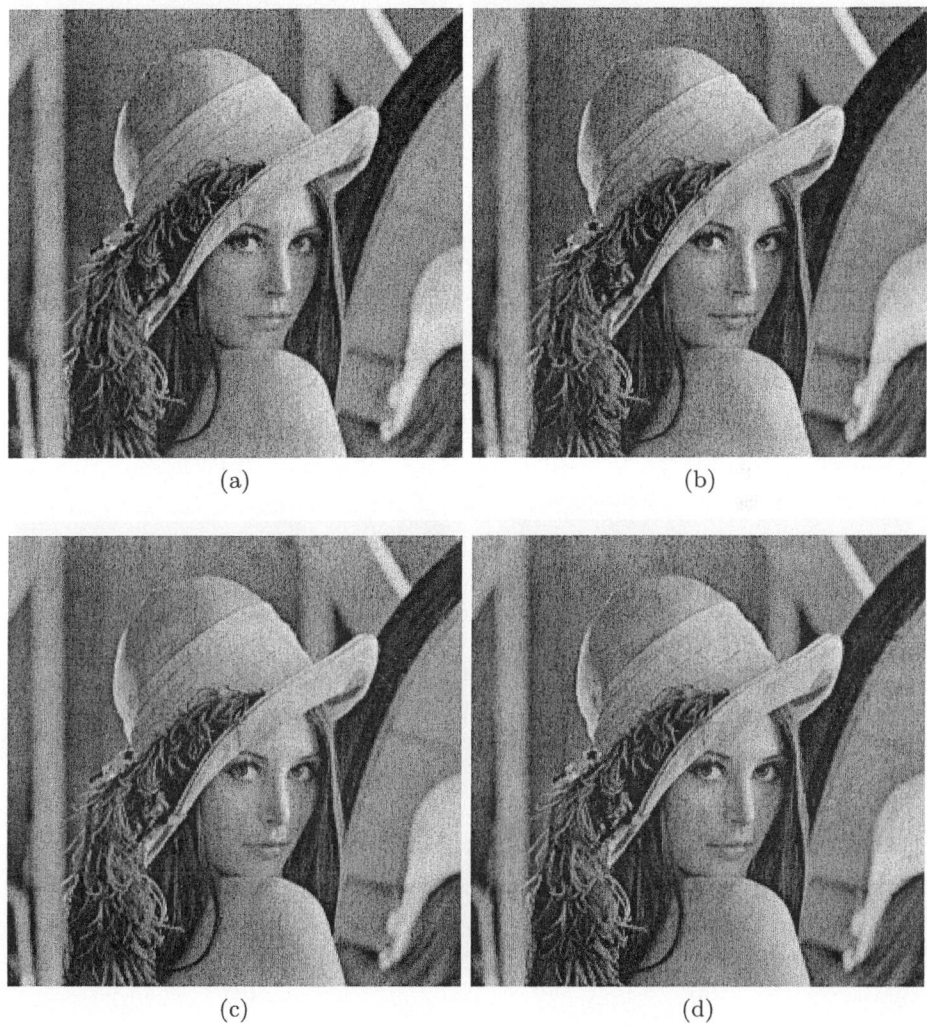

Fig. 1. Experimental results for Lena: (a) original color image, (b) monochrome image, (c) estimated color image using 5×5 references, (d) estimated color image using 20×20 references

excluded from the calculation. In the following experiments, if $|y_{ij+\tau} - y_{ij}| > 0.5s$, where s is the standard deviation of luminance values averaged over four images, $\mathbf{x}_{ij+\tau}^{(p)}$ was excluded from the calculation of $\mathbf{m}_{ij}$. For the covariance matrix $\mathbf{\Sigma}_X$ in (16), the average of normalized covariance matrices (normalized by their maximum components) for four images was used.

Colorization performance for several cases using different numbers of references is shown in Table 1. For each case, the upper row shows performance of initial color estimation and the lower row shows the final result after the itera-

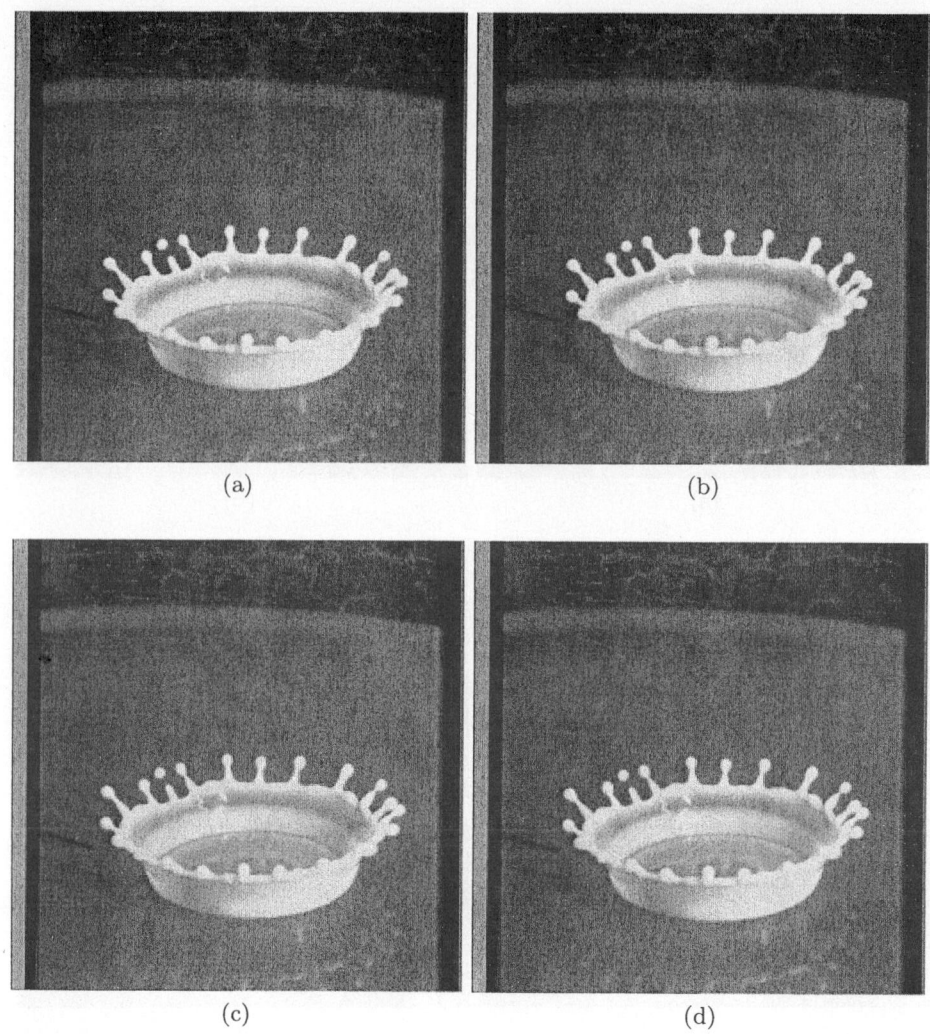

Fig. 2. Experimental results for Milkdrop: (a) original color image, (b) monochrome image, (c) estimated color image using 5×5 references, (d) estimated color image using 20×20 references

tive MAP estimation. Iterations were stopped when the difference of estimated color components averaged over all pixels at a current and the previous iteration became less than 0.5. Computational time to colorize one image was six seconds at most. Comparing with Horiuchi's colorization method [3], where colorization performance for Lena was about 20 dB and 28dB with 1% and 7% of whole pixels, respectively, used as reference pixels, and that for Milkdrop was about 20 dB and 27dB with 1% and 7% used, respectively, the proposed method has outperformed it since 20×20 pixels only amount to 0.6%. Fig. 1 to Fig. 4 show colorization results for four images.

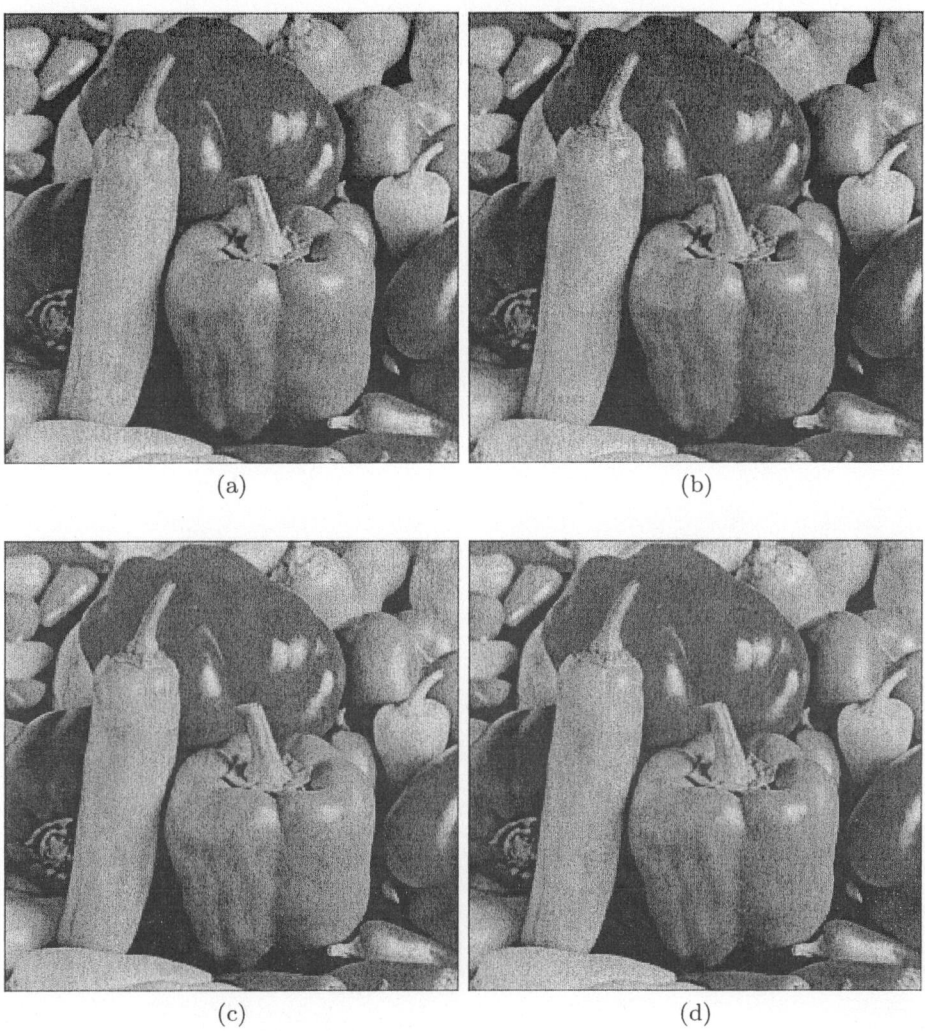

Fig. 3. Experimental results for Peppers: (a) original color image, (b) monochrome image, (c) estimated color image using 5 × 5 references, (d) estimated color image using 20 × 20 references

5 Conclusions

This paper presented a colorization algorithm given some pixels' colors as references. The proposed algorithm is based on the MAP estimation of a color image given a monochrome image, where a color image is modeled by a Gaussian MRF model. The MAP estimation problem for a whole image is decomposed into local MAP estimation problems for each pixel, and the local MAP estimation is reduced to a simple quadratic programming problem with constraints. Using 0.6%

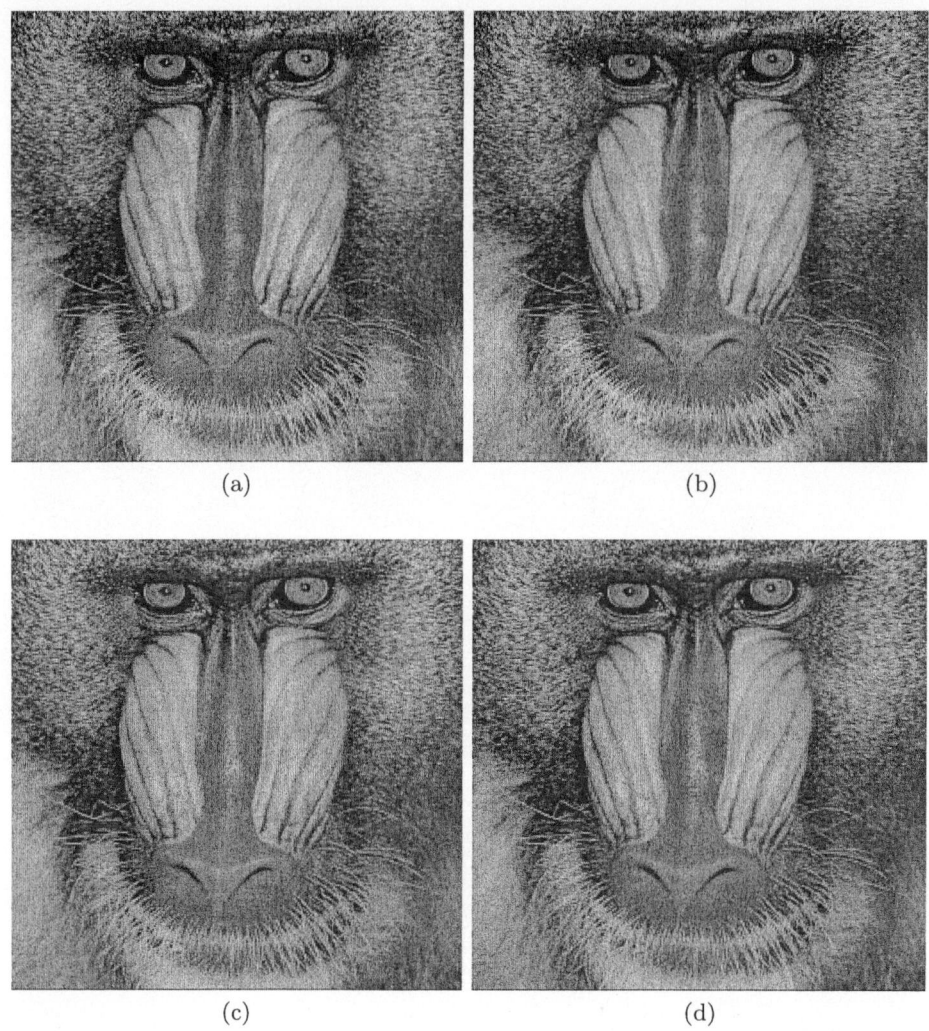

Fig. 4. Experimental results for Mandrill: (a) original color image, (b) monochrome image, (c) estimated color image using 5 × 5 references, (d) estimated color image using 20 × 20 references

of whole pixels as references, the proposed method produced pretty high quality color images with 25.7 dB to 32.6 dB PSNR values for four standard images.

References

1. Welsh T., Ashikhmin M., Mueller K.: Transferring color to greyscale images. ACM Trans. Graphics **21** (2002) 277-280
2. Levin A., Lischinski D., Weiss Y.: Colorization using optimization. ACM Trans. Graphics **23** (2004) 689-694

3. Horiuchi T.: Colorization algorithm using probabilistic relaxation. Image and Vision Computing **22** (2004) 197-202
4. Rosenfeld A., Hummel R.A., Zucker S.W.: Scene labeling using relaxation operation. IEEE Trans. Systems, Man and Cybernetics **SMC-6** (1976) 420-433
5. Geman S., Geman D.: Stochastic relaxation, Gibbs distributions, and the Bayesian restoration of images. IEEE Trans. Pattern Anal. & Machine Intell. **PAMI-6** (1984) 721-741
6. Spitzer F.: Markov random fields and Gibbs ensembles. Amer. Math. Mon. **78** (1971) 142-154
7. Huang K.: Statistical mechanics, second ed. John Wiley & Sons (1987)
8. Noda H., Shirazi M.N., Kawaguchi E.: MRF-based texture segmentation using wavelet decomposed images. Pattern Recognition **35** (2002) 771-782
9. Mittelmann H.D., Spellucci P.: Decision tree for optimization software Web site. http://plato.asu.edu/guide.html

An Efficient Player for MPEG-4 Contents on a Mobile Device

Sangwook Kim[1] and Kyungdeok Kim[2]

[1] Department of Computer Science,
Kyungpook National University, Daegu, 702-701, Korea
swkim@cs.knu.ac.kr
[2] Division of Computer and Multimedia Engineering,
Uiduk University, Gyeongju, 780-713, Korea
kdkim@uu.ac.kr

Abstract. We describe an implementation of an efficient player for MPEG-4 contents on a mobile device. The player uses 3 adaptation methods in order to support high efficiency when it plays MPEG-4 contents. The adaptation methods are composed of a physical adaptation, an event adaptation, and a resource adaptation. The first adaptation resolves the physical difference between the authoring environment and playback environment. The second adaptation resolves some events that cannot support on mobile devices. The last adaptation resolves the load for restricted resource on mobile device. In view of the results of the performance analysis on the player, we could find that the player showed an efficient playback of MPEG-4 contents on a mobile device. The applications for the player are as follows; mobile games, a car navigator, distance learning, etc.

1 Introduction

MPEG-4 contents have been applied to various areas. The MPEG-4 is an international standard for efficient transmission and use of multimedia data and focuses on the content-based encoding that is based on understanding of image contents. Such the content-based encoding splits image contents into object units, transmits the units, and controls and displays split respective units by a user's intention[1, 2, 3]. Currently, their use is very increased by growth of wireless communication.

In MPEG-4 contents, a scene is constructed by the split units that are handled individually, and the scene description language, BInary Format for Scene(BIFS), is used to describe temporal and spatial information for scene changes according to user interaction and temporal flow[1]. Most of MPEG-4 contents authoring tools are suitable to desktop computers, and generated MPEG-4 contents from the tools are most suitable to desk-top players. However, it is especially difficult to present the contents on a PDA device due to a small size of a PDA screen, and shortage of CPU memory usage, electronic power, etc. So conventional MPEG-4 authoring tools need an adaptation method in order to play the contents on a PDA device[6, 8, 9, 10, 18, 19].

In this paper, we describe an implementation of an efficient player for MPEG-4 contents on a mobile device. The player uses adaptation methods in order to support high efficiency on playback. The adaptation methods consist of 3 parts; a physical adaptation, an event adaptation, and a resource adaptation. The physical adaptation resolves the physical difference between the authoring environment and playback environment. The event adaptation resolves some events that cannot use on mobile devices. The last adaptation resolves the load for restricted resource on mobile device. We apply an Inverse Discrete Cosine Transform(IDCT) operation of the Chen-Wang's algorithm[16, 17] to the resource adaptation in order to improve a decoding speed of MPEG-4 contents on a mobile device. We analyze and compare performance of the player on a mobile device in according to pre and post-application of the adaptation method.

This paper is organized as follows. Section 2 introduces related works on MPEG-4 players and adaptation models on a mobile device. Section 3 describes structure and adaptation methods of an MPEG-4 player on a mobile device. Section 4 explains an implementation and performance analysis on the player. Finally, section 5 describes some concluding remarks and presents future plans.

2 Related Works

There are lots of works on MPEG-4 player in desktop environment, but works on a player on a mobile device are not activated yet. We introduce a player, an authoring, and an adaptation on MPEG-4 contents as related works. First, the work of MPEG-4 video decoder[10] describes implementation of the ARM7TDMI processor with an efficient operation for video decoder. The processor improves a speed of the IDCT operation using real number directly, and can play MPEG-4 video efficiently. But, it is difficult for the player to play MPEG-4 contents with user interaction. The work of design and development of MPEG-4 contents authoring system[1] describes an intuitive authoring for users on windows environments. The system supports composing a visual and aural scene using video objects, audio objects, image objects, and text objects, and set up intuitively a scene change by user's clicking a mouse. And the system defines a scene tree to represent the MPEG-4 contents that consists of object units in a scene. The scene tree is used as inner data structure for authoring in the system. It generates a scene descriptor as the form of text, and then finally MPEG-4 contents are created after the scene goes through encoding phase. The work of design and implementation of a visual MPEG-4 scene-authoring tool[4] is developed on windows environment, and the tool can store user's making scene to a data form. Also the authoring tool supports BIFS commands and JAVA scripts in order to support user's interaction. The work of MPEG-4 authoring tool for the composition of 3D audiovisual scenes[5] generates MPEG-4 contents using 3D APIs of the OpenGL library. The tool generates 3D contents and media objects such as a box, a sphere, a cone, video, audio, etc., and then transforms the objects into the BIFS commands. Finally, the tool generates MPEG-4 contents using the generated BIFS file and provides a preview function for a 3D MPEG-4 scene.

There are a few related works with respect to contents adaptation for mobile devices. The work of content model for mobile adaptation of multimedia information[6] proposes a new abstract model to represent and adapt multimedia contents to hybrid environments. The model includes a layered mapping of semantic and physical entities and is combined under the taxonomy of multimedia adaptation to optimize end-to-end service. The adaptation taxonomy consists of two parts; semantic adaptation and physical adaptation. The semantic adaptation is based on users' and service providers' choices and it is affected by the semantic content of a presentation. The physical adaptation is based on physical QoS and the characteristics of media objects consisting multimedia contents. The work of adapting multimedia internet content for universal access[7] presents a system adapting multimedia web documents to optimally match the capabilities of the client device requesting it. The system shows that multimedia contents are adapted by using two components; a representation scheme that provides a multimodal and multi-resolution representation hierarchy for multimedia and a customizer that selects the best content representation to meet the client capabilities while delivering the most value. The scalability for adaptive MPEG-4 contents[9] describes an adapting technique for MPEG-4 contents on various service environments. The adapting technique supports adaptations of each media object in a scene and streaming service using network bandwidth. But the technique doesn't support to author MEPG-4 contents with interactive capability for mobile devices such as a PDA device, and it introduce capability which MPEG-4 contents is reconstructed using media objects in a scene.

Most of above-described works are difficult to suitably support to playback MPEG-4 contents on a mobile device. Besides, most mobile devices use the RISC processor. The processor uses only a few commands very simplified to optimize hardware functions and reduce an execution speed of a program. Also the processor doesn't include a floating point processor and uses software library instead. For reason of using soft-ware library, it is difficult for multimedia data having many floating point operations to encode and decode the multimedia data rapidly. So we use pre-computed integer values instead of computing floating point values for decoding multimedia data. As we use software for a floating point operation, a mobile device is able to overcome hard-ware dependency. Conventional MEPG-4 contents need an efficient player in order to be presented on a PDA device. So, in this paper, we describe the efficient MPEG-4 player that considers characteristics of a PDA device.

3 Structure and Adaptation Methods of an MPEG-4 Player

3.1 MPEG-4 System

MPEG-4 provides an object-based approach to describing and composing an audio-visual scene with user interaction. The most important features of MPEG-4 are the

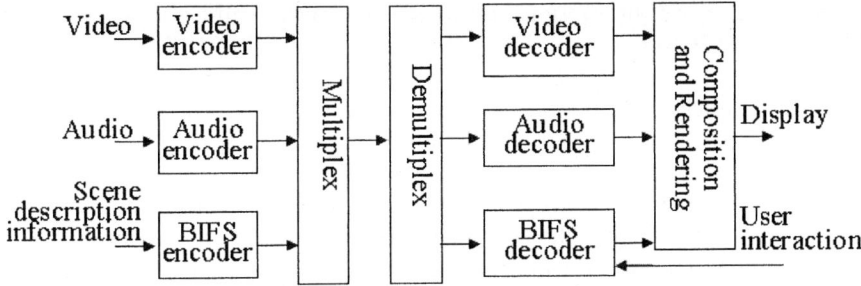

Fig. 1. MPEG-4 system's object based approach

scene description and the object descriptor framework[1, 2, 3]. Figure 1 shows how MPEG-4 system communicates with a multiple object based scene.

An MPEG-4 scene is composed of a set of individual audio-visual objects and the arrangement of the objects, with the scene description specifying the arrangement of multimedia objects. The scene description is mapped into a parametric form called Binary Format for Scenes[1, 2, 3, 18]. Also it declares the spatiotemporal relationship of multimedia objects. In the MPEG-4 scene description, each object included in the scene is specified with its spatiotemporal properties. The scene description has a structure inherited from the Virtual Reality Modeling Language(VRML) for the most part. And MPEG-4 adds distinguishing several mechanisms from the VRML as follows; data streaming, scene updates and compression[20, 21]. The MPEG-4 scene is constructed as a hierarchical structure, which can be represented as directed acyclic graph[3, 21]. Each node of the graph denotes a multimedia object. The event model of BIFS uses the VRML concept of routes to describe how objects behave following to user's event or space and time. Namely, the interactivity mechanisms between user and multimedia object are inte-grated in the form of linked event sources and targets as well as sensor objects, special objects that can trigger events based on specific conditions. Likewise, the media nodes in BIFS are associated with the individual multimedia objects that are carried in separate Elementary Streams[11]. To achieve the mechanism linking Elementary Streams and the scene description, Object Descriptor(OD) is used. The OD identifies the associated Elementary Streams and multimedia object in BIFS[11]. These MPEG-4 contents are encoded and multiplexed into coded binary streams that are either transmitted or stored. For the purpose of presenting the MPEG-4 scene to end users, these streams are demultiplexed and decoded. The decoded multimedia objects are composed according to the scene description information and then rendered on the user's terminal. Finally, a user may interact with the presented scene.

3.2 Structure of an MPEG-4 Player

An MPEG-4 player plays usually the audio-visual scene that consists of various multimedia objects. And the player enables scene to change dynamically according to user's interaction and scene description information described on authoring MPEG-4 contents. Usual playback process of MPEG-4 contents is as follows; first, the header information of MPEG-4 contents becomes to be analyzed. The information is used to separate multimedia objects included in the contents. The system decoder reads a multimedia object, stores it in a decoding buffer, and extracts access units from the buffer at precisely defined points in time. And then it places composition units, the results of the decoding processes, in the scene compositor. The scene compositor arranges the composition units using scene description information. In the scene composition step, a scene tree is generated by analyzing the scene description information. The scene tree is the data structure that represents spatiotemporal relationship of multimedia objects. Also it is used to manage the content of spatially oriented objects which is changed immediately by user's interaction. The changed scene tree has an effect on rendering a scene. Finally, the render displays the arranged composition units on a screen.

In this paper, an MPEG-4 player for a mobile device consists of 6 parts; file format decoder, system decoder, presenter, scene compositor, event processor, and user interface[11]. The File Format Decoder divides the MP4 file into media streams, and transfers them to the system decoder. The decoder reads the MP4 file, and separates each of bit streams and BIFS. And then it gives the unit data having time information, and transmits them to the system decoder. The System Decoder decodes BIFS, OD and each of multimedia streams. The System Decoder transmits each element streams to video, audio or image decoding buffer according to each kind of bit stream. Each decoding buffer is the memory space for each bit streams before decoding. Each decoder decodes the bit stream, and then each decoded stream stores in each composition buffer in the Scene Compositor. Also the System Decoder decodes BIFS streams and extracts the initial information for scene composition. Using the element streams and initial information(BIFS and OD), the scene compositor generates a scene. The scene is rendered on the user interface of a mobile device by the presenter. The event processor affects a scene composition using user's interaction information. The figure 2 presents the structure of an MPEG-4 player using adaptation methods on a mobile device.

The Scene Compositor analyzes the scene description information, and extracts the property information of a multimedia object that is used to render a scene on a screen. To analyze and manage the scene description information in the Scene Compositor need a BIFS parser, an engine to support searching a tree and a rule table for information extraction[19]. The BIFS parser generates the scene tree. The scene tree is used to manage property information of each object in the scene and its content is changed instantly by user's interaction. So change of the scene tree means change of a scene on a screen. To support such rapid change needs a fast search engine to obtain needed data from the scene tree. In this paper, the search engine uses a top-down method and depth-first search mechanism. It receives the scene tree as input, searches property of each object included in a node and judges whether an object is presented in a

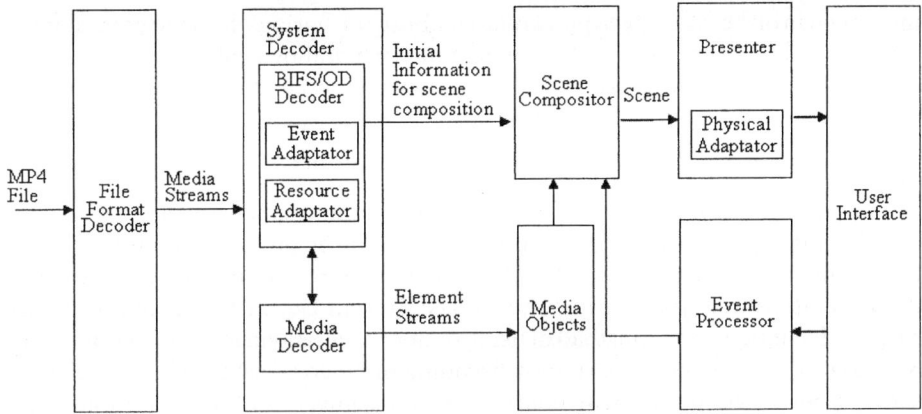

Fig. 2. Structure of an MPEG-4 player on a mobile device

scene according to playback time and drawing order of each object. Also the search engine manages event information describing object's behavior and interactivity. The event information is processed by the ROUTEs mechanism, event model of MPEG-4, to propagate events between objects on scene. The ROUTEs combines with the interpolator that can cause behavior in a scene. The rule table has main properties on each multimedia object. Using the rule table, the search engine gets needed information from the scene tree. For example, the Scene Compositor needs property information to present a video object on screen such as url, whichChoice, center, scale, drawingOrder, translation, etc. In this paper, we consider only video and audio objects on the player. The player supports namely the Simple 2D profile of MPEG-4 standard. So besides the video and audio properties, the rest properties are useless such as AnimationStream, FontStyle, MediaTimeSensor, ScalarInterpolator, etc. Removing useless properties enables the Scene Compositor to reconstruct the scene tree fast and improve a decoding speed of the BIFS.

The Event Processor supports two functions. One manages events happened by the mouse movement of the user in the user interface. The other manages events happened by the flow of time using timer of the MPEG-4 Player. The user's interaction happened by mouse is divided into mouse click, mouse drag and mouse over. And the Event Manager manages each. While the MPEG-4 Player is executed, the MPEG-4 Player examines whether the range of happened mouse events is valid using transform information of each object in the MPEG-4 Player. When the occurred time or user event is valid, the Event Processor searches the related objects and the kind of event. If the suitable event is set up, the Event Processor searches objects to be rendered according to the event. The searched information is transferred to the Presenter.

The Presenter is responsible for rendering scene and consists of a graphic processor and a controller. The graphic processor renders various audiovisual objects using related graphic libraries. The graphic libraries support rendering video, audio and image, and supports a few media formats. The graphic library is independently man-aged in order to easily expand related library on various data formats. The controller has 2 functions as follows; connecting each audiovisual object with related graphic library and supporting synchronization between multimedia objects.

3.3 Adaptation Method for Efficient Playback

For an optimal adaptation of MPEG-4 contents on a mobile device, we consider as following parts; the system decoder module and the presenter module. The system decoder generates essential BIFS information for rendering on a mobile device. Also, the Resource Adaptor included in the System Decoder uses an IDCT algorithm using integer value instead of using cosine values having floating point values. Such IDCT algorithm supports fast decoding of video streams. The Event Adaptor transforms various events(mouse click, mouse over, etc.) into suitable events for a mobile device. When MPEG-4 contents is authored, various events can be included in the contents, but such events doesn't support on a mobile device always. So the events must be adapted on a mobile device. The Physical Adaptor in the Presenter computes coordinate values using a size and location of a media object for rendering media objects on a mobile device. In order to adapt MPEG-4 contents on a mobile device, the adaptation method consists of 3 subadaptations as follows; physical adaptation, event adaptation, and resource adaptation.

The physical adaptation is the technique that adapts a size and location values of media objects in the contents. The adaptation is applied to the Presenter module in the player. Conventional authoring environments make some problems on a displayer due to a difference of a screen size between a mobile device and a conventional device. In addition, width and height rates, a location and a size of visual objects, etc., most visual objects in contents must be adapted according to playback environment of a mobile device[7, 14]. The physical adaptation provides to adapt coordinates of visual objects on an authoring environment into them on playback environment in a mo-bile device. In case of not rendering contents on the mobile device due to its width and height, the procedure transforms coordinates values of visual objects in the contents into them in the mobile device. At this time, drawing information is gathered for rendering. The minimum screen size for playback on a PDA device is computed by using leftmost, rightmost, uppermost, and lowermost location of each visual object in a scene. Also, the size is used to compute a reduction rate. The reduction rate is applied to reduce an external size of each visual object in a scene, and adjusts a coordinates' value of each object. In the case of a text object, a reduction can make user not seeing itself on a PDA device. So, in order to avoid this problem, a reduction rate under a certain font size should be avoided.

The event adaptation is the technique that transforms made events for desktop PC environment in authoring contents into available events on a mobile device. Some of made events in authoring contents are difficult to apply to use them on a mobile de-vice. So, in order to adapt the events on a mobile device, we consider events as follows; mouse click, mouse over, mouse move, mouse drag, mouse out, and mouse right click. Such events map easily to a mobile device through the Event Adapter.

The resource adaptation is the technique that takes playback rate of MPEG-4 contents efficiently on mobile environment with restricted resource. The adaptation is applied to System Decoder module in the player. Conventional MPEG-4 decoding algorithm needs successive operations using real numbers in a DCT algorithm and an IDCT algorithm for encoding and decoding of MPEG-4 contents[12, 13]. So difficulties of conventional algorithm are a low decoding rate and broken playback of the contents. In order to decode video stream efficiently, we use the Chen-Wang's algorithm[15, 16, 17] that provides high efficiency on a mobile device especially. The algorithm provides fast decoding operations for video playback on a mobile device by using integer values which mean pre-computed cosine values with real numbers[15, 16, 17]. In the view of the general IDCT operation (1), we transform 2 cosine operations into integer operation using a table with pre-computed cosine values.

$$f(i,j) = \frac{1}{\sqrt{2N}} \sum_{u=0}^{N-1} \sum_{v=0}^{N-1} C(u) \times C(v) \times F(u,v) \times \cos\left(\frac{(2i+1) \times u \times \pi}{2N}\right) \times \cos\left(\frac{(2j+1) \times v \times \pi}{2N}\right) \quad (1)$$

where $f(i, j)$ denotes a decoded image, $F(u, v)$ denotes an encoded image, $C(u)$ and $C(v)$ denotes coefficients and are less than 1, and N denotes the number of blocks and its value is 8.

Because most of mobile devices doesn't provide a floating point processor. Such floating-point operations are processed by using libraries on a mobile device, and take much time. The floating-point operation needs 12 CPU cycles, and the integer operation needs 2 CPU cycles due to referencing a table with an integer number only. So we can find that the IDCT operation can improve some 6 times by using a reference table instead of computing a floating-point operation for cosine values. In this paper, the pre-computed cosine values is made as follows; first, a cosine value having a floating point value is multiplied by 2n, and then an integer value is derived from adapting a shift operation as a division operation to the multiplied value. And we use 210 as a number to be multiplied. Under condition of a mobile device with 32bit ARM processor of RISC type, the number 10 is a maximum value for reducing resolution error according to a difference between the cosine value and the computed integer value. So the integer value is derived from adapting 10 shift operations to the multiplied value.

Besides, we remove a useless internal data structures as following information; font style, scalar interpolation, etc. As a consequence of the removal of the useless internal data, in parsing BIFS data, a searching and a decoding speed of needed data are improved.

4 Performance Analysis

In this paper, we played back the MPEG-4 contents on a PDA device(HP ComPAQ iPAQ 3850, 206-MHz, 64MB Ram, 32MB FlashROM). For the implemen-

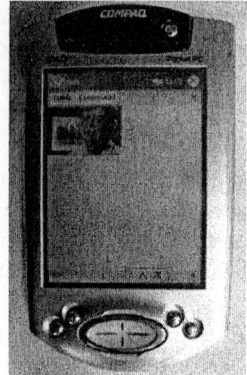 

Fig. 3. Playback of MPEG-4 contents on PC and a mobile device

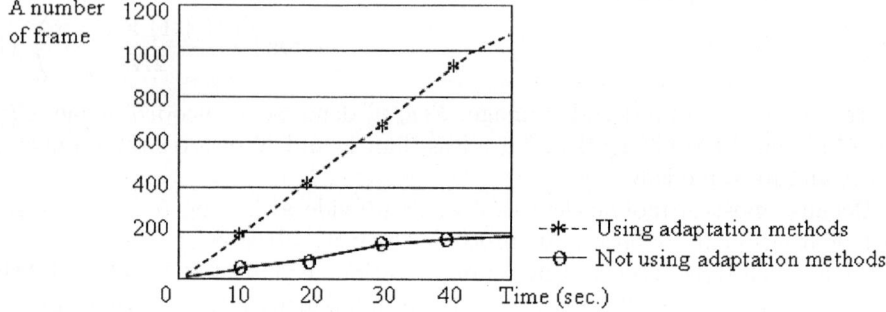

Fig. 4. Playback speed according to using the adaptation methods

tation of the adaptation method and MPEG-4 player on a PDA device, we use Microsoft Visual C++6.0, Microsoft Window for PocketPC 2002 and embedded Visual C++ 3.0.

The figure 3 presents playback of MPEG-4 contents on a PDA device. The MPEG-4 contents on a mobile device can be expanded or reduced according to user's interac-tion. The test data is the MPEG-4 contents including some media objects(video, audio, text, etc.), and is 176 x 144 QCIF format. An audio object that is included in the contents is MEPG-4 AAC format. And we consider MPEG-4 contents using Sim-ple2D as test data. We could find that the player showed an efficient presentation of the MPEG-4 contents on a PDA device.

The figure 4 presents playback speed of pre-application and post-application of the adaptation method on MPEG-4 contents at a PDA device. The figure 5 presents a decoding speed on video according to using integer or real number on computing the IDCT on a PDA(200MHz) and a PC(1.3GHz). In case of applying the proposed adaptation methods, we could find that a speed of decoding video is improved some 6 times.

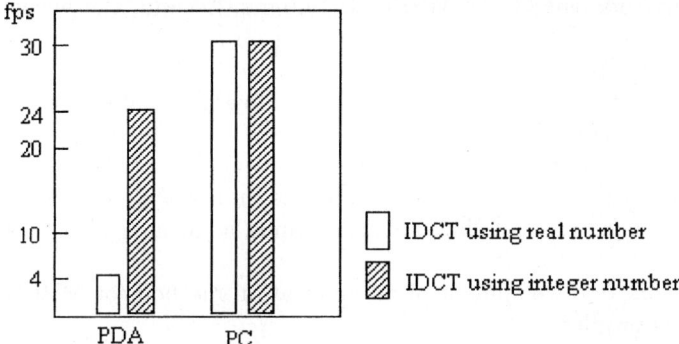

Fig. 5. Decoding speed of video on a PDA device and PC according to an IDCT operation

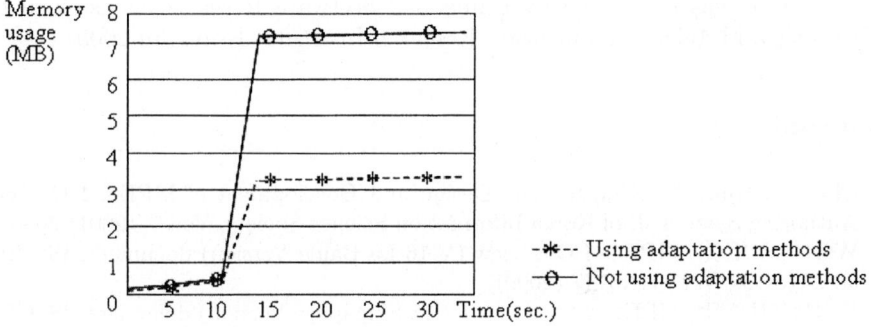

Fig. 6. Memory usage of pre-application and post-application of the adaptation methods

The figure 6 presents memory usage according to pre and post-application of the adaptation methods on MPEG-4 contents. In case of pre-application, a MPGE-4 player needs some 7.3MB. But, in case of post-application, a MPEG-4 player needs about 3MB. We reduced memory usage by using adaptation methods.

In the view of the performance analysis on the proposed MPEG-4 player, we could find that the player showed an efficient playback of MPEG-4 contents on a mobile device.

5 Conclusions

In this paper, we proposed an efficient MPEG-4 player for suitable playback on a mobile device. Most of mobile devices have restricted resource and user interface. In order to overcome such problems, we applied the adaptation methods to the MPEG-4 player in a PDA device. The adaptation methods are physical adaptation, event adaptation, and resource adaptation. Fist, the physical adaptation was used to overcome a physical gap between authoring environment and playback environment of the MPEG-4 contents. Second, the event adaptation was used to transform events not supporting on a mobile device into available events. Finally, the resource adaptation was used to improve playback rate on a mobile device with restricted resource. They affect generally BIFS parser, video decoder, and the rest of player.

We could find that the MPEG-4 player using the adaptation methods showed an efficient presentation of MPEG-4 contents on a mobile device. The applications for the player are as follows; mobile games, a car navigator, distance learning, etc.

Future work is development of an adaptation method for MPEG-4 contents using various profiles.

Acknowledgement

This research was supported by Embedded Software Research Division of the Electronics and Telecommunication Research Institute, Korea, in 2005.

References

1. Cha, K., Kim, H., Kim, S.: The Design and Development of MPEG-4 Contents Authoring System. J. of Korea Information Science Society, Vol. 7. (2001) 309–311
2. WG11(MPEG), MPEG-4 Overview (V.16 La Baule Version) document. ISO/IEC JTC1/SC29/WG11 N3747 (2000)
3. WG11(MPEG), MPEG-4 Overview (V.18 Singapore Version) document. ISO/IEC JTC1/SC29/WG11 N4030 (2001)
4. Shieh, M., Perngand, K., Chen, W.: The Design and Implementation of A Visual MPEG-4 Scene-Authoring Tool. Proc. of Workshop and Exhibition on MPEG-4 (2001) 21–24
5. Daras, P., Kompatsiaris, I., Strintzis, M.: MPEG-4 Authoring Tool for The Composition of 3D Audiovisual Scenes. Proc. of Second Int. Workshop on Digital and Computational Video (2001) 110–117
6. Metso, M., Koivisto, A., Sauvola , J.: Content Model for Mobile Adaptation of Multimedia Information. Proc. of IEEE 3rd Workshop on Multimedia Signal. (1999) 39–44
7. Mohan, R., Smith, J., Li, C.: Adapting Multimedia Internet Content for Universal Access. IEEE Transactions on Multimedia, Vol. 1. (1999) 104–114
8. Lee, S., Cha, K., Kim, S.: An MPEG-4 Contents Authoring for Mobile Devices. Proc. of 2003 HCI (2003) 402-405
9. Cha, K.: A Scalability for Adaptive MPEG-4 Contents. Dissertation for the Degree of Doctor of Philosophy, Kyungpook National Univ., Korea (2003)
10. Ramkishor , K., Gunashree, V.: Real Time Implementation of MPEG-4 Video Decoder on ARM7TDMI, IEEE Proc. of Int. Symposium on Intelligent Multimedia, Video and Speech Processing, Hong Kong (2001)
11. Puri, A., Eleftheriadis, A.:MPEG-4: An Object-based Multimedia Coding Standard supporting Mobile Applications, Mobile Networks and Applications, Vol. 3. (1998) 5–32

12. ITU-T, Draft ITU-T Recommendation H.263: Video Coding for Low Bit-rate Communication (1998)
13. Gonzalez, R. C., Woods R. E.: Digital Image Processing, Prentice Hall, (2002)
14. Prabhakaran B.: Adaptive Multimedia Presentation Strategies, Multimedia Tools and Applications, Vol. 12. No. 2/3. (2000) 281–298
15. Fang, F., Chen, T., Rutenbar, R.: Lightweight Floating-point Arithmetic, Case Study of Inverse Discrete Cosine Transform, EURASIP J. Sig. Proc., Special Issue on Applied Implementation of DSP and Communication Systems, (2002) 879–892
16. Wang, Z.: Fast Algorithms for The Discrete W Transform and for The Discrete Fourier transform, IEEE Trans. Acoust., Speech, Signal Process., Vol. ASSP-32. No. 4. (1984) 803–816
17. Kim., N.: Adaptation Techniques of an Object-based MPEG-4 Player to PDA. Dissertation for the Degree of Master of Science, Kyungpook National Univ., Korea (2005)
18. Cha, K., Kim, K. : MPEG-4 STUDIO: An Object-Based Authoring System for MPEG-4 Contents, J. of Multimedia Tools And Applications, Vol.25, Issue 1, (2005) 111–131
19. Lee., H., Kim.,S. : An Adaptive Scene Compositor Model in MPEG-4 Player for Mobile Device, Proc. of 5th Pacific Rim Conf. on Multimedia, LNCS 3331 (2004) 461–469
20. Signes, J., Fisher, Y., Eleftheriadis, A. : MPEG-4's Binary Format for Scene Description, Signal Processing: Image Communication, Vol. 15, Issues 4–5, (2000) 321–345
21. Herpel, C., Eleftheriadis, A. : MPEG-4 Systems: Elementary Stream Management, Signal Processing: Image Communication, Vol. 15, Issues 4-5, (2000) 299–320

Conversion Mechanism of XMT into SMIL in MPEG-4 System*

Heesun Kim

Division of Electronics & Information Industrial Engineering,
Andong National University, 388 Songchon-Dong, Andong, 760-749, Korea
hskim@andong.ac.kr

Abstract. MPEG-4 system defines a binary format, called BIFS(BInary Format for Scene), and textual format, called XMT(eXtensible MPEG-4 Textual format) to represent the composition information of the scene featuring interactive content. BIFS was proposed for efficient transmission, and XMT based on XML, with the aim to support various playing environments and to enhance the reusability of the contents as it is converted into languages such as VRML, SMIL and etc. To provide interoperability of this XMT, this paper proposes the mechanism to convert XMT into SMIL using XSLT(XML Stylesheet Language Transformation). Further, this paper analyzes XMT and SMIL to propose a conversion method for various nodes, which do not match one to one, and defines XSLT for conversion. In addition, this paper represents various geometric objects that are not supported in the SMIL using SVG(Scalable Vector Graphics).

1 Introduction

The MPEG-4 system[1] defines a scene description language to compose interactive audiovisual scenes. The binary format BIFS(BInary Format for Scene) and the textual format XMT(eXtensible MPEG-4 Textual format)[2] of BIFS describe and define MPEG-4's scene description. Because XMT is composed in the XML format, it is easy to convert it into XML-based scene description language. Therefore, if MPEG-4 authoring system produces audiovisual scenes with the XMT format and converts this into SMIL[3], VRML[4], or BIFS of MPEG-4 according to the user's environment, it can support the reusability and interoperability of the contents[5-7].

XMT defines XMT-A and XMT-Ω. XMT-A corresponds to the scene structure of BIFS one-to-one and is similar to X3D[8]. XMT-Ω is based on SMIL and is a higher-level description language than XMT-A. At present, the following is a study on XMT conversion. IBM Toolkit for MPEG-4[9] is a 2D scene authoring tool producing XMT-A and XMT-Ω through various graphical user interfaces. Related to this, the studies on the production of XMT and the conversion of XMT-A to XMT-Ω are the main stream of the current research in this field.

---

* This work was supported by a grant from 2005 Research Fund of Andong National University.

The MPEG-4 Tools[10], developed by ENST, centers on studying the production of MP4 contents from the alpha format of the XMT file and the conversion of XMT-A into VRML and X3D.

These related studies all emphasize the conversion of audiovisual scenes into XMT-A and XMT-Ω, as well as the conversion of XMT-A format into XMT-Ω or into BIFS by the encoding of XMT-A format. There is still a lack, however, of studies on the conversion of the XMT-Ω file into other formats like SMIL, etc. SMIL has advantages because of its ability to integrate multimedia data and to be generally used with the support of various companies like Adobe, Microsoft, RealNetworks, etc. Since the nodes of XMT-A and BIFS correspond to each other one-to-one, they are easy to convert, and the conversion of the XMT-A format into XMT-Ω is not a problem because they also have corresponding nodes. However, when XMT-Ω is converted into SMIL, there are many nodes that do not support SMIL among the XMT-Ω nodes.

Therefore, this paper presents the system that produces audiovisual scenes as XMT format to provide mutual exchangeability among various scene description languages, which is the original purpose of XMT. This paper also proposes the mechanism to convert the produced XMT file into SMIL. Converting XMT-Ω into SMIL requires a conversion method for the nodes that are not supported in SMIL. To solve this problem, this paper used SVG(Scalable Vector Graphics) [11] within SMIL, and by composing of an XSLT(XML Stylesheet Language Transformation)[12] file for total module conversion, it made xml-based files possible for conversion.

In Chapter 2 of this paper, a comparison is made between the characteristics of tags consisting XMT-Ω and SMIL by module, and proposes a conversion technique for each module. Chapter 3 explains the conversion process of XMT-Ω into SMIL. Chapter 4 shows the development examples and the evaluation, and the paper is concluded in Chapter 5.

2 Comparison and Conversion Mechanism of XMT-Ω and SMIL

XMT-Ω is the description made based on SMIL but there are many tags that do not correspond one-to-one. This is because the expressions, having the original characteristics of MPEG-4, are not expressed in SMIL. This chapter explains the modules' problems in conversion by providing a comparison between each module. Solutions are also proposed.

2.1 Layout

XMT-Ω defines the space layout with the grouping of MPEG-4 and tree structure. XMT-Ω does not basically contain the SMIL layout module, but it is similar to the space layout structure of SMIL. The layout conversion mechanism this paper proposes is as follows.

In SMIL, <region> is used to indicate the location and size of the media. On the other hand, in XMT-Ω, not only <region> but also the attributes of the translation and size of <transformation> displays the location of contents presented in the scene. The <region> used in XMT-Ω is used within the <header> tag, which is similar to SMIL, so that it is easy to convert, but the <transformation> tag is the information that each media own within the <body> tag. Therefore, when the <header> information of SMIL is recorded, the <transformation> information has to be searched by each medium and change the tag name to <region>. Also, there is a slight difference between the coordinate system of XMT and the SMIL. The center of the scene in the coordinate system of the first one is (0,0), while the latter's coordinate system puts (0,0) on the upper left. Therefore, if it wants to display <region> of SMIL by <region> or <transformation> information of XMT-Ω, transformation is required. In the SMIL, the conversion equation for the left and top attributes of the <region> is determined as follows.

$$\text{left} = (\text{scene.width}/2) + \text{translation.x} - \text{media.width}/2$$
$$\text{top} = (\text{scene.height}/2) - \text{translation.y} - \text{media.height}/2$$

2.2 Linking

Basically, XMT-Ω does not link the modules of SMIL, but displays it with the anchor node of MPEG-4. As a single linking factor, XMT-Ω provides <a>. This is similar to the <a> of SMIL and HTML. As <a>'s "href" attributes, xMedia, <group>, and xmtMedia factors can be contained.

2.3 Media

XMT-Ω includes the media module of SMIL, and more extensively includes the media determined in MPEG-4. XMT-Ω includes not only the media formats <img>, <audio>, <video>, <text>, <textstream>, etc., which are defined in the SMIL, but also <rectangle>, <polygons>, <circle>, <lines> and <points>, etc., of 2-D geometric objects. The conversion mechanism of each of them is described below.

1) Image. Presenting an image on the screen in XMT requires only the addressing of the location information because the size of the image addressed on the header can be provided by referring the image included in the process of making MPEG-4 through actual XMT. However, presenting an image on the screen in SMIL is slightly problematic because it requires to clearly indicate the size as well as the starting location of the image in the <region>. To obtain the size of the image, this paper used a method that records the size of image on an "custom" attribute of <img> that is not actually used, and referred this attribute for the actual conversion. The "src" attribute is the path that the actual image used. The image used in the authoring tool is not the image on the Web but has a local path. To use the absolute path in the SMIL, the prefix "file://" is used, and some SMIL players recognize the path, including the blank, but such players do not recognize paths containing Korean characters, only those in English or numbers.

2) **Audio and video.** The audio and video format used in XMT is different from the useable format of SMIL. However, their attributes and structures are similar, causing no problems in simple file conversion. With only the change of the audio and video source used, the file is still playable.

3) **Text.** As a method to present the text, XMT-Ω provides <text> and <string>, and SMIL provides <text> and <textstream>. Although they are used for different purposes, this study changes the two tags of XMT-Ω into SMIL <text>. The size of the text used in the <text> is a little different form the size of font generally used. Comparing to the point unit letters that are normally used, letter height is determined by the size of the text in XMT or SMIL. The contents of the actual text are defined by the attribute "src," used without an attached file, and begin with "data." Also, word spacing is expressed as "%20" in SMIL, and the line chaining in XMT-Ω (";") is indicated as "%0A" so that for special characters used as reading the text contents in the information change of the text, it used them as defining their functions returning their escape code.

4) **2-D geometric object of XMT.** Since SMIL does not support the expression of geometric objects, the geometric objects (rectangle, circle, lines, point, polygon, etc.) in XMT were represented as 2-D geometric objects using SVG. The information recorded in the SVG file includes size, color, and the size and color of the outline. The SVG file is displayed as "src" attribute of <img> in the SMIL. Although the <rectangle> of XMT can be simply presented as <brush> in SMIL, it is more appropriate to display it by SVG due to the insufficiency of the attributes of outline treatment and rotation.

2.4 Timing and Synchronization

SMIL includes comprehensive timing modules. XMT-Ω includes most of these modules. The timing of XMT-Ω and SMIL includes three groups of <seq>, <excl>, and <par>, and because their factors and attributes related to timing are all similar, there is no difficulty encountered during conversion. Since the <group> tag determined in the media module of XMT-Ω includes various media with time information, such was converted as <par> in SMIL, which can be played in parallel. If there is "transformation" information in the <group>, the region values of the media belonging to the <group> are changed during SML conversion. The time groups in the media can have attributes like "begin," "end," "dur," "min," and "max" that the absolute time of those attributes are indicated by the timeline and can be described by user event.

2.5 Time Manipulations

XMT-Ω includes the SMIL time adjustment module that allows for time change. In the time groups of XMT and SMIL, time operation is made possible by attributes like "accelerate," "decelerate," "auto-reverse," and "speed." It is also possible to make the play speed of the media faster or slower because of similar names, which also makes conversion easily done.

2.6 DEFS of XMT-Ω

The <defs> and <use> factors of XMT displays the MPEG-4's reusability through mapping with DEF and USE attributes. As XMT defines the object repeatedly used in the scene in the defs, and writes the ID of defs in the usage value as it is actually used, the scene can be more effectively displayed. However, SMIL does not have any factor to display this characteristic. In the authoring tool, upon conversion into SMIL, if the media used with <use> is found, the media is described referring to the <defs> defined in the header.

2.7 Transitions

SMIL's scene transition consists of three modules, namely BasicTransitions, InlineTransitions, and TransitionModifiers. The scene transition of XMT-Ω includes only BasicTransitions and InlineTransitions modules. BasicTransitions module is made of the two factors of <transition> and <param>. The said module determines the scene conversion type used for authoring on the <transition> factor and registers it in the header, and then used in the media including the ID of the <transition> factor determined in the header through the "transIn" or "transOut" attributes. For items related to transition used in the authoring tool, the module goes through the registration process when it is authored. The InlineTransitions module is presented through the <transitionFilter> factor. This can be determined as it is directly written within the media factor used instead of predetermination. However, because it is not supported in the current SMIL players in many cases, this study takes the method to change the <transitionsitionFilter> used in the XMT to <transition> in the SMIL.

3 Conversion Process of XMT into SMIL

3.1 Production of XSL Document

XMT and SMIL are all XML-based languages in which the conversion of XML language is mainly made by Extensible Stylesheet Language(XSL) document. The XSL document describes where and how to indicate the data file within the XML file exactly, and it is used to make a style definition for an XML document. However, since the conversion mechanism is applied to the XSL document, it takes a long time to define the conversion rule for the whole nodes of the input and output documents and to make this as XSL document.

Therefore, this paper proposes the conversion method to automatically produce the XSL document. For this, several conversion rules are defined for the XSL document according to the defined rules in changing XMT's omega format into SMIL by the XSLT engine provided by "msxml" of Microsoft.

As a process for the conversion in this system, the schema of documents were analyzed before and after the conversion. The patterns of correlation were then defined among the nodes having the same or similar meanings as a rule. Using the defined rule, it automatically produces the XSL document. The resulting

XSL document is used when the XMT-Ω-to-SMIL conversion is done, including the authoring frame producing the contents that can be played in the various multimedia players. The structure of the XSL generator for the production of the XSL document is shown in figure 1.

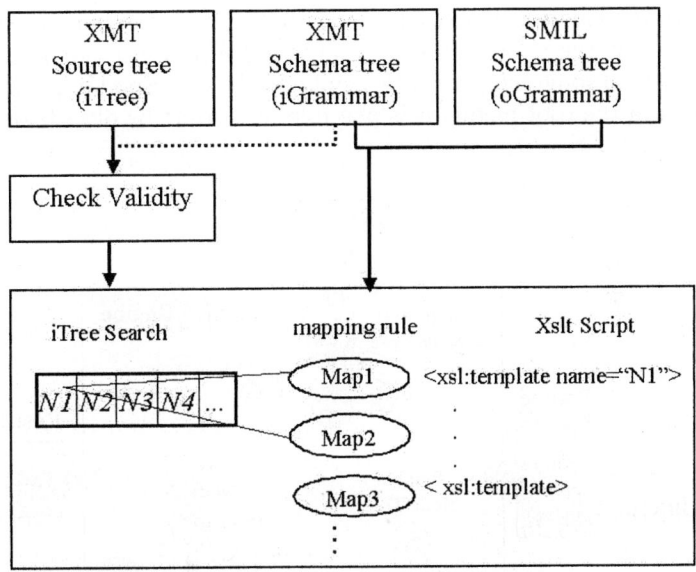

Fig. 1. The structure of the XSL generator for conversion of XMT into SMIL

Defined are the inputting XMT source tree and the XMT schema tree defining XMT's syntax, and the SMIL's schema tree on outing as iTree, iGrammar, and oGrammar, respectively. iTree examines if the scene information made was well-written through iGrammar and if it is effective, it saves the iTree's nodes in order. While iGrammar defines the schema of a document before the conversion, and oGrammar defines the schema of a document after the conversion, if they have similar names and functions, or if they do similar roles in spite of different names, etc., the conversion rules are also determined among the conversional nodes. By taking each node saved in the cue, the XSLT document is produced upon the corresponding conversion rule. The converted document consists of a template unit, and it is a document produced by XML doing the conversion processing for the corresponding nodes.

3.2 SMIL Converter

The SMIL conversion process of XMT-Ω is shown in Figure 2.
The input of the converter is XMT-Ω file and XSL file for the SMIL conversion. These two files are parsed as DOM tree, respectively, by MSXML4. By

applying the parsed DOM tree to the conversion engine, the SMIL file is produced. Actually, the conversion rule mentioned in Chapter 2 is described by an XSL file. An XSL file is largely divided into the part describing the head and the part describing the body. The head part mainly describes the layout information that explains information like the size of the scene, the color of background, the location as an object unit, transition information, meta information, and the switch-related information processing method. The body part describes the conversion rule about the information about the outputted objects. The produced XSL file consists of some templates. By applying the corresponding templates for each media from the root media, it is possible to convert by objects or modules.

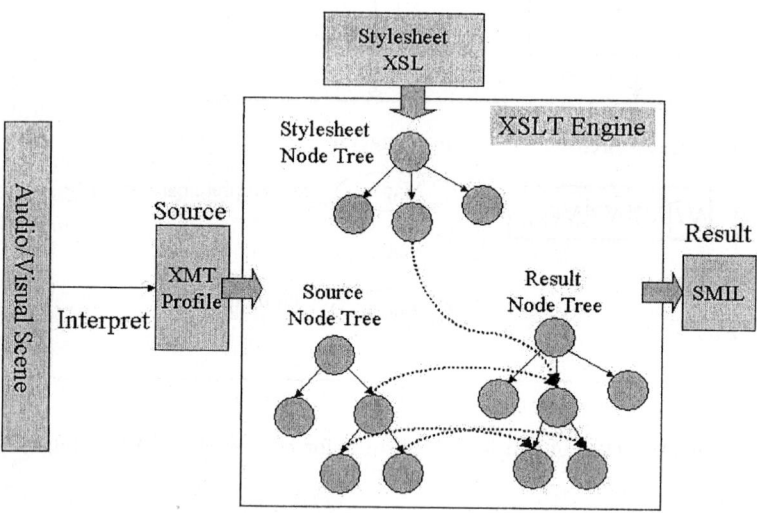

Fig. 2. The SMIL conversion process of XMT-Ω

3.3 Conversion Example of Major Nodes

Figure 3 shows the conversion results of the XMT node into SMIL concerning the major nodes.

As in figure 3, the conversion result of the geometric object node is not made within the SMIL itself, but requires the advanced production of SVG to display the information. The <rectangle> node of SMIL is converted into <img> tag and <rect> tag of SVG. The <transformation> node displays the location information about the upper media node, and there is a sub node of the media node in the XMT's omega profile. But the location information in the SMIL is recorded as an attribute in the <region> node that is the sub node of the <head> node regardless of the media object. The <material> node displays the color information of the media object that exists as an attribute within the media but as a node in SMIL.

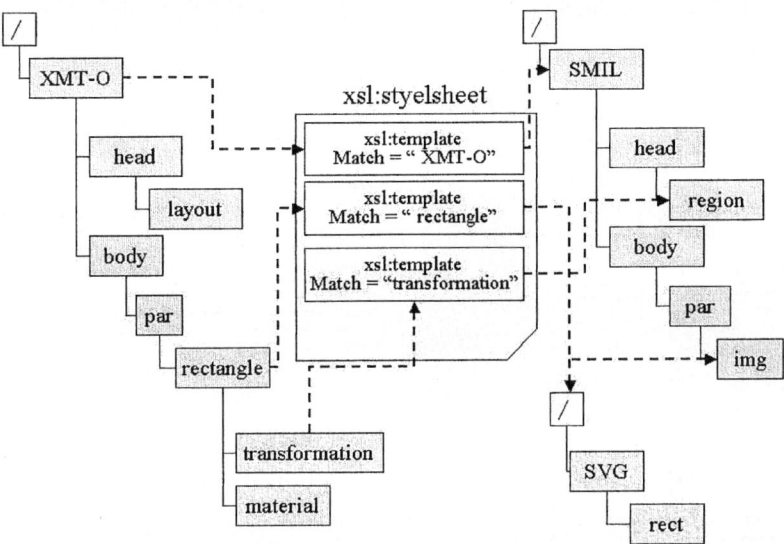

Fig. 3. The conversion example of XMT into SMIL on concerning the major nodes

4 Development and Evaluation

The conversion of XMT into SMIL in this paper was developed using VISUAL C++6.0 of MS WINDOWS. It produced the audio/vidual scene as XMT and converted the resulting XMT file into SMIL. Also, the MSXML 4.0 SP1 was also used to apply XSLT. The figure 4 shows an example of the authoring interface, the generated XMT file, the converted SMIL file, and the play result.

In figure 4, (a) shows an audio/visual authoring system supporting MPEG-4 and XMT. The user interface provides a tool box for the efficient authoring of media objects such as two-dimensional geometrical objects, images, video, audio, text, animation, etc. It also provides authoring environments for event information and for time-space relationships between objects that form scenes. The media to be used in the scene can be added by selecting the icons located at the left hand side of the screen. The basic information about each media is displayed in the attribute window located at the right hand side of the screen.

The (b) shows an example of the XMT-Ω file on audio/visual scene. An authored scene is generated in the form of a scene description tree that maintains the media objects, the event information, and the attributes. To generate the XMT file, this authoring system receives the scene description tree as input and performs a depth first search on the tree before generating the XMT text file. Rules for generating XMT files are defined internally, and the text files are generated according to the rules.

The (c) is a converted SMIL file. The XMT-Ω file is converted into SMIL, using XSL and the XSLT engine. The XSLT engine is predefined for conversion. The XSL

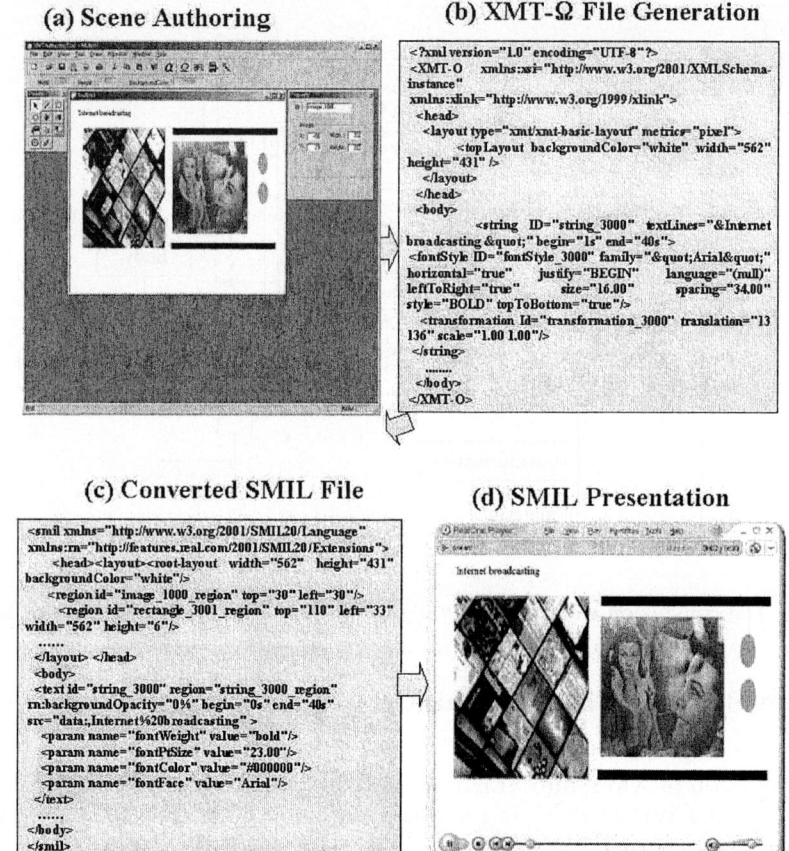

Fig. 4. In this figure, the (a) shows an user interface for authoring XMT. The (b) shows an example of generating the XMT-Ω file on the scene authored in (a). The (c) is a converted SMIL file using XSL and the XSLT engine in this system. The (d) shows the play results of the SMIL file.

file used in this case is based on the SMIL 2.0 schema, which refers to the conversion rule. The rule mentioned in Chapter 2 is described by an XSL file.

The play result of the SMIL file in (c) are shown in (d). Although many SMIL players are available, such as REALONE player of RealNetworks, QUICKTIME of Apple, and GRIN of Oratrix Development VB, this paper used REALONE player version 2.0 as SMIL player, which outputs SVG, which this study used SVG to output 2-D geometric objects. Since the time base authoring of XMT-Ω follows the basic framework of SMIL, it can be played as intended.

Figure 5 shows the converting ratio on each module between XMT and SMIL after applying the proposed converting mechanism.

When only the tags were compared without using any conversion mechanism, only 54% of the tags were identical in both multimedia languages excluding the

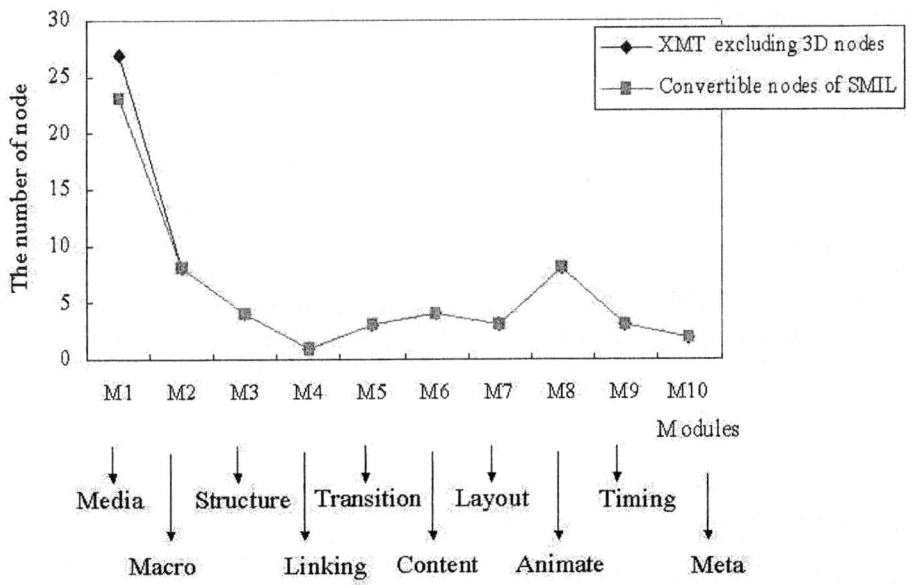

Fig. 5. The conversion ratio on each module between XMT and SMIL after applying the proposed converting mechanism

3-D nodes. This is because most media modules are not supported in SMIL. To solve this problem, the paper made the XMG-omega's tags of <audio clip>, <sound>, and <string> play their roles by changing the names of <audio> or <text> of SMIL, and the XMT tags of <font style>, <material>, <outline>, <transformation> were played as they are changed into the attributes of SMIL's media. Also, 2-D geometric objects such as <circle>, <curve>, <lines>, <points>, <polygons>, and <rectangle> that are not supported in SMIL were converted as SVG to follow the standards of SMIL+SVG, and some of the nodes were converted through the conversion mechanisms proposed in Chapter 2.

In media module M1 of figure 5, 3-D nodes are excluded. This figure represents that proposed SMIL file converter can change 100% of the tags provided in XMT on modules excluding M1. A few nodes that do not converted into SMIL in M1 module is related to converting of XMT-A into XMT-Ω. Therefore, the proposed converting mechanism can support fully semantic conversion between XMT-Ω and SMIL.

5 Conclusion

This paper described the XMT-Ω's conversion mechanism into SMIL in the MPEG-4 system. It proposed the conversion method for the parts where there is no corresponding nodes between XMT-Ω and SMIL by module. The scene information produced by XMT-Ω is produced as SMIL file by predetermined

XSL file and XSLT engine for the conversion. The XSL file used in this study was written based on the schema of SMIL 2.0 and produced based on the conversion rule. Because among the objects consisting XMT-Ω, a part including Material, Outline, Transformation, FontStyle, are determined as attributes in the SMIL, the objects of XMT-Ω was converted as the attributes of SMIL, and the parts of the objects that cannot be presented in the SMIL(rectangle, line, circle, polygon, etc.) were written as SVG and added as the attributes of SMIL media. The proposed conversion method is to find the conversion rule among two scene description languages having different syntaxes, determine them, and produce converted script by the defined rules. This has an advantage that it can confirm the playability of the same scene of MPEG-4 content not only in the MPEG-4 player but also in other generally-used SMIL players. Further, if it is possible to know the syntax definition of other scene description languages, an even more extensive playability can be checked as converting it.

References

1. ISO/IEC JTC1/SC29/WG11 N2201, ISO/IEC FCD 14496-1, Part 1:Systems, Approved at the 43rd Meeting, 1998.
2. ISO/IEC JTC1/SC29/WG11/N4091, Study of ISO/IEC 14496-1:2001/PDAM2:Extensible MPEG-4 Textual Format(XMT), March 2001
3. World Wide Web Consortium, Synchronized Media Integration Language (SMIL 2.0), http://www.w3.org/TR/smil20/
4. ISO/ICE FDIS 14772:200x, Information Technology-Computer graphics and image processing The Virtual Reality Modeling Language (VRML)
5. C. Concolato, J.-C. Dufour "Comparison of MPEG-4 BIFS and some other Multimedia description languages" Workshop and Exhibition on MPEG-4
6. M. Kim, S. Wood, L.T. Cheok, "Extensible MPEG-4 textual format (XMT)," in Proc. on ACM multimedia 2000 workshops, Los Angeles, California, United States, 2000, pp. 717
7. H. Kim, "An XMT Authoring System supporting Various Presentation Environments," Lecture Notes in Computer Science 3331, Springer-Verlag Heidelberg, pp.453-460, 2004.
8. ISO/IEC 19776 X3D February, 2002
9. IBM Toolkit for MPEG-4, http://www.alphaworks.ibm.com/tech/tk4mpeg4/, http://www.research.ibm.com/mpeg4/projects/authoringXMT/index.htm
10. MPEG-4 Tools, http://gpac.sourceforge.net/index.php
11. Scalable Vector Graphics (SVG) 1.1 Specification, W3C Recommendation, http://www.w3.org/TR/SVG11/REC-smil, 2003.
12. Michael Kay, XSLT 2nd Edition:Programmer's Reference, WROX Press, USA, April 2001.

Two-Channel-Based Noise Reduction in a Complex Spectrum Plane for Hands-Free Communication System

Toshiya Ohkubo, Tetsuya Takiguchi, and Yasuo Ariki

Department of Computer and Systems Engineering,
Kobe University, Kobe, Japan
t-ohkubo@me.cs.scitec.kobe-u.ac.jp, {takigu, ariki}@kobe-u.ac.jp

Abstract. For hands-free communication system, this paper describes a noise reduction method using a 2-channel microphone. Recently, the Complex Spectrum Circle Centroid (CSCC) method has been proposed. This method utilizes geometric information and estimates the spectrum of the target signal. The method is advantageous in that no adjustment of the array-processing parameters to the environment is necessary before its operation and it is effective with non-stationary noise. However, the original CSCC method requires at least three microphones to estimate the spectrum of the target signal (center of circle). In this paper, we propose a method which estimates the spectrum of the target signal using only two microphones. In experimental results, the proposed method outperforms the Delay-and-Sum approach and can restore the target signal almost completely in a simulated noisy environment.

1 Introduction

A speech signal is available for hands-free communication system. However, in a real environment, the quality is degraded by the influence of the noise signals that are added to the target speech signal. Thus, it is necessary to reduce the noise signals and to enhance the target speech signals.

A popular method in noise reduction is Delay-and-Sum (DS) [1]-[3]. The advantage of this method is that DS does not require the training of the filter coefficients, but the DS method needs many microphones to improve its performance. Another method is an adaptive type of array processing [4]-[7], such as those proposed by Griffiths-Jim [8], AMNOR [9], where the training of the filter coefficients is required beforehand. The adaptive type methods can achieve better performance than that of DS, but if the test environment is different from the training, the performance decreases severely.

On the other hand, a technique called the Complex Spectrum Circle Centroid (CSCC) method [10] has been proposed recently. This method utilizes the geometric information of the target signal and the observed signal in a complex spectrum plane. This method can reduce noise without training before its operation and also achieve high performance. Furthermore, to process in each frame, this method can be effective with non-stationary noise. However, this method needs at least three microphones to estimate the spectrum of the target signal. This means the method requires a special device, such as microphone array.

In this paper, we propose a method which estimates the spectrum of the target signal using only two microphones. The proposed method can reduce noise with high performance and achieve results as good as the CSCC method.

The organization of the paper is as follows. In section 2, we describe the basis of the CSCC method, followed by an explanation of the estimation process using only two microphones. In section 3, the experimental results are discussed. Finally, in section 4, we summarize the conclusions of this work.

2 Noise Reduction Processing in a Complex Spectrum Plane

2.1 The Layout of Observed Signals in a Complex Spectrum Plane

We assume that two acoustic signals, target and noise, propagate toward the microphones. The configuration of the two-microphone case is shown in Figure 1. The observed signal $m_i(t)$ of the i-th microphone is defined as follows:

$$m_i(t) = s(t) + n(t - \tau_i) \quad (i = 1...M) \tag{1}$$

where $s(t)$ is the target signal and $n(t)$ is the noise signal at time t, and τ_i denotes the time delay at the i-th microphone in respect to the noise signal, and M denotes the number of the microphones. The Fourier transform of the observed signal of the i-th microphone is described as follows:

$$M_i(\omega) = S(\omega) + N(\omega)e^{-j\omega\tau_i} \quad (i = 1...M) \tag{2}$$

where ω denotes angular frequency, and $M_i(\omega)$, $S(\omega)$ and $N(\omega)$ indicate Fourier of $m_i(t)$, $s(t)$ and $n(t)$, respectively. Figure 2 gives a graphic representation of

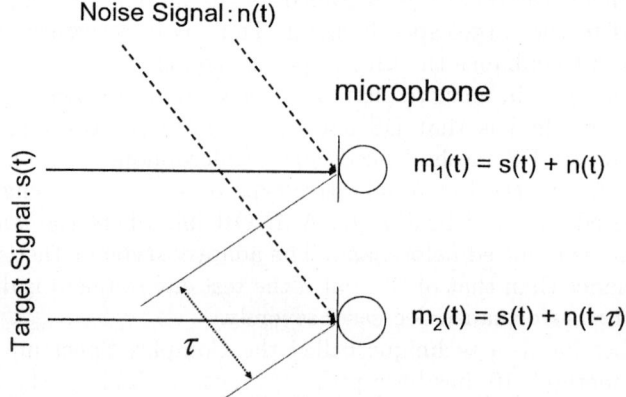

Fig. 1. Signal propagating toward the 2-channel microphone

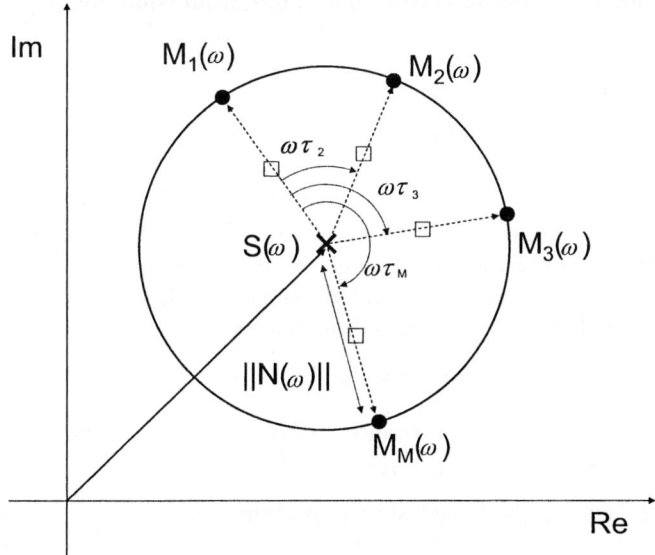

Fig. 2. Distribution of the observed signal by multiple microphones in a complex spectrum plane

Equation (2). Each $M_i(\omega)$ lies on a circle with radius $\| N(\omega) \|$ and at a center $S(\omega)$. The value $\omega\tau_i$ denotes a deflection angle.

In the Complex Spectrum Circle Centroid (CSCC) method [10], the circle location is estimated by using only $M_i(\omega)$, and the center of the circle is the spectrum of the target signal.

2.2 Estimation of the Target Signal Spectrum Using a 2-Channel Microphone

The original CSCC method requires at least three microphones because we need to estimate the location of the circle. This means that the method requires a special device, such as a microphone array.

Here, we propose a method to estimate the spectrum of the target signal using only two microphones. As shown in Figure 1, if the signals propagate as a plane wave, the spectrums of the signal observed using a 2-channel microphone are given as follows:

$$M_1(\omega) = S(\omega) + N(\omega) \tag{3}$$
$$M_2(\omega) = S(\omega) + N(\omega)e^{-j\omega\tau} \tag{4}$$

where $M_1(\omega)$ and $M_2(\omega)$ are the spectrums of the observed signal, $S(\omega)$ and $N(\omega)$ denote the spectrums of the target signal and the noise signal, respectively. The value τ denotes the time delay between the two microphones in respect to the noise signal.

As discussed in Section 2.1, $S(\omega)$ is located at an equal distance from $M_1(\omega)$ and $M_2(\omega)$, and the distance is $\| N(\omega) \|$. Subtracting Equation (4) from Equation (3) gives the value of $N(\omega)$ as

$$\| N(\omega) \| = \frac{\| M_1(\omega) - M_2(\omega) \|}{\| 1 - e^{-j\omega\tau} \|}. \tag{5}$$

Figure 3 shows the process used to estimate $S(\omega)$ using two microphones. First, we draw a perpendicular bisector toward a straight line connecting $M_1(\omega)$ and $M_2(\omega)$ in a complex spectrum plane. Next, we draw a circle with the radius $\| N(\omega) \|$ shown in Equation (5) and its center at $M_1(\omega)$. The coordinates of each spectrum in Figure 3 are defined as follows:

- The spectrum of the observed signal:

$$\begin{cases} M_1(\omega) = (M_{1x}, M_{1y}) \\ M_2(\omega) = (M_{2x}, M_{2y}) \end{cases}$$

- The candidate for the target signal spectrum:

$$\tilde{S}(\omega) = \{S_1(\omega), S_2(\omega)\} \;,\; \begin{cases} S_1(\omega) = (S_{1x}, S_{1y}) \\ S_2(\omega) = (S_{2x}, S_{2y}) \end{cases}$$

- The midpoint:

$$C(\omega) = (C_x, C_y) = (\frac{M_{1x} + M_{2x}}{2}, \frac{M_{1y} + M_{2y}}{2})$$

where subscript x and y denote the coordinates of the real part and the imaginary part, respectively.

The perpendicular bisector and the circle are given as follows:

$$\tilde{S}_y(\omega) - C_y(\omega) = \frac{M_{1x}(\omega) - M_{2x}(\omega)}{M_{2y}(\omega) - M_{1y}(\omega)} (\tilde{S}_x(\omega) - C_x(\omega)) \tag{6}$$

$$(\tilde{S}_x(\omega) - M_{1x}(\omega))^2 + (\tilde{S}_y(\omega) - M_{1y}(\omega))^2 = \| N(\omega) \|^2. \tag{7}$$

The spectrum of the target signal, $S(\omega)$, is located at the intersecting points between the perpendicular bisector and the circle. Hence, $S_1(\omega)$ and $S_2(\omega)$ are obtained by solving the simultaneous equations between Equation (6) and Equation (7). We replace the gradient in Equation (6) with d, which is shown as follows:

$$d = \frac{M_{1x}(\omega) - M_{2x}(\omega)}{M_{2y}(\omega) - M_{1y}(\omega)}. \tag{8}$$

Using this equation, we define the constants as follows :

$$\begin{cases} a = 1 + d^2 \\ b = -2(1 + d^2)C_x(\omega) \\ c = (dC_x(\omega) - C_y(\omega) + M_{1y}(\omega))^2 - \| N(\omega) \|^2, \end{cases} \tag{9}$$

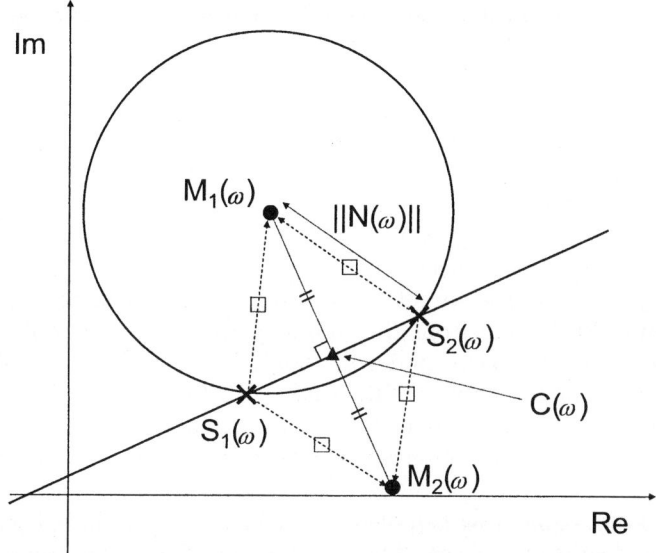

Fig. 3. The estimation process of the target signal spectrum using the 2-channel microphone in a complex spectrum plane

and calculate $\tilde{S}_x(\omega)$ as follows:

$$\tilde{S}_x(\omega) = \frac{-b \pm \sqrt{b^2 - 4ac}}{2a}. \tag{10}$$

Substituting the obtained $\tilde{S}_x(\omega)$ into Equation (6), we are able to obtain $\tilde{S}_y(\omega)$.

Finally, we must choose the proper spectrum from two among the candidates for the target signal. In this paper, we chose the candidate whose spectrum power is smaller, since we considered that the power of the estimated clean signal will be smaller than that of the observed noisy signal. In the case shown in Figure 3, $S_1(\omega)$ is chosen as the target signal spectrum.

3 Experiments

3.1 Experimental Conditions

To evaluate the proposed method, we used two evaluation measures. One is a cross-correlation value (*CC-Value*) between the target signal and the noise removed signal. It is defined as follows:

$$CC\text{-}Value = \frac{\sum_t^T s(t)\tilde{s}(t)}{\sqrt{\sum_t^T (s(t))^2}\sqrt{\sum_t^T (\tilde{s}(t))^2}} \tag{11}$$

where T denotes the length of the signal, and t is the variable of time. $\tilde{s}(t)$ is the noise removed signal.

The other evaluation measure for performance in speech recognition is the cepstrum distance ($CepDist$), which is defined as follows:

$$CepDist = \frac{1}{N}\frac{1}{P}\sum_n^N \sum_p^P (\| S(n,p) - \tilde{S}(n,p) \|) \tag{12}$$

where N and P denote the total number of analysis frames and the dimension of the cepstrum, respectively, and n and p are the variables of the frames and the cepstrum dimension, respectively.

In the experiments, the target source and the noise source were located at 90 degrees and 30 degrees from the line connecting the microphones, respectively. The microphones were uniformly spaced at 2.83-cm intervals. We used 10 Japanese utterances in the "ATR SPEECH DATABASE" as the target signals and three other utterances in the same database as the noise signals, and mixed them to produce the observed signals with a signal-to-noise ratio (SNR) of 0 dB.

The observed signal was sampled at 16 kHz and windowed with a 20-ms Hamming window every 10-ms. Then a 320-point DFT was used to compute 16-order MFCCs (mel-frequency cepstral coefficients). We compared the performance of the conventional method of Delay-and-Sum (using 2 or 14 microphones).

The proposed method requires the noise source direction to calculate $\| N(\omega) \|$ in Equation (5). The direction can be estimated by the inference method of the sound source, such as Cross-power Spectrum Phase analysis (CSP). However, in this experiments, we gave the noise source direction to evaluate the noise reduction performance of the proposed method.

3.2 Simulated Environment

In this experiment, microphone-array data was generated by simulation considering only the time delay. Therefore, the target signals and the noise signals are propagated toward the microphones without degradation. Table 1 and Table 2 show the results for CC-$Value$ and $CepDist$. From these results, we see that the proposed method outperforms the Delay-and-Sum method. An example of the signal waveforms is shown in Figure 4. This example uses an utterance as the noise signal. And another example of the signal waveforms which uses a music as the noise is shown in Figure 5. These result shows that the proposed method is effective for the noise both in speech regions and non-speech regions. In addition, these results lead us to the conclusion that the proposed method can restore the target signal almost completely.

Also an example of the spectrum estimation of the target signal in a complex spectrum plane is shown in Figure 6. In Figure 6, the points of the observed signal spectrum by a 2-channel micorphone are shown as circle symbols, and the candidates of the target signal spectrum which estimated by the observed signal spectrums are shown as square symbols. Here, we chose the bottom-left spectrum as the target signal from the candidates because its power is smaller

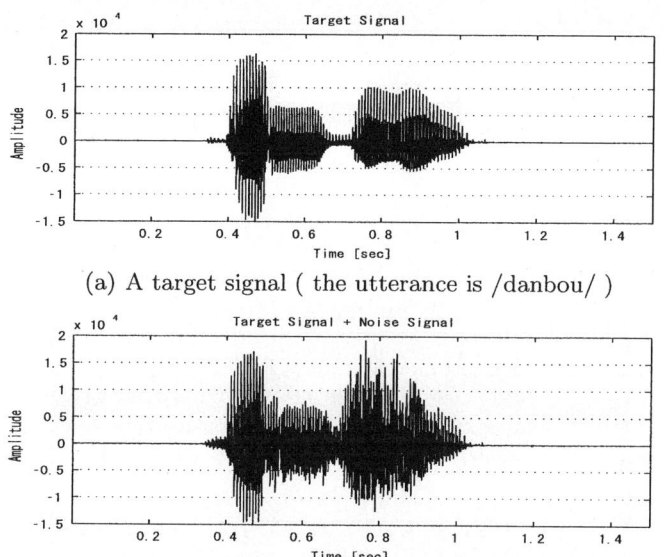

(a) A target signal (the utterance is /danbou/)

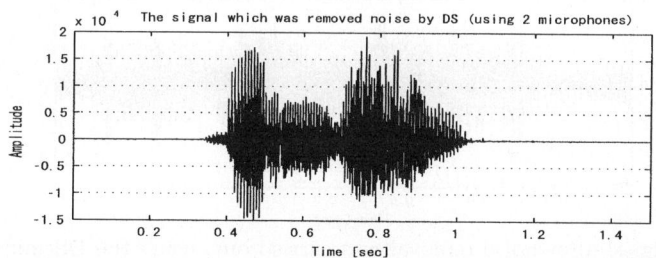

(b) An observed signal (the utterance of noise signal is /shisyuu/) (SNR:0dB)

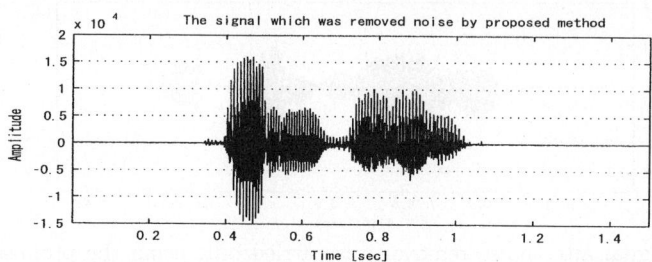

(c) A signal after noise removal was carried out, using the DS(mic:2) method

(d) A signal after noise removal was carried out, using the proposed method

Fig. 4. The waveforms of a target signal, an observed signal and a noise removed signal. (The noise is an utterance.)

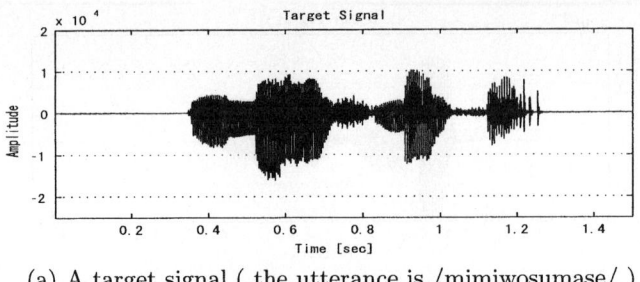

(a) A target signal (the utterance is /mimiwosumase/)

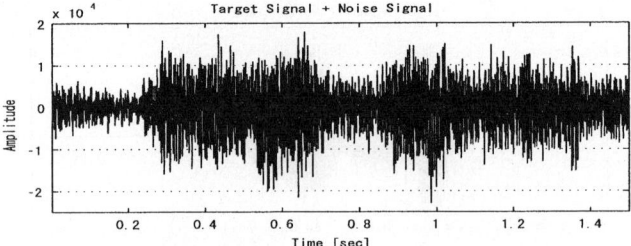

(b) An observed signal (the noise signal is a music) (SNR:0dB)

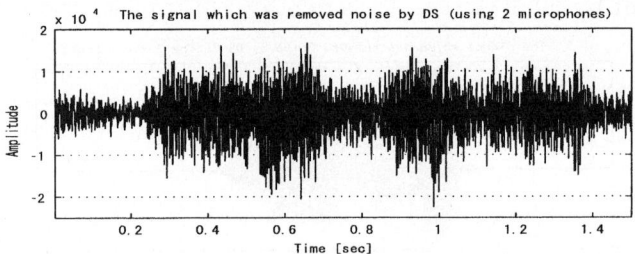

(c) A signal after noise removal was carried out, using the DS(mic:2) method

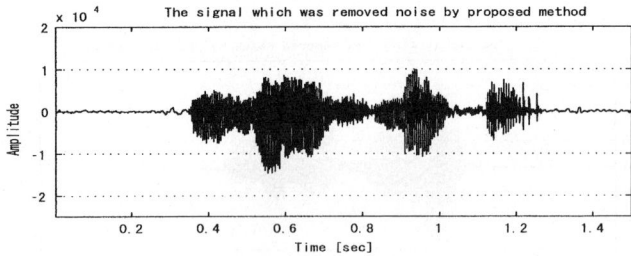

(d) A signal after noise removal was carried out, using the proposed method

Fig. 5. The waveforms of a target signal, an observed signal and a noise removed signal. (The noise is a music.)

than the other, as shown in Figure 6. It should be noticed that the estimated target spectrum located in the almost same location as the spectrum of the real target signal which are shown as the cross symbol.

Table 1. Comparison of cross-correlation value when using simulation data

Data No.	Observed Signal	DS(microphone:2)	DS(microphone:14)	Proposed Method
1	0.69	0.70	0.79	**0.96**
2	0.72	0.73	0.80	**0.94**
3	0.71	0.72	0.84	**0.99**
4	0.66	0.67	0.81	**0.96**
5	0.68	0.69	0.80	**0.97**
6	0.65	0.66	0.81	**0.99**
7	0.71	0.75	0.82	**0.98**
8	0.70	0.74	0.81	**0.99**
9	0.70	0.74	0.81	**0.91**
10	0.69	0.70	0.79	**0.97**
Average	0.69	0.71	0.81	**0.97**

*The figure in () means the number of microphones.

Table 2. Comparison of cepstrum distance when using simulation data

Data No.	Observed Signal	DS(microphone:2)	DS(microphone:14)	Proposed Method
1	9.18	8.88	6.38	**4.44**
2	8.04	7.65	5.61	**4.06**
3	12.46	12.24	11.34	**6.97**
4	8.60	8.62	7.51	**5.68**
5	8.16	8.35	6.73	**5.13**
6	9.28	9.31	8.11	**5.93**
7	9.66	9.26	5.58	**3.40**
8	9.91	9.63	6.69	**4.98**
9	9.38	9.02	5.46	**3.60**
10	8.54	8.12	5.76	**4.01**
Average	9.32	9.11	6.92	**4.82**

*The figure in () means the number of microphones.

3.3 Reverberant Environment

In an experiment in a reverberant environment, we produced the observed signals with reverberant acoustic characteristic using the following steps. First, we convoluted the impulse responses with the target signals and the noise signals. Next, we added the noise signals to the target signals at each microphone. We used impulse responses from "RWCP Sound Scene Database in Real Acoustical Environments" [12], where the reverberation time was 300-ms and the distance between the sound source and the microphone was 2 meters.

Table 3 and Table 4 show the results of $CC\text{-}Value$ and $CepDist$. From these results, the performance of the proposed method degrades below DS. We consider that the failed estimation is attributable to the signal degradation caused by reverberation.

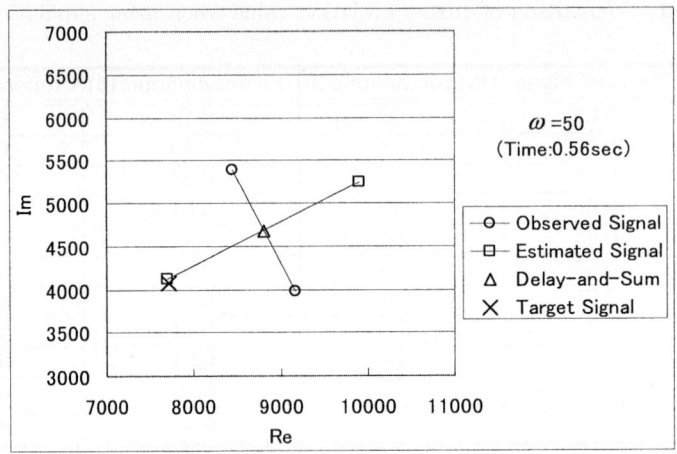

Fig. 6. An example of the target signal spectrum in a complex spectrum plane estimated from the simulated noisy data

Table 3. Comparison of cross-correlation value when using reverberant data

Data No.	Observed Signal	DS(microphone:2)	DS(microphone:14)	Proposed Method
1	0.57	0.57	0.59	0.48
2	0.69	0.69	0.74	0.48
3	0.71	0.72	0.76	0.51
4	0.65	0.66	0.72	0.44
5	0.66	0.67	0.77	0.46
6	0.63	0.64	0.73	0.51
7	0.66	0.68	0.74	0.50
8	0.73	0.75	0.81	0.53
9	0.66	0.68	0.74	0.53
10	0.65	0.65	0.69	0.45
Average	0.66	0.67	0.73	0.49

*The figure in () means the number of microphones.

4 Conclusions

In this work, we have presented a noise reduction method in a complex spectrum plane using only two microphones. The method utilizes the geometric information and restores the target signal to estimate its spectrum. The method is advantageous in that no training time is necessary before its operation and it is effective with non-stationary noise.

The experiment results showed that the proposed method outperformed the Delay-and-Sum method and can restore the target signal almost completely in the simulated noisy environment. On the other hand, in the reverberant environment,

Table 4. Comparison of cross-correlation value when using reverberant data

Data No.	Observed Signal	DS(microphone:2)	DS(microphone:14)	Proposed Method
1	10.52	10.43	9.13	9.90
2	8.30	7.95	6.47	8.29
3	12.22	11.97	11.60	11.64
4	9.68	9.67	8.74	9.82
5	10.28	10.24	9.20	10.06
6	11.33	11.34	10.25	11.08
7	9.48	9.51	7.69	9.47
8	10.07	9.96	7.64	9.81
9	9.29	9.31	7.73	9.56
10	9.37	9.26	7.57	9.13
Average	10.05	9.96	8.60	9.98

*The figure in () means the number of microphones.

the performance degraded. We consider this failed estimation of the spectrum of the target signal was caused by the reverberation and the propagation degradation.

In future work, we will investigate the affects in a reverberant environment, and will try to improve the performance of the proposed method in a real environment. Furthermore, we will investigate a way to estimate the noise propagation direction, as the proposed method requires that we do so.

References

1. J. L. Flanagan, J. D. Johnston, R. Zahn, an G. W. Elko, "Computer-steered microphone arrays for sound transduction in large rooms," J. Acoust. Soc. Am., vol. 78, no. 5, pp. 1508-1518, 1985.
2. K. Kiyohara, Y. Kaneda, S. Takahashi, H. Nomura, and J. Kojima, "A microphone array system for speech recognition," Proc. ICASSP97, vol. 1, pp. 215-218, 1997.
3. M. Omologo, M. Matassoni, P. Svaizer, and D. Giuliani, "Microphone array based speech recognition with different talker-array positions," Proc. ICASSP97, vol. 1, pp. 227-230, 1997.
4. Michael L. Seltzer and Richard M. Stern, "Subband parameter optimization of microphone arrays for speech recognition in reverberant environment," Proc. ICASSP2003, vol. I, pp.408-411, 2003.
5. Alan Davis, Siow Yong Low, Sven Nordholm, "A subband space constrained beamformer incorporating voice activity detection," Proc. ICASSP2005, vol. III, pp.65-68, 2005.
6. W. Herbordt, S. Nakamura and W. Kellermann, "Joint optimization of LCMV beamforming and acoustic echo cancellation for automatic speech recognition," Proc. ICASSP2005, vol. III, pp.77-80, 2005.
7. Xianxian Zhang and John H. L. Hansen, "CFA-BF : A Novel Combined Fixed / Adaptive Beamforming for Robust Speech Recognition In Real Car Environments," Proc. EUROSPEECH2003, pp.1289-1292, 2003.
8. L. J. Griffiths and C. W. Jim, "An alternative approach to linearly constrained adaptive beam forming," IEEE Trans. Antennas Propag., vol. AP-30, no. 1, pp. 27-34, 1982.

9. Y. Kaneda and J. Ohga, "Adaptive microphone-array system for noise reduction," IEEE Trans. Antennas Propag., vol. ASSP-34, no. 6, pp. 1391-1400, 1986.
10. S. Sagayama, T. Okajima, Y. Kamamoto, T. Nishimoto, "Complex Spectrum Circle Centroid for Microphone-Array-Based Noisy Speech Recognition," Proc. ICSLP2004, WeA1705o.5, 2004.
11. M. Omologo and P. Svaizer, "Acoustic Event Localization in Noisy and Reverberant Environment Using CSP Analysis," Proc. ICASSP96, pp. 921-924, 1996.
12. S. Nakamura, "Acoustic sound database collected for hands-free speech recognition and sound scene understanding," International Workshop on Hands-Free Speech Communication, pp. 43-46, 2001.

An Efficient Classifier Fusion for Face Recognition Including Varying Illumination

Mi Young Nam, Jo Hyung Yoo, and Phill Kyu Rhee

Dept. of Computer Science & Engineering,
Inha University, Yong-Hyun Dong,
Incheon, South Korea
rera@im.inha.ac.kr, pkrhee@inha.ac.kr

Abstract. In this paper, we propose an efficient classifier fusion for face recognition under varying illumination environments by taking classifier fusion's advantage of environment context identification. Adaptation to dynamically changing environments is very important since advanced applications become pervasive and ubiquitous. The proposed classifier fusion system, called BCF (Bayesian based classifier fusion), adopts the concept of face context awareness and evolutionary computing. But aside the difference of classifiers the training data performs main role in them consequently the results from the classifiers couldn't be so individual from each other to make decision by considering them. The system working environments are clustered and identified as face environmental context. Majority voting (MV), Maximum based fusion (MX) and Minimum based fusion (MN) are used to explore the most effective action configuration for each identified context. Once the context knowledge is constructed, the system can adapt to varying environment in real-time. The superiority of the proposed scheme is shown using three face image data sets: Inha, FERET, and Yale.

1 Introduction

Classifier fusion methods are illustrated their better reliance on recognition than single classifier and implemented in various ways. Clustering the data set into different regions is added value to recognition systems by finding specific sophisticated system for particular region in ways as selection and fusion of classifiers [1, 2]. Clustering methods discriminate the data by their features so the data vectors in same clusters must be considered similar to each others. In this paper, we discuss about the framework of CAES (Context-Aware Evolvable System) that can behave in an adaptive and robust manner under dynamic variations of application environments. CAES can be thought as an augmented evolvable system framework which provides not only the capability of evolution/adaptation but also that of context-awareness and context knowledge accumulation. The context knowledge of individual environmental contexts and their associated chromosomes is stored in the context knowledge base. The most effective action configuration of the system is determined for a current environment by employing the popular evolutionary computing method, genetic algorithm (GA)[3,4, 5]. Context modeling can be performed by an unsupervised learning method [6] such as Fuzzy Art, SOM, etc. Context identification can be implemented by a normal classification method such as NN, k-nn, etc.

The proposed framework fuses the context-awareness and the evolutionary strategy. The novel strategy make the system adapt itself dynamically under changing and uneven application environments. Similar research can be found in [7, 8, 9]. The main difference of the proposed method from other evolutionary computing methods is that it can optimize action configuration in accordance with an identified context as well as stores its knowledge in the context knowledge. Hence, the proposed method can provide self-growing adaptation capability to the system. That is, once the context knowledge is constructed, the system can react to changing environments in real-time. The proposed method has been tested for the popular vision application, face recognition using three data sets: Inha, FERET, and Yale where face images are exposed to dynamically changing and uneven lighting conditions. We achieve encouraging experimental results showing that the performance of the proposed method is superior to those of most popular methods under uneven environment. This paper is organized as follows. In the section II, we present the model of proposed BCF. In the section III, we discuss about design issues such as context learning, context identification, run-time adaptation using genetic algorithm. Finally, we give experimental results and concluding remarks in the section IV and V, respectively.

2 BCF (Bayesian Based Classifer Fusion)

In this session, we discuss about the model of BCF based CAES with the capability of real-time adaptation and context knowledge accumulation. The goal of BCF based CAES can be described as the provision of optimal services (performances) using given system resources by identifying its working environments (contexts), and the major functionalities of BCF based CAES can be formalized as follows (see Fig. 1):

- Identify the system working environment (Context-awareness),
- Configure its structure using autonomous computing method (Classifier fusion), and Accumulate knowledge from its experience in a manner of self-growing (Context knowledge accumulation).

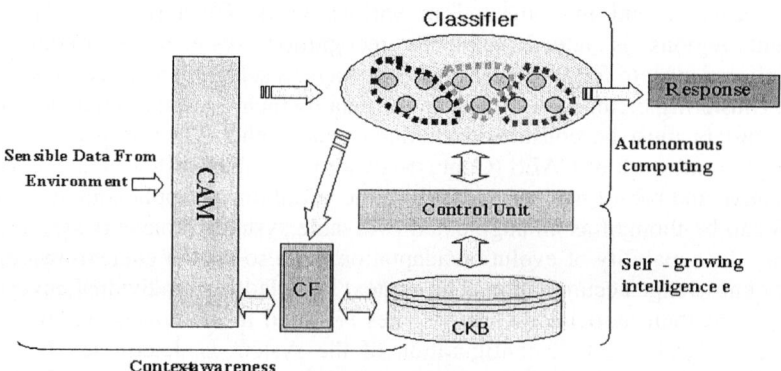

Fig. 1. The system architecture

Two types of data inputs are used: context data and action data inputs in CAES. The action data, denoted by **x**, is a normal data being processed. The context data, denoted by **y**, is used to identify an environmental context of CAES and to construct a proper action (action configuration) based on the identified context. In many cases, the action data itself can be used as the context data. We assume that the context data can be modeled in association with the input action data.

Initially, the scheme learns application's environmental contexts. It accumulates the knowledge of context-action association, and stores them in the CKB. The knowledge of context-action association denotes that of most effective action configurations for the context.

Single classifiers are following:

a) Eigenface
b) Gabor3
c) Gabor13
d) Gabor28
e) Gabor30

Classifier fusion methods are following:

a) Majority voting (MV)
b) Maximum based fusion (MX)
c) Minimum based fusion (MN)
d) Naive Bayes (NB)

BCF (Bayesian Based Classifier Fusion)

We present the recognition system using the table of Trueness using Bayesian rule between clusters for combining the results from the individual clusters. Heretofore fusion methods are aimed on combining the different classifiers, trained on same training data set.

We can restrict the $d_i(x)$ within the interval [0,1] and say $d_i(x)$ is the degree of 'support' given by classifier $\tilde{D}$ to the hypothesis that x comes from class ω_i [most often an estimate of the posterior probability $P(\omega_i | x)$]. But we actually will use classifiers more simple than "soft labels" for implementing Xcor. In a need of making the problem simple we will define the classifier D from $\tilde{D}$ as follows:
$D: \Re^n \rightarrow \Omega \times [0,1]$ is defined as $D(x) = \{\omega'_m, d_m(x)\} \Leftrightarrow d_m(x) = \max_{j=1..c}\{d_j(x)\}$

The set of data used for training the classifier D_i, contains the element of class ω'_i.

$\alpha_i = \frac{p(d_i | True) P(True)}{p(d_i)}$ where $p(d_i) = p(d_i | True) + p(d_i | False)$, $P(True) = m_{ij}$.

For example In Fig.3, training data set consists of four pictures of two people named A and B. Let us assume that we are going to recognize whose picture is the test image. Each similarity of test and trained images measured by classifier (Gabor28) are illustrated in figure. Classifier outputs are usually made comparable by scaling to interval [0, 1]. Most similar one is the fourth element in training data set.

But in this matter, absence of forth image in Training Data Set can bring wrong recognition of test image of B to the third element which belongs to class A. There is no guarantee that training data set should contain features of each class in each cluster. However, if we trained the classifier by only features in cluster 0, that classifier can recognize the test image to class B.

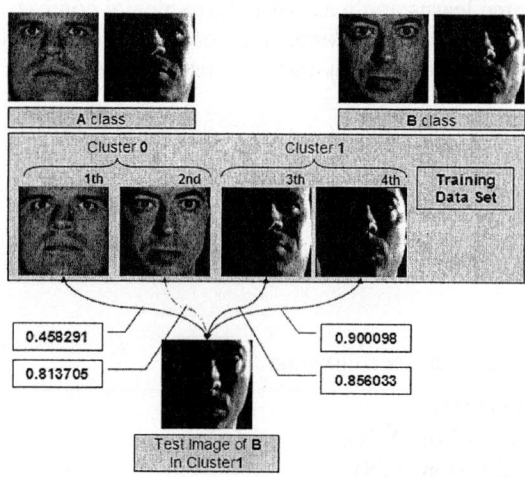

Fig. 2. Two persons' images named A, B classes are clustered by lighting. The similarities measured by Gabor28 are shown.

Classifier outputs are usually made comparable by scaling to interval [0,.1]. We assumed the outputs are also measurable as similarity of feature to classes. By the Fig.1 the features in same cluster are measured more similar by classifiers. In this paper, it is assumed that combination of Classifiers, each fed by data in one cluster is more steady in recognition rate. Classifier fusion assumes that all classifiers are trained over the whole feature space, and are thereby considered as competitive rather than complementary. But some methods as bagging, boosting and ada-boosting made the classifiers individual from each other by selecting different training data sets [9, 10]. Thus, some solutions considered individualism between classifiers by correlation between them for making final decision.

3 Learning and Testing

The assumption that classifiers perform independent of each other might be invulnerable. But methods related to Boosting as Bagging [11], Boosting [2], AdaBoosting [2, 11] considered create each classifier in an ensemble independently of the other classifiers. We can look in way the classifier is simply compares the Test data with trained data. Same idea is introduced here to create the classifiers independent from each other and make the ensemble method fitness correlation more considerable and reasonable. Fig 4 shows the difference of independency of classifiers trained by different data set or whole.

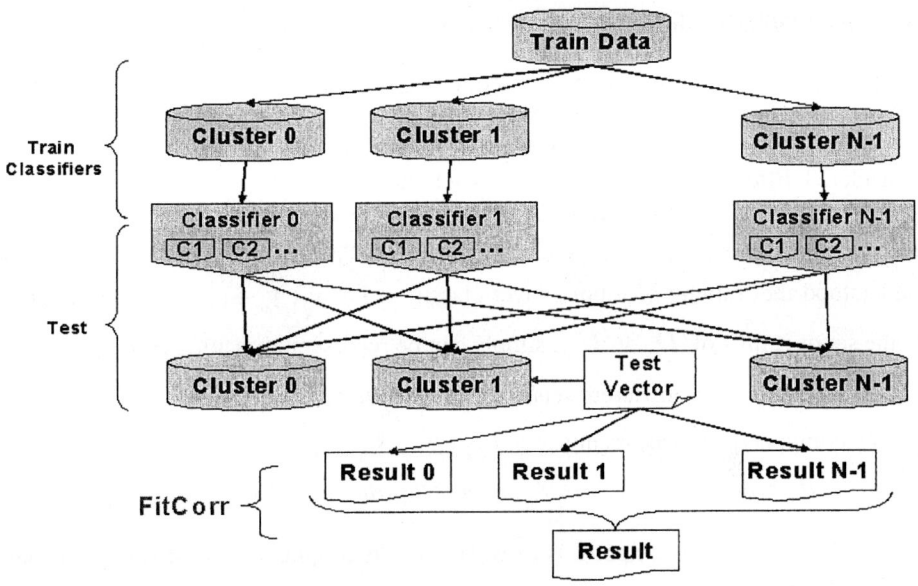

Fig. 3. Classifier decision architecture

3.1 Training Fitness Correlation Table

Let R0, R1 ... RN are regions clustering the feature vector x ∈ R^n data sets and D = {Dij}, i,j ∈ {1,2,3,...,N} are the classifiers. Call a classifier the mapping D: R^n → {h, y}, y is one of {1,2,...,c} c classes and h, h ∈ [0,1] is fitness between x and y measured by classifier. We can look in way the classifier simply compares the Test data set X with trained data set T. Dij is expert on comparing feature vector x, x ∈ Ri, x with training data t, t ∈ Rj.

3.2 Classifying Method

Correlation between Clusters
Training will consists of two main methods "classifier training" and the "Xcor Table training". Each will be accomplished by using Training Data Set T and Xcor Data Set U respectively. $T = \{t_i, t_i \in \Re^n\}$, $U = \{u_i, u_i \in \Re^n\}$

First we will cluster these data sets into K different sets by using clustering methods like k-means. Let $T_1, T_2, ..., T_k$ are the clustered sets of T and $U_1, U_2, ..., U_k$ are the clustered sets of U. Despite the T set contains elements of all classes, there is no guarantee that T_i should contain the elements of all classes. This assumption actually the reason we are adopting Xcor method to keep the recognition rate of classifiers when the training set is not complete at all clusters.

3.3 Xcor Table Training

Train the "simple-soft-label" classifier D by sets $T_1, T_2, ..., T_k$ and let $D_1, D_2, ..., D_k$ are the trained classifiers respectively. ($D_i, i = \overline{1..k}$ can be considered different and individual from each others)

In this method we will create the Xcor Table by using classifiers', $D_1, D_2, ..., D_k$, result of recognition on data sets $U_1, U_2, ..., U_k$. This method would naturally be understood the training of second layer classifier. Let Y_{ij}, $Y_{ij} = \{y, y = D_i(u) \mid u \in U_j\}$ is the set of results of D_i on U_j, simply can be represented as $Y_{ij}^T = D_i(U_j^T)$.

We can define three different sets of soft labels $H_{ij}, \overline{H}_{ij}, \tilde{H}_{ij}$ from Y_{ij}. H_{ij} is set of $d(x)$ components of true results.

$$H_{ij} = \{d \mid \{\omega, d\} = D_i(u) \in Y_{ij} \text{ and } \omega \text{ is the true class of } u \in U_j\} \quad (1)$$

$\overline{H}_{ij}$ is set of $d(x)$ components of wrong results despite T_i contains the true class of $u, u \in U_j$.

$$\overline{H}_{ij} = \{d \mid \{\omega, d\} = D_i(u) \in Y_{ij} \text{ and } \omega \text{ is not the true class of } u, \text{ despite } T_i \text{ contains true class of } u \in U_j\} \quad (2)$$

$\tilde{H}_{ij}$ is set of $d(x)$ components of results when T_i does not contains the true class of $u, u \in U_j$

$$\tilde{H}_{ij} = \{d \mid \{\omega, d\} = D_i(u) \in Y_{ij} \text{ when } T_i \text{ does not contains true class of } u \in U_j\} \quad (3)$$

Suppose that $H_{ij}, \overline{H}_{ij}, \tilde{H}_{ij}$ perform normal distributions. The average and standard deviation of $H_{ij}, \overline{H}_{ij}, \tilde{H}_{ij}$ are denoted by $\{\mu_{ij}, \sigma_{ij}\}, \{\overline{\mu}_{ij}, \overline{\sigma}_{ij}\}, \{\tilde{\mu}_{ij}, \tilde{\sigma}_{ij}\}$ respectively.

The Xcor table, the final result of "Xcor Table training" method, would contain $\{\mu_{ij}, \sigma_{ij}\}, \{\overline{\mu}_{ij}, \overline{\sigma}_{ij}\}, \{\tilde{\mu}_{ij}, \tilde{\sigma}_{ij}\}, m_{ij}, e_{ij}$ where $i, j \in \overline{1..k}$.

		Cluster1	Cluster2	Cluster3	Cluster4	Cluster5
Cluster1	μ_T	0.90009	0.81370	0.80700	0.83618	0.87265
	μ_F	0.85603	0.80367	0.76042	0.81870	0.83755

		Cluster1	Cluster2	Cluster3	Cluster4	Cluster5
Cluster1	$\delta_T{}^2$	0.00120	0.00031	0.00073	0.00050	0.00110
	$\delta_F{}^2$	0.00027	0.00028	0.00027	0.00016	0.00036

Fig. 4. Each cluster's correlation table

3.4 Test Mode

Simply combining method is making final decision when we received number of result from different classifiers. Addition information that we need is trueness of that result and fitness correlation table would help us to find them. The trueness of the classifier's derived result derivate next figure and equation.

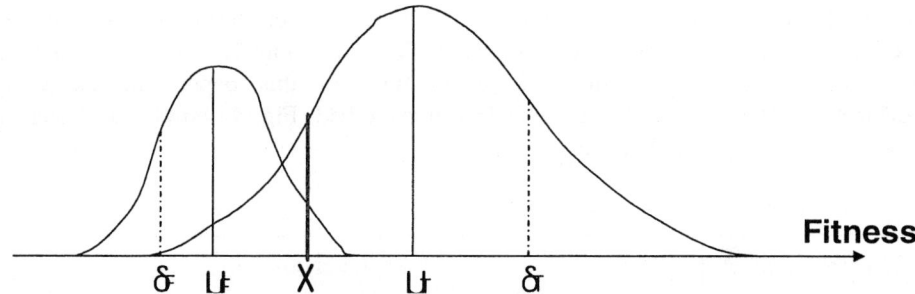

Fig. 5. Classification Reliability

$$ái = P(True | \omega j) = P(True | X) = P(X | True) * P(True) / P(X) \quad (4)$$

$$P(X) = (P(X | True) * P(True) + P(X | False) * P(False) \quad (5)$$

$$P(X | True) = \exp(-0.5 * ((x - \mu_T)/\delta_T)^2) / (\sqrt{2}\eth * \delta_T) \quad (6)$$

- If the Results of 6 Classifiers are
  A B A A B C with Trueness **a01 a1 a2 a3 a4 a5**
  E = {A,B,C}; Ci = (Cluster i ∩ I) = {ωi0, ωi1, ... ωik}

$P(True | A) = \psi A * \varphi B(A) * \varphi C(A)$

$\psi A = a0 * a2 * a3$

$\varphi B(A) = (1-a1)^{D1(A)} * (1-a4)^{D4(A)} * |C1 \cap C4 \cap E| / (|C1 \cap E|*|C4 \cap E|)$

$Di(A) = 1$ if **A** is contained in **Cluster i,** else **0** elsewhere

---

4 Experimental Results

The proposed framework is tested in the area of face recognition and location. Extensive experiments have been carried out using three data sets: Inha, FERET, and Yale. We achieved very encouraging results.

The proposed BCF method has been tested in the area of face recognition. The changes in image data under changing illumination is modeled based on the illumination context. Illumination context may include lighting direction, brightness, contrast, and spectral composition. We adopt lighting direction and illumination as the model of illumination context here.

In the experimental system for the face recognition, the context clusters face data images into five contexts, and constructs the context model of face images for each environmental context using the statistical learning algorithm K-means. The feature space of object instance with uneven illumination must be clustered properly so that the location error can be minimized. However, the clustering of illumination variations is very subjective and ambiguous. Thus, we adopt K-means for achieving an optimal illumination clustering architecture. In this paper, the clustering performance is improved by iterative learning method. Fig. 4 shows the clustering result of face images by K-means.

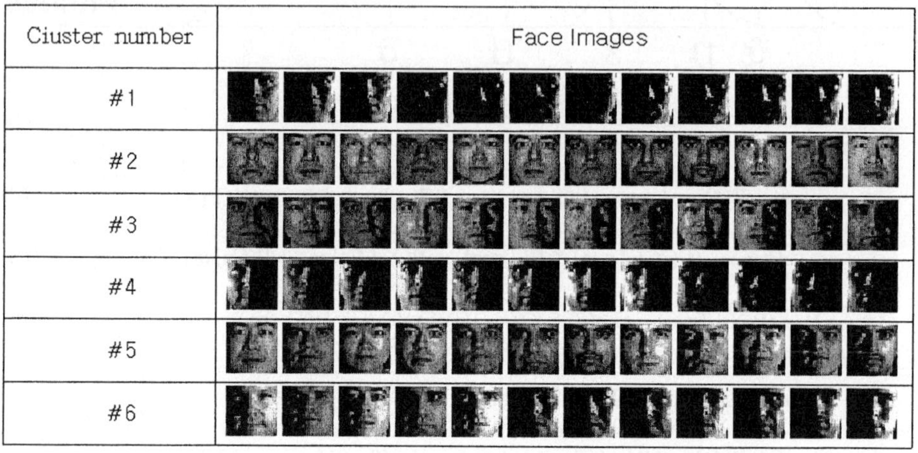

Ciuster number	Face Images
#1	
#2	
#3	
#4	
#5	
#6	

Fig. 6. Examples of face image clustered by the CAM

The action primitives in the feature representation stage are PCA and Gabor representations. Gabor representations are divided into four types. The proposed approach employs Gabor feature vector, which is generated from the Gabor wavelet transform. We adopt four Gabor based feature representation: Gabor3, Gabor13, Gabor28, Gabor30. Thus, we use total five action primitives in the feature representation stage, PCA, Gabor3, Gabor13, Gabor 28, and Gabor30. We adopt two action primitives in the class decision stage: Cosine distance based and cosine distance based action primitives.

Cosine distance is adapted in Gabor vector distance calculate cosine distance is more enhanced the similarity between vector. The proposed paper is the enhanced method more than the other algorithm. The BCF algorithm is interest face database of varying illumination face image. The method has been tested using Inha database,

FERET[12] probe_fafb_expression images and fafc_illumination images, and Yale[13] database. Experiments have been carried out to compare the recognition performance of BCF based face recognition schema and that of other methods.

FERET fafc dataset shows poor performance under bad illumination. Thus, if the working environment of the system can be controlled well, non-evolvable method may perform better than the proposed adaptive method. However, in general we can not predict or control the system working environment. Table 1 shows that varying classifier results for face illumination context. Table 2 is result for cluster number by K-means.

Table 1. Comparison of face recognition rates of BCF based method to those of non-evolvable methods focusing on the feature representation stages in the CF

Method	BCF	PCA	Gabor3	Gabor13	Gaor28	Gabor30
Inha	98.5%	92%	90%	65%	93%	97%
FERRET fafb	95.04%	90%	25%	50.25%	90.25%	94%
FERRET fafc	81.94%	65.5%	20%	26%	65%	68%
Yale	97.5%	85%	10%	30%	85.25%	96.5%
Integrated	93.25%	83.13%	36.25%	42.81%	83.38%	88.88%

Table 2. The proposed method results each cluster number

Database / Result	YaleDB_Del	Feret
Gabor28	96.63%	90.98%
FitCorr[6] G28	93.26%	91.80%
FitCorr[3] G28	98.88%	90.98%
FitCorr[2] G28	96.63%	90.98%
Gabor13	93.26%	90.16%
FitCorr[6] G13	95.51%	91.80%
FitCorr[3] G13	96.63%	90.98%
FitCorr[2] G13	93.26%	90.98%

Table 3 shows the performance of the efficient methods for integration FERET fafb dataset and fafc dataset. The proposed method is higher performance more than other algorithm. Tables are derived the higher performance for bad illumination data.

Table 3 shows the comparative tested performance by Eigenface using Bayesian theory and other classifier. In own experimental results, the proposed method shows recognition rate of over 95.51 % for FERET fafb and fafc dataset, which exceeds the performance of the other popular methods. The context-based classifier fusion method performs better than single classifier method because the image feature is different according context information.

Table 3. Comparison results between classifier fusion (cluster number 5)

	Ferret	Yale	Our Lab
Eigen face	60.35	58.91	94.2
Gabor3	59.59	68.99	93.72
Gabor13	64.96	77.83	94.44
Gabor28	82.06	80.46	95.79
Gabor30	82.06	80.46	95.79
MV	84.58	82.17	98.41
MX	84.66	80.46	97.14
MN	8.38	10.07	8.73
NB	85.16	83.1	97.77
Product	78.62	82.63	90.94
Average	83.74	84.03	97.22
BCF	95.51	95.02	99.20

5 Concluding Remarks

This paper proposes a novel adaptive framework that can be used for adaptive systems under uneven and dynamic environments by employing the concept of context-awareness, BCF, and context knowledge base. Furthermore, it solves the time-consuming problem of the classifier fusion. The system working environments are learned (clustered) and identified as environmental contexts, and BCF is used to explore the most effective action configuration(s) for each identified context. The knowledge of the individual context and its associated chromosomes representing optimal action configurations is accumulated and stored in the context knowledge base. The action mode executes the task of identification using the correlation knowledge between classifier accumulated in the learning mode by Bayesian rule. The major contribution of the proposed method is to achieve real-time evolvable system under varying environments.

Acknowledgement

This work was supported by INHA UNIVERSITY Research Grant.

References

1. L.Lim and C.Y.Suen. optimal combination of pattern classifiers. Pattern Recognition Letters, vol.16 (1995) pp.945-954
2. J.Kittler, M.Hatef, R.P.W. Duin, and J.Matas : On combining classifiers. IEEE Trans. Pattern Analysis and Machine Intelligence, vol.20, no.3 , (1998) pp.226-239
3. Bay, SD.: Nearest neighbor classification from multiple feature subsets. Intelligent Data Analysis. vol.3, no.3 (1999) pp.191-209

4. D. Goldberg, "Genetic Algorithm in Search, Optimization, and Machine Learning, Addison-Wesley, (1989)
5. N. Mori, et. al., "Adaptation to a Dynamic Environment by Means of the ENvironment Identifying Genetic Algorithm," Industrial Electronics Society, 2000. IECON 2000. 26th Annual Confjerence of the IEEE, Vol. 4, (2000) pp.2953 - 2958
6. Ramuhalli, P., Polikar, R., Udpa L., Udpa S. : Fuzzy ARTMAP network with evolutionary learning. Proc. of IEEE 25th Int. Conf. On Acoustics, Speech and Signal Processing (ICASSP 2000), Vol. 6. Istanbul, Turkey, (2000) pp.3466-3469
7. K.Ohkura and K.Ueda: A Genetic Algorithm for Nonstationary Function Optimization Problems, Trans. SICE, Vol.8, No.6, (1995) pp.269-276
8. J.J.Grefenstette : Genetic algorithms for changing environments, Problem Solving from Nature 2, Vol.2, (1992) pp.137-144.
9. Kaenampornpan M, O'Neill E, "Modelling context: An activity theory approach," LECTURE NOTES IN COMPUTER SCIENCE ISSN:3295, (2004) pp.367-374.
10. Feng L, Apers PMG, Jonker W, "Towards context-aware data management for ambient intelligence," LECTURE NOTES IN COMPUTER SCIENCE ISSN:3180, (2004) pp.422-431.
11. P.Phillip: The FERET database and evoluation procedure for face recognition algorithms. Image and Vision Computing, vol.16, no.5, (1999) pp.295-306
12. http://cvc.yale.edu/projects/yalefaces/yalefaces.html

Illumination Invariant Feature Selection for Face Recognition

Yazhou Liu[1], Hongxun Yao[1], Wen Gao[2], and Debin Zhao[1]

[1] School of Computer Science and Technology,
Harbin Institute of Technology, Harbin 150001, P.R. China
{yzliu, yhx, dbzhao}@vilab.hit.edu.cn
[2] Institute of Computing Technology,
Chinese Academy of Science, Beijing 100080, P.R. China
wgao@jdl.ac.cn

Abstract. We propose a novel hybrid illumination invariant feature selection scheme for face recognition, which is a combination of geometrical feature extraction and linear subspace projection. By local geometry feature enhancement technique, neighborhood histogram equalization (NHE) in our experiment, some illegible edges due to week illumination will be enhanced effectively. Then we applied classic linear subspace projection methods, such as Principle Component Analysis (PCA), subspace Fisher Linear Discriminant (FLD), and Direct Fisher Linear Discriminant (DFLD), on these face images to decrease training samples' dimension as well as diminish the effect of noise introduced at the first step. Our methods are evaluated on an elaborate selected subset (with large illumination variation) of YaleB database. Experiments on this data set show that the NHE+DFLD yields the best performance. By using only 3-dimensional features (the original face images are 256×256), error rate can be decreased from 0.73 (by DFLD only) to 0.07.

1 Introduction

Face recognition has been an active research field for it's widen application in automate criminal identification, airport security system and credit card verification. But from a certain point of view, face recognition is a tough task because of generally similar shape and structure of a face combined with numerous variations caused by illumination, facial expression and pose. As stated by Adini in [1], "The variations between the images of the same face due to illumination and viewing direction are almost larger the image variations due to change in face identity." Within recent years, many researches have been focused on diminishing the impact of illumination variation and some promising methods and results have been reported, such as in [2, 3, 4].

A successful illumination invariant face recognition system depends heavily on both the specific features used for classification and the specific classifier being used. So the invariance can be address at these two procedures, feature selection procedure and classification procedure. In [5], Liu proposed two probabilistic reasoning models for face recognition, which is combination of Principle Component Analysis (PCA) and Bayes classifier. His work based on the assumption that the within class densities in reduced PCA subspace are normal distribution. Within class scatter were used to estimate the covariance matrix for each class and Maximum A Posteriori (MAP) decision rule optimized the class separability in the sense of Bayes error. So in his work, the invariance was address in classification procedure. In [2], Chen furthered Liu's work and proposed Adaptive Principle Component Analysis (APCA). He modified the covariance matrix of previous one, and proposed a filter matrix of identity-to-variation (ITV) ratio to capture the main differences between classes (faces) while diminishing the contribution of those that are largely due to the lighting variation (within class differences). In his method the invariance has been addressed in both the APCA feature selection procedure and Bayes classification procedure.

Comparing with above methods, a large number of algorithms deal with the feature selection and classification procedure separately and try to represent the raw image data with some illumination insensitive features. Common used approaches include edge maps and linear subspace projection methods. But edge features generated from shadows are related to illumination changes and may have significant impact on recognition. Also if in the rather weak illumination conditions, the edges may become illegible and difficult to extract. Another effective way is the linear subspace projection method, which base on the assumption that the human face is Lambertian reflected and convex and tries to construct a low dimensional linear subspace for face images taken under different lighting conditions [3]. Within this category, some statistic methods have been proposed for salient features derivation with the purpose of reducing the amount of data used for classification and simultaneously enhancing discriminatory power. These methods often exploit different optimization criteria, such as redundancy minimization and decorrelation (ICA), minimization of the reconstruction error (PCA), as well as maximization of the ratio of the determinants of the projected between-class-scatter matrix and within-class-scatter matrix (FLD).

In our work, the illumination invariance is fully addressed in feature selection procedure. Our goal is to select robust illumination insensitive features for recognition. The method proposed in this paper is a combination of above two approaches, edge enhancement and linear subspace projection, which can integrate the advantages of these two methods as well as avoid their inherent drawbacks. Neighborhood histogram equalization (NHE) can achieve a local contrast enhancement. The edges then become prominent even in some dark regions. So NHE operation can diminish the effect of illumination and yields a face image with strong edges that robust to illumination variation. But the drawback of NHE is that this method also amplified the noise in the "flat" region. Linear subspace methods are powerful techniques that can reduce the amount of data for classification as well as increase the discriminatory capacity of the data. Take Fisher Linear Discriminant for example, it distinguishes the different roles of within and between class scatter by applying discriminant analysis and be relatively robust to noise and mild illumination variation. But the robustness of the FLD depends on whether or not the within class scatter can capture enough variations for a specific class. When the training samples do not include most of the variation due to lighting or the training sample size for each class is small, the FLD leads to deteriorate performance. That's the reason why the FLD doesn't work well in large illumination variation environment. When the illumination variances were diminished by the NHE procedure, FLD's performance can increased essentially.

This paper is organized as follow. In section 2, the local enhancement method Neighborhood Histogram Equalization (NHE) and some of its variations are introduced. Section 3 describes the most common used linear subspace projection methods PCA, FLD and DFLD. In section 4, we evaluate the combinations of these methods on our elaborately selected face dataset from YaleB database.

2 Neighborhood Histogram Equalization

Histogram equalization is a common used method to enhance the contrast of an image. Theoretically the transformed image should have a uniform histogram. This method is considered to produce an "optimal" overall contrast in the image. But the enhancement result highly depends on the gray level distribution of the overall image, and is independent of pixels' spatial distribution at all. So if an image has an almost uniform histogram distribution but most of its informative regions are under week lighting condition, the global histogram equalization will not guarantee more legible visual results for these regions and the information in there region can not be extracted effectively. Another observation is that the geometry structure of an object can be affected dramatically by illumination. Take Fig.1 for example, the region A and region B contain the almost same geometry structure, the edges between face and the background. But due to the weak illumination, the edges in region B are almost imperceptible. So the edge information in region B can not be addressed with the same importance as the one in region A. As a matter of fact, the average gray level difference alone the edges in region B is 6, but the average difference in region A is much stronger, 70. In this case, comparing with the edge in region A, the ones in region B are so week that it maybe neglected if we apply the same criteria on the overall image regardless their local information at all. So the conclusion here is that in order to make the resulting image more legible, the contrast enhancement method should not only depends on the pixels' gray level distribution but also on their spatial distribution. In another word, contrast enhancement makes sense only when it can make spatially adjacent regions become more distinct from each other, and it is almost of no use if we enhance the contrast of two regions spatially far from each other. Based on the above observation, we proposed a sample yet effective local contrast enhancement method, Neighborhood histogram equation, which applies a histogram-equalization like operation in a neighborhood system. Compared with the traditional histogram equalization method, this method takes into account not only the gray level distribution but also the spatial information. It computes the histogram of a local image region centered at a given pixel

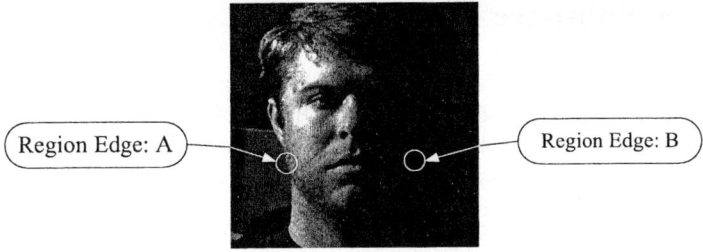

Fig. 1. Illumination can affects the visual result of geometry structure essentially

to determine the mapped value for that pixel; this can achieve a local contrast enhancement. The point mapping function can be state as follows:

$$I'(X) = \frac{D_{max}}{A_{R_X}} \int_0^{I(X)} h(u) du \qquad (1)$$

where

$$h(u) = \sum_{X_t \in R_X} \delta(I(X_t) - u), u = 1, \ldots, 255 \qquad (2)$$

In above two equations, $X = (x, y)$ is the coordinate of current point and $I(X)$ and $I'(X)$ are the pixel values of point X in the original image and mapped image. $h(u)$ is the local histogram of region R_X, which centered at point X. D_{max} and A_{R_X} are the maximum gray scale value and area of region R_X.

Fig.3 shows some local enhancement results of neighborhood histogram equalization (NHE). The images in the Fig.3(a) are are the original ones with very prominent illumination variation. And those in the Fig.3(b) are the enhancement results of NHE. From these examples, we can see that the effect of illumination can be largely removed by NHE and originally very distinct images became very resemble with each others. And also the geometry structures, such as edges, which originally are imperceptible, now can be extracted effectively. Fig.3(c) shows the illumination component removed by NHE, which are the residual images between the ones in Fig.3(a) and Fig.3(b). The definition of pixel value in image $I_{(c)}$ at point X can be expressed as:

$$I_{(c)}(X) = \begin{cases} C_h, & sign(I_{(a)}(X) - I_{(b)}(X)) \geq 0, \\ C_l, & sign(I_{(a)}(X) - I_{(b)}(X)) < 0, \end{cases} \qquad (3)$$

One point should be made clear here is that there also exist other local histogram equalization methods, such as adaptive histogram equalization (AHS) in [6] and block based histogram equalization (BHS) in [4]. These methods also can achieve a regional contrast enhancement, and yield comparable visual results as the algorithm proposed in this paper. All these local contrast enhancement methods share the same drawbacks. They can strengthen the edges even in the quite weak illumination condition, but they also amplified the noise, especially in the "flat" regions. Then linear subspace projection methods can be use to extract the most discriminant features as well as diminish the effects of noise.

3 Linear Subspace Methods

Principal component analysis (PCA) and Fisher Linear Discriminant (FLD) are two well known linear projection methods. Both of them have been applied to the task of face recognition successfully. They have superb ability to reduce the dimensionality of the data as well as diminish the effect of noise.

3.1 Review of PCA Method

Principal Component Analysis (PCA), also known as the Karhunen-Loeve expansion, is a classical technique for signal representation. The projection criterion used in PCA is to choose the direction along which training data has maximum variation to construct the reduced subspace. So any particular face can be economically represented along the eigenpictures coordinate space. Since the eigenpictures are fairly good at representing face images, it is reasonable to use the projections along them as the classification features for face recognition. Turk and Pentland developed a well-known face recognition method, known as egienfaces, which drastically reduces the dimensionality of the original space and face detection and identification are carried out in the reduce space.

The advantage of applying PCA for face recognition (eigenfaces) comes from its generalization ability. PCA's projection axes based on the variations from all the training samples, hence these axes are fairly robust for representing both training and testing images.

3.2 Review of FLD Method

While PCA is a classical technique for signal representation, Fisher Linear Discriminant (FLD) is a classical technique for pattern recognition. It is a class specific method and distinguishes the different roles of within-class variation and between-class variation.

Let the between-class scatter matrix be defined as:

$$S_B = \sum_{i=1}^{c} N_i(\mu_i - \mu)(\mu_i - \mu)^T \quad (4)$$

And the within-class scatter matrix be defined as:

$$S_W = \sum_{i=1}^{c} \sum_{x_k \in X_i} (x_k - \mu_i)(x_k - \mu_i)^T \quad (5)$$

Where μ_i is the mean image of class X_i, and N_i is the number of samples in class X_i. If S_W is nonsingular, the optimal projection W_{opt} is chosen as the matrix with orthonormal columns which maximizes the following ratio:

$$W_{opt} = \arg\max_{W} \frac{|W^T S_B W|}{|W^T S_W W|} \quad (6)$$

But in face recognition problem, the number of images in the learning set N is much smaller than the number of pixels in each image n. And the rank of S_W is at most $N - c$ This means S_W is a singular matrix. To overcome this difficulty, two well- known methods have been proposed. They are subspace Fisher Linear Discriminant (also known as PCA+FLD) and Direct Fisher Linear Discriminant (DFLD).

Subspace FLD. To overcome the singularity of S_W, the most common used method is the subspace FLD (PCA+FLD). In this method, the traditional PCA is exploited firstly to reduce the dimension of the original data. Then the FLD is applied to the samples in the reduced PCA subspace. This is a very popular way to deal with the singular problem, especially in face recognition problem. But the difficulty of this problem is that the PCA criterion may not be compatible with the FLD criterion, thus the PCA step may discard dimensions that contain important discriminative information. So this method may not fully exploit the discriminant potential of FLD.

Direct FLD. Based on the observation that the null space of S_W contains the most discriminative information. Yu [7] proposed a direct implementation of FLD (DFLD). As the traditional FLD, DFLD also simultaneous diagonalize the S_W and S_B. But the key idea here is to discard the null space of S_B, which contains no useful information-rather than discarding the null space of S_W, which contain the most discriminative information. This can be achieved by diagonalizing S_B firstly and the eigenvectors corresponding to the biggest eigenvalues were kept for dimension reduction. Then the S'_W (S_W in reduced space) is diagonalized and the smallest eigenvectors, which corresponding to the null space of S'_W, are kept for extracting the most discriminative features. This implementation gives an exact solution to Fisher's criterion whether or not S_W is singular. So the advantage of Fisher Linear Discriminant can be fully exploited.

4 Experiments

In this section, we make a relatively extensive evaluation on our illumination invariant feature extraction methods, which are NHE+PCA, NHE+subspace FLD and NHE+DFLD. Sine we address the feature selection procedure, we evaluate the validity of these different feature selection methods by nearest neighbor classifier. All the samples used in our experiments are selected from YaleB[8] face database. YaleB contains 10 subjects, 9 poses and 64 illumination conditions in each pose. We use frontal pose (indexed as P00A) for our evaluation.

4.1 Sample Selection

To address the illumination invariant property of our method, we selected the training and testing samples from non overlapping illumination conditions. There are totally 100 training samples and 120 testing samples for ten objects (for each

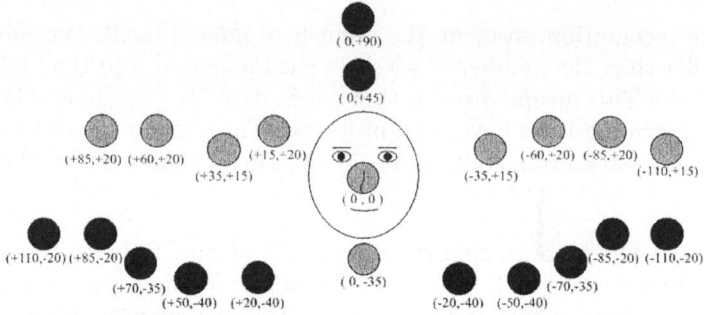

Fig. 2. Training and testing samples' lighting sources distribution, where red points indicate the training samples and the black ones represent the testing samples

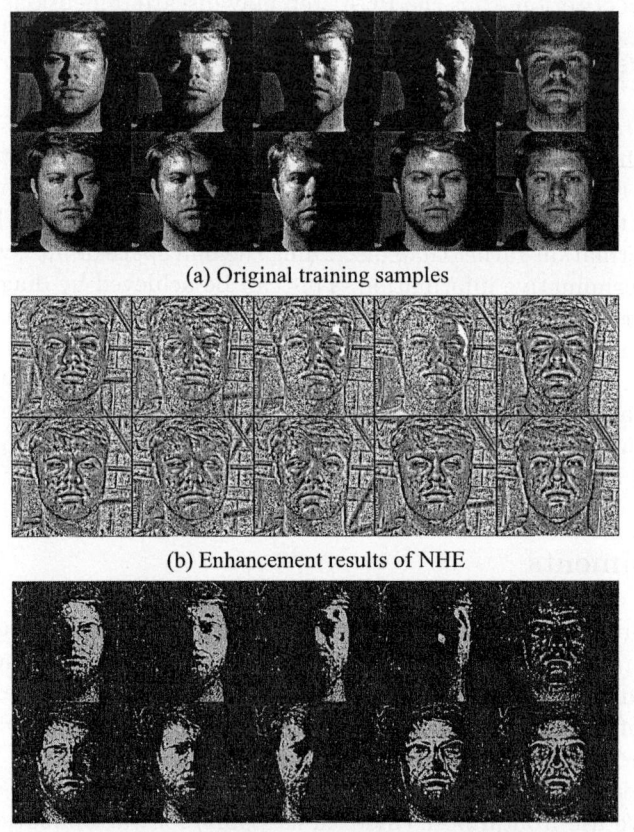

(a) Original training samples

(b) Enhancement results of NHE

(c) Illumination component removed by NHE

Fig. 3. Training samples of object 1

object, 10 frontal picture for training and 12 pictures for testing). All the images are 256×256 pixels. The specific light source direction for each training and testing sample can be stated clearly by Fig.2, where the 10 red points and

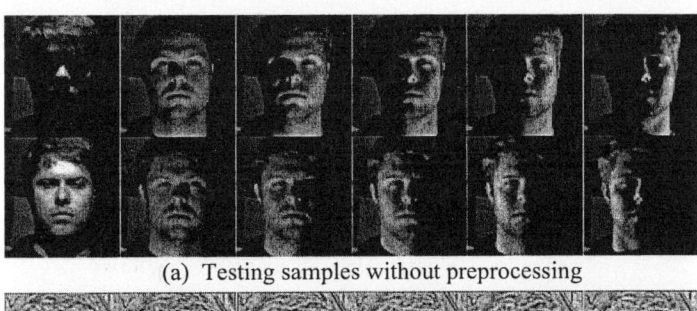
(a) Testing samples without preprocessing

(b) Testing samples processed by NHE

Fig. 4. Testing samples of object 1

12 black points with their corresponding coordinates represents the light source direction of training and testing samples respectively. The coordinate below each colored point in Fig.2 deals with the azimuth and elevation of the single light source direction. Take (+85, +20) for example, in this case the light source direction with respect to the camera axis is at 85 degrees azimuth $'(A+085)'$ and 20 degrees elevation ($'E+20'$). (Note that a positive azimuth implies that the light source was to the right of the subject while negative means it was to the left. Positive elevation implies above the horizon, while negative implies below the horizon.)

From Fig.2, we can see that the training samples (whose light source directions corresponding to red points) for each object are under large illumination variation. The 10 training samples for object1 can be seen in Fig.3(a). And the testing samples, some examples of which can be seen in Fig.4(a), are selected from quite different light conditions, which are non-overlapping with the training samples'. *With this elaborate selection, we are going to verify two key problems: first, if our feature selection methods are so robust to illumination that the training samples for each object with such large illumination variation can be cluster together effectively; second, if there exists over fitting problem (as proposed in [3]) in our method. In another word, weather it will lead to deteriorate performance when these feature selection methods are extended to some unseen samples.*

4.2 Evaluation

In order to provide a more intuitive impression of our methods' illumination invariance, we mapped all the 100 training samples in to the reduced 2-dimensional space. The distribution of these training points can be seen in Fig.5(a) (b) and (c).

Table 1. Evaluation results of our methods

	PCA	Subspace FLD	DFLD
Error rate	0.767	0.767	0.733
	NHE+PCA	NHE+Subspace FLD	NHE+DFLD
Error rate	0.542	0.617	0.067

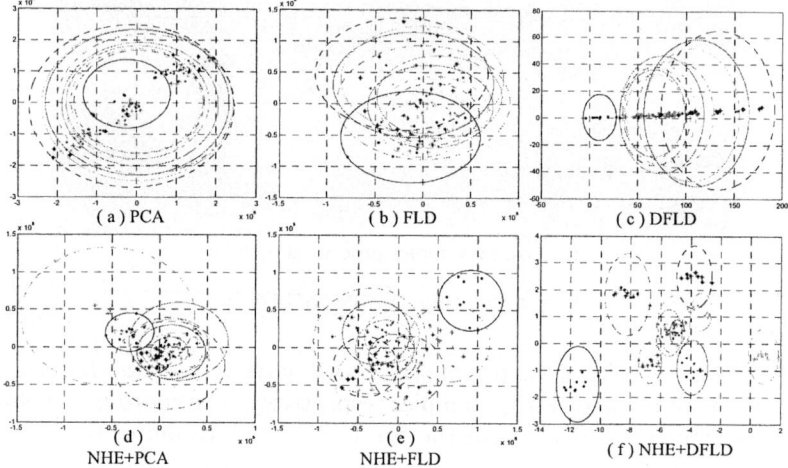

Fig. 5. The cluster results of training samples with features extracted by different methods

They are the mapping results of PCA, subspace FLD and DFLD. We can see that for PCA, its mapping direction corresponding to the largest variance. In our experiments, the largest variances were introduced by illumination rather than by the identity of different objects, so in this reduced space, the samples are almost indiscriminable. Theoretically, the subspace FLD and DFLD will yield better cluster results, but the effects of illumination are so strong in this scenario that both of them can not provide satisfiable cluster results. When we incorporate these linear subspace methods with our local contrast enhancement method NHE (window size is 13×13), the effects of illumination can be diminished essentially. Especially for NHE+DFLD, see (f), which yields a rather satisfiable cluster results according to samples' identity.

We evaluate our methods' generalization capacity by testing them on some unseen samples which selected from quite different illumination conditions. Fig.4(a) shows the original testing images of object 1 without preprocessing and (b) shows the enhancement results by NHE. In our experiments we map the training and testing samples into *3-dimensional* space. The classifier used here is nearest neighbor classifier. Experiment results can be seen in Table.1, which shows that by combining the NHE with the linear subspace methods, error rate

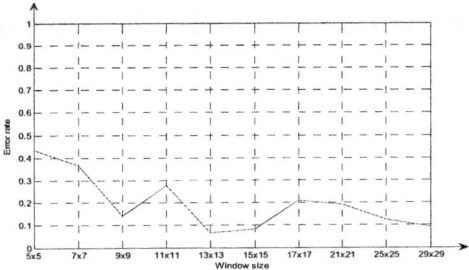

Fig. 6. The error rates of NHE+DFLD at different window size

can be decreased dramatically. Especially for DFLD, it's error rate is only 0.067 even in this extreme low dimensional space.

4.3 About Window Size

The window size of NHE can also affect the robustness of selected features. If the window size is too small, the NHE will introduce more noise and edges extracted are very weak, but a big widow will leads to less noise as well as insufficient illumination removal. We evaluate window size's effect on the performance of NHE+DFLD. The windows size range from 5×5 to 29×29. Results can be seen in Fig.6.

5 Conclusions

In this paper, we proposed an illumination invariant feature extraction method for face recognition, which is a combination of local contrast enhancement and linear subspace projection. The local enhancement can extract the facial geometry features which are resistant to large illumination, as shown in our experiments. But it can also introduce noise into the "flat" region. Then we used subspace projection methods to extract the most discriminant features as well as diminish the effect of noise. By incorporating the advantages of these two kinds of methods, we can decreased the error rate essentially even in very rigorous illumination condition. Another advantage of our methods is that it can reduce the data to very low dimensional space with superb discriminant power. In our experiment, the original data are 256×256-dimensional and the reduced data are only $3 - dimensional$.

References

1. Adini, Y., Moses, Y., Ullman, S.: Face recognition: the problem of compensating for changes in illumination direction. IEEE Trans. Pattern Anal. Mach. Intelligence **19** (1997) 721–732
2. Chen, S., Lovell, B.: Illumination and expression invariant face recognition with one sample image. In: Proc. of the 17th International Conf. on Pattern Recognition. Volume 1. (2004) 300–303

3. Li, Q., Ye, J., Kambhamettu, C.: Linear projection methods in face recognition under unconstrained illuminations: a comparative study. In: Proc. of the 2004 IEEE Computer Society Conf. on Computer Vision and Pattern Recognition. (2004) 474–481
4. Xie, X., Lam, K.M.: Face rcognition under varying illumination based on a 2d face shape model. Pattern Recognition **38** (2005) 221–230
5. Liu, C., Wechsler, H.: Probabilistic reasoning models for face recognition. In: Proc. IEEE Computer Society Conf. on Computer Vision and Pattern Recognition. (1998)
6. Stark, J.: Adaptive image contrast enhancement using generalizations of histogram equalization. IEEE Trans. on Image Processing **9** (2000) 889–896
7. Yu, H., Yang, J.: A direct LDA algorithm for high-dimensional data with application to face recognition. Pattern Recognition **34** (2001) 2067–2070
8. Georghiades, A., Belhumeur, P., Kriegman, D.: From few to many: Illumination cone models for face recognition under variable lighting and pose. IEEE Trans. Pattern Anal. Mach. Intelligence **23** (2001) 643–660
9. Bischof, H., Wildenauer, H., Leonardis, A.: Illumination insensitive recognition using eigenspaces. Computer Vision and Image Understanding **95** (2004) 86–104
10. Sanderson, C., Paliwal, K.K.: Fast features for face authentication under illumination direction changes. Pattern Recognition Letters **24** (2003) 2409C2419
11. Gross, R., Matthews, I., Baker, S.: Fisher light-fields for face recognition across pose and illumination. In: Proceedings of the German Symposium on Pattern Recognition (DAGM). (2002)
12. Sim, T., Kanade, T.: Combining models and exemplars for face recognition: An illuminating example. In: Proceedings of the CVPR 2001 Workshop on Models versus Exemplars in Computer Vision. (2001)
13. Li, Y.M., Chen, J., Qing, L.Y., Yin, B.C., Gao, W.: Face detection under variable lighting based on resample by face relighting. In: Proceedings of International Conference on Machine Learning and Cybernetics. (2004) 3775 – 3780
14. Yang, M.H., Kriegman, D., Ahuja, N.: Detecting faces in images: a survey. Pattern Analysis and Machine Intelligence, IEEE Transactions on **24** (2002) 34 – 58
15. Wei, S.D., Lai, S.H.: Robust face recognition under lighting variations. In: Pattern Recognition, Proceedings of the 17th International Conference on. (2004) 354 – 357
16. Wu, B., Ai, H., Huang, C., Lao, S.: Fast rotation invariant multi-view face detection based on real adaboost. In: Automatic Face and Gesture Recognition, 2004. Proceedings. Sixth IEEE International Conference on. (2004) 79 – 84
17. Wang, H., Li, S., Wang, Y., Zhang, W.: Illumination modeling and normalization for face recognition. In: Analysis and Modeling of Faces and Gestures, 2003. AMFG 2003. IEEE International Workshop on. (2003) 104 – 111
18. Turk, M., Pentland, A.: Face recognition using eigenfaces. In: Computer Vision and Pattern Recognition, 1991. Proceedings CVPR '91., IEEE Computer Society Conference on. (1991) 586 – 591
19. Gao, W., Shan, S., Chai, X., Fu, X.: Virtual face image generation for illumination and pose insensitive face recognition. In: Acoustics, Speech, and Signal Processing, 2003. Proceedings. (ICASSP '03). 2003 IEEE International Conference on. (2003) 776 – 779

20. Garcia, C., Tziritas, G.: Face detection using quantized skin color regions merging and wavelet packet analysis. Multimedia, IEEE Transactions on **1** (1999) 264 – 277
21. He, X., Yan, S., Hu, Y., Niyogi, P.H.J.Z.: Face recognition using laplacianfaces. Pattern Analysis and Machine Intelligence, IEEE Transactions on **27** (2005) 328 – 340
22. Huang, W., Sun, Q., Lam, C.P., Wu, J.K.: A robust approach to face and eyes detection from images with cluttered background. In: Pattern Recognition, 1998. Proceedings. Fourteenth International Conference on. (1998) 110 – 113

Specular Removal Using CL-Projection

Joung Wook Park, Jae Doug Yoo, and Kwan H. Lee

Gwangju Institute Science and Technology (GIST),
Intelligent Design and Graphics laboratory, Department of Mechatronics,
1 Oryong-dong, Buk-gu, Gwangju, 500-712, Korea
{vzo, uranus}@gist.ac.kr, lee@kyebek.gist.ac.kr
http://kyebek9.kjist.ac.kr

Abstract. In this paper we propose a method to remove the specularity of an image using Color Line(CL)-projection. CL-projection is defined as the projection along the direction of color line. In the first step of the proposed procedure, the highlighted region in an image is estimated from two images captured with different camera exposure times. In the second step, the representative color of the neighborhood of each highlighted region is estimated. In the final step, the specular component of color in the neighborhood region is removed using CL-projection and then the highlight is inpainted to recover the original color using a distance transform.

1 Introduction

One of the most significant reasons for discoloration is specularity, which causes saturation or clipping[1]. Several studies have been made on the method to remove this specularity in an image. G.J. Klinker[1] proposed the specular removal method using Shafer's[2] dichromatic reflection model in color space. Robby T. Tan[4] used the relation between the chromaticity and intensity of color in order to separate diffuse and specular components. Although the image without specularity is obtained, generally a polarizer causes reduction of intensity of an image, and it is not able to remove specularity with respect to all directions[5]. In order to solve the problem of polarized images, some researchers considered color as well as polarization[6, 7].

In the case of the consideration of color, it is important to determine the direction of projection in order to remove specularity. Therefore we propose the method of projection along the direction of the color line[8].

Three significant problems have been recognized in the previous works. First, the procedure searching for highlight areas is complicated due to the shortage of information in case of using an image, or difficulty to synchronize images though multiple images are used. Second, in removing the specular component, determination of the projected direction is carried out through heuristics and complicated procedure. Third, to achieve realistic results it was necessary to iterate the inpainting process and to heuristically decide on the terminated condition. Therefore, we proposed a novel method to search for the highlighted area using two images which are obtained using different camera exposure times, and to remove the specular component without consideration of the projected direction. In addition, the method to obtain the realistic inpainting results is also proposed without complicated iteration and heuristic terminated conditions.

This paper is composed of five sections, including an introduction in section 1. Basic concepts are described in section 2 and the proposed procedure is discussed in section 3. Experimental results are presented in section 4. In the last section, conclusions are described.

2 Basic Concept

2.1 Dichromatic Reflection Model and Color Line

Color is composed of a surface reflection component(a specular component) and a body reflection component(a diffuse component) in the dichromatic reflection model. We assume that there exists a single light source and the object has a single color. The color distribution of pixels in an image is similar to a curve in color space such as a skewed L-shape[10]. Omer[8] defined a color line as the curve which is the representative line of similar colors. In this paper, the diffuse color line(DCL) is defined as the portion on a color line, containing colors which are composed of only the diffuse component, and the specular color line(SCL) is defined as the portion on a color line, containing colors which are composed of both the diffuse component and the specular component. In the case of an image composed of only diffuse colors, color lines are generally composed of DCLs without SCLs in color space. Fig.1 shows the concept of the dichromatic reflection model and the color line.

We denote black color(0,0,0) as bp and white color(1,1,1) as wp. $\overline{bw}$ is the straight line between bp and wp. The representative color expressing the

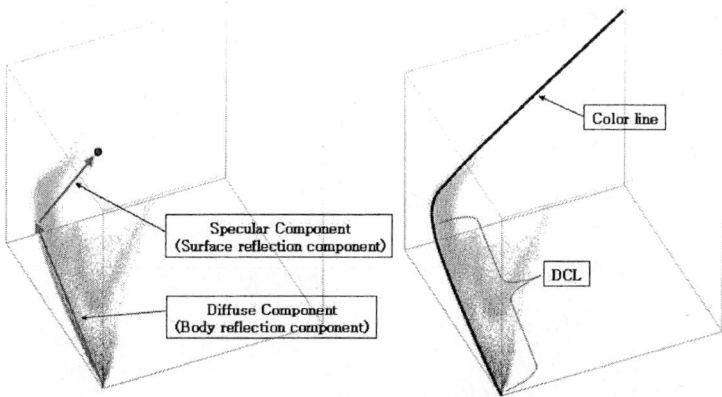

Fig. 1. The concept of dichromatic reflection model(left) and color line(right) in RGB color space

characteristics of the color line is called r_{CL} in color space. We also define r_{CL} as the farthest color on the DCL away from bp, that is, the farthest color on the DCL away from $\overline{bw}$[1]. Therefore, r_{CL} is the brightest color on DCL and does not include a specular component.

2.2 Reduction Ratio of Intensity

Now, let us consider two colors, a_i and b_i, in color space. $Dst(a_i, b_i)$ is the color distance between a_i and b_i. If the $i-th$ camera exposure time is t_i, where i is a positive integer, then an image captured with t_i is denoted as I_{t_i}, where the size of I_{t_i} is $M \times N$, where M, N is the positive integer. Color at the position (x, y) in I_{t_i} is denoted as $I_{t_i}(x, y)$.

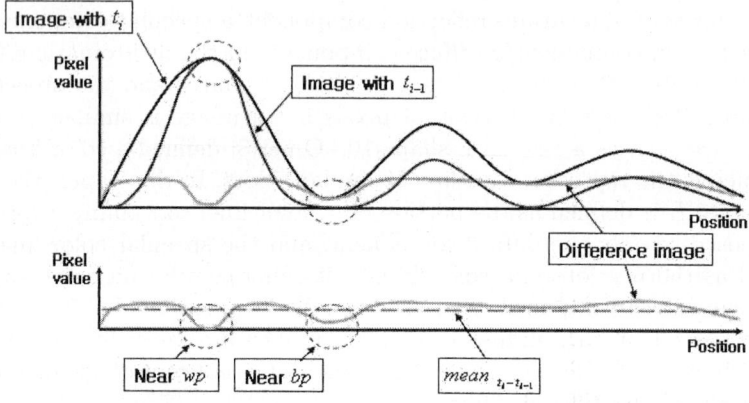

Fig. 2. Reduction ratio of intensity expressed by a difference image

The reduction ratio of intensity between $I_{t_{i-1}}$ and I_{t_i} is defined as $LRR_{t_i-t_{i-1}}$ which is calculated from the color distance of each color at the same position of two images, $I_{t_{i-1}}$ and I_{t_i}. If the reduction ratio is uniform regardless of color, $LRR_{t_i-t_{i-1}}$ is expressed by the mean value of $Dst(I_{t_{i-1}}(x,y), I_{t_i}(x,y))$ (Eq. (1)). In other words, $LRR_{t_i-t_{i-1}}$ is the magnitude of the average of the difference image between $I_{t_{i-1}}$ and I_{t_i}.

$$mean_{t_i-t_{i-1}} = \frac{\sum_{x,y}^{M,N} Dst(I_{t_{i-1}}(x,y), I_{t_i}(x,y))}{M \times N}, \quad (1)$$

where $t_1 < t_2 < \cdots < t_{i-1} < t_i$.

$$LRR_{t_i-t_{i-1}} = mean_{t_i-t_{i-1}} \quad (2)$$

If $I_{t_i}(x,y)$ is close to bp or $I_{t_{i-1}}(x,y)$ is close to wp, $LRR_{t_i-t_{i-1}}$ is smaller than the mean value of $Dst(I_{t_{i-1}}(x,y), I_{t_i}(x,y))$. Therefore, we change Eq. (2) into

Eq. (3). Eq. (3) means that if $Dst(I_{t_{i-1}}(x,y), wp)$ is smaller than $mean_{t_i-t_{i-1}}$, $I_{t_{i-1}}(x,y)$ is not a white color but a color in the highlighted region though the color is similar to white. We use this concept when searching for the highlighted region.

$$LRR_{t_i-t_{i-1}} > mean_{t_i-t_{i-1}} \tag{3}$$

3 Proposed Method

3.1 Adaptive 2-Step Projection

In the case of discoloration due to clipping or saturation, the diffuse component can be estimated by removing the specular component at a color, that is, by projecting a color on the DCL. Therefore, we define color line projection as the projection on the DCL along the direction of the SCL, since the quality of the projected result depends on the estimation of the projected direction. CL-projection will be explained in the next section, and the adaptive 2-step projection, the sub-process of CL-projection, is explained below.

Now, we assume that the color line and r_{CL} are known and the type of color line is a skewed L-shape which is composed of two straight lines, a DCL and a SCL. The color at the highlighted region is considered as the brightest color on DCL after removing a specular component, since the color at the highlighted region is composed of the r_{CL} and the specular component. In other words, if it is necessary to remove the specular component, the color has to move near to the SCL, and then the projected color has to be projected along the direction of the SCL again. We call this projection method a 2-step projection. The 2-step projection in proportion to the ratio of color distance is defined as adaptive 2-step projection to keep the relative characteristics of the color, especially, the ratio of the color distance among colors.

We assume that a_i is a color to project. a_i^{1st} is defined as the projected color of a_i in the direction of the SCL, according to the color distance between the SCL and a_i. Let a_i^{2nd} be defined as the projected color of a_i^{1st} on the DCL along the direction of the SCL, according to the color distance between the SCL and a_i^{1st}. In addition, a_i^{1st} and a_i^{2nd} should be in the range of the radius of the color line as in Eqs. (5), (6), (11), and (12)[1]. Therefore a_i^{1st} and a_i^{2nd} is not on the color line but near the color line after the adaptive 2-step projection.

The projection to obtain a_i^{1st} is called the first projection, and the projection to obtain a_i^{2nd} is called the second projection as in Fig.3. We denote the minimum of the radius as L_o and the maximum of the radius as L_e. The length of $\overline{bw}$, $L_{\overline{bw}}$ is defined as the standard length of the 2-step projection. We denote a_i projected on the SCL as a_i', as in Eq. (4), and a_i^{1st} projected on the DCL along the direction of the SCL as b_i', as in Eq. (10). The result after the adaptive 2-step projection is expressed as in Eq. (14).

$$a_i' = \frac{d \cdot (a_i - wp)}{d \cdot d} d + wp, \tag{4}$$

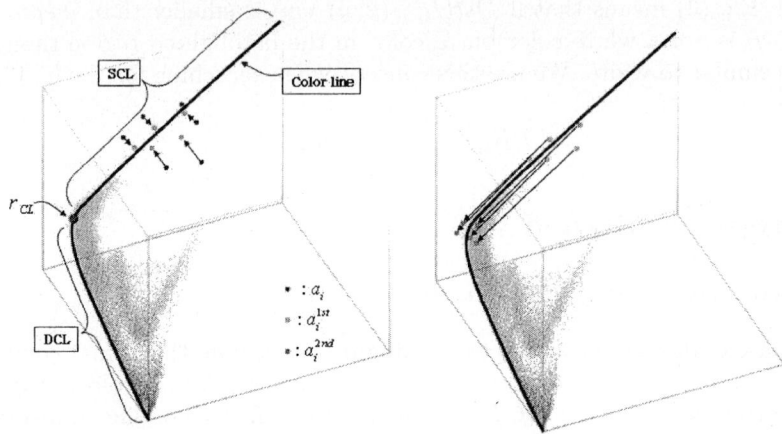

Fig. 3. The adaptive 2-step projection is defined as the first projection(left) and the second projection(right)

where $d = r_{CL} - wp$.

$$a_i^o = \frac{(L_{a_i a_i'} - L_o)a_i' + L_o a_i}{L_{a_i a_i'}} \qquad (5)$$

$$a_i^e = \frac{\beta a_i^o + (\alpha - \beta)a_i'}{\alpha}, \qquad (6)$$

where $L_{a_i a_i'} = Dst(a_i, a_i')$, $L_o = \alpha L_{\overline{bw}}$, $L_e = \beta L_{\overline{bw}}$.

$$a_i'' = \frac{\overline{L_{\overline{bw}}} a_i^o + \overline{L_{a_i a_i'}} a_i^e}{\overline{L_{\overline{bw}}} + \overline{L_{a_i a_i'}}}, \qquad (7)$$

where $\overline{L_{\overline{bw}}} = L_{\overline{bw}} - L_{a_i a_i'}$, $\overline{L_{a_i a_i'}} = L_{a_i a_i'} - L_o$.

$$a_i^{1st} = \begin{cases} a_i'', & \text{if} \quad L_{a_i a_i'} > L_o \\ a_i, & \text{otherwise} \end{cases} \qquad (8)$$

$$b_i = a_i^{1st} \qquad (9)$$

$$b_i' = \frac{(d \cdot d)(b_i \cdot r_{CL}) - (d \cdot r_{CL})(d \cdot b_i)}{(d \cdot d)(r_{CL} \cdot r_{CL}) - (d \cdot r_{CL})(d \cdot r_{CL})} r_{CL} \qquad (10)$$

$$b_i^o = \frac{(L_{b_i b_i'} - L_o)b_i' + L_o b_i}{L_{a_i a_i'}} \qquad (11)$$

$$b_i^e = \frac{\beta b_i^o + (\alpha - \beta)b_i'}{\alpha} \tag{12}$$

$$b_i'' = \frac{\overline{L_{\overline{bw}}} b_i^o + \overline{L_{b_i b_i'}} b_i^e}{\overline{L_{\overline{bw}}} + \overline{L_{b_i b_i'}}}, \tag{13}$$

where $\overline{L_{\overline{bw}}} = L_{\overline{bw}} - L_{b_i b_i'}$, $\overline{L_{b_i b_i'}} = L_{b_i b_i'} - L_o$.

$$a_i^{2nd} = \begin{cases} b_i'', & \text{if } L_{b_i b_i'} > L_o \\ b_i, & \text{otherwise,} \end{cases} \tag{14}$$

where $\overline{L_{\overline{bw}}} = L_{\overline{bw}} - L_{b_i b_i'}$, $\overline{L_{b_i b_i'}} = L_{b_i b_i'} - L_o$.

3.2 CL-Projection

If the shape of the color line does not follow the straight line or the distribution of colors near the highlight is widely spread, the color modified by the general projection is distorted[3]. In order to solve this problem, it is necessary to project along the color line, CL-projection. Instead of complicated calculation, that is, projection along the color line, we use a simple approximation of an adaptive 2-step projection iteratively, as follows.

Firstly, we assume that r_{CL} has been already calculated. A local r_{CL} calculated from the partially extended neighborhood of the highlighted region, is denoted as $l - r_{CL}$ and the initial value of $l - r_{CL}$ is denoted as $init - r_{CL}$. Fig.4 shows the result of the adaptive 2-step projection after three iterations.

Step 1 : $init - r_{CL} = wp$

Step 2 : Extend the area of the neighborhood near the segment of the highlighted region

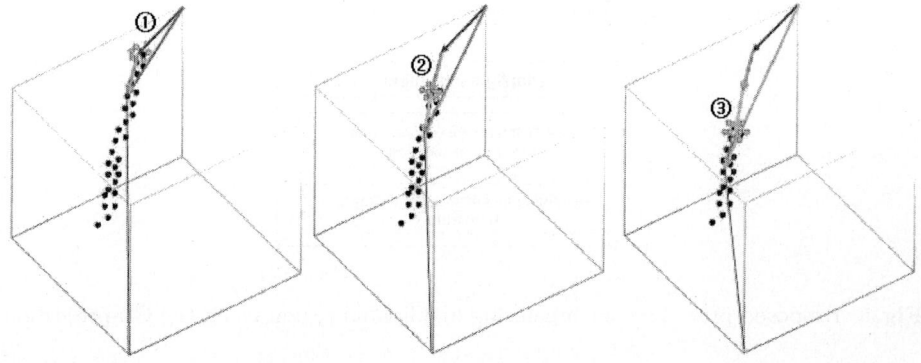

Fig. 4. Concept of CL-projection

Step 3 : Calculate $l - r_{CL}$

Step 4 : Generate the color line from $init - r_{CL}$ and $l - r_{CL}$

Step 5 : Carry out an adaptive 2-step projection

Step 6 : Replace $init - r_{CL}$ with $l - r_{CL}$

Step 7 : Repeat steps from 2 to 6 until r_{CL} and $init - r_{CL}$ are the same

3.3 Removal Procedure of Specularity Using CL-Projection

In this paper, two images are obtained with different camera exposure times. In order to inpaint highlight the method using CL-projection and distance transform is proposed with three steps. In the first step, in order to determine the highlighted region the threshold is calculated from the reduction ratio of intensity, that is, the average of the color distance between two images. In the second step, the highlighted region is segmented and then the representative color of the neighborhood of each segment is determined. In the last step, the specular component of color in the neighborhood region is removed using CL-projection and then the highlight is inpainted by distance transform[9]. The Fig.4 is the whole procedure to inpaint highlighted region using the CL-projection.

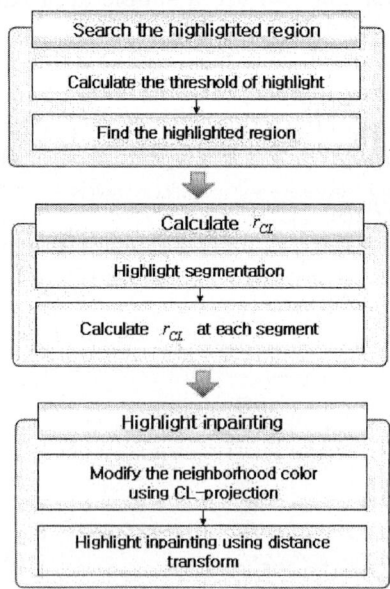

Fig. 5. Proposed procedure for inpainting highlighted region using the CL-projection

4 Experimental Results

The camera, Cannon EOS 300D, is used to capture two images with each exposure time and the lens type of the camera is Cannon EFS(18-55mm). The F-stop number is 5.6 and two kinds of exposure time, 1/100s and 1/500s are used. The color of the light source with diffuse films is white and the color temperature is 5400K. The color temperature of the light source is 5200K by experimental measurement. The captured objects are billiard balls, namely snooker balls.

The results at each step of the proposed method are shown in Fig. 6. Fig. 6(a) is the original image. Fig. 6(b) shows one of segments of the highlighted region, and Fig. 6(c) is the neighborhood of the segment. Fig. 6(d) is the result when the image in Fig. 6(c) is modified by CL-projection. The result of inpainting highlight, using distance transform, is shown in Fig. 6(e). Fig. 6(f) shows the result that the highlighted region and the neighborhood are replaced by each portion in Fig. 6(d) and in Fig. 6(e) in the final step.

Fig. 7(a) shows the image with several color balls. Fig. 7(b) shows the result that specular components in Fig. 7(a) are removed after applying our method. Color distribution is shown in Fig. 7(c) and Fig. 7(d), corresponding to each image Fig. 7(a) and Fig. 7(b). Fig. 7(d) shows the result of removing specular components without changing DCL. Finally, Fig. 7 shows the result of the recovered image generated by the proposed method.

Color distribution differs according to the characteristics of the material, that is, color, surface reflection, coating material and so on. Fig. 8 shows the special case of color line shapes, that is to say, the case in which the modified result can't be better without CL-projection. Fig. 8(a) is the original image, Fig. 8(b) is the result using one directional projection and Fig. 8(c) is that using CL-projection.

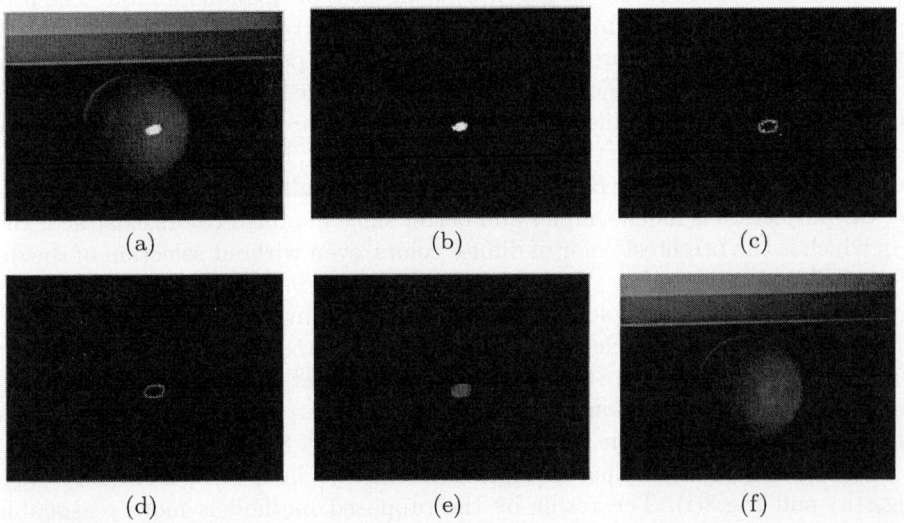

Fig. 6. Results at each step of the proposed method

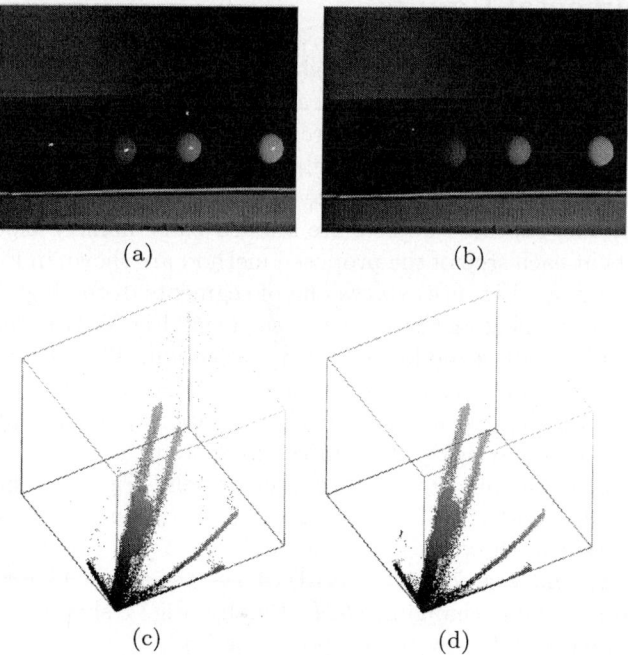

Fig. 7. Results of the image with several color balls

Fig. 8(d) shows the color distribution of the image Fig. 8(a) in color space and color line of the portion corresponding to the brown ball in image Fig. 8(a). Fig. 8(e) and Fig. 8(f) are results of Fig. 8(a) using each projection method. The projection result is expressed in Fig. 8(e), and in Fig. 8(f) by color vectors(black-pink lines), where black points are original points and pink points are projected points. If the single-directional projection is used, colors at the neighborhood of the highlighted region are not modified since projected colors are widely spread. Although the multi-directional projection is applied to Fig. 8(b), it is necessary to make the projection direction of each color determined individually. Therefore the result using CL-projection is much simpler and better since modified colors exist near the r_{CL} which is the brightest color of diffuse colors, even without selection of the direction of projection.

Fig. 8(g) shows RGB color histograms along the line, AA', in the image 8(a). The portion at the dot circle in Fig. 8(g) corresponds to the neighborhood of the highlight area in the image 8(a). Fig. 8(g) explains that all color channels are saturated at the highlight region. Fig. 8(h) and Fig. 8(i) are RGB color histograms at the same position as the line, AA', with respect to Fig. 8(b) and Fig. 8(c).

Fig. 9 shows red channel histograms along the line, AA', from Fig. 8(g), Fig.8(h) and Fig.8(i). The result by the proposed method is more reasonable since the value of modified highlight is similar to that of the neighborhood and is brighter than the other portion.

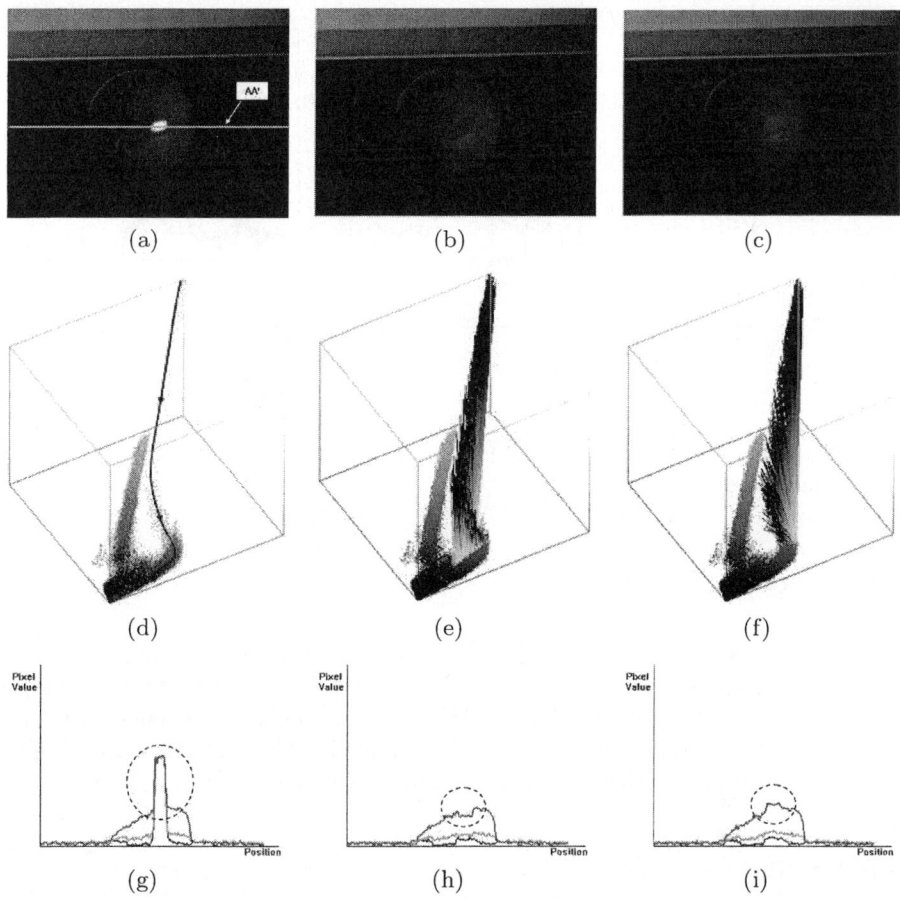

Fig. 8. Comparison of one directional projection and CL-projection

5 Conclusions

The proposed method has several advantages. First, it is easy to find the highlight region by using two images with two different exposure times. Second, the threshold to find the highlight region, is clearly determined due to the reduction ratio of intensity calculated from the two images. Third, although it is an image with a special color distribution, the CL-projection is a simpler and better method to remove the specular component without complicated selection of the projection direction. The proposed method has also limitations. The method can be applied to a region composed of only a single color near the highlight, or to the region which has already been segmented according to color. At present, our method is affected by noise when the color line is similar to $\overline{bw}$. We attempt to solve this problem by applying color density in our future work.

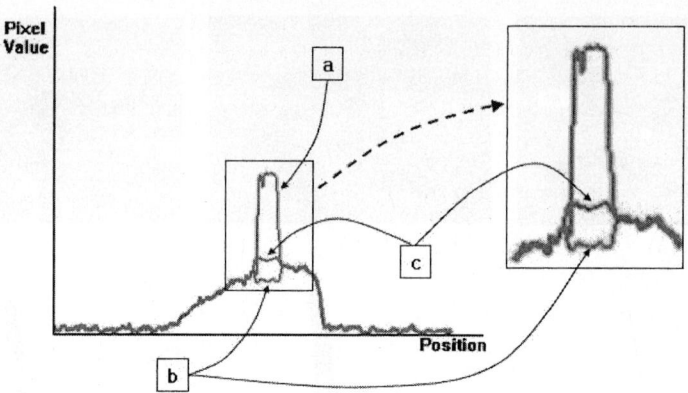

Fig. 9. The histogram of the red channel along the line, AA', corresponding to Fig.8(a), Fig.8(b) and Fig.8(c)

Acknowledgements

This work was supported by the Ministry of Information and Communication (MIC) through the Realistic Broadcasting Research Center (RBRC) at Gwangju Institute of Science and Technology (GIST) and by the Korea Science and Engineering Foundation (KOSEF) through the Immersive Contents Research Center (ICRC) at Gwangju Institute of Science and Technology (GIST).

References

1. Klinker, G.J.: A Physical Approach to Color Image Understanding. A K Peters, Wellesley Massachusetts (1993)
2. Shafer, S.A.: Using color to separate reflection components. COLOR research and application, Vol. 10. (1985) 210–218
3. Tan, P., Lin, S., Quan, L., Shum, H. Y.: Highlight removal by illumination - constrained inpainting. Computer Vision, 2003 Proceedings. Ninth IEEE International Conference on, Vol. 1. (2003) 164–169
4. Tan, R.T., Nishino, K., Ikeuchi, K.: Separating reflection components based on chromaticity and noise analysis. Pattern Analysis and Machine Intelligence, IEEE Transactions on ,Vol. 26, Issue 10. (2004) 1373–1379
5. Wolff, L.B., Boult, T.: Constraining Object Features Using Polarization Reflectance Model. IEEE Trans. Pattern Analysis and Machine Intelligence, Vol. 13, No. 7. (1991) 635–657.
6. Nayar, S.K., Fang, X.S., Boult, T.: Separation of Reflection Components Using Color and Polarization. Int'l J. Computer Vision, Vol. 21, No. 3. (1996)
7. Kim, D. W., Lin, S., Hong, K. S., Shum, H. Y.: Variational Specular Separation Using Color and Polarization. IAPR Workshop on Machine Vision Applications. (2002)

8. Omer, I., Werman, M.: Color lines: image specific color representation. Computer Vision and Pattern Recognition 2004, Proceedings of the 2004 IEEE Computer Society Conference on, Vol. 2. (2004) 946–953
9. Jain, A. k.: Fundamentals of Digital Image Processing. Prentice-Hall, Inc., New Jersey (1989)
10. Gershon, R., Jepson, A.D.,Tsotsos, J.K.: Highlight identification using chromatic information. Proc. 1st Int. Conf. Computer Vision, IEEE, London (1987) 161–171

Oriental Color-Ink Model Based Painterly Rendering for Realtime Application

Crystal S. Oh and Yang-Hee Nam

Division of Digital Media, Ewha Womans University,
11-1 Daehyun-dong, Seodaemun-gu, Seoul, South Korea
osjung8@hotmail.com, yanghee@ewha.ac.kr

Abstract. Automated rendering technique in oriental painting style is demanding in the entertainment industry such as game, animation since this makes their contents more unique. To simulate the oriental painting more vivid, intrinsic color expression is critical. Generally actual artists put 3 colors on the different part of the brush at the same time and they express the volume and diffusion effect with this brush using peculiar color pigments. However most existing works have only focused on black ink painting and they rarely discuss about how to simulate the effect of actual pigments and their layered application. This paper presents a novel algorithm which can express the volume and diffusion of 3D objects using oriental color-ink model constructed from the real artists' standpoint. This model consists of 3 layers according to different color tones. They are combined using Kubelka-Munk (KM) composition model where optical parameters are extracted from the real painting media. We implemented our model on a GPU and the results show real-time rendering performance in arbitrarily given 3D scenes.

1 Introduction

Non-photorealistic rendering researches have investigated aesthetic and stylized element into computer graphics by simulating various artistic styles such as cartoon, watercolor, oil painting. In particular, automated rendering techniques in oriental painting style are demanding in the entertainment industry such as game, animation since they makes the contents more unique.

Among several factors contributing oriental painting style, coloring method is very special. Generally traditional artists put 3 colors on the different parts of the brush at the same time and they express the tone and diffusion effect affected by correct orders and the way of compound application of these 3 colors. Moreover, the oriental color pigments have unique optical properties on account of using natural materials and their resulting form in solution. Most existing works, however, have only focused on the black ink diffusion and the representation of western color pigments. Therefore, their ink models and rendering frameworks are inappropriate for oriental color-ink style painting.

This paper proposes an oriental color-ink model based rendering method which provides an automated way of rendering arbitrary 3D models in oriental style which is also suitable for real-time application such as games and virtual environments. In our approach, we define a novel rendering framework that consists of 4 components for rendering arbitrary 3D models in oriental style : *Color Composition, Volume & Color Diffusion* expression, *Silhouette* expression and *Depth & Paper* expression. To simulate the rich oriental color, we focus on the following two main algorithms :

First, for realistic *Color Composition* effect, we provide how we could simulate the optical effect of superimposed 3 color layers using Kubelka-Munk (KM) compositing model by finding its coefficients from the true representation of real paint media.

Secondly, we propose a color-ink model consisting of 3-layers according to the different color tones (*Base*, *Mid* and *Vivid* tone) from the real artists' standpoints. To meet the requirements of the correct order and methods of applying color layers in oriental painting with KM composition colors, a new algorithm is suggested for expressing *Volume & Diffusion* using this 3-layered color model.

We implemented our oriental color-ink model based framework on a GPU, and we finally show the achievement of real-time rendering results where we can render a 212,452 faces at 21.7 fps on a 3.2Ghz, Intel 4P CPU with NVIDIA GeForce 6800 GPU.

2 Related Works

We will discuss some previous works related to oriental color ink rendering on two topics, which are 3D oriental black ink painting and color representation.

2.1 3D Model Based Oriental Black Ink Rendering

The importance of colors in oriental painting is no less than black ink effects but most previous researches in this area focused on black ink painting. Kang suggested a real time 3D oriental black ink painting using a hardware accelerated rendering algorithm[1]. They represent 5 features of oriental painting as tone, diffusion, brush stroke, depth and paper. Zhang presented diffusion effect for 3D model using a simple behavioral model of ink[2]. It is based on a cellular automaton computation but they can not achieve real-time rendering and their experiment use only tree models so they have limitations to express whole features of oriental painting.

Way presented a methods to automatically draw trees in Chinese ink painting style from 3D polygon models[3]. They define outline rendering and texture generation for oriental painting but they only generate the textures for various trees so they also have limitations. To provide an automated way of rendering 3D models in oriental color ink style, we need to define the novel rendering framework that construct the whole process for oriental color ink painting that focus on the color expressions.

2.2 Color Composition Model

Recently, most NPR researches which express the color composition use the Kubelka-Munk(KM) model to compute a color mixtures of pigments since this model can display the color of the mixed pigments realistically. Curtis used KM model for optically compositing thin glazes of paint in their watercolor simulation[4]. Baxter also used this model in interactive painting system for oils or acrylics styles[5].

But these works were focused on the representation of western color pigments. Lin simulate the oriental color ink diffusion effects based on the flows of water, ink, and pigment on paper, it didn't consider the unique factors of oriental pigments[6]. Since these researches can not reflect the optical parameters of oriental pigment and color composition method, we need to found the KM coefficients and the composition method which is suitable for oriental painting.

3 Artist's Real Process of Oriental Color-Ink Painting

To render arbitrary 3D models in oriental color ink style automatically, it is important to study the characteristics that make oriental painting so unique. In the rest of this section, we'll review some of the most important characteristic expressions of oriental color ink painting from the artists' standpoint [7,8]. Fig.1 shows the general steps of the real oriental color-ink painting.

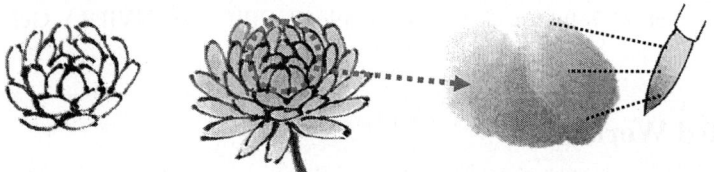

(a) Silhouette Expression (b) Volume Expression (c) Color Diffusion Expression

Fig. 1. Real oriental color-ink painting process

Silhouette Expression. The silhouette expression of the oriental painting explains the object shape and the painter's emotion according to the strength and weakness of stroke.

Volume Expression. In the traditional oriental color painting, artists put 3 colors on the different part of the brush at the same time and they express the volume and diffusion expression with this brush. These colors are applied to objects in the order from dark to light tone. Also they are painted from the center of object to outside in the oriental painting and there's some blank area very close to the outside This empty area is one of the unique factors in oriental style. Since such a coloring method is different from western painting, it is required to develop a novel *Volume* expression algorithm.

Color Diffusion Expression. This is the irregular spreading effect that reveals the color ink diffusion over the oriental paper which is composed of fibers in random position and direction. In particular, the color diffusion effect also occurs among the adjacent color tone layers.

4 3D Rendering Framework Using Oriental Color-Ink Model

Based on the observation on real artist's painting process in the previous section, we define the oriental color-ink model as consisting of 3 color layers : *Base, Mid* and

Vivid. According to this color-ink model, we propose the novel rendering algorithm automatically generating oriental painting style for arbitrary 3D models. Using this framework, users can easily create the oriental scene by just giving 3D input models and choosing 3 colors for each object. Fig. 2 shows the overview of our framework and Fig. 3 shows our color-ink model. We'll explain the main components in the following two subsections.

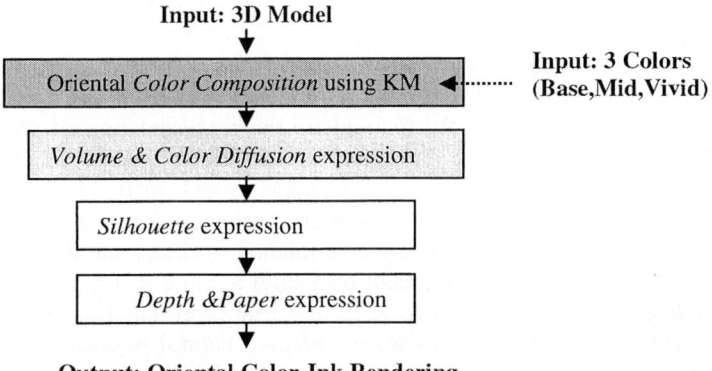

Fig. 2. Overview of rendering framework using oriental color-ink model

4.1 Oriental Color Composition Using Kubelka-Munk(KM) Model

We use the KM compositing model for simulating the optical effect of superimposed 3-color layers and creating realistic *Color Composition* that reflects the characteristics of traditional oriental pigments. The KM model is a two-flux radiative transfer approach which has been suitable for describing reflectance properties of light scattering and absorbing materials. In particular, this model can display the color of mixed pigments realistically [9,10]. Fig.4 shows the steps in our color composition using KM model and the description of these steps will follow.

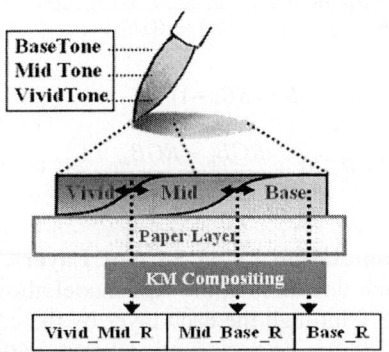

Fig. 3. Color-ink model and KM composition

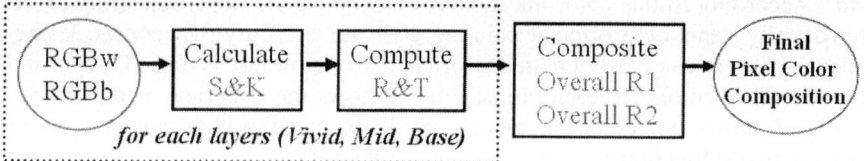

Fig. 4. Steps in Color Composition using KM model

Image-Based Acquisition of the Oriental Pigment Coefficients. Oriental pigment has unique colors on account of using natural materials and solutions. But in previous works using KM theory have only focused on the representation of western color pigments. In our method, we use the image-based acquisition method to reflect the optical parameters of oriental pigments to our KM model. In typical applications of KM theory, each pigment is assigned a set of absorption coefficients K and scattering coefficients S. Curtis proposed an interactive method to determine these coefficients choosing two RGB colors of the pigment over both a white and a black background [4]. In our application, we gain S & K from a true representation of real painting media. We create thick and flat samples of standard natural pigments that use common to artists. Our sample is painted on the Han-ji(oriental paper) as a white background and we used black ink as a black background like Fig.5. From these experimental set-up, we can acquire two colors, RGBw and RGBb respectively, then the K and S values can be computed by the equation (1) and (2).

Fig. 5. Real oriental color pigment samples

$$S = \frac{1}{b} \times \coth^{-1}\left(\frac{b^2 - (a - RGB_w)(a-1)}{b(1 - RGB_w)}\right) \quad (1)$$

$$K = S(a-1)$$

where, $a = \frac{1}{2}\left(RGB_w + \frac{RGB_b - RGB_w + 1}{RGB_b}\right)$, $b = \sqrt{a^2 - 1}$ \quad (2)

Overall Reflectance Computation Using 3-Color Layers. Given S and K for the pigmented 3 layers of given thickness x, the KM model allows us to compute reflectance R and transmittance T through the each layer by the equation (3). We can then determine the overall reflectance of two abutting layers with R1, R2 and T1, T2 respectively by the equation (4). We assume that user can select a desired thickness for each color layer.

In oriental color-ink model, we have two pairs of adjacent pigmented color layers : *Vivid-Mid* and *Mid-Base*. So we need to compute two overall reflectances, *Vivid-Mid_R* and *MidBase_R*. To render final pixel color, we use the 3-KM reflectance values like Fig.3. We use the *Base* layer's R value as it is because it does not have a pigment composition.

$$R = \sinh bSx / c , \quad T = b/c$$
$$\text{where, } c = a \sinh bSx + b \cosh bSx \tag{3}$$

$$OverallR = R_1 + \frac{T_1^2 R_2}{1 - R_1 R_2} \tag{4}$$

4.2 Volume and Color Diffusion Expression

First, to represent the *Volume* expression using 3-KM reflectance colors, we compute the desired *tonelevel* of each vertex using the equation (5). According to this value, we can decide the 4-tone levels for the KM reflectance colors from dark(VividMid_R) to light tone(Blank) like Fig.6. These colors are applied in the order from the center of object to the outside(silhouette) area following the real oriental volume expression which emphasize the center of the object as we described in the previous section.

$$tone\ level = \max(\vec{n} \bullet \vec{l}, 0) \tag{5}$$

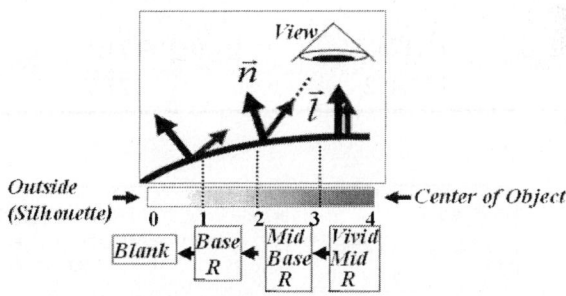

Fig. 6. Generation of tonelevles

Then to render final pixel color, we set the *tonelevels* from 0 to 4 and interpolate each pixel colors with this value. For example, if the tonelevel is 2.8, the final pixel color is decided from the following code. (We use the papercolor for the blank area close to the silhouette.)

```
Final_Pixel_Color = Vivid_Mid_R * 0.8 + Mid_Base_R * 0.2;
```

Second, to simulate the *Color Diffusion* expression, we use the predefined diffusion *valuemap* that represent an irregular spreading pattern (that reveals the color ink diffusion in the oriental paper). This map is pre-rendered by Perlin noise function(like Fig.7 left). Otherwise, we also use the real ink-diffusion image (like Fig.7 right). At runtime, we create the color diffusion expression by blending the final pixel color using the diffusion *valuemap* as their blending rates. We can express the various styles using these predefined diffusion *valuemaps*.

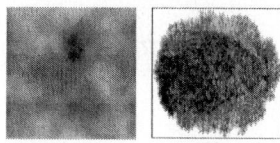

Fig. 7. Diffusion valuemap samples

5 GPU Implementation and Experimental Results

We achieve real-time rendering performance using GPU based implementation to calculate all the processes of our rendering algorithm. Proposed method is implemented

Table 1. Frame rates and sizes of representative models

Model	# of Faces	FPS
Game Character	10,027	69.1
Flower	11,175	71.1
Korean Temple	152,452	21.7

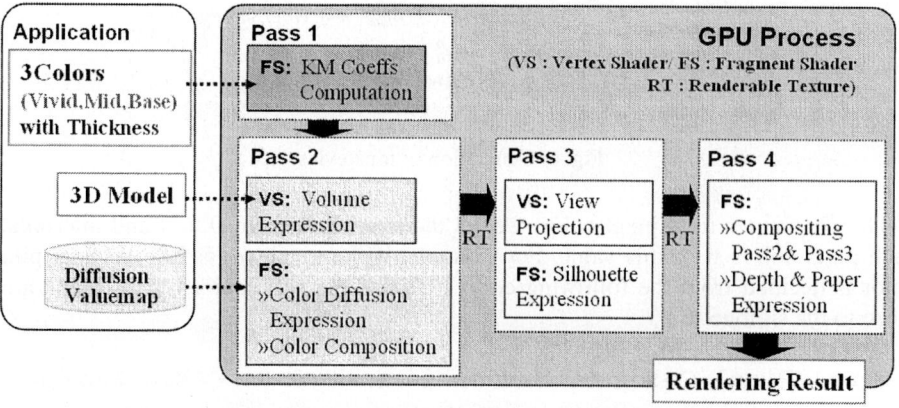

Fig. 8. Implementation architecture of oriental color-ink rendering

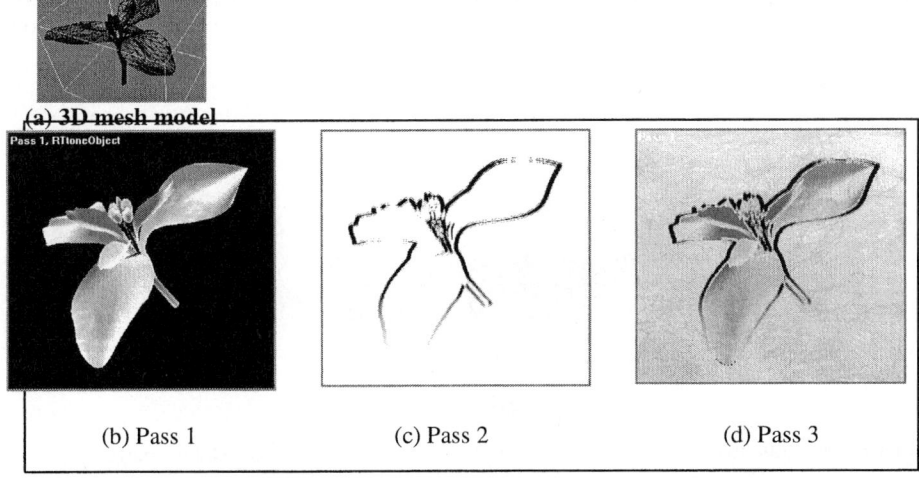

Fig. 9. Oriental color-ink rendering process

using OpenGL and GLSL and we have tested on a 3.2Ghz, Intel 4P CPU with NVIDIA GeForce 6800 GPU. Our frame rates for various models are reported in Table1. Our rendering framework on the GPU follows the stages of Fig. 8 and our pipeline has four GPU rendering passes.

First, when user selects the 3-Colors and each thickness through the application, the fragment shader of pass 1 computes the KM values. Secondly, by importing a 3D input model, the vertex shader of pass 2 computes the *tonelevel* of each vertex, then the fragment shader (of pass 2) blends the multiple diffusion textures and composites the oriental KM color.

Fig. 10. Purple tone flower with minute diffusion texture

Then rendering result of pass 2 transforms into view projection space and we use this image as a reference for pass 3 via render-to-texture extension. In the pass 3, we use the adjusted *Sobel* mask for stylized silhouette expression.

In the pass 4, exponential fogging is used for atmospheric depth effect. Since recent graphics hardware has advantages about the per-pixel computation, most of our algorithms are implemented by the fragment shader.

(a) Diffusion value map   (b) Orange flower   (c) Detail image

Fig. 11. Orange tone flower with smooth brush diffusion texture

Fig. 12. Three example frames selected from the orientally stylized game character scene

Fig.9 ~ Fig.13 show some of the experimental results using our oriental color-ink rendering algorithm. Fig.9 (a) shows the 3D input model and (b)~(c) show the rendering result of each rendering pass, (b) shows the KM color compositing result after tone & diffusion effect, (c) shows our silhouette rendering result and (d) shows the final result after the depth & paper effect.

In the Fig.10 and Fig.11, we observe two different color tone variation and different diffusion texture style. For the Fig.10, we use the 3 purple-tone colors for KM compositing and apply minute diffusion texture. In the case of Fig.11, we use the 3 orange-tone colors and apply more smooth brush diffusion texture.

Fig.12 shows our rendering result for a scene consisting of a 3D game character with a 3D temple model in front of the 2D background image, so that we can see how orientally stylized scene looks like in 3D games or in VR contents. Fig.13 shows three example frames selected from continuous navigation, so that we can observe our frame coherence in real time.

Fig. 13. Three example frames selected from continuous navigation, rendered in oriental style

6 Conclusions and Further Remarks

Our method proposed an automated way of rendering arbitrary 3D models in oriental color ink painting style. We propose a color-ink model consisting of 3-layers according to the different color tones from the real artists' standpoint. For realistic Color Composition effect, we provide how we could simulate the optical effect of superimposed 3 color layers using KM model by finding its coefficients from the true representation of real paint media.

Our novel framework of realtime GPU based oriental painting is different from other existing works in the aspect that this can automatically render 3D models in real-time and our color-ink model is established by reflecting the properties of real pigments and their way of blending. Since this framework is applied to 3D scene that can interactively changes, it is also suitable for real-time application such as animations, games, virtual environments.

As our future work, we can further extend color diffusion expression model using physically based simplified simulation in real time instead of using just a pre-computed diffusion textures.

References

1. Kang, S.J., Kim, C.H.: Real-Time 3D Sumi-e Painting. ACM SIGGRAPH Technical Sketch (2003).
2. Zhang, Q., Sato, Y.: Simple Cellular Automaton-based Simulation of Ink Behaviour and Its Application to Suibokuga-like 3D Rendering of Trees. The Journal of Visualization and Computer Animation (1999), 27-37

3. Way, D.L., Lin, Y.R.: The Synthesis of Trees in Chinese Landscape Painting using Silhouette and Texture Strokes. In Proceeding of Eurographics (2001), 123-131
4. Curtis, C.J., Anderson, S.E., Seims, J.E., Fleischer, K.W., Salesin, D.H.: Computer-Generated Watercolor. In Proceeding of SIGGRAPH (1997), 421-430
5. Baxter, W., Wendt, J., Lin, M.C. : IMPaSTo: A Realistic, Interactive Model for Paint. In Proceeding of NPAR(2004) 45-56
6. Lin, W. J., Shih, Z.C.: Computer-Generated Chinese Painting with Physically-Based Ink and Color Diffusion. In Proceeding of CGW (2004)
7. Sea, J.S: Oriental Color-ink Painting. Hyung-sul publishing co. (1992)
8. An, D.S: Traditional Oriental Painting. Sea-ye publishing co. (1991)
9. Haase, C.S (ed.): Modeling Pigmented Materials for Realistic Image Synthesis. ACM Transaction of Graphics (1992), Vol.11, No.4, 305-335
10. Kortum, G.: Reflectance Spectroscopy. Springer-Verlag (1969)

An Adjusted-Q Digital Graphic Equalizer Employing Opposite Filters

Yonghee Lee[1], Rinchul Kim[2], Googchun Cho[3], and Seong Jong Choi[2]

[1] Mobile Multimedia Lab., LG Electronics Institute of Tech.,
Seoul 137-724, Korea
yongheelee@lge.com
[2] Dept. of Electrical and Computer Eng., University of Seoul,
Seoul 130-743, Korea
{rin chois}@uos.ac.kr
[3] DigitalandAnalog, Co. LTD., AnYang MegaValley 625, AnYang
KyungKi 431-060, Korea
gccho@digitalandanalog.com

Abstract. This paper proposes an adjusted-Q digital graphic equalizer employing the opposite filters. A method for designing the proposed equalizer is also presented. In the proposed adjusted–Q equalizer, we adjust the Q-factor of the equalizer filter depending on the gain, yielding an improved equalizer performance. Also, by increasing the Q-factor of the opposite filters gracefully with increasing gain, the inter-band interference can be reduced effectively in all frequency range in consideration. We shall show that the proposed equalizer can reproduce the user's gain setting faithfully.

1 Introduction

Audio signals may be degraded due to reverberation and filtering process in a listening environment. In this case, subjectively unclear sound may be experienced as some frequency components of the audio signal are attenuated while others are augmented. In order to compensate for the deformation in the frequency domain and to reproduce a sound closer to the original, equalizers [1-4] have been widely employed. The equalizer are also be used to modify the frequency spectrum of input audio depending on the user preferences including the user preferred genre (e.g., pop, classic, etc), or user characteristics [5].

Generally, a graphic equalizer is used as part of an audio system because of its simple structure. In the graphic equalizer, the full audio band is divided into several predefined sub-bands, where each sub-band is separately processed by the corresponding equalizer filter. The equalizer filter is a band-pass filter, typically implemented by the 2nd order infinite impulse response (IIR) filter. It is completely characterized by the three parameters; center frequency, Q-factor, and gain. Note that the Q-factor is inversely proportional to the bandwidth.

The graphic equalizer is constructed by cascading as many equalizer filters as the number of the predefined sub-bands. Each equalizer filter aims to modify the gain of the corresponding sub-band to the user-defined value. However, it leaves a remarkable trail to the neighboring bands because the frequency response of the equalizer filter is not stiff enough. This makes it difficult to achieve the overall response of the graphic equalizer closer to the user setting. In particular, when it is implemented with analog components, the skirt of the filter gets lifted up as the gain decreases, because the Q-factor also decreases in this case. So, the influence becomes larger as the gain decreases. As a solution to this problem, Bohn [2] proposed a constant-Q equalizer, in which the Q-factor was maintained constant over a wide range of gain values. But the improvement is limited since there still remain significant interferences between neighboring sub-bands.

Recently, Azizi [1] proposed the notion of the opposite filters to alleviate the inter-band interferences in an effective manner. In his approach, the effects of the equalizer filter for a given band to the neighboring bands are analyzed. Then, the opposite filters are additionally installed at the neighboring bands to compensate the effects by setting the gains of the opposite filters to the measured amount of interference. It is reported that the Azizi's approach has yielded a significant improvement. Nevertheless, his approach shows a discrepancy between the user setting and the actual response of the graphic equalizer, especially when delicate user settings are applied.

In this paper, we present an adjusted-Q graphic equalizer, in which each filter employs different Q-factors depending on the gain value and sub-band index. In [5], different Q-factors are applied to each equalizer filters depending on the sub-band index. Specifically, the equalizer filters which causes great interferences to neighboring sub-bands take larger Q-factors, while the filters otherwise take smaller Q-factors. In this way, the interferences are maintained below a certain level. But, it is important to note that the Q-factor should be adjusted depending on the gain value in addition to the sub-band index to achieve a faithful equalizer.

In what follows, after reviewing the conventional graphic equalizers in section 2, we describe the adjusted-Q graphic equalizer in section 3. Specifically, the adjusted-Q equalizer employing opposite filters is addressed, and an algorithm to design the proposed equalizer is described. In section 4, we give our simulation results with discussions. Finally, conclusions are given in section 5.

2 Graphic Equalizer

2.1 Equalizer Filter

A 2nd order continuous-time equalizer filter is given by

$$H(s) = \frac{1 + \dfrac{2\pi F_c G^+}{Q} s^{-1} + (2\pi F_c)^2 s^{-2}}{1 + \dfrac{2\pi F_c}{Q G^-} s^{-1} + (2\pi F_c)^2 s^{-2}}, \tag{1}$$

where F_c and Q are the center frequency and Q-factor, respectively. In order to make the frequency response symmetric with respect to the gain, the gain is denoted by two parameters G^+ and G^-. When the gain G is of positive value, $G^+ = G$ and $G^- = 1$. On the other hand, when the gain is of negative value, $G^+ = 1$ and $G^- = G$. In order to convert the continuous-time filter into the discrete-time counterpart, we can resort to the bilinear transform [1, 6], given by

$$s = \frac{2\pi F_c}{\tan(\pi F_c/F_s)} \cdot \frac{(z-1)}{(z+1)}, \qquad (2)$$

where F_s denotes the sampling frequency in Hz. Accordingly, the discrete-time counterpart is given by

$$H(s) = \frac{b_0 + b_1 z^{-1} + b_2 z^{-2}}{a_0 + a_1 z^{-1} + a_2 z^{-2}}, \qquad (3)$$

where the six different filter coefficients are given as follows

$$b_0 = T^2 + \frac{2\pi F_c T G^+}{Q} + (2\pi F_c)^2$$

$$a_1 = b_1 = -2T^2 + 2(2\pi F_c)^2$$

$$b_2 = T^2 - \frac{2\pi F_c T G^+}{Q} + (2\pi F_c)^2 . \qquad (4)$$

$$a_0 = T^2 + \frac{2\pi F_c T}{QG^-} + (2\pi F_c)^2$$

$$a_2 = T^2 - \frac{2\pi F_c T}{QG^-} + (2\pi F_c)^2$$

In (4), T is denoted as

$$T = \frac{2\pi F_c}{\tan(\pi F_c/F_s)Q}. \qquad (5)$$

Fig. 1 shows the magnitude response of an equalizer filter expressed in (3) and illustrates the relationship between the center frequency, the bandwidth, and the Q-factor. Here, the gain is set to 12 dB and -12 dB in Fig. 1(a) and (b), respectively. In Fig. 1(c) and (d), the frequency responses are demonstrated when the Q-factor is set to 1.4 but the gains are varied in the range from -10 dB to 10 dB in a 2 dB step. When the center frequency is set to 1 KHz, as shown in Fig. 1(c), center-symmetric responses are observed. On the other hand, as shown in Fig. 1(d), the magnitude responses at the center frequency of 16 KHz are observed to be deformed toward the sampling frequency. This deformation is caused by the bilinear transform and may give an undesirable effect to the overall equalizer behavior. But, one can alleviate this deformation by increasing the sampling frequency.

2.2 Opposite Filters

The digital graphic equalizer can be formed by cascading k equalizer filters, each of which serves for the respective sub-band. Specifically, one equalizer filter is responsible for making the corresponding sub-band attenuated or augmented by the amount set by the user. At the same time, unfortunately, the neighboring sub-bands also suffer from considerable amount of undesired gain alteration, because the equalizer filter has a relatively long skirt extending to the neighboring sub-bands. Such an undesirable impact of a given equalizer filter on the neighboring sub-bands is called the inter-band interference. Due to the inter-band interference, the actual magnitude response is yielded as sum of both the nominal gain set by the user and the effects coming from the neighboring bands. So, the user's setting may not be faithfully reproduced using such an equalizer.

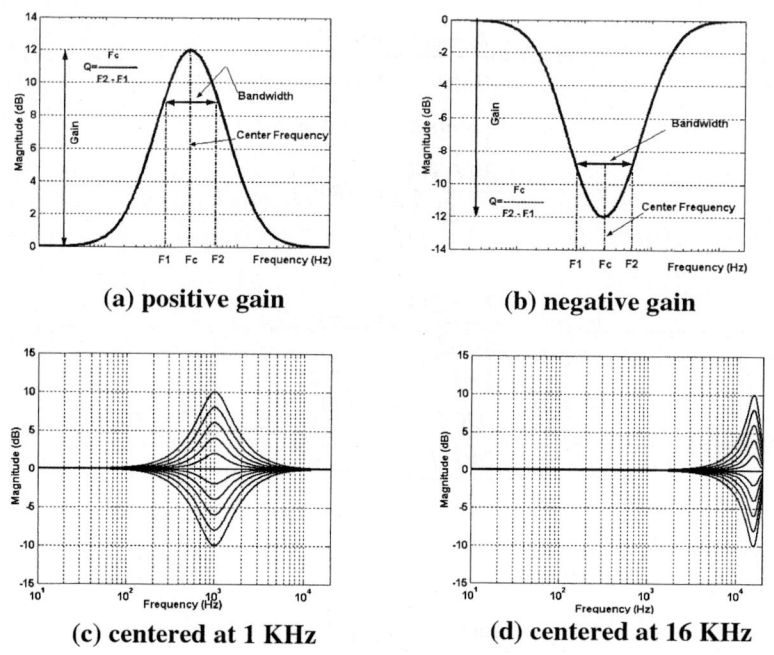

Fig. 1. Frequency responses of the equalizer filters

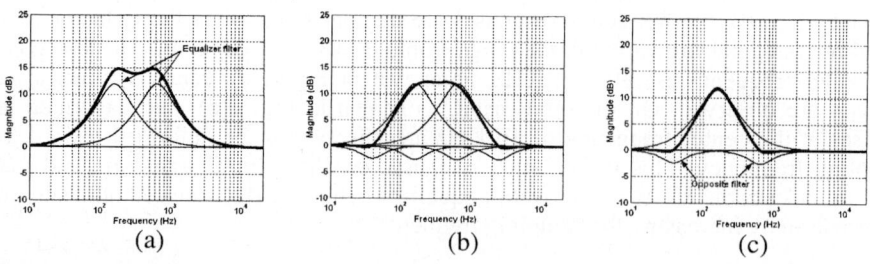

Fig. 2. Frequency responses illustrating inter-band interference; (a) without opposite filters; (b) with opposite filters; (c) sub-band 2 only.

Recently, Azizi [1] proposed the notion of opposite filters to alleviate the aforementioned inter-band interference. Fig. 2 illustrates the advantage of employing the opposite filters. In Fig. 2, the frequency response of a five-band equalizer is shown when the gains are set to 0, 12, 12, 0, and 0 dB from the lowest sub-band. The thin lines denote the frequency responses of the individual equalizer filters, while the thick line denotes the overall response. The frequency response without opposite filters, as shown in Fig. 2(a), reveals actual gains higher than the nominal gains of 12 dB at the second and third sub-bands due to the inter-band interference. When the opposite filters are employed, however, as shown in Fig. 2(b), the frequency response is observed to be very close to the nominal gains. The contribution of the opposite filters is well demonstrated in Fig. 2(c). Fig. 2(c) shows the magnitude responses of the equalizer filter for the second sub-band and its two associated filters called opposite filters. The equalizer filter maintains non-zero gain values at the center frequencies of the neighboring sub-bands, i.e., sub-band 1 and sub-band 3 in Fig. 2(c). Azizi placed the two opposite filters, which were centered at these two frequency locations but have the gains equal to those of the equalizer filter at these locations. Hence, the actual gains at the center frequencies of the neighboring sub-bands would be effectively cancelled out to zero. Azizi also set the Q-factors of the opposite filters to the values equal to the squared Q-factor of the equalizer filter. The Azizi's approach employing the opposite filters is disadvantageous in that there may be relatively large ripples observed where the gains are set to identical values. Furthermore, his approach shows a discrepancy between the user setting and the actual response of the graphic equalizer, especially when delicate user settings are applied.

3 Proposed Equalizer

In this section, the proposed adjusted-Q equalizer is described, by which the user's gain setting can be faithfully reproduced. In section 3.1, the adjusted-Q equalizer is presented. Then, in section 3.2, the adjusted-Q equalizers employing the opposite filters are introduced.

3.1 Adjusted-Q Equalizer

Let us consider an N-band graphic equalizer, which is composed of N equalizer filters with center frequencies $f_1, f_2, \cdots, f_N$. The kth equalizer filter is responsible for the kth sub-band, and is completely characterized by the center frequency f_k, the gain G_k at the center frequency, and the Q-factor Q_k. Among the three parameters, the center frequency is a constant in the graphic equalizer, and the gain is given by the user. So, in the proposed adjusted-Q equalizer, we try to adjust the Q-factor of each equalizer filter so that the actual response of the equalizer is very close to the user's gain setting.

Starting with the definition of the performance measure, let us describe the proposed equalizer in details. In our approach, the performance of the equalizer is measured in terms of the Euclidean distance E_2 between the desired magnitude response $D(f)$ set by the user and the actual magnitude response $|P(f)|$, defined as

$$E_2 = \int_{f_1}^{f_N} \left(|P(f)| - D(f) \right)^2 df . \tag{6}$$

Note that the actual magnitude response $|P(f)|$ of the graphic equalizer is obtained by product of the magnitude responses of the individual equalizer filters given by (3). In (6), the interval of the integration is confined within the range between the first and last center frequencies, since the outside of the range is considered to show a transient behavior. It should be noted that the desired response is generally given as a series of gain values at the N center frequencies. So, we can not compare the actual response with the desired response at all locations within the frequency range in consideration, since the desired response is not fully specified.

In our approach, it is assumed that the desired gain value is denoted as one of M values, $p_1, p_2, \cdots, p_M$. If we set all the gain values to the same value, the desired magnitude response will be $D(f) = p_i$ for all frequencies within the range. This gain setting is advantageous in that we can compute directly the Euclidean distance of (6) and the inter-band interference will be well demonstrated.

Then, assuming that the desired gain is set to p_i for all frequencies, the optimal Q-factor that minimizes the Euclidean distance of (6) can be found by

$$Q_i = \arg\min_{q \in S} \int_{f_1}^{f_N} \left(|P(f,q)| - p_i \right)^2 df , \qquad (7)$$

where S is a set of admissible Q-factors, which is in the range between 0 and 3 in a step of 0.01 in our approach. Here, it is noted that the Q-factor Q_i is a function only of the gain p_i, not of the center frequency f_k. Hence, the equalizer filters with the same gain have the identical Q-factor without respect to their center frequencies. It is observed, however, that we cannot design the equalizer filters for the two highest sub-bands together with the other filters, because the wrapping effect due to the bilinear transform becomes severe as shown in Fig. 1(d). Practically, we design simultaneously the (N-2) lowest equalizer filters for a given gain using (6). Then, the two highest equalizer filters are designed separately. Repeating this process for all M gain values, a complete set of the equalizer filters can be constructed. Now, we can perform the task of the equalizer using equalizer filters chosen properly in the set according to the user's gain setting.

3.2 Adjusted-Q Equalizer Employing the Opposite Filters

The adjusted-Q equalizer employing the opposite filters is composed of equalizer filters together with their associated opposite filters. Since the equalizer filter in (3) shows symmetric magnitude response as shown in Fig. 1, the two associated opposite filters have the same gain and Q-factor. In our approach, the gain of the equalizer filter follows the user's setting. On the other hand, the gain of the opposite filter will be set to the magnitude of the corresponding equalizer filter at the frequency location where the opposite filter is centered. Here, we try to find the proper Q-factors of both the equalizer filter and their associated opposite filters. In order to lead to a simplified design, similar to the description in the section 3.1, we assume that all the gains of the equalizer filters are set to the same value. Then, for a given gain value p_i, the optimal Q-factors Q_i of the equalizer filter and Q'_i of the opposite filter can be found by solving the problem, given by

$$\{Q_i, Q'_i\} = \arg\min_{q,\, q' \in S} \int_{f_1}^{f_N} \left(|P(f, q, q')| - p_i \right)^2 df . \tag{8}$$

In this paper, we design a set of the equalizer filters by performing the following procedure repeatedly for all M gain values. Firstly, for initialization, we try to find the proper Q-factor Q_i of the equalizer filters after setting $Q'_i = 0$. This process is equivalent to the one for the equalizer without opposite filters described in section 3.1. Secondly, we try to find the proper Q-factor Q'_i that can minimize the Euclidean distance of (6) while we leave Q_i unchanged. Thirdly, we try to find the proper Q-factor Q_i while we leave Q'_i unchanged. The last two steps are repeated until the performance measure will not be reduced any longer.

Now, it is worthy of noting that the performance of the equalizer depends on the configuration of the center frequencies of the equalizer filters. In this paper, we consider 3 configurations of the center frequencies, as presented in Table 1. In Table 1, the configuration 1 represents the usual layout of the center frequencies, which are apart by one octave from their neighbors around 1 KHz. In the configuration 2, the full audio band from 20 Hz to 20 KHz is partitioned into 10 equal-sized sub-bands in log scale. While the frequency corrections are made in the configuration 2, the center frequencies are left uncorrected after frequency wrapping by the bilinear transform in the configuration 3. So, it is observed that the higher sub-bands are shifted to lower frequency region.

Table 1. Three configurations of center frequencies in 10-band equalizer (unit: Hz)

sub-band configuration	1	2	3	4	5	6	7	8	9	10
configuration 1	31	63	125	250	500	1000	2000	4000	8000	16000
configuration 2	28	56	112	224	447	893	1782	3556	7096	14158
configuration 3	28	56	112	224	447	892	1774	3494	6643	11419

Table 2 shows an example of the Q-factors of the adjusted-Q equalizer employing the opposite filters, when it is designed using the above procedure. The results on the three different configurations are included in Table 2. Unlike the constant-Q equalizer, the proposed equalizer consists of the equalizer filters having the different Q-factors depending on the gain value. As shown in Table 2, the Q-factor Q of the equalizer filter becomes larger as the gain increases. Such an adjustment of Q-factor helps to reduce the inter-band interference, which grows more severe with increasing gain. For the associated opposite filters, the Q-factor Q' also becomes larger as the gain increases, but the increasing rate is relatively slow. The overvalued magnitude response at the neighboring center frequencies are cancelled out by setting the gain of the opposite filter equal to the value of the magnitude response of the equalizer filter at that frequency location. On the other hand, at the other frequency locations apart from the center frequencies, we can reduce the overvalued magnitude response by adjusting the Q-factor of the opposite filter. In this respect, one can obtain more faithful response by adjusting both the Q-factor of the equalizer filter and that of its associated opposite filters. Note that the opposite filter in the Azizi's approach [1] has the Q-factor equal to the squared Q-factor of the equalizer filter. The performance of the proposed equalizer will be examined in the next section.

Table 2. Example of Q-factors for the adjusted-Q equalizers employing the opposite filters

configuration gain (dB)	configuration 1		Configuration 2		configuration 3	
	Q	Q'	Q	Q'	Q	Q'
12	1.69	1.83	1.85	1.89	2.42	2.24
11	1.59	1.79	1.75	1.85	2.30	2.21
10	1.50	1.75	1.64	1.81	2.18	2.18
9	1.41	1.71	1.55	1.77	2.08	2.17
8	1.33	1.67	1.47	1.75	1.98	2.15
7	1.25	1.63	1.38	1.70	1.89	2.15
6	1.18	1.60	1.31	1.67	1.77	2.09
5	1.11	1.56	1.23	1.63	1.68	2.07
4	1.05	1.53	1.16	1.60	1.59	2.05
3	0.99	1.50	1.10	1.58	1.50	2.02
2	0.92	1.45	1.03	1.54	1.42	2.00
1	0.88	1.45	0.97	1.51	1.33	1.95

4 Simulation Results

In this section, the performance of the proposed adjusted-Q equalizer is compared with those of the conventional equalizers through the MATLAB simulations. In our experiments, audio signals are sampled at 48 KHz and 10-band equalizers are examined, while one can easily apply our approach to other equalizers.

Firstly, Fig. 3 shows the magnitude responses of the constant-Q equalizers when the configuration 1 in Table 1 is employed. The gains are identically assigned to all equalizer filters and varied from -10 dB to 10 dB in a 2 dB step. Also, as the name implies, all the Q-factors of the equalizer filters have the constant value of 1.4. As shown in Fig 3(a), the constant-Q equalizer without opposite filters reveals the actual magnitude response two or more times higher than the desired gain setting. This poor performance results mainly from the inter-band interference. On the other hand, as shown in Fig. 3(b) the equalizer with opposite filters provides the magnitude response close to the desired gain setting. So, we can see that the notion of the opposite filter is very effective in alleviating the inter-band interference. But, we can also observe its shortcoming in Fig. 3(b) that ripples are present when the desired gains are set relatively high. Note that the Q-factor of the opposite filter is also set to the constant of 1.4^2, as was used by Azizi [1].

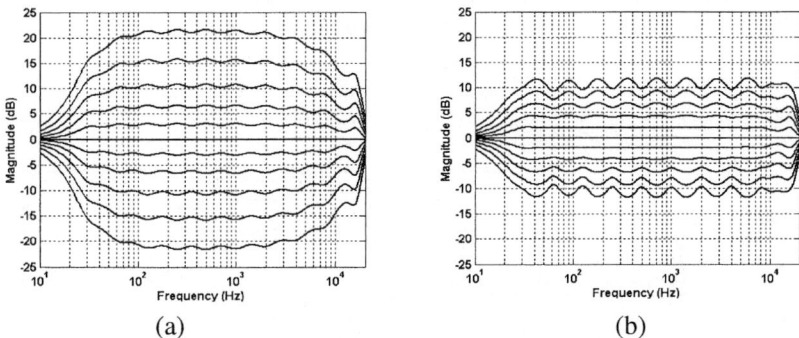

Fig. 3. Magnitude responses of 10-band constant-Q equalizer; (a) without opposite filter (Q=1.4); (b) with opposite filters (Q=1.4)

Next, the performance of the proposed equalizer is demonstrated in Fig. 4. In Fig. 4(a), we provide the magnitude response of the adjusted-Q equalizer without opposite filters, where the configuration 1 is adopted for the layout of the center frequencies and the set of equalizer filters are designed using the procedure described in section 3.1. Fig 4(a) demonstrates well the advantage of the proposed adjusted-Q equalizer. As compared with Fig. 3(a), the adjusted-Q equalizer in Fig. 4(a) reduces significantly the inter-band interference, limiting the magnitude response within about 1.5 times the desired gain setting. But, it shows more pronounced ripples. Fig. 4 (b), (c), and (d) show the magnitude responses of the adjusted-Q equalizers employing the opposite filters, when the configurations 1, 2, and 3 are used, respectively. Here, the corresponding set of the equalizer filters shown in Table 2 is used for each configuration. As shown in Fig. 4 (b)-(d), the adjusted-Q equalizer employing the opposite filters yields much improved performance, as compared with the other equalizers. Like the constant-Q equalizer employing the opposite filters, the overvalued magnitude response is not observed in Fig. (b)-(d). But, the size of ripples is greatly reduced by the proposed equalizer. This good performance comes from the fact that the inter-band interference is significantly alleviated by employing the opposite filters, especially at the frequency locations where the equalizer filters are centered. Furthermore, by adjusting the Q-factors of both the equalizer filter and the opposite filters, we can achieve a much smooth curve, which is observed nearly flat at all frequency range in consideration.

Here, it should be noted that the frequency wrapping due to the bilinear transform causes some degradations in the equalizer performance. Specifically, Fig. 4(d) uses the configuration 3 in Table 1, in which the wrapped center frequencies of the equalizer filters are left uncorrected and are shrunk toward the low frequency. On the other hand, Fig. 4 (b) and (c) use the configuration 1 and 2, respectively, in which the wrapped center frequencies are corrected to maintain the intended frequencies even after the bilinear transform. As shown in Fig. 4(d), the proposed equalizer using the configuration 3 provides the better performance than those using the other configurations. Here, no significant ripples are observed while the magnitude response is nearly identical to the desired gain setting. Hence, it is recommended that the center frequencies of the equalizer filters are left unchanged after the bilinear transform in the applications where the exact layout of the center frequencies is not required.

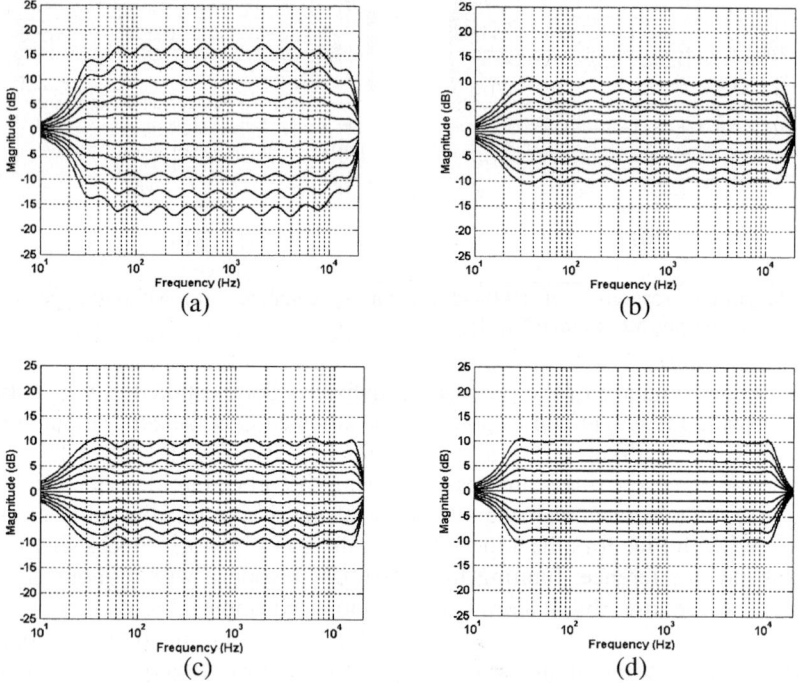

Fig. 4. Magnitude response of 10-band adjusted-Q equalizers; (a) without opposite filter (configuration 1); (b) with opposite filters (configuration 1); (c) with opposite filters (configuration 2); (d) with opposite filters (configuration 3)

Lastly, in order to examine the performance in actual applications, the performance of the adjusted-Q equalizer with the opposite filters is compared, using a realistic gain setting, with those of the constant-Q equalizers with and without opposite filters, and the adjusted-Q equalizer without opposite filters. All the 4 equalizers have the same center frequency layout of the configuration 3. And the desired gains are set to 2, -12, 8, 4, -10, 6, 10, -4, -4, and 0 dB, starting with the lowest sub-band. The results are shown in Fig. 5, where the thin lines indicate the magnitude responses of the individual equalizer filters and the thick lines denote the overall equalizer responses. As is expected, the constant-Q equalizer does not respond to sharp differences in gain between neighboring sub-bands. However, both the constant-Q equalizer with opposite filters and the adjusted-Q equalizer without opposite filters show quite an improved performance. Among the 4 equalizers, the proposed adjusted-Q equalizer employing opposite filters demonstrates the magnitude response nearly identical to the desired gain setting. It is observed in Fig. 5(d) that the proposed equalizer can reproduce faithfully even the small detailed gain values as well as the abrupt differences in gain between neighboring sub-bands.

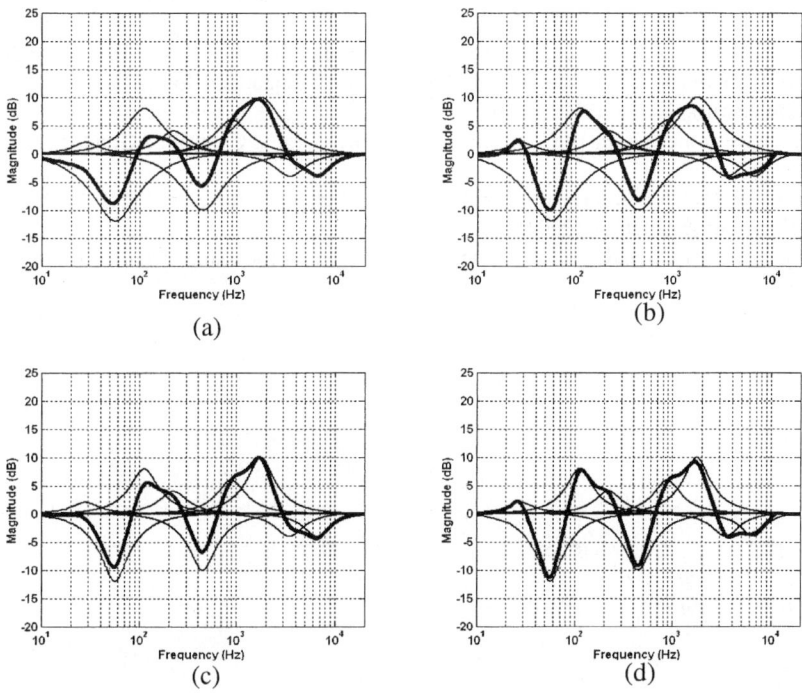

Fig. 5. Performance comparison between the 4 different equalizers; (a) constant-Q equalizer without opposite filter (Q=1.4); (b) constant-Q with opposite filters (Q=1.4, Q'=1.4^2); (c) adjusted-Q without opposite filter; (d) adjusted-Q with opposite filters

5 Conclusions

In this paper, we presented the adjusted-Q equalizer, in which the Q-factor of the equalizer filter was adjusted depending on the gain value. By incorporating it with the notion of the opposite filters, we also proposed the adjusted-Q equalizer employing the opposite filters. The algorithm for designing the proposed equalizer was described. The proposed equalizer was designed with all the gain settings to an identical value, so that the inter-band interference was effectively alleviated in all frequency range in consideration. As a result, it was demonstrated in simulations that the proposed adjusted-Q equalizer employing the opposite filers could reproduce the user's gain settings faithfully even if there existed sharp differences in user's gain settings between neighboring sub-bands. Hence, the proposed equalizer can be effectively applied to audio systems to respond faithfully the user's preference and characteristics.

References

1. Azizi, S. A.: A New Concept of Interference Compensation for Parametric and Graphic Equalizer Banks. 111th AES Convention (2001) 5482
2. Bohn, D.: Constant-Q Graphic Equalizers. J. Audio Eng. Soc., Vol. 34. (1986) 611–626
3. Lee, Y. H., Kim, R. C.: A Variable-Q Digital Graphic Equalizer. Journal of Korea Broadcast Engineering, Vol. 8. (2003) 3–10
4. STMicroelectronics Group of Companies: Five Bands Digital Controlled Graphic Equalizer. Data Sheet (1999)
5. ISO/IEC IS 21000-7: Information Technology-Multimedia Framework (MPEG-21) – Part 9: Digital Item Adaptation. (2004)
6. Oppenheim, A. V., Schafer, R. W.: Discrete-Time Signal Processing. Prentice-Hall (1998)

Interactive Transfer of Human Facial Color

Kyoung Chin Seo[1], Giroo Shin[2], and Sang Wook Lee[1]

[1] Dept. of Media Technology,
Sogang University, Sinsu-Dong, Mapo-Gu, Seoul, Korea
{jiniseo, slee}@sogang.ac.kr
[2] GOMID Co.Ltd., 1005 Daechi-Dong, Gangnam-Gu,Seoul, Korea
grshin@gomid.com

Abstract. This paper focuses on a new and intuitive method for transferring and modifying human skin color based on statistical and photometric clues between two photographs. We construct skin color transfer model for both photographs by clustering pixels along the direction of principal vector as a result of least square fitting. Color and texture features of source skin is transferred to that of target skin by changing Gaussian distribution of each pair of the matched clusters. Discarding or selecting the clusters including specular component also enables to generate various tones of skin color. Interactive tuning of each color cluster adds various effects like weakening the color of flush and exaggerating the traits of face with make-up. We demonstrate realistic skin color transfer results improved from previous works and intuitive handling of skin colors by the skin color transfer model.

1 Introduction

"Color transfer" has been investigated recently to modify the color of a picture (called *target* image) using the color distribution of another image (called *source* image), and a small number of methods have been proposed for general objects and scenes [1]. Most of the existing methods are developed for changing color tone of an entire image rather than modifying the color of a specific object region of interest. In this paper, we focus on the transfer of human facial colors.

Applications of facial color transfer include photograph retouching and image matting. Let us consider the case that we have a photograph of a face (*target*) and like to make its skin colors look like those in another photograph (*source*). We may often find it very difficult to modify the source color distribution to match the target distribution manually using image manipulating software such as Adobe Photoshop^{TM}and GIMP. This is because the source and the target color distributions cannot be made similar simply by adjusting color parameters such as *RGB* or hue, saturation and intensity. The existing color transfer algorithms developed for images with general scenes may not be able to convey the subtle nuance of the target color tones to the source image.

The approach by Reinhard *et al.* is one of the first in image color transfer [1]. It transfers colors using statistical parameters such as the ratio of standard deviations of the source and target images in the $l\alpha\beta$ space. Welsh *et al.* developed a method for coloring gray images from target color image [2]. These approaches do not focus on

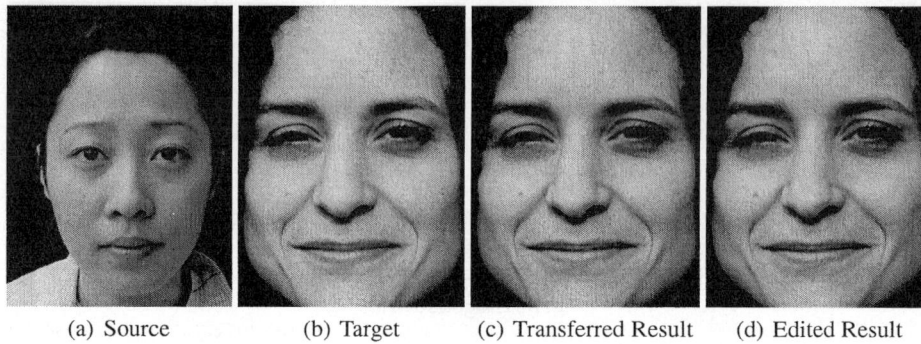

(a) Source　　　　(b) Target　　　(c) Transferred Result　　(d) Edited Result

Fig. 1. Demonstration of a result using skin color transfer and synthesis system

specific object regions but deal with the scene colors of general images. Recently, Levin et al. show interactive coloring of images including multiple textures [3]. They use user-specified lines for initializing regions for segmentation and apply a tracking algorithm to transfer automatically colors onto the next frame.

Other approaches to the transfer of image attributes include texture transfer. Efros et al. presented a simple bit effective method for synthesizing a new texture image from a small texture element [4][5]. This was achieved by transferring a texture element repeatedly in a seamless manner. The "image analogy" method was developed by Hertzmann et al. for transforming image texture using example transformations of other images [6]. The approaches mentioned above are effective for highly varying image textures, but not for gradually shaded regions such as those of human skins.

There have been a few reflectance models for complex human skins. The translucent nature of skin layers was modelled as subsurface scattering by Hanrahan et al. and Jensen et al., but its impact on color appearance has not been investigated [7][8]. Image-based rendering technique is also used to generate realistic skin texture [9][10]. A more biologically oriented approach was given in [11]. In this work, the structure of skin is interpreted as two (melanin and hemoglobin) or three (epidermis, dermis, sub-cutaneous fat) distinctive layers. With this model, Tsumura et al. proposed a layer decomposition method based on the ICA of skin colors [12]. They also presented an approach to color decomposition and synthesis using a linear combination of melanin and hemoglobin pigments [13].

In this paper, we present an interactive color transfer method which is developed specifically for human facial color based on the analysis of skin color distribution in a color space. The presented method utilizes the elongated nature of color clusters from human skins, and determines the statistical parameters for transfer along the major color axes. Furthermore, it lets the human operator interactively adjust the contribution of specular portion in the image irradiance to create varying degrees of shininess and visual impressions of skin surface. We do not explicitly use the multi-layer models for color analysis. Instead, we focus on the specular and diffuse components of surface reflections based on the dichromatic model [14].

The remainder of this paper is organized as follows: Section 2 introduces a model for representing of skin colors. In section 3, we present our skin color transfer and editing methods using the skin color transfer model. Next, we describe editing technique to control the amount of specular component in section 3.1. Section 4 discusses some implementation issues and experimental results and Section 5 concludes the paper.

2 Skin Color Transfer Model

In this section, we define a skin color transfer model to represent color distribution of human skin. Figure 2 depicts the skin color distribution of 6 different people in RGB space. We can see that the skin colors are generally distributed along the lighting direction. We also observe that two groups of colors are distinctively grouped into diffuse and specular component. The amount of diffuse and specular components varies substantially since each face has different distribution of color pigments and the photographs are taken under different lighting conditions with different cameras. Although skin colors form clusters in various shapes, the elongated structure of the clusters is preserved for all skin color images. We use this structural trait for our model.

Another example as illustrated in Figure 3 describes changes of color distribution between skin without make-up and skin with make-up for the same person. The color distribution in a chromaticity space between skin is preserved while its color is changed by cosmetics.

From the distributions of skin color data, it can be seen that the skin color clusters form elongated structures and their slope is determined by illumination and skin colors. As predicted by the dichromatic model, the structure consists of diffuse and specular reflections and the degree of bending results from the dissimilarity of the two reflection components in color [14]. Despite the bend, however, the the overall elongated structure is largely preserved for most skin colors we examined.

In this paper, we define an approximate line to represent the direction of the whole skin color cluster as *the principal line*. The principal line **L** is calculated by least square fitting. Finite numbers of clusters(called *bins*) are formed by dividing the whole clusters

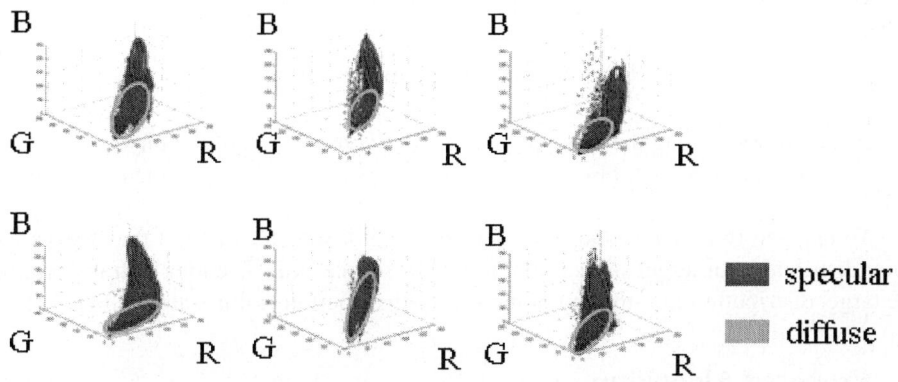

Fig. 2. Color distribution of 6 persons' skin region in RGB space

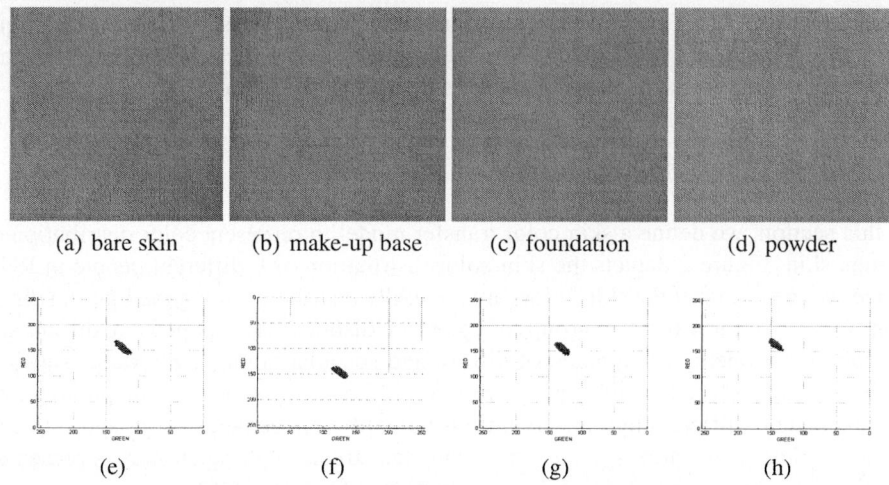

Fig. 3. Color distribution by applying make-up: Three basic cosmetics, make-up base, foundation, and powder are gradually added to bare skin of one person. Lower figures show color distribution of corresponding upper images in chromaticity space.

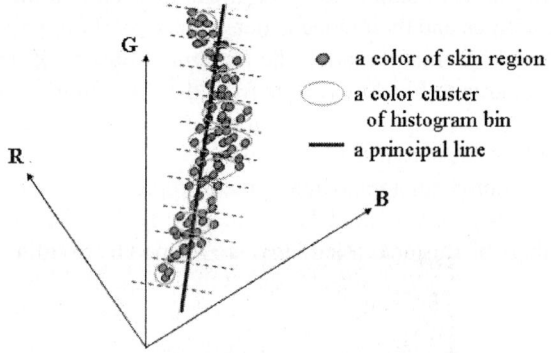

Fig. 4. Illustration of skin color model

in uniform interval along the principal line **L**. The construction of the bins is similar to that of histogram. For each bin, we calculate Gaussian statistical parameters as shown in Figure 4.

We analyze two facial images to develop a color transfer method that makes the color distribution of target skin similar to that of source skin. The idea of transforming the target distribution in imitation of the source distribution is illustrated in Figure 5.

3 Proposed Algorithm

Based on the skin color analysis, we develop a skin color transfer and editing algorithm. The basic idea is:

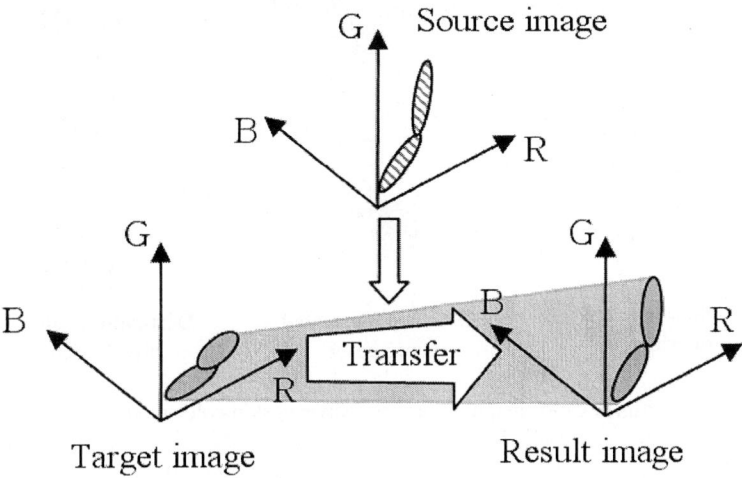

Fig. 5. Basic idea for skin color transfer

1) to divide the source and target color clusters into equal number of bins along the principal line, respectively,

2) to establish artificial correspondences between the source and target color bins in the RGB space, and

3) to warp the target distribution in imitation of the source distribution using the statistical (Gaussian) characteristics of source color clusters such as the principal line and the color variance in the source bins.

We can also vary the appearance of specular reflections by interactively adjusting their contributions to the principal line computation and color bin construction. The most critical stage in our color transfer algorithm for warping the target color distribution is to establish the relationships between the source and target color bins. To deal with the shape of gaussian distribution of each bin, we calculate mapping relationship between divided bins along the principal line for both images. Transferring and editing process are executed using each mapped bins. Figure 6 shows the details of the process for transferring and mapping.

Firstly, we construct skin color transfer model for both images. From source image and destination(target) image, we collect skin color pixels denoted by I_s and I_d, respectively, where s and d denote the source and target images, respectively. Principal lines $\mathbf{L}_s$ and $\mathbf{L}_d$ are calculated by standard least square fitting of I_s and I_d in the RGB space. For each principal line, we find line segments with equal interval. I_s and I_d based on these line segments, which we call bin. The bins for source and destination images are given by:

$$B_s(i) = \{\mathbf{C}_s^t | i = \arg\min \| \mathbf{C}_s^t - z_s^i \|^2, \mathbf{C}_s^t \in I_s, t = 1, \cdots, l\} \tag{1}$$

$$B_d(j) = \{\mathbf{C}_d^t | j = \arg\min \| \mathbf{C}_d^t - z_d^j \|^2, \mathbf{C}_d^t \in I_d, t = 1, \cdots, m\} \tag{2}$$

where z_s^i and z_d^j mean the centroid of each line segment and i and j are the indices of specific segment.

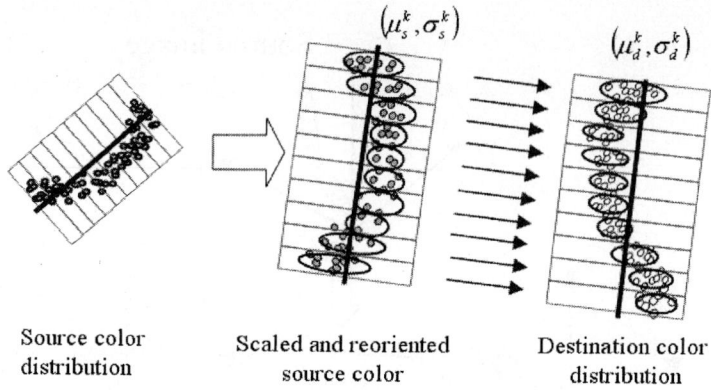

Source color distribution   Scaled and reoriented source color   Destination color distribution

Fig. 6. Color mapping process between skin color models

Secondly, we scale all $B_s(i)$ and $B_d(j)$ to have same number of bins. As a result of scaling, all $B_s(i)$ and $B_d(j)$ are scaled into $\tilde{B}_s(k)$ and $\tilde{B}_d(k)$ with same index k of bins. The number of bins are N. This process facilitates the transfer of color individually between matched bins.

Thirdly, color transfer algorithm is applied between the matched bins. We describe Gaussian distribution of colors in each bin as mean and standard deviation. We denote mean of colors in the bin $\tilde{B}_s(k)$ by μ_s^k and its standard deviation by σ_s^k. For $\tilde{B}_d(k)$, we compute μ_d^k and σ_d^k respectively. To transfer source skin color onto destination(target) skin color, we define a transfer function given by:

$$\mathbf{C}_{r,i}^k = \mathbf{F}(\mathbf{C}_{d,i}^k, \mathbf{C}_{s,i}^k) \qquad (3)$$

where $\mathbf{C}_{r,i}^k$ means transferred result of ith color pixel in kth bin for the target image. We subtract mean μ_d^k of bin $\tilde{B}_d(k)$ of destination skin region from color $\mathbf{C}_{d,i}^k$ in corresponding bin. The difference are scaled by multiplying a weight expressed as ratio of standard deviation:

$$\mathbf{F}(\mathbf{C}_{d,i}^k, \mathbf{C}_{s,i}^k) = \mu_s^k + \frac{\sigma_s^k}{\sigma_d^k}(\mathbf{C}_{d,i}^k - \mu_d^k) \qquad (4)$$

The function $\mathbf{F}$ enables to transfer color distribution from source image to target image while the shading characteristics of the target image are kept. Moreover, the details of skin texture are transferred onto the target image because the transfer function $\mathbf{F}$ is calculated between the matched bins.

3.1 Adjustment of Specular Component

In this section, we propose an editing method for handling specular component of skin color cluster. When we apply conventional color transfer algorithms using photographs taken under different lighting conditions, the algorithms sometimes produce wrong results with saturated colors. The problem is mainly originated from the mismatch of

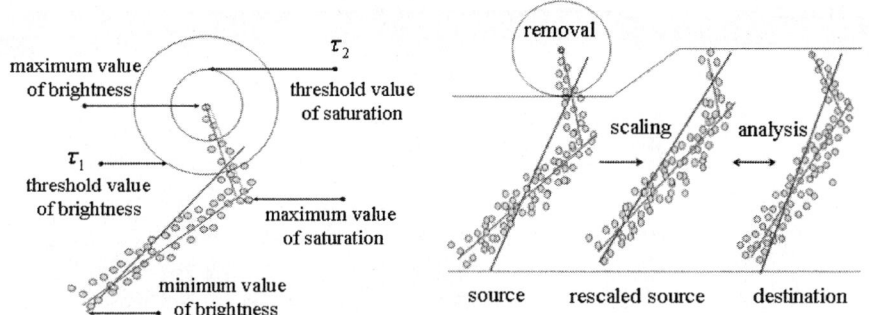

(a) two threshold values for removing specular component (b) processes of adjustment of specular component

Fig. 7. Adjustement of amounts of specular colors

specular components between two skin color transfer models. To avoid this artifact, it is necessary to adjust amounts of specular colors or discard all the specular component.

Under the skin color transfer model, we easily solve this problem by discarding some of clusters(*bins* as described before) including specular component. Figure 7 illustrates our idea to handle this problem. At first, we find the bins including specular colors from source skin color model and then we decide how many bins are discard. After bins including specular colors are discarded, the remained bins are scaled to match the bins of the target(destination) image. Transferring algorithm are executed between two matched clusters after re-scaling bins of the skin color transfer model for source image.

To discard adaptable amounts of specular component interactively, we define two threshold values, τ_1 and τ_2 as depicted in Figure 7(a). τ_1 is denoted as a threshold value for high intensity(Value) in the HSV space. τ_2 is a threshold value for saturation. The reason for choosing these two values is that specular colors have high intensity values and low saturated values in the HSV color space.

Figure 7(b) illustrates how to manipulate specular component using these threshold values. We collect bins which brightness exists from τ_1 to maximum brightness. Among the selected colors, we decide the colors that corresponding saturation value is under τ_2 as specular colors. After removing the selected colors of source skin region, we re-scale bins composed of remained colors to match the bins of target skin color. Newly scaled histogram is applied to the proposed skin color transfer algorithm.

4 Experimental Results

We demonstrate our experimental results generated by our proposed method. We performed experiments with various images captured by digital camera and selected from face database [15]. For comparison, we implemented Reinhard's method[1] in addition to ours. As shown in Figure 10, the results by the proposed algorithm have more detailed color variation compared to those of the previous method because the shading of

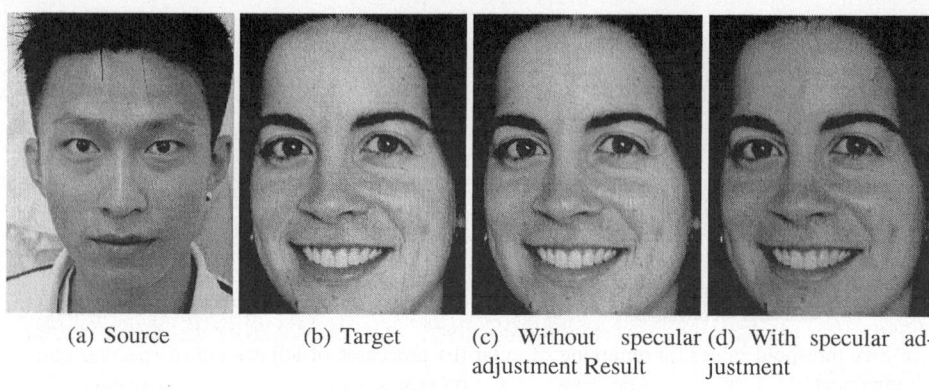

(a) Source (b) Target (c) Without specular adjustment Result (d) With specular adjustment

Fig. 8. Comparison with and without specular adjustment

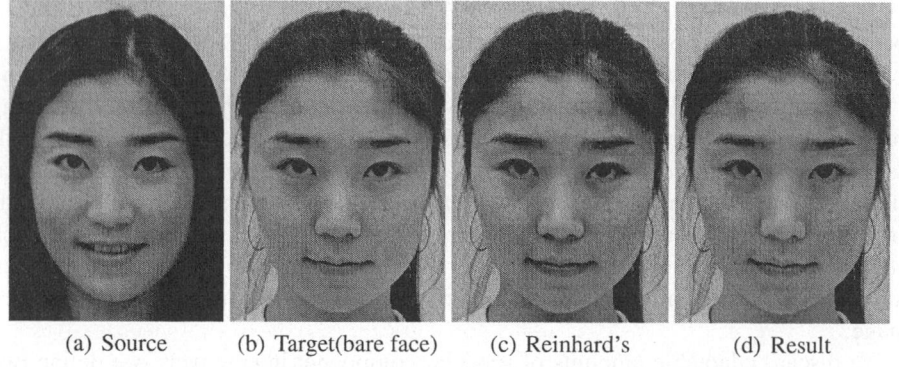

(a) Source (b) Target(bare face) (c) Reinhard's (d) Result

Fig. 9. Color transfer result between skin with and without make-up

destination image is preserved when the source skin colors are transferred. Modified results by adjustment of specular component show that artifacts like blurred red or yellow color in the face is reduced and mixed with other colors.

Figure 8 shows the results adjusting specular colors. By controlling the amount of specularity contribution in the color transfer, we can fine-tune the color appearance in the result. This effect is shown in Figure 8(c) and 8(d). The colors of transferred image are more similar to the source skin color after specularity adjustment.

Color transfer results between bare skin and skin with makeup are shown in Figure 9. Once we have a color transfer model for skin with makeup, we can modify the face of bare skin to create the effect of wearing cosmetics. It may be noted in the results shown in Figure 9(d) that the bluish colors around the eyes in the source image are not properly transferred. This is because our algorithm uses one representative color cluster for transferring all the colors in the whole face regions and the bluish colors are treated as a part of the skin color cluster. Segmentation of this distinctively different colors and independent transfer to a specific region may solve this problem, but this is beyond the scope of this paper.

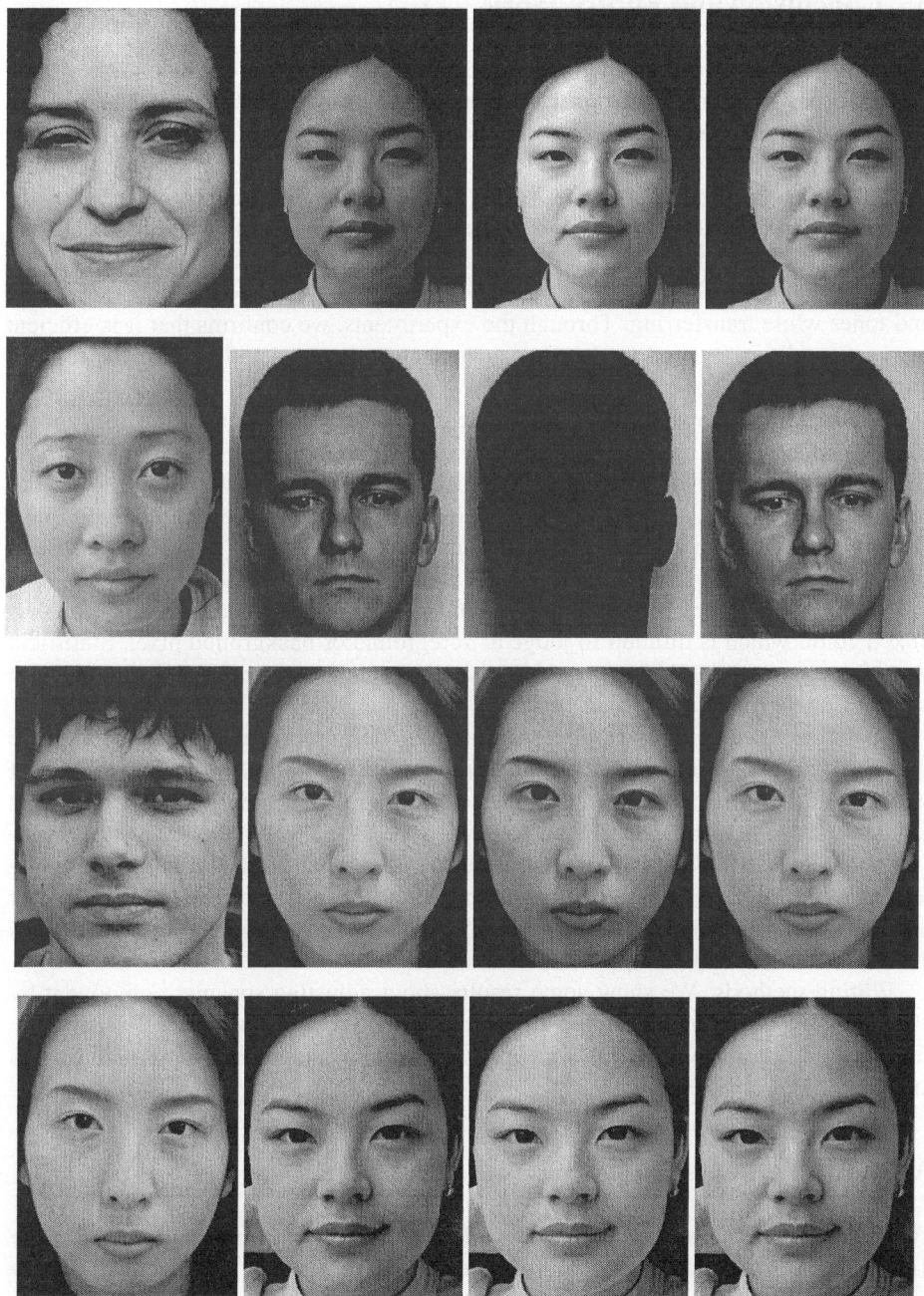

Fig. 10. Results. First column: the source image. Second column: the target image. Third column: Reinhard's method. Fourth column: the proposed method.

5 Conclusion and Future Work

We have been presented an interactive method to transfer skin colors onto new one. First, we design a practical model to represent color characteristics of human skin. Using this model, we propose a new method to manipulate skin colors from example images. Our algorithm shows that more realistic detail of source skin is transplanted to target image compared to previous works. Skin colors under different lighting conditions are easily transferred unlike the previous works since our algorithm has a scaling process along the principal line to protect saturated results.

Under our skin color model, we also develop an editing method to adjust specularity and tones while transferring. Through the experiments, we confirms that it is efficient to use the editing method to decrease specular components and change the tone of transferred results.

In addition to our algorithm, following future works are considered to improve results:

Local principal lines: This paper assumes that the skin has no color make-up to violate skin color model based on the principal line. In many cases, photographs have various color make-up and lighting conditions beyond ideal white light source. Distant color clusters can be processed individually along the the different lines.

Matting techniques: For example, boundary regions between hair and skin has mixed color, which is difficult to judge as foreground or background pixel. Statistical approach presented in [16][17] enable to generate seamless composite results without seam for final production of face image.

Spatial and temporal constraints: Our skin model represented in color space lose spatial information. For preserving local traits of skin texture, we need take care of spatial relationship. For example, the representation model including spatial constraints can be useful to overcome the weakness.

Asymmetric color distribution: In this paper, we use Gaussian distribution for transferring algorithm. The Gaussian distribution can not specify the orientation of the color distribution and the shape of asymmetric distribution. To represent color distributions in detail, we need more complex statistical models.

Editing methods: We show some results about adjusting specular component by discarding bins over the threshold value in the skin color transfer model. Furthermore, advanced editing methods such as picking or discarding some color bins enable users to control color tones efficiently.

Acknowledgments

This work was supported by the Intelligent Robotics Development Program, one of the 21st Century Frontier R&D Programs funded by the Ministry of Commerce, Industry and Energy of Korea.

References

[1] Reinhard, E., Ashikhmin, M., Gooch, B., Shirley, P.: Color transfer between images. In: Computer Graphics and Applications, IEEE. Volume 21(4)., IEEE (2001) 34–41
[2] Welsh, T., Ashikhmin, M., Mueller, K.: Transferring color to greyscale images. In: Proceedings of SIGGRAPH 2002, ACM Press / ACM SIGGRAPH (2002) 277–280
[3] Levin, A., Lischinski, D., Weiss, Y.: Colorization using optimization. ACM Trans. Graph. **23** (2004) 689–694
[4] Efros, A.A., Freeman, W.T.: Image quilting for texture synthesis and transfer. In: Proceedings of SIGGRAPH 2001, ACM Press / ACM SIGGRAPH (2001) 341–346
[5] Efros, A.A., Leung, T.K.: Texture synthesis by non-parametric sampling. In: Computer Vision, 1999. The Proceedings of the Seventh IEEE International Conference on. Volume 2. (1999) 1033–1038
[6] Hertzmann, A., Jacobs, C.E., Oliver, N., Curless, B., Salesin, D.H.: Image analogies. In: Proceedings of SIGGRAPH 2001, ACM Press / ACM SIGGRAPH (2001) 327–340
[7] Hanrahan, P., Krueger, W.: Reflection from layered surfaces due to subsurface scattering. In: Proceedings of the 20th annual conference on Computer graphics and interactive techniques, ACM Press (1993) 165–174
[8] Jensen, H., Marschner, S., Levoy, M., Hanrahan, P.: A practical model for subsurface light transport. In: Proceedings of SIGGRAPH 2001. (2001) 511–518
[9] Marschner, S.R., Westin, S.H., Lafortune, E.P.F., Torrance, K.E., Greenberg, D.P.: Image-based brdf measurement including human skin. In: Proceedings of 10th Eurographics Workshop on Rendering. (1999) 139–152
[10] Debevec, P., Hawkins, T., Tchou, C., Duiker, H.P., Sarokin, W., Sagar, M.: Acquiring the reflectance field of a human face. In: SIGGRAPH '00: Proceedings of the 27th annual conference on Computer graphics and interactive techniques. (2000) 145–156
[11] van Gemert, M., Jacques, S., Sterenborg, H., W.M.Star: Skin optics. IEEE Transactions on Biomedical Engineering **36** (1989) 1146–1154
[12] Tsumura, N., Haneishi, H., Miyake, Y.: Independent component analysis of skin color image. Journal of Optical Society of America **16** (1999) 2169–2176
[13] Tsumura, N., Ojima, N., Sato, K., Shiraishi, M., Shimizu, H., Nabeshima, H., Akazki, S., Hori, K., Miyake, Y.: Image-based skin color and texture analysis/synthesis by extracting hemoglobin and melanin information in the skin. In: Proceedings of SIGGRAPH 2003. Computer Graphics Proceedings, Annual Conference Series, ACM Press / ACM SIGGRAPH (2003) 770–779
[14] Klinker, G., Shafer, S., Kanade, T.: A physical approach to color image understanding. IJCV **4** (1990) 7–38
[15] Marszalec, E., Martinkauppi, B., Soriano, M., Pietikainen, M.: A physics-based face database for color research. Journal of Electronic Imaging **9** (2000) 32–38
[16] Chuang, Y.Y., Curless, B., Salesin, D.H., Szeliski, R.: A bayesian approach to digital matting. In: Proceedings of IEEE CVPR 2001. Volume 2., IEEE Computer Society (2001) 264–271
[17] Sun, J., Jia, J., Tang, C.K., Shum, H.Y.: Poisson matting. ACM Trans. Graph. **23** (2004) 315–321

Panoramic Mesh Model Generation from Multiple Range Data for Indoor Scene Reconstruction[*]

Wonwoo Lee and Woontack Woo

GIST U-VR Lab.,
Gwangju 500-712, S. Korea
{wlee, wwoo}@gist.ac.kr

Abstract. In this paper, we propose a panoramic mesh modeling method from multiple range data for indoor scene reconstruction. The input to the proposed method is several sets of point clouds obtained from different viewpoints. An integrated mesh model is generated from the input point clouds. Firstly, we partition the input point cloud to sub-point clouds according to each camera's viewing frustum. Then, we sample the partitioned sub-point clouds adaptively and triangulate the sampled point cloud. Finally, we merge all triangulated models of sub-point clouds to represent the whole indoor scene as one model. Our method considers occlusion between two adjacent views and it filters out invisible part of point cloud without any prior knowledge. While preserving the features of the scene, adaptive sampling reduces the size of resulting mesh model for practical usage. The proposed method is modularized and applicable to the other modeling applications which handle multiple range data.

1 Introduction

Virtual environment (VE) generation is one of major task in virtual reality (VR) applications. The realism of the VE is important since it increase users' immersion to the virtual world. VE is usually created by computer graphic (CG) modeling software, such as Maya and 3DS Max. However, constructing large VE with 3D CG modeling software requires much time and effort. To create realistic VE, we have to design everything of the environment to be modeled before modeling. In this regard, VE generation by modeling the real scene is one of solutions for constructing realistic VE.

With increasing interest in this area, there have been many researches on VE generation from the real scene. One approach is using range scanners to obtain 3D data from the real environment [1][2][3][12][13][14]. The environment is scanned and 3D information of the environment is obtained as point clouds. Textures obtained from the photos of the environment are mapped to the reconstructed model for realism. Range scanners provide accurate data, however they are designed for scanning objects in short distance. Thus, it is inconvenient for modeling large area. In addition, the

---

[*] This work was supported in part by MIC through RBRC at GIST, and in part by CTRC at GIST.

range scanners are not affordable in general usage and used in few limited purposes. Another approach is reconstructing environment by extracting 3D information from multi-view images [4]. 3D structure of the environment is generated from relationship among the images. Using cameras for 3D reconstruction contains noises compared with the approach exploiting range scanner. Panoramic images of the environment are also used in modeling [5][6][15]. Panoramic images are taken by omni-directional cameras and 3D scene is reconstructed. There are many different approaches of modeling the real scene, however mesh modeling from 3D data is commonly needed to create surface from the 3D point data.

In this paper, we propose a panoramic mesh model generation method from multiple range data for indoor scene reconstruction. We use 3D vision-based modeling method to create mesh models from multiple noisy range data. The 3D point clouds are obtained from multiple viewpoints and all point clouds are registered in 3D space. The input to the proposed modeling method is the registered point clouds and reconstructed camera matrices of all viewpoints. Firstly, we partition the input point cloud to several sub-point clouds according to each camera's viewing frustum. Then, we sample the partitioned sub-point clouds adaptively and generate a mesh model from each sampled point cloud by triangulation. Finally, we merge all triangulated models of all the partitions to represent the whole indoor scene as one model. The modeling sequence of the proposed method is shown in Fig 1.

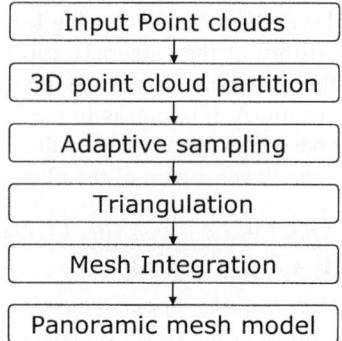

Fig. 1. Panoramic mesh modeling process

Our mesh modeling method considers occlusion between two adjacent views and it filters out invisible part of point cloud without any prior knowledge. While preserving the features of the scene, adaptive sampling reduces the size of resulting mesh model for practical usage. The proposed method is modularized and applicable to the other modeling applications which handle multiple range data.

The rest of this paper is organized as follows. We explain the proposed mesh modeling method in chapter 2. The experimental results and analysis are described in chapter 3. Conclusions and future work are presented in chapter 4.

2 Panoramic Mesh Modeling from Multiple Range Data

2.1 Data Acquisition

In data acquisition step, we obtain 3D data of the indoor environment to be modeled as point clouds using a multi-view camera. The multi-view camera gives a 3D point cloud of a view. To obtain accurate data, we calibrate the multi-view camera and we calculate the instrinsic parameters. The relationship between two adjacent viewpoints is calculated using a co-planar pattern. The data obtained from a viewpoint has its own reference coordinate system. We register all data to locate them in a common reference coordinate system using projection-based registration method [7]. The registered point clouds and the reconstructed camera matrices are input to the modeling process.

2.2 3D Point Cloud Partition

As the first step of the proposed mesh modeling method, we partition input point cloud of the indoor scene into sub-point clouds. Since we obtain 3D points of a view using 3D vision theory, each 3D point of a point cloud corresponds to each pixel of the image captured from a viewpoint. Triangulation of pixels generates naive mesh model of the point cloud. The normal vector of each 3D point is calculated using the triangles around the vertex. We exploit these initial 3D meshes to partition visible points only.

To do partition, we consider each camera's viewing frustum. We discard the points which are outside viewing frustum of the camera. 6 planes surrounding the viewing frustum are calculated and the directions of normal vectors of the planes are set to face inside of the viewing frustum. A 3D point is in the viewing frustum, if the point is upper region of all the planes. This property is evaluated according to equation 1. For a plane L_i, a point p_k is in the lower region of the plane L_i, if γ is negative.

$$\begin{aligned} L_i &= a_i x + b_i y + c_i z + d_i \qquad p_k : (x_k, y_k, z_k) \\ & a_i x_k + b_i y_k + c_i z_k + d_i = \gamma \\ & \gamma \geq 0 : p_k \text{ is in the upper region} \\ & \gamma < 0 : p_k \text{ is in the lower region} \end{aligned} \qquad (1)$$

Then, we determine if a point in the viewing frustum is visible to the camera or not. For the points in the viewing frustum, visibility confidence is calculated as shown in equation 2.

$$Visibility\ confidence = -\frac{Dot(V_{cam}, N_k)}{d^2} \qquad (2)$$

where, V_{cam} is the normalized vector of the camera's viewing direction and N_k is the normalized normal vector of the point. d is the distance between the camera and the point p_k. $Dot(V_{cam}, N_k)$ is dot product between two vectors.

If the point is visible to camera the confidence value is positive. If not, we assume that the point is not visible from current viewpoint. As shown in Fig 2, the point set S_2 is not visible to the camera C_1, but is visible to C_2. Even though it is not visible to C_1, it is in the viewing frustum of C_1. After the confidence value is calculated, the point set S_2 is culled out. Some part of S_3 is visible to C_1 and C_3, simultaneously. In this case the point is assigned to the partition where the point has the largest confidence value. As a result of partitioning, we obtain sub-point clouds S_ks and each sub-point cloud S_k is associated to each camera C_k.

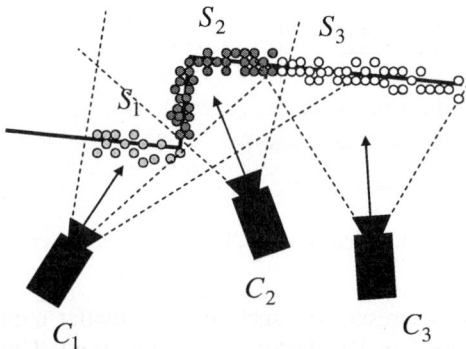

Fig. 2. 3D point cloud partition with viewing frustum

2.3 Adaptive Sampling

There are several points with different coordinates which represent the same point in the real scene in the registered point cloud, since there exist errors in range data and in registration. Thus, we need to remove overlapping points and to sample these points to generate a surface.

For the sub-point cloud S_k, we project it onto the camera's image plane using projection matrix of the camera. We create a grid with resolution of the image used in data acquisition step on the image plane. Each cell of the grid corresponds to a pixel of the image. Then, we search the points which are inside of a kth cell, G_k. Since we know the corresponding 3D coordinates of projected points, the 3D coordinates of the 3D point that corresponds to the cell G_k is calculated from the projected points inside G_k as shown in Fig 3. The (G_{kx}, G_{ky}, G_{kz}) is the 3D point corresponding to the cell G_k.

Median value of each coordinate is calculated and assigned to G_k according to the equation 3.

$$G_{kx} = median(Seq(x))$$
$$G_{ky} = median(Seq(y)) \quad (3)$$
$$G_{kz} = median(Seq(z))$$

where, $Seq(x)$, $Seq(y)$ and $Seq(z)$ are the sequences of the each coordinates of the 3D points that correspond to the projected points inside the cell G_k.

As the resolution of the image used in data acquisition becomes larger, the number of points of the mesh model increases. However, large size mesh model is not desirable to be used in practical usage, since it requires much hardware resource for rendering and may result in low performance. If the surface the point cloud forms has

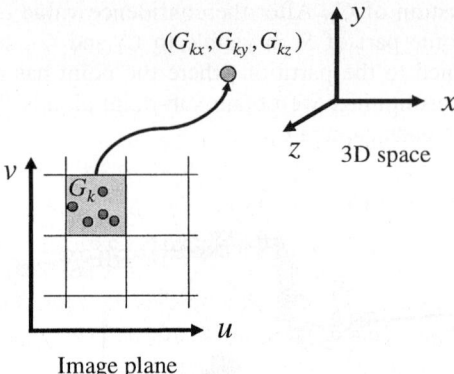

Fig. 3. Calculation of 3D coordinates of a cell

small variation, we can represent the surface with smaller number of points. In this paper, depth information is a key feature to be preserved. Thus, we apply adaptive sampling to simplify the triangulated model while preserving depth information of the scene. To reduce the number of points, we focus on the variation of the z values of the points. We adaptively sample the grid according to the depth variation. The gradient of G_{kz} is calculated with respect to the horizontal and vertical scanline as shown in equation 4. For each scan line, the absolute values of gradient of G_{uz} and G_{vz} are calculated. If δ, the root of squared sum of gradient in horizontal and vertical scanline, is smaller than threshold value, the point is cut out.

$$\frac{\partial G_{uz}}{\partial u} = \left| G_{(u+1)z} - G_{(u-1)z} \right|$$
$$\frac{\partial G_{vz}}{\partial v} = \left| G_{(v+1)z} - G_{(v-1)z} \right|$$
(4)

$$\delta = \sqrt{\left(\frac{\partial G_{uz}}{\partial u}\right)^2 + \left(\frac{\partial G_{vz}}{\partial v}\right)^2}$$
(5)

2.4 Triangulation and Mesh Integration

After adaptive sampling we have 2D point cloud and corresponding 3D point cloud in each partition of a view. To triangulate 3D point cloud, we triangulate 2D point cloud using Dealunay triangulation [10]. The 2D triangulation result is applied to corresponding 3D point cloud. Dealunay triangulation result in convex hull of a 2D point cloud, however, the expected result is not convex hull but the triangulation of 2D point cloud preserving its shape of boundary. Thus, we add 4 extreme points of which coordinates are the 4 corners in image coordinate system before triangulation and remove triangles that contain the extreme points after triangulation. For the realism, we exploit images captured from cameras as textures. For texture mapping the index of a cell in the grid on the image plane is used as texture coordinates of the corresponding 3D point.

After sampled point clouds of all the partitions are triangulated, we merge them to one mesh model to represent whole indoor environment. Since there is no connectivity between two adjacent mesh models, there exist gap between partitions. The points on the boundaries of two adjacent mesh models are triangulated to merge them together. The points on the left and right boundary of a sampled point cloud are the points corresponding to the left-most and right-most cells of the grid on the image plane. For triangulation of two adjacent boundaries, we connect the points which have similar height in 3D space. Then, we triangulate the points the points which have no connection. The mesh integration process is depicted in Fig 4.

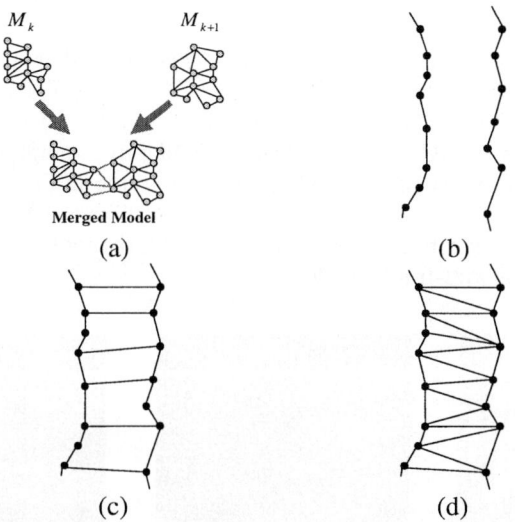

Fig. 4. Mesh integration process (a) Mesh merging of two adjacent models (b) The points on two adjacent boundaries (c) Connection of the points with similar height (d) Triangulation result

3 Experimental Results

To obtain 3D point cloud in each viewpoint, we used Digiclops which is a multi-view camera [9]. In this experiment, we modeled two walls of a room. The point clouds of the room to be modeled were obtained by moving a multi-view camera. There are overlapping areas between cameras' views. When we captured a scene, we used a planar pattern to calibrate the camera.

Fig 5 shows the result of partitioning input point clouds. After the visibility confidence values are calculated, the input point clouds are partitioned to sub-point clouds. Each partition is rendered with different color in Fig 5.

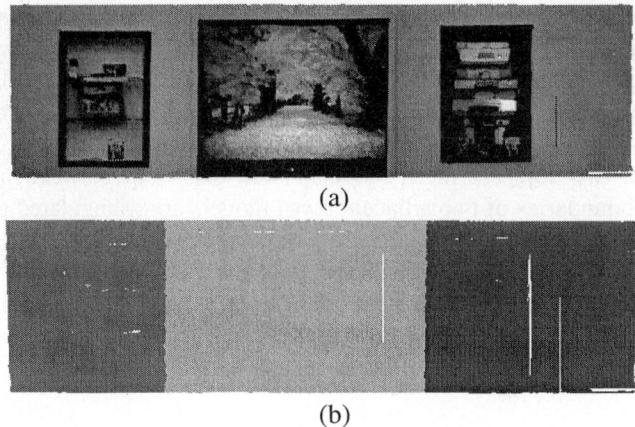

Fig. 5. Partitions of a wall of the room (a) Colored original point cloud (b) Partitioned point cloud

Fig 6 shows a triangulated model to which the adaptive sampling is not applied. The triangulated model is rendered in point and wire-frame in Fig 6(a) and Fig 6(b), respectively. The textured model is shown in Fig 6(c). Since there are many points and the triangles of the mesh model is too small, Fig 6(b) looks like a surface even though it is rendered in wire-frame mode.

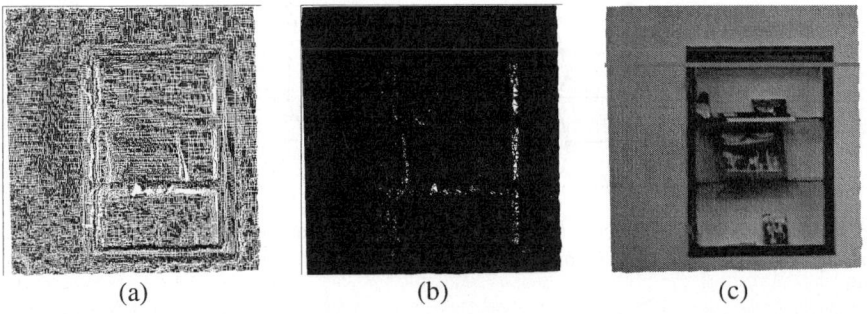

Fig. 6. Triangulated model before adaptive sampling (a) Point model (b) Wire-frame model (c) Textured model

The result of adaptive sampling is shown in Fig 6. Fig 7(a), Fig 7(b) and Fig 7(c) show the point model, wire-frame model and textured model respectively. Note that our key feature, depth information, is preserved and many of points on the smooth area are removed. The adaptive sampling reduces the number of points of the mesh model while preserving the features of the scene. Texture mapping improves the visual quality of the simplified model. Consequently, even though a number of points are removed, the visual quality of the model is not much different from the original model.

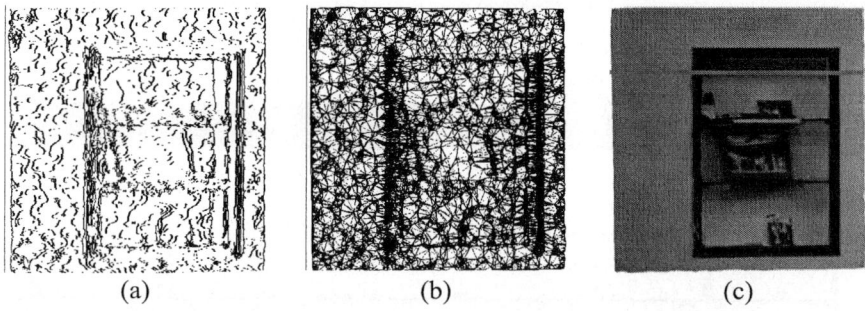

Fig. 7. Triangulated model after adaptive sampling (a) point model (b) wire-frame model (c) textured model

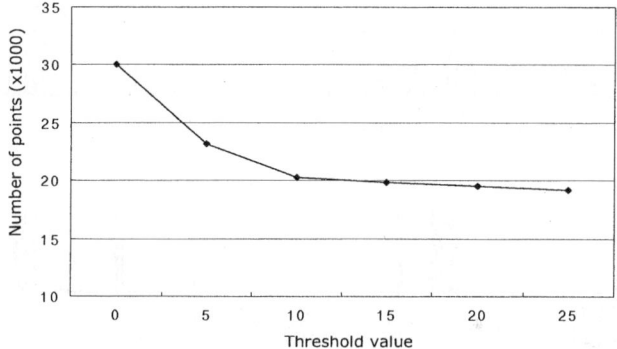

Fig. 8. The number of points of sampled models with different threshold values

Fig 8 shows the number of points with different threshold values. The number of points of the mesh model decreases as the threshold value increases. However, reduction rate decreases as the threshold value increases.

We applied our adaptive sampling algorithm to the red scanline in Fig 6(c) and the result is shown in Fig 9. Fig 9(a) shows the distribution of z axis values of the points on the scanline. Fig 9(b) is the gradient of G_z in horizontal direction. According to the gradient of the z coordinates associated to a grid on an image plane, the points with small gradient values are removed and the points with large variation in z axis are preserved as shown in Fig 9(d). If we select too large threshold value, the precise depth information is lost. We set the threshold value 10cm in this experiment based on our experimental result. In Fig 9, the gradient values are scaled to see the result clearly.

In Fig 10, shows the bookshelf of the scene. Since the reconstructed model has 3D information, we can see that the doll on the bookshelf becomes to be occluded as the rotation angle increases. This is one of major differences from the 2D image-based panorama which is constructed by stitching several 2D images. In 2D image based panorama the scene is static and it is not possible to see different scene according to viewpoint. Thus, users can navigate the reconstructed VE with depth information. This property of 3D panoramic VE provides more realistic feeling to users.

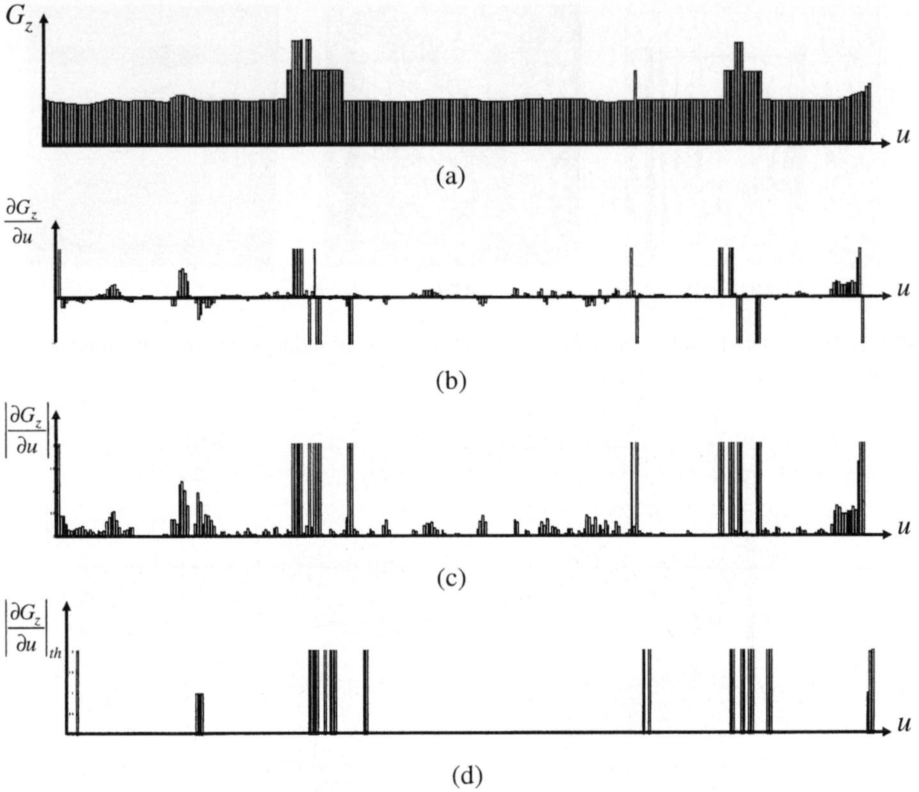

Fig. 9. The result of adaptive sampling of a scan line (a) Raw data of coordinates in z axis (b) Gradient of z coordinates with respect to u (c) Absolute value of gradient (d) Thresholded values

The integrated indoor scene model is shown in Fig 10. The floor is added manually. Fig 11(a) is the bird's-eye-view and Fig 11(b), Fig 11(c) and Fig 11(d) are magnified view of parts of the panoramic VE model. As shown in the magnified views, the reconstructed indoor scene model is photo-realistic enough to be used in virtual reality applications.

(a)

(b)

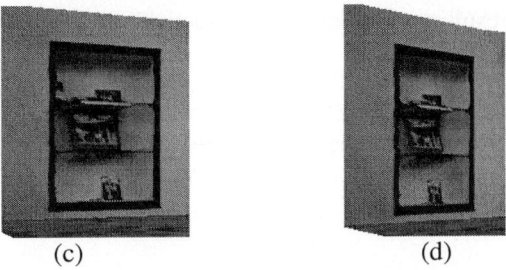

Fig. 10. Depth information of the panoramic mesh model (c) 15° rotation (d) 20° rotation

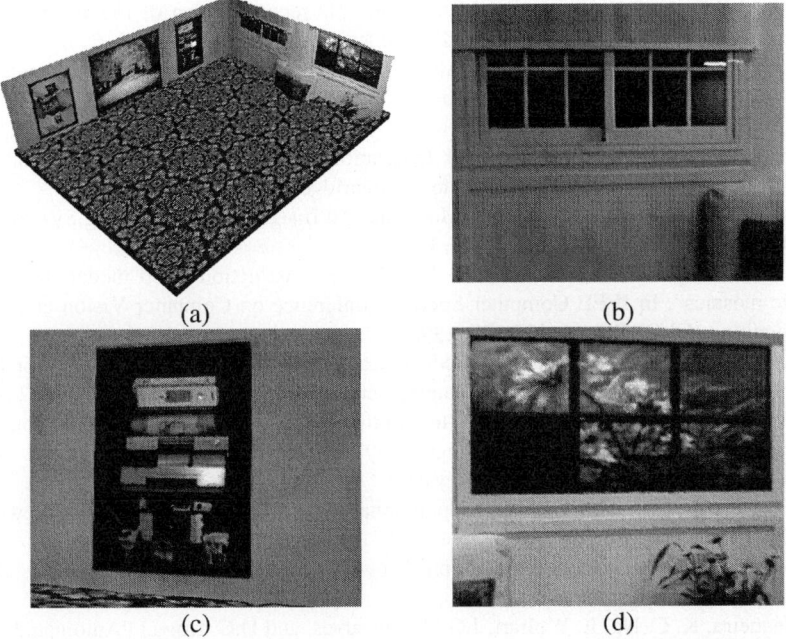

Fig. 11. Modeling result of an indoor scene (a) Bird's-eye-view (b) Window part (c) AV lack part (d) Tiled-display part

4 Conclusions and Future Work

In this paper, we proposed panoramic mesh modeling method from multiple range data for indoor scene reconstruction. The registered 3D point cloud is the input to the algorithm and a panoramic mesh model of indoor scene is generated. The input point cloud is partitioned to sub-point clouds. Each sub-point cloud is sampled and triangulated. After that, we merge all triangulated models of sub-point clouds to represent the whole indoor scene as one model. Our mesh modeling method considers occlusion between two adjacent views and it filters out invisible part of point cloud without any prior knowledge. While preserving the features of the scene, adaptive sampling reduces the size of resulting mesh model for practical usage. Depth information of the scene is preserved. The proposed method is modularized and applicable to the other modeling applications which handle multiple range data. As future work, we are going to improve our adaptive sampling to create smooth surface from point clouds with smaller number of points. The other work to be done is applying our modeling algorithm to complex scene which contains many objects in our daily life.

References

1. Vitor Sequeira, João Goncalves, M.Isabel Ribeiro, "3D Reconstruction of Indoor Environments", ICIP96, pp.405-408, Lausanne, Switzerland, 1996
2. Y.Sun, J.K.Paik, A.Koschan, and M.A.Abidi, "3D reconstruction of indoor and outdoor scenes using a mobile range scanner", Pattern Recognition, vol.3, pp 653–656, 2002
3. Y. Sun, J. Paik, A. Koschan, and M. Abidi, "Surface modeling using multi-view range and color images," Integrated Computer-Aided Engineering, Vol. 10, No. 1, pp. 37-50, February 2003
4. Johnson, S. Kang, "Registration and Integration of Textured 3-D Data" Tech. report CRL96/4, Digital Equipment Corporation, Cambridge Research Lab, 1996
5. McMillan, L., G. Bishop, "Plenoptic Modeling: An Image-Based Rendering System", Proceedings of SIGGRAPH 95, pp. 39-46, 1995
6. H.Y. Shum, M. Han, and R. Szeliski, "Interactive construction of 3d models from panoramic mosaics", In IEEE Computer Society Conference on Computer Vision and Pattern Recognition (CVPR'98), pp 427-433, 1998
7. S. Kim and W. Woo, "Projection-based Registration using Multi-view camera for Indoor Scene Reconstruction," 3-D Digital Imaging and Modeling (3DIM), pp. 484-491, 2005
8. P. Fua. From Multiple Stereo Views to Multiple 3–D Surfaces. International Journal of Computer Vision, 24(1), pp. 19-35, August 1997
9. PointGrey Research, http://www.ptgrey.com
10. H. Edelsbrunner. "Algorithms in Computational Geometry", Springer-Verlag, New York, 1987
11. R. Hartley and A. Zisserman, "Multiple View Geometry in Computer Vision", 2nd Ed. Cambridge University Press(2004)
12. V. Sequeira, K. C. Ng, E. Wolfart, J.G.M Gonçalves, and D.C. Hogg., "Automated 3D reconstruction of interiors with multiple scan-views", Proceedings of SPIE, Electronic Imaging '99, IS&T/SPIE's 11th Annual Symposium, 1999
13. V. Sequeira, J. Goncalves, and M.Isabel Ribeiro, "High-Level Surface Description from Composite Range Image", Proceedings of the 1995 IEEE International Symposium on Computer Vision, Florida, USA, pp.163-168, November 1995
14. S. Elgazzar, R. Liscano, F. Blais, and A. Miles, "3D Data Acquisition for Indoor Environment Modeling Using a Compact Active Range Sensor", Proceedings of IMTC97, 'Sensing, Processing, Networking',Vol. 1, pp 586-592, 1997
15. McMillan, L., and G. Bishop, "Plenoptic Modeling: An Image-Based Rendering System", Proceedings of SIGGRAPH 95, pp. 39-46, 1995

A Novel Low Latency Packet Scheduling Scheme for Broadband Networks

Eric Hsiao-Kuang Wu, Ming-I Hsieh, and Hsu-Te Lai

Department of Computer Science and Information Engineering,
National Central University, Chung-Li, Taiwan
hsiao@csie.ncu.edu.tw, {mihs, xdlai}@wmlab.csie.ncu.edu.tw

Abstract. Adequate bandwidth allocations and strict delay requirements are required for real time flows, such as streaming audio and video data. Most of commonly known packet scheduling algorithms like Weighted Fair Queueing (WFQ) and Start-Time Fair Queueing (SFQ) were mainly designed to ensure the bandwidth reservation function. They only guarantee the queueing delay under a certain threshold. It may cause unsteady packet latencies and introduces extra handling overheads for streaming applications. A few packet scheduling algorithms were proposed in recent years to address this problem like Low Latency Queueing (LLQ) which may suffer from low priority traffic starvation problem. In this paper, we will show the unsteady queueing delay problem, "The buffer underrun problem" for most well known packet scheduling algorithms. We propose a novel packet scheduling algorithm with history support, LLEPS, to ensure low latency and efficient packet scheduling for streaming applications via monitoring the behavior of queues and traffics.

1 Introduction

The number of new IP-based multimedia applications is growing rapidly with the advent of numerous broadband technologies. The traditional best-effort mechanism for data delivery does not provide service differentiation or guarantee for new multimedia flows that have tight bandwidth and delay requirements. A variety of new multimedia applications such as voice over IP, video on demand and teleconferencing rely on network traffic scheduling algorithms in switches and routers to assure performance bounds to satisfy different QoS requirements. Typical VoIP (Voice over IP) applications require low latency and less bandwidth; VoD (Video on Demand) applications require a huge volume of bandwidth, but the acceptable latency of them is higher than VoIP applications'. Unlike bursting data traffic applications, real-time applications usually will not consume all available bandwidth. In most cases, the required maximum bandwidth for a real-time application can be predefined, such as a typical streaming application.

Internet traffic has been growing at an exponential rate. As most of existing routers only provide best-effort services, the traffic of streaming applications will compete with other data traffic like FTP and HTTP. The packets of streaming applications may experience higher delay or packet loss because of the competition among different types of traffic. Therefore, the quality of streaming application can not be guaranteed and new technologies are required to offer quality of service (QoS) for these real time applications.

Differentiated services (DiffServ) [1] [2] and integrated services (IntServ) [3] were proposed to make the IP network to be QoS aware in the mid 1990s. RSVP [4] was proposed for reservation for the IntServ approach and it defined a way to allocate bandwidth hop by hop along the path. Effective bandwidth allocation ensures that each flow can get the bandwidth by the assigned weight. Since real-time applications could acquire bandwidth via RSVP or DiffServ, they do not need to compete with other flows anymore.

GPS offers a concept for multiple tasks (sessions)to share a single processor in an OS. The sessions can get different service rates at the same time, and they are served simultaneously. While applying GPS to the network technologies, it should be noted that the service of GPS is bit by bit. However, the network service is packet by packet. Due to the different service units of GPS (bit-based) and Internet (packet-based), the algorithms WFQ [12] and WF2Q [16] have been developed. They are classified as GPS like algorithms for their simulating GPS discipline. The GPS like algorithms can extend the bandwidth sharing into bandwidth reservation and assure the packet behaviors smooth.

Frame-based packet scheduling algorithms like DRR [20] and NDRR [21] are different from GPS. They service all queues round by round and require no complex control mechanisms. The major advantage of frame-based packet scheduling algorithms is efficiency. The disadvantage is that they only consider the queues which are always backlogged. That makes the latency of packets of the queues not always backlogged unstable.

The rest of this paper is organized as follows. In Section II, we review related scheduling algorithms and introduce their shortcomings for streaming applications. Section III presents the proposed LLEPS scheduling algorithm. In Section IV, simulation experiments are made to compare the effectiveness between LLEPS and other representative scheduling algorithms. We give some further research topics in the field of schedulers and conclude this paper in Section V.

2   Overview of Related Scheduling Algorithms

A *scheduling problem* is often solved as an *optimization problem*, with the objective of maximizing a measure of schedule quality. For example, an airline might wish to minimize the number of airport gates required for its aircraft in order to reduce its operating costs. As mentioned above, different types of packet schedulers carry various merits and this section will summarize their shortcomings for streaming applications.

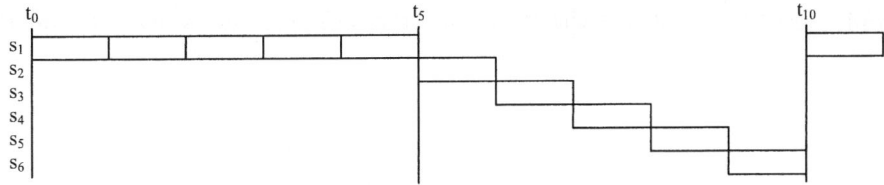

Fig. 1. Service Order of WFQ

2.1 Weighted Fair Queueing (WFQ)

WFQ [12] is a well known sort-based packet scheduling algorithm to approximate GPS. Since dividing a packet into several smaller packets take some extra overheads, packet scheduling algorithms usually determine the service order for packets. WFQ will give a weight for each flow and calculate the departure time of each packet based on the GPS discipline. Fig. 1 shows the service order of WFQ for a well-know case addressed by WF2Q.Since the weight of flow 1 is five times than others, the departure times of packet 1~5 of flow 1 will be equal or smaller than other packets. Thus, they will be sent out first. The departure time of packet 6 of flow 1 is higher than other packets. Thus, it will be sent out until other packets are sent. Hence, the packets of flow 1 were delivered substantially quickly and the variety of the jitter of flow 1 will be significant.

Additionally, an idealized WFQ must work with a precise virtual clock. To implement a precise virtual clock[29] will take a $O(n)$ time complexity in the worst case[1]. Therefore, SCFQ[14] were proposed to solve the virtual clock requirement of WFQ. SCFQ sets the virtual clock to the finish time of last departed packet. Thus, the virtual clock of SCFQ always exceeds the precise virtual clock. Since the virtual clock is exceeding, the real-time flows may take a larger variety of jitter when the flows pass the router with SCFQ. Another WFQ implementation, SFQ[15], was proposed to solve this problem. However, since SFQ always sets the virtual clock as the start time of last departed packet, SFQ still may get a larger variety of jitter for a real-time flow.

2.2 Low Latency Queueing (LLQ)

LLQ is implemented by Cisco in their routers to guarantee the delay of real-time service. LLQ is a combination of Priority of Queueing (PQ) and Class-Based Weighted-Fair Queueing(CBWFQ). It is currently the recommended queueing function for Voice over IP (VoIP) and IP Telephony, and it will also work well with video conferences. However, LLQ only guarantees the low latency for the

---

[1] An undistorted virtual clock implementation must take the rational number library. This means the time complexity of the linear pairwise function of the virtual clock will depend on the weights of flows. And to calculate an undistorted virtual clock may take $O(n^2)$ or higher time complexity.

highest priority queue. As the higher priority queue makes a misbehavior, the lower priority queue will be starving.

In 2003AD, adaptive WFQ[28] tried to address the problem of the variety of queueing delay. However, it still requires to partition the traffic into three class, gold class, sliver class and bronze class. The behavior of adaptive WFQ is similar LLQ. It only could be used to guarantee the queueing delay of the traffics of gold class. If the traffics of gold class makes a misbehavior, the variety of queueing delay of bronze class may not be acceptably stable.

3 LLEPS Packet Scheduling Algorithm

As mentioned above, most well-known algorithms are designed to share the bandwidth resource fairly with a worst case delay bound guarantee. They suffer from either higher complexity for evaluating an enough exact virtual time or unsteady jitter problem. Thus, for addressing these challenges, LLEPS is designed as a sort-based scheduling algorithm with *history support* to compensate the on-going delay difference. The motivation of LLEPS considers a long-term fairness and makes the real-time flows more smooth. Thus, the short-term fairness of LLEPS may not be adorable as some well known sort-based scheduling algorithms like SFQ and WF2Q+. However, LLEPS could make the jitter of real-time application more smooth while assuring the high quality of real-time flow service.

3.1 The Buffer Underrun Problem

Consider a 100kbps real-time CBR traffic over a packet-based QoS network. This packet-based QoS network contains two connected routers, a sender connected to a router, and a receiver connected to another router. The router which the sender connects is a QoS-enabled router. It will guarantee 100kbps for this real-time traffic. In an idealized environment, the jitter of the real-time traffic should be small than $\frac{MTU}{link\ bandwidth}$. However, the interval of real-time packets in the practical cases will not always be a constant like Fig. 2. Fig. 2 shows two typical streams, a perfect CBR stream and a real CBR stream. The perfect CBR stream indicate the idealized delivery of a real-time traffic. However,as Fig. 2 in a practical packet network, the inter-arrival of two packets may be effected by the competitive traffics or others.

Thus, since the interval of a given real CBR stream could be larger than the idealized interval and the corresponding bandwidth reservation just satisfy the requirement of a perfect stream. Thus, the queue for a given real-time traffic

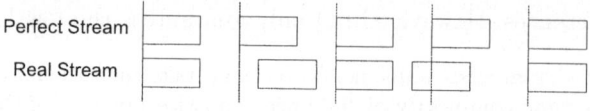

Fig. 2. The difference between prefect real-time traffic and real traffic

in the QoS-enabled router will be empty at some times. In such case, the real-time flow will be handled and regarded as a new flow and the departure time of packets will be set as the current virtual time. Thus, those real-time packets may get more queueing delays because of inaccuracy of virtual time or the queueing delay from competitive traffic at the previous router. Since the extra queueing delay depends on the packet arriving time, and the packet arriving time may be unsteady in real cases, the queueing delay(jitter) is also unsteady. We define this problem as "*the buffer underrun problem*".

Basic Idea of LLEPS. LLEPS maintains multiple queues where each queue is applied only for a session. Upon receiving a packet of a session, LLEPS puts it into a specific queue. The scheduler chooses the queue with the highest priority and forwards packets for the queue. Since the buffer underrun problem occurs in the practical case, LLEPS addresses the problem via flow's history. First, consider a duration from t_s to t_f. Additionally, the bandwidth of link is B and the reservation bandwidth for flow i is r_i. Thus, the relationship could be written as:

$$W = B \times (t_f - t_s), \quad w_i = r_i \times (t_f - t_s) \tag{1}$$

$$w_i^t < r_i(t - t_s), \quad \sum_{i=1}^{n} w_i \leq W \tag{2}$$

where W denotes the total service quote of this link in this duration, and w_i denotes the reserve bandwidth in this duration for flow i. Let w_i^t denote the used bandwidth of flow i from t_s to t. Thus, if Eqn. 2 is satisfied, it denotes flow i does not use the reserved bandwidth in this duration completely. Furthermore, the real-time traffic is a constant bitrate traffic. As the consumed bandwidth of a real-time flow is less than its reserved bandwidth, some packets of the real-time flow may be delayed. Thus, the scheduler should give the higher priority or some credit for such flows. In other words, if the traffic of flow i is more than its reserved bandwidth like Eqn. 3, LLEPS will assign the low priority for it. Thus, we could define the priority of flow i as Eqn. 4.

$$w_i^t \geq r_i \times (t - t_s) \tag{3}$$

$$p_i^t = \frac{w_i^t}{r_i} \tag{4}$$

Let p_i^t denote the utilization of the reserved bandwidth of flow i from t_s to t_f. Thus, the lower value for p_i denotes that the scheduler should give the higher priority for flow i. Specifically, p_i^t denotes the weight of the history of flow i.

The value of p_i can be an indicator to reflect the greedy status for a particular flow. At any moment, p_i of each queue should be similar. As a session is more aggressive than others, its p_i value will be larger than others'. According to the property of p_i, LLEPS only needs to forward packets of the queue with a lower p_i value than others. The behavior of LLEPS is able to keep the p_i value of each queue similar.

3.2 Detailed Algorithm

We have described the key concept of the history for a flow earlier. The implementation for a fixed width history requires a amount of resource to record the information of the departure packets. We will describe how LLEPS implements the history and show the results in next section. First, LLEPS provides the packet forwarding service based on the concept of time slots, like 250ms. Let $Q_i = r_i \times$ (length of time slot) denote the reserved bandwidth for flow i of a time slot in byte units. Let w_i denote the serviced bytes of flow i in current time slot. Thus, the start time of a packet is $\max\left(\frac{w_i}{Q_i}, now - t_s\right)$, where t_s denotes the start time of the current time slot. Assuming a flow i is inactive and a packet for flow i arrives. Thus, we could show the priority for this packet as:

$$p_i = \frac{w_i \times (\text{length of time slot})}{Q_i}$$

Since the length of time slots for all flows are the same, we could rewrite the last equation as:

$$p'_i = \frac{w_i}{Q_i}$$

From another point of view, p'_i denotes the start time of this packet in the current time slot. Thus, to implement the priority, LLEPS sets the start time of packet as $\frac{w_i}{Q_i}$. In other words, LLEPS ignores the part of $now - t_s$ when the time slot is not changed. Additionally, if a time slot is changed, LLEPS will recalculate the w_i to set the priority of each flow according to its information of last time slot. Although, the results for this implementation will not be better the version of SFQ with a fixed width history. However, it is much simply and useful. We will shows the results in the simulation section.

We present the pseudo code of LLEPS. *Enque* function is called when a packet arrives. *Deque* function is called when the link is available. If no packet is available in this time, *Deque* function should return a NULL pointer. *Enque* function and *Deque* function of LLEPS is similar to SFQ. From a technique point of view, LLEPS could be thought as a specific SFQ with time slot-based history support.

Timestamp Update Function. Since the index of LLEPS is composed of a time slot number and a serviced bytes, the *update()* function provides a schema to recalculate the service rate of flow i when a new time slot is available. Additionally, the function sets the priority of flow i to guarantee the low latency for CBR traffic. Let *timestamp* denote the current time slot number, $\left\lfloor \frac{now}{\text{length of time slot}} \right\rfloor$.

Since *update* function is called only when a new time slot is available, we recalculate the current service bytes of flow i, w_i and normalize it into a valid range. The quantum of flow i, Q_i, may not be multiple of the packet size. The value of the serviced bytes of the last time slot, w_i, may be smaller than zero even if the queue i is always backlogged. Thus, we should remain those unserviced reserved bandwidth for flow i. This is why the minimum value of w_i is -MTU.

Table 1. Pseudo code of update timestamp

```
update (Queue_i, nw)
    nts ← ts_i + 1
    if nts < timestamp
        w_i ← nw
    else
        w_i ← min (max (−MTU, w_i − Q_i), Q_i)
    ts_i = timestamp
```

Table 2. Pseudo code of enqueue

```
Enque (packet)
    Queue_i ← find the index i of the queue for packet
    Enque (Queue_i, packet)
    if Queue_i is not in minheap
        if ts_i ≠ ts
            if no queue is active, then update (Queue_i, 0)
            else update (Queue_i, (w_j/Q_j) Q_i) where j is the index of next service flow.
        push Queue_i into minheap
```

Additionally, the nw parameter for update function is a reference if this queue is not active in the last time slice. LLEPS thinks such queue is non-active because of application's behavior, not network behavior. Thus, LLEPS does not give any high priority for such traffic.

Enqueue Function. *Enque* function is similar to most well-known sorted-based scheduling algorithms. First of all, it found the index i of the incoming packet. Then, it push the packet into queue i. If the queue i is not active, *Enque* function will mark it as active. The difference is the mark procedure. Since the index of LLEPS contains a timestamp, it will call *Update* function to update the timestamp first if this flow i is not active in current time slot. Then push it into a minimum heap.

Table 3. Pseudo code of dequeue

```
Deque()
    return NULL if no queue is available in minheap
    Queue_i ← φ
    while Queue_i is empty
        pop first queue from minheap and assign it to Queue_i
    Packet ← pop first packet from Queue_i
    w_i ← w_i + sizeof (Packet)
    if ts_i ≠ timestamp
        update (Queue_i, 0)
    push Queue_i into minheap
    return Packet
```

Thus, the difference of *Enque* function between SFQ and LLEPS is only the timestamp update.

Dequeue Function. *Deque* Function of LLEPS is similar to more well-known sort-based algorithms. If no packet is available, it just returns NULL. Otherwise, it will pop the queue with the minimum index and forward the first packet from the queue. Then, it will update the serviced bytes parameter of queue i, w_i. Since the parameters of index has been modified, it calls *Update* function to recalculate the index of queue i and push it into minheap.

The difference of *Deque* function between SFQ and LLEPS is also the part of *update* function. However, since LLEPS records the virtual time of flow i in current time slot by w_i and Q_i, the update of virtual clock is a little difference with SFQ.

4 Simulations

The simulations are implemented using Network Simulator 2. The topology of this simulation is presented in Fig. 3. The circle with s_i or d_i is a node and it denotes a sender or a receiver. The number i on it denotes that it's i-th pair of a sender and a receiver. The circle with r_s or r_d is a router. The bottleneck of this simulations is the link between the two routers. The bandwidth of the links between nodes and routers is 100Mbps and the propagation delay is 1 msec. The link between two routers is 1Mbps and 15 msec. Since the bottleneck is from router r_s to router r_d, the packet scheduling algorithms are only applied at the link at bottleneck. Other links will be applied DropTail. Additionally, we set the time slots of LLEPS as 250ms for all simulations.

4.1 Queueing Delay Comparison of LLEPS, SFQ, SCFQ, WF2Q+...

In LLEPS section, we have discussed the buffer underrun problem. Thus, we design an simulation to show the variety of queueing delay of those scheduling algorithm. In this simulation experiment, we use nine 1Mbps CBR flows and one 99kbps CBR flow. Additionally, the weights of them are the same, and the

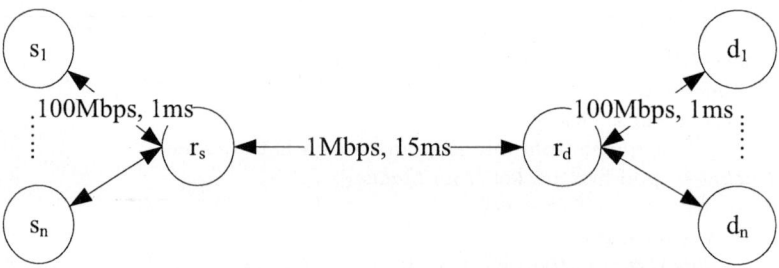

Fig. 3. Topology of Simulation

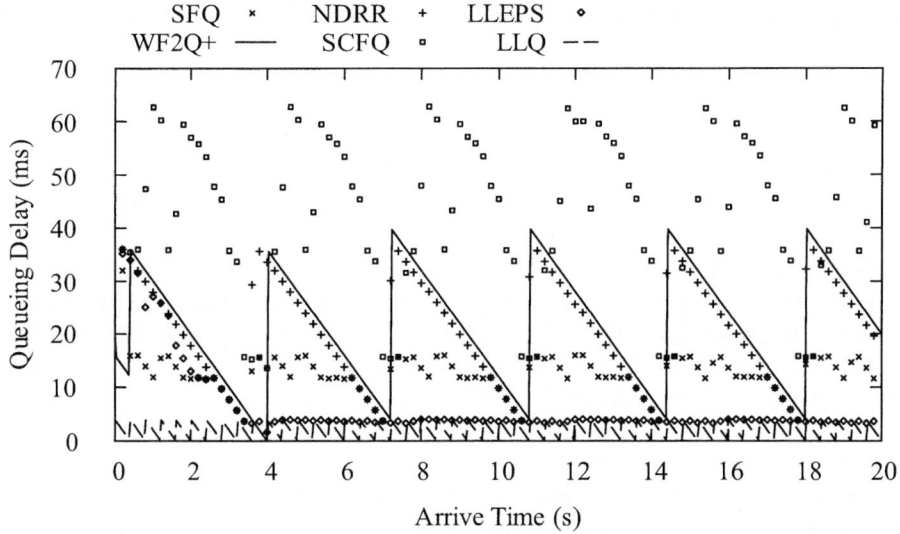

Fig. 4. Queueing Delay

priority of 99kbps CBR flow, flow 10, has high priority for LLQ. Fig. 4 shows the queueing delays of each algorithms in the router of bottleneck link. Since ns2 provides a prefect time-scheduler, it's easy to make the arriving interval of flow 10 slightly larger than the busy period of flow 1. Therefore, if the queueing delay of flow 10 is very small, the queued packet of flow 10 should almost be zero in most time. In other words, a real-time traffic may take an extra delay when: 1. it takes an exceeding virtual clock when it becomes active. 2. if it is ordered at last when all indices of flows are the same. We shows those priorities in Fig. 4.

Since flow 10 is the highest priority of LLQ, the queueing delay of LLQ only effects by the duration from the time of enqueue of this packet to the time of next dequeue of scheduler. Thus, the queueing delay of LLQ is between 0msec and 4msec, MTU÷Bandwidth=500Bytes÷1Mbps=4ms. However, LLQ is a pre-assigned priority algorithm. It should take the better result than other non-preassigned priority algorithms.

SFQ got the best result than other well known algorithms like WF2Q+, SCFQ and NDRR. Since the service order of NDRR is the order of active flows, the queueing delays of NDRR depend on the distance from current service flow to flow 10. Furthermore, the interval of packets of flow 10 is slightly larger than the interval of an inner round of NDRR. Thus, the queueing delays of NDRR in Fig. 4 start at the period of an inner round, MTU× (number of flows - 1) ÷bandwidth= 36ms. Additionally, the distance from current service flow to flow 10 will decrease after each packets of flow 10 until zero. In Fig. 4, the results of NDRR repeats this scenario.

WF2Q+ also got the similar problem. However, we have discussed the virtual clock problem of WF2Q+ and SCFQ before. This is why the queueing delay no.180 packet of flows exceeds the maximum queueing delay of NDRR.

Generally speaking, the queueing delay should be between 0 and the maximum queueing delay of NDRR except that the virtual clock exceeds the precise virtual clock.

Since the policy of virtual clock of SFQ is as the start time of last departed packet. The queueing delay of SFQ only is effected by the number of the same start time packets in scheduler. With the priorities of minimum heap implementation, the maximum queueing delays SFQ is only O (log number of flow) in Fig. 4 .

The queueing delay of LLEPS is interesting. From packet 1 to packet 61, the queueing delay of LLEPS is unsteady. Then, the queueing delay of LLEPS is steady to decrease and is the same with LLQ. We have described the properties of LLEPS before. Since LLEPS will give the higher priority for the flow of non-always backlogged, the queueing delay of the packets between packet 1 and packet 61 of flow 10 may be unsteady because of the small credit. After packet 100, the scenario of LLEPS is the same with LLQ because the credit of flow 10 is more than one packet. Therefore, when a packet is enqueued into flow 10, the flow 10 will get the top position of minimum heap. Although the queueing delay of LLEPS between packet 1 and packet 100 is not perfect like LLQ, LLEPS provides a more fair scheduling algorithm and achieves the better queueing delay than other scheduling algorithms.

5 Conclusion and Future Works

This paper introduces a new scheduling algorithm (LLEPS) to provide bandwidth guarantee service efficiently. In addition to ensuring bandwidth guarantee services, LLEPS does not introduce much delay jitter effects for packets. Since LLEPS always serves the queue with the highest priority, it provides preemption mechanism for packets. However, the service sequence of each queue is constant or is depending on the improper virtual clock in most well known scheduling algorithms.

The continuous work of LLEPS is to design a better way to determine the priority of each session. LLEPS determines the priority of each session based on the corresponding transmission rate. LLEPS estimates the transmission rate of a session in a time interval. When the time interval is too small, the estimation will become very unstable and no meaning for LLEPS. The continuous efforts will address the issue.

References

1. S. Blake, D. Black, M.Carlson, E. Davies, Z. Wang and W. Weiss, "*An architecture for differentiated services*", RFC 2475, December 1998.
2. K. Nichols, V. Jacobson and L. Zhang, "*Two-bit differentiated services architecture for the Internet*", IETF RFC 2638, July 1999.
3. R. Braden and D. Clark, "*Integrated Services in the Internet Architecture: An Overview*", RFC 1633, July 1994.

4. R. Braden, L. Zhang, S. Berson, S. Herzog, and S. Jamin, *"Resource ReSerVation protocol (RSVP) – Version 1 Functional Specification"*, RFC 2205, September 1997.
5. A. K. Parekh, *"A generalized processor sharing approach to flow control in integrated services networks"*, Ph.D. thesis, Dept. Elec. Eng. Comput. Sci., MIT, 1992.
6. A. K. Parekh and R. G. Gallagher, *"A generalized processor sharing approach to flow control in integrated services networks: the single-node case"*, IEEE/ACM Transactions on Networking, June 1993.
7. L. Zhang, *"VirtualClock: A new traffic control algorithm for packet switching networks"*, Proc. ACM SIGCOMM'90, August 1990.
8. G. Xie and S. Lam, *"Delay guarantee of virtual clock server"*, IEEE/ACM Transactions on Networking, December 1995.
9. S. Floyd and V. Jacobson, *"Link-Sharing and resource management models for packet networks"*, IEEE/ACM Transactions on Networking, August 1995.
10. KJ. Loh, I. Gui and KC. Chua, *"Performance of a Linux Implementation of Class Based Queueing"*, Computer Communications and Networks Proceeding, October 1998.
11. K. Cho. *"A Framework for Alternate Queueing: Towards Traffic Management by PC-UNIX Based Routers"*, Annual Technical Conference, USENIX, 1998.
12. A. Demers, S.Keshav and S.Shenker, *"Design and Analysis of a fair queueing algorithm"*, Proceeding of ACM SIGCOMM, September 1989.
13. J. C. R. Bennett and H. Zhang, *"Hierachical packet fair queueing algorithms"*, Proc. SIGCOMM'96, August 1996.
14. S. J. Golestani, *"A self-clocked fair queueing scheme for broadband applications"*, Proceedings of IEEE INFOCOM, June 1994.
15. P. Goyal, H. M. Vin, and H. Cheng, *"Start-time fair queueing: A scheduling algorithm for integrated services packet switching networks"*, TR-96-02, Dept. Comput. Sci., Univ. Texas at Austin, Jan 1996.
16. Jon C.R. Bennett and Hui Zhang, *"WF2Q: Worst-case Fair Weighted Fair Queueing"*, INFOCOM '96, Proceedings IEEE, Mar 1996
17. X. Fei and A. Marshall, *"Delay Optimized Worst Case Fair WFQ (WF2Q) Packet Scheduling"*, ICC 2002, IEEE International Conference, 2002.
18. A. Greenberg and N. Madras, *"How fair is fair queueing"*, J. ACM, July 1992.
19. S. Keshav, *"On the efficient implementation of fair queueing"*, Internetworking: Research and Experience, September 1991.
20. M. Shreedhar and George Varghese, *"Efficient fair queueing Using deficit round-robin"*, IEEE Transactions on Networking, Jane 1996.
21. Salil S. Kanhere and Harish Sethu, *"Fair, Efficient and Low-Latency Packet Scheduling using Nested Deficit Round Robin"*, Proceedings of the IEEE Workshop on High-Performance Switching and Routing (HSPR), May 2001
22. H. Zhang and D. Ferrari. *"Rate-Controlled service disciplines"*, Journal of High Speed Networks, 1994.
23. H. Zhang and D. Ferrari, *"Rate-Controlled static-priority queueing"*, Proc. IEEE INFOCOM '93, September 1993
24. V. Jacobson, *"Congestion Avoidance and Control"*, Proceeding of ACM SIGCOMM, August 1988.
25. S. Floyd and V. Jacobson, *"Random early detection for congestion avoidance"*, IEEE/ACM Transactions on Networking, July 1993.
26. K. Ramakrishnan and S. Floyd, *"A Proposal to Add Explicit Congestions Notification (ECN) to IP"*, RFC 2481, January 1999.

27. S. Floyd, "*A Report on Recent Developments in TCP Congestion Control*", IEEE Communications Magazine, April 2001.
28. A. Sayenko, T. Hamalainen, J. Joutsensal and J. Siltanen, "*On providing bandwidth and delay guarantees using the revenue criterion based adaptive WFQ*", IEEE APCC 2003, September 2003.
29. H. Tayyar and H. Alnuweiri, "*The Complexity of Computing Virtual-Time in Weighted Fair Queuing Schedulers*", IEEE ICC 2004, p1996~2002, vol14, June 2004.

Creative Cartoon Face Synthesis System for Mobile Entertainment

Junfa Liu[1,2,3], Yiqiang Chen[1,3], Wen Gao[1,2], Rong Fu[3], and Renqin Zhou[3]

[1] Institute of Computing Technology,
Chinese Academy of Sciences, Beijing, China, 100080
{jfliu, yqchen, wgao}@jdl.ac.cn
[2] Graduate School of the Chinese Academy of Sciences,
Beijing, China, 100080
[3] Shanghai Institute of Computing Technology, Chinese Academy of Sciences,
Shanghai, China, 201203
{rfu, rqzhou}@shict.cn

Abstract. This paper presents a prototype system, which synthesizes entertainment-oriented cartoon face and translates text message to multimedia animation in mobile phone. While a digital real facial photograph and some text are imputed, a piece of exaggerated facial animation with entertainment will be shown in the phone. Three steps are used to get this entertainment effect: first is the illustration generation of the real face image, General-Scale-Edge (GSE) is adopted to take various scale of the edge into account, which can extract the feature edge on human's face efficiently. The second is the expression warping to produce a caricature. The improved feature based warping method is employed. Finally, we generate the exaggerated facial animation based on the caricature using TTVS method. In addition, we improved modified Active Shape Model to remove the background and control more feature points on the face. Experiments show the system work well with high performance on the PDA.

1 Introduction

In recent years, there is an increasing trend and demand for the digital entertainment on mobile animation. The traditional way for people's communication by mobile device mainly is the speech or the text message. As the advance of 3G mobiles and network, digital multimedia content fall in great demand in daily life. The facial animation plays an important role of it, and there are immense studies focused on it. The researchers from Microsoft Research (Asia) designed systems for the illustration generation. It can even abstract the movement data of a figure in the video stream, and synthesize a new animation. There are also some other studies on auto or semi-auto illustration generation. At current stage, the illustration is created in black-and-white mode. The mobile animation is another active research field. Most of the animation is designed in interactive mode. This paper builds a novel system to synthesize multimedia animation message. The most difference with other systems locates in two points. One is the approach that the caricature is created; the other is that the animation is based on a person's caricature, not on a real face image.

The following parts of this paper are organized as follows: Section 2 describes some related works on the mobile caricature animation system, section 3 gives our system an overview. In section 4, we introduce how to modify the traditional ASM algorithm to fit our system. In the section 5, black-white illustration generation is stated, after that, the illustration is warped into a caricature and animated in section 6. It means the text is translated into facial animation for entertainment purpose. Also in this section, the experiment result is given. At last, in section 7, we draw conclusion for the system and give some ideas to improve the system in the future.

2 Related Work

2.1 Illustration Generation

Illustration generation based on the real face photograph had been a hot topic in NPR (Non-Photorealistic Rendering) field. The traditional way to create photo's illustration is to operate the software such as Adobe Illustrator in interactive mode. But this paper would pay more attention to the automatic way to generate illustration based on people's photos.

Besides the approaches to generate illustrations by the interactive way, there are two ways to auto-create the illustration of the photographs. Bruce Gooch et al [3] present a method for creating black-and-white illustrations. They give a threshold image based on the Blommaert and Martens' model of human first, and generate a threshold luminance image by a simply translating the image to a two-tone one. Then multiply the two images into the result illustration. The other way to create the illustration is represented by the job from [5, 8]. They extract the sketch of the face to construct the illustration.

2.2 Image Warping

This paper tests two image warping approaches, so we briefly give them an introduction here respectively:

Mesh Warping: Mesh warping is a two-pass algorithm that accepts a source image and two 2-D arrays of coordinates S and D. The S coordinates are the control pixels in the source image. The D coordinates specify the location to which the S coordinates map. The final image is the source image warped by means of meshes S and D. The 2-D arrays in which the control points are stored impose a rectangular topology to the mesh. The only constraint is that the meshes defined by both arrays be topologically equivalent i.e. no folding or discontinuities. Therefore the entries in D are coordinates that may wander as far from S as necessary, as long as they do not cause self-intersection. The first pass is responsible for re-sampling each row, while the second pass is responsible for re-sampling each column independently.

Feature Based Image Warping: This method in [11] gives the animator a high level of control over the process. The animator interactively selects corresponding feature lines in the 2 images to be morphed. The algorithm uses lines to relate features in the source image to features in the destination image. It is based upon fields of influence surrounding the feature lines selected. It uses reverse mapping (i.e. it goes through the destination image pixel by pixel, and samples the correct pixel from the source image) for warping the image. A pair of lines (one defined relative to the source image, the other defined relative to the destination image) defines a mapping from one image to the other.

2.3 Mobile Face Animation

There are many works on face animation based on MPEG-4 standard [13, 14]. Generally speaking, such systems define MPEG-4 compatible face topology, using FDP(Facial Definition Parameter), FAPU(Facial Animation Parameter Units) and FAP (Facial Animation Parameter) to recalculate the mesh coordinates and synthesize the new face texture.

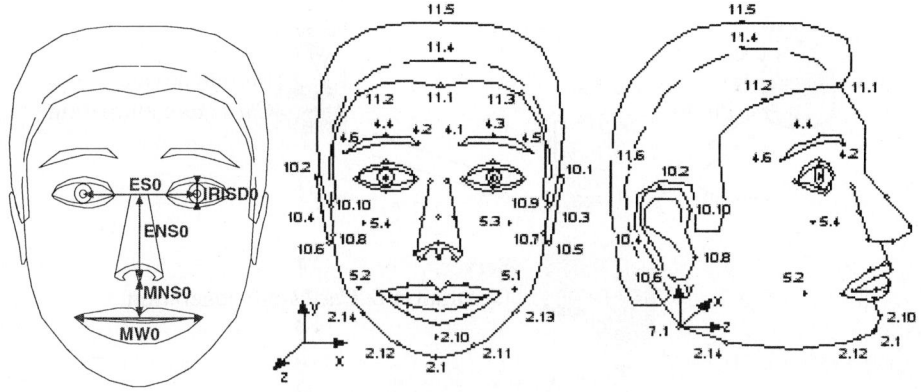

Fig. 1. The MPEG-4 FAPU and FDP definition

All the parameters involving translational movement are expressed in terms of the FAPU. These units are defined in order to allow interpretation of the FAPs on any facial model in a consistent way. They correspond to fractions of distances between some key facial features (e.g., eye distance), and are defined in terms of distances between feature points. Nowadays, since 3D is still not well supported on mobile devices, as reported, many mobile systems realize the animation via 2D way. However, the MPEG-4 FAPs framework provides basic solution for these 2D animation systems, as well as ours.

[1] proposes a model-based and parametric 3D facial animation solution capable of representing and animating real people in a photo-realistic manner on real-time platforms of the future. Their modeling methods allow for modeling new faces from a single 3D scan or even photograph within hours by benefiting facial variations obtained from a large and varied facial database. Resulting heads are animated via MPEG4 data streams extracted from video sequences, thus facial animation data can be sent over low-bandwidth communication channels while the rendering hardware delivers real-time animation on the local mobile platform.

3 System Overview

The system runs on a network with the Server and the Client as the Fig.2. So the work involved in our system can be decoupled into two parts. One is the generation of the caricature, the other is the animation based on the caricature. The former takes place on the server, and comprises 3 steps. The first step is the face auto-location. The Active Shape Model (ASM) approach is adopted here; However, the traditional ASM approach does not output feature points on forehead, so an effort is added to the traditional ASM in order to get a whole shape of the face. The second step is to generate the illustration. General-Scale-Edge (GSE) method is used to obtain adequate contour of the face. The third step is the caricature generation from the illustration.

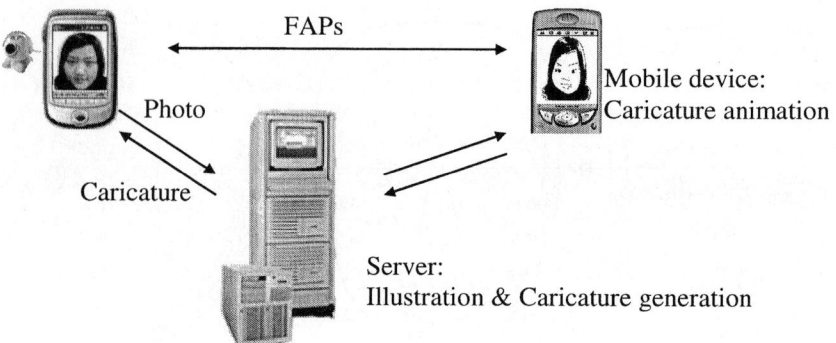

Fig. 2. An overview of the system

The client represents the mobile device (such as phone, PDA etc.). People's photograph is captured there and is sent to the Server for generating the corresponding caricature. Between the clients, the multimedia message is transformed. The content of the message include text and facial animation, and the facial animation content is made up of FAP frames according to the MPEG4, which can decrease greatly the Bytes needed to accomplish the animation by transforming the video stream. Once two clients build contacts, a picture of caricature with MPEG4 parameters will be transformed first. Then, the followed data transformed to the accept is the text and corresponding FAPs, which can animate the caricature.

4 Improved Active Shape Model

ASM is often adopted to get face shape effectively [7, 8]. However, the traditional ASM only considers the feature point array of the cheek, the eyes, the nose and the mouth (see Figure 3(a)). In this work, we improve this method to include some feature points on the forehead (see Figure. 3(b)). This improvement brings two advantages.

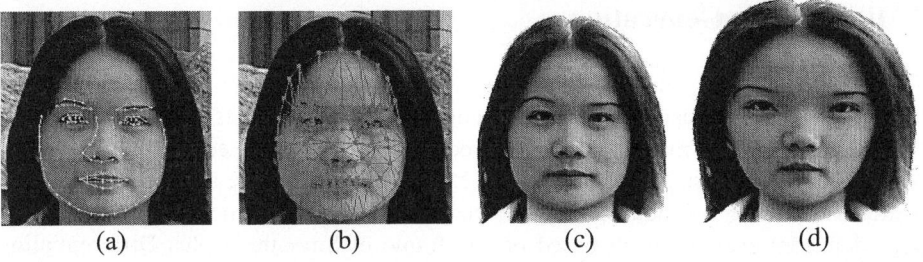

Fig. 3. Advantage of improved ASM. (a) is the feature points extracted by traditional ASM, (b) is the feature points extracted by improved ASM algorithm, and (c) is the image decreased background, and (d) is the image which is warped into a big forehead

One is obtaining pre-knowledge for decreasing the background. In image warping and animating stage, we always avoid the unreality that the object in the background is deformed while the face is warped. For example, a straight pillar is bended after warping. So we tend to remove the background information as much as possible. Meanwhile, we want to keep more hair information. Fortunately, once we get the face area, things becomes easier than ever. We constructed a Gauss function to achieve it. For the hair is always the nearest object around the face area, the function is designed to remove the pixels far away the area, while keep down the hair as much as possible. The collar is the other object that is close to the face area, so it is kept down as the hair. Our processing effect is good (see Figure 3(c)).

The function is constructed as the following:

$$f(d_i) = A \cdot L_i \cdot \exp(-B \cdot (d_i / D)^2), i = 0,1,..., M \times N \qquad (1)$$

$$d_i = \begin{cases} 0 & , P_i \in S \\ \min(\sqrt{(P_i x - P_j x)(P_i y - P_j y)}), j = 0,1,...n, P_i \notin S \end{cases} \qquad (2)$$

where: $f(d_i)$ represents the return gray value; d_i is the distance between pixel i and the face area; L_i is the original gray value of pixel i; D is the half width of the face area; A and B is practical coefficient. M and N are the width and height of the image respectively; S represents the face area obtained by ASM. And $(P_i x, P_i y)$ is the coordinate of pixel i; n is the sum of feature points in the edge of the face area.

The second advantage of improved ASM is to help warping the face automatically. In section 6, the feature based warping method is adopted. However, the feature-based method need specify some feature points artificially, which lead to the disadvantage of this method. The improved ASM can auto-get the feature points, so it can give this method an offset well. Especially, if we want a warping effect like Figure 3(d), we can directly use the feature points on the forehead that the improved ASM can provide. The detail about feature based warping method is given in section 2.2 and section 6.

5 Illustration Generation

We designed an auto-generation approach for illustration based on the job in [12]. In face image, there are usually multi-scale edges. Such as the edges of cheek, it may be considered smooth or medium-large scale edges. In contrast, the edges round eyes and nose are considered small scale ones. To extract the facial edge as more as possible, while keeping the redundancy out, we proposal a method named GSE. Traditional edge detectors are almost all based on the frame of Smoothing plus Differentiating plus Binarizing, some of which such as Canny can not provide rich description for edge information as well as can not make exact edge localization. However, General-Scale-Edge (GSE) takes the various scale of the edge into account, and can extract the feature edge on human's face efficiently. To obtain an effect of hand-drawing style of the photo, in this paper, we first generate a two-tone image by a threshold, and then multiply it with a GSE image, which results in the Figure 4(d). We can find that Figure 4(d) generated by our method look like most a product by hand.

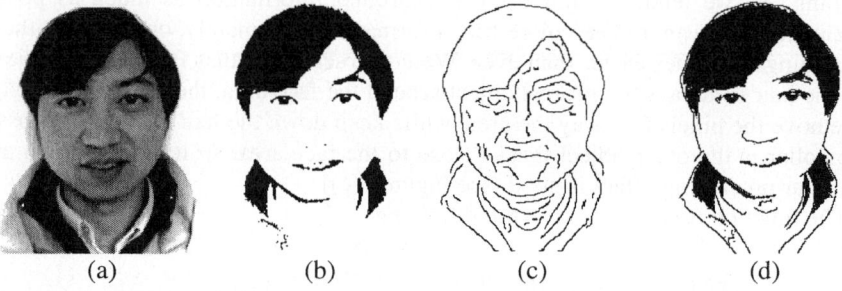

(a)   (b)   (c)   (d)

Fig. 4. Compare of three methods, (a) is the original image, (b) is generated by binary when threshold = 125, (c) is the edges extracted directly from the photo by canny algorithm, and (d) is the GSE image multiplied with the binarizing image

6 Face Warping and Animation

6.1 Compare of Warping Approaches

Now, we compare the performance of two algorithms: Mesh warping and Feature-based Warping. The result shows they behave different in respective aspect. When we evaluate them with computational speed, the Mesh Warping algorithm is the better. For in Mesh Warping, the region is divided into a mesh and each mesh patch essentially has a local influence region., so the computation takes place locally and independently. Moreover, it allows for high level of parallelism. Thus, the mesh warping got high computing speed. Table 1 gives us the average warping time of two algorithms in our experiments. In this paper, The points of the mesh are presented in Figure 3(b).

Table 1. Speed compare of two algorithms

Algorithm Name	Computation Time
Mesh Warping	0.25 s with a 118 mesh
Feature-based Warping	0.85 s with 3 feature lines

However, when we compare them on warping quality, the Feature-based Warping algorithm is the better. For in this case, the image is calculated point by point, which ensures the pixels' transition is smooth enough. Whereas in Mesh Warping, the movement is a block of pixels, so the transition on the region edge is not natural.

It is obvious, to the Feature -based warping algorithm, there is another disadvantage, that is, we must specify the feature lines artificially representing facial features such as eyes, mouth and nose. We use ASM to offset it by auto-providing the feature's coordinates as analyzed in section 4.

6.2 Caricature Generation

To meet the need of mobile entertainment, considering the performance of the two warping method, we choose the second method to generate the caricature from illustration. Through feature based warping, the control pixels specified by us are warped exactly from source position to target position as we want them to. All the other pixels are then blended smoothly based on the positions of the control pixels. This gives us a very high level of intuitive control while morphing. So it is convenient to generate caricature.

As we had mentioned, there is a disadvantage of feature – based warping that we need specify feature lines artificially. But in our system, ASM is carried out first, which means the feature lines are obtained automatically. For example, if we need to warp the nose to a long one, we needn't point out the beginning and end position of the nose. What we should do is to input the serial numbers of the beginning and end points of the nose into warping module. The ASM had located the nose in the face image and can map the serial number into pixel coordinate.

6.3 Caricature Type

For a given face, there are two ways to specify its type to warp, those are the regularity way and the auto-discovery way.

The first one is the regularity way. We provide some types to generate caricature, such as Big Mouth, Big Nose, and Small eyes. User can make a choice according to the characteristic of the input face. The regularities ensure the face will be warped by a set of parameters corresponding to the user's choice.

The second way is to decide the warping type by the computer. Here a mass of statistic work is done. As we know, people perceive the characteristic of a face by comparing the features on the face with those on the average face. Thus, we can equip the computer with experience of average face. In that case, the computer can make compare between the new face and the average face, and decide what type to select for the new face. To do so, we let the computer to do large face observation. In this paper, we collect 200 face photos(100 men,100 women), and compute 19 features to train the computer. The measurement first is the feature's length in terms of the number of pixels. We obtain the fractions between a feature and some stable feature (we use the pupils' distance) to make normalization. Then the mean of each feature is calculated. At the same time ,the CV(Coefficient of Variation) is computed to reflect the feature's distribution. Big CV means the samples is decentralized, and we should give the feature less weight when evaluating its characteristics. Now, the computer can refer to the feature's CV, compare the new face's measurement with the mean feature, and make decision which feature should be warped and exaggerated. Meanwhile, The photos data are divided into man and woman classes to get more exact result. The negative data is the cosine of the angle.

Table 2. The features of average face through faces stat

Features	Man		Woman	
	Mean	CV	Mean	CV
Width of face	2.067604	0.066138	2.022219	0.053108
Height of face	2.222373	0.066138	2.139734	0.060036
Width of forehead	1.947297	0.083178	2.047014	0.058766
Height of forehead	0.893020	0.140041	0.988009	0.094346
Length of left eyebrow	0.688442	0.086718	0.667038	0.058140
Length of right eyebrow	0.677197	0.078372	0.664672	0.062956
Height of left eyebrow	0.165621	0.166543	0.117994	0.136847
Height of right eyebrow	0.166351	0.160293	0.116151	0.139513
Camber of left eyebrow	-0.379079	-0.398787	-0.575628	-0.163348
Camber of right eyebrow	-0.356109	-0.424414	-0.565815	-0.184313
Length of left eye	0.496360	0.065297	0.511017	0.060266
Length of right eye	0.493009	0.074105	0.510733	0.068320
Height of left eye	0.186422	0.172021	0.220795	0.153888
Height of right eye	0.188086	0.180755	0.222637	0.135417
Width of nose	0.673716	0.072458	0.663565	0.063893
Height of nose	1.090492	0.056667	1.107651	0.068989
Width of mouth	0.801977	0.090224	0.816337	0.091548
Height of upper lip	0.148985	0.199987	0.145735	0.171546
Height of lower lip	0.165717	0.179043	0.177072	0.126474

6.4 Text Driven Exaggerated Animation

1. Traditional TTVS System Skeleton

Generally speaking, the framework of the multimodal synthesis system including text, audio and video can be described as Figure.5. In the figure, the white block represents the data in the system, and the grey block represents data processing. The detailed process is as followed:

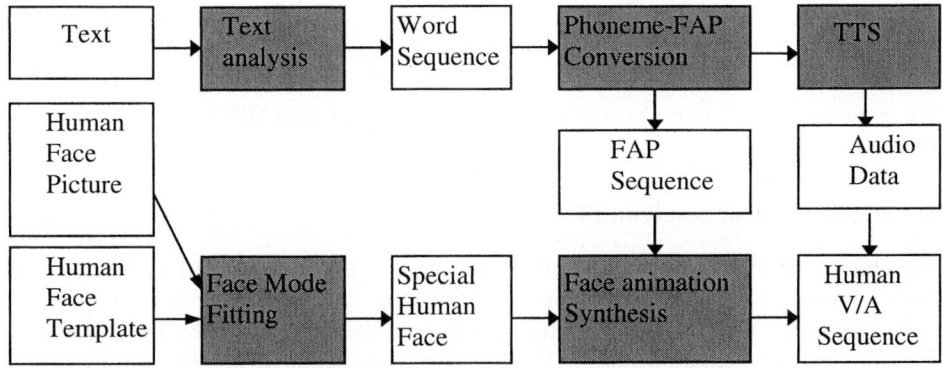

Fig. 5. The framework of a traditional TTVS system

1) After text analysis, the text is processed through TTS, at the same time, system produce the phoneme sequence;
2) The audio data and the duration of each phoneme can be obtained by TTS system;
3) With phoneme sequence and duration sequence, we can get sequence of Face Animation Parameter;
4) With the method of ASM and pre-defined human face template, we can do face detection on the one special human face picture and get the data for special human face model;
5) By the MPEG-4 method for human face, we can synthesize the human face animation by the human face mesh and FAPs;
6) Finally, video and audio data is synchronized according to the time duration information.

2. Text Driven Exaggerated Animation

To make contribution to entertainment, we synthesize animation based on the caricature. So there is a little difference with ever. All affective should be expressed in exaggerated mode. Therefore, we redefined 6 expressions parameters based on MPEG4. Figure 6 gives an example to compare of the smile expression defined in MPEG4 and redefined in our system. We can find that the smile expression in (c) takes more entertainment effect than (b).

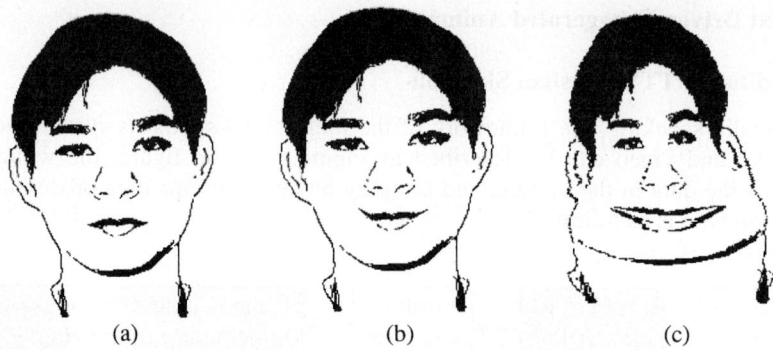

Fig. 6. (a) is a neutral face. (b) is smile expression generated from MPEG4 parameters, (c) is from our system.

3. The experiment result on PDA

We choose the PDA (Personal Digital Assistant) as experiment platform. The hardware condition is lenovo ET560 with Intel 400MHz CPU, 64M memory, and the OS is WindowsCE. We first capture a face photo with the camera in the PDA, then send it to the Server where a processing thread queue is running. A processing thread just deals with one request from the PDA, transforms the photograph into caricature and returns it to the mobile device. On PDA, under WindowsCE environment, when inputting a sentence of text, the caricature is driven to synthesize animation.

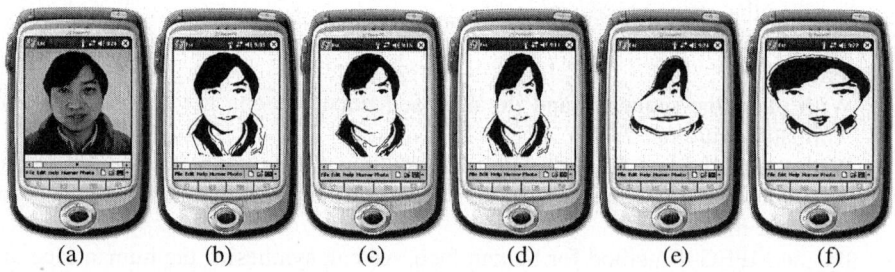

Fig. 7. The experiment result under WindowsCE. (a) is the original photo captured by the mobile camera. (b) is a common illustration. (c) to (f) are different type warped caricatures generated by our system.

7 Conclusion and Future Work

A novel mobile animation system based on local network is presented in this paper. It can transform people's real photograph to caricature and transfer it to the mobile terminal, where the text message is used to synthesize the facial animation. The animation based on the caricature is to bring people mobile entertainment.

This system is in schedule to run on the real 3G network in next years, and at that time, several challenging issues will be studied One is to change the black-and-white face to a color one. As we know, the colorful animation is more attractive. Another important issue is to experiment other warping algorithm to improve the speed of cartoon face synthesis. For in the embedded environment, the calculating resource is limited. The last one is to add gesture content in the animation, which is synchronous with the speech and the mouth movement, so the avatar can express more things to people than ever.

Acknowledgement. This work was supported by the Chinese National Science Foundation(grant 60303018, 60403037). We would like to appreciate Hanbing Dang and Zhang Huiguo, who greatly help collect the data, and thank Prof. Cui Guoqin and Dr. Miao Jun for valuable discussion on this work.

References

1. P. Omedas, F. Berrizbeitia, G. Szijártó, B. Kiss, B. Takács: Model-based Facial Animation for Mobile Communication. 1st Ibero-American Symposium on Computer Graphics (SIACG), Guim arães, Portugal, July 2-5, 2002.
2. M. Gutierrez, F. Vexo, D. Thalmann: The Mobile Animator: Interactive Character Animation in Collaborative Virtual Environments, IEEE Virtual Reality 2004 conference, Chicago, Illinois, March 27-31, 2004.
3. Gooch B., Reinhard E., Gooch A.: Human facial illustrations: Creation and psychophysical evaluation. ACM Trans. Graph.23, 1 (2004), 27–44.
4. Thaddeus Beier, Shawn Neely: Feature-Based Image Metamorphosis. Computer Graphics, 262, July 1992.
5. Hong Chen, Ziqiang Liu, Chunk Rose, Yingqing Xu, Heung-Yeung Shum, David Salesin: Example-Based Composite Sketching of Human Portraits. Proceedings of the 3rd international symposium on Non-photorealistic animation and rendering table of contents, 2004, Annecy, France.
6. Akleman, E., Palmer, J., and Logan, R.: Making extreme caricatures with a new interactive 2D deformation technique with simplicial complexes. In Proceedings of Visual'2000, September 2000.
7. T.F.Cootes, C.J.Taylor, D.Cooper, and J. Graham: Active shape models--their training and application. Computer vision and image understanding, 61(1): pp38-59, 1995.
8. Lin Liang,Hong Chen, Ying-Qing Xu, Heung-Yeung Shum: Example-based Caricature Generation with Exaggeration, IEEE Proceedings of the 10th Pacific Conference on Computer Graphics and Applications, 2002.
9. Zsófia Ruttkay, Han Noot: Animated CharToon Faces, NPAR2000, Annecy , France.
10. Mario Costa Sousa, Faramarz Samavati, Meru Brunn: Depicting Shape Features with Directional Strokes and Spotlighting, IEEE Proceedings of the Computer Graphics International, 2004.
11. BOOKSTEIN, F. L. Principal Warps: Thin-plates splines and decomposition of deformations, IEEE Trans. Pattern Analysis and Machine Intelligence (1989), vol 11(6), pp. 567-585.

12. Jun Miao, Wen Gao, C. Ma and Yiqiang Chen, Image Scale-Smoothing: Scale-Differentiating and Binarizing: A New Frame for General-Scale-Edge (GSE) Extraction, Proc. IEEE International Conference on System, Man and Cybernetics, Tucson, pp.2005-2010,Oct. 2001.
13. Wen Gao, Yiqiang Chen, Rui Wang, Shiguang Shan and Dalong Jiang: Learning and Synthesizing MPEG-4 Compatible 3-D Face Animation from Video Sequence. IEEE Transactions on Circuits and Systems for Video technology. Vol.13, No.11, pp1119-1128,Nov.2003
14. Yiqiang Chen, Wen Gao, Zhaoqi Wang, Changshui Yang, Dalong Jiang: Text to Avatar in Multimodal Human Computer Interface, Asia-Pacific Human Computer Interface (APCHI2002), Vol.2, pp636-643.2002

Concept and Construction of the Caddy Robot

Florent Servillat[1], Ryohei Nakatsu[1,2], Xiao-feng Wu[1], and Kazuo Itoh[1]

[1] Nirvana Technology Inc., Keihanna Plaza Lab Wing, 4F,
1-7 Hikaridai, Seika-cho, Soraku-gun, Kyoto-fu, 619-0237 Japan
{servillat, nakatsu, xiaof-wu, ito}@nirvana.keihanna.ne.jp
http://www.nirvana.ne.jp/
[2] Kwansei Gakuin University
2-1 Gakuen, Sanda, 669-1337 Japan
nakatsu@ksc.kwansei.ac.jp
http://www.nirvana.ne.jp/updatefile/nakatsu/

Abstract. The Caddy Robot is an ambitious project, the purpose of which is to provide a robotic assistant (Caddy) to players on a golf course. This robot will have to deal with its environment (obstacles, hazardous areas, balls), the players (talk with them, advise them), and the rules of golf. Because developing such a robot will take much time, we produced a prototype. First, this paper will deal with the concepts of the final version of the Caddy Robot. We will then address the prototype concept and its construction, describing the architecture and function.

1 Introduction

Research and development of humanoid robots that can behave like humans is being pursued actively in various universities, venture companies and industrial companies [1][2][3][4][5]. So far, however, it seems that the areas in which these robots can be best applied remain unclear. We, however, believe that the "Caddy Robot" for golf is an appropriate application area for such robots. There are several reasons for this. One is that the functions required for a caddy include almost all the functions the humanoid robot should have. Image processing and recognition capability is of course one of the key functions that a caddy robot needs. Furthermore, it should be able to sense environmental conditions such as wind and temperature using various kinds of sensors, and it should possess sophisticated communication capability with golf players. It is easily understood that these capabilities are the keys for the humanoid robot to be accepted by and introduced into our society. On the other hand, it is difficult for many golf courses to hire good caddies and it would be most helpful for them if caddy robots that can work for human caddies could be realized.

Based on the above considerations we have commenced the ambitious project of the "Caddy Robot," the purpose of which is to provide a robotic assistant (caddy) to golf players. This robot will have to deal with its environment (obstacles, hazardous areas, balls), the players (talk with them, advise them,) and the rules of golf. To develop such a kind of robot would take much time. Thus, we have started the research and development of a first demonstration prototype, which can perform some of the main tasks of the final version of the Caddy Robot. In this paper, first we will deal with the concept of the final version of the Caddy Robot. Second, we will explain more precisely the concept and architecture of the prototype. Following that, we will describe the prototype's functions in detail, and finally we will discuss the issues that remain to be solved for the future versions.

2 Concept of a Caddy Robot

2.1 Concept

Caddies are people who work at a golf course. They accompany golfers while they walk and play through eighteen holes of golf. Sometimes the caddy will talk with the players and relax them with conversation, other times they will look for balls the players have hit in the wrong direction. Also, sometimes they will watch the players' swings give them advice if required. In that sense, a caddy can be a secretary, a friend, a coach, and so on. Although there is a tremendous number of golf courses all over the world and a huge number of people who enjoy playing golf, there is unfortunately a shortage of caddies; nowadays it is becoming increasingly common to play golf without them.

Playing golf without caddies is sometimes troublesome, especially when golf players do not know about the golf course on which they are playing. If humanoid robots can take the role of caddies, it could be a real boon for golfers as well as for the robotics industry. Based on this concept, we have commenced the project to develop what we call the "Caddy Robot."

2.2 Functions

The plan for the Caddy Robot is to equip it with various types of information and communication technologies. By utilizing these technologies it is expected that the robot, which would provide real and useful support to golfers at golf courses in the future, would feature the following functions.

Measurement of Natural Conditions and Environmental Conditions.
Using the various sensors fitted to the robot, it can measure a range of natural conditions such as wind strength, wind direction, temperature, moisture, and so on. These data would become a basis of advice the robot would give to the players. Also, by employing visual sensors such as a stereo camera and an omni-directional camera, it can measure or identify a whole variety of data. For example, it can determine the distance from the ball on the fairway to the green, and it can trace the direction of balls hit by the players, making it easier to find balls that have strayed out of bounds. On the green it can measure the distance between the ball and the hole, in addition to checking the roll of the green.

Measuring Playing Positions/Motions of Golf Players (Fig. 1)
Using its visual sensors the robot can check the position of the players when they want to hit or putt the ball. If the position is not appropriate, the robot can assist the players by giving them advice. Furthermore, the robot can watch the motion of the players' golf swing and putting swing, and by comparing their motions with those of

professional players, the robot can detect differences. It would then be able to give some advice to the players.

On the green, the direction and the strength of the putting would vary depending on the lay of the green. Thus, by combining data on green angulation and the golfers' playing motion, the robot would be able to give advice to the players.

Fig. 1. Measurement of playing positions/motions of golf players

Communication with the Golfers (Fig. 2)

One of the most important roles of the caddy is to give the players appropriate advice when required by them. By combining and utilizing measurement data on natural conditions and dynamic environmental conditions as well as data on playing positions/motions, we expect that the robot would be able to fulfill this role. Such advice would be especially relevant when the players are unfamiliar with the course on which they are playing.

Another important role of the caddy is to communicate with golfers. Apart from wanting to know their score, golfers usually want to fully enjoy the sport as a form of entertainment and want to refresh themselves through the game. Since good communication with others relaxes, entertains and refreshes people, the ability of the Caddy Robot to communicate effectively with golfers is essential for its success. When the robot meets new players it can identify them by accessing the face database on the server. While on the course, the robot could tease or relax tense or nervous players by talking to them about current events or something appropriate.

Fig. 2. Entertainment and communication

3 Concept and Architecture of the Prototype Robot

3.1 Concept

The development of a caddy robot that possesses the functions described in the previous section is a great challenging and is expected to take many years. As a first step toward this final goal, we have developed the first prototype robot. The goal of this prototype is not to develop a complete robot but only one that can perform some of the main tasks of the future Caddy Robot. Thus in this section we will only deal with the current functions of the prototype.

3.2 Functions

Moving on the Playground
For this first version, we will restrict the area in which the robot will move. This area is a perfect plane playground, on which there are only balls and a cup. Beside for the color of the ground, we need to ensure that the robot is not confused by any other element. To localize itself, the robot will use four vertical marks on each corner of the playground because we only need three marks to locate the robot's position on the map. The size of the playground has been chosen so that the camera will always be able to detect the cup and the balls (currently, about 5 m x 5 m).

Recognizing Golf Elements

We restrict the number of elements the robot has to detect. There will be only one ball on the ground, and we assume that there are no obstacles on the playground. The robot will always locate elements within its own generalized coordinates, the origin of those coordinates being in the middle of the wheels axis. The x-axis follows the wheels axis and runs from left to right. The y-axis runs from back to front, and the z-axis is vertical.

Dialog with Players

In the first step, we need to restrict the number of subjects with which the robot should be able to communicate with players. Besides, the dialog scheme will be completely predefined and only applied by the robot. The robot will be managed using voice commands.

Playing Golf

The robot needs to understand the basic rules of playing golf in order to know what it has to do. However, in this version, we will express the rules directly in its action scenario; therefore, the playing act will be processed thanks to a script execution, completely defined.

3.3 Construction

The Hardware Architecture

For active detection in its environment, the Caddy Robot uses the PBS sensor. The main purpose of the forwarding camera is to precisely locate the position of the ball just before playing. Thanks to this camera, the robot can reach a convenient position to play golf and then to control the position of the putter relative to the ball. On the other hand, to detect the objects far from the robot and to evaluate a golfer's position in relation to the robot's coordinates, we use a stereovision system. The omnidirectional camera is only used to detect marks on the wall so the robot can ascertain its position in the environment.

Regarding the robot's actuators, we can compare the bottom of the body to a holonomic vehicle with three degrees of freedom (x and y translation and yaw rotation). Each of the end-effectors (hands) has six degrees of freedom, giving the robot the ability to perform many different tasks. Furthermore, the head has five degrees of freedom, and three of these connections are independent of the rest of the body (yaw, pitch and roll rotation for the neck). Because of these rotations, we can control each end-effector independently.

Currently for the hands, we only perform actions previously taught to the robot by a human. The robot is able to greet to players and to play golf. This last action must be taught because currently we are unable to express gestures as an abstract list of actions. Consequently, the robot must attain a suitable posture to play golf (but isn't this the same for humans?).

The Software Architecture

The robot's software architecture consists of two main parts. A low-level software manages the robot's sensors and actuators while a high-level software (the main controller) evaluates current conditions and sends a set of actions to the lower part of the robot. These two parts exchange data using a TCP/IP socket.

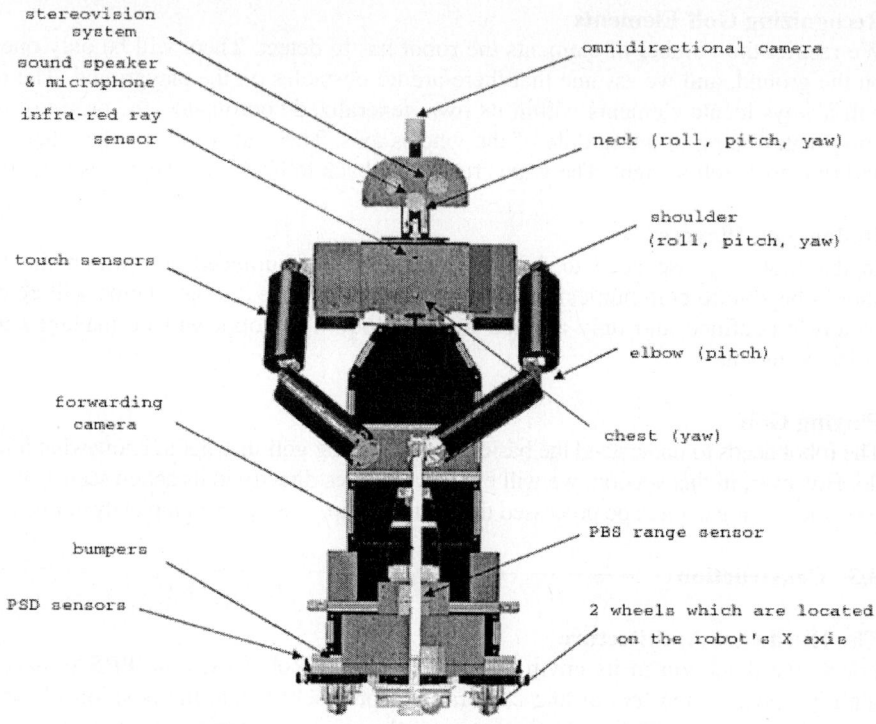

Fig. 3. Caddy robot's hardware architecture

The low-level part only manages the sensors and actuators. When the main controller requests pieces of information to this level, the low-level part will apply the corresponding algorithm and send the answer to the main controller. In addition, some sensors are designed to catch unexpected events (bumpers, touch sensors). Given the results from these sensors, this level sends an interrupt to the main controller and a report on the new situation. These pieces of information enable the main controller to be able to adapt to the robot's goal.

The low-level part actually comprises three processes:

* The main process, which deals with the main controller and applies an algorithm to the data provided by sensors;
* Gtalk, a text-to-speech process that transforms a textual sentence to a sound file;
* The Julian process, which analyzes a user's request.

The last two processes are independent to allow the robot to use its actuators and sensors, while at the same time generating a spoken sentence and analyzing a request.

The main controller has to apply the scenario we defined. It checks the current state of the scenario by using the data received from the low-level part. Once the state of the scenario has been found, the main controller will send back a set of actions to the

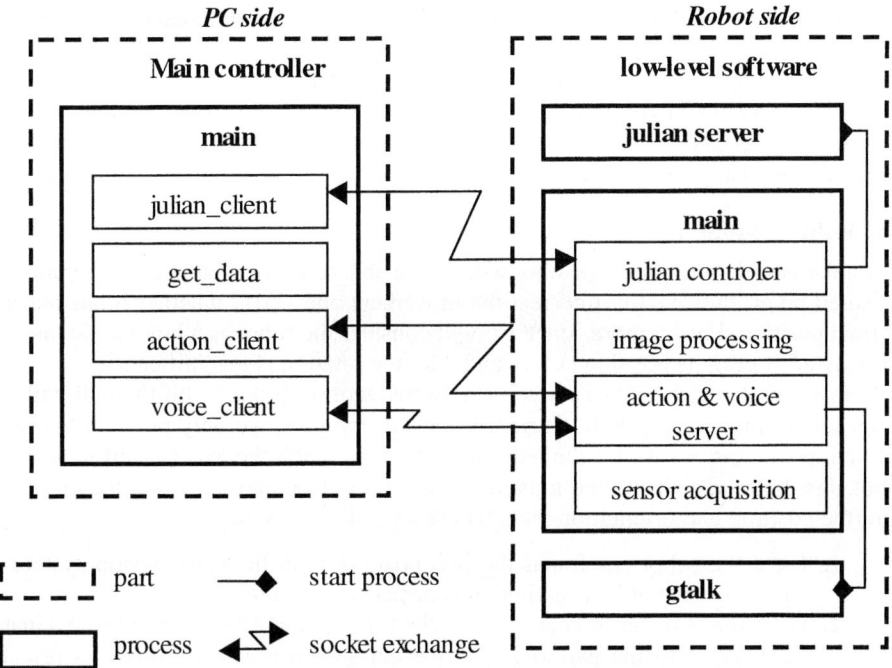

Fig. 4. Caddy robot's software architecture

low-level part. The main controller manages also the Julian (speech recognition) process that performs the voice recognition.

4 Functions of the Prototype Robot

4.1 Image Processing [6][7]

Initially, we need to adapt the image according to the lighting conditions. To so this, we apply only a realignment of the histogram dynamic. Since the objects in an image will have a color completely different to that of the ground, we need not spend more of the processor resources for this task. Therefore, we use a fast color-segmentation algorithm to obtain regions in the image.

The goal of the image-processing package is to recognize objects in an image and evaluate their distance from the robot using the coordinates. The stereovision system determines the distance of elements far from the robot, , while for close objects in the foreground, we use the camera, which is oriented toward the ground, and we evaluate the objects' positions. We assume that the floor will be flat, so we can evaluate the location (within the robots coordinates) of small elements (ball, cup), from their position in the image.

To localize the robot, we employ the omnidirectional camera to detect straight lines in this image. With three markers we can evaluate the position and orientation of the robot with simple geometry. If only two markers can be detected by the system, we will add a stereovisually determined distance for one or two of the markers to complete the localization; otherwise, the robot will not be able to ascertain its location.

When accompanying a golfer, the Caddy Robot looks for the ball's position and evaluates the result of the putting action, then measured the distance and the angle between the cup and the ball. With these data, the robot will be able to comment on the result and also make predictions for the next action.

4.2 Robot's Motion

Given the wheel controller, the robot will not be able to move with enough accuracy to a desired point, thus we must correct the movement and verify whether it has reached its final position. Furthermore, since we will consider the robot as a holonomic one, the difference between its position before and after the rotation is insignificant.

In this prototype, the robot performs only two motion tasks: to hit the ball with the putter and to move to the ball. Currently for the first task, we only perform the same defined movement, so we hit the ball only when we reach the exact position with the robot. Just before this task, we must move the robot to reach the exact playing position (the position and orientation from where the ball will be hit).

1. Once the robot has found the ball position with the stereovision system, it moves in the ball's direction and corrects its heading.
2. Once the ball can be seen through the forward camera, the robot re-evaluates its distance to the ball and with the cup position, it determines its orientation. It then moves to the ball until it reaches the right position. The position is correct when the ball is located in a particular area within the image.
3. From this position the robot is able to execute the action "play golf."

This means that the robot's motion is video controlled since the actuators' controllers are not yet reliable enough.

4.3 Voice Communication

Communication from humans to the robot is performed with the speech recognition tool Julian [8]. Julian is an open-source product written from the open-source program Julius, which is a two-pass, large-vocabulary speech recognition based on word 3-gram and context-dependent HMM. Julian performs grammar-based recognition. This module enables us to add grammar constraints to speech recognition and build a kind of voice command system that uses a small vocabulary.

Because our current goal with this prototype is only to build a rule-based expert system, the Julian recognition system is the most suitable. The recognition system will look for a small number of voice commands and perform the actions attached to these commands. Furthermore, in future versions, we will be able to use Julian to express the meaning of a player's sentences with a more complex model.

In the opposite direction, the Galatea Toolkit [9] performs the communication from the robot to humans. This is an open-source toolkit for anthropomorphic spoken-dialog agents. For the Caddy Robot, we only use the text-to-speech functions provided by Galatea. Currently, replies given by the robot consists of single sentences defined by the programmer where only a few parameters change.

Figure 5 shows some of the robot's photo.

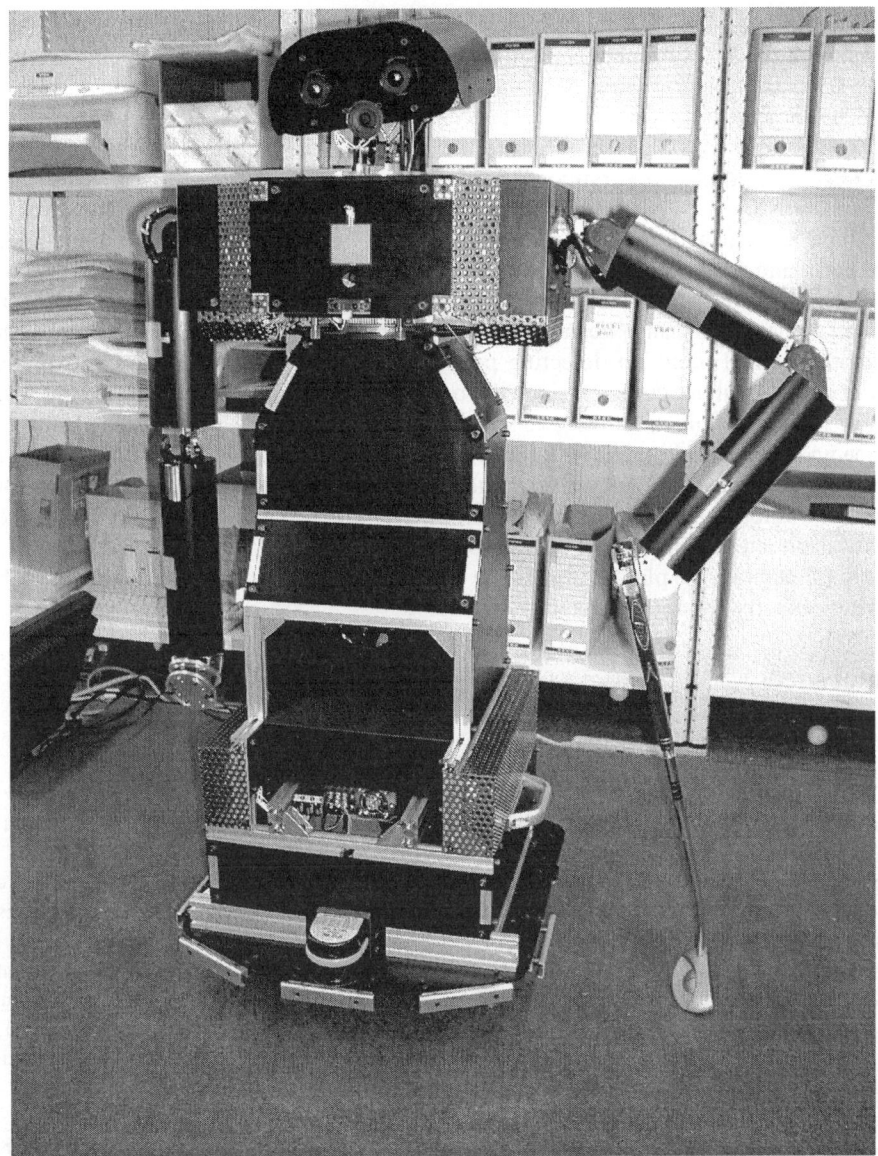

Fig. 5. Caddy robot's photo

5 Conclusion

In this paper we have proposed the concept of a Caddy Robot. First we discussed the functions required for human caddies, followed by a discussion on the final goal of our Caddy Robot. As it is very difficult for us to achieve al the desired functions for the Caddy Robot from the outset, as a first step we have restricted the functions of the first prototype to a few key ones.

The prototype Caddy Robot we have developed is able to putt as one of its key golf plays, with robot vision playing a crucial key role to achieve this. The robot also features a basic verbal communication capability utilizing its speech recognition and speech synthesis functions.

There still remain many problems to be solved before we produce a robot that can deal with a complex environment. For example, currently for the motion task, any movement is only executed within a safe area. In the real-world version, however, we will have to deal with the path-planning problem because a golf course is not a simple, flat plane with no obstacles. We will have to maintain a map with fixed and mobile obstacles to check whether a given element is indeed an obstacle. To date, the recognition task has only been performed for ball and cup detection, but in further versions we will focus on detecting people in order to advise them. Moreover, ball tracking will be more complex since the ball does not usually travel in a straight line.

For the communication task, we will have to increase the ability of the Caddy Robot to understand and to talk with the players. The questions should deal not only with game play and the score but also on other subjects in relation to golf (e.g., the weather forecast). Another issue of communication is for the robot to detect whether a question was directed to itself or to another player.

For game play, we plan to implement a rule-based system that will enable the robot to know exactly what it will have to do.

References

1. http://www.honda.co.jp/robot/
2. http://www.sony.net/SonyInfo/QRIO/
3. http://www.humanoid.waseda.ac.jp/index.html
4. Nakaoka, S., et al.: Leg Motion Primitives for a Dancing Humanoid Robot. Proc IEEE Int. Conf. Robotics and Automation, IEEE (2004) 610-615
5. Wama T., et. al.: Realization of Tai-chi Motion Using Humanoid Robot - Physical Interactions with Humanoid Robot. Building the Information Society, Kluwer Academic Publishers (2004) 59-64
6. M.D. Wagner, D. O'Hallaron, D. Apostolopoulos, and C. Urmson: Principles of Computer System Design for Stereo Perception. Tech. Report CMU-RI-TR-02-01, Robotics Institute, Carnegie Mellon University, January, (2002) http://www.ri.cmu.edu/pubs/pub_3893.html
7. James Bruce, Tucker Balch, and Manuela Veloso.: Real-Time Color Image Segmentation Using Commodity Hardware. In Proceedings of WIRE-2000, (May 2000)
8. http://julius.sourceforge.jp
9. Open-source Software for developing anthropomorphic spoken dialog agent Shin-ichi Kawamoto, Hiroshi Shimodaira, Tsuneo Nitta, Takuya Nishimoto, Satoshi Nakamura, Katsunobu Itou, Shigeo Morishima, Tatsuo Yotsukura , Atsuhiko Kai , Akinobu Lee , Yoichi Yamashita , Takao Kobayashi , Keiichi Tokuda , Keikichi Hirose , Nobuaki Minematsu , Atsushi Yamada , Yasuharu Den , Takehito Utsuro , Shigeki Sagayama,: Open-source software for developing anthropomorphic spoken dialog agent. Proc. of PRICAI-02, International Workshop on Lifelike Animated Agents (Aug 2002) pp.64-69

Rapid Algorithms for MPEG-2 to H.264 Transcoding

Xiaoming Sun and Pin Tao

Computer Science Department, Tsinghua University

Abstract. The bandwidth saving of H.264 compared with MPEG-2 provides a big motivation to migrate to H.264, and this inspires the research on MPEG-2 to H.264 transcoding. We proposed two fast algorithms for MPEG-2 to H.264 transcoding in DCT domain. The first one synthesizes a H.264 integer DCT block for motion compensation from four intersected integer DCT blocks using only a few additions and shift operations. The second algorithm shows our rapid solution on dealing with the difference of scale in the integer DCT domain before and after the quantization procedure and replace the division operations with multiplications and shift operations. They are very useful in MPEG to H.264 DCT domain transcoder designing, especially for embedded RISC processors.

1 Introduction

H.264, also known as MPEG-4 part 10, has become a new international standard recently by the effort of the JVT of ITU. It exceeds other video compressing standards by its highly efficient coding solution. Compared with MPEG-2 video, the H.264 video format gives perceptually equivalent video at 1/3 to 1/2 bit rates of the MPEG-2 format. In spite of its complexity, the actual bandwidth savings compared to MPEG-2 provides a big motivation to migrate to H.264 video coding[1]. The transition from MPEG-2 to H.264 may not accomplish in an action, therefore H.264 and MPEG-2 will coexist for years. In order to conserve the large amount of resources coded in MPEG-2 and convert them into H.264, developing a method of transcoding between the two standards is highly expected.

The existing transcoding methods mainly focus on two aspects, downscaling and format transcoding. The latter one translates syntax format from one standard into another[3], while the downscaling reduces the size of the video pictures in spatial domain or the frequency of frames in temporal domain[4][5]. And sometimes there is a design combining the two above aspects into one transcoder system[4][5].

In this paper we mainly discussed two optimized algorithms necessary in MPEG-2 to H.264 transcoding process. The rest of this paper is organized as follows: Section II demonstrated a brief framework of the DCT domain transcoder. The details of the two optimized algorithms were discussed in Section III and IV respectively. In Section V some conclusions were given.

2 MPEG-2 to H.264 Video Transcoding

The most intuitional way to transcode a video stream is to construct a transcoder by cascading a full decoder and a full encoder with the output of the decoder to be the input of the encoder. However, it leads to a great computational complexity which is the sum of the complexities of the full-functional decoder and encoder. Regarding the similarities in the architectures of the two standards, the computational complexity could be reduced effectively by reusing the original information of the video in the source bit stream. For example, by reusing Motion Vector (MV), the transcoder can omit the step of Motion Estimation (ME) which is usually the part with the greatest computation in the encoder. To minimize the computational complexity, some people proposed trancoding methods in DCT domain which can further avoid DCT and IDCT computation[3][4].

The architecture of a typical DCT domain MPEG-2 to H.264 transcoder is illustrated in figure 1.

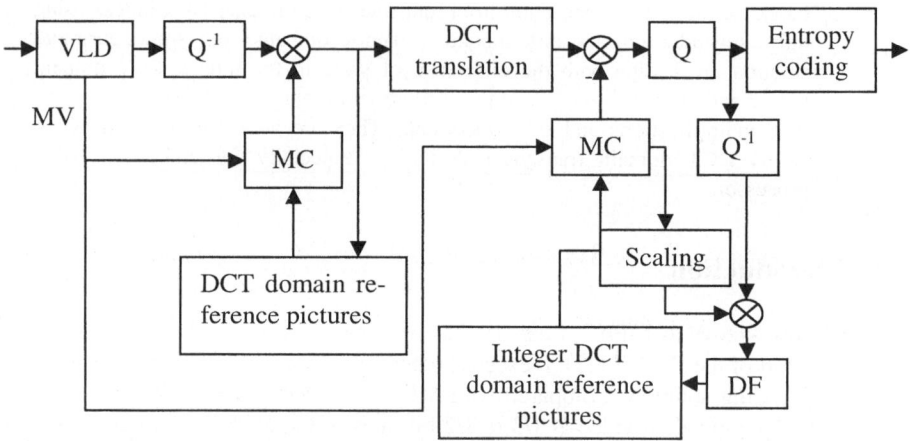

Fig. 1. Transcoding Framework

We take the P picture as an example to describe the procedures of the transcoding as shown in Figure 1. After the VLD (Variable Length Decoding) and Q^{-1}(Inverse Quantization) operations, the DCT coefficients are recovered into MC-DCT domain (Motion Compensated DCT for P or B pictures, e.g. the residual coefficients in DCT domain). Because the direct transcoding in MC-DCT domain introduces error propagation in P pictures[2][3], the coefficients need to be converted into the DCT domain by inverse MC (Motion Compensation). The inverse MC operation adds the MC-DCT coefficients block with the prediction block indicated by the MV pointing to the reference picture in the DCT domain. H.264 adopts an integer DCT transform which differentiates from the traditional DCT method adopted by many previous video coding standards such as MPEG serials, H.263 and so on. So the translation between the above two DCT domains is required. Xin proposed an algorithm to make the translation without converting the coefficients from DCT domain to pixel domain and back to integer DCT domain and further he discovered a rapid method of it[10].

After the translation, a MC operation should be performed with the reference picture in the integer DCT domain to avoid error propagation in P pictures. Since the quantization introduces distortion, a reference picture should be constructed after the H.264 quantization, which is identical to the one constructed in the decoder.

The MC operation needs a prediction reference block which is very easy to acquire in pixel domain but a problem in DCT domain. As the MV usually does not align with the DCT blocks, the prediction reference block will often intersect 4 blocks. In pixel domain, we can re-assemble the pixels to form a prediction reference block very easily. But in DCT domain, the prediction DCT block has to be synthesized from 4 DCT blocks in reference picture because of the edge-effect. Therefore the method of block synthesis in DCT domain has been proposed by Chang[2], but the method for the integer DCT domain is still undeveloped. We proposed an algorithm which operates in integer DCT domain to synthesize a H.264 integer DCT block and further more find out a rapid method for this algorithm with only several addition and shift computations which will be discussed in Section III.

Because H.264 combines the scale adjusting of the integer DCT transform with the quantization and inverse quantization procedure[12], there is difference of scale between the pre-quantization DCT domain and the post-quantization DCT domain. To construct the reference pictures in DCT domain, we have to choose a matrix from the two MC entry matrices and adjust the scale of the coefficients to match another. We proposed an algorithm to satisfy this need and we will discuss the details in Section IV.

3 Prediction Block Synthesis in Integer DCT Domain

As the MC operation can not be performed in MC-DCT domain[2], the block in MC-DCT domain has to be reconstructed into DCT domain before the MC by adding the MC-DCT block with the prediction DCT block indicated by MV. Usually the MV does not point to an exact block partition in the reference picture, and a prediction DCT block has to be synthesized from four DCT block in the reference picture. Chang proposed an algorithm in [2] to solve this problem in DCT domain. We proposed a similar algorithm which can operate in integer DCT domain and developed a rapid computing method using only addition and shift operation from which the embedded systems will benefit a lot.

As shown in figure 2, in the most common case, the prediction block intersects four original block partitions in the reference picture.

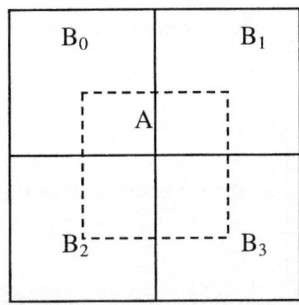

Fig. 2. The prediction block A intersects four original blocks B_0 to B_3

Assume that B_0 to B_3 are the 4 original pixel blocks in the reference frame and A is the pixel prediction block which intersects with B_0 to B_3. Let block A_0 contain the intersection area of block A and B_0 and place the coefficients in the upper-left corner of A_0 as follow:

$$A_0 = \begin{bmatrix} 0 & I_h \\ 0 & 0 \end{bmatrix} B_0 \begin{bmatrix} 0 & 0 \\ I_w & 0 \end{bmatrix} = \begin{bmatrix} b_{3-w,3-h} & \cdots & b_{3-w,3} & 0 \\ \vdots & \ddots & \vdots & 0 \\ b_{3,3-h} & \cdots & b_{3,3} & 0 \\ 0 & 0 & 0 & 0 \end{bmatrix} \quad (1)$$

where subscript h and w stand for the height and width of the intersection area in pixels, respectively. I_h and I_w are the identity matrices with size $h \times h$ and $w \times w$, respectively. Analogously, A_1, A_2 and A_3 are given by:

$$A_1 = \begin{bmatrix} 0 & I_h \\ 0 & 0 \end{bmatrix} B_1 \begin{bmatrix} 0 & I_{4-w} \\ 0 & 0 \end{bmatrix}$$

$$A_2 = \begin{bmatrix} 0 & 0 \\ I_{4-h} & 0 \end{bmatrix} B_2 \begin{bmatrix} 0 & 0 \\ I_w & 0 \end{bmatrix} \quad (2)$$

$$A_3 = \begin{bmatrix} 0 & 0 \\ I_{4-h} & 0 \end{bmatrix} B_3 \begin{bmatrix} 0 & I_{4-w} \\ 0 & 0 \end{bmatrix}$$

and

$$A = A_0 + A_1 + A_2 + A_3 \quad (3)$$

Let $D_m = \begin{bmatrix} 0 & I_m \\ 0 & 0 \end{bmatrix}$, and $B_0^{int\_dct}$ to $B_3^{int\_dct}$ be the corresponding integer DCT blocks of B_0 to B_3 after the inverse quantization operation. Define

$$C_f = \begin{bmatrix} 1 & 1 & 1 & 1 \\ 2 & 1 & -1 & -2 \\ 1 & -1 & -1 & 1 \\ 1 & -2 & 2 & -1 \end{bmatrix}$$

as the transform matrix of integer DCT and

$$C_i = \begin{bmatrix} 1 & 1 & 1 & 1 \\ 1 & 1/2 & -1/2 & -1 \\ 1 & -1 & -1 & 1 \\ 1/2 & -1 & 1 & -1/2 \end{bmatrix}$$

as the inverse transform matrix. Substituting them into equation (3) and noticing that $B_0^{int\_dct}$ to $B_3^{int\_dct}$ have been enlarged 64 times by the inverse quantization procedure[12], equation (3) can be rewritten as:

$$64A = D_h C_i^T B_0^{int\_dct} C_i D_w^T + D_h C_i^T B_1^{int\_dct} C_i D_{4-w} \qquad (4)$$
$$+ D_{4-h}^T C_i^T B_2^{int\_dct} C_i D_w^T + D_{4-h}^T C_i^T B_3^{int\_dct} C_i D_{4-w}$$

Use matrix C_f to transform A into A^{int_dct} which is the corresponding block of A in integer DCT domain:

$$64A^{int\_dct} = C_f [64A] C_f^T$$
$$= C_f (D_h C_i^T B_0^{int\_dct} C_i D_w^T + D_h C_i^T B_1^{int\_dct} C_i D_{4-w}$$
$$+ D_{4-h}^T C_i^T B_2^{int\_dct} C_i D_w^T + D_{4-h}^T C_i^T B_3^{int\_dct} C_i D_{4-w}) C_f^T \qquad (5)$$
$$= C_f D_h C_i^T [B_0^{int\_dct}] C_i D_w^T C_f^T + C_f D_h C_i^T [B_1^{int\_dct}] C_i D_{4-w} C_f^T$$
$$+ C_f D_{4-h}^T C_i^T [B_2^{int\_dct}] C_i D_w^T C_f^T + C_f D_{4-h}^T C_i^T [B_3^{int\_dct}] C_i D_{4-w} C_f^T$$

Let $H_n = C_f D_n C_i^T$, $W_n = C_f D_n^T C_i^T$, and equation (5) can be rewritten as:

$$64A^{int\_dct} = H_h B_0^{int\_dct} H_w^T + H_h B_1^{int\_dct} W_{4-w}^T + W_{4-h} B_2^{int\_dct} H_w^T + W_{4-h} B_3^{int\_dct} W_{4-w}^T \qquad (6)$$
$$= H_h (B_0^{int\_dct} H_w^T + B_1^{int\_dct} W_{4-w}^T) + W_{4-h} (B_2^{int\_dct} H_w^T + B_3^{int\_dct} W_{4-w}^T)$$

where

$$H_1 = \begin{bmatrix} 1 & -1 & 1 & -\frac{1}{2} \\ 2 & -2 & 2 & -1 \\ 1 & -1 & 1 & -\frac{1}{2} \\ 1 & -1 & 1 & -\frac{1}{2} \end{bmatrix} \quad H_2 = \begin{bmatrix} 2 & -\frac{3}{2} & 0 & \frac{1}{2} \\ 3 & -2 & -1 & \frac{3}{2} \\ 0 & \frac{1}{2} & -2 & \frac{3}{2} \\ -1 & \frac{3}{2} & -3 & 2 \end{bmatrix} \quad H_3 = \begin{bmatrix} 3 & -1 & -1 & -\frac{1}{2} \\ 2 & \frac{3}{2} & -4 & -\frac{1}{2} \\ -1 & 2 & -1 & -\frac{3}{2} \\ 1 & -\frac{1}{2} & 3 & -4 \end{bmatrix}$$

$$W_1 = \begin{bmatrix} 1 & 1 & 1 & \frac{1}{2} \\ -2 & -2 & -2 & -1 \\ 1 & 1 & 1 & \frac{1}{2} \\ -1 & -1 & -1 & -\frac{1}{2} \end{bmatrix} \quad W_2 = \begin{bmatrix} 2 & \frac{3}{2} & 0 & -\frac{1}{2} \\ -3 & -2 & 1 & \frac{3}{2} \\ 0 & -\frac{1}{2} & -2 & -\frac{3}{2} \\ 1 & \frac{3}{2} & 3 & 2 \end{bmatrix} \quad W_3 = \begin{bmatrix} 3 & 1 & -1 & \frac{1}{2} \\ -2 & \frac{3}{2} & 4 & -\frac{1}{2} \\ -1 & -2 & -1 & \frac{3}{2} \\ -1 & -\frac{1}{2} & -3 & -4 \end{bmatrix}$$

The forms of H_1 and W_1 are simple. The multiplication and division can be replaced by shift operation. But H_2, H_3, W_2 and W_3 seem not so easy to deal with. To avoid multiplication in computing the matrices, we developed a rapid method for H_2, H_3, W_2 and W_3.

Take H_2 as an example. As we discussed above,

$$H_2 = C_f D_2 C_i^T \qquad (7)$$

D_2 can be decomposed as:

$$D_2 = \begin{bmatrix} 0 & 0 & 1 & 0 \\ 0 & 0 & 0 & 1 \\ 0 & 0 & 0 & 0 \\ 0 & 0 & 0 & 0 \end{bmatrix} = \begin{bmatrix} 0 & 0 & 1 & 0 \\ 0 & 0 & 0 & 0 \\ 0 & 0 & 0 & 0 \\ 0 & 0 & 0 & 0 \end{bmatrix} + \begin{bmatrix} 0 & 0 & 0 & 0 \\ 0 & 0 & 0 & 1 \\ 0 & 0 & 0 & 0 \\ 0 & 0 & 0 & 0 \end{bmatrix} = D_2{'} + D_2{''} \quad (8)$$

Substitute (8) into (7)

$$H_2 = C_f(D_2{'} + D_2{''})C_i^T = C_f D_2{'} C_i^T + C_f D_2{''} C_i^T$$

$$= \begin{bmatrix} 1 & -\frac{1}{2} & -1 & 1 \\ 2 & -1 & -2 & 2 \\ 1 & -\frac{1}{2} & -1 & 1 \\ 1 & -\frac{1}{2} & -1 & 1 \end{bmatrix} + \begin{bmatrix} 1 & -1 & 1 & -\frac{1}{2} \\ 1 & -1 & 1 & -\frac{1}{2} \\ -1 & 1 & -1 & \frac{1}{2} \\ -2 & 2 & -2 & 1 \end{bmatrix} \quad (9)$$

Because the multiplication of two matrices HA can be regarded as the operations upon the rows in matrix A, we take the computation of a single column as an example:

Let $B = \begin{bmatrix} b_1 \\ b_2 \\ b_3 \\ b_4 \end{bmatrix}$, $A = \begin{bmatrix} a_1 \\ a_2 \\ a_3 \\ a_4 \end{bmatrix}$

$$B = H_2 A = [C_f D_2{'} C_i^T + C_f D_2{''} C_i^T] A = C_f D_2{'} C_i^T A + C_f D_2{''} C_i^T A$$

$$= \begin{bmatrix} 1 & -\frac{1}{2} & -1 & 1 \\ 2 & -1 & -2 & 2 \\ 1 & -\frac{1}{2} & -1 & 1 \\ 1 & -\frac{1}{2} & -1 & 1 \end{bmatrix} \begin{bmatrix} a_1 \\ a_2 \\ a_3 \\ a_4 \end{bmatrix} + \begin{bmatrix} 1 & -1 & 1 & -\frac{1}{2} \\ 1 & -1 & 1 & -\frac{1}{2} \\ -1 & 1 & -1 & \frac{1}{2} \\ -2 & 2 & -2 & 1 \end{bmatrix} \begin{bmatrix} a_1 \\ a_2 \\ a_3 \\ a_4 \end{bmatrix} \quad (10)$$

Let $w_1 = a_1 - (a_2 >> 1) - a_3 + a_4$, $w_2 = a_1 - a_2 + a_3 - (a_4 >> 1)$
b_1 to b_4 can be given by:

$$b_1 = w_1 + w_2, b_2 = (w_1 << 1) + w_2, b_3 = w_1 - w_2, b_4 = w_1 - (w_2 << 1), \text{ or}$$
$$b_1 = w_1 + w_2, b_2 = b_1 + w_1, b_3 = w_1 - w_2, b_4 = b_3 - w_2, \text{ e.g.}$$

$$B = \begin{bmatrix} w_1 + w_2 \\ b_1 + w_1 \\ w_1 - w_2 \\ b_3 - w_2 \end{bmatrix} \quad (11)$$

According to this, computation of $H_2 A$ when A is a 4x4 block needs only 40 additions and 8 shift operations and the same for BH_2^T. The computational complexity has been greatly reduced.

For matrix H_3, we use the same strategy and decompose it into three matrices, as follow:

$$H_3 = C_f \left(\begin{bmatrix} 0 & 1 & 0 & 0 \\ 0 & 0 & 0 & 0 \\ 0 & 0 & 0 & 0 \\ 0 & 0 & 0 & 0 \end{bmatrix} + \begin{bmatrix} 0 & 0 & 0 & 0 \\ 0 & 0 & 1 & 0 \\ 0 & 0 & 0 & 0 \\ 0 & 0 & 0 & 0 \end{bmatrix} + \begin{bmatrix} 0 & 0 & 0 & 0 \\ 0 & 0 & 0 & 0 \\ 0 & 0 & 0 & 1 \\ 0 & 0 & 0 & 0 \end{bmatrix} \right) C_i^T \qquad (12)$$

$$= \begin{bmatrix} 1 & \frac{1}{2} & -1 & -1 \\ 2 & 1 & -2 & -2 \\ 1 & \frac{1}{2} & -1 & -1 \\ 1 & \frac{1}{2} & -1 & -1 \end{bmatrix} + \begin{bmatrix} 1 & -\frac{1}{2} & -1 & 1 \\ 1 & -\frac{1}{2} & -1 & 1 \\ -1 & \frac{1}{2} & 1 & -1 \\ -2 & 1 & 2 & -2 \end{bmatrix} + \begin{bmatrix} 1 & -1 & 1 & -\frac{1}{2} \\ -1 & 1 & -1 & \frac{1}{2} \\ -1 & 1 & -1 & \frac{1}{2} \\ 2 & -2 & 2 & -1 \end{bmatrix}$$

To compute $B = H_3 A$, let:
$$w_1 = a_1 - a_3, w_2 = (a_2 >> 1) - a_4,$$
$$w_3 = w_1 + w_2, w_4 = w_1 - w_2, w_5 = a_1 - a_2 + a_3 - (a_4 >> 1)$$

b_1 to b_4 can be given by:
$$b_1 = w_3 + w_4 + w_5,$$
$$b_2 = (w_3 << 1) + w_4 - w_5,$$
$$b_3 = w_3 - w_4 - w_5,$$
$$b_4 = w_3 - (w_4 << 1) + (w_5 << 1)$$

This computation of $B = H_3 A$ needs 60 additions and 20 shift operations when A is a 4x4 matrix and it will need the same for BH_3^T.

For W_2, we got the same result as H_2, and for W_3, the same as H_3.

Finally, the multiplicator 64 on the left of $A^{\text{int\_dct}}$ in equation (6) can be removed by 6-bits right shift operation.

The input of this algorithm is the integer DCT blocks in the post-quantization DCT domain and output is the synthesized DCT block in pre-quantization DCT domain. So there is no need to adjust the scale when computing the residual DCT block by subtracting the reference block. But before the construction for a new reference picture after the inverse quantization, we still need to adjust the scale to turn the reference block from pre-quantization DCT domain to post-quantization DCT domain.

4 Scale Adjusting for DCT Coefficients Before and After Quantization Procedure

According to H.264 standard, the original transform matrix should be like this:

$$\begin{bmatrix} 1 & 1 & 1 & 1 \\ 2 & 1 & -1 & -2 \\ 1 & -1 & -1 & 1 \\ 1 & -2 & 2 & -1 \end{bmatrix} \otimes \begin{bmatrix} a & a & a & a \\ b & b & b & b \\ a & a & a & a \\ b & b & b & b \end{bmatrix} = C_f \otimes E \tag{13}$$

where $a = 1/2, b = \sqrt{1/10}$ and the operator $\otimes$ means the elements in C_f multiply the corresponding elements in E with the same position.

Then the original transform operation should be:

$$Y = (C_f X C_f^T) \otimes E_f = (C_f X C_f^T) \otimes \begin{bmatrix} a^2 & ab & a^2 & ab \\ ab & b^2 & ab & b^2 \\ a^2 & ab & a^2 & ab \\ ab & b^2 & ab & b^2 \end{bmatrix} \tag{14}$$

where C_f is the transform matrix of H.264 and E_f is the transform scale factors matrix.

To reduce the computational complexity, the transform procedure in H.264 does not process the transform scale adjusting with E_f. The scale adjusting is combined with the quantization procedure[12]. There is a similar situation in inverse quantization and inverse transform. Hence, there is a difference in scale between the DCT domain before the quantization and the DCT domain after the quantization.

Here we presented an algorithm to adjust the scale of a DCT matrix between the pre-quantization to post-quantization DCT domain.

Let Y be the integer DCT matrix after the quantization procedure and X be the corresponding pixel domain matrix. We use the inverse transform matrix C_i to convert Y into X:

$$64X = C_i^T Y C_i \tag{15}$$

Let W be the integer DCT matrix with the pre-quantization scale corresponding to X. We use forward transform matrix C_f to convert X into W:

$$64W = C_f [64X] C_f^T = C_f C_i^T Y C_i C_f^T \tag{16}$$

Examine C_f and C_i, and we can find out:

$$C_i = \begin{bmatrix} 1/4 & 1/4 & 1/4 & 1/4 \\ 1/5 & 1/10 & -1/10 & -1/5 \\ 1/4 & -1/4 & -1/4 & 1/4 \\ 1/10 & -1/5 & 1/5 & -1/10 \end{bmatrix} \otimes \begin{bmatrix} 4 & 4 & 4 & 4 \\ 5 & 5 & 5 & 5 \\ 4 & 4 & 4 & 4 \\ 5 & 5 & 5 & 5 \end{bmatrix} = [C_f^{-1}]^T \otimes E_1 = [C_f^T]^{-1} \otimes E_1 \quad (17)$$

where $E_1 = \begin{bmatrix} 4 & 4 & 4 & 4 \\ 5 & 5 & 5 & 5 \\ 4 & 4 & 4 & 4 \\ 5 & 5 & 5 & 5 \end{bmatrix}$

and furthermore we get:

$$C_i^T = C_f^{-1} \otimes E_1^T \quad (18)$$

Substitute equation (17) and (18) into (16),

$$64W = C_f [C_f^{-1} \otimes E_1^T] Y \{ [C_f^T]^{-1} \otimes E_1 \} C_f^T = C_f C_f^{-1} [Y \otimes E_1] \{ [C_f^T]^{-1} \otimes E_1 \} C_f^T$$
$$= C_f C_f^{-1} \{ [Y \otimes E_1] \otimes E_1^T \} [C_f^T]^{-1} C_f^T = Y \otimes E_1 \otimes E_1^T$$

Here we can see W and Y have the relationship as follow:

$$W = Y \otimes E \quad (19)$$

or

$$Y = \frac{W}{E} \quad (20)$$

where $E = \dfrac{E_1 \otimes E_1^T}{64} = \begin{bmatrix} 16 & 20 & 16 & 20 \\ 20 & 25 & 20 & 25 \\ 16 & 20 & 16 & 20 \\ 20 & 25 & 20 & 25 \end{bmatrix} / 64 = \begin{bmatrix} 1/4 & 5/16 & 1/4 & 5/16 \\ 5/16 & 25/64 & 5/16 & 25/64 \\ 1/4 & 5/16 & 1/4 & 5/16 \\ 5/16 & 25/64 & 5/16 & 25/64 \end{bmatrix}$

Here the reason that we didn't combine the factor 1/64 into the matrix at first is if we use the intermediate result $64A^{\text{int\_dct}}$ before the 6 bits shift in equation (6), the factor 1/64 could be removed.

The equation (19) can be performed by multiplications and shift operations. But to compute equation (20), for most coefficients we need to do divisions. We further developed equation (20). Then the division and round operation can be replaced by a multiplication, an addition and a shift operation.

Define $e_{ij}, i = 1...4, j = 1...4$ is the element in matrix E, w_{ij} and y_{ij} are the corresponding elements in matrix W and Y. When $e_{ij} = 1/4$, $i = 1$ or $3, j = 1$ or 3

$$y_{ij} = w_{ij} << 2 \quad (21)$$

When $e_{ij} = 5/16$, we define $\varepsilon_1 = \text{round}\left(\dfrac{2^r}{e_{ij}}\right)$, and

$$|y_{ij}| = (|w_{ij}| \times \varepsilon_1 + 2^{r-1}) >> r \qquad (22)$$

where $r = 14$ and $\varepsilon_1 = 52429$ can guarantee the computational accuracy. The sign of y_{ij} is as the same of w_{ij}.

When $e_{ij} = 25/64$, we define $\varepsilon_2 = round\left(\dfrac{2^s}{e_{ij}}\right)$, and

$$|y_{ij}| = (|w_{ij}| \times \varepsilon_2 + 2^{s-1}) >> s \qquad (23)$$

where $s = 14$ and $\varepsilon_2 = 41943$ can guarantee the computational accuracy. The sign of y_{ij} is as the same of w_{ij}.

We should notice the error propagation in P pictures caused by the utilization of the reference pictures in DCT domain. On decoder side, the constructed reference pictures are in pixel domain. Because a round operation which is non-linear has to be performed on the pixel coefficients after the inverse integer DCT procedure, the DCT domain reference pictures differentiate the ones in pixel domain. This leads to the error propagation in P pictures.

However, the error propagation should be slight. In the worst case, the round operation introduces a difference of 0.5 for each pixel between the reference pictures in DCT domain and pixel domain at most after each DCT reference picture construction. Because B picture is not reference picture, for a typical MPEG-2 GOP which contains 4 P pictures, the accumulated error for each pixel in P pictures should be no more than 2 and will be refreshed immediately by a consequent I picture.

5 Conclusion

We proposed two fast transcoding algorithms for MPEG-2 to H.264 DCT domain transcoding. The first algorithm synthesize the proper prediction reference block from 4 blocks in integer DCT domain, and the second algorithm overcame the scale difference between the pre-quantization and the post-quantization DCT domain. The first algorithm has a rapid method using only additions and shift operations and the second algorithm replaces divisions with multiplications and shift operations. The computational complexity is greatly reduced. This could be useful in various DCT domain MPEG-2 to H.264 video transcoding applications. And especially it will benefit to various embedded processors which have no floating-point unit.

Acknowledgement. This work was supported by National High-Tech Research and Development Plan of China (863) under Grant No. 2004AA1Z2300.

References

1. Hari Kalva: Issues in H.264/MPEG-2 Video Transcoding. IEEE Consumer Communications and Networking Conference, CCNC(2004).
2. Shih-Fu Chang, David G. Messerschmitt: Manipulation and Compositing of MC-DCT Compressed Video. IEEE Journal On Selected Areas in Communications, Vol. 13, No. 1, January 1995.
3. Rong Xie, Jilin Liu and Xingguo Wang: Efficient MPEG-2 to MPEG-4 Compressed Video Transcoding. Proc. SPIE Vol.4671 (2002) 192-201
4. Kwang-deok Seo, Jae-kyoon Kim: Fast motion vector re-estimation for transcoding MPEG-1 into MPEG-4 with lower spatial resolution in DCT-domain. Signal Processing: Image Communication 19 (2004) 299-312
5. Kuniaki Takahashi, Kazushi Satoh, Teruhiko Suzuki and Yoichi Yagasaki: MOTION VECTOR SYNTHESIS ALGORITHM FOR MPEG-2-TO-MPEG4 TRANSCODER. Proc. SPIE Vol. 4310 (2001) 872-882
6. P.A.A. Assuncao, M. Ghanbari: Fast computation of MC-DCT for video transcoding. Electronics Letters, Vol. 33, No. 4 (13th February 1997)
7. Malvar, H.S., Hallapuro, A., Karczewicz, M., Kerofsky, L.: Low-complexity transform and quantization in H.264/AVC. IEEE Transactions on Circuits and Systems for Video Technology, Vol. 13, No. 7 (July 2003) 598-603
8. Jian Lou, Liang Lu, Lu Yu, Jie Dong: Analysis of transform and quantization in H.264. Jounal of Zhejiang University(Engineering Science), Vol. 38, No. 5 (May 2004) 566-570
9. Luthra Ajay, Sulivan Gary J, Wiegand Thomas: Introdution to the special issue on the H.264/AVC video coding standard. IEEE Transactions on Circuits and Systems for Video Technology, Vol. 13, No. 7 (July 2003) 557-559.
10. Jun Xin, Anthory Vetro, Huifang Sun: Converting DCT Coefficients to H.264/AVC Transform Coefficients. IEEE PCM (2004)
11. International Organization for Standardization: Generic Coding of Moving Pictures and Associated Audio. ISO/IEC 13818-2 Amendment 2 (Jan. 1996)
12. Joint Video Team (JVT) of ISO/IEC MPEG & ITU-T VCEG: Draft ITU-T Recommendation and Final Draft International Standard of Joint Video Specification (ITU-T Rec. H.264 | ISO/IEC 14496-10 AVC). DRAFT ISO/IEC 14496-10: 2002 (E), Document: JVT-G050 (March 2003)
13. Jun Xin, Chia-Wen Lin, Ming-Ting Sun: Digital Video Transcoding. Proceedings Of The IEEE, Vol. 93, No. 1, (Jan. 2005)
14. Anthony Vetro, Charilaos Christopoulos, and Huifang Sun: Video Transcoding Architectures and Techniques: An Overview. IEEE Signal Processing Magazine 1053-5888/03/ (Mar. 2003)

A New Method for Controlling Smoke's Shape

Yongxia Zhou, Jiaoying Shi, and Jiarong Yu

State Key Lab of CAD&CG, Zhejiang University, China
`{zhou_yongx, jyshi, yjr}@cad.zju.edu.cn`

Abstract. In this paper we present a novel method for efficiently controlling the smoke's shape. Given the user-specified shape, a geometric model, our method generates a simulation in which smoke flows out somewhere and forms the shape. The geometric model serves as a black hole that applies attraction force to the fluid. The smoke is attracted to flow into the model and prevented from flowing out the model. In additional, an inner driving force term that drives the smoke from the dense region to the thin region in the geometric model, is added to the Navier-Stokes equations. Two force terms we added, need very little cost compared to the ordinary NS equations.

1 Introduction

The simulation of natural phenomena, such as smoke, cloud, water and fire, has widely applications in computer games, special effects, advertisements, visualization in scientific computing, etc. Since the nineties of the last century, a considerable amount of computer graphics researchers has been devoted to the realistic simulation of complex fluid phenomena [5,6,8,9,10](2001-2003). Currently, animations of curling smoke, sparkling fire and splashing water with striking visual realism, are most effectively achieved through physically based numerical simulation. Recent two years, Treuille and McNamara [11](2003), McNamara et al [16](2004), Fattal and Lischinski [17](2004), introduced methods for performing the simulations of controlling the smoke. The method based on keyframes is employed in [11,16], and target-driven method works in [17] which is faster than the former. We discuss their methods in more detail in section 2.

Inspired by the work of Fattal and Lischinski[17], our method is similar to the target-driven one. The target shape, a geometric model, works as an attractor for the simulated smoke, while it is a density keyframe in [17]. Each vertex on the model applies attraction forces to the fluid that carries the smoke towards the target. In the model, an inner driving force that drives the smoke from dense region to the thin, starts to work when the smoke arrives at surfaces of the model. So the main contributions of this paper are:

(i) An attraction force term, designed to induce the smoke to flow towards the user-specified geometric model and to prevent smoke from flowing out the model;

(ii) An inner driving force term, designed to drive the smoke to flow in the model;

(iii) We provide the convenient controlling of smoke, after specifying the shape and a few simple manipulates, our system can nearly automatically generate the animation of the smoke.

The remainder of this paper is structured as follows. In the next section we briefly survey relevant previous work. In section 3 we review the ordinary NS equations and derive our modified flow equations. Section 4 describes the implementation of our simulator. Results are presented in section 5. Section 6 discusses the limitations and future work. Section 7 is the conclusion.

2 Previous Work

Physically based simulation in CG has a short history, but its applications become pervasive. Kajiya and Von Herzen [1](1984) were the first in CG to model 2-D smoke with physically based methods. But the computer power at the time limited the progress. N.Foster and D.Metaxes [2,3] (1996,1997) produced nice swirling smoke motions in 3D. Because of an explicit integration scheme in solving the momentum equation, their simulations are stable only if the time step is chosen small enough, which makes simulations relatively slow. Shortly thereafter, J.Stam[4](1999) introduced an algorithm to break these limitations, by using a semi-Lagrangian treatment of advection combined with an implicit solver, which is adopted by us. In solving the momentum, the simulation suffered from too much numeric dissipation, though he adopted a more accurate method (the Multigrid method) in solving the pressure-Poisson equation. To reduce the numerical dissipation inherent in the semi-Lagrangian scheme, Fedkiw et al [5](2001) proposed a vorticity confinement method, injecting the energy lost due to numerical dissipation back into the fluid using a forcing term. Impressive simulations of water [6,7,10](2001-2003) and fire [8](2002) were generated using level-set methods coupled with fluid solvers. Mostly, in the physically based simulation, the fluid is assumed incompressible and const density. But Yngve et al. [9](2001) modeled explosions with compressible versions.

As to the controlling of fluid flows, Foster and Metaxas[15](1997) provided animators to control the forces. Later Foster and Fedkiw[6](2001) proposed to control the motion of the flow by setting the velocity values at specified grid cells. But none of the above, allow the user to specify smoke shapes until the works of Adrien Treuille, et al [11](2003). Their controlling of smoke simulations is achieved by keyframes technique. Keyframes define desired density and velocity values. An objective function is constructed to measure the difference between the user-specified keyframes and the corresponding simulation states. Then the difference is converted into a set of parameterized wind forces. The process of the simulation is to minimize the amount of the forces and the objective function. This approach produced impressive effects, however, the system is complex, and the computational cost is too expensive.

A.McNamara et al[16](2004) produced controlled fluid simulations with the method inherited in [11]. To accelerate the computing, they introduced the adjoint method for controlling fluid simulations. It is faster than that in [11], however, the process is still slow.

R.Fattal and D.Lischinski [17](2004) generated impressive controlled smoke animations by introducing a driving force term and a smoke gathering term into the standard flow equations. Their methods are faster than those in [11,16], however, the anti-diffusion mechanism by adding a smoke gathering term, does not always result in natural evolution. When choosing keyframes' target states, skill and experience are still required.

In contrast, the approach described in this paper is faster and more convenient than that in [11,16,17]. Our one attraction force term can do the same work that two terms do in [17]: the driving force term and the smoke gathering term. The keyframe in our method is a geometric model, the user doesn't need to convert the mesh to the density keyframe as does in [11,16,17].

3 NS Equations

Physically based simulations follow the fluid dynamics described by Navier-Stokes equations. In general, the fluid is assumed inviscid (but in [17], the viscid term is used to attenuate the momentum) and incompressible, and the controlling equations can be written as:

$$\nabla \cdot \mathbf{u} = 0 \tag{1}$$

$$\frac{\partial \mathbf{u}}{\partial t} = -(\mathbf{u} \cdot \nabla)\mathbf{u} - \nabla p + \mathbf{f} \tag{2}$$

$\mathbf{u} = \mathbf{u}(\mathbf{x}, t)$ is the velocity vector at position $\mathbf{x}$ and time t; $p = p(\mathbf{x}, t)$ is hydrostatic pressure in the flow field; $\mathbf{f}$ is the vector of external forces including gravity, buoyancy(in [17], these two forces is excluded).

$$\mathbf{f} = \mathbf{f}_g + \mathbf{f}_{buoy} \tag{3}$$

$\mathbf{f}_g$ is the gravity, $\mathbf{f}_{buoy}$ is the buoyancy. The smoke is moved (advected) along the fluid's velocity

$$\frac{\partial \rho}{\partial t} = -(\mathbf{u} \cdot \nabla)\rho \tag{4}$$

$\rho = \rho(\mathbf{x}, t)$ is the density of the smoke.

3.1 Modified Equations

We add two external force terms to equation (3).

$$\mathbf{f} = \mathbf{f}_g + \mathbf{f}_{buoy} + \mathbf{f}_a + \mathbf{f}_d \tag{5}$$

$\mathbf{f}_a$ is the attraction force, which is designed to exert forces on the fluid which carries the smoke to the target; $\mathbf{f}_d$ is the inner driving force which is designed to be applied on the fluid in the geometric model so that it looks the smoke flows from the dense region to the thin region in the model.

We only add two terms in the force equation, but in [17], they modify the momentum equation (2) and the density advection equation (4) in addition.

3.2 Black Hole Method

The geometric model, specified by the user as the shape of the smoke, works as a black hole that attracts the smoke and prevents the smoke from flowing out the model. Each point $\mathbf{P}_i$ on the model's surface applies attraction force $\mathbf{f}_{i,j}$ to each grid point $\mathbf{P}_j$ in $\mathbf{P}_i$'s influence range, which is limited in the semi sphere in $\mathbf{P}_i$'s normal direction, centered at $\mathbf{P}_i$ with radius R.(see figure1, here we show in 2D, but the actual simulation is in 3D). To achieve the goal fast, the user can specify the radius R with large value to extend the model's influence range.

$$\mathbf{f}_{i,j} = \mathbf{\Phi}(L_{i,j}) \cdot \xi(\rho_j), \quad i \in [1, M], j \in [1, N] \tag{6}$$

Where M is the total amount of vertexes of the geometric model, N is the total amount of grids in the semi sphere centered at $\mathbf{P}_i$ with radius R, $\xi(\rho_j)$ is the function of smoke density at $\mathbf{P}_j$, here, we define $\xi(\rho_j) = \rho_j$, $\mathbf{\Phi}(L_{i,j})$ is the vector of attraction coefficient,

$$\mathbf{\Phi}(L_{i,j}) = \mathbf{v}\alpha e^{(-\beta L_{i,j}/R)} \tag{7}$$

Where $\mathbf{v}$ is the unit direction vector from $\mathbf{P}_j$ to $\mathbf{P}_i$, $\alpha(> 0)$ is used to control the amount of attraction forces, the greater value of α is, the greater smokes suffer from the attraction force, the earlier smokes form the shape (see figure4). $L_{i,j}$ is the distance between $\mathbf{P}_i$ and $\mathbf{P}_j$, there always has $0 < L_{i,j}/R <= 1$. β ($>= 1$) is used to smooth the force from far to near, in this paper, $\beta = 10$. The attraction force $\mathbf{f}_a$ of a grid point $\mathbf{P}$ at arbitrary location is the sum of forces from all the vertexes of the model:

$$\mathbf{f}_a = \rho_p \sum_{i=1}^{M} \mathbf{\Phi}(L_{i,p}) \tag{8}$$

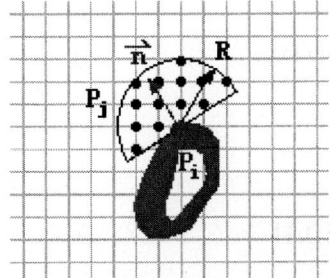

Fig. 1. Influence range of the point on model surface

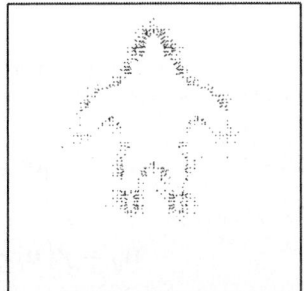

Fig. 2. Vectors of attraction coefficient on the middle cross section ($\alpha=1, R=5$) around the geometric model of a Cartoon man

Where $L_{i,p}$ is the distance from point P_i on the black hole's surface to the grid point **P**. ρ_p is the smoke density at **P**. The term $\sum_{i=1}^{M} \Phi(L_{i,p})$ is precomputed and stored instead of computing iteratively with time. The figure 2 shows the attraction coefficient on the middle across section around the 3-D model of a cartoon man. The whole flow field is partitioned into 81*81*41 grids. Our attraction force term $\mathbf{f}_a$ plays the roles of the driving force term and the smoke gathering term in [17] (see figure 5).

To avoid frequent intersection tests, grids inside the model or on the surfaces of the model are gotten before the computation of the attraction force. These grids are free of the suffering from the attraction force.

3.3 The Inner Driving Force

When the smoke arrives at surfaces of the model, we design an inner driving force to drive the smoke from dense regions to the thin, which causes the smoke to automatically fill the whole model (see figure 8). Note that the gradient of density $\nabla \rho$ always points uphill towards the position with higher density and the smoke is moved along the velocity. So, ideally, the velocity points downhill the thinner region, i.e. if the velocity is along the inverse direction of the gradient of the density, the fluid will carry the smoke from the dense to the thin. Generally, the current velocity **u** at **x** is not in the ideal direction, so we add the inner driving force and get the new velocity **u***(see figure 3):

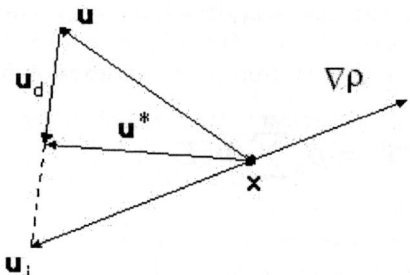

Fig. 3. The inner driving force

$$\mathbf{u}^* = \mathbf{u} + \mathbf{u}_d \tag{9}$$

$$\mathbf{u}_d = \gamma(\mathbf{u}_i - \mathbf{u}) \quad \gamma \in [0,1] \tag{10}$$

$$\mathbf{u}_i = -\frac{\nabla \rho}{|\nabla \rho|} |\mathbf{u}| \tag{11}$$

γ is the coefficient controlling the speed of filling the model with the smoke, the value nearly 1 corresponds to the high speed, and there are no effects if $\gamma = 0$. In equation 2, we abstract the force term:

$$\frac{\partial \mathbf{u}}{\partial t} = \mathbf{f}$$

It can be written as:

$$\frac{\mathbf{u}^* - \mathbf{u}}{\Delta t} = \mathbf{f}$$

$$\mathbf{u}^* = \mathbf{u} + \Delta t\, \mathbf{f}$$

Comparing with the equation 9, we get the inner driving force $\mathbf{f}_d$:

$$\mathbf{f}_d = \frac{\mathbf{u}_d}{\Delta t} \tag{12}$$

Note that this force is only applied to the grids in or on the model.

4 Implementation

To find out the grids in or on the model represented by a triangular mesh, we develop a tool based on OpenGL. We recognize the grids that are out the model in the following steps:

(i) Draw inner grids and the model;
(ii) Call the function of gluProject to transform their 3-D object coordinates into 2-D window coordinates;
(iii) In 2-D space, pick out grids that are out all the triangles, and the picked grids don't need to be drawn later;
(iv) Change the eye's location and repeat the above steps till only the inner grids and the model remain on the screen.

In theory, all the grids out the model can be found out using the above method. The grid out all the triangles can be found as long as we put the eye between the grid and the model and look out at the grid. In fact, it is not necessary to eliminate all the grids that are out the model, because the desired final effect is not the precise shape but the fuzzy one. Generally, the recognition process can be completed after changing the eye location several times by rotating the eye around the scene center (see figure 4). The bound box method is employed to accelerate the process.

Figure 4 shows the recognition process with a dog model. Figure 4-1 is the dog model and the initial 61*61*31 grids. Figure 4-2 is the 14036 inner grids in the bound box. After zooming in and translating, we got figure 4-3. Figure 4-4 is gotten after the first pass of recognition, and the number of inner grids is 3585. After rotating the eye, we got figure 4-5. Figure 4-6 is the result of the second pass of recognition, and the number of inner grids is 2636. And after eight passes of rotating eye and recognition, we got figure 4-7, having 1861 inner grids. Figure 4-8 is all the inner grids without the dog model.

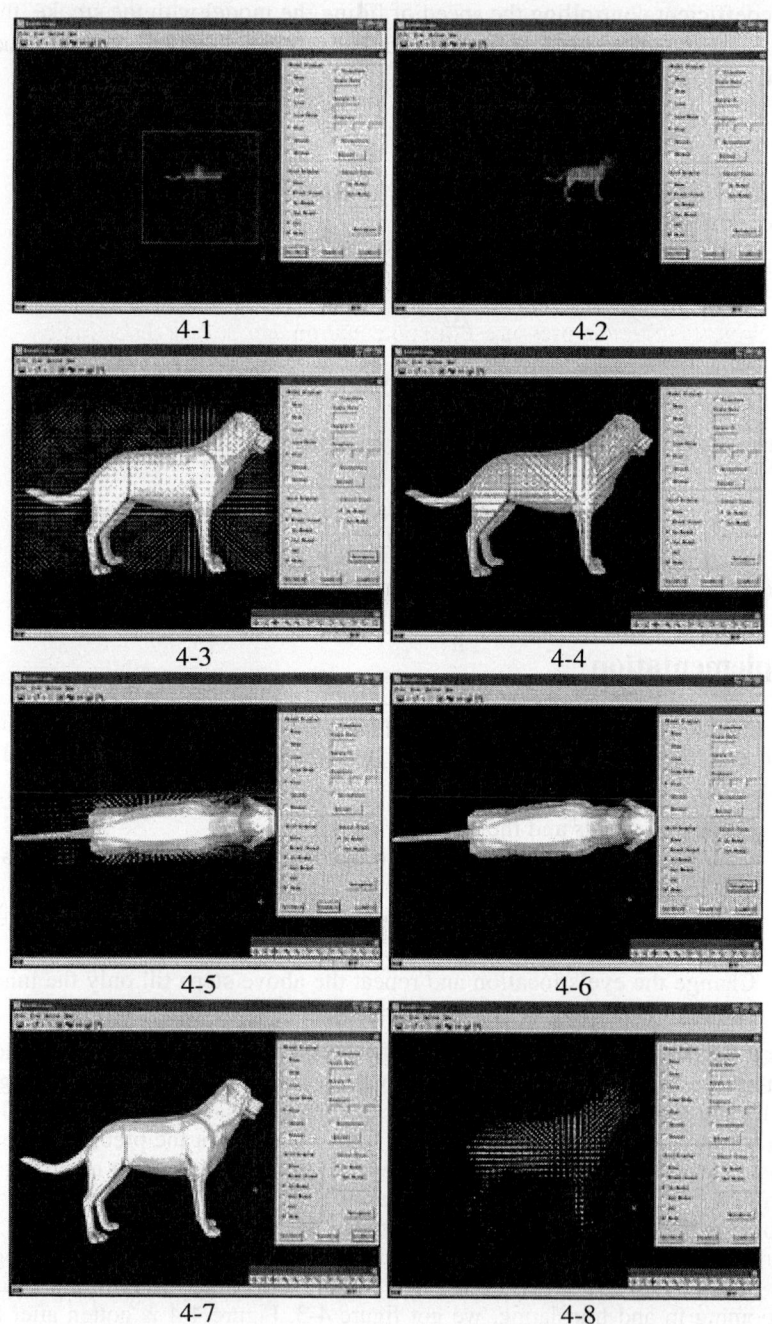

Fig. 4. The process of recognizing the grids in the dog model

To solve the NS equations, we adopt the similar approach used in [4,5]: the advection term is solved by the semi-Lagrangian method [4]. But we employ the non-staggered grids: velocity, pressure and density are all defined at the same location, which is more easier to code than using staggered grids.

In each time step, we perform the following sequence tasks:

1. Advect momentum:

$$\frac{\partial \mathbf{u}}{\partial t} = -(\mathbf{u} \cdot \nabla)\mathbf{u}$$

2. Project: solve the pressure-Poisson equation and update the velocity

$$\Delta p = \frac{1}{\Delta t}\nabla \cdot \mathbf{u}$$

$$\frac{\partial \mathbf{u}}{\partial t} = -\nabla p$$

3. Apply inner driving forces on inner grids:

$$\frac{\partial \mathbf{u}}{\partial t} = \mathbf{f}_d$$

4. Advect smoke:

$$\frac{\partial \rho}{\partial t} = -(\mathbf{u} \cdot \nabla)\rho$$

5. Add forces:

$$\frac{\partial \mathbf{u}}{\partial t} = \mathbf{f}_g + \mathbf{f}_{buoy} + \mathbf{f}_a$$

5 Results

We have used our method to generate several examples. All of the timings reported below were measured on a 1.7GHz Pentium IV with 512MB of RAM running Windows XP.

Figure 5 shows a 3D simulation on 41x41x21 grids, with 430 inner grids that are suffering from the attraction force. The smoke was emitted from left side to form the "D" model that is denoted with finite difference grids. Comparing of the control coefficient α: it is 0.01 in figure A and 0.001 in figure B. The larger α is, the larger attraction force the fluid suffers. At time=0, 0.5, two simulations have little difference. But at time=1.0, 1.5, their appearances are obviously different: the attraction force in B is too small to prevent the smoke from flowing upwards. It is verified that the attraction force has the function of gathering the smoke. Each time step takes 133ms with our method and 139ms with the method in [17]. Our method increases the speed about 4 percent.

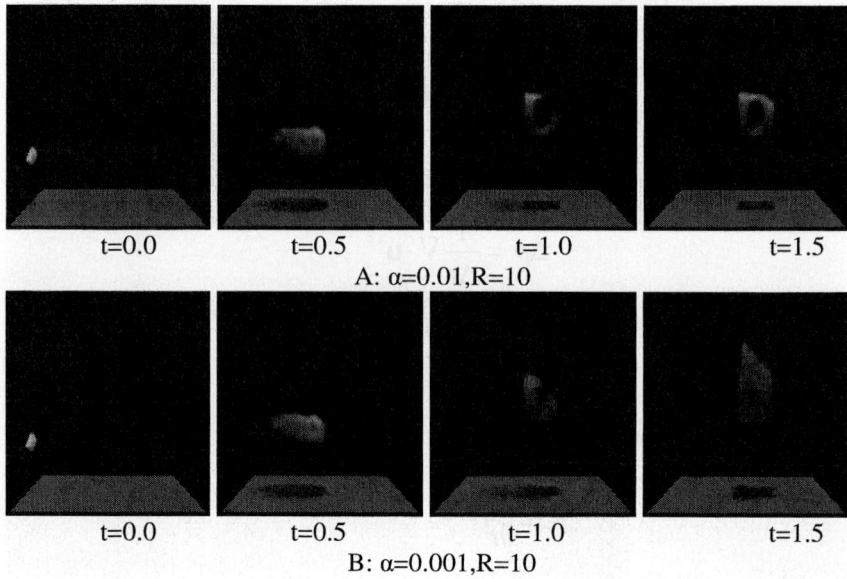

Fig. 5. Smoke was emitted from left side to form the letter "D" model with different value of α

In figure 6, the smoke is emitted from left side and forms a dog on 61*61*31 grids, with 1861 inner grids that are suffering from the attraction force. The geometric model of the dog is represented by a triangular mesh(see figure 7). Each time step takes 452ms with our method and 481ms with the method in [17]. Our method increases the speed about 6 percent.

Figure 8 shows that the smoke forms a cartoon man on 81*81*41 grids, which is represented by a triangular mesh (see figure 7), the corresponding attraction

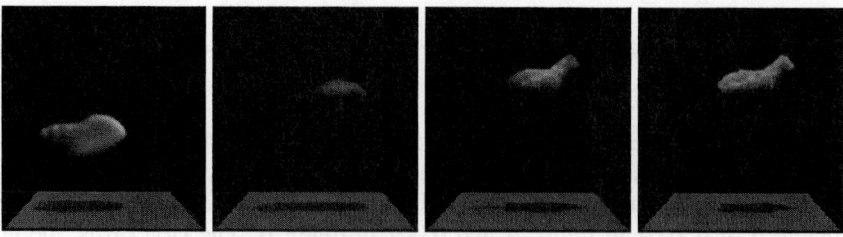

Fig. 6. The smoke forms a dog

coefficient is in figure 2. It has 7270 inner grids. The smoke automatically flows upside and fills the model after the smoke arrives at the feet of the model. Each time step takes 1153ms with our method and 1219ms with the method in [17]. Our method is faster about 5 percent.

Fig. 7. Two geometric models: (left). A dog with 1618 vertexes and 3220 triangles; (right). A cartoon man with 3618 vertexes and 7124 triangles.

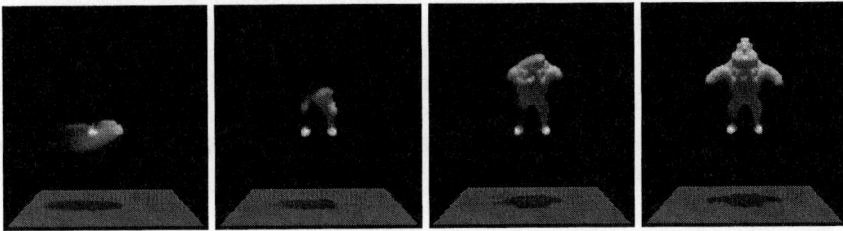

Fig. 8. The cartoon man is formed by smoke emitted from left side

6 Limitations and Future Work

Our current approach suffers from several drawbacks. In figure 6 and 8, dog's legs, tail and the hands of the man are not filled with the smoke, that is, the inner driving force works not well there. In figure 4-8, the inner grids in dog's legs and tail are too few, which causes the precise of the center difference scheme is not enough in calculating the gradient of the density. For example, an isolated inner grid surrounded by outer girds, has larger density than that the outer girds around have. Ideally, three components of density gradient at the inner grid are all zero. But using the center difference scheme, the derivative of the density is independent of the density at the inner grid with larger density, and it only relates to the outer grids with smaller density. The result is obviously wrong. Other current ordinary difference schemes, such as upwind or downwind scheme, have similar problem. To solve the problem, refining the grids is an alternate approach, but it will quickly increase the computational cost. A more accurate difference scheme should compare the density value at current computing grid with that at grids around. I hope there is a better difference scheme or other method to solve the problem in the near future.

Though our system is more automatic than that in [11,16,17], it is not completely automatic and there still have much work to do. After specifying the shape which the smoke will form, the user need to iteratively change eye's location to recognize the inner grids. So, another future work is to increase the automation of the recognition process.

There is a problem in computing the attraction force, too. Vertexes on the model's surface apply the attraction force to the outer grids. However, to smooth the surface, the distribution of vertexes is irregular: planar surface has fewer vertexes than that bumpy surface has. It causes the irrationality of the distribution of attraction forces. The irrationality should be eliminated though it has not prevented us from producing good results.

7 Conclusions

In this paper, we have presented a novel approach for controlling the smoke's shape. Our one attraction force term is equal to two terms in [17]: the driving force term and the smoke gathering term. The inner driving force term causes the smoke to fill the model, this effect is very useful in special effects.

In CG, there are a lot of geometric models, which smoke could form. The user can pick the favorite as the shape to form, and the system will nearly automatically generate the video. It is necessary and requires skill and experience to define the density and/or velocity value on each keyframe in [11,16,17], but it doesn't need to do that in this paper.

In conclusion, I hope the approach presented in this paper will make the simulation faster and more automatic.

References

1. Kajiya, J.T., Von Herzen, B.P.: Ray Tracing Volume Densities. Computer Graphics (SIGGRAPH 84 Conference Proceedings), Vol. 18, No.3 (1984) 165–174.
2. Foster, N., Metaxas, D.: Modeling the Motion of a Hot, Turbulent Gas. SIGGRAPH 97 Conference Proceedings, Annual Conference Series (1997) 181–188.
3. Foster, N., Metaxas, D.: Realistic Animation of Liquids. Graphical Models and Image Processing, Vol. 58, No. 5 (1996) 471–483.
4. Stam, J.: Stable Fluids. SIGGRAPH 99 Conference Proceedings, Annual Conference Series (1999) 121–128.
5. Fedkiw, R., Stam, J., Jensen, H.W.: Visual Simulation of Smoke. SIGGRAPH 2001 Conference Proceedings, Annual Conference Series (2001) 15–22.
6. Foster, N., Fedkiw, R.: Practical Animation of Liquids. SIGGRAPH 2001 Conference Proceedings, Annual Conference Series (2001) 23–30.
7. Enright, D., Marschner, S., Fedkiw, R.: Animation and Rendering of Complex Water Surfaces. SIGGRAPH 2002 Conference Proceedings, Annual Conference Series (2002) 736–744.
8. Nquyen, D.Q., Fedkiw, R., Jensen, H.W.: Physically Based Modeling and Animation of Fire. SIGGRAPH 2002 Conference Proceedings, Annual Conference Series (2002) 736–744.
9. Feldman, B.E., O'Brien, J.F., Arikan, O.: Animating Suspended Particle Explosions. SIGGRAPH 2003 Conference Proceedings, Annual Conference Series (2002) 1–8.
10. Stam, J.: Flows on Surfaces of Arbitrary Topology. SIGGRAPH 2003 Conference Proceedings, Annual Conference Series (2003) 1–8.

11. Treuille, A., McNamara, A., Ppovic, Z., Stam, J.: Keyframe Control of Smoke Simulations. SIGGRAPH 2003 Conference Proceedings, Annual Conference Series (2003)
12. Staniforth, A., Cote, J.: Semi-Lagrangian Integration Schemes for Atmospheric Models: A Review. Monthy Weather Review, Vol. 119 (1991) 2206–2223.
13. Lele, S. K.: Compact Finite Difference Schemes with Spectral-like Resolution. Journal of Computational Physics, Vol. 103 (1992) 16–42.
14. Dexun Fu, Yanwen Ma.: Computational Fluid Dynamics. Higher Education Press. First Edition (2002) 91–94
15. Foster, N., Metaxas, D.: Controlling fluid animation. Computer Graphics International (1997) 178–188.
16. Antoine McNamara, Adrien Treuille, Zoran Popovie, Jos Stam.: Fluid Control Using the Adjoint Method. SIGGRAPH 2004 Conference Proceedings
17. Raanan Fattal, Dani Lischinski.: Target-Driven Smoke Animation. SIGGRAPH 2004 Conference Proceedings

A Scene Change Detection in H.264/AVC Compression Domain

Sung Min Kim, Ju Wan Byun, and Chee Sun Won

Dept. of Electronics Eng., Dongguk University,
Seoul, 100-715, Korea
{smkim112, juwan, cswon}@dongguk.edu

Abstract. This paper presents a novel scene change detection method in H.264/AVC compression domain. We note that, comparing to previous MPEG compression methods, some unique compression schemes such as intra prediction, CAVLC etc. are adopted for H.264/AVC. Therefore, previous scene change detection methods for MPEG-1 or MPEG-2 are not directly applicable to the compressed bit stream of H.264/AVC. To solve this problem, we propose a novel scene change detection algorithm for H.264/AVC, which exploits intra prediction modes of macro block. Since our method requires a simple decoding of the prediction mode, it is quite fast. Also, the precision and recall for various video sequences and bit-rates turn out to be promising.

1 Introduction

With the advent of the digital TV, MPEG compressed digital contents are growing tremendously. This in turn requires automatic and fast digital video analysis schemes. The scene change detection technique is one of the most important and fundamental steps for the video analysis. Previous algorithms for scene change detection can be roughly classified into two groups:

Spatial domain approach: This approach relies on the spatial image features such as color histogram and edge characteristics.
Compressed domain approach: This approach extracts clues for the scene change directly from the compressed bit stream, including DCT coefficient, motion vector, type of macro-block in inter frame, and bit-rate of intra frame.

There are two major methods for the scene change detection in the spatial domain approach. The first one uses color histogram differences [1]. It makes use of the change in histogram bins between consecutive frames for detecting scene changes. The second one observes the change of the edge distribution in the image space [2]. A major drawback of these spatial domain scene change detections, however, is the need of the full decoding of the MPEG compressed bit stream, which is an obvious computational overhead. For this reason, scene change detection methods operating on MPEG-2 compressed data were proposed. There are three major methods for the compressed-domain scene change detection: methods based on

DCT coefficients [3]-[6], motion vectors(MVs) and/or types of macro block(MB) in inter frame [7][8], and bit-rates of intra frame [9]. Note that all methods based on DCT coefficients utilize DC-image(DC coefficient image) as a feature for scene change detection, which requires a simple DC decoding. In [3], the statistical sequential analysis which regards DC-coefficients as a random variable is applied to scene change detection. Similarly, a histogram difference of DC-image is used in [4]-[6]. In particular, in [5], DC-images are extracted from intra frames only, yielding a fast scene change detection. In the second method, MB types and MVs are used as features for the scene change [7][8]. Specifically, the number of intra MBs and forward/backword motion vectors within an inter frame are utilized. Finally, in [9], they make a decision function using bit-rates of each intra frame. The decision function which uses sequence of bit-rates reduces influences of FJP(false jump point) and TP(trend point) [9]. Again, we note that the compressed domain methods directly extract the features from the compressed bit-stream. Thus, there is no need to fully decompress the data, gaining their cost effectiveness [7].

Now, the question is whether the upper-mentioned compressed domain methods are still applicable for H.264/AVC compressed data. According to our investigation, the answer is negative. That is, because the unique encoding methods(e.g., CAVLC, intra prediction etc.) are employed to H.264/AVC, so the features extracted from H.264/AVC bit-stream attenuate the discriminatory capabilities for scene change detection comparing to the features which are used in scene change detection based on MPEG-2 compressed domain. Therefore, we propose a novel scene change detection method for H.264/AVC compressed data in this paper.

The paper is organized as follow: Section 2 presents a relationship between the compressed domain methods mentioned above and H.264/AVC. In Section 3, The characteristics and performance of feature which is used in our proposed method are presented. The proposed scene change detection algorithm is explained in detail in Section 4. The experiment results are presented in Section 5, followed by the conclusion in Section 6.

2   Applying Previous Compressed-Domain Methods to H.264/AVC

2.1   DCT Coefficient-Based Method

As already mentioned, MPEG-2-based scene change detection methods which use DCT coefficient generate DC-images(DC coefficient image). Then, various features are extracted from the created DC-images. Figure 1 illustrates a DC coefficient encoding process of MPEG-2 and H.264/AVC. The DC coefficient which shows an average energy of a block (i.e., 8x8 pixel) can be extracted directly from the compressed data, thank to independent coding of DC coefficient in MPEG-2 [10]. So, it is easy to make DC-image from the extracted DC coefficients. On the other hand, the DC coefficient of H.264/AVC is encoded with AC coefficient [11]. Specifically, unlike the MPEG-2, DC coefficients extracted directly from compressed H.264/AVC data just represent an energy difference

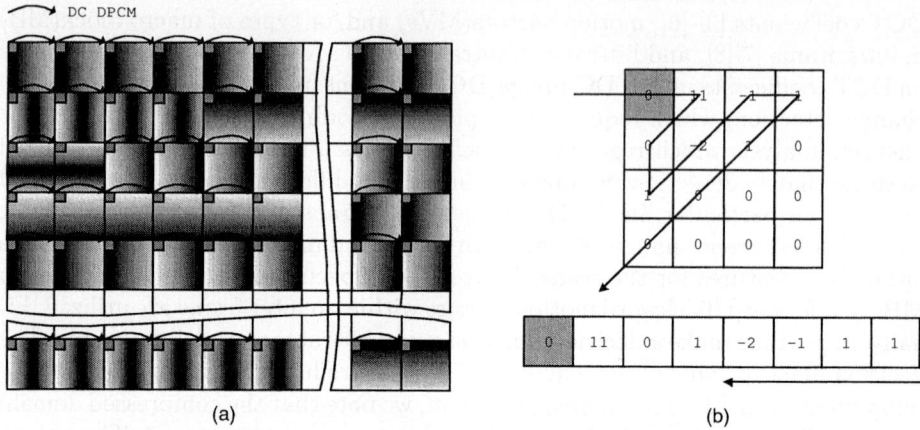

Fig. 1. Differences of DC coefficient encoding methods: (a)DPCM used in MPEG-2, (b)CAVLC used in H.264/AVC

between the current block and the adjacent pixels, since intra prediction is applied to every blocks of 4x4 or 16x16 pixels. Also, it does not use an independent encoding of DC coefficients as in the case of MPEG-2. The H.264/AVC encodes the DCT coefficient in the reverse order according to CAVLC(Context Adaptive Variable Length Coding) strategy. This implies that, if we try to use the previous DC-image based MPEG-2 method to H.264/AVC bit-stream, the inverse transform is required for making DC-images from the compressed H.264/AVC data. Also, we need addition operations for the calculation of predicted energy from adjacent pixels. Therefore, we need almost full decoding to generate the DC-image from the H.264/AVC bit-stream, which deteriorates the advantage of the compressed domain method.

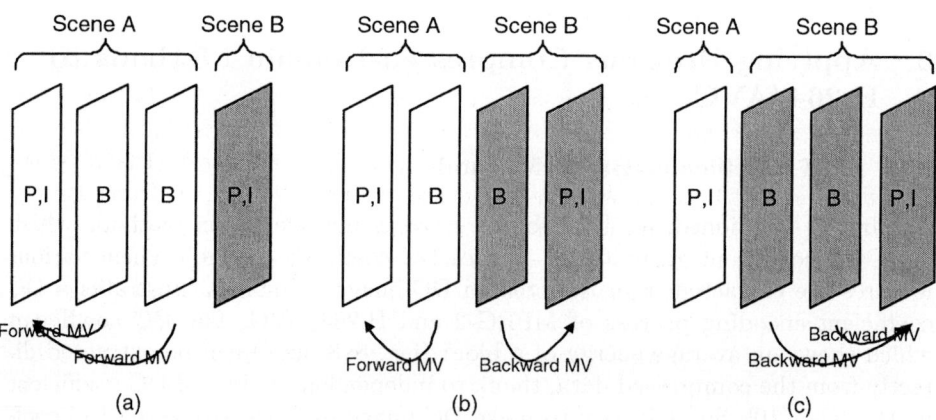

Fig. 2. MV types of inter frames at the scene change: (a) forward/forward motion vector, (b) forward/backward motion vector, (c) backward/backward motion vector

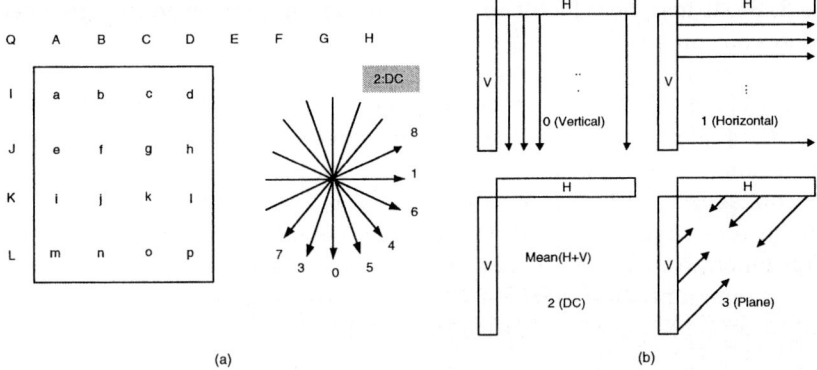

Fig. 3. (a) 4x4 ,(b) 16x16 intra prediction mode of H.264/AVC

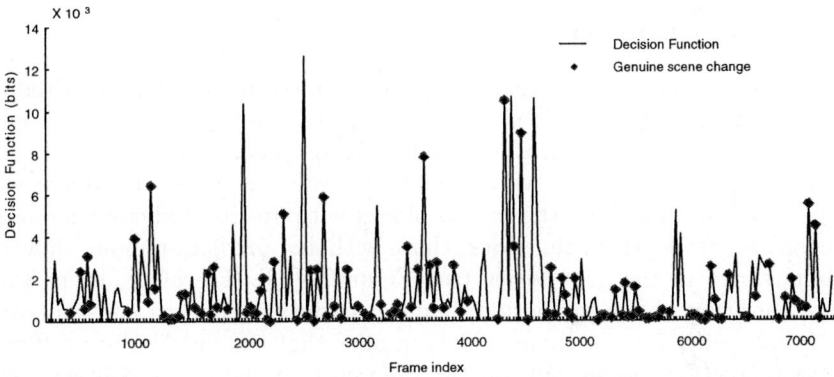

Fig. 4. The performance of decision function used in [9] with regard to H.264/AVC

2.2 Motion Vector-Based Method

In MPEG-2, as shown in Figure 2, forward and backward motion vectors (MV) are used for the scene change detection. The size of macro block(MB) is fixed with 16x16 pixels and also there are only three modes for the prediction frames, namely forward/forward, backward/backward, and forward/backward [10]. However, in the case of H.264/AVC, it is allowed to predict MVs from multiple frames. Moreover, the MBs within inter frame are composed of 7 types, 4x4, 4x8, 8x4, 8x8, 8x16, 16x8, and 16x16 [11]. It also needs to check the DPB(Decoded Picture Buffer), which is to distinguish the direction of forward and backward from the compressed data [11]. These differences make it difficult to directly apply the scene change detection method to the H.264/AVC bit-stream.

2.3 Bit-Rate-Based Method

Note that intra frames of H.264/AVC normally have lower bit-rates than those of MPEG-2, because they have small energy due to intra prediction as shown in

Figure 3. So, it may be difficult to utilize this feature for scene change detection. Also note that bit-rate of intra frame in MPEG-2 normally has larger fluctuations at the scene change occurrences than the H.264/AVC. This is due to the fact that each 8x8 DCT block is encoded independently [11] [12]. However, in H.264/AVC, the fluctuations may not be large enough to detect the scene change, because it adapts an intra prediction for energy reduction. Figure 4 illustrates an example which applies the method proposed in [9] to H.264/AVC. The decision function should have a large value at genuine scene change occurrences. However, the decision function in Figure 4 have no relation to genuine scene change. This is also due to intra prediction in H.264/AVC.

3 Unique Features of H.264/AVC for Scene Change Detection

3.1 Feature Characteristic

Intra prediction is one of the unique features adapted to H.264/AVC. Prediction modes for intra frame are divided into 4x4 and 16x16 modes as shown in Figure 3. Note that the distribution of the intra prediction modes within an intra frame has a close relationship to the variation of pixel value in spatial domain as shown in Figure 5. That is, while the macro blocks with 16x16 prediction mode have monotonous gray levels in the block, those with 4x4 prediction mode show large dynamic range in the gray levels (see Figure 5)[13]. Therefore, there will be a large variation in the prediction mode distribution between consecutive two intra frames with a scene change. This implies that the distribution differences of intra prediction modes can tell the difference of the image contents, which can provide a clue for the scene change. In this paper, we use prediction mode variations between consecutive two intra frames for scene change detection.

3.2 Performance Evaluation

Figure 6 illustrates the method to measure a similarity for scene change detection. As shown in figure 6, the intra prediction modes are extracted from every intra frames, and Δf_i denote feature variation between i^{th} and $i+1^{th}$ frame. Since the total number of 4x4 or 16x16 intra prediction mode within an intra frame do not represent a local characteristic of the corresponding frame, we apply variations of intra prediction modes at the same position between two consecutive intra frames to the similarity measurement. Let $Mode_i^j$ indicate the intra prediction mode for j^{th} MB in the ith frame:

$$Mode_i^j = \begin{cases} 0, \text{ for 16x16 prediction mode} \\ 1, \text{ for 4x4 prediction mode} \end{cases}.$$

Then, for two consecutive i^{th} and $i+1^{th}$ intra frames, we define the normalized feature variation, Δf_i, as follows:

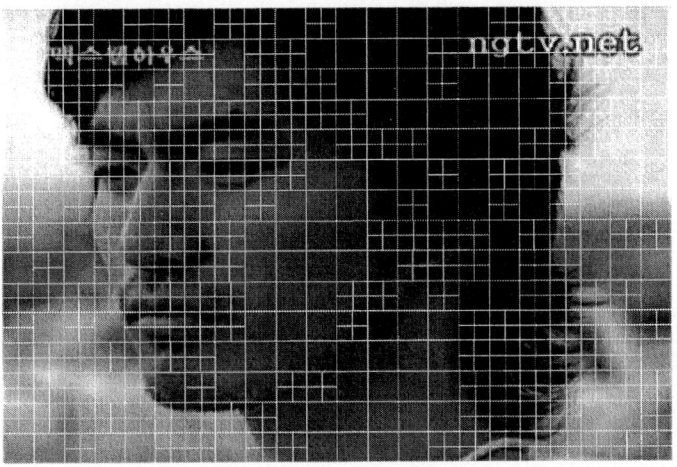

Fig. 5. The distribution of intra prediction modes

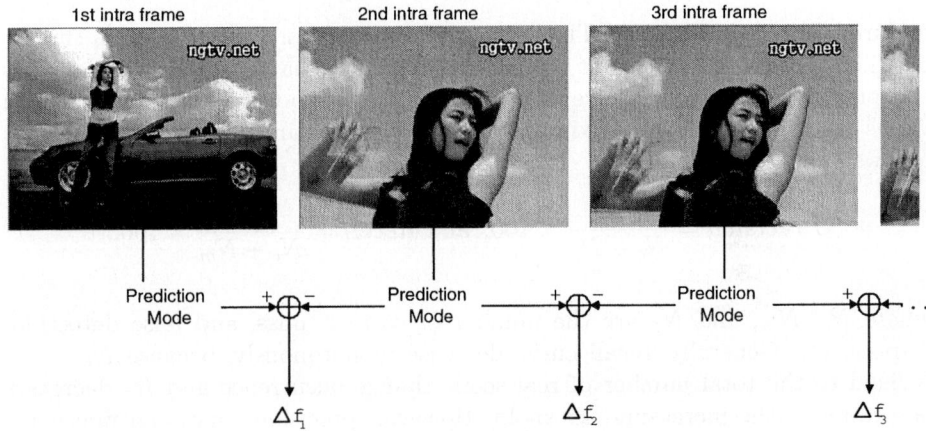

Fig. 6. Similarity measure

$$\Delta f_i = \frac{1}{N_{MB}} \sum_{j=0}^{N_{MB}-1} |Mode_i^j - Mode_{i+1}^j|, \qquad (1)$$

where N_{MB} denote the number of MBs within a frame. Note that Δf_i just represents the normalized number of prediction mode variations at the same position between two consecutive intra frames. Thus, we can justify the decision rule as follow:

Declare "scene change" at $i+1^{th}$ frame, if $\Delta f_i \geq T$,

where T is a threshold. Note that, the similarity measurement of (1) is simple enough to be used in real-time applications. The performance of extracted

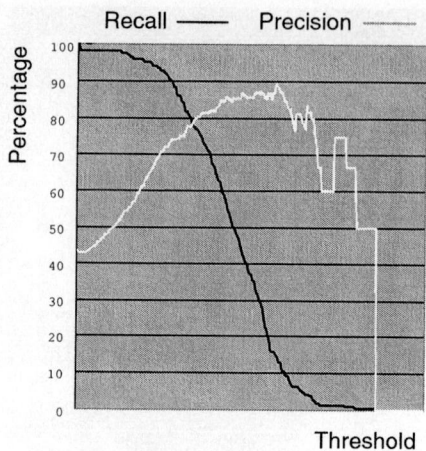

Fig. 7. Precision / Recall curve

feature is shown in Figure 7. The horizontal and vertical axis represent a threshold (i.e., T) and percentage of precision and recall. That is, Figure 7 represents the precision and recall curve of intra prediction mode in terms of T which varies from minimum to maximum value. Precision and recall are defined as follows

$$Precision = \frac{N_c}{N_c + N_f} \times 100, \text{ and } Recall = \frac{N_c}{N_c + N_m} \times 100,$$

where N_c, N_m, and N_f are the number of correct, miss, and false detection, respectively. Generally, recall curve decrease monotonously, because $N_c + N_m$ is fixed to the total number of real scene change occurrence and N_c decreases according to the increasing threshold. However, precision curve can fluctuates according to the variations of N_c and N_f. Specially, precision value can be zero, when the threshold is maximum and N_c is zero as our evaluation shown in Figure 7. Our desired values of N_f and N_m are to be close to zero, which yield large percentage value of precision and recall. However, the precision value is inversely proportional to the recall value. So, we decide the threshold at the intersection point between precision and recall curve shown in Figure 7. The value of precision and recall at the closest point from the intersection in Figure 7 are 77.90% and 78.82%. And the corresponding threshold T is 0.23.

4 Proposed Method

The MB-based similarity measure introduced in Section 3 may generate false alarms whenever there are fast moving objects or fast camera movements in the video, because the comparative unit of prediction mode variation between two consecutive intra frames is the macroblock whose resolution is quite small with 16x16 pixels. To alleviate this problem, we employ a sub-block-based similarity measure. As shown in Figure 8, a sub-block consists of a set of MBs (e.g., there are 20 non-overlapping sub-blocks in Figure 8). Now, let S^k be a set of MBs which are included within the kth sub-block of an intra frame, and also let Δf_i^k indicate the normalized prediction mode variations of each sub-block between i^{th} and $i+1^{th}$ intra frame as follows:

$$\Delta f_i^k = \frac{1}{|S^k|} \ | \sum_{j \in S^k} Mode_i^j - \sum_{j \in S^k} Mode_{i+1}^j |, \qquad (2)$$

where $|S^k|$ is the cardinality of S^k and k is the number of sub-blocks within a frame (e.g., $k \in \{1, 2, 3, ..., 20\}$ in the case of Figure 8). Now, we can define the decision function between i^{th} and $i+1^{th}$ intra frame as follow:

$$d_{i,i+1} = \frac{1}{N_{sub}} \sum_{\forall k} q_i^k \qquad (3)$$

$$q_i^k = \begin{cases} 1, \text{ for } \Delta f_i^k \geq \lambda \\ 0, \text{ for } \Delta f_i^k < \lambda \end{cases}, \qquad (4)$$

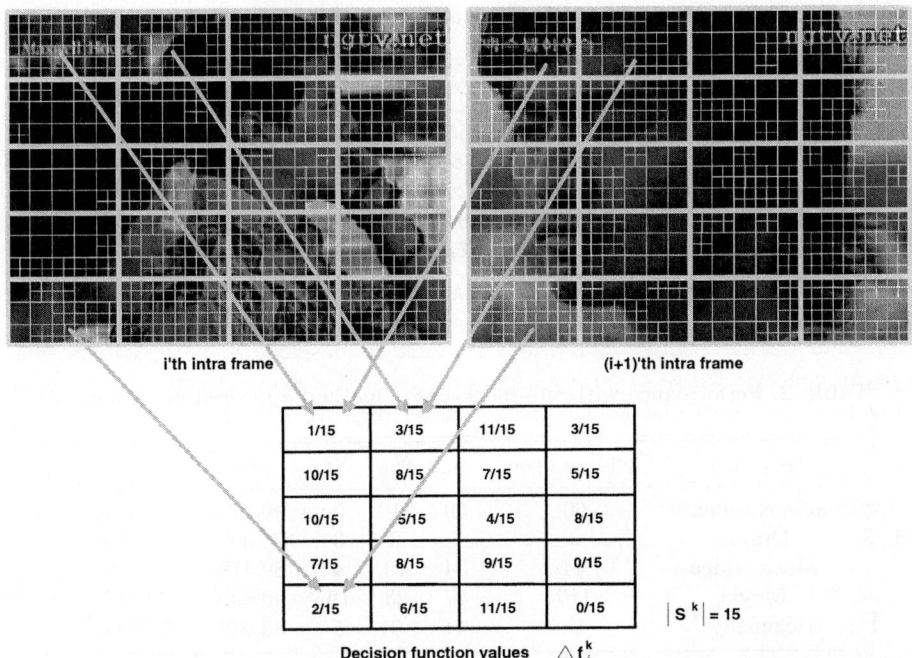

Fig. 8. Definition of sub-block and decision function value

where $N_{sub}(=20$ in Figure 8) represent the number of sub-blocks within a frame, and λ is the predefined threshold which are applied to each sub-block. That is, if $d_{i,i+1}$ is larger than predefined value T', then we declare a scene change. Note that sub-block-based decision rule is robust to the movie that contains fast moving objects or fast camera movement, because the similarity measurement unit of sub-block consists of several MBs and they can absorb such movements.

5 Experiments

Experiments have been carried out on our choice of several TV programs. Each video has a spatial resolution with 320x240, and encoding parameters are baseline profile, level 1.3, one intra period per 30 frames, 30 frame-rate per second and enabled rate control. The performance of proposed scene change detection method is expressed in terms of precision and recall that are defined in Section 3.2. For all our experiments, we fixed the value λ and T' as 0.47 and 0.15. Because the variation of prediction mode between two consecutive intra frames (i.e., Δf_i^k) is normalized by the number of MB within a sub-block, the threshold $\lambda(=0.47)$ represent that the 47 percentage of prediction modes variation within a sub-block at the same position between two consecutive intra frame are guaranteed for scene change. And, the $T'(=0.15)$ represent that the 15 percentage of sub-blocks variation within a frame are guaranteed for scene change. Table 1

Table 1. Performance with MB-based method appeared in section 3

Sequence	Genuine Scene	N_c	N_m	N_f	Precision	Recall
Advertisement	60	55	5	12	82.09%	91.67 %
Drama	9	8	1	4	66.67%	88.89%
Music video	44	28	16	6	82.35%	63.64%
Movie	110	84	26	24	77.78%	76.36%
Comedy	14	12	2	2	85.71%	85.71%
Total	237	187	50	48	79.57%	78.90%

Table 2. Performance with sub-block-based method appeared in section 4

Sequence	Genuine Scene	N_c	N_m	N_f	Precision	Recall
Advertisement	60	59	1	6	90.77%	98.33%
Drama	9	7	2	3	70.00%	77.78%
Music video	44	34	10	4	89.47%	77.27%
Movie	110	87	23	19	90.80%	70.54%
Comedy	14	14	0	5	82.08%	79.09%
Total	237	201	36	37	84.45%	84.81%

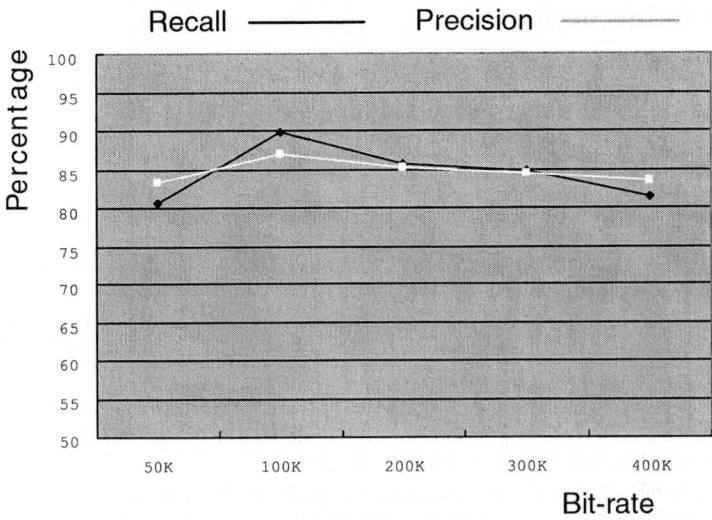

Fig. 9. The variation of Precision/Recall with bit-rate increase

and 2 show results from the video which has a bit-rate of 300Kbps in detail. For all cases, while the abrupt scene changes are detected quite well, false alarms are generated whenever there are fade-in/out and camera zoom-in/out. As shown in Table 1 and 2, the MB-based method addressed in section 3 has many false alarms, but the sub-block-based method addressed in section 4 alleviates this problem with the help of sub-block. Also, the proposed method is applied to the video which has bit-rates of 50K, 100K, 200K, 300K, and 400Kbps. The variation of precision and recall with bit-rate increase is represented in Figure 9. From the Figure 9, the proposed method is performed well on the video which has a low bit-rate with the 84.47% and 84.73% of average precision and recall values.

6 Conclusion

In this paper, we have introduced a scene change detection method in H.264/AVC compression domain. Since the scene change detection methods for previous MPEG, such as MPEG-2 or MPEG-1 are not directly applicable for the compressed bit stream of H.264/ AVC, we propose a prediction mode based scene change detection for H.264/ AVC. In the proposed method, it is easy to extract the prediction modes from compressed data. That is, it has a low computational complexity because it just needs a few addition operations as shown in Figure 6. So, the proposed method will be easily applicable to the real time applications. Moreover, experimental results show that the precision and recall for various video sequences and bit-rates turn out to be promising.

Acknowledgement

This research is supported by Information Technology Research Center (ITRC) funded by Korea IT Industry Promotion Agency (KIPA).

References

1. Zhang, H.J.W., Kankanhalli, A., and Smoliar, S.: Automatic Partitioning of Full-Motion Video, Multimedia System, vol. 1, no. 1, (1995) 10-28
2. Huang, C.L., and Liao, B.Y.: A Robust Scene-Change Detection Method for Video Segmentation, IEEE Transactions on Circuits and System for Video Technology, vol. 11, no. 12, (2001) 1281-1288
3. Lelescu, D., and Schonfeld, D.: Statistical Sequenctial Analysis for Real-Time Video Scene Change Detection on Compressed Multimedia Bitstream, IEEE Transactions on Multimedia, vol. 5, no. 1, (2003) 106-117
4. Edmundo, S., José, I.B., and Nicolás, G.: Reliable Real Time Scene Change Detection in MPEG Compressed Video, IEEE International Conference on Multimedia and Expo, vol. 1, (2004) 567-570
5. Kim, J.R., Suh, S.J., and Sull, S.H.: Fast Scene Change Detection for Personal Video Recorder, IEEE Transactions on Consumer Electronics, vol. 49, no. 3, (2003) 683-688
6. Zhu, Y., and Zhou, D.: Scene Change Detection Based on Audio and Video Content Analysis, Proceedings of the Fifth International Conference on Computational Intelligence and Multimedia Applications, (2003) 229-234
7. Tse, K., and Panchanathan, S.: A Scene Change Detection Algorithm for MPEG Compressed Video Sequences, Canadian Conference on Electrical and Computer Engineering, vol. 2, (1995) 827-830
8. Pei, S.C., and Chou, Y.Z.: Novel Error Concealment Method with Adaptive Prediction to the Abrupt and Gradual Scene Changes, IEEE Transactions on Multimedia, vol. 6, no. 1, (2004) 158-173
9. Li, H., Liu, G., Zhang, Z., and Li, Y.: Adaptive Scene-Detection Algorithm for VBR Video Stream, IEEE Transactions on Multimedia, vol. 6, no. 4, (2004) 624-633
10. Barry, G.H., Atul, P., and Arun, N.N.: Digital Video: Introduction to MPEG-2, International Thomson Publishing, (1997)
11. Richardson, E.: H.264 and MPEG-4 Video Compression, John Wiley, (2003)
12. Report of the Formal Verification Tests on AVC (ISO/IEC 14496-10 — ITU-T Rec. H.264), N6231, (2003)
13. Wiegand, T., Sullivan, G.J., Bjntegaard, G., Luthra, A.: Overview of the H.264/AVC video coding standard, IEEE Transaction on Circuits and Systems for Video Technolgy, vol. 13, issue 7, (2003) 560-576

Author Index

Abdel-Baki, Nashwa II-141
Ahn, Chang-Beom I-489, I-731
Ahn, Sang-Ho II-337
Ahn, Sangjoon II-48
Aizawa, Kiyoharu I-1005, II-584
Ano, Shigehiro II-429
Ariki, Yasuo II-923
Ashourian, Mohsen II-258, II-349
Avilés, Marcos I-61

Bae, MyungJin II-700
Baek, Joong-Hwan I-269
Baek, SeongHo II-688
Bahn, Hyokyung II-1
Basso, Andrea I-524
Beack, Seung-Hwa I-698
Beak, Seungkwon I-742
Belkhatir, Mohammed I-820
Byeon, Okhwan II-441
Byun, Ju Wan II-1072

Cha, Jongeun I-420, II-176
Cernea, Dan I-84
Chae, Jeong-Sook I-922
Chai, Young-Ho I-315
Chang, Chin-Chen I-981
Chang, Chung-Yuan Knight II-394
Chang, Eun-Young I-73
Chang, I-Cheng I-37
Chang, Pao-Chi II-747
Charhad, Mbarek I-820
Chen, Chun-Jen I-512
Chen, Jun-Cheng I-776
Chen, Tsuhan II-665
Chen, Yiqiang II-1027
Cheng, Cho-Chun I-535
Chiang, Huann-Keng I-291
Cho, Choong-Ho II-224
Cho, Googchun II-981
Cho, Hyung-Jea I-922
Cho, Ikhwan I-547
Cho, Jin-Ho I-888
Cho, Yoon Ho I-957
Choi, Byeong Ho II-514

Choi, Han-wool I-315
Choi, In Yong I-709
Choi, Jin Soo I-234
Choi, Jong-Hyun I-731
Choi, JongUk II-153
Choi, Sang Won II-711
Choi, Seong Jong II-981
Chon, Sang Bae I-709
Choudhry, Umar Iqbal II-818
Chou, Yung-Chen I-981
Chu, Wei-Ta I-776
Chu, Xiaowen II-246
Chun, Seong Soo I-168
Chung, Ki-Dong II-382
Cornelis, Jan I-84

Deklerck, Rudi I-84
de Silva, Gamhewage C. I-1005
Driessen, Peter F. I-524

Fan, Liangzhong I-408
Fang, Zhijun II-405
Fei, Hwai-Chung I-512
Fu, Libo I-594
Fu, Rong II-1027

Gao, Wen I-675, I-864, II-550, II-595, II-830, II-946, II-1027
García, Narciso I-61
Gong, Min-Sik II-94
Großmann, Hans Peter II-141

Hahn, Hernsoo I-799
Han, Seung Jo II-489
Han, Seung-Soo I-559
Han, Sunyoung II-48
Har, Dong-Soo I-466, I-500, II-538
Hasegawa, Teruyuki II-429
Hasegawa, Toru II-429
Hayase, Kazuya II-584
He, Wei II-83
He, Weisheng I-809
Hejazi, Mahmoud R. I-910
Hendry II-735

Ho, Yo-Sung   I-179, I-361, I-431,
    I-570, I-687, I-910, II-164, II-176,
    II-258, II-477, II-514, II-617, II-794
Hong, Eon-Pyo   I-500
Hong, Hyun-Ki   II-772, II-782
Hong, Jin Woo   I-212, I-234
Hong, Jun-Hee   I-466
Hong, Jun-Seong   I-731
Hong, Min-Cheol   II-561
Hong, Seung-Wook   I-854
Hong, Tae Chul   II-200
Hoshino, Haruo   II-429
Hsiao, Fu-Jen   II-665
Hsieh, Ming-I   II-394, II-1015
Hu, Bo   II-830
Huang, Chung-Ling   I-37
Huang, Qian   II-550
Huang, Qingming   I-864, II-830
Huang, Shyh-Fang   II-747
Hur, Namho   I-73
Hwang, Eenjun   I-876
Hwang, Gooyoun   II-465
Hwang, Sun-Kyoo   I-280
Hwang, Wen-Liang   I-535
Hwang, Yong-Ho   II-772

Im, ChaSeop   II-688
Itoh, Kazuo   II-1039

Jang, Euee S.   I-73
Jang, Seok   II-782
Jeon, Hyun-Ho   I-524
Jeon, In-Su   I-144
Jeong, Dongseok   I-547
Jeong, Yong-Yeon   I-570
Jhang, Kyoung-Son   I-500
Ji, Kyunghee   I-191
Jiang, Gangyi   I-408
Jin, Xiaogang   I-257, II-270
Jo, Jinyong   II-441
Joe, Hongmi   I-339
Jun, Kyungkoo   I-25
Jung, Cheolkon   I-765
Jung, Chulho   II-36
Jung, Eun-Gu   I-466, I-500, II-538
Jung, Inbum   II-12
Jung, Kyeong Hoon   II-641
Jung, Moon Ryul   I-327
Jung, Young-Kee   I-559

Kamikura, Kazuto   I-96
Kamimura, Kazuhiro   II-429
Kang, Dong Wook   II-641
Kang, Jung Won   I-191, II-129
Kang, Min-Chang   II-538
Kang, Sanggil   I-202
Kawamori, Masahito   I-224
Kawazoe, Katsuhiko   I-224
Kim, Chan Young   I-957
Kim, Daehee   I-843
Kim, Dae-Yeon   I-396
Kim, Daiyong   I-73
Kim, Deok Hwan   I-957
Kim, Dong Hoon   I-25
Kim, Dong-Hun   I-888
Kim, Dongkook   II-12
Kim, Doohan   II-59
Kim, Eui-Jin   I-765, II-129
Kim, Haelyong   II-235
Kim, Hansung   I-384
Kim, Heesun   II-912
Kim, Hong Kook   I-361, I-477
Kim, Hye-Soo   II-71
Kim, Hyon-Gook   II-676
Kim, Hyunjue   II-117
Kim, Jae-Gon   I-202, I-653, I-787, II-129
Kim, Jae-Won   II-71
Kim, Jin-Soo   I-653
Kim, Ji-Yeon   II-877
Kim, Ji-Yeun   I-765
Kim, JongKuk   II-700
Kim, JongSu   II-688
Kim, JongWeon   II-153
Kim, JongWon   I-361, I-443, II-465,
    II-501, II-818
Kim, Jun-Yup   II-477
Kim, Ki-Doo   II-641
Kim, Kwanghoon   II-235
Kim, Kyungdeok   II-900
Kim, Kyung-Ho   II-561
Kim, Mi-Ae   II-371
Kim, Munchurl   I-202, II-735, II-806
Kim, Munjo   I-202
Kim, Rinchul   II-981
Kim, Sangjin   I-843
Kim, Sang-Jun   I-606
Kim, Sang-Kyun   I-765, II-877
Kim, Sang Min   I-350
Kim, Sangwook   II-900
Kim, Sehwan   II-176, II-759

Kim, Se-Jin II-224
Kim, Seong-Whan I-664, II-360, II-676
Kim, Seung-Hwan I-179, II-477
Kim, Seung-Jin I-946, II-337
Kim, Seungjoo II-117
Kim, Seung-Man I-420, I-687, II-176
Kim, Sung-Min II-382, II-1072
Kim, Sung-Yeol I-431, I-687, II-164, II-176, II-794
Kim, Taeseok II-1, II-59
Kim, Tae-Su I-946, II-337
Kim, Tae-Wan II-514
Kim, TaeYong II-688
Kim, Whoi-Yul I-280, I-765, II-129
Kim, Wonjung I-120
Kim, Yong-Deak I-408
Kim, Yong Ho I-234
Kim, Yong Tae II-641
Kim, Yoon II-12, II-489
Kim, Young Yong II-200
Kitahara, Masaki I-96
Kitazawa, Hitoshi I-831
Ko, Hyeongseok I-854
Ko, Ki-Hong I-664
Ko, Sung-Jea II-71
Kodama, Kazuya I-303
Koh, Kern II-1, II-59
Komatsu, Takashi I-246
Kong, Hyung-Yun II-187, II-212
Kong, Xiang-Wei II-301
Kon'ya, Yuko I-224
Korekuni, Hitoshi II-889
Kubota, Akira I-303
Kuo, Jin-Hau I-776
Kuwano, Hidetaka I-224
Kwak, Jaiseung II-441
Kwon, Hyoungmoon II-711
Kwon, Jung-hoon I-315
Kwon, Jun-Sik II-772
Kwon, Kee-Koo I-144
Kwon, Ki-Ryong II-337
Kwon, Yong-Il I-582

Lai, Hsu-Te II-1015
Lai, Shang-Hong I-512
Lee, Beom-Chan I-361
Lee, Cheol-Hoon II-94
Lee, Choong-hoon II-312
Lee, Dai-Boong II-105
Lee, Eun-Kyung I-431

Lee, Eunseok II-36
Lee, Gil Ho I-477
Lee, Gun-Woo II-606
Lee, Gwang-Gook I-765, II-129
Lee, Hae-Yeoun II-312
Lee, Haeyoung I-108
Lee, Han-Kyu I-212
Lee, HeeKyung I-212
Lee, Heung-Kyu II-312
Lee, Hyong-Woo II-224
Lee, HyunRyong I-443
Lee, Jeong-A I-500
Lee, Jeong-in I-315
Lee, Joahyoung II-12
Lee, Jongwan I-327
Lee, Joohun I-799
Lee, Joong Yong II-291
Lee, Jui-Yu II-526
Lee, Jumi II-711
Lee, Jungho I-547
Lee, Jung-Il I-489
Lee, Junhaeng I-843
Lee, Kuhn-Il I-946, II-337, II-606
Lee, Kwan-Heng I-361, I-420, I-687, II-176, II-958
Lee, Kyu-Won I-559
Lee, Moon-Hyun I-606
Lee, Sanghee II-36
Lee, Sang-Rak I-25
Lee, Sang Wook I-339, I-350, II-993
Lee, Seokhee I-361
Lee, Seung-Ik I-888
Lee, Seung-Jun II-641
Lee, Soo In I-73
Lee, Soon-Tak I-269
Lee, Sunyoung I-73
Lee, Tae-Hoon II-382
Lee, Won-Hyung II-371
Lee, Wonwoo II-1004
Lee, Woongho I-547
Lee, Yong-Gu I-361
Lee, Yonghee II-981
Lee, Youngho I-361
Lee, Younjeong I-799
Lee, Yung-Ki I-396
Lee, Yung-Lyul I-396
Lee, Yunsik I-969
Lei, Zhen I-754
Li, Houqiang II-854
Lian, Shiguo II-281

Liang, Dawei   I-864
Liang, Ke   I-455
Liaw, Chishyan   I-291
Lim, Chan   II-688
Lim, Dong-Sun   I-144
Lim, Hoi-Jeong   I-466
Lim, Hyesook   I-120
Lim, Seong-Jae   I-570
Lin, Chuang   II-246
Lin, Chung-Chi   I-291
Liu, Jixue   I-582
Liu, Junfa   II-1027
Liu, Qiang   I-934
Liu, Wen-Feng   II-301
Liu, Yang   I-864
Liu, Yazhou   II-946
Liu, Yonghe   II-572
Liu, Yu-chi   I-754
Liu, Zhengkai   II-854
Liu, Zhongxuan   II-281
Lu, Yan   II-629

Ma, Huadong   II-572
Ma, Siwei   I-675
Ma, Wei-Ying   I-617
Markova, Aneta   I-84
Min, Byeongwook   I-73
Min, Dong Bo   I-384
Min, Geyong   II-246
Min, Kyoung Won   II-514
Mo, Hiroshi   I-303
Moallem, Peyman   II-258
Mohebbi, Keyvan   II-349
Moon, Han-gil   I-742
Moon, Nammee   I-191
Moon, Sung-Kyun   I-854
Moon, Young Shik   II-291, II-865
Morán, Francisco   I-61
Mujahid, Fahad Ali   I-466
Munteanu, Adrian   I-84

Na, Kyung Gun   I-327
Nakatsu, Ryohei   I-373, II-1039
Nam, Hyeong-Min   II-71
Nam, Jeho   II-312
Nam, Junghyun   II-117
Nam, Mi Young   II-935
Nam, Yang-Hee   I-720, II-970
Nam, Yunyoung   I-876
Nascimento, Mario A.   I-582

Neve, Wesley De   I-641
Nguyen, Duc-Hoai   I-698
Niimi, Michiharu   II-889
Noda, Hideki   II-889
Noh, Sung-Ryul   I-13

Oakley, Ian   I-420, II-176
Oh, Crystal S.   II-970
Oh, Han   I-361
Oh, Ha Ryoung   II-94
Oh, Hyung Rai   II-24
Oh, Kwan-Jung   II-617
Oh, Ryong   II-224
Oh, Sejin   I-361
Oh, Seoung-Jun   I-489, I-731
Oh, Yoo Rhee   I-361
Ohkubo, Toshiya   II-923

Paik, Joonki   I-843
Pan, Yunhe   I-993
Pan, Zhigeng   II-325
Pang, Yanwei   II-854
Park, Chul-Man   I-489
Park, Dong-Chul   I-698, I-969
Park, Eunyong   II-48
Park, Hanhoon   I-606, I-854
Park, Hochong   I-489, I-731
Park, Ho-Hyun   I-582
Park, Hyun   II-865
Park, Hyuncheol   II-235
Park, Hyunje   II-48
Park, Jeong-Sik   II-453
Park, Jeung-Chul   I-361
Park, Jong-An   I-899, II-489
Park, Jong-Il   I-606, I-854
Park, Jong-Seung   I-13, I-25
Park, Joung Wook   II-958
Park, Ki Tae   II-291
Park, Minsik   I-234
Park, Sancho   I-698
Park, Sang-Hyun   II-453, II-489
Park, Seong Jun   I-787
Park, Si-Yong   II-382
Park, Sujin   I-108
Park, Youngmin   I-361
Prakash, Edmond C.   I-934
Preda, Marius   I-49
Prêteux, Françoise   I-49
Pyun, Jae-Young   II-453, II-489

Author Index

Qiu, Feng II-246
Quan, Shan Guo II-200

Ren, Zhen II-281
Rhee, Phill Kyu II-935
Rim, Kee Wook II-291, II-865
Ro, Yong Man II-877
Ryu, Byunghan II-417
Ryu, Jeha I-361, I-420, II-176
Ryu, Seungwan II-417

Saito, Takahiro I-246
Sakamoto, Hajime I-373
Salomie, Ioan Alexandru I-84
Schelkens, Peter I-84
Schrijver, Davy De I-641
Seo, Dongmahn II-12
Seo, Hyunhwa II-417
Seo, Jeong-il I-709, I-742
Seo, Kwang-Deok I-787
Seo, Kyong Sok II-877
Seo, Kyoung Chin I-339, I-350, II-993
Seo, Kyung-Sik I-899
Seo, Yang Suk II-877
Seong, Suk-Jeong I-720
Seong, Yeong Rak II-94
Servillat, Florent II-1039
Sha, Jichang II-83
Shahab, Qonita M. II-806
Shen, Jianbing I-257, II-270
Shen, Zuowei I-535
Sheu, Ming-Hwa I-291
Shi, Jiaoying II-1060
Shi, Yuanchun I-809
Shimizu, Shinya I-96
Shin, DongHwan II-153
Shin, Giroo II-993
Shin, Jeongho I-843
Shin, Jitae II-465
Shin, Sangchul II-48
Shin, Yoan II-561
Shin, Yong H. II-59
Shinozaki, Kuniya I-373
Sim, Dong-Gyu I-1
Sohn, Chae-Bong I-731
Sohn, Kwanghoon I-384
Song, Changgeun I-327
Song, Haohao I-629
Song, Hwangjun II-24, II-105
Song, Iickho II-711

Song, Li I-629
Song, Samuel Moon-Ho I-787
Song, Zuman II-653
Suh, Jeong-Jun II-200
Suk, Jung-Youp II-606
Sull, Sanghoon I-168
Sun, Huifang II-550
Sun, Lifeng I-455
Sun, Shusen II-325
Sun, Xiaoming II-1049
Sun, Xiao II-83
Sung, Hyun-Sung II-360
Sung, Koeng-Mo I-709, I-742
Sung, Mee Young I-13, I-25

Takao, Nobuteru II-889
Takiguchi, Tetsuya II-923
Tanaka, Takaho I-373
Tanaka, Toshihisa I-831
Tang, Chih-Wei I-132
Tao, Dan II-572
Tao, Jun II-83
Tao, Pin II-1049
Tran, Chung-Nguyen I-969
Tran, Son I-49
Tung, Yi-Shin II-841

Van Deursen, Davy I-641
Van de Walle, Rik I-641
Van Khuong, Ho II-187, II-212

Wan, Zheng II-405
Wang, Hui II-83, II-653
Wang, Qiang I-675
Wang, Rangding I-408
Wang, Weiqiang I-594
Wang, Wen-Hao II-665
Wang, Yunli II-653
Wang, Zhengyou II-405
Wang, Zhiquan II-281
Weng, Chung-Yi II-841
Wolf, Koen De I-641
Won, Chee Sun II-1072
Won, Chul-Ho I-888
Won, Dongho II-117
Won, Youjip II-59
Woo, Dong-Min I-559
Woo, Woontack I-361, II-176, II-759, II-1004

Wu, Eric Hsiao-Kuang   II-394, II-747, II-1015
Wu, Fei   I-993
Wu, Feng   I-156, II-629
Wu, Ja-Ling   I-776, II-841
Wu, Ling-da   I-754
Wu, Shiqian   II-405
Wu, Wen-Chuan   I-981
Wu, Xiao-feng   II-1039

Xia, Tao   I-535
Xiao, Xin   I-809
Xiong, Hongkai   I-156, I-629
Xu, Feng   I-617
Xu, Jizheng   I-156

Yabuta, Kenichi   I-831
Yamada, Tomokazu   I-224
Yamasaki, Toshihiko   I-1005, II-584
Yang, Seungji   II-877
Yang, Seung-Jun   I-212
Yang, Tian-Lin   I-37
Yang, Ya-Ting   II-841
Yang, Yi   I-993
Yao, Hongxun   II-946
Ye, Xien   I-408
Yeh, Jen-Hao   I-776
Yi, Dong-Hoon   II-501
Yi, Jeong-Seon   I-720
Yim, Changhoon   I-120
Yin, Baocai   II-629
Yin, Hao   II-246
Yoo, Jae Doug   II-958
Yoo, Jo Hyung   II-935
Yoo, Kee-Young   II-723
Yoo, Kil-Sang   II-371
Yoo, Youngil   II-641

Yoon, Eun-Jun   II-723
Yoon, Ja-Cheon   I-168
Yoon, Jae Sam   I-477
Yoon, Seok   II-711
Yoon, Seung-Uk   I-431, II-164, II-176
Yoon, Young-Suk   I-687, II-794
Yoshiyuki, Yashima   I-96
You, Ji-Hyuk   I-489
You, Shingchern D.   II-526
You, Xin-Gang   II-301
Yu, Jiarong   II-1060
Yu, Mei   I-408
Yu, Nenghai   II-854
Yu, Songyu   I-629
Yun, Jae-Woong   II-71

Zeng, Weiming   II-405
Zhan, Yaowen   I-594
Zhang, Daxing   II-325
Zhang, Dongdong   I-156
Zhang, Lei   I-617
Zhang, Mingmin   II-325
Zhang, Nan   II-629
Zhang, Peng   II-830
Zhang, Rong   II-854
Zhang, Wenjun   I-156
Zhang, Xin   II-653
Zhang, Ying   I-754
Zhang, Yu-Jin   I-617
Zhao, Debin   I-675, II-550, II-946
Zheng, Qing-Fang   II-595
Zhong, Yuzhuo   I-455
Zhou, Chuan   I-257, II-270
Zhou, Renqin   II-1027
Zhou, Yongxia   II-1060
Zhuang, Yueting   I-993

Lecture Notes in Computer Science

For information about Vols. 1–3689

please contact your bookseller or Springer

Vol. 3807: M. Dean, Y. Guo, W. Jun, R. Kaschek, S. Krishnaswamy, Z. Pan, Q.Z. Sheng (Eds.), Web Information Systems – WISE 2005 Workshops. XV, 275 pages. 2005.

Vol. 3806: M. Kitsuregawa, E.J. Neuhold, A.H. H. Ngu, J.-Y. Chung, Q.Z. Sheng (Eds.), Web Information Systems – WISE 2005. XXI, 771 pages. 2005.

Vol. 3791: A. Adi, S. Stoutenburg, S. Tabet (Eds.), Rules and Rule Markup Languages for the Semantic Web. X, 225 pages. 2005.

Vol. 3789: A. Gelbukh, Á. de Albornoz, H. Terashima-Marín (Eds.), MICAI 2005: Advances in Artificial Intelligence. XXVI, 1198 pages. 2005. (Subseries LNAI).

Vol. 3785: K.-K. Lau, R. Banach (Eds.), Formal Methods and Software Engineering. XIV, 496 pages. 2005.

Vol. 3784: J. Tao, T. Tan, R.W. Picard (Eds.), Affective Computing and Intelligent Interaction. XIX, 1008 pages. 2005.

Vol. 3781: S.Z. Li, Z. Sun, T. Tan, S. Pankanti, G. Chollet, D. Zhang (Eds.), Advances in Biometric Person Authentication. XI, 250 pages. 2005.

Vol. 3780: K. Yi (Ed.), Programming Languages and Systems. XI, 435 pages. 2005.

Vol. 3779: H. Jin, D. Reed, W. Jiang (Eds.), Network and Parallel Computing. XV, 513 pages. 2005.

Vol. 3777: O.B. Lupanov, O.M. Kasim-Zade, A.V. Chaskin, K. Steinhöfel (Eds.), Stochastic Algorithms: Foundations and Applications. VIII, 239 pages. 2005.

Vol. 3775: J. Schönwälder, J. Serrat (Eds.), Ambient Networks. XIII, 281 pages. 2005.

Vol. 3772: M. Consens, G. Navarro (Eds.), String Processing and Information Retrieval. XIV, 406 pages. 2005.

Vol. 3770: J. Akoka, S.W. Liddle, I.-Y. Song, M. Bertolotto, I. Comyn-Wattiau, W.-J. van den Heuvel, M. Kolp, J.C. Trujillo, C. Kop, H.C. Mayr (Eds.), Perspectives in Conceptual Modeling. XXII, 476 pages. 2005.

Vol. 3768: Y.-S. Ho, H.J. Kim (Eds.), Advances in Mulitmedia Information Processing - PCM 2005, Part II. XXVIII, 1088 pages. 2005.

Vol. 3767: Y.-S. Ho, H.J. Kim (Eds.), Advances in Mulitmedia Information Processing - PCM 2005, Part I. XXVIII, 1022 pages. 2005.

Vol. 3766: N. Sebe, M.S. Lew, T.S. Huang (Eds.), Computer Vision in Human-Computer Interaction. X, 231 pages. 2005.

Vol. 3765: Y. Liu, T. Jiang, C. Zhang (Eds.), Computer Vision for Biomedical Image Applications. X, 563 pages. 2005.

Vol. 3764: S. Tixeuil, T. Herman (Eds.), Self-Stabilizing Systems. VIII, 229 pages. 2005.

Vol. 3762: R. Meersman, Z. Tari, P. Herrero (Eds.), On the Move to Meaningful Internet Systems 2005: OTM Workshops. XXXI, 1228 pages. 2005.

Vol. 3761: R. Meersman, Z. Tari (Eds.), On the Move to Meaningful Internet Systems 2005: CoopIS, DOA, and ODBASE, Part II. XXVII, 653 pages. 2005.

Vol. 3760: R. Meersman, Z. Tari (Eds.), On the Move to Meaningful Internet Systems 2005: CoopIS, DOA, and ODBASE, Part I. XXVII, 921 pages. 2005.

Vol. 3759: G. Chen, Y. Pan, M. Guo, J. Lu (Eds.), Parallel and Distributed Processing and Applications - ISPA 2005 Workshops. XIII, 669 pages. 2005.

Vol. 3758: Y. Pan, D. Chen, M. Guo, J. Cao, J. Dongarra (Eds.), Parallel and Distributed Processing and Applications. XXIII, 1162 pages. 2005.

Vol. 3756: J. Cao, W. Nejdl, M. Xu (Eds.), Advanced Parallel Processing Technologies. XIV, 526 pages. 2005.

Vol. 3754: J. Dalmau Royo, G. Hasegawa (Eds.), Management of Multimedia Networks and Services. XII, 384 pages. 2005.

Vol. 3753: O.F. Olsen, L. Florack, A. Kuijper (Eds.), Deep Structure, Singularities, and Computer Vision. X, 259 pages. 2005.

Vol. 3752: N. Paragios, O. Faugeras, T. Chan, C. Schnörr (Eds.), Variational, Geometric, and Level Set Methods in Computer Vision. XI, 369 pages. 2005.

Vol. 3751: T. Magedanz, E.R. M. Madeira, P. Dini (Eds.), Operations and Management in IP-Based Networks. X, 213 pages. 2005.

Vol. 3750: J.S. Duncan, G. Gerig (Eds.), Medical Image Computing and Computer-Assisted Intervention – MICCAI 2005, Part II. XL, 1018 pages. 2005.

Vol. 3749: J.S. Duncan, G. Gerig (Eds.), Medical Image Computing and Computer-Assisted Intervention – MICCAI 2005, Part I. XXXIX, 942 pages. 2005.

Vol. 3747: C.A. Maziero, J.G. Silva, A.M.S. Andrade, F.M.d. Assis Silva (Eds.), Dependable Computing. XV, 267 pages. 2005.

Vol. 3746: P. Bozanis, E.N. Houstis (Eds.), Advances in Informatics. XIX, 879 pages. 2005.

Vol. 3745: J.L. Oliveira, V. Maojo, F. Martin-Sanchez, A.S. Pereira (Eds.), Biological and Medical Data Analysis. XII, 422 pages. 2005. (Subseries LNBI).

Vol. 3744: T. Magedanz, A. Karmouch, S. Pierre, I. Venieris (Eds.), Mobility Aware Technologies and Applications. XIV, 418 pages. 2005.

Vol. 3740: T. Srikanthan, J. Xue, C.-H. Chang (Eds.), Advances in Computer Systems Architecture. XVII, 833 pages. 2005.

Vol. 3739: W. Fan, Z.-h. Wu, J. Yang (Eds.), Advances in Web-Age Information Management. XXIV, 930 pages. 2005.

Vol. 3738: V.R. Syrotiuk, E. Chávez (Eds.), Ad-Hoc, Mobile, and Wireless Networks. XI, 360 pages. 2005.

Vol. 3735: A. Hoffmann, H. Motoda, T. Scheffer (Eds.), Discovery Science. XVI, 400 pages. 2005. (Subseries LNAI).

Vol. 3734: S. Jain, H.U. Simon, E. Tomita (Eds.), Algorithmic Learning Theory. XII, 490 pages. 2005. (Subseries LNAI).

Vol. 3733: P. Yolum, T. Güngör, F. Gürgen, C. Özturan (Eds.), Computer and Information Sciences - ISCIS 2005. XXI, 973 pages. 2005.

Vol. 3731: F. Wang (Ed.), Formal Techniques for Networked and Distributed Systems - FORTE 2005. XII, 558 pages. 2005.

Vol. 3729: Y. Gil, E. Motta, V. R. Benjamins, M.A. Musen (Eds.), The Semantic Web – ISWC 2005. XXIII, 1073 pages. 2005.

Vol. 3728: V. Paliouras, J. Vounckx, D. Verkest (Eds.), Integrated Circuit and System Design. XV, 753 pages. 2005.

Vol. 3726: L.T. Yang, O.F. Rana, B. Di Martino, J. Dongarra (Eds.), High Performance Computing and Communications. XXVI, 1116 pages. 2005.

Vol. 3725: D. Borrione, W. Paul (Eds.), Correct Hardware Design and Verification Methods. XII, 412 pages. 2005.

Vol. 3724: P. Fraigniaud (Ed.), Distributed Computing. XIV, 520 pages. 2005.

Vol. 3723: W. Zhao, S. Gong, X. Tang (Eds.), Analysis and Modelling of Faces and Gestures. XI, 4234 pages. 2005.

Vol. 3722: D. Van Hung, M. Wirsing (Eds.), Theoretical Aspects of Computing – ICTAC 2005. XIV, 614 pages. 2005.

Vol. 3721: A. Jorge, L. Torgo, P.B. Brazdil, R. Camacho, J. Gama (Eds.), Knowledge Discovery in Databases: PKDD 2005. XXIII, 719 pages. 2005. (Subseries LNAI).

Vol. 3720: J. Gama, R. Camacho, P.B. Brazdil, A. Jorge, L. Torgo (Eds.), Machine Learning: ECML 2005. XXIII, 769 pages. 2005. (Subseries LNAI).

Vol. 3719: M. Hobbs, A.M. Goscinski, W. Zhou (Eds.), Distributed and Parallel Computing. XI, 448 pages. 2005.

Vol. 3718: V.G. Ganzha, E.W. Mayr, E.V. Vorozhtsov (Eds.), Computer Algebra in Scientific Computing. XII, 502 pages. 2005.

Vol. 3717: B. Gramlich (Ed.), Frontiers of Combining Systems. X, 321 pages. 2005. (Subseries LNAI).

Vol. 3716: L. Delcambre, C. Kop, H.C. Mayr, J. Mylopoulos, Ó. Pastor (Eds.), Conceptual Modeling – ER 2005. XVI, 498 pages. 2005.

Vol. 3715: E. Dawson, S. Vaudenay (Eds.), Progress in Cryptology – Mycrypt 2005. XI, 329 pages. 2005.

Vol. 3714: H. Obbink, K. Pohl (Eds.), Software Product Lines. XIII, 235 pages. 2005.

Vol. 3713: L.C. Briand, C. Williams (Eds.), Model Driven Engineering Languages and Systems. XV, 722 pages. 2005.

Vol. 3712: R. Reussner, J. Mayer, J.A. Stafford, S. Overhage, S. Becker, P.J. Schroeder (Eds.), Quality of Software Architectures and Software Quality. XIII, 289 pages. 2005.

Vol. 3711: F. Kishino, Y. Kitamura, H. Kato, N. Nagata (Eds.), Entertainment Computing - ICEC 2005. XXIV, 540 pages. 2005.

Vol. 3710: M. Barni, I. Cox, T. Kalker, H.J. Kim (Eds.), Digital Watermarking. XII, 485 pages. 2005.

Vol. 3709: P. van Beek (Ed.), Principles and Practice of Constraint Programming - CP 2005. XX, 887 pages. 2005.

Vol. 3708: J. Blanc-Talon, W. Philips, D.C. Popescu, P. Scheunders (Eds.), Advanced Concepts for Intelligent Vision Systems. XXII, 725 pages. 2005.

Vol. 3707: D.A. Peled, Y.-K. Tsay (Eds.), Automated Technology for Verification and Analysis. XII, 506 pages. 2005.

Vol. 3706: H. Fuks, S. Lukosch, A.C. Salgado (Eds.), Groupware: Design, Implementation, and Use. XII, 378 pages. 2005.

Vol. 3704: M. De Gregorio, V. Di Maio, M. Frucci, C. Musio (Eds.), Brain, Vision, and Artificial Intelligence. XV, 556 pages. 2005.

Vol. 3703: F. Fages, S. Soliman (Eds.), Principles and Practice of Semantic Web Reasoning. VIII, 163 pages. 2005.

Vol. 3702: B. Beckert (Ed.), Automated Reasoning with Analytic Tableaux and Related Methods. XIII, 343 pages. 2005. (Subseries LNAI).

Vol. 3701: M. Coppo, E. Lodi, G. M. Pinna (Eds.), Theoretical Computer Science. XI, 411 pages. 2005.

Vol. 3700: J.F. Peters, A. Skowron (Eds.), Transactions on Rough Sets IV. X, 375 pages. 2005.

Vol. 3699: C.S. Calude, M.J. Dinneen, G. Păun, M. J. Pérez-Jiménez, G. Rozenberg (Eds.), Unconventional Computation. XI, 267 pages. 2005.

Vol. 3698: U. Furbach (Ed.), KI 2005: Advances in Artificial Intelligence. XIII, 409 pages. 2005. (Subseries LNAI).

Vol. 3697: W. Duch, J. Kacprzyk, E. Oja, S. Zadrożny (Eds.), Artificial Neural Networks: Formal Models and Their Applications – ICANN 2005, Part II. XXXII, 1045 pages. 2005.

Vol. 3696: W. Duch, J. Kacprzyk, E. Oja, S. Zadrożny (Eds.), Artificial Neural Networks: Biological Inspirations – ICANN 2005, Part I. XXXI, 703 pages. 2005.

Vol. 3695: M.R. Berthold, R.C. Glen, K. Diederichs, O. Kohlbacher, I. Fischer (Eds.), Computational Life Sciences. XI, 277 pages. 2005. (Subseries LNBI).

Vol. 3694: M. Malek, E. Nett, N. Suri (Eds.), Service Availability. VIII, 213 pages. 2005.

Vol. 3693: A.G. Cohn, D.M. Mark (Eds.), Spatial Information Theory. XII, 493 pages. 2005.

Vol. 3692: R. Casadio, G. Myers (Eds.), Algorithms in Bioinformatics. X, 436 pages. 2005. (Subseries LNBI).

Vol. 3691: A. Gagalowicz, W. Philips (Eds.), Computer Analysis of Images and Patterns. XIX, 865 pages. 2005.

Vol. 3690: M. Pěchouček, P. Petta, L.Z. Varga (Eds.), Multi-Agent Systems and Applications IV. XVII, 667 pages. 2005. (Subseries LNAI).